W9-BXX-689

Women and Gender

A Feminist Psychology

Women and Gender

A Feminist Psychology

THIRD EDITION

Mary Crawford
University of Connecticut

Rhoda Unger
Brandeis University

Boston   Burr Ridge, IL   Dubuque, IA   Madison, WI   New York   San Francisco   St. Louis
Bangkok   Bogotá   Caracas   Lisbon   London   Madrid
Mexico City   Milan   New Delhi   Seoul   Singapore   Sydney   Taipei   Toronto

McGraw-Hill Higher Education

A Division of The **McGraw-Hill** Companies

WOMEN AND GENDER:
A FEMINIST PSYCHOLOGY, THIRD EDITION

Copyright © 2000, 1996, 1992 by The McGraw-Hill Companies, Inc. All rights reserved.
Printed in the United States of America. Except as permitted under the United States Copyright
Act of 1976, no part of this publication may be reproduced or distributed in any form or by any
means, or stored in a data base or retrieval system, without the prior written permission of the
publisher.

This book is printed on acid-free paper.

2 3 4 5 6 7 8 9 0 QPF/QPF 0 9 8 7 6 5 4 3 2 1 0

ISBN 0–07–039213–7

Editorial director: *Jane E. Vaicunas*
Sponsoring editor: *Beth Kaufman*
Editorial coordinator: *Teresa Wise*
Senior marketing manager: *Daniel M. Loch*
Senior project manager: *Jayne Klein*
Production supervisor: *Laura Fuller*
Coordinator of freelance design: *Rick D. Noel*
Senior photo research coordinator: *Lori Hancock*
Supplement coordinator: *Stacy A. Patch*
Compositor: *ElectraGraphics, Inc.*
Typeface: *10/12 Palatino*
Printer: *Quebecor Printing Book Group/Fairfield, PA*

Cover designer: *Ellen Pettengell*
Cover art: *©SuperStock, Inc.—A Colored Postcard by Patricia Susan Brown*
Interior designer: *Kathy Theis*
Photo research: *Connie Gardner Picture Research*

The credits section for this book begins on page 645 and is considered an extension of the
copyright page.

Library of Congress Cataloging-in-Publication Data

Crawford, Mary (Mary E.)
    Women and gender : a feminist psychology / Mary Crawford, Rhoda
Unger.—3rd ed.
      p. cm.
    Includes bibliographical references and index.
    ISBN 0–07–039213–7
    1. Women—Psychology. 2. Feminist psychology. I. Unger, Rhoda
Kesler. II. Title.
HQ1206.U49   2000
305.42—dc21
          99-32603
          CIP

www.mhhe.com

About the Authors

MARY CRAWFORD is Professor of Psychology and Director of the Women's Studies Program at the University of Connecticut. She has taught the psychology of women and gender for twenty-five years, most of that time at West Chester University of Pennsylvania, where she earned the Trustees' Achievement Award for lifetime professional accomplishment. She has also held the Jane W. Irwin Chair in Women's Studies at Hamilton College, served as Distinguished Visiting Teacher-Scholar at the College of New Jersey, and directed the graduate program in women's studies at the University of South Carolina. Professor Crawford received her Ph.D. in experimental psychology from the University of Delaware. She is a consulting editor of *Psychology of Women Quarterly,* an associate editor of *Feminism and Psychology,* and a Fellow of both the American Psychological Society and the American Psychological Association. Mary Crawford has spoken and written about women's issues for audiences as diverse as the British Psychological Society, *Ms.* Magazine, and the Oprah Winfrey show. Works she has authored or edited include *Gender and Thought: Psychological Perspectives* (1989); *Talking Difference: On Gender and Language* (1995); *Gender Differences in Human Cognition* (1997); *In Our Own Words* (1997); *Coming Into Her Own: Education Successes in Girls and Women* (1999); and a special double issue of *Psychology of Women Quarterly* (1999) on innovative methods for feminist research.

RHODA UNGER is Professor Emerita of Psychology at Montclair State University and Resident Scholar in Women's Studies at Brandeis University. She received her Ph.D. in experimental psychology from Harvard University. Professor Unger was the first recipient of the Carolyn Wood Sherif Award from the Division of the Psychology of Women of the American Psychological Association. She is also the recipient of two distinguished publication awards and a distinguished career award from the Association for Women in Psychology. She has been the president of the Division of the Psychology of Women and, more recently, president of the Society for the Psychological Study of Social Issues. She has lectured extensively in the United States and abroad as a Fulbright scholar in Israel, a distinguished lecturer at the University of British Columbia, and as a visiting fellow of the British Psychological Society. She is currently the book review editor of the international journal *Feminism and Psychology* and is editing a handbook on psychology and gender. Professor Unger is the author or editor of seven previous books, including *Resisting Gender: Twenty-five Years of Feminist Psychology; Representations: Social Constructions of Gender; Women, Gender, and Social Psychology;* and *Female and Male.*

About the Cover

A COLORED POSTCARD, by Patricia Susan Brown. Patricia Susan Brown (b. Patricia Rundgren, Chicago, 1950) earned her B.A. in Studio Arts from the University of Illinois at Chicago in 1984. She writes of her work, "Through painting I am able to freely explore and express the full range of intuitive emotional responses to life situations . . . I embrace abstract expressionism as an opportunity to paint intuitively—not starting with an idea in mind but with the act of painting itself." Though she sometimes feels that her artwork is ignored because she is a woman, Brown says that this fact only causes her to work even harder to gain recognition in the art world. And she is receiving that recognition. Her work has garnered numerous awards, including the 1994 Grumbacher Medal. Patricia Brown lives in Florida where she continues to exhibit her work individually and as a member of the Florida Artists Group.

To our husbands
Roger Chaffin and Burt Unger
for always being there
and to our children:
Mary, Mark, and Ben
Laurel and Rachel
who represent our hopes
for the future.

Contents

PREFACE   xv

1. Introduction to a Feminist Psychology of Women   1

   Beginnings   2
   What Is Feminism?   6
   Methods and Values in Scientific Inquiry   14
   Themes of This Book   21
   Our Goals for Our Students   28
   Suggested Readings   31

2. Images of Women and Men   32

   Images of Women in Cross-Cultural Perspective   34
   Stereotypes: An Overview   36
   Gender Stereotypes in the Mass Media   42
   The Impact of Media Sexism   54
   Women's Quest for Beauty   56
   Language and Women's Place   61
   Stereotypes as Social Demands   65
   Stereotypes and Sexism   67
   Forms of Sexism   73
   Connecting Themes   75
   Suggested Readings   76

3. Doing Gender   77

   Gender as a Social Category   78
   The Social Construction of Gender-Related Differences   86

Gender and Self-Categorization   90
Status and Power   92
Gender Differences as Status Differences   93
The Role of Gender in Boundary Maintenance   98
Women and Men Doing Gender   103
Changing Roles in a Changing Society   105
The Internalization of Gender Norms   109
Connecting Themes   115
Suggested Readings   115

4. The Meanings of Difference   116

A Focus on Similarity: Working for Equality   118
Different or Similar? Gender and Math Abilities   123
The Similarities Tradition: Why It Matters   132
The Differences Tradition: Celebrating Women   135
The Differences Tradition: Why It Matters   145
Can Similarities and Differences be Reconciled?   147
Connecting Themes   148
Suggested Readings   148

5. Biological Bases of Sex   149

What Is Sex and What Are the Sexes?   150
How Is Sex Determined?   151
Prenatal Development   154
Does the Human Brain Have a Sex?   159
Atypical Human Sexual Development   163
Cultural Constructions of Gender   182
Connecting Themes   185
Suggested Readings   185

6. Becoming Gendered: Childhood   186

Acquiring Gender: Some Theoretical Perspectives   187
The Preference for Sons   192
Gender Stereotypes   195
How Does Society Foster Gender Typing?   198
What Is Sex Segregation?   206
Are There Gender Differences in Social Behaviors?   213
Stages in the Development of Gender Understanding   217
Is Gender Nonconformity Different for Boys and Girls?   219
Resisting Gender Rules   225
Factors that Increase Gender Flexibility   226
Connecting Themes   230
Suggested Readings   230

7. Becoming a Woman: Puberty and Adolescence   232

Distinguishing Puberty from Adolescence   234
Female Anatomy and Culture   241
Other Aspects of the Maturing Female Body   245
Schools and Social Power   253
The Silencing of Young Women   255
Parent-Child Relationships   256
Factors Impeding Gender Equality   257
Working Together Toward Gender Equality   262
Connecting Themes   263
Suggested Readings   264

8. Sex, Love, and Romance   265

How Is Sexuality Shaped by Culture?   266
The Scientific Study of Sex   268
Adolescent Sexuality   271
Experiencing Sexuality   275
Sexuality in Social Context   279
Mixed Messages   287
Desire and Pleasure   290
Lesbian and Bisexual Women   295
Gender and Relationship Dynamics   302
What Do Women Want? Satisfaction in Close Relationships   305
Connecting Themes   306
Suggested Readings   307

9. Commitments: Women and
    Long-Term Relationships   308

Marriage   309
Lesbian Couples   324
Cohabiting Couples   328
Never-Married Women   331
Ending the Commitment: Divorce and Separation   333
Remarriage   340
Equality and Commitment: Are They Incompatible Ideals?   341
Connecting Themes   344
Suggested Readings   345

10. Mothering   346

Images of Mothers and Motherhood   347
The Decision to Have a Child   348
The Transition to Motherhood   363
The Event of Childbirth   370
Experiences of Mothering   378

The Future of Mothering   389
Connecting Themes   391
Suggested Readings   392

11. Work and Achievement   393

If She Isn't Paid, Is It Still Work?   394
Working Hard for a Living: Women in the Paid Workforce   402
Doing Gender in the Workplace   410
Women's Career Development: Are There Obstacles from Within?   419
Exceptional Work Lives   422
Putting It All Together: Work and Family   428
Woman, Work, and Social Policy: Models for Change   432
Connecting Themes   435
Suggested Readings   435

12. Midlife and Beyond   436

The Social Construction of Age   436
The Meanings of Midlife   444
Menopause   445
Role Transitions of Midlife and Later Life   457
Caregiver Roles in Later Life   466
Losses Associated with Aging   472
Psychological Well-Being in the Second Half of Life   474
Activism and Feminism among Older Women   477
Connecting Themes   480
Suggested Readings   480

13. Violence Against Women (by Jacquelyn Weygandt
     White, Barrie Bondurant, & Patricia L. N. Donat)   481

Commonalities Among All Forms of Violence Against Women   483
Childhood Sexual Abuse   485
Courtship Violence   491
Acquaintance Sexual Assault and Rape   495
Sexual Harassment   504
Wife Abuse   510
Conclusion   517
Connecting Themes   519
Suggested Readings   520

14. Mental and Physical Health   521

Gender and Psychological Disorders   522
Power Issues   528
Depression   530
The Social Construction of Female Disorders: The View from History   535

Eating Disorders   538
Issues in Treatment   543
Gender and Therapy   549
The Relationship Between Physical and Mental Health   560
Some Unresolved Issues   560
Connecting Themes   561
Suggested Readings   562

15.   Making a Difference: Toward a Better Future
      for Women   563

Transforming Gender   564
Transforming Language   568
Celebrating Diversity   570
Psychology and Social Change   571
Suggested Readings   573

REFERENCES   575

CREDITS   645

NAME INDEX   647

SUBJECT INDEX   658

Preface

We wrote this book to share our excitement about the psychology of women and gender. At the millennium, psychology is in the midst of a transformation into a more balanced and inclusive body of theory, research, and practice. Contemporary feminism has provided psychology with a wealth of new theoretical frameworks and scholarship. In turn, psychological research is being used to further social change to benefit girls and women. This is an exciting time for students to begin their study of women and gender, and an exciting time to be teaching in this dynamic field.

As *Women and Gender* enters its third edition, we feel more confident than ever that it is a thought-provoking and informative text that is also a great read. Through an ongoing process of dialogue with students and teachers who used the earlier editions, we have created a new edition that speaks to today's students without sacrificing the depth and nuance that instructors expect from us.

We believe in introducing students to a variety of perspectives. We try not to oversimplify research findings and social issues. Rather, we respect the intelligence of our student readers. Although many will be new to feminist concepts and psychological methods, all are capable of reasoned analysis. And we have found, along with other instructors who have used the earlier editions, that students appreciate a text that does not talk down to them. The issues are too important, and too complex, to be presented superficially.

We take up the issues students want to know about: media images, women and leadership, transgender activism, male-female differences, relationships, career success, sexuality, date rape, and eating disorders. Students are eager to discuss and debate these topics. We relate the most current and comprehensive research on each. Sometimes, we leave an issue open and unresolved, so the reader may use informed judgment to make up her or his own mind. Feminism has nothing to fear from critical thinking!

Even more than in the earlier editions, *Women and Gender* is grounded in a social constructionist perspective. In other words, we view gender not as an attribute of individuals but as a system of meanings in which we are all immersed. Furthermore, we regard psychology not as an abstract, decontextualized search for truth but a human enterprise shaped by culture. The social constructionist stance opens the way to critical analysis of popular culture, mass media, and everyday understandings of women and men. It also encourages critical analysis of why psychology chooses favored research topics, how it views women as objects of analysis, and how it has treated women in the profession, both historically and in the present.

The consistent social constructionist approach in this text makes it far more than just a compendium of research on sex differences or women's experiences. We draw on a huge variety of research using methods that range from case studies to surveys and experiments, and on theoretical perspectives from anthropology, sociology, and cultural studies, as well as psychology. Our social constructionist perspective organizes this wide-ranging knowledge and fosters the analysis of women and gender in their social, cultural, and historical context.

PLAN OF THE BOOK

Four themes organize this book:

- *Gender is more than just sex.* Gender is a system of meanings related to power and status. It operates at individual, interactional, and cultural levels to structure people's lives. We examine phenomena from each of these levels—individual, internalized aspects such as gender identity and gender typing; interactional aspects such as stereotypes, attributions, and self-fulfilling prophecies; and cultural aspects such as media representations, laws, and religious teachings.
- *Language and naming are sources of power.* Aspects of reality that are named become more visible. Regaining for women the power to name is the first step in personal and social change. We analyze gender bias in naming and language use, both in ordinary language (e.g., the "generic he") and in the specialized language of psychological constructs (e.g., "premenstrual syndrome"). We also show how ongoing language change is making women's experiences more visible. Thinking critically about language can increase understanding of how the gender system works and how it can be changed.
- *Women are not all alike.* Feminist scholars have become increasingly sensitive to the differences among women—in social class, ethnicity, age, sexual orientation, (dis)ability, and culture. Integrating diversity throughout each chapter of the book, we explore how these differences affect women's experiences, including gender socialization, adult relationships, and psychological distress and disorder.

We also make use of a great deal of cross-cultural data, reflecting the transformation of psychological knowledge from its formerly white, North American, middle-class perspective. In discussing cultural differences, we avoid the ethnocentric view that presents other societies as exotic or less developed. Instead we contextualize practices that may seem strange to North American students. This depth of interpretation is especially important when discussing controversial issues such as female genital surgery. Moreover, cross-cultural data provide powerful examples of our first theme, that gender is more than just biological sex. Even phenomena thought to have a strong biological base, such as menarche and menopause, are shaped by culture.

- *Psychological research can foster social change.* Students want more than just information about the problems confronting girls and women. They want to know what is being done to resolve them, and what might be done in the future. Without an emphasis on change, studying the psychology of women and gender could promote a sense of helplessness and pessimism. In every chapter of this text, there are powerful examples of people who have been agents of change.

  Many of the problems that confront girls and women today are the result of social structures that disadvantage them. While changes in individual attitudes and behaviors, traditionally a focus of psychological research and practice, are necessary, they must be linked with changes in societies as a whole. Psychological research and theory can point the way to progressive social change.

NEW IN THIS EDITION

- *Student friendliness.* Written by two active researchers, *Women and Gender* has always been notable for its scholarship. In this edition we have made it more student-friendly while sacrificing none of the authoritative research base that made the earlier editions so popular with instructors.
- *More effective text and chapter organization.* One result of our dual focus on student interest and scholarly depth is that we have developed a new order and organization of chapters. In previous editions, the first three chapters were largely theoretical, and students reported that they found it difficult to connect with the material until well into the book. Moreover, given the changing priorities of feminist psychology, we re-thought the amount of space we had devoted to traditional personality and trait theories. In this edition, the introductory chapter is more student-oriented, and it is immediately followed by a chapter on images of women, then by one on gender processes in social interaction, issues of direct and immediate importance to today's students. Theoretical approaches to personality are integrated into other chapters where relevant.
- *Emphasis on social change.* A third major revision in this edition is the increased emphasis on personal and social change. Although the use of psychological research to foster change has always been a theme of the book, we now make the connections between research and social policy more visible, and we highlight women and men who are agents of change. Each chapter contains a boxed feature, "Making a Difference," which describes one person's efforts to bring about social justice. These features, researched and written by Mykol Hamilton, Associate Professor of Psychology and Psychobiology at Centre College, are an exciting and unique addition to *Women and Gender,* providing models of feminist activism for the new millennium.

- *New and empowering final chapter.* The potential for feminist psychology to foster progressive social change is the focus of an all-new closing chapter. Earlier editions ended with the rather depressing topics of violence against women and psychological disorders, followed only by a short epilogue. The third edition ends by returning the focus to solutions. Chapter 15, "Making a Difference: Toward a Better Future for Women" shows students how psychology can be used outside the classroom and encourages them to become personally empowered to speak out for gender equality.

- *Expanded multicultural coverage.* The new edition expands the multicultural perspective of the previous editions by adding new findings about the interactions of ethnicity, sexual orientation, gender, and social class in women's lives.

- *More coverage of women's health.* Throughout the book there is much greater attention to women's health issues, reflecting the recent increase in research in this area. Rather than isolating health issues in a single chapter, we chose to stress the interaction of physical and psychological well-being, and their sociocultural specificity, by discussing health issues in context. For example, typical and atypical development of the female body is discussed in chapters 5, 7, and 12; reproductive health issues in Chapters 5, 7, 8, and 12; the physical and psychological effects of culturally sanctioned violence against girls and women in Chapters 8 and 13; eating disorders in Chapters 2 and 14; and the social construction of mental health and illness in Chapters 8, 10, 12, and 14.

This edition retains and expands successful features from earlier versions. Each of the four themes is woven throughout the book; each chapter ends with a summary of how the four themes are played out in that particular chapter. This allows students to trace the themes throughout the book and see their relevance across a wide range of topics. In Chapter 15, the themes are summarized and contextualized.

Every page has been revised and updated. There are nearly 600 new references to recent research. The text has more (and livelier) illustrations, boxes, and cartoons. And we have reduced the number of chapters to fifteen for a better fit to semester calendars.

NEW COVERAGE IN EACH CHAPTER

Instructors are invited to take a look at the complete table of contents to see how comprehensive our coverage is. Here, we would just like to point out a few new areas of emphasis in each chapter.

Chapter 1. With its focus on issues relevant to diverse students, Chapter 1 is an engaging introduction to the field. New is expanded coverage of a variety of feminist perspectives, which are contrasted to conservative perspectives on women and gender.

Chapter 2, *Images of Women and Men,* has always been a student favorite. In this new edition issues of high salience to students—gender stereotypes in the mass media, the problematic aspects of women's quest for beauty and their conformity to impossible standards of weight, and new forms of sexism such as covert and ambivalent sexism—are presented earlier, sparking student involvement from the start. New topics include how images of women are nuanced by race and class and how perceptions of being objectified influence women's behavior. Many new illustrations and thought-provoking cartoons are included.

Chapter 3, *Doing Gender,* unique to our text, shows how the belief that women and men are (and should be) fundamentally different is created and sustained in ordinary interaction through such processes as selective attention, selective memory, and self-fulfilling prophecies. In this edition, we look at new studies on perceptions of entitlement, leadership, and legitimacy and how to move beyond the "double bind."

Chapter 4, *The Meanings of Difference,* is new to this edition, replacing Chapter 3 of the earlier editions, which focused on gender differences in cognitive abilities. Students found the earlier chapter too detailed, and we came to agree that the topic no longer warranted the amount of coverage we had given it. Instead, the new chapter asks more general questions about gender differences and similarities and answers them in terms of contrasting feminist perspectives. The debate over gender differences in cognition and personality is connected to current societal issues such as women's under-representation in math and science careers.

Chapter 5, *Biological Bases of Sex,* is the most sophisticated and nuanced discussion of this topic available to students. In this new edition, we critically review recent studies suggesting a genetic basis for sexual orientation as well as new research on the many biological factors that influence human sex. Intersex and transgendered individuals are discussed from ethical as well as scientific perspectives. Finally, there is an increased emphasis on the contribution of culture in determining how sex leads to gender.

Chapter 6, *Becoming Gendered: Childhood,* now includes a synthesis of theoretical and empirical work on the social construction of gender before birth and throughout childhood. New material examines tomboys as examples of gender nonconformity and little girls who participate in beauty pageants as examples of hyperfemininity. New topics include the gendering of emotion, the antecedents of gender flexibility, and how gender segregation in children contributes to the development of male dominance. This chapter integrates cutting edge information on cognitive processes and social interaction.

Chapter 7, *Becoming a Woman: Puberty and Adolescence,* includes new material on the experience of adolescent girls as they encounter their changing bodies and boys' and mens' response to their sexual maturation. We focus on how ethnicity and class interact with situational context to influence girls' response to puberty. New topics include schools and social power, the role of peer culture, and the silencing of young women. The chapter concludes with a discussion of the factors that impede gender equality.

Chapter 8, *Sex, Love, and Romance,* formerly Chapter 9, is another student favorite, with in-depth coverage of the cultural construction of sexual desire, romance, and norms for sexual behavior. New to this edition is coverage of adolescent sexuality, including factors influencing the initiation of sexual activity; safe sex, contraception, and STDs among teens; and the silencing of female desire. Also new is a discussion of female genital surgery in cross-cultural perspective. As in earlier editions, there is comprehensive coverage of lesbian and bisexual women's issues.

Chapter 9, *Commitments: Women and Long-Term Relationships,* updates its survey of heterosexual marriage, cohabitation, divorce, lesbian relationships, and other life patterns for women. Current statistics on these life paths in our own and other societies, as well as new and emerging relationship types such as egalitarian marriage, are presented.

Chapter 10, *Mothering,* expands its analysis of the diverse experiences of women who mother with new sections on teen mothers and single mothers. Another new section, "Is Fathering a Feminist Issue?" discusses the role of fathers in children's development and the changes in social policy needed to encourage responsible fatherhood.

Chapter 11, *Work and Achievement,* reflects the rapid change in women's work roles. The unpaid work of women in their homes is acknowledged, and the domain of employment is analyzed for gender inequality as well as opportunity. A new section, "Leadership: Do Women Do It Differently?" discusses recent research on factors affecting leadership style and effectiveness. The chapter ends with a synthesis of the costs and benefits of juggling work, relationships, and family.

Chapter 12, *Midlife and Beyond,* continues to emphasize the social construction of age and aging. It contains new material on the cultural context and complexity of midlife transitions and how structural factors (past and present) keep many older women in poverty. The chapter concludes with a positive focus on psychological well-being in later life, with new information on sexuality, friendship and social support, and activism and feminism among older women.

Chapter 13, *Violence Against Women,* written especially for this book by Jacquelyn White, Barrie Bondurant, and Patricia Donat, is organized around a model that identifies the commonalities among the various forms of violence against women: child sexual abuse, dating violence, sexual assault, and wife abuse. Its developmental contextual perspective views violence against women as occurring in a sociocultural context that supports male control of women. New to this edition is a discussion of sexual harassment in varied settings. The controversial topics miscommunication and date rape and false memory syndrome are addressed. Most important, there is a wealth of information on what is being done to stop violence against girls and women.

Chapter 14, *Mental and Physical Health,* has a new emphasis on the relationship between physical and psychological health. The section on eating disorders has been expanded to include prejudice and discrimination against overweight women and an examination of the ethnic and class distribution of various eating disorders. An expanded section on feminist therapy discusses the feminist critique of traditional treatment methods, the difference between nonsexist and feminist therapy, issues in therapy with marginalized populations, and the role of culture in the way distress is expressed.

Chapter 15, *Making a Difference: Toward a Better Future for Women,* is new to this edition. Feedback from students and instructors, and our own experience of teaching from the earlier editions, convinced us of the importance of ending a course in the psychology of women and gender with a positive synthesis of the gains that feminist psychology has brought. The new chapter speaks to students about both personal and social change as a result of their involvement in feminist psychology.

At the personal level, Chapter 15 encourages students to continue learning and to expand their knowledge of the psychology of women. It discusses research on the personal changes that occur in students' attitudes toward women, self-esteem, and feminist identity as a result of studying the psychology of women. It acknowledges and encourages increased personal empowerment for students.

At the societal level, Chapter 15 shows students how psychology can be used outside the classroom. It ties together the "Making a Difference" features from earlier chapters and discusses third wave feminism—the work of today's young activists. With examples of successful activism, it demonstrates how much society has changed in response to the first two waves of the women's movement. We are excited about this all-new synthesis and eager to hear feedback about it from our next generation of students and instructors.

USING THIS BOOK

Women and Gender contains a great deal of information and a sophisticated analysis of the field. However, as the wide adoption of the earlier editions at very diverse institutions shows, it is an approachable book. The third edition is even more user-friendly. It can be read by people who have the equivalent of one course in psychology and no previous exposure to women's studies. Students find the wealth of women's own accounts of their experiences compelling. And they like the touches of humor that lighten serious issues.

The book can be used in either a chronological developmental sequence, in social/clinical clusters, or in groupings of topical issues. Each chapter can stand as a unit by itself, allowing maximum flexibility in combining them. Chapters 5–7, 9–10, and 12 have a developmental approach that covers the life span. Chapters 2, 3, and 11 are social psychologically oriented, and Chapters 4, 8, and 14 form a clinical/personality cluster.

SUPPLEMENTS

In our own teaching, we also use *In Our Own Words,* (McGraw-Hill, 1997), a reader we developed specifically to connect the psychological research and theory in textbooks like our own with the voices and experiences of diverse girls and women. *In Our Own Words* is a collection of short (2–20 pages) essays, each with a distinctive personal voice. Some are humorous (Gloria Steinem's "If Men Could Menstruate"), some are poignant (Anna Quindlen's "Birthday Girl"), and all are memorable.

In Our Own Words is organized into six sections: *Making Our Voices Heard; The Making of a Woman: Bodies, Power, and Society; Making Meaning; Making a Living: Women, Work, and Achievement; Making Connections;* and *Making Our Lifepaths.* A section of 5–7 readings and their associated two-page introduction can be read along with a textbook chapter. For example, the section on bodies, power, and society nicely complements the *Women and Gender* chapters on Images of Women or Sex, Love, and Romance. Or, students can write brief reaction papers on selections of their choice. *In Our Own Words* provides a stimulus for student interest and class discussion and an experiential counterpoint to research.

The Instructor's Manual for the new edition, prepared by Mykol Hamilton with Michelle Broaddus, continues our tradition of providing the best teaching resources in the field. It features test items (multiple choice, short-answer, and essay), current video listings, classroom demonstrations and other techniques for stimulating active involvement, sample syllabi, suggestions for using worldwide web resources, course evaluation forms, ideas for integrating additional readings, and much more. Contact your McGraw-Hill representative for further information about supplements that accompany this text.

ACKNOWLEDGMENTS

Like the previous editions, this book came about with the help of colleagues and friends. Jackie White, Barrie Bondurant, and Patricia Donat contributed a compelling chapter on violence against girls and women to each edition. We are grateful to have their expertise on this vitally important topic. Mykol Hamilton contributed not only the Instructor's Manual but the "Making a Difference" feature. We are grateful to Mykol for taking on these sizable tasks. Her superb work will make teaching easier and more rewarding for instructors who choose our book.

We thank Nicole Dolat, of the University of Connecticut Psychology Department staff, and Chris Luberto, Women's Studies staff, for cheerful and skilled help with manuscript preparation; graduate students Julie Konik, Miriam Liss, Jessica Suckle, and Angela Walker and undergraduate intern Anne Levin, for help with library research. Special thanks go to our editors at McGraw-Hill: Jane Vaicunas, Beth Kaufman, and Terri Wise, along with project manager Jayne Klein and photo editor Connie Gardner.

We wish to thank all the instructors and students around the U.S., the U.K., and Canada who so generously gave us feedback on the first two editions. We thank, too, the reviewers for the third edition: Melanie Williams, Humboldt State University; Renee Saris, Ball State University; Ellen G. Friedman, The College of New Jersey; Joan C. Chrisler, Connecticut College; Cindy Ann Hall, The University of Otago; Stephanie Riger, University of Illinois at Chicago; Judi Addelston, Rollins College; Millie Whalen, East Stroudsburg University; Nita McKinley, Allegheny College; Eva Clark, Old Dominion University; and Chieh-Chen Bowen, Cleveland State University.

We consider this book to be truly a collaborative effort. Our respective partners, Roger Chaffin and Burt Unger, have by now put in decades of effort in support of our research and writing, ranging from diaper-changing to computer problem-solving. Their belief in the value of our work and their tangible support has sustained us through the tough spots. Our children, colleagues, students and friends, too, should know that this book would not exist without your cooperation. We are grateful for the network of support that makes our work possible.

Mary Crawford
Rhoda Unger

Introduction to a Feminist Psychology of Women

- **BEGINNINGS**
  How Did Feminist Psychology Get
    Started?
  Has the Women's Movement Affected
    Psychology?
  Voices from the Margins: A History
- **WHAT IS FEMINISM?**
  Feminism Has Many Meanings
  Is There a Simple Definition?
  The Backlash against Feminism
- **METHODS AND VALUES IN SCIENTIFIC
  INQUIRY**

  Toward Nonsexist Research
  Feminist Values in Research
- **THEMES OF THIS BOOK**
  Theme 1: Gender Is More Than Just
    Sex
  Theme 2: Language and Naming Are
    Sources of Power
  Theme 3: Women Are Not All Alike
  Theme 4: Psychological Research Can
    Foster Social Change
- **OUR GOALS FOR OUR STUDENTS**
- **SUGGESTED READINGS**

Consider the following facts and events from the past decade:

- After more than 200 years of U.S. democracy, only 9 percent of U.S. senators and 11 percent of members of Congress are women.
- In Massachusetts, the Back Bay Brewing Company sells "Boston Strangler Stout"—a beer named for a serial killer who raped and murdered thirteen women.
- In the United States, women earn about seventy-four cents for every dollar earned by men.
- On television news, 97 percent of the anchors over the age of 40 are men.
- The United Nations estimates that 100 million women worldwide are missing from the population—dead because, as females, they were unwanted.
- A judge in Rome, Italy, rules against the victim in a rape case on the grounds that it is impossible to rape a woman wearing jeans, because they cannot be removed without her cooperation. In protest, women worldwide stage a "skirt strike," wearing jeans to work.
- One in four U.S. college students believe that the activities of married women should be limited to home and family (down from one in two in 1970).
- The Reverend Jerry Falwell claims that a popular children's toy, the "Tinky Winky Teletubby," is an attempt to make children into homosexuals because it is purple and carries a "purse."

- Women have been heads of state in twenty-three countries around the world, yet in others they lack basic human rights such as voting and going to school.
- Women remain far more likely than men to suffer from serious depression and eating disorders.
- Less than 5 percent of the artists in New York's Metropolitan Museum collections are women, but 85 percent of the nude paintings are of females.
- Mattel Corporation introduces "Butterfly Art Barbie," complete with bikini top, miniskirt, and stomach tattoo, at the same time as "Working Woman Barbie," with a play laptop and cell phone.
- The U.S. public is bombarded with publicity about the Clarence Thomas–Anita Hill hearings, the trial of O. J. Simpson for the murder of Nicole Brown Simpson, the Lorena Bobbit case, the roles of women and gays in the military, the Mitsubishi sexual harassment settlement, the Tailhook scandal, and the Clinton–Lewinsky affair.

What do these facts and events, some of them trivial, some very serious, have in common? Today, ideas about women's roles and the meaning of gender are the subjects of heated debate. Although some things have changed for the better, equality has not yet been achieved. A worldwide wage gap, underrepresentation of women in positions of status and power, and significant problems of violence against girls and women persist. Competing images of femininity abound. Gender, sexuality, and power are at the core of social controversies around the world.

BEGINNINGS

We are living in an era in which nothing about women, sexuality, and gender seems certain. Entering this arena of change, a new branch of psychology has developed research and theory about women and gender. The new branch is a form of *critical psychology*—it questions and challenges the moral, political, and scientific claims of psychology and tries to influence the direction of the field as a whole (Fox & Prilleltensky, 1997). It is usually called *feminist psychology,* the *psychology of women,* or the *psychology of gender* (Russo & Dumont, 1997; Unger, 1998). Those who use the term "feminist psychology" tend to emphasize theoretical connections to women's studies. Those who use "psychology of women" tend to focus on women's lives and experiences as the subject matter. Those who use "psychology of gender" tend to focus on the social and biological processes that create gender differences. In this book, we include all these perspectives, inviting you to explore the social structures that create and maintain gender and give rise to the experiences of girls and women.

How Did Feminist Psychology Get Started?

As the women's movement of the late 1960s made women and gender a central social concern, the field of psychology began to examine the stereotypical thinking and bias that had characterized its knowledge about women. The more closely psychologists began to look at the ways psychology had thought about women, the more problems they saw. They began to realize that women had been left out of many studies. Even worse, theories were constructed from a male-as-norm viewpoint, and women's behavior was explained as a deviation from the male standard. Often, stereotypes of women were unquestioned or considered to be an accurate portrayal of women's behavior. Good psychological adjustment for women was defined in terms of fitting in to gender norms. When women behaved differently from men, the differences were likely to be attributed to biology, instead of social influences (Crawford & Marecek, 1989; Kahn & Jean, 1983; Unger, 1979b).

These problems, though not universal, were very widespread. Psychologists began to realize that most psychological knowledge about women and gender was *androcentric, or male-centered.* They began to rethink psychological concepts and methods and to produce new research with women as the focus of study. Moreover, they began to study topics of importance and concern to women and to develop ways of analyzing social relations between women and men. As a result, psychology has developed new ways of thinking about women, expanded its research methods, and developed new approaches to therapy and counseling.

Women within psychology were a very important force for change. They published many books and articles showing how psychology was misrepresenting women and how it needed to change. One of the first was Naomi Weisstein (1968), who declared that psychology had nothing to say about what women are really like, what they need, and what they want because psychology did not know. Another was Phyllis Chesler, whose book *Women and Madness* (1972) claimed that psychology and psychiatry were used to control women.

Here are a few more examples of the strong critical voices of women who helped develop the new feminist psychology:

Carolyn Sherif, 1964: "Ignorance about women pervades academic disciplines in higher education, where the requirements for the degree seldom include thoughtful inquiry into the status of women, as part of the total human condition." (cited in Sherif, 1979, p. 93)

Mary Parlee, 1975: "The academic discipline (of psychology) . . . has distorted facts, omitted problems, and perpetuated pseudoscientific data relevant to women. Until recently, the body of 'knowledge' developed by academic psychologists happened (apparently) to support stereotyped beliefs about the abilities and psychological characteristics of women and men, and such beliefs happen to support existing political, legal, and economic inequalities between the sexes." (p. 124)

Kathleen Grady, 1981: "The promise of science cannot be realized if . . . certain questions are never asked, or they are asked of the wrong people and in the wrong way, or they are not published because they do not fit accepted theories." (p. 629)

Michelle Fine, 1985: "Women who represent racial and ethnic minorities, working-class and poor women, and disabled women and lesbians, need to be involved in [psychological] research. The lives of these women need to be integrated into this literature, and the assumptions of psychological theories based on white middle-class experiences and beliefs that all persons are (should be?) heterosexual and nondisabled must be challenged." (p. 178)

Rachel Hare-Mustin and Jeanne Marecek, 1990: "We find it curious that psychological thought is still heavily influenced by such nineteenth-century theorists as Darwin, Marx, and Freud. As products of their era, they were primarily supportive of the status quo, of upper-class white male privilege with its limited knowledge of and marginal concern for women. If they were alive today, they would be astonished: What? You are still using those old books? Throw them away." (p. 189)

The growth of feminist psychology can be seen in the number of psychology departments offering courses in the psychology of women or gender. Before 1968, there were virtually none. A recent survey that received responses from 503 psychology departments found that 51 percent listed undergraduate courses in the psychology of women. By 1990, 172 such courses were being taught at the graduate level in colleges and universities in the United States (Women's Programs Office, 1991). Psychology of women courses are often connected to, and have contributed to, the rapid growth of women's studies programs, which began about 1970. Only twenty years later, in 1990, the National Women's Studies Association reported 623 women's studies programs in the United States.

The growth of feminist perspectives can also be seen in the topics of published articles in psychology. In 1974, there was not a single journal article on achievement in women; in 1993, there were 161. Similar growth has occurred for many other topics, including rape and sexual assault, sexual harassment, and feminist therapy (Worell, 1996).

The new field has its own journals focusing on the psychology of women or gender: for example, *Sex Roles*, which began publishing in 1975; *Psychology of Women Quarterly*, published since 1977; and *Feminism & Psychology*, a more recent addition from England.

The new psychology of women and gender is rich and varied. Virtually every intellectual framework from Freudian theory to cognitive psychology has been used in developing new theories and approaches, and virtually every area of psychology, from developmental to social, has been affected by its critical analysis (Crawford & Marecek, 1989; Wilkinson, 1997a, 1997b). This book is an invitation to explore the knowledge and participate in the ongoing debates of the new feminist psychology.

Has the Women's Movement Affected Psychology?

The emergence of interest in women and gender took place in a social context of changing roles for women and the emergence of a feminist social movement in the late 1960s. Questioning psychology's representation of women was very much part of the more general questioning of "women's place" encouraged and led by women's liberation activists.

The women's movement of this era was not the first. A previous women's rights movement had reached its peak more than a hundred years earlier with the Seneca Falls Declaration of 1848, which explicitly rejected the doctrine of female inferiority then taught by academics and clergy (Harris, 1984). However, the women's movement lost momentum in the 1920s, after women had won the vote, because women believed that voting would lead to political, social, and economic equality. Psychology's interest in sex differences and gender waned. The area did not become a major part of psychology's research agenda until a social context of feminist activism again arose.

With the rebirth of the women's movement in the 1960s and with widespread voicing of feminist concerns once again a social force, researchers again became interested in the study of women and gender. Women psychologists and men who supported their goals also began to work toward an improved status for women within the field of psychology. Feminist activism made a big difference for women of this era, who had been openly discriminated against (Unger, 1998). One psychologist, Carolyn Sherif, remembered it this way:

> To me, the atmosphere created by the women's movement was like breathing fresh air after years of gasping for breath. . . . I did not become a significantly better social psychologist between 1969 and 1972, but I surely was treated as a better social psychologist. (Sherif, 1983, p. 280)

Activists—mostly graduate students and newcomers to psychology—formed the Association for Women in Psychology (AWP) in 1969. At about the same time, others—mostly older, more established psychologists—lobbied the American Psychological Association (APA) to form a Division of the Psychology of Women (Unger, 1998). This Division 35 was officially approved in 1973. The courage and vision of those who pioneered the inclusion of women in psychology has built a legacy of effectiveness. AWP continues to thrive as an activist organization with no formal ties to the psychological establishment. Division 35 is now one of the larger divisions of APA, with more than 6,000 members, a more than sixfold increase in two decades (Russo & Dumont, 1997). A recent division president, Janet Hyde, noted, "This division has an exceptional record of getting things done, which is all the more remarkable because many of the things we want to get done are revolutionary and therefore prone to meet with resistance" (cited in Russo & Dumont, 1997, p. 212).

Divisions on ethnic minority psychology and gay/lesbian issues were established later, with the support of Division 35. Progress in incorporating women has also occurred among Canadian psychologists (Parlee, 1985) and the British Psychological Society, where there is now a Psychology of Women Section (Wilkinson, 1997a). These organizational changes have acknowledged the presence of diverse women in psychology and helped enhance their professional identity (Scarborough & Furumoto, 1987). And none too soon—women now earn 60 percent of Ph.D.s awarded in psychology (*Trends in Education*, 1995).

Voices from the Margins: A History

Throughout the history of psychology, there had been criticism of psychology's treatment of women and people of color, most often voiced by members of those groups. As early as 1876, Mary Putman Jacobi had completed a Harvard dissertation challenging the idea that women required special mental and bodily rest during menstruation. Jacobi noted that those who studied the supposed limitations of women were, like those who studied the supposed inferiority of people of color, hardly ever women or people of color themselves, and were very often quick to ascribe differences to nature or biology (cited in Sherif, 1979).

Robert Guthrie's book *Even the Rat Was White* (Guthrie, 1976) examined the history of racism in psychology and anthropology and documented the contributions of early African-American and Mexican-American psychologists in providing less biased views of human nature. In the early 1900s, some of the first scientifically trained women devoted much research effort to challenging accepted wisdom about the extent and nature of sex differences. Helen Thompson Wooley conducted the first experimental laboratory study of sex differences in mental traits, using a variety of innovative measures. In interpreting her results, she stressed the overall similarity of the sexes and the environmental determinants of observed differences, remarking daringly in a 1910 *Psychological Bulletin* article: "There is perhaps no field aspiring to be scientific where flagrant personal bias, logic martyred in the cause of supporting a prejudice, unfounded assertions, and even sentimental rot and drivel, have run riot to such an extent as here" (Wooley, 1910, p. 340). Among the women inspired by her work was Leta Stetter Hollingworth, who challenged the Darwinian view that women are innately less variable (and therefore less likely to be highly creative or intelligent) (Shields, 1982).

The work of a few early women psychologists opened the way for critical empirical research to replace unexamined assumptions about women's "natural" limitations (Rosenberg, 1982). Determined to demonstrate women's capacity to contribute to modern science on an equal basis with men, they chose to measure sex differences in order to challenge beliefs about women's limitations. In a sense, their research interests were dictated by questions chosen by others. Faced with the necessity of proving their very right to do research, these women labored to refute hypotheses that they themselves did not find credible and that they did not believe could account for the inferior social position of women (Unger, 1979a). Moreover, they worked in a social context that denied them opportunities because of their sex and forced them to make cruel choices between work and family relationships (Scarborough & Furumoto, 1987). Their story is one,

> in many ways, of failure—of women restricted by simple prejudice to the periphery of academe, who never had access to the professional chairs of the major universities, who never commanded the funds to direct large-scale research, who never trained the graduate students who might have spread their influence, and who, by the 1920s, no longer had the galvanizing support of a woman's movement to give political effect to their ideas. (Rosenberg, 1982, p. xxi)

The challenges to psychology to develop knowledge about all humanity have been present throughout psychology's history. However, the efforts of women and minorities remained voices from the margins until recently. The existence of AWP, Division 35, women's studies programs, and dozens of feminist journals make it unlikely that interest in the psychology of women and gender will fade away as it did in the 1920s. Because this new psychology so clearly has developed in a social context of feminism, it is important to look closely at the relationship between the two.

WHAT IS FEMINISM?

The writer Rebecca West noted in 1913: "I myself have never been able to find out precisely what feminism is: I only know that people call me a feminist whenever I express sentiments that differentiate me from a doormat" (quoted in Kramarae & Treichler, 1985, p. 160). Exactly what is feminism and what does it mean to call oneself a feminist?

Feminism Has Many Meanings

Contemporary feminist theory has many variants (Tong, 1998). Each can be thought of as a different lens through which to view the experiences of women, and, like different lenses, each is useful for focusing perception on particular phenomena. The diversity of feminist perspectives means that different feminists take different positions on women's issues.

What are the most influential feminist theoretical perspectives? In the United States, they include liberal, radical, socialist, womanist (woman of color), and cultural feminism. Belief in these different branches of feminism has been defined, reliably measured, and shown to predict people's behavior (Henley et al., 1998). Let's look briefly at each.

Socialist feminism emphasizes that there are many kinds of divisions between groups of people that can lead to oppression. Socialist feminists believe that discrimination based on social class, race, and gender are equally wrong. Moreover, it views them as inseparable: sexism, racism, and classism reinforce each other, so that, for example, a poor woman of color is triply disadvantaged. This book presents many examples of relationships among different kinds of disadvantage, from teen mothers (Chapter 10) to social class differences in gender-role learning during childhood and adolescence (Chapters 6 and 7).

Woman of color feminism (womanism) began with criticism of the white women's movement for excluding women of color and the issues important to them: poverty, racism, and needs such as jobs, health care, good schools, and safe neighborhoods for all people. Asian-American, Hispanic, and African-American women and men who are activists often choose to join forces with each other to fight racism and classism, even though the women are aware of their oppression as women (Chow, 1996). In general, women of color do not see men of color as sexist oppressors but as brothers who suffer the effects of racism just as they themselves do. People who adopt this feminist perspective often point out the strengths and positive values of minority communities. For example, African-American family patterns emphasize multigenerational support and closeness (Chapters 10 and 12).

Radical feminism emphasizes male control and domination of women throughout history. This perspective views the control of women by men as the first and most fundamental form of oppression: women as a group are oppressed, not by their biology or their social class, but by men as a group. According to radical feminists, sexist oppression is one thing all women have in common. Radical feminist theory has fostered much research on violence against women and on sexuality, seeking to understand the sources of males' greater power and to examine its consequences (Chapters 8 and 13).

Liberal feminism is familiar to most people because it relies on deeply held American beliefs about equality—an orientation that connects it to political liberalism. From this perspective, a feminist is a person who believes that women are entitled to full legal and social equality with men, and who favors changes in laws, customs, and values to achieve the goal of equality. This perspective has been especially useful in encouraging research on such topics as how people react to others when they violate gender norms (Chapter 3), gender socialization (Chapter 6), and sex discrimination in employment (Chapter 11). It emphasizes the similarities between males and females, maintaining that given equal environments and opportunities they will behave similarly.

Cultural feminism emphasizes differences between women and men. This perspective stresses that qualities characteristic of women have been devalued and should be honored and respected in society. Cultural feminism has been useful in understanding the importance of unpaid work contributed to society by women, such as child care (Chapter 11). It is often used in discussing gender differences in values and social behaviors—for example, the apparent tendency for women to be more nurturing, caring, and oriented toward others' needs.

The diversity of frameworks and values in feminist thought may seem to be a source of confusion, but it is also healthy and productive. The lenses of different feminist perspectives can be used to develop and compare a variety of viewpoints on women's experiences. In writing this book, we have drawn on a variety of feminist perspectives, using the lens of each as we thought it would help clarify a particular topic, sometimes comparing several feminist perspectives on an issue. However, within psychology, liberal and cultural feminism have been more influential and generated more debate and research than any other views. Therefore, Chapter 4 is devoted to contrasting liberal and cultural feminist perspectives on the question, "Just how different are women and men?"

Is There a Simple Definition?

Because of the plurality of definitions and viewpoints, it is perhaps more appropriate to speak of feminisms than feminism. However, feminist perspectives have two important themes in common, and these define feminism in its most general sense. First, feminism places a high value on women. Women are considered important and worthwhile human beings. (For feminist scholars, this means that women are worthy of study in their own right.) Second, feminism recognizes the need for social change if women are to lead secure and satisfying lives. Perhaps the simplest definition of a feminist is an individual who holds these basic beliefs: that women are valuable and that social change to benefit women is needed. The core social change that feminists advocate is an end to all forms of domination, those of men over women and those among women (Kimball, 1995). Therefore, perhaps the simplest definition of feminism is one proposed by bell hooks (1984): It is a movement to end sexism and sexist oppression. These broad definitions allow feminists to work for political change together, while recognizing that ideas about how to reach their goals may differ.

Can men be feminists? Certainly! It should be clear that men can hold the values we have described as feminist; they can value women as worthwhile human beings and work for social change to reduce sexism and sex discrimination. Some men who share these values call themselves feminists. Others prefer to use *profeminist*, believing that this term acknowledges women's leadership of the feminist movement and expresses their understanding that women and men have different experiences of gender. Men, like women, take many different routes to becoming feminist (McLean, Carey, & White, 1996; Stoltenberg, 1989).

Feminist perspectives in general can be contrasted to **conservatism** (Henley et al., 1998). Conservatives seek to keep gender arrangements as they have been in much of the recent past, with males holding more public power and status and women being more or less restricted to home and family. The conservative view has usually been justified on the grounds of biology or religion. The biological justification states that gender-related behaviors are determined by innate and unchangeable biological differences far more than by social conditions. Therefore, women should not be encouraged to try to do things that go against their "nature." For example, if women are biologically destined to be more nurturing due to the fact that they are the sex that gives birth, it is unnatural and wrong for women to limit their childbearing or take on jobs that do not involve nurturing others. The religious justification (often combined with the biological justification) is that female submission and subordination are ordained by a supreme being. For example, some religions teach that women must be obedient to their husbands; others forbid contraception or grant the right to divorce only to men. In the United States the Southern Baptist sect recently created controversy by urging a return to female submission (see Figure 1.1).

Negative attitudes and values about women as a group constitute the form

FIGURE 1.1. Conservative ideas about women are controversial.
Source: Copyright © 1998, The Boston Globe. Distributed by the Los Angeles Times Syndicate. Reprinted by permission.

of prejudice known as *sexism*. Sexist attitudes may lead to sexist behavior, or *sex discrimination*. Over the past thirty years, attitudes toward women have grown less conservative and more liberal. Women have been more liberal than men all along, but this gender difference has decreased in the past decade as men's attitudes have moved in the direction of women's (Twenge, 1997). However, more subtle forms of sexism have emerged (see Chapter 2).

The Backlash against Feminism

Feminism, like other movements for social justice, has often met with resistance. Feminism and conservatism are in opposition, and proponents of each perspective try to gain power and influence for their views.

Each time that feminist perspectives have gained power, there has been a *backlash*—attempts to put women and feminists "back in their place" (Faludi, 1991). The backlash has taken different forms at different times in history, but some characteristic patterns seem to emerge repeatedly. These include stereotyping feminists and their ideas as crazy, outrageous, or trivial; insisting on immutable differences created by God or Nature that make social change impossible; and characterizing feminism as a mere quarrel among women. Let's look more closely at each of these forms of backlash.

Negative Stereotypes of Feminists

When women began organizing to win the right to vote, political cartoonists depicted them in ways that will seem very familiar today. Figure 1.2 shows suffragists as ugly, cigar-smoking, angry women who foist their babies off on men. Their uncontrolled sexuality is represented by the women whose legs are exposed. The text tells us that they are brassy, sharp-tongued man-tamers.

In the 1970s, these stereotypes resurfaced. The image of the feminist circa 1975 was quite negative:

> The moment the women's movement emerged in 1970, feminism once again became a dirty word, with considerable help from the mainstream news media. News reports and opinion columnists created a new stereotype, of fanatics, "braless bubbleheads," Amazons, "the angries," and "a band of wild lesbians." The result is that we all know what feminists are. They are shrill, overly aggressive, man-hating, ball-busting, selfish, hairy, extremist, deliberately unattractive women with absolutely no sense of humor who see sexism at every turn. They make men's testicles shrivel up to the size of peas, they detest the family and think all children should be deported or drowned. Feminists are relentless, unforgiving, and unwilling to bend or compromise; they are single-handedly responsible for the high divorce rate, the shortage of decent men and the unfortunate proliferation of Birkenstocks in America (Douglas, 1994: 7).

By the 1980s, at least some women had made some gains toward equality. The media then turned to declaring feminism outdated, claiming that equal rights have been fully achieved, society is now in a "postfeminist" era, and women are abandoning feminism because it has proved to have terrible costs. In the 1980s version of backlash, everything from infertility to the breakdown of society was blamed on feminism (Faludi, 1991).

Today, the stereotype of feminists has both positive and negative aspects.

Most women do not hold negative views of feminists or see them as unhappy misfits, but generally have a supportive opinion of feminism and the women's movement (Renzetti, 1987). College women describe feminists as strong, caring, capable, open-minded, knowledgeable, and intelligent (Berryman-Fink & Verderber, 1985; Buhl, 1989). On the other hand, being labeled "feminist" clearly holds a certain stigma (see Figure 1.3). In a recent study, women made less positive statements about the "feminist" movement than about the "women's" movement, demonstrating that simply adding the "f-word" (feminist) causes people to think more negatively about a group (Buschman & Lenart, 1996). In an analysis of connotations of the word *feminist*, two views emerged: the positive view encompassed women working together to achieve goals, and the negative view encompassed perceptions of man-hating, masculine-appearing extremists (Alexander & Ryan, 1997). Conservative commentators play to this negative view with terms like "PC" and "feminazis" and by characterizing any criticism of the status quo as "male-bashing" (see Figure 1.4).

Despite attempts to discredit the goals of the women's movement, the majority of women endorse many of these goals. However, they are very reluctant to label themselves feminists. In a recent study, 63 percent of women did not label themselves as feminists but supported feminist goals (Williams & Wittig, 1997). Negative stereotypes seem to have done their work—women

FIGURE 1.2. An early example of backlash.
Source: Collection of The New-York Historical Society.

FIGURE 1.3.
Source: Stone Soup © 1999 Jan Eliot/Dist. by Universal Press Synd. Reprinted with permission.

who support gender justice seem to be quite aware that "feminist" also connotes an angry woman who hates men, and "feminism" connotes an outdated ideology that is no longer necessary and possibly destructive. Gender stereotypes and their effects are further discussed in Chapter 2.

Insisting on Differences

> If combat means living in a ditch, females have biological problems staying in a ditch for 30 days because they get infections and they don't have upper body strength. . . . On the other hand, men are basically little piglets. You drop them in the ditch, they roll around in it, it doesn't matter.

These words were spoken by the former Speaker of the House of Representatives, Newt Gingrich, in 1995. Although it is disturbing that a person in high public office could profess such a simplistic stereotype (one that is demeaning to both sexes), it is not surprising. The more women accomplish in realms formerly closed to them, the more loudly it is proclaimed that they cannot and should not be doing what they are doing. Today, women are astronauts, combat soldiers, coal miners, Supreme Court justices, great artists and musicians, and Nobel Prize–winning scientists, all the while continuing the traditional work of women: bearing and rearing children and caring for the

FIGURE 1.4. Responding to the backlash.
Source: © 1992 by Nicole Hollander. Used by permission of Nicole Hollander.

needs of others. Yet theories and studies that purport to show that women are biologically inferior continue to receive press coverage and are used to justify women's disadvantaged status in society. Throughout this book we will critically examine theories and research claiming that women's minds (Chapter 4), brains (Chapters 4 and 5), and bodies (Chapters 7, 12, and 14) are so different from men's that women are incapable of equal achievements.

Women Against Women: Feminism as a Cat Fight

One of the ways that feminists and their ideas are trivialized is to portray women as fighting with each other (Douglas, 1994). Any woman who attacks the ideals and practices of feminism is almost guaranteed a hearing in the news media. It is even better if she claims to be a feminist, and it seems to matter little if her expertise on the issues is minimal. This prevents male social theorists and political analysts from having to study and consider feminist ideas themselves and allows them to claim that sensible women see through feminism and reject it.

In the 1970s, the media ignored the many groups of women working collectively for women's rights and the opposition they encountered from those in power. Instead, they focused on Gloria Steinem, an attractive feminist journalist and activist, versus Phyllis Schlafly, a conservative activist who called feminists a "bunch of bitter women seeking a constitutional cure for their personal problems." The debate over the Equal Rights Amendment to the U.S. Constitution was described, not as women versus entrenched male power, but as "women versus women." A 1977 network television special on the ERA was even titled "The War Between the Women!"

"The catfight remains an extremely popular way for the news media to represent women's struggles for equality and power" (Douglas, 1994, p. 243). In the 1992 presidential campaign, Barbara Bush and Hillary Rodham Clinton were portrayed as polar opposites—the good wife and mother versus the selfish career woman. Attacks on women's studies, feminism, multiculturalism, "political correctness," and "feminazis" get far more publicity than feminist ideas ever did. The *Wall Street Journal*, not noted for reviewing feminist books or analyzing feminist theories, nevertheless featured a 1995 review of a book critical of feminism, claiming that it showed how feminism "has exhibited from the start a nasty streak of intolerance toward women who don't fall in with the party line," and uses "tactics more ruthless than those that feminists have accused men of using to oppress women." The review suggested that women's studies professors are just cruel and vicious little girls grown up who enforce conformity at the cost of academic integrity (Crittenden, 1995, p. A14). We were recently invited to attend a public lecture in which the speaker, a woman, promised to tell about the "vicious battle" that is "raging" among feminists. Asking "Has feminism become just another racket?," she accused other women of "hijacking" feminism and fabricating their research data. Another way of discrediting feminists is to suggest that today's woman doesn't need to be one.

We invite our readers to think critically about the ways that feminists and feminism are portrayed in our society. It is ironic that feminism, which originated in a challenge to stereotypical assumptions about women, should now have its own negative stereotype. It is absurd that, even as women break new ground, and do it in often hostile environments, they are increasingly labeled different and inferior. It is disturbing that the media focus on the ideas of feminism only through the distortions and attacks of antifeminists (see Figure 1.5). We ask our readers to consider this question: Whose interests does it serve if a movement to end sexism is made to seem irrational, wrong, and futile?

Despite the attacks, feminism is a vital site of theory and research. Far from holding to an inflexible "party line," feminists have always encouraged debate and a plurality of viewpoints. In writing this book, we have tried to present a variety of feminist perspectives with the goal of encouraging critical thinking about them.

METHODS AND VALUES IN SCIENTIFIC INQUIRY

Scientific research is often represented as a purely objective process in which a neutral, disinterested scientist investigates and reveals the secrets of nature. However, as some of the pioneering women psychologists realized, psychology has sometimes been anything but neutral when it came to understanding and explaining the behavior of women. The resurgence of interest in the psychology of women has led psychologists to identify a number of specific methodological flaws in traditional research on women. One major emphasis of feminist psychology has been to analyze sources of distortion in psychological research and propose ways to ensure nonsexist, or gender-fair, research.

Toward Nonsexist Research

Let's look briefly at the research process. The researcher starts by generating a question to be answered by gathering information systematically. The question may originate in a theory, a personal experience, or an observation, or it may be raised by previous research. The next step is to develop a systematic strategy for answering the question—often called *designing* the research. In the design stage, a method is selected, such as experiment, survey, or case study. The research participants are chosen, materials such as questionnaires or laboratory setups are devised, and ways to measure the behaviors in question are decided on.

Next, the data are collected and analyzed so that patterns of results become clear. Statistical techniques are usually used for this task. The researcher then interprets the meaning of his or her results and draws conclusions from them. If reviewers and journal editors judge the research to be well conducted and important, the results are published in a scientific journal where they can influence future research and theory. Some research makes its way from journals into textbooks, influencing teachers and students as well as other researchers. Some even gets reported in the mass media, influencing perhaps millions of readers' and viewers' beliefs about such issues as racial differences in intelligence, sex differences in the brain, and the causes of social problems.

Biases can enter into the research process at any stage. In describing a few common types of bias at each stage, we will focus on gender-related examples.

FIGURE 1.5. Sisterhood is complicated!
Source: © 1994. Used by permission of Lynda Barry.

However, the principles of nonsexist research could also be applied to eliminating biases related to such characteristics as race/ethnicity, social class, or sexual orientation (Denmark, Russo, Frieze, & Sechzer, 1988).

Question Formulation

In the stage of choosing a research question, gender stereotypes related to the topic can bias the question and therefore the outcome of the study. For example, many studies of leadership have defined it in terms of dominance, aggression, and other stereotypically male attributes. A nonstereotypical definition of leadership might include the ability to negotiate, to be considerate of others, and

15

to help others resolve conflicts without confrontation (Denmark et al., 1988). Another example of bias in question formulation is found in the large amount of research on mothers who work outside the home. Much of it focuses on the question of whether the mothers' work endangers their children's psychological welfare. There is much less research on whether fathers' commitment to their work endangers their children's welfare, or on whether mothers' employment might benefit mothers or children (Hare-Mustin & Marecek, 1990).

The process of creating research questions is perhaps the most neglected and undervalued part of the scientific enterprise. Psychology graduate students typically learn a great deal about how to test hypotheses using complex experimental designs and advanced statistics, but textbooks and research courses say very little about where hypotheses come from or how to decide if a question is worth studying (Wallston & Grady, 1985). It is not surprising, then, that unexamined personal biases and androcentric theories often lead to biased research questions.

Designing Research

In the design phase of research, one important aspect is deciding how to measure the behaviors under study. If the measures are biased, the results will be, too. An extreme example of a biased measure comes from a study of women's sexuality. Participants were asked to describe their roles in sexual intercourse by choosing one of the following responses: "passive," "responsive," "resistant," "aggressive," "deviant," or "other." The outcome of this research might have been very different if women had also been allowed to choose from alternatives such as "active," "initiating," "playful," and "joyous" (Bart, 1971; Wallston & Grady, 1985).

Another aspect of the design phase of research is the choice of an appropriate comparison group. The results and conclusions of a study can be very different depending on which groups are chosen for comparison with each other. For example, one group of researchers was involved in an ongoing study of aging among a selected group of college-educated professional men. When they decided to add a sample of women, the biomedical scientists on the research team suggested that they should add the sisters of the men already in the study. Because they had the same parents, these two groups would be similar in physiological characteristics. The social scientists on the research team, however, suggested that the appropriate sample would be college-educated professional women who would be similar in social status. Although one choice is not necessarily right and the other wrong, the choice is a conceptually important one. The conclusions reached about gender differences in aging might be very different depending on which group of women was chosen, and the group chosen depends on assumptions about what kind of explanations (physiological or social) are most important (Parlee, 1981).

Choice of research participants is subject to many possible biases. Since the 1940s psychology has come to rely more and more on college student samples, creating biases of age, social class, and developmental stage (Sears, 1986). Moreover, males have been more likely to be studied than females. Several studies during the 1960s and 1970s found that males were greatly overrepresented in psychological research, perhaps because topics were gender-linked in the minds of researchers, and "male" topics were considered more important (Wallston & Grady, 1985).

The proportion of male-only studies has decreased since the 1970s (Gannon, Luchetta, Rhodes, Pardie, & Segrist, 1992). However, subtler kinds of sex bias persist. Nearly 30 percent of psychological journal articles still do not report the gender of the participants. When researchers use an all-female sample, they are more likely to state it in the article's title, to discuss their reasons for studying women, and to point out that their results cannot be generalized to men (Ader & Johnson, 1994). It seems that psychologists feel it is important to indicate the limitations of an all-female sample, but they see nothing remarkable about an all-male sample—males are still the norm.

Research on ethnic minority people of both sexes is scarce except when they are seen as creating social problems (Reid & Kelly, 1994). There is abundant research on teen pregnancy among African-American women, for example, but little research on their leadership, creativity, or coping skills for dealing with racism.

Poor and working-class women, too, have been virtually ignored (Bing & Reid, 1996; Reid, 1993). Many well-known psychologists, both female and male, have pointed out that psychology, supposedly the science of human behavior, is in danger of becoming a science of the behavior of college sophomores, and white male college sophomores at that. Feminist psychology, with its valuing of women as worthy subjects of research and its recognition of the diversity of social groupings, is providing an important corrective to this type of bias.

Analyzing Data: A Focus on Differences

Psychologists have come to rely on statistical tests in data analysis. Over the past thirty years, both the number of articles using statistics and the number of statistical tests per article have increased. Statistics can be a useful tool, but they also can lead to many conceptual difficulties in research on sex and gender (Wallston & Grady, 1985).

Statistical models lead to a focus on differences rather than similarities. The logic of statistical analysis involves comparing two groups to see if the average difference between them is "statistically significant." Unfortunately, it is not easy to make meaningful statements about *similarities* using statistical reasoning (Unger, 1981). It is also unfortunate that statisticians chose the term "significant" to describe the outcome of a set of mathematical operations. As used by most people the word means *important,* but as used by statisticians it means only that the obtained difference between two groups is unlikely to be due to mere chance. A statistically significant difference does not necessarily have any practical or social significance (Favreau, 1997). The meaning and interpretation of difference will be discussed in more detail in Chapter 4.

Interpreting and Publishing Research Results

Psychology's focus on group differences affects the ways that results are interpreted and conveyed to others. One type of interpretation bias occurs when gender differences in performing a specific task are interpreted as evidence of differences in a more global characteristic. For example, because special samples of highly gifted junior-high boys score higher on SAT math tests than similar samples of girls, some psychologists have argued that there is a biological superiority in math ability for males in general. Another kind of interpretation bias occurs when the performance style more typical of girls or women is given a negative label. For example, girls get better grades in school in virtually every subject, but no one interprets this to mean that females are biologically superior in intelligence. Instead, girls' academic achievement is discounted; they are said to get good grades by being "nice" or "compliant." Biased interpretations of gender differences lead to thinking of men and women as two totally separate categories. But it is simply not true that "men are from Mars, women from Venus." On many traits and behaviors, men and women are more alike than different. Even when a statistically significant difference is found, there is always considerable overlap between the two groups (see Chapter 4).

Problems of interpretation are compounded by publication biases. Because of reliance on the logic of statistical analysis, studies that report differences between women and men are more likely to be published than those that report similarities. Moreover, the editorial boards of journals are predominately made up of white men, who may perhaps see topics relevant to women and ethnic minorities as less important or of lower priority than topics relevant to people more like themselves (Denmark et al., 1988). Until feminist psychology was formed, there was very little psychological research on pregnancy and mothering, women's leadership, violence against women, or gender issues in therapy.

After they are published, some findings are noticed by the media and others are not. Television and the popular press often actively publicize the latest discoveries about gender differences, while similarities are not "news" (Crawford, 1989). The fact that women and men are more similar than they are different is not considered noteworthy either by psychology as a discipline or by society as a whole (Unger, 1990).

In summary, research is a human activity, and the gender biases held by those who do research can affect any stage of the research process. As more diverse people become psychologists, they will bring new values, beliefs, and research questions. They can also question and challenge the biases in others' research. Feminist psychologists have led the way by demonstrating gender bias in psychological research and showing how it can be reduced.

Nonsexist research is not value-free; that is, nonsexist research practices do not eliminate value judgments from the research process. Androcentric research is based on the value judgment that men and their concerns are more important and worthy of study than women and their concerns. In contrast, nonsexist research is based on the value judgment that women and men and their concerns are of equal worth and importance (Eichler, 1988).

Feminist Values in Research

Although feminist psychologists have been critical of psychology, they remain committed to it, expressing feminist values in their work (Grossman et al., 1997). What are some of these values?

Empirical Research Is a Worthwhile Activity

Although feminist psychologists recognize that science is far from perfect, they value its methods. Scientific methods are the most systematic way yet devised to answer questions about the natural and social world. Rather than abandon those methods or endlessly debate whether there is one perfect feminist way to do research, they go about their work using a rich variety of methods, theories, and approaches. Good research on women and gender is necessary and important (Peplau & Conrad, 1989; Worell, 1996).

Research Methods Must Be Critically Examined

Feminist theorists have pointed out that methods are not neutral tools; the choice of method always shapes and constrains what can be found (Crawford & Kimmel, 1999; Marecek, 1989; Unger, 1983). For example, what is the best way to study female sexuality—by measuring physiological changes in the vagina during arousal and orgasm, or by interviewing women about their subjective experiences of arousal and orgasm? The two methods would produce very different discoveries about female sexuality (Tiefer, 1989).

Traditionally, experimentation has been the most respected and valued psychological method. Psychologists like to do experiments because they can control for many outside factors that could affect results and because they can show causation (changing X causes a change in Y). However, experimental methods have been criticized for at least two reasons. First, in an experiment, the researcher creates an artificial environment and manipulates the experience of the participants. Experiments thus strip behavior from its social context (Parlee, 1979). Although laboratory studies isolate variables from the contaminating influence of real-life social processes, gender is played out in exactly those real-life processes (Crawford & Marecek, 1989). Therefore, behavior in the laboratory may not be representative of behavior in more naturalistic situations (Sherif, 1979).

Second, experiments are inherently hierarchical, with "the powerful, all-knowing researchers instructing, observing, recording, and sometimes deceiving the subjects" (Peplau & Conrad, 1989). The inequality of the experimental situation may be particularly acute when the researcher is male and the subject is female, reflecting and reinforcing the dominance of male values and interests (McHugh, Koeske, & Frieze, 1986).

On the other hand, many important advances in understanding women and gender have come about because of experimental results. For example, experimental research has clarified the nature and functioning of stereotypes about women (see Chapter 2). Research on perceptions of leadership, how power influences behavior (Chapter 3), and the evaluation of men's and women's performance (Chapter 11) has demonstrated in detail how sex discrimination occurs. Although psychology has perhaps used the experimental method too much and too unreflectively, it should not be rejected entirely.

Just as any research method can be used in sexist ways, all methods can be used toward the goal of understanding women and gender. When the variety of methods is large, results based on different approaches can be compared with each other, and a richer and more complete picture of women's lives will emerge.

Both Women and Men Can Conduct Feminist Research

Most feminist researchers in psychology are women. The membership of APA's Division 35 is more than 90 percent female, and "women have taken the lead in investigating topics relevant to women's lives and in developing new concepts and theories to explain women's experiences" (Peplau & Conrad, 1989, p. 391). However, it is important not to equate female with feminist and male with nonfeminist. Women who are psychologists work in every area from physiological, perception, and learning, to industrial and clinical psychology. Women psychologists may or may not personally identify as feminists, and even when they do, they may not bring a feminist perspective to their research. Also, male psychologists can identify as feminist. Men can and do conduct research on women and gender, and many conduct research on male gender roles. Of course, all psychologists—male and female, feminist and nonfeminist—should, at a minimum, conduct their research in nonsexist ways and work to eliminate sexism from their professional practices and behaviors.

Science Can Never Be Fully Objective or Value-Neutral

Science is done by human beings, all of whom bring their own perspectives to their work, based on their personal backgrounds. Personal experience sensitizes people to different aspects of problems (Unger, 1983). Because the values of dominant groups in a society are normative, they are not always recognized as values. When others—women and minorities, for example—question the assumptions of the dominant group, the underlying values are made more visible.

One of the most important insights of feminism is that research and the creation of knowledge do not occur in a social vacuum. Rather, each research project or theory is situated in a particular period in history and a particular social context. The psychology of women and gender is not unique in being affected by social currents such as feminism, conservatism, and liberalism. All of psychology is so affected. Moreover, psychology in its turn affects social issues and social policy through providing ways to interpret human behavior. Because psychology is a cultural institution, doing psychological research is inevitably a political act (Crawford & Marecek, 1989).

However, while the effects of values on the scientific process are inevitable, they need not be negative for women. We believe that psychology should admit values, not only as sources of bias, but as a means of evaluating all parts of the research process (Crawford & Marecek, 1989; Unger, 1983). An awareness of the politics of science can help feminist psychologists use science to foster social change and improve women's lives (Peplau & Conrad, 1989).

Human Behavior Is Shaped by Social, Historical, and Political Forces

Because feminists believe that gender equality is possible, although it has not yet been achieved, they are sensitive to the ways that social contexts and forces shape people's behavior and limit human potential. Feminist psychologists try to understand not only the effects of gender, but also the effects of other systems of social classification such as race, social class, and sexual orientation. They tend to be skeptical that psychology will ever discover universal laws of behavior. Rather, they prefer to try to clarify the ways that sociocultural forces, as well as biological and intrapsychic ones, affect behavior.

Feminist psychologists respect the diversity of women and recognize that it is important to study varied groups. For example, U.S. women generally have lower self-esteem than men, but this is not true of African-American women. Differences such as this can show how women's psychology is affected by their social and cultural backgrounds, not just their biology.

THEMES OF THIS BOOK

Because much of psychology's knowledge about women has historically been androcentric, one of the tasks of feminist psychology has been to analyze the implicit assumptions about women embedded in its theories and research practices. Throughout this book, you will find many examples of such critical analyses, in which feminist psychologists have exposed areas of neglect, androcentric concepts and research questions, and faulty reasoning in theory and research about women.

However, feminist psychology does more than just criticize androcentric psychology. It helps create a more comprehensive and adequate psychology of women (Worell, 1996). This book draws on the work of hundreds of psychologists, both women and men, who have contributed to the ongoing process of revising—and transforming—psychology. It also draws on the work of feminist theorists and researchers in other disciplines, including philosophy, history, anthropology, sociology, political science, and literary and cultural studies.

This book, then, provides both a critique of androcentric knowledge about women and a survey of emerging scholarship. Four broad themes are woven through the book. First, we distinguish between sex and gender, conceiving gender as a cultural construction. Second, we emphasize the importance of thinking critically about language and naming. Third, we recognize the diversity of women. Fourth, we emphasize that psychological knowledge about women can and should be used to foster social change that will benefit women. Let's look at these themes in more detail.

Theme 1: Gender Is More Than Just Sex

Researchers who study the psychology of women find it useful to distinguish between the concepts of sex and gender (Unger, 1979b). *Sex* is defined as biological differences in genetic composition and reproductive anatomy and function. All mammalian species have two biological forms, female and male. Human infants are labeled as one sex or the other at birth, based on the appearance of their genitals. It sounds like a simple and straightforward matter (though in fact it can be surprisingly complex—see Chapter 5). Most important, the biology of sex is a very important *social* marker that underlies children's, and some adults', perceptions of women and men (Chapters 3 and 6).

Gender is what culture makes out of the "raw material" of biological sex. All known societies recognize biological differentiation and use it as the basis for social distinctions. In our own society, the process of creating gendered human beings starts at birth. When a baby is born, the presence of a vagina or penis represents sex—but the pink or blue blanket that soon enfolds the baby represents gender. The blanket serves as a cue that this infant is to be treated as a boy or girl, not as a "generic human being," from the start.

Because gender is based on sex, the two terms have sometimes been used interchangeably. However, it is important to distinguish sex from gender for two reasons. First, equating them can lead to the belief that differences in the traits or behaviors of men and women are due directly to their biological differences, when the traits or behaviors actually may be shaped by culture. Second, keeping the concepts of sex and gender distinct can help us to analyze the complex ways they interact in our lives (Unger & Crawford, 1993).

Gender distinctions occur at many levels in society. Their influence is so pervasive that, like fish in water, we may be unaware that it surrounds us. Gender-related processes influence behavior, thoughts, and feelings in individuals; they affect interactions among individuals; and they help determine the structure of social institutions. The processes by which differences are created and power is allocated can be understood by considering how gender is played out at three levels: societal, interpersonal, and individual.

The Social Structural Level: Gender as a System of Power Relations

All known human societies make social distinctions based on gender. In the broadest sense, gender is a classification system that shapes the relations among women and men. The gender system influences access to power and resources (see Chapter 3). In our society and others, for example, many kinds of violence against women are taken for granted (see Chapters 8 and 13). Genital mutilation, sexual harassment, rape, incest, and battering can be seen as culturally "useful" ways of controlling girls and women. The power conferred by gender is pervasive and multidimensional. Men have more public power in most societies, controlling government, law, and public discourse. A quick check on the number of women in Congress and in the judiciary will illustrate that our own society is no exception. By and large, men make and enforce the laws that women and men must obey.

Other ranking systems, such as race, class, and sexual orientation, also influence social power. All women and men can be classified in terms of their race, class, and sexual orientation, in addition to their gender. Feminist research and theory emphasize that these systems are connected—they operate simultaneously in social institutions and everyday interactions, often outside awareness (Weber, 1998). Being white, male, middle class, and heterosexual confers advantages that are often not even noticed by those who have them (Rosenblum & Travis, 1996).

The Interpersonal Level: Gender as a Cue

People use gender cues in deciding how to behave toward others in social interactions. What happens when a person (A) meets someone (B) for the first time? Based on how B appears and acts, A decides that B is either male or female, and behaves accordingly. What happens if A cannot readily identify B's sex? A long-haired person wearing jeans, one earring, and a loose sweatshirt can be very unsettling! Typically, A would search quickly for cues that help to classify B definitely as female or male. (Does B have facial hair? Breasts?) Why is it important to make that classification? Without it, A would not know whether to behave as though he or she were with a woman or with a man.

When people interact, the influences of sex and gender are intertwined.

Not only do people use gender cues to make inferences about sex, they use perceived sex to make inferences about gender. When a man and a woman walk together into a car dealership, the salesperson is likely to direct the sales pitch to the man. Based on their appearance (gender), the salesperson decides that these two are a woman and a man (sex), assumes that they are a heterosexual couple, and acts according to his or her beliefs about which partner is more likely to make decisions about buying a car (gender). These kinds of interactions are so "normal" that they usually pass unnoticed. It is only when people "step out of line" that the gender forces shaping interaction become visible. A couple in which the woman is choosing the new car may feel quite uncomfortable as they violate the unwritten codes of gender.

Although much differential treatment of women and men (and boys and girls) happens outside awareness, research confirms that it is a reality. For example, observations in elementary school classrooms show that although teachers believe that they are treating boys and girls the same, boys receive more attention, both positive and negative, than girls do. Boys are yelled at and criticized more in front of their classmates. Moreover, in some classes a few boys are allowed to dominate class time by interacting constantly with the teacher, while most students remain silent (Eccles, 1989; Sadker & Sadker, 1994).

Research shows that the behavior of men and boys is often evaluated more positively than the behavior of women and girls. Even when a woman and a man behave in identical ways, their behavior may be interpreted very differently. Moreover, gender categorization is not simply a way of seeing differences, but a way of creating differences. When men and women are treated differently in ordinary daily interactions, they may come to behave differently in return. When they do, this re-creates the expectation that men and women *ought* to behave differently, reinforcing continued gender inequality (Risman, 1998). We will look more closely at these processes in Chapter 3.

The Individual Level: Gender as Masculinity and Femininity

To a greater or lesser extent, women and men come to accept gender distinctions visible at the structural level and enacted at the interpersonal level as part of the self-concept. They become *gender-typed*, ascribing to themselves the traits, behaviors, and roles normative for people of their sex in their culture. Women, moreover, internalize their devaluation and subordination. Feminist theories of personality development (see Chapter 4) stress that feminine characteristics such as passivity, excessive concern with pleasing others, lack of initiative, and dependency are psychological consequences of subordination. Members of subordinate social groups who adopt such characteristics are considered well adjusted; those who do not are controlled by psychiatric diagnosis (Chapter 14), violence or the threat of violence (Chapter 13), and social ostracism (Chapter 3).

Much of the psychology of women and gender has consisted of documenting the effects of internalized subordination, and we will see many examples throughout this book. Laboratory and field research, as well as clinical experience, attest that, compared with boys and men, girls and women lack a sense of personal entitlement, expect less pay for comparable work, are equally satisfied with their employment even though they are paid significantly less than men, lose self-esteem and confidence in their academic ability, especially in mathematics and science, as they progress through the educational system, and are more likely to suffer from disturbances of body image, eating disorders, and depression. These differences are not "natural." They are shaped by differential opportunities and maintained in social interaction. They are the product of the gender system.

Although the distinction between sex and gender is an important one, it is relatively new in psychology, and it is not always used consistently from one book or article to another (Deaux, 1993; Gentile, 1993; Unger & Crawford, 1993). For example, differences in the behavior of male and female rats in a maze should be, and almost always are, referred to as sex differences. However, we once came across a study that referred to the rats' gender—perhaps they wore pink and blue hair ribbons as they ran the maze!

Because we (the authors) assume that virtually all human behavior is shaped by culture, we will use "gender" except when referring directly to sexual anatomy or reproduction. Differing social behaviors in women and men, for example, will be referred to as gender differences, because they are probably not directly caused by biological sex. However, terms such as "sex discrimination" that are widely used by researchers will be retained.

Theme 2: Language and Naming Are Sources of Power

Controversies over terminology can sometimes seem like semantic hairsplitting. But language and naming are sources of power. Thinking critically about language can increase understanding of how the system of social classification called gender confers more power on males.

Aspects of reality that are named become "real" and can be talked about and thought about. Names allow people to share experiences and teach others to name their own experiences in the same way. Moreover, when certain aspects of reality are granted names, unnamed aspects become overshadowed and thus more difficult to think about and articulate. Unnamed experiences are less visible, and therefore, in a sense, less real to the social world (Berger & Luckmann, 1966). The idea that language shapes and constrains thought (sometimes called the Whorfian hypothesis) was proposed more than fifty years ago by Benjamin Whorf and Edward Sapir. It still provides many unanswered and interesting questions for psychology (Henley, 1989).

The English language is, unfortunately, rich in linguistic sexism (Adams & Ware, 1989). One example is the traditional practice of using *he, his,* and *him* to represent both women and men—as in "Each student should bring his notebook." How are thinking and understanding affected by this androcentric naming? A great deal of psychological research has shown that the use of "generic" masculine language leads people of both sexes to think more about males (Henley, 1989).

Androcentric language omits important aspects of female experience. The negative physical changes and feelings some women experience in conjunction with the menstrual cycle have the official and scientific-sounding label *premenstrual syndrome*—but the feelings of well-being and heightened competence that some women experience around the ovulation phase of the cycle have no label. Thus, PMS has become widely accepted as "real," is readily discussed everywhere from Oprah to the college classroom, and is a legitimate topic of research. Midcycle well-being is rarely a focus of research or discussion.

Issues of language and naming can divide people. For example, one student described an ongoing feud with her roommate. The student used the term *woman* rather than *girl* for herself and others, believing that to call anyone past the teen years a girl is insulting. The roommate believed just as firmly that it is fine to be called a girl. The issue was important to both because in their choice of words they were claiming different identities. The term *woman*, like *man*, conveys adulthood, power, and sexuality; the term *girl*, like *boy*, conveys youth, powerlessness, and frivolity. The women's movement criticized the practice of calling adult females girls because of these implicit meanings. In this case, "mere words" permanently divided the two roommates (Rosenblum & Travis, 1996).

There is widespread disagreement, too, on whether a woman should take her husband's name upon marriage. Consider these contrasting opinions of women on the subject:

> When I got married, it seemed a bit late in life to get used to a new last name, as I'd had mine for 35 years. I also frankly couldn't see what choosing to share your life with someone had to do with changing your name.

> I feel desperately sorry for all those young women who will never know the joy and/or soaring pride of taking their new husband's name. If it is absolutely imperative for a career title, it might be tolerable in business. But as far as I'm concerned, there are only three acceptable titles for ladies: Miss, Mrs., and Dr. (I think Ms. is a joke and should be avoided).

> When my husband and I decided to give our daughter my last name, it seemed like a sensible plan. Having grown up in a blended family, in which different last names were the norm, keeping my own name at marriage was an easy choice. . . . Little did we know how controversial our decision would be. Routinely, people assume that my daughter is not my husband's—and when it is explained, they look at us in utter shock. They ask my husband, "Didn't you want your kid to have your name?" and say to me, "Your husband must be a really nice guy.". . . The idea that a man would give up the privilege of "passing down his name" is virtually unthinkable; the assumption that women will give up this privilege unquestioned . . . In our age of choices, it is interesting to see how unacceptable this choice still is. (Henry, 1998, p. E6)

Choices about language are controversial because of their symbolic meanings. Linguistic sexism and symbolism will be discussed in detail in Chapter 2. Throughout the book, there are many examples of the importance of language and naming.

Analyzing language critically is not an easy task. Aspects of reality that are unnamed are obscured—made difficult to know and express. However, feminist scholars are analyzing language practices in depth to help understand how ideas about gender are perpetuated. Moreover, they are actively challenging gender bias in language use and have caused some important changes. Psychology as a profession has worked to change its biased language; the APA adopted guidelines for nonsexist language in 1977, and they are now part of the official APA *Publication Manual.*

Language change as a result of feminist activism is evident outside psychology as well. One example is the widespread use of *Ms.* as a parallel title to *Mr.* When Ms. was first proposed, it was considered dangerously radical and subjected to ridicule; now it is the norm (Crawford, Stark, & Renner, 1998). The writer Gloria Steinem perhaps best expressed the importance of the power of naming—and the influence of feminist activism on language change:

> We have terms like "sexual harassment" and "battered women." A few years ago, they were just called "life." (Steinem, 1983, p. 149)

Until recently, the public power to name has been largely in the hands of men. Men controlled the institutions of knowledge, and even if women acquired expertise, they did not acquire legitimacy. History is full of stories about learned women whose work was attributed to their fathers, their brothers, their teachers, or "anonymous."

Such stories can be found in the history of psychology as well. One illustration of how a woman could have outstanding expertise and yet be denied legitimacy is the story of Mary Calkins, one of the first presidents of the American Psychological Association. She attended Harvard University during the latter part of the nineteenth century. But because Harvard was an all-male university, she was permitted to take courses only if she sat behind a curtain or was tutored individually. Despite completing an impressive Ph.D. dissertation with an important psychologist, she was denied a Ph.D. from Harvard because she was a woman.

Mary Calkins taught for many years at Wellesley College, established an experimental laboratory there, and made a number of important contributions to psychology. She was the first woman president of both the American Psychological Association and the American Philosophical Association. In 1927, toward the end of her life, a group of psychologists and philosophers, all Harvard degree holders, sent a letter to the president of Harvard requesting that Mary Calkins be awarded the degree that she had earned in the 1890s. Their request was refused (Scarborough & Furumoto, 1987).

Although Mary Calkins triumphed personally, her life illustrates the way even outstanding women may be marginalized. For example, she taught during her entire life at a women's college where she did not have doctoral students of her own. Under these conditions, her theories and research projects did not receive the continuity of investigation they deserved. Unlike many of her male peers, she did not found a "school" of psychology. Similar stories have been uncovered about other women in the group of early feminist psychologists of the 1920s, including Leta Hollingworth and Mary Jacobi (Scarborough & Furumoto, 1987). The ability to have one's research and theories taken seriously and passed on to the next generation of researchers is part of the power to name.

Theme 3: Women Are Not All Alike

Although gender is an important and universal dimension for classifying human beings and allocating power, it is not the only dimension. As discussed earlier, social class, sexuality, and race/ethnicity also serve as principles of so-cial organization. Therefore, important though gender is, it would be a mis-take to assume that all women necessarily have much in common with each other simply because they are women. A woman who is wealthy and privi-leged may, for example, have as much in common with wealthy and privi-leged men as she has with poor women. African-American and Latina women share with the men of their ethnic groups—and not with white women—the experiences of racism and racial stereotyping. Lesbians share the experience of being in a sexual minority with bisexuals and gay men, not with heterosexual women. Dimensions such as age and (dis)ability are relevant, too. The view-points and concerns of older women and disabled women are not necessarily the same as those of young, able-bodied women.

Studies of different groups of women can help us to understand how bio-logical, social, and cultural factors interact to influence behavior. Physical struc-ture and physiology as well as the timing and form of physical development are, of course, biologically determined. On the other hand, the social reactions to and cultural meaning of physical structure have little to do with biology. It is important to look at different groups of women—both for their own sake and because their differences help us to test the limits of biological determination.

Yet creating a psychology of all women is not an easy task. If women of color are studied only in comparison to a mythical "generic" (white, privi-leged status) woman, researchers are implicitly making white women the norm, just as previous generations of psychologists made men the norm (Greene & Sanchez-Hucles, 1997; Yoder & Kahn, 1992). It is important to study each group of women within their own cultural context. Fortunately, there are new writings by and about Latina, Native-American, African-American, Asian-American, lesbian, poor, older, and disabled women, to name just a few, that can guide understanding of the contexts of their lives.

In writing this book, we have tried to respect and express the diversity of women's experiences. As we worked on the book together, we noticed that feminists have often used metaphors of gender as a lens or prism through which to view the social structure (Bem, 1993; Crawford & Marecek, 1989; Unger, 1990). Viewing psychological and social phenomena through the lens of gender allows us to see aspects of social reality that are otherwise obscured. However, like any lens, gender can reveal only some features of the social landscape. Lenses such as race, class, and age reveal other, equally important features. Feminist psychologists do not wish to copy the limitations of andro-centric psychology by replacing "male as norm" with "white-middle-class-heterosexual female as norm."

Theme 4: Psychological Research Can Foster Social Change

Traditionally, psychology has focused on changing individuals. Psychologists have developed new techniques to bring about attitude change, to increase in-sight and self-understanding, to teach new behavioral skills, and to reduce or eliminate self-defeating thinking and behaviors. These techniques are applied in a variety of educational and therapeutic settings. In this book there are many examples of how feminist psychology has adapted and used the tools of traditional psychology.

However, the new scholarship on women and gender also suggests that there are definite limits to the power of individual change. Many of the issues and problems that confront women today are the result of social structures and practices that put women at a disadvantage and interfere with their living happy, productive lives. Social-structural problems cannot be solved solely through individual changes in attitudes and behavior; rather, the social institutions that permit the devaluation and victimization of women must also be changed. Therefore, throughout this book we discuss the implications of psychological research for changing institutions such as traditional marriage, language use, child rearing, the workplace, and, not least, the institution of psychology itself. Chapter 15 focuses on individual and structural change.

It is clear that personal change does not take place in a social vacuum. It is also clear that equality between women and men cannot occur in the absence of social justice for other marginalized groups. Social change is slow, but as more members of formerly powerless groups gain power in society, they should make further changes in it. They will be able to do so, however, only if they continue to identify with the marginalized groups from which they emerged. People who understand the role of both the individual and the group appear to be most effective in creating social change (Sherif, 1976).

Social changes are not always for the better. Sometimes policies that solve problems for one group create problems for others (McGrath, 1986). For example, the Communist regimes in Eastern Europe reduced the individual freedoms of everyone. These governments were toppled. New, more democratic regimes such as those in Poland, however, have voted to eliminate legal abortion and equal rights for women. Thus, women's freedoms are curtailed in these new democracies. What will be defined as progress here? Of course, it will depend on who is writing the definition.

Psychological research draws on the real world of people living in complex social contexts. It abstracts or isolates aspects of that world for systematic study. When researchers and textbook writers examine the implications of psychological research for changing women's social environments and opportunities, they return the isolated aspects to their context. Thus, a circle is closed, and psychological research is potentially more useful for women.

OUR GOALS FOR OUR STUDENTS

The authors of this book have changed, both personally and professionally, as a result of our involvement in the psychological study of women. Rhoda Unger has written:

> Once upon a time I was a confirmed behaviorist. In principle, this meant that I believed effects derived from orderly determinist causes, that the subjective aspects of behavior were irrelevant, and that the best studies required maximal distance between experimenter and subject. In practice, this meant that my first major research, my doctoral dissertation, involved making lesions in

the caudate nucleus of rats and examining their effects upon temporal and spatial alternation by means of operant conditioning procedures. If I thought of sex professionally at all, I saw it as a variable which could neither be manipulated nor controlled and therefore of very little scientific interest. Even the rats were male. (1989, p. 15)

Like Rhoda Unger, Mary Crawford started out as a psychologist believing that good science demanded a separation of personal or social concerns from scientific problem solving. Her dissertation was an analysis of species-specific reactions in rats and their effects on classical and operant conditioning. She writes:

More and more, my research seemed like a series of intellectual puzzles that had no connection to the rest of my life. In the lab, I studied abstract theories of conditioning, accepting the assumption that the principles were similar for rats and humans. In the "real world," I became involved in feminist activism and began to see things I had never noticed before. I saw sex discrimination in my university and knew women who struggled to hold their families together in poverty. Trying to build an egalitarian marriage and bring up my children in nonsexist ways made me much more aware of social pressures to conform to traditional gender roles. I began to ask myself why I was doing a kind of psychology that had so little to say about the world as I knew it. I turned to the study of women and gender in order to make my personal and intellectual life congruent and to begin using my skills as a psychologist on behalf of social change.

Both of us have worked for social change on behalf of women. We have drawn on our skills and training as psychologists in activism on reproductive rights, gender equity in education, peace and nonviolent conflict resolution, nonsexist marriage and child raising, and gender-fair language. We have helped communicate psychology to the general public through speaking and writing on feminist issues. All these commitments have raised fresh questions and provided us with new insights on women and gender.

Today, we value our early research for teaching us how to go about scientific inquiry systematically and responsibly, but we have changed our views about what the important questions in psychology are and what theoretical frameworks have the most potential. We have chosen to specialize in the study of women and gender, and to write this book, in the hope that we may contribute to the creation of a new, transformed psychology.

A recent study suggests that our experience of professional and personal change through feminism is not unusual. Fifty-one distinguished members of APA's Psychology of Women Division were asked to describe their experience of feminism. Their replies indicated that, to them, feminism meant valuing women and their experiences, a concern with equality of power, the need for change and activism, and the idea of gender as a social construct. To these psychologists, a focus on women and gender in their research and teaching was part of a feminism whose meaning was "much more than the dictionary would suggest . . . a lived, conscious, changing experience" (Kimmel, 1989, p. 145). The researcher, Ellen Kimmel, noted the transformative power of feminist thought among her research participants and in her own life. Her summation can apply to the women who wrote this book as well:

Feminism (whatever it is and all that it is) transformed my life by connecting it to my work and gathering the disparate parts of myself into a whole. (Kimmel, 1989, p. 145)

Rhoda Unger has taught the psychology of women for thirty years and Mary Crawford for twenty-five years. Together, we have introduced thousands of students, both women and men, to feminist psychology. Our students have come from many different racial and ethnic backgrounds, including African-American, white, Asian-American, and Hispanic. In age and experience they have ranged from the traditional young-adult college student to postretirement. Some identified themselves, openly or privately, as gay, lesbian, or bisexual, others as heterosexual. Their personal beliefs and values about feminism, women, and gender varied a great deal. In short, our students have been a diverse group of people. We have welcomed that diversity, and in this book we try to reflect what we have learned from it. Whatever your own background, we welcome you, our newest students, to the study of women and gender.

Perhaps because of our own experience of change through learning about women and gender, our goals for our students involve changes in knowledge, thinking skills, and attitudes. We hope that you, like many of our students before you, will experience growth in at least some of the following areas as a result of your studies:

- *Critical thinking skills.* By studying the psychology of women, you can learn to evaluate psychological research critically and become a more astute, perceptive observer of human behavior.
- *Knowledge and understanding about social inequities.* The focus is on the gender system, sexism, and sex discrimination. However, gender always interacts with other systems of domination such as racism and heterosexism.
- *Empathy for women.* You may come to appreciate the experiences and viewpoints of your mother, your sisters, and your women friends better. In addition, women students may experience a heightened sense of sisterhood with all women.
- *Desire to work toward social change that benefits women*—and a commitment to do so.
- *The ability to see the larger context of women's lives.* The psychology of women is linked to the biology, sociology, anthropology, and cultural representation of women.
- *The understanding that "women" is a complex category.* Women are a diverse group and must be studied in the context of other significant aspects of their lives, not as gendered beings alone.

There is one thing, however, that we cannot offer you as a consequence of studying women and gender: closure. A first course in women and gender, our students tell us, raises as many questions as it answers. Acquiring knowledge about human behavior is an ongoing process, and its outcome cannot be determined in advance. This is true for professional researchers as it is for college students.

Feminist psychology and feminism in general seem to be at the point of trying to piece together the individual parts of a quilt. The overall pattern of the quilt that we want to create is still emerging. No one knows what a feminist psy-

chology will look like any more than we know what equality in a postpatriar-
chal world will look like. We are beginning to piece the separate parts together—to explore the kinds of stitching to use in connecting the pieces and
how to place the separate pieces into the pattern. But we have not stopped
questioning the process of quilting itself (Gentry, 1989, pp. 5–6).

Perhaps most important, the quilt is already useful, and the conversations
around the margins are vibrant.

SUGGESTED READINGS

BAKER, CHRISTINA L., & KLINE, CHRISTINA B. (1996). *The conversation begins: Mothers and
daughters talk about living feminism.* New York: Bantam. Provocative dialogues between two generations of feminists: women who were active in the women's
movement starting in the 1960s, and their daughters who are now adults. Mothers
and daughters explore the meaning of feminism as they see it and how it has affected their lives.

HOOKS, BELL (1981). *Ain't I a woman: Black women and feminism.* Boston: South End Press.
An African-American feminist writes about the impact of sexism on black women
during slavery, the devaluation of black women historically and in the present,
racism among black men and white feminists, and black women's involvement
with feminism.

CRAWFORD, MARY, & UNGER, RHODA. (1997). *In our own words: Readings on the psychology
of women and gender.* New York: McGraw-Hill. A rich collection of diverse voices on
women's lives. A mother whose daughter was stalked and murdered, a "brave
new family" with one child and four gay parents, an Asian-American woman on
the politics of cosmetic surgery, a transgendered person on being a "gender outlaw," feminist Gloria Steinem on "If Men Could Menstruate"—and many more.

CHAPTER 2

Images of Women
and Men

- **IMAGES OF WOMEN IN CROSS-CULTURAL PERSPECTIVE**
  Religious Images of Women
  Similarities and Differences in Images of Women
- **STEREOTYPES: AN OVERVIEW**
  What Are Stereotypes?
  The Measurement of Stereotypes about Women and Men
  Stereotypes and Subtypes
- **GENDER STEREOTYPES IN THE MASS MEDIA**
  Stereotypes Are Everywhere!
  Pictorial Images of Women and Men
  Sexist, Racist, and Class-Biased Images
  Face-ism and Body-ism
- **THE IMPACT OF MEDIA SEXISM**
  Gendered Images and Gender Roles
  Body Image and Self-Esteem
- **WOMEN'S QUEST FOR BEAUTY**
  The Social Importance of Looks
  Learning to Care about Looks
  Impossible Standards of Weight
  Minority Women and White Standards of Beauty
- **LANGUAGE AND WOMEN'S PLACE**
  Verbal Images of Women and Men
  The Case of the Generic "He"
  Sexist Language and Conceptual Distortions
- **STEREOTYPES AS SOCIAL DEMANDS**
  Gender Stereotypes and Social Attributions
  The Social Value of Physical Attractiveness
  Weight and Social Stigma
  Stereotypes About Social Deviance
- **STEREOTYPES AND SEXISM**
  Ambivalent Sexism
  Sexism and Discrimination
  The Persistence of Stereotyping: Cognitive Factors
  Making Meaning
  Cultural Factors
- **FORMS OF SEXISM**
  New Measures of Covert Sexism
  The Future of Change
- **CONNECTING THEMES**
- **SUGGESTED READINGS**

What picture do you see when someone asks you to think of a "woman"? Do you think of the images shown on TV or in the movies? Or do you think of individual women you have known—your mother or a favorite teacher? As you can see from the picture in Figure 2.1, womanhood is not a simple category. Women vary in age, ethnicity, and social class as well as in many other dimensions. Images of women also differ cross-culturally, and they vary within our own culture over time. It would be a mistake, however, to believe that images are either fleeting or trivial. At any given point in time, they are seen as having universal meaning. They are used as models by which women (and men) are judged as worthy members of their sex. These idealized images often become anchors for psychological identity and serve as a basis for self-perception and self-esteem (Gilmore, 1990).

Media images of women differ greatly from the picture of real women in Figure 2.1. In the media, women are portrayed in terms of their bodies much more than men are. They are also judged by more exacting physical and sexual standards. Women who are not sufficiently attractive or are overweight may be stigmatized and shamed. Women who are found deficient or deviant according to media standards may be criticized as immoral and subjected to social penalties. Women who fail to meet minimal standards of femininity (such as older or disabled women) may be denied a gender identity at all. They are invisible to our culture's images of women.

Although images of women are not constructed in the same way by all societies, gender is a category that exists in virtually all cultures. Masculinity and femininity, based on easily observable characteristics, constrict the individual's behavior. Most societies tend to exaggerate biological differences by clearly differentiating gender roles and defining the proper behavior of women and men as opposite or complementary. Images of women convey cultural demands. The way a society pictures its women can never be considered trivial or meaningless. Indeed, the "media are the message."

FIGURE 2.1. Who is the real woman? Women come in all sizes, colors, and varieties.

Images of the ideal women have remained surprisingly consistent over time. For example, the goddesses of ancient Greece embodied qualities still sometimes suggested as desirable in modern women (see Table 2.1). Aphrodite, for example, was seen as every man's sexual fantasy—beautiful, sensual, and infinitely available. Artemis, in contrast, was the chaste athlete—every man's "pal." Athena, the Greek goddess of wisdom, would seem to contradict modern conceptions of ideal femininity, and the Greeks appear to have been aware of this paradox: Athena did not have a normal birth or childhood but sprang full-grown from the head of Zeus, the chief god!

Religious Images of Women

Images of women as part of man can also be found in the creation stories told by the Old Testament. For example, Eve is made from one of Adam's ribs. Interestingly, in Jewish folk tradition, God created Adam and Lilith at the same time, but Lilith refused to be subordinate to Adam and ran away. Lilith became a spirit of evil who seduced men from their wives (Reineke, 1989). In an effort to rehabilitate the image of Lilith as a spirit of independence, a major journal of Jewish feminist thought has been named for her.

Other major religions have also problematized women's sexuality. Mary, the virgin mother of Jesus, is a familiar image; less familiar is Kuan-Yin, the Buddhist goddess of mercy. She became a goddess after earthly tragedies prevented her from becoming a wife and mother (Reineke, 1989). Feminine identity is seen by these religions as formed by childbearing, but female sexuality is seen as polluting. Images of virgin goddesses permit cultures to maintain their negative views of female sexuality and power (Sangren, 1983).

More negative views about women and sexuality are conveyed by Islamic

TABLE 2.1. Mythological Ideals of Women

Goddess	Role	Significant Other	Traits
Artemis	Sister Competitor Feminist	Companions (nymphs) Mother Brother	Goal-oriented Independent Forms friendships with women

Athena	Strategist	Father
		Chosen heroes
			Problem-solver
			Forms strong
			   alliances with
			   men

Hera	Wife	Husband	Commitment Fidelity
Aphrodite	Sensual woman	Lovers	Sensuality Creativity

Source: Adapted from Jean Shinoda Bolen, M. D. 1984. *Goddesses in everywoman.* Copyright © 1984 by Jean Shinoda Bolen, M. D. Reprinted by permission of HarperCollins Publishers, Inc.

imagery. The religion of Islam explicitly argues that social order depends on careful attention being paid to caste differences based on gender. Men live in the public sphere and worship in the mosque, whereas women remain in the private sphere—the home—where they also pray. If a woman finds that she must leave the seclusion of the home to enter the public sphere (such behavior is discouraged in traditional Islam), she must be veiled from head to toe so that no part of her body is exposed (see Figure 2.2).

Extreme fundamentalist views of women in Afghanistan have had tragic consequences for them. Women are no longer permitted to work outside their home or to go to school. Women physicians are not allowed to practice and since male physicians cannot treat a woman outside of their family, women and girls receive virtually no health care. The fundamentalist Islamic sect that has imposed these restrictions has, however, ended Afghanistan's deadly civil war. Would you call this progress?

Similarities and Differences in Images of Women

Religious images of women are reflected in views found in different cultures today. In a twenty-five nation study of gender stereotypes, some adjectives were associated with women in all the countries studied (Williams & Best, 1990). Women were seen as sentimental, submissive, and superstitious. Men were seen as adventurous, forceful, and independent. But the stereotypes were not all alike. For example, they were influenced by the religious composition of various countries. In countries with a high percentage of Catholics, women

FIGURE 2.2. Invisibility at its most extreme. Women in Afghanistan must be completely covered to leave their homes or they may be beaten or, possibly, killed.

were viewed more favorably. They were seen as nurturant parents and sources of order. In Muslim countries, images of women and men were more different from each other and stereotypes about women were more unfavorable than those typically found elsewhere.

Cultural images of women may be internalized and used as sources for individual attitudes and beliefs. Images of women and men are conveyed by myths and fairy tales as well as by pictures and religious beliefs. They are acquired without consent or conscious awareness. In all the countries studied, a general developmental pattern was found. The acquisition of gender stereotypes typically began before the age of 5, accelerated during the early school years, and was completed during adolescence (Williams & Best, 1990). Many people are unaware of stereotypes because they are so pervasive. There are few gender-fair or gender-free images with which to contrast them.

STEREOTYPES: AN OVERVIEW

Gendered images are communicated in virtually every aspect of everyday life, but people pay little conscious attention to most of them. For example, an old nursery rhyme declared:

> What are little boys made of?
> Sticks and snails and puppy dog tails.
> That's what little boys are made of.
>
> What are little girls made of?
> Sugar and spice and everything nice.
> That's what little girls are made of.

One rarely hears anything so explicitly sexist today, although comments about the physical characteristics of women are still more easily found than similar comments about men. When was the last time you heard remarks such as "Beautiful, but dumb!" or "You can never be too rich or too thin"? Did the remarks refer to women or men?

What Are Stereotypes?

Statements of this sort are *stereotypes*. Although the word stereotype has become part of our everyday language, it has some specific meanings when used by a psychologist. This chapter focuses on the cognitive aspects of stereotypes, exploring how stereotypes are measured and how they are put together as cognitive constructs. In this connection we explore the differences between stereotypes about women and men as general categories and stereotypes about various subcategories of men and women. We also look at some sources of stereotypes, particularly mass media and language. Finally, we examine the impact of stereotypes on people's behavior and the question of whether or not gender stereotypes have disappeared or changed.

Surprisingly, the term "stereotype" was not invented by a psychologist. It was first used by Walter Lippmann (1922), a noted journalist of his day, to describe a kind of behavior. He defined stereotypes as culturally determined pictures that intrude between an individual's cognitive faculties and his or her perceptions of the world. Lippmann appears to have borrowed the term from a kind of curved printing press in which the type had to be deformed to fit its structure. Stereotyping is still viewed today as a process that distorts reality. However, such distortions are now seen by most psychologists as part of the normal process of concept formation rather than as a form of irrational thought.

Stereotypes occur whenever individuals are classified by others as having something in common because they are members of a particular group or category of people. The earliest studies of stereotypes by social scientists involved the investigation of attitudes toward religious, racial, or ethnic groups. However, a number of early studies (Fernberger, 1948; Kirkpatrick, 1936; Sheriffs & McKee, 1957) demonstrated that gender stereotypes, defined as consensual beliefs about the different characteristics of men and women, were widely held, persistent, and highly traditional. Gender stereotypes, like other stereotypes, have the following characteristics:

- Groups that are the targets of stereotypes are easily identified and relatively powerless.
- People largely agree about the characteristics of a stereotyped group.
- Stereotypes imply a covert comparison between groups, to the disadvantage of the stereotyped group.
- Stereotypes usually do not represent groups accurately.
- The misperception appears to be the product of information processing; however, motives to preserve one's self, one's group, and the social system in which one lives are also important.
- The misperception is difficult to modify, even when the person who holds the stereotype encounters many disconfirming examples.
- People are largely unaware that they stereotype, and they deny that stereotypes characteristic of their group apply to themselves.

Each of these points will be discussed more fully in this chapter. It is particularly important to keep in mind, however, that it is the consistency and apparent universality of gender stereotypes that makes them so dangerous. They are destructive because they influence perceptions independent of the individual characteristics of members of the stereotyped group. They weigh down these individuals, anchor interactions with them, and hold them back (Fiske, 1993).

Individual beliefs are not the same thing as stereotypes. One of our colleagues, for example, believes that there is an inverse relationship between the length of a woman's fingernails and her grade-point average. Although he obviously has a negative bias against women with long nails, one would not consider this a stereotype because it is probably his own eccentric perception—one that affects, at most, only some women in his classes.

In contrast, stereotypes are defined by their lack of variability: the majority of people in a population choose a particular quality as characteristic of a particular group. For example, most people (including many professors) believe that women are less competent in math and science than men. The extent to which this belief influences the way people perceive and evaluate men and women differently may come to influence their relative abilities in these areas (see Chapter 4). Stereotypes appear to be more like forms of social consensus than individual attitudes. The way psychologists measure sex stereotypes illustrates their social nature.

The Measurement of Stereotypes about Women and Men

The classic studies of stereotypes about women and men were conducted in the late 1960s and early 1970s (Broverman, Vogel, Broverman, Clarkson, & Rosenkrantz, 1972). The researchers developed a questionnaire made up of 122 pairs of adjectives that were antonyms; that is, each member of the pair was opposite in meaning from the other. The pairs consisted of words that are commonly used to describe people's personality traits, such as *sneaky/direct, passive/active, submissive/dominant*, and so forth. Respondents were asked to indicate the extent to which each pair described a normal male, a normal female, and themselves, forcing them to choose between adjectives in describing the target individuals. This methodology was similar to that used in earlier studies of ethnic and religious stereotypes.

If no stereotypes exist, people should assign traits at random and no pattern will emerge. The researchers used a relatively conservative definition of whether or not a trait was gender stereotypic. Items were termed stereotypic only if at least 75 percent of individuals of each sex agreed that the adjective was more descriptive of the average man or woman. Nevertheless, they found high agreement on more than eighty traits about the differing characteristics of women and men. These beliefs were not affected by the age, religion, education level, or marital status of the participants. People from a large variety of different groups, when forced to make a choice, select different traits for men and women.

Some patterns in the content of gender stereotypes emerged that are still relevant today. The researchers found two groups of traits that were highly associated with each other—an *instrumental* dimension that was considered to be characteristic of typical males, and an *affective* dimension considered to be characteristic of typical females. Instrumentality includes traits such as active, objective, independent, aggressive, direct, unemotional, dominant, and competent. These traits appear to describe a person who can manipulate the world effectively. Affective traits include warm, expressive, and sensitive. These traits appear to describe a person who is concerned about and nurturant of others and cares more for people than for things.

More traits were associated with typical males than with typical females, and a greater number of masculine traits were considered socially desirable. Typical feminine traits were also considered more childlike than typical masculine traits, whereas masculine and adult traits were seen as essentially identical in nature. This connection between femininity and immaturity reappears in a number of ways in studies on perceptions of women. It can have a negative impact when people make decisions about women's suitability for managerial careers (see Chapter 11).

The Many Meanings of Being a Woman

When people think about females and males, they are thinking about more than just their personality traits. Other characteristics such as roles, behaviors, and physical appearance are closely related to perceptions about gender in our society (Spence, Deaux, & Helmreich, 1985). Stereotypes about all men and all women may be too general. More differentiated associations are found when researchers examine perceptions about various subtypes of women and men. Such findings are particularly important because most of the target individuals used in such studies are white and middle class. Earlier studies assume not only that "male" and "female" are universal categories but also that beliefs about white middle-class heterosexual women and men were the norm. Other groups of people were rendered invisible.

In the 1980s, researchers turned their attention to subtypes of women and men. Instead of forcing them to choose between two polar opposites in their characterization of men and women, these researchers asked college students to list all the characteristics they thought were pertinent to males and females (Deaux & Lewis, 1984). Students used role behaviors (financial provider, meal preparer), physical characteristics (sturdy, graceful), and occupations (construction worker, telephone operator) as well as personality traits. Perceptions in these different areas were closely associated with each other. For example, women were seen as taking care of children and having small bones, as well as being warm and emotional. Stereotypes about females and males appear to consist of a tight network of associations that extends to virtually all aspects of human beings.

Suppose you were asked to list the attributes of *mother*. What would you say? In a subsequent study, people were asked to list attributes for various subtypes of women and men (Deaux, Winton, Crowley & Lewis, 1985). Instead of views of men and women as general categories, the researchers were interested in perceptions of the sexes in terms of their different roles, such as *mother* and *father;* occupations such as *housewife* or *blue-collar worker;* and physical characteristics such as *strong* or *graceful*. They were trying to answer questions such as: Are women seen as warmer than men because they are perceived as mothers (a social role they occupy) rather than because they are women (the more global category)?

The researchers found that the same number of associations was generated for each label. No one category (gender, social role, etc.) appears to be more perceptually important than any other. By measuring the extent to which the same term appeared on lists with different labels, the researchers were able to calculate the degree of overlap between various images of women and men. For example, they found that there was more overlap between people's perceptions of *mother* and *parent* than *father* and *parent*. Similarly, the terms assigned to *woman* were closer to labels attached to *mother* and *grandmother* than the words used to describe *man* were to *father* or *grandfather*. In fact, there was no relationship between the description of *man* and *grandfather*. Using an entirely different methodology, these studies also suggested that relational roles are very meaningful in conceptions of women but much less so for conceptions about men.

The same technique was also used to measure the beliefs about four sub-types of women and men who had frequently appeared in previous lists generated by college students. The four subtypes of women were housewife, athletic woman, businesswoman, and sexy woman. The four subtypes of men were athletic man, blue-collar working man, businessman, and macho man. The most frequent concepts generated for each type may be found in Table 2.2. Male targets were all viewed as equally unlikely to engage in female occupations or to have female physical characteristics. They were all seen as equally likely to perform masculine role behaviors and *not* to perform feminine role behaviors.

Each of the four female subtypes showed substantial variation from the generic "woman" and from each other. Businesswomen, for example, were viewed as more likely to engage in masculine roles and to have masculine

TABLE 2.2. Most Frequent Attributes Associated with Different Kinds of Women and Men

Woman	*Man*
Attractive	Strong
Feminine	Hides feelings
Smart	Acts macho
Sensitive	Sexy
Emotional	Muscular
Housewife	*Blue-collar working man*
Cleans things	Factories
Cooks	Hard worker
Takes care of kids	Middle-lower class
Motherly	Uneducated
Busy	Union member
Athletic woman	*Athletic man*
Muscular	Muscular
Good body	Healthy
Strong	Strong
Aggressive	In shape
Masculine	Good body
Sexy woman	*Macho man*
Good figure	Muscular
Long hair	Hairy chest
Good dresser	Moustache
Nail polish	Attractive
Pretty face	Self-centered
Businesswoman	*Businessman*
Smart	Wears suits
Nice clothes	Office with view
Unmarried	College education
Hard-working	Smart
Organized	Good appearance

Source: K. Deaux, W. Winston, M. Crowley, & L. L. Lewis (1985). Level of categorization and content of gender stereotypes. *Social Cognition, 3,* 145–167. Copyright © 1985. Reprinted by permission of Guilford Publications, Inc.

traits. At the same time, they were seen as less likely to engage in feminine roles, to have female physical characteristics, or to have feminine traits. In contrast, housewives were seen as high in terms of their possession of feminine role behaviors and low for both male and female occupations and masculine traits. The housewife stereotype appears to bear the closest resemblance to people's global stereotypes about women in general (Eckes, 1994).

Three important conclusions can be drawn from these data. First, stereotypes about particular types of women and men appear to be just as strong as stereotypes about men and women as global categories. Second, stereotypes about women appear to be more strongly differentiated than stereotypes about men. Men are like each other and not like women. Third, perceptions about women and men appear to be conceived in terms of opposites.

Physical characteristics appear to be much more important than traits, roles, or behaviors in triggering stereotypes. This should not be surprising: physical appearance is the first information people have when they meet a new person. Information about appearance is acquired within the first one-tenth of a second of seeing someone (Locher, Unger, Sociedade, & Wahl, 1993). The perception occurs so rapidly that people seem to be unaware of how much information they have acquired. Therefore, they tend to deny the extent to which physical appearance influences their perceptions of others. The importance of first impressions helps explain why there are few important differences among people in terms of the extent to which they stereotype (Wallston & O'Leary, 1981). Women and men appear to be remarkably similar in terms of the extent to which they see men and women as different.

Gendering Race and Class

Much of this work has been done using images of white middle-class women. However, images of women are differentiated by race and class as well as individual qualities. One study provided undergraduates with the labels *white woman, middle-class woman, black woman,* and *lower-class woman* and asked them to assign adjectives to each group in a "manner that best describes society's stereotypes of the group" (Landrine, 1985). Participants offered different stereotypes for each group although all of the adjectives used were stereotypically feminine. White women were rated significantly higher than black women on dependent, emotional, and passive (traits that resemble those identified in earlier studies). Lower-class women were rated significantly higher than middle-class women on confused, dirty, hostile, inconsiderate, and irresponsible. The stereotypes of white women and middle-class women were most similar to the traditional stereotypes of women in general.

Black women are evaluated considerably less positively than white women by white respondents. They are seen as louder, more talkative, and more aggressive than Euro-American women in general, although they are also seen as more straightforward than their white counterparts (Weitz & Gordon, 1993). Black women are rated as more masculine in traits and roles than white women and much more masculine in physical characteristics. There appears to be no difference between black and white women in ratings involving occupations. However, women of both races were seen as closer to each other than either was to men of their own racial category (Deaux & Kite, 1985).

These studies provide evidence that both race and social class are covert aspects of gender stereotyping, but they are too preliminary and too few to do more than conjecture about their meaning. It is important that such studies be continued and extended to include other ethnic groups for a number of reasons. First, the world is not simply white and middle class. Psychologists cannot assume that cognitive processes will be the same no matter what kind of stimulus person is used in their studies. Second, by not examining race and class variables, psychology ignores the extent to which these variables influence behavior. And, last, this kind of neglect makes members of minority groups invisible, with all of the psychological and social consequences that white middle-class women objected to when they were neglected.

GENDER STEREOTYPES IN THE MASS MEDIA

Stereotypes Are Everywhere!

It is easier to describe where gender stereotypes are *not* found than where they are. Since the 1970s researchers have documented the existence of stereotypes in virtually every aspect of the communications media (Busby, 1975). Stereotypes were found in children's picture books, story books, textbooks, in the movies, on television, and in magazine fiction (see Chapter 6). Stereotypes were evident in the disproportionate number of males to females portrayed, the gender-specificity of the traits that males and females displayed, the limited behavioral roles of women compared with the roles of men, the smaller number of occupations in which women could be found, and the different physical characteristics associated with each group (Unger, 1979a).

Unfortunately, things have not changed. An article headlined "Media More Likely to Show Women Talking about Romance Than at a Job" appeared recently in the *New York Times* (1997). It noted that there are still more male characters than female in the movies and on TV; in both the movies and on TV, 49 percent of the men are shown working outside the home versus 28 percent of the women; and women are much more likely than men to talk about romantic relationships. Music videos are the most sexist media in representing women. Seventy-eight percent of their performers are male.

Comic Strips

Sex stereotypes in the comics pages of newspapers may be particularly insidious. Because readers do not take this kind of material seriously, they may be unaware of the sexist messages they are receiving (Figure 2.3). Comics are also one aspect of the media easily accessible to young children. Images of men and women on the comics pages are still seriously distorted. Males appear more frequently as both central and minor characters. The most invisible women of all are ethnic minority women: Black women appear in less than 10 percent of Sunday comic strips; when they do appear they speak little and/or in stereotypic ways (Etter-Lewis, 1988).

Only 4 percent of all women depicted in comic strips are in the labor force, as compared with 69 percent of the men (Chavez, 1985). A much larger num-

FIGURE 2.3. Turning the tables.
Source: Rhymes with Orange. Copyright © 1999. Reprinted with special permission
of King Features Syndicate.

ber of occupations are shown for men. In an analysis of 100 randomly chosen
comic strips, the following occupations were found for men: travel guide, bar-
tender, salesperson, general, information clerk, court jester, vicar, doctor, king,
Viking, sergeant, cook, farmer, wizard, and flutist, as compared with two occupations for women: bank teller and secretary.

One pair of researchers has examined the same three Sunday comics
("Blondie," "The Born Loser," and "Dennis the Menace") over three decades
(Brabant & Mooney, 1986, 1997). These strips were chosen originally because
each included a married couple as central characters. As in the first study in
1974, women and girls continue to appear less frequently than men and boys
and remain at home more than males do. Images of women in passive roles
have declined significantly between 1974 and 1994, but women are still shown
as significantly more passive than men. There was no indication in the first two
studies that any of the women were employed outside the home; however,
Blondie now has a job. The major change over the twenty-year period was that
women were shown wearing aprons less often. Men are never portrayed as
wearing aprons even when Dagwood helps Blondie in her catering business!

The same two researchers have also investigated more contemporary
comic strips in which the wife is portrayed as working outside the home such
as "Hi and Lois," "For Better or Worse," and "Sally Forth," to determine if
these comics differed from more traditional strips in terms of activities, speaking appearances, and images portrayed (Mooney & Brabant, 1987). Even in
these less traditional comic strips, husbands were more likely to be portrayed
outside the home than wives were. Paradoxically, women characters who
work outside the home were also more likely to be shown in both child and
home care than full-time wives and mothers. Conversely, husbands of women
who worked outside the home were shown doing home or child care less often than husbands of nonemployed women. The image of career women in

these comics was not favorable. They were shown as critical, worrying a great deal, and having stressful, sleepless nights.

Women in the News

Women are much less often featured in the news media than men are. One comprehensive survey looked at the front pages of ten major- and ten small-market newspapers in various parts of the United States (Hernandez, 1994). It found that men were referred to or solicited for comment on the newspapers' front pages 75 percent of the time (a decrease from the previous year's 85%). Women were referred to or quoted on the front page only 25 percent of the time (the highest figure recorded during the six years that the survey has been conducted). A more recent survey of both major and minor newspapers found that stories about women had declined from 19 to 15 percent of the front-page stories ("A Survey Finds Bias," 1996). Men dominated the local news and business pages as well. Most of the front-page stories were written by men (67%), as were the op-ed or equivalent pieces (72%).

Women were portrayed negatively much more often than men in both small and large newspapers (30% versus 12%). Even the positive images of women and men were not equivalent. Nearly half of the positive portrayals of women in the major market papers (like the *New York Times* or the *Washington Post*) featured women as entertainers, whereas 82 percent of the positive portrayals of men were as authorities, experts, or opinion makers.

The news media appear to treat women in politics particularly harshly. Sixty percent of all the articles about Hillary Clinton were negative ("A Survey Finds Bias," 1996), although this appears to have changed now that she can be framed as a brave, but ill-used, wife. Some of the political cartoons that portrayed Geraldine Ferraro when she ran for the vice presidency were also quite cruel (Miller, 1993). She was often shown as a threatening or dominating figure who reduced Walter Mondale, the presidential candidate, to helpless submission. Most other women in politics are ignored. For example, little news space has been given to four female senators in their home states ("A Survey Finds Bias," 1996).

When women are mentioned at all, their appearance is commented on more frequently than that of comparable men. News articles treat males and females differently, mentioning the physical appearance and clothing of women much more often than those of men, no matter what the news story is about (Foreit et al., 1980). (See Chapter 3 for more examples of this practice.) As examples of this kind of trivialization of women in the public sphere, the media discussed what length robes Sandra Day O'Connor would wear when she was selected for the Supreme Court and what kind of suits and haircut were appropriate for Geraldine Ferraro in her debates for the vice presidency of the United States. More recently, the news media focused on Ruth Bader Ginsburg's diminutive stature in stories about her Supreme Court nomination. In contrast, it is difficult to recollect any physical feature of the seven male members of the Court.

Women on the Sport Page

Images of women in sports are particularly likely to be distorted by the media when they can be found at all. In 1990, for example, stories on men's sports outnumbered those on women's sports twenty-three to one in four of the top-selling newspapers in the United States (Messner, Duncan, & Jensen, 1993). Male and female athletes were even named differently in stories about them. Women athletes were most likely to be called by their first names, followed by black men athletes. Only white male athletics were routinely referred to by their last names.

Media images of male athletes tend to glorify their strength and power, even their violence. In contrast, media images of women athletes focus on feminine beauty and grace (so they are not really athletes) or on their thin, small, wiry, androgynous bodies (so they are not really women) (Lorber, 1993a). The most disturbing images of female athletes are those of body-builders (see Figure 2.4). In recent years competitions have moved away from the use of identical standards for women and men (involving the definition of the body's muscle groups) to a more feminine standard involving high heels and beauty as well as a 90-second fitness routine. Bulked-up women's bodies call into question beliefs about innate sex differences.

In coverage of the Olympics, detailed attention is paid to women gymnasts, figure skaters, swimmers, and divers rather than women's basketball, speed skating, or track and field.

FIGURE 2.4. Different approaches to women's bodies. The woman on the left meets the same standards as male bodybuilders whereas the woman on the right fits into current more feminine standards.

Extraordinary feats by women athletes who are presented as mature adults might force sports organizers and audiences to rethink their stereotypes of women's capabilities, the way elves, mermaids, and ice queens do not. (Lorber, 1993a, p. 573)

This bias against "mature" females reappeared in the 1998 Winter Olympics when elfin Tara Lipinski (left) won the gold medal against the more sensuous Michelle Kwan (Figure 2.5).

Pictorial Images of Women and Men

Sexism on the TV Screen

Every time you turn on your TV you get a dose of sexism. It has been estimated that the average American adult watches about four hours of television per day (Comstock, 1991). Sexist biases in both children's and adult television programs have been demonstrated repeatedly (Davis, 1990; Signorielli, 1989). Biases take the usual form of a larger representation of men than women. One study found, for example, that 57 percent of all the characters on comedy shows are men, and this figure rises to 71 percent in action/adventure shows (Davis, 1990). Female characters are usually younger than male characters by an average of ten years. This age difference is dramatically illustrated in one of the findings of this study—men are four times more likely than women to have gray hair.

FIGURE 2.5. Girls or women? Images of athletes in the U.S.'s most popular spectator sport involving women.

Television commercials are much more sexist than the programming. Women are about four times more likely to be provocatively dressed on television than men are (Davis, 1990). Women are particularly likely to be presented as sex objects in advertisements delivered during weekend afternoon sportscasts whose audience is primarily men (Craig, 1992). Women in these weekend ads are almost never shown without an accompanying man. When they are not models or sex objects, they are generally shown taking care of men—as hotel receptionists, secretaries, or flight attendants.

One recent Sony commercial produced a large number of complaints from women viewers (Goldman, 1993). It was shown primarily on MTV and all-sports ESPN and featured an emotionless stud draped over a white convertible. As he punched a button on his disc player, female names appeared—each accompanied by a scantily clad attractive woman. The final shot showed all of the women sitting in or lying on the car with a slogan "If you play it, they will come."

There were fewer female main characters in 1980s advertisements than there were in the 1950s, and the majority of women portrayed had no role or job other than "free floating consumer" (Allan & Coltrane, 1996). This study also found some improvements in representations of women. They were much less likely to be shown doing housework and when they were depicted in a job-related activity, a greater variety of occupations were displayed.

One of the most depressing aspects of sexism in TV commercials is the extent to which findings are replicable across cultures. Males predominate in the United Kingdom (Furnham & Bitar, 1993); Portugal (Neto & Pinto, 1998); and Kenya (Mwangi, 1996) as well as in the United States. These same studies also found women to be portrayed as younger than men and as more likely to be shown in traditional, domestic roles. Authoritative voice-overs in commercials also remained a male bastion in all the countries where this was studied.

Sexism in Magazine Advertisements

Several recent studies have shown that, in spite of thirty years of modern feminism, there has been little change in magazine images of women. Only one stereotype of women has declined over the past forty years. As women have entered the labor force in increasing numbers, many more ads show them in work settings outside the home (Busby & Leichty, 1993). But this trend is offset by the trend toward displaying women as decorative and sexualized (73% of all ads). One set of researchers suggested that American women seem to have "exited the home and stepped up to the department store beauty counters" (Busby & Leichty, 1993, p. 259).

Standards of taste seem to be rapidly falling in today's magazine advertisements. For example, the number of women who are shown partially clad or nude has actually increased in recent years (Kong, 1997; Plous & Neptune, 1997). In a current feature, *Newsweek* magazine (1999) discussed the trend toward maximizing breast cleavage with a headline entitled "Finding the Inner Swine." Pornography-like images, such as those in Figure 2.6, have little to do with pictures of real women such as those shown in the beginning of this chapter!

FIGURE 2.6. Fetish or fashion? Pamela Anderson achieved fame and fortune on the TV series "Baywatch," in great measure, because of her implant-augmented breasts. Interestingly, she has since announced that the implants

UR OWN POLYMORPHOUS APPETITES THAT IF HE WERE AROUND TODAY, WINCHELL

would be removed. At about the same time, teenaged singing star Brittny Spears stated that she would have her breasts surgically enlarged.

In addition to scantily clad models, ads in *Vogue, Madamoiselle,* and *McCalls* show a high proportion (over 40%) of women touching or caressing themselves—behaviors associated with the depiction of women as sex objects (Kong, 1997). They are also more likely than men to be portrayed by only part of their body, even when the part has nothing to do with the item advertised (see Figure 2.7). A survey of Israeli magazine ads also found an increase in images of women touching themselves and displays of female body parts (First, 1998). This increase has occurred in spite of the fact that Israel has a conservative state religion (Judaism).

Advertising's images of women are more nuanced than readers may perceive. For example, although white models were twice as likely as other models to be shown in low-status positions (kneeling or lying on the ground), black models wore the majority of animal prints—particularly those patterned after a predatory animal (Plous & Neptune, 1997). There was no difference in the amount of body exposure for black and white models. But both black and white women were nearly four times as likely to be exposed than either African-American or Euro-American men.

Magazines also tailor their images for their audience. Men of all races are more likely to be portrayed in occupational roles than are women (Vigorito & Curry, 1998). Occupational images of men are most likely to be found in magazines aimed at older men with high socioeconomic status whereas nurturing images of men are most likely to be found in magazines read by women. These findings imply that women are being led to have different expectations of men than men have for themselves.

FIGURE 2.7. Another form of gender stereotyping. The ad focuses on the sexuality of the female body rather than the product.

Probably the most overtly sexist images of women and men are presented on video channels. One recent study analyzed the characteristics of men and women on forty videos presented on music television (Sommers-Flanagan, Sommers-Flanagan, & Davis, 1993). Men engaged in significantly more aggressive and dominant behavior; women engaged in significantly more implicitly sexual and subservient behavior; and women were more frequently the object of explicit, implicit, and aggressive sexual advances. Viewers are given the message that romance, sexual attraction, and sexually suggestive activity are only important human activities.

Music videos aimed at predominately African-American rather than white audiences also feature men more than women. The situation may be slightly less dismal for black than for white women. For example, one group of researchers found only 11 percent of the featured singers or band leaders in video aimed at a white audience were women, whereas 19 percent of the videos aired on Black Entertainment Television featured women (Brown & Campbell, 1986). It would be difficult to say, however, that blacks are less sexist in this area than whites. The level of sexual aggression and derogation aimed at women in gangsta rap music (which is more popular with African-Americans) is enormous. Women are frequently called bitches or ho's and images of rape and assault are common. Such lyrics have psychological consequences. For example, when male students who were unfamiliar with this type of music read the lyrics, they expressed more adversarial sexual beliefs than participants who had not read sexually violent material (Wester, Crown, Quatman, & Heesacker, 1997). Many African-Americans are furious about this kind of lyrics and are pressuring rap groups to "clean up their act."

Some of the worst images of women of color are found in pornography. Although pornography treats women in general as mere objects for male sexuality, women of color are treated even more negatively than white women. For example, white women are seen as objects, whereas black women are portrayed as animals. Animals may be treated even more harshly than objects. They can be "economically exploited, worked, sold, killed, and consumed" (Collins, 1993b). In an analysis of X-rated videos, black women received a significantly greater number of verbally and physically aggressive acts than white women did (Cowan, 1995). Asian-American women are also stereotyped in pornography, but their image is one of a "special sexuality" that is both more exotic and more subservient than that of women from other ethnic groups (Root, 1995). Over the past century there have been many portraits of Asian women as prostitutes, ranging from "Madame Butterfly" through "Suzy Wong" to today's "Miss Saigon." The media exploit such images even when they purport to expose them. The *Time* cover in Figure 2.8 received a large number of letters objecting to this image of an Asian prostitute.

Subtle messages about gender roles are also present in both the fiction and nonfiction presented in women's magazines. Although a large number of the women profiled in established magazines such as *Harper's Bazaar*, *Ladies' Home Journal*, *Vogue*, *Cosmopolitan*, *Redbook*, and *Woman's Day* work full-time for pay, they are still more likely to be found in traditional occupations (Ruggiero &

FIGURE 2.8. When photos depict women of color, they may be more brutal than photos of white women. Note the racism and pornography of this cover photograph.

Weston, 1985). They are also less likely than women profiled in newer magazines (*Savvy, Ms, Working Woman,* and *New Woman*) to perceive themselves as having responsibility, power, or influence in relation to their jobs.

The basic message in magazine fiction aimed at women is that sexual relationships are central and all-important in women's lives—more important than family, children, or career at the individual level, and of course, more important than politics, the economy, or war and peace at the societal level (Cantor, 1987). This material is class biased as well as sex biased. For example, Cantor (1987) found in *True Story,* a women's magazine aimed at working-class readers, that 35 percent of the stories were about sexuality. However, sexual drive was portrayed as male, not female, and rape and attempted rape were frequent themes. These stories present a contradictory message. At the same time as they warn women to be careful of men's darker nature, they also tell women they need men to take care of them. In contrast, only one rape story appeared in *Redbook,* a magazine aimed at middle-class women (Cantor, 1987). The fear of rape may be one way to control the behavior of working-class women. In all the stories involving rape the woman was either in the "wrong place," had chosen not to accept advice, or had acted too independently.

These magazines even prescribe specific aspects of female attractiveness such as hair color. Researchers who examined the cover models for two women's magazines (*Ladies Home Journal* and *Vogue*) from the fifties through the eighties found many more blonds than would be found in the normal population (Rich & Cash, 1993). Blonds were even more common in *Playboy*, where they made up 50 percent of the centerfold models. In this magazine blondness seems to be synonymous with sexuality as well as beauty. Of course, it is even more impossible for women of color to attain this standard of beauty than it is for most Caucasian women.

Face-ism and Body-ism

Gender biases are displayed in the way images are presented as well as in their content. Systematic differences in the visual representations of females and males have been demonstrated in a creative series of studies. This phenomenon is called *face-ism* (Archer, Iritani, Kirnes, & Barrics, 1983). Face-ism is determined by measuring the relative size of the head/body in illustrations of women and men to produce an index of relative facial prominence. This index varied from .00 (no face shown) to 1.0 (only the face was shown). The higher this index, the greater the relative emphasis of the head versus the body. (The term *face-ism* shows some androcentric bias. The face-ism of men actually reflects the *body-ism* of women.)

The face-ism index was used to examine 1,750 published photographs from at least twelve issues of each of five American periodicals and a small city newspaper. With *Ms* magazine excluded, more than 70 percent were of men. More women than men were found in ads than in news stories. The average facial index of men was .65, whereas for women it was only .45. In other words, less than one-half of each photo was devoted to the woman's face. In contrast, two-thirds of each photo was devoted to the man's face.

Differential representation of women and men exists cross-culturally and persists over time. A comparison of photos in publications from eleven different countries showed a greater amount of facial prominence in photographs of men. An analysis of paintings from the last six centuries indicated that gender-related differences in face-ism have been present from the seventeenth century and have increased over time. The greatest differences were found in twentieth-century artwork. When men and women students were asked to draw men and women, both sexes drew pictures in which the man's face was significantly more prominent than the woman's face (more facial detail was also provided in drawings of men). Finally, students were asked to rate stimulus photographs of men and women in one of two versions. Photos were identical except for variations in facial prominence. The researchers found that photographs of either women or men with high facial prominence received more favorable ratings on intelligence, ambition, and physical appearance than the same photographs with low facial prominence.

These different visual representations may contribute to people's conception of what is unique about women and men. Concepts of intellect, personality, and character are associated with the face, and the face is given more importance for men than for women. In contrast, qualities associated with the body are weight, physique, and emotion. Women's bodies are more salient than those of men. These images contribute to and perpetuate stereotypes about what is important about men and women.

Stereotypes in the images of women and men have not changed as a result of the women's movement. An examination of *Time, Newsweek, Ms,* and *Good Housekeeping* revealed that men still received greater facial prominence than women in photographs in these magazines (Nigro, Hill, Gelbein, & Clark, 1988). Images convey information about relative power and status as well as gender. For example, photographs in various U.S. news magazines were found to have higher face-ism scores for whites than blacks as well as for men as compared to women (Zuckerman & Kieffer, 1994). Black women had the lowest face-ism scores of all the groups. A similar effect for race was found in European news magazines (although there were not enough photos of black women to compare the effects of sex and race).

The face-ism scores of women were lower than those of men even when differences in status were held constant. Although effects were not produced by status, they do contribute to people's perceptions about the relative importance of various groups. The same individuals were viewed as more dominant when depicted in high face-ism rather than low face-ism photographs. Face-ism may be both a cause and an effect of gender stereotypes. For example, evaluations of women's attractiveness have been found to be based on both their faces and their bodies, whereas evaluations of men's attractiveness appear to be based on their faces alone (Raines, Hechtman, & Rosenthal, 1990).

THE IMPACT OF MEDIA SEXISM

Gendered Images and Gender Roles

Stereotypes are implicit rather than explicit. Images of women in TV commercials appear, nevertheless, to inhibit women's desires for achievement. One experiment dramatically illustrates the impact of sexist advertising. College students of both sexes viewed replicas of either four current gender-stereotypical commercials or four replicas that were identical except that gender roles were reversed, then wrote essays imagining their lives "ten years from now" (Geis, Brown, Jennings, & Porter, 1984). Women who had viewed the traditional commercials de-emphasized achievement in favor of homemaking, more than men and more than women who had viewed the reversed role commercials. Gender-biased commercials influence men, too. Men who watched sexist TV commercials were subsequently more likely than those in the control group to judge a female job applicant as less competent, remember fewer biographical details about her, and remember more about her appearance (Rudman & Borgida, 1995).

Other studies have also found a relationship between TV viewing and acceptance of stereotypical roles. Individuals who watch television heavily have been found to give more sexist responses to questions about the roles of men and women than people who watched less TV (Signorielli, 1989). People who watched a larger number of stereotyped programs also tended to describe themselves in more gender-stereotypic terms (Ross, Anderson, & Wisocki,

1982). This relationship remained even when the frequency of television watching was taken into account.

What can be learned from all these studies of stereotypes in the mass media? Biases in advertising cannot be dismissed as trivial. It has been estimated that advertisements occupy almost 60 percent of all newspaper space, 52 percent of magazine pages, and 17 percent of prime-time television (Collins & Skover, 1993). Negative biases against women in the visual media may be particularly effective both for creating and evoking stereotypes because people are less likely to monitor their responses to pictures than to words. After all, it's just entertainment!

The consistency and stability of images of women and men may lead people to believe that there is a social consensus about gender roles. The universality of these images may help to explain why (as shown later in this chapter) relatively few individual differences in gender stereotyping have been found.

Nontraditional ideology does not appear to protect men from the impact of gendered advertisements. Less traditional males were found to be more susceptible to media influences than their traditionally masculine counterparts. After they had viewed ads featuring males in traditionally masculine rather than androgynous roles, they espoused more traditional attitudes than any other group (Garst & Bodenhauser, 1997).

Body Image and Self-Esteem

Exposure to unrealistic images of women has negative consequences for women and men. In general, women score lower than men on measures of bodily self-esteem. Their scores become even lower after exposure to photos of female models (Grogan, Knott, & Gaze, 1996). In this study, men's self-esteem also fell after exposure to pictures of male models. This may be equality, but is it progress?

In college women, the strongest predictor of dysfunctional views about the importance of physical appearance was the degree to which they accepted stereotypic views about male dominance and female submission in interpersonal relationships (Cash, Ancis, & Strachan, 1997). Women who accepted traditional views of female sexuality showed the greatest investment in their appearance, internalized societal standards of beauty more fully, and endorsed more problematic assumptions about the pivotal importance of their appearance in their lives. Feminist identity was not found to protect women from cultural standards.

Some feminist researchers have argued that the pervasive objectification of women's bodies is a major source of their low body esteem (McKinley, 1998; McKinley & Hyde, 1996). They have found that the relationship between body surveillance, body shame, and body esteem is stronger for women than for men. Those women who were more conscious of body surveillance were also more likely to be ashamed of their bodies, perceive a greater discrepancy between their actual and ideal body weight, and to have lower body esteem. When their objectified body consciousness scores were controlled, however, differences between women and men on these measures disappeared. Following are some of the items from this scale. Would you agree or disagree with them?

- I rarely think of how I look.
- I often worry about whether the clothing I am wearing makes me look good.
- I feel like I must be a bad person when I don't look as good as I could.
- I would be ashamed for people to know what I really weigh.
- A large part of being in shape is having that kind of body in the first place. (McKinley, 1998)

WOMEN'S QUEST FOR BEAUTY

The Social Importance of Looks

The connection between body esteem and traditional views about gender relations should not be surprising given how many cultural messages about female beauty people encounter every day. Good looks are more important to men than to women in evaluating a potential date, and especially important in a prospective sexual partner (Nevid, 1984). The male emphasis on female attractiveness starts early in adolescence. In a study of 11- to 15-year-olds in Iceland and the United States, boys and girls ranked ten characteristics of their "perfect woman" or "perfect man." Both Icelandic and American girls ranked kindness and honesty as most important, while boys from both countries ranked good looks highest (Stiles, Gibbons, Hardardottir, & Schnellman, 1987). Similar results have been found in a great many other research studies using a variety of methods.

The greater importance of attractiveness for women than for men is illustrated by the personal ads that people use to meet new partners. In a 1970s study, women more often mentioned their physical attractiveness in their ads, while men's ads advertised their financial resources. Women who described themselves as attractive in their ads more often mentioned looking for financial security in a mate, and men who described themselves as well-off more often mentioned looking for an attractive mate—the researchers titled their study "Let's Make a Deal" (Harrison & Saeed, 1977)! Men's emphasis on looks had not changed much during the 1980s. An analysis of 800 personal ads for same- and other-sex romantic partners found that men were more concerned with physical characteristics, while women were more interested in psychological factors (Deaux & Hanna, 1984). Neither race, sexual orientation, nor social class affected women's tendency to mention thinness in personal advertisements (Epel, Spanakos, Kasl-Godley, & Brownell, 1996). Do you think this will change as we enter the next millenium?

Beauty may represent a kind of power for women (Unger, 1979a). As the personal ads suggest, women may be able to barter their looks for financial security or other material resources. A study of dating on a southern U.S. campus found that attractive women are perceived by both women and men as deserving better treatment by their romantic partners. Usually, partners are fairly evenly matched on attractiveness. However, the less attractive the woman as compared with the man, the more likely she is to give him her loyalty and affection without his doing anything to "earn" it. Conversely, the more attractive she is in comparison to his attractiveness or social prestige, the more he must compensate by efforts to treat her well. When a man treats a woman well, "her attractiveness is validated and she gains prestige in her social group" (Holland & Skinner, 1987, p. 89).

Attractive women raise the prestige of men. Men are evaluated more highly when they are presented as the boyfriends of attractive rather than unattractive women (Bar-Tal & Saxe, 1976). Curiously, men paired with attractive women are not necessarily seen as more physically attractive—instead, they are seen as better people. People seem to infer that these men must have something going for them to win such an attractive "prize."

Learning to Care about Looks

Girls and women cannot escape the cultural message that a woman's worth is to be judged by her appearance. Learning to care about looks is a lifelong process. Parents of newborns see their daughters as cuter, prettier, softer, and more delicate than their sons, and treat their babies accordingly (see Chapter 6). Currently, elasticized pink ruffled headbands are the height of fashion for bald female infants. Many girls have their ears pierced and wear nail polish before they enter kindergarten. They listen to stories of princesses whose beauty drives men to slay dragons; they play with Barbie dolls and watch Miss America pageants. Throughout elementary school, girls receive more compliments on their appearance than boys do. Their wardrobes are bigger and more elaborate, and girls are especially noticed and admired when they wear dresses (Freedman, 1986).

Images of females in popular magazines also contribute to girls' learned obsession with appearance. Photographs of women and girls are usually subjected to computer retouching, leaving readers with the impression that such flawlessness is real and attainable. Photographs of males, however, tend to show their stubble, scars, and facial lines (Tannen, 1994).

Makeup sets are sold for girls as young as 3, advertised as "the fun way to learn beauty secrets." They include rollers, styling combs, curling irons, hairpieces, and dye for the hair; paint, gloss, shadow, and mascara for the face; and lotions, polish, and decals for the hands and nails (Freedman, 1986). Recently a "workout kit" (jumprope, leotard, exercise mat) was nationally advertised for girls ages 5 and up not as a means of developing coordination, fitness, or athletic skill but as a way to work off that extra chocolate chip cookie. From toys like these, girls learn that feminine beauty requires many faces, that they should impersonate grown-up women by disguising themselves, and that parents approve of spending much time and money on appearance (see Figure 2.9). Perhaps most importantly, each girl learns that her own face and body are inadequate and need to be improved (Freedman, 1986).

Impossible Standards of Weight

As described earlier in this chapter, women in Western cultures are bombarded with images of "ideal women." Women are also exposed to far more media messages about staying slim and keeping in shape than men are. A content analysis of forty-eight issues each of women's and men's magazines found

FIGURE 2.9. Little girls learn to disguise their looks with makeup in order to be "glamorous."
Source: © 1981 by Nicole Hollander. Used by permission of Nicole Hollander.

sixty-three ads for diet foods in the women's magazines—and only one in the men's. At the same time, women were receiving many more messages about eating—the women's magazines contained 359 ads for sweets and snacks, while the men's magazines contained exactly one. Overall, there were 1,179 food ads in women's magazines and 10 in men's magazines. The message for women, then, is that they should stay slim while at the same time thinking constantly about food (Silverstein, Perdue, Peterson, & Kelly, 1986). Women are expected to nurture others, but not themselves, by preparing and serving food.

Girls and women learn that no matter how hard they try, they can never measure up. The definition of what is beautiful has gotten more restrictive over the past few decades. For example, the ideal body shape has (literally) narrowed. An analysis of measurements of Miss America contestants and *Playboy* centerfold models showed that they became steadily thinner after 1960 (Garner, Garfinkel, Schwartz, & Thompson, 1980). There has been no such trend for male models in men's magazines (Petrie et al., 1996).

The curvaceousness of movie actresses and models in women's magazines has been declining since about 1950 (Silverstein et al., 1986), until many models look as though they are starving. Advertisers call this the "waif look." Even Barbie has gotten thinner over time (Freedman, 1986), making the "Barbie look" even more unattainable for women. Researchers who scaled Barbie and Ken to adult height determined that the probability that a real, human woman would have the same proportions as Barbie is about 1 in 100,000. It is more possible for a man to be built like Ken with odds of only 1 in 50 (Norton, Olds, Olive, & Dank, 1996).

Many adolescent girls and women develop distorted perceptions of their bodies. They may believe themselves to be wider or fatter than they really are, exaggerating descriptions of their "huge" thighs, breasts, or stomachs. Increasingly, cosmetic surgery is sold as an acceptable response to normal aging and variation in body shapes (see Figure 2.10).

Girls' and young women's weight is intensely monitored. In a recent survey of more than 800 U.S. college women, 72 percent reported that they were repeatedly teased or criticized about their looks, their weight, or both (Rieves & Cash, 1996). Teasing and/or criticism usually began in late childhood or

FIGURE 2.10. Media messages. The ideal woman is made, not born, with a little help from the surgeon's scalpel.

early adolescence and lasted for an average of 6.6 years. The most commonly ridiculed attributes were features of the face or head (45%) and weight (36%). Peers were named as the most frequent teasers although one-third of the women with brothers named them as the worst offenders. Almost all the women who reported being teased also reported being distressed by it, and 41 percent felt it had been detrimental to their body image. These self-reports were consistent with research that shows a correlation between the frequency of teasing and negative body image (Cash, 1995).

Young women's weight is also intensely monitored on college campuses. One campus fraternity confers a "pig award"—given to the brother who has hooked up with a "fat, ugly" girl during that week (Addelston, 1998). Many women on this and other campuses claim to have heard a myth or legend about a sorority initiation during which fraternity men wrote with red markers on the places on women's nude bodies where they needed to lose weight. The story cannot be verified. It may not matter whether or not it happened since it creates the same effect as if it had. At many colleges, a typical day's diet for women is a bagel and juice for breakfast, salad for lunch, and salad and fruit for dinner. Addelston asks: "What is the real disorder—the Pig Award or the girls who feel forced to pick at their pizzas?"

There is only one other time in this century (the 1920s) when standards of thinness were as extreme as they are now; during that decade, an epidemic of eating disorders appeared among women (Silverstein, Peterson, & Perdue, 1986). Is history repeating itself? Eating disorders among women will be discussed further in Chapter 14.

Minority Women and White Standards of Beauty

In a working-class, predominantly black neighborhood in Philadelphia, a large billboard pictures three glamorous African-American women. All are very light-skinned, thin, and young, with dainty noses and soft-looking hair. The words underneath the picture are "Philadelphia's Faded Beauties"; the billboard advertises skin bleach.

From fairy-tale princesses to movie stars, the idealized image of feminine beauty in Western societies has traditionally been a Caucasian one. Women of color bear a greater burden than their white counterparts as looksism combines with sexism and racism to stigmatize them as unattractive. Black women, even more than white women, describe feeling ugly. In the 1960s, the message that "black is beautiful" began to influence the African-American community, and the white beauty image was displaced by Afro, corn row, and dreadlock hairstyles, along with African-influenced jewelry and clothing. Yet despite these changes, women of color describe being rejected because of their dark skin or curly hair. In one study, 70 percent of black women believed that black men prefer very light-skinned women (Bond & Cash, 1992). For some African-Americans, marrying a lighter-skinned partner is still a mark of status—a legacy of adapting to a racist culture (Freedman, 1986).

On the other hand, the ideal of waiflike slimness seems to be applied more to white women. Within the African-American community, heavier women are not necessarily considered unattractive, and a wider range of body shape and size is accepted. This ethnic-related difference may be related to social class. In one study, African-American women of higher social status valued thinness as much as white women, while those of lower social status perceived a heavier body size as attractive. They did not judge themselves "overweight" unless they were much heavier than the weight that would have triggered such a judgment in the other groups of women (Allan, Mayo, & Michel, 1993).

African-American women may be protected from excessive concern about weight by their conviction that black men prefer small-figured women less than white men do (Molloy & Herzberger, 1998). They are probably correct in this belief. African-American men have been found to be more inclined than Euro-American men to desire larger, heavier women (Cunningham, Roberts, Barbee, Druen, & Wu, 1995). The obsession with overweight is more likely to be found in certain segments of the U.S. population. Individuals who are conservative, individualistic, and who believe in a just world are especially apt to have antifat attitudes (Crandall, 1994). Such individuals are also more likely to be white.

African-Americans are not the only women of color judged by white standards. As North American movies, television programs, magazines, and commercial beauty products are increasingly marketed throughout the world, the North American beauty ideal is becoming an international one, part of a "global culture machine," where each woman is encouraged to aim to be "whiter, more Western, more upper-class." Women factory workers in Malaysia are provided with makeup classes by their employers, and Asian women undergo eyelid surgery to Westernize their eyes (Kaw, 1994). There is also evidence that Mexican women are internalizing U.S. standards of weight. They have begun to report more fear of becoming fat than have Mexican men, although these fears are still less than those of Euro-American women (Crandall & Martinez, 1996).

There is virtually no systematic psychological research on the effects of inappropriate standards of beauty on women of color. At present the effects may only be hypothesized. Oliva Espin, in discussing sources of oppression common to Hispanic and other women of color, suggests that "the inability of most non-white women to achieve prescribed standards of beauty may be devastating for self-esteem" (Espin, 1986, p. 276). In the absence of psychological research, perhaps the best way to understand the oppression of appearances (and how that oppression is internalized by people of color) is to attend to descriptions and analyses by members of the oppressed groups. In Maxine Hong Kingston's book *Tripmaster Monkey*, Asian-American characters discuss eyelid surgery. The African-American novelist Toni Morrison has provided a moving example of a black girl who prays daily for blue eyes and blond hair in her tragic novel *The Bluest Eye*. In his film *School Daze*, Spike Lee analyzes the effects of blacks' internalized racism on young black women's relationships with each other and with black men. Lee's film begins with a scene in which black women call each other names based on skin color.

LANGUAGE AND WOMEN'S PLACE

Verbal Images of Women and Men

The English language contains a large variety of sexist as well as racist words. Analyses reveal persistent negative biases against women. They trace, for example, various forms of debasement that have occurred in female-gender words (Schultz, 1975). The mildest form appears to be democratic leveling whereby the female member of a word pair that was previously reserved for people in high places comes to refer to people at any level of society. Thus, the word *lord* still refers to the deity and a few Englishmen, while anyone may call herself a *lady*. Other examples of this process are *sir/madam* and *master/mistress*. In the last two examples, the female terms have been debased into words with sexual connotations. Whether a woman is a "madam" or a "mistress," her identity is still based on her relationship with men as a sex object.

Terms of endearment addressed to females have also undergone debasement. *Dolly* and *Tootsie*, for example, began as pet names derived from nicknames but eventually acquired the meaning of mistress or prostitute. A *tart* was originally a small pie or pastry, then a term of endearment; next it became a term applied to young women who were sexually desirable, then to those who were deemed careless of their morals, and, finally, it became a word meaning women of the street. Words denoting boys and young men have not been debased in this way.

Metaphors and labels are likely to have wide reference when applied to men and to be narrower, with sexual connotations, when applied to women (Lakoff, 1975). For example, if one states that a man is a professional, one is suggesting that he is a practitioner of a respected occupation. If one calls a woman a professional, one may be implying that she is practicing "the oldest profession." Other terms of the same sort include *tramp* (a male drifter but a female prostitute) and *game* (a male dupe but a female who is seducible).

To a surprising extent, terms referring to women resemble those referring to children. Excluding any negative connotations, words like *doll, honey, pussycat,* and *baby* can apply equally well to women or children (particularly girl children). Our language, like our culture, equates adulthood with manhood (Graham, 1975). The most frequent image of women in popular songs is childlike (Cooper, 1985). There is a clear distinction between the words *boy* and *man* that does not exist between *girl* and *woman*. A boy greatly increases his status when he becomes a man, while a girl is seen as losing status and bargaining power when her youth is lost. Language echoes gender stereotypes when it encourages females to cling to girlhood as long as possible.

Power relationships between men and women are reflected in gender-specific slang vocabulary, too. More sexual slang is used to describe women than men by college students of both sexes (Grossman & Tucker, 1997). The most commonly chosen terms to describe women were *chick, bitch, babe,* and *slut.* The most commonly chosen words to describe men were *guy, dude, boy,* and *stud/homey.* As you can see, the terms used to describe women were more offensive than those used to describe men. Their effects on women's sexuality will be discussed in Chapter 8.

Derogatory names are even more likely to be aimed at women from ethnic outgroups. In a historical inventory of terms for women of various ethnic groups, many negative terms were found that alluded to women of color. These terms often referred to stereotyped physical differences from white women (in terms of skin color, hair texture, or shape of eyes), made derogatory sexual allusions, or used food and animal metaphors (Allen, 1984).

Some of the mechanisms that operate in the linguistic distortion of gender-specific words have been categorized (Graham, 1975):

- Labeling of what is considered to be an exception to the rule—*woman doctor, male nurse, career girl.* The term *feminine logic* is a particularly sexist example of this process.
- Trivializing female gender forms—*poetess, suffragette* (instead of suffragist), and, more recently, women's *libber.*
- "His virtue is her vice"—*mannish attire* or *aggressive female, butch.*
- Exclusion, which may be the most pervasive mechanism of all. The use of *man* in its extended sense, as in *mankind* or "the child is father to the man," may be one of the major sources of the perceived lack of relationship between "woman" and "adult."

The Case of the Generic "He"

One of the issues that have been raised about the English language by feminists is whether the use of nouns such as *mankind* and "generic" pronouns such as *he* for both sexes perpetuates sex biases. It is clear that these supposedly neutral linguistic usages are not perceptually neutral. For example, when undergraduates read sentences aloud that used either *he, he/she,* or *they* and verbally described the images that came to mind, both sexes produced a disproportionate number of male images to the supposedly generic *he* (Gastil,

1990). Male students also gave male images when *he/she* was used. Only *they* appeared to function as a true generic pronoun.

Use of the generic pronoun *he* seems to make men and women think of males first, even when the context implies both sexes (Gastil, 1990; Moulton, Robinson, & Elias, 1978). After examining twenty studies in which people of various ages—from 6 years to adult—were presented with the masculine form used for both sexes, it was concluded that the pictures selected or drawn, the names used for the persons referred to, the subjects of stories, the answers to questions about the sex of the people referred to in stories, or the imagery seen was predominantly, and often overwhelmingly, male (Henley, 1989). In all these studies, females were excluded more easily than males when masculine grammatical forms were used.

It appears that we think of people as males. But do we also think of males as people? One creative study asked students to write a short paragraph about the most typical person they could imagine and then give that person the "perfect typical name" (Hamilton, 1991). The instructions were gender neutral. Nevertheless, only 25 percent of the students in the study described and named a female.

Is any actual harm done by masculine generic usage? After all, such usage may be a grammatical formality devoid of any actual influence on behavior. Newspaper columnists have been ridiculing criticisms of sex-biased language for their triviality for years. One favorite butt of humor is the "personhole cover."

Several studies have documented the behavioral effects of sexist language. An early study found, for example, that women's interest in job positions was

---

Making a Difference ━━━━

Mary Daly (b. 1929), radical feminist theologian, university professor, lesbian philosopher, has been called a thorn in the flesh of Catholic theologians and would undoubtedly be proud to be viewed as such by representatives of all patriarchal religions. Daly sees the women's movement as a spiritual revolution and is fascinated by language and neologisms (newly coined words). "We have not been free to use our own power to name ourselves, the world, or God," she says. One way Daly helps women break free of patriarchal mythology and imagery is by creating new words and giving new meanings to words that have traditionally promoted negative female images (*crone* is defined as "a great hag of history" in her dictionary, *Websters' First New Intergalactic Wickedary*). Despite the fact that Daly has taught theology and women's studies for decades, is the possessor of seven college degrees (three of them doctorates), and is the author of seven books, she remains on the fringes of what she calls "academentia." In January of 1999 the administration of Boston College threatened to force her to stop teaching there after 23 years, because of her refusal to allow men in her classes. Daly is respected among feminists as a fierce fighter and a mother of radical feminist theology.

Source: Griffiths, Sian (Ed.). (1996). *Beyond the glass ceiling: Forty women whose ideas shape the modern world.* Manchester, England: Manchester University Press.
Teacher stands by ban on men. (1999, February 26). AP story.

influenced by the wording of advertisements (Bem & Bem, 1973). This research led to a change in job titles in a major telephone company. Other such changes in language include the shift from *mailman* to *mail carrier* and from *stewardess* to *flight attendant*. The gender ratio of these occupations has changed as well.

Gender bias in language has also been found to influence comprehension and memory as well as self-expectations. The number of correct answers given by women to questions about a science fiction story (presented out loud) was higher when it contained unbiased forms than when it contained masculine forms (Hamilton & Henley, 1982). Both male and female students who read an exclusively male version of the "Ethical Standards of Psychologists" (in contrast to one that used "he or she" or no gender-specific words at all) rated a career in psychology as less attractive for women than for men (Briere & Lanktree, 1983). Some of these effects occur even when participants are unaware that any linguistic manipulation has occurred. Thus, women's memory of essays forty-eight hours later was worse when the essays were written with masculine generics than when they were written with unbiased grammatical forms in spite of the fact that they had not noticed which pronouns had been used (Crawford & English, 1984).

Sexist Language and Conceptual Distortions

Ambiguous language can influence one's understanding in crucial areas. For example, a content analysis of a sample of AIDS coverage in the *New York Times,* the *Los Angeles Times, Newsweek,* and *Time* during the period from 1983 to 1985 found these major news media used the generic terms *homosexuals, gays,* or *bisexuals* in headlines without specifying men (Hamilton, 1988). Did this exposure lead readers to interpret the terms generically and thereby assume that lesbians and gays were at equally high risk for contracting AIDS? To answer this question, college students were asked to rank in order various groups according to what they thought was each group's relative risk for AIDS. Although nearly all the students accurately ranked homosexual men as the number-one risk group, 66 percent of the students incorrectly ranked homosexual women as of higher risk than either male or female heterosexuals. The truth is, of those named, lesbians are the lowest risk group. The amount of perceived risk associated with being a lesbian decreased when the written material was made more specific. This study established a link between language usage in the media and people's lack of understanding about a serious disease. The use of a generic word such as *homosexual* for men also reinforces the pervasive association between being male and being human.

New words acquire stereotypic assumptions similar to words that have been in the language longer. For example, the title *Ms* conveys impressions about a woman who prefers to use it. Women who prefer Ms were seen by Canadian undergraduates as more achievement oriented, socially assertive, and dynamic, but less interpersonally warm than women who preferred the more traditional titles of *Miss* or *Mrs* (Dion, 1987). These attributions were more extreme if the students were told that the woman *chose* Ms rather than simply being told her name and title (Dion & Cota, 1991). The Ms stereotype overlapped the gender stereotype of men with its emphasis on competency and agency. Over time the Ms stereotype has changed to be more positive, probably because it is no longer seen as a radical feminist choice (Crawford, Stark, & Renner, 1998).

STEREOTYPES AS SOCIAL DEMANDS

Gender Stereotypes and Social Attributions

Stereotypes serve as the agents of social messages about the appropriate roles and behaviors of women and men. As you saw earlier in this chapter, gender stereotypes consist of a network of associations involving personality traits, social roles, behaviors, and physical characteristics. Because of their complex interlocking nature, stereotypes can influence assumptions about the behaviors of males and females in a variety of contexts. It is, in fact, difficult to find conditions in which the identical behavior of women and men is viewed similarly by observers. Gender-blind social judgments appear to be quite rare.

Stereotypes reflect the different perceptions people have about women and men. However, stereotypes have a *prescriptive* as well as a *descriptive* function. They inform people about what behavior ought to be as much as they tell them what it is. The prescriptive aspect of stereotypes is conveyed primarily by the different *attributions* people make about others on the basis of their gender. Attributions are assumptions about why people behave the way they do. If one believes that women and men have different causes for the same behaviors, these beliefs can lead to different expectations about future behaviors. It is through such expectations that stereotypes operate as a means of social control (for more about how this can produce discrimination against women, see Chapters 3 and 11). Here we will focus on factors that influence assumptions about the normality, social acceptability, and social deviance of women and men.

The Social Value of Physical Attractiveness

Physical appearance is one of the major sources of information that people use when they are making stereotypic judgments about others. No physical characteristic is too trivial! One recent study found that people rated photos of brunette job applicants as more capable than the same applicants wearing a blond wig (Kyle & Mahler, 1996). This bias can be translated into monetary terms. The suggested average starting salary for blond women was $23,792 versus $27,478 for brunettes. Blondes may be seen as having "more fun," but they are certainly not offered more money with which to do so.

Good looks are an asset for both males and females. So many positive social judgments are made about physically attractive people that researchers coined the phrase "What is beautiful is good!" (Dion, Berscheid, & Walster, 1972). Physical attractiveness is more salient in judgments about females than in judgments about males. As discussed earlier, most images of women are beautiful images. Female bodies are displayed more than male bodies and judged more harshly. How does the cultural emphasis on women as symbols of beauty influence perceptions about women and men?

People appear to be more sensitive to facial differences among women than among men. They make more refined distinctions, offer more extreme positive and negative ratings, and show more consensus about female than about male faces (Schulman & Hoskins, 1986). Facial expression also affects the ratings of women more than men. Women who smiled were seen as more attractive than those who did not. The absence of a smile had a greater effect on perceptions of women than of men. Nonsmiling women were rated as less happy, less warm, less relaxed, and less carefree than the average woman (Deutsch, LeBaron, & Fryer, 1987). These findings illustrate how even minor deviations from social expectations can result in negative social judgments.

Weight and Social Stigma

There is overwhelming evidence that women are much more severely stigmatized for obesity than are men (Crandall, 1995; Crocker, Cornwell, & Major, 1993). Like attractiveness, stigma based on weight can be translated into economic terms. Overweight women earn less money than their nonoverweight counterparts (Sargent & Blanchflower, 1994). They are even less likely to receive support for college from their parents who, nevertheless, support their overweight sons as well as their sons and daughters who are not overweight (Crandall, 1995). Heavyweight women and men are underrepresented in colleges, but in the latter case, it is not because of their parents' prejudices.

Negative attributions about weight are much more likely to be found in white than black populations. When African-American women were asked to evaluate the qualities of professional models dressed in fashionable clothing, they did not stigmatize large women. This was especially true when they rated large black women. In contrast, white women rated heavier models, especially large white women, as lower than average in attractiveness, intelligence, job success, relationship success, happiness, and popularity (Hebl & Heatherton, 1998).

Stereotypes About Social Deviance

Variations in physical attractiveness also influence perceptions about the social deviance of women and men (Unger, Hilderbrand, & Madar, 1982). For example, less attractive women were seen to be more likely to be involved in a radical student organization rather than in student government and as more likely to be lesbian. Less attractive men were also seen to be more likely to be involved in radical politics and to be more likely to be studying for a feminine-typed occupation such as nurse or librarian rather than a traditionally masculine field. There were no important differences between the judgments made by men and women. Respondents appeared to be unaware that their judgments were based on the differential attractiveness of the people in the photographs.

Inferences of homosexuality are made more frequently about women who are perceived to be physically unattractive (Dew, 1985). Women who held conservative attitudes about gender roles were particularly likely to associate homosexuality with those women to whom they had given the worst evaluations on physical appearance. There is a strong relationship between perceived attractiveness and perceived gender. This relationship means that highly attractive women are seen as feminine and highly attractive men are seen as masculine (Gillen, 1981). Thus, attractiveness serves as a mediator between perceptions about appropriate gender roles and assumptions about socially desirable behavior. Less attractive women are perceived as more masculine, and women who are described as masculine are perceived as more likely to be homosexual than women who are described as feminine (Storms, Stivers, Lambers, & Hill, 1981). Homosexual individuals of both sexes are also most frequently described in terms of the stereotypic characteristics of the other sex (Kite & Deaux, 1987). These same perceptual connections probably account for the belief that feminists are more likely to be lesbian.

People appear to have a kind of inversion model involving sex, gender, and sexual orientation. Gay men are sometimes seen as similar to heterosexual women. To a lesser extent, lesbians are seen as similar to heterosexual men. This belief in the inversion of gender-related characteristics in gays and lesbians is, like most stereotypes, quite inaccurate. But this perceptual inversion is very strong (see Chapter 5). Although stereotypically masculine and feminine traits may exist independently within the same individual (defined as **androgyny**), perceptually these characteristics are organized as polar opposites. It is difficult for people to recognize, for example, that a woman can feel sexual desire for another woman and still like makeup, work as a flight attendant, and be timid rather than prefer to wear overalls, work as a mechanic, and be assertive.

Attributions of homosexuality appear to be based on physical appearance cues similar to those that people use to make other inferences about gender. For example, undergraduates assigned higher homosexuality ratings to feminine male and masculine female faces as well as to unattractive female faces (Dunkle & Francis, 1990). Facial maturity affects attributions about a variety of other gender-related traits and roles as well. Baby-faced males were actually seen as lower in power than mature-faced females (Friedman & Zebrowitz, 1992).

STEREOTYPES AND SEXISM

Ambivalent Sexism

Stereotypes about women are particularly complex because they appear to contain both positive and negative judgments. In general, women appear to be liked more than men but are not seen to be as competent (Eagly & Mladinic, 1993). Some men, known as *ambivalent sexists,* appear to compartmentalize these views of women (Glick & Fiske, 1996). Their views have a *hostile sexism* dimension that acknowledges the competence of women who challenge their power in society, but also sees them as manipulative, cold, and aggressive. At the same time, they maintain idealized images of women in their traditional roles as wives and mothers. This idealization (called *benevolent sexism*) is also sexist because it sees women as lovable but unable to take care of themselves. These two views can be illustrated by a few items from the scale devised to measure them. Items that are part of the hostile sexism scale include:

> "Women seek to gain power by getting control over men."
> "Most women fail to appreciate fully all that men do for them."

Items that are part of the benevolent sexism scale include:

> "Women should be cherished and protected by men."
> "Many women have a quality of purity that few men possess."
> (Glick & Fiske, 1996)

Ambivalent sexists generate polarized images of women. Like nonsexist men, they view career women as intelligent, hardworking, and professional, but they also perceive them to have negative interpersonal qualities such as aggression, selfishness, greed, and coldness (Glick, Diebold, Bailey-Werner, & Zhu, 1997). These men reported that they feared, envied, were intimidated by, or felt competitive toward career women. In contrast, nonsexist men viewed career women as confident and honest and expressed admiration for them. Both sexists and nonsexists agreed that homemakers are caring, loving, and nurturant; however, sexist men frequently reported "a wealth of positive emotions toward homemakers—warmth, trust, respect, and happiness" (Glick et al., 1997).

Sexist men cannot always avoid conflicted feelings toward individual women because some women are not easily categorized while others may combine liked and disliked qualities. How would an ambivalent sexist feel about a wife and mother who advocates feminism? Ambivalent sexists may be particularly resistant to attitude change because their favorable feelings toward traditional women enable them to deny their prejudice against women and the power dimension in their relationships with them.

Sexism and Discrimination

Ambivalent attitudes about women who deviate from traditional roles may explain why some women are penalized even when their "deviant" behaviors are appropriate for their occupational role. *Hopkins v. Price Waterhouse* (a case that came before the U.S. Supreme Court a few years ago) illustrates the biasing effect of stereotypes. When Ann Hopkins came up for review for promotion to partner in a major accounting firm, her aggressive (and very successful) strategies were interpreted as "overbearing, arrogant, self-centered, and abrasive." She was denied the promotion, despite the fact that she had brought more money to the company than any other person proposed for partner that year—$25 million (Fiske, Bersoff, Borgida, Deaux, & Heilman, 1991). She was denied the position because of "interpersonal skills problems" that could be corrected, a supporter told her, by walking, talking, and dressing more femininely. In contrast, an opponent suggested she needed to go to "charm school."

A group of researchers in cognitive social psychology served as expert witnesses in this trial. They testified that stereotyping was most likely to occur in situations in which the target person is isolated or few of a kind in an otherwise homogeneous environment. (See the discussions of tokenism in Chapters 3 and 11.) Stereotyping also increases when members of a previously omitted group move into jobs that are nontraditional and when there is a perceived lack of fit between the person's social category and his or her occupation. And, finally, stereotypes are most likely to occur when evaluative criteria are ambiguous (Fiske et al., 1991).

The situation at Price Waterhouse fit these conditions. At the time, the company had 27 women partners out of a total of 900, or 3 percent. Moreover, the traits considered desirable in a manager—aggressive, competitive, driven, and masterful—are still not considered desirable in women (Heilman, Block, Martell, & Simon, 1989). Finally, in the Price Waterhouse partnership process, hearsay information was given equal weight with the opinions of people who had more intensive contact with the candidate. There were no corporate policies prohibiting sex discrimination and no corporate awareness that sex discrimination was inappropriate (Fiske et al., 1991).

The Supreme Court decided in favor of Ann Hopkins. Its ruling stated: "Nor . . . does it require expertise in psychology to know that if an employee's flawed interpersonal skills can be corrected by a soft-hued suit or a new shade of lipstick, perhaps it is the employee's sex and *not* her interpersonal skills that has drawn the criticism" (*Hopkins v. Price Waterhouse* 1989, p. 1793, cited in Fiske et al., 1991). It also stated: "We sit not to determine whether Ms Hopkins is nice, but to decide whether the partners reacted negatively to her because she is a woman" (p. 1795). And, finally, their ruling pointed out the impossible dilemma for women that such stereotypes produce. "An employee who objects to aggressiveness in women but whose positions require this trait places women in an intolerable Catch-22: out of a job if they behave aggressively and out of a job if they don't" (p. 1791). The social processes that create such dilemmas (also known as double binds) are described in Chapter 3.

The Persistence of Stereotyping: Cognitive Factors

Stereotypes about women seem to cluster into two groups involving judgments of competency and likability. Recently, some social psychologists have begun to look beyond their laboratories in their efforts to understand why some rather than other cultural images of women are internalized and used. They argue that perceptions of women's competence are primarily influenced by their status in society, whereas perceptions of their likability are influenced by whether they are seen to compete or cooperate with men (Glick & Fiske, 1999). Thus, women may be divided into *subtypes* on the basis of their social roles. One subtype of women includes housewives and "chicks" who are seen as nice but incompetent. Another subtype includes career women, feminists, lesbians, and some female athletes who are seen as competent but not likable. This group violates conventional gender expectations, does not meet heterosexual needs, and challenges societal power relations.

The existence of subtypes helps explain why stereotypes persist despite the large number of disconfirming examples that people encounter every day. For example, what happens when a person meets a feminine woman who is an excellent athlete or a student leader who is also warm and sensitive? When people encounter individuals who disconfirm their beliefs about members of their group, they often find it easier to reclassify these persons than to change their beliefs about a whole category. A person's response to a member of a social category will, therefore, depend on which subtype of that category is activated.

A recent experiment illustrates the way subtyping works. The researchers examined the attitudes about women of different groups of men (Haddock & Zanna, 1994). They found that right-wing authoritarian men did not share the positive evaluations of women held by other groups of men. This was because the different groups constructed different images in response to the label *woman*. Unlike other men, the term *woman* did not evoke the image of a *housewife* for authoritarian men. Instead, *woman* elicited an image of *feminist* and triggered negative evaluations. The authoritarian men had more negative beliefs about feminists and saw them as possessing a large number of values that they disliked. Ambivalent sexist men are also more likely than nonsexist men to generate a large number of subtypes of women and to make more extreme judgments about different subgroups (Glick et al., 1997).

Some disconfirming cases are better than others. Change in stereotypes is promoted by many examples of otherwise typical group members who engage in one atypical behavior. Change is also facilitated when the disconfirming behavior occurs repeatedly in many different settings. For example, women who are fighter pilots, rock climbers, and construction workers have undermined the stereotype that women cannot do tough, demanding work (Fiske & Stevens, 1993).

Stereotype change is also influenced by the relative power of individuals (Fiske, 1993).

- People pay attention to those who control their outcomes. When people's rewards or punishment depend on someone else, they increase their attention to stereotype-inconsistent information about their partner. For example, Joshua notices and remembers that his boss Susan plays racquetball even though he does not think that racquetball is a feminine activity.
- People make inferences about their partner on the basis of the inconsistent information they have gathered. They construct personality profiles of people on whom they depend, as if to increase their ability to predict their actions. Joshua may infer that Susan is active and assertive because she plays racquetball and decide that being deferential of her authority will pay off for him.
- Interdependence decreases stereotyping regardless of whether it is the result of cooperation or competition. Attention to inconsistent information about one's partner is greatest when the partner has more power. However, when no interdependence is involved, people ignore inconsistent information rather than use it. If Susan is a coworker rather than Joshua's boss, he may not notice that she plays racquetball.

Making Meaning

One of the surprising aspects of gender stereotypes is the extent to which males and females agree about them, even in children as young as 2 years of age

(Cowan & Hoffman, 1986). These findings are consistent with a view of stereotypes as forms of social consensus. This means that stereotypes are not individual opinions, but collective agreements about what constitutes social reality.

Since different groups in our society encounter different versions of social reality, it is not surprising to find ethnic variation in gender stereotypes. Black respondents, for example, differ from white respondents in their stereotypes about women as a group as well as about specific aspects of women's appearance such as weight. One large-scale open-ended survey studied more than 750 African-American and Anglo-American respondents in the Detroit area who differed widely in age, education, and economic status (Smith & Midlarsky, 1985). White respondents had more stereotypical views about women than black respondents did. For example, no black respondent characterized women as passive, although this trait appeared quite often in the responses of the white individuals.

Caution is needed in making statements about the similarities and differences between ethnic groups in gender stereotyping because culture influences both the way one sees and the way one describes social reality. For example, groups of undergraduate women who differed in ethnicity showed few differences in self-evaluations (Landrine, Klonoff, & Brown-Collins, 1992). But they differed in the meaning they attached to the adjectives they used. In other words, they appeared to be more similar than they actually were because they were using the same words with differing meanings. For example, women of color were most likely to define assertive as "Say whatever's on my mind," whereas white women were most likely to define it as "Stand up for myself." These differences would not be apparent if researchers look at self-rating of traits, but not their meaning.

The same word may have different meanings when applied to members of differently stereotyped groups. For example, the word *aggressive* has been found to indicate "physical violence" when applied to a construction worker and "verbal abuse" when applied to a lawyer (Kunda, Sinclair, & Griffin, 1997). When women and men engage in the same activities, they may also be evaluated by shifting standards (Biernat & Kobrynowicz, 1999). Thus, when participants viewed the same five aggressive acts by a man or a woman and were asked to describe them, the most frequent description of the woman was *bitch* or *bitchy*, whereas the most frequent response used to describe the man was *aggressive* (although *asshole* and *jerk* were close behind).

Cultural Factors

To understand the processes that create stereotypes, it is important to explore societies where the meanings associated with maleness and femaleness are different from our own. This kind of cross-cultural exploration has been more the province of anthropology than of psychology. It is difficult to develop standardized instruments in different languages since stereotypes are, by definition, inextricably tied to the language we speak.

One solution to this problem is to use nonverbal or pictorial materials. As discussed earlier, face-ism, or the tendency to portray males as more facially prominent than females, was present in the published materials of all the countries studied (Archer et al., 1983). The greater importance or salience of female attractiveness also seems to be universal in all the countries that have been studied (Buss, 1989). One large-scale study that surveyed attitudes toward men and women in more than twenty-five countries found similar perceptions about women and men in most of the countries surveyed, although some differences between cultures also existed (Williams & Best, 1990). No society examined was gender-blind.

It is important to keep in mind that differences in images of women and men can be much more extreme in some cultures than in the United States. Sometimes researchers find that representations of women simply do not exist. In an important ethnographic museum in Israel, for example, few women were found even in exhibits showing scenes from family life (Izraeli, 1993). One reproduction of a painting of holiday worship even erased the women who had originally stood in the balcony (Figure 2.11). This exclusion of women from history had gone unnoticed by visitors because what is rendered invisible is rarely missed.

It is important to do more cross-cultural studies. But it is also clear that such studies may do little to tell us where the ultimate source of sex stereotypes is to be found. Thus, although women's roles are marginalized in Israel,

FIGURE 2.11. Women are sometimes made invisible. The painting on the right hangs in Israel's Diaspora Museum—a museum devoted to portraying Jewish life in many lands. The original painting by Gottlieb on the "Day of Atonement" (on the left) included women in the balcony. Museum officials have offered no explanation for their erasure.

women are also drafted into its army and hold major public policy positions. Similar contradictions between stereotypes and behavior can be found in other countries as well. For example, although women's bodies and attire are tightly controlled in many Moslem countries, both Pakistan and Bangladesh have had women prime ministers.

FORMS OF SEXISM

New Measures of Covert Sexism

Until recently, few differences had been found between those who hold negative biases against women and those who do not. In part, this was because psychologists had looked at attitudes about women as a group rather than at more nuanced images. Some new studies have revealed correlates of sexism in both women and men. High scorers on a right-wing authoritarianism scale (people who endorse the legitimacy of current civil and moral authority) have traditional gender-role identity and attitudes. They also rate political events associated with women as less important, and see feminists and women as having high power and influence in society (Duncan, Peterson, & Winter, 1997). They also express more antiabortion views in essays and are punitive toward women seeking abortion. Women with this viewpoint are particularly unlikely to attend meetings on women's issues.

Openly admitting that one believes women are inferior to men is not easily done in 2000. Prejudices may continue to exist but in disguised form. One set of researchers devised a neosexism scale that focuses on the conflict between egalitarian values and residual negative feelings toward women (Tougas, Brown, Beaton, & Joly, 1995). Neosexism is related to old-fashioned sexism but predicts attitudes toward symbolically important issues such as affirmative action better than old-fashioned sexism does. Neosexist beliefs appear to be triggered by self-interest. For example, they were stronger among employees of a firm committed to affirmative action than among university students.

There is also some evidence that some individuals who oppose affirmative action do so because they believe that sexual equality already exists. People who score high on a modern sexism scale—a scale designed to measure covert sexism—tend to show such perceptual biases (Swim, Aikin, Hall, & Hunter, 1995). They overestimated the percentage of women in several male dominated occupations. They also believed that gender segregation in the workforce (see Chapter 11) is due to biological or natural differences between the sexes (Swim & Cohen, 1997). Neosexism and modern sexism scales probably measure related biases. Both, for example, predict negative attitudes toward lesbian and gay men as well as feminists (Campbell, Schellenberg, & Senn, 1997).

Is the glass half empty or half full? Are negative attitudes toward women increasing or declining? The answer depends on how change is measured. Scores on the Attitudes toward Women Scale (Spence & Helmreich, 1978)—the first scale to measure attitudes about the political, economic, and social equality of women and men—have become more feminist over the past 20 years

(Twenge, 1997). Men are less liberal in their attitudes than are women, but gender differences have been decreasing since the early 1980s.

On the other hand, changes in behavior lag behind the endorsement of gender-egalitarian beliefs (Spence & Hahn, 1997). Women and men show the greatest resistance to change in the area of male–female relationships. In their relations with men, women admitted to deliberately acting "feminine" as much or more than men admitted to acting "masculine" (Sherman & Spence, 1997). Traditional ideology about gender roles may be linked to social desirability for women. Such "new old-fashioned girls" do not see it as necessarily a bad thing for men to initiate dates, offer women seats on the bus, or offer admiring looks or glances to strange women (Theriault & Holmberg, 1998).

The Future of Change

With the growth of the women's movement, have gender stereotypes declined? The evidence suggests they have changed little over the past thirty years. One study replicated in 1978 a study of gender-role concepts that had first been published in 1957 (Werner & LaRussa, 1985). The researchers used the same 200-item checklist with the same number of respondents at the same university (Berkeley) at which the earlier study had been conducted. They found that 62 percent of the adjectives that had been significantly assigned to men in 1957 were still part of the male stereotype in 1978. Of the adjectives that had been used to describe women in 1957, 77 percent were still part of the current stereotype. In no case did an adjective shift between men and women over the two decades between studies, although some adjectives dropped out and some new ones appeared. The major differences between the two studies was that there were fewer negative stereotypes about women. Roughly equal numbers of favorable and unfavorable adjectives were assigned to women and men. A more recent study which examined the gender stereotypes of college students from 1974 to 1991 also found no substantive change (Lueptow, Garovich, & Lueptow, 1995).

The reduction in negative stereotypes about women should perhaps be a cause for joy. However, this change seems to be due to the assignment of positive communal qualities such as helpfulness, warmth, and understanding to women. Unfortunately, perceptions that women possess these qualities did not influence respondents' attitudes toward the equality of women and men. In other words, women are thought of as very good people but not as worthy as men of equal rights, roles, and privileges (Eagly & Mladinic, 1989). Cross-cultural studies also tend to show this distinction between goodness and other gender-related properties. Overall, neither sex is seen as better than the other, but men are viewed more favorably than women in dynamic terms such as activity and strength (Williams & Best, 1990).

Beliefs about the differences between men and women function at many psychological levels. They help preserve a sense of self, structure interpersonal relationships, and maintain the legitimacy of social systems (Jost & Banaji, 1994). They are maintained by a variety of cognitive and behavioral processes (see Chapter 3).

The connections between perceptions and reality are complex. Biases in information gathering, encoding, and memory processes are important for understanding stereotypes, but so are contemporary societal practices that discriminate against women. For example, although the structure of the work world has changed dramatically, sex segregation of occupations remains strong. If current societal arrangements underlie stereotypes, changes in cognitive biases will not occur (since the current biases are valid in terms of how the real world works). Thus, those interested in social change will have to look beyond cognitive biases.

Some groups are more frequently the target of stereotypes than others. In his landmark book on prejudice, Gordon Allport (1954) attributed being a target to historical as well as psychological circumstances. The difference between believing in stereotypes and being the target of them is closely related to relative power. Groups do not exist in a social vacuum. The issue of power will be discussed more fully in Chapter 3, but it can never be ignored.

Finally, we all have some responsibility for change. Negative attitudes toward feminists have implications for all women—whether or not they label themselves as feminists. Many women understand at some level that if they express complaints about women's status, note some form of inequality, or report sexual harassment, they can expect to be perceived negatively. Negative judgments are likely to focus on aspects of likability—on traits that are important for interpersonal relationships. These perceptions have a silencing effect on women and help maintain the status quo. Will the information in this chapter help you find a voice?

CONNECTING THEMES

- *Gender is more than just sex.* Gender stereotypes exist inside people's heads as forms of cognitive bias. They are maintained through interactive processes involving both the person and society. The consistent and universal representation of women and men as different helps generate these biases. In turn, cultural images of the sexes are used to justify sexist perceptions.

- *Language and naming are sources of power.* Nothing in a culture can be regarded as trivial. Differences in the pictorial and linguistic representations of men and women influence how people perceive and think about the world. Declines in stereotyping are facilitated by naming. Naming brings into focus that which has been invisible.

- *Women are not all alike.* The global stereotypes of "women" and "men" are too broad. Subtypes exist based on physical characteristics, roles, race/ethnicity, and class. It is important to investigate both the similarities and the differences between perceptions about different groups of women and men.

- *Psychological research can foster social change.* Stereotypes are almost "pure" forms of social construction. Cognitive social psychology can help us understand the psychological mechanisms underlying these constructions and how constructs are related to current social realities.

SUGGESTED READINGS

FISKE, SUSAN, & STEVENS, LAURA. (1993). What's so special about sex? Gender stereotyping and discrimination. In S. Oskamp & M. Constanzo (Eds.), *Gender issues in contemporary society* (pp. 173–196). Newbury Park, CA: Sage. A well-written review of the social cognitive approach to stereotyping by a pioneering researcher in the area. It emphasizes the applicability of laboratory research to real life problems.

WEITZ, ROSE (Ed.). (1998). *The politics of women's bodies: Sexuality, appearance, and behavior.* New York: Oxford University Press. A well-chosen set of articles from a social constructionist perspective. It focuses on the way appearance affects all aspects of women's lives.

CONBOY, KATIE, MEDINA, NADIA, & STANBURY, SARAH (Eds.). (1997). *Writing the body: Female embodiment and feminist theory.* New York: Columbia University Press. More postmodern in its perspective than the previous suggested reading, this book presents work by leading feminist theorists that look at the media, sexuality, and violence against women from a broader cultural perspective than that found in most books edited by social scientists.

Doing Gender

- **GENDER AS A SOCIAL CATEGORY**
  The Categorization Process
  The Importance of Gender as a
    Category
  Cognitive Tricks People Use with
    Social Categories
  Behavioral Confirmation and the Self-
    Fulfilling Prophecy
- **THE SOCIAL CONSTRUCTION OF
  GENDER-RELATED DIFFERENCES**
  Who Helps Whom?
  Upsetting Hierarchical Relationships
- **GENDER AND SELF-CATEGORIZATION**
  The Effect of Dominance and
    Subordination
  The Effect of Distinctiveness
- **STATUS AND POWER**
- **GENDER DIFFERENCES AS STATUS
  DIFFERENCES**
  Gender and Nonverbal Behavior
  The Perception of Nonverbal Cues to
    Status
  Gender and the Use of Social Power

- **THE ROLE OF GENDER IN BOUNDARY
  MAINTENANCE**
  Deviance and the Power to Define
  Dealing with Deviance in a Group
    Setting
  The Token Woman
- **WOMEN AND MEN DOING GENDER**
- **CHANGING ROLES IN A CHANGING
  SOCIETY**
  Gender and Leadership
  Gender and Legitimacy
  Moving Beyond the Double Bind
- **THE INTERNALIZATION OF GENDER
  NORMS**
  Women and Personal Entitlement
  The Awareness of Categorical Bias
  Combating Social Myths
- **CONNECTING THEMES**
- **SUGGESTED READINGS**

"Who am I?" This is a question that is much simpler to ask than to answer. Psychologists interested in identity have been asking this question for more than thirty years (Gordon, 1968). People answer it in both predictable and idiosyncratic ways because everyone has many forms of identity—both social and personal. For example, if we, the authors, answered this question, we would probably list woman, feminist, mother, wife, professor, middle-aged, European-American, middle-class, and so on. The order might vary from time to time, and there would be some differences between us, but gender would always be high on the list.

Why is gender such a central part of identity? It is important because it is a major way by which society classifies people. Everyone has a gender although it is noticed more by some people than others. As will be discussed in this chapter, power and status are important determinants of when gender makes a difference. Gender is also more important in some contexts than in others even when people are unaware of how and why it is having an impact. Finally, gender is internalized so that people use its "rules" as a way of defining themselves and evaluating their own behavior. This chapter focuses on the ways gender is created and maintained by social processes. This is why we call the chapter "Doing Gender."

Gender and power are intimately connected. As has been eloquently stated by two early feminist researchers in this area:

> Social interaction is the battlefield on which the daily war between the sexes is fought. It is here that women are constantly reminded of what their "place" is and here that they are put back in their place, should they venture out. Thus, social interaction serves as the locus of the most common means of social control employed against women. By being continually reminded of their inferior status in their interactions with others, and continually compelled to acknowledge that status in their own patterns of behavior, women may internalize society's definition of them as inferior so thoroughly that they are often unaware of what their status is. Inferiority becomes habitual, and the inferior place assumes the familiarity—and even desirability—of home. (Henley & Freeman, 1989, p. 457)

GENDER AS A SOCIAL CATEGORY

In this chapter, we discuss in detail the social processes that maintain women's place. The social processes by which gender is constructed are complex. When women are not treated the same way as men, people can explain these distinctions on the basis of gender-related personality differences, skills, and roles. Experimental research allows one to disentangle the various factors involved. Although they examine behavior in artificial situations, these studies support the arguments of feminists. Interpersonal processes involving gender help to maintain a pattern of male dominance. Moreover, the large number of social mechanisms involved and people's relative unawareness of them help to convince both women and men that androcentric reality has a substantive basis in the natural world.

Experimental analyses are not enough. Although they identify where the problems are, they do not offer solutions. Solutions require both individual and collective action. Thus, the last part of this chapter examines some of the ways strong women have redefined themselves and changed some of the ways of doing gender.

The Categorization Process

Gender may be viewed as a scheme for the social categorization of individuals (Sherif, 1982). It is a lens through which thought and behavior are framed. These thoughts and behaviors have been extensively studied by psychologists as forms of social cognition. Gender is one of the most important social categories. It is relevant even when it seems that it should be irrelevant. Why, for example, do people use a feminine pronoun when they speak of ships?

The following ingenious experiment illustrates how people construct social categories with properties analogous to those of women and men (Hoffman & Hurst, 1990). Participants were asked to imagine a planet that had two kinds of people—Orinthians and Ackmians—who performed different jobs on the planet. Most of the members of one group worked in the industrial centers of the city. Most of the other group stayed home and raised children. Participants were then asked about the personality characteristics of the people in the two jobs. They were also asked why they thought there was an unequal distribution of the two groups in these jobs. Participants reported that they believed each group had personality characteristics that suited them for a particular kind of work.

Pretend that the Orinthians and Ackmians are men and women. Because people have limited experience with men and women in the same roles, they tend to explain gender roles as though they are due to personality differences. They assume that people are in various roles because they wish to be. Roles, however, force people to behave in particular ways regardless of their individual qualities. Nevertheless, people tend to confuse the actor and his or her role (TV actors who play villains often complain about being yelled at in public). Confusion between actor and role explains why people are surprised when a female executive or pro athlete acts "like a man."

Gender as a social category is closely associated with other forms of social distinction. In particular, gender is closely tied to conceptions of power and status. Gender and status may be hopelessly confused in the way people organize social reality (Unger, 1978). Men behave and are behaved toward as high-status people in most situations, whereas women behave and are behaved toward as low-status people. These interpersonal relationships reproduce society's ideology about the greater worth of males.

The Importance of Gender as a Category

People frequently use the perceived sex, race/ethnicity, and age of others as categories by which to organize their ideas about them. Of course, these are not the only categories available. Social psychologists have found that people construct social divisions even when the rationale for doing so is either trivial or arbitrary. For example, students put people into different groups on the basis of whether or not they liked abstract art or whether they consistently overestimated or underestimated the number of dots on a slide (Wilder, 1986).

Such groupings differ from gender, race/ethnicity, and age in several important ways. One must find out something about other people in order to use their behaviors in the construction of categories. Information about gender, race/ethnicity, and age is, however, immediately available. These categories are also relatively permanent. They cannot be changed as easily as one can change a preference in art.

Perhaps because of these properties of visibility and permanence, gender, race/ethnicity, and age appear to be particularly important cues for the perceived categorization of others. Some early studies demonstrated how important sex is for the identification of others (Grady, 1979). These studies revealed that people almost always notice whether another person is female or male.

They also have difficulty ignoring sex in favor of other aspects of the person that may be more useful to them.

To demonstrate that perceived sex is a fundamental category in the identification of others, in one study a situation was chosen in which sex did not appear to have any functional value for the perceiver. People who were waiting at a subway station were asked if they had just purchased a token. If they had, they were told that a study on eyewitness reports was being conducted and would they please describe the token seller by listing characteristics for the purpose of identification. Of the characteristics mentioned, the sex of the token seller—in this case, female—was always included. It was given as a first or second characteristic 100 percent of the time. In fact, it was given first 75 percent of the time and was displaced to second position only by race (in this case, African-American).

> And they never varied—all respondents agreed on female for each of the token sellers. As if to underscore the prominence of sex as a characteristic, the one respondent who couldn't offer any description said, "I can't even remember whether it was a man or a woman." (Grady, 1977, p. 4)

These informants apparently thought that sex was a very important characteristic to mention for purposes of identification. Of course it isn't important in any statistical sense. By naming sex, one only distinguishes a person from about 50 percent of the population. Most people have many more individuating characteristics—glasses, hair color, freckles, and so forth.

The major importance of sex as a social category has been documented by more recent studies, too. These find that people are more likely to categorize others by their sex than by their race (Stangor, Lynch, Duan, & Glass, 1992). They are also more likely to confuse individuals of the same sex than individuals of the same age, race, role, or name (Fiske, Haslam, & Fiske, 1991). And they are more apt to notice when a person breaks a gender prescription than when he or she "fails to act his or her age" (Fiske & Stevens, 1993).

When gender is not available as a social category, people invent it. An ingenious study illustrates the process by which people construct gender. College students were given a story in which two individuals, "Brown Buttons" and "Gray Buttons," took turns furthering the progress of a relationship (John & Sussman, 1984–1985). At various points in the narrative, conversational dominance shifted from one protagonist to the other and back again. At each of these transitions respondents were asked to guess the sex of Gray and Brown Buttons. You can see some of this dialogue in Box 3.1. At each question mark, you may select the sex of the participants.

Did you think Gray Buttons was a man or a woman? How about Brown Buttons? At various points during this dialogue, people in the study changed back and forth between male and female labels as social dominance shifted from one character to the other. They changed labels even when this was at the expense of the logical continuity of the narrative; that is, they had to give up their previous labels and "resex" characters.

Many people seem to have difficulty accepting the idea that people can take turns engaging in gender-inconsistent behaviors during a social encounter. They see sex and gender as one indivisible whole. In addition, they

Box 3.1 Brown Buttons and Gray Buttons at a Singles Bar

The scene is a "singles" bar located in a middle-sized town. Some people are dancing in one section of the room. Others are sitting or standing around the bar drinking and socializing. An individual with brown shirt buttons (Brown Buttons) walks purposefully toward a person with gray shirt buttons (Gray Buttons) and begins a conversation. After a few minutes, Brown Buttons asks Gray Buttons to dance. Gray Buttons agrees, and they begin to move to the dancing area.

?

As they start to dance, Gray Buttons says to Brown Buttons, "You are a good dancer. I don't come across many people who dance this well."

"Thank you" says Brown Buttons with a slightly embarrassed smile. "I think you dance well too."

"What do you do for a living?" asks Gray Buttons.

"I'm a high school teacher," answers Brown Buttons. "And you?"

"I'm a research technician," says Gray Buttons, "but I'm thinking of getting into computers."

As the music comes to an end, Gray Buttons says, "You are a very interesting person. I'd like us to talk some more . . . why don't we sit over here?" motioning to a small table in the corner.

?

They've been sitting for quite a while. Brown Buttons orders drinks again, and they continue to talk. . . . "I'm really fascinated by your life; I'd like to get to know you better."

"That's interesting," says Gray Buttons. "I find you exciting too, but I'm not sure that I'm able to handle too much familiarity now. I'm really interested in pursuing my career. . . ."

?

"I understand your position," says Brown Buttons, "but I'd really like to see more of you."

"I'm going to think about it," says Gray Buttons. "Why don't we stop off at my place? Perhaps we'd both get some perspective over coffee and. . . ."

Source: From John and Sussman, "Initiative taking as a determinant of role reciprocal organization," In *Representations; Social Constructions of Gender;* edited by Rhoda Unger. Copyright © 1989 Baywood Publishing Company, Inc. Reprinted with permission.

perceive masculinity and femininity as complementary aspects of gender that reproduce sex. When one person was perceived as a man, the other was perceived as a woman. No one conceived of the actors as both of the same sex.

People's need for a secure sex identification has been made the subject of humor by the character of Pat in the television show *Saturday Night Live* (see Figure 3.1). Some of the episodes in this series illustrate the extent to which ordinary life is gendered. In one episode, for example, Pat got his/her hair cut and the stylist could not decide whether to charge for the male cut ($15) or the female cut ($18). In another, a druggist tried to figure out whether he should provide Pat with Mennen or Secret in response to a request for deodorant. Pat's fellow employees go to great lengths to determine whether he/she is male or female but are constantly foiled. Pat wins the game of "strip poker" and has an androgynous-looking significant other named Terry. When asked questions such as "Who puts on the condom?," the response is similarly unhelpful— "Why we both do—as part of foreplay." The fact that audiences continue to find Pat hilarious indicates how rigid gender categories are in our society.

Customary representations of reality do not leave any room for ambiguity of sex or gender. For example, in Ursula LeGuin's prize-winning science-fiction novel *The Left Hand of Darkness*—a story that takes place in a world in which people can alternate between sexes—one of her most startling lines is "The king was pregnant."

FIGURE 3.1. Is Pat female or male? And, why do people care so much?

Cognitive Tricks People Use with Social Categories

Stereotypes describe what people think about members of various social categories. They constitute one form of cognitive bias. Such cognitive biases operate inside the head of the observer, and they would be less of a problem if they would stay there. But biased beliefs based on social categories are communicated to others and influence their behavior.

People try to make the world an orderly, predictable place and use a variety of strategies to achieve that end. Popular strategies involve the use of social categories to explain the way people behave. Although often quite functional (they save users time and energy in making decisions about the people they meet), such explanations are usually based on limited information and can lead to broad generalizations that are incorrect. Some of the strategies that people use to create and maintain categories are selective attention and encoding, selective recall, and selective causal attributions.

Selective Attention and Encoding

People encode information about others based on their perceived race and sex. When asked to recall the speakers from a conversation they had heard, students were less accurate in distinguishing between members of the same social category (either race or sex) than they were between members of different categories (Taylor, Fiske, Etcoff, & Ruderman, 1978). All the women (or men) seemed to "look alike." The students did not intend to use these cues as a strategy to remember particular people. In fact, the one student who admitted using race was very apologetic about having done so.

People tend to minimize differences within groups and exaggerate differences between them. Within-group characteristics are also exaggerated in inverse proportion to the size of the minority subgroup present. When few members of the minority subgroup are present, their characteristics are seen as more stereotypic of their social category. Thus, people saw women as more feminine and men as more masculine when there were few other members of their sex present in a group (Taylor et al., 1978). Women and blacks were just as likely to categorize and make social judgments about the minority group as men and whites. In other words, being a member of a less powerful group does not necessarily influence how one sees others who are also marginalized.

Of course, social categories are not equivalent with respect to status and power. Low-status groups are often perceived as more homogenous than higher-status groups (Messick & Mackie, 1989). High-status groups are also much more likely to receive favorable trait evaluations (Jost & Banaji, 1994).

Men and women seem to agree about their relative place in the dominance hierarchy. When they were asked to identify different males and females in a group on the basis of what they had said (other cues were also varied—such as hair length and color of clothing), sex was the primary category used. The mistakes made using gender categories were consistent with the relative status of men and women in our society. Men had more difficulty distinguishing between female target persons than between male target persons under all conditions. Women paid more attention to the environment in which the interactions took place but still confused females more than males (Lorenzi-Cioldi, 1993). Thus, both women and men acknowledged the greater personal distinctiveness and individuality of males.

Selective Recall

People systematically distort their recollections about individuals from a particular category to make them resemble their stereotypes about that category. For example, when students who read a long story about the life of a woman named Betty K. were subsequently informed that she was currently living either as a lesbian or with a male partner, they "remembered" more events that supported their current interpretation of her sexual identity (Snyder & Uranowitz, 1978). Respondents who learned that Betty K. had a lesbian lifestyle remembered more events in her life that reflected stereotypic beliefs about lesbians; for example, that she had not dated in college. Similarly, people were more likely to recall having seen "librarian-like" qualities in the behavior of a stimulus person when she was portrayed as a librarian rather than as a waitress (Cohen, 1981).

It is important to become aware of how perceptions about people are constructed because beliefs have powerful but often unnoticed consequences. "In our quest to see others as stable and predictable creatures, we may cognitively create a world in which erroneous inferences about others can perpetuate themselves" (Snyder & Uranowitz, 1978, p. 949).

Selective Causal Attributions

Attributional biases occur when people try to figure out the causes of behavior and take cognitive shortcuts that speed up the decision-making process. One major form of attributional bias is known as the *fundamental attribution error*. This term refers to the tendency to underestimate the impact of situations on other people's behavior and to overestimate the impact of their individual personality. It is this error that leads people to believe that many behavioral differences between women and men are consistent and stable.

A number of attributional biases based on various aspects of gender have been found. For example, luck appears to be associated with the success of individuals for whom success is not expected. When respondents were asked to explain the rapid rise of attractive women or men as corporate executives, they viewed luck as more responsible for the success of attractive women than for the success of unattractive women. The reverse was true for men. Unattractive men were seen to have needed more luck to succeed (Heilman & Stopeck, 1985). Similarly, a white man with a successful banking career was seen as having greater ability and less luck than a comparable white woman, black man, or black woman (Yarkin, Town, & Wallston, 1982).

One particularly destructive bias is *blaming the victim*. Victim blame may be one form of the fundamental attribution error. Victims are seen as responsible for their misfortunes by people who do not wish to believe that the same random disaster could happen to them. Blaming the victim often occurs when women are raped (see Chapter 13).

Behavioral Confirmation and the Self-Fulfilling Prophecy

Cognitive biases are not just passive perceptions about others. When people interact with someone, they look for information that will confirm their beliefs about that person's social category. For example, when students were informed that they would be interviewing a person who was either an introvert or an extrovert, they chose questions that would confirm the social label they had been given (Snyder & Swann, 1978b). It is only a small step away from generating questions that confirm expectations to acting in such a way as to produce them. This process is part of a phenomenon known as the **self-fulfilling prophecy.**

There are two parts to self-fulfilling prophecies. One part is that people sometimes act to confirm the beliefs that others have about them. This process involves changes in *self-presentation* (behaving in a way that evokes a particular image in others). One of the earliest studies that applied this concept to gender asked women students to describe themselves to a male partner whose stereotype of an ideal woman was said to conform closely to either a traditional or nontraditional type (Zanna & Pack, 1975). The attitudes of these women had been measured on a previous occasion. When the partner was desirable (good-looking and attending an elite university), the women presented themselves more in terms of his ideal type regardless of their actual attitudes. The women performed better on tests of intellectual competence when the desirable partner was portrayed as having nonstereotypic views about women. Women also altered their self-presentation strategies when they believed they were to be interviewed by a sexist rather than a nonsexist potential employer (von Baeyer, Sherk, & Zanna, 1981). When women believed that they were to be interviewed by a sexist man, they wore more frilly clothing, more jewelry, and perfume to the interview.

It seems reasonable that people should choose to change their appearance to maximize the potential rewards in a social interaction. However, these studies demonstrate how sexism is maintained. The participants did not yet know anything about the man's behavior, which exists only in their imaginations. Nevertheless, these women changed their behavior to conform to what they believed to be the expectations of powerful or desirable men.

The other part of the process by which self-fulfilling prophecies are created is known as *behavioral confirmation* (how people's actions produce the behaviors they expect from others). Many traits traditionally associated with men and women may be produced by the combination of self-presentation and behavioral confirmation. In the earliest study on gender and the self-fulfilling prophecy, a label of physical attractiveness was shown to improve women's social competence (Snyder, Tanke, & Berscheid, 1977). Male college students had a short conversation by telephone with women whom they had been led to believe were either physically attractive or unattractive. Photographs had, however, been assigned to their female partners at random. And the women were unaware that their male partners had received any false information about their physical appearance. Nevertheless, judges (who heard only the women's part of the conversation) rated those women who had been labeled as physically attractive as more friendly, sociable, and likable than those who had been labeled as less physically attractive. Presumably, the women were responding to subtle cues in the men's conversations with them.

Even in such a brief encounter, the perceivers created their own social reality. Such behaviors may have long-term effects on the behaviors of those who are categorized as attractive. Attractive people of both sexes have been rated as more socially skillful by people who have only had a telephone conversation with them (Goldman & Lewis, 1977).

Traits traditionally associated with either men or women are also influenced by self-fulfilling prophecies. For example, men who expected to interact in a competitive game with a man who had been labeled as hostile initiated more aggressive interactions with him (Snyder & Swann, 1978a). In turn, their behavior induced more aggression from him than from a supposedly nonhostile partner. When the target individuals in this study were led to believe that their aggressive behavior reflected their own personality characteristics, they maintained their increased level of aggression in their subsequent competition with new partners. If, however, the targets were informed that their behavior in the game reflected their partner's behavior, they did not continue this higher level of aggression with new partners.

This finding illustrates one of the most potent elements of the behavioral confirmation process. If a person internalizes the new behavior generated by the behavioral confirmation process, both that person and the perceiver may come to share perceptions about what he or she is like. "What began in the mind of the perceiver will have become reality not only in the behavior of the target but also in the mind of the target" (Snyder & Swann, 1978a, p. 151).

Self-fulfilling prophecies have been shown to contribute to the perpetuation of stereotypic beliefs about women (Skrypnek & Snyder, 1982).

Unacquainted pairs of men and women were asked to negotiate a division of labor on a series of work-related tasks that differed on their gender-role connotations. Students were located in different rooms and communicated by means of a signaling system. Some of the men were told that they were interacting with a male partner, some with a female partner, and some were not informed about the sex of their partner. During the first part of the study, the men were given the opportunity to make the choices about how the tasks were to be divided between themselves and their partner.

Men were more likely to choose the more masculine tasks when they believed their partner was a woman than when they believed he was a man or had no information about gender. When both partners initially chose the same task, the men were much less willing to let their partner have the preferred task and switch to the alternative when they believed she was a woman.

As long as the men were the initiators in the situation, all their partners provided behavioral confirmation for their beliefs. The "sex" to which they were assigned rather than their actual sex influenced their behavior! "Male" partners chose more masculine tasks and "female" partners chose more feminine tasks. Even when the male initiators no longer had the opportunity to guide the negotiations, many of their partners continued to manifest "gender-appropriate behaviors," for example, behaviors of the sex to which they had originally been assigned. This study clearly shows how one person's beliefs about the sex of another and the corresponding stereotypes associated with this belief actually channel the interaction to confirm stereotypical beliefs. At the same time, this experience probably confirms and strengthens the perceiver's stereotypes about women and men in general—stereotypes that he or she will carry into new situations and act to confirm.

This study also reaffirms the idea discussed earlier in this chapter that people seem unable to tolerate ambiguity in their sexual categories. People whose sex was unlabeled behaved in a manner that was indistinguishable from those who were labeled as male. This is because perceivers adopted similar behavioral strategies for men and for people whose sex was unknown. These results are very consistent with other findings showing androcentric biases (as in Chapter 2). When gender is unspecified, people are assumed to be male. In other words, maleness is the normative condition.

THE SOCIAL CONSTRUCTION
OF GENDER-RELATED DIFFERENCES

Who Helps Whom?

Gender is constructed outside of the laboratory, too. Helping is a particularly useful form of social behavior for demonstrating mechanisms of gender construction because it can be studied unobtrusively. An important question is: Who helps whom? Meta-analyses of helping studies have found a small but consistent difference between men and women (Eagly, 1987). One aspect of this gender difference is not, however, in the direction of traditional stereotypes. Men are only somewhat more helpful than women, although women are, indeed, more likely to be the recipients of help. Like many other social behaviors, helping reflects and maintains gender distinctions.

When are women helped more than men? Many studies show few differences in the way women and men are treated, and some studies show clear discrimination against women. For example, both male and female college students worked less hard in a card-sorting task when they were told that the quota had been set by a woman rather than a man (Sanders & Schmidt, 1980). Men also received service priority in department stores even when they arrived at the same time as a woman customer (Stead & Zinkhan, 1986; Zinkhan & Stoiadin, 1984). The men were assisted first twice as often as the women were. When the salesclerks (mostly women) were asked about this difference, they gave answers that reflected gender stereotypes such as ("Women shop around more," "Men are more serious buyers," "Men need more help than women," or "Men are easier to deal with."

Women are helped more than men in situations where norms about female dependency are evoked. The clearest gender differences were found in studies that involved travel outside the home (Piliavin & Unger, 1985). Women were helped more than men when they needed to change a flat tire; when they had a car break down on the highway and needed someone to relay a call for them; or when they asked for travel directions. Men also helped women more than men when there was some potential danger for the helper, such as assistance with a staged theft. Such conditions are consistent with definitions of help in terms of heroism and chivalry—both aspects of the normative masculine role. Men did not help more than women when the situation called for empathy or social support.

Helping between men and women involves more than empty gestures of courtesy or chivalry. Implicit social demands can be made visible when people violate customary norms for everyday behavior. When, for example, women open the door for men, deference confrontations occur (Walum, 1974). There were delays and confusion about who should do what to whom. The amount of emotion and discussion generated by this apparently slight deviation from routine indicates that more than a violation of the rules of good manners was occurring.

Gender differences in door opening have been compared with encounters between individuals possessing differing amounts of authority: "The doctor ushers in his patient, the mother—her children, the Dean—his faculty, the young and able facilitate the old and infirm. Even reference to the 'gatekeepers of knowledge' symbolically acknowledges the role of authority vested in those responsible for the door" (Walum, 1974, p. 509). Opening a door can be a political act, one that affirms patriarchal ideology.

A study conducted more than twenty-five years ago may seem too out-of-date to explain anything about current gender beliefs. However, this is an investigation that can easily be done. One of us has used it as a class project several times over the last fifteen years and has found behaviors similar to those described. One aspect of men's behavior after a door has been opened for them (not found in the written studies) has been described by our students. Men tend to touch the door after they have passed through it. This behavior is remarkably similar to that found in early studies of public encounters between women and men in which the woman touched the man first (Henley, 1977). Under these conditions, men reciprocated the touch much more frequently than women did. "Touch privilege" appears to be a mark of the dominant group.

Upsetting Hierarchical Relationships

If helping is related to status, what happens when the woman needing assistance has higher status than the man? In one experiment examining this question, men and women college students interacted with a man or woman who was introduced as either their supervisor or their subordinate (Dovidio & Gaertner, 1983). They were told that this individual (actually a confederate) was either higher or lower in ability than they were. Before the students worked with this person on the task that was supposed to be the object of the research, he or she "accidently" knocked a container of pencils to the ground. The researchers unobtrusively measured helping by the number of pencils the students helped the confederate pick up.

Status but not ability influenced the frequency with which women were helped. Both women and men helped women supervisors less than women subordinates but did not discriminate between male supervisors and subordinates. Ability, not status, influenced the degree to which men were helped. Men and women helped high-ability men more than those with low-ability but helped low- and high-ability women partners equally as often. A similar reluctance by white men to help black men who were supposedly supervising them has also been found (Dovidio & Gaertner, 1981). Relative ability had no effect on helpfulness toward black men, although the high-ability white confederate was helped significantly more than his low-ability counterpart.

These studies illustrate some important points about how sex and race function as status variables in our society. First, people in a higher-status group appear to be unwilling to recognize ability differences in individuals with a lower status than their own. White men helped other white men whose abilities were supposedly greater than their own but did not appear to notice superiority abilities in either white women or black men. Second, when traditional role relationships were threatened (by the experimenters conferring supervisory rank on a woman or an African-American man), helping declined. And, third, these studies illustrate that the potential for discrimination is greater than people believe. Discrimination is frequently masked by people's desire to behave in a socially desirable manner. Studies such as these, which use indirect and unobtrusive measures, indicate high levels of covert sexism and racism among college students.

The Effects of Being Helped

Help seeking is also related to roles and status. Women and men with high self-confidence are particularly reluctant to seek help from others (Fisher, Nadler, & Whitcher-Alagna, 1982). They resist being helped by people who have greater resources or power than they do and prefer to be helped by someone who expects to be repaid. Being helped reduces self-esteem, whereas being helpful raises it (Nadler & Fisher, 1986). Men who received unsolicited help from another student actually performed less well on a subsequent task than men who received no such help (Daubman & Lehman, 1993). Both men and women even prefer help from a computer than from another human being (Karabenick & Knapp, 1988).

People who habitually seek help from others appear to trade a short-term gain for a long-term loss. Being helped lowers their self-esteem and increases their sense of dependency, making them more likely to seek help yet again. Learned helplessness has been associated with depression—a disorder that is more common among women than men (see Chapter 14). Depression is not, of course, a result of having a car door opened or having someone's assistance with a coat. However, such "courtesies" help to define and maintain traditional gender roles. Women are socialized into perceiving themselves as helpless and dependent. They are more likely to be helped than men under some circumstances, and this reinforces their belief that they need such help. The long-term consequences may be the creation of gender-biased vulnerability to some forms of emotional distress.

Aggression and Women's Place

Because a discussion on violence against women will appear in Chapter 13, we limit ourselves here to a relatively brief comment about how aggression also acts as a form of social control to maintain social constructions of gender. As this recent high-fashion advertisement shows, it is still socially acceptable to picture men behaving aggressively against women (Figure 3.2).

FIGURE 3.2. Is this man attacking the woman or is she his puppet? This ad from the *New York Times Magazine* is an example of covert messages about male dominance and female subordination.

Female targets are not chosen at random. Women who are "out of place" are more likely to be the targets of male aggression. For example, highly placed women like Margaret Thatcher (the former prime minister of Great Britain), Leona Helmsley (a wealthy hotel owner and tax evader), and Hillary Rodham Clinton have all been the recipients of a number of vicious verbal attacks disguised as "humor."

The willingness to aggress is influenced by the social context. Men are likely to behave more aggressively than women when they are observed by an experimenter or by a single peer or when the aggression is required rather than a matter of choice (Eagly, 1987). Aggressive behavior is very sensitive to social approval. It appears or disappears, depending on whether the societal script says it is "O.K." or "against the rules" (Richardson, Bernstein, & Taylor, 1979). Unfortunately, jokes about powerful women do not seem to be against the rules.

Studies on helping and aggression indicate that women are particularly likely to be the target of sexist behaviors when they violate norms about women's inferior status. Women can violate such norms in a large number of ways. Direct violations include having a position that confers power over men, behaving aggressively, or telling men what to do. All of these violations describe women in positions of authority. It is the subordinate's claim to authority rather than her competence that evokes some men's hostility.

GENDER AND SELF-CATEGORIZATION

The Effect of Dominance and Subordination

If sex is such an important stimulus for interactions with others, it should be an important self-label as well. The use of sex as a self-label is so obvious that there have actually been few studies demonstrating it. In one early study, 156 male and female students responded fifteen times to the question "Who am I?" (Gordon, 1968). The most frequent responses were age (82%) and sex (74%).

People have many different social labels with which to identify. Why did these students choose only two of the many possibilities as an important source of self-identification? The social identities people choose are partly determined by the relationship of these categories to other distinctions made by their society. Individuals who are members of low-status or minority groups seem to identify with these social categories. Thus, women mention their gender category more than men do, African-Americans mention race more than Euro-Americans do, and Jews mention religion more than Christians do (Gordon, 1968). People who belong to the normative group in the United States—white, Christian men—appear to see no need to identify themselves in terms of these categories.

Are these aspects of group identification due to the status of a group? Although researchers cannot change a person's group membership at will, they can manipulate dominance/subordination relationships within a laboratory context. In one clever experiment, a group was given the opportunity of making a choice of the place they wished to occupy. The other group did not have a choice (it was defined for them by the choices made by the first group). This process is analogous to the last moves in a game of tic-tac-toe. When participants were asked "Who am I?" choosers tended to make reference to general categories, such as person, whereas nonchoosers made more positional or relativistic choices, such as student or subject (Deschamps, 1982). Dominant group members did not think of themselves as being determined by their group membership or their social affiliation. The social system is defined by them rather than the other way around.

The Effect of Distinctiveness

Group identification is also influenced by the distinctiveness of a category within its social setting. Schoolchildren, for example, were found to be much more likely to mention sex as an element of their self-concept when their sex comprised the minority in their classroom rather than the majority.(McGuire & Padawer-Singer, 1976). Both boys and girls whose sex was the numerically minority in their household were also more likely to mention sex as part of their self-identification (McGuire, McGuire, & Winton, 1979). Boys who had more sisters were more likely to mention being male than boys who had more brothers. Sex was also more salient for both college men and women when they were asked for self-identification in a just-assembled group in which they were the minority (Cota & Dion, 1986). People focus on their own distinctive personal characteristics because of their value in distinguishing themselves from others.

To understand how gender creates as well as reflects the behavior of men and women, it is important to remember that gender categories are not symmetrical in our society. Women and men are seen not only as different but also as unequal. Men are dominant in our society and are valued more than women. In turn, they exert more power and influence and control cultural definitions that maintain women's subordination. It is not the difference that matters in our society, but the distinction (Tajfel, 1984).

Distinction is the active social process that creates, expresses, and maintains differences. Status differences may also contribute to perceptions about the traits that individuals in high- and low-status groups possess. A recent study illustrates this process (Conway, Pizzamiglio, & Mount, 1996). Participants read anthropological descriptions about a fictional Amazonian society consisting of two groups, the Ngwani and the Gunada. The society was described as stable, peaceful, and cooperative (both groups worked in the same fields). The Ngwani were described as having higher social status (bigger huts), which was justified by their religious belief that they were descendants of the first man and woman. The Gunada had lower religious status and raised the Ngwani's children. When participants were asked to evaluate the traits of each group, the Ngwani were seen as more competent and the Gunada were seen as more interpersonally pleasant. These stereotypes about the traits possessed by the two groups reflected status differences. It is no coincidence that the more powerful group was seen as having a trait traditionally associated with men, whereas the less powerful group was seen to have a more stereotypically female trait.

To understand fully how gender functions to distinguish and stratify people, we must consider concepts such as *social power* (sometimes abbreviated as *power*), ascribed status, and achieved status. Social power is an attribute of relationships, not individuals. It is determined by the control some people have over events or resources that others value (Molm & Hedley, 1992). Because of authority, legitimacy, or expertise, bosses have more power than their employees, teachers have more power than their students, and doctors have more power than their patients. Social power differs from social influence because it implies the use of some kind of force, such as the loss of a salary or a poor grade.

The term *status* is used to refer to a person's potential ability to influence or control others. Sociologists distinguish between two kinds of status: ascribed and achieved. *Achieved status* is based partly on the role one performs in an organization or a family—for example, boss versus secretary, father versus mother, or professor versus student. How well one performs one's role is also a component of achieved status, although this is often difficult to determine because many roles have no explicit criteria by which to evaluate them. Good students are fairly easy to distinguish from poor ones, but within the general range of normality how does one distinguish good fathers from poor ones?

Ascribed status is usually based on inherent characteristics. Status is conferred because of a person's group membership, not their personal characteristics. In the United States, race, age, social class, and sex are all determinants of

---

Making a Difference

Cynthia Cockburn (b. 1934), a sociologist at City University in London, is a pioneer in the study of gender and technology. A recent scholarly article by Cockburn concerns the microwave oven, where "masculine engineering encounters an age-old woman's technology—cooking." Women are excluded from technological expertise as a result of "power-play," not by accident, Cockburn believes. Raised by conservative British parents with little interest in higher education, Cockburn attended secretarial school and spent seven years in the Foreign Service typing pool. Despite lacking university degrees, by the 1960s she became a sociological researcher and has written or contributed to more than forty books and dozens of articles. A

feminist activist, she has also helped to build political and social links among European women and worked against militarism. Cockburn believes it is important to combine activism and intellectualism in "action research—being involved in change but analyzing the process rigorously as it goes along." Regarding her scholarly success, without university degrees, she states, " . . . it's reassuring to find there are people and institutions that are open-minded and willing to judge a researcher on output rather than certification. Perhaps my career could be some encouragement to other women who find their direction late, or want to change track."

Source: Griffiths, S. (Ed.). (1996). *Beyond the glass ceiling: Forty women whose ideas shape the modern world.* Manchester, England: Manchester University Press.

ascribed status. Although some of these characteristics can change, it is not a result of the person's efforts. (The relative value of these characteristics is, moreover, determined by others' definitions rather than one's own.)

Ascribed status is usually described in hierarchical terms—some people possess more or less status than others. Unlike achieved status, these differences are not based on how well people function in their roles. Instead, they are based on cultural norms. Ascribed status describes and predicts relations between categories of people in terms of the rewards, benefits, or compliance they give each other. In other words, ascribed status defines who is supposed to have more social power in society.

Think of a posh restaurant in New York City. A tourist from the Midwest has difficulty getting a waiter's attention no matter how elaborately he gestures. A suave customer from Wall Street obtains obsequious service with a flick of a wrist. Obviously, the latter gentleman has ascribed status. (A gender-relevant example is the tendency for women's suggestions and comments to be ignored until the same idea is proposed by a man.) To get the same amount of recognition women often have to be more persistent and make repeated efforts, sometimes leading to the perception that successful women are "pushy," "mouthy," and "difficult."

In a group or social system, individuals are typically differentiated from one another according to one or more dimensions involving ascribed or achieved characteristics. Gender, as an ascribed characteristic, conveys status and power. It has been argued that "maleness" is a diffuse status characteristic—associated with greater power, prestige, and social value than "femaleness" (Cohen, Berger, & Zelditch, 1972; Unger, 1976, 1978).

Because gender is an ascribed or diffuse status characteristic, it is not easily changed by the behavior of individuals. For example, if women lack power because of their roles as childbearers or child rearers, they should gain power as a result of changes in these roles (e.g., if men had an equal share in child care). If, however, their relative lack of power is a result of who they are, women will continue to lack power even in "male" roles. These competing hypotheses can be tested.

GENDER DIFFERENCES AS STATUS DIFFERENCES

Gender and Nonverbal Behavior

The Use of Space

The study of the relationship between nonverbal behaviors associated with status and the behaviors of women and men began early in the history of the psychology of women (Henley, 1977). Women behave and are treated by others like men with low status in many of the nonverbal behaviors that have been studied (see Table 3.1). (Females' politeness, smiling, emotional responsiveness, smaller personal space, less frequent touching, and greater frequency of being interrupted reflect their subordinate status.)

In one study, for example, pairs of men, pairs of women, and mixed-sex pairs interacted during a ten-minute task in which each pair constructed a

TABLE 3.1. Gestures of Power and Privilege: Some Examples of Nonverbal Behaviors

Nonverbal Behavior	Between Status Nonequals		Between Men and Women	
	Used by Superior	Used by Subordinate	Used by Men	Used by Women
Demeanor	Informal	Circumspect	Informal	Circumspect
Posture	Relaxed	Tense	Relaxed	Tense
Personal space	Closeness (option)	Distance	Closeness	Distance
Touching	Touch (option)	Don't touch	Touch	Don't touch
Eye contact	Stare, ignore	Avert eyes, watch	Stare, ignore	Avert eyes, watch
Facial expression	Don't smile	Smile	Don't smile	Smile
Emotional expression	Hide	Show	Hide	Show
Self-disclosure	Don't disclose	Disclose	Don't disclose	Disclose

Source: Adapted from N. Henley (1977). *Body politics: power, sex, and nonverbal communication.* Copyright © 1977 by Prentice-Hall, Inc.

domino structure for a contest (Lott, 1987). Under these laboratory conditions, women behaved the same way regardless of whether their partner was a man or another woman. Men, however, distanced themselves more from female than male partners by turning their faces or bodies away and by placing the dominoes closer to themselves than to their partners. Among the seventeen mixed-sex pairs in which the structure was closer to one partner than to the other, in fourteen cases it was closer to the man than to the woman. Paper-and-pencil measures had not revealed any evidence of prejudice or gender stereotypes among these college students.

The people with more social power are usually men. Researchers cannot, of course, change people's sex, but they can manipulate assigned roles or levels of achievement to confer status. The question they wish to answer by this research is: Do the ways men customarily behave toward women reflect gender-typed behaviors or their usually superior status in social settings? Status appears to be more important than sex. In one experiment, for example, college women and men were assigned either the high-status position of teacher or the lower status of student (Leffler, Gillespie, & Conaty, 1982). Statuses were reversed on the second trial so that teachers became students and vice versa. In general, high-status men and women claimed more direct space with their bodies, talked more, and attempted more interruptions than low-status men and women. By means of touching and pointing directed to the partner they symbolically intruded on them.

Conversational Dynamics

Gender differences in group settings not only reflect status and power differences but also help to perpetuate them. Women lean away from the group and smile when speaking significantly more than men do (Kennedy & Camden, 1983). People in low-status positions are also more likely to smile in group settings, although their smiles are not connected to positive affect

(Hecht & LaFrance, 1998). People are more likely to be interrupted when they lean away, smile, or do not look at the other person.

By interrupting, higher-status individuals can gain the floor and restrict the contributions of lower-status group members. In most groups, men are more likely than women to interrupt others. Even in groups where men and women attempt to interrupt at roughly the same rate, researchers find that the men are more gender-biased in their interruptions (they interrupt women more than men). Men are also more successful interrupting women than other men (Smith-Lovin & Brody, 1989). These findings illustrate how displays of power by men are socially reinforced.

REINFORCED.

Women who interrupt others cannot be so sure of social support. When students were asked to rate videotapes of interactions between two men, two women, or a man and a woman that were identical in script features, they rated a woman who interrupted a man as ruder, more irritable, and more self-concerned than other interruptors (LaFrance, 1992). Interactions in which a woman interrupted a man received more negative ratings than any other pairing. Male and female raters agreed that there was something wrong with this situation. The woman appeared to have broken more than a conversational rule. She had violated an accepted social policy concerning appropriate behavior by those who have less power. This kind of social regulation makes it less likely that women will emerge as leaders of mixed-sex groups.

There has been no decline in gender differences in conversational interruptions despite the increased presence of women in public life. A recent meta-analysis found that men make considerably more intrusive interruptions than women do (Anderson & Leaper, 1998). Intrusive interruptions are more likely to be found in natural rather than laboratory settings and when participants interact in groups of three or more. Other studies have shown that those who feel most comfortable in social situations are more willing to interrupt others (Campbell, Kleim, & Olson, 1992).

The Perception of Nonverbal Cues to Status

Women are generally better at decoding nonverbal cues than men are (Hall, 1985). This difference is consistent with subordinate status, in which it is important for lower-power individuals to adapt their behaviors to the demands of more dominant individuals (see Chapter 4). When men communicate dominance, their female partners tend to respond with low-power gestures, although men do not show similar accommodation to dominant behaviors in women (Davis & Weitz, 1981). Both women and men seem to have difficulty perceiving that a woman is in a position of high power or leadership. The same nonverbal cues that communicate power for men may not work for women. For example, sitting at the head of the table in a mixed-sex setting was associated with being viewed as the leader of a group for men but had no effect on perceptions of women (Porter & Geis, 1981).

Under some conditions, nonverbal gestures of dominance can affect how others evaluate a woman's social power. Both men and women accurately interpreted different levels of visual dominance displayed by a woman who was interacting with either a man or another woman (Ellyson, Dovidio, & Fehr,

1981). They rated her as more powerful when her use of visual dominance cues was high. Thus, it may be possible to change perceptions of status by changing nonverbal behaviors. However, much more research on how nonverbal cues communicate power is necessary. It is not clear why some cues, such as visual dominance, can enhance perceptions of women's authority while others, such as where she sits at a table, have no effect.

Nonverbal cues involving emotion also regulate the interactions of men and women. In keeping with gender stereotypes, women have been found to encode happiness better than men, whereas men are able to encode anger better than women (Coates & Feldman, 1996). The ability to portray happiness so that people could distinguish it from other emotions was associated with higher popularity for women but not men. In contrast, the ability to demonstrate anger was associated with higher popularity for men but not women. The two emotions appear to play different roles in the social interactions of women and men.

This gendered use of emotional cues is learned in childhood (see Chapter 6). Boys tend to interact in large, status-oriented groups characterized by conflict, competition, and self-promotion. Girls tend to interact in smaller, intimate groups in which conflict is more covert. Open expression of anger is less useful to them. In a large-scale survey of people's responses to feeling angry, men were more likely than women to report that aggressive responses would elevate their mood (Harris, 1992). Since the ability to show anger is a form of social power, it should not be surprising that, by adulthood, the positive relationship between status and anger is found only in men (Keating & Heltman, 1994).

Gender and the Use of Social Power

Any stereotypically masculine form of power may be less effective when used by women than when used by men. It has been found, for example, that women speak more tentatively when interacting with men with whom they disagree than when interacting with other women under the same circumstances (Carli, 1990). This use of tentative speech appeared to be functional for women. Men were influenced to a greater degree by women who spoke tentatively than by those who spoke assertively. Women who spoke tentatively were less effective with other women. Both men and women judged a woman who spoke tentatively to be less competent and knowledgeable than a woman who spoke assertively. The kind of language used, however, had no effect on their judgments of male speakers.

This study illustrates a classic *double bind*. Many double binds are constructed around gender categories. (See Figure 3.3.) They occur when traits or roles are polarized as irreconcilable opposites and it is assumed that a person cannot have both (Jamieson, 1995). Thus, a woman who demonstrates a traditionally male quality such as strength or competence is seen as unfeminine. The double bind is a process that affects those without power much more than those with it. Recently, for example, motherhood has been constructed differently for poor and well-to-do women (see Chapter 10).

When women use tentative language as a subtle influence strategy, it compromises their perceived competence and makes it difficult for them to persuade other women. If they use more assertive language, however, they find it

FIGURE 3.3. A double bind—"damned if you do and damned if you don't." When Fritz Mondale chose Geraldine Ferraro as his running mate in the 1988 presidential election, her femininity was questioned.
Source: Signe Wilkinson. Used by permission of Cartoonists & Writers Syndicate.

difficult to influence men. Since most influence attempts in the real world take place in mixed-sex situations, there is no behavior by which a woman can "win." This study was circulated widely on E-mail networks and sent to one of the authors by her daughter, who was very dismayed at the findings. We find them distressing, too!

One reason women in mixed-sex interactions use indirect power strategies may be their anticipation of unfavorable reactions from men. These assumptions are not unfounded. In a study of emergent leaders in mixed-sex groups, female leaders were found to receive more negative emotional responses when they made the same contributions as male leaders. Negative responses included furrowed brows, tightening of the mouth, and nods of disagreement. Women's contributions to the group also received fewer positive responses such as smiles and nods of agreement (Butler & Geis, 1990).

Reports from "real life" reinforce the message of these laboratory studies. In a random sample of 340 university students, 31 percent of the females versus 10 percent of the males reported being intimidated on the basis of their sex, religion, or academic ability (Sands, 1998). Most of this intimidation came from fellow students. At Yale Law School, women students reported getting anonymous notes (presumably from men) telling them they talked too much in class (Benokraitis, 1997). Similar harassment from fellow students has been reported at the University of Pennsylvania Law School (Guinier, Fine, & Balin, 1997). It is noteworthy that such reports appear to come more frequently from elite institutions that hope to facilitate students' entry into high-status careers.

It is difficult to induce women to behave in a dominant manner in group situations. In one study, for example, groups of two men and two women (with a group leader who received three times as much credit for class participation than the other members of the group) were formed (Ellyson, Dovidio, & Brown, 1992). Groups were either (1) told that the leader had received the unanimous vote of everyone in the group; (2) told that the leader had received more votes than others, but the vote was split; or (3) given no information about leadership selection. Women leaders displayed lower levels of visual dominance except when their leadership was securely mandated (e.g., the result of a unanimous vote). Men, in contrast, displayed high visual dominance even when their position was not secure. The women leaders appeared to underestimate their own power and/or question their own legitimacy.

By behaving in a nondominant manner, the women created a self-fulfilling prophecy. Observers who were not aware of the leadership conditions in the study rated the women in insecure leadership positions as significantly less powerful than comparable men. Only the women who were unanimously authorized in their leadership displayed high visual dominance and were perceived to be as powerful and competent as the men. Similar effects occur even when members of the group have expressed beliefs in egalitarian gender roles. In the majority of the mixed-sex groups observed, men participated more in group discussion and were more likely to be selected as the leader (Sapp, Harrod, & Zhao, 1996).

Women's choice of indirect influence strategies appears to be a function of their lower social power rather than their personality differences from men. Women and men have been found to prefer the same order of influence strategies (White & Roufail, 1989). They both choose more direct influence tactics when they are powerful and more indirect strategies when they have less power (Sagrestano, 1992). Cross-culturally, power predicts what kind of influence tactic is used more than sex does (Steil & Hillman, 1993).

THE ROLE OF GENDER
IN BOUNDARY MAINTENANCE

Gender does far more than tell us about the behavior of women and men. Gender also prescribes the way women and men ought to behave. People who do not conform to perceptions about the way typical and normal individuals of their sex behave are likely to be punished for their nonconformity. Nonconformity is socially defined and punished by means of two social psychological processes—*stigma* and *deviance*. These processes impose social control. Those who have the power to define acceptable behavior in others benefit by labeling others as deviant.

Deviance and stigma are related concepts, although they are not exactly the same. Stigmatization refers to the process of responding to a person in terms of some physically negative or socially undesirable characteristic she or he possesses. Stigma is defined as a trait that intrudes itself on our attention and prevents the person who exhibits it from engaging in normal relationships with others (Goffman, 1963). People react to the characteristic rather than to the person. It is difficult, for example, to ignore the fact that someone is in a wheelchair, is blind, or has an unattractive scar.

Individuals tend to avoid stigmatized people or to deal with them only in terms of their "handicaps" (Asch & Fine, 1988). In daily life, women are often perceived and responded to in terms of their categorical membership—as females, first and foremost. Such a response carries with it a certain degree of social stigma because, relatively speaking, femaleness appears to be a devalued status.

People who fall into a devalued category are typically thought of as comprising a unitary or homogenous group. The number and variety of negative images discussed in Chapter 2 illustrate how women as a group are devalued in society. Women in groups "look more alike" than men do. Women are also objectified more than men are and are disparaged in cultural symbolism; for example, through the pervasive negative stereotypes found in the mass media, pornography, and language itself. Chapter 11 will document the existence of gender inequality within our social and economic system. Highly valued persons are not systematically relegated to lower echelons of the socioeconomic and occupational prestige ladder.

Deviance and the Power to Define

Women are vulnerable to stigmatization because of their social subordination and relatively poor power position. They are not in a good position to define the rules that evaluate their own behavior. Some sociologists have argued that women's social subordination is maintained by defining many of their characteristics and behaviors as deviant (Schur, 1983). "Social groups create deviance by making the rules whose infraction constitutes deviance, and by applying these rules to particular people and labeling them as outsiders" (Becker, 1963, p. 9).

Women's deviance is, like any deviance, a social construct. What most counts socially is how people perceive and react to a given behavior. The very same behavior may be defined or responded to differently when it is associated with a woman rather than a man. For example, there are different names for an unmarried woman or man who has an active and varied sex life. Depending on one's values, such an unmarried woman may be considered "promiscuous" or "liberated." The behavior being described is not different, but the labels are. The same labels do not apply to men. What level or kind of sexual behavior is defined as promiscuity for a man?

Dealing with Deviance in a Group Setting

Several studies illustrate the way a woman may be defined as deviant within a group setting. One important early study examined the role of the lone woman within small groups designed to enhance interpersonal communication (Wolman & Frank, 1975). All participants were of equal status. They were, in fact, peer groups of graduate students or psychiatric residents who participated as part of their professional training. In five of the six groups studied, the lone woman became a deviant or isolated member of the group. In one group she was able to acquire low-status regular membership.

The researchers provide an illuminating description of the techniques used by groups of men to deal with a woman who is "out of place." They found that when the group members began to interact, women were not allowed to compete freely for status. Attempts by a woman to influence the group were ignored, while similar attempts made by a man were heeded and credited to him. A woman who persisted in trying to influence the group after having been ignored received either coordinated reaction against her or further instances of no reaction. Men labeled assertiveness as bitchiness or manipulation and appeared to be more threatened by competition with a woman than with each other. When a woman showed feelings or advocated their expression, emotionality became identified with feminine behavior. The sex of the woman was either virtually ignored or joked about. When the women tried to escape their role as isolates or deviants by increasing their interactions with others, they were increasingly ignored.

Many coping mechanisms carry gender-role labels in our culture. In the Wolman and Frank study, if a woman acted friendly, she was thought to be flirting. If she acted weak, the men tried to infantilize her, treating her as a "little sister" rather than a peer. If she apologized for alienating the group, she was seen as a submissive woman knowing her place. If she asked for help, she earned a "needy female" label. If she became angry or tried to point out rationally what the group process was doing to her, she was seen as competitive, in a bitchy, unfeminine way. "Feminine" coping mechanisms increased her perceived differences; "masculine" ones threatened the men so that they isolated her even more. Any internal ambivalence about her gender role was rekindled by these labels, and increased her anxiety, which increased her coping behavior, which further increased her deviance (Wolman & Frank, 1975).

Men who supported the lone woman in these groups risked being identified with her and sharing her deviance. Similar effects have been found for whites who associated with blacks and heterosexual men who associated with gay men (Neuberg, Smith, Hoffman, & Russell, 1994). The negative qualities associated with those who supported members of stigmatized groups persisted even after attempts to make the heterosexual target seem similar to the respondents and to present him as a person with high achieved status. This generalization of stigma makes it more difficult for those who wish to change the group process to do so.

Since they had been led to expect that the professions were a male sanctuary, the men presumably resented the presence of a woman and acted to prevent her from becoming a regular member in order to retain an almost all-male group. The women tended to give up their efforts after a while, becoming depressed instead. They could almost be termed group casualties. The single characteristic that these women shared (and the apparent explanation for collective hostility) was the fact of being female.

Women who have attained high professional status may also be excluded. Here are some examples in their own words:

> I've attended several dean's conferences where about six out of the seventy participants are women. Women are usually ignored—during panels and informal discussions—because men think they have nothing to learn from women. (Woman vice president at a university)

Several times, my male colleagues used my records of my patients to do research. It's never occurred to them to ask me to participate on these projects or
to ask my opinion about diagnoses. I know I'm doing a good job, but I feel
very isolated professionally.
(Woman physician at a major medical school)

When a team of engineers presented a study, they avoided eye contact with me
and spoke directly to the men on the board. It was so obvious that they were
presenting their findings "over my head" that I decided to take action in order
to demonstrate I had an understanding of the project. I asked a technical question. . . . It made some difference, but I can see that I have to be ever alert to
dealing with subtle discrimination constantly and that I am not being paranoid.
(Only woman on the board of trustees of an electric cooperative)
(From Benokraitis & Feagin, 1986, pp. 92–94)

These processes of exclusion have not completely disappeared. A recent article
in the *Chronicle of Higher Education* quoted Linda Mabry (Figure 3.4) who discussed the reasons for her resignation from her position as a professor at
Stanford Law School:

What finally triggered her resignation, she said, was learning that the law
school was planning to open a new program in her area of expertise—international business law—and hadn't consulted her. She said that oversight reflected a pattern, in which her male colleagues failed to take her scholarship
or her contributions to the law school seriously. She said she first learned of
the new program "when I read a flyer inviting students to a meeting." She
added: "It was demoralizing and embarrassing to be excluded from the discussion. It was as if I were invisible."
(Mangan, 1999, p. A12)

FIGURE 3.4. Linda Mabry resigned from Stanford Law School because "I came to the conclusion that it's just a hostile climate for women and people of color."

A person's sex greatly affects how his or her violation of procedural rules in a group setting is perceived. In one set of studies (Wahrman & Pugh, 1972, 1974), a man or woman (who were confederates of the experimenter) violated rules about turn taking and reward allocation at various times during a series of trials involving problem solving. Early nonconformity by a man led coworkers to consider him more influential and desirable, although the nonconformist was disliked more than one who went along with the group. In contrast, the earlier a woman violated the rules, the less she influenced the group and the more disliked and less desirable as a coworker she became. The best liked of all the confederates was the conforming woman.

A nonconforming woman was least acceptable in these otherwise all-male groups. Even her ability to solve problems well did not affect men's negative evaluations of her. Competent nonconforming women were preferred less than incompetent nonconforming men—even though the group as a whole benefited from competent performance. These findings about the negative evaluations of competent women are similar to those involving female assertiveness and group influence discussed earlier.

The Token Woman

A woman is much more likely to be seen as a representative of the social category "female" when she is the only woman in a group. This situation has become known as *tokenism*. Token women are more visible and isolated than the men who, because of their numerical dominance, determine the culture of the group. Solo women in a group are likely to be seen by themselves and others as representing women's issues rather than the interests of the group as a whole (Izraeli, 1983).

The consequences of having solo status are markedly different for women and men. For example, men who were minorities in their group rated themselves as more masculine than men in groups where they were the majority (Swan & Wyer, 1997). Minority status also increased the masculinity of women's self-ratings. These self-ratings seem to be accurate perceptions of the way they were viewed by their group. Men were seen by others in the group as more masculine when they had solo status, whereas women were perceived to be least feminine when they had solo status (Crocker & McGraw, 1984). These findings can be explained by men's motivation to identify themselves with a higher-status group when they perceive themselves as vulnerable. Women, in contrast, may avoid thinking of themselves in terms of attributes associated with their lower-status social category.

Women do not like being tokens. College women who anticipated being the only female member of their group preferred a different group, wished for a change in the sex composition of their group, and expected more gender stereotyping than nontoken women (Cohen & Swim, 1995). There were no differences in preferences between token and nontoken men. However, token men anticipated more positive stereotypes than token women. Their expectation of stereotyping was positively correlated with their expectation of becoming leader of their group. Women's anticipation of stereotyping, on the other hand, was negatively associated with their belief that they might become the group's leader. These women did not actually have to be tokens for tokenism to affect them. The mere anticipation of being a token (even in a cooperative problem-solving task group) induced negative expectations about the experience.

These expectations appear to be accurate. Various studies have found that solo women were unlikely to be selected as group leaders; overall group satisfaction was lowest when a lone woman was present; and gender-related issues were most likely to be raised in groups that included only one woman (Crocker & McGraw, 1984). Solo men, on the other hand, tended to be integrated into their groups as leader, resulting in smoother group functioning. The gender stereotypes about women and men help explain why lone men are likely to be chosen as group leaders.

Tokenism is not simply a result of numerical dominance. Numerical dominance is situationally dependent (based on who might be available to be part of a group). Tokenism, however, exerts its effects through cultural dominance, which is a constant. Those who dominate a field of action over time come to determine the rules of interaction for strangers who chance to penetrate the boundaries. Neither their culture nor their power is neutralized by numerical reshuffling (Izraeli, 1983).

WOMEN AND MEN DOING GENDER

The extent to which women are discriminated against in groups does not depend only on the percentage of women and men present. Other factors—such as the task in which the group is engaged, whether leaders are elected or emerge, and the position of the group within the general institutional framework—play a role. This means that one cannot simply blame men's prejudice for women's lower power within many groups. The perceptions and behaviors of both women and men interact to maintain male dominance.

As discussed earlier, manipulation of the relative status of women and men can change the nonverbal behaviors customarily displayed by them. Manipulations of perceived competence can also change the way men and women usually perform. For example, researchers observed students interacting in four-person mixed-sex groups (Wood & Karten, 1986). When they were given information only about each other's name and sex, men were perceived by themselves and by other group members to be more competent than women. Men also engaged in a greater amount of active task behavior (giving information and opinions), whereas women showed more positive social behaviors (agreeing and acting friendly).

Women and men in these groups also responded differently to the positive and negative behaviors of others. When a positive act occurred, women were more likely to respond with another positive act (especially if the initiator of the action was another woman), whereas men used the positive action as a cue to begin task-related behavior (Wood & Rhodes, 1992). If, on the other hand, someone behaved negatively within the group, men were much more likely to respond negatively, especially when the initiator was another man. Women rarely responded at all to negative actions. The consequence of these gender-related differences was that the men tended to elevate the level of conflict within a group, whereas the women did not build on conflict and sought to avoid it.

Normative beliefs about greater male competence and social power are difficult to change. Men in one study, for example, did not change their beliefs about their own ability even when they were told that they had less ability than their partner. Women, in contrast, formed either weak or strong expectations about their own ability depending on the experimenters' manipulations (Foschi & Freeman, 1991). The men appeared to be unwilling to accept the authority of others when it conflicted with their standards for themselves.

Men's perceptions of women are also difficult to change. When no experimental intervention took place in problem-solving groups involving spatial judgments, women deferred to men significantly more often than men deferred to women (Pugh & Wahrman, 1983). When researchers used a large number of interventions designed to reduce men's influence, very few worked. Both women and men agreed that men were more competent than women. The only way that the experimenters were able to change this traditional pattern was to rig the task so that women performed better than men. Under these circumstances, women became more influential and men became less. However, these supposedly superior women still did not gain a significant advantage over their male partners. Instead, a woman had to perform much better than a man to be seen as just as good!

The perceptions and behaviors of both men and women must be altered for changes in group processes to occur. In one attempt at such intervention, token women leaders were pretrained with task-relevant information for a stereotypically masculine problem-solving task (Yoder, Schleicher, & McDonald, 1998). But the women's expertise did not, by itself, significantly affect the performance of these otherwise all-male groups. Although outside observers could see no difference between the performance of acknowledged and unacknowledged experts, the women were able to influence their groups only when their expertise was legitimated by a male experimenter.

In contemporary culture, gender and role are intertwined. Roles conferring authority and power are played by men while women occupy subordinate positions. Women, on the other hand, are seen as more likable than men and are assigned roles that emphasize their interpersonal skills (Glick & Fiske, 1999). At present, men and women compete in some roles and cooperate in others. The ambiguity in current images of women (see Chapter 2) has led some men to polarize them more (likable but incompetent or competent but cold and aggressive). Women's awareness of this double bind may explain why some of them are reluctant to change.

There are clearly some rewards for being likable. For example, women were rated by both men and women as being most attractive and powerful when they are trying to be likable (DeBlasio, Angiro, Orbin, & Ellyson, 1993). In contrast, they were rated as less attractive by men when they displayed power. The positive regard of men may also account for the finding that 44 percent of the women surveyed approved of benevolent but not hostile sexism (Kilianski & Rudman, 1998). These "equivocal egalitarians" (women who accepted inequality as long as they saw themselves as benefiting from it) also supported the societal status quo more than those women who condemned all forms of sexism.

It is sometimes difficult for women to distinguish between men's use of power for competitive reasons and their desire for a more affective relationship. Male dominance and female submissiveness remain the core of Western images of romance as well as modern dating scripts (see Chapter 8). In one study, the flirtatiousness of an authority figure significantly reduced women's self-ratings of the creativity of their art projects as compared with women who dealt with a more neutral male authority (Satterfield & Muehlenhard, 1997). The women's self-confidence may have been reduced because they had another rationale (attraction) for his praise of their work.

CHANGING ROLES IN A CHANGING SOCIETY

Figuring out how to effect change is not easy. Traditional perceptions about men and women sometimes disappear when people are reminded about their egalitarian gender-related beliefs (Porter, Geis, Cooper, & Newman, 1985). Explicit messages about gender ideology can also be effective. Women in the United States who were explicitly informed about traditional gender roles requiring feminine modesty about achievement became significantly less modest in their subsequent responses (Cialdini, Wosinska, Dabul, Wheatstone-Dion, & Heszen, 1998). Those women who reacted most strongly to the manipulation also anticipated that they would not be particularly modest about their future achievements. More subtle images of traditional gender roles can have the opposite effect. Sexist messages in the media have a particularly strong impact on women's behavior (see Chapter 2). For example, women who were exposed to advertisements that portrayed women in their traditional role as homemakers subsequently reported less favorable attitudes toward political participation than women who were not exposed to such advertisements (Swarz, Wagner, Bannert, & Mathes, 1987). One contribution of feminist research on politics and the media has been to make such covert messages more visible (cf., Norris, 1997).

Gender and Leadership

Since women are seen to be less competent than men, it is not surprising that they emerge as leaders of groups far less often than men (Eagly & Karau, 1991). The reluctance to select women as leaders is particularly strong in U.S. politics. There have been twenty-three women elected presidents or prime ministers of a nation since 1960 (see Table 3.2), but there has never been a viable woman candidate for the presidency of the United States. There are only nine women in the Senate and fewer than fifty women in the House of Representatives (about 25% of all the legislators in Congress). The scarcity of women in positions of political leadership extends downward to state and local levels. How many women on your campus hold offices other than that of secretary in your student government?

TABLE 3.2. Women Who Have Been Elected Heads of State Since 1960

Leader	Country	Office	Elected
1. Siramavo Bandarannike	Sri Lanka	Prime Minister	1960
2. Indira Gandhi	India	Prime Minister	1966
3. Golda Meir	Israel	Prime Minister	1969
4. Isabel Peron	Argentina	President	1974
5. Margaret Thatcher	United Kingdom	Prime Minister	1979
6. Maria de Lourdes Pintasilgo	Portugal	Prime Minister	1979
7. Lidia Geiler	Bolivia	President	1979
8. Vigdis Finnbogadottir	Iceland	President	1980
9. Eugenia Charles	Dominica	Prime Minister	1980
10. Milka Planinc	Yugoslavia	President	1982
11. Corazon Aquino	Philippines	President	1986
12. Gro Harlem Brundtland	Norway	Prime Minister	1986
13. Benazir Bhutto	Pakistan	Prime Minister	1988
14. Ertha Pascal-Trouillot	Haiti	President	1990
15. Violeta Chamorro	Nicaragua	President	1990
16. Mary Robinson	Ireland	President	1990
17. Khaleda Ziaur Rahman	Bangladesh	Prime Minister	1991
18. Edith Cresson	France	Prime Minister	1993
19. Tamsu Ciller	Turkey	Prime Minister	1993
20. Kim Campbell	Canada	Prime Minister	1993
21. Hanna Suchocka	Poland	Prime Minister	1993
22. Agathe Uwilingiymana	Rwanda	Prime Minister	1994
23. Chandrika Bandaranaike Kumaratunga	Sri Lanka	President	1994

Source: P. Norris (1997). Women leaders worldwide: A splash of color in the photo op. In P. Norris (Ed.). *Women, media, and politics.* NY: Oxford University Press (pp. 149–165) table on p. 150.

It has sometimes been argued that women are not elected to leadership positions because they lack necessary experience and skills. Of course, it will be difficult for them to acquire skills if they are not given the opportunity to learn them. Simulations of the voting process indicate that men will be elected over women who possess the same qualifications for office. In a simulated mayoral election, a black man, a white woman, an older white man, and a younger white man, all with equivalent qualifications, were each pitted in two-candidate races against the same candidate, a middle-aged white man. He was able to win four of the five contests—only the younger white man was able to beat him (Sigelman & Sigelman, 1982).

In another study, undergraduates evaluated six challengers to an incumbent in either a mayoral or a county clerk's race (Sigelman, Thomas, Sigelman, & Ribich, 1986). Men, but not women, consistently discriminated against women candidates. Discrimination against women candidates appears to be independent of other indicators of social or racial awareness. For example, liberals were found to be more likely than conservatives to vote for a black candidate but not for a woman (Hedlund, Freeman, Hamm, & Stein, 1979). African-American men were also significantly less likely to vote for a woman candidate than were African-American women or Euro-American women and men (Sigelman & Welch, 1984).

The news media do not take women candidates seriously. Following are some descriptions of female and male candidates for the U.S. Senate taken from the pages of the *New York Times*:

Ms. [Barbara] Boxer, a 51-year-old Brooklyn transplant . . .

. . . 59-year-old Ms. [Diane] Feinstein . . . faces another race in 1994 . . . no doubt she will rely, as she has done in the past, on the assets of her husband, Richard C. Blum, an investment banker.

The 42-year-old Ms. [Patty] Murray lives in the Seattle suburb of Shoreline, where in addition to her two children, age 12 and 15, she cares for her aging parents.

Ms. [Carol Moseley] Braun who is divorced and the mother of a 15-year-old son . . .

Ben Nighthorse Campbell . . . at age 59, he is striking for his appearance, with steel-gray ponytail and string ties.

Dick Kemphorne, the 41-year-old mayor of Boise . . .

Judd Gregg, 48, is governor of New Hampshire and previously served in the House.

Lauch Fairchild, 64, a businessman and farmer . . .

Russell Feingold, 39, has served in the Wisconsin state senate for 10 years, where he specialized in judicial affairs.

Where occupation is the defining feature of the male candidates, it is a secondary characteristic of the females. Not a single male candidate is identified as married, divorced, or single. By contrast, we learn that Moseley Braun is divorced and Feinstein married.

Two women, but none of the men are identified as parents. Like the women, the male Native American is characterized differently, here by appearance. (Jamieson, 1995, p. 170)

Despite their differential treatment by the media, all of the women candidates except for Moseley Braun were reelected to the Senate in 1998.

Women who assert themselves in mixed-sex groups can be penalized for their behavior. Both men and women associate effective leadership with an authoritarian style (Linimon, Barron, & Falbo, 1984). Such a style is inconsistent with stereotypes prescribing femininity. Men are also more stressed by threats to their status than women are (Brinkerhoff & Booth, 1984). They appear to be

FIGURE 3.5. Equality depends on one's point of view.
Source: Copyright © 1992. Reprinted with special permission of King Features Syndicate.

even more threatened by a woman's authority than by her competence. When a woman is portrayed as having authority over men of the same age and social class, she is seen as reducing their status rather than enhancing her own (Denmark, 1980). (See Figure 3.5.)

Expectations based on gender roles greatly influence a person's ability to be an effective leader. Although men and women leaders appear to be equally effective overall, women do particularly poorly in settings such as the military where leadership is defined in highly masculine terms. Men fare slightly less well than women in educational settings and governmental and social service organizations (Eagly, Karau, & Makhijani, 1995). Both men and women have more difficulty doing tasks in contexts that are seen as incompatible with their gender. Until recently, public settings were much more congenial to men than to women. This situation is changing as the number of women in public life has increased rapidly. As we write this, women are serving as both the secretary of state (Madeline Albright) and attorney general (Janet Reno).

Gender and Legitimacy

In the past, women who have attained high positions of leadership in government and industry have sometimes questioned their own legitimacy. For example, fifty French and Norwegian women leaders interviewed about their accomplishments rarely described them as due to their own efforts, even though they knew how competent they were (Apfelbaum, 1993). Instead, they explained their positions in terms of external circumstances. Many of the older French women leaders mentioned their feeling of being a "token woman" who had achieved power as a result of some male authority. Their loneliness was highlighted by the absence of any mention of family in their lives. Their narratives stressed their marginality and sense of lack of control over their destiny.

The second generation of French women leaders (who had had the first group as role models) and the Norwegian women leaders (who comprised a much larger percentage of the leadership in their country) had a much greater sense of their own legitimacy. Their growing numbers contributed to changes in cultural norms about women in leadership. The positive implications of these findings are clear. Changes in historical/situational circumstances can produce rapid changes in women's lives.

Moving Beyond the Double Bind

Much of the laboratory research on women in mixed-sex groups is quite negative. This is partly because women still face obstacles in the public domain but also because experimental research is better at locating problems than in providing solutions. Most of this research has been conducted with women college students who may be more concerned about being liked than being powerful at this point in their lives.

One important way for women to avoid being defined by others is to recognize the way double binds are constructed and become active agents in defining themselves. Techniques used by successful women politicians include *reframing* (critiquing the conventional rhetoric used to describe women's options). In discussing double binds involving marriage, for example, one female candidate pointed out:

> If we are single, they say we couldn't catch a man. If we are married, they say that we are neglecting them. If we are divorced, they say we couldn't keep him. If we are widowed, they say we killed him. (Jamieson, 1995, p. 190)

Other useful strategies include recovering the stories of strong women (as we have done in the boxes throughout this book) and reclaiming language (words such as *sexism, ageism,* and *homophobia* condemn behaviors that might otherwise be tolerated if unlabeled). Sometimes language can be recast. For example, the word *himbo* was devised by a feminist man to indicate both male images designed for women, such as the model Fabio, and those constructed for men, such as Sylvester Stallone (Kimmel, 1996). Recasting language is particularly effective if one can do it with humor.

THE INTERNALIZATION OF GENDER NORMS

Women and Personal Entitlement

To use strategies similar to those just discussed, women must recognize the extent to which they are still unequal to men. This is a very painful process, and many women prefer to ignore or deny evidence of societal discrimination. The extent to which women accept beliefs and behaviors that are detrimental to themselves is one of the paradoxes of the psychology of women.

The Denial of Personal Discrimination

Many women deny personal discrimination. In one large survey of 400 adults in a Boston suburb, the researcher found no significant differences between employed women and men in measures of job-related grievances, satisfaction, or deservedness (Crosby, 1982). Subjective equality persisted even though employed women made significantly less money than employed men with equivalent jobs. These women reported no sense of personal discrimination, although they were keenly aware of gender discrimination in general. In other words, they knew that discrimination against women existed, but only against "other" women.

There are a number of different explanations for women's denial of discrimination against themselves. Sometimes women lack information with which to make group comparisons (Crosby, 1984). It is often more difficult to get information about the salaries of one's coworkers than about their sexual habits! But people also make more favorable judgments about themselves than about others even when they are using the same information (Unger & Sussman, 1986).

Shifting Standards of Evaluation

Shifting standards of evaluation sometimes make it difficult for individuals to determine whether discrimination has occurred (Biernat & Kobrynowicz, 1999). Many evaluations use subjective language that permits people to judge others with reference to their own gender. Characteristics such as tall or short have different meanings when applied to women or men. When a man and a woman were described as equally tall, they were perceived as having a different height in feet and inches. Tall men were estimated as more than six feet, nine inches, whereas tall women were seen as five feet, nine inches (Biernat, Manis, & Nelson, 1991). In another study, male targets were judged to earn significantly more money than female targets. However, the same women who were objectively judged to earn, on average, about $9,000 less per year than men were seen as more financially successful. They were doing nicely for "someone of their gender."

Categorical Rewards and Procedural Stigma

Women's awareness of their membership in a subordinate category may explain their feeling of undeservedness. In an ingenious experiment, men and women received rewards that they were told were either based on their performance or on their sex (Heilman, Simon, & Repper, 1987). Women's, but not men's, self-perceptions were negatively affected by selection based on sex in comparison to selection based on merit. When given rewards based on sex, women devalued their leadership performance, took less credit for successful outcomes, and reported less interest in remaining as leader of their group. They also characterized themselves as more deficient in general leadership skills.

Reward based on a gender category had no effect on men's view of themselves or their own worth (perhaps because it is a meaningless distinction for them since they are the normative category). This study has obvious implications in terms of affirmative action programs in which members of subordinate groups are told that they have received their positions because of their social category.

Women's devaluation of their own worth appears to be a common response to categorization in terms of gender. Women who attributed their selection as managers mainly to the fact of being a woman were dissatisfied with their work in general and experienced a great deal of work-related role conflict (Chacko, 1982). The term *procedural stigma* has been used to describe how being selected by way of procedures perceived as unfair leaves the person selected feeling stigmatized. These women's perceptions reflect similar perceptions in others. For example, when women undergraduates read a story in which a woman protagonist received a research award, they expected poorer subsequent evaluations when they believed that the selection criteria had included preferential treatment based on sex (Nacoste & Lehman, 1987).

Feelings of lack of entitlement extend to monetary rewards as well as acceptance of personal power. Studies have consistently found that women pay themselves less than men do when allocating rewards between themselves and others (Major, 1994). In the absence of social comparison information, women perceived less money as fair pay for their work and paid themselves less money than men did. Even women at elite universities buy into these beliefs. In a recent study at Yale University, students generated five thoughts to the question: "Do you think it would be better or worse if most shopping were done from home computers rather than in stores?" (Jost, 1997). After writing these essays, the women rated themselves as less sophisticated, less original, and less insightful than the men did. They also gave themselves $1.51 (18%) less pay for work viewed by independent judges as similar in quality and quantity to that of the male students.

Women give themselves lower rewards even when they recognize that their work input was similar to that of men (Major, McFarlin, & Gagnon, 1984). Actually, they had worked longer, did more work, did more correct work, and were more efficient than men for the same amount of pay. Gender differences in personal entitlement do not appear to be related to differences in personal history. Women's willingness to give themselves lower pay for work that is identical to that of men is consistent with a model of cultural sexism. Both men and women are responding to cultural norms about the relative lower worth of women.

The Awareness of Categorical Bias

The information contained in this chapter makes for dismal reading. Women students have sometimes told us that they would rather not know so much about how things are stacked against their gender. However, awareness of the sexist bias of others sometimes reduces its negative effects. For example, when women students believed they were competing against several unseen opponents (who were said to be either men or women) and were informed that they had either failed mildly or severely in this competition, their self-esteem was affected by both the sex of their opponents and the attributions they made about them (Dion, 1975). They were more negatively affected by men's than women's judgments, especially when they had experienced severe failure. However, women who attributed their severe failure at the hands of male opponents to prejudice had stronger self-esteem and more positive feminine identification than women who did not believe in a sexist bias.

Similar effects have been found in other groups such as Asian- and French-Canadian minorities (Dion, Earn, & Yee, 1978). When black students received negative feedback from supposedly prejudiced white evaluators, their self-esteem decreased only when they believed the evaluator could not see them (Crocker, Voelkl, Testa, & Major, 1991). The awareness of social stigma can be self-protective, because it provides an alternative to self-blame as an explanation for failure.

Some men also describe themselves as victims of sex discrimination, although fewer men (8.5%) than women (20%) do so (Kobrynowicz & Branscombe, 1997). Men and women differ in the personality characteristics associated with perceptions of discrimination. For men, reports of personal discrimination were associated with low self-esteem and high personal assertiveness. Reports by women were associated with depression. Women with a high need for approval were also less willing to acknowledge that they had been discriminated against. Drawing attention to discrimination may be particularly difficult for these women because dominant group members have been found to dislike members of devalued groups who report being the victims of discrimination (Dijker, Koomen, van der Heuvel, & Frijda, 1996).

Claims of discrimination meet different needs for men and women. For members of privileged groups, perceptions of discrimination may be an attempt to explain declines in historical privilege (Kobrynowicz & Branscombe, 1997). These men are making a comparison to a better past. In contrast, women are making a comparison to a past that is worse than the present.

Admitting discrimination can mean giving up a sense of control. In one study, when there was any ambiguity in the evaluation process, women avoided making attributions about discrimination (Ruggiero & Taylor, 1995). They did not make this attribution until it was impossible not to do so. Low-status group members (women, African-Americans, or individuals whose status had been manipulated by the researchers) were less likely than members of more privileged groups to blame their failure on discrimination. They were more likely than higher-status group members to blame their failure to perform well on the type of test, quality of their answers, and their ability and effort (Ruggiero & Major, 1998).

Why do members of subordinate groups minimize discrimination? Perceptions of personal discrimination enhanced satisfaction with their performance, but at the cost of lowered social self-esteem. Perceived discrimination resulted in a loss of perceived control as well (Ruggiero & Taylor, 1997). By minimizing discrimination, members of marginalized groups can maintain control over personal events in their lives and preserve their mental health in the context of an unfair reality.

But not all members of devalued groups think alike. An understanding of systemic and contextual factors has been linked with group identification and militancy in both blacks (Forward & Williams, 1970) and women (Sanger & Alker, 1972). These individuals can distinguish between explanations of control for themselves and for the world in general. Feminist activists, for example, appear to believe simultaneously that many structural factors are beyond the individual's control *and* that individuals can change social systems (Unger, 1984–1985). Such a contradictory belief pattern may be particularly adaptive in an ambiguous reality.

Combating Social Myths

Although many gender-related differences in social behaviors are constructed by means of behavioral interactions, people continue to believe in innate gender differences. One could call beliefs about differences *social myths*. The power of deeply entrenched social myths resides in their ability to protect the individual from cognitive conflict. Members of both the dominant and the subordinate group share cultural beliefs. The myths determine views of the world that are conceived to be objectively "true." They are maintained because each person does not create his or her social reality anew but must use cultural beliefs to understand and justify all the forms of inequality in which he or she is involved (Tajfel, 1984).

We believe that the material examined in this chapter gives us reasons for both despair and hope. On the negative side of the ledger, women share cultural assumptions about the lesser worth of women to an astonishing degree. Cultural ideology about gender is conveyed to women every day. It is not surprising that women come to internalize the belief that they are less important than men. "All things being equal, the greater the consistency, duration, and intensity with which a definition is promoted by others about an actor, the greater the likelihood the actor will embrace that definition as truly applicable to himself" (Lofland, 1969, p. 122).

The findings discussed in this chapter are also cause for hope. People are not totally at the mercy of external constraints. They are not passive recipients of social forces. They are also active agents of social change. Women working together have made great changes in social institutions. Just as we were finishing this chapter, the newspapers were full of news about a major breakthrough at the Massachusetts Institute of Technology, or MIT (Goldberg, 1999; Zernike, 1999). The women scientists there had banded together and used their scientific skills to demonstrate pervasive discrimination against women (see Box 3.2). They found differences between men and women in the amount of laboratory space allotted to them, as well as differences in faculty salaries and pensions. The women worked five years on their report, which has been put on MIT's Web site. Their evidence clearly convinced the president, Charles Vest, who said:

> I have always believed that contemporary gender discrimination within universities is part reality and part perception. True, but . . . reality is by far the greater part of the balance. (Zernike, 1999, p. F4)

Ironically, some of the fifteen tenured women who worked on the report secretly worried that they might not be as good as the men. The opposite was true. Forty percent of these women had been named members of the National Academy of Sciences or the Academy of Arts and Sciences (organizations that elect as members the very best scholars in their fields). It was only by talking to one another that they learned that their shared sense of marginality was not due to personal inadequacy. They also found that the men did not dislike women. In making decisions about awards and promotions, they just liked their male buddies more.

This victory should be celebrated, but, as the report notes, things are just as bad at comparable institutions such as Harvard or the California Institute of Technology. It will take communal efforts to make changes there, too. The process of change requires changes in consciousness to make changes in social structures, which, in turn, change attitudes and perceptions. Real social change will take place only when there are changes in both inner and outer reality.

Box 3.2 The Story Behind a Successful Fight on Gender Bias

The story began in 1994 when MIT told Nancy Hopkins, a prominent DNA researcher, that it would discontinue a course that she had designed that was now required for 1,000 students a year. She had worked for five years to develop that course. In the previous two years, a male professor had joined her in teaching it. The man, MIT informed her, was going to turn the course into a book and a CD-ROM without her.

Hopkins drafted a letter to the president of MIT about how she felt women researchers were treated. When she discussed it with a woman colleague, she asked to sign it, too. They decided to poll every tenured woman in the School of Science to see if what they had experienced were individual problems or part of a pattern.

They were surprised to find out how fast they got their answers. Within a day they had talked to all 15 tenured women (there were 197 tenured men) and agreed that there was a problem and that something had to be done. True to their fields, they looked first at the data (see graphs).

Individually, some women said they had sensed discrimination but feared that they would be dismissed as troublemakers or that their work would suffer from the distraction of trying to prove their point. "These women had devoted their lives to science," Hopkins said. "There was the feeling that if you got into it, you weren't going to last; you'd get too angry."

But the hurdles were already costing them time and making them miserable. All fifteen women crowded into the dean's office to ask for an investigation. The dean checked their numbers and became an immediate convert. He boosted the women's salaries an average of 20 percent and eliminated the requirement that they raise part of their salaries from grants. He also appointed a committee that spent five years gathering data. Their report was released in March 1999 and posted on MIT's Web site. It acknowledges that there is evidence of "subtle differences in the treatment of men and women," "exclusion," and, in some cases, "discrimination against women faculty." The inequities included salaries, space, re-

MIT's women scientists

Women faculty in MIT's School of Science compiled a scathing report on unfair conditions they say they work in at the university. Women make up 11.7 percent of the School of Science faculty, the report says.

BREAKDOWN OF SCIENCE FACULTY

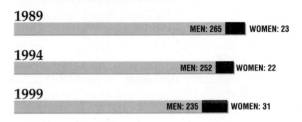

1989 MEN: 265 WOMEN: 23

1994 MEN: 252 WOMEN: 22

1999 MEN: 235 WOMEN: 31

THE SITUATION IN 1994

The faculty and administration of MIT's School of Science began talking about the gender issue in 1994, when women faculty began to realize that the number of female students was increasing, but women faculty were not. Here is the situation in 1994.

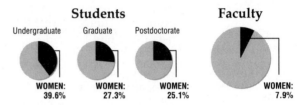

Students

Undergraduate	Graduate	Postdoctorate
WOMEN: 39.6%	WOMEN: 27.3%	WOMEN: 25.1%

Faculty

WOMEN: 7.9%

SOURCE: Study on the Status of Women Faculty in Science at MIT

search, and inclusion of women in positions of power. An underrepresentation of women making key decisions had bred male "cronyism" that for women meant "unequal access to the substantive resources of MIT."

In addition to salary, space, and resource increases, MIT plans to have a 40 percent increase in the number of women with tenure next year, bringing the percentage to above 10 for the first time. The institute also corrected some pensions, one by $130,000 and another by $80,000.

"I was unhappy at MIT for more than a decade," one woman told the committee. "I thought it was the price you paid if you wanted to be a scientist at an elite university. . . . After . . . the dean's response, my life began to change. . . . My research blossomed, my funding tripled. Now I love every aspect of my job. It is hard to understand how I survived—or why."

(Reprinted courtesy of *The Boston Globe,* March 21, 1999.)

- *Gender is more than just sex.* This chapter emphasizes how sex as a category is used to construct gendered distinctions. This process begins with perceptual and cognitive biases that lead individuals to expect different behaviors from women and men. People act to confirm these expectations, which are, indeed, often confirmed by others' self-presentational strategies. These behaviors in turn, reinforce gender-biased views about the differing characteristics of men and women.
- *Language and naming are sources of power.* Naming (in the sense of deviance and stigma) can be used to delegitimize women who exercise social power or possess public authority. However, naming (in the sense of conscious awareness) can also reduce the extent to which gender-biased views of the self are internalized.
- *Women are not all alike.* Sex is not the only social category that is used to produce and maintain distinctions between groups of people. Other categories with similar effects are race/ethnicity, age, and disability. It is important to remember that most of the effect of these categories on behavior is a result of normal cognitive and social psychological processes rather than deliberate discrimination.
- *Psychological research can foster social change.* A model of gender as a social construction is a positive step in the movement for social change. This model argues that gender-related traits and behaviors are situationally constructed and help maintain the societal status quo. As more women move into positions of power in the public arena they will change perceptions about the relationship between gender and status and, therefore, help create more egalitarian social systems.

SUGGESTED READINGS

RIDGEWAY, CECILIA L. (Ed.). (1992). *Gender, interaction, and inequality.* New York: Springer-Verlag. Although the contributions to this book are rather technical in nature, they provide an up-to-date review of the theories and findings of the major sociologists and social psychologists who work in the area of status, power, and gender.

JAMIESON, KATHLEEN HALL. (1995). *Beyond the double bind: Women and leadership.* This is a highly readable book by an expert on the media and politics. It reviews the many double binds that women encounter and suggests strategies for moving beyond them.

SWANN, WILLIAM B., JR., LANGLOIS, JUDITH H., & GILBERT, LUCIA A. (Eds.). (1999). *Sexism stereotypes in modern society: The gender science of Janet Taylor Spence.* Washington, DC: American Psychological Association. This book is the result of a conference to honor the contributions of a woman who has contributed to scholarship on women and gender for nearly thirty years. It includes chapters by a number of experts in the area summarizing and integrating social psychological research on sexism and how it works.

CHAPTER 4

The Meanings of Difference

- A FOCUS ON SIMILARITY: WORKING FOR EQUALITY
  Defining Difference and Similarity
  Measuring Differences
- DIFFERENT OR SIMILAR? GENDER AND MATH ABILITIES
  Are Mathematics Ability and Performance Gender-Linked?
  What Factors Influence Mathematics Performance?
  What Are the Implications for Society?
- THE SIMILARITIES TRADITION: WHY IT MATTERS
  Values and Ideology in Research: What Are the Lessons of History?
  Women, Minorities, and Math/Science Careers

- THE DIFFERENCES TRADITION: CELEBRATING WOMEN
  Nancy Chodorow: A Feminist Perspective on Mothering
  Carol Gilligan: A Theory of Moral Reasoning
  Jean Baker Miller: A Theory of Power and Gender Differences
- THE DIFFERENCES TRADITION: WHY IT MATTERS
  Should Humans Be More Like Women?
  The Politics of Difference
- CAN SIMILARITIES AND DIFFERENCES BE RECONCILED?
- CONNECTING THEMES
- SUGGESTED READINGS

Our language and our stereotypes portray men and women as "opposite sexes." Most people believe that women and men differ in many important ways. But what are the "real" differences between boys and girls or women and men in traits, abilities, and behaviors? Often, students of psychology want "the facts—and just the facts," and they expect the science of psychology to be able to provide those facts.

However, the study of group differences is not just a matter of establishing facts. Many differences between groups of people are related to social power and can be thought of as continuums of domination and oppression. Figure 4.1 shows social distinctions between groups of people. For each dimension, there is clearly a "good" and a "bad" end—for example, society places more value on young people than old people. Some differences do not matter in Western society; it is unlikely that anyone would bother to do research comparing brown-eyed and blue-eyed people. Other differences, like the ones in Figure 4.1, matter very much. These differences have social and political consequences; they represent dimensions of privilege versus disadvantage (Morgan, 1996). In the case of gender, what is male and masculine is valued more highly than what is female and feminine.

In feminist theory and political movements, there have long been two

116

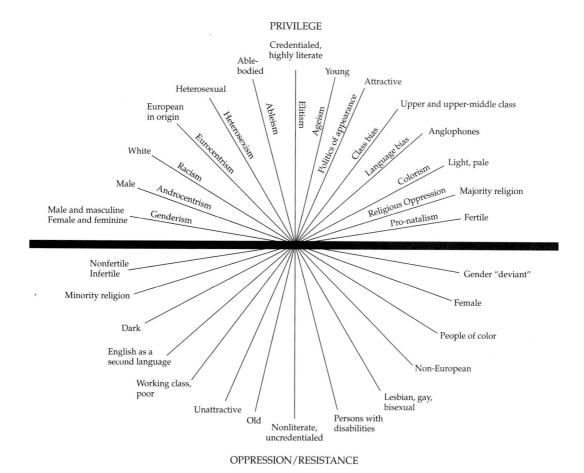

PRIVILEGE

Credentialed, highly literate
Able-bodied
Young
Attractive
Heterosexual
Upper and upper-middle class
European in origin
Anglophones
White
Light, pale
Male
Majority religion
Male and masculine
Female and feminine
Fertile

Ableism
Elitism
Ageism
Politics of appearance
Class bias
Language bias
Colorism
Religious Oppression
Pro-natalism

Heterosexism
Eurocentrism
Racism
Androcentrism
Genderism

Nonfertile
Infertile
Gender "deviant"
Minority religion
Female
Dark
People of color
English as a second language
Non-European
Working class, poor
Lesbian, gay, bisexual
Unattractive
Old
Persons with disabilities
Nonliterate, uncredentialed

OPPRESSION/RESISTANCE

FIGURE 4.1. Intersecting dimensions of privilege and oppression.
Source: From *The Gender Questions in Education: Theory, Pedagogy, and Politics* by Ann Diller. Copyright © 1996 by Westview Press, a member of Perseus Books, L.L.C. Reprinted by permission of Westview Press, a member of Perseus Books, L.L.C.

ways of thinking about gender-related differences (Kimball, 1995). The *similarities tradition* has claimed that women and men are basically very much alike in intelligence, personality, abilities, and goals. This tradition stems from liberal feminism and is used to argue for equality of the sexes. After all, if men and women are far more alike than different, shouldn't they be treated equally under the law and in society generally?

The *differences tradition* has claimed that there are fundamental differences between women and men that should be recognized and honored. This tradition, stemming from cultural feminism, is used to argue that society should give more recognition to the activities, traits, and values of women. After all, if taking care of other people and relationships (traditionally feminine characteristics) were rewarded as much as dominance and personal ambition (traditionally masculine characteristics), wouldn't the world be a better place?

117

Both these ways of thinking have been used to generate research and to form political strategies. Debates about which approach is better—more feminist, more likely to help change society, more scientifically accurate—have gone on for a long time. Because of the influence of contemporary feminism, issues of gender and difference have been studied and debated with new intensity in the past two decades. In this chapter we explore both the similarities and the differences traditions, looking at important research from each. However, the goal is not to decide which tradition is better. Rather, we hope that our readers will decide that there is value in both—that "double visions are theoretically and politically richer and more flexible than visions based on a single tradition" (Kimball, 1995, p. 2).

A FOCUS ON SIMILARITY: WORKING FOR EQUALITY

Psychologists who work within the similarities tradition have tried to show that gender differences in ability or skills are either nonexistent or much too small to explain gender differences in power, prestige, and income (Kimball, 1995). They point out there has been a lack of agreement in *defining* difference, problems in *measuring* difference, and issues of *values and interpretation* in understanding results. This tradition has generated a great deal of research on gender and cognitive abilities, using standard psychological research methods and statistical analysis.

Defining Difference and Similarity

Determining the facts about gender differences sounds relatively easy: a psychologist could just measure a group of women and a group of men for a trait or ability and compute the average difference between the groups. There is a long tradition of this kind of research in psychology. Between 1967 and 1985, for example, *Psychological Abstracts*, which lists published journal articles in psychology, indexed 16,416 articles on human sex differences (Myers, 1986). The tradition continues: between 1991 and 1997 there were more than 15,000 new psychological publications dealing with sex or gender differences!

You might think that with all these studies, some definitive answers would emerge. However, the meaning of "difference" can be very ambiguous. Suppose you were at a party where you overheard someone explain why there are more men than women judges in the United States by saying, "Let's face it, women just don't reason like men. When it comes to reasoning ability, they just don't have what it takes." If you're like us, your first reaction would be that this is just an outdated stereotype. Your second reaction might be to ask yourself what psychological evidence could be brought to bear on this claim.

The speaker (let's call him Mr. Pompous) has asserted that there is a gender-related difference in reasoning, a cognitive ability. But before we examine the evidence, let's consider (using our reasoning ability!) what he might have meant. One interpretation is that all men and no women have the ability to reason—in other words, that reasoning ability is dichotomous by sex. If the entire population of men and women could be measured on a perfectly valid and reliable test of reasoning ability, the two sexes would form two non-overlapping distributions, with the distribution for women being lower. This hypothetical situation is shown in Figure 4.2a. *Despite a hundred years of research on gender-related differences, no one has ever discovered a psychological trait or cognitive ability on which men and women are completely different.*

Since it would be ridiculous to argue that women are totally and categorically inferior, Mr. Pompous probably means something else when he talks about "difference." Perhaps he means that there is a mean, or *average* difference, such that the mean for women is slightly lower (Figure 4.2b) or very much lower (Figure 4.2c) than the mean for men. However, an average difference doesn't tell us very much if taken by itself. Sets of distributions can have the same differences in means but large differences in *variability*, defined as the range or "spread" of scores. Figure 4.2d shows males more variable than females and 4.2e shows females more variable than males. Looking at the areas in which males' and females' distributions do not overlap in each set shows that the meaning of difference is different for each. That is, the proportion of women who score below the lowest-scoring men and the proportion of men who score above the highest-scoring women differ greatly from one set of hypothetical distributions to the next.

Moreover, these are not the only possible population distributions. Women and men could be equal on average, but one sex could be more variable, as shown in Figure 4.2f; here, the area where females and males overlap is larger than those where they do not.

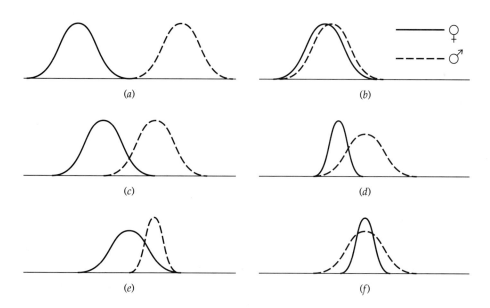

FIGURE 4.2. Some possible distributions of reasoning ability in females and males. *Source:* Unger, R. & Crawford, M. (1996).

Most research on gender-related differences reports a mean (average) difference between a sample of women and a sample of men, with statistical tests to determine whether the difference is *statistically significant* (unlikely to have occurred by chance). The concept of statistical significance is not the same as the ordinary meaning of "significant." A difference may be statistically significant yet be trivially small and useless in predicting differential behavior in other experimental situations or in daily life. In other words, statistical significance is not the same as importance.

How large does a statistically significant difference have to be before we are justified in labeling men and women more different than similar? Should the importance of a difference be judged in terms of average scores or in terms of how much variability exists between scores for each gender, or in how much the distributions for women and men overlap? And how do we compare the results of several studies of the same trait or ability, when the results vary? How many studies are sufficient to settle a question? How consistent must the results be? Is it important to measure the trait or ability in people of different age groups, social classes, ethnic groups, and cultures—or is it safe to assume that what is true for North American college students is true for all people? The answers to these questions involve value judgments about the meaning of difference.

Measuring Differences

Suppose a psychologist wanted to test Mr. Pompous's claim that there is a gender difference in reasoning ability. She might compare a sample of women and a sample of men on a standard test of reasoning, matching (or otherwise equating) the two groups on any other factors that might affect reasoning ability, such as years of education. She would compare the average scores of her two groups with an appropriate statistical test to determine whether the difference she obtained was likely to have occurred by chance.

The logic of experimental design and hypothesis testing leads the field of psychology to put more weight on findings of difference than on findings of similarity. Statistical tests allow psychologists to be fairly confident that when a difference is judged to exist, the conclusion is an accurate one. When a difference is not found, psychologists cannot know for certain that there is no difference in the population; it could always be just a failure of this particular experiment to detect the difference.

Think of an experiment as a microscope for a moment. If a scientist looks through her microscope and sees what she expected to see, she usually concludes that her hypothesis was correct. If she sees nothing or sees only a blurred picture, she may conclude that her instrument or procedures were lacking, and that she should try again, not that her hypothesis was wrong. Relying on similar logic, professional journals are less likely to publish articles that report similarities between women and men (or boys and girls) than they are to publish reports of differences. The possibility of overemphasizing differences is a built-in limitation of hypothesis testing. Sometimes, too, researchers make mistakes in designing, carrying out, or interpreting a study. Problems in research design are common (Deaux, 1984; Grady, 1981; Jacklin, 1981; Maccoby

& Jacklin, 1974; Parlee, 1981; Unger, 1979b), and some researchers in the similarities tradition have charged that many reported gender differences are distorted or exaggerated (Grady, 1981).

What are some of the flaws in difference research? Some studies have measured behaviors of only one sex and erroneously drawn conclusions about differences between the sexes—for example, measuring the relationship between hormonal levels and mood only in women and concluding that only women show such relationships. Of course, it is impossible to demonstrate a gender difference (or similarity) if only one group is studied (Jacklin, 1981). Other flaws include researchers' tendency to overgeneralize from their limited samples to all women and men and to conclude that a gender-related difference is due to innate or biological factors when such factors have not been measured.

Unfortunately, examples of these mistakes are easy to find. The eminent psychologist Harry Harlow, who studied behavior in primates, found evidence that male rhesus monkeys are more aggressive than females. The problem with his research arose when he used this evidence to explain the behavior of boys and girls in biological terms:

> There is reason to believe that genetic variables condition similar differences in human primates. The gentle and relatively passive behavior of most little girls is a useful maternal attribute, and the more aggressive behavior of most little boys is useful preparation for the paternal function of protection. (1971, p. 6)

When Harlow's own research showed that rearing female monkeys in abnormal environments caused them to be much more aggressive toward male monkeys, he was not convinced of the importance of environmental influences on aggression. Instead, his preexisting bias caused him to ignore the implications of his own data, and he resorted to stereotypes:

> Negative feedback, however, quickly suppresses this aggression. Females win their way into male hearts and minds through passive resistance and social sophistication. In our society females usually attempt to combine love and marriage with social security. . . . Young males prefer action and young females prefer active attention. (1971, pp. 90–91)

Not only had Harlow failed to study biological factors in aggression, but he hadn't even studied girls and boys. Instead, he generalized from his research on rhesus monkeys!

One of the most persistent sources of bias in gender-difference research is the difficulty of separating gender from all the other factors it is related to in our society (Jacklin, 1981). The interaction of gender with other factors leads to *confounding*, in which the effects of two or more variables are mixed, and it becomes impossible to decide which variable is causing experimental effects. Because gender is related to many differences in background and status, researchers can rarely know whether their female and male samples are really comparable.

For example, suppose we were matching participants for our imaginary experiment on reasoning ability. We would certainly not choose a male sample with college degrees and compare it with a female sample of high-school graduates. Such a comparison would obviously be unfair because the different backgrounds and experience of the two groups, rather than the fact of their being male or female, could account for differences in reasoning ability. But even when a researcher attempts to measure comparable men and women (or boys and girls), it is often hard to decide what characteristics should be matched. Most researchers would assume that they had solved the comparability problem if they chose to compare, say, female and male college students. But although a sample of male and female college students can be matched on level of formal education, the women and men may have very different backgrounds in mathematics, science, and the liberal arts, starting in high school (Eccles, 1989), and will be concentrated in different courses of study in college. These differences may be irrelevant to some research questions but crucial to others.

Many psychologists believe that a technique called *meta-analysis* can resolve some of the issues of definition and measurement in research on gender differences. What is meta-analysis and how does it work? Basically, it uses quantitative methods to summarize the results of research studies done by different people at different times (Hedges & Becker, 1986). It allows researchers to integrate the results of many studies on a single topic and to assess the magnitude and consistency of difference effects statistically (Hyde & Linn, 1986).

In doing a meta-analysis, the investigator first identifies all the relevant studies on a topic. The next step is to summarize the results of each study in a common unit of measurement. There are different degrees of statistical significance, and the results of some studies may be stronger than others. In meta-analysis, studies can be distinguished from one another in terms of the magnitude of the gender-related difference. Finally, meta-analysis allows researchers to group studies by subcategory and thereby assess the influence of variables other than gender. For example, if a researcher did a meta-analysis of studies on gender and reasoning ability, she might categorize the studies according to the type of task used or whether there was time pressure in the situation. Perhaps the gender difference only occurs when the task is male-oriented or when there is time pressure. A variable that interacts with another variable to change its effect is called a *moderator variable*.

Many psychologists, especially those who work within the similarities tradition, see meta-analysis as a useful technique for studying gender differences (Eagly, 1987; Hyde & Linn, 1986). It helps researchers interpret data from large numbers of studies and allows them to estimate the size of a gender-related difference. It simplifies the study of other variables that interact with gender—which is important because there almost always are other factors involved (Hyde & Linn, 1986).

But meta-analysis cannot wholly compensate for the biases in the original studies or ensure "objective" interpretation (Unger & Crawford, 1989). Reviewers must still rely on their own judgment in deciding which studies are relevant and whether several measures of the same construct (such as different tests of reasoning ability) are measuring the same thing. Moreover, there could be an overlooked source of bias common to all the studies in a meta-analysis, which could lead to an overall conclusion that is biased (Hedges & Becker, 1986). If all the tests of reasoning ability used in research happened to be biased toward men, for example, a false "gender difference" might show up in a meta-analysis.

No statistical technique can resolve all problems of interpreting differences. Meta-analysis can show which variables moderate the occurrence of gender differences, but it does not allow conclusions about the *causes* of the differences. Moreover, there is still room for disagreement about how big a difference must be to count as an important one. The meaning and interpretation of observed differences is still at issue. We now turn to two areas of research where debates about similarity, difference, and their interpretation are ongoing.

DIFFERENT OR SIMILAR?
GENDER AND MATH ABILITIES

The general pattern in cognitive skills is one of gender similarity (Maccoby & Jacklin, 1974). However, math ability and achievement is one of a very few areas where standard psychological research shows consistent gender differences. For this reason, it has generated a great deal of research. In this section we look at ongoing controversies about differences in mathematics performance.

There are two widely used ways to measure math ability and achievement: school grades and performance on standardized tests such as the SAT-M. If ability is measured in terms of school achievement, girls come out ahead. On standardized tests, boys come out ahead. Curiously, girls get better grades than boys even in areas in which the boys score higher in ability tests (Eccles, 1989). Their higher academic achievement is rarely interpreted to mean that girls are more intelligent. Rather, it is argued that girls may get their higher grades by being quiet and neat, following directions, and trying hard to please their teachers. This may be an example of devaluing feminine characteristics.

Are Mathematics Ability and Performance Gender-Linked?

Girls' performance on standardized math tests is better than boys' in the elementary school years, but by high school they have lost their early advantage. Just a relatively short time ago, in the 1940s to 1960s, the differences were much larger and favored boys. Today, however, boys and girls do not differ in basic math skills (Feingold, 1988). Contrary to beliefs that girls don't like math and are not good at it, many studies (summarized by Chipman and Wilson, 1985) show that girls like math just as much as boys do (although it is not a favorite subject for either group) and, through the intermediate high school level, perform similarly.

There is, however, a well-documented difference favoring males in *advanced* mathematics performance as measured by tests. In recent years, boys have scored an average of about fifty points higher on the math portion of the SAT than girls. Among the very highest scorers in two recent test administrations, boys earned 96 percent of perfect 800 scores, 90 percent of scores between 780 to 790, 81 percent of scores between 750 and 770, and 56 percent of scores of 600 (Dorans & Livingston, 1987). In national math talent searches, far more boys than girls are identified as gifted, and the gifted boys score higher than the gifted girls (Benbow & Stanley, 1980; Hyde & McKinley, 1997).

The gender gap in math may be shrinking. In the most recent tests, the SAT gap was forty-one points in favor of boys—still very large, but smaller than in previous years. Asian-American students now score as high on math as white students overall, while other ethnic groups still lag. Ethnic group differences are strongly related to social class: the lower a student's family income and parents' education, the less likely he or she is to do well on the SAT. However, the gender gap has diminished over time in every ethnic group (Shea, 1994). And the gender gap is much smaller than differences due to social class (Hyde & McKinley, 1997).

What a puzzle for psychological research to unravel! Girls start out liking math and believing that girls are better at it than boys (Boswell, 1985). They do better than boys on standardized tests and get better grades in math (as well as in other subjects). Yet, by the time they are in high school, they score lower on advanced math skills. As you might expect, the development of this difference cannot be attributed to one or two isolated variables. Rather, many interacting factors may be responsible for both gender and ethnic differences, especially social class background. Focusing on the gender gap, we examine the effects of in-school and out-of-school opportunities to learn math and on girls' confidence in their math abilities. We also look at stereotypes about math as a male domain. Finally, we consider hypotheses about biologically based differences in ability.

What Factors Influence Mathematics Performance?

Gender in the Classroom

The single biggest influence on math performance is that girls take fewer math courses (Chipman & Thomas, 1985). When course taking is controlled, the differences nearly disappear (Chipman, Brush, & Wilson, 1985). Math course taking is becoming more equal; girls now take algebra and geometry, but not calculus or computer science, nearly as much as boys (AAUW Educational Foundation, 1998; Sadker & Sadker, 1994).

Even when they take the same courses, boys and girls are experiencing different worlds in the classroom. Studies at all grade levels have shown that often a few males are allowed to dominate classroom interaction while other students are silent and ignored (Eccles, 1989) (see Figure 4.3). Gender interacts with race to determine who gets attention from teachers: white males get the most attention, followed by minority males and white females. Minority females get the least attention of any group. And this discrimination takes a toll: classroom interaction studies show that African-American girls become less active, assertive, and visible in class as they move through the elementary grades (Sadker & Sadker, 1994).

Girls are praised for their appearance, boys for their performance. Girls experience sexual harassment from their peers and teachers far more often than boys. Twenty years of research on educational equity has shown such a dismal pattern of deeply ingrained sexism that researchers Myra Sadker and David Sadker titled their 1994 book *Failing at Fairness: How America's Schools*

Doonesbury BY GARRY TRUDEAU

FIGURE 4.3. Sexism in the classroom.
Source: Doonesbury. Copyright © 1992 G. B. Trudeau. Reprinted with permission of
Universal Press Syndicate. All rights reserved.

Cheat Girls. In the voices of the young women they interviewed, the sexism
and its effects on bright girls are evident:

> "In my science class the teacher never calls on me, and I feel like I don't exist.
> The other night I had a dream that I vanished."

> "People are always surprised to learn that I have a 4.0 and I'm a National
> Merit Finalist. Their image of me is 'that *blond* girl who used to go out with
> Scott.' Why can't they understand there's more to me?"

> "I have a teacher who calls me 'airhead' and 'ditz.' I used to think I was smart,
> but now I don't know. Maybe I'm not. What if he's right? The more he treats
> me like an airhead, the more I think maybe I am." (p. 135)

Gender inequity that can affect math and science performance extends to out-of-
school educational experiences as well. Boys are more likely to participate in activities such as chess clubs, math clubs, summer computer courses, and science
camps. In short, boys live in a math-enriched environment that encourages
achievement, and girls in a math-impoverished one that encourages self-doubt.

Low Confidence, Low Self-Expectations

Girls' lower confidence about their abilities is a consistent finding in many
studies (Chipman & Wilson, 1985), although meta-analysis shows that the difference is not large (Hyde, Fennema, Ryan, Frost, & Hopp, 1990). In 1992, the
Mattel Corporation introduced Teen Talk Barbie. Among the words they put in
her mouth: "Math class is tough." Myra and David Sadker noted:

> The national flap over Barbie's "Math class is tough" faux pas is a symptom of
> the inroads females have forged in this formerly male preserve. *The
> Washington Post* dubbed the doll "Foot-in-Mouth Barbie," and the American
> Association of University Women warned that this was precisely the kind of
> role model girls did not need. Math teachers around the country registered
> their dismay. "We've been working so hard at closing the gender gap and
> fighting math anxiety for girls," an Illinois teacher told us. "This is the last
> thing we need." (Sadker & Sadker, 1994, p. 122)

By the time they are in junior high, girls are losing their early confidence that they can do math as well as or better than boys, and their change in attitude is independent of their actual performance (see Figure 4.4). Although their grades remain better than boys' grades, girls rate themselves lower in math ability, consider their math courses harder, and are less sure that they will succeed in future math courses (Eccles et al., 1985). For eighth-graders, math confidence and attitudes toward success in math are more important in determining whether girls will take college preparatory math than their actual math achievement scores are (Sherman, 1983). Among high school girls of equal ability, those who are less confident are more likely to discontinue math (Sherman, 1982). Female college students are also less confident that they can do well in computer courses, and this attitude affects their course enrollment (Miura, 1987). By the time they are in college, doing well in math is unrelated to women's (but not men's) feelings of overall competence (Singer & Stake, 1986). For many young women, math changes from a valued skill to something that is "just not me."

Parents of girls probably play a part in these attitude changes. Parents attribute a daughter's success in math to hard work and effort, and a son's success to natural talent. They view math as more difficult for daughters than for sons, and they believe that math, especially advanced math, is more important for sons. Parents, then, provide an interpretive framework for their sons' and daughters' beliefs about their abilities (Eccles, 1989). Boys learn that they have natural talent in an important area, and girls learn that hard work cannot entirely make up for their lack of ability!

Math as a Male Domain

Close your eyes and visualize a mathematician. Chances are your image is of a cerebral-looking middle-aged man with glasses and an intense but absent-minded air—an Einstein, perhaps. Now visualize a woman mathematician. "Unattractive," "masculine," "cold/distant," and "unfeminine" are the negative stereotypes that women mathematicians perceive others to hold, along with "aggressive," "socially awkward," and "overly intellectual" (Boswell, 1985). When elementary and senior high school students were asked about their perceptions of people in math-related careers such as science, engineering, and physics, they described *men*—who were white-coated loners, isolated

FIGURE 4.4. Math performance depends on the situation!
Source: Foxtrot. Copyright 1995 Bill Amend. Reprinted with permission of Universal Press Syndicate. All rights reserved.

in laboratories, with no time for family or friends (Boswell, 1979). Children learn very early that math is a male domain. By the third grade, they believe that adult women are generally inferior to adult men in math (Boswell, 1985).

In the past, it was thought that the belief that "math is for men" was held largely by girls and women, and that it deterred them from choosing math courses and math-related activities. However, a meta-analysis of math attitudes has shown that *males* hold this belief much more strongly than girls and women do (Hyde et al., 1990). This finding is very interesting because it suggests that gender-related influences on math choices work at the interactional and social structural levels at least as much as at the individual level. In other words, we cannot explain the underrepresentation of girls and women in math courses and math careers by saying that they mistakenly believe that math is for men, an intrapsychic or individual "attitude problem." Rather, if this belief is affecting girls and women, it must be because boys and men hold it, and something in their behavior toward the girls and women they interact with puts subtle pressure on the girls not to achieve in math and science. This is an example of "doing gender" as described in Chapter 3.

The gender incongruence of math for girls is heightened by a lack of role models. Beyond junior high, math and science teachers are predominantly men. Very few girls learn about great women mathematicians like Emmy Noether, who persisted in her research despite blatant sex discrimination and provided the mathematical basis for important aspects of relativity theory (Crawford, 1981). Few young girls have opportunities to offset negative influences through personal contact with women mathematicians and scientists.

Cross-Cultural Effects

As shown by the growing similarity in girls' and boys' cognitive skills over the past thirty years, gender differences in cognitive abilities are certainly not cast in stone. An exploration of situations in which such differences are either smaller or larger than those we've described can tell us much about the sources of differences usually attributed to gender. Different cultures may create, or at least exaggerate or minimize, various cognitive skills.

In Israel, for example, gender differences in cognitive abilities appear earlier than in the United States. Boys surpass girls on verbal as well as mathematical tests by the age of 13 (Lieblich, 1985). Almost identical patterns of performance have been found in both Jewish and Arab children. For both groups, however, socioeconomic class differences in test performance were larger than gender-related differences.

Why do gender differences appear earlier in Israel than in the United States? They may be mediated by the cultural context in which children are raised (Safir, 1986). Israeli society is more patriarchal than our own. For example, in orthodox Judaism, the only branch of Judaism officially recognized in Israel, only men can officiate at religious ceremonies, and only a husband can apply for a divorce. Both Arab and Jewish parents in Israel have been found to value education more for their sons than for their daughters (Alazorov-Por, 1983).

Israel is, however, a young nation whose people continue to explore different ways of living in communities. One study examined students' cognitive performance on standardized tests (similar to the SAT) for groups of young women and men who had been born and educated either in a city, a kibbutz (a communal settlement), or a moshav (an organization of individually owned farms that are worked cooperatively). Kibbutzim are relatively egalitarian. Moshavs, in contrast, are still patriarchal in nature; the father is the legal head of the household, and only he has the right to vote on community issues.

Men tended to score higher than women on both the mathematical and language subtests of these college entrance exams. Gender differences were, however, affected by the ideological conditions under which the students had been raised. Differences were largest between young women and men who had been born and raised in a moshav, and smallest between young women and men who had been born and raised in a kibbutz (Safir, 1986).

This study demonstrates how sensitive cognitive abilities are to cultural context. We predict that as more cross-cultural comparisons are made, gender-related differences in cognitive abilities will be shown to be more sociocultural (and less biological) in origin. Within our own culture, the gender-related difference in math performance is largely a white phenomenon: for African-American and Hispanic students, there is no gender difference, and for Asian-Americans there is a very small difference favoring girls (Hyde & McKinley, 1997).

An Overemphasis on Biology?

Some psychologists believe that differences in mathematics achievement reflect biological influences. As noted earlier, boys are much more likely than girls to be identified as gifted in national math talent searches. Based on this evidence, two prominent researchers concluded: "Sex differences in achievement and in attitude toward mathematics result from superior male mathematical ability which may, in turn, be related to greater male ability in spatial tasks" (Benbow & Stanley, 1980, p. 1264). Although they had not investigated biological variables in any way, they suggested that biology was at the root of the difference because environmental factors were equated: their (junior high) boys and girls had taken the same number of formal math courses.

Researchers in the similarities tradition point out that overgeneralization and a rush to "biologize" results are unfortunately frequent in research on gender-related differences. We have described many sociocultural factors that have been shown to affect math attitudes and performance. As two women mathematics professors pointed out, environmental factors were not ruled out in Benbow and Stanley's study:

> Anyone who thinks that seventh-graders are free from environmental influences can hardly be living in the real world. While the formal training of all students may be essentially the same, the issues of who helps with mathematics, of what sort of toys and games children are exposed to, of what the expectations of parents and teachers are, and of a multitude of other factors cannot lightly be set aside (Schafer & Gray, 1981, p. 231).

More recently, Benbow has reviewed evidence for environmental and biological factors and again concluded that "sex differences in extremely high mathematical reasoning ability may be, in part, physiologically determined" (1988, p. 182). But there is no conclusive evidence for a biological basis for gender differences in math ability. The existence of a sex-linked gene for math ability has been ruled out (Sherman & Fennema, 1978). Possible connections between biological influences such as genetics or hormones and intellectual performance continue to be explored. However, it is important not to overlook sociocultural influences. Even among boys and girls identified as gifted in math and science, the majority do not pursue math and science careers. Clearly, ability alone does not determine intellectual growth and career choice.

Ironically, Benbow and Stanley (1980) may have indirectly (and inadvertently) contributed to the sociocultural causes of math deficits in girls and women. Their article, published in the prestigious journal *Science*, was seized on by the popular press and reported in highly misleading stories and headlines (see Figure 4.5). An interesting field study compared the attitudes of parents who had heard about the article with those who had not (Eccles & Jacobs, 1986). (Because Eccles's research on math attitudes and performance was under way at the time, she had a sample of parents whose attitudes toward their daughters' abilities she had already measured.) Reading about "scientific evidence" for a "math gene" favoring boys led mothers of daughters to lower their estimates of their daughter's abilities. We have already noted the importance of parents in providing an interpretational framework for their children's self-assessments.

Press coverage of research on gender-related differences in math performance is further documentation that theories about the meaning of difference are politically charged. The critical response to Benbow and Stanley's theorizing from the scientific community, such as the rebuttal by Alice Schafer and Mary Gray quoted earlier, received no press coverage. It is encouraging to see recent press coverage presenting the research of Jacqueline Eccles, Janet Hyde, and Marcia Linn with these headlines: "Study: Male, Female Talent Equalizing," and "In Sum: Girls Are Not Bad at Math."

What Are the Implications for Society?

The evidence shows that males are more likely to achieve in advanced (but not elementary or intermediate) mathematics. Researchers in the similarities tradition have sought to minimize the size and importance of this difference. They point out that it is an *average* difference, and the overlap between females and males is much greater than the difference between them. We have also seen evidence that gender-related differences in cognition are decreasing. Girls and young women are increasingly claiming math and science as gender-equal territory.

Researchers in this tradition also emphasize that when differences occur, they are probably the result of differential experiences and socialization. We are all so used to living in a gendered world that it is hard for us to appreciate the pervasiveness of gender differentiation (see Chapter 6). We grow up being given gender-typed toys: dolls and play jewelry for girls; microscopes, building sets, and computers for boys. We read jokes and stories that tell us that boys are better at math, science, and reasoning. Because U.S. society tries so hard to make girls and boys different, it is surprising that cognitive differences are not larger and more general than they are. Research from other societies

Do Males Have a Math Gene?

Can girls do math as well as boys? All sorts of recent tests have shown that they cannot. Most educators and feminists

tude Test normally given to high-school seniors. In the results on the math portion of the SAT—there was no appreciable dif-

Newsweek, Dec. 15, 1980

The Gender Factor in Math

A new study says males may be naturally abler than females

Until about the seventh grade, boys and girls do equally well at math. In early high school, when the emphasis

Julian C. Stanley of Johns Hopkins University, males inherently have more mathematical ability than females.

Time, Dec. 15, 1980

Male superiority

Are boys born superior to girls in mathematical ability? The answer is probably Yes, say Camilla Persson Benbow and Julian C. Stanley, researchers in the department of psychology at the Johns

The Chronicle of
Higher Education,
December, 1980

Are Boys Better At Math?

New York Times,
Dec. 7, 1980

BOYS HAVE SUPERIOR MATH ABILITY, STUDY SAYS

Boys are inherently better at math than girls, according to an eight-year study of 10,000 gifted students. Coun-

Education U.S.A.,
Dec. 15, 1980

SEX + MATH = ?

Why do boys traditionally do better than girls in math? Many say it's because boys are encouraged to pursue

Family Weekly,
Jan. 25, 1981

Study suggests boys may be better at math

WASHINGTON (UPI) — Two psychologists said Friday boys are better than girls in math reasoning, and they urged educators to accept the fact that something more than social factors is re-

Ann Arbor News,
Dec. 6, 1980

FIGURE 4.5. Media messages: Biased reporting of a gender-based difference. *Source:* From Eccles and Jacobs's, "Social Forces Shape Math Attitudes and Performance," *Signs, 11,* pp. 367–389, 1986. University of Chicago Press. Reprinted by permission of Jacquelipine S. Eccles.

shows that gender differences are not universal and that they are reduced by being brought up in a more egalitarian environment.

Research on social influence on math performances suggests that researchers who want to test for gender differences should first match their male and female research participants on relevant background experiences rather than just matching for age or grade in school. Otherwise, a "gender" difference simply reflects the fact that being a boy or a girl is correlated with particular experiences (Crawford & Chaffin, 1997; Hyde, 1981). The studies also suggest that one way to help young girls develop their cognitive abilities is to provide them with computers and "boys' toys." "We may be shortchanging the intellectual development of girls by providing them with only traditional sex stereotyped toys" (Halpern, 1992, p. 215).

Most of the research on cognitive abilities has been based on standard research methods used in rigorous, nonsexist ways. But feminist theorists have questioned some assumptions of standard research methods. One criticism is that psychological research lacks ecological ("real-world") validity because it examines behavior outside its normal social context (Fine & Gordon, 1989; Parlee, 1979). For example, performance on a standardized test may have little relevance to most jobs or everyday thinking skills. If the importance of a task itself is unproven, the importance of a gender difference in the task becomes even more questionable. The belief that stripping behavior from its context results in greater objectivity of observation may be an illusion.

The purpose of standardized tests like the SAT is to predict performance in college. But although women score lower on these tests, they get better grades than men in college. The tests thus underpredict women's performance (Rosser, 1987; Stricker, Rock, & Burton, 1992). Testing activists have charged that a test that underpredicts the performance of more than half the people who take it should be considered consumer fraud (Rosser, 1987, 1992). The consequences for women are serious. Nearly all four-year colleges and universities use test scores in admissions decisions. Because women's college grades are higher than their test scores predict, some women are probably being rejected in favor of male applicants who will do less well in college. Moreover, women lose out on millions of dollars in scholarships based on test performance. More than 750 organizations use test scores in awarding scholarships. Only about one-third of National Merit scholarship finalists are female; proportions in other scholarship programs are similar (Sadker & Sadker, 1994). Young women also lose out on opportunities to participate in special programs for the gifted (we have already noted the overabundance of boys discovered in national talent searches in math). Finally, an individual's test scores affect her self-confidence and her future academic goals (Rosser, 1992; Sadker & Sadker, 1994). For all these reasons, sex bias in testing is an important issue.

Test publishers claim that the tests are not biased. But a review of seventy-four psychological and educational tests documented that girls and women were underrepresented and appeared in stereotyped roles (Selkow, 1984). In math tests, items have tended to be set in contexts more familiar to boys, like sports (Dwyer, 1979). Along with measuring math ability, then, tests may be inadvertently reflecting a bias toward male interests.

Another kind of bias is the topics *not* defined as cognitive abilities by psychologists and test makers. At least one testing specialist maintains that, from a feminist perspective, standardized tests are deeply androcentric:

> Excluded are whole areas of human achievement that contribute to success in school and work. . . . Such characteristics and skills as intuition, motivation, self-understanding, conscientiousness, creativity, cooperativeness, supportiveness of others, sensitivity, nurturance, ability to create a pleasant environment, and ability to communicate verbally and nonverbally are excluded from

standardized tests. By accepting and reflecting the androcentric model of knowledge, standardized tests reinforce value judgments that consider this model of knowledge more valid and important than other ways of viewing the world. Content that is not tested is judged less valuable than that included on tests. (Teitelbaum, 1989, p. 330)

Although standardized tests are supposed to be objective, they are written by subjective human beings who reflect the values of their society. Furthermore, test takers bring to the test different feelings about themselves and the test, and thus interpret items differently. There is no such thing as a value-free test (Teitelbaum, 1989). Because many important decisions are made on the basis of testing in our society, more research is needed on the tests themselves and how they produce similarities and differences among groups.

THE SIMILARITIES TRADITION: WHY IT MATTERS

It is not always easy to see the values and assumptions underlying our cultural practices. Much of what people believe about gender is learned and expressed at a nonconscious level (Bem & Bem, 1971). Students also learn that science is value-free and its practitioners objective, impartial seekers of truth. But values and beliefs related to gender have always affected scientific research (Crawford, 1978; Harding, 1986). A brief review of the history of gender and racial issues in science will help clarify the interconnectedness of values and practice.

Values and Ideology in Research: What Are the Lessons of History?

Throughout most of Western history, the intellectual and moral inferiority of women was seen as self-evident. The first systematic empirical research on women conducted by scientists of the late nineteenth century took women's inferiority as a given and was aimed at uncovering its specific biological determinants (Gould, 1980; Hyde & Linn, 1986; Russett, 1989; Shields, 1975). Looking back at this period with the benefit of hindsight, it is relatively easy to see how the work of scientists was influenced by their beliefs and values about the inferiority of women and people of color. In an era of agitation over slavery and women's rights, members of the dominant social group needed to document the inferiority of other groups in order to defend the status quo. "You are women and hence different," was the message conveyed. "Your differences disqualify you for the worldly roles you seem, most unwisely, to wish to assume" (Russett, 1989, p. 23). Sometimes the scientists' antifeminist bias was expressed directly; one British anthropologist presented a "scientific" paper denouncing the "superficial, flat-chested, thin-voiced Amazons, who are pouring forth sickening prate about the tyranny of men and the slavery of women" (cited in Russett, 1989, p. 27).

Then (as well as now), sexism, racism, and class bias were often intertwined and the brain often was the battle site (Bleier, 1986). First, researchers asserted that the inferiority of women and people of color was due to their smaller brains. One prominent scientist asserted that many women's brains were closer in size to those of gorillas than to the brains of men (cited in Gould, 1981). Similarly, scientists measured cranial size in skulls representing various "races" and concluded that the races could be ranked on a scale of cranial capacity (and hence intelligence) with darker people such as Africans at the bottom, Asians intermediate, and white European men at the top. The brain-size hypothesis foundered when it occurred to scientists that, by this criterion, elephants and hippos should be much more intelligent than people. They then turned to the ratio of brain size to body weight as a measure of intellectual capacity. Little more was heard of this measure when it was discovered that women fared better than men by it.

Giving up on gross differences such as brain size, scientists turned to examining supposed differences in specific regions of the brain. When it was believed that the frontal lobe was the repository of the highest mental powers, the male frontal lobe was seen as larger and better developed. However, when the parietal lobe came to be seen as more important, a bit of historical revisionism occurred. Women were now seen as having similar frontal lobes but smaller parietal lobes than men (Shields, 1975).

When size differences in brain regions proved impossible to document, the debate shifted to the variability hypothesis. It was asserted that men, as a group, are more variable—in other words, that while men and women may be similar on average, there are more men at the extremes of human behavior. Variability was viewed as an advantageous characteristic that enabled species to evolve adaptively. The variability hypothesis was used to explain why there were so many more highly intelligent men than women. Only men could achieve the heights of genius. (It also predicted a greater incidence of mental deficiency among males, a prediction that was virtually ignored.)

The measurement of human abilities began in the nineteenth century with Sir Francis Galton's studies of physical variation and motor skills (cited in Hyde & Linn, 1986). Galton measured height, grip strength, and reaction time because he thought they reflected mental ability. Few questioned his view that these abilities were innate; those who suggested that experiences and opportunity might play a part were usually women, and their views had little impact. When physical abilities failed to correlate with intellectual functioning, the mental testing movement was born.

Although tests of mental ability failed to demonstrate gender differences, the belief in male intellectual superiority was not disrupted. Instead, scientists returned to the variability hypothesis to explain how apparent similarity reflected underlying difference, claiming that men and women might be equal on average, but only men appeared at the upper end of the distribution of mental ability (Hyde & Linn, 1986; Shields, 1982). Although Leta Hollingworth and Helen Montague laboriously examined the hospital records of 2,000 newborn infants to test the variability hypothesis, and others of the first generation of women who became psychologists examined gender-related differences in emotionality and intelligence, few if any differences were found (Unger, 1979b). Widespread beliefs about gender differences in mental abilities persisted into the twentieth century, despite the lack of demonstrable differences in brain structures, variability, or overall performance on intelligence tests. Today, the search for biological differences underlying intellectual functioning continues. For example, some researchers propose that women's brains are less specialized by hemisphere in processing information than men's brains, although the evidence is weak and contradictory (Bleier, 1986). We examine contemporary theories and evidence about biological bases of gender in Chapter 5.

The history of attempts to find biologically based sex differences illustrates some important points about the study of group differences—points that should be kept in mind when evaluating contemporary scientific research. Much of this history shows haphazard testing for a wide variety of differences. Of course, the number of possible group differences is infinite, and demonstrating the existence of one or many gives no information about their causes. Moreover, the "truth" discovered by science is historically and contextually limited. It is easy to see how the racist and sexist prejudices of past eras led researchers to search for justifications of the inferiority of women and people of color. It is less easy to see how personal values affect the work of contemporary scientists, but we can be sure that such influences exist. Although people could be grouped in any number of ways, in practice only a few—such as race and gender—are usually chosen. There seem to be no "separate but equal" classification schemes available. The traits attributed to women and minorities are less positive and socially desirable than the traits attributed to men. Because white men remain the norm by which others are judged, research is easily enlisted in support of the social status quo.

Women, Minorities, and Math/Science Careers

The major political focus of liberal feminism has been to increase the participation of women in male-dominated areas of public life: high-prestige professions such as government, medicine, law, and the media. Math and science are still among the most male-dominated careers (Kimball, 1995). And a working knowledge of math, science, and computers is becoming essential for many different career choices. So it is not surprising that so much research in the similarities tradition has focused on showing that girls and women are not inherently inferior.

Women are now entering science, math, and engineering in greater numbers. However, they are still underrepresented, especially in the physical sciences (25%) and engineering (11%), both math-intensive fields (Farmer & Associates, 1997).

Women's participation in math and science varies greatly cross-culturally. For example, the percentage of Ph.D.s in physics earned by women ranges from a low of 4 to 5 percent (Japan and the Netherlands) to a high of 60 percent (the Philippines). In the United States, women earn less than 10 percent of physics Ph.D.s, and minority women are less than 1 percent of employed Ph.D. scientists in all fields. Despite recent gains, women—both white and women of color—are still far more likely to be found doing the support work of science as technicians and clerical workers than being in charge of a research program (Kimball, 1995).

Women who persevere in scientific careers face discrimination. Although they may start out with similar jobs as their male peers, a gap appears and widens as time goes on. Research (reviewed by Kimball, 1995) shows that women scientists typically earn about 25 percent less than men and are twice as likely to be out of a job. These differences are not due to the women publishing less, or taking time out to have children, or other individual factors. Rather, they seem to reflect built-in structural biases in the scientific professions. The higher the level, the fewer women. Only about 2.5 percent of Nobel Science Prize winners and 3 percent of members of the prestigious U.S. National Academy of Sciences are women.

Researchers in the similarities tradition have tried to demonstrate that, given the same opportunities, women can do math and science as well as men. This tradition has gone on for at least 100 years and generated an enormous amount of research. By questioning the size of cognitive differences and examining how they are socially produced, researchers in the similarities tradition have made a contribution toward equality. Yet, equality has not been achieved, although women, particularly white women, have made some very real gains. The belief persists that math and science are male domains; women of color continue to be extremely underrepresented in science; and discrimination against women persists at the interpersonal and sociocultural levels. (Look back at the MIT example in Box 3.2.)

We have seen that research about gender differences is often distorted in press reports, and that these reports have very real effects on girls and their parents (Beckwith, 1984; Eccles & Jacobs, 1986). We have also seen that hypotheses about female inferiority seem to keep turning up, despite lack of evidence (Shields, 1982). Imagine yourself picking up tomorrow morning's newspaper and reading the following headline: "Reasoning Ability: New Research Shows Boys May Have Genetic Advantage." Using what you have learned so far in this chapter, how would you evaluate this claim? This exercise is not merely academic. Although not every psychology student becomes a psychologist, every student can become a critical thinker when reading reports of scientific research. Gender-difference issues are particularly difficult for psychology and the general public to deal with, since they depend more on interpretation of the evidence than on the evidence itself.

Rather than focus further research effort on debating how big or how real gender differences are, some psychologists have proposed alternative approaches. For example, psychologists could study exceptions to the average, such as girls with very high math abilities, and determine what experiences have influenced them and what cognitive strategies they use (Halpern, 1986). Or they could explore how differences are produced by social causes (Unger, 1979b), or focus on how to equalize opportunity for girls (Hyde & Lynn, 1986). Figure 4.6 shows one attempt to increase girls' interest in science careers.

THE DIFFERENCES TRADITION: CELEBRATING WOMEN

The differences tradition reflects a very different view of what it is to be a woman. Based on theories of personality, this approach claims that there are fundamental differences between the sexes and that the characteristics of women should be honored and respected.

HIGH SCHOOL CHEMISTRY LED HER TO A LIFE OF CRIME.

As Director of the Delaware State Police Crime Lab, forensic microscopist Julie Willey catches murderers, rapists and thieves by analyzing hair and fiber specimens. It's a job she has today because, in high school, she didn't think it was uncool to take chemistry.

There's a whole world of interesting jobs in science out there. Find out how you can turn your daughter on to them.

Call 1-800-WCC-4-GIRLS. Or visit us on the Internet at http://www.academic.org.

EXPECT THE BEST FROM A GIRL. THAT'S WHAT YOU'LL GET.

Women's College Coalition

FIGURE 4.6.

Psychologists working within the differences tradition have focused on positive human characteristics such as being interdependent with others and caring for others' needs. They claim that these characteristics have been underappreciated because they are associated with women and femininity. They stress that if we take seriously women's ways of being in the world, we can imagine—and begin to construct—better worlds for all. Equality within the present system is not the primary political goal of the differences tradition. That is, women should not settle for being equal in a man's world. Rather, the goal is to create "a different, more humane world that incorporates traditional feminine values as a central human focus" (Kimball, 1995, p. 7).

Within the differences tradition, researchers study gender differences and how they are created in particular social contexts. They look closely at women's lives to see how women's experiences create a uniquely feminine psychology. One of the central experiences of many women's lives is motherhood, and this has been closely studied to see how it produces gender differences. For our first example of research in the differences tradition, we look at a feminist psychoanalytic theory of mothering and the development of gender differences. We then turn to a theory of gender and moral reasoning, and finally to a theory of gender and power.

Nancy Chodorow: A Feminist Perspective on Mothering

One of the most influential theorists concerned with women's place in society is Nancy Chodorow (1978, 1979). Her theory attempts to explain why women do most of the child care and nurturing in many societies. How do women develop the skills and the desire to become mothers? Chodorow proposes that the crucial events underlying the development of gender identity and subsequent gender differences in nurturing occur in the first two years of life.

According to Chodorow (and other psychoanalytic theorists) the infant has no "self"—it cannot distinguish between itself and its caretaker (usually the mother). Because the infant is totally helpless and dependent, it is psychologically merged with the mother as she meets its every need. Infants must go through a gradual process of differentiation in which they come to perceive boundaries between themselves and their primary love object (see Figure 4.7).

Developing a self is not automatic or invariable. It requires psychological and cognitive maturation (such as the ability to understand that objects exist independently of the child's presence). Most important, the self develops *in relation to the primary caretaker.* As the mother leaves and returns, meets (or fails to meet) the infant's needs, asserts her own needs, and responds to other people besides her infant, the infant comes to perceive her as separate, to make a "me/not me" distinction:

> Separateness, then, is not simply given from birth, nor does it emerge from the individual alone. Differentiation occurs in relationship, separateness is defined relationally: "I" am "not you." (Chodorow, 1979, p. 67)

Developing a separate sense of self is an essential task for every human infant. What does this process have to do with the development of gender differences? Because most child rearing is done by women, girl infants experience a

FIGURE 4.7. An infant's sense of self develops in relationship with a caring adult.

caretaker who is like them in a very fundamental way. They can define themselves in terms of that similarity; they move from "I and you are one" to "I am like you." Their distinction between self and other ("me" and "not-me") is one of overlap and fluidity, built on their primary sense of oneness with the mother.

Girls grow up with a sense of similarity to and continuity with their mother, and a sense of connection to others in general. Boys, however, must learn the more difficult lesson that their gender identity is not-female, or not-mother. Because mother has been the first object of love, and because fathers are likely to be less available and emotionally involved with their infants, boys have a more precarious gender identity, an identity based on defining themselves in opposition to all that is feminine: femininity becomes negative and masculinity positive.

These gender differences in identity have important consequences for further personality development and adult roles. Boys who define masculinity as the opposite of femininity grow into men who devalue women and believe in the superiority of whatever qualities they define as masculine. They deny and repress their "feminine" needs for closeness and connection with others, which reduces their ability to be warm, loving fathers and leads them to be satisfied with less closeness in relationships.

Women, on the other hand, do not see themselves as separate and independent from others in the way men do. On the contrary, they tend to define themselves in terms of their relationships with others and to feel a need for human connectedness. Their greater relational needs cannot be entirely satisfied by a man (especially one preoccupied with separateness and independence!). So women have babies, satisfying their needs for connectedness in the mother–infant bond.

The cycle is repeated as another generation of boys and girls defines gender in relation to female caretakers. Differences in social roles follow, for as long as women are responsible for children, their opportunities in the wider world will be curtailed. Chodorow titled her book *The Reproduction of Mothering* to indicate her thesis that masculine-feminine identities and roles are not biologically determined but are reproduced in every generation by social arrangements.

Women's experiences as mothers are central to Chodorow's theory; indeed, she views the female practice of mothering as the source of not only gendered personalities but the division of labor in society. The theory does not devalue mothering or suggest that women should try to be more like men. Mothering is viewed as a positive goal for women, one that satisfies important relational needs. Yet the theory does not claim that mothering is instinctive or inherent in women's nature. If men nurtured and cared for young children, they too would develop relationship skills and a sense of connection, and these qualities would be socially reproduced in their sons.

There are, however, some limitations to this approach. First, it assumes that children are all brought up in nuclear families and does not ask how development might differ in other kinds of families. Cross-culturally and historically, a nuclear family pattern is the exception, not the rule. Chodorow acknowledges that there are cross-cultural differences in fathers' and other family members' involvement in child care, but she believes that these differences affect only the details and not the basic process of forming a self.

Another kind of diversity not addressed by Chodorow's theory is sexual orientation. Obviously, not all women are heterosexual. Since the theory claims that women have greater relational needs than men, it implies that women might tend to turn toward each other for friendship, connectedness, and sexual/affectional bonds, rather than to less-satisfying relationships with men. Chodorow, however, glosses over this implication of her theory and views heterosexuality as the only normal outcome of feminine development (Rich, 1980).

Researchers in the similarity tradition also criticize Chodorow's theory for being difficult to test scientifically. Its concepts are abstract, complex, and poorly tied to behavior. The most important processes in gender development are assumed to take place before children can speak and to happen outside conscious awareness. Psychologists who value scientific proof argue that it is difficult or impossible to verify empirically whether an infant experiences itself as separate from its mother or forms attachments differently depending on the gender of its caretaker. Nevertheless, this intriguing theory has stimulated research and scholarship.

Carol Gilligan: A Theory of Moral Reasoning

One of the most important kinds of reasoning and thinking people do in everyday life concerns issues of right and wrong. Psychologists have studied moral reasoning to find out how it develops and how people reach conclusions about moral issues.

Lawrence Kohlberg (1981) suggested that a child's conception of right and wrong should depend on the child's stage of cognitive development, just as other kinds of reasoning and thinking do. He studied moral development in children and adults by posing hypothetical dilemmas like the one in Box 4.1 and carefully analyzing the answers people gave. For Kohlberg, the reasoning behind the solution was more important than the solution itself, because it revealed different levels of moral development.

Kohlberg's research led him to propose a theory of moral development that consists of three levels of moral reasoning, from least to most mature: *preconventional, conventional,* and *postconventional* morality. Within each level, there are two stages. As you can see from Box 4.2, children start out with a moral orientation based on avoiding punishment (e.g., Heinz should not steal because he might get caught by the police). By the time they reach middle childhood, most people have moved to a conventional orientation based on gaining approval from others (i.e., is, Heinz should not steal because it's not nice and people won't like him) and, later, on rules and laws (i.e., Heinz should not steal because there are laws against stealing). Only a few people move beyond conventional morality to the postconventional level, where moral reasoning is based on internalized ethical principles. People at these stages may choose to break laws they believe to be unjust. People who deliberately chose to violate segregation laws during the civil rights movement provide examples of postconventional morality.

In Kohlberg's early research, boys and men tended to achieve at least stage 4 moral thinking, while girls and women were more likely to stop at stage 3. In other words, women seemed to have a less mature and less devel-

---

Box 4.1 How Would You Resolve This Dilemma?

In Europe, a woman was near death from a very bad disease, a special kind of cancer. There was one drug that the doctors thought might save her. It was a form of radium that a druggist in the same town had recently discovered. The drug was expensive to make, but the druggist was charging ten times what the drug cost him to make. He paid $200 for the radium and charged $2,000 for a small dose of the drug. The sick woman's husband, Heinz, went to everyone he knew to borrow the money, but he could get together only about $1,000, which was half of what it cost. He told the druggist that his wife was dying and asked him to sell it cheaper or let him pay later. But the druggist said, "No, I discovered the drug and I'm going to make money from it." Heinz got desperate and broke into the man's store to steal the drug for his wife.

Do you think that Heinz should have stolen the drug? Was his action right or wrong? Why?

Source: Excerpt from *Essays on Moral Development: The Philosophy of Moral Development* (Vol. 1) by Lawrence Kohlberg. Copyright © 1981 by Lawrence Kohlberg. Reprinted by permission of Harper-Collins Publishers, Inc.

oped sense of morality. Carol Gilligan (1982) criticized this conclusion. First, she pointed out, Kohlberg's early research was conducted entirely with male participants and their responses became the norm by which girls and women were later evaluated. Second, the dilemmas posed by Kohlberg may have been easier for boys and men to relate to because they frequently involved men as the principal actor in the moral drama. The hypothetical dilemmas also might not reveal much about moral behavior in real-life situations. For all these reasons, Gilligan proposed, Kohlberg's theory may be an inadequate map of female development.

Gilligan went on to develop her own theory of women's moral development. In one study of real-life moral reasoning, Gilligan interviewed women who were pregnant and considering abortion. She chose the abortion situation because it provides examples of ethical decision making by women and also because it brings up a central conflict for women:

> While society may affirm publicly the woman's right to choose for herself, the exercise of such choice brings her privately into conflict with the conventions of femininity, particularly the moral equation of goodness with self-sacrifice. Although independent assertion in judgment and action is considered to be the hallmark of adulthood, it is rather in their care and concern for others that women have both judged themselves and been judged. . . . When a woman considers whether to continue or abort a pregnancy, she contemplates a decision that affects both self and others and engages directly the critical moral issue of hurting. (1982, pp. 70–71)

Like Kohlberg, Gilligan found preconventional, conventional, and post-conventional levels of moral reasoning in the people she interviewed. However, the basis for each level is different (see Box 4.2). At level I, women are concerned with survival, and their immature responses, derived from their

---

Box 4.2 Levels and Stages of Moral Development According to Lawrence Kohlberg and Carol Gilligan

I. Preconventional morality
 Kohlberg:
  Stage 1: Obeying rules in order to avoid punishment
  Stage 2: Obeying rules to get rewards
  Gilligan: Concern for oneself and survival
II. Conventional morality
 Kohlberg:
  Stage 3: "Good girl" orientation: obeying rules to gain approval
  Stage 4: "Law and order" orientation: rigid conformity to society's laws and rules
  Gilligan: Concern for one's responsibilities; self-sacrifice and caring for others

III. Postconventional morality
 Kohlberg:
  Stage 5: Obeying rules because they are necessary for social order, but with understanding that rules can be changed
  Stage 6: May violate society's rules or laws if necessary to meet one's own internalized standards of justice
  Gilligan: Concern for responsibilities to others and to oneself; self and others as interdependent

Source: Kohlberg, 1981; Gilligan 1982.

feelings of being alone and powerless, may seem selfish. One 18-year-old, for example, saw the decision only in terms of her own freedom. On the one hand, having a baby would provide "the perfect chance to get married and move away from home." On the other hand, it would restrict her freedom "to do a lot of things" (p. 75). At level II, women think primarily in terms of others' needs. The conventional morality of womanhood tells them that they should be prepared to sacrifice all for a lover or a potential baby. When their own and others' needs conflict, they may face seemingly impossible dilemmas. One 19-year-old, who did not want an abortion but whose partner and family wanted her to have one, posed the conflict:

> "I don't know what choices are open to me. It is either to have it or the abortion; these are the choices open to me. I think what confuses me is it is a choice of either hurting myself or hurting other people around me. What is more important? If there could be a happy medium it would be fine, but there isn't. It is either hurting someone on this side or hurting myself." (p. 80)

When women reach the final level of moral development, they resolve the conflicts between their own and other's needs not by conventional feminine self-sacrifice but by balancing care for others with healthy self-care. Because the woman is acting on internalized ethical principles that value relationships, caring is extended both to self and others. A 29-year-old married woman, already a mother, struggled to take into account the strain on herself and her family posed by her pregnancy and her desire to complete her education and concluded:

> "The decision has got to be, first of all, something that the woman can live with, a decision that the woman can live with, one way or another, or at least try to live with, and it must be based on where she is at and other significant people in her life are at." (p. 96)

Gilligan's experiences in listening to what women said about moral issues convinced her that the type of morality studied by Kohlberg (and more common in men) is an ethic of rights, while the type she discovered (more common in women) is an ethic of responsibilities. Rather than judge women as morally deficient by a male norm, Gilligan believes researchers should recognize that women and men have different but equally valid approaches to moral issues. (For this reason, her book on moral development is titled *In a Different Voice.*) For both men and women, the highest levels of development should integrate the moralities of rights and responsibilities.

Carol Gilligan's ideas about moral development have generated a great deal of research and criticism. Some have questioned her use of the abortion dilemma. Comparing women's resolution of real-life abortion dilemmas to men's resolution of hypothetical Heinz-and-the-drug dilemmas may be an invalid "apples-and-oranges" method. Reasoning in the highly stressful abortion situation may not generalize even to women who haven't faced it, let alone to men (Code, 1983). Moreover, viewing this dilemma as only a woman's problem may fail to acknowledge that men should also be responsible for their sexual behavior and may distract attention from the evidence in Gilligan's interviews that many of the women were in exploitative and oppressive relationships (O'Laughlin, 1983).

At a minimum, these critics argue, the moral reasoning of women and men should be assessed in situations that are as comparable as possible. For example, the lovers and husbands of the pregnant women in Gilligan's study could have been interviewed on their moral conflicts about abortion (Colby & Damon, 1983). Other researchers have pointed out that Gilligan did not use well-defined measures or a standard scoring procedure and that she selected parts of the interviews to best illustrate her ideas rather than presenting her data systematically (Broughton, 1983; Nails, 1983).

Gilligan's research did not systematically examine factors other than gender that could be related to differences in moral reasoning. It looked for the "different voice" only as a gender difference, ignoring the question of how a person's social class, ethnic community, or religion might affect her moral orientation (Auerbach, Blum, Smith, & Williams, 1985). Other research suggests that the ethic of care is expressed by African-Americans, both men and women, at least as much as by white women (Stack, 1986). What appears to be a gender difference in moral reasoning could also reflect women's subordinate social position and lack of power; in other words, perhaps the ethic of care and responsibility is expressed by less powerful people generally rather than just by women (Hare-Mustin & Mareck, 1988; Tronto, 1987). Stimulated by Gilligan's and Kohlberg's ideas, other psychologists have examined the existing research more systematically, showing that when women and men are compared directly and factors such as level of education are controlled, moral reasoning does not differ by gender (Ford & Lowery, 1986; Walker, 1984, 1986).

How large does a gender-related difference have to be before we stop calling it a similarity? How can we know that we have controlled all relevant variables such as level of education? These questions stem from the similarities tradition. The debate over theories of difference such as those of Chodorow and Gilligan's is, in part, a debate over which tradition is the best approach. But psychologists from both traditions would probably agree that Carol Gilligan's theory has eloquently described a "different voice"—a moral orientation that Kohlberg's research did not discover. Whether the different voice is a *woman's* voice is still being actively debated.

Jean Baker Miller: A Theory of Power and Gender Differences

Jean Baker Miller (1986) has looked closely at the relationship between power and feminine personality. She proposed that because women are a subordinate group in society, they develop personality characteristics that reflect their subordination and enable them to cope with it.

Miller analyzes the effects of power differences on personality formation. Women have been socially defined as unequals, similar to other "second-class" groups, which are labeled as such because of their race, religion, or social class. Once a group is defined as inferior, the dominant group justifies its inferiority by labeling it as deficient. Just as people of color are stereotyped as less intelligent and poor people are stereotyped as lazy, women are stereotyped as emotional, illogical, and so on.

Dominant groups define acceptable roles for subordinates, which usually involve services that the dominant group members do not want to perform for themselves. Thus, women, minorities, and poor people are relegated to low-status, low-paying jobs that often involve cleaning up the waste products of the dominant group or providing them with personal services. Roles and activities that are preferred in a given society are closed to subordinates. Subordinates are said to be unable to fill those roles, and the reasons given by the dominants usually involve subordinates' "deficiencies" of mind or body. In our own society, the status and pay accorded nurses, teachers, homemakers, and child-care workers versus physicians, attorneys, carpenters, and auto mechanics reflect devaluation of "women's work," and it is easy to find people who believe that women are unsuited for certain prestigious or demanding jobs.

Since dominants control a culture's arts, philosophy, and science, they have the power to define "normal" personality and relationships. Dominants define inequality as normal and justify it in terms of the inferiority of subordinates.

> It then becomes "normal" to treat others destructively and to derogate them, to obscure the truth of what you are doing by creating false explanations, and to oppose actions toward equality. . . . Dominant groups generally do not like to be told about or even quietly reminded of the existence of inequality, . . . if pressed a bit, the familiar rationalizations are offered: the home is "women's natural place," and "we know what's best for them anyhow." (Miller, 1986, pp. 8–9)

When subordinates behave with intelligence, independence, or assertiveness—or even show potential for such behavior—they are defined as exceptions to the rule or abnormal. If women take direct action on their own behalf, they risk economic hardship, social ostracism, and psychological isolation—"even the diagnosis of a personality disorder" (Miller, 1986, p. 10). Moreover, women are controlled by violence and the threat of violence (see Chapter 13).

Being a subordinate has psychological consequences, too, according to Miller. Subordinates are encouraged to develop psychological characteristics that are useful and pleasing to the dominant group, and the ideal subordinate is described in terms of these characteristics, which

> form a certain familiar cluster: submissiveness, passivity, docility, dependency, lack of initiative, inability to act, to decide, to think, and the like . . . qualities more characteristic of children than adults—immaturity, weakness, and helplessness. If subordinates adopt these characteristics they are considered well-adjusted (1986, p. 7).

To survive, women become highly attuned to the dominants, able to "read" and respond to their smallest behaviors—perhaps the origins of "feminine intuition" and women's reputation for using manipulative "feminine wiles." As subordinates, women may know more about men than they know about themselves.

Another consequence of subordination is that women learn to monitor and worry about their relationships, to transmute anger into hurt feelings, chronic fatigue, or depression, and to try to influence others' behavior by indirect or extreme methods. Even if they recognize their anger, they may not act on it. Since direct assertive behavior toward a dominant may be dangerous, devious methods or emotional outbursts may seem preferable (Travis, 1988a). (See Chapter 14.) Moreover, women may come to accept the dominant group's untruths about women. According to Miller, there are a great many women who believe they are less important than men, just as there are people of color who feel inferior to white people. Finally, subordination sets up internal conflicts as women struggle to reconcile their own perceptions of reality with the interpretations imposed on them by men.

THE DIFFERENCES TRADITION: WHY IT MATTERS

Research and theory on women's unique experiences and psychological issues have been very influential in creating the interdisciplinary field of women's studies. This approach has raised interesting and important questions for future feminist scholars.

Should Humans Be More Like Women?

Researchers in the differences tradition argue that women and their characteristic activities must be reappraised (Chodorow, 1979; Gilligan, 1982; Jordan, Kaplan, Miller, Stiver, & Surrey, 1991). Women have been assigned the task of fostering others' development in relationships—of empowering others. In our society, women are expected to be nurturing, to take care of children, old people, ill people, and, of course, men. Women are expected to, and do, use their intellectual and emotional abilities to build other peoples' strength, resources, and well-being. Yet they have not been encouraged to value these interactions and activities, which are just "women's work."

Psychology and its theories have failed women by devaluing their strengths, according to researchers in the differences tradition. Many psychological theories of human development focus on autonomy as the end point. That is, the ideal adult is seen as one whose sense of self is entirely separate from others, and who is independent and self-reliant. Within these theories, close relationships (e.g., the infant–mother relationship) are characterized negatively in terms of dependency and lack of a differentiated self.

But very few people are truly autonomous, and when individuals appear to be so, it is usually because many other people are quietly helping them to survive and function. The idea that psychological development is a process of separating from others may be an illusion fostered by dominant men. Perhaps instead of the John Wayne/Clint Eastwood ideal of the autonomous man, theories of human development should stress human connection and caring. Feminist theorists have articulated alternatives to the notion of the autonomous self, such as the notion of personality development within relationships (Jordan et al., 1991; Miller, 1984b), the self defined in terms of caring and responsibility (Gilligan, 1982), and fluidity in self-development (Kaplan & Surrey, 1984).

From this perspective, the criteria for human development should include the ability to engage in relationships with others that empower others and oneself. Empathy, not autonomy, is the ideal (Jordan et al., 1991). By this measure, women would be revalued, and problems and deficiencies in men's development would become visible. Researchers in the differences tradition believe that the close study of women's experience may lead eventually to a new synthesis that will better encompass all human experience.

The Politics of Difference

Celebrating women's connection to others, their mothering, and their ethic of care seem like very positive ways to think about gender. However, feminist psychologists and philosophers have raised concerns about linking women to caring. Their concerns are about the political consequences of assigning caregiving to women and the relationship of care to women's subordination and oppression (Kimball, 1995).

If we accept the view that women are more connected and caring, it is easy to expect that *all* women *should* show these traits, and that there is something wrong or bad about women who put limits on caring. Yet women have moral responsibility to themselves, as well as others (Gilligan, 1982). The ethic of care may encourage women to sacrifice themselves to others. Should a woman's decisions about an unwanted pregnancy be based only on avoiding distress to her boyfriend or parents? Should a woman stay in an abusive relationship because she feels responsible for her partner's well-being? These dilemmas may produce a loss of self and voice in some adolescent girls (see

---

Making a Difference

Amy Cohen describes her former self as "this nonconfrontational person, just very agreeable." But when Brown University violated Title IX of the Education Amendments of 1972, a federal gender equity law, she came out fighting. In 1991, Cohen, now a second-grade teacher, had just been elected gymnastics team captain at Brown. Suddenly the university declared it was cutting the team due to budget problems. Appeals to the athletic director and team efforts to raise money led to limited reinstatement of the women's team, but also to a series of broken promises ("The athletic trainers can't treat you for injuries [after all] because you're not a varsity team," "you can't use this locker room"). Finally, Cohen and thirteen others brought a lawsuit. As Cohen discovered, only a small percentage of universities are in compliance with Title IX in regard to athletic allocations. Six years and about $3 million later, the Supreme Court agreed that Brown University was in violation of the amendment. Cohen argues that people, whatever their sex, gain incalculably from sports, and that to say that girls' enjoyment of athletics isn't as great as boys' is ridiculous. "If you spend $80,000 recruiting football players and $25 recruiting gymnasts, then should you be surprised if you get 100 football players and 2 gymnasts? Should you then say that people just love football so much more? No. You say you get what you looked for." Fortunately for all of us, due to Cohen's strength and perseverance, women and girls are now a little closer to getting what we're looking for.

Source: Woman of the Year: For Rescuing Title IX for College Women. (1998, January/February) *Ms.*, pp. 52–54.

Chapter 7). Glorifying women's connectedness and caring is problematic if it diminishes women's ability to be responsible for meeting their own needs.

There is another objection to the differences tradition, too. Miller (1986) suggests that women's characteristic traits are the traits of the powerless. Perhaps women have traditionally cared for others because they have had few choices to do otherwise. For example, for the past 100 years, women have entered the caring professions of teaching, social work, and nursing in great numbers, despite their relatively low pay, because these were seen as the only suitable jobs for women, and because they were actively denied admission to other kinds of careers. Of course, many women have found these careers very rewarding—but we can never know how many would have gone in other career directions if they had had the choice. "If the only reason women value care is because they are oppressed, then feminists are in the very awkward political position of glorifying women's oppression if women's caring is valued" (Kimball, 1995, p. 111).

Finally, assigning caregiving to women may prevent men from developing their capacity to nurture, inhibiting them from becoming fully human. Some feminist theorists have suggested that women will never achieve legal and social equality until men become full partners in the nurturing roles so necessary in relationships, families, and society (see Chapter 10).

CAN SIMILARITIES AND DIFFERENCES BE RECONCILED?

Gender differences and similarities are not just attributes of individuals. They are the socially constructed product of a system that creates categories of difference and dominance. One of the themes of this book is that gender is more than just sex. It is a system of social classification that operates at the sociocultural, interactional, and individual levels. Researchers in both the similarities and the differences traditions have recognized that sociocultural aspects of gender govern access to resources; for example, social forces work to keep women out of careers in math and science, and to overvalue the attributes of dominant groups in society. Both traditions also recognize that gender can become internalized—as when women come to think of themselves as bad at math and good at nurturing. The gender system works to sustain social inequality (Crawford & Chaffin, 1997).

Individual feminists, because of their background or experiences, may feel an affinity for either the differences or the similarities tradition (Hare-Mustin & Marecek, 1990). And a particular kind of research may be useful for a specific political goal. For example, if the goal is equal access to merit scholarships, arguing that differences in math ability are socially produced and getting smaller might prove useful. But both traditions have an important place in feminist theory. Rather than try to prove which one is right, perhaps it is best to respect them both and apply each as it seems appropriate. A feminist "double vision" can be theoretically and practically richer than one vision alone (Kimball, 1995). Becoming familiar with both traditions can help address a very important question: How is the gender system made invisible so that socially produced gender seems inevitable, natural, and freely chosen?

- *Gender is more than just sex.* When gender differences in cognitive abilities and performance emerge, they are always preceded by differences in social environments and experiences. The similarities tradition argues that these differences would diminish or disappear with equal opportunity and gender-fair environments.
- *Language and naming are sources of power.* The similarities tradition has demonstrated that what counts as an important difference depends on the values of the observer. The difference tradition, by celebrating feminine qualities, has made previously devalued traits and behaviors the subject of new attention and respect.
- *Women are not all alike.* On every cognitive skill or ability tested, there is much more variability *within* sex than *between* the sexes. Comparisons of different ethnic and social groups within and across cultures suggest that diversity in cognitive skills and personality is strongly related to sociocultural factors.
- *Psychological research can foster social change.* History tells us that "sex differences" have often been created and used to keep women "in their place." The similarities tradition encourages a focus on equity for girls and women in family, work, and educational settings. The differences tradition turns the table by suggesting that women's characteristics are strengths, not weaknesses.

SUGGESTED READINGS

HARE-MUSTIN, RACHEL T., & MARECEK, JEANNE (Eds.). (1990). *Making a difference.* New Haven: Yale University Press. A sophisticated analysis of how psychology has represented male and female as oppositions and an argument that it is time to move beyond conceptualizing gender as difference.

RUSSETT, CYNTHIA E. (1989). *Sexual science: The Victorian construct of womanhood.* Cambridge, MA: Harvard University Press. Gender and racial differences were twin obsessions of Victorian science. In a time when women and people of color were demanding civil rights, science was used to "prove" their biological inferiority. The history of this era is fascinating in itself—and also encourages analysis of the political aspects of contemporary sex difference research.

KIMBALL, MEREDITH. (1995). *Feminist visions of gender similarities and differences.* New York: Harrington Park. By delving into the complexities of research on gender similarities and differences, this book shows how the tension between them can be fruitful. A thoughtful example of good feminist theory, with connections to justice and social change.

CHAPTER 5

Biological Bases of Sex

- **WHAT IS SEX AND WHAT ARE THE SEXES?**
- **HOW IS SEX DETERMINED?**
- **PRENATAL DEVELOPMENT**
  Chromosomal Sex
  Gonadal and Hormonal Sex
  Sexual Differentiation of the Central
    Nervous System
  The Genetics of Sexual Orientation
  Sexual Orientation and the Brain
- **DOES THE HUMAN BRAIN HAVE A SEX?**
  Sex and Neural Laterality
  The Relationship between Biology
    and Behavior

- **ATYPICAL HUMAN SEXUAL DEVELOPMENT**
  Extra or Missing Sex Chromosomes
  Do the Chromosomes Determine Sex?
  Prenatal Hormones and Sex
    Differentiation
  Changing Identity
- **CULTURAL CONSTRUCTIONS OF GENDER**
- **CONNECTING THEMES**
- **SUGGESTED READINGS**

Alex A. was labeled a girl when he was born in 1971, although his genitals were ambiguous. By age one or two Alex's mother noticed that his phallus was enlarged, and by the time he could speak he called it "my penis." At puberty his voice deepened, and he began to be called "he-man" by other kids. He did not develop breasts, but by age thirteen, was menstruating irregularly from his phallus. A rural doctor put him on estrogen, and he developed small breasts and considerable body hair. In his late teens Alex was sent to an endocrinologist who asked him whether he had ever taken hormones. At this point, Alex did not even know what hormones were. The doctor said: "I think you should change to a male" and gave him a prescription for testosterone. But Alex never filled it. He recalls, "We were very religious people. We [mother and I] didn't know what was going on." Alex's mother was encouraging him to "try and grow breasts."

By age twenty-four his breasts were starting to enlarge. Another physician said: "We can make you a girl" and bolstered this suggestion with the argument, "You know, women can even be managers now." Alex was told that his clitoris could be reduced and that ultrasound revealed a uterus. In spite of the doctor's recommendation, Alex does not want to go this route. He is confused because he has always thought doctors were gods. He feels like a male and has no idea what his problem is. (Adapted from Kessler, 1998, p. 1)

What sex is Alex really? The answer to this question depends on how sex is defined. Some of the rules that are challenged by Alex's story (and those of other "intersex" individuals who will be discussed in this chapter) are as follows:

- If an organism has a sex (and some lower organisms do not), it must be either male or female.
- There are only two sexes.
- Within any individual, there are strong and consistent relationships between sexual anatomy, physiology, and sex-related behaviors.
- Within a given individual, sex is always permanent.

In fact, sex, like gender, is much less simple than common sense might suggest.

WHAT IS SEX AND WHAT ARE THE SEXES?

Despite the fact that everyone talks about sex, very few people try to define it. Researchers seem to feel that sex is either too self-evident to require an explanation or so complicated that they feel justified in devoting an entire book to the subject. About all they agree on is that sex represents a division of reproductive labor into specialized cells, organs, and organisms (Bermant & Davidson, 1974). Most definitions of sex stress the separateness and incompleteness of the sexes. They also equate sex with reproduction. This confusion of the ability to reproduce with other aspects of sex and gender has led to some medical decisions about sexually anomalous individuals that have had tragic consequences.

Evolutionary psychologists have also focused on the reproductive aspects of sex. They see organisms as the egg and sperm's way to create other eggs and sperm. Some evolutionary psychologists have tried to reduce almost all complex human social behaviors to reproductive strategies (cf. Buss, 1995). They generalize freely between insects, lower mammals, primates, and human beings. However, different species differ in their reproductive arrangements. There are no clear theories available to help us to determine when a particular animal is a useful model for human reproductive strategies and when it is not.

Animal studies do demonstrate that even the most basic aspects of sex are neither fixed nor universal. Although evolutionary biologists see two sexes as useful for increasing the genetic diversity of a species, two separate sexes do not always exist. Many invertebrate organisms (e.g., earthworms and oysters) have both kinds of *gonads* (the organs that make either eggs or sperm), either at the same time or in sequence. Even among species that have two sexes, sex is not always fixed at birth. Some fish and birds can be made to change sex. These animals produce living eggs or sperm after a period of maturity during which they have produced the kind of germ cells consistent with the other sex (Diamond, 1993). Some fish change spontaneously from fertile female to fertile male in the absence of any males of the species. This transformation is inhibited by the sight of a male even if he cannot be reached by any of the females.

A few vertebrates even manage to reproduce with only one sex. Recently, researchers have begun to examine the reproductive physiology and behavior of an all-female species of whiptail lizards (Crews, 1987a). In this species, there are no males, and the females reproduce from unfertilized eggs that contain the same genes as those of their single parent (this process is sometimes known as *cloning*). This species has separated reproductive biology from reproductive behavior. Although male individuals and their sperm have been lost, courting behaviors supposedly characteristic of males have been retained. The extent to which both malelike and femalelike behaviors are exhibited is influenced by ovarian hormones. The pseudo-male behaviors encourage reproduction much as male courtship behavior does in species with two sexes.

These species are not simply interesting scientific curiosities. Studying them allows scientists to ask, "How fundamental is the relationship between various biological components of sex and sex-related behaviors?" Separating behaviors into "male" and "female" is a false dichotomy, created by ignoring all the exceptions to the rules. This separation may have more political and social than scientific usefulness.

How different are the sexes from each other? Although females in at least one all-female species show the complete range of behaviors associated with males in related species, most biologists and evolutionary psychologists classify many behaviors of males and females as *dimorphic* (characteristic of two forms or bodies). This form of categorization may be misleading because no single behavior can be found exclusively in either males or females. Supposedly dimorphic behaviors such as nurturance or aggression are best viewed in probabilistic terms. These behaviors are more easily elicited or expressed in one sex or the other but may be found in either sex under some conditions. Like gender differences (see Chapter 4), sexual dimorphism is a term based on a judgment call that is not always free of bias.

Even the so-called male and female hormones are not found only in one sex. Nevertheless, many scientists appear to share the biases of the culture as a whole, making absolute distinctions between the sexes (see Figure 5.1). Throughout the nineteenth century, estrogen was known as the female hormone despite the fact that the substance was isolated from the urine of male horses (Laqueur, 1990). The brain and pituitary gland appear to be able to transform the major sex hormones into each other rather easily (McEwen, 1981), but it is only recently that researchers have noted that "male" hormones have normative influences on women's bodies, too (Angier, 1994). However, even within the article that announced this research, the popular press stressed the negative effects on women of excess "male" hormones.

HOW IS SEX DETERMINED?

Alex's story shows that sex is not always an all-or-none phenomenon. Instead, biological sex is determined through an orderly sequence of steps. Each step depends on the one that precedes it. For most people, the first event in this sequence—whether the egg was fertilized by an X or Y bearing sperm—determines all the succeeding steps (see Figure 5.2). Under normal conditions all of these events are consistent with one another. For this reason, it has been difficult to recognize that sex has many components. Experimental research on animals and intense study of humans who are sexually anomalous have made it clear, however, that although most people are sexually consistent, there is no one biological characteristic that always determines sex.

In human beings we must also consider social variables such as the sex to

Baby Blues

FIGURE 5.1. Biologically determinist explanations of different interests in women and men. Cartoons may be funny, but they also reflect cultural beliefs.
Source: Copyright © 1998. Reprinted with special permission of King Features Syndicate.

which the newborn infant is assigned and raised. This is not always the sex with which the individual identifies. Human sexuality is complex. The sexual profile of any individual includes at least five components, which Diamond (1995) abbreviates as *PRIMO* (see Table 5.1). People for whom a sexual profile is being assembled are asked questions about their childhood and adult preferences, the kinds of clothing they wear, what sex their friends are, and so on. These questions are about gender patterns and roles which have everything to do with the society in which one lives and little to do with biology. They are also asked about their sexual identity (either directly or by means of drawings) as well as about the sex (or sexes) of the persons to whom they are attracted erotically. Their reproductive structure is examined, and they are asked about their sexual functioning. For example, some people have little sexual drive whereas others have a great deal. Some women have never had an orgasm whereas others are multiply orgasmic. These aspects of sexuality can be relatively independent of each other even in people who do not, unlike Alex, question their own sex or gender. Some of these characteristics cannot be evaluated until the individual reaches puberty or is completely adult.

The study of people who are sexually inconsistent may reveal a great deal about how various components of sex relate to one another and to gender identity and behaviors. Sexual anomalies are quite common. It has been esti-

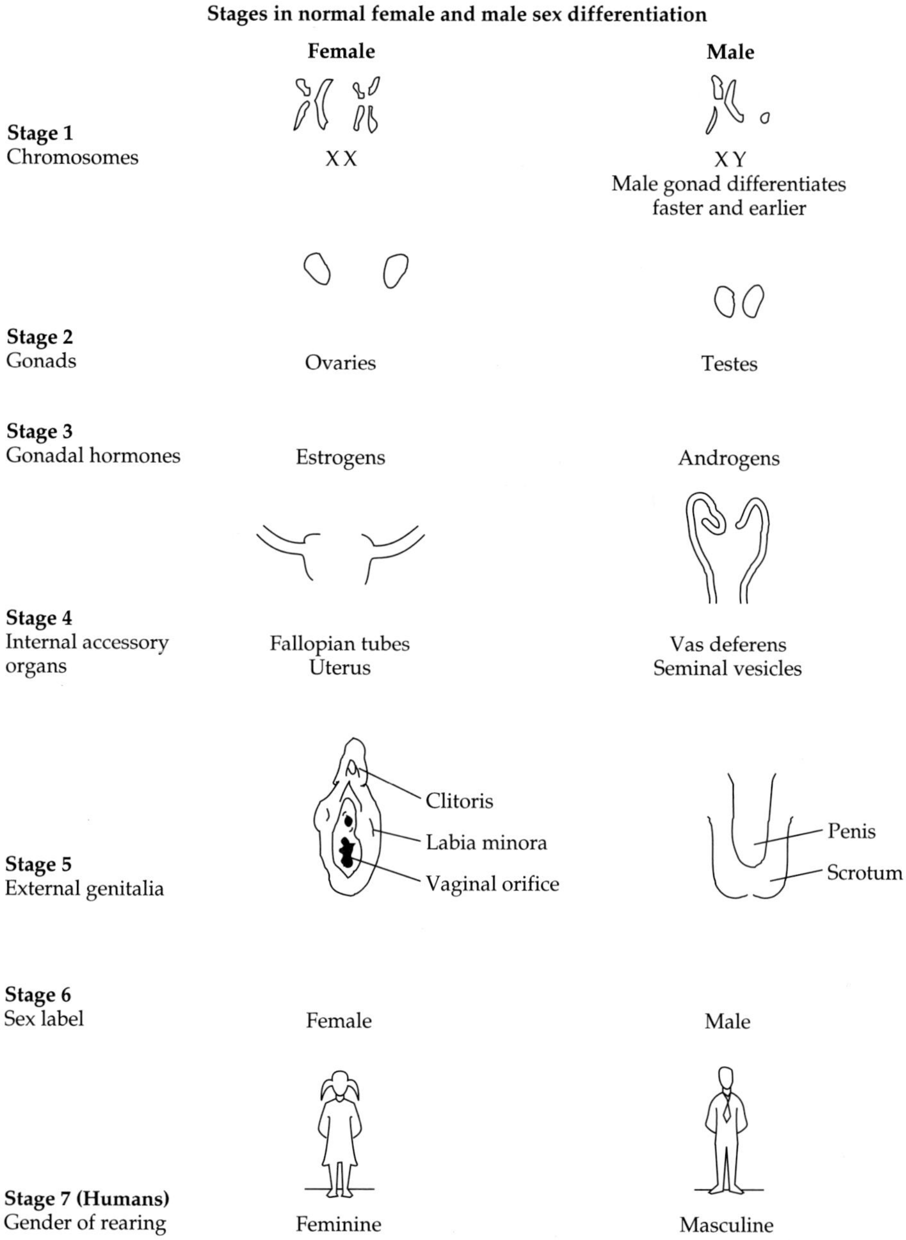

Stages in normal female and male sex differentiation

	Female	Male
Stage 1 Chromosomes	X X	X Y Male gonad differentiates faster and earlier
Stage 2 Gonads	Ovaries	Testes
Stage 3 Gonadal hormones	Estrogens	Androgens
Stage 4 Internal accessory organs	Fallopian tubes Uterus	Vas deferens Seminal vesicles
Stage 5 External genitalia	Clitoris Labia minora Vaginal orifice	Penis Scrotum
Stage 6 Sex label	Female	Male
Stage 7 (Humans) Gender of rearing	Feminine	Masculine

FIGURE 5.2. The many stages of sex determination: (1) chromosomal sex; (2) gonadal sex; (3) hormonal sex; (4) sex of the internal accessory organs; (5) sex of the external genitalia. In human beings the sex label assigned at birth and the socialization associated with that label are also very important for gender identity.
Drawing by Alina Wilczynski.

TABLE 5.1. The Parts of a Sexual Profile (PRIMO)

Name	Examples
Gender Patterns and Roles	Favorite toys; occupational preferences
Reproductive Structure	Kind of phallic structure present; form of accessory structures such as scrotum or labia
Sexual **I**dentity	Perceptions of oneself as male or female
Reproductive **M**echanisms	Subjective perceptions about sexuality such as level of sexual desire or presence or absence of orgasms
Orientation	Sex to which one is erotically attracted

Source: The Psychology of Sexual Orientation, Behavior, and Identity. Copyright © 1995. Reproduced with permission of Greenwood Publishing Group, Inc., Westport, CT.

mated that as much as 2 percent of newborn infants have some inconsistency in the various components of sex (Fausto-Sterling, in press). *Intersex* individuals generate medical, ethical, and social dilemmas. Before we explore such conditions, let's review what is known about typical prenatal development.

PRENATAL DEVELOPMENT

Chromosomal Sex

The first stage in the determination of sex in mammals is the presence of either two Xs or an X and a Y chromosome in the fertilized egg. Human beings have twenty-three pairs of chromosomes, with one of each pair inherited from each parent. Twenty-two pairs of these chromosomes (the *autosomes*) are roughly identical in size and shape. The *sex chromosomes* differ, however, in that females have two X chromosomes that are similar in size and shape to the autosomal chromosomes, whereas males have one X chromosome and a Y chromosome that is only a fraction of the size of the other chromosomes.

In mammals, the Y chromosome contains genes that cause the formation of the *testes*—the male gland that produces sex hormones and sperm (Gordon & Ruddle, 1981). A gene on the Y chromosome (called SRY) regulates the production of a male-specific protein (H-Y antigen), which in turn causes the development of the testes. Other genes on both the X and the Y chromosomes are also involved in sexual differentiation as are genes on some autosomes. For example, one gene on the X chromosome (inherited in men from their mothers) may be related to same-sex orientation in males (Diamond, Binstock, & Kohl, 1996). Other genes regulate the speed of cell replication as well as determining when "chemical factories" within a cell should be turned on or off.

Gonadal and Hormonal Sex

Male and female human embryos develop identically during the first few weeks of gestation. If a Y chromosome is present, however, the gonads begin to grow faster and to develop into testes. Testicular development does not appear to depend on the presence of hormones. Instead, shortly after the testes are formed, they begin to secrete a number of hormones that are collectively called *androgens*. These hormones act on the internal and external genital structures to produce what are considered to be male structures, such as a penis and scrotum. One androgen inhibits the development of female internal organs (the uterus and fallopian tubes). *Testosterone* is responsible for the masculinization of the male internal genital tract, and its derivative *dihydrotestosterone* causes development of the male external genitalia—fusion of the scrotum and growth of the penis (Wilson, George, & Griffin, 1981). All three of these substances must be present prenatally to produce an anatomically complete male.

Predictably, there has been much more investigation of male than female differentiation (Fausto-Sterling, 1992). Although many developmental biologists state that the embryo develops in a female direction if the Y chromosome is absent, this model has been criticized as androcentric. A more balanced model of sex determination argues that parallel genetic pathways for gonadal development exist—one for testis formation and the other for ovarian formation. In fact, a female-determining gene has recently been located on the X chromosome (Angier, 1994). The *ovaries* (the female gland that contains the eggs as well as producing hormones—collectively known as *estrogens*) play little role in the development of a female appearance. In fact, ovarian formation takes place after female external structures are far advanced in development (Wilson et al., 1981). A second X chromosome is necessary, however, for female fertility. Those who lack an X chromosome have nonfunctional gonads and no uterus despite their superficially female external appearance.

A number of different hormones must be present to produce an anatomically typical female or male. In later fetal life androgens are produced primarily by the testes (with a smaller contribution from the adrenal glands), and estrogens and *progestins* (hormones that support pregnancy) are produced mainly by the ovaries. Both sexes are exposed to hormones produced by the mother during pregnancy. Although males and females are exposed to different amounts of each hormone, all three types are found to some degree in both sexes (Collaer & Hines, 1995).

Since these hormones influence various parts of the reproductive system independently of one another, human beings with mixed or ambiguous genitalia are not particularly rare. In fact, so-called normal female and male genitalia are not that different either. Even after the fetal gonads begin to be distinguishable (by the second month of pregnancy), several more weeks are necessary before it is possible to see the differences. Since the reproductive systems of females and males develop from the same embryonic origins, each part has its developmental counterpart, or *homologue,* in the other sex. You can easily identify some of these homologous structures by comparing the male and female internal and external reproductive systems in Figures 5.2 and 5.3.

Sexual Differentiation of the Central Nervous System

The question of sex differences in the human brain is a very controversial one. Researchers cite the same studies to argue that there are no consistent or conclusive differences (Devor, 1996) or that there are many neural sex differ-

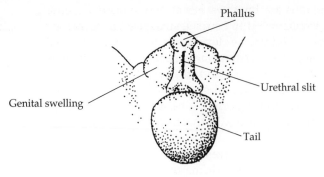

Indifferent stage

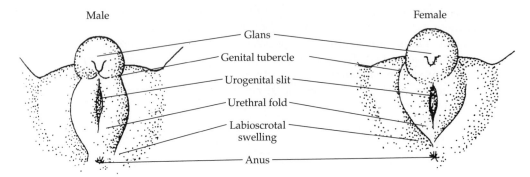

Seventh to eighth week

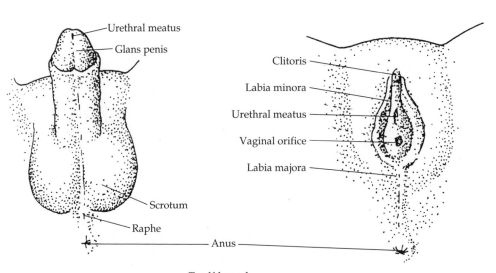

Twelfth week

FIGURE 5.3. The development of the female and male genitalia from the undifferentiated or bipotential gonad during early fetal development.
Drawing by Alina Wilczynski.

ences in human beings similar to those found in lower mammals (Collaer & Hines, 1995). The question is problematic for feminists because biological sex differences are often seen as fixed and used to argue against a need for social change in the roles and statuses of women and men (Unger, 1984–1985) (see Chapter 4). We must be very careful neither to deny the possible importance of biology nor to assume that biology is unaffected by our physical and social environment. Most responsible researchers take an interactional approach, arguing that the environmental-biology distinction is a false dichotomy. One neuroscientist noted in his review of the sexual differentiation of the nervous system that while it is possible to have either biological or psychological measures of a particular behavior, biology operates through psychological mechanisms and any change of behavior must also have an effect on the brain:

> Circumstances that alter behavior must change both the psychology and the biology of an individual. And, because social influences continually alter behavior, it follows that social stimuli must be able to alter biological measures such as brain morphology as well. (Breedlove, 1994, p. 391)

Although rats are not usually thought of as models for maternal behavior, a series of studies on rats has provided a good example of how biology and the social environment can interact to produce sex-related differences (Fausto-Sterling, 1997). Rat mothers have been found to lick the anogenital area of their male offspring more than that of their female offspring. Their licking is stimulated by an odor related to the level of testosterone in the pups' bloodstream. As adults, these rats took less time to ejaculate than pups raised by mothers who had their ability to smell removed and, therefore, did not stimulate their male pups' genital region. Their pups also had fewer motor neurons in a part of their hypothalamus associated with sexuality than did males raised by intact mothers (Moore, Dou, & Juraska, 1992). Is sexual behavior in male rats biologically or socially controlled? The answer is not one or the other, but *both* in a complex pattern of interaction.

Findings on primates also illustrate the importance of early environmental factors on reproductive behavior. Rhesus monkey males raised only with other males showed a lower frequency of *mounting* (climbing on the back of another animal and thrusting with the pelvis) as compared with heterosexually reared males. In contrast, females raised in an all-female environment mounted more than heterosexually reared females (Wallen, 1996). Paradoxically, single-sex environments increased the similarity between males and females in this behavior.

The jury is still out on the source of many so-called sex dimorphisms in the human brain. Researchers do not yet understand the relationship between structure and function in most of the neural areas in which sex differences have been found. Nor do they understand the role that environmental factors play in their development. Remember that the social environment is not sex-neutral even for newborn rats! With the exception of an absolute size difference between the brains of newborn girls and boys (with considerable overlap of the distributions for the two sexes), no sex differences in neural structure have been found at birth (Breedlove, 1994).

The Genetics of Sexual Orientation

Is sexual orientation genetically determined? Much of the recent work on the connection between biology and human behavior has focused on this question. Animal models are of little use here because no experimental treatment has produced animals who show a marked preference for partners of their own sex (Breedlove, 1994). Sexual behavior in lower mammals is largely controlled by hormonal conditions before birth. There is little, if any, relationship between their rigid sexual behaviors and human sexual activity.

Science still does not have a good definition of sexual orientation. Nevertheless, researchers are now looking for evidence of a "gay gene." Strong evidence for a genetic contribution to same-sex desire comes from studies showing that gay and lesbian individuals recur among family members at a rate much higher than chance (Diamond, 1995). If they exist, the genetic determinants of same-sex preference are not the same for women and men. Families with a large number of lesbians do not have a larger than average number of gay men. And families with a large number of gay men do not have an above chance level of lesbians in them.

If one of a pair of identical twins of either sex is lesbian or gay, the other is also likely to be at least 50 percent of the time (Bailey, Pillard, Neale, & Agyei, 1993; Hamer, Hu, Magnuson, Hu, & Pattatucci, 1993). One study even located a set of female triplets in which the two sisters from a single egg were both lesbians and the third sister, who was a fraternal twin, was heterosexual (Whitam, Diamond, & Martin, 1993).

The evidence of a genetic component to male sexual orientation is stronger than that for females. Same-sex orientation in males has been associated with the presence of a gene found on a particular part of the X chromosome. Gay men have been found to be more likely to have gay uncles on their mother's, but not their father's, side of the family (LeVay & Hamer, 1994). And in one study of forty pairs of gay identical twins, thirty-three were found to share a genetic marker on their X chromosome (Hamer et al., 1993). However, even these studies do not indicate complete genetic determinism since seven pairs of gay twins in the study did not share this marker. When both twins do not have the same sexual preference, the heterosexual twin appears to have no same-sex desires at all; for example, he was neither bisexual nor sexually ambiguous (Diamond, 1995). If one brother is gay, adoptive siblings are also gay at a rate higher than chance (Brelis, 1999). Such findings indicate that other factors must be important, too. But it is unlikely that headlines will proclaim: "Environment Modifies Sexual Orientation!"

Sexual Orientation and the Brain

Some researchers believe that the brains and behaviors of gay men resemble those of heterosexual women (this is an example of a *sexual inversion hypothesis,* which is also found in stereotypes about lesbians and gay men as discussed in Chapter 2). Researchers often compare differences between gay and straight men to differences between women and men. Their research has focused on neural areas where sex-related differences are believed to exist.

Several investigators have claimed to have found differences in various parts of the brain between gay and straight men (Allen & Gorski, 1992; LeVay, 1991, Swaab & Hofman, 1990). Besides the hypothalamus, researchers have looked at the corpus callosum—the region of the brain that is concerned with the transmission of information between the two hemispheres (Diamond, 1995).

These studies have been criticized for their small sample size, lack of replicability, and the fact that many of the gays who were studied had died of AIDS (Fausto-Sterling, 1992). These studies are, however, achieving the same kind of media attention that purported sex differences in math genes received (see Chapter 4).

Dramatic headlines followed the publication of LeVay's articles:

The Biology of What It Means to be Gay
—*New York Times*

Zone of Brain Linked to Men's Sexual Orientation
—*New York Times*

What Causes People to Be Homosexual? Study Pinpoints a Difference in the Brain
—*Newsweek*

Are Gay Men Born That Way?
—*Time*

Homosexuality and Biology
—*Atlantic Monthly*

The media's enthusiastic response illustrates the popularity of biologically determinist explanations for any kind of sex-related difference. It also shows the continued assumption that being male equals being human. Although none of the researchers found a difference in the brains of lesbian and heterosexual women (indeed, few have looked for one), several of the headlines generalized the results from gay males to lesbians.

Neural studies based on sexual orientation also illustrate some of the ways sex is oversimplified. These studies ignored the category of *bisexual* (people who have erotic feelings for women and men). When they make comparisons between gay men and heterosexual women, they equate one aspect of a person's sexual profile with the person as a whole. Other than desire, how much of a person's behavior is related to his or her sexual orientation?

DOES THE HUMAN BRAIN HAVE A SEX?

Sex and Neural Laterality

One of the reasons feminist scholars are so cautious about research in this area is that scientists in the past have used supposed differences between the brains of women and men to construct a case for female inferiority in cognitive skills. Attempts to demonstrate differences between male and female brains have been popular since the mid–nineteenth century (see Chapter 4).

Today, the search for biological sex differences underlying intellectual functioning continues. For example, a number of researchers have proposed that female brains are less lateralized than those of males. *Lateralization* refers to the degree to which brain functions are specialized in the right or left hemisphere. In right-handed people, the left hemisphere is usually dominant for language skills as well as motor control. The right hemisphere, on the other hand, is more dominant in spatial activities. The brains of left-handed people appear to be less specialized (or better balanced, depending on your point of view).

Although lateralization differences between males and females are much smaller and more elusive than differences between left- and right-handed people, they are often used to "explain" sex-related differences in cognitive abilities such as mathematics. This "explanation" is a clear example of how processes associated with females are defined as inferior (Unger, 1979b).

This point may be made clearer by looking at the cognitive skills of left- versus right-handed people instead of those of women and men. In normal populations, there is no evidence that left-handers have any more difficulty in acquiring mathematical skills than right-handers. The idea that a left brain/right brain distinction is importantly related to intellectual abilities and personality is selectively used to explain the behavior of normal women but not normal left-handed people. Of course, handedness, unlike sex, is not a distinction of great social and political importance in contemporary American culture.

Despite weak research support, respected scientists and important institutions of scholarship have continued to proclaim the existence of sex differences in neural laterality. Ruth Bleier (1988), a distinguished physician and neuroscientist, documented one such example of the construction of meaning in the neurosciences.

In 1982, Norman Geschwind, a well-known neurologist at Harvard, published a study reporting an association between left-handedness, certain disorders of the immune system, and some developmental learning disabilities, such as dyslexia and stuttering, a complex more common in boys than girls (Geschwind & Behan, 1982). The researchers argued that these disorders were linked by the prenatal effects of testosterone, which slowed down the development of the left hemisphere, resulting in right-hemispheric dominance in males. An important part of their evidence was a study of human fetal brains that reported that two convolutions of the right hemisphere appear one or two weeks earlier during fetal development than their counterparts on the left (Chi, Dooling, & Gilles, 1977). They failed to mention, however, that this study of more than 500 fetal brains failed to find any sex differences (Bleier, 1988). This result completely undermined Geschwind's theory, since testosterone should certainly have had some differential effect on male versus female brains.

Science, one of the most important journals of scholarly research, hailed Geschwind's theory as an elegant explanation of a variety of sex differences. The bold headline "Math Genius May Have Hormonal Basis" prefaced an interview with Geschwind in which he stated that testosterone effects on the fetal brain can produce "superior right hemisphere talents, such as artistic, musical, or mathematical talent" (Kolata, 1983, p. 1312). Another study using Geschwind's theory (which had not examined any physiological variables) received banner headlines such as "Study Shows Male Hormones Multiply Boys' Math Skills" (Bleier, 1988, p. 96). *Science,* however, rejected Bleier's paper showing no differences between the size of the corpus callosum (the structure connecting the two hemispheres) and has, in general, paid little attention to findings that contradict the idea of biological determinism.

The controversy over prenatal testosterone illustrates several points. First, people tend to believe evidence in the "hard" sciences such as physiology and biology more than evidence from the "soft" sciences such as psychology or sociology. Structures are seen as more real than processes. Second, biological effects are believed to be more irreversible than social effects. This belief has major consequences for the way people think about others and the kinds of social policies they espouse. Beliefs in biological determinism, political conservatism, and the inequality of the sexes are associated (Unger, Draper, & Pendergrass, 1986). Although researchers interested in neurology and physiology are aware of the major effects of the environment on biological processes, reports in the popular and professional media de-emphasize the importance of learning (see Figure 5.4). Such biases perpetuate sexist beliefs that, in turn, lead to practices that produce the "evidence" that supports them.

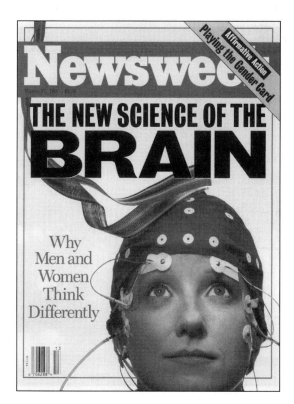

FIGURE 5.4. The article inside this magazine is more balanced than its cover would indicate. However, the cover is far from balanced in its stress on scientific validity. One might also wonder if the connection between the cover and the banner advertising another story on affirmative action is truly accidental.
Source: Newsweek.

The Relationship between Biology and Behavior

To what degree are sex-related differences biologically determined? Surprisingly, this is not as easy a question to answer as you might believe. In most cases, both sexes behave the same way. It is the relative difference in frequency, intensity, or context associated with the display of a particular behavior pattern that is termed a sex difference. In other words, although individuals may display the behavior of the other sex, it is much more likely that they will display behaviors characteristic of their own sex. It might be fair to say, therefore, that behavior has no sex.

Biologically oriented researchers have tended to ignore the role of the social environment in their studies of sex differences in behavior. Recently, however, some of these researchers have begun to stress that "nature needs nurture" (Wallen, 1996). Some of the most interesting work in this area examines the role of environment on sex-related differences in primates. In contrast to earlier work, which viewed primate behavior in terms of human gender stereotypes, this research shows that the early "childhood" experiences of monkeys have an impact on behaviors that are also influenced by hormones and that are usually regarded as sexually dimorphic.

Harry Harlow (1965), an influential comparative psychologist whose ideas were also discussed in Chapter 4, reported that female rhesus monkeys displayed significantly more passivity, rigidity, and withdrawal than young rhesus males. He argued that these behaviors made it easier for juvenile males to learn the appropriate mounting posture. However, males raised under the abnormal conditions he used (alone, with only brief access to other monkeys) rarely achieved normal sexual postures even as adults. When monkeys were studied under more normal group conditions, sex differences in these behaviors were no longer found (Wallen, 1996).

Similarly, high levels of threat behavior by male monkeys were only found in those who had been deprived of their mothers and had limited access to their peers. Aggression was inhibited by either peer socialization or by the moderating influence of parents. The only sex-related behavior that was largely uninfluenced by rearing conditions was rough-and-tumble play. In every environment where play has been examined, male primates engage in more rough-and-tumble play than females do (Wallen, 1996). Levels of such play are also influenced by the presence or absence of prenatal androgens. The role of play in monkey (or human) social development is not known. Recent research suggests, however, that boys' tendency to engage in more rough and active play than girls may help shape gender roles in humans (Maccoby, 1998). (See Chapter 6.)

Other supposedly dimorphic behaviors have also been shown to be influenced by the social environment. One researcher, for example, looked at sex-related differences in the parenting of rhesus monkeys (Gibber, 1981). She found that male and female monkeys looked at, approached, and picked up "stranded" newborn monkeys to an equal extent when they were alone. However, when both a male and a female were present, females did virtually all the parenting behavior. Many of the males who had shown nurturant responses when alone did not do so in the presence of a female.

These studies indicate that monkeys of both sexes are capable of a wide variety of behaviors that have been linked with only one sex. In social situations, however, they appear to "take the easy way out" and let the more experienced sex get involved. Think about this behavior in terms of a human analogy. Most women probably find it easier than most men to change a baby's diaper. Most men will wait for a woman to do the dirty work. However, no one believes that a man would be unable to change a diaper if it was necessary and no women were around.

ATYPICAL HUMAN SEXUAL DEVELOPMENT

We have argued against overgeneralizing from animal to human studies. It is unethical, however, to do experimental studies of human sexual differentiation. Therefore, clinical cases in which the various components of sex are not consistent with each other are the only way to explore the relationship between biological sex and psychological aspects of gender in human beings. However, the use of clinical case material carries with it additional problems, and researchers need to be as careful in generalizing about groups of people whose sexual development differs from the norm as they are in generalizing between animals and people.

Learning about people with sexual anomalies helps show how individuals who do not conform perfectly to dualistic sexual categories deal with a gender-divided world. The major reason for scientists' interest in these individuals is, however, the clues they can provide to the origin of sexual identity and other kinds of gender-related behaviors in typical human beings. By looking at people for whom the various components of sex are inconsistent, researchers can figure out what factors must be present for a particular behavior to occur. They can then eliminate those variables that may be present but are not necessary for that behavior. They can ask questions such as: What is the effect of absent or additional sex chromosomes on sex-related behaviors? Are sex hormones necessary for an individual to identify strongly as a male or female? And what happens to an individual whose external sex is different from that of his or her internal structures?

It is important to be cautious in generalizing from people with sexual anomalies to sexually consistent human beings. People for whom the multiple determinants of sex do not coincide may be more sexually flexible or plastic than other people (Diamond, 1965). It may be easier for them to shift their sexual identities than it is for people whose sexual characteristics are consistent with each other. Individuals who come for clinical treatment may not even be a representative sample of people with the same anomalies. People who seek or are sent for clinical treatment are often more adversely affected than others with the same characteristics.

It is also difficult to determine what is "normal" in this area. People do not carry around signs saying I am a man or I am a woman. It has been estimated that 1 to 2 percent of all live births involve some sort of sexual inconsistency. Many of these cannot be found by simple observation of the genitals (Fausto-Sterling, in press). Figure 5.5 is a photograph of a group of intersex people.

FIGURE 5.5. Moving beyond nude photographs with dots over the faces. Do the intersex people in this photograph look different from anyone else?
Source: Chrysalis: The Journal of Transgressive Gender Identities, Vol. 2, #5 Fall 1997/Winter 1998, p. 57.

What cues could be used to separate them from other people? As Alex's story showed, medical authorities are not always in agreement about an individual's sex. And a person may not always agree with the experts' opinion. The *transgender movement* challenges an obligatory two-sex system and argues that transgender people must be viewed as people rather than as sexual curiosities.

All sex-related characteristics do not necessarily have the same origin. As discussed earlier, at least five different levels of sexual expression—abbreviated as PRIMO—must be assessed to give a complete sexual profile for any individual (Diamond, 1995). Think about each of these categories as we examine different patterns of sexual discordance.

Extra or Missing Sex Chromosomes

Turner's Syndrome: Can One Be a Female without Estrogen?

Under normal circumstances, human beings possess forty-six chromosomes—twenty-two pairs of autosomes and one set of sex chromosomes. During the development of the egg or sperm, however, it is possible for one of these chromosomes to be dropped or for an extra one to be added. One abnormality that affects sexual development is known as *Turner's syndrome.* Individuals with this disorder usually have only one unmatched X chromosome. The incidence of Turner's syndrome is approximately 1:2,000 to 1:5,000 births (Collaer & Hines, 1995).

Individuals with Turner's syndrome usually appear to have normal female genitalia at birth, although they lack ovaries and a uterus. Breasts fail to develop and pubic hair does not grow at adolescence. Their internal reproductive structures are undeveloped, with ovaries represented only by fibrous streaks of tissue. Individuals with Turner's syndrome do not menstruate and, of course, they are completely sterile. They lack ovarian hormones during a critical period of prenatal development. They are also unusually short (rarely reaching more than four and a half feet as adults).

Although the missing chromosome could have been either an X or a Y, people with Turner's syndrome are classified as 45, XO; these individuals are always identified as female on the basis of their external genitalia. People with Turner's syndrome are particularly interesting because they show how development occurs in the absence of any sex hormones except those produced by the mother before birth. Some findings parallel those of animal experiments—in the absence of any gonadal influences differentiation will take a female direction. However, people with Turner's syndrome are not simply unusual females. They are essentially neuter individuals whose external genitalia are similar to those of females. They are defined as females simply because of the inadequacy of our binary classification system for sex.

Individuals with Turner's syndrome provide researchers with an opportunity to examine the psychological effects of the sex of assignment and rearing independent of the biological influences usually associated with that sex. A number of studies have looked at their psychological and behavioral responses, especially in those areas where male/female differences are thought to exist (Collaer & Hines, 1995). People with Turner's syndrome have often been described as being slightly retarded. Their verbal abilities are relatively unimpaired, but their performance on visual and spatial tasks is significantly below normal. They may have difficulty orienting spatially and performing numerical calculations.

The basis for this deficiency is unknown, although it has sometimes been ascribed to the lack of a Y chromosome. The Y chromosome, however, is not known to carry any genes besides those for male sex determination except, possibly, a gene for hairy ears (Hartl, 1983). Recent research suggests that the cognitive difficulties of those with Turner's syndrome may be due to attentional and memory deficits rather than the absence of sex hormones (Collaer & Hines, 1995).

Although their central nervous systems have not been exposed to any gonadal hormones during gestation, individuals with Turner's syndrome identify themselves as female. As children they appear even more feminine than other girls. They show less interest and skill in athletics, fight less, and have a greater interest in personal adornment. In one study, despite the handicap of their stature and infertility, which all of the older Turner girls knew about, all but one explicitly hoped to get married one day. They all reported daydreams and fantasies of being pregnant and wanted to have a baby to care for. All but one had played with dolls exclusively, and the exception preferred dolls even though she played with boys' toys occasionally (Money & Ehrhardt, 1972).

These findings suggest that a feminine gender identity can develop without any help from prenatal gonadal hormones that might influence the brain.

Are gonadal hormones needed to explain these results? The only obvious physical difference, and sometimes the only external sign, of XO individuals is their small size. Other aspects of their physical immaturity may not become obvious until adolescence. It is likely that these children will not be reinforced for their skill in athletics or fighting. Size is also a cue for status and power among children. Since children with Turner's syndrome tend to be consistently much smaller than their peers, they probably have low status and power as well.

Individuals with Turner's syndrome score lower in enthusiasm and impulsiveness than comparable ninth-grade girls (Shaffer, 1963). They also score lower in generalized activity, energy, and masculinity on temperament scales and higher in personal relationships and cooperativeness. There is more uniformity in these traditionally feminine traits among children with Turner's syndrome than among comparable girls. In fact, the degree of overcompliance that the XO individuals showed would be considered a clinical problem in chromosomally normal females.

There is no clear evidence that the personality and behavioral differences between XX and XO individuals are socially determined. But the lack of a second X chromosome may not be directly responsible for these effects, either. Factors such as activity level and body image and its social consequences should be considered in addition to biological variables.

XYY and XXY Males: What Is the Power of the Y Chromosome?

Both scientists and ordinary people tend to overestimate the extent to which biological variables determine behavior. An excellent example of the tendency to overgeneralize biological determinants may be found in the case of the so-called criminality syndrome. Individuals with an extra Y chromosome (47, XYY) were first reported in 1965 among the inmates of institutions for violent, dangerous, and aggressive patients. No physical abnormality was reported except for excessive height. XYY males tend to be tall, averaging over six feet.

More than fifty similar studies have now been carried out in prisons in Europe and the United States, and it has held true that the frequency of XYY males confined for crimes of violence is about ten times greater than the percentage of XYY males found among a sample of newborn infants. This result led a number of investigators to conclude that the extra Y chromosome predisposed these men toward excessive aggression and violence. Such conclusions are an example of an extreme form of biological determinism.

These studies were biased by the fact that they took place in an institutional setting. They had, therefore, no information about the XYY men who are not societal problems (the greater number). Chromosomal factors, moreover, do not rule out social influences as well. Since XYY men tend to be taller than the average, it is possible that their extra height imposes psychosocial stresses that makes violent aggressive behavior more likely. Their height may also make any aggression more effective and reinforcing.

One Danish study of criminality among XYY males is particularly important because it is free of many of the biases found in other studies. The study was possible because of the excellent records kept in the small country of Denmark. The researchers (Witkin et al., 1976) examined *all* available records on almost all men 28 to 32 years of age born in Copenhagen whose height was within the top 15 percent of the height distribution of Danish males. They found twelve XYY and thirteen XXY men in this group. The researchers also obtained information on any crimes committed by these men, the educational level they had attained, and the results of an intelligence test used to screen army recruits.

Individuals with an XXY chromosomal composition (also known as *Klinefelter's syndrome*) served as a comparison group for the XYY males. This group is also taller than average, but the presence of an extra X chromosome produces a smaller penis and testes and feminization of the hips, with some breast development. The testes fail to enlarge at puberty, the voice remains rather high-pitched, and pubic and facial hair remain sparse. Because of the feminizing effects of an extra X chromosome, the researchers expected such men to engage in fewer violent aggressive acts than either XY or XYY males.

They found that chromosomal composition, by itself, was not highly related to the probability that a man would be convicted of a crime. Height was also not related to the probability of being convicted of a crime (criminals were actually shorter than their noncriminal counterparts). Those of low socioeconomic status—irrespective of their chromosomal composition—were more likely to have been convicted.

The most important findings of this study were that both XXY and XYY males had significantly lower army intelligence test scores and lower educational levels than XY males did. For each group, men with criminal records were substantially lower in both measures of intellectual function than men without criminal records. These findings seem to imply that the somewhat higher rate of criminality among XYY males may be due to their moderately impaired mental function. The hypothesis about the relationship of an extra Y chromosome and aggression was definitely not supported. In fact, the only violent crime committed by any man with extra chromosomes was the physical attack on a woman committed by an XXY male.

The case of the so-called criminality syndrome illustrates the danger of overestimating biological causality. At about the time of the first discovery of XYY males among exceptionally violent criminals, a pathological killer, Richard Speck, sneaked into a nurses' dormitory in Chicago and brutally murdered several student nurses. A newspaper claimed that he had been "born to kill" because he was XYY. This turned out to be untrue—he was XY—but the false report was widely disseminated and believed. Several proposals were made for the mass screening of newborn boys to detect those with XYY and to provide them with special education and psychological counseling to counteract their supposed "killer instinct." This could have produced a self-fulfilling prophecy, creating problems for XYY people because others believed them to have severe problems with aggression. The results of the Danish study indicate, however, that the rate of criminality is related more to income and intellectual functioning than to sex-chromosomal composition.

Do the Chromosomes Determine Sex?

Perhaps because the X and Y chromosomes carry relatively little genetic information, missing and extra sex chromosomes appear to be the most common form of chromosomal abnormality in human beings. Many people may be completely unaware of their unusual chromosomal nature. Chromosomal composition appears to have little direct effect on sexual identity or orientation although it may influence characteristics such as intelligence, height, and physique, which, in turn, influence the way people are treated by others.

Society's ignorance about the role of the sex chromosomes has had tragic results for women who compete in world-class athletic events like the Olympics. Women who were found to have a Y chromosome in some of their cells (this is common enough that several such women are usually identified at most major international sports events) were routinely denied the opportunity to participate (Lorber, 1993a). Only women are tested to see if they are "female enough" to compete. Men are not tested. The purpose is to prevent women from having to compete unfairly with individuals who have male advantages in size and strength. However, there is no evidence that chromosomes affect sports prowess (Birrell & Cole, 1990). The International Amateur Athletic Federation has urged that sex be determined by simple genital inspection (Kolata, 1992).

Making a Difference

Cheryl Chase (b. 1956) grew up withdrawn and lonely, stigmatized and harassed by other children. She had been born with a large clitoris, was labeled a boy at birth, and was treated as a boy until age 1 1/2. Then a new set of "expert" physicians relabeled her as a girl and removed her clitoris. Chase, on doctors' advice, was kept in the dark about her intersexuality and history of sex change. In middle age she finally understood that her difficult childhood was likely due to her parents' ambivalent attitude toward her, which had been encouraged by the medical perspective of intersexuality as a shameful secret. Chase then began to speak about her history and soon met others with similar experiences. She founded the Intersex Society of North America (ISNA) in 1993. ISNA holds that cosmetic genital surgery on infants is harmful because: (1) it is sexually mutilating, (2) it conveys that the child is a misfit who would not be acceptable without plastic surgery, and (3) many intersexed people reject the gender assigned by doctors and feel doubly robbed by early surgery. ISNA emphasizes the importance of open and honest disclosure concerning intersexuality as well as peer and professional mental health support for intersexual children and their families. They also believe an intersex person might quite rationally choose not to undergo any medical interventions, considering the body they are born with to be normal for them, a variant rather than an abnormality. Chase and her colleagues at ISNA are working toward the end of the notion that it is monstrous to be different.

Sources: Intersex Society of North America, http://www.isna.org.
Colapinto, J. (1997, December 11). The true story of John/Joan. *Rolling Stone*, 54–97.
Renshaw, D. C. (1999, March 31). Lessons from the intersexed. *Journal of the American Medical Association*, 1137–1138.
Cowley, G. (1997, May 19). Gender Limbo. *Newsweek*, 64–66.

When people are born with a mixture of male/female organs, it is usually due to an excess of or an absence of androgens during critical periods of prenatal development. In turn, the presence or absence of these hormones influences the development of internal reproductive structures and the appearance of the external genitalia. But do these conditions also influence the brain and behavior?

Congenital Adrenal Hyperplasia: What Is a Normal Female?

Individuals with congenital adrenal hyperplasia (CAH) lack an enzyme needed to build certain adrenal steroids. As a result of this missing enzyme, steroids such as testosterone and *progesterone* (a hormone characteristic of pregnancy that has masculinizing properties) build up during prenatal life. The incidence of this genetic disorder is estimated to be between 1 in 5,000 and 1 in 10,000 births (Collaer & Hines, 1995). A related disorder occurs in females whose mothers received doses of progesterone during pregnancy to prevent a threatened miscarriage. The two groups seem to be similar, suggesting that any behavioral effects are due to prenatal androgens.

Females with CAH have two normal X chromosomes, normal ovaries, uterus, and fallopian tubes. However, their external genitalia look more or less like those of male infants (see Figure 5.6). There is usually an enlarged clitoris and a fusion of the lips of the labia, producing a picture of sexual ambiguity. Some individuals have complete closure of the urethral groove and a penis that is capable of becoming erect.

Until rather recently, sex was assigned to newborn infants on the basis of inspection of their genitalia. Thus, two individuals with equivalent ambiguities might have been classified differently. In the United States, at least, this kind of misassignment no longer occurs for individuals with CAH. Advances in knowledge about gonadal structure and chromosomal composition have led to most such individuals being correctly raised as females. In spite of a somewhat enlarged clitoris, their internal structures tend to be normally female and many of them are fertile. If those girls who need it receive proper replacement therapy with other hormones, they experience pubertal development spontaneously at the normal age, and their sexual functioning and fertility are not impaired in adulthood (Ehrhardt & Meyer-Bahlburg, 1981).

Since all such females have received a heavy dose of masculinizing hormones during fetal life, questions about their sexual identity, gender-related behaviors, and sexual orientation are of great interest. Girls with CAH have been found to identify firmly as girls and women. However, they differ from comparison groups (either matched unaffected females, unaffected siblings, or individuals with other clinical disorders) in that they typically showed more intense active outdoor play, increased association with male peers, and long-term identification as a "tomboy" by themselves and others. They preferred "masculine" toys to "feminine" ones beginning in their nursery school years (Berenbaum & Hines, 1992). All of these behavioral differences are probably related to the higher activity levels that they also show from an early age.

They also differed from comparison girls by displaying a lower level of nurturance (doll play or baby care) and less interest in playacting the roles of

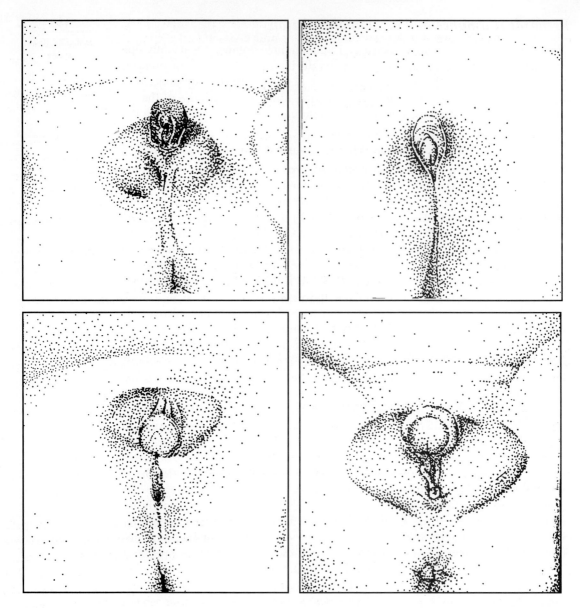

FIGURE 5.6. Genitals are not always clearly "male" or "female." Here are examples of the external genitals of several intersex infants.
Drawing by Alina Wilczynski.

wife and mother. None of their behaviors would be considered abnormal for a girl in our culture. They were not any more aggressive than comparison girls nor did they show what some researchers consider a "malelike" cognitive profile—better spatial-perceptual than verbal abilities (Collaer & Hines, 1995). Despite their childhood characterization as tomboys and their avid interest in high school sports, none of these young women pursued sports as a career or even as a major pastime (Money & Mathews, 1982).

Although most women with CAH are heterosexual, several studies have reported increased same-sex or bisexual fantasies and behaviors in comparison to their unaffected sisters or female relatives. In one study, 44 percent of CAH women 21 years or older had desired or experienced sex with a female partner, but none of their sisters had done so (Dittmann, Kappes & Kappes, 1992). Another study found that CAH women had fewer sexual experiences with men than did their female relatives (Collaer & Hines, 1995). However, many of these women had undergone clitoral reduction and their sexual behavior may have been a result of surgical damage rather than a direct effect of prenatal androgens on sexual orientation.

These studies suggest that the effects of prenatal masculinizing hormones on human females are complex. Most of these women do not question their identity as females. Sexual orientation appears to be more idiosyncratic. Some of these women were heterosexual, some had same-sex preferences, and some were bisexual in orientation, just like women who have not been subjected to masculinizing hormones. Some gender-related behaviors, especially those associated with a high energy level, appear to be influenced by the level of male steroids present prenatally. It is important to stress, however, that most of the women interviewed expressed satisfaction with themselves as females and that even studies suggesting disturbances in gender identity and body image found all the young women with CAH to be within the norms for adolescent girls. These studies show that prenatal androgens do not directly determine gender-related behaviors.

Androgen Insensitivity: What Does the Y Chromosome Do?

Androgen insensitivity (AI) is an inherited condition of individuals with an XY chromosomal composition. It is apparently caused by a genetic defect that prevents embryonic tissues from responding to testosterone either partially or completely. Individuals with complete AI have female external genitalia and an incompletely developed vagina but no uterus or fallopian tubes. Those with incomplete AI have ambiguous genitalia similar to those shown in Figure 5.6 with a structure that could be called either a large clitoris or a small penis. Internally, they are similar to normal males in appearance, although the testes contain unusual cells and are present in the abdominal cavity rather than the scrotum. In the past, individuals with AI were classified as female and raised as girls. Even when the male chromosomal pattern of infants with partial AI was recognized, many physicians continued to argue for "clitoral" reduction and surgical construction of a vagina on the grounds that boys with an inadequate penis would be ridiculed and be unable to function in manly roles (Kessler, 1998).

Individuals with total AI are completely unresponsive to testosterone. However, their bodies (like those of other males) produce estrogens. Without testosterone to counteract them, these estrogens induce breast development and feminine contours at puberty. Individuals with testicular feminization often appear to be very attractive women. The Y chromosome carries information that is not completely mediated by testosterone. Thus, persons with AI tend to have male height. Their breast development is normal and appears to result from the action of estrogens produced by their testes (if they are still present) and their adrenal glands. Pubic and axillary hair tends to be sparse or absent. Of course, having no uterus, these individuals do not menstruate and are sterile.

Since it is a rare disorder, relatively few studies of the behavior of people with AI have been conducted. A survey of the clinical data on ten such individuals reported that they show a high preference for a traditionally feminine role. Eighty percent preferred the role of homemaker over an outside job; 100 percent reported having dreams and fantasies of raising a family; 80 percent reported playing primarily with dolls and other girls' toys. They rated themselves high in affectionateness and fully content with the feminine role (Money & Ehrhardt, 1972). Adults with this syndrome tend to take up occupations that put a high premium on an attractive feminine appearance and behavior, such as modeling and acting. It is disturbing to find that the most attractive female body may be that of a genetic male.

5-Alpha-Reductase and 17-Beta-Hydroxysteroid Dehydrogenase Deficiency: Biology versus Culture?

There have been several studies of individuals who have one of two rare genetic defects with the tongue-twisting names given in the preceding heading. Briefly, affected individuals lack one of several enzymes that aid in the conversion of testosterone to *dihydrotestosterone*—the androgen that masculinizes the external genitalia, including fusion of the scrotum and the growth of the penis. Individuals who lack these enzymes are born with normal testes and male internal structures combined with female-appearing or ambiguous external genitalia that are quite similar to the ambiguous structures of girls who have been exposed to prenatal androgens (see Figure 5.6). When modern scientific methods for determining chromosomal sex are unavailable, they may be identified and raised as girls.

Males with these enzyme deficiencies are, however, masculinized during childhood or at puberty when their normal testes pour increasing amounts of testosterone into their systems. The testosterone produces deepening of the voice, enlargement of the penis and testicles, erections, and ejaculation from a urethral orifice at the base of the penis (Imperato-McGinley & Peterson, 1976; Peterson, Imperato-McGinley, Gautier, & Sturla, 1977). Such males would appear to provide a perfect test case for examining the effect of socialization versus biological factors in the development of sexual identity and gender roles since they are biological males who have been raised as females throughout childhood. The interesting question is: What happens to their identity when their sex of rearing and their physical properties become different at a relatively late point in their lives? Or, how reversible is sexual identity?

One study examined a group of thirty-eight related individuals with the disorder in a rural region of the Dominican Republic (Imperato-McGinley, Peterson, Gautier, & Sturla, 1979). In this isolated group, 5-alpha-reductase deficiency is so common that it has a name: *guevedoce*, or "penis at twelve." In the first nineteen cases, individuals with this disorder were reared unambiguously as girls, but in later cases, persons with the deficiency were recognized early and treated as special. What is surprising is the striking ease with which these people shifted gender at puberty. Seventeen successfully assumed a masculine identity and fifteen were married, suggesting a much later capacity for sexual identity reversal than studies on other sexually ambiguous people would indicate is possible. The researchers believe that the shift was made possible by the prenatal masculinization of the brain in these individuals; that is, their "male" brains were able to overcome easily many years of feminine socialization (Imperato-McGinley et al., 1979).

As you can see, nature versus nurture arguments are still alive and well in the area of sexual development and behavior. Some researchers have challenged that a more intensive analysis of these data suggests that the shift from feminine to masculine identity was not as simple as it first appeared. For example, the individuals are described as realizing that they were different from other girls sometime between the ages of 7 and 12 (Rubin, Reinisch, & Haskett, 1981). This realization took place shortly after the age at which children in this culture are encouraged to segregate by sex for play and domestic tasks. They shifted their gender identity over several years and initiated sexual intercourse with young women at the same age as those affected males who had been raised as boys.

In addition to follow-up studies in the Dominican Republic (Imperato-McGinley, Pichardo, Gautier, Voyer, & Bryden, 1991), other isolated populations of individuals with this disorder have been studied in New Guinea (Herdt & Davidson, 1988) and Gaza (Diamond, 1999). (Groups of individuals with the same recessive genetic disorder tend to accumulate in isolated areas with much intermarriage between relatives.) Unfortunately, it is difficult to test questions of nature versus nurture in these cultures because of linguistic difficulties and differences in sexual norms. In Gaza, for example, close examination of the genitals of newborn infants is not usual even in communities where this intersex condition is fairly common. In Islamic cultures the sexes are segregated, nudity is discouraged, and discussion of sexual matters, even those requiring medical attention, is not considered appropriate (Diamond, 1999). Researchers do not know, therefore, whether anyone recognized differences in these children's genitals at an early age. They also do not know whether assumptions about the stability of one's sex are similar to those found in other cultures where such conditions are rare.

Culture plays a role in the differentiation of sexual identity even in situations where development differs drastically from the norm. There are advantages to living as a male in all of the cultures studied. Anthropological investigations of the Dominican population have indicated, for example, that social class affects how intersexed people take on adult male roles. Individuals from poor families are likely to drift into marginal occupations, including prostitution, whereas similarly affected individuals from well-to-do families marry and purportedly "father" children with their wives (Tobach, personal communication, 1992). As in the Dominican Republic, the genetic abnormality is common enough in parts of New Guinea to have received a colloquial name—Turnim man. This society actually has three linguistic terms for sex: male, female, and an ambiguous compound word that emphasizes a complex relationship between genital anatomy and gender identity (Herdt & Davidson, 1988). People in the third category are not treated like other males. Unlike other boys their age, they are excluded from initiation into male societies, although they are sometimes granted a religious identity as a shaman (Herdt, 1996).

Nevertheless, a strong case may be made for a biological priming of sexual identity in these individuals. Consider the following report on people from Israel and Gaza whose genitals begin to masculinize between ages 3 and 7:

> Intersex persons interviewed claimed to be aware of not being girls/female from an early age on. This was often verbally expressed even before genital masculinization was recognized. Demonstrated male behaviors by an intersexed child were often cause for parents to first become aware of the condition. The older individuals that remained living as women did so due to cultural conditions which prevented their switching. They were fully aware they were male but considered themselves socially restrained from switching to live as men and believed that they were thus also fulfilling the will of Allah. Their sexual orientation, as that of all those that switched to living as males, remained gynecophilic [e.g., attracted to women]. (Diamond, 1999, p. 12 of manuscript)

These findings suggest that prenatal androgens may act on the brains of genetic males to induce a sense of bodily maleness. This combined with the average higher activity level encouraged by prenatal hormones may lead affected boys to see themselves as male in spite of some degree of feminine socialization. Their sexual orientation follows the pattern found in most males with a normal prenatal chemistry.

Cross-Sex Rearing in Prenatally Normal Males

These data would suggest that sexual identity in males, at least, is not easily changed by gender socialization. This conclusion is based on quite new studies that were not available when John Money (1974) began working with a case whose bizarre aspects seem more suited to a science fiction story than to scientific annals. The case involved a set of identical twins whose development before birth was normally male. In infancy, however, an accident during circumcision resulted in near-total destruction of one twin's penis. After much discussion, the parents were advised to reclassify the child as female. This was formally done at the age of 17 months. The sex reassignment was based on the opinion that a child without a penis would be able to function more adequately as a female than as a maimed male. One psychiatrist predicted the twin's emotional future in the following words:

> He will be unable to consummate marriage or have normal heterosexual relations; he will have to recognize that he is incomplete, physically defective, and that he must live apart. (Colapinto, 1997, p. 58)

The decision to change this child's sex of assignment was also supported by clinical studies of *hermaphrodites* (an older term for intersex individuals) suggesting that children identify with the gender in which they are reared if the label is assigned within the first two or three years of life and the child is treated consistently as either a male or a female from then on (Money & Ehrhardt, 1972).

Think about both the conceptual bases and the ethical implications of such a sexual reassignment. First, it reflects our cultural bias about the primacy of the penis. Anyone without a functional penis is not considered to be truly male. Experts were willing to subject this child to additional surgery (including castration or removal of the testes as well as construction of a vagina) and lifelong hormonal replacement therapy because they believed he could not function as a male without a penis. The experts also did not question whether the reassigned "woman" would have sexual pleasure with men or women or whether she would consider herself a "normal" female without menstruation or the ability to bear children.

When a sex change is done for male-to-female transsexuals, it is done with their informed consent. This child was not old enough to give consent and, in fact, as of age 13, had not yet been told about the sex reassignment. Given the higher status of males in our society, it is possible the child might have preferred to remain a male even without a penis. On the other hand, perhaps he would have preferred to be a functional female rather than a maimed male. It is easy to have 20/20 hindsight in this case, but what would you have done?

After the sex change, the parents changed the "girl" twin's clothing and hairdo. "She" was also encouraged to help her mother with housework, in contrast to her brother. Although the "girl" had many tomboyish (a peculiar word to use with reference to this child) traits, she was encouraged to engage in less rough-and-tumble play than her brother and to be quieter and more "ladylike." The boy responded by being physically protective of his "sister" (Money & Ehrhardt, 1972).

This case and two other cases of sex reassignment reported by Money (1974) appeared to provide strong evidence that most traditional gender differences are socially learned. However, when the twin was seen at age 13 by a new set of psychiatrists, she was said to be beset by problems (Diamond, 1982). The reports stated:

> At the present time the child refuses to draw a female figure and when asked to draw a female, refuses, saying it's easier to draw a man.
> The child . . . has a very masculine gait, er, looks quite masculine, and is being teased by each group that she attempts to make overtures toward . . . they will call her cavewoman and they make reference to the fact that she is not particularly feminine.
> At the present time, she feels that boys have a better life. That it's easier to be a boy than it is to be a girl. She aspires to masculine occupations, wants to be a mechanic. (Diamond, 1982, p. 183)

This latter statement might be made by many untreated adolescent girls (see Chapter 7).

This case then disappeared from public scrutiny for many years. It has resurfaced recently in both the medical archives (Diamond & Sigmundson, 1997) and as a somewhat sensational article in *Rolling Stone* entitled "The True Story of John/Joan," which includes interviews of both twins, their parents, and some of the researchers involved in this case (Colapinto, 1997). Contrary to earlier reports of Joan's femininity, her twin reported:

> "I recognized Joan as my sister," Kevin says, "but she never, ever acted the part. She'd get a skipping rope for a gift, and the only thing we'd use *that* for was to tie people up, whip people with it. Never used it for what it was

bought for. She played with *my* toys: Tinkertoys, dump trucks. Toys like this sewing machine she got just sat.

"When I say there was nothing feminine about Joan," Kevin laughs, "I mean there was nothing feminine. She walked like a guy. She talked about guy things, didn't give a crap about cleaning house, getting married, wearing makeup. . . ." (Colapinto, 1997, p. 64)

At 18 years of age Joan sought and received surgery to reconstruct a penis and scrotum. She also had a mastectomy to remove the breasts created by her treatment with estrogens. At age 23 he married a woman three years his senior who had three children. He has successfully maintained his anonymity, works in a well-paid factory job, and enjoys taking his adoptive sons on fishing trips. He has an acceptable sexual life, but unnecessary medical treatment has taken its toll. The original accident prevented John from fathering children without artificial intervention. Subsequent castration made it impossible for him to father children in addition to reducing his sexual pleasure. He resents it now and regrets these losses.

Other cases of XY males assigned and raised as girls have also run into problems (Diamond, 1999). In a long-term follow-up, one researcher stated that two years into his study all six children were closer to boys than girls in their attitudes and behaviors. Two of them spontaneously (without being told about their chromosomal status) switched back to being boys. He commented that it would be wrong to say that these children wished to be boys or felt that they were boys in girl's bodies; they believed they were boys (Reiner, quoted in Colapinto, 1997). In contrast, boys with a very small penis who are reared as boys appear to live sexually satisfactory lives as heterosexual males without surgery (Diamond, 1999). These findings support the view that sexual identity in males is strongly influenced by prenatal androgens. How much does biology and how much does environment influence various aspects of sex and gender? Both are probably important.

Changing Identity

Transsexualism

A substantial number of people firmly believe that they were born with the bodies of the wrong sex. This phenomenon is known as *transsexualism.* Many transsexuals maintain that they have been discontented with their identity from earliest childhood. Their belief is not easily influenced by any form of psychological therapy.

These people are not psychotic. They are not confused about the actual biological condition of their bodies, but believe that their psyches are consistent with the body of the other sex. A number of transsexuals have had successful careers before seeking gender reassignment. One such individual is Jan Morris, a well-known writer, who was James Morris and who wrote the story of her transition from male to female in the best-selling book called *Conundrum* (1974). Another such individual is Rene Richards (previously Richard Raskin), an eye surgeon who made headlines when she attempted (unsuccessfully) to play on the women's professional tennis circuit after having played on the men's circuit. More recently, a well-known economist Donald McCloskey and an important pianist David Buechner made headlines when they became Deirdre McCloskey and Sara Buechner (Jacobs, 1998; Wilson, 1996). (See Figure 5.7.)

It has been estimated that there are 30,000 transsexuals worldwide, 10,000 of whom are believed to live in the United States (Grimm, 1987). Male-to-female transsexuals appear to outnumber female-to-male transsexuals, but this estimate may be inaccurate because many female-to-male transsexuals do not opt for genital surgery (since it is expensive and an acceptable-looking penis is almost impossible to construct). They often self-masculinize by using testosterone (Devor, 1996). Other researchers believe that the reason for this disparity is that primarily androcentric cultures are less accepting of variant masculine role behaviors. Thus, men who deviate in some ways may come to feel that they are not men at all, whereas it is socially acceptable in many countries for women to wear pants, carry briefcases, and enjoy sports. What would people think about a man who wears dresses, carries a purse, and enjoys needlepoint?

People who are *sexually dysmorphic* (whose self-concept does not fit their sexual biology) may range from those who simply dress in the other sex's attire in the privacy of their homes (usually called transvestites) to those who undergo extensive surgery to make their bodies consistent with their psychological sex. Clinics that perform sex-change surgery usually require the individual to live successfully as a member of the other sex for at least a year. "Passing" seems to be more a matter of attire, hairstyle, voice, mannerisms,

FIGURE 5.7. Deirdre McCloskey—a noted economist—who shifted from male to female. Some feminist economists worry whether her egalitarian views on economics will be taken seriously now that she is a woman.

and gestures than any extensive physiological change. In fact, two-thirds of the transsexual population have not gone as far as surgery but are nonetheless living as members of the other sex on a full-time basis (Grimm, 1987). They typically take years to change sex and go through a gradual readjustment to their changing body image and societal reactions to it (Bolin, 1996).

Transsexuals do not necessarily transcend traditional masculine-feminine dichotomies. Until recently, many male-to-female transsexuals often adopted an exaggerated stereotypical version of feminine dress and behavior. They wore more elaborate clothing and makeup than most women. In *Conundrum,* Jan Morris (an ex-war correspondent who went on expeditions to Mount Everest) tells how she liked to be helped on and off trains with her luggage following sex-change surgery.

The medical establishment appears to encourage such stereotyping since the more feminine the appearance and behavior of the applicant, the more likely his request for surgery will be granted. Male-to-female transsexuals are required to divorce their spouse before sex-change surgery to prevent a legal lesbian marriage (Bolin, 1996). Surgical treatment of transsexuals actually confirms traditional social constructions of masculinity and femininity. It opts for massive, permanent changes in the body rather than acceptance of the idea that roles and bodies may be independent and that the connection is imposed by the cultural standards for each sex.

Follow-up reports on sex-change surgery indicate relative satisfaction with the new body. But, for many, there is less consistent change in sexual orientation than has been reported. In one intensive study of seven male-to-female transsexuals, only one was exclusively heterosexual (defined by attraction to biological males). Three were exclusively lesbian and lived with women who did not define themselves as lesbian, one was bisexual living with a self-defined lesbian, and two were living with each other (Bolin, 1996).

Some aspects of sex identity change also illustrate the social meaning of gender. In one recent study, female-to-male transsexuals complained of their difficulty in finding intimacy in their friendships with men although they had no difficulty establishing or maintaining sexual and/or romantic relationships with women (Devor, 1996). Another study found that taking a male body was correlated with higher economic status for women, whereas the change to a female body was associated with lower economic status for men (Blanchard, 1985). Even for the same person, being a man (no matter how it is achieved) is associated with a higher income.

The Transgender Movement

Some transsexual and intersex individuals have moved from personal to societal change. They have begun to challenge what they see as an arbitrary caste system of two sexes based on reproduction and the biological body. They question the idea that there is any necessary relationship between gender, the genitals, and other markers of sexuality. They wish to create a worldview that allows for the possibility of numerous genders and multiple social identities (Bolin, 1996; Califia, 1997).

Some of these people do not wish to call themselves "women," but do not wish to become "men." One of the most visible and articulate proponents of this viewpoint is Kate Bornstein, male-to-female transsexual, who has written a book entitled *Gender Outlaw: On Men, Women and the Rest of Us* (1994). Here is the way she describes herself:

> I know that I'm not a man, about that much I am very clear, and I've come to the conclusion that I'm probably not a woman either, at least not according to a lot of people's rules on this sort of thing. The trouble is, we're living in a world that insists we be one or the other—a world that doesn't bother to tell us exactly what one or the other is. (Bornstein, 1994, p. 8)

Bornstein also calls the idea that "we are trapped in the wrong body" a myth:

> I'll bet that's more likely an unfortunate metaphor that conveniently conforms to cultural expectations, rather than an honest reflection of our transgendered feelings. (Bornstein, 1994, p. 66)

Those in the transgender movement question the need for people to be equipped with penises and vaginas appropriate to their gender and suitable for heterosexual intercourse. They often violate the rules by which sex and gender are constructed in our society. The transgender movement challenges taken-for-granted cultural definitions of sex and gender. Many people find their questioning of the "natural" order disturbing.

Gender Blending and Body Image

The transgendered movement aims to change society. Many individuals who question sex or gender, however, are more concerned about their own personal choices and lives. Women appear to be much more flexible in many aspects of sex than men are. There is, for example, much less evidence for a genetic basis for lesbianism than for gayness. Women also appear to be more able than men to maintain same or bisexual orientations without questioning their fundamental identity as women (Devor, 1996). Of course, they are also permitted much more latitude in gender roles. For these reasons, women appear to be much less active than gay men and male-to-female transsexuals in the transgender movement.

This does not mean, however, that women never alter their gender representations. For example, some women wear clothing and bear themselves in a way that identifies them to others as butch lesbians or men although their identity is that of a lesbian woman (Devor, 1996). Other women may represent themselves as men without engaging in any kind of medical or surgical treatment. An example of this received a great deal of attention recently with the publication of a book about Billy Tipton—a jazz musician who lived as a man until he died (Middlebrook, 1998). Tipton married several times and engaged in sexual activity with his wives who claimed to have been unaware of his femaleness. He also maintained relationships with relatives and colleagues who knew him to have been female. Tipton did not, however, identify himself as a lesbian.

On the other hand, some women are often mistaken for men, but see their sex as female and their gender role as compatible with being a woman. They may or may not be lesbians. These women do not pass as men in a consistent or purposeful fashion. But because of their height, body build, and nonverbal behaviors, they are often mistaken for men or boys during brief encounters of an impersonal and public nature (Devor, 1987). Gender-blending women often explain their gender nonconformity by saying that they oppose traditional standards of femininity and like the advantages they gain through maleness. For example, as men they gain freedom of movement, a feeling of safety on the streets at night, and safety from the threat of rape.

How can women be mistaken for men? Under our current gender schema, men are the unmarked or normative gender. Thus, individuals who do not clearly designate themselves as women by their clothing, cosmetics, and adornment will be perceived as men unless the physical markers of femaleness are overwhelmingly obvious (Devor, 1996). Gender-blending women are unusual in that they have regular experiences of being either male or female. They are in an excellent position to report on the dichotomous response to the two sexes in our society. They also show us how, in everyday life, sex may be irrelevant to the ascription of gender. Assumptions about the separateness of the sexes permit people to explain away any lingering misaligned bodily cues. For example, a prominent chest on a woman who has been identified as a man may be seen as large pectoral muscles or simply fat on the upper body.

Although these women are not transsexuals, their lives may illustrate the social pressures that produce ambivalence about gender. As girls they enjoyed physical activity, and they were tomboys throughout their early years. The majority played mostly with boys or were loners (these stories are similar to those told by female-to-male transsexuals and some lesbians as well). About half came from homes where their fathers acted as though they would have preferred them to be sons. Many of these women were tall—only one was smaller than the average North American woman. This combination of behavioral preferences and physical characteristics appears to have led them to become "gender blenders."

Body image may play an important role in the development of sexual identity. For example, one study found that traditional and nontraditional girls (ages 4 to 12) came from very similar family backgrounds (Green, Williams, & Goodman, 1982). The mothers of nontraditional girls, however, reported that adults commented that their daughters would make handsome boys. Physical attractiveness in childhood is associated with the development of a feminine gender identity in boys (Zucker, Wild, Bradley, & Lowry, 1993). Similarly, girls with a masculine gender identity are perceived as less attractive than feminine girls by raters who are unaware of their gender identification (Fridell, Zucker, Bradley, & Maing, 1996; McDermid, Zucker, Bradley, & Maing, 1998).

You may remember that John/Joan had great difficulty during adolescence because of peers who could not see his gender presentation as consistent with that of a female. Puberty is also reported to be problematic by female gender blenders and female-to-male transsexuals because their developing breasts make it impossible for them to continue to believe that they can be male (Devor, 1997). One of the more obvious (but frequently neglected) truisms in the study of the biological bases of behavior is that one cannot remove the organism from his or her environment. The organism's body structure (and in the case of human beings, social reactions to that structure) forms part of that environment.

If individuals' gender identity conflicts with desirable bodily norms for a member of their sex within a society, they may have gender identity problems. Lack of attractiveness is a major stigma for females in our society. It is significant that girls with CAH who were *virilized* (made more biologically male) showed higher masculinity scores than their less-affected counterparts (Hurtig & Rosenthal, 1987). It should not be surprising, therefore, that unattractive Joan would reject her feminine role. It is a simple fact of binary logic that if you feel everything is wrong the way you are, maybe the correct way is the other way.

Hermaphrodites with Attitude

Intersex individuals have begun to question the rigid two-sex system. Some have joined with the Intersex Society of North America (ISNA), which publishes a newsletter called "Hermaphrodites with Attitude." This group's goal is to "end the idea that it is monstrous to be different" (Colapinto, 1997). Some of its members have publicly acknowledged their genital ambiguities to help others to see them as people rather than as medical curiosities. Members of the group include Cheryl Chase, a leading activist, who was born with a somewhat vaginalike opening behind a male-like urinary tract and a phallic structure that could be described as either an enlarged clitoris (if she was assigned as a girl) or a small penis (if assigned as a boy). See "Making a Difference" on p. 168 for more about Chase.

Other members of ISNA include:

Heidi Walcutt (genetically male, but born with uterine and ovarian tissue and a micropenis, who describes herself as a "true American patchwork quilt of gender") and Martha Coventry, who was born with a penis-sized clitoris but a fully functioning female reproductive system and is the mother of two girls. Kira Triea was assigned as a boy at age 2 and did not learn of her intersexuality until puberty, when she began to menstruate through her phallus. (Colapinto, 1997, p. 95)

A major aim of ISNA is to abolish all cosmetic genital surgery on infants. As noted earlier in the case of John/Joan, newborn infants cannot consent to surgery that may have irreversible effects on their ability to enjoy sex or have children.

Physicians who deal with intersexed infants, like everyone else in our society, have difficulty dealing with gender ambiguity. They assign sexually ambiguous infants to a sexual category based largely on how well they can construct an adequate genital appearance and function for a member of that category. While these physicians recognize that they are assigning and constructing gender, they attempt to make the categorization nonproblematic for the parents and, eventually, for the intersexed persons themselves. They do so by informing their clients that medical science has uncovered the child's real sex and that their manipulations will "improve" this fundamental design (Kessler, 1990).

The decision to assign an infant as a male or a female is largely based on the size of the infant's phallic structure. Figure 5.8 shows the size difference between a medically acceptable penis and clitoris—one and a half centimeters (Kessler, 1998). Most people are not aware of how large a "normal" phallic structure should be. When, for example, college students were interviewed about the normal phallic size of newborn girls and boys, they imagined a much smaller size gap between the largest clitoris and the smallest penis than

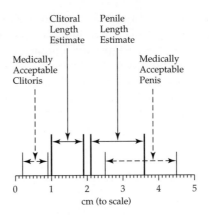

FIGURE 5.8. The size of a normal penis and clitoris at birth and students' estimates of the size of newborns' penis and clitoris.

physicians did. In fact, 35 percent of the students allowed for some overlap between their estimates of clitoral and penile length. The researcher asked: "Would people like these notice that an infant's genitals were the wrong' size unless told so by a physician?" (Kessler, 1998, p. 100).

The language used by physicians to describe the genital anomalies of newborn infants illustrates cultural commitment to a two-sex schema. They describe an overly large clitoris as "disfiguring and embarrassing" or as "a button of unsightly tissue." They state that, "Female babies born with an ungainly masculine enlargement of the clitoris evoke grave concern in their parents." And they indicate that they will attempt to preserve the capacity for erotic stimulation and sexual gratification if it "does not interfere with cosmetic, psychological, social, and sexual adjustment" (Kessler, 1998, pp. 35–37).

Genital anomalies are rarely life-threatening. Newborns are unlikely to be embarrassed by them. The surgery appears to be designed to help parents deal with cultural norms that dictate they must have a boy or a girl. No responsible investigator has suggested that an intersex child should be raised as an "it." Instead, some experts in the field argue that surgery should be withheld until the child has formed a sexual identity and can give his or her informed consent (Diamond, 1999; Kessler, 1998). Whether the person wants genital surgery would then depend on the sexual satisfaction derived from the genitals and, perhaps, the preferred sex of his or her partner.

CULTURAL CONSTRUCTIONS OF GENDER

Not all cultures agree with the idea that all people are either men or women. Earlier in this chapter we discussed the alternative sexual category of "Turnim man." Other traditional societies, such as the Zunis, also see sex as naturally malleable. They believe that a series of interventions, begun before and continuing after birth, are necessary to ensure that the child will have a sex (Roscoe, 1996). Many Native American societies constructed alternative genders, independent of a person's physical body. One such category is called the *berdache*—biological males who adopted the clothes and some of the roles of women and who had sexual relations with other men. They could, however, revert back to the masculine role without penalty or switch back and forth between roles. Male berdaches have been documented in nearly 150 North American Indian societies (Roscoe, 1996).

Attempts to classify such individuals as homosexuals, transvestites, or transsexuals fail because their behavior fits none of these ethnocentric norms (Williams, 1987). Difficulties arise because scholars cannot agree whether sexual orientation, dress, gender role, or even identity is a core characteristic. For example, berdaches do not appear to question their biological maleness, and they do not invariably cross-dress. In their societies, not all homosexuals are berdaches. Moreover, berdaches were not expected to have sex with each other, but only with "normal" males.

One extensive participant-observer study of berdaches concluded that some traditional Native American societies are neither as biologically reductionist nor as bipolar in their gender system as current Western cultures are (Williams, 1986). The berdache can be seen as a third, alternative gender. Instead of by biology, this gender was defined by occupational role. (Berdaches were often involved in creative arts and crafts and were seen to be especially talented and original.) This gender was often conferred by religious authorities before the child was physically mature. Spiritual authorization was more important than cross-dressing, and many berdaches dressed in combinations of male and female attire (Roscoe, 1996).

The berdache role is, however, part of a broader gender system of male and female inequality. In Native American societies in which a positive valuation of the berdache existed, women were also of high status. Men who became berdache had an enhanced status. Because women were valued, androgyny was allowed to men. In contrast, if women were devalued by the society, feminine characteristics in men were denied (Williams, 1986).

There seems to have been less room for a fourth gender category in these societies. Fewer than half the societies that had male berdaches had female berdaches—women who acted out some aspects of the masculine role (Roscoe, 1996). This omission may also be related to status. It is difficult for women to acquire the privileges of maleness.

Interestingly, a category for "social males" exists in isolated rural villages of Albania and Montenegro (part of what used to be Yugoslavia). Under certain special circumstances—for example, when there are no surviving male children—a young woman may be permitted to wear men's clothing and do the work of a man, including military service (Gremaux, 1996). Such women are known as "pledged virgins" rather than "women" (see Figure 5.9). They gain the legal and social status of men by giving up sexual experience.

Alternative cultural arrangements involving differing assumptions about what constitutes sex and the potential of additional sex/gender categories are quite common in non-Western societies. Many Polynesian societies have a category of "gender liminal" persons who are thought to excel in artistic skills such as weaving mats. Although they cross-dress occasionally and have sex with men, their membership in the category is determined by their behavior in domestic and social areas. Like the berdache, they can opt out of the category through marriage (Besnier, 1996).

FIGURE 5.9. Albanian pledged virgin who had served in the military. In a number of cultures, sex is determined by the ability to reproduce, and sex assignment may be more flexible for those who do not engage in sexual activity.

There have also been studies of *hijiras*—a sect found in northern India. Men became hijiras through their impotence with women. Hijiras include individuals defined as intersex, transsexual, or homosexual in our own society. What is important about hijiras is their legitimized role in a society that defines personhood in terms of the ability to reproduce. They are seen as "not men" because their male organ does not work and as "not women" because they cannot bear children. In earlier periods, the group had religious functions and were supposed to castrate themselves and dedicate their "useless male organs" to a mother Goddess. Currently, many hijiras hide the fact that they have kept their genitals (which would make them unfit for religious rituals) and function mostly as prostitutes who take the receptive role with other men. They wear women's clothing, prefer women's occupations, and take female names. Unlike traditional Indian women, however, they also engage in dancing, cursing, and smoking in public (Nanda, 1996).

Varying cultural constructions of sex and gender are intriguing. They provide alternatives to current beliefs about a stable biological core to which one simply adds deviations to broaden the picture. Instead, they show that sex can be unstable and culturally specific (Brod, 1987).

The simple word *sex* hides great complexity. Sex is used to refer to reproductive category, physiological properties, reproductive and nonreproductive behaviors, and, in human beings, our sense of who we are. It also refers to a system of categorization that differs from one culture to another.

But even if discussion is limited to the biological aspects of sex, it is probably impossible to determine what causes a person to be male or female. Instead, think about sex as neither entirely nor permanently male or female. The view that the sexes are opposite to each other is just one of many possible viewpoints. Sexual dichotomies are a result of both androcentric and ethnocentric bias. It may sound strange, but try thinking about "all" the sexes rather than the two sexes for a while!

CONNECTING THEMES

- *Gender is more than sex.* Just as gender is more than just sex, "sex" is more than just sex, too. Studies of various animal species and sexually anomalous human beings indicate that an individual's sex is a composite of biological and social factors. Probably no one single factor determines maleness or femaleness.
- *Language and naming are sources of power.* The assumption that males and females are "opposite" sexes is a good example of the power to name. Beliefs about biologically determined differences between the sexes are maintained by the media's attention to findings about the anatomical bases for such differences and its lack of attention to social and environmental factors.
- *Women are not all alike.* All cultures do not think about sex and gender the same way we do. Human beings with the same biologically induced anomalies may have different experiences based on their culture's beliefs about sex and gender. The connections between biology, physical appearance, social roles, and sexual orientation may be neither stable nor universal.
- *Psychological research can foster social change.* Biology is a double-edged sword in the cause of social change. For example, biological arguments can be used to define homosexuality as morally acceptable (because it is not a matter of choice) or as a reason to commit mass murder (homosexuals were routinely killed by the Nazis because of their alleged biological inferiority). Equality is more a political and social issue than a biological one. Whatever their biology, everyone deserves equal rights under the law.

SUGGESTED READINGS

LEGUIN, URSULA. (1969). *The left hand of darkness.* New York: Ace Books. This award-winning science fiction novel takes place in a world in which the same person can be either male or female. It challenges our assumptions about the relationship between sex and gender.

KESSLER, SUZANNE J. (1998). *Lessons from the intersexed.* New Brunswick, NJ: Rutgers University Press. A brief and clearly written book that takes a critical look at the medical response to intersex infants and the social assumptions that underlie medical and surgical practices.

FAUSTO-STERLING, ANNE. (1999). *Sexing the body: Gender politics and the construction of sexuality.* New York: Basic Books. This book is by a molecular biochemist who is one of the leading critics of reductionist views of sex. It is current, knowledgeable, and clearly written.

Becoming Gendered: Childhood

- ACQUIRING GENDER: SOME THEORETICAL PERSPECTIVES
  Social Learning
  Cognitive Development
  Interactive Models of Gender
    Development
- THE PREFERENCE FOR SONS
  Gender Before Birth
  Selective Mortality: The Missing Girls
- GENDER STEREOTYPES
  Attributions about the Newborn
    Infant
  The Eye of the Beholder: Fathers'
    versus Mothers' Perceptions
  Is Emotion Gendered?
  The Socialization of Helplessness
- HOW DOES SOCIETY FOSTER GENDER TYPING?
  Gender and Children's Clothing
  Gender and Toys
  Gendered Play
  Sexism in Media Messages for
    Children
- WHAT IS SEX SEGREGATION?
  The Development of Social Networks
  The Impact of Peers
  Social Mechanisms for Maintaining
    Boundaries
  Social Dominance and Social
    Influence

- ARE THERE GENDER DIFFERENCES IN SOCIAL BEHAVIORS?
  Aggression
  Instrumentality
- STAGES IN THE DEVELOPMENT OF GENDER UNDERSTANDING
  Cognitions about Gender
  The Behavioral Influence of
    Cognitions about Gender
- IS GENDER NONCONFORMITY DIFFERENT FOR BOYS AND GIRLS?
  The Difference between Sissies and
    Tomboys
  Who Is a Tomboy?
  The Values of Being a Tomboy
  Negative Aspects of Hyperfemininity
- RESISTING GENDER RULES
  Individual Differences in Parental
    Behavior and Its Consequences
  Sociostructural Factors and
    Individual Cognitions
- FACTORS THAT INCREASE GENDER FLEXIBILITY
  Flexibility Begins at Home
  The Effect of Ethnicity and Class
  The Case for Positive Social Deviance
- CONNECTING THEMES
- SUGGESTED READINGS

Early one midsummer's night, Daddy Sam settled on the plush gold carpet in the nursery to play with Baby while the evening bath was being prepared. Reaching for Baby's teddy bear, he slowly and rhythmically bounced it toward Baby, softly saying, "Here comes Teddy! Teddy's coming to see you! Look, look at Teddy. He's coming to play with Baby." Giggling in delight, Baby opens her arms to hug the oncoming teddy bear. Next door, a different Daddy and a different Baby played on the nursery floor. Holding Baby's teddy bear, Daddy John marched the bear resolutely toward Baby in a series of quick, controlled movements, mock growling, "Here comes Teddy! Teddy's coming to *get* you! Better get Teddy, before *he* gets *you!*" Screeching at the challenge, Baby reaches out and tumbles on his now captive Teddy. (Brooks-Gunn & Mathews, 1979, pp. 5–6)

What does this scenario mean? It shows that fathers play with their babies. But it also illustrates the ways that parents can treat infant boys and girls differently even when they are apparently engaged in the same games. And it shows how babies respond to the behaviors of their parents. Even in infancy, gender does not exist in a social vacuum.

How do babies become gendered? At first glance the answer to this question is obvious—infants are born either male or female. That is, they are born not only with the anatomy of their sex, but also with behavioral tendencies that are considered characteristic of that sex. But is this true? Most children can be assigned an unambiguous sex at birth (although there are more exceptions than one might expect); however, it is much more difficult to make the same case for behavioral differences between boys and girls. There is only weak documentation for behavioral differences during the first weeks of life, and few consistent sex-related differences appear during the first year. It takes a long time before a child becomes gendered. Nevertheless, by the age of 3 years, most children can label their own gender correctly, recognize many gender stereotypes, and show traits and behaviors considered appropriate for their own gender.

A number of theories exist that try to explain what happens in the early years that leads to the establishment of gender. Most researchers no longer try to explain the development of gender differences in terms of unconscious psychodynamic processes (cf. Freud, 1933/1965). One exception is Nancy Chodorow, whose ideas were discussed in Chapter 4. The focus in this chapter is on those theories that have generated a great deal of research on how children learn to be boys and girls. Although neither social learning nor cognitive development explains all the processes by which children acquire gender, together they explain a great deal.

ACQUIRING GENDER: SOME THEORETICAL PERSPECTIVES

Social Learning

Social learning theorists explain children's development of gender identity and gender-typed behaviors as the result of moment-to-moment, day-to-day interactions between the developing child and his or her immediate social environment—mother, father, and other caretakers; the media; school; and playmates. This theory proposes that gender typing, just like other social and cognitive behaviors, is learned through reinforcement, punishment, observation, and imitation. There is considerable evidence that parents do reward and punish some behaviors differently for girls and boys. You can probably think of examples from your own experience. Our students tell us that, in their families, boys were less likely to be punished for being messy or careless and more likely to be overtly rewarded for achievement in sports and school. Girls were rewarded for being thoughtful of others' feelings, looking pretty, and taking good care of their possessions and appearance. These students' memories are consistent with systematic research.

Considerable research evidence also exists to support the view that children learn by imitation. A classic study illustrates the operation of both reinforcement and imitation in learning to be aggressive (Bandura, 1965). In this study, children were shown one of three films. In all the films, an adult behaved aggressively by hitting and kicking a large toy clown. In one film, the adult was rewarded; in another, the adult was punished; and in the third, no specific consequences followed the aggression. The children were then given the opportunity to play with the toy clown. Just as social learning theory would predict, children imitated the behavior most when it had been reinforced; that is, children who had seen the first film were more aggressive than those who had seen either of the other films. Overall, boys were more aggressive than girls.

In the next part of the experiment, children were offered small treats for performing as many of the adult model's aggressive behaviors as they could remember. Here, all children were more aggressive, and girls were, overall, nearly as aggressive as boys. The experiment shows that children do imitate adult models even when the children are not directly reinforced for doing so. In particular, they imitate models who are themselves reinforced. Furthermore, children may learn a behavior through observation but show no particular evidence of that learning until the behavior is reinforced—like the girls in the second part of the experiment.

The second major claim of social learning theory is that children identify with (and thus imitate) their same-sex parent in preference to the other parent. Although it sounds intuitively reasonable, little evidence supports this idea (Maccoby & Jacklin, 1974). Children seem to imitate parents fairly indiscriminately, not on the basis of gender.

Cognitive Development

If social learning does not provide a complete explanation for gender typing, what else is going on? Cognitive developmental theorists see children as active participants in gender learning. This theory builds on the idea that children's understanding of gender proceeds through an orderly set of stages (Kohlberg, 1966). Regardless of what stage they have reached, however, children actively strive to interpret and make sense of the world around them. According to this approach, gender identity and gender typing are the outcome of children's active structuring of their physical and social world.

Children understand some things about the concepts of sex and gender long before others. A 2- or 3-year-old child will answer correctly when asked if he or she is a boy or a girl. However, the child may believe that people can change sex by changing their hair styles or clothing. (At age 2, one of our own children maintained stubbornly that the "real" difference between boys and girls was that only girls wear barrettes!) At this stage, children may also believe that boys can grow up to be mommies.

Between the ages of 5 to 7, children develop an understanding of *gender constancy*—they know that gender is permanent. Gender constancy is not a simple result of social learning. Instead it reflects a child's level of cognitive maturity. Once children know that they are, and always will be, one sex or the other, they could turn to the task of matching the cultural expectations for people of their sex.

Thus, children come to value behaviors, objects, and attitudes that are consistent with their sex label. Girls want to do "girl things," wear gender-specific clothes such as frilly dresses, and generally make a sharp distinction between girls and boys. Boys, too, behave as though they are thinking, "I am a boy; therefore I want to do boy things; therefore the opportunity to do boy things (and to gain approval for doing them) is rewarding" (Kohlberg, 1966, p. 89).

Children may begin to exaggerate gender roles at this stage, with boys proclaiming anything remotely associated with girls as "yukky" and girls avoiding "boys'" activities like the plague. Even a child who has been cared for by a female physician may announce that "Only boys can be doctors." This exaggeration may be due to children's need to keep gender categories conceptually distinct (Maccoby, 1980).

According to this theory, identification is an outcome, not a cause, of gender typing. Children tend to model those who are like themselves and who are high in prestige and competence. "For the boy with masculine interests and values the activities of a male model are more interesting and hence more modeled" (Kohlberg, 1966, p. 129). The son's identification with his father thus progresses from identifying with a stereotyped masculine role to identifying with his father's own personification of that role. Feminine identification involves first identifying with a generalized female role, and then with the mother as an example of that role.

External rewards and punishments for gender-typed behavior are relatively unimportant from the cognitive developmental perspective. Rather than being influenced by whatever reinforcers the social environment sends their way, children actively try to fit their beliefs, values, and behaviors to their sex. In their search to become the best possible girl (or boy), children rely on reinforcers only as a guide to how well they are doing. The cognitive developmental perspective does not deny social learning principles; rather, it adds to them by offering the intriguing idea that children willingly socialize themselves to be masculine or feminine.

Much of the research discussed in this chapter supports the idea that children's understanding of gender is related to their cognitive maturity (Fagot, 1985a). However, research does not support the idea that gender constancy is an important foundation for gender typing. Children do not, for example, become gender-typed only after they acquire an understanding of gender constancy. On the contrary, children show a preference for gender-typed objects and activities by the age of 3, while they do not fully understand gender constancy before about the age of 5. In one study, children aged 1 to 4 showed the expected progression from understanding gender labels to understanding gender constancy. However, the children's level of understanding was not related to their adoption of gender-typed behaviors (Fagot, 1985b). Especially for girls, the relationship between understanding gender and becoming gender-typed needs further exploration.

Interactive Models of Gender Development

The processes that mold gender are truly developmental in nature. Both the age of the child and the social environment to which he or she is exposed must be taken into account. Seemingly identical social messages do not have the same meaning at different ages. The child changes in reaction to these messages and, consequently, interprets them differently. In this sense, the meaning of gender is a function of both cognitive level and social learning. Because gender distinctions are everywhere, children acquire a sense of their own gender in quite orderly stages (see Table 6.1).

But societal definitions of what is a gender-appropriate behavior change as the child matures. For example, most people do not expect little girls to wear makeup and high heels, although some think it is "cute" when they do so. But adolescent girls who refuse to wear makeup may be labeled as unfemi-

TABLE 6.1. Percentages of Children Showing Gender-Related Behaviors

Task	Age of child (in months)			
	18 mos.	24 mos.	30 mos.	36 mos.
Cognitive skills				
Gender self-labeling (percentage correct)		68%	88%	93%
Labeling of friend		43%	37%	39%
Nonverbal sorting (placing pictures in boxes)	48%	56%	69%	84%
Sorting to verbal cues	22%	67%	90%	96%
Correct use of gender words				
Mom/Dad		98%	97%	100%
boy/girl		75%	88%	98%
man/woman		53%	79%	94%
he/she		42%	79%	91%
her/him		27%	63%	83%
Stereotype learning				
Clothes (percentage identifying correctly)		37%	59%	74%
Toys		24%	38%	53%
Tasks		—	32%	39%
Occupations		—	27%	35%
Preference behavior				
Percentage of time spent with same-sex toys	32%	42%	45%	62%
Percentage of time spent with other-sex toys	25%	25%	25%	21%
Percentage of same-sex photo choice as playmate			33%	52%
Sex of actual playmates (percentage same sex)		57%	67%	73%

From P. A. Katz, "Raising Feminists," *Psychology of Women Quarterly, 20.* pp. 323–340. Copyright © 1996. Reprinted with the permission of Cambridge University Press.

nine. The process by which gender is constructed is called *interactive* by psychologists. This means that development reflects a continuing interplay between the child and the environment.

Boys and girls are treated differently even before birth. Differential treatment produces behavioral and cognitive differences that, in turn, lead to different social consequences for each sex, making them still more different. You may think of the process of gender construction in terms of the saying "As the twig is bent, so the tree will grow." Little differences become larger as the child grows, until one forgets that the sexes were originally not very different at all.

Children are acutely aware of both their similarities and differences from others (Powlishta, 1995a). They use this information to help construct a sense of self. The media provides many opportunities for children to learn messages about gender-appropriate appearance, roles, and behaviors. Partly because of the repetition of these messages, gender becomes a central dimension in the way children classify themselves and others. Thus, although gender typing may appear to be due to children's cognitive stage, it is also a reaction to the gender distinctions made by everyone around them.

A combination of social and cognitive factors is important because of the need to take into account differences in the ways girls and boys incorporate the various aspects of gender. Female traits, roles, and behaviors are less highly valued in most, if not all, societies. As girls become aware of the categories of masculinity and femininity, they may also recognize the economic, occupational, and status advantages of being male. How then do girls come to value their devalued role enough to want to follow it? Many girls are "tomboys" throughout middle childhood. This identity is a major site of resistance to the devalued aspects of being female.

In the rest of this chapter, we take a closer look at the processes through which children become gendered. Depending on the age of the child, sometimes social learning and sometimes cognitive mechanisms are more important. There is no period in a child's life when he or she is free from messages about gender. And, although the specific mechanisms involved may vary, some themes recur throughout childhood:

Males are the more valued sex, even in our own society.

Pressure for conformity to gender roles occurs earlier for boys and is stronger than that on girls throughout the childhood years.

Parents appear to be largely unaware of the extent to which they treat their young sons and daughters differently.

Differential treatment of boys and girls appears to be consistent with producing a pattern of independence and efficacy in boys and a pattern of emotional sensitivity, nurturance, and helplessness in girls.

The child is not a passive recipient of gender socialization, but actively participates in this socialization by way of his or her views of self, expectations, and behavioral choices.

People are largely unaware of how the culture as a whole mandates dichotomies based on gender and punishes those who do not conform to social expectations.

Look for these patterns from birth through the middle years of childhood. Although the meaning of gender changes as the child grows, not all such changes represent progress. Children acquire more and more gender biases—similar to those of adults—as they mature. This means that the majority of children become increasingly sexist and, thus, fit "better" into a sexist world.

THE PREFERENCE FOR SONS

Gender Before Birth

It may seem strange to think about gender as a characteristic of the unborn child. However, beliefs about the connection between sex and prenatal behavior are quite common. There are many folk recipes for determining whether a pregnant woman is carrying a boy or girl. These predictions are, of course, correct 50 percent of the time. They include:

> The man and woman each take hold of one end of a wishbone and pull it apart. If the longest part comes away in the man's hand, the baby will be a boy.
>
> If you suddenly ask a pregnant woman what she has in her hand and she looks at her right hand first, she will have a boy. If she looks at her left hand it will be a girl.
>
> If a woman is placid during pregnancy she will have a boy, but if she is bad-tempered or cries a lot, she will have a girl.
>
> If her complexion is rosy, she will have a son; if she is pale, a daughter.
>
> If her looks improve, she is expecting a boy; if they worsen, a girl.
>
> If the fetus has started to move by the 40th day it will be a boy and the birth will be easy, but if it doesn't move until the 90th day, it will be a girl. (Brooks-Gunn & Mathews, 1979, pp. 74–75)

You will probably have noticed that girls are symbolized by negative or less desirable characteristics.

The preference for males is not limited to predictions about the pregnant woman. There is still a clear preference for male children in the United States and Canada, although this is beginning to change among women at least. In the late 1960s, 90 percent of the male college students and 78 percent of the female students questioned stated that they would prefer a boy if they could have only one child (Hammer, 1970). A more recent study of 1,045 Canadian women (Krishnan, 1987) found some preference for sons, although the women generally preferred to have children of both sexes.

The most recent studies of college students found that the preference for sons was due primarily to men's responses. Eighty-six percent of the male students surveyed said they would prefer a son if they could only have one child, while only 42 percent of the female students had such a preference (Pooler, 1991). Men preferred sons over daughters for their firstborn child, as the majority in a three-child family, and as their only child (Hamilton & Mayfield, 1999). Like men, women preferred a firstborn son and sons as the majority in three-child families but did not prefer a son as their only child. Only pregnant couples did not indicate this preference for males.

Although the preference for sons may be declining in North America, it is still strong in the developing world. Surveys in Botswana, Tunisia, and Morocco indicated that women, as well as men, prefer sons (Campbell & Campbell, 1997; Obermeyer, 1996). This desire for sons is strongly associated with family size because parents want to ensure the survival of at least one male child. In Israel, when infant survival was ensured, the preference for males and for a larger number of children also declined (Okun, 1996).

Preference for boys is most extreme in Asian countries like Korea and Taiwan. A common Korean saying is "A girl lets you down twice, once at birth and the second time when she marries." Daughters are described as "water spilled on the ground" in Taiwan and as "maggots in the rice" in China. In some Arab cultures, an unexpected pause in the conversation might be followed by the comment, "Why the silence? Has a girl been born?" (Sohoni, 1994). The reasons given for the preference for sons were similar in all the countries investigated: continuation of the family name, economic reasons (including support of parents in old age), and as companions for fathers. In all the countries surveyed, men showed a greater preference for boys than women did (Arnold & Kuo, 1984).

Selective Mortality: The Missing Girls

Probably the most compelling evidence demonstrating the preference for sons are data on voluntary abortion. Because of recent advances in sex determination, parents can be informed about the sex of their prospective offspring during the first few months of pregnancy. In Asian societies, where the preference for sons is most extreme, selective abortion of female fetuses is also extreme. In one study published in the British journal *Nature,* which used statistics provided by an Indian social worker, out of a sample of 8,000 abortions, 7,997 were on female fetuses (Hrdy, 1988). Sex-selective abortion is not officially sanctioned. In fact, more than one state in India has banned prenatal sex determination. Sex-selective abortion is consistent with cultural practices permitting female infanticide. It has been estimated that sex-biased infanticide has been practiced by about 9 percent of the world's cultures, and, more often than not, the unwanted sex has been female (Hrdy, 1988).

Discrimination can also be indirect. In a number of cultures, boys are breast-fed twice as long as girls (see Figure 6.1). In many societies, men and boys eat first, and whatever is left is then distributed to the women and girls. Invariably, women and girls eat less food, which is of inferior quality and nutritive value (United Nations, 1991b). Historical records indicate that among some south Asian groups, four times as many boys survive as girls (Hrdy, 1988). Although more girls survive when agricultural, urban, and industrial development increases, the survival rate of girls does not improve relative to that of boys (Kishor, 1993). Based on demographic information, the United Nations has estimated that more than 100 million females are missing from the world's population (Sen, 1990).

The selective preservation of male infants is beginning to have major social consequences for those countries where it has been practiced most intensively. A recent report from the Chinese Academy of Social Sciences (Agence-

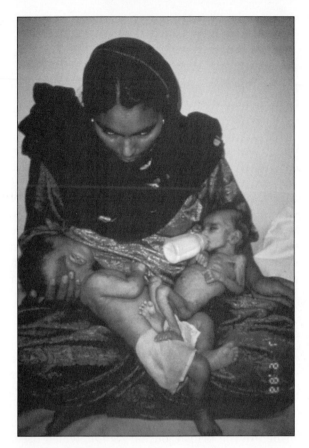

FIGURE 6.1. A mother's grief. This photo from Islamabad, Pakistan, tells a poignant story about the age-old bias in favor of the male child. The child being bottle-fed is a girl. Her twin brother was breast-fed. The woman was told by her mother-in-law that she did not have enough milk for both the children, so she should breast-feed the boy. The infant girl died the next day.

France Press, 1999) revealed that the current gender ratio of males to females is 120:100. This means that 111 million men—a number greater than the entire population of Mexico—cannot hope to find a wife. We presume that this will make daughters more valuable, but it is impossible to predict what other impact such an excess of males will have on this society.

Could this happen here? There is some evidence from our own society that prenatal information about sex can influence the decision about whether to abort a fetus. In an article in *Harvard Magazine* about the ethical issues involved in the ability to evaluate one's children before birth, the author related the following incident:

A genetic counselor at Brigham's and Women's Hospital, Bieber ruefully recalls a seeming lack of communication between two of his clients. Although the expectant father never mentioned the fetus's sex in counseling sessions, he made private efforts to find out whether it was female. It became apparent that the husband would pressure the wife to abort a female fetus. Bieber decided to inform the parents that the fetus was, in fact, female. The couple subsequently decided on an abortion. (Lauerman, 1990, p. 46)

It is obvious that if this girl had been permitted to be born, she would not have entered a gender-blind family.

GENDER STEREOTYPES

Attributions about the Newborn Infant

The sex of a child is his or her most conspicuous feature at birth. One study conducted in English delivery rooms found that 82 percent of the parents' comments within twenty minutes of the baby's birth were made about the infant's sex (Woollett, White, & Lyon, 1982). Fathers more than mothers differentiate between their newborn sons and daughters. One review of the literature on parental interaction with infants showed that in sixteen studies involving mothers, seven found that they treated boys and girls differently. In fifteen studies involving fathers, fourteen showed patterns of gender distinction (Power, 1981).

Popular culture mandates attention to the sex of the newborn. When one of the authors had her first child, she found it impossible to locate a gender-neutral birth announcement. There are many other characteristics besides sex that could be used to describe an infant, such as its size, its coloring, the presence or absence of hair, and so forth. One innovative birth announcement compared the baby to a new model car. Nevertheless, even this relatively ungendered announcement was pink and proclaimed "It's a girl!" rather than "It's a beautiful baby!"

Birth congratulation cards also remain sexist. One recent study looked at girl and boy cards selected from eighteen stores in four municipalities that varied in size, ethnicity, and social class (Bridges, 1993). Visual images of activity were more commonly shown on boy cards, while verbal messages of sweetness and sharing were more likely to be present on girl cards. A few of the cards displayed clear gender-stereotypic messages. For example, two apparently comparable cards (one for girls and one for boys) stated: "Soon she'll be able to say simple two-syllable words: 'ma-ma, da-da, . . . vi-sa'" or "Soon he'll be able to say simple two-syllable words: 'ma-ma, da-da, . . . toyo-ta'."

Despite differential responses to boys and girls, young infants show few, if any, consistent sex-related differences. The differences found are often complex and hard to interpret. For example, differences between boys and girls found at two days after delivery disappeared at four days (Lewis, 1987). Significant gender differences in young infants are more likely to be reported in countries where circumcision rates are high (Richards, Bernal, & Brackbill, 1975). Thus, it is difficult to determine whether reports from the United States of greater activity and irritability among infant boys than among infant girls can be attributed to their gender or the impact of early medical intervention.

The Eye of the Beholder: Fathers' versus Mothers' Perceptions

Although behavioral differences between baby boys and girls are minimal, evidence is accumulating that parents treat their sons and daughters differently from the earliest days of life. The evidence for gender-differentiated socialization is stronger today that it was fifteen years ago. Parents consistently promote differences in activities and interests in their sons and daughters. They also respond differently to girls' and boys' emotional and social behaviors.

Parental stereotyping of their children begins at birth. Parents have been found to rate newborn daughters as finer featured, less strong, more delicate, and more feminine than newborn sons. They did not, however, distinguish between boys and girls when freely describing their firstborn infant (Karraker, Vogel, & Lake, 1995). Mothers used more neutral terms to describe their infant one week later, but fathers continued to use gendered descriptors. The authors concluded that fathers' stereotyping of infants has declined recently but has not disappeared. But the amount of stereotyping found in this study is discouraging when one considers that these fathers were an unusual group. They had been present at their child's birth and had spent thirteen hours with the infant in the week afterward.

One of the reasons that evidence for parental socialization of gender typing has increased in recent years is the greater attention of researchers to the role of fathers. Meta-analysis of a large number of studies indicated that fathers differentiate between their sons and daughters much more than mothers do (Lytton & Romney, 1991). In a sample of parents of 2-year-olds in Great Britain, for example, fathers more than mothers saw their children as conforming to gender stereotypes (McGuire, 1988). Boys, in particular, were stereotyped by their fathers. More than two-thirds of the boys' fathers saw them as very masculine, while only 40 percent of the girls' fathers saw them as very feminine. Even for these very young children, the commonest masculine attribution was physical ability or athletic skill. Feminine attributes for girls usually involved comments about physical attractiveness or appearance (mothers) or nurturant doll play, gentleness, and doing housework (fathers). These 2-year-olds appeared to be receiving some fairly clear information from their parents about how they were supposed to behave.

Is Emotion Gendered?

Consistent with gender-stereotypic beliefs, parents have been found to emphasize different emotions when they talk to their daughters and sons. Parents used a greater number and variety of emotion words when talking to their 40-month-old daughters than when they spoke to sons of the same age. They also mentioned the sad aspects of events more with girls than boys (Kuebli & Fivush, 1992). Although these girls and boys did not differ in their emotional vocabulary at the time of this study, by 70 months of age, these girls used more unique emotional terms than the boys did (Adams, Kuebli, Boyle, & Fivush, 1995).

When children are in preschool, mother-daughter dyads are found to be much more likely to discuss other children and their behaviors than are mother-son pairs (Flannagan, Baker-Ward, & Graham, 1995). Mothers were especially likely to make emotional references when discussing interpersonal relationships and the emotions experienced by their daughters (Flannagan & Perese, 1998). In contrast, the mothers of sons had more emotionally elaborate discussions with them on topics involving learning.

Conversational style influences children's understanding of the relative importance of particular experiences. For example, children whose parents elaborated in conversations about the past (conducted more often with daughters than sons) remembered more about their experiences (Reese, Haden, & Fivush, 1993). Thus, girls may be learning that other people's feelings are an important part of their school day, whereas boys are learning a relatively antisocial focus on achievement.

The messages that mothers convey to their daughters may be particularly powerful because, consistent with Chodorow's theory, mother-daughter pairs appear to be closer emotionally than mother-son dyads. In one observational study conducted in Sweden, for example, mothers of 9-month-old infants displayed significantly more physical and eye contact with their daughters than with their sons (Lindahl & Heimann, 1997). Mothers of daughters were also rated as more sensitive than the mothers of sons. In turn, these girls were rated as more compliant than boys. Videotapes of parent-child pairs of preschoolers engaged in play showed that compared to boys, four- and five-year-old girls remained physically closer to their mothers, engaged in more mutual eye contact, and were rated as higher in general enjoyment (Benenson, Morash, & Petrakos, 1998).

Children acquire beliefs about emotions that are consistent with this pattern of parental socialization. Preschoolers of both sexes were found to believe that females were much more likely to feel sad than males and that men were particularly incapable of expressing sadness (Karbon, Fabes, Carlo, & Martin, 1992). They saw adults of both sexes as capable of becoming angry but believed that men became angry more frequently and intensely than women did.

Are these perceptions correct? There is no consistent evidence that males report being angry more than females do. Social location appears to be a better predictor of anger than gender. Urban children reported more anger in their responses to hypothetical situations such as being hit with a stick by accident or not being invited to a party than did rural youngsters (Buntaine & Costenbader, 1997). However, boys from both locations reported more aggressive responses (such as hitting, kicking, and punching), whereas girls suggested sulking and pouting as responses to the same negative experiences. Boys were also less likely to consider intent. They expressed the same level of anger regardless of whether the negative event was due to an accident or happened on purpose.

Females of all ages (6–12, 14–16, and adults) also reported more fear in response to stories portraying frightening or anger-provoking situations (Brody, Lovas, & Hay, 1995). Both sexes reported more fear of males than females across situations. However, girls' fear of both sexes was more intense than boys' fear of males. The consistent gender differences found were remarkable because the stories were different for each age group. Females of all ages felt more vulnerable than males did. Their sense of vulnerability may be due to their lower status and power, smaller physical size, or their socialization as the "weaker sex."

Beliefs about differences in the emotional responses of boys and girls may lead to different adult responses to identical behaviors. For example, a videotaped snowball fight between two boys was viewed by adults as less aggressive than the same behavior described as being between a boy and a girl or two girls (Condry & Ross, 1985). Those who do not approve of aggression in children might well stop the "girls" from "fighting" while permitting the "boys" to "horse around."

The Socialization of Helplessness

Both parents and other adults appear to believe that girls require more help than boys. Studies in the home have found that fathers are more likely to hold their year-old daughters in contrast to their sons and to give them toys (Snow, Jacklin, & Maccoby, 1983). An observational study made of families visiting a zoo, an amusement park, or a nursery rhyme theme park reported that male toddlers were more likely to be allowed to walk alone than female toddlers were (Mitchell, Obradovich, Herring, Tromborg, & Burns, 1992).

Gender-differentiated beliefs associated with little girls' greater need of help are dramatically illustrated by a clever laboratory experiment entitled "Sex Differences: A Study of the Ear of the Beholder" (Condry, Condry, & Pogatshnik, 1983). While performing an unrelated task, young men and women heard a tape-recording of an infant awakening next door. The infant had previously been labeled a boy or a girl. Although they denied any belief about differences in fragility between girls and boys, the young women responded more quickly to a "girl" than to a "boy." Young men responded equally slowly to infants regardless of their gender.

Such differential responses to little girls and boys may subtly reinforce the distinction between them by means of self-fulfilling prophecies. If girls are seen as more fearful than boys, they will be helped more quickly and more often—especially by their fathers. By being taken care of more, girls learn that they are needier than boys. Greater adult assistance confirms their belief in their own helplessness.

This kind of socialization into helplessness appears to be exaggerated when the toddler is an attractive girl. Adults (mothers, fathers, and caretakers) were more likely to interact with attractive girls aged 12 to 38 months by helping them, telling them what to do and how to do it, and stimulating their interest in the object at hand. These behaviors were not directed toward attractive boys or toward unattractive children of either sex (Leinbach & Fagot, 1991). The adult attention seemed to foster attractive girls' communication skills, but giving them help when they did not need it may also make them less competent and more dependent.

HOW DOES SOCIETY FOSTER GENDER TYPING?

Gender and Children's Clothing

Gender-typed messages are everywhere. Without making the request explicit, researchers have found it is virtually impossible to get parents to provide a neutral environment when dressing their young child. An anecdote from a child development textbook recounts the frustration of one researcher who encountered this problem. The investigator, who was studying perceptions about gender in infants and did not want her observers to know whether they were watching boys or girls, complained that even in the first few days of life some infant girls were brought to the laboratory with pink bows tied to their wisps of hair or taped to their little bald heads. Later, when she made another attempt at concealment of gender by asking mothers to dress their infants in overalls, girls appeared in pink and boys in blue overalls, and as the frustrated experimenter said, "Would you believe overalls with ruffles?" (Hetherington & Parke, 1975, pp. 354–355).

Another investigator made a similar point more recently: ". . . in our laboratory, ruffles on girls' overalls are common, and we have even seen beruffled jogging suits!" (Fagot & Leinbach, 1987, p. 93). Girls' more delicate and restrictive attire can inhibit play and promote gender-stereotypic behavior. A similar point can be made about the ruffles and white furniture found in girls' rooms as compared with the sturdy brown pine found in boys' rooms.

One study demonstrated how clearly young children are "color coded" (Shakin, Shakin, & Sternglanz, 1985). The researchers categorized the clothing found on infants in shopping malls. Baby girls were dressed in pink, puffed sleeves, ruffles, and lace (even on tiny socks), while boys were dressed in blue or sometimes red, but nothing ruffled or pink. Similar gender-related differences in clothing colors have also been found among young children in French-speaking Canada (Pomerleau, Bloduc, Malcuit, & Cossette, 1990). Gender-typed clothing ensures gender-appropriate treatment from strangers. If you wish to see for yourself just how important this aspect of appropriate identification is, deliberately "mis-sex" an infant the next time you are in a public place. At the very least, you can expect a firm correction.

Appropriate distinctions are very important if two genders are to be constructed. Gender-appropriate behaviors must be elicited from the infant and reinforced when they occur. As noted earlier, infant girls and boys have few, if any, behaviors that distinguish between them. In neutral clothing it would be difficult to tell them apart. Knowledge of their sex may not be sufficient to guarantee that strangers react differentially to them. A review of studies involving neutrally clothed infants who were labeled either "male" or "female" indicated that adults did not consistently react differently to them based on their label (Stern & Karraker, 1989).

Gender and Toys

Infancy

Most parents explicitly deny any intention to distinguish between their sons and daughters. In one study of parents of 6-month-old infants, 87.5 percent stated that it was important for infant boys and girls to play with all toys (Culp, Cook, & Housley, 1983). Only two adults (members of the same couple) said there should be different types of toys for girls and boys.

Nevertheless, many social pressures are concentrated on infants and toddlers. One of the earliest studies on children's toys graphically demonstrated that gender stereotyping in toy selection can take place without parental awareness. The researchers examined the furnishings and toys found in the rooms of forty-eight boys and forty-eight girls under the age of 6 on the assumption that whatever differences were found would indicate parental ideology regarding gender (Rheingold & Cook, 1975). They assumed that children under 6 do not control much of their own toy selection. The children in this study were from a highly selected, highly educated university setting in which one might expect that gender differentiation was at a minimum. In fact, the parents denied in a questionnaire that they made any distinctions between sons and daughters.

No gender differences in the number of books, musical objects, or stuffed toys were found in the children's rooms. However, gender differences in several categories of toys were impressive. Summed over age, the number of vehicles for the boys was 375 versus 17 for the girls. No girl's room contained a wagon, boat, kiddie car, motorcycle, snowmobile, or trailer. Conversely, only eight of the boys' rooms contained a female doll, compared with forty-one of the girls' rooms.

A study conducted fifteen years later (Pomerleau et al., 1990) found similar, although somewhat less dramatic, gender differences in these two categories of toys. This study used a sample of younger children ranging from 5 through 25 months of age. Girls had 3.9 dolls as compared with an average of 1.2 for boys. Boys, in contrast, had an average of 10.3 small vehicles each, whereas girls had 3.5. There were no differences between girls and boys in the number and variety of toys.

Toys and Tots

Many children display gender-stereotyped toy preferences and behaviors by 18 to 24 months of age at home and in group settings (Huston, 1983; O'Brien & Huston, 1985a; Perry, White, & Perry, 1984). In one study, by the age of 10 months, girls already showed a preference for dolls and were more likely than boys to offer dolls to their parents (Roopnarine, 1986). At this age, boys and girls were equally likely to play with trucks, blocks, and kitchen utensils. But parental responses to this play were already gender differentiated. Both mothers and fathers were found to be more likely to attend to the block play of their sons than of their daughters.

Parents clearly encourage involvement with toys stereotyped as gender-appropriate and avoidance of toys that have cross-gender connotations. One study videotaped parent-toddler pairs playing with six different sets of toys for four minutes each (Caldera, Huston, & O'Brien, 1989). The parents' initial nonverbal responses to the toys were more positive when the toys were stereotyped for the child's and parent's sex than when they were not. Children showed greater involvement when playing with stereotypically gender-appropriate toys even when parental behavior was taken into account. They were less interested in gender-inappropriate toys even when no alternative toys were available.

Some parents had difficulty complying with the instructions to play with all the toys: "As an extreme example, one father with his daughter opened a box of trucks, said 'Oh, they must have boys in this study,' closed the box, and returned to playing with dolls" (Caldera et al., 1989, p. 75). Different types of toys also elicited different kinds of play regardless of the sex of either parent or child. Stereotypically masculine toys evoked high levels of activity and low physical proximity, whereas feminine toys elicited physical closeness and more verbal interaction.

Even very similar toys can provide cues for gender-different behaviors. In one recent study, parents were provided with two baby dolls and a stuffed clown and asked to play with their 20-month-old toddler for four minutes (Caldera & Sciaraffa, 1998). Parents of girls called more attention to the dolls, whereas parents of boys called more attention to the clown. They also played with these toys differently. Regardless of the sex of the child, baby dolls elicited more nurturance and caretaking from the parents than the clown did. In other words, parents who give their children baby dolls are also providing them with lessons in stereotypic feminine behavior.

By the time they are 3 years of age children are well aware of the socially prescribed nature of the kind of toys with which they play. In keeping with the more rigid demands for gender-role conformity from boys than from girls, three-fourths of all the 3- to 5-year-old boys in one study requested gender-stereotypic toys for Christmas (Robinson & Morris, 1986). A high proportion of slightly older boys (4 to 5 years of age) told interviewers that their fathers would think that playing with feminine toys was "bad" (Raag & Rackliff, 1998). Boys who believed this chose more gender-typed playthings than other boys. The researchers did not have any information about the fathers' actual attitudes, but these boys did not report that anyone other than their father would respond to the gender typing of their toys.

Although the preschool-age child has not yet become completely gender-typed, most children have developed preferences for gender-typed toys and play by this age (see Table 6.1). Girls spend significantly more time playing with stereotypically feminine toys and less with stereotypically masculine toys, whereas the reverse pattern is found in boys (Powlishta, Serbin, & Moller, 1993). There is, however, considerable within-sex variability and between-sex overlap in these play patterns. For example, girls spent 5 to 22 percent of the observed time intervals playing with masculine toys, compared with 5 to 71 percent for boys. In contrast, boys spent 0 to 47 percent of their time playing with feminine toys, compared with 18 to 54 percent for girls.

Girls' toy choices became gender-typed more gradually. Only 29 percent of the girls requested stereotypically feminine toys at age 3 versus 73 percent at age 5 (Powlishta et al., 1993). It is difficult to determine whether gender typing in toy preference among young children is a cause of or a response to parental gift-giving behavior. However, children were less likely to receive toys they requested for Christmas when the toys were atypical for their sex (Etaugh & Liss, 1992).

The Impact of Stereotypic Labels

College students as well as parents are aware of the gender-stereotypic properties of particular toys (Campenni, 1999). The toys rated as most appropriate for girls were those associated with domestic tasks (a toy vacuum cleaner and kitchen center); beauty enhancers (such as a makeup kit and jewelry); and items useful for child care (a cradle, stroller, and dollhouse). Barbie was #2 on the list—just below the makeup kit. The toys rated as most appropriate for boys were, in order, football gear, GI Joe, boxing gloves, a Ninja warrior set, toy soldiers, a gun, and a construction set. What messages about future occupations are being conveyed to boys and girls by these toys?

Children are aware of gender stereotypes about toys at an early age. When preschoolers were exposed to three boxes of gadgets that were labeled for the same sex, for the other sex, or for both sexes by the researcher, they explored the gadgets less, asked fewer questions about them, and recalled their names less frequently when they were labeled for the other sex rather than for their own (Bradbard & Endsley, 1983). The children remembered the objects they had seen and how they had been labeled for at least a week.

Children avoid toys that are considered appropriate for the other sex even when they are very attractive (Martin, Eisenbud, & Rose, 1995). One expert on child development calls this "the hot potato effect." It is probably best illustrated by the following story:

> A boy in their laboratory school had been playing with a racecar and its driver when the driver's helmet fell off revealing long blond hair. The driver was a woman. The boy dropped the racecar like it was a hot potato. (Martin, 1999, p. 49)

In another story about children's responses to gender-inappropriate toys, the researchers who conducted the study reported: "Two boys and six girls overtly reacted to the treatments by (1) seeking reassurance that they could play with the other-sex labeled objects; (2) making negative statements about the other-sex labeled objects ('Yuk, girls!'); and/or (3) refusing to look at, repeat the names of, or move near the table containing the other-sex labeled objects" (Bradbard & Endsley, 1983, p. 257). Such behaviors obviously limit children's opportunities to learn about all aspects of their world.

Boys who engage in cross-gender play are particularly likely to receive less positive attention and more criticism from their peers. They are often ignored and left to play alone. An example of how extreme this isolation can be is provided by an anecdote from another group of researchers on child development:

> . . . case of a boy who spent many hours in his preschool class playing with the doll house and furniture. He played alone. Because of parental concern, the teacher inquired what he was doing, only to learn that he was playing "moving man." No one—children, teachers, or parents—could see the sex-appropriate truck for the sex-inappropriate doll house and furniture. (Wynn & Fletcher, 1987, p. 84)

Not all aspects of gender typing increase at the same rate for all children. Because the focus of research has been on conventional gender-role development, gender-neutral behavior may be underrepresented. For example, preschoolers have been observed to spend a greater proportion of time with neutral toys than with gender-typed toys (Idle, Wood, & Desmarais, 1993).

Gendered Play

It has been suggested that play is the work of children. Different kinds of toys provide children with different opportunities for the rehearsal of adult roles.

Play preferences that become rigidly stereotyped at an early age limit the kinds of experience that children have. Children do not seem inclined to challenge these limits. Toy preferences become increasingly more stereotypic with age. By age 6, 75 percent of the children in one study refused to alter their stereotypic toy choices even after being informed and shown toys that were appropriate for both girls and boys (Frasher, Nurss, & Brogan, 1980).

Toy preferences do not appear to be much influenced by the child's own inclinations either. When forced to choose between the activity level required by a toy and its gender category (e.g., an active boy being forced to choose between a jump rope and an erector set), almost 80 percent of the 3- to 6-year-old children studied based their preferences on the gender appropriateness of the toy (Eaton, von Bargen, & Keats, 1981).

By the time children have reached the age of 3 they have acquired preferences for toys and play based on their experience during their early years. Observations conducted in preschool classrooms have found that boys use the block area much more frequently than girls, whereas girls use the art area much more than boys (Pellegrini & Perlmutter, 1989). Such choices do not reflect an inability to deal with unfamiliar materials. When children are assigned to play areas, they play appropriately with the toys in them.

Little girls and boys also engage in different kinds of fantasy play. One study found that 4-year-old girls spent 73 percent of their fantasy play engaged in domestic activities, as compared with 31 percent of boys' fantasy play (Mathews, 1977). Boys' fantasy play frequently involved interesting and unusual adult roles, such as marching bands, parades, and fireworks displays (none of the girls' play was in these categories). Fantasies with exotic themes such as witches and magic, adventures, spies, ghosts, and wild animals occupied 11 percent of the boys' fantasy play, in contrast to only 1 percent of the girls'. If one thinks of play as a rehearsal for adult roles, what do these gender-related differences in fantasy play tell you about children's idea of men's versus women's worlds?

Although people tend to think of the games of little boys as more active than those of little girls, research suggests that the difference is more one of style than of activity. For example, groups of children have been observed at play throughout their nursery school years (Maccoby, 1988). The children were studied as trios of same-sex playmates in a mobile laboratory equipped with a thick carpet, a child-size trampoline, and a beach ball. Girls spent more time than boys jumping on the trampoline. Thus, the girls' play was not inactive. However, a girl would almost never throw herself on top of another girl who was jumping on the trampoline as some boys did. Boys' play often ended up in bouts of wrestling or mock fighting. Rough play of this sort was seldom seen among trios of girls.

Different kinds of toys encourage different kinds of play. Play with traditionally feminine toys appears to involve more structure and less use of physical space than play with traditionally masculine toys. Toy and play preferences have a great deal of importance when children begin to go to school. The most important consequence of the gender typing of toy and play preferences may be to set limits on the sex of the children with whom a child customarily plays.

Sexism in Media Messages for Children

Stories and the Communication of Gender Roles

Where do children acquire gender stereotypes? You have seen that they are learned from parents and peers. Like adult stereotypes (Chapter 2), they can also be found in every form of media designed for children. The most obvious source of information about the gender appropriateness of toys comes from toy advertisements (Schwartz & Markham, 1985). But toy commercials are only the tip of the iceberg in terms of powerful covert messages about gender-appropriate roles and behaviors.

Traditional fairy tales as well as more modern stories written for children are full of gender stereotypes. In many fairy tales, women are especially desirable when they are passive. In some, like "Snow White" or "Sleeping Beauty," they are most desirable when they are comatose (Dworkin, 1974). Disney's recent feature cartoons for children, like *The Little Mermaid*, *Beauty and the Beast*, and *Aladdin* would appear to provide more positive roles for females. A closer scrutiny, however, reveals a repetition of the old narrative that selfless, beautiful girls are rewarded by the love of a prince they barely know (Douglas, 1994). Disney heroines are a popular theme in Halloween costumes for little girls (see Figure 6.2). Parents need to teach their children that these stories were written many years ago, when men's and women's roles were different from the way they are today.

Analyze some of your favorite fairy tales from a feminist perspective. You may find yourself asking whether anyone in her right mind could possibly want to be a fairy-tale princess. They are either passive victims or decorative

FIGURE 6.2. There may not be quite as much unanimity among real-life girls as is shown in this comic strip, but girls' Halloween costumes clearly differ in meaning from those of boys. Try making your own observations next Halloween.

Source: Cathy © 1996 Cathy Guisewite. Reprinted with permission of Universal Press Syndicate. All rights reserved.

figures, or must die in order to be loved. If they resist these roles, they are punished or portrayed as evil or mad (Sapiro, 1994).

Readers designed for the early school years have improved in the rate at which boys rather than girls are portrayed as main characters, but many gender-appropriate roles have been retained. As in traditional fairy tales, a common theme in these stories is the female main character's need to be rescued. When not rescued by boys or men, the protagonist is shown being rescued by a pet or an animal. "Girls are shown as being very brave while waiting for rescue, but they still cannot help themselves out of trouble" (Purcell & Stewart, 1990, p. 184). Boys, in contrast, almost never have to depend on anyone.

Similar to stereotypes about adults discussed in Chapter 2, these stories seldom show boys engaged in any form of domestic activity. While women are now shown in what were once primarily male-dominated occupations, only men are shown in more adventurous arenas. Women doctors are now common, but women explorers and big-game hunters are still few and far between (Purcell & Stewart, 1990).

Sexism reveals itself in ways other than in frequency counts. It occurs when disparaging statements are made about women or girls or when traits are characterized as different for males and females. A recent analysis of award-winning picture books for children found, for example, that males continue to be portrayed as more powerful and active than females (Turner-Bowker, 1996). Males also appear in greater numbers than females in book titles and illustrations even when there are no differences in the central roles. Girls are portrayed as passive-dependent as often as they were fifty years ago, and boys are portrayed as no less instrumental (Kortenhaus & Demarest, 1993). Young girls are still valued for their beauty while older women are deprecated as hags or witches or given barely visible domestic roles.

Gender Roles and Television Programming for Children

The characters in animated cartoons also model gender stereotypes. In one study, male characters have been found to appear more frequently, to be given more prominence, and to talk significantly more than female characters (Thompson & Zerbinos, 1995). They also displayed more ingenuity, were more often both the perpetrators and victims of physical and verbal aggression, showed more leadership skills, interrupted more, and so on. Female characters were more often shown as attractive, affectionate, and concerned about interpersonal relationships. Males were more likely than females to be shown in some sort of recognizable job (31% of the time as compared with 13% of females). Female characters were shown as caregivers 46 percent of the time, whereas males were never shown in this activity.

The researchers noted that there had been some improvement in the roles of female cartoon characters. Since 1980 the number of main female characters they found was 74 compared with 170 males. Before 1980, researchers counted only 8 female lead characters compared with 121 males. Females also have been portrayed in somewhat less stereotypic ways since 1980, but male characters continue to do everything much more than female characters do because they appear so much more often.

Are children influenced by these stereotypic representations? When children ages 4 through 9 were interviewed, they recognized that there were more males than females in cartoons and that the males talked more as well as engaged in more violent and silly/amusing behavior than females (Thompson & Zerbinos, 1997). Girls were more sensitive to the subtle interpersonal messages being communicated. Boys did not see the violent activities in cartoons as having anything to do with their relationships with girls, whereas girls saw the male characters as teasing and making fun of girls. Girls made comments such as "boys think they are the smartest" and "try to catch girls." Boys described the girl characters as "going out on dates," "follow what boys say," and as saying "I'm pretty."

Learning Occupational Stereotypes

Children who watched the most TV (four or more hours per day) had the most stereotyped views about what household chores should be performed by girls and boys. Their beliefs were not related to the chores they actually did perform (Signorielli & Lears, 1992). Those children who noticed the largest number of stereotypes also selected more gender-stereotypic jobs for themselves (Thompson & Zerbinos, 1997). For boys, the most frequently selected jobs were firefighter, police officer, and athlete. For girls, these jobs were nurse and teacher. Boys whose favorite cartoons were continuing adventures selected more masculine-stereotyped occupations than other boys.

Similar occupational stereotyping has also been found in Australian children (Durkin & Nugent, 1998). Although most children saw most activities as doable by anyone, 5-year-old boys were least likely to indicate that they could be a nurse, wash clothing, or sew (the most stereotypic feminine activities), whereas 5-year-old girls were least likely to indicate that they could fix cars or put out fires (the most stereotypic masculine activities).

Occupational aspirations were found to become more stereotypic for the same boys as they progressed from the second through the sixth grade (Helwig, 1998). By sixth grade, 93 percent of the boys reported that they aspired to a traditionally masculine occupation. In contrast, stereotypic aspirations declined for girls as they grew older. Although 58 percent of the girls reported interest in a traditionally feminine occupation in second grade, by sixth grade, the figure had dropped to 30 percent. In sixth grade, 49 percent of these girls reported interest in a traditionally male, high-prestige occupation such as vet, doctor, and lawyer.

WHAT IS SEX SEGREGATION?

The Development of Social Networks

Beginning at a very young age, children begin to play more with same-sex peers. This may begin as early as 27 months of age (La Freniere, Strayer, & Gauthier, 1984). Observations in day-care centers indicate that at this age girls begin to make friendly overtures to other girls at a level above that of chance. Boys show same-sex preferences about a year later. These same-sex preferences increase steadily during the preschool years (Feiring & Lewis, 1987). We

call this phenomenon *sex segregation* because it appears to be based on perceptions of others' physical sex rather than their gender.

By the age of 35 months, 62 percent of the girls and 21 percent of the boys
were found to be playing with same-sex children above chance levels (Moller
& Serbin, 1996). There appears to be no relationship between children's preference for same-sex playmates and other measures of gender typing such as
preference for masculine or feminine toys or proximity to a teacher (Powlishta
et al., 1993). Preferences may be mediated by behavioral compatibility rather
than cues about gender. Sex-segregating girls were seen by their teacher as
more socially sensitive and segregating boys were seen as more active and disruptive than other children (Moller & Serbin, 1996). Young boys have been
found to become more aroused than girls in highly physical, competitive contexts and have greater difficulty regulating their arousal (Fabes, 1994; Fabes,
Shepard, Guthrie, & Martin, 1997).

By the age of 4 or 5, gender differences in play styles are quite obvious.
When pairs of children were given the opportunity to play with similar toys
that were either stereotypically feminine (a doll house and doll figures) or
masculine (a pirate ship with figures), pairs of girls tended to engage in constructive play (using a plan to reach some goal); pairs of boys were more likely
to engage in repetitive play involving simple muscular movements (Neppi &
Murray, 1997). Boys' play involved adventurous themes with both kinds of
toys while girls had adventures only with the masculine toy. When a girl and
boy were paired, there was a tendency for the boys to refuse to follow the
leads of girls during play with the pirate ship. These pairs tended to engage in
parallel rather than cooperative play, so few attempts at leadership or dominance occurred.

The social networks of girls and boys also support gender differences in
play. Boys tend to play with larger groups of children and at distances farther
from home (Feiring & Lewis, 1987). They use more space and visit settings
outside the home more than girls do (Bryant, 1985). Boys' preference for other
boys is accentuated when children play physically active and competitive
games (Boyatzis, Mallis, & Leon, 1999).

The foundation for sex segregation is laid before children reach elementary school. A critical marker in the development of same-sex social networks
is the so-called birthday party effect. You may remember this phenomenon or
can ask parents of young children about it. During the nursery school years,
playmates of both sexes are invited to birthday parties with equal frequency.
At some point between ages 4 and 6, however, children of the other sex begin
to be excluded. By age 6 both children and mothers report that more same-sex
than opposite-sex friends would be invited by the child to a birthday party
(Feiring & Lewis, 1987).

In one study, nursery schoolchildren were found to spend three times as
much time playing with same-sex playmates as they did with cross-sex playmates, although some play did occur in mixed groups (Maccoby & Jacklin,
1987). By the time the same children had reached the age of 6 1/2, the ratio of
same-sex to other-sex play had increased to eleven to one. You can see from
Figure 6.3 how few children play with children of the other sex. You can also
see that boys maintain more sex segregation than girls do. In one study of 8- to

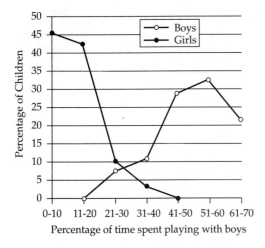

Percentage of children who played with boys as a function of sex of child and percentage of time in social interaction with boys.

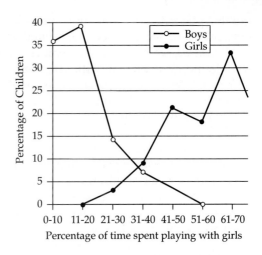

Percentage of children who played with girls as a function of sex of child and percentage of time in social interaction with girls.

FIGURE 6.3. Learning sex segregation. Six-year-old girls stop playing with boys before they begin to play much with other girls, and the pattern for boys is similar. This pattern suggests that the play styles of boys and girls are somewhat incompatible.
Source: From W. B. Swann, Jr., J. H. Langlois, & L. A. Gilbert (eds.). *Sexism and Stereotypes in Modern Society: The gender science of Janet Taylor Spence,* pp. 45–73. Copyright © 1999 by the American Psychological Association. Reprinted with permission.

10-year olds engaged in a puzzle completion task, girls contacted other girls more than twice as often as boys, but boys interacted with other boys by a whopping ratio of forty to one (Powlishta, 1995b). These play patterns are not entirely maintained by different interests in toys and games, because even in sex-segregated groups, children often play with neutral toys and in neutral settings (Martin & Fabes, 1997).

Sex segregation has been found cross-culturally, too (Edwards & Whiting, 1988). As in the United States, it increases from early to middle childhood. Sex segregation is greater when many children are available as potential playmates and when children are in same-age rather than mixed-age groups. The segregation is greatest in situations that have not been structured by adults (Thorne, 1986). By the time children reach the first grade, boys and girls are socialized into two virtually nonoverlapping groups of peers. Preference for same-sex companions does not have to be supported by adults. It is maintained by the social group processes of the children themselves.

The separation of girls and boys in friendships and casual encounters is central to daily life in elementary schools. A series of snapshots taken in varied school settings would reveal extensive spatial separation between girls and boys. When they choose seats, select companions for work or play, or arrange themselves in line, elementary schoolchildren frequently cluster into same-sex groups. At lunchtime, boys and girls often sit separately and talk matter of factly about "girls' tables" and "boys' tables." Playgrounds have gendered spaces: boys control some areas and activities, such as large playing fields and basketball courts; and girls control smaller enclaves, such as jungle-gym areas and concrete spaces for hopscotch and jump rope (Thorne & Luria, 1986, p. 178). In the United States, sex segregation in elementary and middle schools has been found to account for more separation than race does (Graham & Cohen, 1997).

The Impact of Peers

Preference for same-sex peers is associated with deprecating children of the other sex and avoiding activities associated with them as well as favoring one's own sex. Same-sex peers appear to be the most potent agents of gender separation. Both girls and boys patrol gender boundaries. In one study, independent of the kind of activity in which they were engaged, girls responded positively to other girls about twice as often as to boys. Boys responded positively to other boys more than twice as often as to girls, except when the boys were engaged in a traditionally feminine activity (Fagot, 1985a).

When the continuation of the activity was used as the criterion for the effectiveness of the social reinforcement, girls were found to be influenced by other girls and by teachers, but less by boys. Boys were influenced by other boys, but less by girls or by teachers. Boys were not influenced at all by girls or teachers if they were engaged in male-preferred activities (defined from previous studies as rough-and-tumble play, or play with transportation toys, large blocks, or carpentry tools). In other words, boys engaged in male-preferred activities appear to have developed a group structure that resists the social demands of anyone except other boys.

Unlearning the Traits and Behaviors of the Other Sex

Boys actively unlearn those traits and behaviors stereotypically associated with girls. For example, boys' and girls' nurturant responses diverge as they move through early childhood. In one study, children in various day-care facilities were observed interacting with either a young infant or a kitten or puppy in a playpen (Berman, 1980). At age 3, both boys and girls approached the baby human being or baby animal equally closely and were equally affectionate toward it. By age 5, however, boys showed a much greater interest in the animal than in the infant, whereas girls' behavior was unchanged.

These findings suggest that nurturant impulses are present in boys and girls at an early age, but boys learn to withhold responsiveness to young infants because they perceive this behavior to be incompatible with masculinity. In another study, children were shown action sequences of children either diapering or shaving a teddy bear. Afterward, some toddler boys refused to play with the diapering props (Bauer, 1993). They appeared to have a clear idea about who was supposed to be doing the diapering—and it was not them!

Some time between 4 and 6 years of age, both black and white children learn what the "correct" gender-appropriate responses toward infants are. When 5-year-olds were asked to pose for photographs with a same-sex peer and with an infant, girls stood significantly closer, smiled more, and touched the baby more often than boys did (Reid, Tate, & Berman, 1989). The gender differences that appeared when children were asked to enact the same-sex parental role are particularly informative. Girls asked to act as "mommy" moved closer to the infant, while boys asked to act as "daddy" actually stood farther from the infant than when they had posed with the infant without any instructions. This study illustrates the strength of children's gender stereotypes. They influence the way children visualize adult roles as well as their everyday behaviors.

Group Dynamics and Gender Differences

The behaviors of children within same-sex groups also support separation of boys and girls. Male bonding seems to be enhanced by transgressions of adult rules. A particularly titillating form of rule violation involves the use of words with an obscene or sexual connotation. For example, groups of boys were observed playing a "Mad Lib" game in which their rules required filling in the blanks with "dirty" words (Thorne & Luria, 1986). The boys were visibly excited when they broke rules together—they were flushed as they played, they wiped their hands on their jeans, and some looked guilty. These investigators never found groups of girls playing a game of this sort, although some of their young women students recalled having done so in grade school, but giving it up either after being caught by teachers or out of fear of being caught. Both boys and girls may acquire knowledge of the game, but boys repeatedly perform it because their peer group gives them support. The boys play for an audience of other boys.

By the time they are in third or fourth grade, children have developed gender-differentiated speech styles. Boys brag and insult their opponents more during both mixed- and same-sex competition (checkers). They have also been found to be more verbally aggressive during collaborative play with puppets (Leaper, 1991). Girls talk off-topic, interrupt, and laugh more in same-sex dyads than they do in mixed-sex dyads or boys do under any condition. Boys make more demands and use more self-promoting speech in their interactions with girls. Although boys do not appear to dominate their conversations, girls seem to be less happy and less engaged when they are interacting with boys than with other girls (McCloskey & Coleman, 1992).

Social Mechanisms for Maintaining Boundaries

The avoidance of other-sex playmates is closely controlled by group processes, especially among boys. Marginal or isolated boys are verbally taunted with such terms as "sissy" or "fag." Elementary schoolchildren may not be completely aware of the adult meaning of the latter term (which is used essentially as a synonym for "nerd"), but sexual idioms are a major resource that children draw on to maintain sex segregation (Thorne & Luria, 1986). In a context of teasing, the charge that a particular boy "likes" a particular girl (or vice versa) may be hurled as an insult. Children have great difficulty countering such accusations. Here is an example from a conversation with an adult observer in a Michigan school:

> Susan asked me what I was doing, and I said that I was observing the things children do and play. Nicole volunteered, "I like running, boys chase all the girls. See Tim over there? Judy chases him all around the school. She likes him." Judy, sitting across the table, quickly responded, "I hate him. I like him

for a friend." "Tim loves Judy," Nicole said in a loud sing-song voice. (Thorne & Luria, 1986, p. 186)

Sexual and romantic teasing reflect social hierarchies. The most popular children and the pariahs—the lowest status, most excluded children—are most frequently mentioned as targets of "linking." Linking someone with a pariah suggests shared contamination and is an especially vicious tease.

Boundaries between boys and girls are also emphasized and maintained by rituals such as cross-sex chasing. When boys and girls chase each other, they become, by definition, separate teams. Gender labels override individual identities: "Help, a girl's chasing me!" "C'mon, Sarah, let's get that boy." "Tony, help save me from the girls" (Thorne & Luria, 1986, p. 187). Cross-sex chasing is sometimes structured around rituals of pollution, such as "cooties," when individuals or groups are treated as contaminating or carrying germs (see Figure 6.4). Although "cooties" are framed as play, they may have serious implications. Female pariahs—the ultimate school untouchables because of their sex and some added stigma such as being overweight or from a very poor family—are sometimes called "cootie queens" or "cootie girls." On the other hand, "cootie kings" or "cootie boys" do not seem to exist (Thorne & Luria, 1986):

> Gender-marked rituals of teasing, chasing, and pollution heighten the boundaries between boys and girls. They also convey assumptions which get worked into later sexual scripts: (1) that boys and girls are members of distinctive, opposing, and sometimes antagonistic groups; (2) that cross-gender contact is potentially sexual and contaminating, fraught with both pleasure and danger; and (3) that girls are more sexually-defined (and polluting) than boys (pp. 187–188).

FIGURE 6.4. Fear of female pollution can be found in comic strips as well as schoolyards.
Source: Copyright © 1995. Reprinted with special permission of North America Syndicate.

With such social mechanisms operating it is hardly surprising that friendships between girls and boys among 7-year-olds are reported to be very rare (Gottman & Parker, 1987). These rare friendships had been maintained over several years—most commonly since about the age of 3. By age 7 most such friendships had gone underground. The boys and girls seldom acknowledged one another at school but continued to play together mainly in the privacy of their own homes. At what age did you stop associating with the other sex on a regular and public basis?

Social Dominance and Social Influence

Gender differences are also status and power differences. Children learn about gender-related differences in power early. By the age of 3, boys in several Australian day-care centers were found to use powerful strategies in their conflicts with both boys and girls (Sims, Hutchins, & Taylor, 1998). However, while girls used such strategies with other girls, they focused on less powerful strategies when they had conflicts with boys. By the second or third grade, children are well aware of the social hierarchy that exists in their classroom and in their school. In one early study in this area, 70 percent of the children agreed on a dominance hierarchy (Edelson & Omark, 1973). Boys were nominated for the top 40 percent of the positions in the hierarchy, while girls were generally in the bottom 40 percent. Girls agreed with boys on these judgments of peer status.

The characteristics of boys' play promote their dominance in group situations. Researchers examined dominance behavior in groups of four children (two boys and two girls) playing with a movie viewer that was designed to allow only one child at a time to see the movie (Charlesworth & La Freniere, 1983). In these groups, boys generally achieved the dominant position. On the average, boys spent three times as much time in the viewing position as the girls. Another study on all-boy and all-girl groups found that the tactics used to attain dominance differed. Boys usually obtained dominance by shouldering other children out of the way, whereas dominant girls usually managed by greater use of verbal persuasion (Charlesworth & Dzur, 1987). The implication of these studies is that the techniques adopted by dominant girls for gaining control of resources in all-girl groups do not work very well with boys.

Researchers working with a somewhat younger age group (children aged 3 1/2 to 5 1/2) found that both boys and girls make increased attempts to influence their playmates as they grow older (Serbin, Sprafkin, Elman, & Doyles, 1984). Among girls, however, these attempts took the form of an increased number of polite suggestions. Among boys, the attempts took the form of an increased number of direct demands. Over this age range, boys became less and less responsive to polite suggestions. Thus, the girls were developing a style of influence that worked with one another but that was progressively more ineffective with boys. It should not be surprising, therefore, that researchers consistently find that boys are more influential over group decisions than girls (Lockheed, 1985).

What does all this mean? Some researchers have suggested that sex segregation is due to incompatibility between girls' and boys' interactional styles

(Maccoby, 1998). But these interactional styles may reflect status and power differences rather than gender differences. Boys' and girls' groups are actually social categories (see Chapter 3). The major problem is not, therefore, the children's behavior, but the cultural system that supports the existence of these categories (Thorne, 1993). Children learn to make distinctions based on gender as a social category (Powlishta, 1995a). Children's behaviors mimic the gender-different social behaviors of adult men and women. Boys in all-boy groups are more likely to interrupt one another; use commands, threats, and boasts of authority; refuse to comply with another child's demands; heckle a speaker; and call another child names than girls in all-girl groups are (Maltz & Borker, 1983). Boys use at least some of these forms of covert aggression when they play with girls, too. Researchers may have underestimated the extent to which covert forms of aggression regulate male-female contact as well as contact between males.

ARE THERE GENDER DIFFERENCES IN SOCIAL BEHAVIORS?

Aggression

Aggression and Social Learning

Social learning from earliest childhood appears to facilitate the greater use of all forms of aggression by males. Such socialization starts at an early age, beginning with the acceptance of greater assertiveness from sons than daughters. Mothers have been found, for example, to use different ways of dealing with opposition from their 4- to 5-year-old daughters and sons. In turn, their daughters used justifications more and an explicit "no" less than sons did (Eisenberg, 1996). Preschoolers seem to be aware of their parents' gender-differentiated reactions to disobedience. Girls believed that an adult would be more annoyed by a simple no than by defiance, whereas boys believed defiant answers were more annoying (Leonard, 1995). Their beliefs were consistent with mothers' reports of what kind of oppositional behavior would produce a confrontation. Boys learn that they can be forceful as long as they do not overtly challenge maternal authority, whereas girls get into trouble for simple assertiveness.

The line between assertiveness and aggression can be very fine. By the age of 10, boys are reported to expect less parental disapproval for aggression than girls of the same age do (Perry, Perry, & Weiss, 1989). Adolescent boys have also been found to believe more than girls that aggression increases self-esteem and that victims do not suffer (Slaby & Guerra, 1988).

Successful aggression may serve as its own reward. Children who are successful in an aggressive encounter will tend to repeat it (Unger, 1979a). Exposure to violence also increases aggression. Male models of successful aggression are readily available (see Figure 6.5). For example, when men engage in violence on television, they are equally likely to hurt others as to be hurt themselves, but for every ten women who hurt others, sixteen women are hurt (Signorielli, 1989). Greater male aggression is consistent with social learning

Baby Blues

FIGURE 6.5. Toys and other aspects of children's environment influence the development of gender differences in aggression.
Source: Copyright © 1998. Reprinted with special permission of King Features Syndicate.

theory. In one study, although both boys and girls were affected the same way by violence on television at age 3, girls inhibited their aggression in later childhood (Eron, 1980). Findings about gender differences in children's aggression are limited by the narrow range of populations that have been studied—almost entirely white middle-class children in the United States. In a recent paper based on research in Finland, it was argued that psychologists have underestimated levels of female aggression by using the wrong measures as well as the wrong populations (Bjorkqvist, 1994). Physical aggression is replaced by verbal aggression among children as their social skills develop. Anthropological investigations of many societies suggest that adult women use many indirect aggressive strategies, such as locking their husbands out of the house for the night or singing mocking songs about them.

Intensive studies of children outside of the laboratory also reveal a more limited number of gender differences. For example, nursery school boys and girls in Brazil differed only in the amount of bullying (dominant aggression) found. Bullying was, however, more class related than sex related. Middle-class boys engaged in significantly more acts of bullying than did boys from the slums or girls of either social class (Frey & Hoppe-Graff, 1994). Intensive ethnographic studies of children in the United States also indicate relatively few gender differences in aggression (Thorne, 1993). Many acts of aggression were instigated by girls on school playgrounds, including name calling, teasing, and chasing, as well as occasional physical fights. As more models of female aggression become available such as Xena or Buffy the Vampire Slayer, girls may become more aggressive. It is difficult, however, to call this similarity "progress."

Aggression and Computer Games

When various forms of aggressive play are made available to children—for example, violent video games—both boys and girls who played such games showed more aggression in subsequent observations (Kirsh, 1998; Schutte, Malouff, Post-Gorden, & Rodasta, 1988). Boys play computer games more than girls and prefer more violent games (Buchman & Funk, 1996). A recent large-scale study of third- and fourth-graders in a suburban Midwest school district found that boys spent significantly more time playing video games at home as well as in arcades (Funk & Buchman, 1996). Although both boys and girls indicated a preference for games with a violent content, boys preferred those with realistic human violence, whereas girls perferred cartoon and fantasy violence. A majority of the boys and about one-third of the girls agreed that "the fighting games are mainly for boys". Playing video games was related to popularity for boys but not girls. A boy who did not like video games was seen as "not very cool."

Like violence on TV, video games encourage sexism as well as aggression. A recent content analysis of thirty-three of the most popular Nintendo and Sega Genesis games found that traditional gender roles and violence were central to many of the games in the sample (Dietz, 1998). In 28 percent of the games, women appeared as sex objects. They were shown with large breasts and in skimpy clothing. They were also shown as crying and in need of help. The latter images were more likely to be found in videos directed at younger players.

Making a Difference

Natalia Toro, at age 14, is the youngest person ever to win the "Junior Nobel Prize," or the Intel Science Talent Search. The $50,000 scholarship prize, formerly administered as the Westinghouse Science Search, has been given for the past fifty-eight years to the high school senior whose scientific research is judged the year's best. Encouragingly, eighteen of this year's forty finalists for the prize were female, and Toro is the second young woman to win in the past six years. Toro won the prize for her summer physics research at the Massachusetts Institute of Technology on neutrinos, the most elusive of subatomic particles. Her research helps explain shortages in neutrino counts and may have an important impact on high-energy physics. Toro grew up in Boulder, Colorado, with her parents Beatriz, a homemaker with nursing and psychology degrees, and Gabriel, an engineer. Both parents encouraged Natalia to pursue all her interests—she is fluent in Spanish, plays piano and tennis, and tutors middle-school children. Toro has found physics and math fascinating since elementary school, however. "It's just the way that they quantify nature and the ability to describe nature mathematically, to normalize what we see, and answer fundamental questions about the universe," she says. Toro plans to attend MIT, Stanford University, or the California Institute of Technology next year and hopes to obtain a doctorate in physics.

Sources: High achievement. (1999, March 10). *Boulder News.*
Honan, W. H. (1999, March 9). A 14-year-old wins top prize in Intel contest. *New York Times*, p. 17.
Henry, T. (1999, March 9). Colorado girl is youngest to top science contest. *USA Today*, p. 13A.
Announcements of the Institute for the Academic Advancement of Youth, Johns Hopkins University—Institute students take five in Intel science competition!
http://www.jhu.edu/~gifted/news/intel.html.
Boulder Planet. (1999, January 27–February 2). Fairview senior wins national science recognition. Volume 3, Issue 29.
MIT Tech Talk,
http://web.mit.edu/newsoffice/tt/1999/mar17/aandh.html
Science Service website: *http:///www.sciserv.orb./sts/Toro.html*

Of the thirty-three games sampled, only five (15%) portrayed women as heroes or action characters. And even these women wore stereotypically female colors and/or clothing. For example, female power rangers wear pink and yellow and are positioned behind the male power rangers at the beginning of the game. The hero princess in Super Mario II wears a long pink dress and a tiara on her long hair. About the "best" thing that can be said about these videos is that there are no females at all in 41 percent of them.

Instrumentality

By the time children reach the middle-school years, girls seem to have placed limits on their ability to explore both the physical and the intellectual world. At age 11, for example, girls were found to be less likely than boys to use buses for leisure journeys on their own, to go into city centers, or to travel by bus alone for more than one-half hour (Newson & Newson, 1987). These behavioral limits are partly a result of the greater amount of adult supervision given to girls of all ages as well as their realistic and unrealistic fears of sexual victimization (see Chapter 13).

Computers are a new technological development, and one might expect that gender would play little part here. However, boys dominate school computers. In one elementary school observed by researchers, boys monopolized the school computers and actively prevented the girls' access to the machines (Kiesler, Sproull, & Eccles, 1985). When teachers instituted time-sharing rules and, thus, gave the girls "permission" to use the computers, they used them enthusiastically. Apparently, girls can enjoy the computer and do like to use it, but not if they have to fight with boys to get a turn.

Even if girls do not have to compete for the use of a computer, games oriented around masculine interests such as wars, battles, crimes, and destruction lead girls to see computing as a male domain. There have been recent attempts to create video games for girls for whom "shoot 'em up simply won't do" (De Witt, 1997). These games reproduce gender stereotypes about girls' behavior. They include games with names such as "Let's Talk about Me" in which a girl can keep a diary, determine her personality, or alter her wardrobe. Mattel has introduced the "Barbie Fashion Designer," which racked up over a half a million dollars in sales in the three months after it was introduced. Some of the software designed for girls is packaged in pastel colors to make it more attractive to them. This may make some girls more interested in computers, but do you consider this progress?

Gender differences in instrumentality may be enhanced by the kinds of chores boys and girls are asked to do around the home. Researchers who examined a large age range of children (from below 6 years of age through 18) found that, on average, boys had fifty minutes more of leisure time per day than girls did (Mauldin & Meeks, 1990). This difference was largely due to the fact that from the age of 10, girls spent more time doing household chores than boys did. These tasks also differed in terms of the skills involved. Girls spent more time in meal preparation and cleanup, whereas boys were more likely to do miscellaneous tasks, including repairs and home improvements.

A study of 279 Australian families containing a 9- to 11-year-old found similar large gender differences in the construction and repair of objects (Burns & Homel, 1989). Some of the figures given illustrate the extent of these differences: 79 percent of the boys versus 33 percent of the girls made models; 81 percent of the boys versus 33 percent of the girls built something of wood; and 71 percent of the boys versus 23 percent of the girls fixed possessions such as bicycles. These differences illustrate how differential experiences build differences in skill, which, in turn, lead to differential abilities to influence the world. Girls who were given stereotypically feminine chores and toys were found to have more traditional feminine occupational preferences than both girls and boys who were assigned stereotypically masculine chores (Etaugh & Liss, 1992). The physical world promotes active problem solving and mastery because its laws are generally orderly and discoverable (Block, 1983).

STAGES IN THE DEVELOPMENT OF GENDER UNDERSTANDING

Cognitions about Gender

Obviously, gender affects children greatly, but what kind of ideas do children acquire about gender and gender roles? Young children's awareness of gender distinctions may have been underestimated. Recent studies of infants that use perceptual and attention rather than verbal measures show that babies begin to learn some aspects of gender at an early age. One such study found, for example, that 12-month-old infants will look at a slide of a female face associated with a high-pitched voice longer than they will look at slides that mismatch images and voices (Poulin-Dubois, Serbin, Kenyon, & Derbyshire, 1994). By 18 months girls but not boys could match a face with its appropriate gender label "lady" or "man" (Poulin-Dubois, Serbin, & Derbyshire, 1998). And although the children could not match the voices and pictures of children, they understood the label "boy."

Children also develop cognitive connections based on gender that are much broader than simple toy selection and play preferences might indicate. When children were asked whether objects (which were not supposed to be gender-typed) were more likely to be associated with one sex than the other, they believed that bears were for boys and butterflies were for girls (Leinbach, Hort, & Fagot, 1997). They also believed that tall fir trees were for boys and rounded maple trees were for girls. In a different study, typically gender-typed toys were altered according to children's metaphoric rules (Hort & Leinbach, 1993). The researchers painted a tea set brown and put spikes on the teapot. They cut off the mane of a long-haired pastel pony, painted it black, and gave it spiked teeth. With these strong cues, all of the children said they were boys' toys, and several of the boys said they wanted them for Christmas presents.

By the time children learn to speak, they have already acquired *gender labels*. This ability to categorize correctly his or her own sex or that of another person is present in the majority of children by the time they are 26 to 31 months of age (Weinraub et al., 1984). Children are able to make gender distinctions almost as soon as they can use enough language to show that they understand the question. In fact, the distinction between "good" and "bad" and between "boy" and "girl" appear to be the first categories that children learn (Thompson, 1975).

Next, children learn various kinds of *gender schema*. In their simplest forms these schemas involve linking gender labels to objects, traits, and behaviors. When a child learns to "know" that dolls are "girls' toys" or that "boys like to play rough," he or she is using a simple gender schema. Such schemas can be used to organize the child's own preferences for play, toys, and even playmates. By the time children are between 35 and 65 months of age, they show a great deal of knowledge about gender-appropriate toys and clothes and have high preferences for such toys as well as for same-sex playmates (Martin & Little, 1990).

Children's gender schemas are not the same as those of adults. For example, they show a great deal of gender typing before they understand a concept such as gender constancy. Complete gender constancy is said to be attained when the child realizes that gender is constant and invariant despite changes in appearance, clothes, or activity. It is tested by questions such as "If Janie really wants to be a boy, can she be?"; "If Jim put on girls' clothes, what would he be?"; or "Suppose a child like this (picture of a boy) lets his hair grow very long, is the child a boy or a girl?" Gender constancy is usually achieved around 7 years of age (P. Smith, 1987). Below this stage of cognitive development, children cannot understand that a person will remain a member of a particular gender category (1) whether he or she likes it or not, (2) no matter what kind of activities she or he engages in, and (3) no matter what he wears or how she looks.

Children may also differ from adults in terms of their explanations for gender differences. Until the age of 9 or 10, children believe that gender is biologically derived. When children were informed that a baby had been brought up on an island only by members of the other sex, they believed that he or she would still show the traits and behaviors of his or her own sex (Taylor, 1996). In other words, they see gender as similar to physical characteristics—as an intrinsic property of human beings. Only later do they perceive that social factors may influence gender.

The Behavioral Influence of Cognitions about Gender

A child's level of gender understanding does not appear to be well related to his or her degree of gender typing (Hort, Leinbach, & Fagot, 1991; Golombok & Fivush, 1994; Martin, 1999). This lack of relationship between the cognitive and social aspects of gender has been found in several ethnic groups. For example, among both black and white children ages 4 through 9, gender-stereotypical preferences are highly developed prior to the period when gender constancy is fully formed (Emmerich & Shepard, 1984). Although individual differences in gender schemas exist, gender typing appears to be largely independent of how particular children are socialized.

Boys are more influenced by gender distinctions than are girls. They form a greater number of gender stereotypes at an earlier age than girls do. White middle-class boys showed a greater level of such stereotyping than either black middle-class or white working-class boys did (Bardwell, Cochran, & Walker, 1986). Peer acceptance appears to become more closely tied to gender-appropriate play for boys than for girls as they move into the later elementary school years (Moller, Hymel, & Rubin, 1992). Boys show stronger gender-typed preferences than girls at every age. Older girls become more flexible and older boys less flexible than their younger counterparts (Katz & Boswell, 1986). Part of the reason for this difference is that little girls are permitted more latitude in their attire, toy preferences, and behaviors than little boys are.

Ironically, girls and women are probably permitted more latitude because boys and men are seen as the more valuable sex (thus, requiring greater attention to their socialization) and because masculine activities are regarded as having higher status than feminine ones (Feinman, 1981). Both girls and boys assigned more positive attributes to males than to females (Urberg, 1982). People can understand why a little girl might prefer to engage in stereotypically masculine activities, but a boy who prefers stereotypically feminine activities is regarded as doubly deviant. He is engaged in activities that not only are considered gender inappropriate but also are perceived to have low status.

There is more pressure on little boys than on little girls to conform to gender-stereotypic demands. Being told they do anything "like a girl" is a powerful negative message for boys. Here is one story from a man who excelled in high school and college athletics.

> Later, at home, my father informs me that two boys on the team throw like girls, and that I, unfortunately, am one of them! By the next practice, he tells me, we will have corrected that problem. That evening, with glove and cap securely in place, I anxiously face my father on the front lawn. And we play catch, for quite a while. I am concentrating, working hard to throw correctly ("like a man"), pulling my arm back as far as I can and snapping the ball overhand, just past my ear. When I do this, it feels very strange—I really have very little control over the flight of the ball, and it hurts my shoulder a bit—but I am rewarded with the knowledge *"that this is how men throw the ball."* If I learn this, I won't embarrass either myself or my father. When at times I inadvertently revert to what feels like a more natural and more easily controllable throwing style (more of a shot-put style, with hand and ball starting just behind the ear and elbow leading the way), I am immediately rewarded with a return throw that sails far over my head and lands two or three houses down. "Run, Run after that ball! You won't have to chase it anymore when you quit throwing like a girl!" Simple behavior modification, actually. And it worked— I learned very rapidly how to throw properly. But it wasn't really having to run after the ball that taught me; it was the threat to my very fragile sense of masculinity. The fear—oh, the "fear" of being thought a sissy, a "girl"! (Messner, 1994, pp. 29–30)

IS GENDER NONCONFORMITY DIFFERENT FOR BOYS AND GIRLS?

The Difference between Sissies and Tomboys

Children appear to acquire information about the greater importance of gender conformity for boys at an early age. In a study comparing the impact of sex, gender typing of interests, and labels such as tomboy or sissy, 4-year-olds ignored the target child's interests and used his or her sex to determine whether they would like him or her as a playmate (Martin, 1989). By 7 years of age, however, children used interests, labels, and sex to determine a playmate's desirability. Older children disliked children described as sissies more than any other group of potential playmates. Third- to sixth-grade boys have been found to be very intolerant of cross-gendered behaviors in other boys. Girls' ratings of friendship with girls who were portrayed as engaging in an increasing number of masculine activities declined much less sharply (Zucker, Wilson-Smith, Kurita, & Stein, 1995).

When college students were given information about children who played with toys and had personality traits considered more appropriate for the other sex, they also gave more negative evaluations to nonconforming boys than girls (Martin, 1990). They expected such boys to be less well adjusted and more likely to be homosexual when they grew up, but expected tomboys to convert to more traditional behavior when they got older.

Undergraduates saw tomboys as sharing many personality traits and behaviors with boys but did not see sissies and girls to be very similar (Martin, 1995). Sissies were seen as possessing fewer masculine and more feminine traits than traditional girls. The traits that characterized the category were very specific. Sissies were seen as being gentle, neat and clean, crying a lot, and being easily frightened. Preschool teachers have also been found to be less accepting of cross-gender role behaviors and aspirations in boys than in girls (Cahill & Adams, 1997). Like college students, their attitudinal distinction was related to homophobia.

What do you think of when you hear the word *sissy*? It probably does not have the same positive meanings associated with the word *tomboy*. Tomboys are girls who wear jeans, climb trees, and play baseball. Sissies are boys who are absent from these activities. They are defined as much by what they do not do as by what they do. It is not necessary for a boy to play with dolls to be called a sissy. It may be enough if he does not engage in rough-and-tumble games or verbally aggressive horseplay. Judgments about sissies versus tomboys reflect societal judgments about the relative value of traditionally masculine and feminine characteristics.

Who Is a Tomboy?

This question might be more easily answered if we asked "Who isn't a tomboy?" There are many more tomboys than sissies. In fact, tomboyism may be a normal aspect of girls' development. Because it implies some form of gender deviance, it has been suggested that the word be eliminated from our vocabularies. However, it is a label that many women proudly claim. In one questionnaire given to women college students, junior high school students, and a sample of adult women contacted in a shopping mall, more than half of the respondents reported having been tomboys in childhood (Hyde, Rosenberg, & Behrman, 1977). The percentages ranged from 78 percent of those in a Psychology of Women course to 51 percent of randomly sampled women. A high proportion of tomboys has been found in several other studies. For example, more than half the girls surveyed in grades 4, 6, 8, and 10 identified themselves as tomboys (Plumb & Cowan, 1984).

In a recent three-generational study that sampled undergraduates, their mothers, and their grandmothers, 67 percent said that they had been tomboys during childhood (Morgan, 1998). They reported that they became tomboys at an average age of 5.8 years and stopped at an average age of 12.6 years. There were few differences between age groups on the behaviors associated with this label. At least 75 percent of these self-identified tomboys mentioned involvement in sports, active outdoor play, and interest in so-called boys' toys such as trucks, skateboards, and action figures. Their identification was based on doing "boy stuff" rather than a rejection of doing "girl stuff."

Considering the status conferred by our society on masculine activities versus feminine ones, it is surprising that most girls and women do not retain such preferences. Nevertheless, the average age of puberty and the age at which most girls report abandoning tomboyism (12.6 years) are almost exactly the same. Most women did not, however, report puberty as a major factor in their behavioral change. Nor did they report a loss of interest in cross-typed activities. Social pressures were the most important reason given for stopping (Burn, O'Neill, & Nederend, 1996; Morgan, 1998).

The Values of Being a Tomboy

Although there are many benefits for girls who engage in cross-gender activities, the popular media sometimes portray tomboys as oddities. An article in *Allure* magazine on celebrity women who had been tomboys concluded with:

> These days, beautiful celebrities who claim that they spent their childhood climbing trees and scraping knees are about as common as models who own restaurants. Here ten erstwhile tomboys come clean about their dirty past. (O'Connor, 1995, p. 68)

Young girls who identify as tomboys show a more varied set of traits and behaviors than girls who conform to gender-stereotypic norms. They were more likely to have been selected as popular and having leadership skills (Hemmer & Kleiber, 1981). They were also found to be more creative than other girls in a test of the uses for everyday objects (Lott, 1978).

Girls who have been tomboys as young children are more likely to continue their interest in sports in later childhood. Researchers find large differences in the sports participation of boys and girls by the time they are 11 years of age. One study in England found that 57 percent of boys versus 24 percent of girls had active sports interests in addition to those at school or in organized associations (Newson & Newson, 1987). In the United States, it has been estimated that 80 percent of young people withdraw from all levels of organized sport between ages 12 and 17 (Brown, Frankel, & Fennell, 1989). Young women withdraw at an earlier age than young men, often before they reach their peak learning and performance potential.

Girls who continued their involvement in sports reported that they received encouragement to do so from a variety of sources such as mothers, siblings, friends, and coaches (Weiss & Barber, 1995). The encouragement of fathers was reported as more important than that of mothers (Brown et al., 1989). However, the active involvement of mothers in physical activity was also an important determinant of girls' continued involvement. The presence of a physically active mother legitimized participation in norm-violating forms of activity such as competitive sports.

Negative Aspects of Hyperfemininity

The polar opposite of being a tomboy are girls who buy into traditional femininity as it is constructed in the United States and western Europe. There is no name for such girls and, therefore, they may be difficult to recognize. A few examples from recent news sources may help you to recognize them.

The beautiful young woman in Figure 6.6 is actually a child of 5— JonBenet Ramsey—who was found strangled in her wealthy parents' home the day after Christmas in 1996. Because this was a very lurid and visible murder, all of the news media published similar photographs of JonBenet. There were many such photographs available because she had been an active participant in children's beauty pageants for several years before her death. She was a child who had been very successful in the make-believe game of becoming an adult.

Does JonBenet look cute in her photo? We see her premature sexualization

FIGURE 6.6. A 5-year-old femme fatale. JonBenet Ramsey in makeup and costume for a children's beauty pageant. No age seems too young for females to be portrayed as sexually seductive.

as problematic. She was not unique. Stories about beauty pageants in the popular media are full of examples of girls just like her:

> . . . there are endless examples in the media of little girls caked with makeup, adorned with dyed, coiffured helmetlike hair, performing childish, burlesquelike routines under the direction of overbearing parents. There appears to be little concern on the part of many of these parents about the possible negative consequences of dressing their children up in provocative clothing, capping their teeth, putting fake eyelashes on them, and having them perform before audiences in a manner that suggests a sexuality well beyond their years. (Giroux, 1998, p. 272)

The author estimates that the beauty pageant business is a billion-dollar-a-year industry that involves more than 100,000 children under the age of 12 in the United States.

The popular media in the United Kingdom are also full of pictures of highly eroticized alluring little girls often with fair hair and ringlets, usually made up, who look seductively at the camera (Walkerdine, 1998). What do such images mean both to the little girls themselves and to those who look at them? These images are racist as well as sexist. They bear a startling resemblance to images found in child pornography (see Figure 6.7).

Although these little girls claim that they love these activities, it is difficult to make a case that they are truly free agents. In order to win, they require

FIGURE 6.7. Women dressed as schoolgirls have become a sexual turn-on in Japan. This is another example of eroticizing female children.

much coaching as well as the services of professional costumers, hairdressers, makeup artists, dance teachers, and voice coaches. Although we know of no studies of these girls' self-images, it is difficult to believe that they will have high self-esteem when so many body alterations are required to make them "beautiful." Girls, in general, have been found to have higher levels of body dissatisfaction, higher discrepancy between ideal and current self, and lower levels of self-esteem than boys (Wood, Becker, & Thompson, 1996). These findings are consistent with self-esteem differences between adult women and men, which begin around adolescence (Major, Barr, Zubek, & Babey, 1999). Findings of lower self-esteem in females than in males have continued to move downward in age. Premature sexualization of little girls eliminates their childhood and presents an image of beauty that is unattainable by adult women.

Games aimed at girls encourage premature sexualization. In an article in the *Dallas Morning Press* headlined "Toys Aimed at Girls Focus on Boys," the writer described a new board game called "Sealed with a Kiss" (Rosenfeld, 1995). The girls move markers with the picture of a teenage "hunk" around the board and the first girl who receives five kisses wins the game. Another toy marketed during that Christmas season was a pink "Dream Phone" that encouraged girls to dial the phone numbers of "cute guys." The first girl to figure out which one had a crush on her wins. This game also featured penalty cards such as the one that said, "Mom says hang up," with a picture of a crabby-looking woman with a kerchief tied around her head.

Although it may appear xenophobic to Westerners who are used to such images, consumer organizations in some Muslim countries such as Malaysia have called for a ban on the import of Barbie dolls (Assunta & Jallah, 1995). They claim that the doll gives children a warped perception of beauty and attractiveness. They blame Barbie for girls' excessive concerns with fashion and their bodies. Some comic strips in the United States have echoed their concern (see Figure 6.8).

Eating disorders have been documented for younger and younger age girls in the United States (Phillips, 1998). By the time they are 9 years old, white girls had significantly more weight concerns and body dissatisfaction than black girls or boys of either group (Thompson, Corwin, & Sargent, 1997). A recent article in the *Boston Globe* (Rodriguez, 1998) discussed the diets of 10- and 11-year-old girls. They mostly consisted of yogurt, salads, and diet soda.

FIGURE 6.8. Does Barbie make girls want to grow up faster?
Source: Copyright © 1996. Reprinted with special permission of King Features Syndicate.

Many of the mothers interviewed did not seem greatly concerned. It is likely that some of them had eating disorders when they were younger and continue to have unrealistic ideas about what a normal female body should look like.

RESISTING GENDER RULES

Individual Differences in Parental Behavior and Its Consequences

How do girls resist gender socialization? Individual differences in parental ideology about gender roles seem to have some effect. For example, children from egalitarian families (self-identified as sharing parental responsibilities) adopted gender labels later during the second year of life and showed less gender-role knowledge at age 4 (Fagot & Leinbach, 1995). A small relationship between mothers' stereotypes about marriage and child rearing and third- and fourth-grade children's gender-role stereotypes has also been found (Hoffman & Kloska, 1995). Girls whose parents had fewer stereotypic attitudes had a more internal locus of control and showed a trend toward more independent coping skills than daughters from more traditional families. If they were middle class, they showed higher scores on standardized achievement tests.

What a mother does may have an impact on her child's beliefs about gender roles. Mothers who held egalitarian beliefs about the rights and roles of women did not necessarily influence their preschoolers' degree of gender stereotyping. However, mothers in nontraditional occupations seemed to foster nontraditional aspirations in both their preschool daughters and sons (Barak, Feldman, & Noy, 1991). Mothers who have stereotypic beliefs about gender differences have been found to discourage active toy play in their daughters but not in their sons (Brooks-Gunn, 1986). Alarmingly, daughters of mothers who had strong gender-typed beliefs had lower IQ scores at 24 months than did those with less rigidly gender-typed mothers.

Sociostructural Factors and Individual Cognitions

Why does parental behavior have so little to do with children's perceptions about gender? As you saw in Chapter 2, stereotypes are socially mediated messages. It is difficult for children to avoid or evade stereotypic images. Children who watch commercial rather than educational TV have been found to have a greater knowledge about gender stereotypes (Bigler, 1997). Watching commercial TV is also associated with gender-role rigidity in the way children distort or forget stereotype-inconsistent information (Signorella, Bigler, & Liben, 1993).

Psychological interventions designed to counter sexism in children have often been ineffective (Bigler, 1999). Such interventions tend to produce context-specific behaviors that persist for a short time. Girls are usually more responsive to intervention attempts than boys are. This may be because boys have more to lose by a change in the status quo and/or because a majority of intervention attempts have been conducted by female researchers (Katz & Walsh, 1991).

It is also possible that what children take away from an intervention may not be what the investigator intended. Calling attention to gender in a gender-neutral context may increase children's gender stereotyping (Bigler, 1995). Like other stereotypes, cognitions about gender are difficult to change. Here is one example from a study of children's information processing:

> Our cognitive-based intervention taught children decision-making rules for deciding who could perform various occupations. Children then practiced applying the rules in gender-related tasks that permitted the experimenter to monitor the children's information processing. In one trial, children were told the following: "Here is Ann. Ann loves to fight fires, and Ann knows how to drive big fire trucks. Could Ann be a fire fighter?" One young boy enthusiastically replied "Yes!" "How do you know?" the experimenter asked. "Because *he* follows our rules," the boy replied. (Bigler, 1999, p. 137)

Like adults, children may ignore individualizing disconfirming information and maintain their stereotypes (Jones & Bigler, 1996).

FACTORS THAT INCREASE GENDER FLEXIBILITY

It is clear that rules about gender are socially programmed. They are internalized by most children in a fairly orderly sequence. What makes some children resist the impact of gender on themselves? What factors help produce gender-flexible children?

Flexibility Begins at Home

Although parents, particularly fathers, emphasize different behaviors for their sons and daughters, some processes that increase gender flexibility in children begin at home. In almost all cultures surveyed, girls are more likely to be assigned tasks that involve domestic and child-care responsibilities. In less-developed countries both boys and girls are under the supervision of women who use children's labor to assist them in their often heavy work (Bradley, 1993). As they reach middle childhood, however, the boys usually leave home to perform tasks that often involve other boys (Whiting & Edwards, 1973). For example, boys in rural cultures do more of the care and feeding of animals. In urban cultures, they are more likely than girls to run errands or deliver goods and services.

Gender-related differences in task assignment obviously cannot occur if there is only one child in a family or all the siblings are of one sex. Thus, girls who were only children showed a higher preference for masculine activities than other girls, although their level of performance was still well below that of the average boy (Burns and Homel, 1989). It has been known for more than twenty-five years that women who have achieved a high degree of prominence in professions considered nontraditional for women are more likely to have been only children or to have had only female siblings (Anderson, 1973). This effect has been extended to younger women who choose nontraditional careers. A study in England found that young women's choice of science O levels (roughly equivalent to the selection of majors in U.S. colleges) declined as their number of brothers increased (Abrams, Sparkes, & Hogg, 1985).

In the United States, the most gender-flexible preschoolers came from homes where the division of domestic tasks was less stereotyped than on average (Katz, 1996). Their parents granted these children more independence and were less demanding, less authoritarian, and warmer than parents of more gender-typed preschoolers.

The Effect of Ethnicity and Class

Some groups of children are more influenced by gender rules than others. In many studies, the strongest gender-typed patterns are exhibited by white boys (Katz, 1996). These are the individuals who are most privileged by the current status quo. There have been relatively few studies of ethnic differences in gender cognitions. In general, these indicate that black children are less likely to stereotype (Bardwell et al., 1986). They may also have a different definition of appropriate gender roles than white children. Until recently, working outside the home was more a part of the expected feminine role for African-American than for Anglo-American women (McGoldrick, Garcia-Preto, Hines, & Lee, 1989). Black girls have been found to give less-stereotyped responses to questions about adult work roles than white girls do (Gold & St. Ange, 1974). African-American 8- to 10-year-old girls and boys have also been found to be equally responsive to infants, unlike Anglo-American children of the same age (Reid & Trotter, 1993).

Social class differences in gender typing also exist. Findings from a large cross-national study of 3,944 adults in the United States indicated that men, older persons, and poor persons were more gender-traditional in their assignment of household chores to children (Lackey, 1989). Studies in Australia (Burns & Homel, 1989) also indicated that children in homes with a higher socioeconomic level were less gender-typed in terms of chores.

These findings are consistent with older findings indicating that working-class children showed more gender-stereotypical behaviors than middle- or upper-class children did (Unger, 1979a). Girls, however, are less influenced by the social class of their parents than boys are. For working-class girls, resisting gender may also mean resisting other undesirable aspects of their social class. It may be of some interest to you that both authors of this textbook are from working-class families.

Gender, ethnicity, and class intertwine. People of color and people from working-class origins in general have less access to societal rewards. These limits may, however, help them to be more flexible than individuals from dominant groups. White middle- and upper-class males, in particular, have the most to gain by identifying with traditional prescriptions about gender.

The Case for Positive Social Deviance

Short-term manipulations within schools have been ineffective in changing the cultural context that maintains sex segregation. Still, many girls (and some boys) resist conforming. Children who defy societal pressures for gender conformity appear to have had support from a variety of sources over a long period of time. They must also be able to ignore a considerable amount of pressure exerted against them because of their social deviance.

Girls who resist becoming gendered continue to take math and science courses and to compete in sports (see "Making a Difference" on page 215). Such activities help to maintain the high self-esteem needed by girls to fight pressures toward conformity that become stronger as adolescence approaches. It is important, therefore, to reflect on the factors that have helped to produce women who have successfully resisted becoming gendered. Highly creative and achieving women have a high ability to tolerate deviance (Helson, 1978). It was helpful if they did not have brothers. Since fathers seem to be important sources of gender differentiation, their encouragement was also important for the production of independent, self-actualizing girls. But many activist women in psychology also mention the important role of their mothers in structuring their active participation in social causes (Unger, 1998a).

Strong female role models are important. Until recently, few models of high-achieving women were available to most girls (see Chapter 11), although African-American mothers have socialized strong daughters for many years (see Chapter 7). Girls often find meaningful role models in the most improbable places. For example, one of the authors (Unger, 1988) conducted a study examining the childhood heroes of those women who are considered leaders in Division 35 of the American Psychological Association. These women had been recognized for both their professional achievements and their feminism. The role model that was most frequently reported (by almost 50% of those surveyed) as an important influence in their childhood was "Nancy Drew." It seems surprising that such an intelligent and independent group of women would select a series that had such little intellectual merit (the books were written by formula). As a number of these women pointed out, however, Nancy drove her own car, had adventures, and solved mysteries. And, anyway, who else was available?

The kind of books and toys available to children influences their behaviors. It is more difficult to engage in active, adventurous play if one's only toys are dolls. Do not, however, overlook the capacity to subvert gender-appropriate toys that is shown by some girls. The following is a true story that happened to one of the authors of this text. Her 4-year-old daughter demanded a Barbie doll. Since her feminist mother did not want to frustrate her, she reluctantly acceded to the request. You can imagine her delighted surprise when she found her daughter and two friends in the backyard playing with their dolls—they had taken off all the dolls' clothing and were tossing them like darts at a target they had made from a cardboard box.

A series of statements from a group of women writers, artists, scientists, and scholars who were invited to talk about their lives and work brings life to these issues:

> The journey begins, as usual, with my parents—one an attorney and one a teacher. Both were exceptionally able to hand on their experience, their enthusiasms, and their intellectual curiosity. However, they were also "bridge-builders." Firmly committed to the ideal of equality, they did not see a chasm between those who worked with their heads and those who worked with their hands (or between intellectuality and action). "Oh, for goodness sake,"

my mother used to say, "life is not only in books! Put that down, go outside, and look at the world!" My father said, "You will be narrow-minded if you don't work." (Kay Hamod, historian, p. 12 in Ruddick & Daniels, 1977)

The family member who most consistently sustained me was my mother. Though she burdened me with some of her fantasies and expectations about my future, she also freed me from a debilitating pressure to accept the dictates of femininity as usual. She urged me to have a more intellectually gratifying life than she felt she had had. I need not imitate her life, she said, as long as I did something that was both respectable and excellent. If she encouraged me, my father did not discourage me. Indeed, he paid the bills for the ambiguously supportive and straightforwardedly expensive women's college I attended (Catherine Stimpson, literary scholar, p. 74).

My mother and father never doubted my ability to take care of myself. I had been a loved and trusted child. I was a successful and much-admired student. I was not in the habit of asking for help. The realm of art and ideas, a mystery to my parents, was respected, but not basic. I would build my life on these things, but I would take care of the practical side of living, too. (May Stevens, artist, p. 104)

I rejected "women's work," but I rarely considered "men's work"—professional work. Although I imagined future families, I had no comparable fantasy career. When I was already nearly adolescent, I was greatly taken with *Sally Wins Her Wings*—the story of a pilot who, though glamorously attractive, rejects immediate love for the disciplines and adventures of flying. About the same time I cut out advertisements for writers' school, realizing, I suppose, that any wings I might acquire would be far less challenging to health and home than those of the braver Sally. From grade school on I wrote—stories, then poems, then essays—and took my writing fairly seriously. (Sara Ruddick, college professor, p. 132)

As I mentioned, I was not prepared for the discovery that women were not welcome in science, primarily because nobody had told me. In fact, I was supported in thinking—even encouraged to think—that my aspirations were perfectly legitimate. I graduated from the Bronx High School of Science in New York City where gender did not enter very much into intellectual pursuits; the place was a nightmare for everybody. We were all, boys and girls alike, equal contestants; all of us were competing for that thousandth of a percentage point in our grade average that would allow us entry into one of those high-class, out-of-town schools, where we would go, get smart, and lose our New York accents. (Naomi Weisstein, experimental psychologist, pp. 242–243)

As you can see, these women were encouraged by their parents, and their gender-inappropriate traits and behaviors were taken seriously by others and, thus, by themselves. One highly achieving psychologist of our acquaintance used to say that she had been improperly socialized. As this chapter indicates, however, the penalties for girls of "proper" socialization may be severe.

Not all aspects of boys' socialization are good while all aspects of girls' socialization are bad. Internalization of rigid gender roles can lead to psychological distress for men as well as women (see Chapter 14). Psychological disorders appear to be highly gender-specific in our society. While girls are socialized for dependence and passivity, boys are socialized for overindependence and a lack of close ties. Women's problems with achievement (Chapter 11) are paralleled by men's problems with relationships (Chapters 8 and 9). Women's problems may actually be easier to "cure" because they are largely structurally induced.

There is a limit to the amount of change that any one individual can effect. If you choose to become parents, you will (we hope) make every effort to minimize gender typing of both your daughters and your sons. But as long as socialization takes place in a sexist society, boys and girls will have difficulty escaping gender categories. As the number of people who are exceptions to the "rules" continues to increase, however, they may serve as reinforcers of further gender nonconformity in their peers.

CONNECTING THEMES

- *Gender is more than just sex.* Gender is a fundamental factor in the construction of girls' and boys' beliefs and behaviors. Gender determines how one labels oneself and others, what toys and games are considered appropriate, and, somewhat later, serves as a basis for the segregation of boys and girls into largely separate cultures. Gender is acquired as a result of both social learning and cognitive developmental processes that use sex as a basis of categorical distinctions.
- *Language and naming are sources of power.* What is impressive about gender socialization is the lack of awareness of both children and adults of the processes involved. The similarity in stages of gender understanding and the lack of individual variability in gender typing is consistent with the idea that gender socialization is primarily the acquisition of societal norms.
- *Women are not all alike.* Both ethnicity and social class seem to affect gender typing in boys and girls. Those who have the most to gain from the cultural status quo (white middle-class boys) seem to be most rigidly bound by social norms mandating the separation of the sexes.
- *Psychological research can foster social change.* Children take an active part in maintaining gender categories and supporting stereotypically appropriate behaviors for both sexes. Social change in this area requires both individual and structural change. The growing number of young women (and young men) who challenge traditional gender rules indicates that societal change in the direction of greater gender flexibility is possible.

SUGGESTED READINGS

Bem, Sandra L. (1998). *An unconventional family.* New Haven, CT: Yale University Press. A memoir by the pioneer in feminist childrearing. This is a very personal account of the trials and triumphs of raising gender-free children.

Golombok, Susan, & Fivush, Robin. (1994). *Gender development.* New York: Cambridge University Press. An up-to-date integrative review of gender development with a topical organization. The material on cognitions about gender is especially clear.

THORNE, BARRIE. (1993). *Gender play: Girls and boys in school.* New Brunswick, NJ: Rutgers University Press. This book is an engaging and thoughtful account of a series of ethnographic studies on children during their unstructured activities in school. It gathers all the author's previously published material in one place and offers us insightful ideas from outside the laboratory.

JENKINS, HENRY (Ed.). (1998). *The children's culture reader.* New York: New York University Press. A cultural studies perspective on the way popular culture portrays and constructs children's behavior. Includes material on issues that are not usually found in psychology textbooks, such as articles on producing erotic children, reaching juvenile markets, and not so trivial comic books.

Becoming a Woman:
Puberty and Adolescence

- **DISTINGUISHING PUBERTY FROM ADOLESCENCE**
  Puberty in Girls and Boys
  Menarche
- **FEMALE ANATOMY AND CULTURE**
  The Conspiracy of Silence
  Menarche, Menstruation, and Popular
    Culture
  Reports of Subjective Experience
- **OTHER ASPECTS OF THE MATURING FEMALE BODY**
  Breast Development
  Weight and Body Image
  Early versus Late Maturation
  Ethnicity and Class and the Response
    to Puberty
- **SCHOOLS AND SOCIAL POWER**
- **THE SILENCING OF YOUNG WOMEN**
- **PARENT-CHILD RELATIONSHIPS**
- **FACTORS IMPEDING GENDER EQUALITY**
  Femininity and Self-Esteem
  Gender Intensification
  The Role of Peer Culture
  Cultural Constructions: Are They
    Changing?
- **WORKING TOGETHER TOWARD GENDER EQUALITY**
- **CONNECTING THEMES**
- **SUGGESTED READINGS**

"I was nervous about school," Christy said. "I wanted to prove I was as cool as the other kids. I wanted a boyfriend to take me to the parties that the popular girls got invited to. I knocked myself out to get into that crowd. . . . I realized right away that being smart was trouble. I felt like I was 'severely gifted.' I got teased a lot, called a brain, and a nerd. I learned to hide the books I was reading and pretended to watch television. This one guy in my math class threatened to beat me up if I kept breaking the curve. I made B's and C's. My parents were mad at me, but I ignored them. I knew what I needed to do to get by." (Christy, age 14, in Pipher [1994], p. 203)

"All five hundred boys want to go out with the same ten anorexic girls." She said, "I'm a good musician, but not many guys are looking for a girl that plays great Bach preludes. . . . Boys get teased if they even talk to me," she moaned. (Monica, age 15, in Pipher [1994], p. 147)

"I blame my training for my eating disorder," Heidi continued. "Our coach has weekly weigh-ins where we count each others' ribs. If they're hard to count, we're in trouble." (Heidi, age 16, in Pipher [1994], p. 166)

Terra said, "Court would never have hit me if he hadn't been drinking. He apologized and brought me a rose. It won't happen again." (Terra, age 15, in Pipher [1994], p. 227)

"I hate my mother. She's such a witch. Sometimes I think if I have to live with her the next four years till I graduate from high school I'll go crazy. . . . She tries to control my life. She makes me clean my room and go to church on Sunday. She forces me to eat meals." (Jana, age 14, in Pipher [1994], p. 249)

Do any of these girls' words sound familiar? They are a few of the comments made to Mary Pipher, a therapist who specializes in adolescent girls. Although these particular teenagers seem to have more severe problems than many young women do, their brief remarks summarize common conflicts remarkably well. Many of these conflicts are triggered by rapid bodily change. Maturational changes are easily visible to others and seen through gendered lenses. Society (often in the form of one's peers) teaches girls what kinds of bodies are more valued and the adult roles for which they are suitable. These judgments are internalized and become part of one's adult identity. It is no wonder, therefore, that adolescence is a period of anxiety.

Adolescence is more problematic for girls than boys because, on the average, their maturation takes place at an earlier age and results in a greater change from a juvenile to an adult body. Identity is learned through comparisons. Girls compare themselves to other girls as well as to boys. Of course, boys also judge their bodies as they make the transition from childhood to adulthood, but because of biology, most girls must make such comparisons at a younger and more vulnerable age.

Biological events do not take place in a social vacuum. Because of societal ambivalence about the value and meaning of the mature female body, adolescent girls encounter the problematic aspects of female identity for the first time. Apparently individual issues such as excessive concern about bodily appearance and, for some girls, the silencing of an authentic self reflect social ambivalence about the role of women in our society. Adolescent girls frequently have problems with self-esteem, premature sexual objectification, and school achievement. Differences between parental expectations and peer norms also increase conflict as girls attempt to construct their own adult identities. Sexual objectification has an impact on relationships between girls as well as in their relationships with boys.

Other social milestones, such as the transition from elementary to junior/senior high school also take place during these years. In recent years, feminist researchers have begun to look at the situational context of female development during adolescence. They have focused on how home and school environments contribute to the formation of gender stereotypes and the way gender-related behaviors are shaped by peers. Many aspects of feminine and masculine roles are internalized as part of an individual's identity. But definitions of both femininity and masculinity also vary by social groupings such as ethnic group and class. These studies are particularly useful for exploring the social construction of gender. They show that just as males and females may be different in some ways, females may also be quite different from each other.

The physical, sexual, and social changes in girls that occur during early and middle adolescence are so large they produce a discontinuity in their development. Different views of the self emerge between girls and boys that could not be predicted from events that occur during childhood. These self-perceptions come both from the different biological events that occur during puberty in boys and girls and from the different social meanings attached to these events. In particular, contradictory social messages are much more likely to be applied to the mature female than to the mature male body.

DISTINGUISHING PUBERTY FROM ADOLESCENCE

Puberty is the period of most rapid physical growth that human beings experience. The only time in which humans grow faster is during the prenatal period and the early months of postnatal life. And, of course, one is not aware of growth during this early part of life. The word *puberty* is derived from the Latin word *pubescere,* which means "to become hairy." In contrast, the word *adolescence* is derived from the Latin word meaning "to grow up" (Brooks-Gunn & Petersen, 1983a). The origin of these two words emphasizes their different meaning. Puberty involves physical events such as the growth spurt, changes in body composition, and the development of secondary sexual characteristics. (These physical changes and their personal and social significance are discussed in detail later in this chapter.) Every normal individual in every society experiences puberty at some time between their late childhood and middle teenage years.

While puberty involves biological events with social consequences, adolescence is culturally defined. In the United States and western Europe, adolescence is defined as the period between childhood and maturity. Adolescents are a relatively recently created social group: the product of an affluent mid-eighteenth-century society where a falling infant mortality rate, a corresponding growing population, and the need for a smaller workforce resulted in a surplus of young people (Hollin, 1987).

This period has become more important as the age at which one is able to take on adult roles and the age at which one is permitted or expected to do so have moved further apart. We would predict that adolescence will continue to increase in importance as adult work roles become more complex in our increasingly technological society. However, in societies where one is expected to do adult work as soon as one is physically able to do so, there is no such stage as adolescence. Some subcultures, even in our own society, do not recognize adolescence. Without adolescence, there is also no such "social problem" as adolescent pregnancy (see Chapter 8).

Puberty in Girls and Boys

Puberty differs for girls and boys in a number of important ways. First, the timing of pubertal changes is different. On the average, girls begin and complete puberty two years before boys. Second, the quantity and quality of change are different for girls and boys. During puberty, differences in height, body composition, and physical configuration between males and females increase. Teenagers' bodies become increasingly *sexually dimorphic* (literally, two-bodied). In comparison with children's bodies, where it is sometimes difficult to distinguish sex without inspecting the genital area, the physical sex of teenagers is usually quite obvious.

The most important physiological difference between girls and boys that occurs during puberty is *menarche*—the onset of menstruation. Although this is a relatively late event in the process of girls' physical maturation, it has a great deal of personal and social meaning. In purely physical terms, menarche conveys the information that a girl is sexually mature and able to bear children. In many societies, menarcheal rites are designed to publicize this information in order to obtain the greatest amount of economic benefit for a girl's family (Paige & Paige, 1981). Our culture pays little overt attention to the onset of menstruation. However, this does not mean that it is of little personal or social importance.

The Boundaries of Puberty

The ages at which puberty begins and ends differ, depending on which physiological measure we observe. By any measure, however, puberty takes a long time. Some physiological changes begin in the bodies of girls and boys long before they can be seen. For example, the level of *gonadotropins* (hormones produced by the pituitary gland that stimulate the ovaries or testes) in the bloodstream begins to rise around the time children are 7 or 8 years of age. The end of puberty is marked by a stabilization of gonadal hormone levels in the mid to late teens. Thus, in hormonal terms, puberty lasts about ten years.

Puberty is more typically defined in terms of external changes. For girls, the *growth spurt* (produced by the stimulating effect of gonadal hormones on growth centers in the long bones) may begin as early as age 9. Most girls reach their adult height by 14 to 16 years of age. Boys, in contrast, usually start their growth spurt after age 11 and may continue to grow until their late teen years.

Individual Variability

There is a great deal of variation between individuals in the timing of the bodily changes associated with puberty. Girls differ greatly in the age at which their external appearance begins to change and the length of time it takes for the changes to be completed. For example, in some early-maturing girls, the beginning stages of secondary sexual characteristics such as breast buds and pubic and axillary (underarm) hair may appear as early as 8 years of age. However, the average age at which breast buds appear for American girls is 11 and may be as late as 13 years (Brooks-Gunn, 1988).

It takes approximately four and a half years for an average girl to progress from breast buds to complete breast development, but some girls do so in less than a year and a half (see Figure 7.1). Moreover, some girls never reach what is considered the final stage of breast development (large, well-defined, fatty breasts). Given the importance of breasts in our culture, it is difficult to view puberty as "only" a physiological process. Bodily change has very different implications for early-maturing versus later-maturing girls.

The timing, sequence, and duration of pubertal changes may influence teenagers' views of themselves as compared with others of the same age. Remember that girls' and boys' progression through puberty is different in timing as well as in specific physiological events. Girls usually experience their growth spurt and onset of secondary sexual characteristics earlier than boys. Thus, an early-maturing girl is not only different from other girls but is also way ahead of her male classmates. By contrast, a late-maturing girl is in synchrony with her male peers (Brooks-Gunn, 1988).

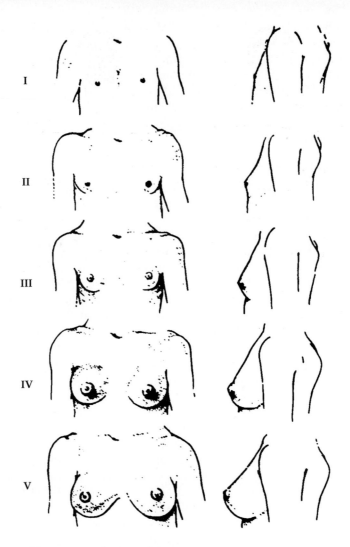

FIGURE 7.1. Breast stages during adolescence.

The Pubertal "Fat Spurt" and Its Implications

Girls experience a rapid gain in fat as well as height around puberty. They experience an average weight gain of twenty-four pounds, which is deposited largely in the breasts, hips, and buttocks (Figure 7.2). Prepubescent boys and girls are similar to each other with respect to lean body mass, skeletal mass, and body fat. By maturity, however, females have twice as much body fat as males (Warren, 1983).

Fatty tissue appears to be necessary for sexual maturation. Menarche usually occurs when about 24 percent of the body mass is composed of fat (Frisch, 1983a). Girls require a critical amount of body fat in order for menarche to occur (Frisch, 1983b). During their adolescent growth spurt, girls' body fat increases 120 percent, compared with a 44 percent increase in lean body weight.

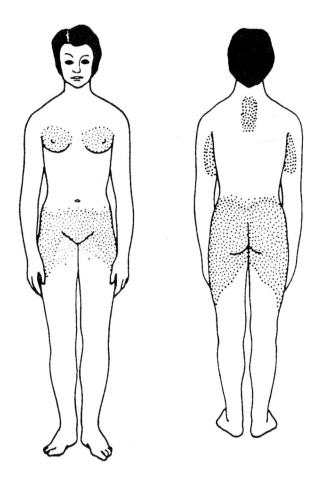

FIGURE 7.2. The places on a girls' body where fat is most likely to be deposited.

(In contrast, boys' bodies mainly increase in amount of muscular tissue.) This increase represents a relative as well as an absolute increase in fatty tissue. At age 18 fat is 27 percent of total body weight.

A number of researchers believe that the tendency for menarche to occur earlier over the past century is due to better nutrition during childhood. Girls simply reach the critical weight sooner. Weight gain is, of course, one of the few pubertal changes over which the teenager has some control. A critical amount of body fat is probably necessary for menstruation to occur. This is why severe dieting or intense athletic activity can delay menarche. Nevertheless, almost every young woman reaches menarche by the age of 16 (Frisch, 1983b).

Menarche

The age at which girls began to menstruate is often noted in diaries, letters, and medical records. These sources show that the average age of menarche has declined over the last 100 years. The average age of menarche in mid-nineteenth-century Britain was $15^1/_2$ to $16^1/_2$ years. Menarcheal age also differed by social class. Upper-class women began to menstruate six months to a year earlier on average than working-class women. The delay among working-class women was explained as due to undernutrition and hard living (Frisch, 1983a).

What is probably more interesting is the fact that girls in the United States in 1871 who began to menstruate at 11 1/2 to 12 1/2 years of age were considered to be cases of precocious puberty (Frisch, 1983a). The average age of menarche today is 12 1/2 years. If one considers menarche the end of childhood and/or the beginning of sexual maturity, this change over the past century represents a significant shortening of childhood for girls.

Menarche is actually only a late step in a long series of changes. It typically occurs after girls have stopped growing at their peak velocity, their breast development is nearly complete, and they have gained a great deal of body fat. All these bodily changes are important determinants of how a girl is viewed by others and, therefore, of the way she feels about herself. However, menarche carries particularly important messages for the individual and society because it is the most sudden and dramatic event that occurs during sexual maturation.

The meaning of menarche in our society is both positive and negative. The messages girls receive and convey are quite contradictory. When girls write about their own menarche, the emotional impact of these messages is evident.

> When I discovered it . . . (my mother) told me to come with her, and we went into the living room to tell my father. She just looked at me and then at him and said, "Well, your little girl is a young lady now!" My dad gave me a hug and congratulated me and I felt grown up and proud that I was a lady at last. (Shipman, 1971, p. 331)

However, even a positive response from one's family can evoke anxiety in some girls. For example, Andrea, a working-class 17-year-old, recently reported to one interviewer that she was "embarrassed" and "felt like an idiot" when her mother told her father and grandparents that she had started her period, and her grandmother congratulated her for being a woman (Martin, 1996).

Girls who had received no information about menstruation report much more negative experiences of menarche:

> I was babysitting and I just like got home. And I just like was screaming! 'Caus, ummm, I ran upstairs and I didn't know what it was 'cause I got home late one night, and I was just going to the bathroom, and I ran upstairs 'cause I didn't know what it was . . . and then she's [my mother's] like, "Don't worry about it, it's just your period." (Martin, 1996, p. 22)

Other research shows, too, that young women are ambivalent about the onset of menstruation. In one study, a group of seventh-graders were shown the beginnings of stories based on passages from Judy Blume's book *Are You There, God? It's Me, Margaret,* a book that is popular with teenage girls and that focuses on puberty. The story about menarche was:

> "Mom—hey, Mom—come quick!" When Nancy's mother got to the bathroom she said: "What is it? What's the matter?" "I got it," Nancy told her. "Got what?" said her mother.

Virtually all the girls recognized that "it" was Nancy's period.

More revealing were their responses to the question "How did Nancy feel?" Half of the girls ranked "scared" first, while 39 percent ranked "happy" first, and no girl ranked "sad" first. Happy and scared were also the most popular second choices. Their responses suggest that girls feel both happy and frightened about menstruation. In including both responses, they were expressing their ambivalence (Petersen, 1983).

Despite their anxiety about menarche, girls also engage in a certain amount of menarcheal competition. This competition is mentioned in fiction as well as in girls' anecdotal accounts of their experiences. The basis for this competition is the status that girls gain when they attain "womanhood." Since womanhood carries more mixed messages than manhood, girls are more ambivalent about maturation than boys are. Contrast these two statements about puberty—one from a 15-year-boy and one from a 15-year-old girl.

> I was glad when I finally got taller and older. Being older you just get to do more, go out and stuff.

> I didn't know what it [puberty] meant. So am I supposed to be like a woman now? Or what? It seemed so awkward to be like a little girl with breasts. I couldn't have both, but I didn't want to be a woman, but like I didn't, it didn't feel right to me. It felt really awkward, but there wasn't anything to do about it. (Martin, 1996, p. 19)

The subjective importance of menarche—in contrast to our society's silence on the subject—is evident from girls' reluctance to discuss menstruation immediately following menarche. The majority do not discuss it with anyone except their mothers (Brooks-Gunn & Ruble, 1983). Only after several periods do they begin to discuss feelings, symptoms, and practical problems with friends.

Menarche appears to focus the adolescent girl's attention on her body. This change in body image is illustrated by human figure drawings collected from girls at two points in time—in sixth and eighth grades (Koff, Rierdan, & Silverstone, 1978). Most of the girls had not reached menarche when they made their first drawings. Some had done so by the time the second drawings were completed. Thus, the researchers were able to compare drawings from comparably aged girls, some of whom had begun menstruating and some whom had not, but all of whom had experienced the same passage of time.

What shifts in body image were reflected in these figure drawings? Postmenarcheal girls, as a group, produced significantly more sexually differentiated drawings than their premenarcheal peers (Figure 7.3). Among those girls who had begun to menstruate during the course of the study, there was a significant increase in the sexual characteristics noted in their drawings from the first to the second occasion. Those girls who had not yet begun to menstruate did not show this change.

Young adolescent girls seem to believe that menarche will produce a sudden and momentous transformation into mature womanhood. In another study, seventh- and eighth-graders responded to the open-ended sentence cue, "Ann just got her period for the first time. When Ann looked at herself in the mirror that night . . ." with statements such as:

1a   1b   2a   2b

3a   3b

FIGURE 7.3. Stage, not age. Girls exaggerate secondary sexual characteristics when they draw female figures after menarche in contrast to their premenarcheal drawings. Drawings 1a and 1b were produced by a girl who was premenarcheal both times. Drawings 2a and 2b were produced by a girl who was postmenarcheal both times. Drawings 3a and 3b were produced by a girl who was premenarcheal at time 1 and postmenarcheal at time 2.

Source: From Koff, E. (1983), *Through the looking glass of menarche: What the adolescent girl sees.* In S. Golub (ed.), *Menarche* (pp. 77–86). Lexington, MA: Lexington Books. Reprinted with permission.

She saw herself in a different way.

She thought she had changed.

She felt very grown-up.

She felt mature.

She thought she looked older. (Koff, 1983, p. 81)

Physical maturity for females in our society carries mixed messages. It is desirable to become an adult, but, as shown in Chapter 2, youthful bodies are more valued for women than for men. And physical maturity can provoke parental fears about premature sexuality and consequent restrictions of girls' behavior (see Chapter 8). It should be no surprise, therefore, that girls are ambivalent about an event they see as the symbol of womanhood.

FEMALE ANATOMY AND CULTURE

The Conspiracy of Silence

Although women spend as much as 25 percent of their adult years menstruating, both menarche and menstruation are still largely taboo as subjects of public discussion.

> We live in a greeting card culture where, for twenty-five cents, we purchase socially approved statements about childbirth, marriage, or death. But Hallmark manufactures no cards that say, "Best Wishes on Becoming a Woman." Rather than celebrate coming-of-age in America, we hide the fact of the menarche, just as we are advised to deodorize, sanitize, and remove the evidence. (Delaney, Lupton, & Toth, 1988, p. 107)

Would you be willing to send such a card?

A survey conducted by Tampax in 1981 found that two-thirds of Americans believe that menstruation should not be talked about at social gatherings or in the office and one-fourth think it is an unacceptable topic even for the family at home (Delaney et al., 1988). Mothers are more reluctant to name the genital organs of their daughters than their sons and tend to do so at a much later age. Many mothers are embarrassed to name the girl's sexual organs except by referring to her "bottom." There is no acceptable word for female sexual parts, which are stereotyped as unpleasant, smelly, and unattractive (Lees, 1997).

Even today, many young women lack subjective body knowledge (Martin, 1996). They know little about their bodies and they are especially ignorant about their genitals. This is particularly true for girls from working-class families. One such young woman reported to an interviewer:

> I never have [looked at my genitals]. Once I started using tampons I was just like "Oops I guess that's the place where everything happens." I never looked. (Martin, 1996, p. 21)

When asked whether she had ever been to a gynecologist, another 17-year-old from a working-class family replied:

No and I want to but I'm afraid to. I don't want to like (spreads her arms apart), you know (giggling) that's gross! I don't know if I should have a man or a woman, I want to go just to make sure nothing's like, that I don't have any like . . . birth defects inside me or something. I don't know. (Martin, 1996, p. 22)

Menstruation is often characterized as an embarrassing event, one that needs to be concealed; and as a hygienic crisis, one that needs to be combated by frequent bathing and napkin changing. Until 1972, ads for sanitary protection products were banned from TV and radio (Delaney et al., 1988). Advertisers are still restricted about what they can say on the air and when they can say it. The ads tend to make generalized statements relating to grooming, femininity, and freshness. Only in 1985 did Tampax break the ultimate taboo and use the word *period* in a TV ad. The absence of specific information about menstrual products can be hazardous to young women's health. For example, many were unaware of the connection between tampons and toxic shock syndrome (a sometimes fatal disease that can be caused by the buildup of toxin-producing bacteria in tampons).

Secrecy also heightens young women's suspicion that menstruation is not a normal event. Girls who mature much earlier than most of their friends appear to have a particularly difficult time coming to terms with menarche. One investigator found that 43 percent of girls in her sample who had menstruated at age 11 denied that menarche had occurred (Petersen, 1983). The mothers of these girls reported the most negative experiences of all mothers of menarcheal girls.

Menarche, Menstruation, and Popular Culture

Neither menarche nor menstruation has received much attention in American literature. Not surprisingly, what people know about initiation into maturity is learned from men writing about the male experience. One of the first explicit references to menarche may be found in *A Tree Grows in Brooklyn*, a novel published in 1943 about growing up Irish, female, and poor in New York City in the early twentieth century. (One of the authors remembers sneaking this novel out of an aunt's bureau drawer a few years after it was published.) The passage exemplifies many of the themes already discussed, such as instant transition to womanhood, pain, secrecy, and the consequences of female sexuality.

She went upstairs to the flat and looked into the mirror. Her eyes had dark shadows beneath them and her head was aching. She lay on the old leather couch in the kitchen and waited for Mama to come home.

She told Mama what had happened to her in the cellar. She said nothing about Joanna. Katie sighed and said, "So soon? You're just thirteen. I didn't think it would come for another year yet. I was fifteen."

"Then . . . then . . . this is all right what's happening?"

"It's a natural thing that comes to all women."

"I'm not a woman."

"It means you're changing from a girl into a woman."

"Do you think it will go away?"

"In a few days. But it will come back again in a month."

"For how long?"

"For a long time. Until you're forty or even fifty." She mused awhile. "My mother was fifty when I was born."

"Oh, it has something to do with having babies."

"Yes. Remember to always be a good girl because you can have a baby now." Joanna and her baby flashed through Francie's mind. "You mustn't let the boys kiss you," said Mama. (Smith, 1943, p. 212)

This scene is very mild compared with the menarche scene in *Carrie*, written by Stephen King more than thirty years later. King's menarcheal counter-ceremony is part of a horror story. Carrie White, the butt of all jokes—the scapegoat—is standing dazed in the shower in the girls' locker room when the book opens. She grunts a "strangely froggy sound," and turns off the water. "It wasn't until she stepped out that they all saw the blood running down her leg" (King, 1974, p. 5).

"Period!"

The catcall came first from Chris Hargensen. It struck the tiled walls, re-bounded, and struck again. "PER-iod!"

It was becoming a chant, an incantation. Someone in the background . . . was yelling, "Plug it up!" with hoarse, uninhibited abandon.

"PER-iod, PER-iod, PER-iod!"

Carrie stood dumbly in the center of a forming circle, . . . like a patient ox, aware that the joke was on her (as always), dumbly embarrassed but unsur-prised.

Sue felt welling disgust as the first dark drops of menstrual blood struck the tile in dime-sized drops. "For God's sake, Carrie, you got your period!" she cried. "Clean yourself up!"

Carrie looked down at herself.

She shrieked.

The sound was very loud in the humid locker room.

A tampon suddenly struck her in the chest and fell with a plop at her feet. A red flower stained the absorbent cotton and spread.

Then the laughter, disgusted, contemptuous, horrified, seemed to rise and bloom into something jagged and ugly, and the girls were bombarding her with tampons and sanitary napkins, some from purses, some from the broken dis-penser on the wall . . . the chant became: "Plug it up, plug it up, plug it. . . ."

The gym teacher . . . slapped Carrie smartly across the face. She hardly would have admitted the pleasure the act gave her, and she certainly would have denied that she regarded Carrie as a fat, whiny bag of lard.

King (1974) emphasizes the fear of blood and of the power that menstruating women were once supposed to possess. Superstitions included the belief that menstruating women could blight green plants, curdle milk or other dairy products, and sour wine (Maddux, 1975). The similarity between the characteristics of menstruating women and those of traditional witches is quite striking. Many of the girls interviewed recently by a British feminist with a psychoanalytic perspective equated menstruation with dying and death (Sayers, 1997). They described puberty in terms of nightmares of bodily change. Films like *Carrie* may contribute to these images.

Men appear to have even more negative views of menstruation than women do. Among the large number of euphemisms used for the event, only one has been found to be used more by males than by females (Ernster, 1975). This phrase is "on the rag." Men interpret the phrase in very negative ways. It is said to imply lack of attractiveness in personality and even in looks. It is sometimes used by men to describe moodiness, easy anger, or irritability in other men.

Reports of Subjective Experience

Reactions to menstruation are usually more negative than reactions to menarche. Many women view it as a secret and, at worst, as a curse. In-depth interviews with women about their menstrual care practices revealed that the central core of their experience involved "making sure"(Patterson & Hale, 1985). The women reported that they had to make sure that they didn't leak, that they were close enough to a bathroom, that they didn't stain, and that they didn't have an odor. In other words, they were concerned about making sure that there was no evidence of menstruation.

The problems of making sure are even greater for adolescents. In junior or senior high school, how does a young woman find time and private space to change pads or tampons so she won't "show"? Here are accounts of some of these problems:

> In school it's hard: teachers don't want to let you out of the classroom, and give you a hard time.

> In seventh grade I didn't carry a pocketbook or anything—wow!—How do you stash a maxipad in your notebook and try to get to the bathroom between classes to change? It was like a whole procedure, to make sure nobody saw, that none of the guys saw. From your notebook and into your pocket or take your whole notebook to the ladies' room which looks absolutely ridiculous! (Martin, 1987, pp. 93–94)

Strategies for dealing with menstruation in school included putting the maxipad up a sleeve, tucking it into a sweatshirt, or slipping a tampon into a sock. These problems have not gone away. They may be intensified by ignorance and disgust with dealing with genitals.

> My sister told me about using tampons. My sister is a lot older than I am. So at first I didn't like the idea of having to go anywhere near touching myself. I thought it was sick! But my sister was like, "You can wear diapers all your life or you can wear whatever you want and wear these." (Martin, 1996, p. 29)

OTHER ASPECTS OF THE MATURING
FEMALE BODY

245

*Becoming a Woman:
Puberty and
Adolescence*

Breast Development

Unlike menarche, which can be hidden or denied, breast development is easily observed by others. Over one-half of elementary or junior high school girls who were in the middle of their breast development reported having been teased about it (Brooks-Gunn, 1987b). The most frequent teasers were mothers, fathers, and girlfriends. When asked to indicate how they felt when teased, 8 percent reported being upset, 22 percent embarrassed, and 22 percent angry. None of the girls reported being pleased!

Some of the teasing about breasts has a ritual quality. A sociologist who observed school culture, reported: "Once in a classroom and several times on the playground I saw a girl or boy reach over and pull on the elastic back of a bra, letting it go with a loud snap followed by laughter" (Thorne, 1993, p. 142). Sometimes this shaming ritual may be followed by little jokes such as "I see you're wearing a Band-Aid!" The adult staff at these schools generally ignored bra snapping.

Some comments of working-class British teenage girls illustrate the discomfort generated by their male peers' gaze:

> I was self-conscious [when I developed breasts], I still am. I don't know. It's just the boys. Some of them, how they react and stuff, just like if you're bigger and stuff like that, some of the boys, I know some. It's aggravating! —Wendy

> I was really self-conscious cause I developed them early. I think it was like fifth grade, and you know guys sometimes would say things.   —Sondra

> When I started to get them and now that I have them, I wish I didn't have them 'cause they're a pain. "'Cause like you have to worry about them when you get dressed in the morning. If you don't . . . well, I'm just, I mean, I am self-conscious about my chest. I wish I was little again where you know, no one really worried about it and guys didn't really care as much and all that stuff. You know now it's the first thing they check out!"
>   —Jill (Martin, 1996, pp. 31–32)

Pubertal girls are often embarrassed or angered by parental discussion of their breast growth or purchase of a bra (Brooks-Gunn & Zehaykevich, 1989). One director of a private elementary school for girls has speculated that fourth- and fifth-graders are much more disturbed about the loss of their childish bodies than grownups think (Delaney et al., 1988). She cited the sloppy big shirts and sweaters common to this age group—no matter what the prevailing style—as evidence of their anxieties.

As in other areas having to do with the body, girls' physical maturation puts them into a double bind. Breasts are viewed as a necessary part of an attractive woman's body, but there seems to be no such thing as "perfect breasts." A recent magazine advertisement illustrates this point clearly. It stated, "Your breasts may be too big, too saggy, too pert, too flat, too full, too far apart, too close together, too A cup, too lopsided, too jiggly, too pale, too padded, too pointy, too pendulous, or just two mosquito bites." With the advertiser's product, however, young women were assured "at least you can have your hair the way you want it." Other advertisements for cosmetic breast surgery show a beautiful small-breasted woman standing naked at a mirror covering her breasts with her hands and saying: "It was the one area in my life where I always felt deprived." With such messages it should not be surprising that some adolescent girls would prefer that the matter not be discussed.

Weight and Body Image

Baggy styles not only hide developing breasts, but they also mask the fact that girls' bodies are becoming increasingly different from those of boys. Puberty involves a considerable increase in fatty tissue in girls both in relative and absolute terms. Although such changes in body composition appear to be necessary to maintain normal reproductive functioning, weight gain cannot be viewed merely as a physiological matter. An increase in weight has severe negative consequences in today's society. First, it accentuates female difference from the normative lean male body. Second, it causes the young woman to deviate from the ideal thin female body. Some young women have begun to reject an excessively thin body ideal. One on-line site for girls called "riotgirls" (www.riotgirl.com) has, for example, begun a feature called "Feed the Supermodel" (Figure 7.4).

Beliefs about what is attractive, gender-appropriate, or erotic vary enormously from one culture to another and from one historical era to another. The "long lithe look" is considered to be the ideal for female beauty today, and it has been so for several decades. Fashion-model sketches and photographs of the female form accentuate the leg length of women and girls more so than that of men and boys. This is especially the case in high-fashion illustrations. Women are depicted with significantly longer legs than men in women's magazines and fashion advertisements in daily newspapers. This portrayal is contrary to actual differences between women and men (Faust, 1983).

Such dimensions are characteristic only of girls in the earliest phases of puberty and Barbie dolls. One researcher, Kelly Brownell of Yale University, whose 7-year-old daughter already owned six Barbies, determined just how impossible this doll's dimensions are. He calculated that if a normal, healthy woman wanted to look like a life-size Barbie, she would have to grow nearly a foot in height, add four inches to her chest, and lose five inches from her waist (Discover, 1996).

What are the consequences for young women of setting up an ideal of beauty that few of them can attain? Puberty is the period in which differences in self-esteem between girls and boys begin to emerge (Major et al., 1999). Dissatisfaction with how one looks begins during puberty and is linked to rapid and normal weight gain that is part of growing up (Attie & Brooks-Gunn, 1989).

These gender-related differences are related to differences in the social meaning of weight for boys and girls (see Figure 7.5). Boys are less likely to be defined by their physical self than girls are. Boys, moreover, gain muscle rather than fat during puberty. The consequences of defining a normal physiological change as unattractive are major in their effects on girls' satisfaction

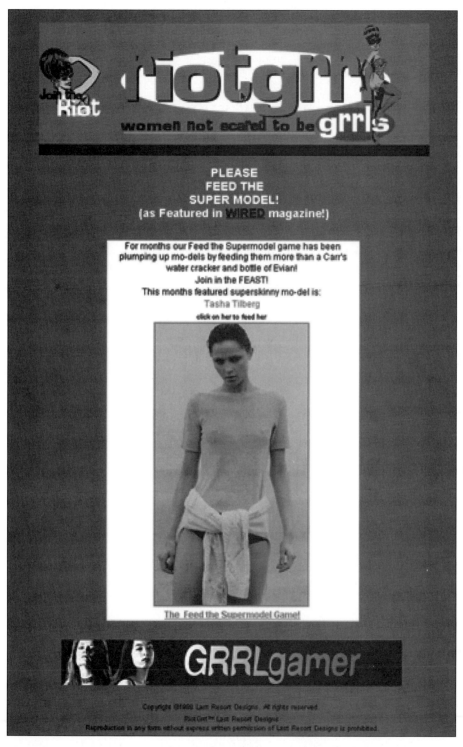

FIGURE 7.4. Making fun of female cultural icons. On this web site girls are invited to feed the supermodel rich, fattening foods.

Calvin and Hobbes

by Bill Watterson

FIGURE 7.5. The different sources of self-esteem for boys and girls: doing versus being.
Source: Calvin and Hobbes © 1990 Watterson. Reprinted with permission of Universal Press Syndicate. All rights reserved.

with themselves. For example, in both seventh and eighth grade, more physically mature girls were found to be generally less satisfied with their weight (Crockett & Petersen, 1987). Boys with greater physical maturity tended to be more satisfied with their weight. They also reported less desire to change their appearance than less mature boys did.

Boys perceived their bodies significantly more positively than girls in terms of overall body image (Tobin-Richards, Boxer, & Petersen, 1983). Pubertal girls were less proud of their bodies than boys, felt more poorly developed, and wished they were thinner. Perceptions about weight produced the largest gender-related differences of any measure. For girls, perceiving oneself as underweight was associated with the greatest amount of satisfaction, followed closely by average weight. A large dip in satisfaction occurred with perceptions of being overweight.

A national survey conducted in 1995 on ninth- through twelfth-grade students found that 34 percent of girls (compared with 22 percent of boys) perceived themselves as overweight (Phillips, 1998). Sixty percent of girls—nearly two out of three—were trying to lose weight at the time of the survey. For many girls and young women, being thin is linked with being in control. Thinness is valued because it signifies triumph over the body and its desire to eat (Malson, 1997). This idea is illustrated by the comments of one group of young women discussing their weight:

Teresa: Passivity is linked in my mind to being fat and to being indulgent, to being out of control.

Zoe: I felt like such a loser because I felt like I couldn't control my weight because I was overweight. So there must be something wrong with me because you know, oh well, I didn't have enough self-control.

Emma: I want to lose the fat. . . . I hate it being in me and it feels completely alien and I just want it away. You know, I want it *off*. It just doesn't feel like it should be part of me . . . you know. It feels all wrong, I . . . just do feel like this big, monstrous sow.

Jane: I just wanted to get rid of all this weight an' it made me feel I was better 'cos there was less fat . . . as if there was less bad. (Malson, 1997, p. 235)

Adolescent girls may attempt to control their weight even when their methods for doing so have serious health consequences (see Box 7.1).

A recent development among girls is to focus on the body as a project. A feminist historian examined the diaries of adolescent women over the past 100 years (Bromberg, 1997). She found that girls in earlier eras described their ideas for self-improvement in terms of more discipline in their studies, learning better manners, or getting along better with their parents. Beginning in the last twenty years, however, self-improvement has been described primarily in terms of bodily change. This time period coincides with the time when the mass media began their narrow focus on thinness as the major determinant of attractiveness in women.

Excessive concern with the control of weight has major implications for young women's health. Consider, for example, the following points made in a recent comprehensive report commissioned by the National Council for Research on Women on what we know about growing up female:

- Girls and women account for 90 percent of all cases of eating disorders. Eating disorders have the highest mortality rate (10 percent) among all types of psychiatric disorders. Girls 7–17 years old are now the heaviest users of diet pills.

- Overall, smoking is on the rise for girls. However, black girls are much less likely to smoke than girls of other races; white girls are more likely to use cigarettes than girls of any other racial group. In 1991, 13 percent of eighth

---

Box 7.1 Study: Diabetic Teenage Girls often Skip Insulin to Stay Thin

Diabetic teenage girls often skip their insulin injections as a way of losing weight, sharply increasing their risk of eye damage, according to a new study.

Canadian researchers found that one-third of the adolescent girls at one hospital diabetes clinic regularly underdosed themselves with insulin.

"It can prevent weight gain, but it is a very dangerous thing to do," said Dr. Gary M. Rodin, a psychiatrist who studied the problem.

Typically, youngsters with diabetes gain about 10 pounds when they start taking insulin shots. However, often they are already underweight because of their disease.

Rodin and colleagues from Toronto Hospital found that while eating disorders—especially binge eating—are common among adolescent teenagers with diabetes, by far the more serious problem is skimping on insulin.

Their study published in today's New England Journal of Medicine found that 86 percent of girls with eating problems had early stages of diabetic retinopathy, a serious eye condition that can lead to blindness.

By comparison, 24 percent of those with normal eating habits had the eye disorder.

The young women were all patients at Toronto's Hospital for Sick Children.

Rodin said the researchers have also studied diabetic boys but found no sign they fail to take enough insulin.

Source: Boston Herald 6/26/97. Reprinted by permission of the Associated Press.

grade girls reported smoking, or more than one in eight. In 1996, the number jumped to 21 percent, or more than one in five. Smoking initiation among girls is strongly associated with weight concerns and dieting. (Adapted from Phillips, 1998, p. 30)

Although the rate of smoking has increased much more rapidly among young women than among young men, very few studies have examined the gender-specific factors associated with this behavior.

Early versus Late Maturation

Because there is a great deal of individual variation in the timing of the events of puberty, these individual differences can be used to examine the impact of social beliefs on psychological functioning. For example, the long lithe look is more attainable by girls who enter puberty later than the average age. Early-maturing girls, on the other hand, weigh more and are slightly shorter than their late-maturing peers even when pubertal growth is complete (Brooks-Gunn, 1987a). Early maturers also have poorer body images related to weight and are more concerned about dieting than late maturers (Attie & Brooks-Gunn, 1989). In contrast, boys who mature early tend to perceive themselves more positively than boys who are either on time or late (Tobin-Richards et al., 1983).

Early-maturing girls have been found to date more than late-maturing girls in middle and junior high school (Brooks-Gunn, 1988). Early-maturing eighth-grade girls were more likely to report having a boyfriend, talking with boys on the phone, dating, and "making out" than their less mature peers (Crockett & Petersen, 1987). They may also engage in "adult behaviors" such as smoking, drinking, and sexual intercourse at an earlier age probably because their friends are older (Magnusson, Strattin, & Allen, 1985).

There is also some evidence that early puberty has negative implications for girls' academic performance. In a large-scale longitudinal study of students in sixth through tenth grade, researchers found that pubertal girls performed less well in both sixth and seventh grade (Simmons & Blyth, 1987). They had significantly lower grade-point averages and poorer reading and math achievement scores than later-maturing girls. These effects are the flip side of these girls' greater popularity and social acceptance (see Figure 7.6). For example, the number of contacts with boyfriends has been found to be negatively related to academic performance for early adolescent girls (Feiring & Lewis, 1991).

The effects of the timing of maturation for girls are complex. This complexity probably reflects the mixed nature of womanhood as constructed by our society. The clear positive social response to the physical maturation of boys does not occur for girls. Becoming an adult in our society does not bring with it the same social advantages for a woman as it does for a man. The social advantages for the maturing boy include athletic competence, an opportunity for leadership roles, and expectations of occupational success. Physical maturation for girls may carry more explicit sexualized meanings. The premature sexualization of early-maturing girls puts them at risk in terms of involvement in activities with peers who are socially more experienced than they are them-

Funky Winkerbean

FIGURE 7.6. The relative importance of dating versus scholastic achievement during the high school years.
Source: Copyright © 1998. Reprinted with special permission of North America Syndicate.

selves. The difficulties of the early-maturing girl in comparison with similarly aged boys and later-maturing girls illuminate the contradictions implicit in being a mature woman in our society.

Ethnicity and Class and the Response to Puberty

Weight concerns among adolescent girls in the United States appear to be virtually universal. Far more women than men diet. In every socioeconomic class studied, the majority of young women, upon reaching full sexual maturity, wished that they were thinner (Dornbusch, Gross, Duncan, & Ritter, 1987). More than 70 percent of white women within normal weight ranges have been on a diet (Thornberry, Wilson, & Golden, 1986). However, more affluent young women are most likely to have bought into the belief that one "can be neither too rich nor too thin." Researchers have found that privileged young women are more likely to wish to be thinner—even after the actual level of fatness of each individual has been controlled for statistically (Dornbusch et al., 1987).

Most of the studies of the impact of puberty have been done on white middle-class populations. A few studies suggest, however, that unrealistic standards of weight have had less of an impact on African-American than European-American women. For example, a survey of fifty-five white and eleven black female dancers in nine regional and national ballet companies in the United States and western Europe found that 15 percent of the white and none of the black American dancers were anorexic. None of the black dancers reported binging or purging, whereas 19 percent of the white dancers reported having done so (Hamilton, Brooks-Gunn, Warren, & Hamilton, 1987).

Although eating disorders in women of color have probably been underreported, these women may have been somewhat protected from the effects of unrealistic weight standards by a racist paradox. The current American standard of thinness applies mainly to white women (Chapter 2). This management of weight is designed to position women within an elite class location (Bordo, 1993). The tight, svelte body reflects material and moral comfort.

Body control may take different forms for adolescents who are neither white nor middle class. For example, while privileged young white women appear to be very familiar with eating disorders, working- and middle-class African-American women are sometimes bewildered at the image of a young woman binging on food and then purging (Fine & Macpherson, 1992). Although eating disorders occur in all ethnic groups, white girls most often develop anorexia and bulimia, followed most closely by Latinas. This is consistent with research findings that black girls report more positive body images than either white or Hispanic girls. A 1996 survey of girls aged 11 to 17 found that 40 percent of the black girls studied considered themselves attractive or very attractive compared with only 9.1 percent of the white girls (Phillips, 1998).

Other studies have found that white adolescent girls have higher self-consciousness, more instability of self-image, and lower self-esteem than black girls of the same age and social class (Simmons & Rosenberg, 1975). For girls of color, culturally and linguistically different girls, working-class girls, and girls living in poverty, gender is not the only site for struggle and negotiation.

What are the experiences that make girls feel good about who they are? In a diverse population of adolescents, girls were most likely to mention athletics as the area that made them feel best (46%). Other aspects of their lives that made them feel good were involvement in arts-related activities (19%), service to others (14%), and simply playing (13%). These preferred activities were, however, influenced by ethnicity, wealth, and where the girls lived. Native American and Asian-American girls were most likely to mention athletics as an activity that made them feel good about themselves. Affluent girls, especially those who lived in cities, were less likely to mention athletics and more likely to mention an arts-related activity such as music, painting, dance, or drama. Urban areas are most likely to provide opportunities for such activities, especially for those whose families can afford to pay for them (Erkut, Fields, Sing, & Marks, 1997).

Ethnicity and class were also related to the reasons girls gave about why an activity made them feel good. Overall, girls from more affluent social classes were more likely to report mastery than those who were less privileged. Class was positively related to mastery, however, only for European-American and Asian-American girls. For Native American girls and Latinas, mastery was inversely related to social class, and there was no relationship between class and mastery in the reports of African-American girls. It seems that social class produces different experiences for girls from various ethnic groups.

Girls from different locations also gave differing reasons for why they enjoyed particular activities. For example, African-American and Asian-American girls were more likely than other groups of girls to say that their enjoyment of an activity was the reason it made them feel good. However, those girls who lived in rural areas or on reservations were more likely to say that the opportunity to be with friends was why an activity made them feel good. Since particular ethnic groups are more likely to be found in some locations rather than others, researchers must take care not to confuse situational context or differential opportunity with ethnic differences.

Situational context interacts with ethnicity in other ways as well. For example, black pubertal girls appear to be less disrupted by moving between elementary and junior high school than white girls are (Simmons, Burgeson, & Reef, 1988). Overall, adolescent girls report much lower self-esteem than girls in grade school, this drop in self-esteem is much larger for girls than boys, and boys in high school report higher self-esteem than their female peers. But research on African-American girls contradicts these findings. This pattern appears to be unique to African-American girls as compared with other ethnic minority populations. Latinas, for example, who express the highest level of self-esteem in elementary school, report less confidence than other girls in their talents, abilities, physical appearance, and relationships with others by the time they reach high school (Phillips, 1998).

SCHOOLS AND SOCIAL POWER

Girls as a group appear to be much more permanently affected than boys by school transitions during their pubertal years. Large-scale longitudinal studies conducted in several cities have shown that the shift from elementary to junior high school and then to high school lowers the self-esteem of girls (Simmons & Blyth, 1987). Girls drop in both school participation and leadership after the transition into a large junior high or middle school. This drop occurs again in high school. Girls who have made two such changes remain impaired when compared with boys and girls who have made one transition from a K–8 elementary to high school.

Why does the transition to a large impersonal environment at an early age have such a major impact on girls? One possibility is that when they make a school transition after sixth grade, girls are being thrust into a social environment for which they are emotionally unprepared. They come into contact with older boys, and, as noted earlier in this chapter, the opportunity to date decreases rather than enhances girls' self-esteem.

Evaluations based on physical attractiveness are more prevalent for women and girls than for men and boys. Nearly 70 percent of the young women surveyed in one study reported being teased or criticized—mostly in terms of their appearance (Rieves & Cash, 1996). See Table 7.1 for a list of the humiliating themes and the most probable teasers. Many strong girls are socially isolated during adolescence because their difference threatens their peers' culture (Pipher, 1994).

Negative evaluations are likely to occur in a school setting. Here are some graphic descriptions by Canadian high school students (Larkin and Popaleni, 1994):

> This guy and his brother went on in their sick way of having fun by rating young women as they passed by in the hallway. I told the guy he was sexist and by rating young women as they passed by . . . he was making them uncomfortable. He said "Just for saying that, I give you a zero."

> I came across a stack of boards in the corner of the art classroom with graffiti written all over them. I expected to read "So and so, 100% true love" or the

TABLE 7.1. The Foci and Perpetrators of Recurrent Appearance Teasing/ Criticism during Childhood and Adolescence

Foci	(%)	Teasers	Ever (%)	Worst (%)
Face and head	45	Mother	30	11
Hair	12	Father	24	6
Lower torso	11	Brother(s)[a]	41 (79)	17 (33)
Mid torso	2	Sister(s)[a]	22 (36)	5 (8)
Upper torso	19	Other relatives	23	4
Muscle tone	1	Friends	47	16
Weight	36	A specific peer	31	13
Height	17	Peers in general	62	28
Clothes/attire	13	Teachers	6	0
Hands/feet	3	Other adults	20	1
General appearance	10			
Miscellaneous	6			

[a]The percentages in parentheses are based on only those participants who have brothers (n = 79) or who have sisters (n = 93) rather than on the entire sample.
Source: Rieves & Cash (1996).

names of people's favorite bands, but as I looked at the graffiti I saw a picture of a naked woman (no arms, head, calves, or knees) with her legs wide open showing her vagina, anal opening and breasts. I was shocked to see such explicit graffiti in my favorite class. I never thought anyone from our school could draw such violent pictures of women in the classroom and not have anyone say or do anything about it. Other people must have seen it because the room is used by three other classes. [To me] that picture says "Rape is OK, sexual abuse is OK," and this is what I'm scared of the most. (p. 220)

Adolescent girls encounter an enormous amount of sexual harassment in school. Harassment often occurs while other people watch. It may be viewed as a public performance conducted primarily by boys for other boys. Teachers and school officials often downplay the significance of sexual harassment among students. Not only may they look the other way, but they may stand by while girls are harassed in front of them in classrooms and school corridors (Stein, 1995). The boys' behavior is frequently dismissed as adolescent pranks, rites of passage, or awkward attempts at sexual teasing. Even when sexual harassment is addressed, intervention seldom occurs at an institutional level. One investigator who spent two years visiting an urban middle school reported that "girls and women in the school found themselves solving the problem of male violence quietly, covertly, and without making any public fuss" (Pastor, McCormick, & Fine, 1996, p. 21). Both girls and boys witness sexist, racist, and homophobic behavior (the latter forms of harassment are used more by boys against other boys) being displayed publicly, in front of adults and peers, without any obvious consequences.

THE SILENCING OF YOUNG WOMEN

Many girls appear to lose their confidence and a clear sense of identity during adolescence. Self-silencing and taking one's knowledge underground are costly strategies adolescent girls employ to remain accepted by others (Brown & Gilligan, 1992, 1993). In repeated interviews, girls from an elite private girls' high school appeared to lose their ability to take seriously their own experience, feelings, and thoughts (Brown & Gilligan, 1993). One girl, for example, used the phrase "I don't know" 112 times in her eighth-grade transcript— more than three times more frequently than in the previous year, although the interviews were of the same length. These girls appear to be struggling with the conflict between authenticity and relatedness. To stay true to themselves they risk being seen as neither "nice" nor "normal" by others.

How general is such silencing? The two adolescent girls focused on by the researchers, Anna and Neeti, both differed from their classmates in important ways. Anna was a working-class scholarship student and Neeti was from an Asian-Indian background. Their perceived need to "fit in" may have had class and ethnic components in addition to problems in making the transition to adulthood. Silencing must also be viewed in a multicultural perspective. In more communal cultures, for example, it would not be considered undesirable

Making a Difference

Teenager *Kelli Peterson* co-founded the Gay Straight Alliance (GSA) at East High School in Salt Lake City, Utah, in 1996, tired of hiding the fact that she was a lesbian and concerned that other high school students were experiencing the same loneliness, shame, and fear. Peterson was not prepared for the subsequent media maelstrom. She became the center of a long-running national news story about the lengths to which conservatives would go to oppose the GSA. The local school board finally voted to ban all clubs from campus rather than allow the GSA to meet, despite unflattering national publicity and massive protest by gay and straight students from many Salt Lake City schools. Peterson appeared on the national news and made the cover of at least one magazine, and was recently featured in a documentary film entitled *Out of the*

Past, which aired on PBS stations around the country. In 1996, Utah's legislature passed a law allowing rental of school property for group meetings, and the GSA has been meeting on campus ever since. This is a victory of sorts, but Peterson's goal was never to prevent other student support or activity groups from meeting. Conservative parents and politicians believe clubs like the GSA are dangerous recruiting tools for homosexuals, but as Peterson stated at a meeting of the Utah Senate and Salt Lake City School Board, "I did not start this group to recruit. . . . I started this group to end the misery and isolation of being gay in high school."

Sources: Sahagun, L. (1996, February 22). Utah board bans all school clubs in anti-gay move. *Los Angeles Times,* p. 1.

Gay alert, drop everything. (1997, April 27). *The Economist,* p. 31.

Dupre, J. (Producer/Director). (1996). *Out of the Past,* [Film.]

for someone (male or female) to submerge their own feelings for the good of the group.

Silencing may represent a form of resistance by young women (Brown & Gilligan, 1993). But this is not the only possible form of resistance. Recent research has suggested that silencing may be more common among European-American teenage girls who have more to gain by "buying into" the gendered status quo. Young urban women of color have been found, for example, to create safe spaces for each other that they do not make accessible to adult authorities whom they believe to be intrusive and controlling. As one young woman commented:

> I think counselors should ask what you want. Sometimes you don't want something to happen in a certain way but they do what they have to do. My friend . . . had an incident with her mother. Her mother has a lot of kids. She is single. She has eight kids. My friend felt neglected. She was not getting attention or nothing like that, so she went to her guidance counselor thinking maybe her guidance counselor could talk to her mother and tell her how she feels because sometimes you don't feel right to tell your mother this, but the guidance counselors reported it to the B.C.W. (Bureau of Child Welfare). That was the last thing my friend wanted. (Pastor et al., 1996, p. 25)

Young African-American women may also resist silencing by becoming "loud" and oppositional in order to counter their invisibility in largely white schools (Fordham, 1993). However, this form of resistance (which is more collectivist than individualistic in nature) can also result in their disengagement from education and the loss of an opportunity to acquire power in white society. Many forms of resistance have both positive and negative consequences.

Young women's assertiveness appears to vary from one situation to another. It is associated with their perception of support for making their opinions known in specific contexts as well as their concern that expressing true opinions might jeopardize particular relationships. Adults may mistake girls' useful, culturally learned strategies for a lack of self-esteem or a tendency to give up on themselves (Phillips, 1998). However, such strategies may be quite realistic. Although there have been few studies of the impact of girls' assertiveness on their peers, one recent study from Israel noted that 10-year-old girls who reported traits and behaviors considered more characteristic of boys were significantly less popular with their peers than more gender-typed girls (Lobel, Stone, & Winch, 1997). Girls, as well as women, may choose to be less assertive in order to be more likeable—not a choice that boys or men have to make (Crawford, 1988).

PARENT-CHILD RELATIONSHIPS

How do girls learn to resist gendering? An obvious site for investigation is a girl's family. Puberty serves as a pivotal point for changes in familial relationships. Time spent with parents and yielding to parents in decision making decrease for both girls and boys from early to middle adolescence (Montemayor & Hanson, 1985). Emotional distance between parents and children also increases during this period. Conflict between parents and children appears to be highest in early adolescence. Although such conflicts are mild in most cases, both parents and children agree that these conflicts are significant. Adolescents perceive them as more frequent than parents do.

In white middle-class families, mother-daughter conflict is pronounced during early puberty (Brooks-Gunn & Zehaykevich, 1989). These conflicts appear to be due more to social than to physiological factors. For example, negative emotions about menarche and pubertal change are common in girls, and girls may attribute them to parents, particularly the mother, who is perceived as not being sensitive to their desire for secrecy. Menarche appears to produce a particularly intense, although temporary, period of family turmoil. Daughters reported more parental control in the first six months after menarche than either premenstrual girls or those whose menarche had occurred more than six to twelve months in the past (Hill & Holmbeck, 1987).

In contrast, mother-daughter relationships appear to remain close after puberty in African-American families (Fine & Macpherson, 1992). Black girls spoke frequently about how much they learned from their mothers. In contrast to the focus on control by European-American mothers, these girls spoke about their mothers' strength, honesty, ability to overcome difficulties, and ability to survive (Joseph & Lewis, 1981). African-American mothers actively teach their daughters to resist the assault of dominant standards about attractiveness and self-worth (Ward, 1996). African-American girls report their mothers as their greatest source of emotional support, and most conflicts between mothers and daughters seem to be about minor everyday issues such as cleaning up around the house (Cauce et al., 1996).

Fathers were largely absent from black adolescent girls' discourse. White fathers were figuratively rather than literally absent. They reported not wishing to talk about body changes or sexuality with their daughters. White fathers also become more assertive or brusque with their postmenarcheal daughters (Hill, 1988). This may be a way of physically distancing themselves, given cultural strictures about father-daughter incest.

FACTORS IMPEDING GENDER EQUALITY

Femininity and Self-Esteem

Freud and other psychodynamic theorists have not had much to say about the dynamics of gender differences after early childhood. They proposed, however, that females are more narcissistic than males, especially after they reach sexual maturity. The events of puberty do appear to focus the child's attention on his or her changing body as well as the body maturity of others (Greene & Adams-Price, 1990). These effects are stronger for girls than for boys. After menarche young women are more apt to draw more sexually explicit female bodies and are more likely to draw a woman before a man when asked to draw a person. In terms of psychodynamic theories, these behaviors suggest an increase in identification with mature femininity (Koff, 1983).

However, psychoanalytic theories have paid little attention to the cultural importance of female attractiveness in constructing differences between women and men. For example, the decline in self-esteem among girls after puberty is partially related to their perceptions about their attractiveness. This relationship between perceived attractiveness and self-esteem has been found only in white adolescents (Tashakkori, 1993). Beliefs about parental closeness were a better predictor of self-esteem for African-American adolescents. Clearly, the demand for thinness contributes to the potential difficulties faced by girls entering puberty. Recent studies have found that such demands are stronger in the white than in the black community (Powell & Kahn, 1995; Thompson, Sargent, & Kemper, 1996).

A longitudinal study that followed girls and boys from the fourth through the twelfth grade indicates that the decline in self-esteem among young women is also related to the declining importance of relationality for their image of themselves (Allgood-Merten & Stockard, 1991). Although self-esteem was significantly associated with perceptions of self-efficacy and relationality for girls in the fourth grade, by the twelfth grade only self-efficacy contributed to their self-esteem. This finding suggests that only stereotypically masculine traits are valued in the world of adolescents.

The devaluing of traits such as expressiveness and relationality contributes to the conflicts experienced by girls entering adolescence. They are coming of age as women while, at the same time, the traits considered characteristic of women decline in importance. It is important to keep this kind of social construction in mind when evaluating theories about the female personality.

Gender Intensification

At puberty, gender roles intensify under pressure from both peers and parents (Hill & Lynch, 1983). Changes in physical appearance may lead to changes in self-views and in the expectations of others. Within each sex, for example, greater height has been found to be associated with higher aspirations and higher expectations in both parents and the young people themselves (Dornbusch et al., 1987). Teachers' assessments of intellectual ability and academic achievement are also associated with height. This effect is actually larger than that for physical maturation.

For boys, early sexual maturation is associated with greater independence in decision making and late maturation with a lower level of independence. The relationship is much weaker in girls. This difference may be due to adult perceptions that early development in girls is more of a problem of sexuality and less a prologue to greater independence and achievement. Since girls also mature, on the average, two years earlier than boys, their chronological status may interfere with the degree of independence their apparent physical maturity confers on them.

Physical development in girls exposes them to dating pressures from older boys. Early dating activity may affect relations with other girls. For example, girls tend to choose best friends who are at the same level of physical maturation as themselves (Brooks-Gunn, Samelson, Warren, & Fox, 1986). Attention from older boys may also intensify self-consciousness and concern about being liked among 12- to 14-year-old girls (Rosenberg & Simmons, 1975). Junior high school girls who were physically mature and who had started dating were found to have the lowest self-esteem of all the girls studied (Simmons, Blyth, Van Cleave, & Bush, 1979). Male-female relationships play an important role in girls' and women's self-esteem (see Chapter 8).

Both girls and boys show trends in the direction of gender-role intensification from grades seven through nine. Not acting like the other sex becomes more important (Simmons & Blyth, 1987). Girls in the higher school grades were much less likely than girls in sixth grade to admit that they could ever act like boys (see Chapter 6). There was little room for boys to change in this measure since even in childhood they are unwilling to admit that they could ever act like a girl.

The Role of Peer Culture

During the teenage years, peer groups increase in size and complexity. Both girls and boys spend more time with their peers than children do. Peer groups can develop a social system that affects the behavior of all their members regardless of the individual's level of physical maturity. For example, an entire group may begin to engage in "pubertal behavior," such as increases in talking on the telephone, frequency of showers, and time spent in front of the mirror (Petersen, 1987). Such group effects may precede individual change at least for some late-maturing adolescents. Grade-in-school effects are often much stronger than maturational timing effects, probably because the adolescents' social world is organized by school grade rather than pubertal development (Brooks-Gunn, 1988).

Some recent ethnographic and observational studies of behavior in the school environment suggest that relationships between the sexes can be quite hostile during adolescence. Extensive research in English schools shows a great deal of verbal abuse of girls by boys (Lees, 1993). A double standard of terminology referring to girls' and boys' sexuality is used to maintain male dominance. The word that illustrates this asymmetry more clearly than any other term is *slag*. Although it is supposed to refer to sexual promiscuity, it is used in many situations that are not related to a girl's actual sexual behavior. Thus, a girl may be called a slag if she wears too much makeup, if her skirt is slit too high, or if her clothes are too tight. On the other hand, unattractive or unfashionably dressed girls are never called slags, although other degrading terms are available for them. The term slag is ambiguous—it implies that the woman is both contemptible and sexually desirable. It is used by both boys and girls as a form of sexual and social control.

English working-class girls are another group who do not lose their voices during adolescence (Lees, 1997). Their most effective forms of resistance involve verbally subverting or challenging the terms of the abuse or collectively resisting the insults. Occasionally girls did take action against the boys as shown in the following account:

> The boys love coming into the girls' changing rooms. This boy, right, we made a decision next time he comes in, grab hold of him and start taking his clothes off and see how he feels. All the girls were watching him. He never comes back. (Lees, 1997, p. 32)

Collective action seems to be an important strategy for girls dealing with a sexist system. Researchers have found, for example, that black girls in the United States were protected from the negative effects of school transitions if they transferred schools with a group of thirty or more peers (Simmons et al., 1988). The size of the peer network had no impact on the negative consequences of school transition for white girls. A more collectivist orientation may protect girls from institutionalized sexism. Evaluations have the greatest impact when an individual enters a new setting (Lerner, Lerner, & Tubman, 1989). Valuation based on looks is problematic for any individual. It involves subjective and unstable criteria. And it places the person at the mercy of outside judges. These judgments may be harder to control in a new school with lesser-known peers.

Cultural Constructions: Are They Changing?

The cultural factors that make adolescent girls more vulnerable to social stress do not appear to have changed as a result of the feminist movement. The studies on the more negative impact of school transitions for girls than for boys were conducted in the late 1970s—well after the feminist movement was under way. Other researchers have found that gender stereotyping among boys and girls was not significantly less in 1982 than in 1956 (Lewin & Tragos, 1987). Boys emphasized gender-role differences and symbols of male dominance more than girls did. They also had more traditional attitudes toward the social, economic, and political rights of women than girls did (Galambos, Petersen, Richards, & Gitelson, 1985). It is noteworthy that boys appear to be more traditional than girls in all national groups sampled in a recent cross-cultural study (Gibbons, Stiles, & Shkodriani, 1991). However, an unusual pattern has been found for African-American adolescent males. They appear to combine traditional attitudes about male gender roles with less conservative attitudes about female gender roles (Pleck, Sonenstein, & Ku, 1994). They are, for example, likely to disagree with the statement that it is better for everyone if the man earns money and the woman takes care of home and family.

Beliefs about women and men can be affected by the social environment. For instance, rural adolescents endorse significantly more traditional attitudes than urban adolescents do. Beliefs are related to individual characteristics as well. Thus, less traditional attitudes toward women were related to higher self-esteem in girls and in one sample of boys (Galambos et al., 1985). Beliefs will not change readily, however, unless significant social change takes place both in adolescent peer groups and in society as a whole. There is little to indicate that such changes are taking place. In fact, one study has indicated that tenth-graders stereotyped various boys' and girls' activities more than children in fourth, sixth, or eighth grades did (Plumb & Cowan, 1984).

The popular media to which young women are exposed certainly do not present images of equality to them. One study examined the number of pages of *Seventeen* magazine that were devoted to various themes for the years 1961, 1972, and 1985 (see Table 7.2). Although the number of pages on male-female relationships decreased and the number of pages on self-development increased in 1972 (possibly as a result of the feminist movement of the late 1960s), by 1985 the percentage had returned to the 1961 figures (Peirce, 1990).

TABLE 7.2. Percentages of Editorial Pages Given to Selected Topics in *Seventeen* Magazine

	1961	1972	1985
Appearance	48.0	52.0	46.0
Home	9.0	10.0	11.0
Male-female relations	7.0	2.7	6.5
Self-development	7.5	16.6	6.8

A further analysis of *Seventeen* by the same researcher (Peirce, 1993) found that more than 60 percent of the articles in each issue were on fashion, beauty, food, and decorating. Most of the fiction showed males and females in gender-traditional occupations. In this example, the heroine, a high school sophomore, suddenly finds herself with a boyfriend:

> "Now I was someone with a future. . . . Until now I'd been a kid, stumbling along. . . . A few weeks ago I'd been a zero and now I had a boyfriend!"

When it turns out that the boy is involved with someone else, the protagonist comments:

> "Now I didn't have a boyfriend anymore, an Ivy-League, advanced math, possible husband-in-a-big-modern-house boyfriend." (Peirce, 1993, p. 64)

"Fortunately" for this young woman, there is another boy waiting in the wings. One could hardly call these images self-actualizing!

Magazines designed for teenagers in Europe do not seem to be much better than those published in the United States. One investigator recently compared the first six issues of a magazine for teenage boys published in the Netherlands with one for teenage girls. She found that 40 percent of the girls' magazine was devoted to such female stereotypic topics as fashion, beauty, love, and romantic fiction. Another 10 percent consisted of "tips" on interior decorating, needlework, and recipes. In contrast, over 30 percent of the boys' magazine was devoted to tips on travel, a regular feature called "Wheels" on cars, motorcycles, and so on and a feature on films, compact disks, and computer games (Willemsen, 1998).

How do certain aspects of the media target adolescents? Twelve- to 17-year-olds are the primary listeners to radio programs during certain parts of the day. Males dominate this programming as DJs, newscasters, voice-overs in advertisements, sportscasters, and weather forecasters. Females are more likely to be found only as traffic reporters and audience participants (Lont, 1990). The terms used to identify males and females in these broadcasts also differ. Women are referred to primarily by family roles such as wife, mother, daughter, or sister (or, sometimes, as ladies). Men are usually referred to as guys, sir, or Mr.

So-called slasher films (which also appeal primarily to adolescents) have a sexist component. Although female and male victims are portrayed equally frequently and are as likely to die in an attack, female nonsurvivors wore significantly more revealing and provocative clothing, were more likely to be shown undressing, nude, or engaging in sexual activity, and were shown as promiscuous more than females who survived (Cowan & O'Brien, 1990). Other studies have found that women who wear heavy makeup are rated as more immoral and more likely to be sexually harassed than those who use less makeup (Workman & Johnson, 1991). However, these women are also seen as more attractive and feminine. These images construct a double bind similar to the one found in the use of the term slag discussed earlier in this chapter. Adolescent girls are being told simultaneously that they should appeal to the sexual fantasies of men, but also that such appeal is dangerous.

Behavior at any age is a complex mix of biological, psychological, and sociocultural forces. Adolescence is a life stage at which many such forces converge and conflict for young women. Contradictory cultural constructions of womanhood are imposed during a period when both girls and boys are negotiating for adulthood. Very few women report that they wish to return to their teenage years. Men appear to have found them more satisfactory. Neither of us would like to be 13 again.

WORKING TOGETHER TOWARD GENDER EQUALITY

Many of the young women discussed in this chapter have developed individual strategies of resistance to sexist constructions that contribute to female inequality. Collective strategies are even more effective. In recent years, girls have become an outspoken voice in the women's movement. Making use of computer technology, there has been a growing number of girls' "zines" that critique mainstream magazines for girls and offer their own, often subversive, images of current culture (see Figure 7.7).

Some of these publications have gone on-line. *Teen Voice Online* is a teen magazine for adolescent girls that encourages audience participation and invites submissions of creative writing and book and music reviews. It can be found at: *www.teenvoices.com*. Another Web site *Club Girl Tech* (*girlstech.com*) contains positive news articles about girls and has a search engine to help viewers find other Web sites for girls. *American Girl Magazine,* found at *www.americangirl.com/ag/ag/cgi,* includes a forum for girls to share ideas, information, and volunteer experience.

A number of women's organizations are also supporting research and action on behalf of girls. These include the American Association of University Women's Educational Foundation, The Ms. Foundation, the Women's College Coalition, and The National Council for Research on Women. The latter organization financed the recent publication of *The Girls Report: What We Know and Need to Know about Growing Up Female* (Phillips, 1998). This publication includes a fourteen-page resource guide to books, media, and programs for and about girls. Thirteen now is not the same as thirteen was in the past or what it will be in the future. Technology offers the promise that young women no longer need to feel isolated in a hostile environment.

FIGURE 7.7. Transgressing cultural rules of gender—girls' zines as a site of resistance.

CONNECTING THEMES

- *Gender is more than just sex.* Adolescence is an excellent example of the way biological sex and the many social aspects of gender interact. The difference in the life experiences of early- versus late-maturing girls shows how perceptions about a young woman's body can influence her in ways that seem largely beyond her control.

- *Language and naming are sources of power.* Adolescence involves both naming and not naming. Recent observational studies demonstrate that the relationships between boys and girls during this period may have a larger power dimension and be much more verbally abusive than researchers had previously thought. Some young women may respond to the ambivalences of being a mature woman in a society that devalues women by silencing themselves.

- *Women are not all alike.* Because adolescence is a socially constructed category (in distinction to puberty, which is a biological event), it is expressed quite differently by young women from different social classes and racial/ethnic groupings in our society. White middle- and upper-class girls appear to be most vulnerable to the stresses produced by normative definitions of mature femininity. For example, they are more affected by school transitions and are more likely to suffer from eating disorders than working-class girls or those from ethnically marginalized groups.

- *Psychological research can foster social change.* Although male dominance is a social norm, strong girls can challenge the normative social structure. Peer groups of assertive young women are very effective agents of change. They are making use of new technologies to critique current cultural systems.

SUGGESTED READINGS

MARTIN, KARIN A. (1996). *Puberty, sexuality, and the self: Boys and girls at adolescence.* London: Routledge. This brief book examines the impact of puberty on both sexes through interviews and analysis. It looks at how adolescents construct their sense of the self and how these constructions are influenced by the social meaning of puberty.

ROSS LEADBEATER, BONNIE J., & WAY, NIOBE (Eds.). (1996). *Urban girls: Resisting stereotypes, constructing identities.* New York: New York University Press. This book presents a large number of studies conducted by experts on adolescence. It is particularly important for its sensitivity to how ethnic group membership and class status influences the experience of being a young female.

PHILLIPS, LYNN. (1998). *The girls report: What we know and need to know about growing up female.* New York: The National Council for Research on Women. This timely and comprehensive report covers important material on health, sexuality, violence, and schooling. It also provides an extensive resource guide for parents, social policy makers, and everyone interested in eliminating gender inequality in the United States.

CHAPTER 8

Sex, Love, and Romance

- **HOW IS SEXUALITY SHAPED BY CULTURE?**
  What Are Sexual Scripts?
  How Do Sexual Scripts Differ Across Cultures?
- **THE SCIENTIFIC STUDY OF SEX**
  A Brief History of Sex Research
  What Are the Strengths and Weaknesses of Sexuality Research?
- **ADOLESCENT SEXUALITY**
  How Does Sexuality Emerge in the Teen Years?
  What Factors Influence the Decision to Have Sex?
  Are Teens Having Safer Sex?
- **EXPERIENCING SEXUALITY**
  First Intercourse: Less Than Bliss?
  How Do Women Experience Orgasm?
  Evils of Masturbation or Joys of Self-Pleasure?
- **SEXUALITY IN SOCIAL CONTEXT**
  Romantic Love as a Cultural Script
  The Experience of Romantic Love
  Controlling Women's Sexuality
  Does Attractiveness Influence Sexual Desirability?
  Does Disability Affect Sexuality?

- **MIXED MESSAGES**
  Is Sex Talk Sexist?
  Studs and Sluts: Is There Still a Double Standard?
- **DESIRE AND PLEASURE**
  Do Romantic Scripts Affect Women's Sexual Experiences?
  Do Romantic Scripts Lead to Sexual Dysfunction?
  Where Is the Voice of Women's Desire?
- **LESBIAN AND BISEXUAL WOMEN**
  A Social History of Lesbianism
  Developing a Lesbian or Bisexual Identity
- **GENDER AND RELATIONSHIP DYNAMICS**
  Are There Power Issues in Heterosexual Relationships?
  Does Gender Affect Influence Strategies?
  Are There Power Issues in Lesbian Relationships?
- **WHAT DO WOMEN WANT? SATISFACTION IN CLOSE RELATIONSHIPS**
- **CONNECTING THEMES**
- **SUGGESTED READINGS**

Sex, love, and romance seem like natural events—instinctive, unlearned, and universal. For an example, think about a kiss. Perfectly natural, right? In Western societies, kissing is seen as an instinctive way to express love and increase arousal and a normal prelude to other sexual activity.

Yet in many cultures, kissing is unknown. When people from these cultures hear about our kissing customs, they agree that these practices are dangerous, unhealthy, or just plain disgusting. Anthropologists reported that when members of one African community first saw Europeans kissing, they laughed and said, "Look at them—they eat each other's saliva and dirt" (Tiefer, 1995, pp. 77–78). Strange as it may seem, sex is not a natural act! In other words, sexuality is not something that can be understood in purely biological terms. Instead, it is a social construct.

HOW IS SEXUALITY SHAPED BY CULTURE?

Individuals develop their own sense of sexual identity and desire in the context of their particular time in history, social class, ethnic group, religion, and prevailing set of gender roles (Foucalt, 1978; Rubin, 1984). Every culture throughout the world controls human sexuality (Hyde & DeLamater, 1997). Because men have more social and political power, this control usually works to their benefit. Sometimes control is quite overt; for example, through the practice of maiming women's genitals in order to "purify" and "tame" their sexuality. (Sexual violence such as rape and incest are discussed in Chapter 13.) Sometimes control is more subtle. We look at how the ideology of romantic love shapes women's understanding of heterosexual relationships. For women, cultural constructions of sexuality lead to an ongoing tension between pleasure and danger (Joseph & Lewis, 1981; Vance, 1984a).

What Are Sexual Scripts?

Each individual has a biological capacity for sexual arousal and physiological limits to the sexual response. But, rather than being "naturally" sexual, people learn rules that tell them how to have sex, with whom they may have it, what activities will be pleasurable, and when the individual is—and is not—allowed to take advantage of the biological potential for sexual enjoyment (Gagnon & Simon, 1973; Radlove, 1983). Together, the repertoire of sexual acts that is recognized by a particular social group, the rules or guidelines for expected behavior, and the expected punishments for violating the rules form the basis of *sexual scripts* (Laws & Schwartz, 1977).

The sexual scripts women (and men) learn can be thought of as schemas for sexual concepts and events. They represent ways of understanding and interpreting potentially sex-relevant situations and plans for action that people bring to such situations. Scripts operate at both a social and a personal level. They are part of cultural institutions (e.g., sexual behaviors are regulated by law and religion), and they are also internalized by individuals (some behaviors come to be seen as exciting and others as disgusting). Table 8.1 shows a familiar script: the first date. Shortly, we will look at love scripts. Throughout this chapter, the psychology of women's sexuality and intimate relationships is considered in terms of both biological potentials and the influences of society's sexual scripts.

How Do Sexual Scripts Differ Across Cultures?

There is tremendous variability in cultural scripts about sex, love, and romance. For example, people in the United States believe that love is necessary for marriage. But in the majority of the world, marriages are arranged by family members, not by the bride and groom. Romantic love is secondary to the

TABLE 8.1. First-Date Scripts

267

Sex, Love, and Romance

What should you expect to do and feel on a first date? When asked to list the typical behaviors they expected from a woman and a man, college students emphasized concerns about appearance, conversation, and controlling sexuality for the female script, and control of planning, paying for, and organizing the date for the male script. The behaviors listed in this table were mentioned by 25 percent or more of those asked.

SCRIPT

A Woman's First Date	A Man's First Date
Tell friends and family.	Ask for a date.
Groom and dress.	Decide what to do.
Be nervous.	Groom and dress.
Worry about or change appearance.	Be nervous.
Check appearance.	Worry about or change appearance.
Wait for date.	Prepare car, apartment.
Welcome date to home.	Check money.
Introduce parents or roommates.	Go to date's house.
Leave.	Meet parents or roommates.
Confirm plans.	Leave.
Get to know date.	Open car door.
Compliment date.	Confirm plans.
Joke, laugh, and talk.	Get to know date.
Try to impress date.	Compliment date.
Go to movies, show, or party.	Joke, laugh, and talk.
Eat.	Try to impress date.
Go home.	Go to movies, show, or party.
Tell date she had a good time.	Eat.
Kiss goodnight.	Pay.
	Be polite.
	Initiate physical contact.
	Take date home.
	Tell date he had a good time.
	Ask for another date.
	Tell date will be in touch.
	Kiss goodnight.
	Go home.

Source: Rose and Frieze, "Young Singles' Script for a First Date," *Gender and Society, 3,* 258–268. Copyright © 1989 by Sage Publications, Inc. Reprinted by permission of Sage Publications, Inc.

decision making. It may be viewed as irrelevant or even destructive. In a study of college students in eleven cultures (India, Pakistan, Thailand, Mexico, Brazil, Japan, Hong Kong, the Philippines, Australia, England, and the United States), participants were asked whether they would marry someone they were not in love with, if the person had all the other qualities they desired. Within each country, male and female respondents were quite similar in their beliefs. In India and Pakistan, about half said yes. Thailand, the Philippines, and Mexico were intermediate, with about 10 to 20 percent agreeing. However, in the other countries, including the United States, only a tiny minority of people said they would marry without love (Levine, Sato, Hashimoto, & Verma, 1995).

Culturally influenced beliefs and expectations about sexuality lead to ethnic group differences in sexual behavior. For example, a comparison of Asian and non-Asian students in a Canadian university showed that the Asian students were more conservative in their behavior (less likely to have had sexual intercourse or to masturbate, fewer different partners if sexually active, etc.) (Meston, Trapnell, & Gorzalka, 1996). In an ethnically diverse sample of young adolescent (grades 6–8) girls in the United States including African-Americans, Hispanics, whites, and Southeast Asians, the girls in each ethnic group expressed somewhat different scripts for their lives. Asked what is the "best" age for a girl to have sex for the first time, the Asian girls gave the highest average age (21.74 years) and the African-American girls the lowest (19.16 years). However, for all groups, the more a girl believed she could succeed in school and work, the less likely she was to predict early sexual activity for herself (East, 1998). Clearly, sexual scripts are part of larger life scripts, both of which are shaped by a person's social group and perceived opportunities.

THE SCIENTIFIC STUDY OF SEX

Starting about 100 years ago, sex came to be seen as an acceptable topic for scientific study. For better or worse, educated people in Western societies can now compare their own sexual behavior with what the "experts" say is normal (see Figure 8.1).

FIGURE 8.1. What does it take to be average?
Source: © 1987 by Nicole Hollander. Used by permission of Nicole Hollander.

Nineteenth-century research on sexuality was conducted mainly by physicians, who frequently reported case studies of people with sexual problems or "pathologies." Some of these pioneer researchers were social reformers who wanted to make society more tolerant of sexual variation; others were judgmental, condemning "deviant" sexual practices. By the early twentieth century, anthropologists like Margaret Mead began to study sexual behavior in other cultures. Evidence of the enormous cross-cultural variability in sexual norms and practices helped create an understanding that there is no single way of being sexual that is "natural" for human beings.

Another important method of studying sexual behavior has been the survey. When Alfred Kinsey and his colleagues conducted surveys of male and female sexual behavior in the 1950s (Kinsey, Pomeroy, & Martin, 1948; Kinsey, Pomeroy, Martin, & Gebhard, 1953), sex became a matter for public discussion. "Whether bought, read, debated, or attacked, the Kinsey reports stimulated a nationwide examination of America's sexual habits and values" (D'Emilio & Freedman, 1988, p. 285). Kinsey (a zoologist whose previous research was on insect behavior) even appeared on the cover of *Time* magazine.

Kinsey's books created a furor because his findings were in conflict with traditional moral values. Among men, virtually every respondent had masturbated, almost 90 percent had engaged in premarital intercourse, and 50 percent had engaged in extramarital sex. Among women, more than 60 percent had engaged in masturbation, 50 percent in premarital intercourse, and 25 percent in extramarital relations. "Kinsey's statistics pointed to a vast hidden world of sexual experience sharply at odds with publicly espoused norms" (D'Emilio & Freedman, 1988, p. 286).

Kinsey also found that masturbation was the most reliable method for obtaining orgasm in women (perhaps partly because sexual intercourse was reported to have an average duration of less than two minutes), and that some women experienced multiple orgasms. Many people refused to believe that women could have more than one orgasm, and this result was widely ridiculed.

Religious leaders disapproved of Kinsey's research—one book, *I Accuse Kinsey,* even claimed that the results must be fraudulent because no decent American woman would take part in such a survey. However, the majority of the public approved of scientific research on sexuality, and other surveys followed.

Kinsey's studies used large (though not random) samples of the American population—5,300 males and 5,940 females. His samples were all white, disproportionately young, and well educated. Other sex surveys, too, have had sampling biases. Obtaining representative samples in sex research is a problem that has no simple solution.

By the 1960s researchers had added another method for gaining information about sexuality: direct observation. In the 1950s, William Masters, a physician, began laboratory research on the physiology of sexual arousal. His first participants were heterosexual female and homosexual male prostitutes. Masters devised ways of measuring physiological changes during sexual activity—using instruments to measure heart rate, muscular contractions, and vaginal lubrication—and developed a laboratory procedure for observing sexual behavior. With Virginia Johnson, he continued the research, using medical and graduate students, his own former patients, and women and men of all ages, both single and married, who volunteered because they needed to earn money or wanted to contribute to medical research (Masters & Johnson, 1966). A later study (Masters & Johnson, 1979) used similar procedures with gay men and lesbians as volunteers. In both studies, the participants were mostly white and well educated. And, of course, people who would feel uncomfortable about having sex under observation in a laboratory were not studied. Masters and Johnson, however, did not consider the representativeness of the sample important because they believed that the basic physiology of sexual behavior is similar in all human beings.

What Are the Strengths and Weaknesses of Sexuality Research?

Sex surveys and observational research provide two different kinds of information about sexuality. Surveys describe normative or typical practices, while direct observation yields descriptions of individual physiological responses to sexual stimulation. Both kinds of knowledge can be useful, but both have their drawbacks.

With surveys, it is difficult to obtain representative samples, and participants may misremember or distort their accounts. There is also a danger that people who read the results of surveys will interpret their own behavior in terms of the supposedly normal behavior reported by others. It is important to remember that no survey is ideologically neutral; the questions asked and the people chosen as respondents can bias toward a particular social construction of sexuality. Kinsey, for example, used a biological-drive model. He thought of sexuality as an instinctual urge demanding satisfaction and maintained that rape and child sexual abuse were the result of denying men the sexual release they needed (Jackson, 1987). Feminists, of course, have developed different explanations of these occurrences (see Chapter 13).

In laboratory studies using direct observation, sex is conceptualized as a set of biological responses to stimulation. But desire and arousal are not simply or directly reducible to blood pressure changes and muscle contractions. An emphasis on biology to the exclusion of subjective experience and social context may imply that biology is (and should be) the primary determinant of social arrangements. Ideally, sex researchers should study *both* subjective experiences and physiological measures to understand sexual activity in social and cultural contexts (see Figure 8.2). Leonore Tiefer, a feminist psychologist and sexologist, has articulated a vision for the future:

> Feminist research on sexuality would begin by adopting a collaborative stance, using participants' subjective perceptions to enrich objective measurements, and planning research to benefit the participants as well as the researchers. Research would be contextualized to as great a degree as possible, since no understanding of sexuality can emerge from any study that ignores the social, demographic, and cultural features of participants' lives. . . . The

"NOT BAD, PHILLIP. CLOUD EIGHT."

FIGURE 8.2. A subjective measure of sex?
Source: Copyright © Martha F. Campbell.

assumption would be that we are studying sexualities, and looking for ways
that all women are alike would play no part. (Tiefer, 1988, p. 24)

ADOLESCENT SEXUALITY

How Does Sexuality Emerge in the Teen Years?

With puberty comes a surge in sexual interest and behavior. During the last
forty years, there have been large changes in patterns of sexual activity in the
teen years, both in the United States and around the world:

- more teens are having sexual intercourse outside of marriage;
- the increase has been greater for girls;
- first intercourse is occurring at an earlier age, on average, than ever before;
- there are ethnic group differences in the United States in age of first intercourse;
- there are large variations from one country to another (Hyde & Delamater, 1997).

In the 1940s, only about 33 percent of females and 71 percent of males had
intercourse outside marriage by the age of 25 (Kinsey et al., 1948, 1953). In

1990, about 79 percent of males and 74 percent of females were sexually experienced by age 19 (Hyde & DeLamater, 1997). The gender gap in sexual experience has almost disappeared. (However, boys still have first sex at an earlier age than girls despite reaching puberty at a later age.) African-American teens have first-time sex at around 15.5 years of age, and whites at around 17 years; Latinos vary, with Cuban-Americans and Puerto Ricans at 16.6, and Mexican-Americans at 17. More than one in five teens experiences first intercourse between the ages of 11 and 14 (Becker et al., 1998).

Comparisons of countries around the world show that the average age of first intercourse is similar (around 16–17 years in most countries). However, the percentage of unmarried women who have intercourse is lower in Latin American countries than the United States or Africa, due to the influence of Catholicism. Increasingly, the influence of North American mass media around the world is contributing to changing sexual values and behavior, so that intercourse outside marriage is becoming more widespread globally (Hyde & DeLamater, 1997).

What Factors Influence the Decision to Have Sex?

Many factors, both biological and social, are implicated in adolescents' choice to become sexually active. Puberty is occurring earlier, and marriage is occurring later (see Chapters 7 and 9), so there is a longer time between biological readiness for sexual activity and society's approval of it.

The initiation of sexual behavior and the form it takes are highly associated with beliefs about sexual activity in one's peer group (Furstenberg, Moore, & Peterson, 1986). For both boys and girls, one of the strongest predictors of sexual activity is *perceived* level of sexual activity of their best friends (DiBlasio & Benda, 1992; Miller et al., 1997). In a recent study of more than 1,300 poor, urban middle schoolers, those who became active during sixth grade were more likely to believe that their peers were sexually active and that joining in would make them more popular (Kinsman, Romer, & Schwarz, 1998). But it is not just poor urban youth who are influenced by their beliefs about others' sex lives—most teens are. In other words, teens start having sex partly because they think their friends are doing it. In fact, perceptions about what peers are doing are more important predictors than the peers' actual behavior (Brooks-Gunn & Furstenberg, 1989).

Although adults are quick to attribute teens' behavior to "raging hormones," the relationship between hormones and sexual activity is complex. Hormonal levels have been found to have a strong effect on the level of a girl's sexual interests but only weak effects on her sexual behaviors (Udry, Talbert, & Morris, 1986). An earlier age of menarche has been associated with earlier sexual activity among both black and white adolescents (Smith, 1989; Zelnick, Kantner, & Ford, 1981), probably due to dating frequency. In other words, girls who have reached menarche and have more mature bodies become more attractive as dates; girls with high rates of dating are equally likely to have intercourse, regardless of their age at menarche.

Late-developing girls are more likely to become sexually active sooner after menarche than earlier-developing girls (Cusick, 1987). Although both

groups of girls are presumably at the same level of hormonal development at
menarche, late-developing girls are in a social environment where sexual activity has already become normative for girls of their age.

COMMON

Peer pressure is probably more important than parental influences on girls'
sexual behavior. Although both African-American and white girls who feel
closer to their parents and talk to them about sexual issues engage in less sexual behavior than girls who do not (Murry-McBride, 1996; Westney, Jenkins, &
Benjamin, 1983), parents have much less influence than peers on an adolescent's sexual involvement (Miller et al., 1997). Good parent-child communication may even have different effects, depending on whether the teenager is a
boy or a girl. For example, one study found that while mothers' ability to communicate with sons and daughters was associated with later intercourse, sons'
discussions with their fathers were related to earlier intercourse (Kahn, Smith,
& Roberts, 1984). This effect may be due to the double standard for sexuality in
our society. Fathers may encourage sexual activity in their sons in response to
sexual scripts endorsing masculinity and potency. In one Midwestern U.S.
study, 70 percent of the fathers surveyed wanted their sons to feel that premarital sex was acceptable (Beckstein, Dahlin, & Wiley, 1986). Only 2 percent, however, had ever mentioned contraception to their sons.

Cultural factors seem to play a part in adolescent sexual initiation, too.
Low socioeconomic status is associated with an early age of intercourse for
girls (Zelnik et al., 1981). This is especially true for African-American  STATUS
teenagers. But is this difference one of cultural norms or economic class? Black
and white adolescents still mostly attend racially segregated schools with their
own peer cultures. School segregation is an indirect measure of low socioeconomic status among blacks and reflects the pervasive conditions of disadvantage that characterize poor neighborhoods. When social class is controlled in
local studies, little variation in the sexual behavior of black and white adolescents has been found (Nettles & Scott-Jones, 1987).

The belief that low-income black women are sexually promiscuous is a
racist assumption. African-American teenagers are, in fact, less likely than
Anglo teenagers to have had a number of sexual partners, and they report
having intercourse less frequently. To avoid pressures to engage in sexual activities, African-American teenage girls who are educationally ambitious tend
to seclude themselves socially, backed by strong, achievement-oriented mothers (Chilman, 1983). Recent studies show that the long-term trend toward earlier intercourse in the United States has halted for African-Americans and for
whites who are religious conservatives, but continues for all other whites
(Cooksey, Rindfuss, & Guilkey, 1996).

Are Teens Having Safer Sex?

Because traditional sexual scripts focus on men's needs and condone more
male power and control in relationships, women often may be unable to assert
a claim to safety during sexual activity (Gomez & Vanoss-Marin, 1996). The
consequence is an increased risk of unwanted pregnancy (see Chapter 10) and
sexually transmitted diseases (STDs). These include bacterial infections such
as chlamydia and gonorrhea, and viral infections such as herpes, genital

warts, and the human immunodeficiency virus (HIV), which causes AIDS. All these STDs are transmitted by genital, anal, or oral sexual contact. Although STDs are a risk for sexually active people in any age group, teens are particularly vulnerable because they may have more partners and because they are inconsistent in using protection. One in four sexually active teens acquires an STD (Becker, Rankin, & Rickel, 1998; Hyde & DeLamater, 1997).

The number of women being infected with HIV is rising rapidly. In parts of Africa, more women than men carry the virus. In the United States, the most common means of transmission for women is intravenous drug use, but the second most common, and the fastest growing, is sexual intercourse with infected men. A single act of unprotected sex with an infected man carries up to a 20 percent risk of infection for a woman. Black and Hispanic women who have sex with men are at greater risk than white women because of higher rates of infection among their sexual partners, most of whom are Black or Hispanic (Hyde & DeLamater, 1997). Heterosexual contact accounts for 46 percent of all AIDS cases in adolescent women. The other cases are largely accounted for by intravenous drug use.

Condoms are the most effective means of preventing HIV infection during heterosexual contact. But adolescents do not use condoms consistently even when they know about their effectiveness in reducing AIDS risk. In a study of ninety-eight African-American women college students, 17 percent had never used condoms, and 48 percent only rarely. Less than one-fourth insisted on using condoms as a means of reducing their risks for sexually transmitted diseases like AIDS, despite the fact that they knew about condom effectiveness (Mays & Cochran, 1988). In a study of white college students, 38 percent never used condoms (Boyd & Wandersman, 1991).

Despite educational campaigns that urge condom use, studies in many cultures show that large proportions of young heterosexuals still engage in unprotected sex. For example, a Nigerian study of a large sample of adolescents showed that only 21 percent of the girls and 36 percent of the boys used condoms, although they knew about condom effectiveness in STD prevention, and their average age for first intercourse was less than fifteen years (Araoye & Adegoke, 1996).

Among teens, the main reason for not using protection seems to be an emotional one: safer sex is inconsistent with the romantic, spontaneous sex of scripted fantasies. In a study of 162 Australian students, 39 percent never used condoms even for casual sex with new partners, although they rated this activity as high risk. The strongest factor determining both men's and women's condom use was their concern that it would destroy the romance and their fear of negative implications ("What will he/she think of me if I start talking about condoms?") (Galligan & Terry, 1993).

College students underestimate their AIDS risk because they use personal decision rules that are inaccurate (Malloy, Fisher, Albright, Misovich, & Fisher, 1997). For example, many believe that it is OK to have unprotected sex with someone they know well and like (Williams et al., 1992). They may judge their risk of AIDS based on their partners' appearance ("He doesn't look sick" or "She is too good-looking to have AIDS"). And while they may use condoms for first-time sex with a new partner, they believe that when they are in a relationship, they do not have to worry about protection from STDs (Hammer, Fisher, Fitzgerald, & Fisher, 1996; Misovich, Fisher, & Fisher, 1997). Of course, all these beliefs are dangerous. Young people tend to have a number of different partners during the college years; even if they are monogamous in each relationship, their partners may have engaged in risky behavior over time and are unlikely to have been tested for AIDS. In relationships, people are in effect having sex with every other person their partner has had sex with. Even if they do not have intercourse, other activities such as oral sex can transmit STDs (Schuster, Bell, & Kanouse, 1996). Because people value relationships, and want to trust their current partner, they may refuse to recognize the risks (Joffe, 1997; Misovich et al., 1997).

What can be done to reduce risky sexual behavior? Fortunately, psychologists have developed strategies that work for a wide variety of groups, including urban minority teenagers and college students (Fisher & Fisher, in press; Fisher, Fisher, Misovich, Kimble, & Malloy, 1996; Fisher, Williams, Fisher, & Malloy, in press). Successful strategies depend on giving people *information* about how AIDS is transmitted, increasing their *motivation* to reduce their own risk, and teaching them *specific skills and behaviors*. These skills and behaviors might include practice in talking about condoms with a partner, avoiding drinking or drug use before sex, or learning how to buy and use condoms. What works depends on the cultural and social norms of the group under study; general appeals to "Practice Safer Sex" simply do not change behavior.

EXPERIENCING SEXUALITY

First Intercourse: Less Than Bliss?

North American culture is more ambivalent and restrictive about women's sexuality than some European cultures, and this may affect how American young women experience their first sexual encounter. In a study of more than 400 American and Swedish college women, the Americans expressed significantly more negative reactions to their first experience of sexual intercourse (Schwartz, 1993). In a study of 1,600 American college students, women reported more guilt and less pleasure than men. When asked to rate the pleasure of their first sexual intercourse on a 1 to 7 scale, the women gave it an average score of 2.95 (Sprecher, Barbee, & Schwartz, 1995).

The gap between the ideal and the real is highlighted in the following two accounts. The first is from a Harlequin romance novel. The second is from a sexual autobiography written by a college sophomore, reproduced here exactly as she wrote it.

> For a long timeless moment Roddy gazed down at the sleeping figure, watching the soft play of moonlight on her features. The expression on his own face was unreadable as he slipped the toweling robe from his shoulders, letting it fall unheeded to the floor. Gently he pulled back the blankets and lay down beside the motionless girl. She turned in her sleep, one hand flung out towards him. Tenderly he stroked a dark strand of hair from her face, then pulled her into his arms. . . . Still half drugged from brandy and sleep, she found herself stroking his hair. "Such a perfect dream," she murmured, her eyes already beginning to close again.

"No dream, my lady," and Roddy's mouth found hers, silencing her words. Tenderly he slipped the ribbon straps of her nightdress over her shoulders, and her body arched up towards him as his fingers traced a burning path across her breast. A groan vibrated deep in her throat as he threw her nightdress to the floor. Then his body was pressed along hers and she gasped at the feeling of skin on naked skin, the soft hair on his chest raising her sensitivity to such a pitch she felt she couldn't bear it any longer . . . his hands played across her skin, turning her into a creature of pure feeling. It all seemed so real, so right. . . .

Driven now only by pure instinct, she moved against him, raining kisses down on his hair-roughened skin, tracing her fingers down the hard strength of his muscled chest. His breathing became ever more ragged, his hands slipping under her to pull her closer still, and she gave a tiny cry of surrender as he finally claimed her body, her fingers digging his shoulders as they moved together in frenzied rhythm. A vast well seemed to surge up within her, and as the room exploded into fragmented light she heard a voice crying "I love you"——but never knew which one of them had spoken. Afterwards they lay in silence . . . she felt herself slipping back into sleep, secure in the knowledge that his arms were holding her close. (Elliot, 1989, pp. 116–118)

I don't think I will ever forget the night that I did lose my virginity. It was this past September (September 7th to be exact). My boyfriend and I had been going out for six months. I met him at a party late that night, but, by the time I had gotten there, he was extremely drunk. We came back to my room because my roommate was not going to be there. We always slept together without making love so, it wasn't like we had those intentions on that night. Well, my boyfriend was very drunk and very amorous to say the least. Once we got into bed, I knew exactly what he had in mind, he was all hands and lips. I figured that we might as well have sex. . . . So, I made the decision to let him do whatever he wanted. For the actual act of sex itself, I hated it the first time. Not only was it painful but, it made a mess on my comforter. I hated my boyfriend at that time. I actually kicked him out of my room and sent him home. I was upset for a lot of reasons: My boyfriend was too drunk to remember the night so, I had made the wrong decision in letting him do whatever he wanted; there had been no feelings involved; I hadn't enjoyed it in the slightest; I had lost my virginity and betrayed my parents. I was upset for just a couple of days.

After that first night, the sex between my boyfriend and myself has been great. (Moffat, 1989, pp. 191–192)

How Do Women Experience Orgasm?

Describing orgasm (and other aspects of sexual response) in terms of frequency or physiology hardly gives a complete picture. The subjective, emotional response is equally important. Women who do not have a great deal of sexual experience are sometimes unsure about whether they have had an orgasm because they do not know how it is supposed to feel. Men, with their visible erections and obvious ejaculatory response at orgasm, need have no doubt when the event occurs.

One way to get an idea of the subjective experience of orgasm is to ask women to describe their own behaviors and sensations. Shere Hite (1976) collected lengthy surveys from more than 3,000 women. Although this is a large sample, it represents only about 3 percent of the questionnaires she distributed, and there is no way to know how accurately the women who chose to respond represent all women. The major strength of Hite's work is that she used open-ended questions. Many of her respondents wrote lengthy, detailed answers that give a picture of the experience of sexuality, at least for the individual writers. A few sample descriptions of orgasm are given in Box 8.1.

Is the experience of orgasm different for women and men? Asking this question would seem to require comparisons of apples and oranges! However, research suggests that the experiences are similar. In a study in which college students were asked to write descriptions of their orgasms, judges (psychologists and physicians) could not reliably distinguish women's and men's descriptions (Vance & Wagner, 1976). In another study, students chose adjectives from a list to describe their experiences of orgasm (Wiest, 1977). Again, there were no significant differences in responses by women and men. These similarities fit well with Masters and Johnson's (1966) emphasis on male-female similarities in the physical sexual response cycle.

Evils of Masturbation or Joys of Self-Pleasure?

Stimulating one's own genitals is a very common sexual practice (Hyde, 1990). Traditionally, this practice was given the clinical term *masturbation*, which made it seem like a disorder. Indeed, masturbation was thought to cause everything from dark circles under the eyes to insanity. However, the majority of young people today believe that it is neither harmful nor wrong (Hunt, 1974). Women

---

Box 8.1 Women's Accounts of Orgasms

"There are a few faint sparks, coming up to orgasm, and then I suddenly realize that it is going to catch fire, and then I concentrate all my energies, both physical and mental, to quickly bring on the climax—which turns out to be a moment suspended in time, a hot rush—a sudden breathtaking dousing of all the nerves of my body in Pleasure—I try to make the moment last—disappointment when it doesn't."

"Before, I feel a tremendous surge of tension and a kind of delicious feeling I can't describe. Then orgasm is like the excitement and stimulation I have been feeling, increased, for an *instant*, a hundred-fold."

"It starts down deep, somewhere in the 'core,' gets bigger, stronger, better, and more beautiful, until I'm just four square inches of ecstatic crotch area!"

"The physical sensation is beautifully excruciating. It begins in the clitoris, and also surges into my whole vaginal area."

"It's a peak of almost, almost, ALMOST, AL-MOSTTTT. The only way I can describe it is to say it is like riding a 'Tilt-a-Whirl.'"

"Just before orgasm, the area around my clitoris suddenly comes alive and, I can't think of any better description, seems to sparkle and send bright dancing sensations all around. Then it becomes focused like a point of intense light. Like a bright blip on a radar screen, and that's the orgasm."

"There is an almost frantic itch-pain-pleasure in my vagina and clitoral area that seems almost insatiable, it is also extremely hot and I lose control of everything, then there is an explosion of unbelievable warmth and relief to the itch-pain-pleasure! It is really indescribable and what I've just written doesn't explain it at all!!! WORDS!"

Source: Reprinted with the permission of Simon & Schuster, Inc. from The Hite Report by Shere Hite. Copyright © 1976 by Shere Hite.

usually masturbate by stimulating the clitoris, either by hand or with a vibrator. Other methods include pressing the clitoral area against a pillow or using a stream of water while in the bath or shower. Most women who masturbate engage in sexual fantasies while doing so (Hite, 1976; Hunt, 1974). Hite's survey respondents described both their techniques and their fantasies (see Box 8.2).

There is a persistent gender difference in masturbation experience. Kinsey's survey showed that virtually all males, but only about 60 percent of females, reported having masturbated to orgasm. Not only were women less likely to have masturbated, but also those who did began at a later age than the men. A recent meta-analysis has confirmed that this difference persists. Curiously, women do not report more negative attitudes toward masturbation, but they are definitely less likely to do it (Oliver & Hyde, 1993).

More positive terms for masturbation include *self-pleasuring* and *self-gratification*. Feminists have suggested the use of these positive terms to encourage women to explore the activity of self-stimulation. Experience in self-pleasuring has positive effects on women's sexual satisfaction. For example, Kinsey et al. (1953) found that women who had masturbated to orgasm before

---

Box 8.2 Women's Accounts of Masturbation

"To masturbate, I almost always need to be turned on by something like pornographic literature (and believe me it's hard to find anything halfway decent). I lie in bed, on my back, slide out of my panties or pajama bottoms because I like to be free to move. I rub my two middle fingers up and down and around the clitoral area. Sometimes I put two fingers of my other hand into my vagina. I rub for a few seconds and tense up my body. I can usually feel a definite fuzzy feeling when I know the orgasm is coming on and then I rub harder, mostly up and down. My legs are apart. The vaginal area is usually moistened as a result of my pornographic reading, otherwise I use spit or, very rarely, cold cream. I usually arch my back slightly when I am really turned on, at which point I take the fingers of my other hand out of my vagina and I push down on the uterine area just above the pubis."

"I lie down and begin to fantasize in my mind my favorite fantasy, which is a party where everyone is nude and engaging in group sex, lovely, lovely sex, all positions, kissing, caressing, cunnilingus, and intercourse. After about five minutes of this I am ready, very lubricated. I lift one knee slightly and move my leg to one side, put my middle finger on or around the clitoris and gently massage in a circular motion. Then I dream of being invited to this party and all those delicious things are happening to me. I try to hold out as long as possible, but in just a minute or two I have an orgasm. It is very simple, all in the mind. After the first orgasm I do not fantasize any longer, but concentrate entirely on the delicious feeling in my vagina and surrounding areas, continuing the same movement of my finger, but slightly faster and in about one minute I have another orgasm. I am very quiet, but do moan some during each orgasm. After several orgasms in this manner I start thinking of what's for dinner and the party is over."

"I don't masturbate like anybody else I ever heard of. I make a clump in the bedding about the size of a fist (I used to use the head of my poor teddy bear, but since I became too old to sleep with a teddy bear, a wad of the sheets has to suffice) and then lie on my stomach on top of it so that it exerts pressure on my clitoris. I then move my hips in a circular motion until I climax—very simple. It works with legs apart or together—either one, although when I am in a particularly frenzied state, together sometimes feels better. I usually end up sort of with my weight on my knees and elbows, so I can't do too much else with my hands."

Source: Reprinted with the permission of Simon & Schuster, Inc. from The Hite Report by Shere Hite. Copyright © 1976 by Shere Hite.

marriage were more likely to enjoy orgasm during intercourse in the first years of marriage than those who had not. In a recent study of married women aged 18 to 30, those who had experienced orgasm through self-gratification had more orgasms with their partners, greater sexual desire, more rapid arousal, higher self-esteem, and greater marital satisfaction than those who had not (Hurlbert & Whittaker, 1991).

Self-pleasuring can be an important way for a woman to learn about her own pattern of sexual arousal and satisfaction. Through practice, she can learn what fantasies are most arousing, what kinds and amounts of stimulation are most enjoyable, and what to expect from her body. For these reasons, sex therapists frequently use a program of education (and "homework") in self-pleasuring for women who are unable to experience orgasm with a partner (LoPiccolo & Stock, 1986). If a woman has learned to know and love her own body and her own sexual impulses, she is better prepared to help her partner learn about her. Equally important, feminist writers have encouraged women to use self-gratification as a route to erotic skill and sexual independence (Dodson, 1987). The woman who can enjoy solo orgasms is not dependent on a partner for sexual pleasure and can enjoy sexual satisfaction without risk of pregnancy or STDs.

SEXUALITY IN SOCIAL CONTEXT

Romantic Love as a Cultural Script

In virtually every supermarket and shopping mall bookstore in America a rack of romance novels is prominently displayed. Each of their covers features a woman (always young, always white, always beautiful) gazing rapturously up into the eyes of a tall, strong, handsome man. Their titles and their plots tell women that "Love Is Everything."

According to their publishers, romance novels are read by more than 50 million American women. They account for 46 percent of mass-market paperback sales in the United States, forming a $1 billion industry each year (Associated Press, 1996). More than 120 new titles are published every month. Many readers subscribe to their favorite series (Harlequin, Candlelight Ecstasy, Second Chance at Love) by mail so that they can be sure to get every new volume (Brown, 1989). Romance novels aimed specifically at adolescents were developed through market research by Scholastic Press and have been sold through school book clubs since about 1980, gaining in popularity every year. Although most romance novels are published in the United States, England, and Canada, their readership is global (Puri, 1997).

No one would claim that these novels are great literature. They follow a predictable script: "Woman meets (perfect) stranger, thinks he's a rogue but wants him anyway, runs into conflicts that keep them apart, and ends up happily in his arms forever" (Brown, 1989, p. 13). But their enduring popularity and appeal suggest that many women still believe (or want to believe) that love conquers all.

In romance novels, the heroine attracts the hero without planning or plotting on her part. In fact, she often fights her attraction, which she experiences as overwhelming, both physically and emotionally—her knees go weak, her head spins, her heart pounds, and her pulse quickens. The hero is often cold, insensitive, and rejecting, but by the end of the novel the reader learns that his coldness has merely been a cover for his love. The independent, rebellious heroine is swept away and finally gives in to the power of love and desire.

What do young women learn from reading teen romances? A close analysis of a sample of thirty-four teen romances showed that the novels portrayed girls' sexuality as dangerous and needing to be channeled into heterosexual pairing. Readers also learn that their bodies are the site of a struggle for control among boyfriends, themselves, and their parents, and that they should appear passive. Girls respond to boys' cues but never take the lead themselves (Christian-Smith, 1998). In these novels, the lives of the heroines are made meaningful only by their heterosexual relationships.

Why do so many women enjoy these fantasies? For adolescent girls, they provide a way to make sense of one's own emerging sexuality (Christian-Smith, 1998). For older women, they provide an escape from humdrum reality and a time when hardworking wives and mothers can treat themselves to solitude and leisure (Radway, 1984). They also provide a reassuring fable of women transforming men. Although the hero is initially cold, patronizing, sometimes even brutal, he actually loves the heroine, and it is the power of her love that transforms him into a sensitive, passionate, and caring lover. In reading the romance, women may learn to interpret the insensitivity of their own boyfriends and lovers as "evidence" that underneath the gruff exterior is a manly heart of gold, and thus to make the limitations of their (un) romantic relationships more bearable (Radway, 1984).

Some feminist scholars believe that by escaping into romances women are encouraged to learn to tolerate oppressive aspects of gender relations. However, other feminists point out that one should not blame the novels or their readers:

> An understanding of Harlequin romances should lead one to condemn not the novels but the conditions which have made them necessary. Even though the novels can be said to intensify female tensions and conflicts, on balance the contradictions in women's lives are more responsible for the existence of Harlequins than Harlequins are for the contradictions. (Modleski, 1980, p. 448)

Romance novels are one of the many ways that women learn the cultural script that love defines and redeems a woman's existence. From earliest childhood, girls are encouraged to identify with heroines who are rescued by a handsome prince from poverty and the cruelty of other women (Cinderella), who are awakened from the coma of nonbeing by the love of a good man (Sleeping Beauty), or who transform an extremely unpromising prospect into a handsome prince through their unselfish devotion (Beauty and the Beast). College students (and young adolescents, too) get their sexual information largely from mass consumer culture: movies, popular music, advertising, TV; Dr. Ruth and sex manuals; *Playboy, Penthouse, Playgirl*, and so on; and romances (Moffat, 1989).

Moreover, romantic love is seen as sufficient reason for sexual activity. Regardless of race, religion, socioeconomic class, and urban or rural background, teenagers believe that love makes sexual activity more permissible.

One study showed that although only 3 percent approved of a teenage girl having sex with a stranger, and 10 percent with a date, 41 percent approved if the girl was "in love"—and about two-thirds of the teens interviewed said they had been in love at some time, including 52 percent of 13-year-old girls (Coles, 1985).

What meanings do romantic scripts have for women who read romance novels in other cultural contexts? In India, dating is usually unacceptable, and women are expected to be virgins when they marry. Romantic love has little or nothing to do with choosing a life partner; most marriages are arranged by the couple's families. Yet India, where many middle-class women read English, may be the world's largest sales outlet for romance novels. A study of more than 100 young, single, middle-class Indian women suggested that reading romance novels is a form of cultural resistance. In them, women explored alternative, more "liberated" kinds of relationships with men. They also admired the spunky, feminine-but-strong heroines. And they gained information about sexuality. As one woman said, she had learned about the biology of sex at school, but it was from romance novels that she learned there is nothing wrong with sex—indeed, that it is pleasurable. For better and for worse, romance novels are part of the globalization of Western culture (Puri, 1997).

The Experience of Romantic Love

Given that the ideology of romance is directed largely at women, it might be expected that women are more romantic in their beliefs about relationships than men. The opposite seems to be true (see Figure 8.3). Studies (reviewed by Peplau and Gordon, 1985) show that, at least among the young, predominantly white college students studied by most researchers, men are more likely to believe that true love comes only once, lasts forever, and overcomes obstacles such as religious differences. They are more likely to believe in love at first sight and to be "game players," enjoying flirtation and pursuit. Consistent with their beliefs, men report falling in love earlier in a new relationship. They also feel more depressed, lonely, and unhappy after a breakup and are less likely to initiate the breakup than their female partners. Women

FIGURE 8.3. Not what she bargained for.
Source: © 1987 by Nicole Hollander. Used by permission of Nicole Hollander.

are more likely to report feeling joy or relief after breaking up (Choo, Levine, & Hatfield, 1997).

Women, on the other hand, report more emotional symptoms of falling in love—feeling giddy and carefree, "floating on a cloud," and being unable to concentrate. And once a relationship has moved beyond its first stages, they may become more emotionally involved in it than their male partners.

The reasons for these differences in the experience of romantic love are unclear (Peplau & Gordon, 1985). Men may fall in love more readily because they rely more on physical attractiveness to decide whom to love—a characteristic that is easy to see at the start of a relationship. They may also react more quickly because the cultural script says that men should initiate a dating relationship. Women traditionally may have been more pragmatic because, in choosing a mate, they were choosing a provider as well as a romantic partner. Yet they may be more "emotional" because cultural norms allow them to admit to having feelings. Gender-related differences in the experience of romantic love are not large, and there is a great deal of overlap in the beliefs and self-reported behaviors of women and men. But the differences are interesting because they do not always fit stereotypical expectations. Perhaps future researchers will examine them in more detail.

Controlling Women's Sexuality

Radical feminist perspectives suggest that male dominance is fundamentally sexual. In other words, the power of men over women in society is expressed and acted out not only in sexual violence (see Chapter 13) but also in male control of the very definition and meaning of sexuality (MacKinnon, 1994). An example of overt control of women's sexuality is the practice of *female genital mutilation* (also termed *female circumcision*, although it involves much more drastic procedures than male circumcision).

Female genital mutilation is a common practice in at least twenty-eight African countries and among some ethnic groups in Asia. It is usually done to young girls between the ages of 4 and 12. It may involve removal of part or all of the clitoris (*clitoridectomy*), cutting away the clitoris plus part or all of the inner lips of the vagina (*excision*), or in addition to excision, sewing the outer lips of the vagina together to cover the urinary and vaginal entrances, leaving only a small opening for the passage of urine and menstrual blood (*infibulation*). A woman who has undergone infibulation must be cut open for childbirth and resewn afterward (Abusharaf, 1998).

The genital surgery is usually done by a midwife with no medical training under unsanitary conditions. Complications such as infection and hemorrhaging are common. Long-term health consequences, especially for infibulated women, include chronic pelvic and urinary tract infections, childbirth complications, and depression. Because the clitoris is damaged or removed, circumcised women feel little or no sexual pleasure and do not have orgasms. "Circumcision is intended to dull women's sexual enjoyment, and to that end it is chillingly effective" (Abusharaf, 1998, p. 25).

Between 100 million and 130 million women living today have been subjected to genital surgery, and each year another 2 million girls are cut. Why does this custom persist? It is seen as necessary to "purify" women and control their sexuality. Women who remain uncut are disrespected, considered promiscuous, and may become social outcasts.

The practice of genital surgery has been very resistant to change. However, studies show that the more educated women are, the less willing they are to allow their daughters to be cut. As African women make gains toward social equality, becoming less dependent on marriage for survival, their attitudes toward circumcision may change.

The custom of genital mutilation in African countries is an example of a cultural construction of sexuality that may seem barbaric to Westerners. However, it was actually a common practice in England and the United States only a century ago, where clitoridectomies were done by physicians to "cure" upper-class women of masturbation and "excessive" sexuality. And some current Western practices seem barbaric to outsiders, too, because what counts as normal in the pursuit of love and marriage depends on one's cultural standpoint:

> Today, some girls and women in the West starve themselves obsessively. Others undergo painful and potentially dangerous medical procedures—face lifts, liposuction, breast implants, and the like—to conform to cultural standards of beauty and femininity . . . people in the industrialized world must recognize that they too are influenced, often destructively, by traditional gender roles and demands. (Abusharaf, 1998, p. 24)

Clearly each culture exerts its own pressures. Even within the United States, Western (European) ideas about sexuality and love are not shared by people from all ethnic backgrounds. Because almost all psychological research on romantic beliefs and behavior has relied on white heterosexual college students, there is much more to learn about the experiences of other groups of people.

Religion and social class separate cultural groups within the United States. Like their white peers, African-American girls learn different lessons about sex and love, depending on their social class and religion. They may be brought up in strict homes, receiving explicit warnings from their mothers about men and sex, or in quite permissive ones where sexual activity is regarded as good, pleasurable, and expected (Joseph & Lewis, 1981). Behaviorally, African-American women are more conservative than white women—less likely to masturbate, for example, or to engage in oral sex (Hyde & DeLamater, 1997). Attitudes may differ, too; some writers have suggested that black women may be less likely than their white counterparts to believe in romantic love as a woman's reason for living and more likely to maintain strong feelings of autonomy and independence (Williams, 1997).

Like black women, Latinos in the United States are a diverse group with respect to social class. In addition, their families come from many different countries, including Cuba, Puerto Rico, Guatemala, and Mexico. Despite this diversity, there are some commonalities affecting romantic and sexual attitudes and behaviors (Espin, 1986). Because of historical influences and the Catholic religion, virginity is an important concept. In Hispanic cultures, the honor of a family depends on the sexual purity of its women. The Virgin Mary is presented as an important model for young women. Traditionally, an unmarried woman who had "lost" her virginity was automatically perceived as promiscuous and evaluated very negatively. Hispanic women who immigrate to the United States soon encounter the idea that all American women are immoral; to become "Americanized" is to become sexually promiscuous.

The traditional Hispanic ideal for men is one of *machismo*—men are expected to show their manhood by being strong, demonstrating sexual prowess, and asserting their authority and control over women. Women's complementary role of *marianismo* (named after the Virgin Mary) is to be not only sexually pure and controlled but submissive and subservient. Of course, not all Latino men endorse the values of machismo, and when they do it may be at least partly in response to the oppression they themselves suffer from white society. And Latinas do have some sources of power, especially in their roles as mothers and among other women. Nevertheless, the cultural imperatives of virginity, martyrdom, and subordination continue to exert influence over the experience of love for Hispanic women (Espin, 1986).

Traditional Asian cultures, especially Chinese, have suppressed sexual expression. Today, Asian-Americans tend to be more sexually conservative than people of other ethnic groups in some ways. For example, they are the least likely to have had several different sex partners. However, Asian-Americans are in general more liberal about abortion. Although Asian-Americans come from a variety of cultural backgrounds including Vietnamese, Thai, Korean, and others, the majority are of Chinese origin and from non-Christian religions. From their perspective, abortion is viewed as an ethical, socially responsible decision to avoid overpopulation and poverty (Hyde & DeLamater, 1997).

Cross-cultural and ethnic group differences in attitudes toward sexuality and sexual practices remind us that there is no "right" way to think about sexuality. Rather, sexuality, including beliefs, values, and behavior, is always ex-

Making a Difference

Fauziya (Fah-ZEE-ya) Kassindja fled the West African country of Togo alone at age 17, to avoid her aunt's plans for her—marriage to a 45-year-old stranger and female genital mutilation (FGM). Girls and women in the Middle East, Africa, Southeast Asia, and elsewhere have been subjected to FGM, which often results in deadly infection, problems in childbirth, and lifelong pain. Kassindja, with the support of her sister and mother, fled Togo hours before she was to undergo FGM. She reached the United States only to be imprisoned with other refugees for more than a year, at times with mur-

derers and other violent criminals. She finally gained political asylum in 1996, when due to her lawsuit, it was ruled that the Immigration and Naturalization Service must recognize FGM as a form of persecution. Kassindja has since coauthored a book, *Do They Hear You When You Cry?*, which not only exposes the horrors of FGM, but also reveals the poor treatment of refugees in the United States. She says of her homeland, "I love my people, but this is a part of my culture I don't like." She dreams that some day no girl will have to fear the horrors of female genital mutilation.

Source: Associated Press.

pressed in cultural context. It is social, emergent, and dynamic (White, Bondurant, & Travis, in press).

Does Attractiveness Influence Sexual Desirability?

In earlier chapters, we discussed how physical attractiveness is important in triggering stereotypical thinking and affecting attributions about others. Attractiveness is an important factor in relationships as well. Good looks are especially important to men choosing a prospective sexual partner or mate, as shown by research in many cultures and societies (reviewed by Pratto, 1996) (see Figure 8.4). When U.S. college students were asked to rate physical, personal, and background characteristics they consider important in a sexual relationship, males emphasized their partners' physical characteristics, and females emphasized personal qualities. However, when rating characteristics they considered important in a long-term, meaningful relationship, both men and women emphasized personal qualities more than looks (Nevid, 1984).

Because attractiveness is more important to men, variations from attractiveness norms are more stigmatizing for women. In one study, college students received a description of an obese or normal-weight person and then evaluated the person on aspects of sexuality. Students believed that the sexual experiences and desirability of an obese or a normal-weight man would be about the same; however, they viewed an obese woman as less sexually attractive and likable, and less likely to have pleasurable sexual experiences (Regan, 1996). Clearly, the women's sexuality, more than the men's, was being evaluated in terms of their physical attractiveness.

Once a girl starts to develop a mature female body, she becomes vulnerable to sexual objectification and its effects (see Chapter 2). She learns that she will be treated as a body or a collection of body parts—breasts, thighs, "butt"—and valued primarily by how she measures up on unrealistic standards of beauty (Fredrickson & Roberts, 1997).

Of course, very few women can meet these standards, and no woman can do so as she grows older. Increasingly, women are resorting to drastic measures. Cosmetic surgery is one of the fastest-growing medical specialties in the

FIGURE 8.4.
Source: © Lynn Johnston Productions, Inc./Dist. by United Feature Syndicate, Inc.

United States. Its patients, 60 to 80 percent of whom are female, seek "cures" for aging and perceived defects through techniques such as liposuction, breast implants, collagen injections, face-lifts, eye-lifts, and nose shaping. Although changing one's appearance is presented as an individual choice to make the most of one's unique looks, the result is to make people look more alike—and to enforce a white beauty norm (Haiken, 1997; Morgan, 1998). The objectification of women is implicated in a variety of psychological problems such as anxiety, depression, and eating disorders (see Chapter 14).

Does Disability Affect Sexuality?

Disabled girls and women, like nondisabled women, are judged by their attractiveness. Additionally, they are judged against an ideal of the physically perfect person who is free from weakness, pain, and physical limitations. Women who are "less than perfect" may be seen as not entitled to be sexual (Galler, 1984). In a study of attitudes about the sexuality of disabled and nondisabled women, Australian college students expressed much more negative attitudes about the disabled women's sexuality, and men were more negative than women (Chandani, McKenna, & Maas, 1989).

Women with disabilities confront stereotypes that sexual activity is inappropriate for them; that people with disabilities need caretakers, not lovers; that they cannot cope with sexual relationships; that they are all heterosexual and should feel grateful if they find any man who wants them; and that they are too fragile to have a sex life. When people around them express these stereotypical beliefs, it is difficult for women with disabilities to see themselves as potential sexual and romantic partners. Many are concerned that they will not find loving relationships or will be forced into restrictive roles (Corbett, 1987). In a national survey that compared women aged 18 to 83 with and without disabilities, the disabled women were less satisfied with the frequency of dating and perceived personal and societal barriers to dating relationships (Rintala et al., 1997). Indeed, disabled women are less likely to be married than disabled men, and ongoing relationships frequently end with the onset of the disability (Fine & Asch, 1988).

Parental attitudes and expectations for daughters with disabilities can have important effects on daughters' sexual development. In a study of forty-three women with physical and sensory disabilities (including cerebral palsy and spinal cord injury), many of the parents had low expectations of heterosexual involvement for their daughters because they saw them as unable to fulfill the typical role of wife and mother. Some of these daughters became sexually active partly out of rebellion and a desire to prove their parents wrong, while others remained sexually and socially isolated. In contrast, other parents saw their daughters as normal young women, with the disability only one of many unique characteristics. These young women became socially and sexually active as a matter of normal growing up. One interviewee reported:

> In childhood, I was led to believe that the same social performance was expected of me as of my cousins who had no disabilities. I was a social success in part because my mother expected me to succeed. In fact, she gave me no choice. (Rousso, 1988, p. 156)

Is Sex Talk Sexist?

A negative evaluation of female sexuality is deeply embedded in language. An analysis of terms for *prostitute* found more than 200 in English novels (Stanley, 1977). Linguists agree that languages develop an abundance of terms for concepts that are of particular interest or importance to a society. The fact that English has many terms describing women in specifically sexual ways, and that most of these are negative, leaves women in the position of being defined in terms of a sexuality that is considered ugly and distasteful (Adams & Ware, 1989).

Absences in language are also revealing. For men, *virile* and *potent* connote positive masculine sexuality, as do other, more colloquial terms such as *stud*, *macho man*, and *hunk*. However, there is no English word for a sexually active woman that is not negative in connotation. Words such as *nympho, whore, tramp,* and *slut*, when applied to women who are sexually assertive or choose many partners, function as a means of social control.

Slang words for sexual intercourse (*hump, bang, nail, lay*) suggest that it is something violent and mechanical done to women rather than an equal and reciprocal act. The same verb can even be used to describe harm and sex—as in "she got screwed." One anthropologist who studied college students in their "natural habitat" (the dorm), reported that about one-third of the young men he studied talked of women, among themselves, as "chicks, broads, and sluts." Their "locker-room style" was characterized by "its vulgar Anglo-Saxon vocabulary, by its focus on the starkest physicalities of sex itself, stripped of any stereotypically feminine sensibilities such as romance, and by its objectifying, often predatory attitudes toward women" (Moffat, 1989, p. 183).

In a recent study, a group of New Zealand psychology students made observations of any talk about sex in their daily life settings for a week and then analyzed the metaphors used. The four most common kinds of metaphor were food and eating (*munching rug; tasty; fresh muffin; meat market*); sport and games (*muff diving, getting to first base, chasing, scoring*); animals (*pussy, spanking the monkey, hung like a horse*); and war and violence (*whacking it in, sticking, pussy whipped, launching his missile*). Males were two and a half times more likely to be the actor (*"He scored her sister"*) than females (*"She turns my crank"*) or both partners (*"They've been bonking away"*), reflecting the cultural tendency to objectify women and portray men as active agents (Weatherall & Walton, in press).

It is easy to see how women might become ambivalent about sexual pleasure when the very language of sex suggests that the female role is synonymous with being exploited, cheated, or harmed and the female body is dirty and disgusting. The Whorfian hypothesis, discussed in Chapter 1, asserts that language reinforces, as well as reflects, social reality. Talking in negative ways about women and women's part in sexual acts probably encourages both women and men to view women and their sexuality in these ways. By making it hard to imagine alternatives, sexist language also inhibits social change.

Studs and Sluts: Is There Still a Double Standard?

Traditionally, a double standard of sexual behavior was widely endorsed: Women were severely sanctioned for any sexual activity outside of heterosexual marriage, while for men such activity was expected and tolerated. Boys had to "sow their wild oats," while girls were warned that a future husband "won't buy the cow if he can get milk for free." Because sexual activity before marriage was viewed as wrong for women, fewer young women than young men were sexually active. For example, a 1959 study (cited in DeLamater & MacCorquodale, 1979) found that 59 percent of men and only 14 percent of women had engaged in premarital intercourse. Moreover, men were most likely to have sex with casual acquaintances, and women with men they expected to marry.

For women, the double standard was often connected with a Madonna/whore dichotomy. Women were either "the pure, virginal, 'good' woman on her pedestal, unspoiled by sex or sin" or "her counterpart, the whore . . . consumed by desires of the flesh . . . dangerous and inherently bad" (Ussher, 1989, p. 14). A woman could not belong to both categories, and women who sought out or enjoyed sex were relegated to the "bad." Oliva Espin (1986) describes this dichotomy in Latin culture:

> To enjoy sexual pleasure, even in marriage, may indicate lack of virtue. To shun sexual pleasure and to regard sexual behavior exclusively as an unwelcome obligation toward her husband and a necessary evil in order to have children may be seen as a manifestation of virtue. In fact, some women even express pride at their own lack of sexual pleasure or desire. (p. 279)

By the 1970s, sex researchers announced the death of the double standard (Coles, 1985). Teenagers, college students, and young adults had come to hold virtually the same sexual standard for men and women. Young people judged it equally acceptable for a girl or for a boy to engage in sex if they were going with each other (24%), in love (46%), or planning marriage (61%). While sex with affection was the new norm, a substantial minority of young adults thought that casual sex without affection was also acceptable (DeLamater & MacCorquodale, 1979).

However, the death announcement for the double standard was premature. Although today people are about equally accepting of sexual activity for females and males when asked about it in general, and more women are sexually active outside marriage, the double standard is still used to control girls and women's sexual autonomy. Acceptable behaviors in boys and men—having many partners, taking the sexual initiative, openly talking about sex—are definitely less acceptable in girls and women.

When middle-school students (ages 11–14) were observed in their daily interactions, the researchers reported that girls were often labeled whores, bitches, and sluts:

> Joe and Hank walked over to a girl sitting at a table and repeatedly called her "slut-face" and "whore." They asked if her rates had gone down, or if they were still a quarter. They also told her they knew she'd "fuck any guy in the school" . . . She finally said, "Fuck you," at which point Hank and Joe backed off and left her alone. (Eder, Evans, & Parker, 1995, p. 130)

Middle-school girls use sexual labels to insult each other, and they try to avoid associating with other girls who have been labeled. By participating in the routine sexual insults, girls end up reinforcing the constraints placed upon them, even though they may disagree with the double standard (Eder et al., 1995). As one 16-year-old put it, "Guys can go around and screw a lot of girls, and they look macho, but when a girl does it, she looks like a slut" (Coles, 1985, p. 168). In a study of college students, over half the women and about half the men believed that women and men should follow different moralities. They thought of sex as a bargain, a game, or a battle, between (aggressive) men and (reluctant) women. Women and men agreed that women came in two types: "good women" and "sluts." (There were no corresponding categories for men.) The researcher summed up the men's attitudes:

> I am a man and I need sex. Most women want it more than they admit. Men have the right to experiment sexually for a few years. There are a lot of female sluts out there with whom to so experiment. And once I have gotten this out of my system, I will then look for a good woman for a long term relationship (or for a wife). (Moffat, 1989, p. 204)

In one study, simply asking college students to judge the sexual behavior of a woman versus that of a man produced little evidence of a double standard. However, more subtle evidence of a double standard emerged. Highly sexually active women, but not men, were seen as more assertive and liberal, suggesting that sexuality is more important in evaluating women than men (Gentry, 1998). Shere Hite's surveys of college students reveal a double standard among men (see Box 8.3).

Box 8.3 College Men Vote on the Double Standard

Between 1983 and 1987, more than 2,500 college men were asked the following series of questions by sex researcher Shere Hite, with the following responses:

1. Do you believe the double standard is fair? *No, according to 92 percent of men.*
2. If you met a woman you liked and wanted to date, but then found out she had had sex with ten to twenty men during the preceding year, would you still like her and take her seriously? *Most men were quite doubtful they could take her seriously; only 35 percent could.*
3. If one of your best male friends had sex with ten to twenty women in one year, would you stop taking him seriously and see it as a character flaw? *Definitely not—according to 95 percent of the men.*

4. Isn't this a double standard? And to equalize it, what should be done? Do you believe (a) men should stop being so "promiscuous" or (b) women should have as much sex as men do, with no negative feedback? *Most men found this a very difficult choice, but could see the logic of the question; the majority, approximately two-thirds, voted for (b), preferring giving women "equal rights" to changing their own view regarding sex. But many men also commented that of course the woman they would marry would probably not be one of those women who had chosen to have sex with that many men!*

Source: From Women and Love: A Cultural Revolution in Progress by Shere Hite. Copyright © 1987 by Shere Hite. Reprinted by permission of Alfred A. Knopf, Inc.

Young women, especially those of the dominant white culture, are exposed to many messages that tell them love is everything to a woman. At the same time, they learn that finding fulfillment and self in the love of a man is outside their control. In the romantic script, it is always the man who actively initiates and pursues; the woman passively offers token resistance but finally gives in to his desire.

Do Romantic Scripts Affect Women's Sexual Experiences?

These beliefs inform the sexual scripts of young adults. College students stereotype men as using interpersonal strategies in dating situations to have sex and women as strategizing to avoid sex. Moreover, when asked their own strategies, they reported that they behaved according to stereotype: Men said they tried to influence their dates to have sex and women said they tried to control their "turned on" dates (LaPlante, McCormick, & Brannigan, 1980). This finding is consistent with other research on dating couples and marital partners, showing that men are more likely to initiate sex. People are especially vulnerable in sexual encounters; the woman who wants to initiate sex and the man who wants to say no may fear being rejected as future dates and labeled as deviants. It feels more comfortable and secure to follow familiar patterns.

When the woman in a dating situation wants to respond positively to a man's sexual initiative, she may still feel that she ought to offer *token resistance*—in other words, to say no when she actually intends to have sex. Both women and men engage in token resistance for a variety of reasons: they want to test their partner's response, add interest to a boring relationship, or prevent being taken for granted (Muehlenhard & Rodgers, 1998). However, saying no when they really mean yes may have serious negative consequences for women. It discourages honest communication and perpetuates restrictive gender stereotypes. Most important, it may teach men to disregard women's refusals. If men learn from experience that no is often only a prelude to yes, they may become more aggressive with dates. Token resistance may provide a context of ambiguity that encourages date and acquaintance rape (Muehlenhard & Hollabough, 1988). Of course, some men are sexually aggressive despite a woman's clear, unambiguous no (see Chapter 13).

Romantic scripts also encourage people to think of lovemaking as something that "just happens." However, although sex may seem "perfectly natural," it is not naturally perfect (Tevlin & Leiblum, 1983). Women who take responsibility for their own pleasure and who take an active role in sex are much more likely to experience pleasure than those who are passive. Satisfying sex depends on communication, learning, and initiative on the part of both partners.

Women are encouraged to view sex in rosy, romantic terms, focusing on candlelight dinners, courtship, and soft caresses. Since many men do not require a romantic context for arousal, they may initiate intercourse with little romantic prologue. Romance novels portray men as the "experts" who make "their" women come alive sexually. But men are likely to be expert only in the techniques and behaviors that bring them pleasure. Though men could benefit from learning about women's desires, sexual scripts can impede their development. Women who have not learned to acknowledge their own arousal and who do not feel entitled to initiate or direct sex are not in a good position to teach their male partners how to give them pleasure.

Do Romantic Scripts Lead to Sexual Dysfunction?

Because our society does not give women the same permission to be fully sexual that it gives men, women may learn to repress sexual desire and need (Radlove, 1983). A meta-analysis of studies of self-reported sexual attitudes and behavior showed that women express somewhat more anxiety, fear, and guilt about sex than men and are less accepting of casual and extramarital sex (Oliver & Hyde, 1993). However, the women and men did not report any overall difference in sexual satisfaction. Most of the participants in these studies were college-age students. Other research suggests that adult women in heterosexual relationships experience less pleasure in sexual activity than their partners. Survey data show that more than 50 percent of women are dissatisfied with some aspect of their sexual lives (Morokoff, 1990). In a study of couples, 35 percent of the women (and only 16% of the men) reported difficulty in experiencing sexual desire. Moreover, 47 percent of the wives (and 12% of husbands) said they had trouble relaxing during sex (Frank, Anderson, & Rubenstein, 1978).

Acceptance of traditional sexual scripts is implicated in women's sexual dysfunction and suppression of desire. One scripted message is that the "good" woman experiences no desire of her own. However, sexual pleasure and orgasm require an awareness of one's own needs plus a feeling that one is entitled to express those needs and have them met. Women's recognition of themselves as sexual beings is blocked in many ways, related to the cultural influences described earlier in this chapter. Women are more likely to feel guilty and ashamed about their bodies ("I look too fat in this position"; "I shouldn't ask my partner for oral sex or to touch my 'dirty' genitals"; "I don't smell good"). They may feel guilty about having needs and fear their partners' disapproval if they express their needs ("I shouldn't be taking so long to climax"; "He'll get angry if I suggest a new position") (Tevlin & Leiblum, 1983, p. 134). Guilt, fear, and shame inhibit sexual arousal.

Another script is that women are sexually passive, men sexually aggressive. As noted earlier, adolescents and college students believe that males almost always want to have sex and females almost always want to avoid it. The effect of accepting this script is that sexual behaviors may proceed on his, not her, timetable, and the woman's pleasure is reduced. Because both sexes believe that it is "natural" for the man to initiate a sexual encounter and take the lead throughout, it is he who decides what activities the couple will (and will not) try, the duration of intercourse, and the sequence of events. With such little control, it is unlikely that the woman will have her needs met. If the man prefers only brief foreplay, the couple may proceed to penile penetration before the woman is aroused, making intercourse painful and unpleasant for her. (The term *foreplay* itself implies that penis-in-vagina is the main event, with hugging, kissing, talking, genital touching, and all other sexual activities merely a prologue.) Women typically need more stimulation to have an orgasm than men do. If intercourse seems to be over almost before it has begun, the woman who has accepted a passive role may be reluctant to ask for more stimulation. Repeatedly engaging in sex when one is not aroused and not satisfied may lead to clinical sexual problems (Tevlin & Leiblum, 1983).

That passivity is a learned script rather than a natural mode for women is shown by comparing the behavior of the same women with both female and male partners. When bisexual women were with a male partner, they were much less active and initiating than when they were with a female partner (Masters & Johnson, 1979). Women who take an active, autonomous, and assertive part in sexual expression are more likely to be orgasmic (and multiorgasmic) (Radlove, 1983).

Another aspect of sexual scripts is the idea that women should be oriented primarily toward their partner's pleasure. Among best-selling sex manuals, some have advocated that women should fake orgasm in order to gratify their male partners. *The Sensual Woman*, purportedly written anonymously by a woman, "instructs the reader in great detail how to fake an orgasm convincingly" and states that no woman would refuse to make love to a man she cares about just because she doesn't feel like it (cited in Altman, 1984). Some sex manuals instruct women to "act like prostitutes" or perform specific acts (such as strip routines or oral sex) to arouse and please their partners. Faking arousal, pleasure, and orgasm may become so ingrained that the woman may not be able to distinguish between her own sexual desire and her desire to please, and her sex life may come to feel like a part she is acting rather than an expression of herself (Morokoff, 1990).

Where Is the Voice of Women's Desire?

As we learned earlier in this chapter, American attitudes toward girls' sexuality are mixed. Coupled with the attention given to girls' ornamentation and "improvement" of face and body is a relative silence about the normal physical aspects of being a girl or woman. Nearly three-quarters of the African-American and white women participating in one community study reported that they had wanted more sex education when they were growing up (Wyatt & Riederle, 1994). In a British study, only 44 percent of a sample of more than 3,000 high school students considered their school sex education satisfactory. They thought it should start earlier, be taught in mixed-sex groups, and provide information on STDs and contraception. They did not want sex education left up to parents (Mellanby, Phelps, Crichton, & Tripp, 1996).

What role do parents play in educating girls about their sexuality? Unfortunately, many parents do not know enough about the physiological aspects of sexuality to be of much help. In one study, adolescents and their mothers were asked to define in their own words seven terms about sexual development, including ejaculation, hormones, puberty, and menstruation. Although mothers were high school graduates and averaged 38 years in age, only 57 percent could define ejaculation, 10 percent could define hormones, and 36 percent could define puberty. Eighty-eight percent of the mothers could accurately define menstruation (Hockenberry-Eaton, Richman, DiIorio, Rivero, & Maibach, 1996). This study did not ask about definitions of female arousal and orgasm.

Unfortunately, many parents mislabel sexually important parts of the body or simply give them no names at all—especially for girls. Mothers are more reluctant to name the sexual parts of their daughters' anatomy than their sons' and do it at a later age. Few girls know they have a clitoris or that it is a separate organ from the vagina; many confuse the urinary opening with the vagina, thus associating sexuality with the taboos and shame surrounding elimination. In contrast, the more visible and more readily named organs of boys are a source of pride. Boys learn to personify their penises with names like *peter* or *dick,* to ascribe power and strength with names like *cock* and *tool,* or to make everyday comparisons (testicles are *nuts, balls,* or, in Spanish, *eggs).* Girls learn to talk about their genitals, if at all, with terms such as *down there, privates, between your legs, nasty,* or *bottom.* In sum, "Boys learn to perceive their genitals as a source of pride and pleasure, girls mainly develop a sense of shame, disgust and humiliation about theirs" (Ussher, 1989, p. 19). It is not surprising that after years of societal attention to their looks and shamed silence about their sexual embodiment, many young women are far more prepared to look sexy than to be sexual.

Can schools fill the education gap? Many U.S. schools avoid sex education because of pressures from some parents and conservative religious groups who believe that knowledge about sexuality encourages sexual activity. At best, girls are taught that they should avoid being victims—of teen pregnancy, STDs, or selfish males. They also learn that "good girls just say no" to sex. But nowhere do they hear the suggestion that girls and women might like, want, need, seek out, or enjoy sexual activity (outside of heterosexual marriage). While boys are seeing educational films about wet dreams, erections, and penis size, girls see films about menstruation.

This kind of sex education does not allow young women to come to terms with their own feelings of sexuality. It "allows girls one primary decision—to say yes or no—to a question not necessarily their own" (Fine, 1988, p. 34). By emphasizing to girls the many ways that they can be victimized, it may also convey the idea that women are always weak and vulnerable, undermining their self-confidence and sense of their own power (Marecek, 1986). Suddenly, a young girl's male companions, with whom she previously may have played freely, are transformed into slightly dangerous strangers. The neighborhood itself is no longer safe for her. bell hooks (1989) has poignantly described the consequences of this fear:

> I no longer felt the intimate sweet companionship with strange black men and even the old familiar faces. They were the enemies of one's virginity. They had the power to transform women's reality—to turn her from a good woman into a bad woman, to make her a whore, a slut. Even "good" women suffered, were somehow always at the mercy of men, who could judge us unfit, unworthy of love, kindness, tenderness, who could, if they chose to do so, destroy us. (p. 149)

The acceptable conditions for a girl to become sexually active are narrowly prescribed in our society. It must be done to please her partner (certainly not herself), must be because she is "in love," and must be unexpected and unplanned (Cusick, 1987). This social construction of sexuality gives young women little opportunity to learn how to say no at whatever stage of sexual activity suits them, and no chance to learn when they would rather say yes. And it leaves no room for them to become initiators of sexual activity. By assuming that girls and women are not active agents in their own sexuality, sex education contributes to muting women's desires:

> The naming of desire, pleasure, or sexual entitlement, particularly for females, barely exists in the formal agenda of public schooling on sexuality. When spoken, it is tagged with reminders of "consequences"—emotional, physical, moral, reproductive, and/or financial. . . . A genuine discourse of desire would invite adolescents to explore what feels good and bad, desirable and undesirable, grounded in experiences, needs, and limits. (Fine, 1988, p. 33)

There is resistance to this silencing. Some girls mock scripts about love and sexuality when they are around boys (Eder et al., 1995). Among some African-American and Puerto Rican girls in one study, their comments often combined a sense of danger and desire. As one of them explained to the researcher: "Boys always be trying to get into my panties. . . . I don't be needin' a man who won't give me no pleasure but takes my money and expect me to take care of him" (Fine, 1988, p. 35).

Women's sexual agency and desire also have been relatively invisible in sex education materials for adults. The sex manuals of the first half of this century constructed a model of sexuality that "purported to be objective and scientific but in fact reflected and promoted the interests of men in a sexually divided society" (Jackson, 1987, p. 52). Female sexuality was defined as passive or even as nonexistent outside the actions of men. Thus, women were characterized as slow to become aroused, needing to be "given" orgasms, and capable of being sexually awakened only by the skill of their husbands in the security of marriage. Musical metaphors abounded, with women characterized as harps or violins that the male master musician could cause to give forth beautiful melodies. The sex manuals of the 1960s and 1970s sexual revolution urged women to be sexually free, but still on others' terms. After analyzing their contents, one feminist researcher asked, "Clearly, the new liberated woman is 'sensuous' and sexy—but is she sexual, on her own behalf?" (Altman, 1984, p. 123).

Even in feminist theorizing, it is hard to find positive accounts of erotic experiences. A large proportion of feminist writing about sexuality has come from a radical perspective that views men and heterosexuality as oppressive. These writers explore sexual domination by focusing on graphic depictions of sexual violence against women and making connections among forms of violence from pornography to rape. At the extreme, heterosexual intercourse is seen as inherently coercive, the prototype of male domination (Dworkin, 1987). This approach implies that women who experience heterosexual desire and pleasure are suffering a kind of false consciousness (Joseph & Lewis, 1981).

In the midst of the pressures to experience sex on others' terms, it is well to remember that in spite of social pressures from all sides, some women, some of the time, do manage to have good sex! Where can the missing discourse of women's sexual desire, action, and pleasure be found? Women's accounts of their sexual experiences, relationships, adventures, and fantasies offer possibilities (Friday, 1973; Hite, 1976, 1987; Vida, 1978). Celebrities such as Dr. Ruth, Susie Sexbright, and Nancy Friday speak openly of the joys of sex. New guides to women's bodily health and sexual functioning such as *Our Bodies, Ourselves* have been written by women. Works of fiction and poetry by women explore their naming and claiming of desire. Powerful and playful voices emerge from women's music, too, from the blues (Bessie Smith singing "You've Been a Good Ole Wagon") to Janis Joplin ("One Night Stand") and Ani DiFranco ("In or Out").

Researchers can also explore how women act on their own sexual choices within gender constraints—for example, how they use "feminine" flirting behaviors to choose a partner (McCormick & Jones, 1989). Such records of women's experiences remind us that the terms of sexual attraction and erotic arousal are not merely programmed into us. Often, they may even be contradictory to the cultural stereotypes that surround us. Future research on female (and male) sexuality needs to develop ways of understanding how, "in spite of the patriarchal contours separating and opposing men and women, women do still desire and even celebrate sexual pleasure with men, and men still can renounce some of the . . . oppressive sexual practices which the sexual power divisions of our society produce and encourage in them" (Joseph & Lewis, 1981, pp. 238–239).

LESBIAN AND BISEXUAL WOMEN

So far, the discussion in this chapter has been about heterosexuality, because it is the dominant, socially approved form of sexual expression and the one that has clear, pervasive scripts. We turn now to other sexual identities and experiences. First, we look at sexual orientation in historical and social context. Next, we describe the process of developing a personal identity as a lesbian or bisexual woman.

A Social History of Lesbianism

The term *homosexual* was coined in the mid–nineteenth century. Although the term was applied to both women and men, it was defined as the inability to have a "normal" erection—a notable example of androcentrism in scientific thinking (Money, 1987b)! Throughout the nineteenth century, many women in North American society had intense friendships, in which they spent weeks at each others' homes, slept in the same beds, and wrote passionate and tender letters to each other describing the joys of perfect loving harmony and the agonies of parting. These relationships sometimes were part of a lifelong commitment. Yet no one labeled these women homosexuals or lesbians (Faderman, 1981; Smith-Rosenberg, 1975). Of course, we have no way of knowing how many of these relationships involved genital sex. They certainly involved romance, attachment, and intimacy.

By the early twentieth century, lesbianism came to be seen as a serious form of pathology. The lesbian was "sick" with a grave "disease." The change in attitude may have come about because women were beginning to demand political and social equality with men. The first wave of feminists were campaigning for women's education and the vote, and more women were entering the workforce. When women's friendships and attachments to other women had the possibility of leading to real alternatives to heterosexual marriage and dependence on men, they were stigmatized and controlled. Feminists in particular were likely to be diagnosed as suffering from the newly invented disease of lesbianism (Kitzinger, 1987). One writer (cited in D'Emilio & Freedman, 1988) claimed: "The driving force in many agitators and militant women who are always after their rights is often an unsatisfied sex impulse, with a homosexual aim" (p. 193).

The medical and psychiatric establishment continued to evaluate lesbianism as pathological until the second wave of feminism in the late 1960s. Responding to pressure from women's liberation and gay liberation activists, the American Psychiatric Association conceded that there is no evidence that homosexuality in itself is a disorder and removed this "sexual deviation" from its official manual of psychiatric diagnoses in 1973. Overnight, millions of people who had had a psychiatric disorder became normal, a compelling example of the power of social institutions to construct—and reconstruct—reality.

Contemporary definitions of lesbianism reflect the political and social complexities of the category. Some definitions focus on lesbianism as a refusal to accept male dominance:

> Lesbian is a label invented by the Man to throw at any women who dares to be his equal, who dares to challenge his prerogatives . . . who dares to assert the primacy of her own needs. (Radicalesbians, 1969, cited in Kitzinger, 1987, p. 43)

Others focus on intimacy and attachment:

> . . . a woman who loves women, who chooses women to nurture and support and to create a living environment in which to work creatively and independently, whether or not her relations with these women are sexual. (Cook, quoted in Golden, 1987, p. 20)

Still others emphasize the individual's self-definition, as well as her behavior:

> . . . a woman who has sexual and erotic-emotional ties primarily with women or who sees herself as centrally involved with a community of self-identified lesbians whose sexual and erotic-emotional ties are primarily with women and who is herself a self-identified lesbian. (Ferguson, quoted in Golden, 1987, p. 21)

Lesbianism may be thought of as a continuum rather than a category. Sexual relationships are only one point on the continuum, which encompasses "women's passion for women," as well as "women's choice of women as allies, life companions, and community" (Rich, 1980, p. 232).

Definitions of bisexuality are equally complex. A bisexual woman is capable of emotional and sexual attachment to both women and men. However, traditionally some researchers and clinicians have maintained that there is no such thing as a "true" bisexual, implying that they are just confused or indecisive and will eventually decide to be either gay or straight.

Bisexuals may feel that they fit in with neither gay nor straight culture. They may be accused by the gay community of wanting to avoid the stigma of the homosexual label and of using cross-sex relationships to hide from their own homosexuality (Ault, 1996; Blumstein & Schwartz, 1993; Rust, 1993). The heterosexual community devalues both bisexual and lesbian women: One spokesperson for a conservative religious group recently called bisexualism "the ultimate perversion" (Ault, 1996).

Some feminists argue that bisexuality is a revolutionary concept because it challenges the "little boxes" of sexual orientation and allows society to move beyond dualistic thinking about sexuality (Firestein, 1998). By definition, bisexuals defy categorization. "There is no bisexual prototype; that is the center of both their significance and their challenge" (Shuster, 1987, p. 57). Nevertheless, individuals identifying as "bi" face difficult choices about how to present themselves in everyday life (Ault, 1996).

Research has tended to echo society's model of lesbianism and bisexuality. When lesbianism was labeled a form of pathology, professional research by physicians, psychiatrists, sexologists, and psychologists supported that view not only by lending it the weight of professional authority but also by focusing on theories of causes (note that there is little research on the causes of heterosexuality), on juicy details of the deviant behaviors, and on various approaches to "curing" the disorder (Kitzinger, 1987).

In this context, it is not difficult to see why the results of the first survey and experimental research on lesbians were controversial and shocking. Kinsey et al. (1953) found that 28 percent of the women he interviewed had engaged in some sort of lesbian sexual activity at some time in their lives. As adults, 13 percent had had at least one sexual experience with another woman leading to orgasm. About 3 percent had had sexual relationships only with other women. This is quite a lot of "pathological" women.

Kinsey's approach emphasized that every human being has the capacity to respond sexually in both heterosexual and homosexual ways. Indeed, later laboratory research showed that the pattern of physiological change in the sexual response cycle is the same regardless of whether one's partner is a woman or a man (Masters & Johnson, 1979). No longer a deviant and inherently unsatisfying act, lesbian sex now came to be seen as more satisfying than heterosexual sex. Kinsey noted that his respondents reported greater consistency in having orgasms in lesbian sex than in heterosexual sex. Masters and Johnson (1979) suggested that women are better at making love to women than men are, and that lesbians have more satisfying relationships.

The effects on individuals of these rapid changes in the social construction of lesbianism can only be guessed at. Women born in the first decades of the twentieth century have seen lesbianism transformed from an official psychiatric disorder to a "lifestyle choice" in their own lifetime. In 1995, a *Newsweek* cover featured the "new sexual identity" of bisexuality.

Still, societal attitudes about gays and lesbians are generally negative. About two-thirds of Americans believe that sexual relations between two same-sex adults are always wrong; the percentage expressing that opinion has dropped only slightly since 1973 (Hyde & DeLamater, 1997). In a recent random sample survey of U.S. households, 67 percent of the men and 58 percent of the women viewed homosexuality as unacceptable (Kane & Schippers, 1996). At the extreme, some people endorse the death penalty for lesbian and gay sexual acts (Lewis, 1979), and, as the 1998 murder of Matthew Sheppard showed, some are willing to murder out of hatred. The ideology that denies or denigrates any nonheterosexual behavior has been termed *heterosexism* (Herek, 1993). Just as racist ideology is used to justify prejudice and discrimination against people of color, heterosexist ideology is used to justify antigay prejudice and discrimination and to discourage lesbians and gay men from becoming socially visible.

Developing a Lesbian or Bisexual Identity

Most people still assume that the sexual orientation of others can be placed neatly in categories—"straight" or "gay," with bisexual and asexual for the leftovers. Assuming that others' behavior consistently fits these tidy boxes, they assume that there is always a sexual identity that matches the behavior. It seems logical to assume that a person who has sex with both male and female partners is a bisexual, and one who has sex only with same-sex partners is a homosexual, and that they will apply these labels to themselves as part of their identity. But sexual identity and sexual behavior are not always so simple (Golden, 1987).

The process of coming out, or accepting lesbianism as a part of one's identity, may be slow and erratic. Gay and lesbian students do not have an easy time in high school. They are at higher risk for low self-esteem, emotional isolation, poor school performance, dropping out, and a variety of other problems. The suicide rate for lesbian and gay youths is two to three times higher than for other adolescents (Black & Underwood, 1998).

Coming out can take place at any time from middle childhood to late middle or old age. When it occurs later in life, it has been likened to a "second adolescence." One woman, who came out as a 56-year-old grandmother, explained: "I simply did not know there was any other way to live than heterosexual. I knew I was pretty miserable, but I just accepted that as part of the way things had to be" (Lewis, 1979, p. 19).

Women may first come into contact with lesbians or the idea of lesbianism in many ways. They may read about the topic or hear it discussed in the media and connect it with their own feelings even though they have had no actual sexual contact with other women. They may discover the existence of a lesbian community, perhaps through a friend or perhaps by being interested in gay activism or politics. Or they may engage in same-sex activity, without at first labeling it as lesbian:

> I think . . . I was 16 when I first got sexually involved for about four years on and off. . . . Then she came to college, we were in different sororities. . . . It really tapered off because she got interested in a guy who she married. . . . Our sexual relationship we kept to ourselves, and I was more excited about it than anything else. I just thought it was a delicious secret. And at the same time, I had a mad crush on a guy. I didn't think of it as being anything weird. I just thought of it as being neat, really something terrific. . . . I thought it was a unique thing we were doing. (Ponse, 1978, p. 187)

Accepting a stigmatized social identity may occur in stages (Cass, 1979). The woman may move from identity confusion and uncertainty (when she initially realizes that she is unlike the heterosexuals around her) through a stage of feeling alienated and alone, to an increasing tolerance of her orientation. She gradually comes to accept her lesbian identity, making contacts with others like herself, and then to take pride in her identity. Finally, she may develop a network of lesbian friends, patronize women-owned businesses, attend a gay and lesbian religious congregation, join civil-rights groups for lesbian and gay people, and so forth, finding her place in a lesbian community.

However, the stage theory of lesbian identity may oversimplify matters. There seems to be no inevitable or "correct" process or outcome in matters of sexual identity (Bohan, 1996). Rather, women's sexual identity seems to be (at least potentially) very fluid and changeable (Golden, 1987; Rust, 1993). Some women identify first as heterosexual, then as lesbian, later as bisexual. Others go through these "stages" in reverse. And labels and behaviors don't necessarily match. Some women say they are lesbians although their actual behavior is heterosexual or bisexual; still others say they are heterosexual although their behavior is lesbian or bisexual. Some women experience their sexual orientation as freely chosen, while others see it as beyond their control. Women's racial or ethnic identification is also intertwined with their development of a sexual identity.

In interviews with women college students, every possible grouping of feelings and activities existed within sexual identification categories (Golden, 1987, p. 30). Among women who identified themselves to the researcher as lesbians, there were some who were sexually inexperienced, some whose sexual behavior was exclusively with other women, some with heterosexual experience, and some with bisexual experience. In response to an anonymous in-class survey of ninety-five psychology-of-women students, 65 percent identified as heterosexual, 26 percent as bisexual, and 9 percent as lesbians. However, their actual sexual experiences were 72 percent exclusively heterosexual; 20 percent, bisexual; 4 percent, lesbian; and 4 percent, inexperienced. These results show that sexual identity is not perfectly congruent with sexual experience. They also suggest that bisexuals are a larger, yet more hidden, group than lesbians. The researcher noted that while lesbian issues were frequently discussed in class, bisexual identities and issues were not, because bisexuals felt less comfortable about revealing their orientation than lesbians did.

Like those who identify as lesbian, women who identify themselves as bisexual show a diversity of actual experience. In a poll of members of a bisexual organization, about 4 percent described their sexual behavior as exclusively with other women, 7 percent as mostly with other women, 23 percent as more with women than men, 38 percent as both equally, 7 percent as mostly with men, and none as exclusively with men (Shuster, 1987). In a study of young urban lesbians and bisexuals aged 14 to 21 years, self-identification had changed over time for many of the young women; more than half who identified as lesbian had identified as bisexual at some time in the past, and the majority had had sexual activity with both other women and with men (Rosario et al., 1996).

It is clear that women do not always mean the same things when they say "I am a lesbian" (or bisexual). A study done in England compared the accounts—explanations or stories about the woman's subjective experience of her lesbianism—given by a sample of forty-one self-identified lesbians ranging in age from 17 to 58 (Kitzinger, 1987). Five viewpoints emerged from a close comparison of the accounts. The first was the idea of lesbianism as personal fulfillment. Women who viewed themselves primarily in this way were sure of being lesbians, were unashamed of their orientation, and thought of themselves as happy, healthy individuals:

> I have never stopped feeling relief and happiness about discovering myself and, you know, accepting about myself and finding all these other women, and it means that I'm happy almost every day of my life. . . . I've never regretted being a lesbian, or becoming a lesbian, if you want to put it that way, or coming out, or whatever. I mean, at least one was alive, you know, and doing things one was meant to do, doing things that were natural to one. (Kitzinger, 1987, p. 99)

A second viewpoint defined sexual preferences in terms of love: lesbianism was seen as the result of falling in love with a particular person, who just happened to be a woman. Though defining themselves as lesbian, these women felt that they could or would have a heterosexual relationship if they fell in love with a man. A third viewpoint had to do with the feeling of being "born that way," yet resisting sexual labeling:

> I'm me. I'm . . . a social worker; I'm a mother. I've been married. I like Tschaikowsky; I like Bach; I like Beethoven; I like ballet. I enjoy doing a thousand and one things, and oh yes, in amongst all that, I happen to be a lesbian; I love a woman very deeply. But that's just a *part* of me. So many other lesbians seem to have let it overtake them, and they are lesbians first and foremost. (Kitzinger, 1987, p. 110)

The fourth view identified women who came to lesbianism through being radical feminists:

> It was only through feminism, through learning about the oppression of women by men and the part that the enforcement of heterosexuality, the conditioning of girls into heterosexuality plays in that oppression, it was through that I decided that whatever happens I will never go back to being fucked by men. My resolution to choose sexual partners from among women only, that decision was made because I'm a feminist, not because I'm a lesbian. I take the label "lesbian" as part of the strategy of the feminist struggle. (Kitzinger, 1987, p. 113)

A final view identified women who saw their sexual orientation as a sin or weakness—a "cross to bear." These women were sometimes ashamed of being lesbians, said they would not have chosen it, and would be happier if they were heterosexual.

This study explores the multiple meanings women give to their sexuality and its relationship to the rest of their lives, including their political beliefs. Each of the ways these women subjectively experience their sexuality has both costs and benefits for the woman's understanding of who she is and where she fits into her society.

Almost all the research on lesbian and bisexual women has relied on all-white or predominantly white samples. How does identity development differ for women of different ethnic and racial backgrounds? Focusing on Latina lesbians, one researcher noted that

> coming out to self and others in the context of a sexist and heterosexist American society is compounded by coming out in the context of a heterosexist and sexist Latin culture immersed in racist society. Because as a Latino she is an ethnic minority person, she must be bicultural in American society. Because she is a lesbian, she has to be polycultural among her own people. The dilemma for Latina lesbians is how to integrate who they are culturally, racially, and religiously with their identity as lesbians and women. (Espin, 1987a, p. 35)

Latina lesbians are perhaps more likely to remain in the closet, keeping their orientation secret from family and friends, than white lesbians because most members of their ethnic group strongly reject and disapprove of lesbians. However, families who become aware of a daughter's lesbianism are unlikely to openly reject or disown her. They will remain silent, tolerating but never openly accepting the situation.

In a questionnaire study of sixteen Latina (Cuban-born) lesbians, the respondents, like white participants in previous research, showed a wide range of subjective understandings of their lesbianism. They also wrote eloquently about the difficulty of integrating their ethnic and sexual identities. This woman had earlier said that being a Cuban and being a lesbian were equally important to her:

> I guess that if the choice were absolute, I would choose living among lesbians . . . but I want to point out that I would be extremely unhappy if all my Latin culture were taken out of my lesbian life. I had a hard time with all the questions that made me choose between Cuban and lesbian, or at least, made me feel as if I had to choose . . . it is a very painful position because I feel that I am both, and I don't want to have to choose. (Espin, 1987a, p. 47)

In interview studies, African-American lesbians also have described issues of integrating multiple identities and group memberships: as lesbians, as members of the black community, and as part of the larger culture with its racism, sexism, and heterosexism:

> Diane (hesitated) to discuss her lesbian feelings while in college. The college she attended was predominantly White, and Diane relied a great deal on the Black community there for support. She considered that coming out to these individuals might jeopardize her acceptance in this group. Although Diane continued to explore her lesbian feelings internally, she also continued to date men. Several years later, as she did begin to come out to others, she feared that identification as a lesbian might pull her away from what she considered her primary reference group—Black Americans. (Loiacano, 1993, pp. 369–370)

Some writers have speculated that lesbianism is even more invisible in black communities than white ones (Joseph & Lewis, 1981). This may be due to the strong influence of organized religion, with African-American religious groups keeping silence on issues of sexual orientation, as well as to community values that emphasize childbearing as a central role for women (Hatton,

1994). The very small samples used in interview research to date make it difficult to generalize about African-American lesbians and underscore the need for more study of homosexuality in the black community (Hatton, 1994).

Asian-American lesbians, too, face issues of multiple identity. Within Asian cultures, being a lesbian is viewed as a rejection of women's most important role, that of wife and mother. Moreover, the implication is that the lesbians' parents have failed and that the child is rejecting not only family values but Asian culture. In a study of nineteen Asian-American lesbians, the majority felt more comfortable in the lesbian community than the Asian-American one, and reported that they had experienced more frequent discrimination as Asians than as lesbians. The researcher speculated that perhaps the stereotype of the passive but exotic Asian woman is so strong that the possibility that an Asian woman could be a lesbian is rarely considered; therefore, Asian lesbians experience more discrimination as women and Asians than as lesbians (Chan, 1993).

In a cross-cultural study of identity development, women aged 18 to 35 in Brazil, Peru, the Philippines, and the United States were asked "At what age did you realize that you would be heterosexual (or homosexual)?" In all four countries, lesbians reached this point of identity development at a later age than heterosexuals, suggesting that the prevalence of heterosexual social norms and scripts impeded lesbian identity development (Whitam, Daskalos, Sobolewski, & Padilla, 1998).

More research is needed on how women integrate sexual identity with other aspects of their sense of self. One model for integrating identities comes from Native American culture, where sexuality, ethnicity, and gender are seen as interconnected and where there is a tradition of accepting different sexualities. Anthropologists have used the term *berdache* (see Chapter 5), but some gay, lesbian, and bisexual Native American people use the term "two-spirit" to describe themselves. Traditionally, two-spirit people were a part of the community; by taking the traditional name, Native Americans who are gay, lesbian, or bisexual feel that they are returning to their communities (Wilson, 1996).

GENDER AND RELATIONSHIP DYNAMICS

Relationships involve power and influence as well as love and intimacy. Because the normative script for relationships is a heterosexual one, the patterns of power can be seen most clearly in heterosexual dating and courtship. Recent research has also examined power and influence in lesbian couples, providing a basis for comparison and new information about the dynamics of being a couple.

Are There Power Issues in Heterosexual Relationships?

The traditional script for a date says that the man should take the lead. He should ask the woman out, offer her a selection of activities, provide transportation, and pay the bills (Peplau & Campbell, 1989). Today, the traditional date, with its clear spheres of power, is disappearing. Along with changes in dating patterns have come changes in power relationships. Actively indicating interest in a man and even taking the sexual initiative are not as frowned on as in the past (McCormick & Jesser, 1983). However, as shown in Table 8.1, people are still very much aware of the traditional script. Expectations of male control can affect perceptions of behavior. For example, male college students perceived women who asked for a date as more flexible and agreeable, more of a casual dater, and more sexually active than women who did not ask for a date (Muehlenhard & Scardino, 1985).

Gender-related power differentials continue to affect dating relationships. In a large study of predominantly white college students, both partners in more than 200 heterosexual dating couples independently completed a questionnaire about their relationship three times over a two-year period. (The average couple had been dating for about eight months at the start of the study.) The couples held a strong belief in egalitarian relationships: When asked which partner should have more say in the relationship, 95 percent of women and 87 percent of men felt that each partner should have "exactly equal" power. However, when asked specific questions about decision-making power (e.g., who has more say in what the partners do together), a less egalitarian pattern emerged. Fewer than half the students reported equal-power relationships. In the unequal ones, it was usually the man who had more power. The large difference between the proportion of people who felt that power should be equal and those who felt their relationship was equal suggests that many couples who want equality do not achieve it.

What factors predict a balance of power in dating relationships? Not surprisingly, couples with less traditional attitudes toward male-female roles tended to have more egalitarian relationships. The woman's career goals were especially relevant. The higher her educational aspirations, the less likely she was to be in a male-dominant relationship (Rubin, Peplau, & Hill, cited in Peplau & Campbell, 1989).

Equality is also more likely if the partners are about equally involved. If one partner is deeply in love or dependent on the relationship for self-esteem and the other is only casually interested, the balance of power tips toward the least involved partner. This factor seems to be especially important for women: The less they love relative to their partners, the more power they see themselves as having (Sprecher, 1985).

Does Gender Affect Influence Strategies?

Gender stereotypes about how to get one's way in a relationship are very clear. Women are believed to use indirect and manipulative strategies—pouting, crying, sulking, and accusing the partner of being insensitive. Men are believed to express anger directly, to call for a logical, unemotional assessment of the problem, and to avoid exploring feelings. Dating partners not only express these beliefs but say that their own behavior fits the stereotypes (Kelley et al., 1978). These results reflect the power structure of heterosexual relationships. Since men have more power, they may have little to gain by displaying and exploring feelings and may retain their power edge by avoidance. Since women have less power, they may have more to gain from negotiation and manipulation of feelings (Peplau & Gordon, 1985).

Indirect power strategies are gentler and less confrontational. They are also the strategies of the weak. The "woman's" strategies of silence, withdrawal, and sulking are "last resort" tactics used by people of both sexes when they perceive themselves as less powerful than their partner. Cross-cultural research shows that women from the United States use more direct interactional ("men's") influence tactics than women from Mexico, who have relatively less economic power and more restrictive gender roles (Belk, Garcia-Falconi, Hernandez-Sanchez, & Snell, 1988).

Are There Power Issues in Lesbian Relationships?

In general, most lesbians (like most heterosexuals) desire egalitarian relationships. In a study using matched samples of lesbians, gay men, and heterosexuals, all groups (and especially women, both lesbian and heterosexual) said that having an equal-power relationship was very important. However, only 59 percent of lesbians reported that their current relationship was exactly equal—a higher proportion than among the heterosexual women but still short of their expressed desires (Peplau & Cochran, 1990). In another study, lesbians characterized their relationships as more intimate and equal, and less gender-stereotyped, than heterosexual relationships. In fact, these relationship characteristics, along with sexual attraction, were cited as their main reasons for choosing a lesbian rather than a heterosexual relationship (Rosenbluth, 1997). Lesbian college students also report a higher level of trust in their current relationship than heterosexual women students (Zak & McDonald, 1997).

Lesbian relationships are similar to heterosexual ones in that if partners are equally interested, committed, or in love, power tends to be equal. However, when one partner is more dependent, committed, or involved than the other, the less involved person tends to have more power (Caldwell & Peplau, 1984).

In discussing influence strategies among heterosexual couples, we noted that "weak" influence tactics are stereotyped as typical of women and "strong" tactics as typical of men. This stereotype would suggest that both partners in lesbian couples would use similar tactics of withdrawal and emotionality. However, it was also noted that "women's" strategies are the strategies of low-power partners. This analysis would suggest that strategies used by lesbian (and gay male) couples would be related more to the power differential within the particular couple than whether they were males or females. Research tends to confirm this view. In a study comparing self-reported influence strategies used by lesbians, gay men, and heterosexuals in their relationships, gender affected the type of strategy only among heterosexuals. Heterosexual women expressed negative emotions or withdrew; heterosexual men bargained or appealed to reason. Gay men and lesbians did not use gender-differentiated strategies. Regardless of whether they were gay or straight, people who saw themselves as the more powerful partner in their relationship used direct, interactive strategies (the prototypical heterosexual male strategies) and low-power partners used indirect and noninteractional tactics (Falbo & Peplau, 1980).

Power in relationships is frequently abused, leading to sexual aggression and violence. Violence against women in relationships is a major social problem connected to other forms of violence against girls and women (see Chapter 13).

WHAT DO WOMEN WANT? SATISFACTION IN CLOSE RELATIONSHIPS

Most women, regardless of their sexual orientation, want intimacy and equity in relationships. They want to share feelings; do things together as a couple; be sexually close, safe, and comfortable with their partner; and to be respected as persons.

What factors affect relationship intimacy? In a study of women in lesbian and heterosexual couples, the two groups were similar in their capacity for intimacy. However, a woman's capacity for intimacy made a difference only if her partner was a woman, when it led to a more intimate relationship and more direct communication strategies. In heterosexual couples, the woman's capacity for intimacy had no connection with how intimate her relationship actually was, probably because men's greater power allows them to set the intimacy limits (Rosenbluth & Steil, 1995).

Bookstores are flooded with advice manuals aimed at teaching heterosexual women how to have satisfying relationships with men. Some of them tell us, quite falsely, that women and men are from different planets and can never really understand each other (see Crawford, 1995). Others, with titles such as *The Rules; Women Who Love Too Much; Women Men Love, Women Men Leave;* and *Smart Women, Foolish Choices,* carry a clear message that women are responsible for their relationships and have only themselves to blame if they are unhappy or unsatisfied.

In these books, women are portrayed as ignorant in relationships—as not knowing what they want or what they need to be happy. They are also shown as incompetent—lacking the skills or techniques that would allow them to initiate or maintain satisfying relationships. Are women really ignorant and incompetent about relationships? There is a great deal of psychological research on close relationships; this research shows that women know very well what they want and need in a relationship: intimacy and equality. However, they may have difficulty meeting those needs within heterosexual relationships and may settle for less than they would prefer (Worell, 1988).

Nor are women (as a group) in any way deficient in relationship skills. On the contrary, they often give much more social support to others, especially boys and men, than they receive in return. They are named as confidante, friend, or intimate more often than men by children, friends, spouses, and kin. They communicate clearly and listen to others. (Gender differences in communication skills are small, but they are in favor of women.) Nevertheless, the pop psych books "recognize a valid relationship issue for women, and then place the blame on the woman for having allowed herself to become involved in this painful situation" (Worell, 1988, p. 480). Such books foster illusions by dichotomizing women and men—portraying them as fundamentally different and opposed in their personalities and needs. And they tell women that it is their responsibility to "fix" themselves, their relationships, and the men involved as well.

The demands of providing social support to many people may be a significant source of stress for women, and one of the reasons they turn to psychological counseling. Moreover, women are often expected to use their communication skills to help lovers and partners understand themselves and to mediate among other people. Pop psych books that tell women they are incompetent may compound stress and add to women's belief that they are to blame when their own and their friends' relationships are unhappy. However, satisfaction in close relationships depends on both partners and their social context.

CONNECTING THEMES

- *Gender is more than just sex.* In the study of sexuality and relationships, it is important to view the "facts of life" as socially and politically constructed. What appears to be natural and normal—female passivity, male aggression, the suppression of female desire, power differentials in relationships—may be neither. Human sexuality is constructed within the gender system.
- *Language and naming are sources of power.* Women are defined negatively by their sexuality. The language of sex portrays women as objects and sexual activity as something aggressive done to a female. Women are viewed in terms of a Madonna/whore dichotomy. Their sexual body parts and their sexual agency remain unnamed, leading to shame and suppression of desire. But names can change. One of the clearest examples of the power of a label is the reclassification of lesbianism from a psychiatric disorder to a normal sexual orientation.
- *Women are not all alike.* Sexuality and relationship norms are shaped by culture. How important is virginity before marriage? How will a family react to a daughter coming out as a lesbian? What is a woman's risk of HIV infection? The answers to all these questions depend on the social class, ethnicity, religious background, and disability status of individual women. Moreover, women's sexual identity is fluid and changeable across the life span, adding to the diversity of ways that women experience their sexual selves.
- *Psychological research can foster social change.* Sexual norms have been changing rapidly in Western societies, and these changes have global impact. The increasing acceptance of same-sex and extramarital sexual behavior have been liberating in some ways, but a sexual double standard remains, and women's sexuality is still suppressed, both overtly (genital mutilation) and covertly (the double standard). Social change efforts should focus on developing nonsexist sex education, enlarging cultural images of women's sexuality, and empowering women to make sexual choices without coercion and shame.

SUGGESTED READINGS

HYDE, JANET S., & DELAMATER, JOHN. (1997). *Understanding human sexuality* (6th e
New York: McGraw-Hill. A matter-of-fact, nonsexist college text on human sexu
ity. This book, written with wisdom and humor, provides a great deal of factual
formation.

D'EMILIO, JOHN D., & FRIEDMAN, ESTELLE B. (1988). *Intimate matters: A history of sexual
in America.* New York: Harper & Row. Changing values and practices througho
the history of American society. Reading about the meanings of sexuality (inclu
ing homosexuality) over time shows how individual desire and social judgment
interact.

VANCE, CAROL S. (Ed.). (1984). *Pleasure and danger: Exploring female sexuality.* Boston:
Routledge and Kegan Paul. A rich collection of essays reflecting feminist views
from sociology, anthropology, psychology, and literary and cultural studies. The
diversity of women's sexual identities and expression is evidenced here.

Commitments: Women and Long-Term Relationships

- **MARRIAGE**
  Who Marries and When?
  Who Marries Whom?
  "Marrying Up" and "Marrying Down": The Marriage Gradient
  Varieties of Marriage
  Are There Biases in Research on Marriage?
  Power in Marriage
  Happily Ever After? Marital Satisfaction and Psychological Adjustment
  What Makes a Marriage Last?
- **LESBIAN COUPLES**
  Who Are Lesbian Couples?
  What Are the Characteristics of Enduring Lesbian Relationships?
  Power in Lesbian Relationships
  Satisfaction in Lesbian Relationships
  Are There Biases in Research on Lesbian Couples?
- **COHABITING COUPLES**
  Who Cohabits and Why?

Do Cohabitors Play Gender Roles?
Does Living Together Affect Later Marriage?
- **NEVER-MARRIED WOMEN**
  The "Old Maid": Still a Stereotype?
  Who Stays Single and Why?
  Rewards of the Single Life
- **ENDING THE COMMITMENT: DIVORCE AND SEPARATION**
  How Likely Is Divorce?
  What Are the Causes and Consequences of Divorce?
  Breaking Up: When Relationships End without Divorce
  Are There Biases in Research on Divorce?
- **REMARRIAGE**
- **EQUALITY AND COMMITMENT: ARE THEY INCOMPATIBLE IDEALS?**
  How Can You Have an Egalitarian Relationship?
- **CONNECTING THEMES**
- **SUGGESTED READINGS**

She gave a gasp as he slid her underneath him. . . . By now Merril didn't want to talk any more. She simply wanted to fly, wherever Torrin chose to pilot her into the upper reaches of the seventh heaven.

But he lifted his head one last time. "Now will you tell me what it is I haven't asked you yet?"

"It's all right, I think you already have—" she breathed.

"And will you? Marry me, I mean?" he asked tenderly.

"Torrin, what are you doing?"

His voice was husky. "I'm giving you a lesson in love."

"Let it last forever, my dream lover," she whispered, moving sensually beneath his touch. "Like our marriage."

"And like my love for you," he murmured in velvet tones beside her head.

And as she moved against him, all notion of holding back now gone, she knew that, like love, their dream would last forever—because it was the real thing.

—The ending of Fantasy Lover, a Harlequin Romance
(Heywood, 1989, p. 187).

Happy endings like this one appeal to women's hopes of finding the "real thing" and settling down to a lifetime of happiness. The romantic relationships discussed in Chapter 8 lead—at least sometimes—to a desire to make a commitment to one partner. In our society that commitment usually leads to marriage, and when people marry they almost always hope it will last a lifetime. Not all enduring commitments to a partner take the form of marriage. Some lesbian couples choose long-term commitment, although they do not have the right to legal marriage. Some heterosexual couples choose to live together without formal marriage. The desire to be part of a couple is so strong that when marriages (or other long-term relationships) fail, most partners try again with someone else.

Psychologists study long-term relationships for many reasons. Clearly, relationships are important in people's lives. Social changes such as the rising divorce rate have challenged traditional views of marriage. Moreover, the emergence of feminist psychology has encouraged researchers to question common assumptions about marriage and love relationships (Peplau & Gordon, 1985). In this chapter we explore the kinds of commitments couples make to each other and the consequences of these commitments for women.

MARRIAGE

As a very old joke puts it, "Marriage is an institution—but who wants to live in an institution?" This joke recognizes that marriage is a way that societies legalize and regulate private relationships between couples. Laws and statutes stipulate who may marry whom—for example, same-sex couples and some biological relatives are prohibited from marrying, and in the past, interracial marriages have been prohibited. Laws also regulate the minimum age for marriage, the division of property when marriages dissolve (indeed, whether they are permitted to dissolve), and the responsibilities of each partner within the marriage (e.g., what behaviors constitute grounds for divorce).

In cultures in which written law is less important, religious codes or powerful social norms may serve the same regulatory function. For example, cross-cultural studies of preindustrial hunter-gatherer societies show that 79 percent of these societies allow men to have more than one wife. Few prohibit divorce and remarriage, but most punish married people for having sexual relations outside the marriage (Gough, 1984).

Although people in Western societies are aware that marriage is a legal contract subject to regulation by the state, they rarely think of it that way in relation to themselves. Rather, they are influenced by the ideology of romance, choosing their partners as individuals and expecting to live out their married lives according to their own needs and wishes. Nevertheless, the formal definitions of rights and responsibilities imposed by the state may have consequences for both partners—especially when the marriage ends, with divorce or the death of a spouse.

Behaviors and attitudes are importantly shaped by the institutional aspects of marriage. Because the definition of marriage is an institutional one, there are cultural scripts that inevitably affect individuals:

> An institution is a way of life that is very resistant to change. People know about it; they can describe it; and they have spent a lifetime learning how to react to it. The *idea* of marriage is larger than any individual marriage. The *role* of husband or wife is greater than any individual who takes on that role. (Blumstein & Schwartz, 1983, p. 318)

Marriage, then, is both a personal relationship and a scripted social institution.

Who Marries and When?

The great majority—over 90 percent—of people in Western societies will marry at some time in their lives. However, marital patterns are diverging among ethnic groups. The marriage rate among African-Americans is declining. By the early 1990s, African-American women were the least likely of any group to be married, and it is estimated that about 25 percent will never marry (Dickson, 1993; Steil, 1997). Over all ethnic groups, the timing of marriage has changed. Both women and men are waiting longer to marry. In the 1990s, the typical first-time bride was nearly four years older than her 1970s counterpart. A similar trend is occurring in other industrialized countries. Teenage marriages are becoming much less common, and at least half of all women have not yet married by the age of 24. Scandinavian countries lead the way in the trend to later marriage; for example, only 15 percent of 24-year-old Swedish women are married (Bianchi & Spain, 1986; Norton & Moorman, 1987). In contrast, women in developing areas of the world marry very young. In many parts of Africa and Asia, the average age at first marriage is under 18 (United Nations, 1991a).

What is the cause of these changes? There are probably several. In the United States, many young women have been influenced by feminism's emphasis on choices for women. Even though not all young women label themselves feminists, the idea that women can have goals other than being a wife and mother has been widely accepted. Advances in contraception methods have made premarital sex and living-together arrangements more practical, and these practices have become more acceptable to many. For black women, there is a shortage of marriageable men, due to a number of socioeconomic forces. In the African-American community, marriageable men are a scarce resource (Dickson, 1993) (see Chapter 10 for more on African-American family patterns). Economic factors may play a part, too; some young people find it difficult to become financially independent of their parents (Bianchi & Spain, 1986; Taylor, 1997).

Whatever the causes, the tendency to marry later has important implications for women, because the increased time between high school and marriage offers opportunities to broaden experience. A woman who enters her first marriage at an older age is less likely to exchange dependence on her parents for dependence on a husband. She is likely to have had some experience of independent living; has probably held paid jobs and perhaps has supported herself with her work; and has had time to get more education, which exposes her to a variety of viewpoints and experiences and also increases her employment opportunities. All in all, she is more likely than a younger woman to enter marriage with a well-developed sense of self and broad horizons for her life.

Who Marries Whom?

In a cross-cultural study, more than 9,000 people from thirty-seven nations representing every part of the world were asked to assess the importance of thirty-one characteristics in a potential mate (Buss et al., 1990). The diverse characteristics included good health, chastity, dependability, intelligence, social status, religious background, neatness, ambition, and sociability. The participants in this study were young (their average age was 23) and typically urban, well educated, and prosperous—in other words, they are not representative samples from their countries. Nevertheless, their answers give an interesting picture of what women and men from diverse cultures look for in a potential marriage partner.

No two samples ordered the characteristics in exactly the same way. The biggest difference across cultures was in a cluster of characteristics that reflect traditional values such as chastity (the potential husband or wife should not have had previous sexual intercourse), being a good cook and housekeeper, and desire for a home and children. Samples from China, Indonesia, India, and Iran, for example, placed great importance on chastity, while samples from Scandinavia considered it irrelevant.

Overall, cultural differences were much more important than gender differences. Men and women from the same culture were more similar in their mate preferences than men to other men, or women to other women, from different cultures. In fact, men's and women's rankings were virtually identical overall, with a correlation of +.95. This gender similarity suggests that each culture—whether Bulgarian, Irish, Japanese, Zambian, Venezuelan, or whatever—socializes men and women to know and accept its particular script for the institution of marriage. Of course, such scripts may include different marital goals for women and men. In this study, women were similar to each other across cultures in being slightly more likely to emphasize a mate's earning capacity and ambition, and men in emphasizing good looks and physical attractiveness.

When all thirty-seven cultures were considered together, an overall picture of an ideal mate emerged. Women and men agreed, rating mutual attraction and love, dependable character, emotional stability, and pleasing disposition as the four most important characteristics in a potential marriage partner. In the U.S. sample, women and men also agreed on the importance of education and intelligence.

Many other studies have focused on spouse choices in the United States, providing a detailed picture of who marries whom in America (reviewed by Peplau & Gordon, 1985). In general, these studies, like the cross-cultural one just described, show that the desires of men and women are more similar than different.

However, some differences in Americans' marital expectations and desires are related to gender and social class. The high value that women of all social classes place on affection and companionship is shared more by middle-class than by working-class men. The partner's capacity for self-disclosure (sharing thoughts, beliefs, dreams, and emotions) in a relationship appears to be more important to women than to men across all social classes. And middle-class women express concerns about keeping their independence and autonomy in relationships more than men or working-class women do (Peplau & Gordon, 1985).

Men tend to be somewhat more traditional in their thinking about marital scripts and roles. They are more likely than their wives to believe that traditional gender roles are innate and unchangeable (Mirowsky & Ross, 1987). Several studies in the 1970s and 1980s (reviewed by Peplau & Gordon, 1985) showed that men are more likely to believe husbands should be the primary family wage earner and women should be in charge of home and family. In a recent study of college students, the men were more conservative than the women on issues such as whether a mother should stay at home with an infant and willingness to move for a spouse's career (Novack & Novack, 1996). Overall, women appear to expect and desire more flexible marital patterns than men.

"Marrying Up" and "Marrying Down": The Marriage Gradient

Individual couples usually end up being fairly closely matched on social class and ethnic/racial group as well as on characteristics such as height, SAT scores, attractiveness, and age. Couples are similar in values, too: Religious people tend to marry other religious people, traditionalists marry other traditionalists, and feminists marry other feminists. When there are differences within a couple, it is usually the man who is older, is better educated, and has a more prestigious occupation (Peplau & Gordon, 1985), and this is true cross-culturally (United Nations, 1991a).

The tendency for women to "marry up" and men to "marry down" by sorting themselves into couples in which the man has higher prestige and income potential is called the *marriage gradient* (Bernard, 1972). Historically, the marriage gradient probably came about because women had little access to education and high-status occupations in their own right and could only achieve economic security through marriage. In the United States, women's tendency to marry up has decreased as women have become more equal to men in earning power and educational opportunity. It also varies among groups of women. Black women, for example, are less likely than white women to marry up with respect to education (Schoen & Wooldredge, 1989). The marriage gradient has important implications for power in marriage, which will be discussed later in this chapter.

Varieties of Marriage

In the United States, many different marriage patterns coexist, from the most traditional to the most experimental (Blumstein & Schwartz, 1983). We classify marriage patterns in terms of three important characteristics: the division of authority, how spousal roles are defined, and the amount of companionship and shared activities they provide (Peplau, 1983; Peplau & Gordon, 1985; Scanzoni & Scanzoni, 1976; Schwartz, 1994).

Traditional Marriage

In traditional marriage, both husband and wife agree that the husband has (and should have) greater authority; he is "the head of the family," or "the boss." Even in areas in which the wife has some decision-making responsibility (e.g., household shopping), he retains veto power over her decisions. In traditional marriages, the wife is a full-time homemaker who does not work for pay. Clear distinctions are made between the husband's and wife's responsibilities. She is responsible for home and child care, and he is the breadwinner. Couples in these marriages may not expect to be "best friends"; rather, the wife finds companionship with other women—neighbors, sisters and other kin, or members of her church. The husband's friendship networks are with male kin and coworkers, and his leisure activities take place apart from his wife.

Most studies of traditional couples have focused on working-class families, and traditional marriage may be more common in this group. However, it is not confined to one social class. In middle- and upper-class families, traditional wives may serve as hostesses for elaborate social functions or become active in community volunteer work. However, they do not work for pay, and husbands' authority outweighs theirs.

Attitudes toward traditional marriage have changed a great deal in the past few decades (Steil, 1997). A comparison of national opinion polls over the years (cited in Bianchi & Spain, 1986) shows that in 1937 only 18 percent of the population approved of a married woman working for pay if her husband was capable of supporting her. By the 1990s, more than half the population said that an ideal marriage is one where both spouses hold jobs and share housework and child care (DeStefano & Colasanto, 1990, cited in Steil, 1997).

Throughout this century, black women have been less economically dependent and more likely to work for pay than white women. Black women and men have more liberal views about women's appropriate roles, and there is less of a gap between men's and women's views than there is among whites. Attitudes in the black community, like those of the population in general, have grown more liberal over time (Crovitz & Steinmann, 1980). However, these changes do not mean that marriages based on traditional beliefs and values are entirely a thing of the past. Even in the 1990s, a significant minority—37 percent of a national sample—maintain that the traditional roles of man as provider and woman as homemaker are best (DeStefano & Colasanto, 1990, cited in Steil, 1997). And conservative religious groups such as the Promise Keepers and Nation of Islam insist that submission by the wife to her husband is necessary for marital and societal stability (Hewlett & West, 1998; Mathews, 1996).

Modern Marriage

In modern marriage, the spouses have a "senior partner–junior partner" or "near-peer" relationship. Modern wives work outside the home, but, by mutual agreement, the wife's job is less important than the husband's—he is the breadwinner, and she is working to "help out" or to provide "extras." Moreover, it is expected that her paid employment will not interfere with her responsibilities for housework and child care, which she is expected to fit in around it. Within modern marriage, the paid work of husbands and wives may be equal in the amount of time it takes, but it has different meanings because the belief that the "real" provider is, and should be, the man remains unchanged (Steil, 1997).

Modern couples emphasize companionship and expect to share leisure time activities. They value "togetherness" and may discuss husband/wife roles rather than taking them for granted as more traditional couples do. Modern marriage may seem to be a relationship of equality when compared with traditional marriage, but the equality is relative (see Box 9.1). Husbands still have more financial responsibility, and women have more responsibility for the home and the children. (See Figure 9.1.) Modern wives do a *second shift* every day—they put in a day's work for pay, and another day's work when

---

Box 9.1 Equality or Inequality? The Role-Reversal Test

Read the following paragraph about modern marriage:

> Both my wife and I earned Ph.D. degrees in our respective disciplines. I turned down a superior academic post in Oregon and accepted a slightly less desirable position in New York where my wife could obtain a part-time teaching job and do research at one of the several other colleges in the area. Although I would have preferred to live in a suburb, we purchased a home near my wife's college so that she could have an office at home where she would be when the children returned from school. Because my wife earns a good salary, she can easily afford to pay a maid to do her major household chores. My wife and I share all other tasks around the house equally. For example, she cooks the meals, but I do the laundry for her and help her with many of her other household tasks.

Sandra Bem and Daryl Bem have suggested that gender is a largely unconscious ideology of inequality. Both women and men are socialized to believe that equality exists where it does not, and inequality is hard to recognize. If it represents a truly gender-neutral arrangement, the paragraph you just read should have the same tone and implications when the roles are reversed. As a test for hidden inequality, here is the paragraph with the roles reversed:

> Both my husband and I earned Ph.D. degrees in our respective disciplines. I turned down a superior academic post in Oregon and accepted a slightly less desirable position in New York where my husband could obtain a part-time teaching job and do research at one of the several other colleges in the area. Although I would have preferred to live in a suburb, we purchased a home near my husband's college so that he could have an office at home where he would be when the children returned from school. Because my husband earns a good salary, he can easily afford to pay a maid to do his major household chores. My husband and I share all other tasks around the house equally. For example, he cooks the meals, but I do the laundry for him and help him with many of his other household tasks.

Source: Bem & Bem "Training the woman to know her place: The power of a nonconscious ideology." In M. H. Garskof (Ed.); *Roles women play: Readings toward women's liberation*, pp. 84–94. 1971, Brooks Cole. Reprinted by permission of the authors.

FIGURE 9.1. Let's make a deal . . .
Source: 1997 by Nicole Hollander. Used by permission of Nicole Hollander.

they get home (Hochschild, 1989). Men are considerably more satisfied than women with this arrangement (Baker, Kiger, & Riley, 1996). As one marital researcher put it, the men in these couples "support female equality but only up to the point it collides with their privilege" (Schwartz, 1994, p. 9). Women may be content with this arrangement because they want to be closely involved with their children, or they may put up with it because they do not know how to change it.

Egalitarian Marriage

Egalitarian marriage, once relatively rare, is becoming more common (Schwartz, 1994). In egalitarian marriages, the partners have equal power and authority. They also share responsibilities equally without respect to gender roles. For example, one partner's paid job is not allowed to take precedence over the other's. In practical terms, this would mean that either the husband or the wife might relocate to accommodate the other's promotion; either would be equally likely to miss work to care for a sick child or to work part time to accommodate household responsibilities. The ever-present tasks of running a household—cleaning, cooking, bill paying, errands—are allocated by interest and ability, not because certain jobs are "women's work" and others are "men's work." Such marriages are "postgender" relationships, where the partners have moved beyond using gender to define their marital roles. Although partners may be very involved in their careers, they may make career sacrifices to meet each others' and their children's needs because they believe in equity (Risman & Johnson-Sumerford, 1998).

Egalitarian marriage is much more than just a 50-50 division of labor. More than any other type of marriage, an egalitarian relationship provides the couple with profound intimacy, intense companionship, and mutual respect. Egalitarian couples put their relationship first, ahead of work and other relationships (even family and children). Because they share a great deal (housework, financial responsibility, child care) they understand each other, communicate well, and choose to spend a lot of time together. Often, each says that the other is their "best friend," believes that the other is precious and irreplaceable, and says that their relationship is unique (Risman & Johnson-Sumerford, 1998; Schwartz, 1994).

Are There Biases in Research on Marriage?

Marriages in which both spouses work for pay have been around for a long time, especially among working-class, immigrant, and rural couples, for whom two jobs were often necessary for economic survival. Farm wives sold butter, eggs, and homemade foods; immigrant women earned money in garment factories and textile mills, or worked alongside their husbands in small mom-and-pop stores and businesses. Wives also took in boarders and did laundry, sewing, and cleaning for wealthier families (Aldous, 1982). During World War II, women held factory and industrial jobs of all kinds. These patterns are not just a matter of history; rural, immigrant, and working-class women continue to contribute to their families' economic survival in these ways.

However, working-class dual-earner families have not been studied systematically by social scientists; neither have Asian-American, Puerto Rican immigrant, or African-American dual-earner families. Instead, research has focused on white, upper-middle-class professional couples. There is a need for research on the lives of working couples who do not have high-prestige careers, especially since the number of such couples is increasing rapidly (Pleck, 1987). For the present, however, most of psychology's insight into dual-worker marriage comes from studies of professional couples.

One reason dual-career couples have been considered more interesting and important than dual-earner couples may be that the values of both partners resemble the male ideal in our society. Also, many researchers who study dual-career couples are themselves part of a dual-career marriage (Aldous, 1982). These observations serve as a reminder of how social norms and values can influence a research agenda.

Thinking about marriage in terms of distinct types may oversimplify the varieties that exist. But it helps to illustrate the importance of the dimensions of role differentiation, companionship, and authority. Different marriage types reflect different beliefs about what the duties of husband and wife should be and how they should view each other. In traditional, modern, and dual-career marriages, men have more power and authority. Completely egalitarian marriages are still relatively rare. Although Americans like to think of marriage as an equal partnership, men end up having more say. We now take a closer look at the power dimension. Why is it that the end result of a stroll down the aisle and the words "I do" is often a long-term state of inequality?

Power in Marriage

Studying marriages in terms of power is not an easy task. Many people do not like to think or talk about their relationships in such "crass" terms. Couples may construct a *myth of equality,* refusing to acknowledge how gender socialization and social forces have steered them toward traditional roles (Knudson-Martin & Mahoney, 1996). For example, when a sample of highly educated dual-career couples were asked about other couples' relationships, they defined equality in terms of task-sharing. However, when asked about their own relationships, they talked less about who did the cooking and cleaning than about mutual respect and commitment (Rosenbluth et al., in press, cited in Steil, 1997). In fact, most of the couples had not achieved their ideal of equality: the women did more household work and their careers were definitely secondary to their husbands' careers. But they did not focus on adding up who did what around the house, perhaps because it would make inequality painfully apparent. In another study, couples reported that decisions about work and family issues were made together, but in fact husbands were far more likely to get their way. "Agreement" seemed to mean agreeing that the husband was right (Zvonkovic, Greaves, Schmiege, & Hall, 1996).

Marital privacy makes it difficult for researchers to see the power dynamics involved in a couple's life together. In addition, it is not always clear just what the word *power* means in a marriage. In spite of these difficulties, psychologists and sociologists have conducted studies of marital power for at least the past thirty years.

One definition of power is "the ability to get one's way, to influence important decisions" (Blumstein & Schwartz, 1983, p. 62). Accordingly, researchers have often compiled lists of the sorts of decisions that must be made in families and asked one or both partners who usually makes the final decision about each type of issue. In the best known of these studies (Blood & Wolfe, 1960), more than 900 urban, suburban, and rural wives were asked who had the final say on whether the husband should change jobs (90% said husbands always did) and on how much to spend on food (41% reported that wives always did). Only 39 percent of the wives had decision-making power over whether or not they themselves should hold a paying job. Of course, some decisions are much more important to the family's welfare than others. Note that the decision with the most far-reaching consequences, the husband's job, is one where husbands had virtually uncontested power.

Another approach is to ask couples who the "real boss" is in the family or who usually "wins out" when there's a disagreement on a really important decision. In a sample of 336 Canadian households, 76 percent of wives said that the husband was the boss and only 13 percent said both had equal power (Turk & Bell, 1972). More recent research confirms that the norm has not changed. Even in dual-career marriages, which are often claimed to be the most egalitarian marriage form and the vanguard of future trends, there is a consistent pattern of inequality; the roles and responsibilities are more balanced than in traditional marriages, but "despite an essentially supportive orientation, both partners seem to endorse some level of male dominance" (Steil, 1983, p. 53).

What Are the Sources of Men's Greater Power?

Many factors are associated with husband dominance in marriage (Steil, 1983, 1997). Social class and ethnicity make a difference: Black and working-class couples have less of a power differential than white middle- and upper-class couples. Wives who are employed have more power than those who work only at home. White middle-class women in traditional marriages may have less marital power than any other group of women.

One reason the power balance in marriage is weighted in favor of men is the influence of traditional beliefs and social norms (Steil, 1994). In a major study of American couples (Blumstein & Schwartz, 1983), couples were asked whether they agreed or disagreed that it is better if the man works to support the household and the woman stays home. In couples where either spouse agreed, the husband was more powerful, regardless of how much money each partner actually earned. For example, Marlene and Art have been married for thirty years. She is an executive with the telephone company and he is a farm-equipment dealer; their incomes are about equal, although sometimes she earns more:

> Marlene: Art makes the major economic decisions in our household. We are as consulting of one another as possible, but I realize that in the final push comes to shove that he is the one who shoulders the responsibility for this family . . .

> Art: I would say that I make the decision when it comes to money and I guess I would also say that if there is an argument and we cannot totally work it out so that we both agree, then I have more to say . . . someone has to finally make a decision and we have always done it this way. (Blumstein & Schwartz, 1983, pp. 57–58)

Another explanation for greater male power in marriage comes from *social exchange theory* (Thibault & Kelley, 1959). This theory proposes that the partner who brings greater outside resources to the relationship will have the greater influence in it. The partner who has less to offer, be it status, money, or knowledge, will inevitably take a back seat. Money establishes the balance of power in heterosexual relationships, even though this reality conflicts with American beliefs about equality:

> Most people like to think that the right to affect decisions is based on the demands of daily events, on which partner is wiser on a certain issue, or on special gifts of persuasion. They do not like to think that income, something that comes into the relationship from the outside, imposes a hierarchy on the couple. But it does. (Blumstein & Schwartz, 1983, p. 53)

Do Two Incomes Lead to Equality?

Dual-career marriages often contain unrecognized inequalities. For example, housework is not a mutual and equal responsibility. In a national sample of more than 1,500 dual-career, dual-earner, and traditional couples, it was found that wives in all three categories spent considerably more time in housework each week than their husbands. Dual-career husbands did not spend any more time each week doing housework than other men (Berardo, Shehen, & Leslie, 1987).

Another way in which dual-career marriages often fall short of being truly egalitarian is in the relative importance attached to each partner's career. Imagine a situation in which one partner is a psychologist and the other is also engaged in a demanding career. Which spouse would be more likely to move to a different location to advance the career—husband or wife? Which would be more likely to relocate because the spouse had a job offer in a different place? When male and female members of the American Psychological Association were asked about their own choices, 42 percent of the men and only 19 percent of the women said they had moved for an increase in salary. However, 25 percent of the women and only 7 percent of the men had moved because of their partners' relocation. (Incidentally, these couples also said that the women spent more time on housework and child care. The researcher [Gutek, 1989] noted that gender typing seems to be alive and well among psychologists!)

In American marriages, husbands usually bring more of three very important resources: money, education, and prestige. Husbands usually earn more than wives, even when both are employed full time, and are likely to have higher status jobs. (This is true for a variety of reasons that we will look at more closely in Chapter 11.) As already noted, wives who have no income or employment of their own have the least power of any group of married women. Moreover, because of the marriage gradient, the husband in most marriages has a higher level of education than the wife. In American society, educational attainment brings status and prestige in itself and is also associated with higher income.

When the husband earns more, couples agree that he automatically has the right to make important financial decisions for the family. But the money he brings in also may give the husband the right to make other important decisions that have nothing to do with money. One wife described how a husband can dominate family decision making by appealing to his earning power. Gordon and Leanna have been married twelve years. He is a highway patrol officer and she works in a delicatessen:

> Gordon is aggressive, and me I'm somewhat passive. And while that has equalized some over the years, Gordon still has to have the last word on everything. We get annoyed with each other over that, but when I start to push back, he reminds me just who supports me and the children. He doesn't always bring that up, but if I start to win an argument or to make more sense about something we should do, I think he gets frustrated and so he gives me his big final line which is something like, "If you're so smart, why don't you earn more money?" or how dumb I am 'cause if I had to go out and support myself I'd be a big fizzle. . . . He's only lousy like that when he thinks I'm winning and he gets threatened. (Blumstein & Schwartz, 1983, p. 59)

Social exchange theory implies that if husband and wife have equal external resources, marital interaction will also be equal. But we have noted that even in dual-career families, where the resources are fairly well matched, husbands still have more weight. Social exchange theory is too limited; it has focused on economic exchange while ignoring the symbolic value of gender roles. For example, the "good provider" role, still more important for men than women, means that men's capacity to earn money is more highly valued than their capacity to nurture children. For women, on the other hand, "being there" to provide emotional nurturance to husband and children is more valued than the ability to earn money. Even if a wife brings in as much money as her husband, she may not have equal power because her success is seen as undermining his provider role and interfering with her nurturing role. In other words, the same resource (in this case, earned income) may function differently for husband and wife (Howard & Hollander, 1997; Steil, 1994; Steil & Weltman, 1991).

Just how central is earning power to marital equality? And does its influence work the same way for husbands and wives? To answer these questions it is necessary to study couples in which the wives have achieved incomes equal to or greater than that of their husbands. These couples are "rare birds," indeed. However, one intriguing study (Steil & Weltman, 1991) managed to find thirty couples in which the wife earned at least 33 percent more than the husband and matched them with an equal number of couples in which the husbands earned at least 33 percent more than the wives. All partners were employed full time, all couples were white, and family incomes ranged from $25,000 to more than $75,000 annually.

Respondents were asked questions about the relative importance of careers ("Whose career is more important in the relationship?") and decision-making power ("Who has more say about household/financial issues?"). Consistent with social exchange theory, spouses who earned more saw their careers as more important and also had more say at home than spouses who earned less. Nevertheless, wives overall had less say in financial decisions, had more responsibility for children and housework, and felt that their husbands' careers were more important than their own. In other words, equal access to money can be an equalizer of power in marriage—but even when wives earn more money than their husbands, beliefs about the appropriate roles of women and men still influence the balance of power in favor of men. Social resources and social norms are both important.

Happily Ever After? Marital Satisfaction and Psychological Adjustment

"Happily ever after," as romance novels remind us, is our society's romantic ideal of marriage. However, in her influential book *The Future of Marriage* (1972), Jessie Bernard maintained that marriage is not good for women. She suggested that every marriage is really two marriages, "his" and "hers"—and "his" is much more advantageous. Which is closer to reality, the romantic ideal or the social scientists' seemingly cynical view? Does marriage bring happiness and fulfillment? We can examine the issue by looking at research on whether women (and men) are generally satisfied with the marriages they make, and whether marriage has any relationship to psychological adjustment.

Does Marital Happiness Change Over Time?

The happiness and satisfaction of married women (and men) varies greatly across the life course of a marriage. Almost all studies of marital satisfaction over time show an initial "honeymoon period" followed by a substantial decline in happiness with the birth of the first child. Satisfaction often hits its lowest point when the children are school-aged or adolescents. Some studies have shown that the happiness of the early years is regained or even surpassed in later life, when the children have grown and left home. In other studies, the happiness trend has been all downhill (Feeney, Peterson, & Noller, 1994; Schlesinger, 1982; Steinberg & Silverberg, 1987).

What accounts for the changes in marital happiness over time? One possibility is that the birth of children ends the happy honeymoon because of the increased work and responsibility children bring (Veroff, Young, & Coon, 1997). This may be especially true for wives; as we discussed earlier, even in relatively nontraditional marriages, women do more child care than their partners. However, it seems that it is not the increased workload itself but rather the increased inequality that makes mothers less satisfied with their marriages than nonmothers. When more than 700 women were studied during pregnancy and three months after the birth of their first child, they reported doing much more of the housework and child care than they had expected. Their negative feelings about their marriages were related to the violation of their expectancies of equal sharing. In other words, it was not the tedious domestic chores that made these new mothers less happy than they had been earlier, but their feeling that the new division of labor was unfair. The more they had expected equality, the more dissatisfied they were (Ruble, Fleming, Hackel, & Stangor, 1988).

Even when couples have been married thirty years or more, they look back at the child-rearing years as their least happy (Finkel & Hanson, 1992). When children leave home, couples have fewer demands on their money and time. Many couples experience the postchildren stage of their marriage as a time of greater freedom and flexibility, and therefore of increased marital happiness (Schlesinger, 1982).

How Does Marriage Affect Psychological Well-Being?

Studies in the 1970s showed that married women were more likely than married men to have psychological disorders and problems. Single women, on the other hand, had fewer disorders and problems than single men. In fact, for every type of unmarried person (ever-single, divorced, and widowed), most studies showed higher rates of psychological adjustment disorders for men than women. Only married women had more disorders than their male counterparts (Bernard, 1972; Gove, 1972; Steil & Turetsky, 1987b). This pattern was one reason Bernard (1972) made the "his and her" marriage distinction; it seemed to show that marriage is not good for women's mental health. Recent research shows that marriage seems to be good for both women and men; it is associated with better psychological adjustment in both. However, the benefits are unequally distributed: men are more satisfied than women with their marriages and receive greater mental health benefits from being married (Fowers, 1991; Steil, 1997).

Why do husbands enjoy better psychological adjustment and well-being than wives? To answer this question we need to consider the different types of marriage. Several studies have shown that full-time homemakers have the poorest psychological adjustment, employed husbands have the best, and employed wives are intermediate (Steil, 1997; Steil & Turetsky, 1987b)—suggesting that something about being a homemaker contributes to the occurrence of psychological disorders.

We will look at women's work in homemaking and child care more closely in Chapters 10 and 11 and at psychological disorders in Chapter 14. For now, it is important to note that some of the unpaid work that women do in marriage is low status and boring. It may provide valuable social and emotional resources for others, while the woman herself has less support (Peplau & Gordon, 1985). Wives usually keep up contacts with friends and relatives, care for family members when they are ill, and encourage their husbands and children to take good care of themselves. They are likely to be available to listen to their husbands' troubles and problems.

In one study of more than 4,000 married persons aged 55 and over, husbands said they were most likely to confide in their wives, while wives were less likely to confide in their husbands and more likely to turn to a friend, sister, or daughter. Both men and women who confided in their spouses had markedly higher marital satisfaction and overall psychological well-being than those who did not (Lee, 1988). The work of caring and emotional support that married women do is an important resource for others' well-being and may partly account for their husbands' better psychological adjustment.

Does Inequality Affect Well-Being in Marriage?

A great deal of research suggests that equality is beneficial for relationships (Steil, 1997). Couples who see their marriage as equal are more satisfied than more traditional couples, report better sexual adjustment and communication, and are less likely to use manipulative and indirect influence tactics with each other (Aida & Falbo, 1991; Steil, 1994, 1997). Perhaps it is not marriage per se that is bad for women's mental health but marriages in which women have little power and status (Steil, 1983). Inequalities of power and status are also related to physical and sexual abuse in marriage (see Chapter 13).

A study of more than 800 dual-career professional couples tested the hypothesis that marital power is related to psychological well-being (Steil and Turetsky, 1987a). The researchers gathered information on each woman's earned income, her influence and responsibilities within the marriage, and her symptoms of psychological disorders. Because of earlier research connecting the presence of children to lowered marital happiness, they also compared childless women and mothers.

For childless women, the more equal a woman's marital relationship, the more satisfied she was with her marriage—and marital satisfaction was an important factor in overall psychological well-being. The mothers experienced their marriages as significantly less equal than the childless women did, and the perceived inequality was directly related to psychological symptoms. Although the dual-career professional couples in this sample are not representative of all married couples, this study suggests that relative power and equality play an important role in married women's well-being.

What Makes a Marriage Last?

What are the "secrets of success" of husbands and wives in enduring marriages? Despite the importance of marriage in people's lives, there is very little research on long-lasting marriages. However, a few studies exist, and they suggest that marriages change across time. In one study of 581 adults who had been married an average of eighteen years, participants were asked to remember how they had felt about their partner at the beginning of their love relationship, and to describe how they felt now. They reported less erotic feelings and game-playing, an equal amount of friendship-based love, and (among the men) an increase in selfless, nurturing love (Grote & Frieze, 1998). In a study of 129 Canadian couples who had been married an average of twenty-five years and had at least one child, more than half the women said that they had started out their married lives with traditional expectations; only 23 percent had expected to share domestic and workforce responsibilities. However, only 20 percent still had traditional expectations at the time of the study; over the course of their marriages their expectations had evolved to an ideal of shared responsibilities and more independence for themselves. Wives and husbands were asked to indicate the factors that had contributed to their staying together. Although they were interviewed separately, spouses agreed almost perfectly (Schlesinger, 1982). More recently, 147 U.S. couples who had been married at least twenty years were asked similar questions (Fenell, 1993). The factors both sets of couples thought were most important are shown in Table 9.1.

Of course, not all marriages that last a long time are happy marriages. In the Canadian study, about 10 percent of women and men indicated dissatisfac-

TABLE 9.1. Longtime Married Couples Cite Factors That Make Marriage Last

Canadian Couples	U.S. Couples
Respect for each other	Lifetime commitment to marriage
Trusting each other	Loyalty to spouse
Loyalty	Strong moral values
Loving each other	Respect spouse as best friend
Counting on each other	Commitment to sexual fidelity
Considering each others' needs	Desire to be a good parent
Providing each other with emotional support	Faith in God and spiritual commitment
	Desire to please and support spouse
Commitment to make marriage last	Good companion to spouse
Fidelity	Willingness to forgive and be forgiven
Give and take in marriage	

Source: Fenell, 1993; Schlesinger, 1982.

tions with their relationships; for women, the dissatisfactions centered around sexual relations, finances, the husband's workload, and children (Schlesinger, 1982). Chronic marital dissatisfaction is related to problems of mental and physical health for older women (Levenson, Carstensen, & Gottman, 1993). Because marriage is an institution supported by the society as a whole, some marriages endure despite unhappiness and lack of fulfillment. One major study of couples found that those who were living together (but not legally married) were likely to break up when there was a pattern of inequality in the relationship; however, for married couples, inequality had no effect on whether the couple stayed together (Blumstein & Schwartz, 1983). Although marital inequality may lower marital satisfaction and fulfillment, social norms may keep some unhappy marriages together.

Psychological research on happiness in marriage points up some interesting discrepancies between the romantic ideal and the psychological and sociological realities. Our society tells us that marriage and parenthood are more important routes to fulfillment for women than for men. Women are thought to be eager to catch a husband and men are thought to be caught reluctantly. Women may invest a great deal of energy in planning their weddings and their married lives—have you ever seen a *Grooms* magazine on the newsstand? Yet research on marital satisfaction and the psychological adjustment of married people suggests that Jessie Bernard was right when she proposed that there are two marriages in every marital union, his and hers, and that his is better than hers. Perhaps it would make more sense for men than for women to be investing their time in dreaming and planning for the day they will marry and begin to live happily ever after.

LESBIAN COUPLES

Lesbian couples have been a largely invisible minority of people in long-term committed relationships. However, lesbian and gay relationships are increasingly becoming visible. This change is due to many factors, including the active civil rights movement for lesbian, gay, and bisexual people, the move to urban centers that helped create lesbian and gay communities, and the destigmatization of lesbian/gay identity by the APA (see Chapter 8) (Allen, 1997).

Who Are Lesbian Couples?

In surveys of lesbians conducted over the last two decades, about 75 percent of respondents were currently in a steady relationship, with the range between 45 percent and 80 percent in different samples. Not all steady relationships involved living with the partner. Women not currently in committed relationships were unattached for a variety of reasons—some had been through a recent breakup or the death of a partner, others were actively looking, and others did not want a relationship (Peplau & Gordon, 1983).

When two women make a commitment to live together as lovers and friends, their relationship has some similarities to conventional marriage—but without the institutional aspects or the label. Lesbians (and gay men) do not have access to the predictable features of marriage that make it seem desirable to become a couple and difficult to break up. For example, there is no standard way for them to have an engagement ritual or public wedding ceremony or to establish reciprocal legal rights and responsibilities. There are no tax advantages or spousal insurance benefits. Lesbian partners may even be legally forbidden to see each other in the event of serious accident or hospitalization if their families of origin do not approve. Ending the relationship is not hampered by complicated laws regulating divorce; nor does society urge gay couples to work at their relationships and remain loyal through the hard times.

This lack of institutional and societal support can give people the freedom to make their own rules, but it can also lead to instability. Some lesbian couples have written their own wedding ceremonies; occasionally one partner legally adopts the other or the other's children. Many include each other in their wills and insurance policies, buy homes together, or draw up contracts delineating rights and responsibilities to each other. All these are ways of giving the relationship some institutional and legal status (Blumstein & Schwartz, 1983; Cabaj & Purcell, 1998). Organizations such as P-FLAG (Parents and Friends of Lesbians and Gays) provide social support, and the Metropolitan Community Church, as well as some Protestant ministers and Jewish rabbis, perform ceremonies of union to bless the relationships of same-gender couples.

Making a Difference

Ninia Baehr and *Genora Dancel* met in 1990 and have been trying to get married ever since. What started as a private romantic relationship, however, soon turned public. When the couple inquired at the local gay community center about domestic partnership options, they were asked to join two other same-sex couples applying for marriage licenses in the state of Hawaii. The couples were denied licenses, but despite fears of job loss and other repercussions, Baehr and Dancel fought for same-sex marriage rights alongside gay and lesbian activists for the next seven years. In 1993, an Hawaiian court ruled that denial of marriage licenses to the three couples constituted gender discrimination and declared that Hawaii must allow same-sex marriage or show compelling reason not to. It seemed that Hawaii would become the first state to marry same-sex couples. At this point, conservatives, led by a group called "Save Traditional Marriage," campaigned aggressively and finally derailed the issue in Hawaii. In November of 1998, Hawaiian voters ratified a constitutional amendment permitting the legislature to restrict marriage to male-female couples. The Hawaiian Supreme Court may ultimately rule in favor of same-sex marriage, but most gay activists believe that the battle has been lost in Hawaii, and they plan to focus their efforts in other states. Dancel and Baehr are not defeated, however, declaring that even if they find they can never be legally married, at that point, "we'll just accept that we know we are married, and live our lives."

Sources: Ness, C. (1995, April 27). Lesbian couple leads fight for right to marry, http://polyamory.org/~howard/Poly/news/lesbian_couple.html. Davis, N. (1996). Love's Labors Won, http://bi.org /~ndavis/ninia.htm.

What Are the Characteristics of Enduring Lesbian Relationships?

For many years, researchers and the public alike assumed that lesbian couples mimic traditional heterosexual roles, with one partner being the "husband" ("butch") and the other the "wife" ("femme"). This belief applied a heterosexual script to lesbian relationships. No one bothered to ask lesbians if the script was meaningful to them. When a researcher recently asked a sample of 235 self-identified lesbians to define these concepts for themselves, the majority did identify as butch (26%) or femme (34%), with 40 percent of the sample being neutral. The higher a woman's education and income, the more likely she was to have an independent (not butch/femme) gender identity (Weber, 1996).

However, these women did not use butch/femme to represent husband/wife roles. To them, "butch" signified that they did not enjoy "girly" things such as makeup, dresses, and elaborate hairdos. "Femme" signified the freedom to enjoy makeup and other feminine aspects of personal style, while still being committed to loving women. They stressed that butch did not mean they were dominant, acted like men, or disliked being women, and femme had nothing to do with being submissive. In summary, the butch/femme dimension is important to some lesbians, especially working-class women, but it is not related to relationship dominance.

Lesbian relationships can be described on the same dimensions as heterosexual marriages: roles and the division of labor, companionship and communication, power and authority, and satisfaction. Most lesbians actively reject gender roles (Peplau & Gordon, 1983). In one study of more than 1,500 lesbian couples, 75 percent expressed the belief that both should work for pay (Blumstein & Schwartz, 1983). Fewer than 1 percent of these couples lived in a one-earner situation. Because same-sex couples cannot assign the breadwinner role on the basis of gender and because they tend to value independence in their relationships, the importance of the work or career interests of each partner is much more likely to be fairly equal than in heterosexual marriages.

Just as they balance work roles, lesbians are highly likely to share household duties (Kurdek, 1993). Perhaps because they resist being defined in terms of traditional (and low-status) "women's" work, they assign housekeeping chores on the basis of preference and ability, with each partner adjusting her responsibilities to fit her paid-work schedule. The basic principle is fairness, and couples negotiate changes in work and home responsibilities. In one couple interviewed, the speaker is an investment officer at a bank and her partner is a medical student:

> She feels very strongly about having an equitable situation and I think that comes from her having lived with men and feeling taken advantage of in the past, so she definitely feels it ought to be equitable. It's easy to slip into something where she does more because I am the only one working full time . . . but we see the dangers of that and we are keeping things in line so she doesn't get stuck with too much. (Blumstein & Schwartz, 1983, p. 150)

Same-sex couples tend to share more leisure activities than heterosexual couples. They are more likely to socialize with friends together, belong to the same clubs, and share hobbies and sports interests. There are probably several reasons for this. Perhaps, due to socialization, two women are more likely to have interests in common than a woman and a man; or perhaps most people need same-sex "best friends," and only lesbians and gay men can find a same-sex friend and a spouse in the same person. Whatever their sexual orientation, women are more likely than men to say that they value emotional expressiveness, sharing feelings, and having egalitarian relationships (Peplau & Cochran, 1980). The majority of lesbian couples want their relationship to be central to their lives, and they value companionship and communication (Blumstein & Schwartz, 1983).

Power in Lesbian Relationships

When there are power differences in a lesbian relationship, they are usually due to the same factors that influence power in heterosexual relationships, such as one partner having greater resources of money, status, or education, or one partner being more committed than the other (Peplau & Gordon, 1983). However, the egalitarian ideal may be more important than status and money in determining power relations among lesbians. In one study of seventy couples, power sharing was *un*related to age, income, and education of the partners (Reilly & Lynch, 1990).

Many of the other factors that influence power, such as traditional beliefs, are much less likely to be present in lesbian relationships. Therefore, we might expect that lesbian couples will typically have a more equal balance of power—more egalitarian relationships—than heterosexual married couples. Research bears out this expectation. Unlike heterosexual couples, many of whom believe that the man should be the head of the family, the lesbian ideal is a relationship "where two strong women come together in total equality" (Blumstein & Schwartz, 1983, p. 310). In one study of seventy-seven women currently involved in lesbian relationships, seventy-five thought that both partners should have exactly equal power (Caldwell & Peplau, 1984).

Satisfaction in Lesbian Relationships

Several studies have compared the self-reported satisfaction and happiness of lesbian and heterosexual committed couples. In general, these studies show that there are few differences between the two types of couples in scores on marital adjustment measures (Cardell, Finn, & Marecek, 1981; Peplau & Gordon, 1983). When matched samples of lesbians and heterosexuals were compared on liking and loving scales, the lesbians, like the heterosexual women, reported that they both loved and liked their partners—in other words, were high in attachment, caring, and intimacy, as well as affection and respect (Peplau & Cochran, 1980). Like heterosexual women, lesbians are likely to be more satisfied when the relationship is egalitarian (Caldwell & Peplau, 1984). When the two partners have different levels of career commitment, satisfaction is lower (Eldridge & Gilbert, 1990). However, lesbians may be more likely to establish egalitarian relationships than heterosexual women (Caldwell & Peplau, 1984; Schneider, 1986; Steil, 1994); therefore, their relationship satisfaction may be greater on the average.

External pressures affect relationships, too. Women who love women have to cope with being labeled deviant and with having heterosexist behavior directed at their relationship. This may include rejection or "disowning" by a woman's parents, removing the lesbian daughter from a will or denying her an inheritance, refusing to acknowledge the partner or the relationship, exclusion from family gatherings, active encouragement to break up, and forbidding all contact between partners. One important determinant of relationship satisfaction for lesbians is having a social support network. Women who are "out" (identified as homosexual) to significant others in their lives (parents, best friends, siblings, employees) report more satisfaction with their partners. Receiving social support from friends and family is related to individual psychological adjustment as well as happiness in the relationship for both lesbian and gay male couples (Berger, 1990; Kurdek, 1988).

Are There Biases in Research on Lesbian Couples?

Although psychology has come a long way in the past twenty years in studying lesbian relationships, the research is limited in several important ways. Like research on heterosexual couples, it frequently relies on self-reports (interviews or questionnaires), which may be biased because people want to look well adjusted to researchers or because they lack insight into their relationships. The pressure to appear normal may be greater for lesbians, and some may want to present a rosy picture of their relationships to make their sexual orientation more acceptable to others.

Research has also depended heavily on samples of volunteers that are not representative of the general population of gay and lesbian people. Lesbians who have volunteered for research tend to be young, white, and middle class. Therefore, comparing them with more heterogeneous heterosexual couples may involve hidden race, class, and age biases. Much more research is needed on older couples, women of color, working-class women, and relationships that cross barriers of class, color, and ethnicity (Garcia, Kennedy, Pearlman, & Perez, 1987; Weber, 1996). Yet it may be all but impossible to study a truly representative sample of lesbians as long as the dominant culture stigmatizes lesbianism (Peplau & Gordon, 1983).

COHABITING COUPLES

Today many heterosexual couples choose to live together without being legally married. Sociologists give this arrangement the unromantic name *cohabitation*. Couples who do it usually call it "living together"—not a very good distinguishing term since roommates or parents and children can be said to live together, too. A generation ago, the extreme social disapproval directed at cohabitation was expressed in the term "shacking up." None of the tags seems quite right. The absence of a suitable everyday term is one clue that the cohabitation relationship is not yet an institution in society. (A similar problem exists in naming the living-together relationships and roles of gay men and lesbians. "Marriage" implies a legally sanctioned unit, "husband" and "wife" aren't

quite right, "lover" is too sexual, "significant other" is too formal, and "partner" can sound too much like a law firm.)

Who Cohabits and Why?

Whatever the label, the practice of heterosexual couples living together without being officially married is more popular than ever in the United States (see
Figure 9.2). In the 1990s, about half of all first marriages were preceded by living together (Forste & Tanfer, 1996). Black and Hispanic women are more
likely than white women to cohabit, but there are differences among subgroups of Hispanic women. Mexican-Americans, for example, are more disapproving of living together without planning to marry than are Puerto Ricans
(Oropesa, 1996). Cohabiting women are generally young; nearly 40 percent are
under the age of 25. Living together is especially popular among college students: about 25 percent of undergraduates have cohabited, and another 50 percent say they would if the situation were right; only 25 percent object on moral
or religious grounds (Bianchi & Spain, 1986; Spanier, 1983).

Although the increase in cohabitation is a dramatic social trend, the United
States still has a lower proportion (about 4% of all couples) than many other industrialized countries. Estimates for France are about 13 percent; for the
Netherlands, 7 percent; and for Sweden, about 25 percent (Popenoe, 1987).
Cohabitation in Sweden is almost as much an institution as conventional marriage (Trost, 1996). As one couple explained to a researcher, they moved in together two years after they met, exchanged rings four years later, when their first
child was born, and married four years after that. When asked what anniversary
they celebrated they responded, "The day we met" (Popenoe, 1987, p. 176).

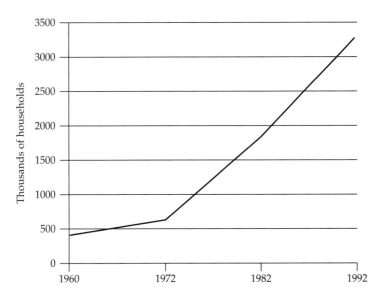

FIGURE 9.2. Cohabitation trends in the United States.
Source: Adapted from *Bianchi & Spain,* 1986, Figure 1.1, p. 20; Costello & Stone, Table 1.4,
p. 260.

Virtually all Swedes cohabit before marriage, and a growing number never marry at all. Cohabitation is accepted both legally and morally even for couples who have children. As a result, half of all Swedish children are born to unmarried women (Trost, 1996). Swedes believe that cohabitation is a way of liberating oneself from oppressive traditions about marriage and from state control of a private relationship. A common attitude is, "Why marry? It's our love that counts" (Popenoe, 1987).

In the United States, people choose to cohabit for a variety of reasons (Murstein, 1986). For some, it is a prelude to marriage or a "trial marriage" in which the couple assesses its compatibility. Some cohabitants have previously been married and divorced. They may cohabit because they are not yet ready to remarry or because they feel soured on marriage. Some young people cohabit to show their independence from their parents. Some cohabiting arrangements are more a matter of convenience than deep commitment (it's easier for two to pay the rent).

People who choose cohabitation tend to be more sexually experienced and active than those who do not. Their relationships are less likely than married relationships to be monogamous. In a national sample of more than 1,200 women aged 20 to 37, cohabitors were five times more likely than married women to have sex with someone other than their partner—about one in five had sex with someone else while cohabiting. This was true for all ethnic groups studied (Forste & Tanfer, 1996).

Do Cohabitors Play Gender Roles?

Cohabitors tend to be liberal in attitudes about gender roles. Cohabiting women generally value their independence and autonomy; they say they prefer to be thought of as an individual rather than half of a couple (Blumstein & Schwartz, 1983; Murstein, 1986).

Cohabiting couples usually have a division of labor similar to modern marriage. They almost always expect that both partners will work outside the home. However, as with most married couples, the division of labor at home is still more or less traditional, with women doing much more housework than men (Blumstein & Schwartz, 1983). Liberal attitudes about gender roles do not always lead to liberated behavior.

Though many cohabiting women have egalitarian ideals (and choose to cohabit rather than marry partly because of those ideals), their goals of independence and autonomy within a relationship are usually only partly fulfilled. As with married couples, issues of money, power, and the division of labor inside and outside the home can be sources of conflict. Nevertheless, most cohabitants report high satisfaction with their arrangement, and a large majority plan to marry someday, though not necessarily their current partner (Murstein, 1986).

Does Living Together Affect Later Marriage?

One obvious potential outcome of living together is that the woman becomes pregnant. National data show that cohabitation is associated with premarital pregnancy among all ethnic groups, and the likelihood of pregnancy during cohabitation is greater for Puerto Rican than white or African-American women. Does pregnancy push cohabitors toward marriage? This, too, depends on one's ethnic and cultural group. White women who get pregnant while cohabiting are very likely to marry; there is no effect for African-American women; and for Puerto Rican women, pregnancy lowers the odds of marrying before the birth of the child. These differences reflect cultural patterns; for example, there is a long tradition of cohabiting in Puerto Rico, and having a child may solidify the union without leading to marriage. The data show that cohabiting has different meanings to different ethnic groups (Manning & Landale, 1996).

Does cohabitation affect later marital satisfaction? It would seem that if people use living together as a trial marriage, those who do go on to marry should be better adjusted and less likely to divorce. However, in the United States, Sweden, and Canada, research studies show a greater tendency for former cohabitants to divorce, though their total time together is as long as the average married couple spends before divorcing (Teachman & Polenko, 1990). There may be ethnic and racial differences, too. In a study of about 200 black and 175 white couples in their first year of marriage, living together before marriage was unrelated to marital happiness for whites, but negatively related for blacks (Crohan & Veroff, 1989). Of course, a higher divorce rate for people who had previously cohabited is not necessarily an indication that cohabitation is a social problem. Part of the reason may be that women who cohabit (and their partners) are more unconventional, independent, and autonomous than those who do not; therefore they may be more likely to leave a marriage that does not meet their expectations (Murstein, 1986).

NEVER-MARRIED WOMEN

At any time, about one-third of the adult women in the United States are single. Most of these are women under 25, cohabitants, or older women who have been divorced or widowed. An unknown proportion are lesbians, living alone or with other women. Many are mothers. Widows, divorced women, and single mothers are discussed elsewhere; here we focus on never-married women without children.

The number of women who remain single throughout their lives is probably increasing, although exact statistics are not available. The majority of never-married women maintain their own independent households (Bequaert, 1976; Bianchi & Spain, 1986).

The "Old Maid": Still a Stereotype?

Negative judgments of never-married women are certainly easy to document. The goal of a perennial children's card game is to avoid being stuck with the "Old Maid" card. Poets and authors write of "maidens withering on the stalk" or "the tasteless dry embrace of a stale virgin with a winter face"; or they belittle a male character by comparing him to a fussy old maid. In advertising, spinsters are symbols of penny-pinching, prissiness, timidity, and overly proper behavior. Barbara Levy Simon (from whose 1987 book these examples are taken) concludes that "In Anglo-American culture, the never-married old woman is a stock character, a bundle of negative personal characteristics, and a metaphor for barrenness, ugliness, and death" (p. 2). Never-married men, or bachelors, are rarely the targets of such negative assessments.

Clinical psychology and psychiatry have reinforced the notion that remaining unmarried is due to being psychologically unable to form long-term committed relationships. This view assumes that unmarried women do not have close relationships. It supports the harmful fallacy that there is one psychological norm that exemplifies good adjustment and social value. Because of such stigma, unmarried women must cope with judgments about their supposedly deficient psyches that may lower their self-esteem. They also are subjected to psychological tactics that question their motives. For example, when an unmarried woman asserts that she is single by choice, she may be accused of rationalization or denial due to unconscious conflicts and pent-up sexual energy (Adams, 1976).

Who Stays Single and Why?

In contrast to these stereotypes and social judgments, it is generally true that women who remain unmarried have better physical health and greater economic resources than those who marry. Earlier, we discussed research showing that unmarried women have fewer serious psychological disorders than married women. Single women are better educated, are more intelligent, and achieve greater occupational success than their married counterparts. The lower marriage rate of highly capable women has been explained in terms of the marriage gradient discussed earlier in this chapter. Because men prefer to marry women who are slightly below them in education, occupational status, and income (and women prefer to "marry up"), the women who are at the top of the social scale are likely to be the "leftovers," with nobody sufficiently "superior" to them to want to marry them! (The marriage gradient idea also implies that men who do not marry are more likely to be those at the very bottom of the social scale.) However, it is important to remember that data about who marries whom are correlational, and causation cannot be determined. Whether highly educated, intelligent women are unattractive to men, whether they are less likely to marry because they have alternatives that are more appealing, or whether other factors not yet analyzed are involved is an open question (Unger, 1979a). Maybe some unmarried women held out for equality in a relationship and never found one that came close enough.

Rewards of the Single Life

What are the advantages and disadvantages of a permanently single way of life? Because never-married women have seldom been studied, the evidence is scarce. However, a few researchers have completed interview studies, and their results give a descriptive picture of a single woman's life (Bequaert, 1976; Simon, 1987). In the largest of these studies, 50 elderly women reflected on their lives in in-depth interviews in their homes (Simon, 1987). All these women had supported themselves, and many had helped support their parents in old age. Work and financial independence were important aspects of their lives.

Sixty-eight percent of the women stressed the importance of autonomy and freedom from the role expectations of marriage: "You see, dear, it's *marriage* I avoid, not men. Why would I ever want to be a wife? . . . A wife is someone's servant; a woman is someone's friend" (Simon, 1987, pp. 31–32). More than three-fourths of the group had consciously and deliberately chosen to be single:

> I dated four men over the years who wanted me as a wife. They were darlings, each of them. I spent huge amounts of time with them. But I never for a moment considered marrying one. Well, why would I? I had their company and their attention without all the headaches a wife bears. I knew all about birth control from the time I was a girl, so I didn't worry about getting pregnant. (Simon, 1987, pp. 41–42)

Rather than being socially isolated, the women were closely involved with their families and had many friendships with coworkers and neighbors, both women and men. The women in this study were of an age group and era that did not tolerate discussion of sexuality, and they refused to answer interview questions about lesbianism. However, many spontaneously described their friendships with women as especially rewarding, and some had intimate relationships with female life partners:

> There is nothing I did that Joyce didn't know about . . . I shared everything with her. She did the same with me. We got to be friends in high school. . . . We stayed roommates for fifty-seven years, until her heart gave out suddenly six years ago. . . . I'm still reeling from that loss. She leaned on me all those years just like I relied on her. In selfish moments, I wish that I had gone before her. Now I come home to silence and to memories. (Simon, 1987, p. 92)

Of course, people looking back on their lives in retrospect may remember selectively. Nevertheless, the voices of the never-married women in these studies give reason to challenge the stereotype of the frustrated, unfulfilled "old maid." In an era when marriage was very restrictive for middle-class women, they rejected it for largely positive reasons.

ENDING THE COMMITMENT: DIVORCE AND SEPARATION

The rise in divorces has probably gained more attention and caused more concern than any other social trend of our times. While psychologists and sociologists analyze causes and consequences, the popular media dramatize its effects in movies (*When a Man Loves a Woman, War of the Roses, The Favor*) and TV shows (*Civil Wars, Grace under Fire*). Divorce is an everyday occurrence—even in the funnies (see Figure 9.3).

How Likely Is Divorce?

The United States has the highest divorce rate of any industrialized nation, a rate that more than doubled between 1960 and 1980 and has only recently lev-

FIGURE 9.3.
Source: Copyright © 1997. Reprinted with special permission of King Features Syndicate.

eled off or in some groups, declined slightly (Costello & Stone, 1994; Taylor, 1997). By the 1970s, for the first time in American history a marriage was more likely to end in divorce than in the death of a spouse. Black women are considerably more likely than white women to end a marriage through divorce or prolonged separation, and Hispanic women less likely. Based on earlier age groups, it is projected that between 40 percent and 50 percent of Americans who marry will proceed to divorce, and the Department of the Census predicts that the U.S. divorce rate will continue to be among the world's highest. Other countries have experienced similar increases in divorce rate, though none as extreme as the United States (Bianchi & Spain, 1986; Norton & Moorman, 1987; Price & McKenry, 1988; Taylor, 1997).

What Are the Causes and Consequences of Divorce?

At the societal level, several factors have been correlated with rising divorce rates. Divorce rates rise along with women's participation in the paid workforce, both in the United States and in many other countries (Trent & South, 1989). Wives' paid employment is not usually a direct cause of divorce; rather, it seems that when women have alternatives for economic survival other than dependence on a husband's income, they are less likely to stay in unsatisfactory marriages (Bianchi & Spain, 1986; Price & McKenry, 1988). Age at first marriage is also highly correlated with later separation and divorce: The younger the man and woman are when they marry, the more likely they are to divorce (Norton & Moorman, 1987). Other factors related to the rising divorce rate are changes in laws and attitudes; divorce is no longer the social disgrace it once was, and "no-fault" laws make it easier.

At the personal level, people who divorce give a variety of reasons. Of course, these reasons are hardly objective; rather, they indicate how women and men try to make sense of what has happened to their dreams of a happy marriage. Interview studies of divorcing women in the 1940s and 1950s generally showed that their reasons had to do with their husbands failing to support the family or being excessively authoritarian. In contrast, lack of communication and companionship are more common reasons given in recent studies (Price & McKenry, 1988). This suggests that the ideal marriage that divorcing women are using as a yardstick by which to judge their own marriages has changed over time and is now closer to the modern than the traditional type.

Women and men tend to give somewhat different reasons for the breakup of their marriages. In one study (Cleek & Pearson, 1985), more than 600 divorcing persons were asked to indicate which of eighteen possible causes of divorce were applicable to their own situation. (The eighteen causes had been derived from counseling sessions with other divorcing spouses.) Table 9.2 shows the causes and the percentage of people who perceived each as applicable. Women were more likely than men to stress basic unhappiness, incompatibility, emotional and physical abuse, and their husbands' alcohol abuse and infidelity as causes of their divorce. Men were more likely to indicate that their own alcohol abuse and "women's lib" were responsible for their divorce. It would be interesting to explore the different meanings that women and men in this sample gave to the term "women's lib," a negative term for feminism, since men considered it to be more of a contributor to marital breakdown.

TABLE 9.2. Perceived Causes of Divorce: Women's and Men's Accounts

Cause	Women (%)	Men (%)
Mentioned significantly more often by women:		
Basic unhappiness	60	47
Incompatibility	56	45
Emotional abuse	55	25
Alcohol abuse (spouse)	30	6
Infidelity (spouse)	25	10
Physical abuse	22	4
Children	9	4
Mentioned significantly more often by men:		
Women's lib	3	14
Alcohol abuse (self)	1	9
No significant difference between men and women:		
Communication problems	70	59
Financial problems	33	29
Sexual problems	32	30
In-laws	11	12
Religious differences	9	6
Mental illness	5	7
Drug abuse (spouse)	4	1
Infidelity (self)	4	6
Drug abuse (self)	–	1

Source: Adapted from *Journal of Marriage and Family, 47,* Table 3, p. 181. Percentages have been rounded to nearest whole number.

Whatever the reasons for its occurrence, divorce has serious and long-lasting consequences for women. Three types of consequences can be distinguished, each intertwined with the others in its effects. We examine, in turn, psychological adjustment, economic effects, and responsibility for children.

How Do People Psychologically Adjust to Divorce?

A considerable number of divorcing women (from 17% to 33% in different samples) describe their divorces as causing little or no psychological disturbance or pain. These women view their divorces as ending a stressful or unbearable situation (e.g., physical or emotional abuse) and leading to increased feelings of freedom and competence. For most women, however, adjustment to divorce includes feelings of anger, helplessness, and ambivalence. Stress during divorce is related to a variety of physical health problems. (As with all correlational research, it is not possible to determine cause and effect in these studies.) Compared with married people, divorced people of both sexes have higher rates of illness and death, alcoholism, and serious accidents.

The adjustment to divorce seems to be more difficult for men than women. Although both divorced men and women are more likely to commit suicide than their married counterparts, divorced men are 50 percent more likely to do so than divorced women. They are also more likely to show serious psychological disturbances (Price & McKenry, 1988). Women appear to be better at building and maintaining networks of close friends and family during and following divorce (Gerstel, 1988), and men may miss their partner's caretaking more (see Figure 9.4). However, women and men are quite similar in their responses to divorce in many other ways (Gove & Shin, 1989). The question of whose divorce is worse, his or hers, is not easily resolved. Some researchers have suggested that men are more negatively affected in the short term, while women have more long-term problems to resolve (Price & McKenry, 1988).

Women whose marriages and personal values are traditional may have a more difficult time adjusting to divorce than those whose values and marriages are more egalitarian. Women who have devoted themselves to nurturing others and furthering their husbands' careers may find that their life's work is devalued when they must seek paid employment. The divorce rate for older couples continues to rise (Taylor, 1997). Many older women entered marriage with the expectation that they would be lifelong homemakers, their husbands the family providers. When these *displaced homemakers* lose their source of financial support, they have few marketable skills and "face triple jeopardy of discrimination; because they are women, because they have been homemakers, and because they are older" (Greenwood-Audant, 1984, p. 265). Moreover, they are likely to suffer from low self-esteem because their sense of self is heavily invested in being a good wife and mother. The displaced homemaker is especially likely to view her divorce as a personal failure and a negation of all she has worked for.

What Are the Economic Effects of Divorce?

Divorce in the United States has been characterized as an economic disaster for women. It has been documented repeatedly that the economic status of

"*That's right, Phil. A separation will mean—among
other things—watching your own cholesterol.*"

FIGURE 9.4.
Source: © The New Yorker Collection 1992 Michael Maslin from cartoonbank.com. All
Rights Reserved.

men improves upon divorce, while the economic status of women deteriorates
(Price & McKenry, 1988). Moreover, modern "no-fault" divorce laws, designed
to ensure equitable division of assets, have actually made the situation worse
for women.

Why do women lose out financially with divorce? There are several reasons. Women's sense of guilt and failure during the breaking-up period may
prevent them from asserting financial needs. However, structural factors are
probably more important than individual ones. The majority of state property
laws assume that property belongs to the spouse who earned it. Since husbands usually have had greater earning power during the marriage, these
laws result in men being awarded more of the couple's assets. The economic
value of the wife's unpaid labor may not be considered. When courts decide
what an equitable share is, the divorcing wife usually receives only about one-
third of the couple's property (Price & McKenry, 1988).

In other states, attempts to make divorce fairer for women have led to
laws that order equal division of property. However, most divorcing couples
(especially younger ones) have very little in the way of valuable property—

perhaps a car (complete with loan payments), household furnishings, and a modest bank account, offset by credit card debt. Fewer than half have equity in a house. The biggest assets for the large majority of couples are the husband's education, pension benefits, and future earning power.

As we discussed earlier, the husband's career usually takes priority in both single-earner and dual-earner marriages. Couples invest their time, money, and energy in his advancement; frequently the wife will postpone her education or career plans in order to put him through school, and she will do the unpaid work at home that allows him to concentrate on his paid job. Courts have been slow to recognize that the benefits husbands gain from traditional and modern marriage patterns translate into economic advantages upon divorce.

Contrary to the stereotype of the ex-wife leading a life of ease on her ex-husband's money, only about 15 percent of all divorced women in the United States are awarded spousal support. Most awards are for a period of about two years; and in the past, less than half of the men ordered to provide such support have actually complied (Faludi, 1991; Price & McKenry, 1988).

Who Is Responsible for the Children?

The presence of children is an important factor in adjustment to divorce for women. This is because women of all social classes and marriage types are likely to be left with the financial responsibility and the day-to-day care of children when a marriage ends. The benefit of awarding custody to women is that most divorced women stay connected with their children and receive the emotional rewards of parenting more than most divorced men do. However, current custody arrangements also have costs for women.

Two-thirds of divorces involve children. More than half of all children in the United States will experience their parents' divorce before the age of 18, and they will then spend an average of about five years in a single-parent home, the great majority with their mothers (Arendell, 1997). Being a single parent is not easy. The single mother may feel overwhelmed with responsibility, guilty at having separated the children from their father, and compelled to be a "supermom" (L'Hommedieu, 1984).

The lack of a male's income is a big handicap for divorced women and their children (Cherlin, 1981). About 75 percent of divorced mothers with custody of their children are awarded child support. However, the average amount paid as of the early 1990s was only about $3,600 a year (Arendell, 1997). Child support payments clearly do not cover the actual costs of bringing up a child.

Moreover, the majority of women entitled to child support do not receive it. Several national studies from the 1970s to the 1990s have shown that only 25 percent to 50 percent of men ordered to pay child support did so. No study has ever found that more than half of the fathers complied; many who comply do it irregularly and pay less than the designated amount; and one-fourth to one-third of fathers never make a single payment despite court orders. Black women are half as likely as white women to receive support, and the poorest, least educated women are the least likely of all. Only 10 percent of welfare clients receive child support (Arendell, 1997; Costello & Stone, 1994; Price & McKenry, 1988).

Divorced women and their children must adjust to a lower standard of living. A woman's standard of living declines by about 30 percent to 40 percent on average (Duncan & Hoffman, 1991; Morgan, 1991). More than 25 percent of divorced women fall into poverty for some time within five years of divorce. Many more "balance on the brink of poverty" (Morgan, 1991, p. 96). For many women with children, the financial hardship that comes with divorce becomes the central focus of their lives, dictating where they can live, determining whether they and their children can afford health care, and affecting their psychological well-being (Arendell, 1997).

Breaking Up: When Relationships End without Divorce

In contrast to the large amount of research on divorce, few studies have examined the process or consequences when relationships end without a formal divorce. This can happen in several ways. Some husbands simply desert their families, leaving their wives and children without a division of assets or child support. Little is known about how these families fare.

The ending of relationships between cohabiting men and women or lesbian couples have not been studied much, perhaps because they lack the institutional and legal status of marriage. As we discussed earlier, heterosexual cohabiting couples are more variable in their degree of commitment than married couples. Overall, then, one would expect that the breakup rate for cohabitors would be higher than the divorce rate for married couples, and this is true cross-culturally—for example, in the United States, Australia (Sarantakos, 1991), and Sweden. One study of Swedish couples attempted to sample only highly committed cohabiting couples by selecting only those who had had a child. Still, their breakup rate was three times the rate for comparable married couples (Popenoe, 1987).

For U.S. couples, the best comparisons of breakup rates come from a study in which couples were recontacted a year and a half after participating in the original study and asked if they were still together (Blumstein & Schwartz, 1983). Figure 9.5 shows the percentage of married, cohabiting, and lesbian couples who had separated. Lesbians were the most likely to break up, a surprising finding given the lesbian couples' emphasis on commitment and equality, but not so surprising when lack of social support for lesbian relationships is considered. People rarely talked about a breakup without sadness, anger, or regrets. Whether the relationship is heterosexual marriage, cohabiting with a man or with another woman, the emotional consequences are probably similar. When gay, lesbian, and heterosexual individuals who had broken up with a partner were asked why their relationship ended and how they felt about it, they gave similar reasons and reported similar levels of distress (Kurdek, 1997).

Are There Biases in Research on Divorce?

Research on divorce usually treats it as a personal and social tragedy; "broken" families are stigmatized. This perspective reflects an androcentric bias in which the only normal family is a traditional, patriarchal nuclear unit. From a feminist perspective, resistance to marriage can be positive for women, and di-

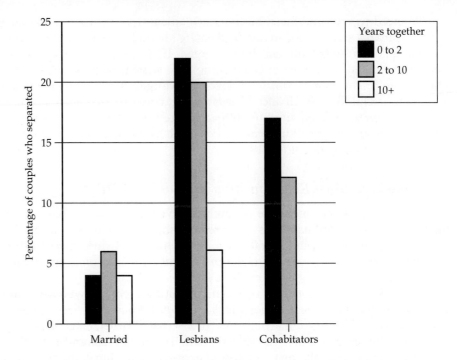

FIGURE 9.5. Percentage of couples who separated.
Source: Blumstein & Schwartz, 1983. Adapted from Figure 53, p. 308, and Figure 54, p. 315.

vorce may be an important way that women counter marital inequality. As we have seen, women are likelier to divorce when they can earn a living on their own; they cite abuse and unhappiness as major causes; and they adjust to divorce psychologically better than men, despite reduced income and increased responsibility for children. Despite its costs, divorce, as a way out of an oppressive situation, may be an affirmative choice for many women (Rice, 1994). In a study of successful egalitarian marriages, almost half were not first marriages, and most of the women said they had left their first marriage because of inequitable treatment (Schwartz, 1994). Divorce is a painful family transformation, but also a potential opportunity for growth and change (Stewart, Copeland, Chester, Malley, & Barenbaum, 1997).

REMARRIAGE

About two-thirds of women who get divorced remarry, about half of them within three years of the divorce. White women are more likely to remarry than black or Hispanic women. More than 40 percent of all marriages involve at least one partner who was previously divorced (Arendell, 1997; Ihinger-Tallman & Pasley, 1987). A cynic might say that remarriages represent a triumph of belief over experience; women (and men, who are even more likely to remarry) do not question the institution of marriage after they have been divorced. Rather, they believe that they chose the wrong partner last time and now know how to choose the right one.

Women may remarry partly to escape divorce-induced poverty. Research shows that women with lower levels of education and income are more likely to remarry than those with more economic options. However, given the importance of power relations in marriage, the consequences of entering a new marriage from an impoverished "one-down" position are unlikely to be positive. Economic discrepancies may be related to the higher rate of spouse abuse in remarried families (Crosbie-Burnett & Giles-Sims, 1991). And a Norwegian study of sixty-three blended families showed that women did more housework and child care regardless of whether they were the mother or the stepmother of the children in the family (Levin, 1997).

Are second marriages more successful? In general, the level of satisfaction in second marriages is about the same as in first marriages; as in first marriages, husbands are more satisfied than their wives (Ihinger-Tallman & Pasley, 1987). However, self-reported satisfaction is only part of the picture. Several studies have shown that second marriages are more likely to end in divorce than first marriages (Cherlin, 1981). Researchers predict that over half of women in their thirties who remarry will experience a second divorce (Dolan & Lown, 1985).

The complex family structures and dynamics of second marriages ("his," "hers," and "their" children, stepparents, ex-spouses, in-laws, and ex-in-laws) may be a source of stress. Financial problems may be increased by lack of support payments from former husbands, and many families have conflicts over how to allocate money to various household members (Ihinger-Tallman & Pasley, 1987). (Who should pay Tiffany's college tuition—mother, father, or stepparent?) Second marriages may also be less stable because, once having violated the societal and religious ideal of lifelong marriage, people are even less inclined to stay in unsatisfying relationships.

Some of the special problems of remarried couples—and the unshaken belief in the ideal—can be seen in the words of one couple, married less than two years at the time of the interview. She is a homemaker and he is a carpenter:

> Wife: I feel anyone thinking about marrying a person who has been previously married should think very seriously about it. There are definitely special problems that accompany this type of marriage. I feel the couple should have counseling before and not marry until *all* doubts about the marriage are gone. I feel my husband and I will always have his previous marriage overshadowing our marriage. My husband also feels guilty for not having his children with him. I in turn feel guilty and feel if it wasn't for me, maybe my husband would get back with his ex-wife and kids and live happily ever after.

> Husband: I think everyone should find the right spouse the first time. I found mine the second time and the only thing that stops it from being perfect is my previous marriage. (Ihinger-Tallman & Pasley, 1987, p. 60)

EQUALITY AND COMMITMENT: ARE THEY INCOMPATIBLE IDEALS?

Throughout this chapter we have focused on women in long-term relationships with men and with other women. A recurrent theme has been that close relationships are important and beneficial to both women and men. Another theme has been that women in relationships with men almost always have less power than their partners. Even when both partners believe in equality and want to work toward it, and even when both take on paid employment, the division of labor in the home remains relatively traditional, his job or career is given more importance than hers, and he has greater decision-making power.

This pattern seems to suggest that commitment and equality are incompatible, at least in heterosexual relationships. But egalitarian marriage and cohabitation are not impossible. Studies of power in marriage have consistently found that a small number of couples do manage to have long-term egalitarian relationships. Although their numbers may be small, their existence tells us that the ideal is not beyond human power to achieve. Egalitarian marriage may be emerging as a new way to be married—a life pattern of the future (Risman & Johnson-Sumerford, 1998; Schwartz, 1994) (see Figure 9.6). The voices of women and men in relatively egalitarian relationships tell us that these relationships can work. Here, the speaker is a man married for sixteen years:

> I started out pretty traditional. But over the years it made sense to change. We both work, and so we had to help each other with the kids, and pretty soon they start asking for you—so only you will do, so you do some of that. And we worked together at church, and we both went whole hog into the peace program. So that got shared. I don't know; you can't design these things. You play fair, and you do what needs doing, and pretty soon you find the old ways don't work and the new ways do. (Schwartz, 1994, p. 31)

It is tempting to believe that equality in marriage or long-term cohabitation can be achieved simply by being willing to work at it. This belief is related to the ideology of romantic love discussed in Chapter 8, a variation of "Love conquers all." How many times have you heard people express the belief that "If two people love each other enough, and if they're both willing to compro-

FIGURE 9.6. Life in an egalitarian family.
Source: Sally Forth by Greg Howard. Copyright © 1995. Reprinted with special permission of North America Syndicate.

mise, they can have a good marriage"? A related belief is that if the husband does not *intend* to oppress or dominate the wife, oppression and domination will not occur. Happy marriage, then, should be mainly (or entirely) a matter of picking the right person. But one major conclusion that can be drawn from the research reviewed in this chapter is that power differentials between husbands and wives are *not* solely the result of individual differences. Rather, they are strongly related to social-structural aspects of gender. The institution of marriage has been organized around gender inequality and attempts to change it have been only partially successful. "Even couples who willingly try to change traditional male and female behavior have difficulty doing so" (Blumstein & Schwartz, 1983, pp. 323–324). To understand how equality in marriage might become the rule rather than the exception, we need to look at both personal and structural factors.

How Can You Have an Egalitarian Relationship?

To have an egalitarian marriage, both wife and husband must be willing to integrate their work and family responsibilities despite social pressures to conform to more traditional roles (Gilbert, 1987). Women who value their work outside the home and set limits on the sacrifices they make for husbands and children may be perceived as cold, unfeminine, and selfish; men who do housework and child care and set limits on their career involvement may be perceived as weak and unmasculine. (One of our children once begged his father not to wear an apron in front of the child's friends!) Fortunately attitudes toward the work and family roles of women and men have changed a great deal in the past thirty years and continue to become more flexible. A large majority of women express nontraditional, profeminist attitudes about gender roles, and the popularity of these views is increasing over time. Though men remain more conservative than women, they also have become considerably more liberal across time (Mason & Lu, 1988). Blacks are slightly more liberal than whites on family issues.

The fact that women have more profeminist attitudes suggests that they will be more likely than men to take the lead in initiating change within their families. Moreover, women must lead the way to more egalitarian relationships because men are unlikely to fight a status quo that gives them many benefits. However, only when women perceive gender roles in relationships as unequal and unjust can they begin to change them. To recognize their position as unjust, women must be aware that other possibilities exist, must want such possibilities for themselves, must believe they are entitled to them, and must not feel personally to blame for not having them (Crosby, 1982; Steil, 1997).

Change involves negotiation. Roles are not engraved in stone, nor are they totally defined by society. Rather, they are expressed in day-to-day activities and can be negotiated between partners:

> Human beings are not just robots programmed by society. They are also willful actors, capable of choosing nonconformity and altering social structure if they so wish. . . . [There are] enormous possibilities for negotiation, compromise, and innovation [in marriage]. Individuals can construct their own realities to a surprising extent. (Thoits, 1987, p. 12)

What social factors give women more negotiating power in relationships with men? If the wider society allows for more flexible commitments to paid work by both women and men, there will be less likelihood that the man's job or career will take precedence. It is encouraging that many social critics are calling for corporations to be more flexible and adaptable to the needs of dual-worker couples (Guinn & Russell, 1987). In Norway, the women's movement has endorsed the idea of a universal six-hour workday as a way to reduce marital inequity (Haavind, 1983), based on the idea that work within the home is more likely to be shared equally if neither partner has an excessive commitment to paid work. The interaction of work and family life will be discussed further in Chapter 11.

Economic power is a key social factor. We have seen that equality is most likely when the partners' economic resources are most balanced. The single biggest obstacle to egalitarian marriage and cohabiting relationships is men's greater earning power, which steers couples into investing in his career and leaving the work at home to her (Schwartz, 1994).

It is important for couples who are trying to find new postgender ways to live together to build networks of like-minded people. Couples who spend time with other nontraditional couples can learn from each other, provide havens from the criticism that more traditional people may aim their way, and provide role models of healthy alternatives to male dominance for themselves and their children. As the number of couples who are consciously trying to build egalitarian relationships increases, it should be easier for them to find each other and build supportive networks. Nontraditional arrangements are coming to be seen as legitimate, normal, and even routine (Thoits, 1987). Similar needs can be met for lesbian couples by being part of a lesbian community (Krieger, 1982).

The movement toward egalitarian relationships will bring benefits for both women and men. Men will be relieved of some of the economic burdens of traditional marriage and be freer to become involved with their children's growth and development. Women will experience better psychological adjustment. For both men and women, equality is linked to more satisfying relationships and greater intimacy (Schwartz, 1994; Steil, 1997; Steil & Turetsky, 1987b). Equality and role flexibility in committed long-term relationships offer both women and men a chance to become more fully human.

CONNECTING THEMES

- *Gender is more than just sex.* Women and men in enduring relationships often have "his" and "her" experiences, such as differential workloads and roles, relationship satisfaction, and psychological adjustment. This is not because women and men are fundamentally different in needs and goals, but because differences in power and status structure different roles for them.
- *Language and naming are sources of power.* Marriage is an institution with a name and a script. The life paths of lesbians, unmarried women, and het-

erosexual cohabitants are either not named or given negative labels. Within marriage, inequality is so much the norm that it may be invisible.

- *Women are not all alike.* Women who do not enter heterosexual marriages are a diverse group. Lesbian couples form a largely invisible minority, and ever-single women are rarely studied. Even within heterosexual marriage, there is great diversity along lines of ethnicity, social class, and marriage type (traditional, modern, egalitarian).
- *Psychological research can foster social change.* The disadvantages women suffer in long-term relationships—and when those relationships end through death or divorce—cannot be remedied by individual efforts. Restructuring the gendered domain of relationships requires restructuring the domains of work and public power that support it. However, individual couples can develop strategies to support egalitarian relationships.

SUGGESTED READINGS

LERNER, HARRIET G. (1985). *The dance of anger.* New York: Harper & Row. Subtitled "A Woman's Guide to Changing the Patterns of Intimate Relationships," this book encourages the reader to recognize that anger and dissatisfaction are signals that something is wrong in a relationship and can provide a starting point for the renegotiation of roles.

BOSTON LESBIAN PSYCHOLOGIES COLLECTIVE (Eds.). (1987). *Lesbian psychologies: Explorations and challenges.* Urbana: University of Illinois Press. This book, winner of an award from the Association for Women in Psychology, has sections on lesbian identity, psychological adjustment, and community. Of special interest to this chapter is a section on lesbian relationships and families.

SCHWARTZ, P. (1994). *Peer marriage: How love between equals really works.* New York: Free Press. A sociologist reports on interviews with couples in egalitarian marriages and suggests that this kind of relationship is becoming more widespread.

CHAPTER 10

Mothering

- IMAGES OF MOTHERS AND
  MOTHERHOOD
  Is There a Motherhood Mystique?
- THE DECISION TO HAVE A CHILD
  Why Do Women Choose to Have
    Children?
  Is There a Mandate for Motherhood?
  Childless by Choice or Circumstance?
  How Does Society Restrict Women's
    Choices?
  Technology and Choice
- THE TRANSITION TO MOTHERHOOD
  How Does Motherhood Change Work
    and Marital Roles?
  Do Mothers Face Impossible Ideals?
  Are Sexuality and Motherhood
    Incompatible?
  What Are the Psychological Effects of
    Bodily Changes During
    Pregnancy?
  How Do Others React to Pregnant
    Women?
  Does Motherhood Change Women's
    Identity?

- THE EVENT OF CHILDBIRTH
  How Is the Meaning of Childbirth
    Socially Constructed?
  Is Childbirth a Medical Crisis?
  Can Childbirth Be Family Centered?
  Depression Following Childbirth:
    Why?
- EXPERIENCES OF MOTHERING
  Teen Mothers
  Single Mothers
  Black Mothers and the Matriarchal
    Myth
  Lesbian Mothers
  Commonalities
- THE FUTURE OF MOTHERING
  Why Blame Mom?
  Is Fathering a Feminist Issue?
- CONNECTING THEMES
- SUGGESTED READINGS

M*other* is one of the most fundamental archetypes of woman, and motherhood has been regarded as women's ultimate source of power and fulfillment. In our society, motherhood is viewed as central to a woman's life and identity, a natural and unchanging aspect of being a woman. However, those aspects of society that seem most natural often are the ones most in need of critical examination.

Like marriage, motherhood is an institution. Its meaning goes beyond the biological processes of reproduction, encompassing many customs, traditions, beliefs, attitudes, rules, and laws. Like other institutions, it also has a powerful symbolic component. Yet women who become mothers, though they mother in the context of the social and symbolic meanings of motherhood, are individuals. "Mother is a role; women are human beings" (Bernard, 1974, p. 7).

Motherhood raises troubling questions for feminist analysis. It is a key topic in debates between feminists who want to pursue equality on the basis of gender similarity and those who want to claim the value of women's bodies and women's work (see Chapter 4). Liberal feminists have stressed that the institution of motherhood has been used to exclude women from public life. They have called for publicly financed child care and better access to abortion, contraception, and reproductive health care. They have also exposed how the myths and mystique of motherhood keep women in their place. Some radical and cultural feminists, on the other hand, have explored the experiences of women who mother, studied how motherhood changes women, and pointed out that motherhood is a woman-centered model of how people can be connected and caring (McMahon, 1995).

The diversity of feminist opinion on motherhood need not be a problem. Motherhood has different meanings to different women. Just as there is no single meaning of motherhood, there is no unified feminist position on it. In this chapter, we ask many questions about mothering, using a variety of feminist perspectives. What are the images and scripts that define mothers and motherhood? How do women go about choosing whether or not to have children—and to what extent are they allowed to choose? How does the transition to motherhood change women? What are women's experiences of birth and mothering? We also examine mother-blaming and ask whether fathering is a feminist issue.

IMAGES OF MOTHERS AND MOTHERHOOD

Is There a Motherhood Mystique?

Western society has strong beliefs about motherhood. The ideology of motherhood has been termed the *motherhood mystique.* It includes the following myths (Hays, 1996; Hoffnung, 1989; Oakley, 1974):

1. Ultimate fulfillment *as a woman* is achieved through motherhood. Motherhood is a natural and necessary experience for all women. Those who do not want to mother are psychologically disturbed, and those who want to but cannot are fundamentally deprived.
2. Women are naturally good at caregiving and should be responsible for infants, children, elderly parents, home, and husband. A woman who experiences conflicts among these demands is maladjusted or poorly organized.
3. A mother has infinite patience and the willingness to sacrifice herself to her children. If she does not put her own needs last, she is an inadequate mother.

4. A woman's intense, full-time devotion to mothering is best for her children. Women who work are inferior mothers.

Although these beliefs may seem outdated, the motherhood mystique lives on in advice to mothers from (usually male) experts, media portrayals of mothers, and attitudes toward working mothers (see Figure 10.1). A recent analysis of three best-selling child-rearing manuals showed that all the authors hold mothers primarily responsible for child care, prescribe intensive mothering, and glorify self-sacrifice to the needs of the child—this despite the fact

FIGURE 10.1. The motherhood mystique internalized!
Source: Copyright © 1989. Reprinted with special permission of King Features Syndicate.

that in the 1990s, the majority of mothers work for pay (Hays, 1996). During the 1990 Gulf War, a *People* magazine cover story, "Mom Goes to War," featured a woman in uniform embracing her sad-eyed toddler, with the question, "Mommy, what if you die?" Though the military is 89 percent male, there were no heartrending stories of "Dad Goes to War." Media representations such as these reinforce the view that motherhood is the sole important aspect of women's identity (Flanders, 1992).

The mystique persists because it has important functions for *men* (Hays, 1996; Lorber, 1993b). Assigning caretaking to women creates economic dependence on men and is used to justify women's lower status and pay at work. "The social order that elevates men over women is legitimated by women's devotion to child care, since it takes them out of the running for top-level jobs and political positions and defuses their consciousness of oppression" (Lorber, 1993b, p. 170). The mystique may persist also because it is the one area where Western society values connectedness and caring over individual gain. But glorifying motherhood, and defining it in ways that make many women feel guilty and burdened by it, benefits groups that have the most power economically and politically.

THE DECISION TO HAVE A CHILD

Having a child profoundly changes a woman's life. And in our society, children are more a liability than an asset in material terms. They are not expected to produce much useful work or income for their parents or to support them financially in their old age. The cost of bringing up even one child is high. Yet the great majority of women have children.

Why Do Women Choose to Have Children?

There are practical reasons for having children, particularly in traditional societies. Children are necessary as a source of family income, as domestic workers, as a path for passing on property and a traditional way of life, and sometimes as a form of personal immortality. In postcolonial and underdeveloped societies, many children are lost to disease and malnutrition in infancy and childhood. Five or more children may have to be conceived for two to live to adulthood; these children may provide the only form of economic support available for their parents' old age.

As third world countries adopt Western industrialized ways of life, the birthrate drops. The best predictor of smaller families is not modernization itself, but attitudes toward modern science and medicine. As people begin to believe that science and medicine can deal with social problems, they may feel that it is not necessary to bear many children in order to have a few grow up. Nevertheless, attitudes change more slowly than material conditions, so that there is a considerable lag between the development of better medical conditions and smaller family size.

In industrialized societies, children have little economic value—in fact, they are a big liability—and psychological reasons are given more weight. One traditional explanation for childbearing is the existence of a "maternal instinct" (Bernard, 1974). This idea has been criticized by anthropologists and sociologists. If wanting children is instinctive, they ask, why are so many powerful socialization forces directed at instilling this "instinct" in girls? (For example, recall the "girls' toys" in Chapter 6.) And why have abortion and infanticide been features of so many human societies throughout history? At the species level, it is necessary for women and men to reproduce. But there are no inherent physiological benefits of motherhood for women, and there is no instinctive drive for pregnancy.

Another theory is that women have a psychological need to care for a child and men do not. In Chapter 4, we discussed the approach of Nancy Chodorow (1978), who stresses the importance of psychological differentiation in infancy. Because girls' separation from their mothers differs from boys', girls grow up defining the self in terms of relationship and connectedness. Having babies satisfies deep relational needs. Unfortunately, it also leads to dependence on and subordination to men.

Chodorow's theory has been criticized along several dimensions. First, it takes white middle-class family patterns as the norm. In the African-American community, motherhood and self-sufficiency are seen as compatible (Joseph, 1991). Second, even among white middle-class mothers, many women feel isolated and unfulfilled by mothering. In a qualitative interview study, these mothers were aware of their own needs for autonomy but found little social support (Kaplan, 1992).

A third criticism is that men can mother very well when they have to. Virtually all studies of single fathers show that when men cannot depend on women for child care (because of death, desertion, or a divorced spouse who did not want custody), they develop skills and behaviors very much like those of women. In addition, they come to see themselves as nurturing, compassionate, and sensitive to the needs of others, all stereotypically feminine traits (Risman, 1998). Biological theories assume that women are "programmed" to care for children; socialization theories assume that women are more nurturing because of early learning. But it is just as likely that a "nurturing personality" is created by being put into a nurturing role as an adult. The process of mothering is a kind of "doing gender" that produces womanly persons (McMahon, 1995).

The reasons for choosing to become a mother are different for women of different social classes. In an in-depth study of fifty-nine white Canadian women, all employed full time and mothers of a preschool child, the middle-class women talked about being ready to have a child only *after* they had met certain goals: maturity, the right relationship with a man, and career achievement. In contrast, the working-class women saw themselves as achieving adulthood *through* having a child. Their pregnancies, typically not planned, provided the opportunity for these women to claim an identity as a mature, loving, and responsible person (McMahon, 1995).

R's for Mom.

Among the reasons our students mention when we discuss motherhood in our classes are the desire to experience pregnancy and birth, to participate in the growth of another human being, to please a husband or partner, to have a child's love, to strengthen a relationship, to prove oneself an adult, to be needed and loved by someone, and to pass on a family name, or one's genes, or one's values. Which of these reasons seems most compelling to you? What do you think your own mother's answer would be?

Is There a Mandate for Motherhood?

There is considerable social pressure on women to have children. Moreover, one child is not enough; "real" women have at least two. This pressure to have children has been called the *motherhood mandate* (Russo, 1979) (see Figure 10.2).

The motherhood mandate has a long tradition in American society. More than eighty-five years ago, one of the first women psychologists, Leta Hollingworth, analyzed the social techniques used to persuade women to

FIGURE 10.2.
Source: Cathy © 1996 Cathy Guisewite. Reprinted with permission of Universal Press Syndicate. All rights reserved.

Box 10.1 Mothers Are Made, Not Born

In 1916, Leta Hollingworth wrote a powerful article entitled "Social Devices for Impelling Women to Bear and Rear Children." Asserting that it is necessary to "clear our minds of the sentimental conception of motherhood and to look at facts," she went on:

> The facts, shorn of sentiment, then, are: (1) The bearing and rearing of children is necessary for tribal or national existence and aggrandizement. (2) The bearing and rearing of children is painful, dangerous to life, and involves long years of exacting labor and self-sacrifice. (3) There is no verifiable evidence to show that a maternal instinct exists in women of such all-consuming strength and fervor as to impel them voluntarily to seek the pain, danger, and exacting labor involved in maintaining a high birth rate.

Hollingworth described ways in which societies ensure that women will choose to have and care for children.

Leta Hollingworth

Personal Ideals. The "normal," or "womanly," woman is proclaimed by experts to be one who enthusiastically engages in maternity. Citing medical and psychological authorities, Hollingworth shows how women are told that "only abnormal women want no babies."

Law. Child rearing is ensured by restrictions on abortion. "There could be no better proof of the insufficiency of maternal instinct as a guaranty of population than the drastic laws which we have against birth control, abortion, infanticide, and infant desertion."

Belief. Religions, for example, may "regard family limitation as a sin, punishable in the hereafter."

Art. "The mother, with children at her breast, is the favorite theme of artists. Poetry abounds in allusion to the sacredness and charm of motherhood . . . fiction is replete with happy and adoring mothers. Art holds up to view only the compensations of motherhood, leaving the other half of the theme in obscurity."

Illusion. "One of the most effective ways of creating the desired illusion about any matter is by concealing and tabooing the mention of all the painful and disagreeable circumstances connected with it. Thus there is a very stern social taboo on conversation about the processes of birth. . . . The drudgery, the monotonous labor . . . are minimized."

Education. Women's education is aimed at making them better wives and mothers, not at enabling them to achieve independence or public achievement.

"Bugaboos." Women are told by experts that they must have their children before the age of 30 or they are highly likely to face grave complications. They are told that motherhood increases happiness and longevity. Finally, it is claimed that only children grow up selfish and disturbed.

Are the social devices described by Hollingworth valid today?

Source: Hollingworth, 1916.

have babies (see Box 10.1). Americans surveyed in the 1950s showed overwhelming approval of motherhood for married women, describing childless people as "selfish" and "bad" (Baruch, Barnett, & Rivers, 1983). Studies during the 1960s and 1970s (reviewed in Unger, 1979a) also showed a strong social norm against childlessness and one-child families. Deliberately choosing not to have children was viewed as a sign of psychological maladjustment in women; stereotypes of the woman who declined to be a mother represented her as selfish and neurotic. Stereotypes of the "only child" represented him or her as maladjusted, socially inadequate, self-centered, unhappy, and unlikable. (There is no evidence that only children actually possess these characteristics.)

Has the motherhood mandate decreased because of the influence of feminism? Surveys in the late 1970s showed an increased tolerance for people who chose not to have families. This change may have reflected the influence of the women's movement or increasing concerns with the environment and overpopulation. However, in the 1980s, the media rediscovered motherhood, announcing all of the following (sometimes contradictory) "trends":

- Women's chances of marrying decrease drastically each year.
- There is an infertility epidemic, and women's careers are to blame.
- There is a "baby boomlet," as women rediscover motherhood.
- Women are fleeing the workforce and abandoning career paths to devote themselves to full-time motherhood.
- Employed mothers and full-time mothers are enemies.
- Single women are so desperate to marry and have children that they are stealing husbands by the millions.
- Day-care centers are dangerous, and women are afraid to leave their children in them.
- Women have achieved equality, but at a terrible cost (home and family).

These "trend stories" claimed to show huge shifts in women's attitudes and behavior. However, they were based on biased anecdotes and sweeping generalizations and had little basis in reality. Each "trend" was a way of telling women that they must return to traditional roles or suffer dire consequences. "For women, the trend story was no news report; it was a moral reproach" (Faludi, 1991, p. 80).

In this social context, the decision to have a child may not represent a free choice as much as an inability to escape the pressure to conform. One feminist remembers her own decision in these words: "I had no idea of what *I* wanted, what *I* could or could not choose. I only knew that to have a child was to assume adult womanhood to the full, to prove myself, to be 'like other women'" (Rich, 1976, p. 25).

Childless by Choice or Circumstance?

Throughout history, the childless woman has been regarded as a failed woman (Phoenix, Woollett, & Lloyd, 1991; Rich, 1976). Our language provides no ready positive term for her. Traditionally, she was labeled *barren*. The more neutral term *childless* still defines her in terms of a lack. Recently, the term *child-free* has been suggested as a more positive alternative. Even in the 1990s, college students judged that women who remained childless by choice (even though they were happily employed) were less fulfilled, less acceptable role models, and more likely to be unhappy in later life (Mueller & Yoder, 1997). Given the negative stereotype, why do some women choose not to have children, and what effects does this choice have on their psychological development and adjustment?.

Studies comparing women who express a preference for remaining childless with those who express a preference for having children suggest that there are factors in personality and attitudes that distinguish the two groups. Women who want to be child-free are more individualistic, more independent of their families during adolescence, more inclined to identify with the women's movement, more interested in vocational success, and more aware of the disadvantages of motherhood. They are high in autonomy, androgyny, and achievement orientation (Gerson, 1980; Houseknecht, 1979; Landa, 1990; Unger, 1979a).

Some women make the decision not to be mothers at an early age, even before they marry. Others decide through a process of repeated postponement, finally realizing that there probably never will be a "right time" for them. Women's reasons include financial considerations, a desire to pursue their education or career, the dangers of childbirth, the possibility of bearing a defective child, concerns about overpopulation, and a belief that they are not personally suited to nurturing and caring for children (Landa, 1990). Regardless of when the decision is made, the choice to remain child-free is definitely a minority choice, and it is important for the woman to have a supportive social environment. Like couples trying to create egalitarian marriages (Chapter 9), women who are childless by choice need to know that they are not the only ones making this decision (Houseknecht, 1979).

Of course, childlessness is not always a matter of choice. In a Canadian study of childless women and men over the age of 55, 72 percent attributed their childlessness to circumstance. Some people said they had not married because they had to take care of sick or elderly parents; others married late in life; others reported infertility or repeated miscarriages; and for others, it seemed to be simply fate: "It just didn't turn out that way" (Connidis & McMullin, 1996).

In the United States, about one woman in six experiences fertility problems, and only about half who seek medical treatments are able to conceive. Accepting childlessness is a gradual process. In a study of women who had given up trying to conceive a child after up to fifteen years of treatment, participants reported coming to a point where they realized that further efforts were futile. After years of treatment, they felt "exhausted" and "worn out." They felt profound grief and loss, and a sense of emptiness. At the same time, however, they felt relief at being out of the "medical machinery" and recognized an opportunity to take back their lives, moving on to other goals (Daniluk, 1996).

Does not having children (by choice or by chance) lead to unhappiness? As discussed in Chapter 9, marital satisfaction drops with the birth of the first child and may not return to its original level until children leave home. In a major study of women at midlife, whether a woman had children had no relationship to her psychological well-being. The women in this study grew up in an era when the motherhood mandate was in full force, yet their well-being at midlife did not suffer because of childlessness. These results contradict the belief that children are central to a woman's happiness, the researchers pointed out. They concluded that "many supposed truths about women are based simply on myth and misinformation. . . . There is an urgent need to build a new vision about women's lives that is based on reality, not on stereotypes, assumptions, or wishful thinking" (Baruch et al., 1983, p. 107).

How Does Society Restrict Women's Choices?

Women's choices about child rearing do not take place in a social vacuum. Most societies regulate women's rights to have—and choose not to have—children. Moreover, practical and economic factors restrict women's options.

Feminists advocate *reproductive freedom* for women. This concept includes a range of issues, such as the right to comprehensive and unbiased sex education, access to safe and reliable contraception, an end to forced sterilization and birth control for poor and minority women, and access to safe and legal abortion (Baber & Allen, 1992; Bishop, 1989).

At the heart of the concept of reproductive freedom is the idea that all choices about reproduction should be made by the woman herself: it is her body and her right to choose. For this reason, feminist perspectives on reproductive freedom are often termed *pro-choice*. Because reproductive freedom affects every aspect of a woman's life, it has been a key component of every feminist movement throughout history. "Without the ability to determine their reproductive destinies, women will never achieve an equal role in social, economic, and political life and will continue to be politically subordinate to and economically dependent on men" (Roberts, 1998). Restrictions on reproductive freedom are more severe for poor and minority women. Poverty limits women's options—for example, a poor woman, but not a middle-class one, may have to choose her birth control method by its cost. Women who receive government benefits are more vulnerable to government monitoring, supervision, and control of their reproductive choices. Because they have less access to lawyers and the media, and less of a public voice, they may be less able to challenge government restrictions of their rights. And they are more likely to be coerced into having (or not having) children (Roberts, 1998). Our discussion of current issues in contraception and abortion will show that reproductive freedom for all women is a feminist ideal that has not yet been achieved.

Contraception

Accidental pregnancies can be the result of a number of factors: contraceptive failure, lack of contraceptive knowledge or skill, lack of access to contraceptives, failure to use contraception, and unplanned or coerced sexual activity. Moreover, although women are expected to take most of the responsibility for safer sex, psychological factors, lack of power within heterosexual relationships, and sexual scripts make it difficult for many women, particularly young and inexperienced ones, to take control in this area (see Chapter 8).

Every form of contraception has drawbacks. Some methods are messy, inconvenient and interfere with spontaneity (foam, condoms, diaphragms). Some may cause nausea and weight gain, require daily remembering, or have the potential for long-term side effects (the pill). The most effective methods of preventing pregnancy, such as the contraceptive pill, offer no protection against STDs (see Chapter 8). Some are expensive and not covered by insurance (see Box 10.2). Problems with using contraceptives effectively are compounded for poor women and women in developing countries. For example, some methods cannot be used by women who are breastfeeding; in countries without hygienic water supplies, breastfeeding is the only safe way to nourish an infant. Other methods require supervision by medical professionals, which is prohibitive for the majority of the world's women (Owen & Caudill, 1996).

Recently, hormonal contraceptives that can be implanted under the skin to ensure infertility for up to five years have been developed. This is the first contraceptive method (other than sterilization) that does not require the use of contraception to be connected to the act of intercourse or remembered and acted upon daily. By separating contraception from both sexual encounters and daily behavior patterns, the implant method provides important new psychological advantages. A major drawback at present is its high cost. Like other hormonal methods, it may have possible long-term side effects as yet undetermined (Hardon, 1992). Even more important, this type of contraceptive can be implanted without the woman's consent (see Box 10.3). Already, six states have proposed mandatory implantation for some women. The National Black Women's Health Project and the American Medical Association have both denounced the punitive use of birth control on poor women and women of color (Long-Scott & Southworth, 1992).

Information about contraception is widely available to middle-class women, everywhere from *Glamour* magazine to Planned Parenthood and the *New York Times*. However, some groups of women are much less likely to get

---

Box 10.2 Viagra Bias

Viagra bias? The initial rush of some insurers to pay for Viagra, the so-called erection pill, is leaving women (and their doctors) crying foul. Nearly 40 years after the advent of the birth control pill, only 56 percent of Pill prescriptions are covered by insurers. Why the disparity? The American College of Obstetricians and Gynecologists (ACOG) says the fact that the financial burden of birth control is borne by women, not insurers, is a clear case of gender discrimination. In fact, the cost of covering contraception would more than pay for itself in savings on abortion, prenatal care and delivery. "Contraception isn't optional," says Anita Nelson, an associate professor of obstetrics and gynecology at UCLA School of Medicine. "Women need it to protect their health and quality of life, and the prohibitive cost is partly to blame

for the high number of unintended pregnancies in this country." Indeed, most Americans favor mandatory coverage of prescription contraceptives: A new survey of 1,000 adults by the Kaiser Family Foundation found that 73 percent believe insurers should foot the bill for these methods, even if it means an increase in premiums. (By comparison, only 49 percent feel that Viagra should be covered.) The Equity in Prescription Insurance and Contraceptive Coverage Act (EPICC), now being considered in Congress would require insurers who pay for prescription drugs to cover all FDA-approved contraceptives, as well as related doctor visits.

Source: Courtesy of Glamour, Conde Nast Publications, Inc., Glamour, September 1998.

┌───┐
│   │
│ *Box 10.3 Reproductive Control in the News: Coerced Contraception*   │
│   │
└───┘

JUDGE ORDERS NORPLANT IN A
CHILD-ABUSE CASE

A California judge has ordered a woman convicted of beating her children to have the recently
approved Norplant birth-control device implanted in her arm for three years. . . . Darlene
Johnson, a 27-year-old pregnant mother of four,
was found guilty of beating her children with a
belt. As part of a plea bargain with her court-
appointed attorney on Wednesday, Broadman
sentenced Johnson to one year in county jail and
three years of probation.

But on the day of sentencing, Broadman also
ordered Johnson to have six plastic Norplant
tubes inserted into her upper arm by June.
Johnson agreed to the conditions, but her attorney
now says that Johnson did not understand that
Norplant must be surgically implanted.

"She had a gun to her head. She was told she
agrees or she goes to state prison" instead of
county prison, said Johnson's attorney. "She
didn't understand what was involved. She had
never heard of this procedure before. I had never
heard of this procedure before."

The enforced contraception marks the first
time a judge has ordered a woman to use the implantable device.

. . . Johnson is black and Judge Broadman is
white.

"The use of Norplant for any kind of coercive
purpose is something I am totally against," said
Sheldon Segal of the Rockefeller Foundation, the
originator of implantable contraceptives and the
driving force behind the development of Norplant.
"I consider it a gross misuse of the method."

"I told you so," said Arthur Caplan, director
of the center for biomedical ethics at the
University of Minnesota. "I am not surprised by
this, but I find it troubling when reproductive capacity is manipulated as a form of punishment. It
sure didn't take long."

. . . Segal and others agreed that ordering
Norplant would set a dangerous precedent because Norplant is a prescription drug with possible side effects, such as headaches and irregular
menstrual bleeding, and could be wrong for some
women.

"The judge really appears to be going beyond
his expertise," Segal said.

[Ms. Johnson's attorney] said his client, who
has diabetes and a heart ailment, may not even be
an appropriate candidate for Norplant. He said he
will try to overturn the order.

"I think it is an effort by government to say to
certain people, 'You shouldn't have children,'" he
said.

Source: © 1991 *The Washington Post.* **Reprinted with permission.**

the information they need and want. Young women just beginning to be sexually active are disadvantaged: only thirteen states mandate sex education in
the schools, and not all of these programs discuss contraception. Ads for contraceptives do not appear on TV, the medium teens use most. Non-English-
speaking women are disadvantaged, too; virtually no information is available
in diverse languages, even in areas where there are large numbers of recent
immigrants and ethnically diverse populations (Watson, Trasciatti, & King,
1996).

Abortion

Abortion is a reproductive option that many women find necessary at some
time in their lives. In the United States, about 1.5 million abortions take place
each year, representing about 30 percent of pregnancies; 91 percent of these
abortions take place within the first three months of pregnancy. Women choosing abortion tend to be young: 57 percent are under 24 years of age, and girls

under 15 are the most likely of any age group to end a pregnancy through abortion. The great majority (81%) of those having abortions are unmarried. Minority women comprise approximately one-third of those choosing to have an abortion (Albert, 1993; Bishop, 1989; Henshaw, 1998; Hyde & DeLamater, 1997).

Abortion has been legal in the United States since 1973, when the Supreme Court, ruling in *Roe v. Wade,* affirmed that women have a right to decide whether to terminate their pregnancies on the basis of the constitutional right to privacy. Abortion, the Court ruled, is a matter to be decided between a woman and her physician. Although the principle of choice was affirmed by this ruling, in practice there are many limitations and legal restrictions on women's choices with respect to ending unwanted pregnancies.

In 1976, Congress passed the Hyde Amendment, which prohibited the use of federal Medicaid money to pay for abortions except in the few cases in which the mother's life is (medically) endangered. Since Medicaid provides health care for low-income families, poor women were left with the bitter choice of paying for an abortion out of their own inadequate incomes or carrying an unwanted fetus to term. The Medicaid restriction has resulted in some poor women delaying abortion until they can afford to pay for it, or even resorting to illegal abortion, leading to more risk of complications (Bishop, 1989; Miller, 1996). In 1994, a law was passed ordering states to pay for abortions for poor women who were victims of incest or rape. However, this law met with immediate protest from six states that had laws prohibiting the use of state Medicaid funds for abortions (Hall, 1994). Since 99 percent of the money spent annually on abortions for poor women comes from state (rather than federal) funds, state compliance with the 1994 law will be necessary for it to have any beneficial effect on poor women (Daley & Gold, 1993).

Recent Supreme Court decisions give more power to individual states to set abortion regulations, and many states have responded with very restrictive laws requiring the consent of a husband or partner, parental consent for young women, mandatory waiting periods, and "educational" requirements that are designed to discourage women from seeking abortions (Lublin, 1998). Abortion is safest when it is performed early in the pregnancy; laws that delay it affect women's health (Miller, 1996).

Harassment and violence at abortion clinics have had wide societal impact. The number of doctors who perform abortions has dropped 18 percent since 1982, partly because of stalking, death threats, and murders of physicians and clinic staff (Cozzarelli & Major, 1998; Vobejda, 1994). Picketing, bomb threats, and demonstrations affect clients, too. Studies of women who encountered antiabortion protesters as they went to a clinic show that the encounters made women feel angry, intruded on, and guilty. However, they had no effect on the women's decision to have an abortion (Cozzarelli & Major, 1998).

Women in some European countries face even greater restrictions on their abortion option (see Box 10.4). Poland had readily available abortions until 1994, when the legislature passed one of the most restrictive policies in Europe. This complete reversal came largely from pressure from Polish Catholic Church leaders. Although 95 percent of the population are Catholic, public opinion polls indicate that the majority wants a freer abortion policy.

Box 10.4 Reproductive Control in the News: The Uterus Inspectors

A UNITED GERMANY IS DIVIDED
OVER ABORTION

BERLIN—From the start, Kathrin K. was suspect to the federal German border police. She was female, she was young, and she and her husband were driving back to Germany from the Netherlands, where each year thousands of West German women seek the abortions their own land outlaws.

So the police searched her car. They searched her bag.

And finally, when she wouldn't answer to interrogation, they searched her womb: They forced the 22-year-old mother of one to submit to a vaginal exam by a doctor at a nearby Catholic hospital.

Kathrin now stands charged with obtaining a first-trimester abortion abroad, a crime punishable by a year in prison.

. . . Abortion inquisition is standard practice at the border crossing at Gronau, where Kathrin was stopped. In one earlier case, a woman was prosecuted after a car search turned up a bill from an abortion clinic. Another became a criminal suspect because she was bleeding and asked police for help. Some women unthinkingly made themselves vulnerable to prosecution by volunteering information about their abortions after police accused them of traveling to the Netherlands to buy drugs. . . . For Kathrin K., a nightgown and two sanitary napkins packed in an overnight bag were considered enough evidence of crime for police to follow through with the forced gynecological exam. . . . The West German law forbids abortion except when the woman's life is endangered, the fetus is deformed, or the woman can prove to medical counselors that the abortion is necessary because of "extraordinary social circumstances." In former East Germany, abortion in the first trimester remains legal and unrestricted. . . .

Source: Nina Bernstein, Staff Writer, "Germany Still Divided on Abortion," *Newsday*, March 11, 1991. New York Newsday, Inc., copyright 1991. Reprinted with permission.

Other European countries have implemented high fees, waiting periods, and requirements for women to have two doctors' opinions before obtaining an abortion (Darnton, 1993). Ireland has a complete ban on abortions. In Germany, a liberal law providing free abortions with few limitations was declared invalid. Counseling is strongly antiabortion (Kinzer, 1993). Women in abortion-restrictive countries have few options regarding their pregnancies. More than 200,000 women die each year from illegal abortions; most of these deaths occur in Asia, Africa, and Latin America (United Nations, 1991a).

However, the abortion debate does not center solely around countries that prohibit or restrict availability. A proposed law in China advocates abortion and sterilization to prevent the birth of children with mental or physical disabilities. Although the government claims to offer women the final decision regarding their fetuses with abnormalities, prenatal counseling for these women gives strong persuasion for abortion. Chinese officials wish to prevent the birth of children of "inferior quality" (World Wire, 1993). Because China restricts the number of children a woman may have to one, most women abort the abnormal child in hopes of carrying a healthier child in a later pregnancy. In the United States, federal guidelines encourage routine HIV testing for "at-risk" pregnant women. The potential for coercing these women, most of whom are poor women of color, to have abortions or to be sterilized is a major concern for feminist health-care activists (Amaro, 1993).

Most women contemplating an abortion have mixed feelings about it. Living in societies where many people condemn abortion, women feel conflicts over sexuality and their right to make decisions on the basis of their own needs. Moreover, the decision to bear a child has irrevocable, long-term effects. It is easy to see why ambivalence is the norm. "There is no painless way to deal with either an unwanted pregnancy or an intended pregnancy and the knowledge that one is carrying a genetically defective fetus. Abortion is rarely a decision taken lightly, even by pro-choice women" (Lemkau, 1988, p. 461).

One of the arguments used in efforts to restrict abortion is that it has harmful psychological consequences (Miller, 1996). Although psychology cannot resolve moral or ethical differences of opinion about abortion, empirical research can readily be used to answer questions of psychological well-being. Does abortion cause psychological damage and decreased psychological well-being for women?

To determine the effects of abortion on women's mental health, the American Psychological Association commissioned a study of all the scientific research published in the United States since abortion was legalized in 1973. This research review established that the legal termination of an unwanted pregnancy does not have major negative effects on most women. Measurements of psychological distress usually drop immediately following the abortion and remain low in follow-ups after several weeks (Public Interest Directorate, 1987). Other reviews, too, agree that psychological problems caused by abortion are rare (Miller, 1996). When a woman freely chooses a legal abortion, the typical emotion that follows is one of relief (Lemkau, 1988).

Research studies assessing psychological problems over a range from one week to ten years following abortion show negative effects for anywhere between 0.5 percent and 15 percent of clients. Several risk factors, both internal and external, have been identified. A woman is more likely to have postabortion psychological problems if she has a history of prior emotional problems, has received little support from her family or friends, felt pressured into the abortion decision, has strong religious beliefs that abortion is immoral, or believed in advance that she would have problems in coping (Public Interest Directorate, 1987). When a woman obtaining an abortion had a partner who did not support her choice, her likelihood of psychological problems was higher only if she did not firmly believe in the integrity of her own decision (Major, Cozzarelli, Testa, & Mueller, 1992). Encounters with antiabortion demonstrators at the time of the abortion also have negative effects. The more intense the protest outside the clinic when a woman tried to enter, the more depressed she was after the abortion (Cozzarelli & Major, 1998).

Women who experience severe distress following abortion may want to obtain psychological counseling. However, women should not have to deny their conflicts for fear of being labeled emotionally disturbed:

> Women may (and are entitled to) have many conflicting feelings about abortion, including guilt and grief as well as relief, either at the time or later in their lives. Abortion, like other moral dilemmas, does cause suffering in the individuals whose lives are impacted. That suffering does not make the choice wrong or harmful to the individual who must make the choice, nor should the

individual be pathologized for having feelings of distress. In fact, the shouldering of such suffering and of responsibility for moral choices contributes to psychological growth. (Elkind, 1991, p. 3)

Choices about whether, when, and how often to bear children are complex ones. Although our society expects women to accept most of the responsibility for caring for children, it has been less willing to entrust them with the freedom to make responsible reproductive choices. Steeped in the motherhood mystique, many people still view reproductive rights as unnatural and maternal sacrifice as women's lot in life.

Technology and Choice

Controversies about contraception and abortion show that the development of new reproductive technology does not always result in increased choices for women. Although each technological change is presented as an advance in scientific progress to benefit women, the reality is that the new reproductive technologies have introduced many troublesome questions of ethics, morality, power, and choice. The birth of septuplets and octuplets in 1998 to women who had been taking fertility drugs added to the publicity and controversy surrounding medical manipulation of women's bodies. Indeed, the body may be the major battleground of women's rights for decades to come. The most difficult issues include the following.

Selective Abortion

Blood tests, amniocentesis, and other new technologies allow selective abortion of "defective" fetuses. The great majority of women who find that they are carrying a Down syndrome fetus, for example, choose to abort, and a majority of Americans endorse that choice (Wertz, 1992). Is abortion justified for disorders that cause mental retardation? What about those that may cause social (but not cognitive) problems, such as the sex chromosomal variations discussed in Chapter 5? Some women feel that they do not have the right to end a potential life simply because the child will be less than perfect (Rothman, 1988). On the other hand, it is women who bear the burden of child rearing. Disability activists argue that disability is in large part socially constructed. If social supports were available, parenting a disabled child would not involve the sacrifices it now does. And what counts as a "disability"? Consider the use of amniocentesis so that female fetuses can be aborted, described in Chapter 6.

Fetal "Rights"

The monitoring of women's behavior during pregnancy is increasing (Baber & Allen, 1992; Kline, 1996; Pollit, 1998). In at least seventeen states, women have been charged with child abuse for using drugs or alcohol during pregnancy, although fetuses are not children under the law. Meanwhile, media reports blame the woman and ignore the fact that there are almost no treatment programs available for pregnant women who are addicted to drugs. This form of social control falls more heavily on poor women—those who can afford private health care are not monitored or tested against their will. (One physician pointed out that if these were middle-class women, they would be referred to the Betty Ford Clinic, not sent to jail.) Feminist health-care activists are concerned about the "slippery slope"—will women soon be jailed for smoking, failing to take their medication, or not getting enough exercise during pregnancy? And they point out that the concept of fetal rights places responsibility solely on women instead of on both parents and their community. Medical resources should be used to help ensure healthy babies without treating women as though they were only vessels for fetal development. The best way to foster infant health is to help pregnant women by providing low-cost prenatal care, drug treatment programs, and social support services—not by punishing women for being less than perfect incubators.

Infertility Technology

Couples who are unable to conceive a child can now make use of new technologies such as *in vitro fertilization,* or IVF, commonly known as the "test-tube baby" procedure. A woman's ovaries are stimulated with strong fertility drugs so that they produce multiple eggs, which are then surgically removed. Her partner's sperm (obtained by masturbation) is combined with the eggs in a glass dish. If fertilization occurs, the embryos are inserted into the woman's uterus to develop into full-term fetuses (Williams, 1992). Many feminists argue that women are at risk for exploitation by this revolutionary change in the reproductive process. Men control the technology, but it is women's bodies that are manipulated and experimented on. More than ever, women may be viewed solely as egg providers and incubators (Baber & Allen, 1992; Raymond, 1993). IVF carries many risks. The fertility drugs and surgeries can lead to unpleasant and dangerous side effects and complications. The emotional costs are high, as women put their lives and careers on hold to concentrate on getting pregnant, and the attempt can fail at any time. The success rate is low (less than 10% per attempt), the procedure is very expensive ($3,000 to $7,000 per attempt), and most couples make several attempts (Baber & Allen, 1992).

Women who choose to undergo IVF describe themselves as desperate to have children at any cost. Their strong desire to become biological mothers is usually seen as natural and is taken for granted by physicians and the general public alike. The popular press frequently features heartrending stories of a woman's quest for a child, with physicians as techno-heroes who can fulfill her deepest needs. Rarely do these stories analyze how the need to have children is socially constructed. In an analysis of 133 news articles on IVF, 64 explicitly endorsed the belief that bearing children is the single most important accomplishment of adult life, and only 2 articles countered that belief (Condit, 1996). "To what extent does our society *create* a market for IVF by placing so many important meanings on fertility that to be infertile indeed becomes an unbearable problem?" (Williams, 1992, p. 262).

Studies exploring women's motivations for seeking IVF suggest that these women have been strongly influenced by the motherhood mandate: the majority believe that having children is natural and instinctive and that parenthood is an essential part of marriage and women's roles in life. Moreover, they report having experienced strong external pressures to bear children (Williams,

1992). Indeed, some women may undergo IVF partly because it proves how much they desire to bear children. Only after IVF fails can they be accorded the socially acceptable identity of a woman who is childless because of fate, not choice (Koch, 1990).

Contract Motherhood

Because new reproductive technologies separate genetic and physiological aspects of pregnancy, it is now possible for people to pay others to breed children for them. Many feminists believe that these practices exploit women physically, emotionally, and economically (Baber & Allen, 1992; Raymond, 1993). Others argue that contract pregnancy can have substantial benefits to all parties, but only if it is stringently regulated to protect women's interests (Purdy, 1992). As currently practiced, contract pregnancy raises seemingly insoluble ethical dilemmas. The following are descriptions of actual cases:

> Robert M. contracts for a baby with Elvira J. without telling her that he is considering divorcing his wife Cynthia M. On learning of the coming divorce, Elvira refuses to give up the baby for adoption, although she allows the Ms to take the baby home with them on the condition that they seek marriage counseling. Six months later, Robert M. files for divorce, triggering a three-way custody battle between biological father, biological mother, and caretaker mother. Who is being exploited here? Does the fact that Elvira is a Latina with only a seventh-grade education make a difference? (Nelson, 1992)

> Mark C. and Cristina C. hire Anna J. to gestate an embryo grown from their sperm and egg. Finding herself attached to the child, Anna seeks visitation rights. A judge rules that Anna is not the child's mother (although it is she who has given birth), but merely a temporary foster mother, and denies her request. Anna is a black single mother; the Cs' are white and Asian-American, respectively. (Purdy, 1992)

These cases illustrate the ethical and social dilemmas created by reproductive technologies, dilemmas involving fetuses, women, couples, biomedical researchers, and health-care providers. In these conflicts, who will represent the needs of women?

Brave New Families

Scientific knowledge about reproduction is not inevitably a source of oppression for women. Women (and men) are using novel reproductive methods in ways that increase their options for parenthood, creating unconventional new families. In one case, two longtime lesbian partners, D. and B., were approached by a cousin of B.'s with a request to bear a child for her and her husband. (The cousin was unable to conceive.) D. and B. believed that the couple would be loving parents, and D. decided to bear the child. Using sperm donated by B.'s adult son, D. became pregnant and gave birth to a healthy baby daughter. B. had the opportunity to support her partner during the pregnancy and throughout the birth of B.'s (genetic) grandchild, and the cousins were able to bring up a child that was genetically related to them. D. described the process as deeply satisfying.

In another case, a lesbian couple had a child with sperm donated by one partner's father to the other partner. Both genetic and social ties of grandparent to grandchild were thus created. In many such cases, the methods are decidedly "low tech," with the kitchen turkey-baster the favored means of insemination. Most important, the couples themselves are in control of the technology and its outcome.

THE TRANSITION TO MOTHERHOOD

Becoming a mother changes a woman's life perhaps more than any other single event. Yet surprisingly, there has been little psychological research on pregnancy and the transition to motherhood until recently. It is as though psychology has been indifferent to this major life transition that affects women: "Women are supposed to get pregnant; it is their lot; why make a fuss about it?"

Pregnancy, birth, and the transition to motherhood include both biological and social events. These events interact to produce changes in life circumstances, lifestyle, and involvement in paid work, as well as changes in relationships with significant others such as partner and parents. Each additional child also has further effects, as a new pregnancy is added to caring for young children. Once a woman becomes a mother, the role is hers for life, and she will be defined largely through that role, much more than men are defined through their roles as fathers. It is not surprising that motherhood profoundly affects a woman's sense of self (Ussher, 1989). Let's look more closely at some of the changes that occur with pregnancy and motherhood and their effects on women's identities.

How Does Motherhood Change Work and Marital Roles?

More than twenty longitudinal studies have shown that the birth of a child can negatively affect family relationships, reducing psychological well-being and marital satisfaction (Walzer, 1998). Husbands and wives become more different from each other; studies using large national samples show that parenthood results in bigger changes in women's lives than in men's, as women take on more child care and housework (Sanchez & Thomson, 1997) (see Figure 10.3).

FIGURE 10.3.
© 1991 by Nicole Hollander. Used by permission of Nicole Hollander.

Many women experience the change from paid worker to unpaid at-home mother as stressful. The changes from a nine-to-five schedule to being on call twenty-four hours a day, from adult company to isolation with an infant, from feeling competent to feeling overwhelmed with new tasks, all require adjustments. The difficulties may be offset by the rewards of getting to know one's growing baby, the belief that caring for one's children is worthwhile and important, and the sense of mastery that comes from learning how to do it well. Women who return to paid work have their own stresses, juggling many demands. For both groups, conflicts occur.

A major source of conflict is that women's expectations of their partners' involvement do not coincide with men's actual behavior once the child is born. Studies suggest that although many men are positive about the idea of becoming a father, they do not follow through with a fair share of the work (Nicolson, 1990). In one study, new mothers kept time-use diaries and were also interviewed twice. Their workdays ranged from eleven to seventeen and a half hours a day, and they spent an average of six hours a day alone with their babies. Although they cited the babies' fathers as their main source of support, fathers actually contributed only zero to two hours a day of primary care (Croghan, 1991).

In another study of eighty-six new mothers, 77 percent said that their partners were their single biggest source of help. However, husbands definitely did not contribute equally, as evidenced by the women's descriptions of the kinds of help they received: "If I'm at the end of the rope, he'll step in and take over." "At dinner time he pitches in . . . entertains the baby." Husbands expressed understanding but did not offer to change the situation: "He doesn't make me feel there's something wrong with me if I can't cope perfectly" (Rhoades, 1989, pp. 131–141).

These studies suggest that new mothers are stressed by inequality in marital roles. Women may enter motherhood with expectations of equality in parenting, but these expectations collide with reality (Ruble et al., 1988). It is difficult for women and men to change parenting relationships because cultural images and social structures constantly reinforce the idea that mothers, not fathers, should have day-to-day responsibility for children (Walzer, 1998). Myths of motherhood still imply that women should be happy and fulfilled through self-sacrifice. A partner's contribution is an optional extra for which they should be grateful, however small it is (Croghan, 1991).

Do Mothers Face Impossible Ideals?

Mothers are encouraged to evaluate themselves against images of ideal mothers such as the radiant, serene "Madonna," and the "superwoman" who juggles the demands of house, children, husband, and job, while providing her children with unfailing love and plenty of quality time (Ussher, 1989). Women often are not prepared for negative and ambivalent feelings and may feel like failures when they occur. It is likely that a majority of women experience decreased emotional well-being at some point during pregnancy and early motherhood (Condon, 1987; Ruble et al., 1988; Ussher, 1989; Wells, Hobfall, & Lavin, 1997). The best strategies for coping with role changes during pregnancy seem to be active assertion and seeking communal relationships with other women. In a study of white employed pregnant women, these were associated with reduced depression and anger (Wells et al., 1997). In another study, women who received social support during pregnancy showed many beneficial physical and psychological outcomes that persisted through the first year of motherhood (Oakley, 1992).

Some women have described the conflicts that come from experiencing negative feelings they knew did not live up to the ideals:

> Motherhood wasn't what I expected—unadulterated wonder. The shock of the isolation and much of the sheer slog and boredom were exacerbated by the fact that I felt I wasn't supposed to feel dissatisfied. (Wandor, 1980, cited in Ussher, 1989, p. 84)

> I was haunted by the stereotype of the mother whose love was "unconditional"; and by the visual and literary images of motherhood as a single-minded identity. If I knew parts of myself existed that would never cohere to these images, weren't those parts then abnormal, monstrous? (poet Adrienne Rich, 1976, p. 23)

> Being brought up in the traditional way, I always feared something terrible would happen if I went away, like the house would burn down. I felt I would be punished for leaving the children, even to go to work. Especially to go to work. (A single mother; Hall, 1984, pp. 17–18)

> I couldn't seem to do anything right; I felt so tired, the baby kept crying, and I kept thinking that this was supposed to be the most fulfilling experience of my whole life. It felt like the most lonely, miserable experience. (A mother three weeks after the birth of her first child, cited in Ussher, 1989, p. 82)

Are Sexuality and Motherhood Incompatible?

"During pregnancy and motherhood, one of the fundamental aspects of a woman's identity which is oppressed is sexuality" (Ussher, 1989, p. 92). When women become pregnant, they are confronted with many of the contradictions about sexuality that characterize Western society. The Madonna ideal—pure, serene, the image of peace and wholeness—exists at the cost of desire: the Madonna must be a virgin (Young, 1998). The idea of a mother who has sexual desires and acts on them conflicts with the ideal of maternal selflessness. Becoming pregnant and giving birth highlight a woman's sexuality, at the same time society denies its existence in the pregnant woman or the mother; this perpetuates a split between body and self for women (Ussher, 1989, p. 92).

One example of this split is the disconnection between desire and behavior during pregnancy. Many women experience increased sexual desire while pregnant, especially in the middle three months (Kitzinger, 1983). This may reflect physical changes such as an increased blood supply to the pelvic area, as well as psychological factors. (For one thing, the woman and her partner needn't worry about contraception!) Yet women may engage in sexual activities less often, out of fear of harming the fetus, feelings of being unattractive, or physical awkwardness.

Research has shown that in a normal pregnancy, intercourse and orgasm are safe until four weeks before the due date; these activities do not harm the fetus or cause miscarriage (Masters & Johnson, 1966). When women were surveyed about their physicians' advice, however, 60 percent had received no information at all, and another 10 percent were told they should not have intercourse after their seventh month (Gauna-Trujillo & Higgins, 1989). Perhaps the medical profession perpetuates the myth of the asexual mother because doctors, themselves influenced by the myth, are reluctant and embarrassed to discuss sex with pregnant women (Ussher, 1989).

What Are the Psychological Effects of Bodily Changes During Pregnancy?

The hormonal changes of pregnancy are much greater than those of the menstrual cycle. The levels of the hormones progesterone and estrogen in pregnant women are many times higher than in nonpregnant women and drop precipitously after birth.

Besides these major changes in gonadal hormones, there are other alterations in levels of substances that may be associated with the functioning of the central nervous system. The level of the neurotransmitter norepinephrine is lower during pregnancy, while the levels of stress-associated adrenal cortical hormones increase (Treadway, Kane, Jarrahi-Zadeh, & Lipton, 1969). Norepinephrine and progesterone have both been related to depression in nonpregnant people. In a study of mood changes during pregnancy, women were interviewed both before and during their pregnancies and compared with a control group of women who did not become pregnant. For the pregnant group, changes in mood increased compared with their prepregnancy baseline and also in comparison with the control group, mainly during the first third of the pregnancy (Striegel-Moore, Goldman, Garvin, & Rodin, 1996).

Psychologists have virtually ignored the social effects of changes in women's bodies during pregnancy. Throughout this book we have discussed the social importance of slimness and attractiveness in evaluating women. Pregnancy may be viewed as a progressive loss of these valued attributes. It should not be surprising if pregnant women feel unfeminine or moody, even apart from hormonal causes.

Many women feel extremely ambivalent about the dramatic changes in body shapes and size that accompany pregnancy (Ussher, 1989). Reactions include feeling temporarily free from cultural demands to be slim, feeling awe and wonder, feeling afraid and disgusted by their size, and feeling alienated and out of control (see Box 10.5). In a study of more than 200 women, changes in body image were among the most frequently reported stressors of pregnancy and early motherhood, second only to physical symptoms (Affonso & Mayberry, 1989). Recent research suggests that body image concerns are increasing; some women are choosing not to become pregnant because of fears about how it would change their bodies (Garner, 1997).

Indeed, pregnancy can be viewed as a time of loss of control over one's body. Changes will occur to the pregnant woman no matter what she does (see Figure 10.4). She is helpless (short of terminating the pregnancy) to govern her own body, and yet she remains defined to society largely through her body.

Box 10.5 *"A Brand New Body": One Woman's Account of Pregnancy*

Suzanne Arms (1973) kept a journal during her first pregnancy. Her reactions to her changing body are captured in these journal entries, ranging from early to late in her pregnancy.

> I have the feeling that I brought a brand new body home from the doctor's office. I'm a new me. Nobody else would look at me and call me pregnant, but it's wonderful to know that I really am, and I look for every tiny sign to prove it's true. My developing breasts are encouraging, and my nipples have become much larger. My nipples stand erect at times, and they're at least three shades darker. (p. 13)

> I have never felt beautiful but I've always liked my face and filled-out body. . . . But looking at pictures of me crying last week really hurt. They're so un-me. Just a pudgy woman. Today I don't feel like that at all. I've tied my hair back, vowed not to wear those baggy farmer jeans till after the baby comes, and put on a dress; I really do feel beautiful. In fact, I feel like I'm a pretty good place for a baby to stay and grow in. Nice, round, firm, with just enough fat all over to make it really soft and safe for the baby. (p. 29)

> . . . I've been getting more and more pleasure from my sensual feelings. There's some old tightness in me that seems to be losing its hold at last, and I feel all of me expanding. (p. 35)

> I rub cocoa butter on my tummy and breasts every morning after showering. The skin has become pink and smooth and I can't help feeling it all the time. The other day we were in the bookstore, and I was absent-mindedly rubbing myself and staring into space. A young woman with a child called to me from across the store, "That's a lovely belly you have there!" (p. 40)

> . . . I've begun to feel huge. I remember hearing other pregnant women hassle themselves about getting fat. I never could figure it out. To me they looked beautiful, round and blooming. I assured myself that I would never feel that way, and I would love my tummy and all the extra pounds. Well, that's great in theory—but suddenly the day comes when I look in the mirror and my face is round and I really do look like an orange! even holding my stomach in. So yesterday I spent the whole day feeling fat, ugly, and unlovable. Despite every nice thing John has said, I knew he would soon see how unappealing I am. (p. 44)

> A very full feeling today, I'm thick and stuffed like a bulging cabbage. (p. 59)

> I never thought it would come to this. I can't reach over my stomach to get to my feet. John has to lace up my hiking boots! (p. 63)

> Sometimes it seems as though I've been pregnant all my life. I can't remember being un-pregnant. (p. 64)

Suzanne Arms' pregnancy was planned and wanted, and she was in a stable relationship with a supportive male partner. How might the reactions of women to their changing bodies differ in differing social circumstances?

Source: From Suzanne Arms, *A Season to be born.* Copyright © 1993. Reprinted by permission of the author.

Moreover, society encourages a more general helplessness. Pregnant women (at least those who are white and middle class) are thought to be delicate and frail. Until quite recently, pregnant women were expected to remain secluded within the home. If a woman comes to view herself merely as a vessel for the forthcoming generation, it would be surprising if she did not experience depression!

How Do Others React to Pregnant Women?

Pregnant women are powerful stimuli for the behavior of others. "A woman begins to assume the identity of mother in the eyes of society almost as soon as

FIGURE 10.4. Suzanne Arms, pregnant.

she is visibly pregnant, ceasing to be a single unit long before the birth of her child" (Ussher, 1989, p. 81). Her body symbolizes the eternal power of women:

> As soon as I was visibly and clearly pregnant, I felt, for the first time in my adolescent and adult life, not-guilty. The atmosphere of approval in which I was bathed—even by strangers on the street, it seemed—was like an aura I carried with me, in which doubts, fears, misgivings, met with absolute denial. *This is what women have always done.* (Rich, 1976, p. 26)

On the other hand, pregnancy is a kind of stigma: people react very differently to pregnant and nonpregnant women, and their reactions may lead to change in the women's behavior in return. This was illustrated in an intriguing experiment (Taylor & Langer, 1977). In it, two female experimenters alternated between appearing pregnant (with the help of a little padding) or carrying a box the same size as the "pregnancy." The women stood in elevators and measured the distance that other passengers stood from them. Both men and women stood closer to the "nonpregnant" woman. Men, especially, avoided the "pregnant" woman. She was also stared at more; both men and women spent considerable time furtively looking at her stomach, so much so that both experimenters felt very uncomfortable when playing the pregnant role. Differences in treatment could be quite extreme:

> A large curious dog was wrenched away from the pregnant confederate by his master so abruptly and so far that he spent the remainder of the ride sitting on the feet of the nonpregnant experimenter, a fact completely unnoticed by his owner, who was still apologizing to the pregnant experimenter. (Taylor & Langer, 1977, p. 30)

In another part of the study, people were given the chance to interact in a laboratory situation with either a pregnant or a nonpregnant woman. Women

preferred the pregnant woman more if she had been passive, rather than assertive, in a previous group discussion. However, they also preferred not to interact with the passive pregnant woman in the future.

The study we've described was done in the 1970s. Since then the public
presence of pregnant women has become more acceptable. One indication of
attitude change is changes in maternity clothing styles. Until quite recently,
maternity clothes were tentlike and infantilizing, aimed at both concealing the
pregnancy and making the woman look as childlike as possible, with ruffles,
bows, and polka dots. Today, one can buy maternity T-shirts with a bold BABY
logo and an arrow pointing to the protruding abdomen, maternity tights and
sweaters, and business clothes for the pregnant executive. And actress Demi
Moore appeared nude and very pregnant on the cover of *Vanity Fair* in 1991.
Are pregnant women still stigmatized? With the help of a little padding, perhaps some intrepid female researchers will conduct another study.

Does Motherhood Change Women's Identity?

The process of pregnancy and mothering affects women's sense of self. In a
Canadian study, for example, the women experienced themselves as profoundly changed. Middle-class women described the changes in terms of personal growth and self-actualization; working-class women described a process
of "settling down." For both groups, motherhood involved a moral transformation in which they became deeply connected to their babies. However, the
flip side of such connectedness—feeling responsible for the child—was described as one of the hardest things about motherhood (McMahon, 1995).

In another study that followed newly married couples over a three-year
period, the birth of a child changed both parents' identities: men became more
masculine and women more feminine on dimensions that defined masculinity
and femininity for themselves as individuals. In other words, the changes in
marital roles and activities following the birth of a child affected their sense of
themselves as feminine women and masculine men (Burke & Cast, 1997).

An intensive case study of one woman's pregnancy illustrates the experience of change (Smith, 1991). Clare's identity change during early pregnancy
involved imagining the child-to-be:

> In one respect, it's—it's a person, a whole person that just happens to be in
> there, and in another way, it's something different. (p. 231)

In the middle phase, Clare experienced a growing sense of psychological relatedness with others—partner, mother, sister. In defining herself and the child-
to-be, Clare sought social confirmation; the process of constructing a family
was beginning. Near the end of the pregnancy, Clare sees herself as very
changed:

> I'm one of two and I'm one of three. . . . An irrevocable decision, the steps
> have been made that mean that my other identities, if you like as a mother
> and a partner, make up that essential me now. (p. 236)

The transition to motherhood involves losses as well as gains. The woman
ceases to be seen as an autonomous individual and is instead viewed as an

"expectant mother" and then "mother." It is not surprising that feelings of loss are experienced. It is hard to change from being "Joy Williams, secretary/jogger/painter/daughter/spouse and more" to being "Timmy's mom." One of the authors remembers her feelings of sadness and loneliness when the nurses in the hospital following the birth of her first child referred to all the women in the obstetric unit as "Mother" ("Mother, are you ready for your lunch tray?") rather than by our names. It seemed as if everything that had gone before was now to be put aside for the all-encompassing identity and job of Mother. One of the ways our cultural constructions of motherhood may oppress women is that they are not allowed to mourn or grieve the old, lost self (Nicolson, 1993; Ussher, 1989).

Because these feelings of loss of identity conflict with the motherhood mystique, women may be ashamed of them, label themselves as ill or abnormal, or believe that "baby blues" are inevitable and biologically determined. Rather than pathologize women's experiences, feminist psychology looks for explanations in the sociopolitical context of mothering (Ussher, 1989).

So far, we have been talking about the transition to motherhood mainly as it has been constructed for white, middle-class women exposed to the motherhood mystique. Poor women have been expected to bear and bring up children while struggling for survival; for them, the identity of mother has a different meaning. One of the most eloquent expressions of class and color differences in ideals of womanhood and motherhood comes from a famous speech attributed to Sojourner Truth, a crusader for abolition and suffrage and an ex-slave, to the Akron Convention for Women's Rights in 1852:

> That man over there says that women need to be helped into carriages, and lifted over ditches and have the best place everywhere. Nobody ever helps me into carriages, or over mud puddles or gives me any best place, and ain't I a woman? Look at me! Look at my arm! I have ploughed, and planted, and gathered into barns, and no man could head me! And ain't I a woman? I could work as much and eat as much as a man—when I could get it—and bear the lash as well! And ain't I a woman? I have borne thirteen children, and seen them most all sold off to slavery, and when I cried out with my mother's grief, none but Jesus heard me. And ain't I a woman? (Adapted from Ruth, 1990, pp. 463–464)

Attitudes toward pregnant women still vary by social class. Middle-class women in heterosexual marriages may be treated as delicate and special, but poor single women are labeled "welfare moms," undeserving of respect. Middle-class mothers are urged to stay home and give intensive, full-time mothering to their children, while poor mothers are forced to look for paid employment (see Figure 10.5). Heterosexual women's connectedness with their children is seen as positive, while lesbians' connectedness with theirs is pathologized. Identity is affected not only from within, but by the social context of mothering.

THE EVENT OF CHILDBIRTH

If a woman were training to run a marathon, climb a mountain, or go on an "Outward Bound" trek, she would probably think of the upcoming event as a challenge. She would acknowledge that her body would be worked hard and

FIGURE 10.5.
Source: Copyright © 1997. Reprinted with special permission of King Features Syndicate.

stressed, her courage tested, and her life at some risk. Yet she could feel in control, prepared and accepting of the challenge. She might undertake such an experience as a way of knowing her own psychological and physical self or of developing her strengths and resources. Childbirth is a normal physical process with some of the same potential for empowerment, yet women are rarely encouraged to think of it in this way (Rich, 1976). Instead, they are taught to think of it as an event in which they will be dependent, passive, subject to authority, and in need of expert medical intervention.

How Is the Meaning of Childbirth Socially Constructed?

In virtually all cultures, the event of birth is associated with fear, pain, awe, and wonder; it is viewed as both "the worst pain anyone could suffer" and as "peak experience." Yet there are surprisingly few accounts of childbirth *by women*. Instead, birth is described in the words of men. When male anthropologists visit preindustrial cultures, they are rarely allowed to see the women's work of attending birth and instead rely on men to tell them about the local customs. Margaret Mead noted, "I have seen male informants writhe on the floor, in magnificent pantomime of painful delivery, who have never themselves seen or heard a woman in labor" (cited in Rich, 1976, p. 156).

Women's experiences of childbirth are invisible in Western art. Artist Judy Chicago has noted that images of war and death are innumerable, but images of birth are nonexistent (Chicago, 1990). Instead, there are images of the blissful Madonna or virgin with child. Chicago's Birth Project is a collective effort by women artists and crafters to represent images of birth (see Figure 10.6).

Popular culture gives us its own version: Rhea Perlman (*Cheers*), Meredith Baxter-Birney (*Family Ties*), Markie Post (*Night Court*), and Candace Bergen (*Murphy Brown*) have all been depicted giving birth. A study of books, magazines, newspaper articles, TV shows, and movies in the 1980s and early 1990s showed that these media usually portrayed a woman giving birth as a passive patient, not an active agent who can participate in making decisions about what is best for her and her baby. They also showed a very strong preference for hospital births over birthing centers or home births. (When Opal on *All My Children* gave birth at home, it was because of a snowstorm, and Palmer was coached by a doctor over the phone) (Sterk, 1996). It seems that birth is a matter where women are in charge only in science-fiction novels (see Box 10.6).

Is Childbirth a Medical Crisis?

In some countries, birth is considered a natural phenomenon that needs no medical intervention in the majority of cases. For example, in the Netherlands the laboring woman is believed to need only "close observation, moral support, and protection against human meddling." A healthy woman can best accomplish her task of birthing her baby if she is self-confident, in familiar surroundings—preferably her own home—and attended by a birth specialist such as a midwife. Women at risk of complications are hospitalized, but most

FIGURE 10.6. Judy Chicago's image "Crowning" represents the moment the baby's head first becomes visible at the vaginal opening.

Box 10.6 Takver Gives Birth

In this passage from her novel *The Dispossessed*, acclaimed science-fiction writer Ursula LeGuin movingly describes the work and the triumph of giving birth.

Takver got very big in the belly and walked like a person carrying a large, heavy basket of laundry. She stayed at work at the fish labs till she had found and trained an adequate replacement for herself, then she came home and began labor. Shevek arrived home in midafternoon. "You might go fetch the midwife," Takver said. "Tell her the contractions are four or five minutes apart, but they're not speeding up much, so don't hurry very much."

He ran to the block clinic, arriving so out of breath and unsteady on his legs that they thought he was having a heart attack. He explained. They sent a message off to another midwife and told him to go home, the partner would be wanting company. He went home, and at every stride the panic in him grew, the terror, the certainty of loss. . . .

Takver had no time for emotional scenes; she was busy. She had cleared the bed platform except for a clean sheet, and she was at work bearing a child. She did not howl or scream, as she was not in pain, but when each contraction came she managed it by muscle and breath control, and then let out a great *houff* of breath, like one who makes a terrific effort to lift a heavy weight. Shevek had never seen any work that so used all the strength of the body.

He could not look on such work without trying to help in it. He could serve as handhold and brace when she needed leverage. They found this arrangement very quickly by trial and error, and kept to it after the midwife had come in. Takver gave birth afoot, squatting, her face against Shevek's thigh, her hands gripping his braced arms. "There you are," the midwife said quietly under the hard, engine-like pounding of Takver's breathing, and she took the slimy but recognizably human creature that had appeared. A gush of blood followed, and an amorphous mass of something not human, not alive. The terror he had forgotten came back into Shevek redou-

bled. It was death he saw. Takver had let go of his arms and was huddled down quite limp at his feet. He bent over her, stiff with horror and grief.

"That's it," said the midwife, "help her move aside so I can clean this up."

"I want to wash," Takver said feebly.

"Here, help her wash up. Those are sterile cloths—there."

"Waw, waw, waw," said another voice.

The room seemed to be full of people. . . .

Somehow in this extreme rush of events the midwife had found time to clean the infant and even put a gown on it, so that it was not so fishlike and slippery as when he had seen it first. The afternoon had got dark, with the same peculiar rapidity and lack of time lapse. The lamp was on. Shevek picked up the baby to take it to Takver. Its face was incredibly small, with large, fragile-looking, closed eyelids. "Give it here," Takver was saying. "Oh, do hurry up, please give it to me."

He brought it across the room and very cautiously lowered it onto Takver's stomach. "Ah!" she said softly, a call of pure triumph.

"What is it?" she asked after a while, sleepily.

Shevek was sitting beside her on the edge of the bed platform. He carefully investigated, somewhat taken aback by the length of gown as contrasted with the extreme shortness of limb. "Girl."

The midwife came back, went around putting things to rights. "You did a first-rate job," she remarked, to both of them. They assented mildly. "I'll look in in the morning," she said leaving. The baby and Takver were already asleep. Shevek put his head down near Takver's. He was accustomed to the pleasant musky smell of her skin. This had changed; it had become a perfume, heavy and faint, heavy with sleep. Very gently he put one arm over her as she lay on her side with the baby against her breast. In the room heavy with life he slept.

Source: Excerpt from *The Dispossessed* by Ursula K. LeGuin. Copyright © 1974 by Ursula K. LeGuin. Reprinted by permission of HarperCollins Publishers, Inc.

babies are born at home (MacFarlane, 1977, p. 29). The Netherlands has the world's lowest infant mortality rate (Nelson, 1996).

In contrast, virtually all U.S. births take place in hospitals. As recently as 1935, the majority of babies were born at home, but by the end of the 1970s, 99 percent of births took place in hospitals attended by physicians (Nelson, 1996). Even the language of childbirth has come to reflect the centrality of the physician: People routinely speak of babies being *delivered* by doctors instead of *birthed* by women.

Is the medical model of birth best for women? Many of the customary procedures surrounding birth in the United States are virtually unknown in other societies and are not necessarily in the best interest of mother or baby. For example, in hospital births the woman lies on her back during delivery, while in most cultures women give birth in a squatting or semiseated position. The supine position puts pressure on the spine, may slow labor, works against gravity, increases the risk of vaginal tearing, and makes it more difficult for the woman to push actively during the process. Why, then, do hospitals insist on this position? It is easier for the physician, who can view the birth more conveniently.

American women have experienced childbirth with feet in the air, drugged, shaved, purged with an enema, denied food and water, hooked up to machines and sensors, and psychologically isolated to a degree that is virtually unknown in other parts of the world (Nelson, 1996). Research shows that giving birth in an unfamiliar environment, being surrounded by strangers, and being moved from one room to another late in labor adversely affect the birth process even in nonhuman animals, yet these practices are routine in medicalized childbirth (MacFarlane, 1977; Newton, 1970).

In the United States, women have also been routinely taught that they will need pain relief during normal birth. When anesthetics were first introduced in the mid–nineteenth century, clergymen opposed their use in childbirth on the grounds that the Bible prescribed that women *should* suffer while giving birth, and physicians claimed that they were unnatural. Queen Victoria endorsed the practice of pain relief during childbirth by using an anesthetic for the birth of one of her own children in 1853, thus silencing religious opposition (Hyde & DeLamater, 1997). Today, the use of tranquilizers, barbiturates, and anesthetics is routine during childbirth.

The use of drugs in childbirth is controversial. On the one hand, it is argued that modern technology can spare women unnecessary pain. On the other hand, there are "a number of well-documented dangerous effects on both mother and infant" (Hyde & DeLamater, 1997, p. 162). For example, anesthetics in the mother's bloodstream are passed to the infant and may slow development for up to four weeks. Anesthetics may prolong labor by inhibiting contractions and making the mother unable to help push the baby through the birth canal. Psychologically, they reduce the woman's awareness and her ability to control one of the most challenging and awesome events of her life.

The medical model of birth encourages physicians and pregnant women to focus on possible complications and emergencies and may cause them to react to even remote possibilities with drastic medical interventions. In the past twenty-five years, there has been a dramatic increase in the number of cesarean births in the United States, from about 4 percent to 24 percent of all births (Nelson, 1996). One of every four babies is now surgically removed from its mother's body. This rate is much higher than in comparable countries such as Great Britain and is *not* associated with lower infant mortality.

The reasons for the epidemic of surgical intervention are unclear. Some critics have rather cynically suggested that scheduled surgical births are more convenient and profitable for physicians. Others have attributed the increase to physicians' fear of malpractice suits. When birth is defined as a medical event, helping and supporting the laboring woman seems inadequate, and heroic medical measures seem desirable. It has also been suggested that the high rate of surgical deliveries is an attempt by the medical profession to keep its dominant role in childbirth, despite women's increasing insistence on viewing birth as a normal process.

Can Childbirth Be Family Centered?

The medicalization of birth reached its height in the United States in the 1950s and 1960s. After undergoing male-managed childbirth, many women began to write about their experiences and work toward more woman- and family-centered birthing practices. Women organizers founded the International Childbirth Education Association in 1960. Widely read books such as *Our Bodies, Ourselves; Immaculate Deception; Of Woman Born;* and *The Great American Birth Rite* helped change public attitudes in the 1970s.

At about the same time, methods of *prepared or natural childbirth* were introduced to the American public. The most popular type of prepared childbirth is the Lamaze method, named after a French obstetrician. Women who use this approach learn techniques of relaxation and controlled breathing. Relaxation helps to reduce tension and the perception of pain and conserves energy during labor. Controlled breathing helps the woman work with, not against, the strength of each uterine contraction. The Lamaze method does not rule out the use of pain-relieving drugs, but it emphasizes that with proper preparation they may not be needed, and it leaves the choice to the laboring woman.

Another important part of the Lamaze technique is the presence of a "coach," or trusted partner—usually the baby's father—during labor and birth. Men had been banished from the delivery room at the heyday of the medical model, regarded as unhygienic, superfluous, and likely to get in the way of the physician (MacFarlane, 1977). The coach helps the mother with relaxation and controlled breathing and provides emotional support and encouragement. Research shows benefits of the father's presence to the mother, including a more positive emotional reaction to the birth (MacFarlane, 1977). Many men feel that participating in the birth of their child is an important part of being a father.

Studies comparing women who used Lamaze and other methods of childbirth education and training with women who had no special preparation have shown that there are definite benefits associated with prepared childbirth. These include shorter labor, fewer complications, less use of anesthetics, more positive attitudes after birth, less reported pain, and increased feelings of self-esteem and control (Hyde & DeLamater, 1997). These studies, while they do suggest that childbirth education and preparation are important, must be interpreted carefully. Perhaps women who sign up for Lamaze training are largely those who are motivated to experience childbirth positively under any circumstances. In other words, the studies do not rule out self-selection.

One study of support during childbirth does rule out self-selection effects (Kennell, Klaus, McGrath, Robertson, & Hinkley, 1991). More than 600 pregnant women, mostly Hispanic, poor, and unmarried, were randomly assigned to one of three groups. One group received emotional support during labor from a specially trained woman helper. The helpers, who were recruited from the local community, stayed with the laboring women to provide encouragement, explain the birth process, and offer soothing touch and handholding. A second group had a noninteractive female observer present, and the third group had standard hospital care.

Women in the emotional support group had a cesarean rate of 8 percent, compared with 13 percent in the observed group and 18 percent in the standard procedure group. They experienced less pain in labor: the standard group were almost seven times as likely to need anesthesia as the emotional support group. Moreover, their labor time was shorter, and they and their babies spent less time in the hospital. Clearly, emotional support made a large difference. The study's director estimated that investing small amounts of money in providing this kind of support would save $2 billion a year in costs of high-tech interventions. However, we suspect that hospitals will continue to invest in "advanced" technology more than the helping wisdom of women.

Women's efforts to regain control of the event of birth have resulted in many changes from the extreme medical model of thirty years ago. Today, fathers are more likely to be with the birthing woman. More births are taking place in homelike birth centers, attended by nurse-midwives. Women and their partners are far more likely to be educated about the normal processes and events in pregnancy and birth. Such knowledge reduces fear and helplessness, and thus reduces discomfort. Learning techniques to use during labor can replace passive suffering with active involvement and coping. However, new technology is continually being introduced, and each new intervention can readily be overused.

The family-centered birth movement continues to grow. Women's struggle for choice and control in childbirth parallels women's struggle for self-determination in general and is part of a social revolution that is not yet complete. The medical model of birth illustrates the way social institutions can decrease the power of women. When real control is lacking, women perceive themselves as helpless and passive, and this perception in turn contributes to their continued powerlessness. Treating birth as a normal, woman- and family-centered event, rather than a medical one, could prove very beneficial to women, their partners, and their children.

Depression Following Childbirth: Why?

The first weeks following childbirth (the *postnatal period*) have often been characterized as a time of mood swings and depression. For the first few days after giving birth, most women feel elated: the labor is over and the baby has arrived. Soon, however, they experience depression and crying spells. These mood swings range from minor to severe. Between 50 percent and 80 percent of women experience them for only a day or two. Longer-lasting depression (six to eight weeks) occurs in about 20 percent of women; it includes feelings of inadequacy and inability to cope, fatigue, tearfulness, and insomnia. The most severe form, a clinical psychosis, affects one-tenth of 1 percent of new mothers (Hyde & DeLamater, 1997; Mauthner, 1998).

Are postpregnancy mood disorders due to hormonal changes? The event of birth is followed by dramatic decreases in the high levels of estrogen and progesterone that characterize pregnancy. However, hormone changes have not been shown to be the *cause* of depression; in fact, there is no direct link between hormone levels and mood (Hopkins, Marcus, & Campbell, 1984). In one study, pregnant women were assessed six weeks before their due date and during the postnatal period. Compared with a matched sample of women who had not been pregnant, the new mothers were more depressed and cognitively slower. However, there was no relationship between hormonal state and mood; some mothers with progesterone-related changes were depressed and some were not (Treadway et al., 1969). Moreover, postnatal depression is virtually unknown in many countries, including India, China, Mexico, and Kenya (Mauthner, 1998), suggesting that the causes are more cultural than physiological.

The hormonal changes of pregnancy and the postnatal period are real; like the smaller changes of a normal menstrual cycle, they give rise to bodily changes and sensations that must be interpreted by the woman who is experiencing them. Countries where postnatal depression is rare offer a period of rest and special care for the new mother, practical and emotional support from other women, and positive social recognition of the mother's new status (Mauthner, 1998). These practices may help the new mother interpret her bodily changes and sensations more positively.

Feminist scholars have documented the importance of the social and cultural conditions that women face as mothers, linking depression to women's inferior status in society, the medicalization of childbirth, inadequate parental leave and child care, isolation, and the unfair allocation of housework. They view postnatal depression more as a social construction than a medical condition (Mauthner, 1998).

Many social and interpersonal factors may contribute to depression and mood swings among new mothers: dissatisfaction with body size and shape, feeling incompetent in the tasks of caring for a newborn, a sense that one's real self is lost in the role of mother, disappointment with a partner's lack of support, and so on. In an intensive study of a small sample of English women experiencing postnatal depression, a key factor was conflicts between their expectations of motherhood and their actual experiences. Different mothers resolved these conflicts in different ways, but in all cases recovery was a process of accepting themselves and rejecting the impossible ideals of motherhood. Often, this came about through talking with other women (Mauthner, 1998). Women who find it difficult to relate to others because of their personality styles or their past experiences may experience more depressive symptoms (Lutz & Hock, 1998).

One factor obvious to the authors of this book, both mothers, but often overlooked by researchers, is sleep deprivation. During the last weeks of pregnancy, a woman may not sleep well due to the discomfort caused by the heavy, restless fetus. Next, the hard physical work and stress of birthing a child are followed by many consecutive nights of disturbed sleep. Babies rarely sleep for an unbroken six- to seven-hour period before they are 6 weeks old, and some take much longer to "settle down." We know of no studies of postnatal depression that have examined sleep deprivation as a factor or compared moodiness in new mothers with moodiness in a sleep-deprived comparison group. The lack of attention to this possibility is a striking example of how socially influenced variables are often overlooked in studying women's lives.

EXPERIENCES OF MOTHERING

The realities of mothering are as different as the social circumstances of women who mother. In this section, let's look at what motherhood involves for diverse groups of women.

Teen Mothers

Each year in the United States more than a million young women under the age of 20 become pregnant. Most of these teens are unmarried. About half of teen pregnancies result in the birth of a child; 30 percent to 40 percent are terminated by abortion; and the rest end in miscarriage (Hyde & DeLamater, 1997).

The rate of teen pregnancy has been dropping throughout the 1990s, and fewer teen mothers go on to have a second baby (U.S. Department of Health & Human Services, 1998). However, the teen pregnancy rate in the United States is still much higher than in comparable countries. U.S. girls under 15 are five times more likely to give birth than girls of the same age group in other developed countries (Hayes, 1987). U.S. teens are not more sexually active than their European counterparts, but they are much less likely to use contraception reliably and effectively.

Contrary to popular belief, girls who have early and unprotected sex are more likely to accept feminine socialization than rebel from it. For example, adolescents who hold traditional attitudes about gender were found to be *more* likely to become sexually active and less likely to employ effective contraception on a regular basis (Jorgensen & Alexander, 1983). Nonpregnant teenagers described themselves as having more "masculine" characteristics than similarly sexually active teenagers who became pregnant (Crovitz & Hayes, 1979). Black pregnant teenagers were found to have the most traditional ideas about feminine roles of all the groups studied (Blum & Resnick, 1982).

A long-term study of public high school girls in New York City indicated that many who got pregnant were not those whose bodies, dress, and manner evoked sensuality and experience. The pregnant girls were more likely to be those who were quite passive and relatively quiet in their classes. Traditional notions of what it means to be a woman did little to empower them (Fine & Zane, 1988).

Though teen pregnancy is seen as a huge social problem, rates were actually higher in the 1950s than they are now (Nettles & Scott-Jones, 1987). It was less of an issue then, because most teen mothers were married, or got married on becoming pregnant. Even today, a teenage girl's pregnancy may not be considered a problem if it occurs in the context of marriage. As one high school administrator said about a student:

> Don't worry. She's dropping out, but it's a good case. She's fifteen, pregnant, but getting married. She'll go for a G.E.D. (Fine & Zane, 1988, p. 20)

The birthrate among Latina teenagers gets less negative publicity than that of other ethnic minorities, although it is higher than that of white teenagers. In 1985, more than 25 percent of Latina girls aged 15 to 19 were married—usually to considerably older men (Lopez, 1987). Marriage does not, however, protect Latinas from the academic consequences of teenage pregnancy. In 1982, only 26 percent of Latina teenage mothers had completed high school, as compared with 41 percent of white and 36 percent of black teenage mothers (Cusick, 1987).

More unmarried teenage mothers are white than black. However, the rate of pregnancy outside of marriage is higher among black than among white teenagers (Furstenberg et al., 1989). African-American teenagers often expect to bear children before they marry (Cusick, 1987). They are likely to report an expected age at parenthood that is less than or equal to their expected marriage age (Furstenberg et al., 1986).

Most African-American teenage mothers remain within their extended families (Field, Widmayer, Stoller, & de Cubas, 1986). Family members provide support, companionship, and role models for them. Later on, daughters provide domestic support for their mother when she is employed outside the home. Girls as young as 9 may have primary responsibility for taking care of younger siblings (Reid, 1982).

We are not arguing that early childbearing is desirable. But its meaning and consequences depend on its cultural context. Among some Latino cultures, for example, the concept of adolescence as a stage between girlhood and womanhood is not accepted. "Chicano girls, in particular, argue for a close temporal relation between the generations and against the concept of adolescent development. Adolescence, they have guessed, is a construct, a notion that seems to them synonymous with a waste of ripe time" (Thompson, 1986, p. 33).

Statistics alone do not convey the meaning of teen pregnancy in our society. Teen pregnancy has become a symbol of moral and social decay. Teen mothers are castigated for undermining family values and gender norms. The meaning of teen pregnancy is further complicated by the fact that the rate of adolescent pregnancy is higher for women of color; blaming teen mothers for society's ills is racist as well as sexist.

Adolescent motherhood does have serious consequences for the young women involved, their children, and society as a whole. These include health problems such as low-birth-weight babies, interrupted education and lowered job opportunities for the mothers, and the costs of public assistance (Elise,

1995). Young mothers need access to programs to help them learn parenting skills, complete their education, and take control of their contraceptive use. Moreover, they need a great deal of support from their families (Elise, 1995; Henly, 1997). With help, the negative effects of early childbearing can be overcome (Furstenberg et al., 1989).

Single Mothers

The number of families headed by single women is increasing dramatically; over 8 million U.S. children live with their mothers alone (Atwood, 1997). The main reason for this increase is the high separation and divorce rate (see Chapter 9). A secondary reason is a rise in births to single women, which now make up nearly one-fourth of U.S. births. Minority children are more likely to grow up in single-parent families; 16 percent of white, 27 percent of Hispanic, and 55 percent of African-American children are in women-headed households (Dickerson, 1995; Sapiro, 1994).

Families headed by women are far more likely to be poor than families with a male wage-earner. The link between single motherhood and poverty is especially strong for minority families. Over half of all black and Hispanic woman-headed families, and about one-third of white families, are living in poverty. Poverty among women and children is one of the most serious social problems in the United States today (Polakow, 1993).

Why are women-headed households so likely to be poor? Some of the reasons for women's poverty are the same as men's: they may lack education or job skills, or live in an area in which there are few jobs. But women are poor for gender-related reasons as well: because they are expected to both care for and provide for their children, and because they are underpaid and underemployed (see Chapter 11) (Polakow, 1993). Perhaps most important of all, public policy does not reflect the needs of women and children.

Even women who have full-time employment may not be able to earn enough to keep themselves and their families out of poverty. The story of one single working mother illustrates the dilemmas of being both nurturer and provider. Lori P. worked full time as a secretary at a university, earning about $800 a month. When her partner left her and their 4-year-old son, she was unable to pay her monthly bills, which included $500 for child care. Although Lori started out with advantages—health care coverage, good child care, safe housing, occasional child support contributions from the absent partner, and middle-class respectability—she barely manages to survive on her own with her young son:

> I don't know what I'm going to do. My dad helped last month, but rent's due next Wednesday and I don't have any money. I mean I don't. I just paid all my bills. It's the end of the month now and I don't get paid for two more weeks. I have $2.50 in my account; two dollars and fifty cents! Rent's $545—I get paid in two weeks again, but that will only be $400 . . . I need help—I feel like I'm sinking. (Polakow, 1993, pp. 82–83)

Ashamed to be "on welfare," Lori wants to get her college degree so that she can get a better job, but she cannot afford to pay for child care while she attends night classes. For now, she is relying on another poor single mother, who baby-sits for $2.00 an hour.

The failure of divorced men to provide child support (see Chapter 9) is a major source of single mothers' economic burdens. Former partners appear to provide little support of any kind. In a study of the social networks of long-term single mothers, ex-partners were most often reported to be either absent or harmful (Malo, 1994). In addition, the lack of publicly subsidized child care makes it impossible for a mother to get ahead. Even if she works full time at minimum wage, child care for one child will consume between 37 percent and 78 percent of her income (Polakow, 1993). Of all the Western industrialized nations, only the United States fails to provide family support benefits as a matter of public policy (Lorber, 1993b).

Although single mothers, especially those who have never married, are stigmatized as "welfare queens," most single mothers want to work (Youngblut, Singer, Madigan, Swegart, & Rodgers, 1997). Since 1996 welfare reform legislation has mandated that mothers of young children who receive benefits find paid employment. However, finding good child care is a worry. In a study of low-income African-American single mothers who were former welfare recipients, concerns about child care were linked with mothers' depression and negative feelings about their children (Jackson, 1997). The transition from welfare to work is stressful because many low-income mothers are raising their children in high-risk environments where the need for quality care is crucial.

The primary response to the feminization of poverty in the United States seems to be to blame the victims. Women who accept welfare benefits are accused of causing the very problems they are trying to cope with. In President Ronald Reagan's 1986 State of the Union address, he blamed the "welfare culture" for the breakdown of the family, child abandonment, women and children's poverty, crime, and the deterioration of the public schools (Polakow, 1993). Throughout the 1980s, public aid programs to help people help themselves out of poverty were repeatedly cut (Polakow, 1993; Sapiro, 1994), and the current political climate is even more harsh.

The moral panic over teen mothers and single mothers may represent a fear of women who are not under the control of men. Many conservative policymakers assume that marriage is the answer to poverty in women and children. However, second marriages are even more likely than first marriages to end in divorce (Chapter 9). The majority of women who have children outside of marriage are poor before they become pregnant. Even if these women married the fathers of their babies, they would still be poor, because the fathers are likely to be unemployed and living in economically depressed areas (Dickerson, 1995).

But there is more to single-mother families than poverty and despair. When they are considered a legitimate kind of family, and studied for their strengths, it becomes apparent that they may have some advantages (Smith, 1997). Studies show that single mothers express a positive attitude of being proud that they are surviving and handling a difficult job well. They are just as satisfied with motherhood as married mothers are.

Among white families, single-parent homes seem to be less gender-typed than two-parent homes. They encourage more gender-neutral play in children and create more flexible attitudes about gender roles (Smith, 1997). This result makes sense when we consider that fathers are more prone than mothers to treating children in gender-stereotypical ways (Chapter 6), and that children of single moms see their mothers filling both the provider and nurturer roles. Among African-American families, too, there are strengths that offset the disadvantages of being brought up in a single-parent family. These include role flexibility (e.g., many adults may "mother" a child), spirituality (relying on inner strength rather than material possessions for happiness), and a sense of community ("It takes a village to raise a child") (Randolph, 1995).

In the United States, the great majority of single parents are women and, as we have seen, their economic disadvantage is a big part of their problems. Little research has been done on single parents in other countries. In a recent study of more than 300 single parents in China, one-third were men; the majority had arrived at single parenthood through divorce, and the others through the death or desertion of a spouse. (Parenthood outside of marriage is extremely rare in China.) Virtually all were employed, and they had an average of one child. In this sample, the psychological adjustment of both single mothers and fathers was positively related to the amount of emotional and practical support they received. This study shows that the social context of single parenthood differs across cultures and suggests that the same factors influence psychological well-being in single moms and dads when they are in comparable situations (Cheung & Liu, 1997).

Black Mothers and the Matriarchal Myth

African women were brought to the United States to work as slaves and to produce more slaves, sometimes through rape and forced breeding. If they were given a few days off from slave labor after childbirth, it was more to protect the owner's investment than to allow them to rest and recover. They were able to care for their own children only after all their other work was done and, as Sojourner Truth eloquently testified, were likely to see their children sold away from them (Almquist, 1989).

African-Americans are the only minority group in the United States to have had the experience of systematic, widespread destruction of their families. In addition to this legacy of slavery, there has since been a scarcity of black men to be providers and husbands. The causes for this scarcity include migration from the South, high death rates from poor health care, and the effects of poverty and discrimination, leading to drug use, imprisonment, and violent death. Thus, black women have been (and still are) more likely than white women to be bringing up families without a resident father/husband. For African-American women, motherhood is not equated with being dependent on a man (Collins, 1991; Dickerson, 1995).

Black women have coped with oppression in many ways. They often form extended households, with two or three generations living together and sharing resources. Grandmothers, sisters, cousins, and aunts care for the children of young mothers. Black families are less likely than white ones to give children up for adoption by strangers, and more likely to take in the children of friends and relatives. In the black community, these informal adoptions are seen as better than stranger adoption, because they allow continued contact with the child's mother, and the child is with people she knows and trusts (Almquist, 1989). This collective, cooperative child rearing may reflect a West African heritage (Collins, 1991; George & Dickerson, 1995; Greene, 1990).

Unfortunately, the strengths and coping strategies of black mothers have often been interpreted negatively (Dickerson, 1995; Greene, 1990). Black women have been judged against a white middle-class norm of female submission and traditional marriage arrangements (Collins, 1991). Sociologists and psychiatrists have accused them of "castrating" their husbands and sons by being "unfeminine" (Giddings, 1984). The infamous *Moynihan Report* (Moynihan, 1965) attributed the problems of the urban black community to the "matriarchal" social organization of black families.

Black mothers' extended households and woman-centered child rearing appear to be problems only if the implicit norm is traditional (white) middle-class marriage. Blaming black women for social problems and labeling their resourcefulness and strength as "dominance" avoids confronting the real problems of racism, classism, and sexism. Moreover, it obscures the unique social contributions of African-American family patterns. Black women's involvement in social activism often stems from their definition of motherhood: A good mother does not just take care of her own biological offspring, she works to meet the needs of her entire community (Collins, 1991; Naples, 1992).

Lesbian Mothers

Not all mothers are heterosexual; about one lesbian in six is a mother (Strommen, 1993). Some women who marry or cohabit with men and have children within these relationships later identify as lesbian and bring up their children in lesbian households. Other lesbians, both single and in relationships, have a child through adoption or artificial insemination. What are the special issues and stresses that confront lesbian mothers?

One of the biggest potential problems is the reaction of others. The lesbian couple's own parents may react negatively, while celebrating the grandchildren provided by their "straight" daughters and sons. Although there is increasing acceptance of lesbians, we still live in a heterosexist culture in which many people consider a lesbian family unnatural:

> Vicky's parents had a party to introduce their grandchild to the family, but they refused to acknowledge me as the other parent; rather, they chose to identify me as a very good friend who is helping Vicky raise the baby. I wept for hours and knew that I would never again hide the nature of our relationship. At a particularly vulnerable time in our union, the birth of our child, I was asked to deny my identity, connection, and contribution. It would have been easier if I had not been there. (Mercer, 1990, p. 233)

Economic problems and strains exist. Like single mothers, lesbian mothers have to manage without a man's greater earning power. Their income is often so low that lack of money is a source of daily stress. If the mother has to deal with a welfare department, there is the added strain of a state agency making judgments about her lesbian lifestyle (Crawford, 1987).

Lesbian families may experience isolation. Children must live in the larger heterosexual world, but their lesbian mothers may feel little in common with the families of their children's friends. Turning to the lesbian community for support, they may find that the lives of their child-free lesbian friends are very different from their own on a practical, day-to-day level. As more lesbians decide to have children, support groups and networks of lesbian families are growing.

Finally, lesbian mothers may confront problems of internalized homophobia:

> Lesbians should not be surprised or ashamed to find themselves grappling with questions such as: Is this natural? Is it okay for lesbians to have kids? Am I hurting my children . . . is it unfair to bring them into a homophobic world? Am I a woman who is able to mother like other women? These old questions are important to take seriously; they are questions that have been answered in positive ways by many lesbian mothers over the years (Crawford, 1987, p. 197).

Do lesbians raise children differently than heterosexual mothers, and do their children turn out differently? Research suggests that the children of lesbian families are remarkably similar to those of heterosexual families.

One study compared the attitudes of a sample of twenty-six heterosexual and twenty-six lesbian mothers, all black women, to assess similarities and differences in their approaches to child raising. The two groups were similar in the value they placed on independence and self-sufficiency for their children, and how open and candid they saw themselves as being in general. The lesbian mothers, however, were more tolerant about rules and more accepting of children's sexuality (less restrictive of sex play, less concerned with modesty, and more open in providing sex education and information to children). They also viewed boys and girls as more similar to each other than the heterosexual mothers did and expected more traditionally masculine activities from their daughters (Hill, 1987). Given the costs of feminine socialization for girls, these may be healthy attitudes.

In the United Kingdom, a unique study followed seventy-eight children, half raised by lesbian mothers and half by heterosexual single mothers, from middle childhood to young adulthood. As young adults, these participants were asked to look back on their family life. There were no negative effects of growing up in a lesbian household on family or peer relationships; in fact, children of lesbians were more positive about their family life than children of heterosexuals, especially if their mother was open about her sexual orientation and active in lesbian politics. Children of lesbians were no more likely to identify as gay or lesbian, but those who did were more likely to be involved in a relationship than were gay children of heterosexuals.

Children raised by lesbians reported that their mothers had been more open and comfortable communicating with them about sexual development and sexuality as they were growing up. There was no difference in psychological adjustment in the two groups. Both had normal rates of anxiety and depression, and they did not differ in how often they had sought psychological help (Tasker & Golombok, 1997).

On the whole, it seems that lesbian family life produces children who are very much like children from heterosexual families. A review of research (Falk, 1993) found no detrimental effects of lesbian parenting on children's psychological adjustment or gender-role development. Despite this evidence, courts have often assumed that lesbians are unfit mothers who are liable to molest their children, interfere with their becoming "appropriately" gender-typed, or cause them to become homosexual.

In 1993, the American Psychological Association, the National Association of Social Workers, and other professional organizations argued in a Virginia court case that there is no specific evidence that lesbians are worse parents than heterosexuals or that the children of lesbians are at risk for psychological disorders. The court had awarded custody of a 2-year-old boy to his grandmother solely because his mother is a lesbian. There was no evidence that Sharon Bottoms was a poor mother or that her son Tyler was suffering any problems; her relationship with another woman was the only custody issue. This case is not atypical; "admitted" lesbians stand a fifty-fifty chance of losing their children in custody disputes (Falk, 1993). In a 1975 case, Mary Jo Risher—a college graduate, nurse, Sunday school teacher, and PTA president—lost custody of her 9-year-old son to her ex-husband and his new wife. There was no question that Mary Jo Risher was demonstrably a "good mother"; yet as a lesbian she was deemed unfit (Pollack, 1990). In Sharon and Tyler Bottoms' case, an appeals court, influenced by the APA brief and psychologists' expert testimony, overturned the earlier verdict and returned Tyler to his mother and her partner (Sleek, 1994).

Commonalities

With the experiences of women who mother being shaped by social class, sexual orientation, economic status, and many other factors, are there any overall similarities? Do most mothers have at least some things in common? In writing this chapter, we read many accounts by mothers of their feelings and thoughts about motherhood. Several themes emerged in these accounts. Here, we illustrate each of five themes we perceived with the words of some of the women who chose to write their stories in *Balancing Acts*, a book edited by Katherine Gieve (1989).

1. *Becoming a mother results in large, significant, and permanent changes in identity and life circumstances.*

   Daniel is seven, Matthew, five, and when I think about the past seven years I feel like a person watching the dust begin to settle after an earthquake. Seismic tremors still shoot through my life, but perhaps not so frequently nor quite so catastrophically as they did in earlier years. (p. 41)

   I did not imagine the force or the excitement—nor how I would willingly be taken over by my children. . . . I look at the world with different eyes and inward with a new vision. I feel riven, torn apart, and made again. (p. 51)

   I am not where I was before—not in a single detail. I have learned to pride myself on new abilities, some I had never considered of value. I was blown wide open by motherhood and by the emotions that came with it. . . . I had no idea that I could love that well. . . . Conversely, other abilities by which I had set great store, producing words on time, selling an idea, keeping myself fired up . . . seem useful but little more than that. (pp. 127–128)

2. *Motherhood can involve feelings of intense love, competence, and achievement.*

The rewards of motherhood were immediate and lasting. I have established a relaxed physical intimacy with both my children which tolerates anger and laughter, built up over a decade of washing them, reading to them, and tumbling about with them. The relationship I have with my children is the single most important part of my present life. (p. 114)

Pregnancy had suited me, I enjoyed giving birth, but nothing prepared me for the reality of the new baby. I was almost paralyzed by the joy that shot through me as I looked through the plastic (hospital crib) that morning . . . and caught a glimpse from the bright little eyes which, wide open, were waiting to engage mine. I have never felt emotion like it . . . it's just impossible to put into words . . . I was transported. (p. 124)

My mother was proud and confident of her role and people came to her for advice. The kitchen was always full of the children of neighbors and aunts, and, by the time of my own adolescence, the children of my own older sisters. My mother has an ample bosom and a sense of rhythm which can reduce any infant to a coma within minutes. She knows nursery rhymes you have never heard and old wives' tales that would make your hair stand on end. . . . I absorbed from her an overwhelming sense that childbirth was miraculous, that having children was at the core of being a woman. . . . I was left in no doubt that I, too, wanted children. I wanted the experience which had made her life so worthwhile and I wanted, like her, to be good at it. (pp. 1–2)

She's brought into a room. . . . Not much hair, toothless, a fat bald child in a scratchy pink dress. It is love at first sight. . . . I feel as if I've been waiting all my life for this moment, for this child. . . . The "I" who adopts this four-month-old baby is forced to recognize that, physically and symbolically, she is another being, formed by other bodies, in relationships I know nothing of. But in my imagination, she is the missing part of myself, at last returned. I am complete. . . . There is gratitude, passion, absorption—above all gratitude—to the birth mother whose child I swear to love and cherish, to my own mother who gave me existence, to my newly found daughter who has given me this feeling. (pp. 138–139)

3. *Motherhood is a constantly changing relationship, as both child and mother grow and develop. Mothers and children move from a relationship of profound inequality, with the child literally dependent on the mother for life itself, to one of (ideally) equality. Throughout the process, the mother moves from meeting physical needs to meeting intellectual ones; yet, emotional demands remain a constant.*

It was not the hard work of child care that I found so difficult (probably because I shared it with others) but the constantly changing relationship which continued in terms not chosen by me at an unpredictable and changeable pace. It required constant reassessment and with it pain, anger, and remorse, as well as excitement and pleasure. Daniel elicited from me both my greatest love and generosity and my darkest anger and frustration. (p. 45)

As our children grow and change, and new pleasures, new battles, take the place of the early ones, I feel I live in a constant state of surprise and suspense. It is like reading the best of novels, combined with being in love; I want things to stand still yet can't wait to see what will happen next. And, above all, I don't want the story to end. (p. 159)

4. *Both child and mother must confront the limitations of love and care.*

To be kissed better is the child's expectation of the mother and to kiss better is the mothers' hope of herself; to take away the pain and bring peace in its place is to be a good mother. Why do all those baby care manuals not tell us how difficult it is? We cannot kiss better all the suffering even in our own homes. (p. 45)

My (adopted) daughter came from a white mother and a black father. I can be a white mother to her but I cannot represent either that maleness or that blackness. . . . With all my love, I cannot be everything she wants and needs any more than I can shield her from pain . . . indeed I must add to her pain. . . . My fantasy, that if I love her enough nothing else matters, has to give way. I see that it matters to her, being black, to have two white parents and that I am not powerful enough in the real world, where black is different from white, to undo this. This is one of the things I cannot change. (p. 140)

"You are not my real mother," says my daughter to me. I did not feel either that my mother was my real mother, perhaps every daughter, every child, has this doubt. . . . The gap between the ideal Mother, and the mother we actually have, is perhaps always there. If the Mother is the fixed perfect image of the ideal, a mother (small m) is always what falls short of that image. (pp. 143–144)

Making a Difference

Candy Lightner has suffered more sadness and anger than any mother should ever have to. Her daughter Serena was cut and bruised at age 6 when a drunk driver rear-ended Lightner's mother's car. Her son Travis was run over by a drugged driver when he was 4. And her 13-year-old daughter Cari was thrown 120 feet and killed when she was hit by a drunk driver. Police told Lightner Cari's killer was unlikely to serve time, even though he had a long record of drunk driving convictions. Lightner fought back. She founded Mothers Against Drunk Drivers (MADD), a group she headed until 1985, and she continues to speak out against driving under the influence of alcohol and drugs. In fact, Lightner has probably been the strongest individual force behind the 30 percent decline in drunk driving since the 1960s, behind the fact that every state raised the drinking age to 21 by the time she left MADD, and behind the drop in drunk driving–related deaths from 25,000 in 1980 to under 18,000 in 1992. Lightner was able to turn a mother's love and grief into an irresistible force. MADD now has over 3 million members, a staff of 300 plus, and a budget of $53 million. Thanks to Lightner's courage and determination, the United States continues to make progress against this deadly behavior, drunk driving.

Sources: Encyclopedia of Associations (32nd ed.) Vol. 1, Part 2, entry # 11710. Griffin, K. (1994, July). MADD again. *Health,* 62. *Time,* 1–7–85, p. 41.

5. *Mothers and children must adapt to a society that is structured as though children did not exist and does not provide necessary support for those who care for the young* (see Figure 10.7).

The world suddenly became a much more dangerous place once I had a baby dependent on me for his very life. For the first time I was thrown into a world that did not recognize my physical, emotional, social, and political needs. This applied to design, architecture, roads, public transport, dangerous machinery; not to mention lack of community child care facilities. . . . it isn't the child that makes your life hard, it is the adult world and the powers that be. Usually, it is the very people who sentimentalize and idealize motherhood who stop listening. (pp. 53–54)

Motherhood . . . has made me aware of time in many different ways. In particular how women's time is taken for granted so that there is little concordance between the way time is structured in the so-called public world and the rhythm of time associated with caring for a young child. (p. 77)

If men had to travel with children in buggies on public transport as often as they had to carry briefcases, I suspect they would have devised a rather different transport system and invented escalators and steps on which it was possible to take children in buggies easily. (p. 87)

These five commonalities emerged for us as we read the writings of diverse women about their experiences of motherhood. Perhaps you can think of others.

FIGURE 10.7. After security guards ordered a woman to leave the premises when she was discovered discreetly nursing her baby, mothers staged a "nurse-in" at a New York shopping mall.

Bringing up children is an awesome responsibility. Traditionally, in Western societies it has been divided into a nurturing role, assigned to women, and a provider role, assigned to men. We have seen that this arrangement has many limitations. It does not allow for individual differences in personality and ability—some men might make better nurturers than providers, and some women better providers than nurturers. It keeps women and children economically dependent on men; when men default, families live in poverty. It keeps children dependent solely on their mothers for love and care. It overlooks the diversity of families, and changes in roles. Single-parent families, gay and lesbian families, and families from different cultural traditions do not conform to the patriarchal ideal. In most families, women now participate in the provider role much more than men participate in nurturing. It also leads to blaming mothers for just about everything that can go wrong, and overlooking fathers' potential for involvement with their children.

Why Blame Mom?

Our society has myths about both the Perfect Mother and the Bad Mother (Caplan, 1989). The Perfect Mother is an endless fount of nurturance, naturally knows how to raise children, and never gets angry. The measure of her success is a perfect child; a less than perfect child is seen as proof of a bad mother. Perfect Mother myths establish standards that every woman fails to meet. Bad Mother myths (see Figure 10.8) exaggerate mothers' limitations or faults and transform them into monstrous flaws: in these myths, mothers are bottomless pits of neediness, their power is dangerous, and closeness between mother and adult children is unhealthy.

"Mother-blaming is like air pollution"—so pervasive that it often goes unnoticed (Caplan, 1989, p. 39). The societal tendency to scapegoat mothers extends to mental health researchers and practitioners. A review of articles published in major mental health journals between 1970 and 1982 found a strong tendency to blame mothers for clients' problems among psychoanalysts, psychiatrists, psychologists, and social workers (both female and male). In fact, in

FIGURE 10.8.
Source: By permission of Mell Lazarus and Creators Syndicate, Inc.

the 125 articles reviewed, mothers were blamed for seventy-two different kinds of problems in their offspring. The list included aggressiveness, agoraphobia, anorexia, anxiety, arson, bad dreams, bedwetting, chronic vomiting, delinquency, delusions, depression, frigidity, hyperactivity, incest, loneliness, marijuana use, minimal brain damage, moodiness, schizophrenia, sexual dysfunction, sibling jealousy, sleepwalking, tantrums, truancy, inability to deal with color blindness, and self-induced television epilepsy (Caplan & Hall-McCorquodale, 1985)!

Our society has assigned mothers responsibility not only for their children's physical care but also for their psychological well-being to an extent that few other cultures around the world or throughout history have done. It has asked them to fulfill their responsibilities in relative isolation, and often without the material and social support they need. Moreover, it has created myths that disguise the realities of parenting. Perhaps, for each of us, one task of growing up is to look beyond the myths of motherhood at the human being who is our mother, to see her as a complex, multifaceted individual, and to stop blaming her for being only human (Caplan, 1989; Howe, 1989).

Is Fathering a Feminist Issue?

Where are the fathers when blame is handed out? They seem to be invisible. In popular advice books about parenting, mothers are represented as being dangerously emotional, and their (inevitable) failure to control their emotions is claimed to cause their children's problems. Emotional expressiveness, which is part of women's caregiving roles, is portrayed as inherently dangerous (Shields, Steinke, & Koster, 1995). However, fathers, even single fathers, are not blamed. Rather, their children's problems are presented as outside their control.

Psychology has contributed more than its share to the father-invisibility problem. A review of 544 empirical research studies of children's psychological disorders published between 1984 and 1991 found that only 1 percent focused exclusively on fathers, while 48 percent focused exclusively on mothers. Another 25 percent included both parents but did not analyze for sex differences or interactions (Phares & Compas, 1993). When the studies including fathers were examined separately, clear effects were found: Fathers do play a role in children's psychopathology. The evidence is clearest in children whose fathers sexually molest them, abuse alcohol, or are depressed.

Fathering is being recognized as a feminist issue. Redefining what it means to be a good father is essential to the achievement of equality for women and the psychological wholeness of men (Silverstein, 1996). As long as a good father is defined simply as a good provider, men will have more privilege both at home and in public life. Moreover, this narrow definition deprives men of the chance to recognize and satisfy their needs for intimacy and emotional connection with their families. At present, women are performing double roles as nurturers and providers, but men are less likely to do so. Societal institutions do not support women in either role. Only when men, too, play dual roles, will public policy wake up to the needs of families.

What kind of changes would be beneficial to families? At present, public life is structured as though children did not exist. Public spaces and public transport are designed without regard to the safety and comfort of children or their caretakers. Food and clothing stores, which depend on the business provided by women who shop for their families, rarely provide play areas for children. Commuter trains and airports make special provisions for smoking and dining but provide no facilities for children's play. Although women's breasts can be seen exposed on magazine covers at every newsstand, there are very few places where women can comfortably nurse their babies outside their homes, and seeing women breast-feed in public is widely considered disgusting (see Figure 10.7). Public institutions plan schedules as though all women were available for full-time child care—for example, nursery schools and kindergartens with half-day programs assume a mother will be free at midday to retrieve her child, and the hours of service provided by day-care centers frequently are inadequate for women on shift work. These are just a few examples of socially created obstacles that make motherhood into a kind of disability. If men took care of children, too, these things would change. In England, for example, airports and train stations feature equipment for diapering babies in both the women's restroom and the men's.

Public policy on families in the United States lags behind every other industrialized country in the world (Lorber, 1993b). The United States needs better paid parental leave, subsidized child care, and flexible working hours. The political activism to bring about these changes is unlikely to be effective until the changes are as relevant to men as to women (Silverstein, 1996).

What are the payoffs for redefining parenthood? Studies (reviewed by Silverstein, 1996) have shown that father involvement is good for children, who show better cognitive and emotional development. It is good for couples, leading to greater marital satisfaction, and for mothers, who report decreased stress. And it is good for fathers themselves, who report higher self-esteem and satisfaction with their role as parent. Redefining parenting is a revolution that is past due. What is needed is not a return to the patriarchal world of traditional marriage, but a postgender definition that allows for flexibility and diversity of family patterns.

CONNECTING THEMES

- *Gender is more than just sex.* The ability to bear children is a biological capacity unique to women. However, birth, child rearing, and motherhood occur within a gender system that controls and regulates women's sexuality and fertility. Sexual biology becomes a gendered experience.
- *Language and naming are sources of power.* The motherhood mandate decrees that all women should be mothers, and the motherhood mystique defines the approved way to do it. Deviant mothers are stigmatized by labels such as "working mother" and "welfare mom." Accounts of motherhood in women's own language and images have been conspicuously absent from art, literature, and history.
- *Women are not all alike.* Experiences of mothering are shaped by social class, ethnicity, sexual orientation, and many other factors that define a women's

social position. Rather than generalize about a mythical motherhood, we should recognize the diverse experiences of women who mother.

- *Psychological research can foster social change.* The United States is virtually alone among industrialized nations in its failure to develop public policy that recognizes the needs of today's families. Poverty among women and children is a major social issue. Women's reproductive rights are contested, and new medical technologies complicate issues of ethics, choice, and power. Redefining fatherhood would benefit families.

SUGGESTED READINGS

BELL-SCOTT, PATRICIA, GUY-SHEFTALL, BEVERLY, JONES ROYSTER, JACQUELINE, SIMS-WOOD, JANET, DeCOSTA-WILLIS, MIRIAM, & FULTZ, LUCILLE P. (1991). *Double stitch: Black women write about mothers and daughters.* New York: HarperCollins. This rich collection of poems, stories, and essays explores and analyzes black mother-daughter relationships through a beautifully developed quilt-making metaphor.

REDDY, MAUREEN T., ROTH, MARTHA, & SHELDON, AMY. (1994). *Mother journeys: Feminists write about mothering.* Minneapolis: Spinster Ink. Poetry, art, and essays on the experience of mothering by an ethnically and culturally diverse group of women.

LUBLIN, NANCY. (1998). *Pandora's box: Feminism confronts reproductive technology.* New York: Rowman & Littlefield. Is reproductive freedom furthered or hampered by technological advances? This book unites feminist theory and activism in an original analysis.

CHAPTER 11

Work and Achievement

- **IF SHE ISN'T PAID, IS IT STILL WORK?**
  "Just a Housewife?"
  Relational Work: Keeping Everybody
    Happy
  The Two-Person Career
  What Are the Costs and Benefits of
    Invisible Work?
- **WORKING HARD FOR A LIVING: WOMEN
  IN THE PAID WORKFORCE**
  Sex Segregation and Sex Stratification
  Women's Work as Extension of
    Family Roles: "It's Only Natural"
  The Wage Gap
  What Are the Costs of
    Underemploying Women?
- **DOING GENDER IN THE WORKPLACE**
  Attributions for Success and Failure
  Devaluing Women's Performance
  Discrimination in Hiring and
    Promotion
  Social Reactions to "Uppity Women"
  Mentors and Role Models
  Leadership: Do Women Do It
    Differently?
- **WOMEN'S CAREER DEVELOPMENT: ARE
  THERE OBSTACLES FROM WITHIN?**
  Do Women Have Limited
    Expectations?

Do Women Have Different Values
    and Interests?
  Math and Computing: Still Barriers?
  Are Women Less Motivated to
    Achieve?
- **EXCEPTIONAL WORK LIVES**
  Achievement in the Professions: From
    Pink Collar to White
  What Factors Affect Women's Career
    Development?
  Nontraditional Occupations: From
    Pink Collar to Blue
- **PUTTING IT ALL TOGETHER: WORK AND
  FAMILY**
  What Are the Costs of the Balancing
    Act?
  What Are the Benefits of the
    Balancing Act?
- **WOMEN, WORK, AND SOCIAL POLICY:
  MODELS FOR CHANGE**
- **CONNECTING THEMES**
- **SUGGESTED READINGS**

Work is a part of virtually every woman's life. But the world of work is a gendered world; often, women and men do different kinds of work, face different obstacles to satisfaction and achievement, and receive different, unequal rewards. In this chapter we examine the unpaid and paid work of women, women's values about work and achievement, explanations for the differing work patterns of women and men, and factors affecting women's achievement in both traditional and nontraditional professions and trades. We listen to the voices of women as they talk about their work: its problems, its satisfactions, and its place in their lives.

IF SHE ISN'T PAID, IS IT STILL WORK?

The phrases *working woman* and *working mother* suggest that a woman is not really a worker unless she is in the paid workforce. Much of the work women do is unpaid and not formally defined as work. Listen to one full-time homemaker talking with a psychologist conducting a study of adult identity:

Q. What is your current employment status?
A. Do you mean am I working? No, I'm just a housewife.
Q. Do you consider yourself to be a full-time homemaker?
A. Yes.
Q. How important to you is your work as a homemaker?
A. Very important. It's all I do. (Whitbourne, 1986, p. 161)

This conversation captures some of the contradictions of the homemaker role. The homemaker works full time in an unpaid job that is low in status, especially in comparison to the idealized image of the "career woman." Scrubbing floors and toilets; shopping for food and cooking meals; changing beds; washing, ironing, and mending clothes; doing household planning, scheduling, and recordkeeping—all the chores required to keep a household functioning—certainly qualify as work. She may justifiably feel that her work is necessary and important, yet she labels herself "just a housewife."

"Just a Housewife?"

Feminist scholars and researchers are examining the experiences and activities hidden behind the phrase "just a housewife" (e.g., Oakley, 1974). Because it is invisible to the larger society, there are misconceptions about women's work in the home (Vanek, 1984). For example, some people believe that couples today share housework equally, that labor-saving appliances and modern conveniences have made housework easy, and that housework is trivial, with little monetary value. Let's look at each of these beliefs more closely.

Is Housework Shared?

Chapters 9 and 10 documented that equality in the domestic realm is rare. Although gender roles are changing in many ways, housework and child care remain largely the responsibility of women (Baber & Allen, 1992; Ferree, 1987; Hochschild, 1989; Lorber, 1993b; Phillips & Imhoff, 1997) (see Figure 11.1). For

FIGURE 11.1.
Source: Reprinted with special permission of King Features Syndicate.

example, a study of more than 3,000 U.S. couples showed that women worked more than twice as many hours per week (33.10) than men (14.44) on household chores (Blair & Lichter, 1991). Chores are still assigned by gender: men do outside work, women do inside work, and women tend to do the chores that come up most often. For example, a recent survey of more than 1,200 U.S. households showed that 93 percent of the women usually did the meal planning, 88 percent usually did the food shopping, and 90 percent usually did the cooking—percentages that had not changed much since the 1970s (Harnack, Story, Martinson, Neumark-Sztainer, & Stang, 1998). Women's chores are also more psychologically stressful because often they have to be done on a tighter schedule—you can put off washing the car until it's convenient, but it's not so easy to put off making dinner (Barnett & Shen, 1997).

When wives work outside the home, some studies show that husbands' participation in housework changes little. The *proportion* of total housework they do goes up, but this is because wives are doing less. Other studies suggest that men are beginning to do somewhat more (Baber & Allen, 1992; Dancer & Gilbert, 1993), but a recent survey of a national sample of more than 2,700 U.S. couples showed that only when both husbands and wives share egalitarian beliefs and values do husbands pitch in and do more than the minimum (Greenstein, 1996). For most women, work outside the home is followed each day by a "second shift" at home (Hochschild, 1989).

The prevailing pattern—overworked women and resistant to moderately involved men—is quite consistent across cultures and ethnic groups. In a study of sixty-three dual-earner African-American families, husbands spent about half as much time as wives on household labor—they were involved, but hardly egalitarian (Hossain & Roopmarine, 1993). In Mexican-American families, women do more housework even when they are professionally employed, and, especially in working-class families, traditional roles prevail (Hartzler & Franco, 1985; Williams, 1990). In an Australian study of 128 wives' attempts to get their husbands more involved in housework, only 4 wives experienced any lasting success (Dempsey, 1997). Comparisons of couples in Indonesia, the Philippines, Taiwan, South Korea, and the United States showed that women did more housework regardless of their own income or their country's level of economic development (Sanchez, 1993).

Is Housework Easy?

Surprisingly, women today spend as many hours each week in housework as women did in 1900—between fifty-one and fifty-six hours a week for married women with no employment outside the home (Vanek, 1984). Housework demands more hours each day than many paid jobs. Labor-saving devices such as automatic washers and technological advances such as household electricity and running water have made the work less dirty and arduous than it used to be, and the smaller size of modern families means less work, but new tasks have taken the place of old ones. Travel for errands, shopping, and transporting children takes up many hours each week. Household equipment must be maintained and serviced. Moreover, the modern middle-class homemaker is much less likely to have paid help than her grandmother.

Research shows that women today are just as concerned with home cleanliness as they were in 1975 (Robinson & Milkie, 1998). But standards of housekeeping have risen. Today's homemakers are encouraged to go far beyond past standards in cleanliness, food preparation, and a warm, welcoming emotional climate for husband and children. Homemakers often take pride in their high standards. For example, one homemaker told an interviewer that her children "don't know what it is to eat store-bought cookies. They won't eat them. Because they're so used to me doing it" (Whitbourne, 1986, p. 164). Another described her duties as follows:

> I know every day when I get up that I have "x" amount of things to do in the house, and I just do 'em. . . . They like a clean house. You know, they like it vacuumed, picked up, cleaned . . . clothes, they like their clothes washed and things like that. . . . They like decent meals every night. It's not Burger King. Or, you know, Kentucky Fried Chicken. They like to eat at home, they like a good meal . . . I have a lot of conveniences, too . . . microwave oven . . . so, it's not really that hard a task (laughs). (Whitbourne, 1986, p. 171)

Today, housework has higher standards of achievement than our grandmothers could have imagined, and it is just as time-consuming as it was in their day.

Is Housework Trivial?

What is the value to society of the unpaid domestic work of women? Within individual families it is often accorded very little value:

> The garbage could overflow and no one would dump it, or the dog may need to be fed . . . and everybody relies on mother to do it . . . some days I feel that they're taking me for granted. They know I'm not going out into the work force, and every once in a while I hear one of my sons say, "Well, you don't do anything all day long." . . . If they didn't have clean clothes or their beds weren't changed or something like that they might realize that their mother does do something. But most of the time they don't. I don't think men feel that a woman does a day's work. (Whitbourne, 1986, p. 165)

The devaluation of housework is also apparent at the societal level. Unpaid housework is not listed in the U.S. Department of Labor's *Dictionary of Occupational Titles*. Its monetary value is not computed into the gross national product—an example of androcentrism and an "official denial that this work is socially necessary" (Ciancanelli & Berch, 1987). One official Labor Department ranking put *homemaker* at the same level of complexity and skill as *parking lot attendant* (Baruch et al., 1983).

Obviously, families could not live as comfortably and cheaply without the services of a homemaker. But exactly how much is her work "worth"? It is difficult to compute the monetary value of women's work in the home. One way is to estimate the cost of replacing her services with paid workers—cook, chauffeur, babysitter, dishwasher, janitor, and so forth. Another is to calculate the wages the homemaker loses by staying at home. If she could earn $250 a week as a bank clerk, for example, that is the value of her housework. But neither method really captures the unique characteristics of homemaking.

Many women feel that their services could not be replaced with paid workers because the work demands loving care and an intimate knowledge of the family. Who could calculate the appropriate pay for planning a small child's birthday party—or the "overtime" involved when a woman cooks and serves an elegant dinner for her husband's boss? These tasks require organizing, scheduling, shopping, cooking, and so forth, plus loving personal involvement. Calculating lost wages from a paid job also presents problems. By this method, housework done by a woman who could earn $140 an hour as an attorney is worth twenty times as much as the identical chores done by a woman who could only earn $7 an hour as a food server (Vanek, 1984). Because housework does not fit a definition of work derived from male experience, it resists classification.

Once we begin to think of the homemaker's job as work rather than as "doing nothing all day," contrasts with paid work become even more apparent. Imagine how a "help wanted" ad for a homemaker might look:

> WANTED: Full-time employee for small family firm. DUTIES: Including but not limited to general cleaning, cooking, gardening, laundry, ironing and mending, purchasing, bookkeeping, and money management. Child care may also be required. HOURS: Avg. 55/wk but standby duty required 24 hours/day, 7 days/wk. Extra workload on holidays. SALARY AND BENEFITS: No salary, but food, clothing, and shelter provided at employer's discretion; job security and benefits depend on continued goodwill of employer. No vacation. No retirement plan. No opportunities for advancement. REQUIREMENTS: No previous experience necessary, can learn on the job. Only women need apply.

The homemaker's job looks unattractive indeed in this description. Women do find it unsatisfying in many ways. They dislike the boring, repetitive, and unchallenging nature of much of the work. They frequently feel lonely and isolated from others—unlike paid employment, household work is performed without the companionship of coworkers, and there is no built-in source of feedback on how well you are doing. Women also express concern about not bringing in income:

> I never wanted to be a helpless person economically—and I'm probably about as helpless now as I could be in that respect, because I'm not making anything and don't really have many ideas about a lucrative job that I could go and get. If anything happened to my husband I'd be very worried. . . . The family is completely dependent on him. (Baruch et al., 1983, p. 199)

On the other hand, full-time homemakers appreciate the freedom to make their own schedules rather than to punch a time clock or answer to a supervisor. They like having time to pursue interests and hobbies and to do creative tasks such as decorating. (If this seems unrealistic given a 55-hour workweek, remember that the homemaker is comparing herself to employed women, who usually work at both housework and their paid jobs.) And they enjoy the rewards that come from being emotionally and physically available to their children and husbands (Baruch et al., 1983). In the rare cases in which men take primary responsibility for housework and child care, their feelings about the job are similar to women's. Interviews with sixteen "househusbands" showed that they rated increased involvement with their children as the best aspect of their unusual situations—and doing housework as the worst (Rosenwasser & Patterson, 1984–1985).

Relational Work: Keeping Everybody Happy

Women are largely responsible for caring for others' emotional needs. Keeping harmony in the family has long been defined as women's work (Parsons & Bales, 1955). In a study of marital interaction in which more than 100 couples kept diaries about their communication patterns, wives did more relational work than husbands. They focused on their husbands, friends, and family; spent time talking and listening with them; talked about relationships more; and kept up with their household tasks to keep harmony in the family (Ragsdale, 1996). The time and energy necessary for this work may be considerable, as everyone relies on "Mom" to smooth emotional crises:

> The hardest part of my life is having to deal with two college-age kids and a husband who has professional needs and an eighty-year-old mother who is going through great difficulties. . . . I sometimes feel put upon by all the demands made on me by others, that's all. And I think that's a difficulty, but being a concerned mother, that may not change. (A 51-year-old homemaker, quoted in Baruch et al., 1983, p. 190)

Part of the reason mothers do more child care than fathers (see Chapter 10) may be because they are believed to be the "relationship specialists" (see Figure 11.2). And this does not change when mothers work for pay. When a sample of full-time homemakers and full-time paid workers were surveyed, the employed women were doing just as many child-care activities as the homemakers, except for watching TV with their children. Working mothers were equally likely to read to their child, play games, offer praise, and stop their own activity to play with the child (DeMeis & Perkins, 1996).

Relational work goes beyond a woman's immediate family to a wider network of relatives (Baruch et al., 1983; Di Leonardo, 1987). Women are in charge of visits, letters, and phone calls to distant family members. They buy the presents and remember to send the card for Aunt Anna's birthday. They organize family reunions and holiday celebrations, negotiating conflicts and deciding who will host the dinner.

Although the specifics of the family rituals vary according to social class and ethnic group, families' dependence on women's labor is similar, whether

FIGURE 11.2.
Source: Jump Start reprinted by permission of United Feature Syndicate, Inc.

they are upper-class Mexican, working-class African-American, middle-class Italian-American, migrant Chicano farm workers, or immigrants to America from rural Japan (research reviewed in Di Leonardo, 1987). Like housework, the relational work of women is largely ignored in traditional definitions of work. But it requires time, energy, and skill, and it has economic and social value. Exchanging outgrown children's clothes with a sister-in-law or sending potential customers to a cousin's business firm are ways of strengthening relationships that also help families maximize financial resources (Di Leonardo, 1987).

The Two-Person Career

Women's unpaid work benefits the career development of their husbands. The term *two-person career* describes situations in which wives serve as unofficial (and often unacknowledged) contributors to their husbands' work (Papanek, 1973). The two-person career has been studied most extensively in the case of the corporate wife (e.g., Kanter, 1977), but it is not limited to corporate life. The male graduate student whose wife supports him by working for pay, typing his papers, and keeping mundane household problems out of his way so he can study is receiving the benefits of a two-person career. So is the politician, whose wife must be able to "give the speech when he can't make it but to shut her mouth and listen adoringly when he is there" (Kanter, 1977, p. 122). The clergyman's wife and the college president's wife are highly visible examples.

The role of helper to a prominent man may be quite rewarding. But at the same time, the woman's freedom of action is strictly controlled and her fate is tied to her spouse's. Consider that Hillary Rodham Clinton, who did not take her husband's name when she married, was later pressured into doing so for political reasons (Marshall, 1997). Although she was a graduate of Yale law school with a distinguished legal career, she was expected to engage in a cookie recipe contest with Barbara Bush to help her husband get elected. When she took on the important task of health care reform, it seemed that the press was more interested in her hairstyle than her health care plan. And, as First Lady, she was subjected to hostile jokes and public humiliation over her husband's sexual activities.

What kinds of work do women do in the service of their husbands' careers? The specific tasks vary, depending on the husband's job and career stage (Kanter, 1977). She may serve as a hostess, entertaining clients or customers in her home; make friends with and socialize with people who can be useful in advancing her husband; and engage in other aspects of image building for him. She is expected to be available at any time for complete care of their children, so that he can travel or work evenings and weekends. She often participates in volunteer or community service related to his position—the faculty wives' club raises money for scholarships, and the ladies' auxiliary at the hospital raises money for equipment for their physician husbands. She may also contribute direct services in place of a paid employee—typing, taking business or sales calls, keeping books or tax records for his small business, or scheduling his travel arrangements. Finally, she provides emotional support. She is expected to listen to his complaints, help him work through problems at work, cheerfully accept his absences and work pressures, avoid burdening him with domestic trivia, and motivate him to achieve to his fullest potential. She is, indeed, "the woman behind the man."

What Are the Costs and Benefits of Invisible Work?

Obviously, housework, relational work, and the ladies' auxiliary do not provide a paycheck. The traditional homemaker is expected to be rewarded for her services indirectly, through a sense of *vicarious achievement* (Lipman-Blumen & Leavitt, 1976). In other words, she is supposed to identify with her husband and feel rewarded and gratified by his successes. Many women do report this kind of gratification; they are glad to be the woman behind the man. Others feel exploited and powerless to change the system. One corporate wife complained to an interviewer, "I am paid neither in job satisfaction nor in cash for my work. I did not choose the job of executive wife, and I am heartily sick of it" (Kanter, 1977, p. 111).

Women who achieve through their husbands are vulnerable. If the marriage ends through the husband's death or divorce, or if despite her efforts he does not achieve fame and glory, she may have little to put on a résumé and few skills that prospective employers would regard as valuable. As discussed in Chapter 9, such women may become displaced homemakers, lacking the protection of a successful man and without marketable skills. Increasingly, women are insisting that divorce courts recognize that their unpaid work is vital to their husband's success (see Box 11.1).

The availability of some women as unofficial employees for their husbands' companies also has implications for women who are employed and competing with men. There is no "corporate husband" position to match that of the corporate wife. Indeed, the world of work assumes that workers are men and that these men have wives to take care of them (Wajcman, 1998). The female employee may appear less talented and motivated than her male colleague because she lacks his invisible support staff and therefore cannot accomplish as much. If she is married, her husband is unlikely to invest his future in vicarious achievement. A study of more than 1,600 U.S. corporate employees showed that men at the highest executive levels were significantly more likely to have spouses who were full-time homemakers than men at lower levels and women at all levels (Burke, 1997). Similar results were found in a U.K. study of high-level managers: 88 percent of the married women, and only 27 percent of the married men, had partners who were employed full-time. In other words, the career success of men is given an invisible boost by their at-home support staff. Corporations know this very well; men are seen as bringing two people to their jobs, and women, because of their family duties, as bringing less than one (Wajcman, 1998).

Gay men and lesbians also are disadvantaged in the workplace by the expectation that everyone has a wife at home. Remember that many lesbians are mothers, and their partners almost always have paid work, too (Fassinger, 1996). A gay friend of ours in graduate school shared the feelings of many career-oriented women both lesbian and heterosexual, single and married, when he observed, "I need a wife!"

Box 11.1 It's Her Job Too

ONCE UPON A TIME, A GOOD CORPORATE WIFE was to be seen and not heard. She was to make sure nothing, but nothing, came between her man and his work. She was to shield him from the tedious and distracting details of domestic life. She was to raise beautiful, well-mannered children and maintain a beautiful, well-appointed home, making it look effortless. She was to work the charity circuit—to be the belle of the charity ball and also its unpaid CEO. She was to smile through scores of business dinners. And she was never, ever, to make a stink. Even in the worst of times, even when things unraveled, she was expected to know her place and, if need be, to slip quietly offstage. Lorna Wendt did all of these things except the last. When her 32-year marriage to GE Capital CEO Gary Wendt came apart two years ago, she raised a big ruckus. She wanted half of the $100 million she estimated he was worth. She wanted to tap what she considered her rightful share of the treasure-trove of stock options and pension benefits accumulated during the marriage but not due until later in his career. She wanted respect. She wanted acknowledgment, just once and writ large, that society valued all those things she'd done on the home front. As with executive pay, the amount one needs to live on wasn't the issue. The money was merely a way of keeping score.

And Lorna Wendt did score. . . . She came away with $20 million—far less than the $50 million she'd sought, but far more than the $8 million plus alimony that Wendt had originally offered. She got half the hard assets—breaking the glass ceiling that often exists in uppercrust divorces, where wives are more likely to get what the judge thinks they need according to a practice known in the divorce bar as "enough is enough."

The Wendt case has launched a thousand cocktail-party conversations and struck fear in the hearts of primary breadwinners everywhere. A lot of men are still incredulous of her demands. In a big-bucks case like hers, "the question becomes, Is the person who is making the money—is that person's contribution greater than the person who stays at home and runs the house?" says Robert Stephan Cohen, a New York divorce lawyer. "I'll tell you, having represented a number of high-net-worth individuals—they think the contribution of the at-home spouse is important, but not equal." Yet Lorna Wendt has elicited cheers from lots of career women and stay-at-home women alike. No matter the unlikelihood of this very proper, soft-spoken, 54-year-

What's A Corporate Wife Worth?

GE spouse Lorna Wendt got her $20 million. Now executive divorce is a whole new deal.

http://fortune.com

old woman straight out of another era becoming a feminist symbol. Her case has struck a chord.

Lorna Wendt is rich, privileged, hardly Everywoman. But as the woman behind the success story, she has come to stand for the many things that wives still mostly end up doing and that society seems mostly to take for granted: child rearing, tending a family's emotional and spiritual needs, and the unglamorous stuff like car pools, doctor's appointments, sympathy notes. Lorna Wendt has become a lightning rod for the tensions that swirl around what has traditionally been called women's work. "I complemented him by keeping the home fires burning and by raising a family and by being the CEO of the Wendt corporation and by running the household and grounds and social and emotional ties so he could go out and work very hard at what he was good at," she says. "If marriage isn't a partnership between equals, then why get married? If you knew that some husband or judge down the road was going to say, 'You're a 30% part of this marriage, and he's a 70% part,' would you get married?"

Source: Reprinted by permission from "It's Her Job Too," by Betsy Morris, *Fortune*, February 2, 1998, pp. 65–67. Copyright © 1998 Time Inc. All rights reserved.

WORKING HARD FOR A LIVING: WOMEN IN THE PAID WORKFORCE

More women are working outside the home than ever before, a worldwide social change (United Nations, 1991a). About 95 percent of American women work outside the home at some time in their adult lives. The U.S. Department of Labor predicts that the average woman can expect to spend more than twenty-nine years in the labor force (Betz & Fitzgerald, 1987). A majority of American women, including most mothers of young children, now work for a living; women are 46 percent of the total U.S. workforce (National Committee on Pay Equity, 1998).

In the United States, women from minority ethnic groups have historically been much more likely to work outside the home than white women, but white women have now caught up to them. Today, ethnic differences in employment rates are small. In the mid-1990s, 59 percent of white women, 59 percent of black women, and 53 percent of Hispanic women (compared with 75% of all men) were working for pay.

Employment patterns differ by ethnic subgroup. For example, women of Puerto Rican background had the highest employment rate of any group of women in the 1950s (39%, compared with 37% for black and 28% for white women), but opportunities in the garment industry, where many urban-dwelling Puerto Rican women worked, have declined; now, they are less likely than other groups of women to be employed. Nearly two-thirds of all Asian-American women are in the paid workforce (Kim, 1986). Filipino-American women have the highest employment rate for any ethnic group and are frequently found in medical professional roles, while Chinese- and Japanese-American women are concentrated in clerical jobs and food service (Bose, 1987; Kim, 1986).

Sex Segregation and Sex Stratification

In 1900 the three main occupations available to women were schoolteacher, factory worker, and domestic servant (Perun & Bielby, 1981). Though women's job options have expanded a great deal since 1900, the American workplace is still characterized by *sex segregation.* There are few occupations in which the proportion of women and men is about equal. Instead, there are women's jobs and men's jobs (Lorber, 1993b). Ninety-eight percent of all secretaries, 93 percent of nurses, and 86 percent of elementary schoolteachers are women (Benokraitis, 1997). Men are about six times as likely as women to be in skilled trades like carpentry (Ciancanelli & Berch, 1987). As Figure 11.3 shows, in 1997 nearly 60 percent of all employed women worked in service, clerical, administrative support, technician, and sales fields. Fewer than one-third of employed women were in the higher-paying managerial and professional occupations. Although researchers still use the traditional term "sex segregation," the fact that workplaces tend to be "his" or "hers" is a product of the gender system.

Some occupations have an overall equal ratio of women and men but remain segregated at the level of the individual workplace or task (England & McCreary, 1987; Lorber, 1993b; Nieva & Gutek, 1981). For example, in retail sales, men sell appliances, computers, and cars (the "big-ticket items"), while

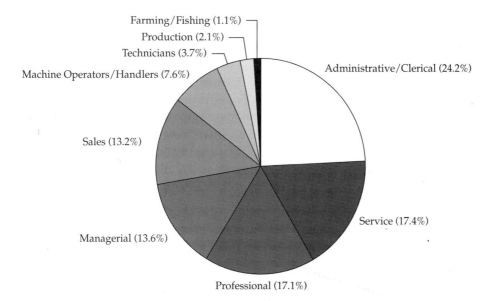

FIGURE 11.3. Women by occupation, 1997. Women are clustered in low-wage service, clerical, and sales jobs.
Source: National Committee on Pay Equity.

women sell clothing. Women are more likely to work in fast-food chains, men are more likely to be waiters and chefs in expensive restaurants.

Sex segregation has begun to decline as more women are entering formerly male jobs. This change is happening for both white women and women of color, at all job levels—women are now more likely to be bus drivers, bartenders, janitors, and insurance agents than they were in 1970. However, sex segregation at the level of specific jobs does not seem to be decreasing. Women bus drivers are more likely to hold part-time school bus employment and men to hold more lucrative long-distance routes; women pharmacists tend to work in hospitals and men in higher-paying retail stores (England & McCreary, 1987).

There is also a great deal of *sex stratification* within general occupational categories: Men tend to occupy higher status and better paid positions (Lorber, 1993b). In the field of education, women are 51 percent of college instructors (the lowest rank) and only 5 percent of full professors; 86 percent of elementary school teachers and only 6 percent of school superintendents (Bell & Chase, 1996; Betz & Fitzgerald, 1987). In health care professions, women are nurses' aides, abortion clinic workers, social workers, laboratory technicians, and nurses, while men are much more likely to be physicians and hospital administrators.

The closer to the top of the corporate hierarchy, the fewer women. In a recent study of more than 500 companies in the UK, 92 percent of top executives were male; in the United States, although women occupy up to 40 percent of managerial positions, only about 5 percent of senior executives are women, and this has hardly changed within the past decade (Valian, 1998; Wajcman, 1998). Men are twice as likely as same-aged women to hold supervisory jobs; women workers who have authority are disproportionately white and usually supervise only a small number of other women. Only 9 percent of women have decision-making power over others' pay or promotions (D'Amico, 1986). Even among a carefully matched sample of senior managers of multinational companies, the men were more than twice as likely as the women to oversee large numbers of employees (Wajcman, 1998). It is difficult to think of any jobs or professions in which women typically hold the authority to determine over-all work conditions and policies (Needleman & Nelson, 1988). In other words, women are still not hiring, firing, and promoting others (Wajcman, 1998). Sex segregation and stratification are worldwide phenomena (United Nations, 1991a).

As more women enter traditionally male occupations, it would seem that sex stratification would decrease. However, the path to the top of a professional hierarchy is not always a smooth one. Although women are not totally excluded, they find it difficult to move past midlevel positions in business and the professions. The pervasive phenomenon of women being blocked from advancement has been termed the *glass ceiling:* The woman can see her goal, but she bumps into a barrier that is both invisible and impenetrable (Lorber, 1993b). Women on their way up perceive the glass ceiling as very real, but men in power do not agree. In one survey of women corporate vice presidents, 71 percent said there was a glass ceiling for women in their organization. However, 73 percent of the male chief executive officers in the same organizations said there was not (Federal Glass Ceiling Commission, 1998).

Making a Difference

Dolores Huerta (b. 1930) has been an activist in the farm workers' movement since 1955, fighting for the rights of California's migrant workers. With César Chavez in 1962, she founded a group now called the United Farm Workers (UFW), famous for their grape boycott and other strikes and political actions. Huerta has incredible stamina—she gave birth to eleven children, the first when she was 20 and the last at age 46, while carrying on a punishing schedule of union activities. And she rarely felt she had to make a choice between work and family. She loaded up her kids and took them with her whenever possible. Huerta's strength was never tested more than in 1988 when a 6'7" police officer brutally beat her at a political demonstration. She lost so much blood she was expected to die.

Largely because she is female, Huerta's role in the founding and success of the UFW has never been acknowledged in history books. Nevertheless, Huerta continues to struggle for workers' rights, bringing women's issues to the forefront now. In the early days of the UFW, Huerta kept a tally of the number of sexist remarks and jokes made by the male leaders at meetings. "At the end of the meeting, I'd say, 'During the course of this meeting you men have made 58 sexist remarks.' Pretty soon I'd have them down to 25, then 10, then 5." While there is still far to go, both men and women workers' rights have made substantial progress in the last thirty-five years, due in no small part to Huerta's efforts.

Source: Woman of the Year: For a lifetime of labor championing the rights of farmworkers. (1998, January/February) *Ms.*, 46–49.

Women's Work as Extension of Family Roles: "It's Only Natural"

The qualities valued in women—service, empathy, caretaking, sexual and intellectual flattery of men—keep women out of the top ranks of business, government, and professional life. These characteristics are feminine, but they are also subordinating (Lorber, 1993b; Miller, 1986). Many women's paid jobs are characterized by service to others in ways that are extensions of the unpaid work wives and mothers do (Nieva & Gutek, 1981). For example, secretaries were traditionally expected to provide personal services, such as serving coffee. In many ways, they were treated like "office wives" (Kanter, 1977). Many secretarial and clerical workers have protested employers' expectations of personal service and insisted that their jobs be defined in terms of skills.

Women provide food and cleaning services as waitresses and as staff in hotels, restaurants, and hospitals. Nurses are expected to provide tender loving care to patients, manage the unit like good housekeepers, and serve as subservient handmaidens to physicians (Cassell, 1997; Corley & Mauksch, 1988). Teachers provide emotional nurturance to young children, and social workers care for the poor and needy. The caring required in these jobs is usually stressed more than the skills (Nieva & Gutek, 1981).

Even when women and men are in equivalent jobs, such as corporate management, women are expected to be more caring and supportive than men, creating extra demands on their time and energy (Wajcman, 1998). Though it is expected, their caring is simultaneously devalued. For example, one psychologist who received excellent teaching evaluations was described by her department chair as being "mama-ish" and "charming" in the classroom—hardly the qualities valued by the tenure and promotion committee (Benokraitis, 1997)! Because caring fits into a feminine stereotype, it is often seen as a natural by-product of being female rather than an aspect of job competence. This contributes to the devaluation of women's work. If women perform certain functions "naturally," the reasoning goes, virtually any woman can do them, and they need not be rewarded by employers (Needleman & Nelson, 1988).

People who take care of zoo animals earn, on average, $2,500 a year more than those who take care of children in child-care centers. In 1993, the *highest* paid teachers at these centers, most of whom have college-level training in early childhood education, earned $15,488 a year. Ninety-five percent of child-care workers are women, and 33 percent are women of color (Murray, 1997; Noble, 1993). Because child care is seen as natural for women, and unnatural for men, male child-care workers are frequently questioned about why they chose this line of work and are suspected of being gay (Murray, 1997). But excluding men contributes to the continuing devaluation of caring. One researcher who studied women in social work, nursing, and education noted societal indifference to women's caring functions and asked about the future of these professions, "How much do we care about caring? And are we willing, as a society, to offer respect and a living wage to those who do it for us?" (Collins, 1988).

The Wage Gap

Women earn less money than men. This generalization holds for full- and part-time workers and white, African-American, Asian-American, and Hispanic women (Betz & Fitzgerald, 1987; England & McCreary, 1987; Kim, 1986; Nieva & Gutek, 1981; Russo & Denmark, 1984). Indeed, as Figure 11.4 shows, no group of women has a median income that comes close to the median income of white men. The difference holds for every level of education. Although young people are urged to get a college education to increase lifetime earnings, the financial payoff of education is much greater for men. Overall, women college graduates earn about $13,788 less annually than college-educated white men (National Committee on Pay Equity, 1998) (see Figure 11.5).

The gender gap in wages has decreased slightly over the past forty years. As shown in Figure 11.6, this is partly because women are earning more, and partly because men are earning less. Women now earn 74 cents for every dollar of men's earnings, and the earnings of African-American women are catching up to those of white women. But although these gains are encouraging, the gap between all women's earnings and those of white men is still very large (National Committee on Pay Equity, 1998). And 26 cents out of every dollar has huge life-time costs to women. If the current wage gap continues, a woman who is now 25 and works full-time for the next forty years will earn a lifetime total of $523,000 less than the average 25-year-old man. (You can check out your own loss on the Internet: go to *www.aflcio.org/woman,* key in your age, education, and current income, and the consequences of your personal wage gap will be calculated for you. But be careful—the numbers may be hazardous to your health!)

Why this large and persistent inequity in earnings? Many possible causes have been suggested. One traditional explanation is that women invest less in

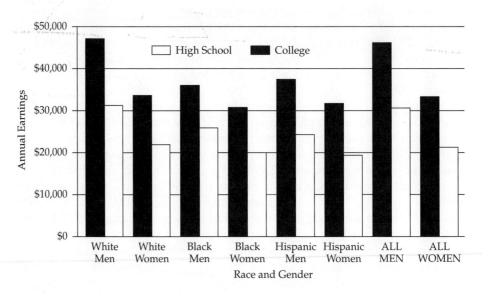

FIGURE 11.4. 1997 Median annual earnings by race, gender, and education.
Source: National Committee on Pay Equity, 1998.

FIGURE 11.5.
Source: © Steve Kelley. Used by permission of Copley News Service and Steve Kelley.

their work roles than men—they are less committed to their work, less likely to obtain extra training and education, more likely to be absent or to quit a job. However, little evidence exists to support these claims. On the contrary, the gender gap in earnings remains substantial when a number of variables such as education, absences, and years on the job are controlled (Betz & Fitzgerald, 1987; England & McCreary, 1987; Tsui, 1998; Valian, 1998; Wajcman, 1998). The individual investment hypothesis also does not explain why women's jobs that require high levels of education and skill pay less than men's jobs with lower requirements (Betz & Fitzgerald, 1987).

Another explanation focuses on the jobs rather than the gender of the worker—secretaries and clerks are paid less than electricians and truck drivers, and since more women choose to be secretaries and clerks, they earn less on average. It is certainly true that women are clustered in a few low-paying job sectors, but is this entirely a matter of choice? Moreover, there are substantial wage differences when women and men do exactly the same jobs. Female marketing managers earn 31 percent less; female elementary school teachers, 9 percent less; female sales clerks, 32 percent less; and female economists, 27 percent less than their male counterparts (National Committee on Pay Equity, 1998).

It is hard to escape the conclusion that men are paid more for whatever they do quite simply because they are men (Betz and Fitzgerald, 1987). The income discrepancy between women and men is part of a larger pattern of

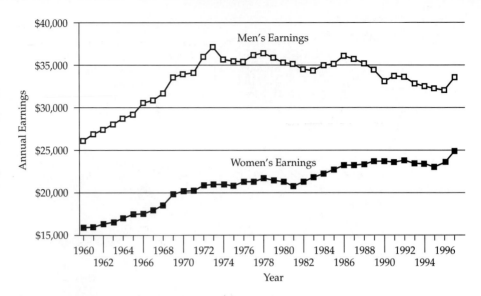

FIGURE 11.6. Median earnings of year-round full-time workers by sex, 1960–1997.
Source: National Committee on Pay Equity, 1998.

overvaluing whatever is male and undervaluing whatever is female (see Figure 11.7). A United Nations study (cited in Landrine & Klonoff, 1997) of 140 people who had sex-change operations even found that all the women who changed to men had higher salaries after the change, while all but two of the men who changed to women had much lower salaries!

What Are the Costs of Underemploying Women?

Workers are classified as underemployed when they are in jobs that do not fully use their education, skills, and abilities (Feldman, 1996). *Underemployment* in women has been little studied, although it is widespread (Nieva & Gutek, 1981). The sex-segregated and sex-stratified world of women clerical and service workers has been termed *pink-collar employment* (Howe, 1977). Most of the top ten occupations for women are low in status, are poorly paid, and offer few opportunities for advancement. This lack of opportunity translates into lower pensions and Social Security income for women in later life and contributes to a high poverty rate for older women (see Chapter 12).

Pink-collar work is frequently monotonous and unchallenging. Moreover, the worker has little decision-making power or autonomy; her task is to follow directions and complete her work to a supervisor's satisfaction. Pink-collar jobs do have some compensations or positive aspects. Many women report that they enjoy the company of coworkers and develop close friendships with them. Office birthday parties and sharing of family news and photographs are among the ways that women humanize the workplace and create solidarity with one another (Ferree, 1987).

The "women's professions" of nursing, social work, and teaching are very important to society and require both skill and dedication. More than most

FIGURE 11.7. Sex discrimination—the power of a good allegory.
Source: Copyright © 1993. Reprinted with special permission of North America Syndicate.

other jobs held by women, they offer intellectual challenge and the rewards of doing socially valued work. However, their educational requirements do not lead to high pay; rather, they are characterized by "learning without earning." Moreover, like other occupations with a high proportion of women they tend to lack clear avenues for advancement and autonomous working conditions (Betz & Fitzgerald, 1987).

When women (and people of color) are channeled into a narrow range of occupations that do not allow the full development of their unique skills or abilities, there is loss both to individuals and to society (Betz & Fitzgerald, 1987). Underemployment leads to poor job attitudes and lowered psychological well-being. Individuals may come to believe that the job they are "stuck" in is all they deserve and to suffer from decreased motivation to work (Feldman, 1996; Kanter, 1977). Society in general comes to accept the clustering of women into a few occupations as natural and inevitable, making future change difficult. And society loses much needed talent.

One of the most poignant examples of societal loss associated with underemployment of women comes from a well-known study of gifted children (Terman & Oden, 1959). More than 1,500 children with measured IQs over 135 were followed as they grew into adulthood. The boys almost invariably became prominent, respected professionals—as adults, they were scientists, authors, and college professors. The girls were most likely to become full-time homemakers; only about half held paid jobs, and the greatest number of these were schoolteachers and secretaries.

The researcher, Louis Terman, came to recognize the waste of talent that his results demonstrated, remarking of the gifted women in his study that "After marriage they fall into the domestic role. . . . The woman who is a potential poet, novelist, lawyer, physician, or scientist usually gives up any professional ambition she may have had and devotes herself to home, husband, and children . . . robbing the arts and sciences of a large fraction of the genius that might otherwise be dedicated to them. My data strongly suggest that this loss must be debited to motivational causes and limited opportunity rather than to lack of ability" (Seagoe, 1975). Terman's sample reached adulthood in the 1950s. Would gifted girls growing up today still be less likely than gifted boys to achieve their fullest potential? Unfortunately, research done in the 1980s and 1990s still shows that substantial numbers of gifted and talented young women underrate their own ability, lower their career goals during high school and college, and are less likely to achieve a high-status professional career than gifted boys (Reddin, 1997).

DOING GENDER IN THE WORKPLACE

Women's position in the workplace is not just a static aspect of social structure. Rather, it is continually enacted and remade as people make workplace decisions influenced by gender. Sexism in the world of work operates in many ways, both subtle and overt. Psychological research contributes to our understanding of the dynamics of gender in the workplace by providing experiments and field studies that identify the conditions and circumstances of discrimination.

As described in Chapter 3, judgments about other people are affected by gender in many ways and affect others' behavior in turn:

- *Attributional biases* lead to different explanations of women's and men's behavior.
- Gender functions as a *status cue,* with men being accorded higher status.
- Gender distinctions maintain social boundaries.

Let's look at how these cognitive and social processes affect working women.

Attributions for Success and Failure

When faced with an example of a woman or man who has succeeded at some achievement, people very often come up with different reasons to explain her or his success. As described in Chapter 3, men's success is more likely to be seen as the result of high ability—"He succeeded because he's talented or smart." Women's success is more likely to be attributed to luck (Deaux & Emswiller, 1974). When the task is one that can't be attributed entirely to luck (e.g., becoming a physician), people are still reluctant to judge women equal to men in ability. Instead, they attribute the woman's success more to hard work (Feldman-Summers & Kiesler, 1974).

How do people explain situations in which a male or female attempts achievement but fails? Several studies show that they are likely to blame a woman's failure on lack of ability and a man's failure on bad luck or the quirks of the situation, such as an unusually difficult task (Cash, Gillen, & Burns, 1977; Etaugh & Brown, 1975). Sexism seems to interact with racism when people make judgments about others' success (Yarkin et al., 1982).

Sexism and racism in explaining others' achievements is not universal. Managers (both female and male) who have more positive attitudes toward women in business generally are less likely to make attributions based on stereotypes (Garland, Hale, & Burnson, 1982). Nevertheless, it is easy to see how the typical pattern of attributing males' successes to ability and females' to luck disadvantages women in the workplace. A manager is probably far more likely to hire or promote someone who is perceived as highly able than someone who just got lucky. Similarly, an employer might view an isolated failure as a confirmation of a woman's lack of ability but as only a temporary setback for a man. The assumption behind the typical pattern of attribution seems to be that men are basically competent; whether they succeed or fail, that belief remains intact. Women and people of color, on the other hand, are basically incompetent, and that belief, too, can be maintained whether they succeed or fail.

Devaluing Women's Performance

"Are women prejudiced against women?" is a question asked in a study that set off a wave of research on how people judge the performance of women versus men (Goldberg, 1968). Female college students were asked to rate several professional articles on their quality and importance to their field. Some of the articles were from stereotypically female professions, such as dietetics; others from stereotypically male professions, such as city planning; and others from relatively gender-neutral areas. Each article was prepared in two versions, as though written either by "John MacKay" or "Joan MacKay." Except for the authors' names, the two versions of each article were identical.

The students rated the articles more highly when they thought they had been written by a man, including even the articles from "feminine" fields. Other researchers found that male raters showed similar prejudice (Paludi & Bauer, 1983; Paludi & Strayer, 1985). Gender bias isn't always found—it interacts with other factors, and sometimes the work of women and men ends up being evaluated similarly (Nieva & Gutek, 1981; Wallston & O'Leary, 1981). Sometimes highly competent performance by a woman may actually be evaluated more positively than comparable performance by a man—as though female competence has more value because it is unexpected (Abramson, Goldberg, Greenberg, & Abramson, 1977). (This has been called the *talking platypus phenomenon*. The platypus is not judged by how well it talks, but by the fact that it can talk at all.)

In general, though, many laboratory studies from the 1960s to the present make a convincing case that devaluation of work attributed to a woman is common. Studies in real job settings, too, report this problem. Combined with the attributional biases just discussed, it affects how women are treated every day at work. "Over and over again in many studies, women report that their comments and suggestions are ignored or ridiculed; that men making the identical comments receive praise whereas they do not, and that they are excluded from meetings, networks, lunches and other activities that are part of the 'old boy' network and of the road to career advancement" (Landrine & Klonoff, 1997, p. 11). Even women in positions of power experience this kind of sexism; studies of women who work as professors, surgeons, attorneys, police officers, and firefighters show that they face hostile and dismissive treatment at work (Cassell, 1997; Haslett & Lipman, 1997; Lott & Rocchio, 1997) (see Chapter 3). For women of color, sexism may be compounded by racism. In a study of a matched sample of 200 African-American and white women in professional and managerial positions, the majority of both groups reported differential treatment at work due to their gender, and a majority of the African-American women also perceived differential treatment due to their race (Weber & Higginbotham, 1997).

Discrimination in Hiring and Promotion

Sex discrimination in employment has been illegal since 1964, when the Civil Rights Act was passed. Before that time, many employers discriminated as a matter of policy. For example, AT&T allowed women to work only up to certain levels and in a limited range of tasks (Gutek & Larwood, 1987). Although employers may no longer refuse to hire or promote applicants because of race or gender, a great deal of informal discrimination still occurs. For example, 37 percent of women in a recent Australian study said they had been discriminated against in promotion decisions (Snizek & Neil, 1992). In a U.S. sample of more than 1,200 women, over 40 percent said that at some time in their lives they had been denied a raise, a promotion, or some other deserved reward at work because they were women. One in five (and more women of color than white women) had experienced such discrimination within the past year (Landrine & Klonoff, 1997). Sexism today is unfortunately alive and well; however, unlike sexism of the past, it is more likely to be subtle than blatant. Often, it is not even intentional (Benokraitis, 1997).

A classic study of gender bias in hiring used psychologists themselves as the participants. Fictitious sets of credentials for psychologists were sent to psychology department chairpersons, who were asked to indicate how likely they would be to hire the individual described and what level of job they might offer. Although the chairpersons were not aware of it (each saw only one set), the fictitious credentials were identical except for the gender of the applicant. When the chairpersons thought they were evaluating a female psychologist, "she" was rated less favorably and considered qualified for a lower-level position than when "he" was evaluated (Fidell, 1970). Many other studies have shown similar biases; equally qualified women are less likely to be hired or are offered lower-paying, less desirable jobs (Betz & Fitzgerald, 1987; Fitzgerald & Betz, 1983; Nieva & Gutek, 1981).

In addition to gender discrimination, lesbians may also face discrimination on the basis of sexual orientation. They may be fired, not hired, or not promoted due to stereotypes about lesbians being maladjusted, mentally ill, or child molesters. In a survey of 203 lesbians in a metropolitan area (mainly white collar, middle class, and highly educated), 25 percent reported specific instances of formal or informal discrimination, including being fired or forced to resign when their personal life became known. Others were denied raises or promotions. Informal discrimination included taunts, gossip, ridicule, social rejection, and even physical violence (Levine & Leonard, 1984). In several large-sample surveys, between 13 percent and 62 percent of lesbian and gay adults reported that they had experienced employment discrimination (Badgett, 1996).

Because of heterosexism, the majority of lesbians remain "in the closet" at work (Levine & Leonard, 1984). Being "out" in the workplace is linked to greater job satisfaction: Lesbians and gay men who are out to their coworkers are more satisfied with their jobs and interpersonal relationships at work than those who are not (Driscoll, Kelley, & Fassinger, 1996; Ellis, 1996). On the other hand, it may lead to increased discrimination, even losing a job (Croteau, 1996; Fassinger, 1996). Staying closeted also constrains gays and lesbians from speaking out against heterosexual privilege in the workplace. The "out-or-not" decision is a classic double bind!

Progress is being made in this area. Employers ranging from Microsoft to Ben & Jerry's (and including the American Psychological Association) are increasingly providing health insurance and other benefits for same-gender couples (Spielman & Winfeld, 1996). However, gay and lesbian civil rights and workplace equity are by no means assured (Baber & Allen, 1992).

Unfortunately, patterns of discrimination are often very hard to see. For example, if you are a woman with a bachelor's degree who has been with a company for five years and you are not promoted, you might compare yourself with a male coworker who was promoted. Suppose this man has been with the company for only three years but he has a master's degree: It's hard to decide whether or not you have been discriminated against. But suppose you look further in the company and find a man who was promoted with only a high school diploma and ten years of service and a woman who was not promoted with two years of college and eight years of service. A pattern begins to form. But that pattern is apparent only when many cases are averaged, and discrimination is usually examined one case at a time (Crosby, 1994; Crosby, Clayton, Alksnis, & Hemker, 1986).

Even when people know that their group as a whole is discriminated against, they often persist in believing that they themselves have never been affected (see Chapter 3). This is true not only for women in general but for other disadvantaged groups like lesbians and working-class people. Like ostriches who keep their heads in the sand, people often deny that gender bias and discrimination affect them (Crosby, Pufall, Snyder, O'Connell, & Whalen, 1989).

Discrimination is not inevitable or invariable. It depends on a complex set of influences that have been studied systematically by psychologists and *can* be changed. By showing how discrimination works, psychological research can help point the way to change.

How can gender bias in hiring and promotion be eliminated? Both individuals and organizations must change (Valian, 1998):

- Ensure that women's performance is accurately evaluated by teaching people about attributional biases.
- Develop clear, specific criteria for performance evaluation and make people responsible for meeting the criteria.
- Allow enough time and attention for performance evaluations. The quicker and more automatic the decision making, the more people rely on cognitive biases that disadvantage women.
- Increase the number of women in the pool, which reduces the salience of gender.

- Appoint leaders who are committed to gender equity. Employees do "follow the leader." Consistent organizational messages that fair play is expected decrease gender discrimination in organizations.
- Develop clear institutional policies about gender equity, and make sure they are consistently implemented.

Parallel changes are also needed to eliminate bias due to race, ethnic group, sexual orientation, age, disability, and other dimensions of disadvantage.

Social Reactions to "Uppity Women"

Women in corporate management and professional careers are likely to work mostly with men. What is it like to be virtually the only woman on the job?

As discussed in Chapter 3, how women are treated in male-dominated work settings may have as much to do with their rarity as their gender (see Figure 11.8). The social construction of women as different from men is a major way of maintaining male power in the workplace (Wajcman, 1998). The same dynamics work for other disadvantaged groups, too. The "odd person," whether black, Hispanic, disabled, or female, encounters a predictable set of problems. She or he becomes a *token*, a symbol of all members of her group.

Marian Pour-El, a mathematician, described her reception as a graduate student in the math department at Harvard in the 1970s:

> I recall very vividly my first day in class: three seats in front of me, three seats in back of me, and two seats on either side were left vacant. I was a complete pariah in that social setting. . . .
>
> My first colloquium at Harvard University was a memorable event. The tea, which preceded the actual lecture, was held in the library and was a rather formal affair. As I entered, all eyes sank lower into the teacups in a great effort not to seem to notice me. Needless to say, no one talked to me at all. At the end of the tea the chairman . . . turned to me and said with a twinkle in his eye, "Your presence is noted here." (Pour-El, 1974, p. 36)

Another woman, a medical school student in the 1980s, described her first encounter with her faculty adviser:

> My first day in the OR with him, I walked in. . . . So he was in this big surgery and I stood behind him and I didn't want to bother him, you know. . . . He has a big reputation for being an excellent surgeon. . . . I had been sitting back there for half an hour watching him and he suddenly turns his head but doesn't look at me and he says, "Who are you?" So I introduced myself. . . . He says, "Dammit, another woman!" and then he says, "And a Chink, too! . . . Killed a lot of them in the war." (Reddin, 1997, pp. 113–114)

Because tokens are highly visible in the organization, they feel a great deal of performance pressure. The token woman or black management trainee may be deliberately and publicly displayed to prove that the company is complying with affirmative-action policies or asked to give speeches about the progress made by women and blacks in industry. One woman commented about this treatment, "If it seems good to be noticed, wait until you make your first major mistake" (Kanter, 1977, p. 213).

FIGURE 11.8. Affirmative distraction.
Source: NOW Times.

When a white male employee makes a mistake, it is interpreted as an individual error and no more; if the token woman or minority makes a similar mistake, it is taken as evidence that "those people" should not have been hired and are bound to fail. Paradoxically, tokens must also worry about being too successful. Since all eyes are on the token, if she performs well enough to "show up" members of the dominant group she will be criticized for being a workaholic or "too aggressive." Tokens are usually very eager to fit in, so they do not challenge the values and practices of the men in power—indeed, they may outdo the men in enforcing the status quo, becoming "queen bees" who reject other women (Lorber, 1993b). To sum up, the token position is highly stressful and ambivalent (see Box 11.2).

Box 11.2 The Effects of Tokenism: A Case Study

Social psychologist Janice Yoder has written a moving description of her experiences as a visiting faculty member at a U.S. military academy. Yoder's token status was extreme on several dimensions: She was one of sixteen women among 545 faculty members, 97 percent of whom were military officers. Her visibility, isolation, and relegation to negative roles were correspondingly extreme:

My differences as a civilian, a researcher, and a woman created uncertainty among my colleagues and threatened to disrupt the team. . . . I frequently was isolated from group discussions. . . . One subgroup (of the department) dubbed itself the "Wolf Gang," used "We eat sheep!" as their motto, and howled when called upon to make group presentations. The departmental theme song chosen was "Macho Man," hardly appropriate for an academic department that included two female officers and myself. The gossip about my sexuality ranged from lesbian to heterosexually promiscuous. . . .

I was assigned to one of two female roles: "wife" or "feminist/libber." In the former role, I was invited to a luncheon for wives. . . . While this was mildly amusing, the effects of my second label as "feminist/libber" were not. . . . I watched as my colleagues began to get restless when I raised my hand, rolled their eyes as I spoke, and concluded by ignoring. . . . I became totally ineffectual, yet unwilling to keep quiet and thus implicitly condone these actions. My role as a deviate became predictable, unwelcome, and ignored. (pp. 64–65)

Yoder described the psychological effects of token treatment in a journal entry made after only three months of such treatment:

What does happen to the deviate? The deviate can convert, but short of a sex-change operation . . . and a personality overhaul, conversion seems out of the question for me. . . . What can I do? Yet, the failure is placed squarely on my shoulders. "What's wrong with you?" "Why can't you get along?" These questions haunt me, undermining my self-image to a point where I am reduced to crying at home alone at night. . . . I feel impotent, I can't sleep, but I am never clear-headed and fully awake. I have an eye infection. Daily problems have become insurmountable difficulties. . . . I can't work. I can't go out and have fun. . . . I have become bad in my eyes; the attributions of blame have been internalized. (p. 66)

Janice Yoder resigned from her visiting professorship after one semester.

Source: From Yoder, "An academic woman as a token: A case study," *Journal of Social Issues, 41,* 61–72. Copyright © 1985 Plenum Publishing Corporation. Reprinted with permission.

Women and minorities are much more likely than white men to experience token status. However, as noted in Chapter 3, when white men are the tokens, they do not encounter negative treatment. Male nursing students did not differ from females on measures of social isolation, performance pressure, and so on (Snavely & Fairhurst, 1984). In a field study of work groups in an amusement park, only female tokens were negatively evaluated. In fact, male tokens advanced more quickly than nontokens (Yoder & Sinnett, 1985). These results are intriguing—is there a double standard even for tokenism?

How can women tokens become more respected and effective? A recent study reaffirms that just getting the job and having the expertise to do it are not enough. When women were appointed leaders of all-male task groups and supplied with task-relevant expertise to help them lead the groups, they still were not very successful or appreciated as leaders. Only when a male experimenter specifically told group members that the woman leader had special training and useful information for their task was the woman able to be effective (Yoder, Schleicher, & McDonald, 1998). This study suggests that women's leadership still needs to be given legitimacy by high-status men.

Mentors and Role Models

Role models are members of one's own reference group who are visibly success-ful (Yoder, Adams, Grove, & Priest, 1985). Just knowing that other women have managed to overcome the obstacles to success may help the newcomer deal with her conflicts and prepare for the challenges to come (Basow & Howe, 1980; O'Connell & Russo, 1980). For example, female graduate students who had female professors as role models described themselves as more ca-reer oriented, confident, instrumental, and satisfied with their student role than those who had male role models (Gilbert, Galessich, & Evans, 1983).

While white men are exposed to many role models, women and minority men have had few. Lack of role models probably contributes to loneliness and feelings of deviance. Adding a few token women to the workplace does not solve the role model problem. In fact, pressures to be role models for others add to the other pressures on the token. One woman, who was the only female faculty member in a fifty-member university department of economics, put the dilemma clearly: "I feel I can't do anything wrong because it will be attributed to my sex and not to me. I know that in schools where there are women econo-mists on the faculty, more women major in economics and more go on to grad-uate school. But I can't be a role model for everybody, and I can't do it alone" (Crawford, 1978, p. 93).

Role models may be admired from afar, while *mentors* are people who take a personal interest in the newcomer (Yoder et al., 1985). Knowing the formal rules in a workplace is rarely enough. Whether you are working in a corpora-tion, factory, hospital, or office, there is inside knowledge about how to get ahead that is never written down in the employee manual. Instead, workers rely on informal social networks to work "the system" to their advantage (Lorber, 1993b). Successful older men frequently serve as mentors to young men on their way up, providing them with introductions to important people, special training, and hints on how to bypass the bureaucracy. They may also stand up for the young man if he makes a controversial decision and empower him simply by associating with him.

Women workers lack access to this *old-boy network,* with its "bands of brothers" who look out for each other's interests (Lorber, 1993b). As one fe-male corporate executive put it:

> It's always been men at the top of this company and the top of the company I was in before. They all know each other. They've all come up the same route together, all boys together. Now the only way to get into senior management is to know people in the senior management clique, but how can you know them when you are invisible? (Wajcman, 1998, p. 97)

Having a mentor increases job satisfaction and success. For example, a study of 171 female attorneys showed that those who had had mentors were more successful and satisfied in their careers than those who had not (Riley & Wrench, 1985). Having a white man as mentor is especially beneficial. In one study, graduates of business administration (MBA) programs who had established a mentoring relationship with a white man earned $16,840 more annually than those who did not. Having a woman or a minority man for a mentor had no effect on salary. Not surprisingly, African-American and Hispanic graduates of both genders, and white women, were less likely to have white male mentors (Dreher & Cox, 1996).

High-status men are reluctant to mentor women. Quite simply, they feel more comfortable with people they perceive as similar to themselves. Also, young women may not always have realized the importance of finding mentors, believing instead that hard work and playing by the rules will guarantee success (Kanter, 1977; Nieva & Gutek, 1981). What about women mentoring other women? In the past, only a few women were in positions that would allow them to be mentors for other women, and the pressures of their own token status may have prevented them from reaching out (Yoder et al., 1985). The scarcity of mentors is probably easing, as *old-girl networks* have grown to provide women with advantages traditionally available to men. For example, the Psychology of Women Division of the American Psychological Association has a volunteer program that matches beginning researchers with accomplished ones for mentoring and encouragement. And a national E-mail mentoring network, "MentorNet," now offers opportunities for women in engineering, math and science to connect with supportive experts of both genders in their fields *(http://www.mentornet.net)*. Although female and male mentors may provide much the same practical benefits and advantages to women, women may be better mentors for women in the areas of creating a professional self-image, empowerment, and supportive personal counseling (Burke & McKeen, 1997; Gaskill, 1991; Gilbert & Rossman, 1992).

Leadership: Do Women Do It Differently?

Stereotypes, cognitive biases and social structural factors make it harder for women to achieve positions of leadership. But once they are in leadership positions, do women lead differently from men? This question is grounded in more general debates about difference (see Chapter 4). If women are indeed more relationally oriented, that fundamental gender difference may affect the style and effectiveness of their leadership. Let's look at the research.

Research on leadership style indicates that, contrary to stereotype, there are no large, dramatic gender differences. In a meta-analysis of 370 previous comparisons, women were somewhat more democratic and participative leaders than men. However, the difference was dependent on the situation—for example, it was larger in laboratory studies than real-life settings (Eagly & Johnson, 1990).

Are women more effective as leaders? Effectiveness is usually defined as how well the leader helps the group reach its stated goals. A meta-analysis of seventy-six studies of leadership effectiveness showed that there were no gender differences except in the military, where men were more effective (Eagly et al., 1995). Again, the effect of situation is apparent—military leadership takes place in an extremely masculine-stereotyped realm where women are a small minority of each work group. In another measure of effectiveness, studies of woman-owned businesses (reviewed by Hooijberg & DiTomaso, 1996) show that they are equally likely to survive and thrive as businesses owned by men.

In summary, the evidence suggests that, once women are legitimated as leaders, they behave similarly to men in the same kinds of positions and they are equally likely to succeed. As more and more women enter formerly masculine domains such as management, the professions and public service, the salience of gender will diminish in leadership contexts. Already, women have served as presidents or prime ministers of countries as diverse as Sri Lanka, Turkey, Ireland, Great Britain, Bangladesh, and Norway. In the United States, although there has never been a woman president, public officials such as Secretary of State Madeleine Albright and Attorney General Janet Reno offer visible evidence of women's leadership abilities.

WOMEN'S CAREER DEVELOPMENT: ARE THERE OBSTACLES FROM WITHIN?

So far our discussion of obstacles to women's job and career satisfaction has focused on forces in the social environment. We now turn to psychological factors—individual differences in beliefs, values, motives, and choices.

Do Women Have Limited Expectations?

In Chapter 3, we noted that women often do not feel *entitled* to equality. They know that gender discrimination is pervasive but deny that it has ever happened to them (Crosby, 1984). They pay themselves less than men in laboratory experiments, even though they do equal or better work (Jost, 1997; Major, 1994). When they achieve positions of power, they may continue to question the legitimacy of their authority even though they know they are competent (Apfelbaum, 1993). In an interesting real-life example of entitlement, professional tennis player Monica Seles in 1991 proposed that the prize money in tennis tournaments should be the same for women and men. However, two other women pro players responded for the press: Steffi Graf said, "We make enough, we don't need more," and Mary Jo Fernandez, "I'm happy with what we have; I don't think we should be greedy" (Bailey, 1991, cited in Valian, 1998). These two women interpreted simple equality as "more than enough" and "greedy." Compare this with the entitlement of male professional athletes!

Why do women have low expectations for their career options? The answer may lie partly in early gender socialization. Restrictive, gender-stereotyped ideas about what kinds of jobs are appropriate for women are formed very early and reinforced by media bias. The good news is that gender-linked perceptions about jobs are decreasing and can be reduced by educational programs for children and teens (Phillips & Imhoff, 1997). Also, low expectations probably occur partly because women are aware of the social obstacles described earlier. If a woman suspects that her attempt at a career may lead to devaluation of her competence, the stresses of being a token, sexual harassment, discrimination, and social rejection, she may give up her high aspirations. These effects are compounded for women of color, who also may experience racism (Mays, Coleman, & Jackson, 1996).

Women's low expectations may also reflect the fact that people learn to aspire to what they see around them. With few role models of women scientists, executives, and public leaders, girls and women may find it difficult to aim for these goals (England & McCreary, 1987). If women do not feel entitled to equality, it is because they are responding to pervasive cultural norms.

Do Women Have Different Values and Interests?

Perhaps women and men differ in their work roles because they have different values. Do women workers want and need different rewards than men? Do they end up in feminized occupations because these occupations fit with their personal values? A great deal of research (reviewed by Betz & Fitzgerald, 1987; Nieva & Gutek, 1981) has attempted to answer these questions.

In general, women and men in similar jobs do not differ in their need for *intrinsic* rewards (those that come from actually doing the job, such as a sense of accomplishment and feeling that the work is meaningful). Both women and men, especially those employed in high-status occupations such as medicine and management, report that it is important that their careers meet these needs. However, when women and men are compared on *extrinsic* rewards (those that come after the job is done or as a by-product of the job), there are some differences. Men are more likely to say that pay and promotion are important, while women place higher value on a pleasant working environment—friendly coworkers, comfortable surroundings, ease of transportation, and so forth; often, they create a work environment of interpersonal caring and involvement by sharing aspects of their personal lives with coworkers (Ferree, 1987). Perhaps women value comfort and friendliness on the job more than men because many women leave paid work at the end of the day for a second full-time job of homemaking and child care. A more comfortable and pleasant day in paid work may help them stretch their energy for the second shift.

Women's and men's values seem to be becoming less gender differentiated, especially when they occupy similar positions. In a recent study of senior managers of multinational corporations, women and men agreed that "a sense of achievement" and "enjoying the job" were their most important motives. In fact, they were in agreement on every motive they were asked about—respect from colleagues, developing other people, meeting goals, and so on. The only gender differences were that women were slightly more likely than men to care about having power and slightly less likely to care about money (Wajcman, 1998). Other studies, too, show that women and men in the same occupation or profession are remarkably alike in their values and motives about work (Valian, 1998).

While values may help determine one's occupational setting, the occupational setting may also affect one's values. When a person is given opportunities to advance, he or she is likely to develop positive attitudes and values, such as a strong work commitment and high aspirations for promotions and raises. A person placed in a job with little upward mobility tends to become indifferent, to complain, and to look for extrinsic satisfactions. Thus, the social structure of the workplace is a powerful force in shaping values and behavior. But its effects are often overlooked. When women in dead-end jobs develop poor attitudes, these attitudes are sometimes seen as characteristic of women as a group instead of a human response to blocked opportunities. As one organizational researcher put it, "What the clerical worker with low motivation to be promoted might need is a promotion; what the chronic complainer might need is a growthful challenge. But who would be likely to give it to them?" (Kanter, 1977, p. 158).

Math and Computing: Still Barriers?

Many of the best career opportunities in American society today require a background in mathematics and computer technology. These include jobs in engineering, science and medicine, computer science, business, technical fields, and skilled trades (Betz & Fitzgerald, 1987). As discussed in Chapter 4, math is stereotyped as a male domain, and many girls lose confidence and interest in doing it. Girls are also socialized to like computers less than boys do (see Chapter 6). People who lack a math/technology background tend to be limited to a small range of potential career fields. Possible remedies for this problem include educating girls to understand that math is necessary to many careers, including ones that offer high pay and challenging work; requiring four years of math in high school for all students; special math, science, and computer conferences for junior high and high school girls to stimulate interest; educating girls in all-girls' schools; providing girls with stories and pictures of female role models in math and computing; and helping teachers create a positive classroom climate for girls (Betz & Fitzgerald, 1987; Eccles, 1989; Sadker & Sadker, 1994).

In a study of more than 700 workers in university faculty, clerical and administrative jobs that require computer and technology-related skills, the male faculty had more computer experience, used more different applications, and were less anxious and intimidated by computers. However, among the clerical workers, these gender differences were reversed, suggesting that it is not computer use in itself but the gendered meaning of computers in different jobs that creates difficulties for women (Harrison, Rainer, & Hochwarter, 1997).

Are Women Less Motivated to Achieve?

For more than forty years, psychologists have explored the question of why some people strive for success in situations involving a standard of excellence (McClelland, Atkinson, Clark, & Lowell, 1953). A person who is high in achievement motivation will strive to excel when the motivation is aroused. Achievement behaviors of any sort—from running a marathon to winning a beauty contest—could theoretically be predicted by one's score on an achievement-motivation measure. For research purposes, however, scores were used to predict performance in academic settings and competitive games in the laboratory.

Early research showed that achievement-motivation scores were able to predict the achievement behavior of men but not women. Reflecting the strong masculinist bias of research at that time, the intriguing question of why women behaved less predictably than men was not explored further (Unger, 1979a). Do women and men really differ in achievement motivation? Although the different response patterns of women were interpreted as a lack of motivation (Veroff, Wilcox, & Atkinson, 1953), the issue is more complex. Achievement motivation is now thought to have several dimensions: *mastery,* or liking challenge; *work,* liking to work hard; and *competitiveness* (Helmreich & Spence, 1978; Spence & Helmreich, 1983). Both women and men who are instrumentally oriented score higher on all dimensions, especially competitiveness. In other words, people of both genders whose backgrounds lead them to be oriented toward acting on the environment tend to be higher in all aspects of achievement motivation. This sort of background is, of course, more often provided for males in our society, so it is not surprising that overall, men score higher on mastery and competitiveness. Women score higher on the desire to work hard. These differences are small, however, compared with the differences between people in different occupational groups.

An alternative way to study achievement motivation is to interview people in depth about their goals and their efforts to achieve them. This approach has the advantage of allowing research participants to define achievement in their own terms. Women's and men's own definitions of achievement are much broader than just employment or academic success (Gravenkemper & Paludi, 1983). In one study using biographical interviews of women ranging in age from their twenties to their eighties, the women's goals reflected their age and life stage. In addition to academic success, many mentioned "being independent" and "having successful relationships." Although they valued achievement, 96 percent of the women reported that they had wondered whether their achievements were worth the costs to themselves and their families (Paludi & Fankell-Hauser, 1986).

Today, researchers in achievement motivation recognize that men and women have similar motives overall. However, those motives are channeled and expressed within a gendered society. Rather than showing that women are less motivated to achieve than men, the research has shown that the complexities of motivation cannot be understood without considering gender socialization in both women and men (Canter, 1982; Sutherland & Veroff, 1985).

EXCEPTIONAL WORK LIVES

Achievement in the Professions: From Pink Collar to White

Until recently, women professionals were largely found in education, social work, and nursing. One woman remembered that "It never occurred to me to be anything but a teacher; medicine and law were not for girls. But I have often wondered why I did not consider medicine. I remember being in the top of the class in physiology and anatomy, competing with boys who later became M.D.s"(Peterson, 1974, p. 78). Like this woman, who later became a university teacher, many women have built careers of distinction after being channeled into "women's" professions (Collins, 1988). Today many women continue to enter these professions. Meanwhile, others are entering formerly masculine professions—law, medicine, psychology, science and engineering, the military, and business management (Jacobs, 1992; Stevens & Gardner, 1987). Between 1980 and 1990, women went from a minority to earning nearly 60 percent of the Ph.D.'s awarded in psychology, for example (Farmer, 1997). Women have gone from 3 percent of all attorneys in the 1970s to about 25 percent in the 1990s (Valian, 1998). The most dramatic increase is in the number of African-American women in white-collar and professional corporate jobs. They are entering management at almost twice the rate of African-American men (Gaiter, 1994).

What Factors Affect Women's Career Development?

Because of the obstacles, relatively few women have achieved professional success. Yet, despite the odds, some women do. How are these women different? What factors in their personalities and backgrounds make the difference between them and their nonachieving peers? Researchers have been interested in answering these questions. Although high-achieving women are few in number, they are an important group. They provide potential role models for other women. Their backgrounds suggest ways to bring up girls without limiting their aspirations and development, and their achievements represent the possibility of breaking down sex segregation and sex stratification in the workplace. If a few women can "make it," a world of equal power and status for all women and men becomes easier to imagine.

In general, high-achieving women come from backgrounds that provide them with a relatively unconstricted sense of self and an enriched view of women's capabilities (Lemkau, 1979, 1983). Their families and their upbringing are unusual in positive ways, as shown in Table 11.1. As social learning theory would predict, girls who are exposed to less gender-stereotyped expectations are more likely to become high achievers. Attending all-girls' schools and women's colleges can provide role models, opportunities for leadership, and a woman-centered learning environment. Not surprisingly, parents play

TABLE 11.1. Characteristics Associated with Achievement in Women

Individual variables	*Background variables*
High ability	Working mother
Liberated sex role values	Supportive father
Instrumentality	Highly educated parents
Androgynous personality	Female role models
High self-esteem	Work experience as adolescent
Strong academic self-concept	Androgynous upbringing
Educational variables	*Adult lifestyles variables*
Higher education	Late marriage or single
Continuation in mathematics	No or few children
Girls' schools and women's colleges	

Source: From Betz & Fitzgerald, *The Career Psychology of Women*, p. 143. Copyright © 1987 Academic Press. Reprinted by permission.

an important role. Employed mothers—especially when they enjoy their work and are successful at it—provide an important model for achievement. Since fathers usually encourage gender typing in their children more than mothers do and usually have more family power, a father who supports and encourages his daughter's achievements may be especially influential (Weitzman, 1979). One black woman who became a distinguished physician has provided an eloquent description of her parents' belief in her:

> As a woman, I was told, I would be able to do whatever I wanted. I was taught that my skin had a beautiful color. This constant, implicit reinforcement of positive self-image was my parents' most valuable gift to me. I grew up loving my color and enjoying the fact that I was a woman. . . . In school, I performed well because my mother and father expected it of me. When I entered high school, I elected the college preparatory program as a matter of course.
>
> What happened next is, tragically even today, all too familiar to blacks. A faculty adviser called me in. In her hand was the (college prep course schedule). The courses I had elected were crossed out, and substituted with a Home Economics curriculum. I took the paper home. . . . When my mother saw it she was outraged. Together, we went back to the school to face the adviser . . . (who) attempted to placate my mother. "Mrs. Texiera," she pleaded, "what is a colored girl going to do with college? If she learns cooking and sewing, she can always get a good job." But when we left the office, I was enrolled in the college course. (Hunter, 1974, pp. 58–59)

Setting high goals and persisting despite setbacks are important factors in women's career development. In a longitudinal study, high school girls (of diverse ethnicities) who expressed interest in math/science careers in 1980 were followed up to thirteen years later. Those who had achieved their goals had taken more elective math and science in high school, set high goals for themselves, and stressed how important it is to "hang in there" when difficulties arise. Those who had experienced their parents' divorce were especially motivated to be financially independent because they had seen what happens to women who have to support their children on their own. Among the group that had not achieved their goals, some were stopped by family socialization (they were taught that the most important goal for a woman is marriage) or critical life events such as an unplanned pregnancy (Farmer et al, 1997). In a survey of more than 200 African-American women attorneys, 80 percent said that their families and teachers had encouraged them to work hard and set high goals. They also said they had benefited from having access to black women role models and to equal opportunity programs (Simpson, 1996).

The personalities and values of high-achieving women are nontraditional. They have a high and healthy level of self-esteem and liberal opinions about women's roles. They describe themselves as independent, assertive, and rational. The latter traits, of course, are labeled masculine in our society. But these women do not fit the stereotype of the aggressive masculine woman who sacrifices femininity for success. They also see themselves as warm, expressive, and nurturing.

The research summarized in Table 11.1 has been very useful in helping psychologists understand the dynamics of achievement in women, but it does have limitations. Obviously, all these characteristics are not true of all high-achieving women. Some women who do not have any of them manage to succeed anyway, and some even report having been spurred on by a disapproving parent or an attempt to hold them back (Weitzman, 1979). In one study, black and white women who came from poor families where neither parent had finished high school were extensively interviewed. Despite their disadvantaged backgrounds, these women had achieved extraordinary success in business, academia, or government service. The biggest difference between them and a comparison group of women from middle-class backgrounds with similar achievement levels was that the "odds-defying" achievers had an unusually strong belief in their ability to control their lives. They believed that "You can do anything if you put your mind to it" (Boardman, Harrington, & Horowitz, 1987).

Studying the factors leading to success by looking at successful women is an example of *retrospective research* in which participants look back at factors influencing them at an earlier time. It can show us what characteristics successful women tend to share. However, it can also lead us to assume that we know the *causes* of success when we may be observing its *results*. In other words, women who—for whatever reason—have the opportunity to test themselves in a demanding career may develop high self-esteem, assertiveness, independence, and achievement motivation as a *consequence* of their success. From this perspective, opportunity creates a "successful" personality, rather than vice versa (Kanter, 1977). Retrospective memory is not always accurate, either. Successful women may remember more achievement emphasis in their backgrounds than nonachieving women simply because this dimension is relevant to them as adults (Nieva & Gutek, 1981).

As they are growing up, girls and young women continually make choices, both consciously and unconsciously, about how they will spend their time and efforts. Achievement-related choices are made in a complex social context. They are affected by many factors, from outright discrimination to gender socialization. The individual's *expectations of success* (If I take this math course, will I pass?) and the *subjective value* of various options (Do I enjoy English more than math? Will I really need math for my chosen career?) strongly affect decision making. Such expectancies and values are shaped by parental attributions (My daughter got an A in math because she works hard, my son because he's bright), gender-role beliefs (scientists are nerdy guys), and self-perceptions (I can't do physics). Because gender-role socialization affects values, definitions of success, and the kinds of activities seen as crucial to one's identity, it affects virtually every aspect of achievement-related decision making (Eccles, 1994).

It will be fascinating to see the results of future studies as researchers attempt to find out more about how some women resist or rebel against socialization pressures. The growing number of midlife women returning to college and taking up new careers provides a chance for researchers to study factors affecting achievement across the life span (Weitzman, 1979). Nontraditional students often experience increased self-esteem and life satisfaction with their commitment to academic achievement (Astin, 1976).

Research on high-achieving women has been done mostly on white women. Racial and ethnic differences in family background and gender socialization probably affect Hispanic, Asian-American, and African-American women differently. For example, black women generally grow up expecting to support themselves rather than to rely on a male breadwinner, while traditional Asian-American culture discourages women from independence and rewards subservience. In a cross section of 161 employed Asian-American women, those who were more instrumentally oriented or androgynous had higher self-esteem, had higher status jobs, and were more satisfied with their work than their more traditional peers (Chow, 1987). More research is needed on diverse groups of women achievers to give a complete profile of successful women.

It is likely that racism and sexism interact to impede the career development of women of color. Black women, for example, have higher aspirations than black men or white women during high school, but, like white women, their career goals decline during college. Black women are more likely than black men, but less likely than white women, to achieve success in a profession. In comparison to white women in the professions, they are even more likely to be in a traditional "woman's" profession, especially teaching (Betz & Fitzgerald, 1987). More than 82 percent of the highly educated and productive Hispanic women professionals in one survey reported that they had experienced discrimination (Amaro, Russo, & Johnson, 1987).

Models of career development based on heterosexuals may have limited applicability to lesbian and bisexual women. Recent research suggests that the process of coming out and accepting a lesbian identity (see Chapter 8) is personally demanding and, in some cases, may delay career development. However, coming out is a normal, positive developmental phase for lesbian and bisexual women, one that should be taken into account in career counseling (Boatwright, Gilbert, Forrest, & Ketzenberger, 1996).

Nontraditional Occupations: From Pink Collar to Blue

Increasingly, women are entering *blue-collar work.* They are enrolling in apprentice programs in the skilled trades and taking jobs as coal miners, police officers, truck drivers, welders, carpenters, and steelworkers (Braden, 1986; Deaux & Ullman, 1983; Hammond & Mahoney, 1983; Martin, 1988). Employers have responded to federal affirmative-action guidelines, sex-discrimination suits from workers, and union pressure by opening up opportunities for women in these fields (Harlan & O'Farrell, 1982).

Who are these women and why do they choose these particular kinds of "men's work"? How do they feel about their unusual way of making a living, and how well do they perform in their jobs? They are an important group to study because they challenge stereotypes and because their choices represent one way of breaking out of the pattern of lower earnings for women.

Most women who became skilled blue-collar workers in male-dominated areas did not specifically plan to do so (Deaux & Ullman, 1983; Martin, 1988). Rather, they often started out in other occupations and changed to meet perceived opportunities. Those who pioneered in entering the trades before affirmative-action mandates have been described by themselves and their coworkers as "fighters": brave, rugged, tough, aggressive, confident, and willing to take risks (Harlan & O'Farrell, 1982). Even today, women entering blue-collar work are more assertive, less gender-typed, and more likely to use active, direct problem-solving strategies than women in pink-collar work (Nash & Chrisler, 1995). They have a strong sense of self and a desire to be independent (Greene & Stitt-Gohdes, 1997).

In one study of 470 women, African-American, white, and Hispanic women who entered programs in which more than 80 percent of the students were male were compared with women who entered programs with a preponderance of female students. The biggest difference between the two groups of students was that women in the nontraditional group (regardless of ethnic background) had received more support and encouragement from female and male friends, family, teachers, and counselors. They were also more instrumentally oriented (Houser & Garvey, 1985). These factors, interestingly, correspond to background and personality factors influencing professional women. Another study of 325 white and black workers showed that economic need was the biggest factor in women's decision to move from traditionally female (white-collar) to traditionally male (blue-collar) jobs, and this was especially true for black women (Padavic, 1991). Thus, individual background, personality factors, and current contexts may interact to influence women's employment choices.

Blue-collar women generally report a high level of satisfaction with their jobs. They like the high pay and the variety and challenge of the work. They take pride in feelings of competence and autonomy, have high levels of self-esteem, and often aspire to promotion and advancement (Deaux & Ullman, 1983; Ferree, 1987; Hammond & Mahoney, 1983; O'Farrell & Harlan, 1982). Being well paid is an important part of job satisfaction for blue-collar women because they need to provide for their families. In one study, two-thirds of a sample of black, white, and Hispanic women steelworkers had children at home, and 61 percent of these were the sole wage earners for their families (Deaux & Ullman, 1983). In a study of twenty-five women coal miners, twenty-two were the primary or sole breadwinners for their families. The miners were aware that they could always get low-status, low-paying "women's" jobs but rejected them. One woman remembered her experience as a waitress: "I thought there must be a better way—here I am making $1.45 an hour and $1.00 an hour in tips. Jesus, there's gotta be another way." She described her decision to become a coal miner to support her family in vivid terms: "I can wash off coal black but I can't wash off those damn bill collectors" (Hammond & Mahoney, 1983, p. 19).

Of course, we have no way of knowing whether the woman shapes the job or the job shapes the woman—a problem with retrospective research discussed earlier. It does seem that proving oneself in a job that requires physical strength and endurance is empowering. One woman mechanic/shipfitter described her early fears but also reported how she learned to deal with "static" from male coworkers, one of whom told her "This is no place for a woman, you ought to be outside taking care of your kids."

> I got angry one day, and I told one of the guys that I had to feed my damn kids just like he did, that's why I was there, and I never had too much trouble after that. (Braden, 1986, p. 75)

Blue-collar women do face some disadvantages in their jobs. As the foregoing example illustrates, male coworkers and supervisors may feel threatened by their presence. Physical strength, endurance, and courage are central components of manhood. If mere women can handle their jobs, how are these men to distinguish themselves as men? Because blue-collar women are a very small minority numerically—for example, they constitute only about 6 percent of police officers and less than 1 percent of miners—they suffer the high visibility and isolation of tokens (Martin, 1988). Sexual harassment is particularly prevalent in blue-collar jobs (Gruber & Bjorn, 1982; Lembright & Riemer, 1982; O'Farrell & Harlan, 1982). Women may be taunted and ridiculed, subjected to physical hazing, threatened with physical injury, deliberately given unsafe equipment, and exposed to hostile, violent pornography on the job (Fitzgerald, 1993).

A survey of blue-collar women (compared with school secretaries) showed that they experienced more sexual harassment and gender discrimination, more adverse working conditions, higher stress levels, and lower satisfaction. The black women in the sample also reported more racial discrimination than their counterparts who were secretaries (Mansfield et al., 1991). On-the-job stress creates psychological symptoms for blue-collar women (Goldenhar, Swanson, Hurrell, Ruder, & Deddens, 1998). Clearly, the satisfaction of doing a tough job and getting paid well for it can be offset by the burden of working in a hostile environment. (For more on workplace sexual harassment, see Chapter 13.)

Other job disadvantages include the often dirty and dangerous working conditions and the fact that, as the "last hired, first fired" employee group, women are subject to layoffs and plant closings (Deaux & Ullman, 1983; Ferree, 1987). Despite these obstacles, research suggests that women perform similarly to men and are no more likely to quit their jobs than blue-collar men (Deaux & Ullman, 1983).

PUTTING IT ALL TOGETHER: WORK AND FAMILY

Despite society's efforts to keep work and family roles separate (e.g., people say that "You shouldn't bring your work home from the office" or "You shouldn't let personal problems affect your work"), they do affect each other. Men's and women's work and family roles function as a system, with each component affecting every other (Lorber, 1993b; Pleck, 1977). A woman's involvement in her paid work may depend not only on whether she has young children but also on whether she has a partner. If so, how flexible is her partner's work role (can he/she stay home with a sick child?), and how do both partners define housework responsibilities? Each partner's involvement in paid work depends on the other. If one earns a high salary, the other may feel less tied to a particular job; if one job is only part time, the other may put in overtime.

Today, women are highly likely to combine mothering with paid work. As discussed in Chapters 9 and 10, many mothers are unmarried or divorced and must provide all or most of the financial support of their children. Even married mothers, however, increasingly work outside the home as well as in it. According to U.S. Census data, in 1970 only 30 percent of women with children under the age of 6 worked outside the home; by the mid-1990s, 62 percent of these women were working (Steil, 1997).

Unlike most research on work, which focuses on men, research on the problems of combining work and family has focused almost exclusively on women, especially on white, upper-middle-class women who are pursuing careers in business and the professions. It has emphasized the social and personal costs of multiple roles, rather than their rewards (Crawford, 1982; Gilbert, 1994). For example, researchers have frequently investigated whether women's work involvement is detrimental to their mental health or their marriages. They have been much less likely to ask whether family involvement or a happy marriage may make one a better and more productive worker.

In a way, focusing on women (and on costs) is a rational research strategy, because multiple roles have different consequences for women and men. Men's main family responsibility, to be a good provider, is compatible with being heavily involved in work roles (Bernard, 1981), whereas women's many responsibilities as primary parent, emotional nurturer, and housekeeper are not. However, the research emphasis on women may lead to seeing working women as a social problem and leave important questions unexamined.

There is a need for more research on how family and personal life affect work for women *and* men, on benefits to women *and* men of juggling work and family, and on multiple roles among women who are not heterosexual, financially privileged, or white. It is interesting that women's work became a research issue only in the 1970s, when middle-class white women began entering the workforce in greater numbers. The fact that working-class, black, and some groups of Hispanic women had always held both types of roles had not been considered worthy of psychological research. Fortunately, researchers are now examining work and family from a broader perspective.

Combining the multiple obligations of spouse, parent, and worker has often been described as a "balancing act" for women. Here we look at some costs and benefits of the balancing act for working women and their families.

What Are the Costs of the Balancing Act?

There is no doubt that the combination of paid and unpaid work done by many women is difficult and demanding. *Role conflict* refers to the psychological effects of being faced with two or more sets of incompatible expectations or demands; *role overload* describes the difficulties of meeting these expectations. The secretary who is asked to work overtime on short notice and must scramble to find child care may experience both conflict (feeling guilty and torn between her two obligations) and overload (as she calls baby-sitters while typing the overdue report). Because her mother and worker roles are incompatible, there is no really satisfactory resolution of the conflict, and it may lead to guilt, anxiety, and depression. Chronic overload may lead to fatigue, short temper, and lowered resistance to physical illness.

Research has consistently shown that most women workers experience role conflict (Crosby, 1991; Gilbert, 1993; Wajcman, 1998). For example, in a group of

232 married women who were doctors, lawyers, and professors, the majority said that they often experienced strains between work and family (Gray, 1983). Compared with women who were not in paid employment, married women workers in a variety of jobs experienced more irritating or frustrating "hassles" in everyday life (Alpert & Culbertson, 1987). In a study of more than 300 Hispanic women professionals, managers, and business owners, on-the-job stress and the amount of support provided by the spouse were important factors influencing the stress of balancing work and family roles. Having young children led to less satisfaction with one's professional life, and high income was related to less stress and more satisfaction (Amaro et al., 1987).

Although working lesbians engage in the same roles as heterosexual women and experience similar conflicts and strains, the very fact of being a lesbian can become an issue at work, providing an added source of conflict (Fassinger, 1996). In a study of seventy lesbians, most of whom currently had a relationship with a partner, 41 percent reported conflicts between their relationship and work roles—usually problems in allocating time and energy to each. Moreover, 33 percent reported conflicts at work in feeling socially unacceptable in a heterosexist and male-dominated work environment. They felt unable to "be themselves" or to discuss their partner or home life, and they reported pressure to dress and act in stereotyped heterosexual ways (Shachar & Gilbert, 1983). In another recent study, lesbians reported less satisfaction with their interpersonal relationships at work than heterosexual women did (Peters & Cantrell, 1993).

What Are the Benefits of the Balancing Act?

Effects on Women

Side by side with research showing widespread problems with role conflict and overload is a great deal of research showing *benefits* associated with multiple roles (reviewed in Betz & Fitzgerald, 1987; Crosby, 1991; Gilbert, 1993; Gutek, Repetti, & Silver, 1988; Nieva & Gutek, 1981; Steil, 1997). Studies from the 1970s onward show that married working women are likely to have fewer psychological problems and better physical health than married homemakers (Barnett, 1997; Bernard, 1972; Steil, 1997). In a study of 300 dual-career couples, higher job quality was related to lower psychological distress in both women and men (Barnett, Marshall, Raudenbush, & Brennan, 1993). In short, working at a satisfying job is beneficial to well-being.

People who are happier at home also tend to be happier on the job and experience less job stress. Married women consistently report higher job satisfaction than single women (see, e.g., Bersoff & Crosby, 1984). In a systematic study of more than 200 middle-aged women, having both a job and a family was related to feelings of greater competence, mastery, and pleasure. In fact, the women who had the overall best psychological adjustment were those who had husbands, children, *and* high-prestige, demanding jobs (Baruch et al., 1983). Other studies show comparable results: Handling more roles is related to higher self-esteem, happiness, and job satisfaction (Beatty, 1996; Miller, Moen, & Dempster-McClain, 1991; Pietromonaco, Manis, & Frohart-Lane, 1986).

Why does involvement in many roles benefit psychological well-being? One reason may be that paid work in itself is generally a source of increased self-esteem, more social involvement, and an independent identity (Steil, 1997). When women make it part of their lives, they gain more than just an income. Another reason is that success in one domain may help people keep a sense of perspective about the others (Crosby, 1982, 1991). In a recent study of more than 200 managers, both women and men believed that their roles as parents and active members of their community had more positive than negative effects on their performance at work (Kirchmeyer, 1993). Being passed over for promotion might seem less of a disaster if one is happily involved in leading a Girl Scout troop; dealing with a difficult teenager at home may be made easier by being in charge and well rewarded at the office. Women who juggle home and work develop good coping strategies, such as choosing the most rewarding aspects of each job and delegating the others. Having a paid job can provide a handy excuse for a woman not to do things she didn't want to do in the first place (Baruch et al., 1983). Employment also increases women's power in the family (see Chapter 9).

There are limitations to the research in this area, however. Research samples are *self-selected*—people have sorted themselves into employed and non-employed groups before being studied. It is possible that multiple roles and happiness go together simply because better-adjusted people are more likely to attempt multiple roles in the first place. Furthermore, most of the research on the benefits of multiple roles has been done on women who have the advantages of high income and professional status. Role conflict and overload may contribute to "burnout" in less prestigious women's jobs such as nursing and teaching (Greenglass & Burke, 1988; Statham, Miller, & Mauksch, 1988).

Effects on Children

What about the children? Do they suffer when both parents work outside the home? Articles in the popular press on day care versus home care for children are largely negative about nonmaternal care, presenting mothers' work as a problem for children (Etaugh, 1980). And employed mothers are still viewed as second-class mothers. After reading a brief description of a mother of an infant who was either employed or not, college students gave the employed mother lower approval ratings and saw her as lower in communal (feminine) traits. She was especially seen as less communal if her motive for working was personal fulfillment rather than financial necessity (Bridges & Orza, 1992).

However, research does not confirm the popular wisdom. The effects of mothers' paid work on children are generally neutral or positive (Farel, 1980; Silverstein, 1991; Steil, 1997). In general, children in day care do not suffer from disruption of their affectional bond with their mothers; they may actually experience increased intellectual growth and development, especially if they come from low-income homes where families cannot provide an enriched environment; and they are at least as socially skilled as home-care children (Scarr, 1998; Scarr, Phillips, & McCartney, 1990). Because researchers have most often chosen to ask questions about possible problems or pathologies created by mothers working, they may have overlooked potential benefits—an example of bias in the framing of research questions. Child care can provide enrichment and foster intellectual and social development, while family care can be neglectful and abusive. In some cases, good child care may help offset poor parenting (Scarr, 1998; Scarr et al., 1990; Silverstein, 1991). One benefit of maternal employment that has rarely been considered by researchers is that in many families, mothers' incomes are a matter of necessity. Two-thirds of mothers are working to keep their families out of poverty, and, with welfare reform, this proportion is increasing (Scarr, 1998).

Employed mothers also provide alternative role models for their children. Several studies have shown that daughters of employed women are more independent and self-confident. Both daughters and sons of employed women hold more egalitarian attitudes about women and view women (including their own mothers) as more competent (Steil, 1997). The benefits of a mother who models many areas of competence may be especially great for girls. As adults, daughters of employed women are more likely to become high achievers (Betz & Fitzgerald, 1987).

It is time for a new agenda in child-care research (Scarr, 1998; Scarr et al., 1990; Silverstein, 1991). Instead of starting with the assumption that "mother care is good and other care is bad," researchers should acknowledge that most mothers *do* work outside the home, and that the risks involved in child care are small compared with the damage caused by the unavailability of the kinds of child-care support today's families desperately need (see Figure 11.9). "We must tie research on child care to the negative consequences of the lack of affordable, government subsidized, high-quality programs" (Silverstein, 1991, p. 1030).

WOMEN, WORK, AND SOCIAL POLICY: MODELS FOR CHANGE

Clearly, the world of work presents women with many problems. Alexis Herman, chair of the National Commission on Working Women, eloquently expressed some of them:

> The 34 million women who are in the pink- and blue-collar work force—sales workers, service workers, factory and clerical workers—have a simple agenda. They want decent wages and benefits; they want affordable child care . . . ; they want training and education for advancement in their jobs; and they want decent and dignified working conditions. They have said it over and over again—with different accents and in different ways, but it is always the same. As Bella Abzug says, "It is shocking that as women, we have to beg to contribute our labor to society. We have to beg for family support systems, decent wages, and the dignity to do what men have always done." (Herman, 1988, p. x)

The problems may seem large and unsolvable, but equity for women workers, whether pink collar, blue collar, or professional, is not an impossible dream. How to go about achieving that dream is, however, an open question. Different ideas about the causes of inequity lead to different proposed solutions. Some researchers and policymakers focus on the individual level, others on the interpersonal or intergroup level, and still others on the structural level (Nieva & Gutek, 1981).

At the individual level, there is an emphasis on problems within women themselves: Women fail to achieve because they lack achievement motivation

FIGURE 11.9. Day-care fantasies and realities.
Source: Doonesbury © G.B. Trudeau. Reprinted by permission of Universal Press Syndicate. All rights reserved.

or are socialized early in life to value vicarious achievement and nurturing rather than autonomy. According to this model, the best way to change women's work situation is to provide self-improvement and training programs to help women overcome their deficiencies. An example is the popular assertiveness training courses for women (Crawford, 1995). Individual change efforts may be helpful for some women, but, as we have seen, there is little evidence that women *as a group* lack ability or motivation. The individual-deficit model runs the risk of blaming the victim by ignoring social factors that are beyond the control of the individual (Henley, 1985; Ryan, 1971).

Recently, a "mommy track" for corporate women has been proposed (and highly publicized in the popular media) (Schwartz, 1989). The idea is that corporations should identify "fast track" women—those whose career is primary—early in their careers and treat them just like men. Other women would be placed on a "mommy track" of lower job prestige in return for such advantages as parental leave, flexible schedules, and so on. The idea created a great deal of controversy. What are the advantages and disadvantages of classifying women workers into two tracks? Objections raised by feminists are that this solution presents women (but not men) with an impossible choice between sacrificing a family life for success on the one hand and having a family but underachieving on the other (Lorber, 1993b; Makosky, 1989). It leaves the

433

"choice" at the individual level, without questioning the male values of corporate culture or the assumption that only women are part of a family.

A structural-level approach focuses on the impact that organizations have on the people in them. It proposes that the situation a person is placed in shapes and determines her or his behavior. Thus, when women are discriminated against in hiring and promotion and confined to dead-end, unrewarding jobs, they will not display initiative or ambition. When a few women are made into tokens, their performance will be negatively affected by the stresses of high visibility and isolation.

From this perspective, women's low expectations and lack of ambition are adaptive adjustments to reality and will change if real opportunities for advancement become available. This approach implies that the system, not the individual, must change for equity to be achieved. Rather than viewing women as unique, it sees their problems as similar to problems faced by other disadvantaged groups such as racial and ethnic minorities. Legislation for equal opportunity and affirmative action is one route to change. However, affirmative action is currently being undermined and eliminated. Evaluating jobs on the basis of comparable worth is another route to change (Lowe & Wittig, 1989). According to the structural approach, equal opportunity leads to equal performance. Family leave policies and affordable, high-quality child care are important structural changes, too.

A final approach is based on intergroup power. From this perspective, when men have more social power, women inevitably become the outgroup. This model explains why women's work is devalued, why male career patterns and definitions of work and achievement are taken as the norm, and why occupations so frequently end up in a pattern of sex stratification, with women at the bottom. Stereotypes about differences between women and men serve to reinforce the ingroup-outgroup distinction. The intergroup power model has been stressed throughout this book and is the focus of Chapter 3.

The intergroup perspective views change in the workplace as dependent on societal change. Educating people about stereotyping might help in the short run, but fundamental change would depend on altering the power structure of society. Power-oriented strategies include passing and enforcing equal-opportunity legislation, increasing women's political power, and forming women's organizations and networks to exert pressure for social change. Many women today are engaged in these strategies.

The information and analysis in Chapters 9 to 11 show that women's experiences in relationships, families, and workplaces are interdependent. Much recent feminist analysis recognizes these interrelationships (Baber & Allen, 1992; Lorber, 1993b). Women who cannot achieve economic parity at work are disadvantaged by having less power in their marriages. Much of the work women do is unpaid and undervalued. Sex discrimination at work affects productivity and quality of life. If women are to have the same career opportunities as men, they must be able to decide if and when they will bear children. Families suffer when social policy is based on myths of motherhood instead of the realities of contemporary life. These are just a few examples of the complex relationships among family roles and workplace issues. Models of change that focus on gendered social structures and power inequities are more useful than those that stress changing women's attitudes and values.

- *Gender is more than just sex.* Women and men have very different experiences in the workplace, and these differences both reflect and perpetuate the gender system. The gendered world of work encompasses structural factors (such as sex segregation and stratification), interactional factors (such as tokenism), and individual-level differences (such as feelings of entitlement).
- *Language and naming are sources of power.* Because work has been defined in terms of a male norm, much of the work that women do—housework, child care, emotional maintenance of families, and building the careers of their male partners—has remained largely invisible. A feminist perspective names all the work women do and places women's paid work in the context of multiple roles and obligations.
- *Women are not all alike.* Most research on women and work has focused on upper-middle-class women who have professional careers. However, the majority of women are underemployed in low-paying clerical and service jobs. Discrimination is based not only on sex/gender but also on race/ethnicity, social class, and sexual orientation.
- *Psychological research can foster social change.* Women are engaged in a complex balancing act as they try to integrate work and family. However, solutions depend not only on individual efforts but also on developing public policy that recognizes the realities of women in the workforce. Women and their families need social supports such as child-care options, paid parental leave, wage equity, and effective sanctions against sex/gender discrimination.

SUGGESTED READINGS

STATHAM, ANNE, MILLER, E. M., & MAUKSCH, H. O. (Eds.). (1988). *The worth of women's work: A qualitative synthesis.* Albany: State University of New York Press. A close look at the experience and working conditions of women who work in traditional occupations (teaching, nursing, social work) and less traditional ones (policewoman).

HASLETT, BETH J., GEIS, FLORENCE L., & CARTER, MAE R. (1992). *The organizational woman: Power and paradox.* Norwood, NJ: Ablex. This compilation of research from social psychology argues that gender stereotypes and self-fulfilling prophecies interact with power, verbal and nonverbal behavior, and leadership to lead to sex discrimination in the workplace. Chapter summaries and hypothetical case studies clarify theoretical points.

GILBERT, LUCIA ALBINO. (1993). *Two careers/one family: The promise of gender equality.* London: Sage. An exploration of societal gender expectations as they affect young dual-career couples. Changes in the workplace that affect employed parents balancing work and family are discussed, and predictions about future challenges are presented.

CHAPTER 12

Midlife and Beyond

- **THE SOCIAL CONSTRUCTION OF AGE**
  Images of Age and Aging
  The Double Standard of Aging
  Cultural Differences in the Images
    of the Aging Woman
  The Consequences of Women's
    Invisibility for Psychological
    Research
- **THE MEANINGS OF MIDLIFE**
- **MENOPAUSE**
  The Aging Woman's Body and Its
    Social Meaning
  Signals of Menopause or Signals
    of Aging?
  The Medicalization of Menopause
  Language about Menopause and
    Popular Consciousness
  Other Voices: Nonclinical Views
    of the Menopausal Experience
  Correlates of Positive and Negative
    Menopausal Transitions
  Menopause, Power, and Status

- **ROLE TRANSITIONS OF MIDLIFE AND
  LATER LIFE**
  Cultural Context and Midlife
    Transitions
  The Complex Nature of Midlife Role
    Transitions
  Older Women and Poverty
- **CAREGIVER ROLES IN LATER LIFE**
  Being a Grandmother
  Care for Aging Parents
- **LOSSES ASSOCIATED WITH AGING**
  Widowhood
  Loss of a Lesbian Life Partner
- **PSYCHOLOGICAL WELL-BEING IN THE
  SECOND HALF OF LIFE**
  The Reentry Woman
  Sexuality at Midlife and Beyond
  Friendship and Social Support
- **ACTIVISM AND FEMINISM AMONG
  OLDER WOMEN**
- **CONNECTING THEMES**
- **SUGGESTED READINGS**

THE SOCIAL CONSTRUCTION OF AGE

What is age? If someone asks a person's age, he or she will have little difficulty in providing a number. Does this number mean that a person is young, middle aged, or old? The significance of age as a number is relatively new. In northern Europe, for example, it was not until the mid–sixteenth century that numerical age had any social significance. Indeed, few people knew their age (Cole, 1992).

Stating a number implies that age can be objectively measured. However, the meaning of this number is quite relative especially when one applies labels to an age such as "midlife" or "old." People define these boundaries differently depending on their own age. Thus, middle age is seen to begin at 35 when people are in their twenties and to begin at 50 when they are two decades older. People's understanding of these boundaries also depends on

436

how long they expect to live in a given time and place. In the United States, what used to be considered old age is now the realm of midlife (Lachman & James, 1997).

There is also a double standard for aging in many societies that depicts women as older than men of the same age. For Freud, women as young as 30 were unfit for analysis because of their psychological rigidity and inability to change. At the same age, men were seen as youthful and pliable (Markson, 1997). As will be shown later in this chapter, this double standard remains alive and well in today's media.

Research on aging has traditionally compared people of different chronological ages on measures of physical health or emotional adjustment. This approach treats age as a simple biological variable. As in studies of gender differences, people are chosen for study on the basis of their membership in a (biologically defined) group. Like gender, however, age is a social classification system that organizes identity and social roles. Age is connected to differences in power, prestige, and opportunities (Markides, 1989). To the extent that age is a source of inequality, it affects people over and above any biological realities. Therefore, to understand the effects of age and aging, one must consider both biological and social factors. Because of the large number of variables involved, people become more different from one another as they age.

A society's beliefs and attitudes about aging provide a powerful cultural context for growing older. In a society where the old are seen as wise elders or keepers of valued traditions, the stress of aging is less than in a society where they are seen as mentally slow and socially useless. To understand the meaning of age and aging for women in contemporary Western societies, we start by examining stereotypes about the old in general and old women in particular. The absence of images is also important for determining when women and men are seen as old as well as their perceived value in society.

Images of Age and Aging

Age and Gender

In Western cultures, aging has long been viewed negatively or at best ambivalently (Kimmel, 1988). Even the word *old* is avoided, as though to be old is so terrible that it should not be mentioned in polite company. Instead, people use a variety of euphemisms, such as "senior citizen," or "golden ager." One woman wrote that when she mentioned the activist group OWL, the Older Women's League, to a friend, the friend's immediate response was, "What an awful name!" (Healy, 1986, p. 59).

Language researchers have noted the ambivalence and negativity of words used to describe older people. Viewed through slang, old people are weak, foolish, and pathetic (see Table 12.1). Although some terms for old men connote respect (an "old salt," for example, refers to an experienced sailor), terms for old women have almost always focused on evil powers, repulsiveness, and disagreeableness (Covey, 1988). Stereotypes about old women portray them as "sick, sexless, uninvolved except for church work, and alone" (Payne & Whittington, 1976).

TABLE 12.1. Terms for Old People from the Late Eighteenth Century to the Present

Male or Gender-Neutral	Female
Old buzzard	Little old lady
Old coot	Granny
Old salt	Old hag
Old duffer	Old maid
Gay old dog	Old bag
Old crock	Old biddy
Old fogey	Old crow
Dirty old man	Old cow
Gramps	Old bird
Grandpa	Crone
Old codger	Old hen
Fuddy-duddy	
Fossil	

Source: Republished with permission of Gerontological Society of America, from Covey. "Historical terminology used to represent older people," *Gerontologist, 28,* 1988, 291–297, and conveyed through Copyright Clearance Center, Inc.

When college students and adults were asked to list the characteristics of 35-year-old and 65-year-old women and men, age stereotypes were more pronounced than gender stereotypes (Kite, Deaux, & Miele, 1991). For example, same-age persons were seen as more similar to each other than were women and men in general. The stereotypes about 65-year-olds were not uniformly negative. Older people were seen as experienced, interesting, physically active, and friendly, as well as wrinkled, hard of hearing, rigid, grouchy, and lonely. Both men and women were seen as losing masculine characteristics as they age with no change in feminine traits. These beliefs seem to depict older women and men as both more similar to one another and less competent than younger people of either gender.

Sexism and Ageism

Negative attitudes toward the aged as a group have been labeled *ageism.* Ageism, like sexism, includes not only beliefs and attitudes but the discriminatory practices that follow from such prejudices (Butler, 1980). There is evidence that ageism is a common prejudice (Kimmel, 1988). Both younger and older respondents evaluated identical behavior differently, depending on the age of the actor; for example, an episode of forgetfulness was viewed more negatively in a 75-year-old than in a 35-year-old (Rodin & Langer, 1980). Psychologists are not exempt from ageism either! One research study found that clinical psychologists evaluated a case study more negatively and were more likely to diagnose psychosis when the client was older (Settin, 1982).

Several parallels can be drawn between ageism and sexism. Both involve the negative categorization of people on the basis of their membership in a group. Both are reflected and perpetuated in language about the devalued groups. Both are pervasive in our society (see Figure 12.1). Finally, they are prejudices that are frequently shared by members of the devalued groups themselves.

The Double Standard of Aging

Differential Views of Aging Women and Men

Feminists have argued that images of old women, which are often more negative than those of old men, are a logical extension of sexist beliefs that "women are only valuable when they are attractive and useful to men" (Healy, 1986, p. 59). Discrimination based on sex adds to discrimination based on age to put older women in double jeopardy. Those women who are from ethnic minority groups, such as Latinas, Asian-American women, or African-American women, and who are also economically deprived are in "quadruple jeopardy." If being female is a devalued status in itself, to be female, black, old, and poor is to be multiply devalued (Padgett, 1988).

FIGURE 12.1. This cover manages to be sexist and ageist at the same time. Note the contrast between the young postfeminist, Ally McBeal (whose fictional name is used rather than that of the actress, Calista Flockheart) and the three real feminists who are portrayed as both aging and literally colorless. Only Ally McBeal was pictured in color; the others were in black, white, and tones of grey.

Because women live longer than men, the majority of old persons are women. In 1990, for example, there were 149 women for every 100 men over age 65 and 259 women for every 100 men over age 85 (Hatch, 1995). The majority of those caring for old persons are also women. The effects of ageism on older men are often cushioned by the women who care for them. However, older women may have no such cushion (Kimmel, 1988). Though our society does not reward or honor older people generally, the costs of ageism seem to be greater for women.

A double standard of aging can be seen in many ways. For example, the physical changes of age are viewed very differently in men and women: The middle-aged man's wrinkles and gray hair are seen as evidence of character and distinction, while the middle-aged woman is urged to conceal all signs of growing older with makeup, hair dye, and cosmetic surgery. Jokes about older women are more frequent and negative than those about either younger women or older men. Most of the jokes about age concealment involve women. One such joke says "It's terrible to grow old alone—my wife hasn't had a birthday in six years" (Palmore, 1997). Jokes such as these reinforce the idea that all older women are ashamed of their age, while older men are not.

Men are also perceived as becoming old later than women. Men are seen as old between 60 and 64, whereas women are seen as old between 55 and 59 (Seccombe & Ishu-Kuntz, 1991). Women are also seen as losing their sexual attractiveness at a younger age than men. Men's sexual value is defined mainly in terms of personality, intelligence, and social status. Women's sexual value is defined almost entirely as physical attractiveness. One of the most overt ways in which this double standard is conveyed to women is that when middle-aged and older men remarry following divorce or widowhood, they show an increasing tendency to choose women younger than themselves. It is socially acceptable for men to marry women as much as twenty years younger than themselves, while older women–younger men combinations are rare (Bell, 1989).

Changes in aging men's level of sexual desire and performance are not publicly acknowledged. It is not uncommon for middle-aged men to blame their diminishing sexual drive or problems in sexual functioning on their partners. Women may accept the blame, believing that their aging bodies are no longer sexually desirable (Daniluk, 1998). Media images of romance legitimize the idea that aging men are sexually virile and attractive to much younger women.

Ageism and Sexism in the Media

The gendered double standard is evident in the movies and on TV, where male actors play romantic leads into their fifties and sixties, often paired with females a generation younger. Recent films included the following romantic partners: Harrison Ford (age 56) and Anne Heche (age 29); Robert Redford (age 61) and Kristin Scott Thomas (age 31); Michael Douglas (age 53) and Gwyneth Paltrow (age 25); and Jack Nicholson (age 60) and Helen Hunt (age 34) (Taylor, Lambert, Perry, & Tobin, 1999). One movie critic commented that he wasn't sure whether the men were going to adopt these women rather than make love to them.

Romantic leading roles for middle-aged women are almost nonexistent. At 40, Jane Fonda told an interviewer that she could find no good roles because "Who wants to look at a 40-year-old woman?" Other middle-aged actresses opt to play older parts. Sally Field was Tom Hanks's lover in *Punchline* in 1988 and his mother in *Forrest Gump* six years later (Weinraub, 1994). Film is an insidiously powerful tool for telling women what they aren't and what they should be.

> So conditioned for shame about our bodies as they age, we watch portraits of once-vital women degenerate before our eyes while the men they support, each his own Dorian Gray, retain supernatural youthfulness. (Kozlowski, 1993, p. 7)

An analysis of the Academy Awards illustrates the differential impact of aging on women and men. From 1927 through 1990, women over the age of 39 accounted for 27 percent of the nominations for best actress, whereas men over the age of 39 accounted for 67 percent of the nominations for best actor (Markson & Taylor, 1993). Katherine Hepburn, who won three Oscars for best actress, accounted for half the awards made to women over 60.

Ageist images are not limited to starring roles. A recent analysis of 100 top grossing movies from the 1940s through the 1980s (20 from each decade) charged that aging women in popular movies were "underrepresented, unattractive, unfriendly, and unintelligent" (Bazzini, McIntosh, Smith, Cook, & Harris, 1997, p. 531). This study found that female characters were consistently younger than male characters over all five decades. Older women were almost invisible. Under the age of 35, 46 percent of the characters were female and 55 percent of the characters were male. Over the age of 35, only 19 percent of the characters were female and 81 percent were male. Although both men and women were seen to be less attractive as they aged, the effect was stronger for women than men. Older women were also portrayed as less good and poorer than comparably aged men.

Older people make up only 3 percent of the characters on prime-time TV, and older men are generally portrayed more positively than older women (Vernon, Williams, Phillips, & Wilson, 1991). Among the "Golden Girls," only two had gray hair (Gerike, 1990). Even *Lear's*—a now defunct magazine that portrayed itself as being "for the woman who wasn't born yesterday"—rarely published photographs of gray-haired women (see Figure 12.2).

Editors of women's magazines admit that signs of age are routinely airbrushed from photographs through computer imaging so that 60-year-old women can be made to look 45 (Chrisler & Ghiz, 1993). The absence of women over 40 in advertising is striking. Unless their images are used to sell laxatives or denture adhesives or to give homey advice about cooking, older women are usually ignored.

Cultural Differences in the Images of the Aging Woman

It is not surprising that women more than men are concerned about growing older since ageism has always been more of a problem for them. Early images of middle-aged women in Western culture focused on their ability to bear chil-

FIGURE 12.2. Do you know many women over 40 who look like these women?

dren. In the biblical story of Sarah, for example, a woman is celebrated for her ability to conceive a child long past her normal time. A similar story is told about Saint Elizabeth, the mother of John the Baptist. Both women were stigmatized by their society for their barrenness and honored for their belated fertility. They symbolize motherhood as the highest calling for a woman. Age was seen as no barrier to a woman with enough faith. Medical scientists have recently announced a breakthrough that allows less exalted postmenopausal women to bear children. We are not sure this is progress!

Barren and/or powerful old women were likely to be transformed into witches by way of a false logic that argued that because good power is fertile, unfertile power must be evil (Kincaid-Ehlers, 1982). Other older female archetypes have been recast in a similar way. For example, the term *crone* once meant a wise elder woman, but changed to mean a malevolent old woman (Mantecon, 1993), until feminists reclaimed it as a symbol of experience and wisdom. The goddess Kali in India was once seen as a source of transformation. Although her image implied both creation and destruction, she is generally portrayed to Western eyes as an image of chaos and death.

Non-Western cultural images of old women can be quite positive. Native American legends include many powerful old women. The Navajo's "Changing Woman" is responsible for all new life and successful crop growth. In the Cheyenne legend the "Old Woman of the Spring," it is the old woman who has the knowledge and power to restore the buffalo. "Grandmother Spider" is a particularly well-drawn figure who, despite her infirmities, succeeds in bringing fire to the world after the younger men had failed and teaches the art of pottery making and weaving to many American Indian tribes (John, Blanchard, & Hennessy, 1997). Such figures help create strong self-images for Indian women and enhance their position in Native American society. For example, only older women can perform certain kinds of medicine work (Cypress, 1993).

In traditional Japanese culture, age denotes wisdom, authority, and a hard-won freedom to be flexible and creative (Lock, 1998). Even in the entertainment media, older women are often portrayed as respected and admired, not only for their artistic skills, but for their beauty. When asked about aging, several older women said that they were looking forward to old age because they would no longer have to "keep a low profile" and display feminine reserve (Lock, 1993).

In contrast, traditional Indian views of old women and men may be even more negative than those found in Western Europe and the United States. One popular saying about aging in Hindi uses "teesi-kheesi" to describe women. This means that when a woman reaches age 30 (tees), her face caves in and teeth fall out (khees). Men, on the other hand, are described as "satha-patha" which means that even at age 60 (sath), a man remains a virile youth (patha) (Kakar, 1998). Hindu movies portray middle-aged women (who are now mothers-in-law) as witches, snakes in human form, or malevolent female ghosts. Although older women are given power and authority by this role, it is shadowed by the resentment of the daughters-in-law and their desire to replace her.

Our own culture gives women few reasons to celebrate their age. Birthday cards for older women allude to failing memory, decreased sexual abilities, and diminished vigor and attractiveness, all in the guise of humor (Adolph, 1993). Clearly our culture views getting older to be a cause for mourning. The double standard of aging encourages women to deny their age to themselves and others. Even professional women, for whom age represents professional experience and maturity, are rarely candid about it. In the official membership directory of the American Psychological Association, women are ten times as likely as men not to list their age (Bell, 1989).

The double standard may be less relevant to lesbians. In a comparison of personal advertisements written by lesbians and heterosexual women, 98 percent of the lesbians and 76 percent of the heterosexuals specified their age in their ad. Heterosexual women were also more likely than lesbians to specify the desired age of a prospective partner. These results suggest that age is less of a stigma and a less important dimension in choosing a romantic partner among lesbians than among heterosexual women (Laner, 1979).

The Consequences of Women's Invisibility for Psychological Research

Women have been largely invisible in psychological research on aging. Much research on older people has either used all-male samples or failed to analyze results by sex, so that possible differences between men and women are obscured. Moreover, biases based on stereotypes of women have affected researchers' choice of participants. For example, researchers have equated aging for women with the end of the childbearing years, while for men it is seen in terms of retirement from paid work. Thus, the importance of work in women's lives is often underestimated (Bumagin, 1982). In one major study of the effects of menopause, women who worked outside the home were excluded, apparently because they were considered deviant. In an important early study of retirement, married women were excluded on the grounds that their husbands' retirement, and not their own, was the most important influence (cited in Barnett & Baruch, 1978). Omissions and biases such as these result in research that has little validity for understanding the lives of today's aging women.

The bias against including women and gender is widespread and slow to change. For example, two widely respected research handbooks on aging published in the 1980s list no index entries for *women, men, sex differences,* or *gender.* Books on aging published in the 1990s have taken gender into account but still look at gendered aging in terms of heterosexist norms. For example, one important handbook on women and aging neither has a chapter on lesbians nor includes them in its chapter on single women in later life.

Omitting women and gender from the study of aging seems to be based on the assumption that gender becomes less important as people grow older. However, gender is as important a lens for understanding midlife and elderly people as it is for any other age group. The omission of women is especially ironic since women make up a majority of the aging population.

THE MEANINGS OF MIDLIFE

Before people are considered old in today's culture, they pass through a period called midlife—usually defined as the years from 45 to 65. It should not be surprising that there has been little research on this life stage, because it appears to be a twentieth-century invention. The term *midlife* cannot be found in older dictionaries and is a result of a cultural obsession with youth (Gullette, 1997). Aging men as well as women are targets for advertisements that emphasize magic potions that will regain or maintain a youthful appearance. Nevertheless, women are more affected by midlife because they "age" sooner than men and are more dependent on appearance for social success.

The transition to midlife can be particularly problematic for women. Based on her clinical practice, one psychologist has described a phenomenon she termed "late midlife astonishment" (Pearlman, 1993). She found that between the ages of 50 and 60, many women suddenly become aware of an acceleration of aging and an increasing stigmatization based on its visible signs. Passing as younger is no longer possible for them. They fear being discriminated against in the workplace and rejected or abandoned by romantic partners or mates. These fears produce a sense of heightened vulnerability, shame, and loss of self-esteem.

Such fears are a realistic product of the combination of sexism and ageism of our society, which focuses on women's bodies more than those of men. Women appear to have a shorter period of presentability in the labor market than men do. For example, one manager was quoted as saying "We have two good secretaries with first-rate skills who cannot move up because they dress like grandmothers" (Rodeheaver, 1990, p. 57). The most frequent compliment given to older women is: "You don't look your age." Think about the unstated assumptions in this remark! "If you looked your age, you would look ugly" (Healy, 1993).

MENOPAUSE

The Aging Woman's Body and Its Social Meaning

The word *menopause* (physiologically, the end of menstruation and, therefore, fertility) did not even exist in English until the last quarter of the nineteenth century (Kincaid-Ehlers, 1982). Nevertheless, this event is the one glaring exception to the omission of women from the study of aging. Menopause has been the subject of great attention from both the medical profession and the media. In fact, aging and menopause are treated as almost synonymous in women. As discussed in Chapters 7 and 10, women are defined by their reproductive functions more than men are. This is especially true for the phases of life that appear to have no parallels for males, such as menarche, pregnancy, and menopause. Many researchers in these areas believe that women's behavior during these life stages is determined by the direct influences of hormones on their brains. Beliefs about biological causality have led to the neglect of other psychological and social events that occur at the same stage of life.

Since biological and physiological explanations are usually viewed as primary, menopause has been used to explain much of women's behavior at midlife. Menopause—or what is sometimes known as the "change of life"—occurs in most women between the ages of 45 and 55. The average age of menopause—around 50—has not changed since the medieval period. This average age seems to be relatively constant across cultures despite a wide range in levels of nutrition and health. These facts would seem to indicate that menopause is a purely biological phenomenon. Indeed, menopause is biologically caused by a decrease in the production of estrogen and progesterone by the ovaries. Natural menopause is a gradual process. It is defined as having occurred when a woman has not menstruated in a year.

Menopause is not, however, treated as a normal life event in our society. Instead it is used as a metaphor for disparaging the aging female body (see Figure 12.3). Menopause coincides with many other life events such as children leaving home; changes in domestic, social, and personal relationships; changes in identity and body image; possible divorce or widowhood; new experiences of retirement; and increasing anxiety about aging, dying, and losing friends, loved ones, and financial security. Rather than analyzing women's responses to these events, however, menopause is portrayed as a fundamental cause of women's loss of prestige, status, visibility, and value during their last quarter century of life (Zita, 1993).

> By defining menopause as an illness, all middle-aged and old women are characterized as ill—a Y chromosome has become a necessity for well-being. (Gannon, 1998, p. 296)

FOR BETTER OR FOR WORSE by Lynn Johnston

FIGURE 12.3. Elly's husband is certainly expecting the worst from menopause.
Source: © Lynn Johnston Productions, Inc./Dist. by United Feature Syndicate, Inc.

Although media descriptions have changed over the past three decades, they continue to accentuate the negative. The symptoms stressed during each decade document changes in cultural attitudes toward women. In the 1960s, for example, the focus of the articles in popular magazines was on beauty and femininity. Symptoms such as weight gain, sagging breasts, wrinkles, loss of femininity, and loss of sexuality were noted more frequently in this decade. In succeeding years, the number of emotional symptoms and psychiatric conditions mentioned also declined. The 1980s woman was not warned to fear for her sanity. Instead, she was told to worry about such health issues as osteoporosis and heart disease (Chrisler, Torrey, & Matthes, 1990). The major trend in the 1990s is to portray menopausal symptoms as occurring at an earlier age. For example, a recent special issue of *Newsweek* on women's health, featured an article on *perimenopause* (defined as the ten years before menopause), which is said to cause physical problems for women early in their fourth decade. In large bold type, the article begins:

> It can masquerade as insomnia, moodiness, or depression. But physicians now understand that in the years before menopause, women ride a hormonal roller coaster. The grab bag of symptoms that it brings has a single underlying cause, so you don't have to take it lying down. (Begley, 1999, p. 31)

Despite the extensive lists for menopause and, now, perimenopause, there are few consistent signs of menopause. The only symptom that is found in *all* women is the end of menstruation. Other signals of the end of menstrual life are, however, found in some women. Although all of these effects have been attributed to a decline in ovarian hormones, no relationship has been found between hormone levels and the number and severity of symptoms.

What evidence supports the medicalization of midlife for women? Although there has been a recent dramatic increase in popular publications on menopause, there has been no increase in new medical findings. The percentage of articles on menopause in the medical literature has remained at the same low rate of 1 to 2 percent a year since the 1970s (Gannon, 1997). Media descriptions of menopause advocate hormone replacement for preventing heart disease, depression, sagging breasts, wrinkled skin, loss of sexual desire, and marital discord. Similar symptoms in men are said to be due to natural aging rather than lower levels of testosterone. Only women are seen to be victims of their biology. Each so-called symptom of menopause will be discussed separately. In summary, it is clear that each is influenced by social and cultural variables as well as biological ones.

Signals of Menopause or Signals of Aging?

The Hot Flash

The most consistently found symptom during menopause is the *hot flash*. Hot flashes are usually described as sensations of heat, often limited to the face and upper torso, that persist for some minutes. Hot flashes are now considered physiological phenomena, although they were at one time considered to be "all in a woman's head" (Travis, 1988b). They usually begin during the years before menopause and gradually decline after menopause has occurred. Researchers believe that hot flashes are caused by a reduction in estrogen that influences the temperature regulation centers of the hypothalamus. Hot flashes are among the few menopausal symptoms that are successfully treated by estrogen replacement therapy (Gannon, 1998).

Evidence suggests, however, that hot flashes are not completely controlled by hormones. For example, hot flashes begin before menopause in many women—frequently before their level of estrogen has declined to a critical level (Kronenberg, 1990). Moreover, although women vary enormously in the severity of this symptom, no relationship has been found between hormone levels and the number or intensity of hot flashes reported (Gannon, 1985). Researchers do not know why hot flashes last only a few months in some women, while in others they persist for years or never occur at all. They are unrelated to employment status, social class, age, marital status, domestic workload, and number of children (Kronenberg, 1990).

The percentage of women who report having hot flashes around menopause varies widely. The prevalence rate also varies widely from culture to culture. For instance, Japanese and Indonesian women report far fewer than women from Western societies do (Flint & Samil, 1990; Goodman, 1982; Kaufert, 1990). One study, using comparable data-gathering techniques, found that 69.2 percent of Caucasian women reported having experienced a hot flash at some time, while only 20 percent of a sample of Japanese women reported having had one (Lock, 1986). In the most extreme case, Mayan women in the Yucatan did not report any symptoms at menopause except menstrual-cycle irregularities (Beyene, 1989).

These cross-cultural findings illustrate how biological determinism can produce overly simplistic causal explanations. Hot flashes may be partly a function of a reduction in female hormones during menopause, but other factors also play a role. For example, hot flashes have been successfully treated using stress reduction techniques (Freedman & Woodward, 1992) and are also influenced by weight and diet. Women from cultures whose diet includes plants that contain natural estrogens (yams in the Yucatan and soy products in the Far East) report fewer hot flashes. Cultures also vary in terms of the age at which a woman has her last child; diets vary in terms of the amount of animal fat eaten; and so on. All these factors illustrate the interaction between biological and social variables.

Most women do not find hot flashes incapacitating, but many women do find them embarrassing:

> I can remember being very embarrassed talking with a fellow worker and my face turned very red. I was sure it was written all over my face what the cause of that redness was and there was nothing for me to be blushing about, nothing in the conversation that was embarrassing, so I remember those little embarrassing episodes. (Martin, 1987, p. 168)

When asked what she did about this incident, the woman replied, "Nothing, just prayed he wouldn't notice it."

Many women are unable to explain why they are embarrassed by hot flashes. They associate them with situations in which they are nervous or especially want to make a good impression. Hot flashes may be embarrassing because they are an outward public sign of an inner body process associated with the uterus and ovaries, which is supposed to be kept private and concealed. They reveal indisputably that a woman is of a "certain age." They also reveal a woman's difference from men, with a focus on her reproductive system—a system that may be devalued even more because it is now "failing" (Martin, 1987). Although a small percentage of women (perhaps 10 to 15%) report being seriously bothered by them, hot flashes have never totally incapacitated or killed anyone. They may, however, produce fatigue and loss of energy, which is sometimes misdiagnosed as depression (Voda, 1997).

Osteoporosis

Osteoporosis is characterized by a decrease in skeletal mass or in the quantity of bone. This reduction in mass is regarded as a major factor in the bone fractures found in older people. It is generally believed that menopause is at least a contributing factor, and possibly the primary factor, in the development of osteoporosis. The characterization of this disorder as menopausal may, however, be another example of the confusion between menopause and the normal processes of aging.

Loss of skeletal mass with age is not found only in women. Both men and women begin to lose bone mass after age 35. Women are usually more prone to fracture because of thinning of their bones since they have less massive skeletons to begin with. But gender reversal can occur. For example, among the Chinese in Singapore, the rate of bone loss is greater for men than for women (Brown, 1988). Men who live long enough for their skeletons to reach a critically thin level are also prone to osteoporotic fractures.

There is also no evidence that loss of estrogen is directly associated with the development of osteoporosis. Loss of bone mass in women normally begins during the fourth decade of life, or well before menopause. No difference has been found in the level of estrogen in the blood between postmenopausal women with osteoporotic fractures and age-matched women without fractures (Edman, 1983b).

Factors other than menopause have been implicated in osteoporosis. Diet and exercise appear to be extremely important. For example, the risk of osteoporosis is five times greater in thin than obese women (Gannon, 1985). Women who have been anorexic are particularly prone to this problem. Some interesting ethnic differences have also been found. Black and Puerto Rican women in the United States have a lower incidence of vertebral atrophy and fractures than white women (Gannon, 1985). The less affected women had a higher level of calcium in their diet. Asian women also appear to have a lower rate of osteoporosis than white North American women. In fact, risk for this disorder appears to be related to skin color—the fairer the complexion, the greater the risk (Doress-Worters & Siegal, 1994). In the last twenty years, osteoporetic fractures have increased in urban areas of Scandinavia to the highest rate in the world (Johansson, Mellstrom, Lerner, & Osterberg, 1992). Factors associated with osteoporosis, besides those just discussed, include low lifetime calcium intake, consumption of alcohol and caffeine, and smoking.

Women from a lower socioeconomic bracket, with jobs that were more physically demanding, also have lower amounts of bone loss. Exercise has been found to reduce the loss of bone mass (Doress-Worters & Siegal, 1994). It is possible that the traditional gender-role differences in levels of physical activity accounts for the greater risk of osteoporosis in women. The connection between osteoporosis and menopause may also be mediated by traditional gender roles. For example, men begin to lose bone mass in their sixties rather than in their forties. This is the age at which men retire and drastically reduce their level of physical activity. An equivalent reduction in physical activity for women may take place in their forties, when their children leave home (Gannon, 1985).

The effectiveness of estrogen replacement therapy for osteoporosis is quite controversial. There is no consensus about how estrogen works, what the mechanisms are, and even the reliability and validity of the measures used to evaluate bone loss (MacPherson, 1985). Not all postmenopausal women need long-term estrogen therapy. The individuals most at risk are thin, small-framed, white women who smoke and who weigh less than 120 pounds (Edman, 1983b). It does not appear to be good medical practice to place all menopausal women on medication to protect 25 percent to 30 percent of them. Calcium supplements and daily exercise are less risky alternatives.

Coronary Heart Disease

Loss of female hormones is also assumed to increase the risk of coronary heart disease. Some physicians argue that because death from coronary heart disease is rare in premenopausal women and relatively high in men under 50, estrogens must protect premenopausal women. The incidence of cardiovascular disease appears to increase disproportionately in women following menopause. However, the logic of this argument is flawed. The gender reversal is not due to a rapid acceleration of death among women after menopause, but to a decline in male deaths with age. The drop may be due, in part, to a high incidence of early death in men who are genetically predisposed to fatal coronary heart disease (Edman, 1983). In fact, women never catch up to men in risk for coronary heart disease. Women in their forties and fifties have disease rates approximately 45 percent lower than men of the same age. This same 45 percent difference is found for people in their sixties and seventies as well.

It would seem to be a contradiction that more women die from coronary heart disease than men although they have a lower rate of risk. The contradiction is explained by the fact that women, on the average, develop the disease seven to eight years later than men. Since there are substantially more older women than men, more women actually die of coronary heart disease, but always at a lower rate (Bush, 1990).

The erroneous connection between hormones and heart disease in women is a good example of the extent to which health problems in women are overly attributed to their reproductive functions. This emphasis on reproductive events leads researchers to ignore important social and cultural factors. For example, the ratios of males to females who die from coronary heart disease at ages 45 to 54 are two to one in Italy and one to one in Japan (Edman, 1983b). Gender-related differences are also smaller among blacks in the United States than among whites.

Excessive attention to biology leads to less attention to other important risk factors. For example, smoking increases the rate of coronary heart disease for women as much as it does for men. It has been said that "women who smoke like men die like men who smoke" (Bush, 1990, p. 226). The influence of smoking (as well as other health-related behaviors) may account for the tendency of some large-scale studies to find a connection between hormone replacement and a lower level of cardiovascular disease. Hormone users are also less likely to smoke, more likely to exercise, to have had their cholesterol measured in the last year, to have higher incomes, more education, and less body fat (Derby et al., 1993). In the United States, the wives of men who develop coronary heart disease are twice as likely to suffer from heart disease than women whose husbands are free of heart disease. Unless coronary heart disease is contagious, this suggests a powerful role for environmental influences (Strickland, 1988).

The Myth of Emotional Instability

Little evidence supports a connection between menopause and psychoneurotic disorders (Doress, et al., 1987; Edman, 1983; Gannon, 1998a). There is also little evidence that postmenopausal women are more depressed than younger women. Two large-scale community surveys have, for example, failed to find a higher rate of depression among menopausal women (Lennon, 1987).

Part of the reason for the perceived association between menopause and depression may be an emphasis on women who seek treatment for psychological problems during menopause. These women appear to have significantly lower levels of estrogens than women who do not seek medical help (Ballinger, 1990). They experienced more environmental stress and coped less well with it than a comparable nonclinical population. A British study also found a relationship between premenopausal and postmenopausal mood (Hunter, 1990). Premenopausal depression, holding a negative stereotype about menopause, and being unemployed (combined with a low socioeconomic status) accounted for more than half the variance in postmenopausal depression.

Although no relationship between measures of mood and the level of hormones has been found, popular culture (as interpreted in comic strips) supports the use of estrogen for a variety of psychological and physical disturbances (see Figure 12.4). The media take their cue from medical and scientific "expertise." In a survey of medical and science-based journal articles on menopause from 1984 to 1994, the researchers found that both the presence and absence of women's hormones are assumed to make them crazy (Rostosky & Travis, 1996). Women are socialized to attribute their midlife feelings and reactions to menopause and the aging process, rather than to other stressful life events.

The Medicalization of Menopause

The Effect of Medical Views on Treatment

Physicians and nurses see menopausal symptoms as more severe and pathological than menopausal women see them (Cowan, Warren, & Young, 1985). This is probably because medical personnel encounter only 10 percent to 30 percent of all menopausal women. These women probably have more severe symptoms than most women do.

Women who seek treatment have more negative attitudes about menopause than other women. They complain about its unpredictability, their inability to control symptoms, and the loss of a sense of continuity in their lives. In one study conducted in England, women patients at menopausal clinics saw themselves as having completely changed with the onset of menopause—both physically and in terms of their personalities. They viewed their symptoms as some sort of mystery over which they had little control (Ussher, 1989).

Physiological signs and symptoms can be interpreted in a number of ways. Symptoms can also be experienced differently, depending on how medical authorities react to them. Physicians do not create actual physiological symptoms but can define which symptoms are important, which are to be disregarded, which should be treated, and which should not (Zimmerman, 1987).

FIGURE 12.4. Estrogen is stressed for all kinds of women's disorders—real and unreal. *Source:* Us & Them © 1995. Dist. by Universal Press Syndicate. Reprinted with permission. All rights reserved.

The creation of a diagnostic category such as "menopausal syndrome" can lead physicians as well as women themselves to assign symptoms of stress to menopause rather than social causes.

Many women express a strong sense of dissatisfaction with their physicians and the medical advice that they have been offered (Logothetis, 1993). Physicians tend to view women's health problems, whatever their type, location, or symptoms, in terms of reproductive function. This preoccupation of physicians with the menopausal status of their patients has persisted for more than a century:

> Women are treated for diseases of the stomach, liver, kidneys, heart, lungs, etc.; yet, in most instances, these diseases will be found on due investigation, to be, in reality, no diseases at all, but merely the sympathetic reactions or the symptoms of one disease, namely, a disease of the womb. (Dirix, 1869; cited in Zimmerman, 1987, p. 448)

> A woman is a uterus surrounded by a supporting organism and a directing personality. In advancing this proposition I am neither facetious nor deprecatory of womankind. I am biologically objective. (Galdston, 1958; cited in Zimmerman, 1987, p. 448)

Culture and Medical Treatment

The definition of women's reproductive system as a source of illness and disability has ignored findings about poor women and women of color. These groups are absent from most of the studies on the medical risks of menopause. For example, a review of 108 papers cited in an important article on menopause found that only two looked at ethnicity as a variable (Kaufert, 1990). When populations that are *not* middle-class white Americans are considered, they often contradict hypotheses about the direct relationship between hormones and symptoms.

The medicalization of menopause is not yet universal. In Japan, for example, the pattern of symptoms is completely different from those found in North America. Typical symptoms include shoulder stiffness, headaches, and dizziness. These symptoms are considered part of the normal aging process and women are expected to "ride over" their physical distress. Recently, however, a menopausal syndrome has been recognized by some physicians. They believe it is common in urban centers and is a result of a loss of traditional values and the embrace of individualism (Lock, 1998). It is unlikely that estrogen replacement will be seen as a remedy for this problem.

Defining the normal changes of midlife as a hormone deficiency disease has serious consequences for women. For women to be physically and psychologically healthy, they cannot subscribe to the belief that only the first forty years of their lives are important and worthwhile. There is a tremendous gap in health care for midlife women. They stay away from available health care providers because they find their experience medicalized in ways that they cannot tolerate (Kaufert & Gilbert, 1986). They also tend to resist using estrogens prescribed by physicians for long periods of time. Instead, they prefer to use them for a short time to ease transient symptoms such as hot flashes.

Women in the United States are urged to use estrogen replacement therapy at menopause to prevent all of the symptoms discussed earlier in this chapter. Although there is fairly good evidence that estrogen is helpful in treating hot flashes and vaginal thinning, it is more controversial as a treatment for osteoporosis and for reducing the risk of cardiovascular disease. And, estrogens are useless in dealing with anxiety, irritability, and so on.

Surgical menopause appears to produce more physical symptoms than natural menopause (Gannon, 1985). Many studies on menopause combine groups of women whose menopause has been prematurely caused by surgery with those who have reached menopause naturally. While estrogens are necessary to prevent osteoporosis and hot flashes in women who lose their ovaries at an early age (usually because of a surgery), they are potent substances that carry a number of risks. In the past estrogen was implicated in an increase in uterine cancer (Edman, 1983b). Estrogen is now combined with progesterone and does not seem to carry the same risk as it did in the 1970s. It may, however, increase the risk of breast cancer in some women. Women who have diabetes, high blood pressure, high cholesterol, or who are obese are advised not to take it, as are women who smoke (Voda, 1997).

Estrogens should be thought of as a treatment for a specific set of symptoms experienced by a minority of women. These symptoms usually disappear gradually after menopause or can be treated by less potent medications. Some experts on menopause have called for the abandonment of the term *estrogen replacement therapy*. They argue that women are not estrogen deficient unless they are made that way surgically or medically. The term estrogen replacement softens the risks involved in using such a potent substance and heightens the benefits while reinforcing the idea that menopause is a disease (Voda, 1997).

Physicians and drug companies promise women a safe, symptom-free menopause. The majority of doctors are more likely to prescribe hormones to menopausal women than to consider any other form of advice, supplement, or intervention. This excessive use of hormones continues despite a report of the World Health Organization that challenged the use of estrogens in treating menopausal symptoms. This report stated that in 70 percent to 80 percent of postmenopausal women the level of circulating estrogens is sufficient (Ussher, 1989):

> Convincing women that their normal and natural development is flawed and requires intervention—that they should have large breasts, be safe sex partners, and have premenopausal levels of estrogen at the age of 70—engenders feelings of inadequacy and low self-esteem. When women internalize this negative self-image, they become vulnerable to a quick fix or fountain of youth. (Gannon, 1997, p. 262)

How useful is estrogen for most women? Although 95 percent of all women have undergone menopause by age 55, less than 11 percent develop cardiovascular disease by this age. The mortality rate for women from heart disease does not reach 1 in 100 until after age 70. By this age the average woman has been postmenopausal for fifteen to twenty years (MacPherson, 1993).

There are 20 million women over the age of 65 who represent a potentially lucrative market for hormones if women and their physicians can be convinced that hormones are a way of treating the ills of aging and staying feminine forever. It seems advisable, in the light of the lack of information about the long-term effects of hormone therapy, to look at these claims with a healthy degree of skepticism (Doress et al., 1987).

Language about Menopause and Popular Consciousness

It is not surprising that women will seek drugs to stave off aging at any cost. The equation of aging and menopause has no parallel in men. The language used to describe menopause is particularly hostile. It is in sharp contrast to the language used to describe changes men experience during this part of the life cycle: For example, there is no term "testicular insufficiency" to match "ovarian insufficiency" or "senile scrotum" to match "senile vagina." In the *Merck Manual of Diagnosis and Therapy* (the common physician's handbook), the description of premature menopause gives directions for "preservation of a serviceable vagina." When a doctor injects testosterone into a man, it isn't for the purpose of preserving or creating a "serviceable penis . . . men do not serve. Women do. The purpose is to increase his libido, to raise his hormone level" (Reitz, 1981, p. 73).

The language of loss leads some women to believe that all midlife changes are negative, inevitable, and debilitating (Ussher, 1989). The following quotes are representative of the comments of the many women who dread the approach of menopause:

> I look at every new wrinkle, every grey hair and think of the time when I won't be able to cope with anything: when I'll probably finally go mad. Isn't it true that women who are going through the change are out of their minds for most of the time? (Melanie, aged 30, in Ussher, 1989, p. 109)

> I guess it's more of a fear, not of post-menopause, just the actual process. You're not really in control of your body. That much is not predictable, that's what scares me about it. (Tania Parrish, aged 20, in Martin, 1987, p. 174)

> My grandmother almost went insane, she almost didn't make it through menopause at all. (Marcia Robbins, aged 19, in Martin, 1987, p. 174)

These comments were all made by women who were far from the age of menopause. They are in sharp disagreement with the comments of older women who see menopause as "no big deal." The comments of the younger women, however, echo the views of some physicians:

> I cannot help feeling that the reason so few women being [sic] found in leading positions is to be at least partly explained by the mental imbalance in these years around the time of the menopause. It is around the age of 50 that men take the final step to the top, a step that women with equal intellectual capacities rarely take. I know that many aspects are involved, but the climacteric may well be an important one. (cited in Martin, 1987, p. 175)

> . . . is the trigger for the powder keg of emotions slowly smoldering somewhere in the hypothalamus. (Dunlop, 1968, p. 45)

> The assumption has been put forward that women's ability to work reduces to a quarter of the normal by menopause. (Achte, 1970, p. 13)

One gynecologist even described menopausal women as "a caricature of their younger selves at their emotional worst" (Bart & Grossman, 1978). It should not be surprising that negative images about menopause abound. What is surprising is the number of women who reject the model of menopause as illness.

Other Voices: Nonclinical Views of the Menopausal Experience

Studies that examine women's accounts of their experiences find relatively little distress. Over and over, women described menopause by saying, "It was nothing"; "Nothing. Never had any problem. It just stopped, it slowed up"; and "Nothing. Just stopped and that's about it" (Martin, 1987, p. 173). The vast majority of older women respondents saw menopause in a positive light. They felt pleasure at avoiding whatever discomfort they had felt during menstruation and relief from the nuisance of dealing with bleeding, pads, or tampons. For those women who were sexually active with men, menopause meant delight in freedom from the fear of pregnancy.

A more recent study that asked women between the ages of 40 and 60 to write about menopause found similar results. The women's unconstrained responses were overwhelmingly positive (Logothetis, 1993). Most of them placed menopause in the overall context of their reproductive lives. Here are some of their remarks (Logothetis, 1993, pp. 128–129):

> It's like your period—it's what you make of it, good or bad. I had more discomfort from periods than from menopause. No more fear of getting pregnant.

There was no indication of the *empty nest syndrome* (depression following the departure of the last child from home) among these women. Instead, they frequently communicated a sense of freedom from the responsibility of bearing and nurturing children. Women do not appear to experience menopause as if it were a separate episode in life similar to a major illness (Martin, 1987). Instead, interviewers report that they had difficulty keeping older women respondents on the topic because they wanted to wander off from menopause to talk about many other aspects of their lives.

Women's negative reports about menopause may be influenced by the kinds of questions they are asked. In a creative study of how both women and men may be influenced by the social setting in which questions are asked, attitudes were examined in the context of medical problems, life transitions, or symbols of aging (Gannon & Ekstrom, 1993). For example, one group of people expressed their attitudes toward a broken leg, a stomach ulcer, and menopause. Another group expressed their attitudes about menopause in the context of puberty and leaving the parental home, and a third group responded to questions that included attitudes toward gray hair and retirement. The researchers found that the medical context elicited significantly more negative attitudes than the other two contexts. In general, women's attitudes were more positive than those of men, and their attitudes became increasingly positive with age and experience.

Attitudes about menopause have many similarities to other gender-related stereotypes (see Chapter 2). For example, women believe others have more problems than they themselves do. Like another reproductive milestone, menarche, attitudes are most negative among those women who have not yet experienced the event. Negative views of menopause may be a response to popular stereotypes—to what is perceived as the expectations of others about this life stage.

Correlates of Positive and Negative Menopausal Transitions

The emotional states supposedly associated with menopause have been found to vary with women's level of education and their socioeconomic status. Upper-middle-class women, in particular, minimized the importance of menopause (Bart & Grossman, 1978). A similar social-class effect was found in an analysis of a large representative sample of married women in Belgium who ranged from 46 to 55 years of age (Severne, 1982). Those women who worked outside the home reported the least impact of menopause. In a smaller U.S. study, researchers examining the attitudes of women and their families also found that the women's level of education had an effect. For women who had completed high school, and their families, the changes of menopause were seen as a part of a time of life when things were getting better (Dege & Gretzinger, 1982). They saw the midlife period as a time when there was more opportunity for outside employment. These data on the impact of education and social class demonstrate that the emotional responses associated with menopause cannot be separated from other aspects of women's lives.

Menopause, Power, and Status

Women who have the most positive attitudes about menopause perceive that it has given them more power to direct their own lives. When people age in our society, they often lose power and status. Many feminist researchers have argued, therefore, that the negative consequences of middle age for women are a result of U.S. society's attitude toward aging rather than the menopause per se. Since women in all societies go through menopause but cultures vary in their response to aging women, it is possible to infer whether there is a relationship between menopausal symptoms and the status and power of aging women by examining a number of cultures. Indeed, certain structural arrangements and cultural values appear to be associated with an increase in women's status after the childbearing years (Bart & Grossman, 1978). (See Table 12.2.) These arrangements have major consequences in the lives of middle-aged women in many non-Western societies. For example, the end of fertility and/or responsibility for child rearing may give them greater opportunity for geographic mobility, the right to exert authority over certain members of the younger generation (usually daughters or daughters-in-law), and recognition beyond the household unit (Brown, 1982). In contrast, relatively weak bonds between women and their adult children, minimal menstrual taboos (giving women no more freedom after menopause than before it), and the high value placed on youth and sexual attractiveness decrease the power of middle-aged women in the United States.

TABLE 12.2. The Structural Arrangements and Cultural Values Associated with Increases and Decreases in Women's Status after Childbearing Years

Increased Status	Decreased Status
Strong tie to family of orientation (origin) and kin	Marital tie stronger than tie to family of orientation (origin)
Extended family system	Nuclear family system
Reproduction important	Sex an end in itself
Strong mother–child relationship reciprocal in later life	Weak maternal bond; adult-oriented culture
Institutionalized grandmother role	Noninstitutionalized grandmother role; grandmother role not important
Institutionalized mother-in-law role	Noninstitutionalized mother-in-law role; mother-in-law doesn't train daughter-in-law
Extensive menstrual taboos	Minimal menstrual taboos
Age valued over youth	Youth valued over age

Source: From P. B. Bart & M. Grossman (1978). Menopause. In M. T. Notman & C. C. Nadelson (Eds.). *The Woman Patient: Medical and Psychological Interfaces,* pp. 351–352. Copyright © 1978 Plenum Publishing Corporation. Reprinted with permission.

Women in non-Western societies suffer fewer physical and psychological problems during menopause than do women in the United States. For example, no evidence of depression in menopausal women was found in fifteen non-Western cultures (Kaiser, 1990). Older women in these societies enjoyed enhanced social status and political power. They were freed from taboos involving menstrual pollution; they had seniority in their domestic unit, new role opportunities, permission to participate in traditional male domains of power, greater decision-making authority, and the respect and responsibility accorded to the elderly. Arab women in Israel also appear to gain power as they grow older (Friedman & Pines, 1992). In contrast, a similar shift with age is not found among poor women in either the United States or Kenya (Todd, Friedman, & Kariuki, 1990).

ROLE TRANSITIONS OF MIDLIFE AND LATER LIFE

In the United States, women are typically identified by an adjective referring to the menopause—*menopausal, postmenopausal,* or *premenopausal*—rather than by a reference to their social situation, such as *widowed, newly promoted,* or *empty nester* (Parlee, 1990). Physical symptoms are stressed, but women's experiential accounts are ignored. The reliance on biomedical causality leads researchers to ignore social context and to exaggerate differences between women and men. Gender differences are seen as important because other differences, such as ethnicity, class, and culture, are ignored (Unger, 1990). Cultural factors are critical for understanding the value and importance of midlife transitions.

Cultural Context and Midlife Transitions

> Irrevocable decisions of childhood, adolescence, and young adulthood shape the social context of middle age determining whether a woman will be surrounded by many children or one or two; whether she will be surrounded by grandchildren while she still has small children of her own at home; whether her family will be her primary concern or if she is likely to seek an outside job; if she does seek work outside the home whether she can hope for white-collar work or will be restricted by illiteracy to menial jobs. (Datan, Antonovsky, & Maoz, 1981, pp. 2–3)

The preceding quotation is from a pioneering study of midlife transitions for women in five subcultures in Israel. The participants ranged from a modern city-living population, similar to most women in the United States, to women living in an extremely traditional nomadic tribal society. Other groups of women in the study were in various stages of the process of modernization; that is, they had been born or raised in a traditional society but were now living in a more modern one. The basic question asked by the researchers was, "How is a woman's response to the changes of middle age shaped by the culture in which she has grown?"

The researchers had expected that attitudes about the end of fertility would be shaped by the value placed on childbearing in a woman's cultural group. They hypothesized that middle age would be perceived most negatively by women in the most traditional groups, since their cultural role is defined largely by their reproductive and mothering roles. Surprisingly, the study found that few of the women in any of the groups mourned their loss of fertility. Menopause was welcomed by women of all five subcultures, regardless of whether they had borne fifteen children (as was likely in the most traditional group) or one or two (as was probable in the most modern subculture). Psychological well-being at middle age was found to be highest for the most modern and the most traditional subcultures. Women in the transitional groups were least satisfied because they saw no choices for themselves among possible roles, although they recognized the broadened horizons open to other women. Women in the most traditional group appeared to gain power after menopause. The researchers suggested that Western biases may have led some previous researchers to confuse tradition for passivity. For example, one traditional Arab woman described the measures she took to deal with menopause: She made use of free medical help in Israeli clinics, traveled to a gynecologist for the sake of the excursion, and consulted a faith healer.

Cohort Effects

Sometimes women change cultures through the passage of time rather than moving from one place to another. Women who grew up during different historical periods differ in their response to midlife and aging. An examination of *cohort* effects allows researchers to explore the interaction between biological changes and social roles. Cohort refers to a group of persons born in the same close time period—for example, within the same year or the same decade. Individuals of the same cohort will tend to be exposed to the same broad societal events, which shape their life prospects and values similarly.

Would you expect the following cohorts to have responded the same way to life changes?

Women now in their 80s were born earlier than 1920. They were infants during World War I and young adults during the Great Depression. Their educational attainment is considerably lower than that of younger cohorts. These women are usually widowed, living alone or with relatives, and typically have insufficient incomes. Women born in the 1920s were adults during World War II. If they did not enlist in the military, they worked in war industries filling traditionally male jobs. Many returned to their homes after the war, but some juggled jobs, homemaking, and children. Many experienced drastic changes in family structures and social networks as a result of mass migration from rural areas to northern cities. They are likely to have limited access to pension programs as a result of interrupted and uneven work histories. Women born in the 1930s are a privileged group benefiting from a booming postwar economy. Many entered professions, reaching maturity at a time when women had begun to combine work with families. Feminist ideas were discussed if not realized. Now reaching retirement age, some plan to continue working outside the home. Others are caring for husbands or parents with chronic illnesses (Crose, Leventhal, Haug, & Burns, 1997).

A person's cohort provides a better prediction of her beliefs, values, and behavior than her chronological age does. A 40-year-old woman in 1940 cannot be readily compared with a 40-year-old woman of 1990. Research on women is particularly influenced by cohort effects, because women's roles in the past few generations have changed more dramatically than men's roles.

Old age is not an isolated stage of life. The resources available to older women derive from the opportunities and constraints they have experienced over a lifetime. In the United States, for example, women now in their middle years were the first cohort legally able to control childbearing through effective contraception and legal abortion. Thus, they are the first generation of women who could plan a career without a high probability that it would be disrupted by an unplanned pregnancy (Grambs, 1989).

Many of those who are currently very old probably never expected to live as long as they have. When they were born, life expectancy was 49. Death was a part of life for all age groups; a majority of this cohort had lost a parent, brother, or sister by the time they were 15. They grew up with a constant fear of killer childhood diseases, and they survived an influenza epidemic in 1917 to 1918 that killed millions of people. The great majority of people in this cohort did not finish high school.

In contrast, members of the current middle-age cohort usually have both parents living and may also have grandparents. Medical advances have made direct experience with death rare in their lives. The great majority are high school graduates, and a substantial number have college degrees. For women of the earlier cohort, divorce was a shame and a scandal; today it is an acceptable personal decision. They were also much less likely to have lived alone or been financially independent as young adults than today's women. The importance of all these differences in cohort experiences should demonstrate why it is impossible to generalize about aging across cohorts.

Race and Ethnicity

Women from ethnic minority groups have shorter life spans and may be functionally old well before age 65. The burden of poverty is also greater for aging women of color. Eighty percent of older black women and 50 percent of older Latinas live in poverty compared with 20 percent of older women as a whole (Padgett, 1988). The median income for older Asian-American women is also less than that of older Euro-American women (Yee, 1997).

Although older women of color suffer a greater relative decline in health as they age than Anglo-American women, their relative deprivation in income and health is not necessarily linked to less satisfaction in life. Blacks actually report greater life satisfaction than whites during their late middle age (Carlson & Videka-Sherman, 1990). African-American women have consistently been found to have the lowest rate of suicide of all age/ethnic categories (Padgett, 1988). Despite a lifetime of racism and poverty, they seem to view old age as a reward. Older women of color may be survivors who expect less than older women from more privileged groups.

These ethnic differences are more than just the effect of selection bias. Social networks within minority communities play an important role in life satisfaction that has largely been overlooked by mainstream researchers. Investigators conducting an in-depth examination of aging African-Americans living in low-income high-rise public housing found, for example, that almost everyone had received help from family, friends, and/or neighbors (Faulkner & Heisel, 1987). Women were significantly more likely to both give and receive favors than men. Much of this support occurred in the context of religious activity. Older Native-American women were also more likely to attend church and perform volunteer activities than either Anglo or Latina women (Harris, Begay, & Page, 1989).

Ethnic minority families place great importance on interdependence and the needs of the family over the needs of the individual. These values mean that increasing dependency in old age is not viewed as negatively as it is within dominant cultures (Yee, 1990). The majority of Asian-American women over age 65 are widowed, but they are less likely to live alone than non-Asian women. Like Mexican-American women, they are likely to share housing and receive help from an adult child (Yee, 1997). Social support can be both a comfort and a burden. Black single women who have dependent children or other relatives living with them are more likely to have economic problems than those who live alone (Ralston, 1997). Nevertheless, families are also the most dependable source of aid.

Communal values may contribute to a feeling of entitlement among older individuals so that they do not lose their sense of self-worth when their needs are met by others (Faulkner & Heisel, 1987). This sharing of limited economic and social resources is a positive adaptation to the pressures of poverty.

The Complex Nature of Midlife Role Transitions

Midlife is characterized by a series of role transitions. *Roles* are clusters of expectations placed on people who occupy a position in the social structure. Most people have many roles. These roles may be relational, such as the role of daughter, mother, wife, or grandmother, or they may be work related, such as the role of nurse, truck driver, or salesperson. As is obvious from these examples, many roles carry with them assumptions about the gender of the person occupying them as well as about his or her gender-related traits and behaviors.

During midlife, many roles begin to be redefined, resulting in permanent changes in an individual's life. Although every individual is embedded in many roles, researchers have focused on different midlife transitions in women and men. Until recently, changes in women's relational roles have been examined much more than changes in their work roles, whereas the opposite has been true for men. The different numbers of studies are due largely to unexamined assumptions about what roles are important for women and men.

When one role is singled out for attention, other roles may be neglected. Roles are not, however, acted out in isolation from each other. For the midlife woman, the departure of her last child from home; loss of a spouse or other longtime companion; entry into, reentry into, or departure from the labor market; or acquisition of a college degree is not an isolated event. Although each of these role transitions will be examined separately, they all influence one another. These transitions also interact with other events that are likely to occur in middle age, such as the aging of one's parents, the birth of grandchildren, and the new freedom to explore alternative lifestyles offered by retirement.

The consequences of life transitions are also influenced by their timing. Individuals are judged as being *on time* if their role behavior accords with cultural prescriptions for their age/sex category and *off time* if it does not. Ironically, for a midlife woman, a lifetime of on-time events such as marriage and childbearing in early adulthood means being vulnerable to economic declines throughout the latter half of the life span. Being off time, as in completing a college degree, entering an occupation early in one's work life, and postponing marriage and childbearing so as to advance in one's career, usually predicts economic security in later years (Long & Porter, 1984).

Since psychologists have tended to focus on women who are on time in their roles, they may have developed an overly negative image of women at midlife. These misperceptions have not been corrected because theories about women at midlife tend to be based on Freudian tradition. These theories focus on reproductive heterosexual womanhood. Thus, work on older women represents them as mourning the loss of reproductive and sexual functions (Gergen, 1990). Little attention has been paid to older women in general and even less to women in deviant off-time roles. The next part of this chapter looks at both traditional and non-traditional midlife roles.

The Empty-Nest Syndrome: Myths and Realities

For women who have followed a traditional lifestyle of early marriage and childbearing, midlife is usually the period when their last child leaves home. This period has been thought to be characterized by depression. A combination of unrealistic fears, loneliness, and crying bouts was even named "Mama Portnoy's complaint" by one early feminist researcher (Bart, 1970). Other psychologists and sociologists have labeled the phenomenon the *empty nest syndrome*. It is considered to be related to the arrival at adulthood of a woman's youngest child and her sense that she is no longer needed by her family. Such depressive reactions are said to be more common among women in ethnic groups that traditionally place great value on motherhood and the family (e.g., Jewish- and Italian-Americans).

In considering the empty nest as a cause of middle-age depression it is important to remember that when the empty nest is experienced, it appears to be quite idiosyncratic. One woman reported that she felt the strongest impact when her youngest child went to kindergarten, others when their first or last child went to college, and still others reported sadness when their child moved his or her personal belongings out of the family home after college (Black & Hill, 1984). The majority of midlife women who have developed other interests do not experience severe trauma when their last child departs from the home. On the contrary, most mothers positively anticipate freedom from child-rearing responsibilities and look forward to the opportunity to pursue their own interests and to spend more time with their peers (Black & Hill, 1984; Long & Porter, 1984). These mothers appear to view motherhood more as an episode than a lifelong occupation.

The concept of an empty nest syndrome seems to have been the result of psychologists' focus on women who had been socialized in traditional beliefs about motherhood. An interesting study illustrates how changes in early socialization patterns can influence role transitions much later in life. The researchers found that the empty nest was more likely to be a negative experience among the cohort of women who had reached adulthood during a period of strong societal emphasis on women's maternal role. Those women who had come of age in the 1950s (during the height of the so-called feminine mystique) reacted more negatively to the empty nest than women who had come of age during World War II (when women were encouraged to enter the labor market). These comparisons were done on successive twenty-year samples so that the women were the same age when they were surveyed. They demonstrate that the empty nest syndrome is more an effect of socialization during young adulthood than an inevitable response to maternal loss. In fact, the researchers argue that the current group of midlife women—who reached their young adulthood during the feminist movement—should experience the departure of their last child from home as positively as their grandmothers did (Adelmann, Antonucci, Crohan, & Coleman, 1989)!

It seems likely that the empty nest syndrome is class based as well as time bound. For example, in two successive samples of the alumnae of a private women's college, women in their early fifties often described their lives as "first-rate" and rated their quality of life as high (Mitchell & Helson, 1990). Empty nests, better health, and higher incomes were correlated with a positive quality of life. These respondents reported that after the children left home, life at home became simpler, and the energy that went to the children was redirected to the partner, work, the community, or self-development. The women reported a greater sense of control over their lives than they had previously.

These women were, however, in an excellent position to make use of the life opportunities that became open to them when their children left home. For example, 43 percent of the older cohort and 78 percent of the younger cohort in this study were in the workforce at least part time. Studies conducted in Israel, Kenya, and the United States have also indicated that only women with higher economic and social status gain greater power with age (Todd et al., 1990).

The departure of children from home may result in major economic losses for some women. For example, eligibility for public assistance such as Aid to Families with Dependent Children or survivor's benefits (if the woman is a widow with dependent children) ends when children reach age 18 (Long & Porter, 1984). At this time of a woman's life, opportunities for job training and career placement are few.

There is no evidence that being a mother necessarily enhances a woman's well-being. In a study of women over 50, researchers found no difference in happiness or satisfaction between mothers and childless women once income and employment status were controlled (Glenn & McLanahan, 1981). Attitudes about the gains and losses of retirement have also been found to be unrelated to the presence or absence of children (Anson, Antonovsky, Sagy, & Adler, 1989). Even for widows aged 60 to 75, who would seem to be most in need of children, children had only very slight effects on measures of life satisfaction (Beckman & Houser, 1982). One pair of researchers concluded:

> Best evidence now available indicates that the present young adult should not choose to have children on the basis of expectations that parenthood will lead to psychological rewards in the later stages of life. The prospects of such rewards seem rather dim at best. (Glenn & McLanahan, 1981)

Other sources of social support can make up for a lack of children.

Retirement

Retirement is a major life transition and a conspicuous marker of age. Stereotypes of retired people include both positive images—of freedom, travel, hobbies, and leisure—and negative ones of boredom, withdrawal, and feelings of uselessness. As with other developmental stages, the norm has been a male one. When people think of retirement, it is the stereotypical male pattern of leaving at the top of a lifelong career that comes to mind. For women, whose work patterns and life goals may be different, this stereotype does not always fit.

Research on women's decision to retire, adjustment to retirement, or its meaning in women's lives has lagged in comparison to research on men. Until recently, few women had enough years of continuous employment to afford the luxury of retirement. A majority of nonemployed older women did not describe themselves as retired, even up to age 74 (Bernard, Itzin, Phillipson, & Skucha, 1995). Older women continue to have domestic and family responsibilities so that retirement with its implication of freedom from the obligation to work does not describe the reality of their lives.

In keeping with androcentric biases about the world of work, few studies have examined women's decision to retire. Women are more likely to retire at an earlier age than men and for different reasons. Men are more likely to leave for work-related reasons, whereas women are more likely to leave for family reasons often involving the care of a spouse or parent. Married women are also sometimes pressured to retire at the same time as their usually older husbands (Carp, 1997).

Role reversal in paid employment (when the wife works and the husband does not) threatens traditional gender roles in several ways. The woman's employment enhances her status and power and may put pressure on her husband to take on some of her household tasks. Among British couples aged 55 to 69 where only one partner was employed, in about one-third of the cases this was the wife. These couples may not have been attempting to challenge traditional norms but were constrained by their circumstances. Wives who worked longer than their husbands tended to live in poorer households (presumably more dependent on their income), have children under the age of 21, and to be married to men with health problems (Arber & Ginn, 1995).

In many countries, women are required to leave the workforce at a younger age than men. For example, in Italy and Japan, women retire at age 55 and men at age 60. In the United Kingdom, women retire at 60 and men at age 65. It seems ironic to require women to leave the workforce before men do when they are likely to live many years longer. Such patterns also disadvantage women economically by allowing them less time to accumulate pension benefits (Grambs, 1989).

In general, the limited data comparing women's and men's experiences of retirement suggest that women do it differently. Women do less financial planning and less adequate planning than men do (Carp, 1997). Although this pattern could be due to women's traditional reliance on their husbands' income, divorced women and those who are newly widowed also do not try to acquire financial planning skills (Hayes & Anderson, 1993). Money matters have lagged behind labor force participation and remain the domain of men.

The experience of retirement varies greatly among different groups of women. Homemakers often find their husbands' retirement problematic. They often complain about the men's intrusion into their domain at home (Vinick & Ekerdt, 1992). One commonly heard "joke" is "I married him for better and for worse, but not for lunch." Women who worked at jobs with low salaries have more adjustment problems after retirement than women in more highly paid occupations. The loss of the work role often results in poor self-esteem, feelings of uselessness, loneliness, and isolation (Perkins, 1992). Professional women were found to have more trouble adjusting than nonprofessional women and, unlike men, high job satisfaction prior to retirement resulted in poorer adjustment to it (Carp, 1997).

Older women who chose the dual role labels of homemaker and retiree had higher self-esteem and less depression than those who labeled themselves either homemaker or retiree (Adelmann, 1993). However, those women who identified themselves with both roles were less likely to be married and had more education than women in the other groups. Most women still retire from low-paid, low-status, and relatively unrewarding jobs, not from careers.

Older Women and Poverty

Whether a woman is able to lead a satisfying and rewarding life in her middle and later years depends on a combination of material and psychological factors. Not surprisingly, money is an important material factor. Women who earned more in their paid work are happier with their retirement than those who earned less (Grambs, 1989). Poverty in old age remains a critical issue for women (see Figure 12.5). In 1992, the median annual income for women over age 65 was $8,189 versus $14,548 for men of the same age (Rubin, 1997). These figures include social security benefits, other pensions, and the income from investments. These income differentials are the consequence of lifetime inequalities. Few women or African-Americans of either sex have the same number of work years at the same pay level as white men. Only 27 percent of U.S. women over 65 receive a pension (one-half the pension rate for men), and the average pension income for women is only slightly more than half of men's average pension (Schulz, 1992).

There has been much discussion of the "feminization of poverty" in the United States. Much of this poverty is due to the poor economic situation of older women. In 1993, 16 percent of women over age 65 had incomes below the poverty level. Women make up 75 percent of the elderly poor. Widows have the lowest income of any demographic group in the United States (Rubin, 1997). Older lesbian couples are often unprotected by social policies that provide heterosexual couples with a safety net through social security, pensions, and health insurance (Motenko & Greenberg, 1995). Poverty makes older people dependent on their families for survival.

Since younger cohorts of women have had more years of work experience than the currently retired, one might expect that poverty in old age will be less likely for them. However, the income gap for retired men and women has actually widened in the last two decades because of gender inequities in income

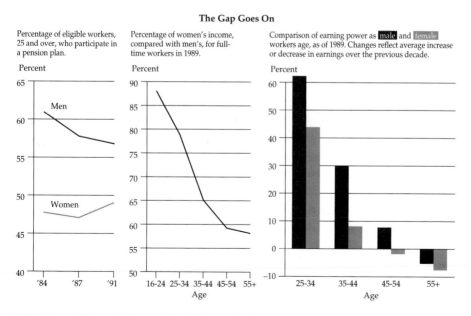

FIGURE 12.5. Women's financial well-being declines more than men's with age.
Source: Copyright © 1994 by the New York Times. Reprinted by permission.

from pensions and financial investments. "Midlife women need to be vigilant lest when they reach old age they will be no better off than their mothers and grandmothers before them" (Grambs, 1989, p. 179).

CAREGIVER ROLES IN LATER LIFE

Being a Grandmother

Becoming a grandmother in her fifties is a probable event for a woman who has led a traditional on-time lifestyle of early marriage and motherhood. This is a positive event for most women, who may look forward to having a less stressful relationship with their grandchildren than they had with their own children.

> Being a grandmother is one of the great experiences of life, especially today, when women cannot take this experience for granted. There is no question that having a grandchild come to visit is demanding physically, mentally, and emotionally, especially when the grandmother is still employed.
>
> Our three-year-old granddaughter has just left after a four-week visit. As the wildflowers in the juice glass fade, I try to decide which of the twenty-one crayon and watercolor pictures to keep taped to the banister. I rescue a 1950 miniature trailer truck her father used to play with from under the bed and hear her say proudly, "I'm bigging!" I see the world anew through her eyes and hope I'm still bigging too. (A woman in her seventies, in Doress et al., 1987, p. 133)

Today's grandmothers want to define for themselves the specific relationship they have with their grandchildren (Doress et al., 1987). Few want to babysit regularly or be responsible for child care:

> I have an unwritten understanding with my children. I do not babysit my grandchildren, I entertain them. I invite them—but I am not called in as a babysitter. I think babysitting damages the relationship. They know when I'm with them I'm there because I want to be and because I enjoy their company. And I invite them on that basis too. I don't want to be considered a babysitter because that's not the relationship I want to establish with my grandchildren. (A 74-year-old woman, in Doress et al., 1987, p. 135)

These women appear to have more power in their relationship with their family than many older women do. Relationships between mothers and their adult daughters are not always close or positive. The younger women can act as gatekeepers determining the extent of the older women's involvement in the lives of their grandchildren (Henwood, 1993).

For some women, however, being a grandmother involves more than a short-term commitment. Economic factors may limit their ability to make choices. Many midlife women take on substantial responsibility for the care of grandchildren because of the illness, incapacity, or death of the child's parents (Long & Porter, 1984).

In some ethnic groups, active grandmothering is common and considered normative. Black women, for example, commonly experience raising their children's children, whether as their own or as their grandchildren. Young girls may also be singled out by their grandmothers for a special socialization into the family's history and cultural traditions (Ralston, 1997).

Grandmothers are seen as the center of the Native American family and as the people who hold it together. It is common for women to be grandmothers by the age of 40. Children are often cared for by their grandmothers who are unwilling to let adverse circumstances such as the youth of the mother or poverty affect the child (John et al., 1997).

In most Hispanic cultures, grandmothers are ever present and highly involved in family affairs. Chicana grandmothers are usually considered to be the backbone of family endurance and the symbol of cultural survival (Facio, 1997). They are presumed to have a great deal of practical knowledge and are seen as the family's advice giver and chief storyteller. The positive value attached to motherhood in this group legitimates the status of grandmother. Older women have more status and power than their white American counterparts.

On the other hand, some older Chicana women find their role confining. They object to becoming convenient baby-sitters and make a distinction between "raising" children and providing child care (Facio, 1997). They do not want the caregiver role to be taken for granted:

> I love it, but I'm not the kind of grandma where I'm going to sit down and only knit little things for my grandkids or nothing. (Facio, 1996, p. 92)

Lack of involvement in an extended family appears to be peculiar to white middle-class culture. In one survey of women over 60 in the American Southwest, 50 percent of the Native American and 32 percent of Latina respondents reported taking care of children versus only 14 percent of the Anglo respondents (Harris et al., 1989). African-American women tend to report significant familial networks even when they are single and living alone (Spurlock, 1984). In fact, having a spouse had little influence on the number of socially supportive relationships or the most important sources of financial assistance reported. The major role of marriage is to privatize helping relationships. Married older women have been found to give less help to their friends and more help to their kin in comparison to the help provided by widows (Gallagher & Gersler, 1993).

Care for Aging Parents

The Impact of Sexism

In our culture, women are expected to tend to their elderly parents when they are ill, provide transportation to the doctor's office, and be on call for any emergency (Stueve & O'Donnell, 1984). In a phone survey of 315 adults living in western Alabama, such gender-stereotypic assumptions were confirmed. Both women and men agreed that it was more appropriate for an employed son to help his infirm parent with yard work, whereas it was more appropriate for a similarly employed daughter to assist with housework and to bring meals to her mother's home (Roff & Klemmack, 1986). Consider the amount of time and effort that will have to be spent by daughters versus sons in their gender-appropriate caretaking tasks!

Daughters provide more support to older parents than sons do. They help by running errands, giving custodial care, and taking older parents into their home. In a study in Quebec, daughters also had more contact with formal authorities on behalf of the elderly. For these women, other obligations did not reduce their amount of assistance, although it did reduce the amount of time that they spent providing it. Employed women provided as much care as unemployed women. For men, in contrast, other obligations reduced both helping and time. The group that spent the least time on caregiving were single men with children and married men without children (Jutras & Veilleux, 1991).

When there are no daughters, sons do not necessarily step in. Daughters who were only children were found to be twice as likely as only sons to become caregivers (Coward & Dwyer, 1990). When sons did involve themselves in the care of their elderly parents, they were likely to wind up as care managers (Montgomery & Kamo, 1989). Widows without daughters tended to receive support from daughters-in-law, sisters, female kin, or friends and neighbors (O'Bryant, 1988). These gender differences probably stem from the lower expectation of involvement of both the sons themselves and others.

The Impact of Class

Daughters from working-class backgrounds were more likely to live with or near parents and to have built up patterns of interdependence and helping out. By contrast, middle-class daughters, particularly those women who left home to attend college, were more likely to draw strict boundaries between their own nuclear families and those of their parents and to have constructed lives that were separate from those of parents and siblings (Stueve & O'Donnell, 1984). For working-class women, parents are seen as part of the immediate family, and their needs are seen as part of the fabric of daily life. The following case study illustrates how unaware these women may be about the amount of elder care they are providing:

> Nora Dubchek lives two miles away from her widowed father. She works part time as a hairdresser, and her husband is a self-employed gardener. When she was first asked if her father had come to rely on her, she replied, "No, no. Only when he doesn't feel well. You know, I will sometimes take him to the post office, or drive him here, or go over and do a few things in the house." When asked how often she saw her father, however, she went on to say, "Oh, I see him every day. I was there this morning. This morning I did the dishes for him because he has a bad hand. And I just talked to him." Later in the conversation, it came out that Mrs. Dubchek did many other things for her father—she tends to home repairs, makes sure his house is properly cleaned, takes him places in bad weather, and nudges her brothers and children to make regular visits. She has thought about her father's advancing age and the possibility that at some point he may not be able to live alone. She anticipates becoming more involved in his life, even to the point of establishing a joint residence. (Stueve & O'Donnell, 1984, p. 217)

In the same study, middle-class parents and daughters believed more than those from the working class that parents can be taken care of by people other than family members. Parents were seen as having the financial resources to purchase needed services and were also perceived as being accustomed to making arrangements without the help of their children. Among daughters who lived within an hour's drive of parents, full-time employed women provided less assistance and visited less often (Stueve & O'Donnell, 1984).

The Woman in the Middle: Myths and Realities

Longer life spans have made it increasingly likely that adult children will need to care for aging parents. Only 45 percent of the oldest group of women surveyed (born between 1905 and 1917) had ever been caregivers. For the youngest group surveyed (born between 1927 and 1934), 64 percent were caregivers (Moen, Robison, & Fields, 1994). Because of smaller families, the number of daughters per mother has also decreased. A new version of the problems associated with women's involvement in multiple roles is the conception of *the woman in the middle* (Brody, 1981). This label describes the middle-aged woman who must cope simultaneously with the needs of elderly parents and teenaged children. Her burdens have been richly detailed by the popular media (see Figure 12.6).

This concept of the "woman in the middle" may be a construction of mainstream society's preoccupation with autonomy and independence. Ethnic minority groups seem to have a more interdependent view of relationships

FIGURE 12.6. An example of negative images of the caretaking role.

between the generations. African-American women take relatives into their homes at twice the rate of their Anglo-American age peers (Beck & Beck, 1989). Black middle-aged women provide both economic and social support for both older and younger relatives. Black elders are also more likely to be supported by a variety of helpers rather than one child as in white elder care (Doress-Worters, 1994). While these practices are probably partly a result of economic necessity, they also provide psychological benefits for the elderly that help explain why older African-Americans are more satisfied with their lives than older white peers.

Periods of simultaneous heavy demands appear to be relatively rare (Baruch, 1984). The assumption that elderly parents are typically needy and dependent is also not correct. The majority of older people are in good health. In a survey conducted in 1975, almost 70 percent of people over 65 rated their health as excellent or good (Stueve & O'Donnell, 1984). Moreover, women— who comprise the largest part of the population over 65—report sizable networks of women their own age who provide mutual support (O'Bryant, 1988). Little attention has been paid to how this society of women functions to facilitate adjustment to the problems of aging.

Gender and Care

Women constitute 75 percent of family caregivers (Mathews & Campbell, 1995). While elder care may not be as bad as it is portrayed by the media, it takes an emotional toll in addition to the economic toll of premature workforce departure (much more common among women than men). A meta-analysis of gender differences in caregiving outcomes found a greater impact on women. The effect was not explained by how well the dependent individual functioned nor the caregiver's degree of involvement, although women were more likely than men to perform personal care and household tasks (Miller & Cafasso, 1992). In another study, women felt much more burdened than men and had more health complaints despite being younger than the male caregivers (Pushkar-Gold, Franz, Reis, & Senneville, 1994). Caregivers have twice the depression rate of the general population, and depression is greatest for those taking care of a cognitively impaired relative (Tennstedt, Cafferata, & Sullivan, 1992).

There are fewer gender differences in elder care between employed women and men. Sons and daughters who are still employed tended to provide primarily instrumental care such as transportation, shopping, laundry, and help with finances. Male caregivers who provided personal care were likely to be doing so by default—they were not financially well off and were less likely to have siblings, especially female ones. They provided fewer hours of personal care than their female counterparts, but only about one hour less per week. Both men and women caregivers reported lost opportunities for promotion and career advancement (Mathews & Campbell, 1995). It is important to recognize men's involvement, because it is middle-aged women who are seen as less reliable or more problematic employees.

Our society assumes that wives will care for their incapacitated husbands (see Figure 12.7). Indeed, they may have little choice about the matter, and little attention has been paid to their emotional or physical needs.

I cry a lot because I never thought it would be this way. I didn't expect to be mopping up the bathroom, changing him, doing laundry all the time. I was taking care of babies at twenty; now I'm taking care of my husband.

People tell me he deserves all the care I can give him because he's such a nice person and was always so good to me. Well, I'm a nice person and have always been good to him—what do I deserve? (Doress et al., 1987, pp. 199–200)

Caregiving when a woman resents it or is overwhelmed by economic and social responsibilities is a great burden—one that our society has preferred to ignore. Even those who are very aware of societal constraints on women to function in multiple roles requiring care can be overcome by stress. Following is a quote from Mary Pipher, a noted psychotherapist, whose work on the psychological issues of adolescent girls was discussed in Chapter 7. Her remarks are from a recent book in which she discusses relationships between midlife women and their aging parents. It refers to her experiences during the year she was responsible for the care of her dying mother:

That year, no matter where I was, I felt guilty. If I was with my mother, I wasn't caring for my own kids or my clients. If I was working, I was ignoring my family. When I was with my children, I thought of my mother alone in a

FIGURE 12.7. "Your husband is lucky to have you to take care of him at home, Mrs. Jacobs."
Source: Cartoon by Maggy Krebs from Paula B. Doress-Worters and Diana Laskin Siegal. *The New Ourselves Growing Older: Women Aging with Knowledge and Power* (NY: Simon & Schuster, 1994). Copyright © Paula B. Doress-Worters and Diana Laskin Siegal. Used by permission of the authors.

faraway hospital. I got depressed and crabby. My husband and I fought more and my children didn't get the supervision and nurturing they needed. I got a speeding ticket. (Pipher, 1999, p. 9)

On the other hand, some women find satisfaction in caring for someone they love.

> My mother never had any joy, only hard work and struggle. I tried to make it up to her, to do things for her and to give her things, and felt guilty because I couldn't take away the old pains and troubles and make her into a happy person. But at least I was able to take care of her in her old age. I have no guilt about that. And she died at home, in my house, where I could say goodbye to her in my own way and in my own space. That was five years ago, and as I get older I see more and more of my mother in myself, and that's okay because she was a wonderful woman and I love her. (A woman in her fifties, in Doress et al., 1987, p. 203)

Caring for and losing a parent when a woman is older can seem like a part of the natural timing of events. Women who were born when their parents were young may find transitions such as the aging and death of their parents easier. They have friends and acquaintances who have had similar experiences (Stueve & O'Donnell, 1984).

Feelings about the personal costs of caregiving are very different from one woman to another. It is important that society permit women to have as many choices as possible. These include the availability of full- and part-time support systems to relieve the primary caregiver. Pressures on women who are not employed outside the home are particularly intense. They often feel they must be endlessly available to others, and when they do feel resentful or overwhelmed about their obligations, they feel they have failed (Baruch, 1984). These feelings result from societal assumptions that only women should and can provide care.

LOSSES ASSOCIATED WITH AGING

Widowhood

Differences in the life expectancy of women and men, combined with a marital pattern in which women marry men older than themselves, mean that women are more likely to be widowed than are men. Almost half of all the women over age 65 are widows. In contrast, only 14 percent of all men over 65 are widowers (Bradsher, 1997). Men who lose their wives are more apt to remarry than women who lose their husbands.

The experience of widowhood varies according to the time of life when it occurs. Younger women usually recover from their loss better than older women do. The older women may be in ill health themselves or in economically straitened circumstances. One study of 226 women between the ages of 60 and 89 who had been widowed from seven to twenty-one months found that positive feelings were associated with greater religious involvement, a larger number of siblings, and support from children and families (McGloshen & O'Bryant, 1988). Negative feelings were associated with additional deaths among family or friends, housing dissatisfaction, and a history of employment outside the home during marriage. No explanation was given for the latter finding. Depression in widows was also associated with financial strain. For men, depression was associated with the strain of household management (Umberson, Wortman, & Kessler, 1992).

One might expect black women and women from other groups with close relational networks to be less devastated by widowhood, but little attention has been paid to race and class differences in this area. Spousal relationships appear to play a comparatively less important role in black women's than in white women's lives (Brown & Gary, 1985). Black women may rely less on male support because the greater vulnerability of black men to poor health makes it likely that these women will face middle age as a widow or with the added responsibilities of a chronically ill spouse (Spurlock, 1984).

Ethnicity and class difference are, of course, intertwined with economic need. In the United States, social security pays a widow with dependent children a caretaker's allowance, but only until the children reach age 18. This system docs not supplement a widow's income again until she reaches age 60 (50 if she is disabled). Private pensions and life insurance contribute to widows' economic well-being in only a small percentage of cases. Moreover, if a woman has followed a traditional life path, the time she has spent out of the labor force reduces the number of years used to compute her retirement benefits (Long & Porter, 1984). One study found that, on average, widowhood reduced women's living standards by 18 percent and pushed 10 percent of the women whose prewidowhood income was above the poverty line below it (Bound, Duncan, Laren, & Oleiniek, 1991).

Nevertheless, women cope better with the loss of a spouse than men do. Widowed women have higher levels of happiness, life satisfaction, and home life satisfaction than widowed men (Gove & Shin, 1989). These data are consistent with findings showing that widowhood is a much higher predictor of suicide for older men than for older women (Canetto, 1992). Older men depend on their wives for emotional support, personal care, and running of the home. These losses appear to be psychologically more devastating than the economic losses sustained by women who have lost their husbands.

Loss of a Lesbian Life Partner

Lesbians who have lost their companions may suffer additional stress because the relationship is not publicly acknowledged. Women who have lost a lover may have to carry on without the usual social supports offered to widows. Even when the relationship is an open one, friends may not be aware of the depth of the loss. As one woman recounted:

> Recently, I vacationed with friends who had been friends also with my deceased partner-in-life. A guest arrived with slides of earlier vacations, including pictures of my lover. I objected that if I had been a man who had been recently widowed, they surely would have asked if I would object to showing the pictures. One friend responded that she wanted very much to see them. She blanched when I suggested she might feel differently after the death of her husband. Clearly, she thought that my relationship with Karen differed

from her marriage; she evidently also thought my love differed from her friendship with Karen only by degree. Heterosexuals really do not understand what lesbians feel for their partners, even when they know us well. All of these friends had known Karen and me as lovers and had sent me bereavement condolences when Karen died. (In Doress et al., 1987, p. 139)

The loss of a significant other—female or male—to whom a woman has not been married is multiplied by the lack of legal acknowledgment of such relationships. The lover of the departed person may find herself deprived of economic resources she has long shared. And, of course, she receives no spousal benefits of any kind.

PSYCHOLOGICAL WELL-BEING IN THE SECOND HALF OF LIFE

The Reentry Woman

Life at midlife and beyond should not be considered merely a catalog of losses. "Women's history is filled with stories about women for whom life began at 40—or thereabouts. Grandma Moses's late start was somewhat excessive—at age 78—but the fact that her serious work began late is not atypical for her sex" (Alington & Troll, 1984, p. 196). In some cases, personal misfortune serves as a catalyst for new kinds of achievement. For example, divorced women are disproportionately represented among the ranks of adult students, and they are noticeably more committed, both as students and workers, than any other group (Alington & Troll, 1984).

Midlife achievement may be due to a reduction in family responsibilities or because the woman did not have an opportunity to indulge her passions for personal achievement earlier in life. Two-thirds of all adults who have returned to school (the majority of whom are women) reported that they had wanted to enroll sooner than they actually did (Schlossberg, 1984). They were impeded by institutional barriers, such as requirements that students take at least twelve credits during a semester or the lack of evening courses.

Contrary to assumptions that an older life stage is one of limited choice and few opportunities, many women choose to do new things and expose themselves to new experiences. An exciting catalog of achievements was provided by one group of fifty-six women between the ages of 60 and 70 (Siegel, 1993):

Emalu has published a book of her newly written poems: Betty and Laura took a study tour to Antarctica; Charlotte and her husband attend a different Elder Hostel every year; Bev gave herself a cruise in Norwegian waters for her 60th birthday; Laci is taking piano lessons and has given two recitals; Carol learned Italian before taking a sabbatical year in Rome. . . .

Shevy Healy and Vera Martin took on leadership roles in creating the Old Lesbians Organizing Committee. Lydia Peyton tutors children in her granddaughter's elementary school. Lucille Parker, an African-American civil service retiree, helped create new projects at her senior center. (p. 181)

Midlife achievement may also be a result of a personality change in the direction of assertive independence that occurs in midlife women. Midlife brings with it a sense that there is still much to do and options are diminishing; it is now or never, but not yet too late (Lachman & James, 1997).

As life expectancies continue to increase and health care helps women to live healthier lives in their fifties and beyond, we can expect that the ranks of those who are off time in their years of peak achievement will continue to grow. Already such women can be found as the deans of law schools (Barbara Aronstein Black, Columbia University), the authors of best-selling books (Belva Plain), and at the forefront of organizations for social change (Marian Wright Edelman). One recent study has found that more women in their early fifties rated their lives as first-rate than either younger or older women in their sample (Mitchell & Helson, 1990). For economically advantaged women, midlife may indeed be prime time.

Sexuality at Midlife and Beyond

Most studies of midlife sexuality are limited to married women with little attention to those who are not partnered or who are partnered with a woman. Although changes in sexual activity are thought to be a result of aging, they may also reflect women's difficulty in finding a suitable partner or lack of privacy in living arrangements (Daniluk, 1998). A woman's past sexual patterns of desire and behavior appear to be the best predictors of sexual patterns as she grows older. For women who never, or rarely, enjoyed sex, menopause may be experienced as relief from having to be sexually available and active (Barbach, 1993).

The equation of youth and sexuality may also contribute to women's lessening sexual activities. Middle-aged women see themselves as less attractive than any other age group (Stevens-Long & Commons, 1992). Although midlife lesbians are less influenced by cultural pressures than heterosexual women,

Making a Difference

Maggie Kuhn (1905–1995), a lifelong social activist, was forced to retire at age 65 in 1970, but her most important work was about to begin. She met with five friends in similar circumstances and together they began an alliance called Consultation of Older and Younger Adults for Social Change, later renamed the Gray Panthers. Kuhn was a Gray Panthers leader until her death in 1995 at age 89. She and her organization took on issues ranging from pension rights and the hearing aid industry to the Vietnam War. Kuhn's charisma and speaking ability—she gave thousands of speeches around the country including several on Capitol Hill—attracted media attention and helped the Panthers achieve "a contemporary cultural revolution" in the form of nursing home and health care reform and ending forced retirement provisions. Two weeks before her death, Kuhn picketed with striking transit workers. In her own words, "Well-aimed slingshots can topple giants."

Sources: Mority, C. (Ed.) (1978). Current biography. New York: The H. W. Wilson Co.; Graham, J. (Ed.) (1995). Current biography yearbook. New York: The H. W. Wilson Co.

they are not free from them. They reported to one interviewer that their ability to be comfortable with the changes of age involved a conscious process of rejecting cultural messages that blame women for their failure to retain the appearance of youth. The changes of midlife also enabled some women to recognize their attraction to women. Almost half the sample of more than 100 midlife lesbians had heterosexual relationships at some point in their lives and had one or more children (Sang, 1991).

There are even fewer studies of sexuality in older women than in middle-aged women. It is difficult to predict what sexuality at old age will be like for the current generation of young women because of cohort problems. Today's older women grew up with different values and more restrictive norms. "They were taught that sex was disgusting, nasty, or bad. It was restricted by the church, warned against by mothers, and relegated to hushed, forbidden discussions" (Daniluk, 1998, p. 217). Nevertheless, some older women retain their interest. Good sex for women over 70 has been linked to good health and an interesting and interested partner.

Like many of the other topics discussed in this chapter, sexuality is linked to financial well-being:

> Sexual pleasure may be very low on the priority list of women who cannot afford to feed themselves or their families. For some elderly women who are struggling to survive, sexuality is simply irrelevant. (Gannon, 1994, p. 121)

Sexism as well as racism and classism affect women's interest in sex. It is not uncommon for middle-aged men to blame their diminishing sexual drive or problems in sexual functioning on their partners. Women may accept the blame, believing that their aging bodies are no longer sexually desirable (Daniluk, 1998).

Older women can find no validation of the normality of their erotic desires in the media. Sean Connery, a man in his midsixties, was recently voted the "Sexiest Man Alive" by readers of *People* magazine. Photos of Sophia Loren and Elizabeth Taylor may be presented in the media as images of aging beauty, but it is difficult to imagine either of these women, or others of their cohort, receiving the designation of "Sexiest Woman Alive" (Daniluk, 1998).

Thus, even well-off aging women may decide to "go it alone." The stories of 90 never-married, divorced, and widowed women between the ages of 40 and 55 told of freedom, adventure, self-satisfaction, ease, and an increasing capacity to appreciate moments of joy and discovery. They also reported feelings of spiritual regeneration or transformation in their lives (Anderson & Stewart, 1994). Many have found it quite challenging to include safe and satisfying sexual activities into their lives. Some have no desire for sexual intimacy and others have found outlets for sexual and creative energy in masturbation and fantasy, dance, art, and music.

Friendship and Social Support

Perhaps the most important psychological factor in satisfaction during later life is connections with other people. Loneliness is one of the most feared consequences of aging. It is a major problem for women who live alone, especially if they live in small towns or rural areas (Adams, 1997). Nevertheless, older women seem to have an advantage over men in creating and sustaining networks of friends. Women's support networks are a valuable resource in aging. Their friendships help to maintain physical health, increase psychological adjustment and satisfaction, and contribute to continued psychological growth in old age.

Women of all ages are more likely to have close friends, to confide intimate matters to their friends, and to have a varied circle of friends than are men (Adams, 1997; Grambs, 1989). Women have closer networks of relatives as well (Antonucci & Akiyama, 1997). Friends appear to be more important than relatives for many groups of elderly women. For example, elderly widows' contact with their adult children was found to be unrelated to morale, while contact with friends and neighbors was correlated with decreased loneliness, less worrying, and feeling useful and respected (Grambs, 1989). Ever-single elderly women are healthier than their widowed, divorced, or separated counterparts probably because they have maintained relationships with a supportive peer group of friends. Those who have been married report that their spouse is their preferred provider of most types of informal social support, followed by adult children. The effect of this dependency may be a less effective support system for the formerly married at a time when it is needed (Newtson & Keith, 1997).

Relationships with friends may be important because they are voluntarily chosen and based on common interests. Interacting with friends is a boost to one's sense of efficacy and self-esteem in old age. Women maintain and widen their friendship networks even when they are limited in their mobility. In a study of elderly residents in a retirement home, it was found that the women relied on the telephone to keep in touch with old friends and made new friends in nearby rooms (Hochschild, 1978). Women are probably being socialized for affiliation no less today than they ever were. We can predict that younger cohorts of women will continue to rely on their connectedness with friends as they grow older, and we can speculate that they will find keeping in touch easier with advances in communication technology. If it seems farfetched to imagine Great-Grandma logging onto her international computer network from her bedside chair in a retirement home, remember that future cohorts of elderly women will have grown up with such technology.

ACTIVISM AND FEMINISM AMONG OLDER WOMEN

Midlife is a time when many women feel freed from the constraints of femininity. The so-called empty nest is usually experienced with relief and joy and menopause is not a major health crisis for most women. Just at they outgrow their early roles and definitions, midlife women may also outgrow a need to conform to social pressures to be passive and self-sacrificing. In general, women in their early 50s saw themselves as assured, oriented in the present rather than the future, cognitively broad and complex, well adjusted, and smooth in relationships, although they were aware of aging (Helson & Wink, 1992). Women physicians reported some of the same changes as professional men, such as a greater sense of their leadership potential and better judgment and impulse control. These women also reported less concern for validation from others (Cartwright & Wink, 1994).

Another view of the freedom of middle and later life for women is shown in Figure 12.8. Elizabeth Layton began her life as an artist in 1977 at the age of 68. Her work, exhibited nationally since 1980, has won many honors. Although depicting aging is taboo in the art world, "Layton is able to tackle such difficult content because she doesn't give a damn about the art world. She has unself-consciously mastered the fusion of personal and political that so many progressive artists strive for." In this radiant self-portrait, *Her Strength Is in Her Convictions,* Layton shows off a chestful of political buttons (Lippard, 1986).

As family and job pressures recede for midlife women, activism and political involvement of all kinds may increase. This will probably be especially true of cohorts of women now entering middle and later life, because they have grown up with important social movements like the civil rights movement, the women's movement, the antinuclear and antiwar movements, and environmental activism.

People aged 55 to 64 are now more likely to exercise political power by voting than any other segment of the population. The percentage of elderly in the American population is larger than at any time in history and is still increasing (Grambs, 1989). Thus, simple demographics suggest an increasingly important role in public life for older women.

FIGURE 12.8. Older women as activists: an alternative view.

The political activism of older people is often focused on the position of the elderly in society. Activist Maggie Kuhn founded the Gray Panthers after she was forced to retire at the age of 65. The Older Women's League (OWL) lobbies effectively on policy issues affecting older women. The American Association of Retired Persons, another powerful lobbying group, has a special program on women's concerns. Senior Action in a Gay Environment (SAGE) provides services and information for older gay men and lesbians (Macdonald & Rich, 1983). As women become more sensitive to their vulnerability in old age and more educated in public affairs, more participation and more leadership from older women can be expected.

Among women who become activists against social injustice, many see their activism as connected to their feminism. Interviews have chronicled the activism of women leaders on issues such as toxic waste, neighborhood community life, education for disadvantaged children, auto safety, and nuclear weapons. These women are a diverse group ranging from well-to-do white Jewish suburbanites to a former Catholic nun working in Appalachia and the black daughter of a Virginia sharecropper. They conceived of their feminism broadly, believing that "everything is connected," and that social activism is a form of nurturing others. One reported that she had started seeing the nuclear issue in terms of her children; another said that she had never thought of herself as a feminist, but

> when I have to fight for my children, I do, and I guess I've always been a feminist in my own way; I've always fought for what I think is important. To me, that's what it means to be a feminist—being able to fight for your rights, your community, your children, and other women. (Garland, 1988, p. xxi)

Though psychologists are beginning to view midlife as a time of growth and expansion of roles for women, rather than a time of loss and decline, there is little psychological research on the political consciousness and activism of midlife women. To begin understanding the meaning that political and social events have for women, feminist psychologists recommend the use of intensive case studies. In one such study of three women who had graduated from college in 1964, several factors that seemed to have influenced political consciousness in later life were found (Stewart & Gold-Steinberg, 1990). These included growing up in a politically aware family; political activity in adolescence and young adulthood; the desire to make a contribution to the world; experiences as a parent; and access at midlife to time, energy, and resources. Interviews and case studies can help researchers conceptualize this new area of research in ways that are meaningful to women.

In a powerful message to feminists of all ages who want to be active on behalf of older women, one older feminist cautioned that activism must be based on a real knowledge of women in all their diversity, not on stereotypes or a person's own fears of aging (Macdonald & Rich, 1983). Women are advised not to talk about "the woman's movement" until all the invisible women are present—all races and cultures, and *all ages* of all races and cultures. One is reminded that an old woman has not always been old. She is in the process of discovering what 70, 80, and 90 mean. As more and more old women talk and write about the reality of this process, in a world that negates them, we will all discover how revolutionary that is.

CONNECTING THEMES

- *Gender is more than just sex.* Women's and men's lives are different because of sexism rather than sex. It is more difficult to make generalizations about people as they age because the cumulative effect of biological, social, and cultural forces creates differences within groups as well as between them. Both the timing and kind of roles available differ greatly, so that aging has very different implications for women and men. The gendered nature of these roles accounts for most of the inequalities between women and men found in later life.
- *Language and naming are sources of power.* The power to name is particularly clear in the identification of menopause as synonymous for aging. This has made aging appear to be more destructive for women than for men and has put women at risk for many medical procedures that cannot cure aging.
- *Women are not all alike.* Models of aging are based almost entirely on white middle-class women in the United States. Studies that look at aging across class, ethnicity, and culture indicate that gender differences in aging are not biologically determined but are socially constructed by a variety of social forces.
- *Psychological research can foster social change.* Social change is impeded by U.S. views of individualism and independence. Successful transitions from midlife to beyond are facilitated by social support systems and collectivistic philosophies. Middle-aged women's renewed sense of personal freedom and defiance of societal constraints can provide an important source of energy for effective social change.

SUGGESTED READINGS

DATAN, NANCY, ANTONOVSKY, AARON, & MAOZ, BENJAMIN. (1981). *A time to reap: The middle age of women in five Israeli subcultures.* Baltimore: Johns Hopkins. In analyzing how the meaning of the empty nest is socially and culturally constructed, this book goes beyond the particular cultures studied to show how researchers' beliefs about women influence the questions they can ask and the answers they can find. A wise blend of anthropology, sociology, and psychology.

DORESS-WORTERS, PAULA, & SIEGAL, DIANA S. (1994). *The new ourselves growing older.* New York: Simon & Schuster. A new edition of the popular book by and for women, this work relies on an excellent base of scholarship and research, yet avoids jargon. It has many excellent and practical suggestions for understanding and coping with the physical and social changes of the second half of life.

COYLE, JEAN M. (Ed.). (1997). *Handbook on women and aging.* Westport, CT: Greenwood Press. An excellent source book for information on diverse populations of women. Chapters are written by experts in each area and include many citations for further research.

GULLETTE, MARGARET M. (1997). *Declining to decline: Cultural combat and the politics of the midlife.* Charlottesville, VA: The University Press of Virginia. Although this prize-winning book is about midlife for men and women, it is important reading nevertheless. This book wittily exposes the cultural construction of midlife and moves attention away from "midlife crisis" as a private psychological condition to a collective problem.

Violence Against Women

This chapter was contributed by Jacquelyn Weygandt White,
Patricia L. N. Donat, and Barrie Bondurant.

- COMMONALITIES AMONG ALL FORMS OF VIOLENCE AGAINST WOMEN
- CHILDHOOD SEXUAL ABUSE
  Defining Childhood Sexual Abuse
  Frequency of Childhood Sexual Abuse
  Who Commits Childhood Sexual Abuse?
  Who Are the Victims?
  Consequences for the Survivor
  Steps to Protect Children and Treat Victims
- COURTSHIP VIOLENCE
  Defining Courtship Violence
  Frequency of Courtship Violence
  Who Inflicts and Sustains Courtship Violence?
  When Does Courtship Violence Occur?
  Consequences of Courtship Violence
  What Is Being Done?
- ACQUAINTANCE SEXUAL ASSAULT AND RAPE
  Defining Sexual Assault

Frequency of Sexual Assault
Who Is at Risk?
Who Does This?
Consequences for the Victim
What Is Being Done?
- SEXUAL HARASSMENT
  Defining Sexual Harassment
  Frequency of Sexual Harassment
  Who Is at Risk?
  Who Sexually Harasses? The Interaction of Individual and Organizational Factors
  Consequences of Sexual Harassment
  What Is Being Done?
- WIFE ABUSE
  "Wife" Abuse versus "Spouse" Abuse
  Frequency of Wife Abuse
  Who Commits Wife Abuse?
  Who Are the Victims?
  Consequences for the Victim
  Steps to Take
- **Conclusion**
- **Connecting Themes**
- **Suggested Readings**

every 3 minutes a woman is beaten
every five minutes a
woman is raped/every ten minutes
a lil girl is molested
yet i rode the subway today
i sat next to an old man who may have beaten his old wife
3 minutes ago or 3 days/30 years ago
he might have sodomized his
daughter but i sat there
cuz the young men on the train
might beat some young women

later in the day or tomorrow
I might not shut my door fast
enuf/push hard enuf
  very 3 minutes it happens . . .
    ery three minutes
     ry five minutes
      y ten minutes
       y day

—NTOZAKE SHANGE, *1978, pp. 114, 117.*

There is no difference between being raped
and being pushed down a flight of cement steps
except that the wounds also bleed inside.

There is no difference between being raped
and being run over by a truck
except that afterward men ask if you enjoyed it.

There is no difference between being raped
and being bitten on the ankle by a rattlesnake
except that people ask if your skirt was short
and why were you out alone anyhow.

There is no difference between being raped
and going head first through a windshield
except that afterward you are afraid
not of cars
but of half the human race.

—MARGE PIERCY, *1976;*
In Living in the open, *88–89, New York: Knopf.*

Reading this chapter may be a distressing experience for many students. Some may realize, perhaps for the first time, that they or someone they know has been a victim of one of the forms of violence we discuss in this chapter. Feelings of despair and anger may arise. This is natural. As authors, we too have experienced despair, sadness, and anger while researching and teaching this material. But we are learning to turn our emotions into activism. Students can learn to do likewise.

Though the magnitude of violence against women is alarming, awareness of the problem is the first step toward prevention. People cannot stop something they cannot see. Once named, violence against women, in its various forms, is no longer socially and culturally invisible. As noted in Chapter 1, naming is power.

One of the most, if not *the* most, devastating consequences of gender inequality is violence toward women. Women are victimized by criminal violence (i.e., robbery, burglary, aggravated assault, forcible rape, and murder) and intimate violence (i.e., child abuse, incest, stalking, courtship violence, acquaintance rape, battering, marital rape, and elder abuse). For many reasons, the risk of intimate, but not nonintimate, victimization is significantly greater for women than men. Violence takes many forms, from psychological intimidation and coercion through name-calling, sexual harassment, stalking, moderate physical violence (pushing, shoving, slapping) to severe physical violence (beating, using weapons) and sexual assault. Although women are victimized by strangers, they are much more likely to be victimized by someone they know: an acquaintance, coworker, friend, or relative, including a father, brother, or husband.

Consequences are psychological and physical, short term and long term. Furthermore, assaults committed by someone known to the woman are often more violent and result in more physical trauma than those committed by strangers (Stermac, DuMont, & Dunn, 1998). In all analyses of violence against women a disturbing conclusion is unavoidable: We live in a society that tolerates and even sanctions men's authority and entitlement to subdue and control a woman against her will. Until quite recently women shunned reporting, and society failed to acknowledge, the extent of intimate victimization.

> Although most intimate violence qualifies as crime, a historical tradition that has condoned violence within the family has created strong forces toward secrecy that oppose disclosure of such incidents into public record. . . . Coverup may be facilitated by the forced secrecy that is almost uniformly demanded by perpetrators of abuse. That victims were silent is attested by the small proportion of victims who informed authorities. In fact, only 2% of intrafamilial child sexual abuse, 6% of extrafamilial sexual abuse, and 5% to 8% of adult sexual assault cases were reported to police according to recent victimization studies. By comparison, 61.5% of the robberies and 82.5% of the burglaries were reported. (Koss, 1990, pp. 374–375)

The evidence documenting violence against women is so compelling that many experts have suggested that the United States is experiencing an epidemic. Experts also suggest that the largest single group of posttraumatic stress disorder sufferers are female sexual abuse and assault victims (Foa, Olasov, & Steketee, 1987). Taken together, it is not surprising that violence against women is one of the top three priorities identified in a report establishing a national mental health agenda for women (Russo, 1985).

COMMONALITIES AMONG ALL FORMS OF VIOLENCE AGAINST WOMEN

Jacquelyn White and Robin Kowalski (1998) proposed a model to integrate a wide range of factors across various forms of violence against women and which reveals their commonalities. Their contextual developmental model (see Figure 13.1) describes *five levels of interacting factors:* sociocultural (including historical and cultural values), interpersonal (i.e., social networks), dyadic, situational, and intrapersonal.

This perspective examines individual behavior in context. It assumes that patriarchy operating at the historical/sociocultural level affects the power dynamics of all relationships. Shared patterns of ideas and beliefs passed down from generation to generation define one's social networks. Historical and sociocultural factors create an environment in which the growing child learns rules and expectations, first in the family network, and later in peer, intimate, and work relationships. Early experiences define the context for later experiences (Huesmann & Eron, 1992; Olweus, 1993; White & Bondurant, 1996).

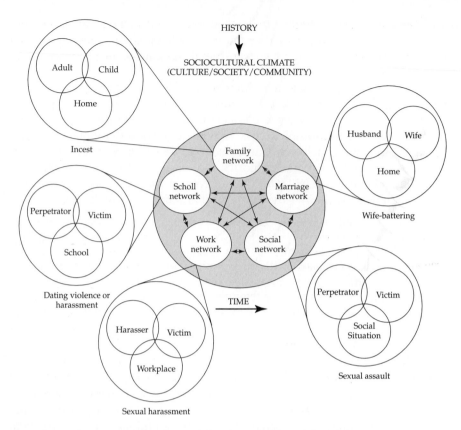

FIGURE 13.1. An integrative contextual developmental model of violence against women.

Embedded in these social networks are characteristics of the personal relationships in which individuals act violently. Power dynamics become enacted at the interpersonal level and result in the internalization of gendered values, expectations, and behaviors. Thus, cultural norms governing the use of aggression as a tool of the more powerful to subdue the weaker combines with gender inequalities to create a climate conducive to violence against women. Violence against women is inextricably bound to the social context of male domination and control. The patriarchal view of society gives men a higher value than women. It is taken for granted that men should dominate in politics, economics, and the social world, including family life and interpersonal relationships. This is seen as normal and natural. Violence against women is an assertion of the power and control men have over women.

Using this model as a framework, White and Kowalski (1998) identified key factors that distinguish various types of violence against women: the nature of the relationship, the ages of the perpetrator and victim, and the form the violence takes. For example, sexual activity between relatives is labeled incest; between unrelated adults and children it is called child sexual abuse; forced sexual intercourse between nonrelated adults is labeled rape. Similarly, beating up one's wife is called spouse abuse, whereas beating up one's dating partner is called dating or courtship violence. In a work relationship, coerced sexual intercourse in exchange for job security is called quid pro quo sexual harassment, but in a dating relationship it is called acquaintance rape. In all cases, the violence varies on a severity continuum and may be psychological, verbal, or physical and may be episodic or continuous.

Intimate violence is learned and maintained within a broader social context that has tolerated violence against women. Following White and Kowalski's (1998) contextual developmental perspective, this chapter begins with childhood sexual abuse. This is followed by discussions of courtship violence, acquaintance rape, sexual harassment and wife battering.

CHILDHOOD SEXUAL ABUSE

The sexual victimization of children is an abuse of interpersonal power and a violation of trust. What makes the statistics even more tragic is that most children are victimized by people they know and trust to protect them. Almost 90 percent of children who are raped arc victimized by someone known to them; 43 percent by family members (Greenfeld, 1997). Betrayal of the trust vested in those who have power is central to the understanding of childhood sexual abuse, its consequences, and the systems that sustain it (Freyd, 1997). The feminist viewpoint states that "sexual abuse, because it is an element of patriarchy, can be found everywhere" (Brown & Burman, 1977, p. 14). As survivors of sexual abuse have spoken out about their victimization, their voices have been heard. By refusing to be silent, these women have challenged the patriarchal system that once kept victims silent about their abuse (Brown, 1997).

Making a Difference

In 1990, **Katie Koestner** was raped by a young man she was dating at the College of William and Mary. After an unsuccessful attempt to bring the man to justice, Koestner began speaking out publicly against this crime of silence. She presents her program, "He Said She Said," at campuses and conferences around the country, spotlighting the little understood crime of date/acquaintance rape. Koestner has appeared on "Oprah," "Larry King," and dozens of other television shows. She graced the cover of *Time* magazine in June of 1991. In 1993, HBO produced the docudrama, "No Visible Bruises: The Katie Koestner Story." Koestner coauthored the book *Sexual Assault on Campus: What Every College Needs to Know About Protecting Victims, Providing for Just Adjudication, and Complying with Federal Laws* (1995). Her lobbying efforts on Capitol Hill helped convince Congress and President Bush to pass the 1992 Victim's Bill of Rights. Since Koestner's graduation from William and Mary in 1994, her message has been heard by hundreds of thousands of students at almost 700 colleges. Through her activism, Katie Koestner has made, and continues to make, great progress in raising awareness about the damage of sexual violence and what we can all do to prevent it.

Sources: Profile: Katie Koestner, Founder of COS, http://www.campusoutreachservices.com/katieProfile.htm., *Time*, June 3, 1991.

Defining Childhood Sexual Abuse

Although definitions of *childhood sexual abuse* vary, a commonly accepted definition involves either physical contact or noncontact (e.g., exhibitionism) sexual interactions between a child and an adult, or between two nonadults in which coercion is used (Rind & Tromovitch, 1997). A specific form of exploitative sexual behavior occurring between relatives is labeled incest. *Incest* occurs "when a child of any age is exploited by an older person for his [the perpetrator's] own satisfaction while disregarding the child's own developmental immaturity and inability to understand the sexual behavior" (Steele, 1986, p. 284).

Frequency of Childhood Sexual Abuse

In recent years, society has become more aware of child sexual abuse, including incest. "Social and personal denial and suppression of such abuse have begun to give way to acknowledgment and validation" of victimization (Courtois, 1988, p. 5). This increased awareness and concern has prompted research efforts to learn more about the frequency, characteristics, and patterns of child sexual abuse. Estimates of the frequency of childhood sexual abuse vary, depending on the sampling method and definition of victimization used by the researcher. Despite the differences in cited statistics, two things remain clear: (1) childhood sexual victimization is a serious concern, and (2) girls are far more likely to be its victims. The best information to date comes from three published national probability samples. One found that 27 percent of women and 16 percent of men reported childhood sexual abuse in a telephone interview (Finkelhor, Hotaling, Lewis, & Smith, 1990). In a telephone survey of children between the ages of 10 and 16, researchers found that 15 percent of girls and 6 percent of boys reported being victimized (Boney-McCoy & Finkelhor, 1995). A study using face-to-face interviews found similar results, using a more restrictive physical contact definition; 17 percent of women and 12 percent of men reported childhood sexual abuse (Laumann, Gagnon, Michael, & Michaels, 1994).

The relationship between racial ethnicity and victimization is currently being studied. Although no statistical differences between the percentages of black (57%) and white (67%) women reporting childhood sexual victimization have been reported, white women were more likely to have experienced sexual abuse earlier in their childhood (Wyatt, 1985). Similarly, no significant differences in the prevalence of childhood sexual abuse among Hispanic and non-Hispanic women have been reported (Arroyo, Simpson, & Aragon, 1997). Using a restrictive definition of childhood sexual abuse, 27.1 percent of Hispanic women and 33.1 percent of non-Hispanic white women reported victimization as children (Arroyo et al., 1997). Rates of childhood sexual abuse among Native American tribal members also appear to be similar (Robin, Chester, Rasmussen, Jaranson, & Goldman, 1997); 49 percent of the women in a Southwestern American Indian tribal community reported childhood sexual victimization. Thus, all girls appear to be at risk for becoming a victim of sexual abuse.

Who Commits Childhood Sexual Abuse?

Most sexual abuse of girls (91%) involves men as sole perpetrators, with an additional 4 percent of abuse involving women as coperpetrators with a male partner (Laumann et al., 1994). Only 7 percent of sexual contacts between adults and children involve strangers. The most commonly identified perpetrators are family friends and relatives. Within the family, 7 percent of women reported incestuous contact by a father, 7 percent by a stepfather, 9 percent by an older brother, and 29 percent by another relative (e.g., cousin, uncle) (Laumann et al., 1994).

Parent-child incest has been considered the most harmful not only because the child is exposed to age-inappropriate sexual behavior, but also because the parental role of protector and nurturer is violated (Courtois, 1988; Roth & Lebowitz, 1988). In addition, given that the children usually live in the same home as their parents, the privacy of the home provides greater opportunity for incestuous contact to be of longer duration, greater frequency, and greater severity (Courtois, 1988). Given these circumstances, the child is more likely to be entrapped in a continuing cycle of abuse if the abuser is a parent (Summit, 1983).

Adult survivors of parent-child incest typically describe their fathers as authoritarian, punitive, and threatening. The victim of incestuous abuse tends to feel overwhelmed by her father's authority and unable to resist. This may result in a conspiracy within the family to keep the abuse a secret. The family refuses to see the abuse, and the daughter may feel she cannot talk about the abuse for fear of betraying the family secret. The perpetrator also may convince the child that others will be angry with her, that they will not believe her if she tells, and/or that the abuse is her fault.

David Finkelhor (1984) proposed a model that described the preconditions for abuse. For abuse to occur, the individual must possess a motivation to offend and an ability to overcome internal barriers, external barriers, and the resistance of the child. There may be a cyclical pattern in perpetrator-victim incestuous relationships (Simon-Roper, 1996; Wolf, 1985). Prior to an abusive incident, the perpetrator may engage in nurturant, *grooming behaviors* (i.e., buying the child toys, tucking her into bed at night, asking the child to spend time with him). Following the abusive incident, the perpetrator may experience transitory guilt and promise to himself and to the child that he will not victimize her again. This pattern of violation mixed with contrite, loving behavior perpetuates the cycle of abuse.

Who Are the Victims?

Although specific intrapersonal characteristics of the perpetrator have been identified by researchers, the risk factors for who will be victimized are situational ones, outside the child's control, rather than victim characteristics. Any child may be victimized by an adult family member, but several studies have identified family variables associated with childhood sexual abuse (Carson, Gertz, Donaldson, & Wonderlich, 1990; Edwards & Alexander, 1992; Jackson, Calhoun, Amick, Maddever, & Habif, 1990; Yama, Tovey, & Fogas, 1993).

In a recent review of the literature, three key factors present in sexually abusive families have been identified (Draucker, 1996). Incest is more common in families in which members are emotionally distant. Open displays of affection often are absent, and the family system lacks intimacy and cohesion. There is little mutual affection displayed between family members. Incest also is more common in families with a rigid, traditional family structure. Fathers are the head of the household and women are viewed as subordinate to their husbands and children as subordinate to their parents. Obedience and control permeate all aspects of the parent-child relationship. Last, incest is more common in families with a number of conflictual relationships between family members, particularly between parents.

Several risk factors relate specifically to the father or stepfather in the family. Children living without a father or with a stepfather are more likely to become the victims of incest (Finkelhor, 1984). Not only are girls who have stepfathers more likely to be abused by the stepfather himself, but they are also more vulnerable to abuse perpetrated by other men if there is no father in the home. Girls may have greater exposure and potentially greater risk from a variety of unfamiliar men prior to as well as following the mother's remarriage as the new spouse introduces his friends to the family.

Until recently, mothers often have been blamed for incestuous relationships within the family (Green, 1996). This view was often based on the invalid assumption that mothers colluded in their children's abuse. Recent clinical and research studies do not support the concept of collusion (e.g., Deblinger, Hathaway, Lippman, & Steer, 1993; Peterson, Basta, & Dykstra, 1993). Mothers of children who have been sexually abused do not display higher levels of psychopathology and often are proactive in responding. A recent review of the research finds that most mothers believe their children's reports of abuse and take action to protect them (Joyce, 1997). Future research may need to consider social and cultural factors that enhance or limit a mother's ability to believe and protect her child from abuse.

Consequences for the Survivor

Children who are victimized often feel powerless to stop the abuse and feel they have nowhere to turn for help, comfort, and support. The child's ability to confront and refuse sexual contact is overwhelmed by the feelings of loyalty and trust that the child may have developed for the perpetrator. The adult is in a position of authority (and often one of trust as well) and communicates to the child that the behavior is part of an exclusive, secretive, and special relationship. The perpetrator may even come to believe and attempt to convince the child that the relationship is a mutually loving and caring one (Gilgun, 1995). For children who may otherwise be neglected and emotionally isolated, the special attention and inappropriate sexual contact with the adult may be confusing and complicates the coping process.

The responses to sexual abuse vary as children develop *coping strategies* to deal with their abuse. Some children develop highly successful strategies for isolating the abuse; other children develop self-destructive strategies to cope with their pain. The immediate effects of sexual abuse may be seen in children's emotional, social, cognitive, and physical functioning. For example, children who are victims of sexual abuse may have difficulty in school. They may wet the bed, may fear going to bed at night, and may have nightmares. They may fear being alone and may cry hysterically when left with the perpetrator. They may feel ashamed, guilty, and isolated. Moreover, the child may feel responsible for holding the family together and avoiding conflict and pain by keeping her victimization secret (Breines & Gordon, 1983).

Although survivors may remain silent as children, the abuse may resurface in adulthood. (See Box 13.1.) Adult survivors may be reminded of their abuse when seeing a family member again, looking at pictures, watching a movie about incest, being sexually victimized again, or having children reach the same age they were when they were abused. "Abuse is not destiny, but it does make progress toward successful social, interpersonal, and intrapsychic functioning in adult life more difficult" (Mullen, 1993, p. 431).

Many women (70%) report that their experience of childhood abuse significantly affected their lives since it happened (Laumann et al., 1994). Approximately 40 percent of all survivors suffer aftereffects serious enough to require therapy in adulthood (Browne & Finkelhor, 1986). The most commonly reported psychological effects include shame and guilt, fear, disgust, distrust, feelings of isolation or marginalization, hostile and aggressive feelings toward

---

Box 13.1 Recovery of Repressed Memories

Recently, controversy has flared in the media regarding whether repressed memories of childhood sexual abuse can be recovered years after the abuse. On one side of the debate, reports of childhood sexual abuse uncovered during the course of psychotherapy are accepted as truth. On the other side of the debate, accused abusers are claiming that these recovered memories are, in fact, false memories created by highly suggestive therapeutic techniques, such as hypnotism and age regression, and that the clients of therapists who used these techniques are suffering from a false memory syndrome.

Unfortunately, there has not been enough research to date to resolve the controversy. Moreover, real cases of childhood sexual abuse may be discounted amid the controversy. Laboratory studies show that, depending on the circumstances, memories can be recalled accurately, memories can be distorted, or memories can be created. However, for ethical reasons, laboratory research cannot deal with memories of the same traumatic nature as childhood sexual abuse. Before the possibility of false memory syndrome can be accepted, further research is needed to

- determine whether a distinction between repression and ordinary forgetting is meaningful and what the nature of the differences is;
- clarify the diagnostic criteria for a "false memory syndrome" and determine its clinical usefulness; at present, such a syndrome does not exist in the *Diagnostic and Statistical Manual of the American Psychiatric Association;*
- evaluate the legal criteria for establishing the validity of repressed memories; for example, a therapist may be more interested in how a person interprets what has happened while the legal system is more interested in observable, verifiable behaviors;
- explore repression and ordinary forgetting in accused perpetrators as well as abuse survivors; and
- explore the effects of an unequal distribution of power in child abuse relationships on memory.

the perpetrator, and anxiety (Rind & Tromovitch, 1997). Some studies also have found that childhood sexual abuse can result in impairment in adult relationships and sexual functioning for some women (Finkelhor, Hotaling, Lewis, & Smith, 1989). Although the abuse was in the past, the effects for some survivors remain part of their lives.

> People have said to me, "Why are you dragging this up now?" Why? WHY? Because it has controlled every facet of my life. It has damaged me in every possible way. It has destroyed everything in my life that has been of value. . . . It's prevented me from being able to love clearly. . . . I don't care if it happened 500 years ago! It's influenced me all the time, and it does matter. It matters very much. (Lavender in Bass & Davis, 1988, p. 33)

Although the psychological impact of incest can be very serious, many victims are able to use coping and adaptation strategies that allow them to protect their personal integrity (DiPalma, 1994). In in-depth interviews with incest survivors, many survivors demonstrated great inner strength and determination. As child victims, these women used realistic, future-oriented fantasies to find relief from their pain and to escape their identity as a victim. Some focused their energy toward academic achievements, finding validation and personal affirmation through their educational pursuits. Others used creative outlets (e.g., writing, drama, music, dance) to enhance their ability to cope. Together, these strategies suggest a holistic view of incest survivors, acknowledging survivor strengths as well as vulnerabilities.

Steps to Protect Children and Treat Victims

Protection of children from abuse is a focus of national attention in recent years. Schools are beginning to educate teachers about the signs of physical and sexual abuse. They also are beginning to teach children what is appropriate touch, to teach children that their body is their property and they have the right to say no to someone who is abusive, and to encourage children to tell a teacher, parent, or adult friend when someone touches them inappropriately (Crewdson, 1988), although in some cases a child may be powerless to say no. Doctors also are being trained to identify signs of child sexual abuse in their patients and to conduct the necessary tests to verify sexual abuse.

Many adult survivors also are becoming aware of their victimization and are seeking help from private therapists, support groups of other survivors, and books. Even though the memory of the abuse may not be completely forgotten, many women have found ways to heal and to come to terms with their history.

> I don't know if I will ever be completely healed. It's like there was a wound and it healed over, but it was still infected in there. It needed to be lanced and cleaned out so that a good healthy scar tissue could grow over it. I knew that once that scar tissue grew, it wouldn't be very pleasant to look at, but it wouldn't hurt anymore. It would be raised, and you would know it was there, but you could touch it and it wouldn't be painful. And I think that's how it is. I have scars, but they don't hurt. They're cleaned out now. (Bass & Davis, 1988, p. 167)

Young people usually begin dating in high school, though children as young as kindergartners talk about having boyfriends and girlfriends. The idea of being paired with a member of the other sex is pervasive in our society. Traditionally, it has been assumed that children's "playing house" and, later, dating provide a context for socialization into later roles, including wife, lover, and confidante (Rice, 1984). Dating also offers opportunities for companionship, status, sexual experimentation, and conflict resolution. However, courtship has a different meaning for young women and men (Lloyd, 1991). Whereas for men courtship involves themes of "staying in control," for women, themes involve "dependence on the relationship." Inevitably, as a relationship develops, conflicts arise. No two people are always going to agree on everything. How do young people deal with conflicts? Unfortunately, the research evidence is clear. Violence is a failure to constructively resolve conflict (Billingham & Sack, 1986) as well as a failure to communicate effectively (Carey & Mongeau, 1996). It is a frequent reaction to the confusion and anger young people experience in heterosexual conflicts. Violence is also a tactic used to gain control in a relationship. (See Box 13.2.)

Defining Courtship Violence

When I was 16 my boyfriend of two years began to hit me. . . . I spent most of my time covering up for him—putting makeup on my bruises, going into the hospital under an assumed name (for a cracked rib). I was afraid to tell my

---

Box 13.2 Teenager Glad She's Rid of Abusive Boyfriend

Dear Ann Landers: I know you've written a lot about battered women, but most people aren't aware that teenage girls can be battered, too.

I began dating a terrific-looking guy when I was 16. He was really cool and had his own car. A year later, I was scared to death of him. I didn't dare tell my family for fear they'd make me stop seeing him, and I didn't want to. If I broke one of his rules, he would beat me up. Once, when I wore my jeans too tight (according to him), he locked me in the trunk of his car. I thought I would suffocate to death. It was a horrible experience.

My family knew nothing of the hell he put me through. He made an effort to put the bruises where no one would see them. On the rare occasion when they were visible (like a black eye), I would tell people I had had an accident.

I was the ideal child—I had straight As, got home on time, did all my household chores, and never gave my parents any trouble. It wasn't until

I attempted suicide at the age of 18, and then got some great counseling, that I began to understand how he had taken control of my life.

Ann, please print this letter and alert teenage girls and their parents to this potentially dangerous situation. No one would have guessed such a thing was going on in my life. I realized that I wasn't alone when I met other girls in the support group who were just like me.—Lucky to Be Out of It.

Dear Lucky: This is not the first letter I've printed from a teenager who was battered by her boyfriend. My advice has been to get out at once. No guy is worth it.

There is no national support group for battered teenage girls, but they can call the Domestic Violence Hotline for help. The number is 1-800-333-SAFE.

Source: Permission granted by Ann Landers and Creators Syndicate.

friends because I was embarrassed. I didn't want to tell my father because I knew he would fight violence with violence. I couldn't tell my mother because she was beaten by my father when she was younger. I felt helpless and alone. (Anonymous student)

Courtship violence, dating violence, and *premarital violence* are all terms researchers have used to refer to acts of aggression occurring between unmarried women and men. Researchers have studied the gamut of aggression, from verbal aggression, such as screaming, yelling, name-calling, criticism, and threatening, to stalking and severe physical violence involving the use of weapons. Depending on which measure of aggression one uses, rates of courtship violence range from a low of 6 percent, when the definition focuses exclusively on severe forms of physical aggression, to a high of almost 90 percent, when the definition includes all forms of aggression.

Frequency of Courtship Violence

A national survey of approximately 2,600 college women and 2,100 college men revealed that within the year prior to the survey 81 percent of the men and 88 percent of the women had engaged in some form of *verbal aggression,* either as perpetrator or victim (White & Koss, 1991). Approximately 37 percent of the men and 35 percent of the women inflicted some form of *physical aggression,* and about 39 percent of the men and 32 percent of the women sustained some physical aggression. In this survey all types of heterosexual relationships were included, from the most casual to the most serious, thus providing a comprehensive estimate of the scope of courtship violence. The measures of verbal aggression included arguing heatedly, yelling, sulking, and stomping. Physical aggression included throwing something at someone, pushing, grabbing, shoving, or hitting.

Studies also indicate that courtship violence during the teen years is pervasive, with as many as 35 percent of female and male students surveyed reporting at least one episode (O'Keeffe, Brockopp, & Chew, 1986), with fewer experiencing recurring violence (Burcky, Reuterman, & Kopsky, 1988). As with college students, not all high school students experience physical violence (15.7% of female students and 7.8% of male students, according to Bergman, 1992).

Who Inflicts and Sustains Courtship Violence?

The ubiquity of courtship violence among college students is apparent in that comparable rates of violence have been observed across gender, ethnic group, and type of institution of higher learning, such as private or public, religious or secular (Clark, Beckett, Wells, & Dungee-Anderson, 1994; White & Koss, 1991). All the evidence to date suggests that it would be unusual to find a high school or college student who had not been involved in some form of verbal aggression, and it appears that the same people who report inflicting some form of violence are the same ones who report experiencing violence. Clearly, violence begets violence.

The finding that women and men do not appear to differ in the frequency with which they engage in aggressive acts should not be taken to mean there are no gender-related differences in aggression. On the contrary, when the motives for violence and the consequences are considered, gender-related differences are clear. Most data suggest that women are more likely to engage in aggression for self-defense, whereas men report that they aggress to instill fear and to intimidate. However, some data suggest that at least for dating relationships, women are often the initiator (DeMaris, 1992). When women do initiate courtship violence, it is clear that they are more likely than men to sustain serious injury. Men are two to four times more likely to use the severe forms of violence, and women are three to four times more likely to report injuries (Makepeace, 1986; Sugarman & Hotaling, 1989).

Finally, the underlying processes involved in courtship violence for women and for men appear different. The results of these studies are quite consistent. Although the best predictor of being aggressive is having an aggressive partner (Bookwala, Frieze, Smith, & Ryan, 1992), other predictors are different for women and men. Men who are quick to react to anger, who believe that violence will aid in winning an argument, and who have successfully used violence in other situations are likely to do so again (Riggs & Caulfield, 1997; White, Koss, & Kissling, 1991). Similarities between men who engage in courtship violence and who are wife batterers have been found (Ryan, 1995). Drug use, divorced parents, stressful life events, beliefs that violence between intimates is justifiable, and less traditional sex role attitudes also have been identified as predictors (Bookwala, Frieze, Smith, & Ryan, 1992; Mason & Blankenship, 1987; Tontodonato & Crew, 1992).

For women, on the other hand, a history of parent-child abuse (Sappington, Pharr, Tunstall, & Rickert, 1997; Tontodonato & Crew, 1992), as well as anxiety, depression (White et al, 1991), and drug use (Tontodonato & Crew, 1992), have been related to courtship violence. However, it is likely that these latter factors are reactions to childhood experiences with violence, rendering women more vulnerable to being the target of a violent partner, which in turn increases the likelihood of being violent. Learning about violence in the home and associating with peers who endorse the use of violence may provide a backdrop of social norms that legitimate violence. Violence is learned as a tactic of dealing with interpersonal conflict (Gwartney-Gibbs, Stockard, & Brohmer, 1983; Reuterman & Burcky, 1989; Thompson, 1991; Worth, Matthews, & Coleman, 1990).

Romantic relationships may become *destructive traps* for women when they feel they must put maintenance of the relationship above their own self-interests (Carey & Mongeau, 1996). Women who experience ongoing victimization are often more committed and in love with their partner, less likely to end the relationship because of abuse, and also allow their partner to control them. These women also report more traditional attitudes toward women's roles, justify their abuse, and tend to romanticize relationships and love (Follingstad, Rutledge, McNeill-Hawkins, & Polek, 1992).

When Does Courtship Violence Occur?

Courtship violence is most likely to occur in private settings (Laner, 1983; Roscoe & Kelsey, 1986) and on weekends (Olday & Wesley, 1983). Several researchers have found that violence is more likely to occur in serious than in casual relationships (Pedersen & Thomas, 1992), suggesting that violence in more *committed relationships* may reflect the acceptance of violence as a legitimate mode of conflict resolution (Billingham, 1987). On the other hand, violence in a *developing relationship* may be a way of "testing the relative safety of a relationship before movement to greater commitment is risked" (Billingham, 1983, p. 288). In a large percentage of committed, violent relationships, the violence occurs more than once, the couples stay together, and some even feel the relationship improved as a result of the violence—some interpret violence as a sign of love (Cate, Henton, Koval, Christopher, & Lloyd, 1982). This is not surprising given the romantic scripts discussed in Chapter 8. Many students believe dating violence is more acceptable in serious relationships (Bethke & DeJoy, 1993), and not sufficient grounds for ending the relationship (Bethke & DeJoy, 1993; O'Keeffe et al., 1986). Violence is more likely in relationships plagued by problems, which include jealousy, fighting, interference from friends, lack of time together, breakdown of the relationship, and problems outside the relationship (Riggs, 1993), as well as disagreements about drinking and sexual denial (Roscoe & Kelsey, 1986). These are the conflicts young people report most frequently leading to feelings of confusion and anger, and resulting in violence (Sugarman & Hotaling, 1989).

A recently developed *model of courtship aggression* consists of two components (Riggs & O'Leary, 1989, 1996). The first component consists of background factors, including the observation of interparental physical aggression and the receipt of child physical abuse. These model aggression and contribute to the establishment of a pattern of aggressive behavior. These early childhood experiences also contribute to attitudes accepting of aggression, as well as to the development of an impulsive, aggressive personality style. The second component consists of situational factors associated with the relationship (such as relationship satisfaction and communication patterns), expectations about the outcome of aggression, stress, alcohol use, and partner's use of aggression. Situational factors increase the likelihood of conflict in relationships, which in turn increases the likelihood that aggression will be used to resolve the conflict. Related work suggests that personal history may be more important for women than for men, because women need more life experiences with violence to overcome the traditional sociocultural sanctions against female violence (O'Leary, Malone, & Tyree, 1994).

Consequences of Courtship Violence

Most victims and offenders experience at least some mild emotional trauma, and as many as half may experience physical injury (Makepeace, 1984). The consequences tend to be more severe for the women involved. Women are three times as likely as men to experience a major emotional trauma (Makepeace, 1986). Victims are most likely to experience, anger, fear and/or surprise (Matthews, 1984), whereas offenders experience sorrow. Although few victims (only 4%) seek professional help in resolving their feelings, most tell a friend about the incident. Other factors associated with dating violence include disciplinary problems in school, lower grade averages, and not attending college, as well as frequent dating and drug use (Reuterman & Burcky,

1989). It also has been suggested that dating violence is particularly problematic for ethnic minorities who may need to "rely on the family as a protective buffer against racism and oppression" (Clark et al., 1994, p. 265).

A further serious consequence of courtship violence is a possible increased risk of marital violence either with the same or a different partner. Little systematic research on this has been conducted. For example, it is not known what percentage of women who were victimized during courtship also is victimized in marriage, but for women who are victimized in marriage there is evidence that some were victimized during courtship. In 25 percent of the violent marriages, the violence began before marriage (Gayford, 1975). More recently, interviews with eighty-two clients at domestic violence shelters found that 51 percent of the clients had experienced previous physical abuse in a dating relationship (Roscoe & Benaske, 1985). Battered women revealed, in a series of interviews, that the key factor linking marital battering with earlier courtship violence was the women's acceptance of traditional gender roles as a result of being raised in a patriarchal home (Avni, 1991).

What Is Being Done?

Courtship violence has not received the public attention that other forms of violence against women have, in particular incest, rape, sexual harassment, and wife battering. Given the current climate of concern about violence in the school and in youth in general, interpersonal violence is receiving more attention than in the past. However, it is encouraging to know that students who are involved in courtship violence will turn to community resources in the absence of campus resources (Bogal-Allbritten & Allbritten, 1987). A recent program for Canadian secondary schoolchildren was successful in altering attitudes, knowledge, and behavioral intentions after six weeks. The program consisted of a large group presentation followed by classroom discussion led by community professionals (Jaffe, Suderman, Reitzel, & Killip, 1992).

At present, it appears that the prevalence of courtship violence and its consequences are not seen widely as the real problems they are. It may be that young people are so accustomed to witnessing and experiencing behaviors such as arguing, yelling, pushing, and slapping that these actions seem normal. They do not label these experiences as problems. It appears that a major educational effort to change attitudes toward courtship violence is needed to sensitize persons to the consequences of their aggressive interactions with others. (See Figure 13.2.)

ACQUAINTANCE SEXUAL ASSAULT AND RAPE

At age 17 I lost my virginity on a squeaky hotel bed—against my will. It scared the hell out of me. I didn't want to be touched by any man for months. Worse yet, it was my boyfriend—someone I had trusted. I got pregnant—a scared 17-year-old who couldn't even afford a pregnancy test. I confided in

FIGURE 13.2. Information table at the Port Authority Bus Terminal in New York City, educating the public about violence against women.

only one person, my best friend. I told her that if I really was pregnant I was going to kill myself. My period was about one month and a half late already—a week later I miscarried.

Approximately 85 percent of all sexual assaults are perpetrated by someone at least casually known to the victim. Romantic partners commit as many as 57 percent of all assaults (Koss, 1990).

Defining Sexual Assault

Sexual assault, sexual coercion, and *sexual aggression* are all terms used to refer to instances in which one person engages in sexual behavior against another's will. These terms encompass acts that range from unwanted sexual contact, such as forced kissing or the fondling of breasts and/or genitals, to *attempted rape* and *rape.* In research, the term sexual assault often is used rather than rape. An inclusive term such as sexual assault reminds us of the continuum of sexual activity, ranging from consensual to violent acts. A man's tactics may range from psychological pressure (i.e., threatening to end the relationship, saying things he does not mean, such as falsely professing love), verbal persuasion ("if you loved me, you'd let me"; "you owe it to me"), verbal threats of harm, use of alcohol and drugs, physical intimidation, mild physical force (pushing, slapping, holding down), severe physical force (beating, choking), to displaying or using a weapon.

Although the legal definition of rape appears straightforward, it is a label some are reluctant to apply to certain acts of forced sexual intercourse. Both the social meaning of the term rape and the circumstances surrounding an act of forced sexual intercourse make using the term rape difficult. The term rape has been shown to have different meanings for women and men, as well as different segments of the community such as police officers and mental health counselors. Some people are hesitant to label forced sex between acquaintances as rape, particularly if any of the following circumstances were present: the man initiated the date; he spent a great deal of money; the couple went to his place; there had been drinking, kissing, and petting; the couple had been sexually intimate on previous occasions; the woman had had sex with other men (Goodchilds, Zellman, Johnson, & Giarrusso, 1988); or "no" was not explicitly verbalized (Sawyer, Pinciaro, & Jessell, 1998). College students in general, and sexually aggressive men in particular, believe that *sexual precedence* (i.e., a past history of sexual intercourse) reduces the legitimacy of sexual refusal. This reluctance is apparent in recent criticisms appearing in the popular press (i.e., trade books, newspaper articles, and magazine features) questioning the veracity of rape statistics. These critics suggest that if young women do not label their experiences as rape, then they are not victims. Of course, this is illogical. Although a woman may not realize that forced sexual intercourse by an acquaintance during a date is rape, this does not change the legal definition of the act as rape, nor does it reduce the culpability of the perpetrator (Koss & Cleveland, 1997). Furthermore, whether or not a sexual assault is labeled rape does not alter the consequences (discussed later). There is clearly an incongruity between legal and social definitions of what constitutes "real rape." Susan Brownmiller (1975) in her groundbreaking book *Against Our Will* noted,

> . . . the question of "What is a rape?" is not answered by a powerful legal litmus test but through a system of beliefs that drive from a misogynistic social context, the "rape culture." (p. 436)

Frequency of Sexual Assault

Rape is the crime least likely to be reported and, if reported, the least likely to result in a conviction, particularly if committed by an acquaintance. Not only do many women not report their assault to the authorities, many never tell anyone. Thus, crime statistics greatly underestimate the frequency of rape. Researchers must rely on large-scale surveys of women to obtain accurate estimates of victimization rates. Women are asked about a number of sexual experiences that may have involved force or threat of force, some of which meet the legal criteria for rape, rather than being asked directly "Have you ever been raped?" This is important because many victimized women (73%) never label forced sexual intercourse as rape. This approach has suggested that the actual rape victimization rate is ten to fifteen times greater than corresponding FBI estimates (Koss, 1992). Because most of these unlabeled, unreported rape experiences are perpetrated by acquaintances, acquaintance rape has been labeled a *hidden crime* (Koss, 1985).

A comprehensive survey asked more than 3,000 college women from thirty-two institutions of higher education across the United States about sexual experiences since the age of 14 (Koss, Gidycz, & Wisniewski, 1987). Of those surveyed, over half (53.7%) had experienced some form of sexual victimization; 15.4 percent had experienced acts by a man that met the legal definition of rape (though only 27% labeled the experience rape), and 12.1 percent, attempted rape. An additional 11.9 percent had been verbally pressured into sexual intercourse, and the remaining 14.4 percent had experienced some other form of unwanted sexual contact, such as forced kissing or fondling with no attempted penetration. More recent studies confirm these high numbers among Canadians (DeKeseredy, 1997), as well as among a probability sample of 8,000 women in the United States (Tjaden & Thoennes, 1998).

Community-based surveys have found that 25 percent of African-American women, 20 percent of white women (Wyatt, 1991), and 8 percent of Hispanic women (Sorenson & Siegel, 1992) reported at least one sexual assault experience in their lifetime. High school women also appear to be at greater risk for rape than previously thought. A recent survey of 834 entering college students found that 13 percent reported being raped between the ages of 14 and 18, and an additional 16 percent reported being victims of an attempted rape (Humphrey & White, in press).

Who Is at Risk?

Numerous studies have been conducted to identify *risk factors for sexual victimization*, most with little success. The greatest risk factor is being female. Although men are also sexually victimized, the likelihood is less than for women. Age is also a risk factor, with adolescence being the period of greatest vulnerability; during adolescence the risk of first being victimized increases steadily from age 14 to 18 and declines thereafter (Humphrey & White, in press). Another risk factor is being a college student; sexual victimization rates are about three time higher among college students than in the general population (Aizenman & Kelley, 1988; Koss et al., 1987), although recently the opposite has been found (Zweig, Barber, & Eccles, 1997). Other risk factors have been difficult to determine. Several researchers have confirmed that the best predictor of victimization is past victimization; typically childhood victimization increases the risk of adolescent victimization, which in turn increases the risk of victimization as a young adult (Collins, 1998; Gidycz, Coble, Latham, & Layman, 1992; Mills & Granoff, 1992; White & Humphrey, in press; Wyatt, Guthrie, & Notgrass, 1992). Additionally, childhood victimization has been related to an earlier age of menarche and sexual activity (Vicary, Klingman, & Harkness, 1995), as well as alcohol use. It is likely that alcohol is implicated in several ways. Women with a history of victimization may turn to alcohol as a means of coping. Unfortunately, alcohol use may also make it more difficult for women to read the danger cues present in an impending assault, and more importantly her alcohol use may suggest, erroneously, to the perpetrator that she is sexually available and/or that she is a "safe" victim, that is, she will be less able to resist an assault. (See Box 13.3.)

Who Does This?

The Koss survey (Koss et al., 1987) described earlier also examined the sexual experiences of more than 2,900 college men. Of this group, 4.4 percent admitted to behaviors meeting the legal definition of rape, 3.3 percent admitted to

---
Box 13.3 Gang Rape

Most research on acquaintance rape has focused on instances involving a single attacker. However, gang rape is a phenomenon that is beginning to receive attention (O'Sullivan, 1991). Looking at police records, Amir (1971) found that 26 percent of the reported rapes had involved three or more perpetrators, and that 55 percent of convicted rapists had been involved in a gang rape. The rate of conviction for gang rape is probably higher than the rate for rapes by single perpetrators because a victim of a gang rape is more likely to label the rape as a crime and report it than a victim of a single perpetrator, especially if he is an acquaintance. However, because not all gang rapes are reported, we need to consider data sources that assess unreported gang rapes. On the Koss survey described earlier (Koss et al., 1987), data revealed that multiple offenders were involved for 5 percent of the women who had been raped. The survey also revealed that for 16 percent of the men who reported having committed rape, at least one other male was involved. O'Sullivan (1991) noted that, "Of the twenty-three documented cases of alleged gang-rape by college students in the last ten years, thirteen were perpetrated by fraternity men, four by groups of basketball players, four by groups of football players, and only two men unaffiliated with a formal organization" (p. 11). She feels that the cohesiveness of all-male groups that promote macho values of sex as adventure may challenge men to perform in a group situation to prove they belong. According to O'Sullivan, victims of gang rape are usually first-year students who are naive, but have a reputation among the men for being promiscuous.

attempted rape, 7.2 percent to sexual coercion, and 10.2 percent to forced or coerced sexual contact, indicating that 25.1 percent of the college men admit to some form of sexual aggression. Similar rates have been reported in college samples (Calhoun, Bernat, Clum, & Frame, 1997; White & Humphrey, 1995) and in a community college sample (White et al., 1998).

The typical acquaintance rapist appears to be a "normal" guy. He is not a crazed psychopath, although he may display *psychopathy-related traits* (Kosson, Kelly, & White, 1997). Among college students, alcohol use (Koss & Gaines, 1993; White & Humphrey, 1994), athletic affiliation (Frintner & Rubinson, 1993; Koss & Gaines, 1993), and fraternity membership (Frintner & Rubinson, 1993, but not Koss & Gaines, 1993) have been associated with sexual aggression toward women. Other significant correlates of sexual assault include a history of family violence; an early and varied sexual history, including many sexual partners; a history of delinquency; acceptance of rape myths; an impulsive personality; hedonistic and dominance motives for sex; lower than average sense of self-worth; and lower religiosity; as well as peers who condone and encourage sexual conquests (White & Koss, 1993). Finally, sexually aggressive men are more likely to perceive a wider range of behaviors as indicative of sexual interest than do nonsexually aggressive men (Bondurant & Donat, in press) and are attracted to sexual aggression (Calhoun et al., 1997). (See Box 13.4.)

It appears that sexual promiscuity and hostile attitudes combine to characterize sexually aggressive men (Malamuth, Sockloskie, Koss, & Tanaka, 1991). Furthermore, these two factors are most likely to result in sexual aggression in men who tended to be self-centered and had little regard for others (i.e., were low in empathy) (Dean & Malamuth, 1997).

Sexually aggressive men tend to be more domineering with women. In an unstructured, five-minute get-to-know-each-other conversation with a female

Box 13.4 Is Acquaintance Sexual Assault a Result of Miscommunication?

Miscommunication has been put forth as a way of understanding the social process that results in a young woman being forced into sexual activity by her date. The term *miscommunication* implies that the problem lies in the communication skills of the two people involved, particularly the woman. Many young women on college campuses across the nation are admonished in "rape awareness workshops" to communicate more clearly their refusal to have sex; the implication is that if the woman believes she has communicated her nonconsent and sexual intercourse occurs, the failure is hers. Researchers frequently study women's verbal and nonverbal cues that may suggest sexual interest on the assumptions that the man's motive is sexual, and he is looking for cues from the woman that may communicate sexual interest. This work also assumes that if these cues are present, any man would interpret them as indicators of a woman's willingness to engage in sex with him. However, these assumptions are incorrect.

Men who self-report sexually aggressive behaviors have been found to perceive nonverbal cues, especially cues that others perceive as reflecting little sexual interest, as connoting more sexual interest than nonaggressive men (Bondurant, 1994). Furthermore, sexually aggressive men claim that their victims were more sexually interested in them than sexually nonaggressive men involved in consensual sex do, and they base this perception on the presence of behaviors that previous research has found to indicate low sexual interest (Kowalski, 1992). These behaviors include eye contact, smiling, accepting a date, and slow dancing. In contrast, sexually nonaggressive men base their inferences of their partner's sexual interest on the presence of behaviors such as kissing the man, undressing him, removing her top,

and suggesting they spend the night (White & Humphrey, 1994a).

Sexually aggressive men may also believe that a woman's no does not always mean no. The term *token resistance* has been used to describe the situation in which a woman says no but is really *game-playing*. In an early study, Charlene Muehlenhard and Lisa Hollabaugh (1988) found that about one-third of the women she surveyed indicated that they had said no at least once when they really wanted to have sex. Many people latched onto this finding as evidence that women are deceptive and that maybe men are justified in their belief that they ought to pursue sexual activity in spite of the no. However, in a follow-up study and, Carrie Rodgers Muehlenhard (1998) discovered that women who say no in spite of desiring sex genuinely meant no; they were not manipulating or teasing. Rather, although they were interested in sexual activity, they decided to refrain for a variety of reasons, including moral beliefs, fear of sexually transmitted diseases, or fear of pregnancy.

Whereas the language of miscommunication suggests that a sexual assault occurs because a normal guy understandably misunderstands his date's intentions on the basis of how she looks or what she does, the language of aggression and violence suggests a more negative view of men who commit acts of sexual aggression. It is sexually aggressive men's perception rather than a woman's actions that drives the inference of sexual interest. The language of miscommunication tends to reduce the culpability of the perpetrator and diverts attention from a study of perpetrator characteristics and factors that contribute to perpetrators' attitudes and behaviors, such as sexism and the glorification of violence in the media.

confederate, these men used more "one up" messages aimed at "gaining control of the exchange" (e.g., bragging about oneself and criticizing the other person) than they did with a male confederate (Malamuth & Thornhill, 1994). Domineeringness in conversation may be a test sexually aggressive men use to identify vulnerable targets. A woman who resists the domination may be seen as unavailable, but a subordinate response from a woman may indicate that she is a potential target. Furthermore, it is likely that a woman experiencing the helplessness and powerlessness associated with a previous victimization will be less likely to resist the man's domineering behavior than women without a victimization history. This may help us understand why and how perpetrators target vulnerable women.

Consequences for the Victim

Emotional reactions to the assault include fear and anxiety, phobias, depression, diminished self-esteem, sexual dysfunctions, nightmares, and *posttraumatic stress disorder* (see Chapter 14). Behavioral reactions can include alcohol/drug use and dependency and behavioral deviancy, including sexual promiscuity, and an increased risk of future victimization. Physical difficulties, including psychosomatic symptoms, can arise from injuries associated with the assault itself and the attendant violence, as well as from the emotional trauma. Risk of contracting any one of several sexually transmitted diseases, including AIDS, and/or pregnancy also are associated with rape. Finally, for many rape victims, their relationships with family members, friends, and intimate partners (i.e., husbands or boyfriends) frequently become severely strained. In some instances, the victim is blamed; in others, the assault is trivialized—often with the well-meaning intention of trying to make her feel better.

Victims go through various phases during their recovery. According to Taylor (1983) they struggle initially with the meaning of the assault. Subsequently, they attempt to gain a sense of control, which can include self-blame, that is, "What did I do wrong?" "How could I have avoided this situation?" Following this, victims may tend to minimize the seriousness of the experience as a means of self-enhancement; for example, they are grateful they lived through the attack. As victims go through this process of redefining the meaning of the assault and their lives, and as they develop a greater sense of mastery, positive outcomes emerge; the victim progresses from being a victim to being a survivor (Koss & Burkhart, 1989).

In spite of the tendency for the public to consider stranger rape as "real rape" and acquaintance rape as something less serious, mental health data clearly suggest otherwise. Several studies have shown that the psychological impact of nonstranger rape may be worse than that of stranger rape (Karp, Silber, Holmstrom, & Stock, 1995; Katz, 1991); however, people persist in their belief that stranger rape is much worse (Roth, Wayland, & Woolsey, 1990; Stacy, Prisbell, & Tollefsrud, 1992) and are more likely to hold the victim responsible for the acquaintance rape (Kanekar & Seksaria, 1993). It appears that a woman's strong negative psychological reactions to acquaintance rape are due to feelings of betrayal by a trusted acquaintance and self-blame, that is, uncertainty about her role in the assault (Frazier & Seales, 1997; Pitts & Schwartz, 1997).

Many victims are unable to acknowledge their victimization for months to years following the assault. A recent survey of women at three midwestern universities found that only 28 percent of the sexual assault victims sought any type of help, and of those who did, 75 percent turned to a friend (Ogletree, 1993). Acknowledged or not, symptoms develop, with 31 to 48 percent of rape victims eventually seeking professional help (Koss & Burkhart, 1989). Also, the impaired well-being (anger, depression, low self-esteem, anxiety, social isolation, and poor coping) appears to be the same for college and noncollege women (Zweig et al., 1997). Unfortunately, rapid recovery is not likely for the majority of victims. Interviews with rape victims four to six years after the sexual assault revealed that only 37 percent felt they had recovered within a few months of the assault; 26 percent did not yet feel recovered. Although recovery is often slow, the good news is that recovery is possible.

What Is Being Done?

Most larger communities now have twenty-four-hour hot lines and rape crisis centers. Law enforcement, medical, mental health, and judicial personnel increasingly are receiving training to facilitate treatment of the victim and adjudication of the perpetrator.

Beginning in the mid-1970s most states began to revise their rape laws. It was hoped that changes in (a) the definition of rape as assault, (b) statutory age offenses, and (c) evidentiary reforms (such as ruling a woman's past sexual history or manner of dress inadmissible evidence) would result in increases in the reportage, prosecution, and conviction of rape cases, and improvement in the treatment of rape victims by the criminal justice system (Searles & Berger, 1987). However, analyses of the effects of these legal reforms provide little optimism that the plight of victimized women has improved.

At the institutional level, experts encourage schools and universities to espouse a philosophy condemning sexual assault, to develop policies, and to offer services congruent with their policies (i.e., escort services; rape prevention programming for students, faculty, and staff; counseling/treatment services; strict judicial procedures and punitive consequences).

Several types of rape prevention programs have been aimed at the individual. These programs may be for women only, men only, or mixed-sex groups and involve videos and films depicting acquaintance rapes, group discussions, consciousness-raising activities, theatrical productions, and education about counseling services available.

Programs for women, in addition to providing general information about sexual assault, especially acquaintance rape, offer tips for day-to-day conduct that may help reduce one's risk for sexual assault and may teach self-defense (Cummings, 1992). There are at least five problems with these types of programs. First, they are deterrence programs rather than true prevention programs (Lonsway, 1996); that is, these programs may deter the likelihood of a perpetrator assaulting a particular woman but will not prevent him from seeking another victim. Second, the recommendations offered in these programs result in a life full of restrictions (e.g., don't go out alone; watch what you wear; don't drink on dates; don't take any man for granted) and precautionary behaviors (e.g., walk with a friend or a dog; take a flashlight, whistle, and/or mace; dress for easy escape; learn self-defense). All these restrictions, while obviously contributing to one's safety, may interfere with the quality of one's life. Third, the research suggests that the best predictor of engaging in precautionary behaviors is fear and, paradoxically, women fear stranger assault far more than acquaintance assault (Hickman & Muehlenhard, 1997). Fourth, some programs espouse physical resistance, based on evidence that resistance is associated with escaping a rape attempt; however, more information about the situation-specific features of rapes is needed to fully understand the relationship between the likelihood of completed rape and physical injury to victims (Ullman & Knight, 1995). Finally, rape prevention programs may not work equally well for all women. For example, Kimberly Hanson and Chris Gidycz (1993) found that the program reduced the incidence of sexual assault among women with no prior history of sexual assault, but it was ineffective for women with a sexual assault history.

Aiming rape prevention programs at women places the responsibility for rape prevention solely on women. However, the recognition that men are ultimately responsible for their aggressive behavior has led some to direct educational efforts at men. (See Box 13.5.)

Initially, many of these programs were implemented without an effort to evaluate their effectiveness. This is changing for two reasons. First, recent evaluative studies suggest that most intervention programs either do not work or may result in attitude change, such as decreased acceptance of rape myths (Lonsway, 1996). However, most programs have not assessed whether they effectively reduce the likelihood of victimization among women and the likelihood of perpetration among men. Attitude change in the absence of behavior change cannot reduce the risk of sexual assault.

Second, it has become apparent that some types of programs may produce a *boomerang effect*. In particular, some men with deeply entrenched hostile attitudes about women and who accept rape myths may actually have their attitudes strengthened as a result of a rape awareness program (Wilson, Linz, Donnerstein, & Stipp, 1992; Winkel & DeKleuver, 1997). For example, Barbara

---

Box 13.5 Fraternity Violence Education Project

A Statement by West Chester Fraternity Men Against Violence Against Women

We believe that it is important for men to struggle against the sexism in themselves and other men. Our goal is to challenge the attitudes and dispel the myths that perpetuate sexism and violence against women. This requires taking risks, being willing to listen, and speaking out.

Violence against women is often viewed as a woman's problem. Women are told to take self-defense classes, not to walk alone at night, and to dress conservatively. We feel that restricting the behavior of women ignores the responsibility of some men to not only accept their role as perpetrators, but for all men to be spokespersons against it. We believe that violence against women is an issue that both men and women must confront.

It is a common belief that women bring violence on themselves, while in fact, we live in a culture that permits violence toward women. Men are socialized through their upbringing, the media, and the educational system to assume a more dominant role in relation to women. This leads to the belief that men can control women through physical means and that these actions are justifiable.

To date, women have provided the leadership and direction to stop violence against women. Since men are the perpetrators of these acts of violence, we feel that men must also take action.

Source: From D. Mahlstedt and K. Kohat (August 1991), Fraternity violence education project: When men take action. Paper presented at the American Psychological Association convention, San Franscisco. Reprinted by permission of Dr. Deborah Mahlstedt.

Wilson, along with her colleagues, found that older men exposed to a TV movie about acquaintance rape actually attributed more blame to women in date rape situations after viewing the film than before, whereas women and younger viewers showed an increased sensitivity to date rape as a result of viewing the film.

SEXUAL HARASSMENT

Defining Sexual Harassment

Although *sexual harassment* has a long history, it was not until the 1970s that the term was created (Fitzgerald, 1996); the first legal definition of sexual harassment did not appear until 1980 (Equal Employment Opportunity Commission [EEOC], 1980). There is a great deal of confusion about what constitutes sexual harassment for a number of reasons. First, many behaviors that are now defined as sexual harassment were once seen as more socially acceptable. In the United States, television shows, movies, and comic strips often provide favorable depictions of men making sexually suggestive comments to their female employees and clients. Redefining social behavior as unacceptable and, in some cases, illegal, generates confusion and disagreement. (See Box 13.6.)

Second, the legal definition of sexual harassment is somewhat ambiguous and Supreme Court rulings continually change what behaviors and circumstances qualify as sexual harassment. In 1998 alone, the Supreme Court made three important rulings on sexual harassment (Laabs, 1998). To further entangle the situation, the definitions used by the legal system and by researchers don't always agree. Some research definitions are broader and rely on individuals' self-reports of their psychological experience (Fitzgerald et al., 1997).

Finally, although researchers have documented that sexual harassment is a widespread problem, many people do not label themselves as victims of sexual harassment (Cortina, Swan, Fitzgerald, & Waldo, 1998). Many times women will not label an event as sexually harassing because these behaviors have been normalized by our culture. Women are encouraged to minimize violence by men or risk being stigmatized for "being too fussy" or "uptight" (Giuffre & Williams, 1994; Kelly & Radford, 1996). Thus, women are caught in a no-win situation; they simultaneously express outrage about abusive events and discount them by saying "nothing happened" or "it didn't matter" (Kelly & Radford, 1996). Women who do not label an event as sexual harassment, however, have psychological consequences just as serious as women who do name their experiences (Cortina et al., 1998; Schneider, Swan, & Fitzgerald, 1997).

In the United States, sexual harassment is a form of sex discrimination that violates Title VII of the Civil Rights Act of 1964 and is legally defined as

> unwelcome sexual advances, requests for sexual favors, and other verbal or physical conduct of a sexual nature constitute sexual harassment when (1) submission to such conduct is made either explicitly or implicitly a term or condition of an individual's employment, (2) submission or rejection of such

Box 13.6 Organizational Climate Affects Experience of Sexual Harassment

Louise Fitzgerald and her colleagues (Fitzgerald, Swan, & Magley, 1997) provide two examples, based on actual sexual harassment cases, to illustrate how the consequences of sexual harassment depend not only on the incident, but on the reactions of others to the harassment and the victim's past experiences.

Victim A works as a waitress in a popular restaurant where the manager and other male employees routinely engage in the crudest type of sexual commentary concerning the waitresses, the female busers, and the customers. This occurs virtually every day, all day, and has since the beginning of A's employment. A, who was raped as a young girl, was horrified to learn that the manager had recently forced one of the other waitresses to have oral sex. Although several women have complained to the owner about the behavior of the male employees, he seems unconcerned, saying, "There are always two sides to every story." The restaurant has no sexual harassment policy. Victim A, who is the sole support of her two daughters, and has no salable skills besides waitressing, has no option but to remain employed. At the time she was assessed, she was seriously depressed and had suffered a recurrence of the nightmares and flashbacks that followed her previous victimization.

In contrast, Victim B was employed as a secretary in a high-technology software firm. The firm, which had a well-developed human resources program, had an extensive sexual harassment policy and offered periodic training; the president made many public statements to the effect that harassment would not be tolerated, and the few problems that arose were dealt with immediately, usually informally, and effectively. B was thus caught off guard one night when, working late to finish a proposal, her new supervisor followed her into the women's restroom, turned out the light, locked the door, and attempted to have sex with her. Terrified, she managed to evade him, ran out of the building, and drove home; despite several frantic phone calls from her assailant protesting that he "didn't mean anything" and had thought she was interested in him, she filed a formal complaint with the director of human resources the following morning. After a brief investigation, the manager was summarily fired; the company apologized to B, offered her time off with pay, and offered to pay for counseling. At the time of her assessment, B, who had never previously been victimized, was experiencing anxiety and mild phobic reactions to public restrooms. She was diagnosed with adjustment disorder, from which she subsequently recovered rapidly and fully.

---

by an individual is used as a basis for employment decisions affecting such individual, or (3) such has the purpose or effect of substantially interfering with an individual's work performance or creating an intimidating, hostile or offensive work environment. (EEOC, 1980, p. 33)

Students who are sexually harassed by professors are protected under Title IX of the Education Amendment of 1972, which prohibits sex discrimination in higher education (Watts, 1996). There are two broad categories of sexual harassment: quid pro quo and hostile environment. *Quid pro quo sexual harassment* (conditions 1 and 2 in the preceding definition) occurs when some kind of sexual conduct is implicitly or explicitly required for a person to maintain or advance their position in an employment or educational setting. People often think of quid pro quo examples when they think of sexual harassment.

Hostile environment sexual harassment (condition 3 in the preceding definition) occurs when one or more people create a noxious working environment. The hostile environment can involve offensive sexual language or graphics or can single a person or persons out for abuse because of their gender. Common hostile environment behaviors that can qualify as sexual harassment include putting up sexual signs or posters in a work environment, making sexist comments, making sexual comments, and singling a person out for negative remarks because of their sex.

One common concern with hostile environment sexual harassment is the fear that any ill-thought comment or slip of the tongue can result in a person being accused of sexual harassment. To establish hostile environment sexual harassment, a number of incidents of harassment must have occurred to demonstrate a pattern of behavior (Paetzold & O'Leary-Kelly, 1996). A person cannot charge hostile environment sexual harassment for one incident unless it is severe, such as a sexual assault. Furthermore, the conduct must meet a "reasonable person" standard of offensiveness (Paetzold & O'Leary-Kelly, 1996). Finally, the behavior must in some way interfere with the person's work or education.

Frequency of Sexual Harassment

Sexual harassment can happen to anyone, young or old, lesbian or heterosexual, feminist or not, in any kind of job. It even happens to clergywomen; 70 percent of a sample of 140 female rabbis had been sexually harassed (Cowen, 1993). In about half the cases, the harasser is a supervisor but may also be a peer, coworker, or client (American Association of University Women [AAUW], 1993; Gutek, 1985; Maypole, 1986; Maypole & Skaine, 1983; Rosenberg, Perlstadt, & Phillips, 1993). A nationwide study of sexual harassment in a representative sample of more than 20,000 federal employees found that 42 percent of the women had experienced some form of sexual harassment (U.S. Merit Systems Protection Board [USMSPB], 1981, 1987). Other studies support this figure, suggesting that one out of two women will experience sexual harassment during their career (Fitzgerald, 1996; Gutek, 1985). On college campuses, one out of two female students experience sexual harassment while at college (Brooks & Perot, 1991; Cortina et al., 1998). The American Association of University Women (1993) surveyed 1,632 eighth- to eleventh-graders in seventy-nine different schools across the United States. Of the girls, 85 percent had experienced sexual harassment. White girls reported the greatest sexual harassment (87%), followed by African-American (84%) and Latina girls (82%). *Gender harassment,* a subcategory of hostile environment harassment consisting of generalized sexist remarks and behavior that convey hostile or degrading attitudes about women, is the most frequent form of sexual harassment (AAUW, 1993; Cortina et al., 1998; Gutek, 1985; Houston & Hwang, 1996; USMSPB, 1981, 1987).

The United States has somewhat higher rates of sexual harassment than Europe, especially Scandinavia, which has achieved greater workplace gender equality (Gruber, 1997). A cross-cultural review of sexual harassment concluded that sexual harassment is a common problem in all cultures, although the form of sexual harassment may differ from culture to culture (Barak, 1997). Whereas research has focused on the workplace and education, sexual harassment also happens to women in public areas (Bernard & Schaffler, 1983; Gardner, 1995), and on the telephone (Smith & Morra, 1994).

Although sexual harassment against men is an important concern, it happens much less often (USMSPB, 1981, 1987). Men are at least as likely to be harassed by a man, and when harassed, men report fewer negative reactions (Waldo, Berdahl, & Fitzgerald, 1998).

Who Is at Risk?

Sexual harassment can be seen as an abuse of power, a reflection of the low status of women, and a means of social control (Fitzgerald, 1993; MacKinnon, 1979). Because men have greater authority, status, and material power in the workplace, they are able to force their sexual attentions on women. They justify their behavior by claiming that women invite harassment or use it to "sleep their way to the top." Male-dominated organizations legitimize harassment by claiming that it is a minor problem and by treating women who complain as though they were crazy (e.g., a U.S. senator suggested that Anita Hill was schizophrenic for reporting sexual harassment by a Supreme Court nominee in 1991). Sociocultural and organizational power are two important types of power that influence who is sexually harassed (Tangri, Burt, & Johnson, 1982).

Sociocultural Power

Our culture marks women as having lower status than men and young, unmarried people as having lower status than older, married persons (Fain & Anderton, 1987). Young women and women who are unattached to men (lesbians, single women, and divorced women) are more likely to be harassed than any other group (Fain & Anderton, 1987; Gruber, 1997). Black and Latina women college students were more likely to report sexually harassing experiences than Asian/East Indian Americans, who were least likely to report sexually harassing behaviors (Cortina et al., 1998). Not only are people with less power more likely to be harassed, but the greater the difference in power between two people at work, the more likely sexual harassment will occur (Gruber, 1997). Lesbian workers may face harassment based on their sexual orientation (Gelwick, 1984; Levine & Leonard, 1984). Accusations of lesbianism are also used to keep heterosexual women "in line."

> I worked with some very chauvinistic men. They thought women were sex objects. They would make sexual jokes and I was expected to respond to the jokes in a favorable way or else they would call me a dyke or a lesbian. (Gutek, 1985, p. 89)

Similarly, a West Point cadet, Nicole Galvan, said she was targeted as a lesbian after charging sexual harassment (Moss, 1997).

Organizational Power

Sexual harassment is not inevitable or natural. Lower rates of sexual harassment and less severe cases are reported when workplaces have clear, well-publicized policies on sexual harassment, and when supervisors support sexual harassment policies, encourage women to report, and punish harassers (Bond, 1991; Fitzgerald, Dragow, Hulin, Gelfland, & Magley, 1997; Gutek, 1985). John Pryor studied sexual harassment of U.S. military personnel and found that women's reports of sexual harassment were highest when the commanding officer was perceived as encouraging or supporting sexual harassment and lowest when the commanding officer actively discouraged sexual harassment (cited in Pryor, Giedd, & Williams, 1995). Similarly, sexual harassment of graduate students was found to be less likely to occur if the department had an unfavorable attitude toward professor-student relationships (Bond, 1991). Clearly, social norms, as set by workplace supervisors, are related to sexual harassment.

Women in male-dominated jobs or workplaces encounter more sexual harassment than workplaces with an equal gender ratio (Fitzgerald et al., 1997; Gruber, 1997). Many women (75%) in male-dominated jobs have experienced sexual harassment (Lafontaine & Tredeau, 1986). Workplaces that are male dominated are more likely to emphasize sexual aggression, sexual posturing, and belittling femininity (Kauppinen-Totopainen & Kandolin, 1992; cited in Gruber, 1997). A national survey of African-American women firefighters found that all but one had suffered sexual harassment; the harassment was prolonged, sometimes lasting years, and had the effect of making the women feel excluded from their coworkers and less valued as employees. Importantly, these women did not let the harassment reduce the sense of commitment and accomplishment they felt in their job (Yoder & Aniakudo, 1996).

Who Sexually Harasses? The Interaction of Individual and Organizational Factors

Men who associate power with sexuality have a greater *predisposition to sexually harass* women (Bargh & Raymond, 1995; Pryor et al., 1995). These men may be more likely to view women as objects. In one study, male college students train female college students to play poker or putt a golf ball (Pryor, 1987). The men believed that their evaluations of the women would influence how many experimental credits they received. Men with a greater predisposition to sexually harass, as measured by a likelihood-to-harass scale, engaged in more sexual touching and sexual language but only when acting as a golf instructor, indicating that both personality factors and the situation can contribute to sexual harassment. This research also suggests that men in the workplace or educational settings may use situational excuses to engage in sexual harassment, such as a boss who leans on a secretary when she is typing or a coach who continually touches players to explain how to improve their stance.

A similar study involved male students teaching female students a new computer program. The male students were exposed to a graduate student who modeled either professional behavior or sexually harassing behaviors, including flirting, leering, and touching. Men with a predisposition to sexually harass engaged in more touching, sexual comments, and nonverbal behaviors than other men when exposed to the harassing role but did not when given the professional role model (Pryor, La Vite, & Stoller, 1993). This research suggests that the climate set by supervisors in work and educational settings can influence whether men predisposed to engage in sexual harassment suppress or emit those behaviors.

Consequences of Sexual Harassment

Women frequently describe the experience of harassment as degrading, disgusting, and humiliating. They feel shamed and helpless. One woman described her experiences with workplace sexual harassment as follows:

> He was a gross man. That was his manner toward everyone in the office. He thought it was cute that he could have every woman in the office. He was executive vice president and he thought this would give him special privileges. I thought it was disgusting how he acted. He acted real macho, like he was God's gift to men. I quit. (Gutek, 1985, p. 80)

Women who are sexually harassed report more negative psychological symptoms than do other women (Dansky & Kilpatrick, 1997; Fitzgerald et al., 1997; Schneider et al., 1997), including anxiety, depression, decreased satisfaction with life, and greater symptoms of posttraumatic stress disorder. They may also suffer lowered self-esteem, self-blame, impaired social relationships, and overall lowered satisfaction with their lives (Gruber & Bjorn, 1982; Maypole, 1986). Students in the eighth to twelfth grade reported feeling embarrassed, self-conscious, less confident, scared, confused about who they were, and less popular in response to sexual harassment (AAUW, 1993).

Sexual harassment does not need to be severe to have negative consequences (Schneider et al., 1997). College women who were sexually harassed, even at "low levels," reported feeling more negative feelings about themselves, their peers, their professors, and the campus (Cortina et al., 1998). Significantly, women who were sexually harassed felt less competent academically and were more likely to leave school.

The economic costs of sexual harassment can be quite high. In a study of sexual harassment in a large West Coast utility company, harassment was associated with higher levels of absenteeism and a greater desire to leave the company (Fitzgerald et al., 1997). Women who are sexually harassed have been found to be less satisfied with work, their coworkers, and their supervisors (Schneider et al., 1997). More than 20 percent of women have quit a job, been transferred, been fired, or quit trying to get a job because of harassment (Gutek, 1985). In a large-scale study of federal employees, 56 percent of the women harassed by a supervisor and 30 percent of the women harassed by a coworker felt that their work conditions would suffer if they did not comply (USMSPB, 1981).

What Is Being Done?

To fight sexual harassment, schools and businesses are adopting clear policies on sexual harassment that are well publicized and easily accessible. As most victims of sexual harassment do not report the incidents, policies and educational programs need to encourage women to label incidents as offensive, provide support when they do report sexual harassment, and protect them from retribution by the accused harasser(s) (Biaggio & Brownell, 1996). Ethnic minority women's concerns may differ from other women and care should be taken to understand their perspectives (Paludi, 1997). It is important for organizations to recognize that sexual harassment often happens to those with little power who are unable to defend themselves from retribution. Therefore, supervisors, peers, and coworkers should be educated so they can support efforts to reduce it (Biaggio & Brownell, 1996; Paludi, 1997).

Although many institutions have implemented polices and educational programs, none have been shown to reduce sexual harassment (Grundmann, O'Donohue, & Peterson, 1997). This ineffectiveness may be the result of institutions adopting policies merely to reduce legal liability. The research reviewed in this section indicates that organizational climate is associated with rates of sexual harassment. If schools and businesses adopt sexual harassment policies "in name only," then the important organizational factors that support sexual harassment may remain unchanged. To really combat sexual harassment, those in power need to be committed to creating an environment where harassment is not tolerated.

WIFE ABUSE

Partner abuse is the maltreatment of one partner in an intimate relationship by the other. Partner abuse includes psychological abuse, such as intimidation, threats, public humiliation, and intense criticism, as well as physical force, which can range from a slap or push to the use of a weapon. For many *battered women,* psychological abuse is more devastating than physical abuse and usually accompanies physical abuse (Tolman, 1989). Furthermore, the terror and control associated with battering can persist even after the physical abuse has stopped. However, physical abuse is more frequently studied (Smith, Smith, & Earp, 1999).

"Wife" Abuse versus "Spouse" Abuse

Partner abuse occurs between married and unmarried partners, including lesbian and gay couples (Renzetti, 1997). (See Box 13.7.) The majority of cases, however, involve heterosexual couples where the woman is at greater risk of physical injury and sexual abuse (Romkens, 1997; Zlotnick, Kohn, Peterson & Pearlstein, 1998). Although women often engage in aggressive acts toward their partners, in many cases, they act in self-defense (Barnett, Lee, & Thelen, 1997; Langhinrichsen-Rohling, Neidig, & Thorn, 1995). Thus, the evidence suggests that *wife abuse* is a much more frequent and serious social problem than husband abuse. In fact, it has been argued that terms such as *partner abuse, spouse abuse,* and *domestic violence* obscure the central issue in wife abuse of men physically harming women (Bograd, 1988). Wife abuse is a more specific term that raises questions about the economic, political, and social context in which the violence occurs.

Feminists point to the patriarchal structure of society as encouraging and supporting wife abuse. For instance, it has been suggested that a woman's second-class status in society makes her more likely to be economically dependent and unable to leave an abusive situation (Bograd, 1988; Browne, 1993). By leaving the relationship, a woman may lose her house, car, and insurance. She may need to relocate and find new employment. If she has been out of the job mar-

Box 13.7 Lesbians and Battery

Relationship abuse is not limited to heterosexual relationships. Although men engage in more violent acts against women (rape, attempted rape, courtship violence, or nonconsensual infliction of pain during sexual activities) than women do against men or women, this does not hold true for committed relationships (Brand & Kidd, 1986). For homosexual women, the rate of relationship abuse was not significantly different than for heterosexuals (27% and 25%, respectively). Apparently, violence in committed relationships is not simply a gender issue. Issues of power and control arise in all relationships and provide the basis for battering in heterosexual and homosexual relationships.

Lesbians face discrimination from police, counselors, and shelters who assume a battered woman is a heterosexual. If revealed as a victim of lesbian battering, many counselors and police officers have homophobic reactions (Suh, 1990). Although slow to surface, shelters and organizations are beginning to assimilate information on the issue; for example, Minnesota now has a full-time staff person to deal specifically with lesbian battering (Suh, 1990).

ket raising a family, she may lack needed skills. Furthermore, if children are involved, she must contend with day care and the economic demands of single parenthood. Poverty is a real threat for women who leave abusive husbands.

Women who have been battered often report that their partner taking control of them is a major part of the violence (Yllo, 1993). One battered woman, who eventually lost her unborn child in a battering incident, recounts the relationship between control and violence:

> I didn't even realize he was gaining control and I was too dumb to know any better. . . . He was gaining control bit by bit until he was checking my pantyhose when I'd come home from the supermarket to see if they were inside out. . . . He'd time me. He'd check the mileage on the car. . . . I was living like a prisoner. (Yllo, 1993, p. 57)

The *power and control wheel,* developed by the Domestic Abuse Intervention Project in Duluth, Minnesota, has been used with batterers and women's support groups around the country because it clearly links power and control to physical, sexual, and psychological violence (see Figure 13.3). Each spoke of the wheel represents a different tactic used by abusive men to dominate their partner.

Social acceptance of wife beating has been common in the United States until recent years (Goldstein, 1983). People with more traditional attitudes toward male and female roles tend to blame the victim more and the perpetrator less for wife assault (Hillier & Foddy, 1993). Moreover, clergy who counsel women often hold traditional attitudes that blame women for their abuse (Wood & McHugh, 1994). There is some evidence that attitudes that support wife abuse are declining in the United States (Straus, Kaufman, Kantor, & Moore, 1997). The situation is not as optimistic in some other countries where patriarchal views are stronger. For men and women in Israel, the West Bank, and the Gaza Strip, acceptance of patriarchal values is associated with acceptance of wife beating. Despite growth in educational and career opportunities for women in Arab countries, religious and family values condone wife abuse and provide women few avenues for escape (Haj-Yahia, 1996). Women

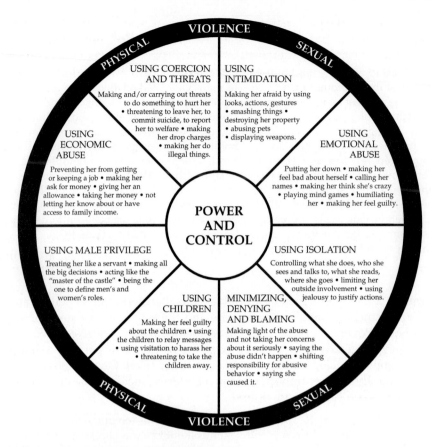

FIGURE 13.3. The power and control wheel.
Source: From R. J. Gelles & D. R. Loseke (eds.). *Current Controversies on Family Violence,* pp. 47–62. Used by permission of the Minnesota Program Development, Inc.

in many countries such as Bangladesh and India also suffer (Fernandez, 1997; Schuler, Hashemi, Riley, & Akhter, 1996). Economic, social, cultural, and psychological factors may not be addressed in a discussion of "spouse" abuse but become obvious when the topic is defined as "wife" abuse.

Frequency of Wife Abuse

"Police Say Woman, 21, Is Killed by Ex-Husband ("Police Say," 1998). Headlines like this frequently appear in the news. In fact, wife abuse is one of the most common causes of injury for women in the United States. It is estimated that one-third of all women will be battered at some time in their lives (Straus & Gelles, 1990). In one study, more than 33 percent of the female patients admitted to an urban emergency room were suspected victims of spouse abuse, and 22.5 percent were confirmed victims (Stark & Flitcraft, 1996). In a study of women at a community-based family practice clinic, 25 percent of 351 women reported physical injuries inflicted by their partner, and 15 percent reported injuries in the past year (Hamberger, Saunders, & Hovey, 1992). Most researchers agree that wife abuse is probably underreported due to shame, guilt, and the belief that wife beating is a normal part of marriage (Browne, 1993).

Wife abuse may result in homicide. Sometimes a woman's death is the result of a severe beating; other times her death is the result of wounds inflicted by a gun or knife. Two-thirds of partner homicides are women killed by their male partners, and more than one-half of all murders of women are committed by current or former partners (Browne & Williams, 1993). In contrast, only 6 percent of male murder victims are killed by wives or girlfriends (Federal Bureau of Investigation, 1985).

Who Commits Wife Abuse?

Wife abuse is a complex phenomenon; there do not appear to be any easy explanations or solutions. Some social factors that may contribute to wife abuse are a general societal acceptance of violence, devaluation of women, and acceptance of men's right to dominate women. The finding that men who earn less than their wives are more likely to engage in wife abuse supports the idea that battering is related to patriarchal beliefs (Anderson, 1997). While removing patriarchal values might eradicate wife abuse, the fact that not all men in our society batter their partners suggests that factors other than culture should be examined.

Social scientists have looked for differences between men who batter and men who do not. Men who batter are more likely to be diagnosed with a personality disorder (Dutton, 1996). Early experiences shape an abusive personality (Dutton, Starzomski, & Ryan, 1996). Men who are rejected by their parents in childhood while suffering verbal and physical abuse are more likely to develop an abusive personality.

Frustration, stress, and a lack of coping skills may explain why some men are violent toward their partners (Howell & Pugliesi, 1988). Abusive men are more likely to have a history of alcohol abuse, to have more life stress, and to lack coping skills (Barnett & Fagan, 1993; Hale, Duckworth, Zimostrad, & Nicholas, 1988). Other characteristics are low self-esteem, a need to dominate, depression, dependency on others to meet emotional needs, and hostility toward women (Dewhurst, Moore, & Alfano, 1992; Hale et al., 1988). Age, ethnicity, education, and income have been associated with domestic violence (Sorenson, Upchurch, & Shen, 1996). Factors such as being under age 30, being an urban dweller, being black, having less than a high school education, and earning less than $40,000 a year are associated with violence against wives. Wife abuse occurs, however, in all social classes (Gelles & Straus, 1988).

Who Are the Victims?

When the phenomenon of wife abuse first became widely publicized, the masochism theory, which states that women who enjoy pain are likely to seek out and stay in abusive relationships, was offered as an explanation for wife abuse (Goldstein, 1983). This theory has found no support and is now seen as a mechanism for blaming the victim. Contrary to the masochism theory, it is now believed that the majority of women who suffer from wife abuse do not remain in the relationship because they enjoy the pain of battering (Bowker,

1993). Furthermore, studies of abusive couples have found little evidence that battered women have certain personalities that put them at risk (Russell, Lipov, Phillips, & White, 1989).

Asking women why they stay in abusive relationships rather than asking men why they abuse assumes that women are weak, unable to protect themselves, and responsible for the abuse (Schwartz, 1989). Because research typically focuses on women who are married or in relationships with abusers, women who *do* leave abusive relationships often are not studied. A follow-up study of fifty-one battered women found that after two and a half years, only 25 percent of the previously battered women were still in a violent relationship (Schwartz, 1989). More research is needed to investigate the many ways women respond to abusive incidents, including leaving the relationship.

Consequences for the Victim

A person who lives with someone who physically and emotionally abuses them develops a stress response when attacked. If the attack is repeated or the threat of attack is present, a chronic set of symptoms develops. Many battered women suffer from depression (Zlotnick et al., 1998) and posttraumatic stress disorder (Weaver, Kilpatrick, Resnick, Best, & Saunders, 1997). The *battered woman's syndrome* is a special case of posttraumatic stress disorder and explains how the psychological effects of battering create feelings of helplessness (Walker, 1984, 1993). When repeatedly degraded and ridiculed by their husbands over a period of time, wives can come to believe the husbands' accusations. Women's self-esteem and confidence erode. They may actually come to believe that they deserve their husbands' abuse and that they are incapable of caring for themselves and their children.

In contrast, the *survivor theory* emphasizes women's active attempts to seek help and cope with violence (Gondolf & Fisher, 1998). Battered women seek help from family, clergy, police, lawyers, counselors, and social service agencies, but often their active responses to abuse are undermined by the responses of others (Dutton, 1996).

Social and economic pressures frequently prevent battered women from taking effective action. African-American battered women who may perceive themselves as having fewer options because of racism are less likely to call the police or use social services, perhaps due to a mistrust of these institutions (Joseph, 1997; Sorenson, 1996). It is not unusual for abused women to be blamed for their husbands' behavior or have their stories discounted. Women are often told to "try and be a better wife," to "be thankful for what you have," or to "think of the children." Furthermore, many women are economically dependent on their husbands, lacking money or job skills to provide for themselves and their children. Without financial and social supports women may be very accurate in feeling that they have nowhere to go.

Battered women are often afraid to leave their husbands because they fear that their husbands will follow them, intensify their abuse, perhaps killing them, their children, or other family members. Indeed, women who leave a relationship are at greater risk for battering (Dearwater, Coben, Campbell, Nah, et al., 1998; Wilson & Daly, 1994), as the following cases illustrate:

FIGURE 13.4. This photo, from a series taken by Donna Ferrato, shows one of many actual abusive episodes between Garth and Lisa. Their marriage, which had the appearance of being ideal, ended after many bouts of violence when Lisa divorced Garth and moved away with their children. Garth continued to deny that he ever hit Lisa (Ferrato, 1991).

> Sharon had been separated from Roy for over two years and was divorcing him, yet he continued to harass her. He broke into her home, destroyed her furniture, poured acid in the motor of her car, and slit the seats with a knife. He cut power and phone lines to her house, set small fires, and bragged to others about how he was going to kill her. He attacked and severely injured her at work, and she finally took a leave of absence from her job. She had unlisted phone numbers, but he always got them. She repeatedly called the police for protection. (Browne, 1987, pp. 120–121)

> Every time Karen would have ugly bruises on her face and neck. She would beg me for a divorce, and I would tell her, "I am sorry. I won't do it again. But as for divorce, absolutely not. If I can't have you for my wife, you will die. No one else will have you if you ever try to leave me." (Browne, 1987, p. 114)

Steps to Take

Historically, women have had fewer rights than men (Steil, 1989). Prior to the American Civil War, husbands had the right to control their wives' property, collect and spend their wages, and punish their wives for transgressions. The abuse of women was tolerated, if not accepted, by many men and women (Gordon, 1988). Recently, increased education and awareness of battering may be changing people's attitudes (Straus et al., 1997). Although it is encouraging that acceptance of wife abuse may be declining in the United States, there are still many areas of the world where this is not the case.

Not only may some people still consider wife abuse a normal and acceptable behavior, it is suggested that our society supports wife abuse with a male-dominated family structure and economic system. As discussed in Chapter 9, husbands usually have more power than wives in a society in which men make most of the money and many of the important family decisions. This unequal distribution of power leads men to feel entitled to dominate and leads women to feel vulnerable. Battering has been linked with other social problems: "Battering is rooted in a culture of domination, a culture that does not celebrate our differences in race, age, sexual preference, physical and mental abilities, and gender, but instead uses these differences to exploit and dehumanize" (Pence & Shepard, 1988, p. 296).

From this perspective, the way to end battering is to change our social structure. The battered women's movement over the past two decades has begun this process through public education, legal reform, and programs designed to aid battered women. The first battered women's shelter in the United States opened in 1974, largely in response to the growing awareness of battered women's needs. Now there are shelters in most large cities and many smaller towns in America. The staff at shelters work to educate the public about the difficulties of battered women and can be successful in informing young people about the seriousness of wife abuse (Tulloch & Tulloch, 1992). These shelters, largely through volunteer effort, provide temporary emergency housing, emotional support, and information about legal and social services. Women report that shelters are often cited as the most helpful intervention when dealing with abuse (Gordon, 1996). Battered women in South Africa reported that access to a shelter enabled them to escape abuse and transform their lives (Angless, Maconachie, & Van Zyl, 1998). The importance of shelters in protecting battered women is underscored by the economic upheaval in Russia, which has resulted in housing restrictions and a lack of shelters. These problems have been associated with the fact that Russian women have the highest rates of spousal homicide in the industrialized world (Gondolf & Shestakov, 1997).

In many states, police departments are now trained to deal with men who batter. In the past, police have been reluctant to arrest male batterers and have discouraged women from pressing charges. Due to education programs, officers are now more likely to respond to calls and make arrests. Some localities have adopted programs to arrest an abusive person without waiting for the abused person to press charges. Acknowledging that a woman may have trouble pressing charges against her partner, the police take the decision away from her. It is not yet apparent whether arresting the abuser is helpful (Berk, 1993; Buzawa & Buzawa, 1993). In many states, such as North Carolina and Rhode Island, women can now get temporary restraining orders against their abusers without a lawyer. It is unclear how effective these orders may be. Some research suggests that contacting police may intensify abuse (Gordon, 1996).

Psychologists have designed programs targeted toward the men in our society who batter their wives. These programs focus on teaching men to change their attitudes and behavior (Edleson, 1996). The men have to want to change and be willing to undergo lengthy counseling. The success of these programs has yet to be fully evaluated but appears promising (Edleson, 1996).

Although these steps have not changed society enough to eradicate wife abuse, it is obvious that some movement has been made. Unfortunately, many areas still need shelters for battered women, and many shelters suffer from lack of funds and space to meet the needs of the large number of battered women seeking help. In addition, programs that treat male batterers are still in their infancy, and it is difficult to solicit participants unless under court order. Clearly, the battle to end wife abuse is not over.

CONCLUSION

This brief review makes clear the common themes underlying all these forms of violence against women. The levels of analysis approach described at the beginning of this chapter shows how these themes relate.

The sociocultural level reflects sexual inequalities, gender-role prescriptions, and cultural myths about women, men, children, family, sex and violence, as well as scripts for enacting relationships. Whether discussing childhood sexual abuse, sexual harassment, courtship violence, sexual assault, or wife abuse, a common underlying theme is societal endorsement of male dominance. Cultural norms governing aggression as a tool of the powerful to subdue the weak interact with gender inequalities to create a context conductive to violence against women.

The social network level of analysis helps show how gendered norms and expectations are transmitted through the various social networks of which we are all a part, including the family, peer groups, and school, church, and work groups. Witnessing or experiencing family violence as a child is related to the various forms of violence against women we have studied. Indeed, roughly a third of individuals who witness or experience violence as children become violent as adults. Many households in which violence occurs are characterized by patriarchal family structures where traditional gender roles are encouraged.

The dyadic level of analysis calls our attention to the power and status differences between the perpetrator and victim. Stemming from historical and sociocultural traditions, women and children are regarded as weaker and more passive than men, and, thus, rightfully should be dependent on men. Such culturally prescribed dependence affects communication patterns and other relationship dynamics to increase women's vulnerability to abuse.

However, in order for male violence against women to occur, the situation must be conducive to the violence. A number of situational variables have been examined, including time, place, and the presence of social inhibitors or disinhibitors (i.e., the presence of others or the presence of alcohol). Regardless of the type of violence under investigation, features of the situation influence the likelihood that violence will occur by affecting the opportunity for the violent acts (i.e., times when privacy is available and detection minimal) and/or by contributing to the ambiguity of the situation.

Finally, similar intrapersonal variables appear to underlie various forms of male violence toward women. These attitudinal, motivational, and personality characteristics include endorsement of traditional gender-role stereotypes, acceptance of cultural myths about violence, and a need for power, dominance, and control over women and children. Other characteristics include antisocial tendencies and nonconformity, as well as impulsivity, irresponsibility, hypermasculinity, affective dysregulation, and self-centeredness coupled with insensitivity to others. The extent to which these specific intrapersonal variables influence the incidence of violence against women depends on the degree to which cultural norms and the influence of social groups affect individual mental representations of the situation and the relationship with the woman.

Analysis of violence against women from a feminist perspective emphasizes the sociocultural level. Our culture teaches men to protect women and women to look to others for safety and security. Ironically, in a chivalrous society, men are both those who commit violence and those who protect. "In the system of chivalry, men protect women against men . . . chivalry is an age-old protection racket" (Griffin, 1971, p. 30) that depends on male violence for its very existence. Chivalry promotes the man as the protector and the woman as the protected, the man as the aggressor and the woman as the victim.

A key aspect of chivalrous behavior in men is to protect women's chastity and vulnerability from involuntary defilement and violent attacks. The protection, however, has its own costs for women in our culture by prescribing a code of appropriate behavior called femininity. The characteristics of traditional femininity may make women perfect victims and vulnerable to attack. Women have the right to protect and defend themselves.

If a woman is attacked, she may be accused of noncompliance with the traditional codes for feminine behavior and blamed for her victimization. The culture in general, and men specifically, may accuse her of teasing and dressing provocatively in a sexual attack or of nagging and being disrespectful in a physical attack. Within the patriarchal system, a woman is both bound by rules for feminine behavior and accused when she is attacked and cannot protect herself even though it is the culture who discouraged her from learning how to defend herself.

"Each girl as she grows into womanhood is taught fear. Fear is the form in which the female internalizes both chivalry and the double standard" (Griffin, 1971, p. 33). Her fear results in a passive rather than active response to male aggression. She may become paralyzed with fear, restrict her behavior (i.e., not go out alone, not do anything without her partner's permission), try to appease her attacker, and worry about how *she* can prevent a future attack. "The passive woman is taught to regard herself as impotent, unable to act, unable even to perceive, in no way self-sufficient" (Griffin, 1971, p. 33) To confront violence in our patriarchal society, women must use their own strength as an energy source for reform.

> Social movements, feminism included, move toward a vision; they cannot operate solely on fear. It is not enough to move women away from danger and oppression; it is necessary to move toward something: toward pleasure, agency, self-definition. Feminism must increase women's pleasure and joy, not just decrease our misery. (Vance, 1984, p. 24)

In addition, men must be included in the fight to end violence against women. Men are secondary victims as their girlfriends, sisters, wives, mothers, and daughters face the threat of attack. Men are also the victims of the codes that demand accountability for protecting women in a society where it is impossible to do so. By recognizing women as equals, refusing patriarchal demands for men to be dominant and aggressive, and fighting for legal and societal reforms, men will be liberated and our society transformed.

Feminist analyses of patriarchy and violence have given women and men a basis for combating violence against women. Though the evidence of violence against women is distressing, documentation of the problem provides the first step toward eradication. Public demand for treatment facilities, legal reforms, explicit institutional policies condemning sexual misconduct of all forms, and educational programs for young people signal hope that future generations of women, in equal partnership with men, will enjoy a life free from the fear of violence.

CONNECTING THEMES

- *Gender is more than just sex.* The pattern of intimate violence, where women are the victims and men are the perpetrators, is not due to biological destiny. Women are not born victims and men are not biologically predetermined to be aggressors. Rather, stereotypes of how women and men are supposed to behave, experiences that reinforce stereotypical behaviors, and a social structure that supports power inequities between women and men all contribute to violence against women.
- *Language and naming are sources of power.* Traditionally, secrecy and myths regarding male-female relationships trivialized and/or justified male violence against women. The women's movement has done much to bring to public awareness the extent of the harm done to women by men and has prompted redefinitions that acknowledge the violence. Thus, for example, no longer is rape defined as a sexual act, sexual harassment as standard working conditions, and wife abuse as a legitimate way to "show the little lady who is boss"; rather, each is seen as an act by men intended to dominate and control women.
- *Women are not all alike.* Violence against women is influenced by social and cultural factors that affect the occurrence of and responses to intimate violence. Although violence against women is a problem throughout the world, the incidence of violence and the forms it takes, as well as societal attitudes, can vary greatly across cultures.
- *Psychological research can foster social change.* Violence against women, in its various forms, is now recognized as a public health and social problem. Hence, research has moved from focusing on individual psychopathology to identifying the sociocultural factors that contribute to such violence. Also, communities, institutions, and organizations are combating violence against women by developing interventions that not only help individuals but also promote change in values and attitudes at the societal level.

SUGGESTED READINGS

BERGEN, RAQUEL KENNEDY. (1998). *Issues in intimate violence.* Thousand Oaks, CA: Sage. This is a comprehensive and accessible anthology that prepares the foundation for understanding a wide range of violence that commonly occurs in families and between intimates. Many articles offer a feminist perspective that addresses the gendered nature of violence and the consequences of power inequality in our society.

KOSS, MARY, GOODMAN, LISA, FITZGERALD, LOUISE, RUSSO, NANCY, KEITA, GWENDOLYN, & BROWNE, ANGELA. (1994). *No safe haven.* Washington, DC: American Psychological Association. A comprehensive review of current psychological research on the prevalence, causes, and effects of forms of violence against adult women is presented. Recommendations for effective intervention, treatment, and public policy initiatives are given.

SHRIER, DIANE K. (1996). *Sexual harassment in the workplace: Psychiatric issues.* New York: American Psychiatric Press. Experts provide a practical guide to identification, treatment, and advocacy for individuals, particularly women, who have been sexually harassed. Case vignettes are presented that illustrate the damaging psychological, medical, social, and economic consequences of sexual exploitation and discrimination.

WARSHAW, R. (1988). *I never called it rape: The Ms. report on recognizing, fighting, and surviving date and acquaintance rape.* New York: Harper & Row. This book provides a good overview of acquaintance rape from the victim's perspective, includes firsthand accounts, and contains suggestions for combating the problem.

CHAPTER 14

Mental and Physical Health

- **GENDER AND PSYCHOLOGICAL DISORDERS**
  The Social Construction of Mental Illness
  Problems of Psychological Diagnosis
  Gender Differences: A Review of Explanations
  The Social Construction of Symptoms
- **POWER ISSUES**
  The Case of Dora
  Personal Consequences and Social Circumstances
- **DEPRESSION**
  Depression and the Developmental Process
  Gender Roles
  Power and Depression
  Blaming Women: Reproductive Function as a Source of Depression
- **THE SOCIAL CONSTRUCTION OF FEMALE DISORDERS: THE VIEW FROM HISTORY**
  Nervous Disorders
  Gender, Class, and Social Control
- **EATING DISORDERS**
  The "Normal" Desire for Thinness
  Prejudice and Discrimination Against Overweight Women
  Disordered Eating as Pathology

The Demographics of Eating Disorders
A Feminist Perspective
- **ISSUES IN TREATMENT**
  The Politics of Labeling
  The Double Standard in Diagnostic Categories
  Gender Bias in Practitioner Attitudes
  Gender Biases in Treatment: The Use of Medication
  Institutional Biases in the Treatment of Women and Men
- **GENDER AND THERAPY**
  The Feminist Critique of Traditional Treatment Methods
  Feminist Therapy
  The Difference between Nonsexist and Feminist Therapy
  The Impact of Therapist Characteristics
  Race/Ethnicity
  Therapy with Marginalized Women
  Culture-Bound Syndromes
- **THE RELATIONSHIP BETWEEN PHYSICAL AND MENTAL HEALTH**
- **SOME UNRESOLVED ISSUES**
  Invisible Groups of Women
  Invisible Values
- **CONNECTING THEMES**
- **SUGGESTED READINGS**

Why is gender central to any discussion of mental and physical health? Gender differences are very evident in these areas. Women are more likely than men to seek psychotherapy and, despite their longer life span, they are more likely to seek medical help as well. Are women actually sicker than men? If not, what accounts for these gender differences? As in many other aspects of women's lives, some theories focus on women's biological vulnerabilities. Others focus on women's roles and their life circumstances. Some of these factors are shared by all women and others are a result of their membership in other social categories such as ethnicity and social class. Still others are a result of each woman's unique experiences. One of the connecting themes of this book is particularly relevant to this chapter—women are not all alike. Each woman has a mixture of strengths and weaknesses that contribute to her psychological and physical well-being.

It is becoming more and more difficult to separate physical and mental health. For example, stress produces problems for both mind and body. The ways people cope with stress also influence how it affects them. Because of their traditional roles, women and men encounter different forms of stress and because of traditional socialization, they have also developed different coping strategies. Feminist therapists and health psychologists have examined many of the problematic areas of women's lives. They argue that the greater social power and dominance of men are major contributors to women's mental and physical health problems. Women of color must deal with other forms of oppression as well. This focus on the social context of women's lives is in sharp contrast to earlier theories that focused on women's psychological weaknesses.

GENDER AND PSYCHOLOGICAL DISORDERS

Feminist researchers have been actively engaged in exploring biases in the diagnosis and treatment of women for nearly thirty years. Compared with men, women are overrepresented in some areas and underrepresented in others. Stereotypical beliefs about women and men influence both diagnosis and treatment. Feminist researchers have, therefore, called for greater attention to women's lived experience.

Feminists have also raised many unresolved questions. Do women and men manifest different kinds of psychological disorders or do they show different symptoms of the same disorders? If some disorders are found to be more prevalent in women than men, how much of this difference can be explained by biological sex? How important are gender roles and situational context in producing gender differences in psychological and physical distress? Can a person's social environment create psychological disorders as well as influence their expression? Are traditional methods of diagnosis and treatment intrinsically sexist? And, finally, how can the psychological and medical treatment of women be improved? All of these questions will be addressed in this chapter.

The Social Construction of Mental Illness

Beginning in the 1970s, feminist therapists have charged that the social system makes women "mad" (Chesler, 1972). Psychological distress is seen as a social as well as a personal event. Societal norms define what traits and behaviors are considered acceptable and unacceptable in women and men. Norms are social constructions and, as such, they may change over time. As norms change, ideas about what is a mentally healthy person change, too. Thus, definitions of mental illness in women have also changed over time.

Norms are not applied to everyone the same way. People who have little power in society are more likely to be punished for engaging in undesirable behaviors than are more powerful people. This is because the less powerful do not have the ability to define themselves. Feminist psychotherapists are very concerned about how the politics of gender intersect with those of class and ethnicity (Brown, 1994). Power greatly influences how psychological diagnoses are created, applied, and treated. The power to name is also the power to control.

Problems of Psychological Diagnosis

Sampling Bias

Psychological diagnoses are much more problematic than diagnoses of physical illness because few objective standards can be applied. How, for example, does one take a psychological temperature or do a psychological blood test? Therapists are usually limited to information given by the client and/or the observations of others with whom the client is in close contact. From this limited information, they must infer causes and offer a psychological label.

Most mental health professionals (psychiatrists, psychologists, and psychiatric social workers) currently use the fourth edition of the *Diagnostic and Statistical Manual of Mental Disorders*, or DSM-IV, in making their diagnoses. This large and impressive-looking book was published by the American Psychiatric Association in 1994. It includes descriptions of the symptoms of 125 psychological disorders and also provides information on prevalence rates for males and females for 101 of these disorders (Hartung & Widiger, 1998). Relatively few disorders have equal rates for women and men, and many show large gender differences.

What is the source of these differences? Several potential sources of sampling bias have been identified: Women and men may differ in their willingness to seek treatment. They may differ in their ability or willingness to acknowledge that they have a disorder. People's differential reactions to the same symptoms in a man or woman may influence the willingness to acknowledge a disorder and seek treatment for it (e.g., depression is inconsistent with the traditionally masculine role). Finally, an additional disorder or condition may be present that affects the likelihood of seeking and receiving treatment (e.g., alcoholism, more often diagnosed in men, may mask depression).

Gender Bias in Diagnosis

Therapists are taught to give individuals a psychological label based on how well their symptoms fit one of the diagnostic categories in the DSM-IV. Here are some behavioral descriptions of two disorders:

- This person is depressed most of the time, tending to feel sad, blue, down in the dumps, and "low."
- The person doesn't seem to be interested in his/her usual activities and doesn't get pleasure out of them anymore.
- The person feels inadequate, or feels worthless, and has a very low opinion of himself/herself.

- The person passively allows others to assume responsibility for major areas of his/her life because of a lack of self-confidence and an inability to function independently.
- The person subordinates his/her own needs to those of others on whom he/she is dependent in order to avoid any possibility of having to be self-reliant.
- The person is unwilling to make demands on the people he/she depends on for fear of jeopardizing the relationships.
- The person tends to belittle his/her abilities and assets by constantly referring to himself/herself as "stupid."

The first three symptoms describe mild depression, and the last four describe a dependent personality.

What kind of people do these descriptions bring to mind? Do you think they are male or female? Young or old? Rich or poor? Psychological symptoms are not evaluated in a social vacuum. When lists including such descriptions were shown to students, who were asked what kind of person was being described, they tended to agree on the individual's gender, ethnicity, and social class (Landrine, 1988, 1989). A large majority agreed that the individuals described above would be white, middle class, and female.

Perceptions of psychological symptoms are inextricably associated with social characteristics. They involve assumptions about social roles (married or

---

Making a Difference

Phyllis Chesler (b. 1935), psychotherapist, professor, public lecturer, and author, is best known for her 1972 book, *Women and Madness.* This volume, which has sold 2.5 million copies, told the world that women aren't crazy—they're oppressed—and their trauma is only increased when they are misdiagnosed and mistreated by the psychological and psychiatric professions. Chesler argued that a double standard of mental health exists for women and men; women are medicated, put in mental institutions, and pathologized for behaviors that would be considered normal in men. Women's status as second-class citizens and the frequency with which they are physically and psychologically abused add to their difficulties. Yet, when they respond assertively, they are deemed mentally ill. The twenty-fifth anniversary edition of *Women and Madness,* with its new in-troduction on the trauma of psychiatric labeling, is unfortunately still quite relevant to women's lives.

Since 1972, Chesler has written several other important books. These include *With Child: A Diary of Motherhood* (1979) and *Sacred Bond: The Legacy of Baby M* (1986). Chesler was also a founder, in 1969, of the Association for Women in Psychology. She was recently named the first research scholar to the International Institute for Research on Jewish Women at Brandeis University. Phyllis Chesler is a founding mother of feminist therapy, and it has been said that she enjoys "a reputation as one of America's most ar-ticulate and thoughtful feminist writers, [whose] activism in representing women who are marginalized by illness, poverty, and exploitation has not diminished despite personal hardship."

Source: About Dr. Chesler, http://www.phyllis-chesler.com/biography.htm. *Contemporary Authors.* (1998). New Revision Series, Volume 59, pp. 85–86.

single) as well as about class, race, age, and gender. Although it is impossible to do a similar study with professionals (who are familiar with DSM categories), clinicians have been found to show a strong connection between gender stereotypes and diagnostic labels. For example, they labeled a stereotypical description of a single, middle-class white woman as a hysterical personality and the stereotype of a married, middle-class woman as depressed (Landrine, 1987). Neither the therapists' gender nor their clinical orientation had any effect on their labels.

Why are gender stereotypes and diagnostic categories connected? Some theorists conclude that such beliefs reflect actual differences in the incidence of various disorders (Hartung & Widiger, 1998). Others argue that some disorders are identified in some people just because they are members of a particular gender, race, or class category (Chesler, 1972; Kaplan, 1983). In other words, under some circumstances, simply being a woman is a sufficient reason to be considered "crazy" (Caplan, 1995).

Psychological symptoms probably have more than one cause. Individual, social, and cultural factors all play a role. Some disorders considered characteristic of women may be induced by the demands placed on them by their social circumstances. However, not every woman shows the "appropriate" symptoms. A weaker version of the idea that society creates madness is the view that society shapes symptoms, but other, more individual, factors determine who is most susceptible to these social forces. This point of view recognizes that men's symptoms are also shaped by gender stereotypes.

The identification and treatment of gender-characteristic disorders are not value free. Many signs of psychological distress are both vague and highly subjective in nature. Stereotypic beliefs can lead to different labels being attached to the same symptoms, different opinions about the severity of such symptoms, and different views about the nature of effective treatment for women and men. Women and men may internalize these beliefs so that they themselves view their symptoms differently and seek treatment at differing rates. Gender biases in the DSM are particularly troubling because this book is used by most therapists. Feminists charge, moreover, that the research base of this manual is weaker than the psychiatrists who constructed it claim (Caplan, 1995). The association of psychiatry with medicine may give DSM categories more power and legitimacy than they deserve.

Sexist assumptions about symptoms can either increase or decrease a person's possibility of receiving help. Some women may be treated needlessly, whereas others (both women and men) may not receive the help and support they need.

Gender Differences: A Review of Explanations

Clinical researchers generally agree about the kinds of disorders that are more likely to be diagnosed in women than in men. These include depression and eating disorders. Most mental health surveys indicate a two to two and a half times greater incidence of depression among women. It has also been estimated that 95 percent of those suffering from eating disorders are women (Franks, 1986). Although it is easy to give statistics about the different incidence of various disorders in men and women, it is not easy to explain why such differences exist. We will briefly review the major explanatory theories. Because some of these theories explain some disorders better than others, we will refer to them again in discussing specific gender-related disorders.

Medical Models

Medical models assert that women are biologically more vulnerable to certain disorders, especially depression. As discussed in Chapters 7, 10, and 12, women are regarded as being particularly at risk during periods of hormonal change such as menstruation, following childbirth, and at menopause. A major problem with such medical models is that they define women almost entirely in terms of their reproductive functions. In effect, they see a direct connection between the uterus and the mind!

A higher rate of mental illness in women appears to be a recent development in the United States. Before World War II, more men than women were admitted to mental hospitals. Moreover, while more recent surveys report a higher incidence of psychological symptoms among women than men, the converse was true in earlier studies (Unger, 1979a). In developing countries, such as India, Iraq, New Guinea, and Rhodesia, more men than women are diagnosed as being depressed (Rothblum, 1983). One recent study that explored the rates of mental disorders among various ethnic groups in Los Angeles County found no gender differences in depression for Asian-Americans (Root, 1995). Asian-American men had higher depression rates than men from other ethnic groups, including African-Americans, Latinos, and Anglo-Americans. Such historical trends and ethnic/cultural differences suggest that biological vulnerability is too simplistic an explanation for gender differences.

Stereotypes and Gender Roles

An alternative explanation for gender differences in the prevalence of some psychological disorders is the idea that traditional gender roles increase the risks for some disorders. In other words, behaving like a feminine woman increases a woman's chance of developing depression, *agoraphobia* (fear of being outside of one's home), or some form of eating disorder. All these disorders show a high degree of overlap between symptoms and stereotypes about women. They are characterized by passivity, dependence, and concern for pleasing others. In contrast, disorders that appear to be more prevalent among men, such as alcoholism and aggressive acting-out behavior, are more consistent with stereotypes about men. Gender-role conformity appears to be pathological for both women and men (Huselid & Cooper, 1994).

Women who have internalized characteristics traditionally considered feminine by society seem to be most at risk. For example, *learned helplessness* (a belief that nothing one can do will matter) has been associated with depression (Blechman, 1984). Dependency has been associated with agoraphobia (Chambless & Goldstein, 1980). This kind of linkage tends to place the blame for an illness within the woman. She is expected to use therapy to assist her to change her maladaptive characteristics. Little attention is paid to the role of her family and society as a whole in rewarding these same characteristics.

Living in a sexist society may contribute to women's psychological distress. Recently, researchers constructed a scale called "The Schedule of Sexist Events," which measures women's recent (in the past year) and lifetime experience with sex discrimination in four areas of their lives: in their close relationships, in their distant relationships, in the workplace, and in encounters involving sexual degradation (Klonoff & Landrine, 1995). The latter category included having to listen to sexist jokes (reported by 94% of the women as having occurred at least once in their lives), being sexually harassed (reported by 82%), and being discriminated against by people in service jobs (77%). An alarmingly high number of the women sampled (56%) reported that they had been picked on, hit, shoved, or threatened with harm because they were women.

A woman's score on this scale was related to her level of psychological and physical distress (Landrine, Klonoff, Gibbs, Manning, & Lund, 1995). The number of discriminatory events reported was related to premenstrual discomfort; depression; obsessive, compulsive, and somatic symptoms; as well as the total number of psychiatric and physical symptoms. Sexist discrimination contributed more to women's symptoms than other stressors such as family problems did. A sexist society can truly make some women "crazy."

Sexist discrimination does not occur randomly. For example, never-married women reported more sexist treatment in every domain but work. Women of color reported more incidents of sex discrimination than white women did. And younger women reported more sexism than older women. The prototypic woman who reported the fewest incidents was a 32-year-old married white woman (Klonoff & Landrine, 1995).

The Social Construction of Symptoms

Society not only makes women sick, it also tells them what the signs of their sickness should be. Stereotypes function as prescriptions for women's behavior rather than accurate descriptions of that behavior (see Chapter 2). Social systems can create many behaviors that are considered maladaptive. A major mechanism in this constructive process is the *double bind* (also discussed in Chapter 3). A double bind exists when mutually contradictory assumptions exist within the same social context. For example, it is almost impossible for a woman to be seen as feminine and instrumentally competent at the same time because society's definition of competence excludes so-called feminine characteristics such as sensitivity and dependence. For a woman to gain the rewards of femininity, she must forgo rewards for competence and vice versa. No such dilemma exists for men because the definitions of masculinity and competence coincide.

Double binds are the result of social definitions. They are more likely to be imposed on individuals who are relatively powerless. But they are not merely a consequence of that person's life choices. Because of contradictory demands, a woman is likely to incur some social penalty no matter how she behaves. For example, what is the appropriate reaction of a woman who is the target of street remarks? Or what does a woman do when her promotion is assumed to be a result of "sleeping with the boss"?

Many so-called female disorders may be a response to covert control mechanisms like the double bind combined with a lack of socially acceptable behavioral options. Whatever a woman does under such circumstances may be labeled "sick." Socially defined feminine illness may be the only way that some women can find to rebel against social constraints. Conversely, the label of psychological disorder can serve to control rebellious women as well.

Social construction theories emphasize the situational context of women's lives. They advance understanding of some of the trends and changes in women's mental health that will be discussed later in this chapter. They do not, however, explain why some women acquiesce in their roles, others develop effective coping mechanisms, and still others develop maladaptive behavioral patterns.

POWER ISSUES

The Case of Dora

In general, women have less power than men do. The lack of specific criteria for psychological disorders is a great problem for individuals who are marginal within a society. Throughout the history of clinical psychology, women have been the patients and men the practitioners. Examples of the effect of power differentials on clinical diagnosis and treatment may be found in the earliest psychoanalytic annals. One case (see Box 14.1) that has been reconstructed by feminist scholars is that of Dora (Hare-Mustin, 1983; Lakoff, 1990).

This case history illustrates the abuse of therapeutic power. Freud did not see himself as his patient's advocate or agent, but as her father's (who was paying for the therapy). He did not see his task as to make Dora happy or productive, but to "bring her to reason"—to make her stop pestering her father and his friends. Freud and his followers (mostly men) were able to define Dora's view of her reality as a form of fantasy. She, rather than her family, was seen as the source of her problems. Freud, of course, wrote the case history. Until recently, women have had little power to define themselves.

Freud's analysis of Dora represents therapy in its most adversarial form (Lakoff, 1990). In Freud's notes, for example, he indicated that he "forced her to acknowledge" certain truths; she "confessed that she had masturbated"; and her objections to his interpretations were "easy to brush aside." In case histories with male patients, Freud noted that they "discovered" such facts together or that he "explained" his hypothesis. With Dora, in contrast, Freud's interpretations were used as weapons to convince her to submit.

Personal Consequences and Social Circumstances

The impact of power in therapy is not limited to issues involving gender. Psychologists' perceptions of people's situations are influenced by their own ethnicity, class, and relatively affluent circumstances. Clinicians may be unaware of culturally diverse coping strategies and insensitive to the negative consequences of so-called healthy coping strategies under some circumstances. Such biases can affect therapy. Following is a candid account of a rape-counseling

Box 14.1 The Dora Case

In 1899, an acquaintance and former patient brought his 18-year-old daughter, known as Dora, to Freud. She suffered from a number of hysterical symptoms, which were making life annoying for her family and, in particular, for her father. The father requested that Freud "bring her to reason." Freud was acting on the father's behalf. He saw it as his job to persuade Dora that—however correctly she may have analyzed her family's situation—she had to admit that her neurosis was self-induced and that, in order to be "cured," she must renounce her own perceptions in favor of those of her father's and Freud's.

For many years, Dora's family had been friends with another family, the Ks. Herr K. was like Dora's father (and Freud): an ambitious and successful man in his forties. Frau K. and Dora, not yet out of childhood, became confidantes, and Dora came to realize that her father and Frau K. were having an affair and that the families were making vacation plans to facilitate it. Since no one wanted Dora's mother, Herr K. was the odd man out.

From the time Dora was 7 or 8, Herr K., the busy, successful businessman, found the time to take long walks with her and to buy her expensive gifts. At the age of 14, Dora went by invitation to Herr K.'s office to watch a festival from the window. Herr K.'s family was supposed to be there too. When she arrived, Herr K. was alone and the curtains were drawn. He grabbed the child when she went up the stairs and gave her a deep kiss. She felt his erection and pulled away in horror and disgust. Her symptoms began with this incident. There were a couple of similar, but more serious, incidents, and after each, her symptoms increased. Dora eventually tried to tell her father about the incidents. He confronted Herr K., who denied everything, and Dora was accused of creating fantasies in order to make trouble. Dora ultimately came to the conclusion that the two men were using her as an item of barter: my wife for your daughter. The only problem with the arrangement was that, although the other three were consenting adults, Dora's preferences were never consulted. Freud acknowledged that Dora's perceptions had validity but felt that it would be an error for him to tell her because it would just encourage her in her willful and disruptive ("neurotic") behavior.

Dora remained in analysis with Freud for only three months. Freud offered several reasons for her ending treatment. She was taking revenge on him for not responding sexually to her or she was incapable of relating to him because of her homosexual attraction to Frau K. There is no explicit evidence for either argument in Dora's own recollections or associations.

Source: From "Talking Power" by Robin Tolmach Lakoff. Copyright © 1990 by Robin Tolmach Lakoff. Reprinted by permission of Basic Books, a member of Perseus Books, L.L.C.

session between a volunteer counselor, Michelle Fine, and a black woman who lived in poverty, Altamese Thomas. Altamese did not want to prosecute her attackers or talk with social workers or counselors. She disrupted the counselor's white middle-class views about taking control in the face of injustice.

> Fine: Altamese, the police will be here to speak with you. Are you interested in prosecuting? Do you want to take these guys to court?
>
> Thomas: No, I don't want to do nothin' but get over this. . . . When I'm pickin' the guy out of some line, who knows who's messing around with my momma, or my baby. Anyway nobody would believe me. . . .
>
> Fine: Do you think maybe you would like to talk with a counselor, in a few days, about some of your feelings?
>
> Thomas: I've been to one of them. It just made it worse. I just kept thinking about my problems too much. You feel better when you are talking, but then you got to go back home and they're still there. No good just talking when things ain't no better. (Fine, 1983–1984, pp. 253–254)

Altamese Thomas had little power to change the causes of her problems—racism, poverty, and violence. Individualistic strategies could have made matters worse for others in her family. They would do little to improve oppressive economic and social arrangements.

One can, of course, argue that Altamese Thomas's passivity represents a form of psychological surrender. It is obvious that her behavioral patterns cause her great pain. They will not help her, nor will they help others like her in a similar situation. But if her social circumstances are not taken into account, she may be blamed for her own victimization. Self-knowledge without the power to change her circumstances will do little for her.

This discussion of coping and power illustrates the dilemmas produced by limitations in the range of options available. It helps explain why psychological distress is expressed in gender-specific ways. It may also help put the question of whether women are "sicker" than men in perspective. Any therapeutic system that looks at individual behavior in isolation from sociocultural circumstances is fundamentally flawed. Psychological symptomology is closely tied to what normative roles are available. Because of the general inequality between women and men, it is inevitable that their psychological distress will be acted out differently.

DEPRESSION

The disorder that has received the most attention in terms of gender issues is depression. This is because mild to severe depression is a common problem in U.S. society today. On the surface, depression appears to be an exaggeration of normal sadness. Depressed individuals describe their emotional state in highly negative terms, they may have a sad facial expression, and they may experience loss of appetite, insomnia, and fatigue. Other signs include stooped posture, slow speech, indecisiveness, hopelessness, and feelings of inadequacy and guilt. It has been estimated that as many as 28 percent of women in the United States and 14 percent of men will suffer from depression at some point in their lives (Hankin et al., 1998).

Depression and the Developmental Process

The so-called gender gap in depression is not found at all ages. In a recent national survey of more than 12,000 Norwegian adolescents, no gender difference was found at age 12 (Wichstrom, 1999). However, more girls than boys became depressed between 13 and 14 years of age. A gender gap in depression in Norway is particularly disheartening because this country seems to have considerable social equality: it has had a female prime minister for a long time, half of the other ministers are also female, and more young women than young men pursue a university degree. Nevertheless, the gender differences found among Norwegian adolescents were very close to those found in the United States. Girls' rate of serious depression (7.7%) was nearly three times that of boys the same age (2.8%).

Dissatisfaction with body parts and overall physical appearance was associated with depression for both girls and boys, but girls were much more dissatisfied with their bodies. The researcher attributed girls' higher risk of depression during adolescence to *gender intensification* (see Chapter 7). After puberty, femininity becomes more important to girls and the association of femininity and an attractive appearance increases some girls' risk for depression. Since masculinity is less associated with physical appearance, puberty has a smaller impact on boys' mood. Girls' depression appears to be triggered when their bodies take on a more mature appearance.

Body dissatisfaction has also been found to be more highly correlated with low self-esteem for girls than boys (Wichstrom, 1998). There appears to be a stronger connection between self-esteem and body satisfaction during adolescence than at any other age (Harter, 1990). Low self-esteem is also linked to depression.

The gap between males and females continues to grow throughout most of the teenage years. Significantly more females than males become depressed for the first time between the ages of 15 and 21 (Hankin et al., 1998). During this period, the female rate for clinical depression rises to twice that of males, where it remains unchanged until old age. Adolescence is also the life stage in which more girls than boys attempt suicide (Canetto, 1997).

Other aspects of women's and men's life paths are also related to depression. As shown in Chapter 9, married women consistently report more depression than married men, even when they are matched on age, income, and number of children. Single women report less depression than single men (Mirowsky, 1996). Full-time homemakers are particularly at risk for depression because of the low value that society places on their role.

Gender Roles

Self in Relation and Self-Silencing

Some researchers have suggested that women's need for relationship is linked to their higher risk of depression. Women's sense of self is thought to be related to their need to be connected with others (see Chapter 4) (Miller, 1991). When their relational needs are not met, women tend to see this as their own failure—they see themselves as not caring enough or not doing enough. A lack of mutuality in relationships has been found to be a significant predictor of depression in women (Genero, Miller, Surrey, & Baldwin, 1992).

Maintaining relationships with men is an important part of the socialization of Euro-American girls (see Chapter 8). To do so in a patriarchal society, they must silence their authentic self and deny that their needs are not being met. Self-silencing has been linked to depression in young white women (Jack & Dill, 1992). Young white women are also more likely to make suicide attempts for relational conflicts than for any other reasons (Canetto, 1997).

Although young black women may silence themselves in their relationships with men, this does not lead to depression (Carr, Gilroy, & Sherman, 1996). Instead, depression, as in other marginalized groups of women, is linked to economic and social disadvantage (Azocar, Miranda, & Dwyer, 1996).

Gender Roles and Depressive Symptoms

Do gender roles affect how women and men experience depression as well as whether or not they become depressed? Gender roles may be more important than biological sex in affecting behaviors associated with depression. For example, male and female college students with the same level of depression reported symptoms consistent with gender stereotypes. Depressed men reported physical symptoms such as sleep disturbance and loss of sexual drive. They also reported more social withdrawal and suicidal thoughts. Depressed women tended to report more emotional symptoms such as crying, sadness, and a sense of failure (Oliver & Toner, 1990). Similar stereotypic differences have also been reported in patients who have been hospitalized for severe depression (Vredenburg, Krames, & Flett, 1986).

The degree of identification with traditional gender roles also influences the way depression is expressed. For example, depressed feminine-identified women reported more self-dislike and weight loss and less insomnia than equally depressed but less gender-typed women. Depressed gender-typed men reported more withdrawal than other depressed men (Oliver & Toner, 1990).

Instrumental traits (associated with traditional masculinity) may protect both men and women from depression. A meta-analysis of studies of the relationship between gender-role orientation, depression, and general adjustment supported a masculinity model of adjustment (Whitley, 1985). "Masculine" people (both females and males) showed higher adjustment and less depression than "feminine" people. Mental health was *not* associated with being gender typed. In other words, highly masculine men and highly feminine women were not better adjusted than others with more atypical gender patterns.

On the other hand, emotionality (stereotypically associated with traditional femininity) may prolong depression and/or make it more severe. Women in whom a depressed mood had been induced were found to be more likely to think about emotions than similarly treated men, even though this prolonged their depressed mood. Cognitive style rather than gender actually predicted depressive outcomes. Once the tendency to dwell on particular thoughts was controlled, gender differences in the length or severity of the depressed mood disappeared (Butler & Nolen-Hoeksema, 1994).

Before everyone decides that women would be better adjusted if they were just like men, it is important to recognize the role that self-esteem plays in the relationship between traditional masculinity and mental health. The relationship between masculinity and adjustment disappears when level of self-esteem is taken into account (Feather, 1985; Whitley, 1985). High self-esteem protects individuals against depression. Of course, self-esteem reflects the values considered important by the culture as a whole. In Western society, these values are androcentric and their expression is controlled by gender categorization. Signs of psychological disturbance may occur whenever people are denied an opportunity to engage in behaviors that enhance their self-esteem.

Power and Depression

In addition to body dissatisfaction, adolescence may bring with it the recognition of women's and men's unequal status and power. Depression is lower among women who are employed full time, have jobs that allow autonomy, and who have little difficulty affording and arranging child care or have partners who do a large share of the housework and child care (Mirowsky, 1996). In contrast, rates of depression are very high among less-privileged groups of women. For example, 35 percent of the Mexican-American women who came to a community health center were found to be clinically depressed (Tazeau & Gallagher-Thompson, 1993). And 83 percent of the women who used a domestic violence shelter were depressed (Campbell, Sullivan, & Davidson, 1995). Only 58 percent were still depressed ten weeks later, probably because the shelter experience reduced their sense of powerlessness and increased their sense of social support.

Contrary to the opinion that modern women are "stressed out" and depressed by juggling work, family, and relationships, research reviewed in Chapter 11 indicates that multiple roles are good for women's physical and mental health. Employment gives women more power, and power is linked to psychological well-being for both women and men. In fact, a great deal of the gender gap in depression may actually be due to power differences. Individuals who are younger, are less educated, have lower incomes, or are unemployed are at high risk for depression regardless of whether they are female or male (Golding, 1988). Many of these factors are associated with being female. When they are all taken into account, gender differences become insignificant.

A report of a Task Force on Women and Depression of the American Psychological Association highlights how women's place in the social structure depresses them. It found, for example, that the prototypic depressed individual was a woman with a young child who was living in poverty (McGrath, Keita, Strickland, & Russo, 1990). It also found that the sexual and physical abuse of women was much greater than previously suspected and that victims were very vulnerable to depression. When one looks at social context, it is difficult to view depression as an indicator of psychopathology unless it is the psychopathology of society rather than that of individual women.

Blaming Women: Reproductive Function as a Source of Depression

Despite the considerable evidence suggesting social causes for depression, explanations based on women's body chemistry still have an important place in medical texts. Women are regarded as being particularly vulnerable during critical points in their reproductive cycle. Many forms of depression are labeled in terms of women's reproductive stages, for example, premenstrual syndrome (PMS), postpartum depression, and menopausal syndrome. These labels illustrate the power that social constructions have to define women's experience.

A *syndrome* is a constellation of symptoms associated with a particular cause. Syndromes associated with women's reproductive lives appear to be particularly poorly defined. For example, no single symptom or pattern of signs is required for a diagnosis of PMS. There is no agreed-upon standardized test to determine its existence or its cure (Ussher, 1989). Nevertheless, claims have been made that from 25 to 100 percent of women suffer from some form of premenstrual or menstrual emotional disturbance (Laws, 1983).

Medical and pharmaceutical interests have helped to create PMS (Parlee, 1989). Careful empirical research has produced little evidence to support the idea that most women have a negative premenstrual phase. In one study, the same percentage of women who said they had PMS (about 50%) as those who said they did not, actually met the criteria for such a diagnosis (about 10% of each group) (McFarlane & Williams, 1994). Since the researchers found that most participants (men as well as women) experienced a cyclic fluctuation of moods, they suggested that those women who believe they have PMS are attending to actual physiological changes but mislabeling them.

Social labels have an important impact on the way women view their bodily changes. In another recent study, female college students completed either a "Menstrual Joy Questionnaire" or a "Menstrual Distress Questionnaire" before responding to a measure of menstrual attitudes. Those who first encountered "menstrual joy" reported more positive attitudes and cyclic changes (Chrisler, Johnston, Champagne, & Preston, 1994). Participants also reported that they were surprised by these findings because they had never before considered positive aspects of the menstrual cycle.

More recently, researchers have demonstrated that "a little psychiatric knowledge may be a dangerous thing" (Nash & Chrisler, 1997). When participants read the description of "Premenstrual Dysphoric Disorder" (a new category in the DSM-IV) with the label attached, they were more likely to perceive that premenstrual changes were a problem for women than if they read the same description with the label "Episodic Dysphoric Disorder." The premenstrual label did not influence women's perception of their own menstrual changes but made them more likely to attach a psychiatric label to women they knew who had symptoms. Men had a more negative response to symptoms when they were associated with the menstrual cycle than with a more gender-neutral label. The presence of this diagnostic label in a major resource book for the mental health community provides a legitimate, "scientific" tool for those who wish to devalue women's power, position, and emotional reactions.

Premenstrual syndrome has been popularized in women's magazines as a hormonal problem (Markens, 1996). In these magazines, women's experiences are used to show what is wrong with women's bodies. The focus on women's bodies allows the structure of work organizations to go unchallenged and naturalizes gender roles just when inequities of power and privilege are being contested.

Stories about PMS focus on problems for professional women. They have little to say about women who work in low-wage jobs. Even the self-help instructions such as "changing jobs" or "closing the office door" are implicitly class biased. There has been very little coverage of PMS in magazines aimed at African-American women (Markens, 1996).

Postpartum depression is said to affect between 3 and 25 percent of women (see Chapter 10) (Elliot, 1984). Like PMS, it is difficult to find a consistent description of this disorder, as there is little agreement between different researchers and practitioners (Ussher, 1989). A similar situation exists for menopausal depression (discussed in Chapter 12). There is a lack of agreement about what symptoms are required for diagnosis, no medical tests that differentiate sufferers from nonsufferers, and no effective medical treatment.

Feminists have charged that biologically determinist explanations are being used to ignore the historical and political context of women's reproductive experiences (Brown, 1994; Ussher, 1989). As shown in Chapters 7 and 12, menstruation and menopause carry many negative values in our society. Pregnancy is a more mixed event. Thus, it is the postpartum period that is seen as dangerous.

The vagueness of what constitutes the risk period after birth makes it easy to confuse depressive responses to child rearing with those of childbearing. For example, a substantial percentage of women with children under the age of 5 years have been diagnosed as depressed (Oakley, 1986). The role of a parent with young children may be particularly stressful. In fact, men who are the primary caregivers for young children have been shown to suffer more severely from depression than their female counterparts (Jenkins, 1985).

The existence of so-called reproductive syndromes helps to justify beliefs in the biological inferiority of women. The view that their reproductive cycle makes women vulnerable to psychological problems helps to limit women, to define them as dangerous and deviant, and to exclude them from a role in society equal to that of men. Biological determinism—or anatomy as destiny—causes people to neglect other, more social sources of women's unhappiness. Rather than social change, unhappy women are offered chemicals in the form of hormones or psychotropic drugs. At best, these substances are ineffective and, at worst, they may be habit forming and/or medically harmful. Although there is little evidence to support the existence of hormonal imbalance syndromes, they support a thriving industry of physicians, psychiatrists, and drug companies.

THE SOCIAL CONSTRUCTION OF FEMALE DISORDERS: THE VIEW FROM HISTORY

This is not the first time that scientific classification has been used to legitimate internal explanations for women's distress. Beginning in the mid–nineteenth century, an epidemic of nervous disorders labeled anorexia nervosa, hysteria, and neurasthenia raged in England and the United States.

Nervous Disorders

The first of the female nervous disorders to be labeled during this period was *anorexia nervosa*—identified in 1873 as a new clinical syndrome among adolescent girls in both England and France. It was characterized by extreme emaciation, loss of appetite, lack of menstruation, and restless activity (Showalter, 1987). The years between 1870 and World War I were also the "golden age" of *hysteria*. Classic hysteria had two defining characteristics—seizures or fits and sensations of choking (the latter was believed to be caused by the rising of the uterus within the body). However, attention soon moved from fits, paralyses, and anesthesias to traits, moods, and personality. By the end of the nineteenth century, "hysterical" had become almost interchangeable with "feminine"

(Showalter, 1987). Hysterical women were described as highly impressionable, suggestible, and narcissistic (Smith-Rosenberg, 1985).

Neurasthenia, like hysteria, had a wide range of symptoms, from blushing, vertigo, and headaches to insomnia, depression, and uterine irritability. It was seen to be caused by increased mental activity in women, which sapped their strength (Showalter, 1987). All these disorders were especially frequent among well-to-do, intellectual women, including those in the professions. Physicians attributed these nervous conditions to the weakness of the female reproductive system and the strains put on that system by women's ambition. As late as 1900, one physician pictured the female reproductive cycle in the following melodramatic terms:

> Many a young life is battered and forever crippled in the breakers of puberty; if it crosses these unharmed and is still not dashed to pieces on the rock of childbirth, it may still ground on the ever-recurring shallows of menstruation, and lastly, upon the final bar of the menopause ere protection is found in the unruffled waters of the harbor beyond the reach of sexual storms. (Smith-Rosenberg, 1985, p. 184)

Others declared that mental breakdown would occur when women defied their "nature" by competing with men instead of serving them or by seeking alternatives or even additions to their maternal functions. One physician "concerned about 'the danger of solitary work' for girls 'of nervous family' studying at home, forbade the fifteen-year-old Virginia Woolf to continue her lessons and ordered her to spend four hours a day gardening" (Showalter, 1987, p. 126).

Many well-known women suffered from these disorders. Alice James, the sister of Henry and William James, began her career as an invalid at the age of 19. There is no way to know if Alice James's lifelong illness had a "real" organic basis. However, unlike her brothers, she was never encouraged to go to college or to develop her gift for writing (Ehrenreich & English, 1979).

Psychiatric treatment of nervous women has been described as ruthless. Physicians assumed that patients were shamming. Their goal "was to isolate the patient from her family support systems, unmask her deceitful stratagems, coerce her into surrendering her symptoms, and finally overcome her self-centeredness" (Showalter, 1987, p. 137). The standard treatment was a "rest cure" developed by a noted American neurologist named Silas Weir Mitchell. During this treatment, the patient was isolated from her family and friends for six weeks, confined to bed, and forbidden to sit up, sew, read, write, or do any intellectual work.

One of Mitchell's patients was Charlotte Perkins Gilman, who wrote a fictionalized account of her experiences in "The Yellow Wallpaper." Gilman's heroine went mad, although Gilman herself recognized that she was being brainwashed and left treatment. Among Mitchell's other patients were Jane Addams and Edith Wharton. These women were exceptions in that they went on to live full and active lives. Most cases were more like that of Alice James—neither fatal nor curable (Ehrenreich & English, 1979).

Feminist scholars have attempted to explain this epidemic of nervous diseases. They emphasize the limited roles that upper-class women were permitted during the Victorian era. These women had no serious productive work in the home; tasks such as housework, cooking, and child care were left as much as possible to domestic servants. Women were expected to exchange sexual and reproductive duties for financial support (Ehrenreich & English, 1979).

Nervous disorders such as neurasthenia and hysteria provided a socially acceptable way for a woman to remove herself from her self-sacrificing role as a wife or mother. This escape from emotional and sexual demands was, however, purchased at the personal cost of pain and disability and the social cost of an intensification of stereotypes about women's passivity and dependence (Smith-Rosenberg, 1985).

The diagnosis of hysteria was limited to women, and when large numbers of men began to suffer from "shell shock" in response to the intolerable conditions of World War I, their "hysterical" behavior was labeled a functional neurosis (Showalter, 1987). Other assumptions about what causes deviance in men and women persist. When they engage in socially undesirable behavior, men tend to be labeled as "bad," whereas women are labeled as "mad." The relative distribution of men and women in prisons versus mental institutions reflects these assumptions (Burns, 1992).

The differential labeling of similar symptoms for women and men illustrates one of the ways that psychological disorders were socially constructed. Disorders were also constructed in terms of social class. Working-class women did not have the time or money to support a cult of invalidism. Because they were not potential patients, nineteenth-century experts ignored their health. These experts blamed education for the greater weakness of affluent women. Their arguments were both sexist and racist:

> At war, or at play, the white man is superior to the savage, and his culture has continually improved his condition. But with woman the rule is reversed. Her squaw sister will endure effort, exposure, and hardship which will kill the white woman. Education which has resulted in developing and strengthening the physical nature of man has been perverted through folly and fashion to render women weaker and weaker. (Dr. Sylvanus Stall, in Ehrenreich & English, 1979, p. 114)

Social constructionism does not deny the reality of women's suffering. However, it does point out how some parts of women's experience may be expressed while others may not. In the nineteenth century, educated women were permitted to be sick or mad, but they were not allowed to be angry or to protest their limited choices. It is possible that some twentieth-century female disorders, such as anorexia and PMS, also involve social construction. If the unacceptable parts of one's personality can be labeled PMS and be seen as the result of an unfortunate hormonal imbalance, a woman can retain her self-definition as a good woman. PMS can also be used to deny responsibility for one's actions; for example, women are never violent, aggressive, and antisocial, but women with PMS are (Laws, 1983).

The issue here is not whether women make up their symptoms. Clearly, so-called female disorders refer to real experiences. What is important is how one is taught to describe and label these experiences and how these labels fit socially acceptable roles. The boom in PMS may be a response to the second wave of feminism (Laws, 1983). Like nineteenth-century nervous disorders, PMS attempts to define women's consciousness of discontent in medical terms.

EATING DISORDERS

Hysteria and neurasthenia probably seem like quaint old-fashioned diseases. Anorexia, another major nineteenth-century female malady, is alive and well today. Professional journals and the popular press have proclaimed the existence and growth of an epidemic of eating disorders. Estimates of the incidence of eating disorders vary widely, but it is clear that the vast majority of people with anorexia and bulimia are women. In fact, the extent of dieting and concern about weight control among women is so high today that it has been termed a "normative discontent" (Rodin, Silberstein, & Striegel-Moore, 1984).

The "Normal" Desire for Thinness

Differential standards for weight in women and men have been discussed in Chapters 2 and 7 in terms of stereotypes and ideals of attractiveness. The results of one survey of college students illustrate the extent of gender differences in satisfaction with body weight. The researchers surveyed 176 undergraduates from several midwestern colleges and found that a similar percentage of college men and women were in the normal weight category (McCaulay, Mintz, & Glenn, 1988). Fifty percent of the male students perceived themselves to be of normal weight, compared with 40 percent of the female students. The other 50 percent of men were equally divided in perceiving themselves as either overweight or underweight, whereas the majority of women perceived themselves as overweight. The women wanted to lose an average of 8.4 pounds, while men wanted to gain an average of 2.9 pounds. Gender differences were even larger in the slightly overweight category. In this group, men wanted to lose an average of 5.5 pounds, whereas women wanted to lose 24 pounds. Even slightly underweight women wanted to lose an average of 1.4 pounds (see Figure 14.1).

Prejudice and Discrimination Against Overweight Women

The importance of thinness for feminine attractiveness is not merely a stereotype. Overweight girls and boys are stigmatized. As adults, however, women are much more harshly punished than men for failing to achieve slenderness. Overweight high school girls are less likely to be accepted to college than their thinner peers with comparable credentials. Obese women, but not men, have lower academic and economic attainments than their parents (Wooley &

FIGURE 14.1. Dying to be thin.
Source: © Lynn Johnston Productions, Inc./Dist. by United Features Syndicate, Inc.

Wooley, 1980). Overweight women frequently report that they have been subjected to job discrimination and feel that they have been the butt of unsavory jokes because of their weight (Snow & Harris, 1985). In contrast, overweight men are more likely to mention that they were not asked to join social clubs and sports activities.

Insults about fat people in the media usually have women as their targets. For example, many articles about Roseanne mention her weight as much as her personal crudity. Overweight women have virtually disappeared as models in women's magazines over the last thirty-five years (Snow & Harris, 1986).

Although concerns about weight are justified on the basis of health, most of the data relating mortality and health risks to weight refer to men:

> Weight is of greatest concern to and weight loss is pursued most avidly by women, who are actually least affected in terms of health and survival. Among women the actual/expected mortality ratio rises negligibly from underweight women to women who are markedly obese. . . . Among women with marked overweight (average height 5'3" to 5'6" and weights 195 to 254 lbs.) the mortality rates are still lower than among men in the most favorable build category, i.e., underweight. (Gubner, 1974, in Wooley & Wooley, 1980, p. 140)

As indicated in Chapter 2, cultural standards about weight have become more demanding in recent years. Even the term *obesity* is a twentieth-century word.

Social control of weight in women even involves control of their eating behavior. In one intriguing study, entitled "Women, But Not Men, Are What They Eat," male and female undergraduates read a food diary and rated the person who had written it (Chaikin & Pliner, 1987). In the diary, either a young woman or young man was portrayed as eating either a small breakfast and lunch or a large breakfast and lunch. Ratings of the man were not affected by the size of the meals he ate. In contrast, both men and women saw a woman who ate smaller meals as significantly more feminine and more expressive (emotional, kind, and understanding of others) than a woman who ate larger meals. They also saw the woman who ate less as more concerned about her appearance and significantly better looking than the woman who ate more. In a similar study using videotapes of college women and men consuming the same large or small meal, the female who ate the smallest "feminine" meal (a salad) was rated as more socially appealing than the same woman when she ate the larger "masculine" hoagie (Basow & Kobrynowicz, 1993).

College-age women appear to be aware of the effect that eating less has on perceptions of their femininity. They have been found to eat a smaller snack during a "get-acquainted" study when they interacted with a desirable male confederate than when they interacted with an undesirable male or any female (Mori, Chaikin, & Pliner, 1987). Their behavior indicates that they are aware of stereotypes that label overweight people as low in self-esteem, unlikely to be dating, unerotic, and more deserving of a fatter, uglier partner than normal-weight individuals (Harris, 1990).

Disordered Eating as Pathology

Anorexia

It is unclear at what point the desire for thinness translates into the pathological behaviors associated with *anorexia, bulimia,* or *binge-eating disorder* (a condition newly defined in the DSM-IV). Anorexia is defined as the refusal to maintain a weight that is minimally normal for an individual of that age and height, intense fears of gaining weight or becoming fat, body image disturbance, and a denial of the seriousness of the current low weight (Pike & Striegel-Moore, 1997). Anorexics may use dieting, fasting, and excessive exercise to lose weight, or they may induce vomiting and abuse laxatives and diuretics.

Anorexia usually emerges between puberty and 17 years of age. Girls and women account for more than 90 percent of the reported cases, and the disorder may be present in 1 percent of adolescent males (Walters & Kendler, 1995). It has been estimated that 40 percent of individuals with anorexia recover, 30 percent improve, and symptoms become chronic in 20 percent. As many as 10 percent may die (Pike & Striegel-Moore, 1997). (See Figure 14.2.)

Bulimia

Bulimia is characterized by episodes of binge eating that may last two hours or more during which the person feels a loss of control. Bulimics feel that they cannot stop eating or control what or how much is eaten. Weight is regulated by excessive purging or use of laxatives and diuretics. Males account for about 10 percent of all bulimics. Between 1 to 2 percent of adult women have the disorder with a greater incidence among those women born after 1960.

Binge-Eating Disorder

This disorder is defined by recurrent episodes of binge eating without regular attempts to control weight by the excessive use of laxatives and purging. People with this disorder also eat faster than normal, eat until they are uncomfortably full, eat a large amount of food when they are not physically hungry, and eat alone because they are embarrassed about the amount of food they eat. They feel disgusted, depressed, or guilty after overeating. About 2 percent

FIGURE 14.2. The consequences of anorexia. Photographs of Karen Carpenter "before" and "after."

of adult females in community surveys meet the criteria for binge-eating disorder, and about 30 percent of the obese individuals who participate in university weight control programs have the disorder (Yanovski, 1993). It is only slightly more common in women than it is in men.

Many women with eating disorders appear to be able to function reasonably well despite their extreme preoccupation with weight. Most anorexic women deny that they have any problem at all. Bulimic women are also unwilling to disclose their "disgusting and wasteful" food practices. Since our culture so highly values thinness, excessively low weight may be ignored or even socially rewarded. Women in treatment are often those who still reside within the parental home, where the abnormal food habits and excessive exercise cannot escape notice.

The Demographics of Eating Disorders

Age

As early as the fifth grade, girls begin to show evidence of eating disorders. Significantly more girls than boys reported spending more time dieting, wishing they were thinner, feeling pressured to eat, and feeling guilty after eating sweets (Keel, Fulkerson, & Leon, 1997). Lower self-esteem and depression are associated with negative attitudes about weight and disordered eating behavior. Approximately two-thirds to three-quarters of high school girls in the United States report dieting to lose weight despite being of normal weight or underweight (Pike, 1995). Between 5 and 15 percent of adolescent girls engage in more extreme forms of weight control such as vomiting and purging (Phelps, Andrea, Rizzo, Johnston, & Main, 1993).

Ethnicity

The "typical" anorexic woman is usually portrayed as upper or middle class, and white. Recent evidence suggests, however, that eating disorders are increasing among girls and women of color (Ofosu, Lafreniere, & Senn, 1998; Striegel-Moore & Smolak, 1996). African-American adolescents tend to exhibit body-image dissatisfaction and abnormal concern about dieting and weight at about half the rate of their Euro-American peers (Root, 1990). Older urban black women are also less likely to use extremely restrictive dieting practices than their white counterparts are. However, a substantial percentage did report fasting (25%), use of diuretics (11.9%) and laxatives (8.8%), and self-induced vomiting (2%) for weight control (Thomas & James, 1988).

Eleven percent of the girls in a rural public high school primarily serving a low-income Hispanic and Native American population reported eating habits consistent with clinical criteria for bulimia (Snow & Harris, 1989). High levels of anorexia and bulimia were also reported in a recent study of Mexican-American adolescent girls regardless of their degree of acceptance of dominant cultural norms (Joiner & Kashubeck, 1996). Similar to findings for white girls and women, disordered eating was associated with low self-esteem.

It has been argued that the cultural context that equates beauty with whiteness "protects" ethnic minority women from eating disorders. These recent findings suggest, however, that cultural demands for thinness have extended beyond the original target group. It is also possible that prevailing stereotypes of the white, upper-middle-class victim may have conspired against the early recognition of eating disorders in people of color (Root, 1990). Women of color who seek treatment for anorexia have lower weights at the start of their treatment, suggesting that the disorder may go undetected or untreated longer in ethnic minority women (Pike & Striegel-Moore, 1997).

"Fat Talk"

In-depth interviews of a group of high school girls reveals the extent of their concern with weight. The girls engaged in a form of discourse among themselves that has been termed "fat talk" (Nichter & Vuckovic, 1994). The statement "I'm so fat" was frequently repeated throughout the school day. It was not used, however, by girls who are actually overweight or those who had attempted to change their weight over sustained periods of time. The phrase appears to be a request for reassurance from one's peers rather than an actual statement about weight. At least one 14-year-old informant seemed to be aware of this. Here is her response to the interviewer's question, "What usually happens when someone says I'm so fat?"

> Jamie: About six or seven girls go "No, you're not!" Probably it's just because, you know, you like to hear that people don't think you're fat. And it's mostly like in gym, cuz when you change into your gym clothes those are so bunchy anyway they make you look fat. And, uh, but I'd say, I'd say that not very

many of them mean that, mean it when they say it. They just want to hear "Oh no you're not." (Nichter & Vuckovic, 1994, p. 114)

A confusion between thinness and a perfect life appears to be common among white adolescents. Researchers reported being struck by the uniformity of teenage girls' descriptions of the ideal girl (tall, thin, and usually with long blond hair) regardless of the girls' own physical characteristics (Nichter & Vuckovic, 1994). The responses of African-American adolescents were much more varied. They often began with a list of personality traits rather than physical attributes (Parker et al., 1995). They described the ideal girl as having it "going on." This meant having what they had work for them: long nails, pretty eyes, big lips, nice thighs, whatever.

A Feminist Perspective

Obviously, some people are more susceptible to eating disorders than others. We have focused on social risk factors rather than individual ones because it is important to keep individual behavior in cultural perspective. Why do people in some groups develop some symptoms at a much higher rate than others? This question is particularly important in considering a disorder that has become increasingly common in recent years.

The characteristics of women who resist becoming obsessed with weight also provide information about cultural messages. These women seem to be less vulnerable to self-objectification—they do not look at their bodies from another's perspective (Noll & Fredrickson, 1998). They are more likely to identify with feminist values such as commitment to nonsexist roles and personal empowerment (Snyder & Hasbrouck, 1996). Several studies indicate that lesbians have less negative views of their bodies than heterosexual women do (Bergeron & Senn, 1998; Siever, 1994). A lesbian identity buffers them from the impact of social norms. It does not, however, completely protect them from pressure to be thin. For all groups of women, internalization of societal norms predicted negative attitudes about their bodies.

A feminist focusing of questions moves the problem away from blaming the victim to issues of social and cultural change. Feminists ask: Why are standards for women's attractiveness under such tight social control and who in society benefits from these standards? Feminist therapists also argue that a person's behavior cannot be changed without considering her situational context. In the case of eating disorders, situational refers to political and economic as well as personal circumstances.

ISSUES IN TREATMENT

Most psychological therapy is designed to help change the individual. Beginning with Freud, therapy has been more often used to reconcile the powerless to their circumstances than to assist them in creating social change. We turn now to the contributions of feminist theory, research, and practice in dealing with issues of personal and social change.

The Politics of Labeling

Treatment begins with diagnosis. However, psychological diagnoses are not easy to make. Most recently, mental health practitioners have been assisted in their diagnoses by the DSM-IV, discussed earlier. Although the manual is periodically updated by a panel of experts—primarily white male psychiatrists—it continues to perpetuate myths about women and femininity. This concerns feminist practitioners because the manual is used to determine which individuals are worthy of treatment and how they should be treated. DSM categories even determine whether government agencies or private insurance companies should pay for the therapist's services.

While the previous edition of the manual (DSM-III-R) was being revised, feminist therapists realized that several new categories were being considered for inclusion that had negative implications for women. One of these categories—late luteal phase dysphoric disorder—appears in the fourth edition as "premenstrual dysphoric disorder," which has already been discussed. The other category—self-defeating personality disorder, which corresponds to what is popularly known as **masochism**—is not in DSM-IV. Feminist objections to this diagnostic category illustrate once again the political uses and consequences of the power to name.

Self-Defeating Personality Disorder

Feminist psychologists noted that the concept of masochism derives from psychoanalytic theory (Committee on Women in Psychology, 1985). It fails to consider sociocultural variables that might yield similar behaviors in the absence of any personality disorder. For example, victims of interpersonal violence have a high rate of psychiatric illness (Brown, 1986). Nevertheless, the researchers who conducted the field trial of more than 300 patients used in the development of the diagnosis of self-defeating personality disorder never questioned them about their past or current experiences of sexual, physical, or emotional abuse. Moreover, many of the behaviors associated with this diagnostic category decrease or disappear when the victimized individual is removed from the abusive context for as short a period as six months.

Ignoring a history of abuse and its behavioral consequences results in blaming the victim. Her personality may be seen as the source of the violence in her life rather than vice versa. Diagnosis of her behavior as pathological also illustrates the way double binds operate. Women are labeled as "sick" if they won't leave an abusive situation, although they are encouraged to keep their families together. And they are censured by the conservative press as selfish and foolish if they try to combine work and home life (see Chapter 10). A label such as masochistic personality allows both clinicians and society to blame women for their "failures" without requiring anyone to question the cultural context and its effects on psychological functioning (Brown, 1986).

Ignoring an abusive situation within the home can have devastating consequences. Sexual and physical abuse contribute to serious mental illness in women. For example, several studies of chronically psychotic women patients in mental institutions have indicated that a high proportion of those who appear to be irresponsive to treatment were the victims of childhood abuse.

Childhood incest appears to produce the most intractable disorders (Beck & van der Kolk, 1987). The severity of hospitalized women's symptoms has also been linked with the amount of other sexual and physical abuse to which they were exposed as children (Bryer, Nelson, Miller, & Krol, 1987). These studies demonstrate how important it is for therapists to recognize and respond to the violence in an individual's home (see Chapter 13).

Posttraumatic Stress Disorder

An increasing number of feminist therapists have suggested that a diagnostic label that appears in the DSM-IV—*posttraumatic stress disorder*, or PTSD—is applicable to battered women (Brown, 1994; Koss et al., 1994). The criteria for a diagnosis of PTSD include recurrent and intrusive memories and dreams, distressful experiences when exposed to events symbolizing the trauma, persistent avoidance of thoughts and feelings associated with the trauma, and persistent and heightened arousal symptoms such as irritability, hypervigilance, and exaggerated startle responses (American Psychiatric Association [APA], 1994). Any of these symptoms taken out of the context of battering can lead to a different diagnosis, such as depression or paranoia.

As it is currently written, PTSD does not fully describe the complexity of battered women's experience. This is because the diagnosis was originally conceptualized to deal with the traumatic impact of war on men. Unlike the abrupt ending of a war or act of terrorism, the ongoing and intimate nature of the violence that women experience in the home may lead to a different set of reactions. Moreover, the traumatic situation may still be present when battered women enter the mental health system seeking assistance. This negates the "post" aspect of the diagnosis (Gondolf, 1998). Although battered women's symptomology was proposed for inclusion in the DSM-IV, it was not accepted.

The Double Standard in Diagnostic Categories

How are diagnostic categories determined? One feminist clinical psychologist's questions include: How does this construct figure in our accounts of otherwise unaccountable behavior? How is the boundary drawn between disorders on the one hand and crime, eccentricity, or alternative lifestyles on the other? Who is part of the negotiations that fix the boundaries, and who polices them? What kinds of claims-making activities surround the birth of new categories of disorders and the death of old ones? (Marecek, 1993, p. 7). One may also ask who gains by gender-biased diagnostic labels. Unfounded diagnoses do not advance research or make clinicians more empathetic. Labels can cause people to believe that a particular disorder *really* exists, but they do not make ambiguous data stronger, and they do not help women (Alagna & Hamilton, 1986).

While researchers are aware that vague diagnostic descriptions promote gender stereotyping and bias in diagnosis, other androcentric biases involving diagnostic categories have received less attention. The "experts" who construct these categories are predominantly powerful men with a psychodynamic perspective. The content of the DSM at any given time is the codified opinions of those in power (Brown, 1994).

Androcentric biases have led to a number of important omissions. The subjective experience of the victim has been ignored and, thus, the degree to which individuals feel able to leave an exploitative or abusive situation is overrated (Committee on Women in Psychology, 1985). The diagnostician may lack adequate information about life circumstances of individuals different from himself. Such ignorance can lead to ethnic and class as well as gender biases. A psychodynamic orientation leads inevitably to the neglect of social context. This may result in pathologizing the individual without considering outside forces.

Androcentric biases include presumptions that autonomy and individualism are healthier than dependency and concern with relationships. These assumptions may also be flawed. What might happen if gender biased definitions of dependency were reversed? Here is one feminist's answer:

> Suppose dependency were defined as letting someone else choose one's underwear, clean one's clothing, cook one's meals, arrange details of one's vacation? Men who do not become competent in these spheres or exert energy in fulfilling these tasks are not perceived as dependent or having failed to separate. They are not thought to suffer psychologically or emotionally from the condition, nor perceived to be less developed as individuals. Rather men are thought to be exhibiting their independence of women and home by pursuing public activities. (Travis, 1988b, p. 20)

In a similar ironic vein, a new diagnostic category called "delusional dominating personality disorder" has been proposed by another feminist therapist (Caplan, 1991). This diagnostic category describes the psychopathology of men who conform to social norms for the "real man." Its behavioral criteria include the following:

> The presence of any one of the following delusions: (a) the delusion of personal entitlement to the services of (1) any woman with whom one is personally associated, (2) females in general for males in general, (3) both of the above; (b) the delusion that women like to suffer and be ordered around; (c) the delusion that physical force is the best method of solving interpersonal problems; (d) the delusion that sexual and aggressive impulses are uncontrollable in (1) oneself, (2) males in general, (3) both of the above; (e) the delusion that pornography and erotica are identical. . . .
>
> A pathological need to affirm one's social importance by displaying oneself in the company of females who meet any three of the following criteria: (a) are conventionally physically attractive; (b) are younger than oneself; (c) are shorter in stature than oneself; (d) weigh less than oneself; (e) appear to be lower on socioeconomic criteria than oneself; (f) are more submissive than oneself.
>
> A distorted approach to sexuality, displaying itself in one or both of these ways: (a) a pathological need for flattery about one's sexual performance and/or the size of one's genitalia; (b) an infantile tendency to equate large breasts on women with their sexual attractiveness.
>
> A tendency to feel inordinately threatened by women who fail to disguise their intelligence. (Caplan, 1991, p. 173)

Caplan's new diagnostic category may or may not be taken seriously, but it demonstrates the extent to which social norms and individual pathology can be confused, as well as the effect values have on what is considered normal.

Gender Bias in Practitioner Attitudes

Some of the earliest studies on gender stereotypes found that clinical practitioners completely shared popular beliefs about the appropriate and normative characteristics of men and women (Broverman et al., 1972). More recent studies have found that clinical practitioners have become more willing to see human traits in less gender-biased ways. Nevertheless, clinicians still classify more stereotypically masculine than feminine characteristics as socially desirable. For example, while practitioners made no distinctions between healthy adults and healthy males, they still believed that there were differences between a healthy female and a healthy adult (Phillips & Gilroy, 1985).

Both female and male clinicians have been found to be more likely to view a female client more positively than a male with identical symptoms (Hansen & Reekie, 1990). In contrast, male physicians like male patients better than female patients even when the patients' age, education, income, and occupation are taken into account (Roter & Hall, 1997). These biases increase the likelihood that females will be treated for psychological disorders whereas physical causes will be explored for males. Such biases also influence decisions about appropriate treatment. For example, therapists are likely to recommend more medication and less psychotherapy for elderly depressed female clients than for younger women or men of any age (Ford & Sbordone, 1980; Ray, McKinney, & Ford, 1987).

Gender Biases in Treatment: The Use of Medication

One alternative to psychotherapy is the use of what are known as *psychotropic drugs*—substances that alter mood, thinking, or behavior. Such drugs include tranquilizers, antidepressants, and sedatives that have a variety of generic and trade names (Valium, Librium, Elavil, Seconal, etc). In the United States at the end of the 1970s, more than two-thirds of all prescriptions for psychotropic drugs each year were written for women. Women comprised 63 percent of those for whom tranquilizers were prescribed, 71 percent of those given stimulants, and 71 percent of those receiving antidepressants (Carmen, Russo, & Miller, 1981). (See Figure 14.3.)

Translation of these percentages into actual numbers of prescriptions shows that women received 53 million prescriptions for psychotropic drugs versus 26 million for men (Travis, 1988b). This gender difference is not simply due to the fact that women go to the doctor more often than men. Women received such prescriptions at a higher rate (if 100 people visit a physician, approximately eight women versus six men will receive a prescription). Once women received a prescription, there was a tendency for it to be continued over several years, whereas the pattern among men was to receive psychotropic drugs for a more limited time (Travis, 1988b).

No differences between men and women in the use of over-the-counter drugs have been found. Instead, women disproportionately used and abused prescription drugs, which are stronger and which require the cooperation of a physician. Although great attention has been paid to the abuse of illicit drugs, more people use psychotropic drugs. In addition to being female, these people are more likely to be older, richer, and whiter than illicit drug users (Fidell, 1982).

"Since you are a damsel, I understand your natural predisposition to distress. Therefore, I'm going to prescribe a strong anti-depressant. ...Try to think of it as your own little "Knight-in-Shining-Armor-in-a-Bottle."

FIGURE 14.3.
Source: By permission of Leigh Rubin and Creator's Syndicate.

A number of factors help to explain why women are likely to abuse psychotropic drugs. Most important, physicians are simply more likely to prescribe such medication to them than to men. Gender stereotypes among physicians lead them to perceive that women are likely to be depressed or to have anxiety reactions. Such stereotypes even carry over into the medications prescribed to women and men after life-threatening surgery. For example, male patients were administered more pain medication after a coronary artery bypass and female patients were administered more sedatives (Calderone, 1990). These differences are consistent with the belief that women are more emotional than men and more apt to exaggerate complaints about pain. Stereotypic beliefs are especially likely to affect behavior toward older women. The prescription rate for psychotropic drugs is quite similar for women and men until age 45. After age 45, women have a substantially higher rate than men (Travis, 1988b).

Drug advertisements play a major role in supporting differential patterns of prescription use, because their images support traditional gender stereotypes. One drug advertisement, for example, stressed the image of the troublesome woman. It depicted a woman seated in a chair with her head and arms fading into the back and arms of the chair, while the caption asked, "Is this patient becoming a fixture in your office?" Advertisements also encourage the adaptation of women to traditional roles and responsibilities. One advertisement illustrated a harassed housewife caged behind bars made of brooms and mops. The caption read, "You can't set her free, but you can make her feel less anxious." Another stated that the physician could help an entire family by tranquilizing the mother so that she would be able to cook and serve their meals. This caption read, "Treat one—six people benefit" (Travis, 1988b).

Feminist therapists consider many women's problems as structural rather than intrapsychic. However, most psychotropic drug prescriptions are written by general practitioners and internists, not psychologists (Fidell, 1982). Social changes are harder to make than advances in drug therapy, although adequate child care, decent wages, or more responsive husbands might make many women less depressed.

Women's traditional roles have also been found to have negative consequences for their physical as well as their mental health. In one study of female cardiac patients, those women who were high on *unmitigated communion* (defined as a tendency to get overly involved in others' problems) had greater difficulty in adjusting to their illness (Helgeson, 1994). It was particularly hard for them to reduce their household activities even when they had been instructed to do so by their physician. In another study of adolescent girls with diabetes, those who scored high on unmitigated communion had poorer metabolic control partly because they coped badly with relationship stress (O'Leary & Helgeson, 1997).

Institutional Biases in the Treatment of Women and Men

Perceptions about gender differences in psychological disorders influence all aspects of treatment. Women's disorders may be characterized as "acting in," whereas men's disorders may be characterized as "acting out." There is a double standard in the way women and men are treated when they violate normative standards of acceptable behavior in these gender-typed ways. Women are more likely to be defined as mentally ill and are treated by clinical practitioners. Men are more likely to be seen as engaging in antisocial activities and are dealt with by the criminal justice system. Thus, they are not counted as suffering from psychological disorders. This kind of definitional difference helps make it appear that more women than men are mentally ill.

Is it better to be defined as ill than as a criminal? The standards of what is criminal behavior are clearer than definitions of mental instability (every society has, for example, a set of laws and penalties for breaking them). Definitions of criminality are applied to behavior, whereas mental illness is perceived as more internally based and less under the individual's control. Psychological treatment, in contrast to a criminal's sentence, has no time limits or criteria for termination. Thus, society's institutionalized responses to gender-typed deviance may contribute to social myths about women's greater weakness and instability.

GENDER AND THERAPY

The Feminist Critique of Traditional Treatment Methods

The use of drugs instead of psychotherapy and support for social change is probably the most negative aspect of a medical model of women's mental health. The medical model has encouraged women to seek individual solutions to many problems that may not best be solved individually—or may not be responsive to individual remedies at all. It has discouraged women from finding more social or collective avenues of self-help. For people with less power—people whose emotional problems are most often rooted in social arrangements and practices that have severely restricted their life options—the medical model can be destructive. The belief that they can solve by themselves problems over which they have no control as individuals can have severely depressing consequences.

Powerless individuals are also more likely to be treated with drugs, electroshock, or medical hospitalization than with long-term individual psychotherapy (Greenspan, 1983). In Great Britain, for example, black women are more likely than white women to be diagnosed as having a chronic rather than an acute mental health problem and to be institutionalized for mental illness (Watson & Williams, 1992).

Psychologists generally view psychotherapy as a positive alternative to drugs or imprisonment for helping people cope with their problems. Feminist therapists have charged that traditional therapies often lead practitioners to make the fundamental attribution error (discussed in Chapter 3). The locus of causality is placed within individuals rather than in their circumstances. People are, therefore, viewed as ultimately responsible for their own distress. Because of this perspective, traditional therapists are more likely to see pathology in normal behavior. This is especially true when they are evaluating people whose life circumstances are most different from their own.

Traditional therapy can also be viewed as a form of social control because it focuses on personal rather than social change. Women are often labeled as disordered when the true diagnosis should be an unjust society (Kaplan, 1983). As one feminist therapist has pointed out:

> As long as basic structural inequities of power exist in society, large numbers of women will manifest symptoms of this inequality. Working to correct social inequities is, in the long run, the only final cure for most forms of female emotional distress. Therapy can help people cope with certain intolerable social conditions, but it cannot improve those conditions unless it contributes to raising the consciousness of patients so that they will be less likely to tolerate them. On the one hand, this points to the necessity to demystify therapy so that people are no longer encouraged to believe that only individual psychological "treatment" can cure what ails them. On the other hand, this points to the by-and-large unexplored potential of therapy to be an instrument of social change. (Greenspan, 1983, p. 36)

Feminist therapists support the idea of "giving psychology away." Their ultimate goal is to help clients understand the ways in which they collude with their own oppression and to recognize their own power, both as individuals and as members of a community of women.

Feminist therapists have criticized the process of therapy as well as its assumptions and goals. The myth of the detached and neutral expert has tended to cloud the fact that every therapist offers a worldview to his or her clients—the terms by which they are to understand themselves and their world. As is shown in the case of Dora, the therapist's choice of words, his choice of what to go after in therapy, what to analyze, what to stress and what to ignore, are all political acts laden with meaning. There is nothing the least bit neutral about this process (Greenspan, 1983).

Feminist Therapy

The theoretical principles of feminist therapy are hard to summarize. Unlike many other schools of therapy, feminist therapy does not have a single "founding mother." It arose in response to needs recognized by a number of pioneering practitioners. Feminist therapy has focused on the solution of practical problems facing women: discrimination, violence, oppression, and marginalization (Brabeck & Brown, 1997). It is based on the lived experience of women (Lerman, 1986). Theory building has taken second place to finding ways to empower women to make changes in their lives.

Although the principles of feminist therapy have evolved over time and continue to change, feminist therapists agree about some basic principles. These principles are summarized in Box 14.2. Some of the most important involve awareness and use of power. Unlike other schools of therapy, feminist therapy is concerned about the world outside of people's heads. A key issue is how to devise ways to call attention to women's oppression and its debilitating effects without losing sight of women's agency (Marecek & Kravetz, 1998).

Gender is seen as the primary focus for understanding oppression and power imbalances. Gender is not, however, the only site of oppression. Feminist therapists call for attention to each individual as both oppressor and oppressed—as a part of dominant culture and marginal to it (Brabeck & Brown, 1997). They also call for a recognition that clients' behaviors are adaptive responses to an unhealthy society rather than forms of pathology for which they must be blamed (Wyche & Rice, 1997).

On a practical level, feminist therapists try to avoid using diagnostic labels as a means of stigmatizing women who do not conform to the dominant culture's gender-role stereotypes. They try to assist their clients' understanding that many personal problems are a result of social inequality and common to many women. But they also help them use their own personal resources to challenge and alter their circumstances in ways that are consistent with their own values (Greene, 1994).

The goal of feminist therapy is personal *empowerment*—defined as helping women to become more independent and assertive about attaining their goals and achieving psychological growth (Wyche & Rice, 1997). Empowerment is a complex phenomenon involving changes at the personal, interpersonal, and sociopolitical level (Morrow & Hawxhurst, 1998). To become empowered, individuals must seek permission, enablement, and information at each of these levels (see Table 14.1). They must determine, for example, what sources of power they have, whether it is all right for them to use power, whether they will be able to use it, and what will happen to themselves and others if they choose to use their power.

Notice that we have shifted from the word *patient* to the word *client* in describing feminist therapy. Because of their concerns about power and hierarchies,

Box 14.2 Summary of Tenets of Feminist Theory of Psychological Practice

1. Feminist theory of psychological practice is consciously a political enterprise, and its goal is social transformation in the direction of feminist consciousness.

2. We are trying to change women's understanding of their reality to include the oppression of the patriarchal society and to create feminist consciousness. *Feminist consciousness* is a process of becoming, a way of seeing and sensing the world, a familiar lens, "another mother tongue." Feminist consciousness leads one to be response-able to self and others, attend to one's own and collective well-being; it is un-numbing and re-integrating of all experiences and leads to social transformation. A goal of feminist practice is the creation of a feminist consciousness that becomes as unconscious as patriarchal consciousness is currently.

3. The capacity to create theory comes from experience and human connections through any form or medium: human communication, written word, political action, group solidarity, community activism. In this way, the personal is political because experience is connected to transformation and change.

4. Gender is an important locus of women's oppression and intersects with other important loci of oppression including, but not limited to, ethnicity, culture, class, age, sexual orientation, ability, and linguistic status. The practitioner of feminist theory is self-reflective regarding her positions in these various hierarchies.

5. Feminist theory of feminist practice embraces human diversity as a requirement and foundation for practice. Diversity (ethnicity, sexual orientation, able-bodiness, religion, language) not only is a goal in its own right, but also is neces-sary for feminist theory to be complete and re-flective of the total range of human experience.

6. Feminist theory affirms, attends to, and authorizes the experience of the oppressed in their own voices. This is an interactive process in which our role as oppressor must be considered a part. Feminist therapists–psychologists are self-reflective about their own experience, which informs this process.

7. Feminist practitioners expand the parameters of conceptions of identity or personhood. Feminist theorists and practitioners seek models of human growth and development that describe a variety of ways that people have a sense of identities and multiple subjectivities.

8. Feminist theory of practice leads to an appreciation of the complex and multidetermined causations of distress, with particular attention to the sociopolitical context. Within this context, persons are viewed as capable of acting (response-able) to effect change, and each person is viewed as responsible for participating in the process of change. As part of the process of change, those practicing a feminist theory contextualize behavior as occurring within a patriarchal system. Women are viewed as agentic and powerful but not entirely responsible for the pathology of sexism. Feminist theory of practice challenges assumptions of men as whole and center and women as broken and marginalized.

9. Feminist theory building is not static. Feminist theory of psychological practice is evolving and in process.

Source: J. Worell & N. G. Johnson, Eds. (1997). *Shaping the future of feminist psychology: Education, research, and practice.* Copyright © 1997 by American Psychological Association, p. 32. Reprinted with permission.

feminist therapists strive for an egalitarian relationship with their clients. The client is encouraged to take a consumer attitude in seeking out psychological services and asking questions (Gilbert, 1980). The therapist is encouraged to disclose some aspects of her own life and to see the relationship as one between two adult women (Greenspan, 1986). This decrease in therapist distance helps to demystify the therapeutic process and to divest the client of her fantasies of rescue by another from her problems.

**TABLE 14.1. Conditions and Dimensions of Empowerment
in Feminist Therapy**

Dimensions of Empowerment

	Personal (Power within)	Interpersonal (Power with others)	Sociopolitical (Power in society)
Permission (May I? Am I worthy?)	Individual rights and freedoms	Approval or permission from another	Legal rights
Enablement (Can I? Am I able?)	Personal resources	Support and advocacy from others	Access to resources
Information (What do I need to know?)	"Know thyself"	Sharing stories, breaking silences	Questioning "the truth"

Conditions for Empowerment

Source: S. L. Morrow & D. M. Hawxhurst. (1998). Feminist therapy: Integrating political analysis in counseling and psychotherapy. *Women & Therapy, 21,* p. 43. Used by permission of The Haworth Press, Inc., Binghamton, N.Y.

The Difference between Nonsexist and Feminist Therapy

How does feminist therapy differ from nonsexist therapy, which advocates the equal treatment of women and men? Feminist therapy incorporates the political values and philosophy of feminism in its therapeutic values and strategies (Brown, 1994). It may be considered revolutionary for psychology because it insists that internal change is not enough.

> We would question here the increasingly accepted notion that changes in inner experience constitute a positive outcome for women in therapy. Given the cultural and institutional prejudices against women, it is not enough that the woman client leave therapy with an increase in self-esteem, regardless of the nature and extent of behavior change. We question whether it can be considered a "successful" therapy when the client "adjusts" to the cultural, societal, and familial contexts in which she lives without an awareness and understanding of their impact on her. (Kaplan & Yasinski, 1980, p. 192)

> People without power, people who look around at the world and do not see themselves reflected in it, learn to feel marginal, unimportant. People for whom the social order shows contempt learn to hate themselves. Powerlessness breeds depression. (Greenspan, 1983, p. 194)

These statements show that feminist therapists view internal power and external power or oppression and domination as intermeshed.

The Impact of Therapist Characteristics

Female versus Male Therapists

Although empirical studies do not clearly demonstrate the impact of therapists' gender on the outcome of therapy, we suggest that women consider a woman therapist. First, if men need more experience to understand the social context of women's lives, how does one select the women they should practice on? Second, there is evidence that a greater number of similarities between client and therapist is associated with a more satisfactory therapeutic outcome (Lerman & Porter, 1990). Female therapists can provide role models of strong effective women for their clients (Gilbert, 1980; Greenspan, 1983). They have also been found to be better able to express feelings in interactions with clients than male therapists (Marecek & Johnson, 1980).

One of the most problematic aspects of therapy between a female client and a male therapist is the possibility of sexual involvement between them. Although female-female relationships among therapists and clients have become increasingly visible in the past few years, sexual involvement is still overwhelmingly a problem of violations by male therapists with female clients (Bouhoutsos, Holroyd, Lerman, Forer, & Greenberg, 1983; Pope, 1994). The typical pattern is one in which sexual relations occur during therapy sessions while psychotherapy supposedly continues.

Such behavior totally violates the ethical code of the American Psychological Association. A therapist will be expelled from the APA if he is found to have engaged in sexual relationships with a client. It is considered to be a major abuse of the unequal power relationship between therapist and client.

Sexual Orientation

Lesbian clients may encounter dilemmas during psychotherapy when the therapist is heterosexual. Heterosexual therapists may have conscious or unconscious prejudices about a "homosexual lifestyle." They may be unaware of the extent of abuse and violence that lesbians experience. It is difficult to estimate how many lesbians have been assaulted or raped because they are lesbian. Many lesbians are unwilling to go to authorities because they fear that they will be victimized again by the police or others who might learn of their sexual orientation (Ellis & Murphy, 1994). Heterosexual therapists may also lack knowledge of lesbian communities.

Some questions have been devised that are designed to stimulate therapists' self-awareness (Rigby & Sophie, 1990):

1. Do I believe a heterosexual woman has a better chance at a happy life?
2. How do I respond to two women publicly showing affection in a manner that has obvious sexual overtones? How does this compare to the way I feel when a heterosexual couple shows similar public behavior?
3. How do I react when a female shows that she is sexually attracted to me?
4. Should a mother tell her children she is a lesbian? Why or why not?

You and your friends may want to answer these questions to explore your own level of awareness and/or discomfort about lesbians.

Lesbian therapists may also encounter issues that are not problematic for heterosexual women in our society. For example, feminist principles require therapists to tell clients some important things about themselves. But self-disclosure as a lesbian can put some therapists at professional risk (Ellis & Murphy, 1994). This is a situation in which clinical belief systems may collide with social reality.

When both therapist and client are lesbian or bisexual, there is the possibility of sexual relationships between them. In such female-female relationships, the therapist is likely to terminate the therapy, refer the client elsewhere, and then enter a long-term relationship with her that frequently involves their living together. Such actions have great potential harm for the client and are unethical. True informed consent for any kind of sexual relationship is not possible, regardless of the client's expressed wish, because of the carryover from the unequal power of the therapist-client relationship (Lerman & Rigby, 1990). Despite these problems, many lesbians feel it is important to have a lesbian therapist.

Race/Ethnicity

Issues of lifestyle differences between therapists and clients are particularly salient when they differ in race and/or ethnicity. The likelihood that any African-American woman will find a therapist who is also black, a woman, *and* a feminist is extremely small. Only a decade ago, fewer than 100 black women psychologists listed themselves as clinicians in an APA directory, and, among these, fewer than ten mentioned women's issues as a psychological interest (Childs, 1990). The number of African-American therapists has grown enormously in the past decade, but it is still likely that a combination of white therapist–black client will occur, particularly in public health clinics and hospitals (Greene, 1986).

Most therapists have had little training in the treatment of patients of color. For example, they may have difficulty distinguishing between the opportunity to work and having to work out of necessity. For many women of color, work is neither forbidden nor a novelty—it is burdensome and inescapable (Greene & Sanchez-Hucles, 1997). Women of color are also likely to live in environments where racism is pervasive. Encounters with racism are stressful and potentially traumatic and may have long-term psychological effects (Henderson-Daniel, 1994).

Information on women of color is not readily available even in journals that focus on women and psychotherapy. In a survey of such journals between 1990 and 1992, only 43 out of more than 700 articles addressed the concerns of women of color (Hall & Greene, 1996). Most of these articles did not look at social class differences between women nor mention the impact of poverty on mental and physical health. Although race and class are confounded in the United States, a substantial number of women of color are middle or upper class. Class does not have the same meaning, however, for black and white women. African-American women are more vulnerable to unemployment because they lack the accumulated assets that many European-American women possess (Wyche, 1996). They also suffer more stress than comparable white middle-class women because they are likely to be one of the few minority group members in their place of employment and because social class does not necessarily protect black Americans from the stress of racist encounters.

If therapists know little about African-American women, they know even less about Asian- and Latin-American women. The Asian-American community has become much more diverse in recent years, as large numbers of

Vietnamese, Koreans, East Indians, Cambodians, Hmong, Thai, and Tibetans have joined the Chinese-, Japanese-, and Filipino-Americans who were the predominant Asian-American groups during the last fifty years. These groups vary from one another as well as from dominant U.S. culture although most of them share traditional values that relegate women to subordinate roles (Bradshaw, 1994).

Asian-American women may not seek therapy because silence is supposed to convey pain and suffering (Bradshaw, 1994). When they are seen in community clinics, they tend to have a high rate of depression (Homma-True, 1990). Women in all these groups lack power, but some are especially oppressed. In the Khmer culture, for example, women are supposed to "stay in the shadows and in the home" (Ho, 1990). They are particularly at risk for domestic violence, which is considered acceptable if the woman refuses sexual overtures from her husband or refuses to tolerate his extramarital affairs.

The U.S. Census Bureau reported that there were 22.4 million Latinos in the United States in 1990—a 53 percent increase since 1980. The largest group includes those of Mexican origin followed by South and Central Americans, Puerto Ricans, and Cubans. There is great diversity among the groups categorized by the single label "Latino." For example, Cuban Americans have achieved higher levels of education and occupational attainment than individuals from other Latin American countries. Puerto Ricans, Chicanas, and Cuban Americans also differ in terms of their acceptance of traditional values and gender roles (Ginorio, Gutierrez, Cauce, & Acosta, 1995).

A major factor that contributes to differences between various Latina populations is the conditions under which they immigrated to the United States (Espin, 1987b; Ginorio et al., 1995). Immigration is probably more stressful to women than to men because women are held responsible for maintaining family ties and ethnic traditions. It is particularly stressful when migration has been forced by war or other forms of state-supported violence (Lykes, Brabeck, Ferns, & Radan, 1993). Some Asian-American populations (e.g., Vietnamese and Cambodians) have also been forced to immigrate by war (Root, 1995). And many Native American groups have engaged in a kind of internal immigration because of the poverty and lack of opportunities available on their reservations (LaFromboise, Choney, James, & Running Wolf, 1995). Women in all these groups may show symptoms of multiple loss.

Although it might appear that they are protected by their extended family networks, Latinas are at high risk for mental health problems. Their families are both a source of strength and of problems. Latinas usually come to therapy angry and discouraged and feeling that they have little control over their lives (Vasquez, 1994). Therapy requires the recognition of both their subordinated family roles and their worth as caregivers and nurturers.

As with gender, racial/ethnic similarity between therapist and client is probably a positive feature in therapeutic relationships. However, there has been little research in this area partly because of the low number of ethnic minority therapists. Feminist therapists feel, therefore, that it is particularly important that therapists from the dominant group sensitize themselves to the experiences and values of many diverse cultural groups. They also advocate that attention be paid to women who belong to several oppressed categories, such as disabled women of color or lesbians from ethnic minority groups (Greene & Sanchez-Hucles, 1997). The needs of poor older white women (especially if they are from rural areas) have also been neglected.

Therapy with Marginalized Women

Groups that are marginalized and stigmatized by society have special problems in therapeutic situations. These problems are primarily due to therapists' inability to "get inside the skin" of individuals whose life circumstances are very different from their own. Sometimes therapists invent "stories" to explain behaviors they do not understand. One social worker reported the following story about a mother:

> [She] waited four hours with her children for a clinic appointment and then finally acceded to the demands of her youngest for a snack. When the doctor eventually appeared, the mother hadn't yet returned and her absence was taken as a sign of irresponsibility. Filing for neglect was initiated. (Schnitzer, 1996, p. 574)

This woman was held to a standard of care for her children that did not take into account the economic and social circumstances in which poor mothers struggle (see Chapter 10).

When those in charge say "They don't come in!" to clinics, the statement raises concerns about personal unreliability and irresponsibility rather than social problems such as lack of transportation or money for child care. Minority women may also be charged with "disorganization" if they are unwilling to offer information that is socially stigmatizing (e.g., different fathers for several children). Health professionals may also label these women as uncaring because they do not show emotions when family members are seriously ill. They fail to ask what kind of living conditions would make disease and death "just one more thing" (Schnitzer, 1996).

Psychotherapy is based on the philosophical assumption that all members of society deserve life, liberty, and happiness. However, therapy is not equally available to all members of society. A user of therapy is more likely to be a middle-class person with discretionary income, as well as values that include being able to spend money on oneself rather than on family or children (Faunce, 1990). Moreover, therapy is not equally effective for all members of society. For clients in poverty, the concern may not be so much how to express anger but whether or not to express it at all (Faunce, 1990). For women with little power, the expression of anger may have extremely negative consequences in terms of physical and social abuse (see Chapter 13).

Poor clients may also have a very different set of priorities than their middle-class therapists. The words of one participant in a black woman's support group illustrate this point:

> When I heard about this group I asked my therapist (a white woman) if I could attend. It seemed like all she was concerned about was the fact that I got raped. Hell! I know that was important, but that bastard got my last twenty-five dollars. That was all the money I had, till payday. I can deal with the rape later, but I won't have a job if I can't get back and forth to work. (Boyd, 1990, p. 156)

Therapists must be attentive to clients' material as well as personal needs. It is easy to confuse dire social circumstances with personal pathology.

Some groups of women have been almost entirely ignored even by feminist psychologists. Poor women in psychological research are shut up and shut out (Reid, 1993). When researchers do examine neglected populations such as homeless women, they often find surprising results. For example, homeless women did not differ psychologically from a population of women who were not homeless from the same neighborhood (Jackson-Wilson & Borgers, 1993). Neither group of women had a high rate of psychological or physical disability. Instead, women in both groups were likely to be black and single and to have a higher than average number of children, an educational level of less than twelve years, and severely limited work histories. Social rather than intrapsychic variables appear to be the source of the homeless women's vulnerability. They had fewer sources of social support during a period of need.

White feminist therapists may have a particular problem in dealing with African-American women clients because they tend to see gender as the primary issue in the lives of all women, independent of their race, class, or color. They may be unaware of the powerful effect that being white has had on their own lives. As one feminist therapist of color has pointed out: "Many white feminist therapists forget that they were white long before they chose to become feminists or therapists. Being a feminist therapist does not negate the societal privilege that is inherent in being born white" (Boyd, 1990, p. 163).

White therapists' lack of awareness of the pervasive effects of racism can harm their black clients. For example, skin color variations within African-American families can be a source of conflict between family members. An African-American therapist is more likely to inquire about the skin color of family members, particularly those about whom there are intense feelings (Greene, 1992). Following is a vivid account of how intrafamily conflict may be driven by perceived color differences:

> When I was growing up, calling someone black was worse than calling them nigger. We sat on the porch steps, and in a terrible game of degradation, compared our colors. Who was the darkest? Who was "it"? I was, more times than not. I fought my sister and my brother because they called me black. I generally got beaten up in those fights, and then beaten up again by my light-skinned mother for my loud, violent, attention-getting behavior. (Harris, 1994, p. 10)

Colorism (which is found among some Asian-American groups as well) is a consequence of the internalization of the dominant culture's standard of beauty. Until recently, however, it had gone unnamed and unrecognized.

Color is a salient and usually obvious characteristic. It often predicts where people will work, live, socialize, attend school, and receive health care, and how much money they may earn. Black women live in a culture that frequently reminds them of their skin color and the label of ugliness and inferiority that accompanies it. To ignore race is to fail to acknowledge the individual's complete experience (Greene, 1986).

Culture-Bound Syndromes

The rules for female behavior vary considerably from one culture to another. Groups differ, for example, on the distance women are allowed to go beyond the confines of their family, on what work is considered acceptable, and on how roles are distributed within the home (McGoldrick et al., 1989). The issues for many ethnic groups (such as Arab-American, Italian-American, or Jewish-American women) are too varied to deal with in depth here. To illustrate the importance of culture in therapeutic practice, we will focus on issues involving Latina women.

In most Spanish-speaking countries, women learn how to be female in a man's world. They are taught to repress or sublimate their sexual drives and to be extremely modest while, at the same time, enhancing their sexual attractiveness to obtain a good husband. Traditionally, Latina women have been expected to be responsible for taking care of the home and children and for keeping the family together. They often feel obligated to sacrifice themselves for this goal, relying on other women within the extended family for support and strength. This sacrificial role is rewarded by the community; when they perform it well, women are admired (McGoldrick et al., 1989).

As might be expected from this pattern of extreme feminine socialization, rates of depression are high among some populations of Hispanic women. In Puerto Rico, for example, the ratio of mild depression for women versus men in one study was 4.75 to 1 (Canino et al., 1987). The high rates of depression among Puerto Rican women remain even when age, marital status, employment, and health factors are taken into account. These findings suggest that depression would be relieved more easily by social rather than personal change. The researchers suggested remediation through affirmative action, social legislation, and education through the mass media.

Just as cultural norms affect rates of depression in some Latina groups, they probably also determine how distress is expressed. A number of Latina psychologists have, for example, discussed the existence of a "Puerto Rican syndrome" (Comas-Diaz, 1987; Ramos-McKay, Comas-Diaz, & Rivera, 1988) that includes hyperventilation, mutism, hyperactivity, and violence. This syndrome resembles the hysterical "fits" observed in nineteenth-century American women (discussed earlier in this chapter). Like the earlier hysteria, these symptoms may represent an effort to resolve contradictions between the need to be soft, yielding, and submissive while fulfilling a strong maternal role requiring self-reliance and good managerial skills. Culturally unique sets of symptoms have been found in other ethnic groups as well.

Such findings reinforce the point that cultural forces create symptomology. Examination of culturally diverse populations reveals cultural construction in action. Many women from ethnic minority groups are unwilling to seek out mental health practitioners because they fear that such practitioners will not share their values and will devalue important aspects of their culture. For example, religion and spirituality are often more important than they are in dominant secular society. Communality and the subordination of individual needs to group needs are also valued. Feminist emphasis on the context of behavior can help therapists distinguish between cultural practices and individual pathology.

There are many differences in the life experiences of white women and women of color in the United States. For example, women of color have always worked outside the home in greater numbers than white women. They are also overrepresented in occupations that pay low wages, have inadequate or no health insurance, and carry high risks of occupational injuries (Chrisler & Hemstreet, 1995). These include injuries that result from exposure to dangerous chemicals (laundry workers and hairdressers) as well as from repetitive movement (factory workers). Even though unionized automotive workers and college professors may earn the same amount of money, they are exposed to very different levels of stress. Worrying about "How am I going to find the time to write that journal article?" is quite different from worrying "Will I come home from work today with both my hands?" (Baker, 1996).

The ability of women of color to endure and survive has not left them unscarred. Survival has come at the cost of adaptation to high levels of stress and, not infrequently, moving from crisis to crisis with little respite (Greene, 1986). Black and Latina women have a higher mortality rate from coronary heart disease than white women do (Chrisler & Hemstreet, 1995). Their increased vulnerability to heart disease is probably due to a combination of physiological and behavioral factors. For example, coronary heart disease has a strong inverse relationship with socioeconomic status (Adler & Coriell, 1997). The highest mortality rates are among women with the least amount of education who are also exposed to more stress than well-educated women. However, lower mortality is also linked with positive aspects of lifestyle such as not smoking, regular exercise, and a low-fat diet. African-American women are less likely to smoke than European-American women but are more likely to eat a high-fat diet and to be overweight.

Excessive weight may also contribute to African-American women's high risk of diabetes which is the fourth leading cause of death in this group (Torrez, 1997). Poor diets may be a result of poverty as well as cultural preference. Poorer individuals not only have less disposable income for healthy food, but these foods are also harder to find and more expensive relative to less healthy foods in the same market (Adler & Coriell, 1997). As a result of coronary heart disease, hypertension, a greater mortality from breast cancer, and greater risk of diabetes and some autoimmune diseases such as lupus, the life expectancy of African-American women is nearly six years shorter than that of European-American women (Torrez, 1997).

SOME UNRESOLVED ISSUES

Invisible Groups of Women

Feminist research on ethnically diverse populations has increased in recent years (cf. Landrine, 1995). However many groups are still invisible. There are, for example, many different Native American cultures whose members speak more than 200 indigenous languages (LaFromboise, Berman, & Sohi, 1994). Even more invisible are those women who live (as does half of the Native American population) in urban environments separated from their tribal communities.

Other invisible populations are not part of any particular ethnic group. They include homeless women, lesbians, and disabled women. Since the latter group is often denied both the traditional feminine nurturing role and the role of independent worker, disabled women may feel that they have no role to play in society (Prilleltensky, 1996). Minimizing a client's disability or overemphasizing its impact on her life are common therapeutic pitfalls (Esten & Willmott, 1993). Dealing with disabled women may be particularly difficult for feminist therapists because these women do not fit their ideal of strong, independent, self-sufficient women (Barshay, 1993).

Invisible Values

There has been much discussion about ethnic minority women in this chapter, partly because adding ethnic discrimination to gender subordination multiplies negative effects on mental and physical health. But the relatively abundant research on ethnic minority women also reflects psychology's biases. Psychologists are much more likely to focus on weaknesses rather than on strengths. Thus, the value of women's coping strategies may be ignored or their difference from strategies used by men seen as evidence of individual pathology. Similarly, differences from the dominant culture can be either unseen or misinterpreted.

Because of psychology's biases, women who deviate from cultural stereotypes about their weakness and need may also be ignored. Not all women of color are poor, some old women make important contributions to society, and lesbians vary as much as heterosexual women in terms of their need for therapy. A focus on diversity should not be used to promote stereotyping.

Finally, although gender represents one way to organize social reality, it is not the only way to do so. Age, class, sexual orientation, ethnicity, and culture can also serve as organizing principles. They are all closely interwoven with gender. None of these categories is politically neutral or value free. Each (separately and in combination) can serve as a tool for oppression. They can serve as sources of strength as well (see Chapter 15).

CONNECTING THEMES

- *Gender is more than just sex.* Women's psychological disorders are more closely related to their status and roles (in other words, aspects of gender) than they are to their biological sex. Emphasis on gender differences in psychological disorders is a consequence of lack of attention to the social context of people's lives.
- *Language and naming are sources of power.* Diagnostic categories are clear examples of the power to name. Feminist critiques stress the need to question the economics and politics of diagnostic labels. Feminist therapists

have been active in renaming. Terms such as *client* instead of *patient* or *coping strategies* rather than *symptoms* do much to break down traditional views that most women are either "sick" or "crazy."

- *Women are not all alike.* Mental and physical well-being largely depend on an interplay of social structures and individual experience. Women from many different groups respond to discrimination and subordination by developing similar psychological and physical disorders. However, the buffering effect of education and income reveals that women's so-called weaknesses are often the product of social construction.
- *Psychological research can foster social change.* Feminist theory stresses social change in addition to personal change. Since therapy is an individual process, the contradiction between theory and practice is an ongoing problem for feminist therapists. Nevertheless, feminist practitioners have made great strides in empowering women from many diverse groups to make constructive changes in their lives.

SUGGESTED READINGS

COMAS-DIAZ, LILLIAN, & GREENE, BEVERLY (Eds.). (1994). *Women of color: Integrating ethnic and gender identities in psychotherapy.* New York: Guilford Press. This book contains a wealth of information about the lives and needs of many groups of ethnic minority women. The contributors are mainly working therapists—many women of color—who interweave theory and practice.

WORELL, JUDITH, & JOHNSON, NORINE (Eds.). (1997). *Shaping the future of feminist psychology: Education, research, and practice.* Washington DC: American Psychological Association. This book is the result of a conference organized by the Division of the Psychology of Women of the American Psychological Association. The contributors explore a wide variety of issues derived from therapeutic practice from a diverse set of perspectives.

GALLANT, SHERYLE, KEITA, GWENDOLYN, & ROYAK-SCHALER, RENEE (Eds.). (1997). *Health care for women: Psychological, social, and behavioral influences.* Washington DC: American Psychological Association. Psychologists have only begun to recognize the importance of integrating the mind and the body. The contributors to this book (also the result of an APA-sponsored conference) examine women's health in terms of their social context, lifestyle, and stage of life cycle.

Making a Difference: Toward a Better Future for Women

- **TRANSFORMING GENDER**
  Transforming Ourselves
  Transforming Interpersonal Relations
  Transforming Society
- **TRANSFORMING LANGUAGE**
- **CELEBRATING DIVERSITY**
- **PSYCHOLOGY AND SOCIAL CHANGE**
- **SUGGESTED READINGS**

What do women want? This is an especially important question to ask of young women, since they are the future. The first wave of feminist activists included the suffragists who achieved the vote for women in the early 1900s. The second wave, whose activism began in the 1960s, worked on issues such as reproductive rights, workplace equality, sexism in the media, and an end to violence against women. Despite media claims that feminism is dead, many young women identify as *third-wave feminists* who are defining their own goals for the next round of social change. Third-wave feminists are a diverse group (on dimensions of ethnicity, social class, religion, etc.), and they consider feminism as only one part of their identity—a part they try to integrate with other aspects of who they are:

> Young feminists are constantly told that we don't exist. It's a refrain heard from older feminists as well as in the popular media: "Young women don't consider themselves feminists." Actually a lot of us do. And many more of us have integrated feminist values into our lives, whether or not we choose to use the label "feminist." This is an important barometer of the impact of feminism, since feminism is a movement for social change—not an organization doing a membership drive. (Findlen, 1995, p. xv)

Other young women believe that feminism has failed because it did not allow women to "have it all":

> If there is a troublesome legacy from the feminism that has come before, it's the burden of high expectations—of both ourselves and the world. Many young feminists describe growing up with the expectation that "you can do anything," whether that message came directly from parents or just from seeing barriers falling. But there's a point where you realize that while you may indeed feel capable of doing anything, you can be stopped—because of sexism. Maybe you played Little League baseball but found yourself relegated to girls' softball at age thirteen. Maybe you were the smartest kid in your high school class, and were stunned the first time you heard a college professor say

563

that women couldn't be great artists or mathematicians or athletes. Maybe your mother gave you *Our Bodies, Ourselves* and taught you to love your body, but that didn't stop you from being raped. (Findlen, 1995, pp. xv–xvi)

But is the message that "you can have it all" or "you can do anything" what feminism promised? There are many different kinds of feminism, and feminists have had different goals. For example, among second-wave activists, a liberal feminist might be concerned with gaining equality for women in education and employment; a cultural feminist might focus on achieving respect for women's traditional work of mothering; a radical feminist might work to expose the systemic nature of violence against women; and a womanist might focus on social change through valuing ethnic diversity and multiculturalism. This diversity of feminisms is a strength, not a weakness, because it encourages people to work for social change in many important areas and to use many different strategies.

Despite their diversity, feminists also have shared values and goals. Feminists believe in the worth and value of women. As a 1970s bumper sticker proclaimed, "Feminism is the radical notion that women are people." Moreover, feminists recognize that social change is necessary and that no one can create social change by herself. And they believe that people should work together to change society so that women can lead more secure, satisfying, and fulfilling lives. This belief in *collective action*, or group solidarity toward social change, is part of what differentiates feminism from just individual women achieving success.

How can feminist goals be achieved? Four themes have been traced throughout this book:

- Gender is more than just sex.
- Language and naming are sources of power.
- Women are not all alike.
- Psychological research can foster social change.

Let's look at each of these themes one last time, with a focus on how they relate to making a difference for women.

TRANSFORMING GENDER

Gender is a system of power relations that affects individuals, relationships, and society. Changes can be fostered at each of these levels.

Transforming Ourselves

Most women have internalized at least some of the sexist messages of our culture. Some feel shame about their bodies, their sexuality, or the normal changes of aging. Some doubt their abilities or do not feel entitled to equal treatment, whether at work or at home. Many women feel guilty about not being perfect mothers or blame themselves for having been subjected to rape, incest, or sexual harassment. This self-hatred is fostered by exposure to media images, gender socialization in childhood and adolescence, and the experience of having lower status and power in everyday interactions and relationships.

What can women do to change these beliefs and attitudes? In the 1970s, second-wave feminists developed *consciousness-raising (C-R) groups,* where women met informally to talk about their lives as women. One of the benefits of these groups was that women who took part in them began to see that their problems were not just individual deficiencies but were related to society's devaluation of women. Consciousness-raising groups encouraged social action, leading to such activities as opening shelters for battered women and protesting against sexist advertising. However, as women made some social progress in the 1970s and 1980s, many of these groups became more individually focused and then disappeared altogether (Kahn & Yoder, 1989; Rosenthal, 1984). Nevertheless, many organizations working for social change have incorporated the values and norms of C-R groups into their process.

Consciousness raising became a model for feminist therapy because it offered women an opportunity to share experiences without being treated as patients who needed expert psychiatric help and because C-R groups assumed that the environment plays a major role in women's problems and difficulties (Brodsky, 1973). C-R groups often led to positive changes for the women in them, including an altered worldview, greater awareness of sexism, positive changes in self-image, increased self-acceptance, and increased awareness of anger (Kravetz, 1980). Today, although C-R groups no longer exist, feminist counseling and therapy empower women who want to make changes in their lives. Nonsexist or feminist therapies may be particularly valuable for people who have a history of physical or sexual abuse, eating disorders, or depression—all of which are more likely to affect women and which are due in part to gender-related social influences.

For women who are students, the growth of women's studies programs and the increasing interest in single-sex education for girls and women may be filling some of the gap left by the disappearance of C-R groups (Davis, Crawford, & Sebrechts, 1999). Women's studies classes, whether single-sex or coed, often provide powerful consciousness raising (James, 1999). In one study, taking a single women's studies course led to a decrease in the passive acceptance of sexism. By the end of the course, students were less likely to believe that marriage and motherhood would fulfill most women, that a woman should relocate for her husband's job, and that rape is sometimes the woman's fault (in comparison with their answers at the beginning of the course and also to a group of students taking other courses). The students also increased in their active commitment to feminism, integrating their personal identity as a feminist with plans for social activism (Bargad & Hyde, 1991).

Women's studies courses have a positive influence partly because they make women and gender their main focus, countering the androcentric bias of other courses. When students take these courses, they read about women's activism throughout history; study the work of women writers, artists, and scientists; and learn about women's lives across cultures. In addition, women's studies teachers often use feminist teaching principles: They encourage class participation, teach critical thinking, and help young women find their own voice and set their own goals (James, 1999; Kimmel, 1999). A frequent student response after a first women's studies course is, "This should be required for everyone!"

Do women's studies courses change men's attitudes? There has been less research on this question, and results are mixed. Men who are conservative and very gender typed when they enroll may change little (Vedovato & Vaughter, 1980). Changes may be subtle, becoming evident only through in-depth interviews (Crawford, McCullough & Arato, 1983). In one study, the attitudes of male students changed in a profeminist direction, but not as much as the attitudes of female students (Steiger, 1981).

As women redefine gender expectations, other girls and women have more models of different ways to be a woman. This seems to have a beneficial effect. For example, female graduate students who had female professors as role models were more empowered and satisfied than those who had male role models (Gilbert et al., 1983). Cynthia Cockburn (Chapter 3) has expressed the hope that her own life path from secretary to sociologist might inspire other women. Indeed, all the women in the "Making a Difference" boxes throughout this book can serve as models of women's strengths. Consider how a young girl like Natalie Toro (Chapter 6) can be a role model. By showing that a girl can be very good at math and science while still being a well-rounded, "normal" person, she may inspire other girls to persist in their educational goals.

Transforming Interpersonal Relations

Sexism is reproduced in everyday interactions with others. The cognitive processes that lead to devaluing women usually occur outside awareness. Even the most well-meaning people can make sexist attributions, and sexist patterns of interaction lead to self-fulfilling prophecies. The interactional level may be the most important one to change precisely because gender processes are largely invisible and taken for granted.

Stereotyping exerts control over people in several ways. First, stereotypes describe how people in a certain group supposedly behave: Women are emotional, Asian-Americans are academically motivated, old people are always talking about the past, and so forth. These stereotypes exert pressure to conform among group members. They are prescriptive as well as descriptive—in other words, they tell members of stereotyped groups how they *should* behave. People who do not conform may be penalized. A woman who does not show much emotion, for example, may be harshly judged as cold, unfeminine, and controlling.

"Doing gender" can be disrupted when people treat others as individuals, not as members of a stereotyped group. One important strategy for change is to become aware of how we often respond to others as members of a category. In general, people with more power engage in stereotyping of people with less power. Powerful people do not need to pay attention to the powerless, because their well-being does not depend on it. For example, a worker would have to pay more attention to the moods and demands of the boss than the boss would have to pay to the worker's, because the worker does not control important outcomes for the boss (Fiske, 1993). Knowing how power affects stereotyping can help change these processes. For example, psychological research on power and stereotyping was influential in the Supreme Court decision in the *Price-Waterhouse v. Ann Hopkins* case, where Hopkins won a partnership that had been denied because of stereotyped judgments about her femininity (Fiske et al., 1991).

When awareness of sexism is raised, small acts of resistance can follow. Gloria Steinem, a founding editor of *Ms.* magazine, calls this kind of resistance "outrageous acts and everyday rebellions" (Steinem, 1983). For example, while not everyone personally can run for the Senate or aid Afghani refugee women, each of us can give money or time to those who do. We can unite with others who may be devalued for their differences, just as Kelli Peterson supported lesbian and gay students by forming a student association at her school (Chapter 7). Even though she lived in a very conservative community, Kelli received encouragement from many family members, school administrators, and friends (Bohan & Russell, 1999). Both women and men can support others who work for change; in particular, women can choose to support and mentor each other. One feminist organization that provides leadership seminars for women in administration has as its motto, "Lift as you climb."

Doing gender is also disrupted when people refuse to be cooperative or silent in the face of sexism. Humor can be an effective tool. *Not* laughing at sexist jokes undermines their aggressiveness. And women often defuse hostile situations with their own take-charge humor. When Britain's former prime minister Margaret Thatcher received the backhanded compliment from a member of the opposing political party, "May I congratulate you for being the only man on your team?," she responded with "That's one more than you've got on yours." When actress Judy Holliday was being sexually harassed by a casting director who was literally chasing her around the room, she reached into her bra, pulled out the foam rubber pads, and said calmly, "I believe it's these you're after" (Barreca, 1991). Women's self-aware use of humor can be a powerful tool in challenging gender-based power plays (Crawford, 1995).

More seriously, activist Dolores Huerta effectively stopped sexist talk in farm workers' union meetings by counting how often it happened and speaking up about it (Chapter 11). Another example of an effective "everyday rebellion" occurred at Cornell University. Four male students electronically posted a list of "Top 75 Reasons Why Women (Bitches) Should Not Have Freedom of Speech." The list included items such as "She doesn't need to talk to get me a beer"; "If my dick's in her mouth she can't talk"; and "If she can't speak she can't cry rape." When women protested, the men defended the list as "Humor, that's all. Humor, Humor, Humor."

A group of women students decided to take a different course of action. Instead of creating an equally derogatory list about men, they posted a list of "75 Reasons Why Angry Cornell Women (Your Worst Nightmare) Are Exercising Their Freedom of Speech." The list consisted of evidence about women's lives, such as "In the U.S. four women are killed every day by their husbands or boyfriends" and "45% of underweight women think they are too fat." By moving the dialogue to a more serious level, these women effectively showed how truly unfunny the men's "humor" was (Women's Action Collective, 1992).

Transforming Society

Transforming gender at the social structural level is linked with the individual and interactional transformations just described. When people are empowered as individuals, they can speak out against injustice, and they can begin to change the institutions, laws, customs, and norms that harm girls and women. The effect is reciprocal, as speaking out leads to greater feelings of self-efficacy and empowerment.

Feminist activists of the 1970s achieved many important goals, and third-wave feminist activists are building on them. For example, Amy Cohen (Chapter 4) thought of herself as "nonconfrontational" and "agreeable," but because 1970s feminists had achieved the passage of Title IX, she could use it to achieve more equitable resources for college women athletes. Dolores Huerta cofounded the United Farm Workers; Maggie Kuhn (Chapter 12) lobbied for the elderly; Candy Lightner (Chapter 10) organized Mothers Against Drunk Driving; and Katie Koestner (Chapter 13) organized a movement to end acquaintance rape. All these women transformed personal hardship and suffering into powerful collective action, so that others might not have to endure their pain. Their activism reflects women's traditional roles as nurturers of others and celebrates the power of connectedness and caring.

Social change is not easy; attempts to change power relations almost always provoke backlash. Certainly, there has been a strong backlash against each wave of feminist activism throughout history. Today, the backlash ranges from repeated media claims that "feminism is dead" to the murder of people connected with women's health clinics. Moreover, change does not always result in progress. Feminist activists worked for no-fault divorce laws, only to find that they worsened the economic consequences of divorce for women (Weitzman, 1985). When more women entered the workforce, one result was the "second shift" of paid work followed each day by child care and housework (Hochschild, 1989). When Title IX legislated equality in sports opportunity in schools and colleges, it had costs for women coaches. By increasing the number of sports programs for women, Title IX increased the number of coaching positions for women's sports—but men were the main beneficiaries of the change, taking 75 percent of the new jobs (Valian, 1998). Attempts to change society must be reevaluated periodically to judge whether they have had their intended effects and also whether they have had unanticipated negative effects. Fortunately, social science research can help find the answers to these questions.

TRANSFORMING LANGUAGE

The women's movement has provided a powerful force for change in how women are talked about, what problems can be named, and who can speak and be heard. Mary Daly (Chapter 2) reclaims names that have been used to derogate women and uses them to celebrate women instead. Reflecting Daly's influence, at the annual meetings of the Association for Women in Psychology, a "croning ceremony" now celebrates the wisdom of the older women present. We even know a group of middle-aged in-line skaters, all women, who called themselves "Crones on Wheels."

Women are now more free to keep their own names if they marry, use Ms, and assign gender-neutral names to their children. Textbooks and professional journals no longer refer to all humans as *he, him,* and *man.* Terms like *battered* woman, *date rape,* and *sexual harassment* have entered the language. *Victim* (as in rape victim, breast cancer victim) has been replaced by *survivor,* a change that emphasizes women's strength and coping skills in adversity. In all these ways and more, women are claiming the right to name.

Even more important, women are speaking out about injustices that they used to suffer in silence and shame. Within psychology, Phyllis Chesler (Chapter 14) was among the first to draw attention to the misuse of psychiatric power; Paula Caplan (1989, 1991) fought mother blaming and the misuse of DSM labels by mental health professionals; and Lenore Walker (1979) brought the experiences of battered women to public attention. When Fauziya Kassindja (Chapter 8) was threatened with forced marriage and genital mutilation, she had the courage not only to save herself by fleeing but to write about these forms of control and work for political change to protect women. Ninia Baehr and Genora Dancel (Chapter 9) dared to say that lesbian couples should have the right to marry. And Katie Koestner went public as a victim of acquaintance rape, educating thousands of people about the problem.

Along with positive language change influenced by the women's movement, there is also a new language of backlash. Terms like *bra-burners* and *feminazis* diminish women's rights activists. And, unfortunately, the word *feminist,* tainted by the backlash, is not part of many young women's identity. Activist Rebecca Walker is working to change the negative perception of feminism by encouraging young women to learn about the "herstory" and accomplish-

Making a Difference

Contemporary Authors says of **Rebecca Walker,** "Through both her activism and her writing, Rebecca Walker has become a role model for a new generation of feminists attempting to reinterpret the legacy of the women's movement as we approach the twenty-first century." Walker (b. 1970), daughter of novelist Alice Walker, graduated from Yale University in 1992 and soon thereafter co-founded Third Wave Direct Action Corporation, a group whose goal is to encourage activism among young women. In its first year of existence, TWDAC won the Feminist of the Year award from the Fund for the Feminist Majority for its efforts in registering young women to vote. In 1995, Walker edited a volume of essays by young writers, called *To Be Real: Telling the Truth and Changing the Face of Feminism.* In this inspiring volume, each writer an-

swers the question, "Is there more than one way to be a feminist?" The answer is clearly yes, and Walker believes that there is therefore a need for a "third generation" feminist movement. Many young women have been misled by the media's narrow, negative stereotypes of feminism into believing that feminism has nothing to offer contemporary young women, and that they owe nothing to the women's movement of the 1960s through 1990s. Before young women disavow feminism altogether, Walker asserts, they should become better informed about the past feminist movement's contributions to their own lives and think about ways in which they can shape today's feminism to fit their own needs.

Sources: Rooney, T. M. (Ed.). (1997). *Contemporary Authors,* Vol. 154, pp. 455–457.
Changing the face of feminism (1996, January). *Essence,* p. 123.

ments of the first and second waves of the women's movement. While the accomplishments of our foremothers are important, each generation must define its own goals. With knowledge of past victories, backlash, and defeats, today's women can shape third-wave feminism to their own goals.

CELEBRATING DIVERSITY

Women are not all alike. The problems faced by a working-class woman such as Dolores Huerta are quite different from those faced by college students such as Amy Cohen or Katie Koestner. Older women experience different forms of sexism than younger women, as Maggie Kuhn showed. Anyone whose sexual orientation is different from the heterosexual norm may encounter prejudice and discrimination on that basis, as the stories of Baehr, Dancel, and Peterson testify. People whose bodies are marked by difference are beginning to claim a right to their own dimensions of diversity, as shown by Cheryl Chase's activism for the rights of intersex people to determine their own bodily form and gender label (see Chapter 5).

Making the women's movement, and feminist psychology, more inclusive is not an easy task. Much of feminist theory has assumed that gender is the primary source of oppression for all women. If this were true, being inclusive would consist simply of studying how sexism affects women of color, disabled women, and any other defined group of women. However, many women do not consider gender the primary source of oppression in their lives. They urge other women to become more aware of how sexism varies or interacts with other kinds of oppression and privilege (Greene & Sanchez-Hucles, 1997).

Women of color argue that feminist theory and research should go beyond analyzing the position of white women in relation to white men. It should also analyze the position of white women in relation to women of color, white women to men of color, and people of color to white men. These analyses would help white feminists confront and change their own unacknowledged racism and ethnocentrism. As a start, each white feminist might ask herself, "What privileges does my white skin give me?" (Fine, Weis, Powell, & Wong, 1997; McIntosh, 1988). Similarly, each heterosexual feminist might ask, "How has my heterosexuality affected my feminist politics?" (Wilkinson & Kitzinger, 1993).

The importance of women of color perspectives is eloquently stated by one Asian-American third-wave feminist, Jee Yeun Lee:

> Women of color do not struggle in feminist movements simply to add cultural diversity, to add the viewpoints of different kinds of women. Women of color feminist theories challenge the fundamental premises of feminism, such as the very definition of "women," and call for recognition of the constructed racial nature of *all* experiences of gender. . . . These days, whenever someone says the word "women" to me, my mind goes blank. What "women"? What is this "women" thing you're talking about? Does that mean me? Does that mean my mother, my roommates, the white woman next door, the checkout clerk at the supermarket, my aunts in Korea, half the world's population? . . . Sisterhood may be global, but who is in that sisterhood? None of us can afford to assume anything about anybody else. This thing called "feminism" takes a

great deal of hard work, and I think this is one of the primary hallmarks of young feminists' activism today: We realize that coming together and working together are by no means natural and easy. (Lee, 1995)

571

Making a Difference: Toward a Better Future for Women

The womanist perspective in feminism was articulated by women of color who believed that white women had omitted recognition of their issues. In response, white women have tried harder to overcome the racism that is part of our society and to work together with women of color. Similarly, lesbians and bisexual women criticized feminist organizations for focusing on straight women's issues, and older women wrote about ageism within the women's movement. As a result of these criticisms, the women's movement has made respect for differences a cornerstone of feminist philosophy and activism.

As feminism becomes a more global movement, the issues of women in other cultures become more visible. These include the loss of human rights in Afghanistan, restrictions on reproductive rights in Eastern Europe, sexual slavery and sweatshop labor in Asian countries, genital mutilation in African countries, and mass rape as a tactic of war in the former Yugoslavia. Some psychologists, such as Brinton Lykes, have worked tirelessly to support the struggle of indigenous women and children who are victims of state-supported violence (Lykes et al., 1993). Yet global feminism may bring troubling questions of who is entitled to define a problem and whose viewpoint should determine what constitutes a solution. For example, white Western feminists may be appalled by female genital surgery, but the women who perpetuate it may see themselves as protecting their daughters from social ostracism. Whose viewpoint should prevail?

New women's issues, reflecting the differences in women's positions in diverse cultures, continue to emerge. The Internet is a powerful tool for connecting activists around the world and creating dialogue among diverse groups of women. For example, the Feminist Majority (*http://www.feminist.org*) and Women Leaders Online/Women Organizing for Change (*http://www.wlo.org*) draw attention to human rights abuses and provide information on how women can make their voices heard in protest.

PSYCHOLOGY AND SOCIAL CHANGE

The second wave of the women's movement has had important effects on psychology. Only a few short years ago, psychologists who happened to be women could not get hired into high-status universities and were rarely taken seriously as scientists or theorists (Unger, 1998). Today, women earn the majority of higher degrees in psychology, lead well-established professional organizations, produce many books and journals on the psychology of women, and participate in every aspect of psychological research, education, and practice.

One of the authors saw a good example of change just recently. At our university, there are regular lunch-time talks for faculty and graduate students. At one recent meeting, the speakers were a married couple (with different last names) from a nearby college, who do their research jointly. With them were their two children, a 4-year-old son and a 1-month-old infant. The man in the couple started their research presentation, while Mom took the children to play outside. Sexist? Not exactly. Halfway through the talk, she returned, Dad took the kids outside, and she concluded the presentation and discussion of their research. Afterward, another male professor arranged for the older child to join a play group with his own 4-year-old daughter. A lunch-time psychology program became an example of collaborative research, shared parenting, and the "balancing act" of multiple roles for both women and men.

Progress is uneven, however. It will probably be a while before such a scene occurs regularly enough that it is taken for granted, and even longer before it happens in business settings. And there are more subtle signs that women and feminist perspectives have not yet been fully integrated into psychology. Publishing one's research in a psychology of women journal still may have less impact than if it were published in a "mainstream" journal. Despite the wealth of feminist books and journals, college textbooks and course syllabi too often still exclude gender, women, ethnicity, and diversity (Chin & Russo, 1997).

The continued lack of integration of feminist scholarship is a serious problem, because throughout history, women's contributions have often been curtailed by their exclusion from powerful positions and erased by their omission from the history books. The life and work of Mary Calkins, discussed in Chapter 1, is only one example (Furumoto, 1979). Women have been re-placed in the history of psychology due to feminist efforts, but sustained attention to a more inclusive psychology is needed (Bohan, 1990; Chin & Russo, 1997; Landrine, 1995; Scarborough & Furumoto, 1987). This inclusiveness must extend to social class (Reid, 1993; Walkerdine, 1997) ethnicity (Fine et al., 1997; Wyche & Crosby, 1996) sexual orientation (Bohan, 1996), and other dimensions.

What can a student do? Students can make a difference by contributing to research and by using their knowledge of women's issues to work for change. When you have a choice of topic, you can write term papers on women or gender in your psychology, history, and literature courses. You can do an independent study or thesis on women and gender. You can ask questions in class when women are excluded or trivialized in readings and lectures. These strategies do not add much to the time and effort you put into your education, but they can help raise consciousness for yourself and others.

You can join an organization for women or volunteer at the women's center on your campus. If your campus has no women's center or women's studies program, start asking why. By taking courses that focus on women and gender, you can show the administration that there is a demand for this knowledge.

In 1999, students at the University of Connecticut formed a group called the Coalition for Multicultural Undergraduate Education. Their goal was to enlarge the general education requirements to include more courses on diversity (gender, sexual orientation, ethnicity, and culture). Because of their persistent, informed leadership, the administration agreed to endorse their effort publicly and to form a long-term committee of supportive faculty and students who will continue their mission even after the original members graduate. Their success shows that student activism can bring about change that will continue to benefit the next generation of students.

If you are planning to apply to graduate schools in psychology (or any other area), look carefully at the number of women faculty in the programs you consider, and how many have tenure. Look for courses on women and gender in the catalog, and find out whether there are women's studies and ethnic studies programs and a women's center. When visiting, ask about the level of support for feminist scholarship on campus. Psychology students can find information and support on a variety of gender issues by joining the Association for Women in Psychology or Division 35 of APA as student affiliates. These organizations allow students to become part of networks of people with similar concerns. Such coalitions provide meaningful personal relationships as well as sites of social change (Unger, 1998).

If you are seeking employment after graduation, look carefully at the gender and family sensitivity of the companies you consider. Do they have flextime, on-site day care, parental leave, benefits for same-sex partners? What proportion of management are women? How often do women get promoted from inside the company? Is there ethnic and racial diversity? What is the company's record on sexual harassment complaints? Ask questions based on your knowledge of the psychology of women and gender.

One of the most important things students can do is to educate themselves on the issues facing girls and women. Overcoming androcentrism in education helps people think critically about what they read and hear in their textbooks, classes, and from the popular media. It also helps them become effective employees and responsible citizens after graduation. The students who formed the Coalition for Multicultural Undergraduate Education were effective because they had "done their homework"—they presented evidence for their position logically and systematically. The Cornell women who responded to aggressive humor did the same. Like the women faculty who fought sex discrimination at MIT, discussed in Chapter 3, they knew that evidence and reason do count.

Psychological research and theory have provided a wealth of evidence and reason on why women want and deserve full human rights. We offer the research and theory in this book as a resource and a gift. This gift is unusual in that it can be made meaningful only by the recipient. How will you use psychology to make a difference?

SUGGESTED READINGS

UNGER, RHODA. (1999). *Resisting gender*. London: Sage. The title says it all. A pioneer second-wave feminist discusses the history of feminist psychology over the past 25 years and argues for feminist coalitions toward future social change.

VALIAN, VIRGINIA. (1998). *Why so slow? The advancement of women*. Cambridge, MA: MIT Press. Studies from sociology and psychology document that equality in the professions has not yet been achieved. Most important, this book suggests practical, concrete ways to increase personal and social power.

FINDLEN, BARBARA (Ed.). (1995). *Listen up! Voices from the next feminist generation*. Seattle: Seal Press. This collection reflects the passion and vibrancy of third-wave feminists. It shows how they fight feminist struggles in their own creative and diverse ways. Plus, it is fun to read!

References

AAUW Educational Foundation. (1998, October). *Gender Gaps: Where Schools Still Fail Our Children*. Washington, DC: Author.

Abrams, D., Sparkes, K., & Hogg, M. A. (1985). Gender salience and social identity: The impact of sex of siblings on educational and occupational aspirations. *British Journal of Educational Psychology, 55,* 224–232.

Abramson, P. E., Goldberg, P. A., Greenberg, J. H., & Abramson, L. M. (1977). The talking platypus phenomenon: Competency ratings as a function of sex and professional status. *Psychology of Women Quarterly, 2,* 114–124.

Abusharaf, R. M. (1998, March/April). Unmasking tradition. *The Sciences,* pp. 22–27.

Achte, K. (1970). Menopause from the psychiatrist's point of view. *Acta Obstetrica et Gynecologica* (Suppl.), *1,* 3–17.

Adams, K. L., & Ware, N. C. (1989). Sexism and the English language: The linguistic implications of being a woman. In J. Freeman (Ed.), *Women: A feminist perspective* (4th ed., pp. 470–484). Mountain View, CA: Mayfield.

Adams, M. (1976). *Single blessedness.* New York: Basic Books.

Adams, R. C. (1997). Friendship patterns among older women. In J. M. Coyle (Ed.), *Handbook on women and aging* (pp. 400–417). Westport, CT: Greenwood Press.

Adams, S., Kuebli, J., Boyle, P. A., & Fivush, R. (1995). Gender differences in parent-child conversations about past emotions: A longitudinal investigation. *Sex Roles, 33,* 309–323.

Addelston, J. (1998). *The pig award and other acts of gender terrorism.* Unpublished manuscript, Rollins College, Winterpark, FL.

Adelmann, P. K. (1993). Psychological well-being and homemaker versus retiree identity among older women. *Sex Roles, 29,* 195–212.

Adelmann, P. K., Antonucci, T. C., Crohan, S. E., & Coleman, L. M. (1989). Empty nest, cohort, and employment in the well-being of midlife women. *Sex Roles, 20,* 173–189.

Ader, D. N., & Johnson, S. B. (1994). Sample description, reporting and analysis of sex in psychological research: A look at APA and APA division journals in 1990. *American Psychologist, 49,* 216–218.

Adler, N. E., & Coriell, M. (1997). Socioeconomic status and women's health. In S. J. Gallant, G. P. Keita, & R. Royak-Schaler (Eds.), *Health care for women: Psychological, social, and behavioral influences* (pp. 11–23). Washington, DC: American Psychological Association.

Adolph, M. A. (1993). The myth of the golden years: One older woman's perspective. In N. D. Davis, E. Cole, & E. D. Rothblum (Eds.), *Faces of women and aging* (pp. 55–66). Binghamton, NY: Harrington Park Press.

Affonso, D. D., & Mayberry, L. J. (1989). Common stressors reported by a group of childbearing American women. In P. N. Stern (Ed.), *Pregnancy and parenting* (pp. 41–55). New York: Hemisphere.

Agence-France Press. (1999). China reportedly has 20 percent more males than females.

575

Media Resource Service, Sigma Xi home page (www.sigmaxi.org).

Aida, Y., & Falbo, T. (1991). Relationships between marital satisfaction, resources, and power strategies. *Sex Roles, 24,* 43–56.

Aizenman, M., & Kelley, G. (1988). The incidence of violence and acquaintance rape in dating relationships among college men and women. *Journal of College Student Development, 29,* 305–311.

Alagna, S. W. & Hamilton, J. A. (1986). *Science in the service of mythology: The psychopathologizing of menstruation.* Paper presented at the meeting of the American Psychological Association, Washington, DC.

Alazarov-Por, N. (1983). Giftedness across cultures: A study of educational values. In B. Shore, S. Gagne, S. Tarievee, R. Tali, & R. Tumbey (Eds.), *Face to face with giftedness.* New York: Nillian Books.

Albert, J. L. (1993, August 18). Who is getting abortions. *USA Today,* p. A11.

Aldous, J. (Ed.). (1982). *Two paychecks: Life in dual-earner families.* Beverly Hills, CA: Sage.

Alexander, S., & Ryan, M. (1997). Social constructs of feminism: A study of undergraduates at a women's college. *College Student Journal, 31,* 555–567.

Alington, D. E., & Troll, L. E. (1984). Social change and equality: The roles of women and economics. In G. Baruch & J. Brooks-Gunn (Eds.), *Women in midlife* (pp. 181–202). New York: Plenum Press.

Allan, J. S., Mayo, K., & Michel, Y. (1993). Body size values of White and Black women. *Research in Nursing and Health, 16,* 323–333.

Allan, K., & Coltrane, S. (1996). Gender displaying television commercials: A comparative study of television commercials in the 1950s and 1980s. *Sex Roles, 35,* 185–203.

Allen, I. L. (1984). Male sex roles and epithets for ethnic women in American slang. *Sex Roles, 11,* 43–50.

Allen, L. S., & Gorski, R. A. (1992). Sexual orientation and the size of the anterior commissure in the human brain. *Proceedings of the National Academy of Sciences, 89,* 7199–7202.

Allgood-Merten, B., & Stockard, J. (1991). Sex role identity and self-esteem: A comparison of children and adolescents. *Sex Roles, 25,* 129–139.

Allport, G. W. (1954). *The nature of prejudice.* Cambridge, MA: Addison-Wesley.

Almquist, E. M. (1989). The experiences of minority women in the United States: Intersections of race, gender, and class. In J.

Freeman (Ed.), *Women: A feminist perspective* (4th ed., pp. 414–445). Mountain View, CA: Mayfield.

Alpert, D., & Culbertson, A. (1987). Daily hassles and coping strategies of dual-earner and nondual-earner women. *Psychology of Women Quarterly, 11,* 359–366.

Altman, M. (1984). Everything they always wanted to know. In C. S. Vance (Ed.) *Pleasure and danger: Exploring female sexuality* (pp. 115–130). Boston: Routledge & Kegan Paul.

Amaro, H. (1993). Reproductive choice in the age of AIDS: Policy and counselling issues. In C. Squire (Ed.), *Women and AIDS: Psychological perspectives* (pp. 20–41). London: Sage.

Amaro, H., Russo, N. F., & Johnson, J. (1987). Family and work predictors of psychological well-being among Hispanic women professionals. *Psychology of Women Quarterly, 11,* 523–532.

American Association of University Women (AAUW). (1993). *Hostile hallways: The AAUW survey on sexual harassment in America's schools.* Washington, DC: The American Association of University Women Educational Foundation.

American Psychiatric Association (APA). (1994). *Diagnostic and statistical manual of mental disorders* (4th ed.). Washington, DC: American Psychiatric Association.

Amir, M. (1971). *Patterns of forcible rape.* Chicago, IL: University of Chicago Press.

Anderson, C. M., & Stewart, S. (1994). *Flying solo: Single women in midlife.* New York: Norton.

Anderson, J. V. (1973). Psychological determinants. In R. B. Kundsin (Ed.), *Successful women in the sciences: An analysis of determinants.* New York: New York Academy of Sciences.

Anderson, K. J., & Leaper, C. (1998). Meta-analysis of gender effects on conversational interruptions: Who, what, when, where, and how. *Sex Roles, 39,* 225–252.

Anderson, K. L. (1997). Gender, status, and domestic violence: An integration of feminist and family violence approaches. *Journal of Marriage and the Family, 59,* 655–670.

Angier, N. (1994, May 3). Male hormone molds women, too, in mind and body. *New York Times,* pp. C1, 13.

Angless, T., Maconachie, M., & Van Zyl, M. (1998). Battered women seeking solutions: A South African study. *Violence Against Women, 4,* 637–658.

Angrist, S., Dinitz, S., Lefton, M., & Pasamanick, B. (1968). *Women after treatment.* New York: Appleton-Century-Crofts.

Anson, O., Antonovsky, A., Sagy, S., & Adler, I. (1989). Family, gender, and attitudes toward retirement. *Sex Roles, 20,* 355–369.

Antonucci, T. C., & Akiyama, H. (1997). Concern with others at midlife: Care, comfort, or compromise. In M. E. Lachman & J. B. James (Eds.), *Multiple paths of midlife development* (pp. 147–169). Chicago: University of Chicago Press.

Apfelbaum, E. (1993). Norwegian and French women in high leadership positions: The importance of cultural contexts upon gendered relations. *Psychology of Women Quarterly, 17,* 409–429.

Araoye, M. O., & Adegoke, A. (1996). AIDS-related knowledge, attitude and behaviour among selected adolescents in Nigeria. *Journal of Adolescence, 19*(2), 179–181.

Arber, S., & Ginn, J. (1995). Choice and constraint in the retirement of older married women. In S. Arber & J. Ginn (Eds.), *Connecting gender and aging: A sociological approach* (pp. 69–86). Buckingham, UK: Open University Press.

Archer, D., Iritani, B., Kimes, D. D., & Barrios, M. (1983). Faceism: Five studies of sex differences in facial prominence. *Journal of Personality and Social Psychology, 45,* 725–735.

Arendell, T. (1997). A social constructionist approach to parenting. R. Arendell (Ed.), *Contemporary parenting: Challenges and issues* (pp. 1–44). Thousand Oaks, CA: Sage.

Arms, S. (1973). *A season to be born.* New York: Harper & Row.

Arnold, F., & Kuo, E. C. (1984). The value of daughters and sons: A comparative study of the gender preferences of parents. *Journal of Comparative Family Studies, 15,* 299–318.

Arroyo, J. A., Simpson, T. L., & Aragon, A. S. (1997). Childhood sexual abuse among Hispanic and non-Hispanic White college women. *Hispanic Journal of Behavioral Sciences, 19,* 57–68.

Asch, A., & Fine, M. (1988). Introduction: Beyond pedestals. In M. Fine & A. Asch (Eds.), *Women with disabilities: Essays in psychology, culture, and politics* (pp. 1–37). Philadelphia: Temple University Press.

Associated Press. (1996, October 27). Some facts about the $1 billion romance fiction industry from Harlequin.

Assunta, M., & Jalleh, M. (1995, April 16). Consumer organization calls for Barbie doll ban. *Third World Network Features,* PNEWS.

Astin, H. S. (1976). A profile of the women in continuing education. In H. Astin (Ed.), *Some action of her own: The adult woman and higher education.* Lexington, MA: Lexington.

Attie, I., & Brooks-Gunn, J. (1989). The development of eating problems in adolescent girls: A longitudinal study. *Developmental Psychology, 25,* 70–79.

Atwood, J. D. (Ed.). (1997). *Challenging family therapy situations: Perspectives in social construction.* New York: Springer.

Auerbach, J., Blum, L., Smith, V., & Williams, C. (1985). On Gilligan's In a different voice. *Feminist Studies, 11,* 149–161.

Ault, A. (1996). Ambiguous identity in an unambiguous sex/gender structure: The case of bisexual women. *The Sociological Quarterly, 37*(3), 449–463.

Avni, Noga. (1991). Battered wives: characteristics of their courtship days. *Journal of Interpersonal Violence, 6*(2), 232–239.

Azocar, F., Miranda, J., & Dwyer, E. V. (1996). Treatment of depression in disadvantaged women. *Women & Therapy, 18,* 91–105.

Baber, K. M., & Allen, K. R. (1992). *Women and families: Feminist reconstructions.* New York: Guilford.

Badgett, M. V. L. (1996). Employment and sexual orientation: Disclosure and discrimination in the workplace. In A. L. Ellis and E. D. B. Riggle (Eds.), *Sexual identity on the job: Issues and services* (pp. 29–52). New York: Harrington Park Press.

Bailey, M. J., Pillard, R., Neale, M., & Agyei, Y. (1993). Heritable factors influence sexual orientation in women. *Archives of General Psychiatry, 50,* 217–223.

Baker, N. L. (1996). Class as a construct in a "classless" society. *Women & Therapy, 18,* 13–23.

Baker, R., Kiger, G., & Riley, P. J. (1996). Time, dirt, and money: The effects of gender, gender ideology, and type of earner marriage on time, household-task, and economic satisfaction among couples with children. *Journal of Social Behavior and Personality, 11*(5), 161–177.

Ballinger, S. (1990). Stress as a factor in lowered estrogen levels in the early postmenopause. In M. Flint, F. Kronenberg, & W. Utian (Eds.), *Multidisciplinary perspectives on menopause. Annals of the New York Academy of Sciences, 592,* 95–113.

Bandura, A. (1965). Influence of model's reinforcement contingencies on the acquisition of imitative responses. *Journal of Personality and Social Psychology, 1,* 589–595.

Barak, A. (1997). Cross-cultural perspectives on sexual harassment. In W. O'Donohue (Ed.), *Sexual harassment: Theory, research, and treatment* (pp. 263–300). Boston: Allyn & Bacon.

Barak, A., Feldman, S., & Noy, A. (1991). Traditionality of children's interests as related to their parents' gender stereotypes and traditionality of occupations. *Sex Roles, 24,* 511–524.

Barbach, L. (1993). *The pause: Positive approaches to menopause.* New York: Dutton.

Bardwell, J. R., Cochran, S. W., & Walker, S. (1986). Relationship of parental education, race, and gender to sex-role stereotyping in five-year-old kindergartners. *Sex Roles, 15,* 275–281.

Bargad, A., & Hyde, J. S. (1991). Women's studies: A study of feminist identity development in women. *Psychology of Women Quarterly, 15,* 181–201.

Bargh, J., & Raymond, P. (1995). The naive misuse of power: Nonconscious sources of sexual harassment. *Journal of Social Issues, 51,* 85–96.

Barnett, O. W., & Fagan, R. W. (1993). Alcohol use in male spouse abusers and their female partners. *Journal of Family Violence, 8,* 1–25.

Barnett, O. W., Lee, C. Y., & Thelen, R. E. (1997). Gender differences in attributions of self-defense and control in interpartner aggression. *Violence Against Women, 3,* 462–481.

Barnett, R. C. (1997). Gender, employment, and psychological well-being: Historical and life course perspectives. In M. E. Lachman & J. B. James (Eds.), *Multiple paths of midlife development* (pp. 323–344). Chicago: The University of Chicago Press.

Barnett, R. C., & Baruch, G. K. (1978). Women in the middle years: A critique of research and theory. *Psychology of Women Quarterly, 3,* 187–197.

Barnett, R. C., Marshall, N. L., Raudenbush, S. W., & Brennan, R. T. (1993). Gender and the relationship between job experiences and psychological distress: A study of dual-earner couples. *Journal of Personality and Social Psychology, 64*(5), 794–806.

Barnett, R. C., & Shen, Y-C. (1997). Gender, high- and low-schedule-control housework tasks, and psychological distress: A study of dual-earner couples. *Journal of Family Issues, 18*(4), 403–428.

Barreca, G. (1991). *They used to call me Snow White . . . but I drifted: Women's strategic use of humor.* New York: Viking.

Barshay, J. M. (1993). Another strand of our diversity: Some thoughts from a feminist therapist with severe chronic illness. *Women & Therapy, 14,* 159–169.

Bart, P. (1970). Mother Portnoy's complaint. *Transaction, 8,* 69–74.

Bart, P. B. (1971). Sexism and social science: From the gilded cage to the iron cage, or, the perils of Pauline. *Journal of Marriage and the Family, 33,* 734–735.

Bart, P. B., & Grossman, M. (1978). Menopause. In M. T. Notman & C. C. Nadelson (Eds.), *The woman patient: Medical and psychological interfaces* (pp. 337–354). New York: Plenum.

Bar-Tal, D., & Saxe, L. (1976). Perceptions of similarly and dissimilarly attractive couples and individuals. *Journal of Personality and Social Psychology, 33,* 772–781.

Baruch, G. K. (1984). The psychological well-being of women in the middle years. In G. Baruch & J. Brooks-Gunn (Eds.), *Women in midlife* (pp. 161–180). New York: Plenum.

Baruch, G. K., Barnett, R. C., & Rivers, C. (1983). *Lifeprints: New patterns of love and work for today's women.* New York: New American Library.

Basow, S. A., & Howe, K. G. (1980). Role model influence: Effects of sex and sex-role attitude in college students. *Psychology of Women Quarterly, 4,* 558–572.

Basow, S. A., & Kobrynowicz, D. (1993). What is she eating? The effects of meal size on impressions of a female eater. *Sex Roles, 28,* 335–344.

Bass, E., & Davis, L. (1988). *The courage to heal: A guide for women survivors of child sexual abuse.* New York: Harper and Row.

Bauer, P. J. (1993). Memory for gender-consistent and gender-inconsistent event sequences by twenty-five-month-old children. *Child Development, 64,* 285–297.

Bazzini, D. G., McIntosh, W. D., Smith, S. M., Cook, S., & Harris, C. (1997). The aging woman in popular film: Underrepresented, unattractive, unfriendly, and unintelligent. *Sex Roles, 36,* 531–543.

Beatty, C. A. (1996). The stress of managerial and professional women: Is the price too high? *Journal of Organizational Behavior, 17*(3), 233–251.

Beck, J. C., & van der Kolk, B. (1987). Reports of childhood incest and current behavior of chronically hospitalized psychotic women. *American Journal of Psychiatry, 144,* 1474–1476.

Beck, R. W., & Beck, S. J. (1989). The incidence of extended households among middle-aged black and white women. *Journal of Family Issues, 10,* 147–168.

Becker, E., Rankin, E., & Rickel, A. U. (1998). *High-risk sexual behavior: Interventions with vulnerable populations.* New York: Plenum Press.

Becker, H. S. (1963). *Outsiders.* New York: Free Press.

Beckman, L. J., & Houser, B. B. (1982). The consequences of childlessness for the social-psychological well-being of older women. *Journal of Gerontology, 37,* 243–250.

Beckstein, D., Dahlin, M., & Wiley, D. (1986). Overview of sexuality education for young men. In C. H. Gregg & S. Renner (Eds.), *Sexuality educational strategy and resource guide: Programs for young men.* Washington, DC: Center for Population Options.

Beckwith, B. (1984). How magazines cover sex differences research. *Science for the People, 16,* 18–23.

Begley, S. (1999, Spring/Summer). Understanding perimenopause. *Newsweek: Health for Life,* pp. 30–34.

Belk, S. S., Garcia-Falconi, R., Hernandez-Sanchez, J., & Snell, W. E. (1988). Avoidance strategy use in the intimate relationships of women and men from Mexico and the United States. *Psychology of Women Quarterly, 12,* 165–174.

Bell, C. S., & Chase, S. E. (1996). The gendered character of women superintendents' professional relationships. In K. D. Arnold & K. D. Noble (Eds.), *Remarkable women: Perspectives on female talent development. Perspectives on creativity* (pp. 117–131). Cresskill, NJ: Hampton Press.

Bell, I. P. (1989). The double standard: Age. In J. Freeman (Ed.), *Women: A feminist perspective* (4th ed., pp. 236–244). Mountain View, CA: Mayfield.

Bem, S. (1993). *The lenses of gender.* New Haven: Yale University Press.

Bem, S. L., & Bem, D. J. (1971). Training the woman to know her place: The power of a nonconscious ideology. In M. H. Garskof (Ed.), *Roles women play: Readings toward women's liberation* (pp. 84–96). Belmont, CA: Brooks Cole.

Bem, S. L., & Bem, D. J. (1973). Does sex-biased job advertising "aid and abet" sex discrimination? *Journal of Applied Social Psychology, 3,* 6–18.

Benbow, C. P. (1988). Sex differences in mathematical reasoning ability in intellectually talented preadolescents: Their nature, ef- fects, and possible causes. *Behavioral and Brain Sciences, 11,* 169–132.

Benbow, C. P., & Stanley, J. C. (1980). Sex differences in mathematical ability: Fact or artifact? *Science, 210,* 1262–1264.

Benenson, J. F., Morash, D., & Petrakos, H. (1998). Gender differences in emotional closeness between preschool children and their mothers. *Sex Roles, 38,* 975–985.

Benokraitis, N. V. (Ed.). (1997). *Subtle sexism: Current practice and prospects for change.* Thousand Oaks, CA: Sage.

Benokraitis, N. V., & Feagin, J. R. (1986). *Modern sexism: Blatant, subtle, and covert discrimination.* Englewood Cliffs, NJ: Prentice-Hall.

Bequaert, L. (1976). *Single women alone and together.* Boston: Beacon.

Berardo, D. H., Shehen, C. L., & Leslie, G. R. (1987). A residue of tradition: Jobs, careers, and spouses' time in housework. *Journal of Marriage and the Family, 49,* 381–390.

Berenbaum, S. A., & Hines, M. (1992). Early androgens are related to childhood sex-typed toy preferences. *Psychological Science, 3,* 203–206.

Berger, P. L., & Luckmann, T. (1966). *The social construction of reality: A treatise in the sociology of knowledge.* Garden City, NY: Doubleday.

Berger, R. M. (1990). Passing: Impact of the quality of same-sex couple relationships. *Social Work, 35,* 328–332.

Bergeron, S. M., & Senn, C. Y. (1998). Body image and socio-cultural norms: A comparison of heterosexual and lesbian women. *Psychology of Women Quarterly, 22,* 385–401.

Bergman, L. (1992). Dating violence among high school students. *Social Work, 37,* 21–27.

Berk, R. A. (1993). What the evidence shows: On the average, we can do no better than arrest. In R. J. Gelles & D. R. Loseke (Eds.), *Current controversies on family violence* (pp. 323–336). Newbury Park, CA: Sage.

Berman, P. W. (1980). Are women more responsive than men to the young? A review of developmental and situational variables. *Psychological Bulletin, 88,* 668–695.

Bermant, G., & Davidson, J. M. (1974). *Biological bases of sexual behavior.* New York: Harper & Row.

Bernard, C., & Schlaffer, E. (1983). The man in the street: Why he harasses. In L. Richardson & V. Taylor (Eds.), *Feminist frontiers: Rethinking sex, gender, and society.* New York: Random House.

Bernard, J. (1972). *The future of marriage.* New York: World.

Bernard, J. (1974). *The future of motherhood*. New York: Penguin.

Bernard, J. (1981). The good provider role: Its rise and fall. *American Psychologist, 36*, 1–12.

Bernard, M., Itzin, C., Phillipson, C., & Skucha, J. (1995). Gendered work, gendered retirement. In S. Arber & J. Ginn (Eds.), *Connecting gender and aging: A sociological approach* (pp. 56–68). Buckingham, UK: Open University Press.

Berryman-Fink, C., & Verderber, K. S. (1985). Attributions of the term feminist: A factor analytic development of a measuring instrument. *Psychology of Women Quarterly, 9*, 51–64.

Bersoff, D., & Crosby, F. (1984). Job satisfaction and family status. *Personality and Social Psychology Bulletin, 10*, 79–84.

Besnier, N. (1996). Polynesian gender liminality through time and space. In G. Herdt (Ed.), *Third sex, third gender: Beyond sexual dimorphism in culture and history* (pp. 285–328). New York: Zone Books.

Bethke, T. M., & DeJoy, D. M. (1993). An experimental study of factors influencing the acceptability of dating violence. *Journal of Interpersonal Violence, 8*, 36–51.

Betz, N. E., & Fitzgerald, L. E. (1987). *The career psychology of women*. New York: Academic Press.

Beyene, Y. (1989). *From menarche to menopause: Reproductive lives of peasant women in two cultures*. Albany: State University of New York Press.

Biaggio, M., & Brownell, A. (1996). Addressing sexual harassment: Strategies for prevention and change. In M. A. Paludi (Ed.), *Sexual harassment on college campuses: Abusing the ivory power* (pp. 215–234). Albany: State University of New York Press.

Bianchi, S. M., & Spain, D. (1986). *American women in transition*. New York: Russell Sage Foundation.

Biernat, M., & Kobrynowicz, D. (1999). A shifting standards perspective on the complexity of gender stereotypes and gender stereotyping. In W. B. Swann, Jr., J. H. Langlois, & L. A. Gilbert (Eds.), *Sexism and stereotypes: The gender science of Janet Taylor Spence* (pp. 75–106). Washington, DC: American Psychological Association.

Biernat, M., Manis, M., & Nelson, T. E. (1991). Stereotyping and standards of judgment. *Journal of Personality and Social Psychology, 60*, 485–499.

Bigler, R. S. (1995). The role of classification skill in moderating environmental influences on children's gender stereotyping: A study of the functional use of gender in the classroom. *Child Development, 66*, 1072–1087.

Bigler, R. S. (1997). Conceptual and methodological issues in the measurement of children's sex typing. *Psychology of Women Quarterly, 21*, 53–69.

Bigler, R. S. (1999). Psychological interventions designed to counter sexism in children: Empirical limitations and theoretical foundations. In W. B. Swann Jr., J. H. Langlois, & L. A. Gilbert (Eds.), *Sexism and stereotypes in modern society: The gender science of Janet Taylor Spence* (pp. 129–151). Washington, DC: American Psychological Association.

Billingham, R. E. (1987). Courtship violence: The patterns of conflict resolution strategies across seven levels of emotional commitment. *Family Relations, 36*, 283–289.

Billingham, R. E., & Sack, A. R. (1986). Courtship violence and the interactive status of the relationship. *Journal of Adolescent Research, 1*, 315–325.

Bing, V. M., & Reid, P. T. (1996). Unknown women and unknowing research: Consequences of color and class in feminist psychology. In N. R. Goldberger & J. M. Tarule (Eds.), *Knowledge, difference, and power: Essays inspired by "Women's Ways of Knowing"* (pp. 175–202). New York: Basic Books.

Birrell, S. J., & Cole, S. L. (1990). Double fault: Renee Richards and the construction and naturalization of difference. *Sociology of Sport Journal, 7*, 1–21.

Bishop, N. (1989). Abortion: The controversial choice. In J. Freeman (Ed.), *Women: A feminist perspective* (4th ed., pp. 45–56). Mountain View, CA: Mayfield.

Bjorkqvist, K. (1994). Sex differences in physical, verbal, and indirect aggression: A review of recent research. *Sex Roles, 30*, 177–188.

Black, J., & Underwood, J. (1998). Young, female, and gay: Lesbian students and the school environment. *Professional School Counseling, 1*(3), 15–20.

Black, S. M., & Hill, C. E. (1984). The psychological well-being of women in their middle years. *Psychology of Women Quarterly, 8*, 282–292.

Blair, S. L., & Lichter, D. T. (1991). Measuring the division of household labor: Gender segregation of housework among American couples. *Journal of Family Issues, 12*, 91–113.

Blanchard, R. (1985). Gender dysphoria and gender reorientation. In B. W. Steiner (Ed.),

Gender dysphoria: Development, research, management. New York: Plenum.

Blechman, E. A. (1984). Women's behavior in a man's world: Sex differences in competence. In E. A. Blechman (Ed.), *Behavior modification with women* (pp. 3–33). New York: Guilford Press.

Bleier, R. (1988). Science and the construction of meanings in the neurosciences. In S. V. Rosser (Ed.), *Feminism within the science and health care professions: Overcoming resistance.* Elmsford, NY: Pergamon Press.

Bleier, R. (Ed.). (1986). *Feminist approaches to science.* Elmsford, NY: Pergamon Press.

Block, J. H. (1983). Differential premises arising from differential socialization of the sexes: Some conjectures. *Child Development, 54,* 1335–1354.

Blood, R. O., & Wolfe, D. M. (1960). *Husbands and wives.* New York: Free Press.

Blum, R. W., & Resnick, M. D. (1982). Adolescent sexual decision-making: Contraception, pregnancy, abortion, and motherhood. *Pediatric Annals, 11,* 797–805.

Blumstein, P., & Schwartz, P. (1983). *American couples.* New York: William Morrow.

Blumstein, P. W., & Schwartz, P. (1993). Bisexuality, Some social psychological issues. In L. D. Garnets & D. C. Kimmel (Eds.), *Psychological perspectives on lesbian and gay male experiences* (pp. 168–184). New York: Columbia University Press.

Boardman, S. K., Harrington, C. C., & Horowitz, S. V. (1987). Successful women: A psychological investigation of family class and education origins. In B. A. Gutek & L. Larwood (Eds.), *Women's career development* (pp. 66–85). Newbury Park, CA: Sage.

Boatwright, K. J., Gilbert, M. S., Forrest, L., & Ketzenberger, K. (1996). Impact of identity development upon career trajectory: Listening to the voices of lesbian women. *Journal of Vocational Behavior, 48,* 210–228.

Bogal-Allbritten, R. B., & Allbritten, W. L. (1987). Availability of community services to student victims of courtship violence. *Response to the Victimization of Women and Children, 10,* 22–24.

Bograd, M. (1988). Feminist perspectives on wife abuse: An introduction. In K. Yllo and M. Bograd (Eds.), *Feminist perspectives on wife abuse* (pp. 11–26). Berkeley, CA: Sage.

Bohan, J. (1990). Contextual history: A framework for re-placing women in the history of psychology. *Psychology of Women Quarterly, 14,* 213–227.

Bohan, J., & Russell. (1999). Support networks for lesbian, gay, and bisexual students. In S. Davis, M. Crawford, & J. Sebrechts (Eds.), *Coming into her own: Encouraging educational success in girls and women,* pp. 279–294. San Francisco: Jossey-Bass.

Bohan, J. S. (1996). *Psychology and sexual orientation: Coming to terms.* New York: Routledge.

Bolin, A. (1996). Transcending and transgendering: Male-to-female transsexuals, dichotomy, and diversity. In G. Herdt (Ed.), *Third sex, third gender: Beyond sexual dimorphism in culture and history* (pp. 447–485). New York: Zone Books.

Bond, M. (1991). Division 27 sexual harassment survey: Definitions impact and environmental context. In M. A. Paludi & R. B. Barickman (Eds.), *Academic and workplace sexual harassment: A resource manual.* Albany: State University of New York.

Bond, S., & Cash, T. F. (1992). Black beauty: Skin color and body images among African-American college women. *Journal of Applied Social Psychology, 22,* 874–888.

Bondurant, B. (1994, March). *Men's perceptions of women's sexual interest: Sexuality or sexual aggression?* Paper presented at Southeastern Psychological Association 40th Annual Meeting, New Orleans.

Bondurant, B., & Donat, P. L. N. (in press). Perceptions of women's sexual interest and acquaintance rape: The role of sexual overperception and affective attitudes. *Psychology of Women Quarterly.*

Boney-McCoy, S., & Finkelhor, D. (1995). Psychosocial sequelae of violent victimization in a national youth sample. *Journal of Consulting and Clinical Psychology, 63,* 726–736.

Bookwala, J., Frieze, I. H., Smith, C., & Ryan, K. (1992). Predictors of dating violence: A multivariate analysis. *Violence and Victims, 7,* 297–311.

Bordo, S. (1993). *Unbearable weight: Feminism, western culture and the body.* Berkeley, CA: University of California Press.

Bornstein, K. (1994). *Gender outlaw: On men, women, and the rest of us.* New York: Routledge.

Bose, C. E. (1987). Dual spheres. In B. B. Hess & M. M. Ferree (Eds.), *Analyzing gender: A handbook of social science research* (pp. 267–285). Newbury Park, CA: Sage.

Boswell, S. L. (1979). *Nice girls don't study mathematics: The perspective from elementary school.* Presented at the meeting of the American Educational Research Association, San Francisco.

Boswell, S. L. (1985). The influence of sex-role stereotyping on women's attitudes and achievement in mathematics. In S. F. Chipman, L. R. Brush, & D. M. Wilson (Eds.), *Women and mathematics: Balancing the equation* (pp. 175–198). Hillsdale, NJ: Erlbaum.

Bouhoutsos, J., Holroyd, J., Lerman, H., Forer, B. R., & Greenberg, M. (1983). Sexual intimacy between psychotherapists and patients. *Professional Psychology, Research and Practice, 14,* 185–196.

Bound, J., Duncan, G. J., Laren, D. S., & Oleiniek, L. (1991). Poverty dynamics in widowhood. *Journal of Gerontology: Social Sciences, 46,* S115–S124.

Bowker, L. (1993). A battered woman's problems are social, not psychological. In R. J. Gelles & D. R. Loseke (Eds.), *Current controversies on family violence* (pp. 154–166). Newbury Park, CA: Sage.

Boyatzis, C. J., Nallis, M., & Leon, I. (1999). Effects of game type on children's gender-based peer preferences: A naturalistic observational study. *Sex Roles, 40,* 93–105.

Boyd, B., & Wandersman, A. (1991). Predicting undergraduate condom use with the Fishbein and Ajzen and the Triandis attitude-behavior models: Implications for public health interventions. *Journal of Applied Social Psychology, 21,* 1810–1830.

Boyd, J. A. (1990). Ethnic and cultural diversity: Keys to power. In L. S. Brown & M. P. P. Root (Eds.), *Diversity and complexity in feminist therapy* (pp. 151–167). New York: Harrington Park Press.

Brabant, S., & Mooney, L. (1986). Sex role stereotyping in the Sunday comics: Ten years later. *Sex Roles, 14,* 141–148.

Brabant, S., & Mooney, L. A. (1997). Sex role stereotyping in the Sunday comics: A twenty year update. *Sex Roles, 37,* 269–281.

Brabeck, M., & Brown, L. (1997). Feminist theory and psychological practice. In J. Worell & N. G. Johnson (Eds.), *Shaping the future of feminist psychology: Education, research, and practice* (pp. 15–35). Washington, DC: American Psychological Association.

Bradbard, M. R., & Endsley, R. C. (1983). The effects of sex-typed labeling on preschool children's information-seeking and retention. *Sex Roles, 9,* 247–260.

Braden, A. (1986). Shoulder to shoulder. In J. B. Cole (Ed.), *All American women: Lines that divide, ties that bind* (pp. 74–80). New York: Macmillan.

Bradley, C. (1993). Women's power, children's labor. *Behavior Science Research, 27,* 70–96.

Bradshaw, C. K. (1994). Asian and Asian American women: Historical and political considerations in psychotherapy. In L. Comas-Diaz & B. Greene (Eds.), *Women of color: Integrating ethnic and gender identities in psychotherapy.* New York: Guilford.

Bradsher, J. E. (1997). Old women and widowhood. In J. M. Coyle (Ed.), *Handbook on women and aging* (pp. 418–429). Westport, CT: Greenwood Press.

Brand, P. A., & Kidd, A. H. (1986). Frequency of physical aggression in heterosexual and female homosexual dyads. *Psychological Reports, 59,* 1307–1313.

Breedlove, S. M. (1994). Sexual differentiation of the human nervous system. *Annual Review of Psychology, 45,* 389–418.

Breines, W., & Gordon, L. (1983). The new scholarship on family violence. *Signs, 8,* 490–531.

Brelis, M. (1999, February 7). The fading "gay gene." *The Boston Sunday Globe,* pp. C1, C5.

Bridges, J. S. (1993). Pink or blue: Gender-stereotypic perceptions of infants as conveyed by birth congratulations cards. *Psychology of Women Quarterly, 17,* 193–205.

Bridges, J. S., & Orza, A. M. (1992). The effects of employment role and motive for employment on the perceptions of mothers. *Sex Roles, 27,* 331–343.

Briere, J., & Lanktree, C. (1983). Sex-role related effects of sex bias in language. *Sex Roles, 9,* 625–632.

Brinkerhoff, D. B., & Booth, A. (1984). Gender, dominance, and stress. *Journal of Social and Biological Structures, 7,* 159–177.

Brod, H. (1987). Cross-culture, cross-gender: Cultural marginality and gender transcendence. *American Behavioral Scientist, 31,* 5–11.

Brodsky, A. (1973). The consciousness-raising group as a model for therapy with women. *Psychotherapy: Theory, Research, and Practice, 10,* 24–29.

Brody, E. (1981). "Women in the middle" and family help to older people. *Gerontologist, 21,* 471–485.

Brody, L. R., Lovas, G. S., & Hay, D. H. (1995). Gender differences in anger and fear as a function of situational context. *Sex Roles, 32,* 47–78.

Bromberg, J. J. (1997). *The body project: An intimate history of American girls.* New York: Random House.

Brooks, L., & Perot, A. (1991). Reporting sexual harassment: Exploring a predictive model. *Psychology of Women Quarterly, 15,* 31–47.

Brooks-Gunn, J. (1986). The relationship of maternal beliefs about sex typing to maternal and young children's behavior. *Sex Roles, 14*, 21–35.

Brooks-Gunn, J. (1987a). The impact of puberty and sexual activity upon the health and education of adolescent girls and boys. *Peabody Journal of Education, 64*, 88–112.

Brooks-Gunn, J. (1987b). Pubertal processes and girls' psychological adaptation. In R. M. Lerner & T. T. Foch (Eds.), *Biological-psychosocial interactions in early adolescence* (pp. 123–153). Hillsdale NJ: Erlbaum.

Brooks-Gunn, J. (1988). Antecedents and consequences of variations in girls' maturational timing. *Journal of Adolescent Health Care, 9*, 365–373.

Brooks-Gunn, J., & Furstenberg, F. F., Jr. (1989). Adolescent sexual behavior. *American Psychologist, 44*, 249–257.

Brooks-Gunn, J., & Mathews, W. S. (1979). *He & she: How children develop their sex-role identity.* Englewood Cliffs, NJ: Prentice-Hall.

Brooks-Gunn, J., & Petersen, A. C. (1983). (Eds.), *Girls at puberty: Biological and psychological perspectives.* New York: Plenum.

Brooks-Gunn, J., & Ruble, D. N. (1983). Dysmenorrhea in adolescence. In S. Golub (Ed.), *Menarche* (pp. 251–261). Lexington, MA: Lexington Books.

Brooks-Gunn, J., Samelson, M., Warren, M. P., & Fox, R. (1986). Physical similarity of and disclosure of menarcheal status to friends: Effects of age and pubertal status. *Journal of Early Adolescence, 6*, 3–14.

Brooks-Gunn, J., & Zehayhevich. (1989). Parent-daughter relationships in early adolescence: A developmental perspective. In K. Kreppner & R. Lerner (Eds.), *Family systems and life-span development.* Hillsdale, NJ: Erlbaum.

Broughton, J. M. (1983). Women's rationality and men's virtues: A critique of gender dualism in Gilligan's theory of moral development. *Social Research, 50*, 597–642.

Broverman, I. K., Vogel, S. R., Broverman, D. M., Clarkson, F. E., & Rosenkrantz, P. S. (1972). Sex-role stereotypes: A current appraisal. *Journal of Social Issues, 28*, 59–78.

Brown, B. A., Frankel, B. G., & Fennell, M. P. (1989). Hugs or shrugs: Parental and peer influence on continuity of involvement in sport by female adolescents. *Sex Roles, 20*, 397–409.

Brown, D. R., & Gary, L. E. (1985). Social support network differential among married and nonmarried black families. *Psychology of Women Quarterly, 9*, 229–241.

Brown, E. A. (1989, June 9). Happily ever after. *Christian Science Monitor*, p. 13.

Brown, J. D., & Campbell, K. (1986). Race and gender in music videos: The same beat but a different drummer. *Journal of Communication, 36*, 94–106.

Brown, J. K. (1982). A cross-cultural exploration of the end of the childbearing years. In A. M. Voda, M. Dinnerstein, & S. R. O'Donnell (Eds.), *Changing perspectives on menopause* (pp. 51–59). Austin: University of Texas Press.

Brown, L. M., & Gilligan, C. (1992). *Meeting at the crossroads: Women's psychology and girls' development.* Cambridge, MA: Harvard University Press.

Brown, L. M., & Gilligan, C. (1993). Meeting at the crossroads: Women's psychology and girls' development. *Feminism & Psychology, 3*, 11–35.

Brown, L. S. (1986). *Diagnosis and the Zeitgeist: The politics of masochism in the DSM-III-R.* Paper presented at the meeting of the American Psychological Association, Washington, DC.

Brown, L. S. (1994). *Subversive dialogues: Theory in feminist therapy.* New York: Basic Books.

Brown, L. S. (1996). Politics of memory, politics of incest: Doing therapy and politics that really matter. *Women & Therapy, 19*, 5–18.

Brown, L. S., & Burman, E. (1997). Feminist responses to the "false memory" debate. *Feminism & Psychology, 7*, 7–16.

Brown, S. (1988, July–August). Osteoporosis: Sorting fact from fallacy. *The Network News: National Women's Health Network*, pp. 1–2.

Browne, A. (1987). *When battered women kill.* New York: Macmillan.

Browne, A. (1993). Violence against women by male partners: Prevalence, outcomes, and policy implications. *American Psychologist, 48*, 1077–1087.

Browne, A., & Finkelhor, D. (1986). Impact of sexual abuse: A review of the research. *Psychological Bulletin, 99*, 66–77.

Browne, A., & Williams, K. R. (1993). Gender, intimacy, and lethal violence: Trends from 1976 to 1987. *Gender & Society, 7*, 78–98.

Brownmiller, S. (1975). *Against our will: Men, women, and rape.* New York: Simon & Schuster.

Bryant, B. K. (1985). The neighborhood walk: Sources of support in middle childhood. *Monographs of the Society for Research in Child Development, 50*, 11985.

Bryer, J. B., Nelson, B. A., Miller, J. B., & Krol, P. A. (1987). Childhood sexual and physical abuse as factors in adult psychiatric illness. *American Journal of Psychiatry, 144*, 1426–1430.

Buchman, D. D., & Funk, J. B. (1996). Video and computer games in the 90s: Children's time commitment and game preferences. *Children Today, 24,* 12–16, 31.

Buhl, M. (1989, September/October). The feminist mystique. *In View,* p. 16.

Bumagin, V. E. (1982). Growing old female. *Journal of Psychiatric Treatment and Evaluation, 4,* 155–159.

Buntaine, R. L., & Costenbader, V. K. (1997). Self-reported differences in the experience and expression of anger between girls and boys. *Sex Roles, 36,* 625–637.

Burcky, W., Reuterman, N., & Kopsky, S. (1988). Dating violence among high school students. *School Counselor, 35,* 353–358.

Burke, P. J., & Cast, A. D. (1997). Stability and change in the gender identities of newly married couples. *Social Psychology Quarterly, 60*(4), 277–290.

Burke, R. J. (1997). Alternate family structures: A career advantage? *Psychological Reports, 81*(3, Pt. 1), 812–814.

Burke, R. J., & McKeen, C. A. (1997). Gender effects in mentoring relationships. In R. Crandall (Ed.), *Handbook of gender research* (pp. 91–104). Corte Madera, CA: Select Press.

Burn, S. M., O'Neil, A. K., & Nederend, S. (1996). Childhood tomboyism and adult androgyny. *Sex Roles, 34,* 419–428.

Burns, A., & Homel, R. (1989). Gender division of tasks by parents and their children. *Psychology of Women Quarterly, 13,* 113–125.

Burns, J. (1992). Mad or just plain bad? Gender and the work of forensic clinical psychologists. In J. M. Ussher & P. Nicolson (Eds.), *Gender issues in clinical psychology* (pp. 106–128). London: Routledge.

Busby, L. J. (1975, Autumn). Sex-role research on the mass media. *Journal of Communication,* 107–131.

Busby, L. J., & Leichty, G. (1993). Feminism and advertising in traditional and nontraditional women's magazines, 1950s–1980s. *Journalism Quarterly, 70,* 247–264.

Buschman, J. K., & Lenart, S. (1996). "I am not a feminist but . . .": College women, feminism, and negative experiences. *Political Psychology, 17,* 59–75.

Bush, T. L. (1990). The epidemiology of cardiovascular disease in postmenopausal women. In M. Flint, F. Kronenberg, & W. Utian (Eds.), *Multidisciplinary perspectives on menopause. Annals of the New York Academy of Sciences, 592,* 263–271.

Buss, D. M. (1989). Sex differences in human mate preferences: Evolutionary hypotheses tested in 37 cultures. *Behavioral and Brain Sciences, 12,* 1–49.

Buss, D. M. (1995). Psychological sex differences: Origins through sexual selection. *American Psychologist, 50,* 164–168.

Buss, D. M., et al. (1990). International preferences in selecting mates: A study of 37 cultures. *Journal of Cross-Cultural Psychology, 21,* 5–47.

Butler, D., & Geis, F. L. (1990). Nonverbal affect responses to male and female leaders: Implications for leadership evaluations. *Journal of Personality and Social Psychology, 58,* 48–59.

Butler, L. D., & Nolen-Hoeksema, S. (1994). Gender differences in responses to depressed mood in a college sample. *Sex Roles, 30,* 331–346.

Butler, R. N. (1980). Ageism: A foreword. *Journal of Social Issues, 36,* 8–11.

Buzawa, E. S., & Buzawa, C. G. (1993). The scientific is not conclusive: Arrest is no panacea. In R. J. Gelles & D. R. Loseke (Eds.), *Current controversies on family violence* (pp. 336–356). Newbury Park, CA: Sage.

Cabaj, R. P., & Purcell, D. W. (Eds.). (1998). *On the road to same-sex marriage: A supportive guide to psychological, political, and legal issues.* San Francisco: Josey-Bass.

Cahill, B., & Adams, E. (1997). An exploratory study of early childhood teachers' attitudes toward gender roles. *Sex Roles, 36,* 517–529.

Caldera, Y. M., Huston, A. C., & O'Brien, M. (1989). Social interactions and play patterns of parents and toddlers with feminine, masculine, and neutral toys. *Child Development, 60,* 70–76.

Caldera, Y. M., & Sciaraffa, A. (1998). Parent-toddler play with feminine toys: Are all dolls the same? *Sex Roles, 39,* 657–668.

Calderone, K. L. (1990). The influence of gender on the frequency of pain and sedative medication administered to postoperative patients. *Sex Roles, 23,* 713–725.

Caldwell, M. A., & Peplau, L. A. (1984). The balance of power in lesbian relationships. *Sex Roles, 10,* 587–599.

Calhoun, K. S., Bernat, J. A., Clum, G. A., & Frame, C. L. (1997). Sexual coercion and attraction to sexual aggression in a community sample of young men. *Journal of Interpersonal Violence, 12*(1), 392–406.

Califia, P. (1997). *Sex changes: The politics of transgenderism.* San Francisco, CA: Cleis Press.

Campbell, B., Schellenberg, E. G., & Senn, C. Y.

(1997). Evaluating measures of contemporary sexism. *Psychology of Women Quarterly, 21,* 89–101.

Campbell, E. K., & Campbell, P. G. (1997). Family size and sex preferences and eventual fertility in Botswana. *Journal of Biosocial Science, 29,* 191–204.

Campbell, K. E., Kleim, D. M., & Olson, K. R. (1992). Conversational activity and interruptions among women and men. *Journal of Social Psychology, 132,* 419–421.

Campbell, R., Sullivan, C. M., & Davidson, W. S. II. (1995). Women who use domestic violence shelters: Changes in depression over time. *Psychology of Women Quarterly, 19,* 237–255.

Campenni, C. E. (1999). Gender stereotyping of children's toys: A comparison of parents and nonparents. *Sex Roles, 40,* 121–138.

Canetto, S. S. (1992). Gender and suicide in the elderly. *Suicide and Life-Threatening Behavior, 22,* 80–97.

Canetto, S. S. (1997). Meanings of gender and suicidal behavior during adolescence. *Suicide and Life Threatening Behavior, 27,* 339–351.

Canino, G. J., Rubio-Stipec, M., Shrout, P., Bravo, M., Stolberg, R., & Bird, H. R. (1987). Sex differences and depression in Puerto Rico. *Psychology of Women Quarterly, 11,* 443–459.

Canter, R. (1982). Achievement in women: Implications for equal employment opportunity policy. In B. A. Gutek (Ed.), *Sex role stereotyping and affirmative action policy* (pp. 9–64). Los Angeles: Institute of Industrial Relations, University of California.

Cantor, M. G. (1987). Popular culture and the portrayal of women: Content and control. In B. B. Hess & M. M. Ferree (Eds.), *Analyzing gender* (pp. 190–214). Newbury Park, CA: Sage.

Caplan, P. J. (1989). *Don't blame mother.* New York: Harper & Row.

Caplan, P. J. (1991). Delusional dominating personality disorder (DDPD). *Feminism & Psychology, 1,* 171–174.

Caplan, P. J. (1995). *They say you're crazy: How the most powerful psychiatrists decide who's normal.* Reading, MA: Addison-Wesley.

Caplan, P. J., & Hall-McCorquodale, I. (1985). Mother-blaming in major clinical journals. *American Journal of Orthopsychiatry, 55,* 345–353.

Cardell, M., Finn, S., & Marecek, J. (1981). Sex-role identity, sex-role behavior, and satisfaction in heterosexual, lesbian, and gay male couples. *Psychology of Women Quarterly, 5,* 488–494.

Carey, C. M., & Mongeau, P. A. (1996). Communication and violence in courtship relationships. In D. D. Cahn & S. A. Lloyd (Eds.), *Family violence from a communication perspective.* Thousand Oaks, CA: Sage.

Carli, L. L. (1990). Gender, language, and influence. *Journal of Personality and Social Psychology, 59,* 941–951.

Carlson, B. E., & Videka-Sherman, L. (1990). An empirical test of androgyny in the middle years: Evidence from a national survey. *Sex Roles, 23,* 305–324.

Carmen, E. H., Russo, N. F., & Miller, J. B. (1981). Women's inequality and women's mental health: An overview. *American Journal of Psychiatry, 138,* 1319–1330.

Carp, F. M. (1997). Retirement and women. In J. M. Coyle (Ed.), *Handbook on women and aging* (pp. 112–128). Westport, CT: Greenwood Press.

Carr, J. G., Gilroy, F. D., & Sherman, M. F. (1996). Silencing the self and depression among women: The moderating role of race. *Psychology of Women Quarterly, 20,* 375–392.

Carson, D. K., Gertz, L. M., Donaldson, M. A., & Wonderlich, S. A. (1990). Family-of-origin characteristics and current family relationships of female adult incest victims. *Journal of Family Violence, 5,* 153–171.

Cartwright, L. K., & Wink, P. (1994). Personality change in women physicians from medical student year to mid 40s. *Psychology of Women Quarterly, 18,* 291–308.

Cash, T. F. (1995). Developmental teasing about physical appearance: Retrospective descriptions and relationships with body image. *Social Behavior & Personality, 25,* 123–130.

Cash, T. F., Ancis, J. R., & Strachan, M. D. (1997). Gender attitudes, feminist identity, and body images among college women. *Sex Roles, 36,* 433–448.

Cash, T. F., Gillen, B., & Burns, D. S. (1977). Sexism and "beautyism" in personnel consultant decision making. *Journal of Applied Psychology, 62,* 301–310.

Cass, V. C. (1979). Homosexual identity formation: A theoretical model. *Journal of Homosexuality, 4,* 219–235.

Cassell, J. (1997). Doing gender, doing surgery: Women surgeons in a man's profession. *Human Organization, 56*(1), 47–52.

Cate, C. A., Henton, J. M., Koval, J., Christopher, F. S., & Lloyd, S. (1982). Premarital abuse: A social psychological perspective. *Journal of Family Issues, 3,* 79–90.

Cauce, A. M., Hiraga, Y., Graves, D., Gonzales, N., Ryan-Finn, K., & Grove, K. (1996). African American mothers and their adolescent daughters: Closeness, conflict, and control. In B. J. R. Leadbeater & N. Way (Eds.), *Urban girls: Resisting stereotypes, creating identities* (pp. 100–116). New York: New York University Press.

Chacko, T. I. (1982). Women and equal employment opportunity: Some unintended effects. *Journal of Applied Psychology, 67,* 119–123.

Chaikin, S., & Pliner, P. (1987). Women, but not men, are what they eat: The effect of meal size and gender on perceived femininity and masculinity. *Personality and Social Psychology Bulletin, 13,* 166–176.

Chambless, D. L., & Goldstein, A. J. (1980). Anxieties: Agoraphobia and hysteria. In A. M. Brodsky & R. Hare-Mustin (Eds.), *Woman and psychotherapy: An assessment of research and practice* (pp. 113–134). New York: Guilford Press.

Chan, C. S. (1993). Issues of identity development among Asian-American lesbians and gay men. In L. D. Garnets & D. C. Kimmel (Eds.), *Psychological perspectives on lesbian and gay male experiences* (pp. 376–388). New York: Columbia University Press.

Chandani, A. T., McKenna, K. T., & Maas, F. (1989). Attitudes of university students towards the sexuality of physically disabled people. *British Journal of Occupational Therapy, 52,* 233–236.

Charlesworth, W. R., & Dzur, C. (1987). Gender comparisons of preschoolers' behavior and resource utilization in group problem-solving. *Child Development, 58,* 191–200.

Charlesworth, W. R., & LaFreniere, P. (1983). Dominance, friendship utilization and resource utilization in preschool children's groups. *Ethology and Sociobiology, 4,* 175–186.

Chavez, D. (1985). Perpetuation of gender inequality: A content analysis of comic strips. *Sex Roles, 13,* 93–102.

Cherlin, A. J. (1981). *Marriage, divorce, remarriage.* Cambridge, MA: Harvard University Press.

Chesler, P. (1972). *Women and madness.* New York: Doubleday.

Cheung, C., & Liu, E. S. (1997). Impacts of social pressure and social support on distress among single parents in China. *Journal of Divorce & Remarriage: International Studies, 26*(3/4), 65–82.

Chi, J. G., Dooling, E. C., & Gilles, F. H. (1977). Gyral development of the human brain. *Annals of Neurology, 1,* 86–93.

Chicago, J. (1990, March). *The birth project.* Women's History Month Lecture, Trenton State College, Trenton, NJ.

Childs, E. K. (1990). Therapy, feminist ethics, and the community of color with particular emphasis on the treatment of black women. In H. Lerman & N. Porter (Eds.), *Feminist ethics in psychotherapy* (pp. 195–203). New York: Springer.

Chilman, C. S. (1983). *Adolescent sexuality in a changing American society* (2nd ed.). New York: John Wiley & Sons.

Chin, J. L., & Russo, N. F. (1997). Feminist curriculum development: Principles and resources. In J. Worell & N. G. Johnson (Eds.), *Shaping the future of feminist psychology* (pp. 93–102). Washington, DC: American Psychological Association.

Chipman, S. F., Brush, L. R., & Wilson, D. M. (Eds.). (1985). *Women and mathematics: Balancing the equation.* Hillsdale, NJ: Erlbaum.

Chipman, S. F., & Thomas, V. G. (1985). Women's participation in mathematics: Outlining the problem. In S. F. Chipman, L. R. Brush, & D. M. Wilson (Eds.), *Women and mathematics: Balancing the equation* (pp. 1–24). Hillsdale, NJ: Erlbaum.

Chipman, S. F., & Wilson, D. M. (1985). Understanding mathematics course enrollment and mathematics achievement: A synthesis of the research. In S. F. Chipman, L. R. Brush, & D. M. Wilson (Eds.), *Women and mathematics: Balancing the equation* (pp. 275–328). Hillsdale, NJ: Erlbaum.

Chodorow, N. (1978). *The reproduction of mothering.* Berkeley, CA: University of California Press.

Chodorow, N. (1979). Feminism and difference: Gender relation and difference in psychoanalytic perspective. *Socialist Review, 46,* 42–64.

Choo, P., Levine, T., & Hatfield, E. (1997). Gender, love schemas, and reactions to romantic break-ups. In R. Crandall (Ed.), *Handbook of gender research* (pp. 143–160). Corte Madera, CA: Select Press.

Chow, E. N. (1987). The influence of sex-role identity and occupational attainment on the psychological well-being of Asian-American women. *Psychology of Women Quarterly, 11,* 69–82.

Chow, E. N-L. (1996). The development of feminist consciousness among Asian American women. In E. N-L Chow, D. Wilkinson, & M. B. Zinn (Eds.), *Race, class, & gender:*

Common bonds, different voices (pp. 251–264). Thousand Oaks, CA: Sage.

Chrisler, J. C., & Ghiz, L. (1993). Body image issues of older women. In N. D. Davis, E. Cole, & E. D. Rothblum (Eds.), *Faces of women and aging* (pp. 67–75). Binghamton, NY: Harrington Park Press.

Chrisler, J. C., & Hemstreet, A. H. (1995). The diversity of women's health needs. In J. C. Chrisler & A. H. Hemstreet (Eds.), *Variations on a theme: Diversity and the psychology of women* (pp. 1–28). Albany: State University of New York Press.

Chrisler, J. C., Johnston, I. K., Champagne, N. M., & Preston, K. E. (1994). Menstrual joy: The construct and its consequences. *Psychology of Women Quarterly, 18,* 375–387.

Chrisler, J. C., Torrey, J. W., & Matthes, M. A. (1990). Brittle bones and sagging breasts, loss of femininity and loss of sanity: The media describe the menopause. In A. M. Voda & R. Conover (Eds.), *Proceedings of the eighth conference of the Society for Menstrual Cycle Research* (pp. 23–35). Salt Lake City: Society for Menstrual Cycle Research.

Cialdini, R. B., Wosinska, W., Dabul, A. J., Wheatstone-Dion, R., & Heszen, I. (1998). When social role salience leads to social role rejection: Modest self-presentation among women in two countries. *Personality and Social Psychology Bulletin, 24,* 473–481.

Ciancanelli, P., & Berch, B. (1987). Gender and the GNP. In B. B. Hess and M. M. Ferree (Eds.), *Analyzing gender: A handbook of social science research* (pp. 244–266). Newbury Park, CA: Sage.

Clark, M. L., Beckett, J., Wells, M., & Dungee-Anderson, D. (1994). Courtship violence among African American college students. *Journal of Black Psychology, 20*(3), 264–281.

Cleek, M. G., & Pearson, T. A. (1985). Perceived causes of divorce: An analysis of interrelationships. *Journal of Marriage and the Family, 47,* 179–183.

Coates, E. J., & Feldman, R. S. (1996). Gender differences in nonverbal correlates of social status. *Personality and Social Psychology Bulletin, 22,* 1014–1022.

Code, L. B. (1983). Responsibility and the epistemic community: Woman's place. *Social Research, 50,* 537–555.

Cohen, B. P., Berger, J., & Zelditch, M. (1972). Status conceptions and interactions: A case study of developing cumulative knowledge. In C. McClintock (Ed.), *Experimental social psychology.* New York: Holt, Rinehart, & Winston.

Cohen, C. E. (1981). Person categories and social perception: Testing some boundaries of the processing effects of prior knowledge. *Journal of Personality and Social Psychology, 40,* 441–452.

Cohen, L. L., & Swim, J. R. (1995). The differential impact of gender ratios on women and men: Tokenism, self-confidence, and expectations. *Personality and Social Psychology Bulletin, 21,* 876–884.

Colapinto, J. (1997, December 11). The true story of John/Joan. *Rolling Stone,* pp. 54–97.

Colby, A., & Damon, W. (1983). Listening to a different voice: A review of Gilligan's In a different voice. *Merrill-Palmer Quarterly, 29,* 473–481.

Cole, T. R. (1992). *The journey of life: A cultural history of aging in America.* New York: Cambridge University Press.

Coles, R. (1985). *Sex and the American teenager.* New York: Rolling Stone Press.

Collaer, M. L., & Hines, M. (1995). Human behavioral sex differences: A role for gonadal hormones during early development? *Psychological Bulletin, 118,* 55–107.

Collins, M. E. (1998). Factors influencing sexual victimization and revictimization in a sample of adolescent mothers. *Journal of Interpersonal Violence, 13,* 3–24.

Collins, P. H. (1991). The meaning of motherhood in Black culture and Black mother-daughter relationships. In P. Bell-Scott, B. Guy-Sheftall, J. J. Royster, J. Sims-Wood, M. DiCosta-Willis, & L. P. Fultz (Eds.), *Double stitch: Black women write about mothers and daughters* (pp. 42–60). New York: HarperCollins.

Collins, P. H. (1993b). The sexual politics of Black womanhood. In P. B. Bart & E. G. Moran (Eds.), *Violence against women: The bloody footprints* (pp. 85–104). Newbury Park, CA: Sage.

Collins, R. K. L., & Skover, D. M. (1993). Commerce and communication. *Texas Law Review. 71,* 697–746.

Collins, S. K. (1988). Women at the top of women's fields: Social work, nursing, and education. In A. Statham, E. M. Miller, & H. O. Mauksch (Eds.), *The worth of women's work: A qualitative synthesis* (pp. 187–201). Albany, NY: State University of New York Press.

Comas-Diaz, L. (1987). Feminist therapy with mainland Puerto Rican women. *Psychology of Women Quarterly, 11,* 461–474. APA.

Committee on Women in Psychology. (1985,

October). Statement on proposed diagnostic categories for DSM-III-R. *American Psychological Association,* Washington, DC.

Comstock, G. (1991). *Television and the American child.* San Diego: Academic Press.

Condit, C. M. (1996). Media bias for reproductive technologies. In R. L. Parrott & C. M. Condit (Eds.), *Evaluating women's health messages* (pp. 341–355). Thousand Oaks: Sage.

Condon, J. (1987). Psychological and physical symptoms during pregnancy: A comparison of male and female expectant parents. *Journal of Infant and Reproductive Psychology, 5,* 207–220.

Condry, J. C., Jr., & Ross, D. F. (1985). Sex and aggression: The influence of gender label on the perception of aggression in children. *Child Development, 56,* 225–233.

Condry, S. M., Condry, J. C., Jr., & Pogatshnik, L. W. (1983). Sex differences: A study of the ear of the beholder. *Sex Roles, 9,* 697–704.

Connidis, I. A., & McMullin, J. A. (1996). Reasons for and perceptions of childlessness among older persons: Exploring the impact of marital status and gender. *Journal of Aging Studies, 10*(3), 205–222.

Conway, M., Pizzamiglio, M. T., & Mount, L. (1996). Status, communality, and agency: Implications for stereotypes of gender and other groups. *Journal of Personality and Social Psychology, 71,* 25–38.

Cooksey, E. C., Rindfuss, R. R., & Guilkey, D. K. (1996). The initiation of adolescent sexual and contraceptive behavior during changing times. *Journal of Health and Social Behavior, 37*(1), 59–74.

Cooper, V. W. (1985). Women in popular music: A quantitative analysis of feminine images over time. *Sex Roles, 13,* 499–506.

Corbett, K. (1987). The role of sexuality and sex equity in the education of disabled women. *Peabody Journal of Education, 64,* 198–212.

Corley, M. C., & Mauksch, H. O. (1988). Registered nurses, gender, and commitment. In A. Statham, E. M. Miller, & H. O. Mauksch (Eds.), *The worth of women's work: A qualitative synthesis* (pp. 135–150). Albany, NY: State University of New York Press.

Cortina, L. M., Swan, S., Fitzgerald, L. F., & Waldo, C. (1998). Sexual harassment and assault: Chilling the climate for women in academia. *Psychology of Women Quarterly, 22,* 419–441.

Costello, C., & Stone, A. J. (Eds.). (1994). *The American woman 1994–1995: Where we stand–Women and health.* New York: Norton.

Cota, A. A., & Dion, K. L. (1986). Salience of gender and sex composition of ad hoc groups: An experimental test of distinctiveness theory. *Journal of Personality and Social Psychology, 50,* 770–776.

Courtois, C. A. (1988). *Healing the incest wound: Adult survivors in therapy.* New York: W. W. Norton.

Covey, H. C. (1988). Historical terminology used to represent older people. *Gerontologist, 28,* 291–297.

Cowan, G. (1995). Black and White (and blue): Ethnicity and pornography. In H. Landrine (Ed.), *Bringing cultural diversity to feminist psychology: Theory, research, practice* (pp. 397–411). Washington, DC: American Psychological Association.

Cowan, G., & Hoffman, C. D. (1986). Gender stereotyping in young children: Evidence to support a concept-learning approach. *Sex Roles, 14,* 211–224.

Cowan, G., & O'Brien, M. (1990). Gender and survival vs. death in slasher films: A content analysis. *Sex Roles, 23,* 187–196.

Cowan, G., Warren, L. W., & Young, J. L. (1985). Medical perceptions of menopausal symptoms. *Psychology of Women Quarterly, 9,* 3–14.

Coward, R. T., & Dwyer, J. W. (1990). The association of gender, sibling network composition, and patterns of parent care by adult children. *Research on Aging, 12,* 158–181.

Cowen, J. R. (1993, October). *Survey finds that 70% of women rabbis sexually harassed.* Moment, 34–37.

Cozzarelli, C., & Major, B. (1998). The impact of antiabortion activities on women seeking abortions. In L. J. Beckman & S. M. Harvey (Eds.), *The new civil war: The psychology, culture, and politics of abortion* (pp. 81–104). Washington, DC: American Psychological Association.

Craig, R. S. (1992). The effect of television day part on gender portrayals in television commercials: A content analysis. *Sex Roles, 26,* 197–211.

Crandall, C. S. (1994). Prejudice against fat people: Ideology and self interest. *Journal of Personality and Social Psychology, 66,* 882–894.

Crandall, C. S. (1995). Do parents discriminate against their heavyweight daughters? *Personality and Social Psychology Bulletin, 21,* 724–735.

Crandall, C. S., & Martinez, R. (1996). Culture, ideology, and anti-fat attitudes. *Personality and Social Psychology Bulletin, 22,* 1165–1176.

Crawford, M. (1978, November). Climbing the ivy-covered walls: How colleges deny tenure to women. *Ms.*, pp. 61–63, 91–94.

Crawford, M. (1981, August). Emmy Noether: She did Einstein's math. *Ms.*, pp. 86–89.

Crawford, M. (1982). In pursuit of the well-rounded life: Women scholars and the family. In M. Kehoe (Ed.), *Handbook for women scholars* (pp. 89–96). San Francisco: Americas Behavioral Research.

Crawford, M. (1988). Gender, age, and the social evaluation of assertion. *Behavior Modification, 12,* 549–564.

Crawford, M. (1989). Agreeing to differ: Feminist epistemologies and women's ways of knowing. In M. Crawford & M. Gentry (Eds.), *Gender and thought* (pp. 128–145). New York: Springer Verlag.

Crawford, M. (1995). *Talking difference: On gender and language.* London: Sage.

Crawford, M., & Chaffin, R. (1997). The meanings of difference: Cognition in social and cultural context. In P. J. Caplan, M. Crawford, J. S. Hyde, & J. T. E. Richardson, *Gender differences in human cognition* (pp. 81–130). New York: Oxford.

Crawford, M., & English, L. (1984). Generic versus specific inclusion of women in language: Effects on recall. *Journal of Psycholinguistic Research, 13,* 373–381.

Crawford, M., & Kimmel, E. (1999). Promoting methodological diversity in feminist research (pp. 1–6). In M. Crawford & E. Kimmel (Eds.), *Innovations in feminist research* (special issue). *Psychology of Women Quarterly, 23,* 1.

Crawford, M., & Marecek, J. (1989). Psychology reconstructs the female. *Psychology of Women Quarterly, 13,* 147–166.

Crawford, M., McCullough, M., & Arato, H. (1983, June). *Do women's studies classes change attitudes in women but not men?* Paper presented at the annual meeting of the National Women's Studies Association, Bloomington, Indiana.

Crawford, M., Stark, A. C., & Renner, C. (1998). The meaning of Ms.: Social assimilation of a gender concept. *Psychology of Women Quarterly, 22,* 197–208.

Crawford, S. (1987). Lesbian families: Psychosocial stress and the family-building process. In Boston Lesbian Psychologies Collective, *Lesbian psychologies* (pp. 195–214). Urbana, IL: University of Illinois Press.

Crewdson, J. (1988). *By silence betrayed: Sexual abuse of children in America.* New York: Harper and Row.

Crews, D. (1987a). Diversity and evolution of behavioral controlling mechanisms. In D. Crews (Ed.), *Psychobiology of reproductive behavior: An evolutionary perspective* (pp. 89–119). Englewood Cliffs, NJ: Prentice-Hall.

Crittenden, D. (1995, January 25). Sisterhood vs. new-wave thought. *Wall Street Journal, 225,* A14.

Crocker, J., Cornwell, B., & Major, B. (1993). The stigma of overweight: Affective consequences of attitudinal ambiguity. *Journal of Personality and Social Psychology, 64,* 60–70.

Crocker, J., & McGraw, K. M. (1984). What's good for the goose is not good for the gander: Solo status as an obstacle to occupational achievement for males and females. *American Behavioral Scientist, 27,* 357–369.

Crocker, J., Voelkl, K., Testa, M., & Major, B. (1991). Social stigma: The affective consequences of attributional ambiguity. *Journal of Personality and Social Psychology, 60,* 218–228.

Crockett, L. J., & Petersen, A. C. (1987). Pubertal status and psychosocial development: Findings from the early adolescent study. In R. M. Lerner & T. T. Foch (Eds.), *Biological-psychosocial interactions in early adolescence* (pp. 173–188). Hillsdale, NJ: Erlbaum.

Croghan, R. (1991). First-time mothers' accounts of inequality in the division of labour. *Feminism & Psychology, 1,* 221–246.

Crohan, S. E., & Veroff, J. (1989). Dimensions of marital well-being among white and black newlyweds. *Journal of Marriage and the Family, 51,* 373–383.

Crosbie-Burnett, M., & Giles-Sims, J. (1991). Marital power in stepfather families: A test of normative-resource theory. *Journal of Family Psychology, 4,* 484–496.

Crosby, F. (1982). *Relative deprivation and working women.* New York: Oxford University Press.

Crosby, F. (1984). The denial of personal discrimination. *American Behavioral Scientist, 27,* 371–386.

Crosby, F. J. (1991). *Juggling: The unexpected advantages of balancing career and home for women and their families.* New York: Free Press.

Crosby, F. J. (1994, April 2). *Gender, justice, and the meritocratic ideal.* Invited address at the meeting of the Southeastern Psychological Association, New Orleans.

Crosby, F. J., Clayton, S., Alksnis, O., & Hemker, K. (1986). Cognitive biases in the perception of discrimination: The importance of format. *Sex Roles, 14,* 637–646.

Crosby, F. J., Pufall, A., Snyder, R. C., O'Connell, M., & Whalen, P. (1989). The denial of personal disadvantage among you, me, and all the other ostriches. In M. Crawford and M. Gentry (Eds.), *Gender and thought: Psychological perspectives* (pp. 79–99). New York: Springer-Verlag.

Crose, R., Leventhal, E. A., Haug, M. R., & Burns, E. A. (1997). The challenges of aging. In S. J. Gallant, G. P. Keita, & R. Royak-Schaller (Eds.), *Health care for women: Psychological, social and behavioral influences* (pp. 221–234). Washington, DC: American Psychological Association.

Croteau, J. M. (1996). Research on the work experiences of lesbian, gay, and bisexual people: An integrative review of methodology and findings. *Journal of Vocational Behavior, 48,* 195–209.

Crovitz, E., & Hayes, L. (1979). A comparison of pregnant adolescents and non-pregnant sexually active peers. *Journal of the American Medical Women's Association, 34,* 102–104.

Crovitz, E., & Steinmann, A. (1980). A decade later: Black-white attitudes toward women's familial role. *Psychology of Women Quarterly, 5,* 171–176.

Culp, R. E., Cook, A. S., & Housley, P. C. (1983). A comparison of observed and reported adult-infant interactions: Effect of perceived sex. *Sex Roles, 9,* 475–479.

Cummings, N. (1992). Self-defense training for college women. *Journal of American College Health, 40,* 183–188.

Cunningham, M. R., Roberts, A. R., Barbee, A. P., Druen, P. B., & Wu, C. (1995). Their ideas of beauty are on the whole the same as ours: Consistency and variability in the cross-cultural perception of female physical attractiveness. *Journal of Personality and Social Psychology, 68,* 261–279.

Cusick, T. (1987). Sexism and early parenting: Cause and effect? *Peabody Journal of Education, 64,* 113–131.

Cypress, A. (1993). Men were taught more than women. In S. Wall (Ed.), *Wisdom's daughters: Conversations with women elders of Native America* (pp. 85–90). New York: HarperCollins.

Daley, D., & Gold, R. B. (1993). Public funding for contraceptive, sterilization, and abortion services, fiscal year 1992. *Family Planning Perspectives, 25,* 244–251.

D'Amico, R. (1986). Authority in the workplace: Differences among mature women. In L. B. Shaw (Ed.), *Midlife women at work: A fifteen-year perspective.* Lexington, MA: D. C. Heath.

Dancer, L. S., & Gilbert, L. A. (1993). Spouses' family work participation and its relation to wives' occupational level. *Sex Roles, 28,* 127–145.

Daniluk, J. C. (1996). When treatment fails: The transition to biological childlessness for infertile women. *Women & Therapy, 19*(2), 81–98.

Daniluk, J. C. (1998). *Women's sexuality across the life span: Challenging myths, creating meaning.* New York: Guilford.

Dansky, B. S., & Kilpatrick, D. G. (1997). Effects of sexual harassment. In W. O'Donohue (Ed.), *Sexual harassment: Theory, research and treatment* (pp. 152–174). Boston: Allyn & Bacon.

Darnton, J. (1993, March 11). Tough abortion law provokes dismay in Poland. *New York Times,* p. A13.

Datan, N., Antonovsky, A., & Maoz, B. (1981). *A time to reap: The middle age of women in five Israeli subcultures.* Baltimore: Johns Hopkins Press.

Daubman, K. A., & Lehman, T. C. (1993). The effects of receiving help: Gender differences in motivation and performance. *Sex Roles, 28,* 693–707.

Davis, D. M. (1990). Portrayal of women in prime-time network television: Some demographic characteristics. *Sex Roles, 23,* 325–332.

Davis, M., & Weitz, S. (1981). Sex differences in body movements and positions. In C. Mayo & N. Henley (Eds.), *Gender and nonverbal behavior* (pp. 81–92). New York: Springer-Verlag.

Davis, S., Crawford, M., & Sebrechts, J. (Eds.). (1999). *Coming into her own: Encouraging educational success in girls and women.* San Francisco: Jossey-Bass.

Dean, K. E., & Malamuth, N. (1997). Characteristics of men who aggress sexually and of men who imagine aggressing: Risk and moderating variables. *Journal of Personality and Social Psychology, 72,* 449–455.

Dearwater, S. R., Coben, J. H., Campbell, J. C., Nah, G., et al. (1998, August 5). Prevalence of intimate partner abuse in women treated at community hospital emergency departments. *Journal of the American Medical Association, 280,* 433–438.

Deaux, K., (1984). From individual differences to social categories: Analysis of a decade's research on gender. *American Psychologist, 39,* 105–116.

Deaux, K. (1993). Commentary: Sorry, wrong number–A reply to Gentile's call. *Psychological Science, 4,* 125–126.

Deaux, K., & Emswiller, T. (1974). Explanations

of successful performance on sex-linked tasks: What's skill for the male is luck for the female. *Journal of Personality and Social Psychology, 29,* 80–85.

Deaux, K., & Hanna, R. (1984). Courtship in the personals column: The influence of gender and sexual orientation. *Sex Roles, 11,* 363–375.

Deaux, K., & Kite, M. E. (1985). Gender stereotypes: Some thoughts on the cognitive organization of gender-related information. *Academic Psychology Bulletin, 7,* 123–144.

Deaux, K., & Lewis, L. L. (1984). The structure of gender stereotypes: Interrelationships among components and gender labels. *Journal of Personality and Social Psychology, 46,* 991–1004.

Deaux, K., & Ullman, J. C. (1983). *Women of steel.* New York: Praeger.

Deaux, K. Winton, W., Crowley, M., & Lewis, L. L. (1985). Level of categorization and content of gender stereotypes. *Social Cognition, 3,* 145–167.

DeBlasio, C. L., Argiro, L. G., Orbin, J. A., & Ellyson, S. L. (1993, April). *Gender strategies in displaying power and attractiveness.* Paper presented at the annual meeting of the Eastern Psychological Association, Arlington, VA.

Deblinger, E., Hathaway, C. R., Lippman, J., & Steer, R. (1993). Psychosocial characteristics and correlates of symptom distress in nonoffending mothers of sexually abused children. *Journal of Interpersonal Violence, 8,* 155–168.

Dege, K., & Gretzinger, J. (1982). Attitudes of families toward menopause. In A. M. Voda, M. Dinnerstein, & S. R. O'Donnell (Eds.), *Changing perspectives on menopause* (pp. 60–69). Austin: University of Texas Press.

DeKeseredy, W. S. (1997). Measuring sexual abuse in Canadian university/college dating relationships: the contribution of a national representative sample survey. In M. D. Schwartz (Ed.), *Researching sexual violence against women: Methodological and personal perspectives* (pp. 43–53). Thousand Oaks, CA: Sage.

DeLamater, J., & MacCorquodale, P. (1979). *Premarital sexuality.* Madison: WI: University of Wisconsin Press.

Delaney, J., Lupton, M. J., & Toth, E. (1988). *The curse: A cultural history of menstruation* (rev. ed.). Urbana, IL: University of Illinois Press.

DeMaris, A. (1992). Male versus female initiation of aggression: The case of courtship violence. In E. C. Viano (Ed.), *Intimate violence: Interdisciplinary perspectives* (pp. 111–120). New York: Hemisphere Publishing Corp.

DeMeis, D. K., & Perkins, H. W. (1996). "Supermoms" of the nineties: Homemaker and employed mothers' performance and perceptions of the motherhood role. *Journal of Family Issues, 17*(6), 776–792.

D'Emilio, J., & Freedman, E. B. (1988). *Intimate matters: A history of sexuality in America.* New York: Harper & Row.

Dempsey, K. (1997). Trying to get husbands to do more work at home. *Australian and New Zealand Journal of Sociology, 33*(2), 216–225.

Denmark, F. L. (1980). Psyche: From rocking the cradle to rocking the boat. *American Psychologist, 35,* 1057–1065.

Denmark, F. L., Russo, N. F., Frieze, I. H., & Sechzer, J. A. (1988). Guidelines for avoiding sexism in psychological research: A report of the ad hoc committee on nonsexist research. *American Psychologist, 43,* 582–585.

Derby, C. A., Hume, A. L., Barbour, M. M., McPhillip, J. B., Lasater, T. M., & Carleton, R. A. (1993). Correlates of postmenopausal estrogen use and trends through 1980s in two southeastern New England communities. *American Journal of Epidemiology, 137,* 1125–1135.

Deschamps, J-C. (1982). Social identity and relations of power between groups. In H. Tajfel (Ed.), *Social identity and intergroup relations.* Cambridge, England: Cambridge University Press.

Deutsch, F. M., LeBaron, D., & Fryer, M. M. (1987). What is in a smile? *Psychology of Women Quarterly, 11,* 341–351.

Devor, H. (1987). Gender blending females: Women and sometimes men. *American Behavioral Scientist, 31,* 12–40.

Devor, H. (1996). Female gender dysphoria in context: Social problem or personal problem? *Annual Review of Sex Research, 6.*

Devor, H. (1997). *MTF: Female-to-male transsexuals in society.* Bloomington, IN: University of Indiana Press.

Dew, M. A. (1985). The effect of attitudes on inferences of homosexuality and perceived physical attractiveness in women. *Sex Roles, 12,* 143–155.

Dewhurst, A. M., Moore, R. J., & Alfano, D. P. (1992). Aggression against women by men: Sexual and spousal assault. *Journal of Offender Rehabilitation, 18,* 39–47.

De Witt, K. (1997, June 23). Girl games on computers, where shoot 'em up simply won't do. *The New York Times,* p. D3.

Diamond, M. (1995). Biological aspects of sexual orientation and identity. In L. Diamant & R. McAnulty (Eds.), *The psychology of sexual orientation, behavior, and identity: A handbook* (pp. 45–80). Westport, CT: Greenwood Press.

Diamond, M. (in press). Pediatric management of ambiguous and traumatized genitalia. *Journal of Urology.*

Diamond, M., Binstock, T., & Kohl, J. V. (1996). From fertilization to adult sexual behavior. *Hormones and Behavior, 30,* 333–353.

Diamond, M., & Sigmundson, H. K. (1997). Management of intersexuality: Guidelines for dealing with persons with ambiguous genitalia. *Archives of Pediatric and Adolescent Medicine, 151,* 1046.

Diamond, M. A. (1965). A critical evaluation of the ontogeny of human sexual behavior. *Quarterly Review of Biology, 40,* 147–175.

Diamond, M. A. (1982). Sexual identity, monozygotic twins reared in discordant sex roles and a BBC follow-up. *Archives of Sexual Behavior, 11,* 181–186.

Diamond, M. A. (1993). Some genetic considerations in the development of sexual orientation. In M. Haug, R. E. Whalen, C. Aron, & K. L. Olsen (Eds.), *The development of sex differences and similarities in behavior* (pp. 291–309). Dordrecht: Kluwer Publishing Company.

DiBlasio, F. A., & Benda, B. B. (1992). Gender differences in theories of adolescent sexual activity. *Sex Roles, 27,* 221–239.

Dickerson, B. J. (Ed.). (1995). *African-American single mothers.* Thousand Oaks, CA: Sage.

Dickson, L. (1993). The future of marriage and family in Black America. *Journal of Black Studies, 23,* 472–491.

Dietz, T. L. (1998). An examination of violence and gender role portrayals in video games: Implications for gender socialization of aggressive behavior. *Sex Roles, 38,* 425–442.

Dijker, A. J., Koomen, W., van der Heuvel, H., & Frijda, N. H. (1996). Perceived antecedents of emotional reactions in interethnic relations. *British Journal of Social Psychology, 35,* 313–329.

Di Leonardo, M. (1987). The female world of cards and holidays: Women, families, and the work of kinship. *Signs, 12,* 440–453.

Dion, K. K., Berscheid, E., & Walster, E. (1972). What is beautiful is good. *Journal of Personality and Social Psychology, 24,* 285–290.

Dion, K. L. (1975). Women's reaction to discrimination from members of the same or opposite sex. *Journal of Research in Personality, 9,* 292–306.

Dion, K. L. (1987). What's in a title? The Ms stereotype and images of women's titles of address. *Psychology of Women Quarterly, 11,* 21–36.

Dion, K. L., & Cota, A. A. (1991). The Ms. stereotype: Its domain and the role of explicitness in title preference. *Psychology of Women Quarterly, 15,* 403–410.

Dion, K. L., Earn, B. M., & Yee, P. H. N. (1978). The experience of being a victim of prejudice: An experimental approach. *International Journal of Psychology, 13,* 197–214.

DiPalma, L. M. (1994). Patterns of coping and characteristics of high-functioning incest survivors. *Archives of Psychiatric Nursing, 8*(2), 82–90.

Discover Magazine. (April, 1996). Laws of Physiques, p. 22.

Dittmann, R. W., Kappes, M. E., & Kappes, M. H. (1992). Sexual behavior in adolescent and adult-females with congenital adrenal hyperplasia. *Psychoneuroendocrinology, 17,* 153–170.

Dodson, B. (1987). *Sex for one: The joy of self-loving.* New York: Crown.

Dolan, E. M., & Lown, J. M. (1985). The remarried family: Challenges and opportunities. *Journal of Home Economics, 77,* 36–41.

Dorans, N. J., & Livingston, S. A. (1987). Male-female differences in SAT-verbal ability among students of high SAT-mathematic ability. *Journal of Educational Measurement, 24,* 65–71.

Doress, P. B., Siegal, D. L., & the Midlife and Old Women Book Project (1987). *Ourselves, growing older.* New York: Simon & Schuster.

Doress-Worters, P. B. (1994). Adding elder care to women's multiple roles: A critical review of the caregiver stress and multiple roles literature. *Sex Roles, 31,* 597–616.

Doress-Worters, P. B., & Siegal, D. L. (1994). *The new ourselves growing older.* New York: Simon & Schuster.

Dornbusch, S. M., Gross, R. T., Duncan, P. D., & Ritter, P. L. (1987). Stanford studies of adolescence using the national health examination survey. In R. M. Lerner & T. T. Foch (Eds.), *Biological-psychosocial interactions in early adolescence* (pp. 189–205). Hillsdale, NJ: Erlbaum.

Douglas, S. J. (1994). *Where the girls are: Growing up female with the mass media.* New York: Times Books/Random House.

Dovidio, J. F., & Gaertner, S. L. (1981). The effects of race, status, and ability on helping behavior. *Social Psychology Quarterly, 44,* 192–203.

Dovidio, J. F., & Gaertner, S. L. (1983). The effects of sex, status, and ability on helping behavior. *Journal of Applied Social Psychology, 13,* 191–205.

Draucker, C. B. (1996). Family-of-origin variables and adult female survivors of childhood sexual abuse: A review of the research. *Journal of Child Sexual Abuse, 5,* 35–63.

Dreher, G. F., & Cox, T. H., Jr. (1996). Race, gender, and opportunity: A study of compensation attainment and the establishment of mentoring relationships. *Journal of Applied Psychology, 81*(3), 297–308.

Driscoll, J. M., Kelley, F. A., & Fassinger, R. E. (1996). Lesbian identity and disclosure in the workplace: Relation to occupational stress and satisfaction. *Journal of Vocational Behavior, 48,* 229–242.

Duncan, G. J., & Hoffman, S. D. (1991). A reconsideration of the economic consequences of marital dissolution. *Demography, 22,* 485.

Duncan, L. E., Peterson, B. E., & Winter, D. G. (1997). Authoritarian and gender roles: Toward a psychological analysis of hegemonic relationships. *Personality and Social Psychology Bulletin, 23,* 41–49.

Dunkin, K., & Nugent, B. (1998). Kindergarten children's gender role expectations for television actors. *Sex Roles, 38,* 387–402.

Dunkle, J. H., & Francis, P. L. (1990). The role of facial masculinity/femininity in the attribution of homosexuality. *Sex Roles, 23,* 157–167.

Dunlop, E. (1968). Emotional imbalances in the premenopausal woman. *Psychosomatics, 9,* 44–47.

Dutton, D. G. (1996). Patriarchy and wife assault: The ecological fallacy. In L. K. Hamberger, & C. Renzetti (Eds.), *Domestic partner abuse* (pp. 125–151). Springer.

Dutton, D. G., Starzomski, A., & Ryan, L. (1996). Antecedents of abusive personality and abusive behavior in wife assaulters. *Journal of Family Violence, 11,* 113–132.

Dutton, M. A. (1996). Battered women's strategic response to violence. The role of context. In J. L. Edleson, & Z. C. Eisikovits (Eds.), *Future interventions with battered women and their families* (pp. 105–124). Thousand Oaks, CA: Sage.

Dworkin, A. (1974). *Woman hating.* New York: E. P. Dutton.

Dworkin, A. (1987). *Intercourse.* New York: Free Press.

Dwyer, C. A. (1979). The role of tests and their construction in producing apparent sex-related differences. In M. A. Wittig & A. C. Petersen (Eds.), *Sex-related differences in cognitive functioning: Developmental issues* (pp. 335–353). New York: Academic Press.

Eagly, A. H. (1987). *Sex differences in social behavior: A social role interpretation.* Hillsdale, NJ: Erlbaum.

Eagly, A. H., & Johnson, B. T. (1990). Gender and leadership style: A meta-analysis. *Psychological Bulletin, 108,* 233–256.

Eagly, A. H., & Karau, S. J. (1991). Gender and the emergence of leaders: A meta-analysis. *Journal of Personality and Social Psychology, 60,* 685–710.

Eagly, A. H., Karau, S. J., & Makhijani, M. (1995). Gender and the effectiveness of leaders: A meta-analysis. *Psychological Bulletin, 117,* 125–145.

Eagly, A. H., & Mladinic, A. (1989). Gender stereotypes and attitudes toward women and men. *Personality and Social Psychology Bulletin, 15,* 543–558.

Eagly, A. H., & Mladinic, A. (1993). Are people prejudiced against women? Some answers from research on attitudes, gender stereotypes, and judgments of competence. In W. Strobe & M. Hewstone (Eds.). *European review of social psychology* (pp. 1–35). NY: Wiley.

East, P. L. (1998). Racial and ethnic differences in girls' sexual, marital, and birth expectations. *Journal of Marriage and the Family, 60,* 150–162.

Eaton, W. O., von Bargen, D., & Keats, J. G. (1981). Gender understanding and dimensions of preschooler toy choice: Sex stereotypes versus activity level. *Canadian Journal of Behavioral Science, 13,* 203–209.

Eccles, J. S. (1989). Bringing young women to math and science. In M. Crawford and M. Gentry (Eds.), *Gender and thought: Psychological perspectives* (pp. 36–58). New York: Springer-Verlag.

Eccles, J. S. (1994). Understanding women's educational and occupational choices: Applying the Eccles et al. model of achievement-related choices. *Psychology of Women Quarterly, 18,* 585–610.

Eccles, J. S., Adler, T. F., Futterman, R., Goff, S. B., Kaczala, C. M., Meece, J. L., & Midgley, C. (1985). Self-perceptions, task perceptions, socializing influences, and the decision to enroll in mathematics. In S. F. Chipman, L. R. Brush, & D. M. Wilson (Eds.), *Women and mathematics: Balancing the equation* (pp. 95–122). Hillsdale, NJ: Erlbaum.

Eccles, J. S., & Jacobs, J. E. (1986). Social forces shape math attitudes and performance. *Signs, 11,* 367–389.

Eckes, T. (1994). Features of men, features of women: Assessing stereotypic beliefs about gender subtypes. *British Journal of Social Psychology, 33,* 107–123.

Edelson, M. S., & Omark, D. R. (1973). Dominance hierarchies in young children. *Social Science Information, 12,* 1.

Eder, D., Evans, C. C., & Parker, S. (1995). *Gender and adolescent culture.* Rutgers: Rutgers University Press.

Edleson, J. L. (1996). Controversy and change in batterer's programs. In J. L. Edleson & Z. C. Eisikovits (Eds.), *Future interventions with battered women and their families* (pp. 154–169). Thousand Oaks, CA: Sage.

Edman, C. D. (1983a). The climacteric. In H. J. Buchsbaum (Ed.), *The menopause* (pp. 23–33). New York: Springer-Verlag.

Edman, C. D. (1983b). Estrogen replacement therapy. In H. J. Buchsbaum (Ed.), *The menopause* (pp. 77–84). New York: Springer-Verlag.

Edwards, C. P., & Whiting, B. B. (1988). *Children of different worlds.* Cambridge, MA: Harvard University Press.

Edwards, J. J., & Alexander, P. C. (1992). The contribution of family background to long-term adjustment of women sexually abused as children. *Journal of Interpersonal Violence, 7,* 306–320.

Ehrenreich, B., & English, D. (1979). *For her own good: 150 years of the experts' advice to women.* Garden City, NY: Anchor Books.

Ehrhardt, A. A., & Meyer-Bahlburg, H. F. L. (1981). Effects of prenatal sex hormones on gender-related behavior. *Science, 211,* 1312–1318.

Eichler, M. (1988). *Nonsexist research methods.* Boston: Allen & Unwin.

Eisenberg, A. R. (1996). The conflict talk of mothers and children: Patterns related to culture, SES, and gender of child. *Merrill-Palmer Quarterly 42,* 438–458.

Eldridge, N. S., & Gilbert, L. A. (1990). Correlates of relationship satisfaction in lesbian couples. *Psychology of Women Quarterly, 14,* 43–62.

Elise, S. (1995). Teenaged mothers: A sense of self. In B. J. Dickerson (Ed.), *African American single mothers* (pp. 53–79). Thousand Oaks: Sage.

Elkind, S. N. (1991, Winter). Letter to the editor. *Psychology of Women, 18,* 3.

Elliot, R. (1989). *Song of love.* New York: Harlequin.

Elliot, S. (1984). Pregnancy and after. In S. Rachman (Ed.), *Contributions to medical psychology 3* (pp. 93–116). New York: Pergamon Press.

Ellis, A. L. (1996). Sexual identity issues in the workplace: Past and present. In A. L. Ellis & E. D. B. Riggle (Eds.), *Sexual identity on the job: Issues and services* (pp. 1–16). New York: Harrington Park Press.

Ellis, P., & Murphy, B. C. (1994). The impact of misogyny and homophobia on therapy with women. In M. P. Mirkin (Ed.), *Women in context: Toward a feminist reconstruction of psychotherapy* (pp. 48–73). New York: Guilford.

Ellyson, S. L., Dovidio, J. F., & Brown, C. E. (1992). The look of power: Gender differences and similarities in visual dominance behavior. In C. L. Ridgeway (Ed.), *Gender, interaction, and inequality* (pp. 50–80). New York: Springer-Verlag.

Ellyson, S. L., Dovidio, J. F., & Fehr, B. J. (1981). Visual behavior and dominance in women and men. In C. Mayo & N. Henley (Eds.), *Gender and nonverbal behavior* (pp. 63–79). New York: Springer-Verlag.

Emmerich, W., & Shepard, K. (1984). Cognitive factors in the development of sex-typed preferences. *Sex Roles, 11,* 997–1007.

England, P., & McCreary, L. (1987). Gender inequality in paid employment. In B. B. Hess and M. M. Ferree (Eds.), *Analyzing gender: A handbook of social science research* (pp. 286–320). Newbury Park, CA: Sage.

Epel, E. S., Spanakos, A., Kasl-Godley, J., & Brownell, K. D. (1996). Body shape ideals across gender, sexual orientation, socioeconomic status, race, and age in personal advertisements. *International Journal of Eating Disorders, 19,* 265–273.

Equal Employment Opportunity Commission (EEOC). (1980). Guidelines on discrimination because of sex. *Federal Register, 45,* 74676–77.

Erkut, S., Fields, J. P., Sing, R., & Marks, F. (1997). Diversity in girls' experiences: Feeling good about who you are. In B. J. R. Leadbeater & N. Way (Eds.), *Urban girls: Resisting stereotypes, creating identities* (pp. 53–64). New York: New York University Press.

Ernster, V. L. (1975). American menstrual expressions. *Sex Roles, 1,* 3–13.

Eron, L. D. (1980). Prescription for reduction of aggression. *American Psychologist, 35,* 244–252.

Espin, O. M. (1986). Cultural and historical influences on sexuality in Hispanic/Latin women. In J. Cole (Ed.), *All American women: Lines that divide, ties that bind* (pp. 272–284). New York: Free Press.

Espin, O. M. (1987a). Issues of identity in the psychology of Latina lesbians. In Boston Lesbian Psychologies Collective (Ed.), *Lesbian psychologies: Explorations and challenges* (pp. 35–55). Urbana: University of Illinois Press.

Espin, O. M. (1987b). Psychological impact of migration on Latinas: Implications of psychotherapeutic practice. *Psychology of Women Quarterly, 11,* 489–503.

Esten, G., & Willmott, L. (1993). Double bind messages: The effects of attitude toward disability on therapy. *Women & Therapy, 14,* 29–41.

Etaugh, C. (1980). Effects of nonmaternal care on children: Research evidence and popular views. *American Psychologist, 35,* 309–319.

Etaugh, C., & Brown, B. (1975). Perceiving the causes of success and failure of male and female performers. *Developmental Psychology, 11,* 103.

Etaugh, C., & Liss, M. B. (1992). Home, school, and playroom: Training grounds for adult gender roles. *Sex Roles, 26,* 129–147.

Etter-Lewis, G. (1988). *Power and social change: Images of Afro-American women in the print media.* Paper presented at the annual meeting of the National Women's Studies Association, Minneapolis, MN.

Fabes, R. A. (1994). Physiological, emotional, and behavioral correlates of gender segregation. In C. Leaper (Ed.), *The development of gender and relationships* (pp. 19–34). San Francisco: Jossey-Bass.

Fabes, R. A., Shepard, S. A., Guthrie, I. K., & Martin, C. L. (1997). Roles of temperamental arousal and gender-segregated play in young children's social adjustment. *Developmental Psychology, 33,* 693–702.

Facio, E. (1996). *Understanding older Chicanas: Sociological and policy perspectives/*Thousand Oaks, CA: Sage.

Facio, E. (1997). Chicanas and aging: Toward definitions of womanhood. In J. M. Coyle (Ed.), *Handbook on women and aging* (pp. 335–350). Westport, CT: Greenwood Press.

Faderman, L. (1981). *Surpassing the love of men: Romantic friendship and love between women from the Renaissance to the present.* New York: William Morrow.

Fagot, B. I. (1985a). Beyond the reinforcement principle: Another step toward understanding sex role development. *Developmental Psychology, 21,* 1097–1104.

Fagot, B. I. (1985b). Changes in thinking about early sex role development. *Developmental Review, 5,* 83–98.

Fagot, B. I., & Leinbach, M. D. (1987). Socialization of sex roles within the family. In D. B. Carter (Ed.), *Current conceptions of sex roles and sex typing: Theory and research* (pp. 89–100). New York: Praeger.

Fagot, B. I., & Leinbach, M. D. (1995). Gender knowledge in egalitarian and traditional families. *Sex Roles, 32,* 513–526.

Fain, T. C., & Anderton, D. L. (1987). Sexual harassment: Organizational context and diffuse status. *Sex Roles, 17,* 291–311.

Falbo, T., & Peplau, L. A. (1980). Power strategies in intimate relationships. *Journal of Personality and Social Psychology, 38,* 618–628.

Falk, P. J. (1993). Lesbian mothers: Psychosocial assumptions in family law. In L. D. Garnets & D. C. Kimmel (Eds.), *Psychological perspectives on lesbian and gay male experiences* (pp. 420–436). New York: Columbia University Press.

Faludi, S. (1991). *Backlash: The undeclared war against American women.* New York: Doubleday.

Farel, A. (1980). Effects of preferred maternal roles, maternal employment, and sociodemographic status on school adjustment and competence. *Child Development, 51,* 1179–1186.

Farmer, H. S., et al. (Eds.). (1997). *Diversity & women's career development: From adolescence to adulthood.* Thousand Oaks, CA: Sage.

Fassinger, R. E. (1996). Notes from the margins: Integrating lesbian experience into the vocational psychology of women. *Journal of Vocational Behavior, 48,* 160–175.

Faulkner, A. O., & Heisel, M. A. (1987). Giving, receiving, and exchanging: Social transactions among inner-city black aged. In H. Strange & M. Teitelbaum (Eds.), *Aging and cultural diversity* (pp. 117–130). South Hadley, MA: Bergin & Garvin.

Faunce, P. S. (1990). Women in poverty: Ethical dimensions in therapy. In H. Lerman & N. Porter (Eds.), *Feminist ethics in psychotherapy* (pp. 185–194). New York: Springer.

Faust, M. G. (1983). Alternative constructions on adolescent growth. In J. Brooks-Gunn & A. C. Petersen (Eds.), *Girls at puberty* (pp. 105–125). New York: Plenum.

Fausto-Sterling, A. (1992). *Myths of gender: Biological theories about women and men* (rev. ed.). New York: Basic Books.

Fausto-Sterling, A. (1997). Beyond difference: A biologist's perspective. *Journal of Social Issues, 53,* 233–258.

Fausto-Sterling, A. (in press). How sexually dimorphic are we? Review and synthesis. *American Journal of Human Biology.*

Favreau, O. E. (1997). Sex and gender comparisons: Does null hypothesis testing create a false dichotomy? *Feminism and Psychology,* 7(1), 63–81.

Feather, N. T. (1985). Masculinity, femininity, self-esteem, and sub-clinical depression. *Sex Roles, 12,* 491–500.

Federal Bureau of Investigation. (1985). *Uniform crime report.* Washington, DC: U.S. Department of Justice.

Federal Glass Ceiling Commission. (1998). Working women face barriers to advancement. In M. E. Williams (Ed.), *Working women: Opposing viewpoints* (pp. 64–72). San Diego: Greenhaven Press.

Feeney, J., Peterson, C., & Noller, P. (1994). Equality and marital satisfaction in the family life cycle. *Personal Relationships, 1,* 83–99.

Feingold, A. (1988). Cognitive gender differences are disappearing. *American Psychologist, 43,* 95–103.

Feinman, S. (1981). Why is cross-sex-role behavior more approved for girls than for boys? A status characteristic approach. *Sex Roles, 7,* 289–300.

Feiring, C., & Lewis, M. (1987). The child's social network: Sex differences from three to six years. *Sex Roles, 17,* 621–636.

Feiring, C., & Lewis, M. (1991). The transition from middle childhood to early adolescence: Sex differences in the social network and perceived self-confidence. *Sex Roles, 24,* 489–509.

Feldman, D. C. (1996). The nature, antecedents and consequences of underemployment. *Journal of Management, 22*(3), 385–407.

Feldman-Summers, S., & Kiesler, S. J. (1974). Those who are number two try harder: The effects of sex on attributions of causality. *Journal of Personality and Social Psychology, 30,* 846–855.

Fenell, D. L. (1993). Characteristics of long-term first marriages. *Journal of Mental Health Counseling, 15,* 446–460.

Fernandez, M. (1997). Domestic violence by extended family members in India. Interplay of gender and generation. *Journal of Interpersonal Violence, 12,* 433–455.

Fernberger, S. W. (1948). Persistence of stereotypes concerning sex differences. *Journal of Abnormal and Social Psychology, 43,* 97–101.

Ferree, M. M. (1987). She works hard for a living: Gender and class on the job. In B. B. Hess & M. M. Ferree (Eds.), *Analyzing gender: A handbook of social science research* (pp. 322–347). Newbury Park, CA: Sage.

Fidell, L. S. (1970). Empirical verification of sex discrimination in hiring practices in psychology. *American Psychologist, 25,* 1094–1098.

Fidell, L. S. (1982). Gender and drug use and abuse. In I. Al-Issa (Ed.), *Gender and psychopathology* (pp. 221–236). New York: Academic Press.

Field, T., Widmayer, S., Stoller, S., & de Cubes, M. (1986). School-age parenthood in different ethnic groups and family constellations: Effect on infant development. In B. A. Hamburg & J. B. Lancaster (Eds.), *School age pregnancy and parenthood* (pp. 263–272). New York: Aldine De Gruyter.

"Finding the inner swine." *Newsweek,* February 1, 1999, p. 51–52.

Findlen, B. (Ed.). (1995). *Listen up! Voices from the next feminist generation.* Seattle: Seal Press.

Fine, M. (1983–1984). Coping with rape: Critical perspectives on consciousness. *Imagination, Cognition, and Personality, 3,* 249–267.

Fine, M. (1985). Reflections on a feminist psychology of women: Paradoxes and prospects. *Psychology of Women Quarterly, 9,* 167–183.

Fine, M. (1988). Sexuality, schooling, and adolescent females: The missing discourse of desire. *Harvard Educational Review, 58,* 29–53.

Fine, M., & Asch, A. (1988). *Women with disabilities: Essays in psychology, culture, and politics.* Philadelphia: Temple University Press.

Fine, M., & Gordon, S. M. (1989). Feminist transformations of/despite psychology. In M. Crawford & M. Gentry (Eds.), *Gender and thought* (pp. 146–174). New York: Springer-Verlag.

Fine, M., & Macpherson, P. (1992). Over dinner: Feminism and adolescent female bodies. In M. Fine (Ed.), *Disruptive voices: The possibilities of feminist research* (pp. 175–203). Ann Arbor: University of Michigan Press.

Fine, M., & Zane, N. (1988). Bein' wrapped too tight: When low income women drop out of high school. In L. Weis (Ed.), *Dropouts in schools: Issues, dilemmas, solutions.* Albany: SUNY Press.

Fine, M., Weis, L., Powell, L. C., & Wong, L. M. (Eds.). (1997). *Off white: Readings on race, power, and society.* New York: Routledge.

Finkel, J. S., & Hanson, F. J. (1992). Correlates of retrospective marital satisfaction in long-lived marriages: A social constructivist approach. *Family Therapy, 19,* 1–16.

Finkelhor, D. (1984). *Child sexual abuse: New theory and research.* New York: Free Press.

Finkelhor, D., Hotaling, G. T., Lewis, I. A., &

Smith, C. (1989). Sexual abuse and its relationship to later sexual satisfaction, marital status, religion, and attitudes. *Journal of Interpersonal Violence, 4,* 379–399.

Finkelhor, D., Hotaling, G., Lewis, I. A., & Smith, C. (1990). Sexual abuse in a national survey of adult men and women: Prevalence, characteristics, and risk factors. *Child Abuse and Neglect, 14,* 533–542.

Firestein, B. A. (1998, March 7). *Bisexuality: A feminist vision of choice and change.* Paper presented at the annual meeting of the Association for Women in Psychology, Baltimore, MD.

First, A. (1998). Nothing new under the sun? A comparison of images of women in Israeli advertisements in 1979 and 1994. *Sex Roles, 38,* 1065–1077.

Fisher, J. D., & Fisher, W. A. (in press). Theoretical approaches to individual-level change in HIV-risk behavior. In J. Peterson & R. DiClemente (Eds.), *HIV prevention handbook.* New York: Plenum.

Fisher, J. D., Fisher, W. A., Misovich, S. J., Kimble, D. L., & Malloy, T. E. (1996).Changing AIDS risk behavior: Effects of an intervention emphasizing AIDS risk reduction information, motivation, and behavioral skills in a college student population. *Health Psychology, 15*(2), 114–123.

Fisher, J. D., Nadler, A., & Whitcher-Alagna, S. (1982). Recipient reactions to aid. *Psychological Bulletin, 91,* 27–54.

Fisher, W. A., Williams, S. S., Fisher, J. D., & Malloy, T. E. (in press). Understanding AIDS risk behavior among sexually active urban adolescents: An empirical test of the information–motivation–behavioral skills model. *AIDS and Behavior.*

Fiske, A. P., Haslam, N., & Fiske, S. T. (1991). Confusing one person with another: What errors reveal about the elementary forms of social relations. *Journal of Personality and Social Psychology, 60,* 656–674.

Fiske, S. T. (1993). Controlling other people: The impact of power on stereotyping. *American Psychologist, 48,* 621–628.

Fiske, S. T., Bersoff, D. N., Borgida, E., Deaux, K., & Heilman, M. E. (1991). Social science research on trial: Use of sex stereotyping research in Price Waterhouse v. Hopkins. *American Psychologist, 46,* 1049–1060.

Fiske, S. T., & Stevens, L. E. (1993). What's so special about sex? Gender stereotyping and discrimination. In S. Oskamp & M. Constanzo (Eds.), *Gender issues in contemporary society* (pp. 173–196). Newbury Park, CA: Sage.

Fitzgerald, L. F. (1993). Sexual harassment: Violence against women in the workplace. *American Psychologist, 48,* 1070–1076.

Fitzgerald, L. F. (1996). Sexual harassment: The definition and measurement of a construct. In M. A. Paludi (Ed.), *Sexual harassment on college campuses: Abusing the ivory power* (pp. 25–47). Albany: State University of New York Press.

Fitzgerald, L. F., & Betz, N. E. (1983). Issues in the vocational psychology of women. In W. B. Walsh & S. H. Osipow (Eds.), *Handbook of vocational psychology,* Vol. 1. Hillsdale, NJ: Erlbaum.

Fitzgerald, L. F., Drasgow, F., Hulin, C. L., Gelfland, M. J., & Magley, V. J. (1997). Antecedents and consequences of sexual harassment in organizations: A test of an integrated model. *Journal of Applied Psychology, 82,* 578–589.

Fitzgerald, L. F., Swan, S., & Magley, V. J. (1997). But was it really sexual harassment? Legal, behavioral, and psychological definitions of the workplace victimization of women. In W. O'Donohue (Ed.), *Sexual harassment: Theory, research, and treatment* (pp. 5–28). Boston: Allyn & Bacon.

Flanagan, D., Baker-Ward, L., & Graham, L. (1995). Talk about preschool: Patterns of topic discussion and elaboration related to gender and ethnicity. *Sex Roles, 32,* 1–15.

Flanagan, D., & Perese, S. (1998). Emotional references in mother-daughter and mother-son dyads conversations about school. *Sex Roles, 39,* 353–367.

Flanders, L. (1992). Mothers and other soldiers: The media's "woman warrior." *Extra,* Special Issue, p. 23.

Flint, M., & Samil, R. S. (1990). Cultural and subcultural meanings of the menopause. In M. Flint, F. Kronenberg, & W. Utian (Eds.), Multidisciplinary perspectives on menopause. *Annals of the New York Academy of Sciences, 592,* 134–155.

Foa, E. B., Olasov, B., & Steketee, G. S. (1987). *Treatment of rape victims.* Paper presented at the conference, State of the Art in Sexual Assault, Charleston, SC.

Follingstad, D. R., Rutledge, L. L., McNeill-Hawkins, K., & Polek, D. S. (1992). Factors related to physical violence in dating relationships. In E. C. Viano (Ed.), *Intimate violence: Interdisciplinary perspectives* (pp. 121–135). New York: Hemisphere.

Ford, C. V., & Sbordone, R. J. (1980). Attitudes of psychiatrists toward elderly patients. *American Journal of Psychiatry, 137,* 571–575.

Ford, M. R., & Lowery, C. R. (1986). Gender differences in moral reasoning: A comparison of the use of justice and care orientations. *Journal of Personality and Social Psychology, 50,* 777–783.

Fordham, S. (1993). "Those loud black girls": (Black) women, silence, and gender "passing" in the academy. *Anthropology and Education Quarterly, 24,* 3–32.

Foreit, K. G., Agor, A. T., Byers, J., Larue, J., Lokey, H., Palazzini, M., Patterson, M., & Smith, L. (1980). Sex bias in the newspaper treatment of male-centered and female-centered news stories. *Sex Roles, 6,* 475–480.

Forste, R., & Tanfer, K. (1996). Sexual exclusivity among dating, cohabiting, and married women. *Journal of Marriage and Family, 58,* 33–47.

Forward, J. R., & Williams, J. R. (1970). Internal-external control and black militancy. *Journal of Social Issues, 26,* 75–92.

Foschi, M., & Freeman, S. (1991). Inferior performance, standards, and influence in same-sex dyads. *Canadian Journal of Behavioral Sciences, 23,* 99–113.

Foucault, M. (1978). *The history of sexuality.* New York: Pantheon.

Fowers, B. J. (1991). His and her marriages: A multivariate study of gender and marital satisfaction. *Sex Roles, 24,* 209–221.

Fox, D., & Prilleltensky, I. (1997). *Critical psychology: An introduction.* London: Sage Publications.

Frank, E., Anderson, C., & Rubenstein, D. (1978). Frequency of sexual dysfunction in "normal" couples. *New England Journal of Medicine, 299,* 111–115.

Franks, V. (1986). Sex stereotyping and the diagnosis of psychopathology. In D. Howard (Ed.), *The dynamics of feminist therapy* (pp. 219–232). New York: Haworth Press.

Frasher, R. S., Nurss, J. R., & Brogan, D. R. (1980). Children's toy preferences revisited: Implications for early childhood education. *Child Care Quarterly, 9,* 26–31.

Frazier, P. A., & Seales, L. M. (1997). Acquaintance rape is real rape. In M. D. Schwartz (Ed.), *Researching sexual violence against women: methodological and personal perspectives* (pp. 54–64). Thousand Oaks, CA: Sage.

Fredrickson, B. L., & Roberts, T. (1997). Objectification theory: Toward understanding women's lived experiences and mental health risks. *Psychology of Women Quarterly, 21*(2), 173–206.

Freedman, R. (1986). *Beauty bound.* Lexington, MA: D. C. Heath.

Freedman, R., & Woodward, S. (1992). Behavioral treatment of menopausal hot flushes: Evaluation of ambulatory monitoring. *American Journal of Obstetrics and Gynecology, 167,* 439–449.

Freud, S. (1933/1965). *New introductory lectures on psychoanalysis.* New York: Norton.

Frey, C., & Hoppe-Graff, S. (1994). Serious and playful aggression in Brazilian girls and boys. *Sex Roles, 30,* 249–268.

Freyd, J. (1997). Violations of power, adaptive blindness and betrayal trauma theory. *Feminism & Psychology, 7,* 22–32.

Friday, N. (1973). *My secret garden: Women's sexual fantasies.* New York: Simon & Schuster.

Fridell, S. R., Zucker, K. J., Bradley, S. J., & Maing, D. M. (1996). Physical attractiveness of girls with gender identity disorder. *Archives of Sexual Behavior, 25,* 17–31.

Friedman, A., & Pines, A. M. (1992). Increase in Arab women's perceived power in the second half of life. *Sex Roles, 26,* 1–9.

Friedman, H., & Zebrowitz, L. A. (1992). The contribution of typical sex differences in facial maturity to sex role stereotypes. *Personality and Social Psychology Bulletin, 18,* 430–438.

Frintner, M. P., & Rubinson, L. (1993). Acquaintance rape: The influence of alcohol, fraternity membership, and sports team membership. *Journal of Sex Education and Therapy, 19,* 272–284.

Frisch, R. E. (1983a). Fatness, menarche, and fertility. In S. Golub (Ed.), *Menarche: The transition from girl to woman* (pp. 5–20). Lexington, MA: Lexington Books.

Frisch, R. E. (1983b). Fatness, puberty, and fertility: The effects of nutrition and physical training on menarche and ovulation. In J. Brooks-Gunn & A. C. Petersen (Eds.), *Girls at puberty* (pp. 29–49). New York: Plenum.

Funk, J. B., & Buchman, D. D. (1996). Children's perceptions of gender differences in social approval for playing electronic games. *Sex Roles, 35,* 219–231.

Furnham, A., & Bitar, N. (1993). The stereotyped portrayal of men and women in British television advertisements. *Sex Roles, 29,* 297–310.

Furstenberg, F. F., Jr., Moore, K. A., & Peterson, J. L. (1986). Sex education and sexual experience among adolescents. *American Journal of Public Health, 75,* 1221–1222.

Furumoto, L. (1979). Mary Whiton Calkins (1863–1930): Fourteenth president of the American Psychological Association. *Journal of the History of the Behavioral Sciences, 15,* 346–356.

Gagnon, J. H., & Simon, W. (1973). *Sexual conduct: The social sources of human sexuality.* Chicago: Aldine.

Gaiter, D. (1994, March 8). The gender divide: Black women's gains in corporate America outstrip Black men's. *Wall Street Journal, 223*, 1.

Galambos, N. L., Petersen, A. C., Richards, M., & Gitelson, I. B. (1985). The Attitudes toward Women Scale for Adolescents (AWSA): A study of reliability and validity. *Sex Roles, 13*, 343–356.

Gallagher, S., & Gersler, N. (1993). Kinkeeping and friend keeping among older women: The effect of marriage. *Gerontologist, 33*, 675–681.

Galler, R. (1984). The myth of the perfect body. In C. S. Vance (Ed.), *Pleasure and danger: Exploring female sexuality* (pp. 165–172). Boston: Routledge & Kegan Paul.

Galligan, R. F., & Terry, D. J. (1993). Romantic ideals, fear of negative implications, and the practice of safe sex. *Journal of Applied Social Psychology, 23*, 1685–1711.

Gannon, L. (1994). Sexuality and menopause. In P. Y. L. Choi & P. Nicolson (Eds.), *Female sexuality: Psychology, biology, and social context* (pp. 100–124). New York: Harvester/Wheatsheaf.

Gannon, L. (1997). Perspectives on biological, sociological, and psychological phenomena in middle- and old-age women: Interference or intervention? In S. M. C. Dollenger & L. F. DiLalla (Eds.), *Assessment and interventions issues across the life span* (pp. 239–266). Mahwah, NJ: Erlbaum.

Gannon, L. (1998). The impact of medical and sexual politics on women's health. *Feminism & Psychology, 8*, 285–302.

Gannon, L. R. (1985). *Menstrual disorders and menopause: Biological, psychological and cultural research.* New York: Praeger.

Gannon, L. R., & Ekstrom, B. (1993). Attitudes toward menopause: The influence of sociocultural paradigms. *Psychology of Women Quarterly, 17*, 275–288.

Gannon, L. R., Luchetta, T., Rhodes, K., Pardie, L., & Segrist, D. (1992). Sex bias in psychological research: Progress or complacency? *American Psychologist, 47*, 389–396.

Garcia, N., Kennedy, C., Pearlman, S. F., & Perez, J. (1987). The impact of race and culture differences: Challenges to intimacy in lesbian relationships. In Boston Lesbian Psychologies Collective (Ed.), *Lesbian psychologies: Explorations and challenges* (pp. 161–174). Urbana: University of Illinois.

Gardner, C. B. (1995). *Passing by: Gender and public harassment.* Berkeley, CA: University of California Press.

Garland, A. W. (1988). *Women activists: Challenging the abuse of power.* New York: Feminist Press.

Garland, H., Hale, K. F., & Burnson, M. (1982). Attributions for the success and failure of female managers: A replication and extension. *Psychology of Women Quarterly, 7*, 155–162.

Garner, D. M. (1997, February). The 1997 body image survey results. *Psychology Today*, pp. 30–44.

Garner, D. M., Garfinkel, P. E., Schwartz, D., & Thompson, M. (1980). Cultural expectations of thinness in women. *Psychological Reports, 47*, 483–491.

Garst, J., & Bodenhausen, G. V. (1997). Advertising's effect on men's gender role attitudes. *Sex Roles, 36*, 551–572.

Gaskill, L. R. (1991). Same-sex and cross-sex mentoring of female proteges: A comparative analysis. *Career Development Quarterly, 40*, 48–63.

Gastil, J. (1990). Generic pronouns and sexist language: The oxymoronic character of masculine generics. *Sex Roles, 23*, 629–643.

Gauna-Trujillo, B., & Higgins, P. G. (1989). Sexual intercourse and pregnancy. In P. N. Stern (Ed.), *Pregnancy and parenting* (pp. 31–40). New York: Hemisphere.

Gayford, J. J. (1975). Wife-battering: A preliminary survey of 100 cases. *British Medical Journal, 1*, 194–197.

Geis, F. L., Brown, V., Jennings, J., & Porter, N. (1984). TV commercials as achievement scripts for women. *Sex Roles, 10*, 513–525.

Gelles, R. J., & Straus, M. A. (1988). *Intimate violence: The definitive study of the causes and consequences of abuse in the American family.* New York: Simon & Schuster.

Gelwick, B. P. (1984, September). Lifestyles of six professional women engaged in college student development careers. *Journal of College Student Personnel*, 418–429.

Genero, N. P., Miller, J. B., Surrey, J., & Baldwin, L. M. (1992). Measuring perceived mutuality in close relationships: Validation of the Mutual Psychological Development Questionnaire. *Journal of Family Psychology, 6*, 36–48.

Gentile, D. A. (1993). Just what are sex and gender, anyway?: A call for a new terminological standard. *Psychological Science, 4*, 120–122.

Gentry, M. (1989). Introduction: Feminist perspectives on gender and thought: Paradox and potential. In M. Crawford & M. Gentry (Eds.), *Gender and thought* (pp. 1–16). New York: Springer-Verlag.

Gentry, M. (1998). The sexual double standard. *Psychology of Women Quarterly, 22*(3), 505–511.

George, S. M., & Dickerson, B. J. (1995). The role of the grandmother in poor single-mother families and households. In B. J. Dickerson (Ed.), *African American single mothers* (pp. 146–163). Thousand Oaks: Sage.

Gergen, M. M. (1990). Finished at 40: Women's development within the patriarchy. *Psychology of Women Quarterly, 14,* 471–493.

Gerike, A. E. (1990). On gray hair and oppressed brains. *Journal of Women & Aging, 1,* 35–46.

Gerson, M. (1980). The lure of motherhood. *Psychology of Women Quarterly, 5,* 207–218.

Gerstel, N. (1988). Divorce, gender, and social integration. *Gender & Society, 2,* 343–367.

Geschwind, N., & Behan, P. (1982). Left-handedness: Association with immune disease, migraine, and developmental learning disorder. *Proceedings of National Academy of Sciences, 79,* 5097–5100.

Gibber, J. R. (1981). Infant-directed behaviors in male and female rhesus monkeys. Unpublished doctoral dissertation. Department of Psychology, University of Wisconsin–Madison.

Gibbons, J. L., Stiles, D. A., & Shkodriani, G. M. (1991). Adolescents' attitudes toward family and gender roles: An international comparison. *Sex Roles, 25,* 625–643.

Giddings, P. (1984). *When and where I enter: The impact of black women on race and sex in America.* New York: Morrow.

Gidycz, C. A., Coble, C. N., Latham, L., & Layman, M. J. (1992). Relation of a sexual assault experience on adulthood to prior victimization experiences: A prospective analysis. *Psychology of Women Quarterly, 7,* 151–168.

Gieve, K. (1989). *Balancing acts: On being a mother.* London: Virago.

Gilbert, L. A. (1980). Feminist therapy. In A. M. Brodsky & R. Hare-Mustin (Eds.), *Women and psychotherapy: An assessment of research and practice* (pp. 245–265). New York: Guilford Press.

Gilbert, L. A. (1987). What makes dual-career marriages tick? ERIC Document Reproduction Service No. ED 289 135.

Gilbert, L. A. (1993). *Two careers/One family: The promise of gender equality.* London: Sage.

Gilbert, L. A. (1994). Reclaiming and returning gender to context: Examples from studies of heterosexual dual-earner families. *Psychology of Women Quarterly, 18,* 539–558.

Gilbert, L. A., Galessich, J. M., & Evans, S. L. (1983). Sex of faculty role model and students' self-perceptions of competency. *Sex Roles, 9,* 597–607.

Gilbert, L. A., & Rossman, K. M. (1992). Gender and the mentoring process for women: Implications for professional development. *Professional Psychology: Research and Practice, 23,* 233–238.

Gilgun, J. F. (1995). We shared something special: The moral discourse of incest perpetrators. *Journal of Marriage and the Family, 57,* 265–281.

Gillen, B. (1981). Physical attractiveness: A determinant of two types of goodness. *Personality and Social Psychology Bulletin, 7,* 277–281.

Gilligan, C. (1982). *In a different voice.* Cambridge, MA: Harvard University Press.

Gilmore, D. D. (1990). *Mankind in the making: Cultural concepts of masculinity.* New Haven: Yale University Press.

Ginorio, A., Gutierrez, L., Cauce, A. M., & Acosta, M. (1995). Psychological issues for Latinas. In H. Landrine (Ed.), *Bringing cultural diversity to feminist psychology* (pp. 241–263). Washington, DC: American Psychological Association.

Giroux, H. A. (1998). Stealing innocence: The politics of child beauty pageants. In H. Jenkins (Ed.), *The children's culture reader* (pp. 265–282). New York: New York University Press.

Giuffre, P. A., & Williams, C. L. (1994). Boundary lines: Labeling sexual harassment in restaurants. *Gender and Society, 8,* 379–401.

Glenn, N. D., & McLanahan, S. (1981). The effects of offspring on the psychological wellbeing of older adults. *Journal of Marriage and the Family, 43,* 409–421.

Glick, P., Diebold, J., Bailey-Werner, B., & Zhu, L. (1997). The two faces of Adam: Ambivalent sexism and polarized attitudes toward women. *Personality and Social Psychology Bulletin, 23,* 1323–1334.

Glick, P., & Fiske, S. T. (1996). The ambivalent sexism inventory: Differentiating hostile and benevolent sexism. *Journal of Personality and Social Psychology, 70,* 491–512.

Glick, P., & Fiske, S. T. (1999). Sexism and other "isms": Interdependence, status, and the ambivalent content of stereotypes. In W. B. Swann, Jr., J. H. Langlois, & L. A. Gilbert (Eds.), *Sexism and stereotypes: The gender science of Janet Taylor Spence* (pp. 193–221). Washington, DC: American Psychological Association.

Goffman, E. (1963). *Stigma*. Englewood Cliffs, NJ: Prentice-Hall.

Gold, A. R., & St. Ange, M. C. (1974). Development of sex role stereotypes in Black and White elementary school girls. *Developmental Psychology, 10,* 461.

Goldberg, C. (1999, March 23). M.I.T. acknowledges bias against female professors. *The New York Times,* pp. A1, A16.

Goldberg, P. A. (1968). Are women prejudiced against women? *Transaction, 5,* 28–30.

Golden, C. (1987). Diversity and variability in women's sexual identities. In Boston Lesbian Psychologies Collective (Eds.), *Lesbian psychologies* (pp. 18–34). Urbana: University of Illinois Press.

Goldenhar, L. M., Swanson, N. G., Hurrell, J. J., Ruder, A., & Deddens, J. (1998). Stressors and adverse outcomes for female construction workers. *Journal of Occupational Health Psychology, 3*(1), 19–32.

Golding, J. M. (1988). Gender differences in depressive symptoms: Statistical considerations. *Psychology of Women Quarterly, 12,* 61–74.

Goldman, K. (1993, August 23). Sexy Sony ad riles a network of women. *Wall Street Journal,* B5.

Goldman, R., & Goldman, J. (1982). *Children's sexual thinking*. London: Routledge & Kegan Paul.

Goldman, W., & Lewis, P. (1977). Beautiful is good: Evidence that the physically attractive are more socially skillful. *Journal of Experimental Social Psychology, 13,* 125–130.

Goldstein, D. (1983). Spouse abuse. In A. Goldstein (Ed.), *Prevention and Control of Aggression* (pp. 37–65). New York: Pergamon Press.

Golombok, S., & Fivush, R. (1994). *Gender development*. New York: Cambridge University Press.

Gomez, C. A., & Vanoss-Marin, B. (1996). Gender, culture, and power: Barriers to HIV-prevention strategies for women. *Journal of Sex Research, 33*(4), 355–362.

Gondolf, E. W. (1998). *Assessing women battering in mental health services*. Thousand Oaks, CA: Sage.

Gondolf, E. W., & Fisher, E. R. (1998). *Battered women as survivors: An alternative to treating learned helplessness*. Lexington, MA: Lexington.

Gondolf, E. W., & Shestakov, D. (1997). Spousal homicide in Russia versus the United States: Preliminary findings and implications. *Journal of Family Violence, 12,* 63–74.

Goodchilds, J. D., Zellman, G. L., Johnson, P. B., & Giarrusso, R. (1988). Adolescents and their perceptions of sexual interactions. In A. W. Burgess (Ed.), *Rape and sexual assault,* Vol. II (pp. 245–270). New York: Garland.

Goodman, M. J. (1982). A critique of menopause research. In A. M. Voda, M. Dinnerstein, & S. R. O'Donnell (Eds.), *Changing perspectives on menopause* (pp. 273–288). Austin: University of Texas Press.

Gordon, C. (1968). Self-conceptions: Configurations of content. In C. Gordon & K. Gergen (Eds.), *The self in social interaction*. New York: Wiley.

Gordon, J. S. (1996). Community services of abused women: A review of perceived usefulness and efficacy. *Journal of Family Violence, 11,* 315–329.

Gordon, J. W., & Ruddle, F. H. (1981). Mammalian gonadal determination and gametogenesis. *Science, 211,* 1265–1271.

Gordon, L. (1988). *Heroes of their own lives: The politics and history of family violence*. New York: Penguin.

Gottman, J. M., & Parker, J. G. (Eds.). (1987). *Conversations of friends: Speculations in affective development*. New York: Cambridge University Press.

Gough, K. (1984). The origin of the family. In J. Freeman (Ed.), *Women: A feminist perspective* (3rd ed., pp. 83–99). Palo Alto, CA: Mayfield.

Gould, S. J. (1980). *The panda's thumb*. New York: Norton.

Gould, S. J. (1981). *The mismeasure of man*. New York: Norton.

Gove, W. R. (1972). The relationship between sex roles, marital status, and mental illness. *Social Forces, 51,* 34–44.

Gove, W. R., & Shin, H-C. (1989). The psychological well-being of divorced and widowed men and women: An empirical analysis. *Journal of Family Issues, 10,* 122–144.

Grady, K. E. (1977, April). *The belief in sex differences*. Paper presented at the meeting of the Eastern Psychological Association, Boston.

Grady, K. E. (1979). Androgyny reconsidered. In J. H. Williams (Ed.), *Psychology of women: Selected readings* (pp. 172–177). New York: Norton.

Grady, K. E. (1981). Sex bias in research design. *Psychology of Women Quarterly, 5,* 628–636.

Graham, A. (1975). The making of a nonsexist dictionary. In B. Thorne & N. Henley (Eds.), *Language and sex: Difference and dominance*. Rowley, MA: Newbury House.

Graham, J. A., & Cohen, R. (1997). Race and sex as factors in children's sociometric ratings and friendship choices. *Social Development, 6*, 355–372.

Grambs, J. D. (1989). *Women over forty: Visions and realities.* New York: Springer.

Gravenkemper, S. A., & Paludi, M. A. (1983). Fear of success revisited: Introducing an ambiguous cue. *Sex Roles, 9*, 897–900.

Gray, J. D. (1983). The married professional woman: An examination of her role conflicts and coping strategies. *Psychology of Women Quarterly, 7*, 235–243.

Green, J. (1996). Mothers in "incest families": A critique of blame and its destructive sequels. *Violence Against Women, 2*, 322–348.

Green, R., Williams, K., & Goodman, M. (1982). Ninety-nine "tomboys" and "nontomboys": Behavioral contrasts and demographic similarities. *Archives of Sexual Behavior, 11*, 247–266.

Greene, A. L., & Adams-Price, C. (1990). Adolescents' secondary attachments to celebrity figures. *Sex Roles, 23*, 325–347.

Greene, B. (1994). Diversity and difference: The issue of race in feminist theory. In M. P. Mirkin (Ed.), *Women in context: Toward a feminist reconstruction of psychotherapy* (pp. 333–351). New York: Guilford.

Greene, B., & Sanchez-Hucles, J. (1997). Diversity: Advancing an inclusive feminist psychology. In J. Worell & N. G. Johnson (Eds.), *Shaping the future of feminist psychology: Education, research, and practice* (pp. 173–202). Washington, DC: American Psychological Association.

Greene, B. A. (1986). When the therapist is white and the patient is black: Considerations for psychotherapy in the feminist heterosexual and lesbian communities. In D. Howard (Ed.), *The dynamics of feminist therapy* (pp. 41–65). New York: Haworth Press.

Greene, B. A. (1990). Sturdy bridges: The role of African-American mothers in the socialization of African-American children. In J. P. Knowles & E. Cole (Eds.), *Motherhood: A feminist perspective* (pp. 205–225). New York: Haworth.

Greene, B. A. (1992). Still here: A perspective on psychotherapy with African American women. In J. C. Chrisler & D. Howard (Eds.), *New directions in feminist psychology: Practice, theory, and research* (pp. 13–25). New York: Springer.

Greene, C. K., & Stitt-Gohdes, W. L. (1997). Factors that influence women's choices to work in the trades. *Journal of Career Development, 23*(4), 265–278.

Greenfeld, L. A. (1997, February). *Sex offenses and offenders: An analysis of data on rape and sexual assault.* U.S. Department of Justice. Office of Justice Programs. Bureau of Justice Statistics. (NJC-163392). http://www.ojp.usdoj.gov/bjs.

Greenglass, E. R., & Burke, R. J. (1988). Work and family precursors of burnout in teachers: Sex differences. *Sex Roles, 18*, 215–229.

Greenspan, M. (1983). *A new approach to women and therapy.* New York: McGraw-Hill.

Greenspan, M. (1986). Should therapists be personal? Self-disclosure and therapeutic distance in feminist therapy. In D. Howard (Ed.), *The dynamics of feminist therapy* (pp. 5–17). New York: Haworth Press.

Greenstein, T. N. (1996). Husbands' participation in domestic labor: Interactive effects of wives' and husbands' gender ideologies. *Journal of Marriage and the Family, 58*(3), 585–595.

Greenwood-Audant, L. M. (1984). The internalization of powerlessness: A case study of the displaced homemaker. In J. Freeman (Ed.), *Women: A feminist perspective* (3rd ed., pp. 264–281). New York: Mayfield.

Gremaux, R. (1996). Woman becoming man in the Balkans. In G. Herdt (Ed.), *Third sex, third gender: Beyond sexual dimorphism in culture and history* (pp. 241–281). New York: Zone Books.

Griffin, S. (1971). Rape: The all-American crime. *Ramparts, 10*, 26–35.

Grimm, D. E. (1987). Toward a theory of gender: Transsexualism, gender, sexuality, and relationships. *American Behavioral Scientist, 31*, 66–85.

Grogan, S., Knott, J. A., & Gaze, C. E. (1996). The effects of viewing same gender photographic models on body esteem. *Psychology of Women Quarterly, 20*, 569–575.

Grossman, A. L., & Tucker, J. S. (1997). Gender differences and sexism in the knowledge and use of slang. *Sex Roles, 37*, 101–110.

Grossman, F. K., Gilbert, L. A., Genero, N. P., Hawes, S. E., Hyde, J. S., & Marecek, J. (1997). Feminist research: Practice and problems. In J. Worell & N. G. Johnson (Eds.), *Shaping the future of feminist psychology: Education, research, and practice* (pp. 73–91). Washington, DC: American Psychological Association.

Grote, N. K., & Frieze, I. H. (1998). 'Remembrance of things past': Perceptions of marital love from its beginnings to the present. *Journal of Social and Personal Relationships, 15*(1), 91–109.

Gruber, J. E. (1997). An epidemology of sexual

harassment: Evidence from North America and Europe. In W. O'Donohue (Ed.), *Sexual harassment: Theory, research and treatment* (pp. 84–98). Boston: Allyn and Bacon.

Gruber, J. E., & Bjorn, L. (1982). Blue-collar blues: The sexual harassment of women autoworkers. *Work and Occupations, 9,* 271–298.

Grundman, E. O., O'Donohue, W., & Peterson, S. H. (1997). The prevention of sexual harassment. In W. O'Donohue (Ed.), *Sexual harassment: Theory, research and treatment* (pp. 175–184). Boston: Allyn & Bacon.

Guinier, L., Fine, M., & Balin, J. (1997). *Becoming gentlemen: Women, law school, and institutional change.* Boston: Beacon Press.

Guinn, S., & Russell, L. G. (1987). Personnel decisions and the dual-earner couple. *Employment Relations Today, 14,* 83–90.

Gullette, M. M. (1997). *Declining to decline: Cultural combat and the politics of the midlife.* Charlottesville: University Press of Virginia.

Gutek, B. A. (1985). *Sex and the workplace.* San Francisco: Jossey-Bass.

Gutek, B. A. (1989). Relocation, family, and the bottom line: Results from the Division 35 survey. *Psychology of Women Quarterly, 16,* 5–7.

Gutek, B. A., & Larwood, L. (Eds.). (1987). *Women's career development.* Newbury Park, CA: Sage.

Gutek, B. A., Repetti, R. L., & Silver, D. L. (1988). Nonwork roles and stress at work. In C. L. Cooper & R. Payne (Eds.), *Causes, coping, and consequences of stress at work* (pp. 141–174). New York: Wiley.

Guthrie, R. V. (1976). *Even the rat was white: A historical view of psychology.* New York: Harper & Row.

Gwartney-Gibbs, P. A., Stockard, J., & Brohmer, S. (1983). Learning courtship violence: The influence of parents, peers and personal experiences. *Family Relations, 36,* 276–282.

Haavind, H. (1983). Love and power in marriage. In H. Holter (Ed.), *Patriarchy in a welfare society* (pp. 136–167). Oxford, England: Oxford University Press.

Haddock, G., & Zanna, M. P. (1994). Preferring "housewives" to "feminists": Categorization and the favorability of attitudes toward women. *Psychology of Women Quarterly, 18,* 25–52.

Haiken, E. (1997). *Venus envy: A history of cosmetic surgery.* Baltimore: Johns Hopkins University Press.

Haj-Yahia, M. M. (1996). Wife abuse in the Arab society in Israel. Challenges for future changes. In J. L. Edleson & Z. C. Eisikovits (Eds.), *Future interventions with battered women and their families* (pp. 87–101). Thousand Oaks: Sage.

Haj-Yahia, M. M. (1998). *Beliefs about wife beating among Palestinian women: The influence of their patriarchal ideology.* Violence Against Women, 4, 533–558.

Hale, G., Duckworth, J., Zimostrad, S., & Nicholas, D. (1988). Abusive partners: MMPI profiles of male batterers. *Journal of Mental Health Counseling, 10* (4), 214–224.

Hall, J. A. (1985). *Nonverbal sex differences: Communication accuracy and expressive style.* Baltimore: Johns Hopkins University Press.

Hall, M. (1994, March 31). Feds, states clash on abortion. *USA Today,* A3.

Hall, N. L. (1984). *The true story of a single mother.* Boston: South End Press.

Hall, R. L., & Greene, B. (1996). Sins of omission and commission: Women, psychotherapy, and the psychological literature. *Women & Therapy, 18,* 5–31.

Halpern, D. F. (1986). *Sex differences in cognitive abilities.* Hillsdale, NJ: Erlbaum.

Halpern, D. F. (1992). *Sex differences in cognitive abilities* (2nd ed.). Hillsdale, NJ: Erlbaum.

Hamberger, L. K., Saunders, D. G., & Hovey, M. (1992). The prevalence of domestic violence in community practice and rate of physician inquiry. *Family Medicine, 24* (4), 283–287.

Hamer, D. H., Hu, S., Magnuson, V., Hu, N., & Pattatucci, A. M. L. (1993). A linkage between DNA markers in the X chromosome and male sexual orientation. *Science, 261,* 321–327.

Hamilton, L. H., Brooks-Gunn, J., Warren, M. P., & Hamilton, W. G. (1987, December). The impact of thinness and dieting on the professional ballet dancer. *Journal of Medical Problems of Performing Artists,* 117–122.

Hamilton, M. C. (1988). Masculine generics and misperceptions of AIDS risk. *Journal of Applied Social Psychology, 18,* 1222–1240.

Hamilton, M. C. (1991). Masculine bias in the attribution of personhood: People = male, male = people. *Psychology of Women Quarterly, 15,* 393–402.

Hamilton, M. C., & Henley, N. M. (1982, March). *Detrimental consequences of generic masculine usage: Effects on the reader/hearer's cognitions.* Paper presented at the meeting of the Western Psychological Association, Sacramento, CA.

Hamilton, M. C., & Mayfield, B. (1999). Son-daughter preferences of primiparous married couples, nonpregnant married couples, and college students. Paper presented at the meeting of the Association for Women in Psychology. Providence, RI, March.

Hammer, J. C., Fisher, J. D., Fitzgerald, P., & Fisher, W. A. (1996). When two heads aren't better than one: AIDS risk behavior in college-age couples. *Journal of Applied Social Psychology, 26*(5), 375–397.

Hammer, M. (1970). Preference for a male child: Cultural factor. *Journal of Individual Psychology, 26,* 54–56.

Hammond, J. A., & Mahoney, C. W. (1983). Reward-cost balancing among women coalminers. *Sex Roles, 9,* 17–29.

Hankin, B. L., Abramson, L. Y., Moffott, T. E., Silva, P. A., McGee, R., & Angell, K. E. (1998). Development of depression from preadolescence to young adulthood: Emerging gender differences in a 10-year longitudinal study. *Journal of Abnormal Psychology, 107,* 128–140.

Hansen, F. J., & Reekie, L. (1990). Sex differences in clinical judgments of male and female therapists. *Sex Roles, 23,* 51–64.

Hanson, K. A., & Gidycz, C. A. (1993). An evaluation of a sexual assault prevention program. *Journal of Consulting and Clinical Psychology, 61,* 1046–1052.

Harding, S. (1986). *The science question in feminism.* Ithaca, NY: Cornell University Press.

Hardon, A. (1992). Norplant: Conflicting views on its safety and acceptability. In H. B. Holmes (Ed.), *Issues in reproductive technology.* New York: Garland.

Hare-Mustin, R. T. (1983). An appraisal of the relationship between women and psychotherapy: 80 years after the case of Dora. *American Psychologist, 38,* 593–601.

Hare-Mustin, R. T., & Marecek, J. (1988). The meaning of difference: Gender theory, postmodernism, and psychology. *American Psychologist, 43,* 455–464.

Hare-Mustin, R. T., & Marecek, J. (Eds.). (1990). *Making a difference: Psychology and the construction of gender.* New Haven: Yale University Press.

Harlan, S. L., & O'Farrell, B. (1982). After the pioneers: Prospects for women in nontraditional blue-collar jobs. *Work and Occupations, 9,* 363–386.

Harlow, H. (1971). *Learning to love.* New York: Albion.

Harlow, H. F. (1965). Sexual behavior in the rhesus monkey. In F. A. Beach (Ed.). *Sex and behavior,* pp. 234–265, NY: Krieger.

Harnack, L., Story, M., Martinson, B., Neumark-Sztainer, D., & Stang, J. (1998). Guess who's cooking? The role of men in meal planning, shopping, and preparation in U.S. families. *Journal of the American Dietetic Association, 98*(9), 995–1000.

Harris, B. J. (1984). The power of the past: History and the psychology of women. In M. Lewin (Ed.), *In the shadow of the past* (pp. 1–5). New York: Columbia University Press.

Harris, M. B. (1990). Is love seen as different for the obese? *Journal of Applied Social Psychology, 20,* 1209–1224.

Harris, M. B. (1992). Beliefs about how to reduce anger. *Psychological Reports, 70,* 203–210.

Harris, M. B., Begay, C., & Page, P. (1989). Activities, family relationships and feelings about aging in a multicultural elderly sample. *International Journal of Aging and Human Development, 29,* 103–117.

Harris, V. R. (1994). Prison of color. In E. Featherston (Ed.), *Skin deep: Women writing on color, culture, and identity* (pp. 8–15). Freedom, CA: The Crossing Press.

Harrison, A. A., & Saeed, L. (1977). Let's make a deal: An analysis of revelations and stipulations in lonely hearts advertisements. *Journal of Personality and Social Psychology, 35,* 257–264.

Harrison, A. W., Rainer, R. K., Jr., & Hochwarter, W. A. (1997). Gender differences in computing activities. *Journal of Social Behavior and Personality, 12*(4), 849–868.

Harter, S. (1990). Self and identity development. In S. S. Feldman & G. R. Elliott (Eds.), *At the threshold: The developing adolescent* (pp. 352–387). Cambridge, MA: Harvard University Press.

Hartl, D. L. (1983). *Human genetics.* New York: Harper & Row.

Hartung, C. M., & Widiger, T. A. (1998). Gender differences in the diagnoses of mental disorders: Conclusions and controversies of the DSM-IV. *Psychological Bulletin, 123,* 260–278.

Hartzler, K., & Franco, J. N. (1985). Ethnicity, division of household tasks and equity in marital roles: A comparison of Anglo and Mexican American couples. *Hispanic Journal of Behavioral Sciences, 7,* 333–344.

Haslett, B. B., & Lipman, S. (1997). Micro inequities: Up close and personal. In N. V. Benokraitis (Ed.), *Subtle sexism: Current practice and prospects for change* (pp. 34–53). Thousand Oaks, CA: Sage.

Hatch, L. R. (1995). Gray clouds and silver linings: Women's resources in later life. In J.

Freeman (Ed.), *Women: A feminist perspective* (5th ed., pp. 182–196). Mountain View, CA: Mayfield Publishing Co.

Hatton, B. J. (1994, March). The experiences of African American lesbians: Family, community, and intimate relationships. Poster presented at the Southeastern Psychological Association Convention. New Orleans, LA.

Hayes, C. D. (Ed.). (1987). *Risking the future: Adolescent sexuality, pregnancy, and childbearing.* Washington, DC: National Academy Press.

Hayes, C. L., & Anderson, D. (1993). Psychosocial and economic adjustment of midlife women after divorce. *Journal of Women and Aging, 4,* 83–99.

Hays, S. (1996). *The cultural contradictions of motherhood.* New Haven: Yale University.

Healy, S. (1986). Growing to be an old woman: Aging and ageism. In J. Alexander, D. Berrow, L. Domitrovich, M. Donnelly, & C. McLean (Eds.), *Women and aging* (pp. 58–62). Corvallis, OR: Calyx.

Healy, S. (1993). Confronting ageism: A must for mental health. In N. D. Davis, E. Cole, & E. D. Rothblum (Eds.), *Faces of women and aging* (pp. 41–54). Binghamton, NY: Harrington Park Press.

Hebl, M. R., & Heatherton, T. F. (1998). The stigma of obesity in women: The difference in black and white. *Personality and Social Psychology Bulletin, 24,* 417–426.

Hecht, M. A., & LaFrance, M. (1998). License or obligation to smile: The effect of power and sex on amount and type of smiling. *Personality and Social Psychology Bulletin, 24,* 1332–1342.

Hedges, L. V., & Becker, B. J. (1986). Statistical methods in the meta-analysis of research on gender differences. In J. G. Hyde & M. C. Linn (Eds.), *The psychology of gender: Advances through meta-analysis* (pp. 14–50). Baltimore: Johns Hopkins.

Hedlund, R. D., Freeman, P. K., Hamm, K. E., & Stein, R. M. (1979). The electability of women candidates: The effects of sex role stereotypes. *Journal of Politics, 41,* 513–524.

Heilman, M. E., Block, C. J., Martell, R. F., & Simon, M. C. (1989). Has anything changed? Current characterizations of men, women, and managers. *Journal of Applied Psychology, 74,* 935–942.

Heilman, M. E., Simon, M. C., & Repper, D. P. (1987). Intentionally favored, unintentionally harmed? Impact of sex-based preferential selection on self-perceptions and self-evaluations. *Journal of Applied Psychology, 72,* 62–68.

Heilman, M. E., & Stopeck, M. H. (1985). Attractiveness and corporate success: Differential causal attributions for males and females. *Journal of Applied Psychology, 70,* 379–388.

Helgeson, V. S. (1994). Relations of agency and communion to well-being: Evidence and potential explanations. *Psychological Bulletin, 116,* 412–428.

Helmreich, R. L., & Spence, J. T. (1978). The work and family orientation questionnaire: An objective instrument to assess components of achievement motivation and attitudes towards family and career. *JSAS Catalog of Selected Documents in Psychology, 8,* 35.

Helson, R. M. (1978). Creativity in women. In J. Sherman & F. Denmark (Eds.), *Psychology of women: Future directions of research* (pp. 553–604). New York: Psychological Dimensions.

Helson, R. M., & Wink, P. (1992). Personality change in women from the early 40s to the early 50s. *Psychology and Aging, 7,* 46–55.

Helwig, A. A. (1998). Gender-role stereotyping: Testing theory with a longitudinal sample. *Sex Roles, 38,* 403–423.

Hemmer, J. D., & Kleiber, D. A. (1981). Tomboys and sissies: Androgynous children? *Sex Roles, 7,* 1205–1211.

Henderson-Daniel, J. (1994). Exclusion and emphasis reframed as a matter of ethics. *Ethics and Behavior, 4,* 229–235.

Henley, N. (1985). Psychology and gender. *Signs, 11,* 101–119.

Henley, N. M. (1977). *Body politics: Power, sex, and nonverbal communication.* Englewood Cliffs, NJ: Prentice-Hall.

Henley, N. M. (1989). Molehill or mountain? What we do know and don't know about sex bias in language. In M. Crawford & M. Gentry (Eds.), *Gender and thought* (pp. 59–78). New York: Springer-Verlag.

Henley, N. M., & Freeman, J. (1989). The sexual politics of interpersonal behavior. In J. Freeman (Ed.), *Women: A feminist perspective* (4th ed., pp. 457–469). Mountainview, CA: Mayfield.

Henley, N. M., Meng, K., O'Brien, D., McCarthy, W. J., & Sockloskie, R. (1998). Developing a scale to measure the diversity of feminist attitudes. *Psychology of Women Quarterly, 22,* 317–348.

Henly, J. R. (1997). The complexity of support: The impact of family structure and provisional support on African American and white adolescent mothers' well-being. *American Journal of Community Psychology, 25*(5), 629–655.

Henry, C. (1998, May 10). Community voices—women in the '90s: Names. *The Philadelphia Inquirer*, p. E6.

Henshaw, S. K. (1998). Barriers to access to abortion sources. In L. J. Beckman & S. M. Harvey (Eds.), *The new civil war: The psychology, culture, and politics of abortion* (pp. 61–80). Washington, DC: American Psychological Association.

Henwood, K. L. (1993). Women and later life: The discursive construction of identities within family relationships. *Journal of Aging Studies, 7,* 303–319.

Herdt, G. (1996). Mistaken sex: Culture, biology, and the third sex in New Guinea. In G. Herdt (Ed.), *Third sex, third gender: Beyond sexual dimorphism in culture and history* (pp. 419–445). New York: Zone Books.

Herdt, G. H., & Davidson, J. (1988). The Sambra "Turnim-man": Sociocultural and clinical aspects of gender formation in male pseudohermaphrodites with 5 alpha-reductase deficiency in Papua New Guinea. *Archives of Sexual Behavior, 17,* 33–56.

Herek, G. M. (1993). The context of antigay violence: Notes on cultural and psychological heterosexism. In L. D. Garnets & D. C. Kimmel (Eds.), *Psychological perspectives on lesbian and gay male experiences* (pp. 89–108). New York: Columbia University Press.

Herman, A. (1988). Foreward. In A. Statham, E. M. Miller, & H. O. Mauksch (Eds.), *The worth of a women's work: A qualitative synthesis* (pp. ix–xi). Albany, NY: State University of New York Press.

Hernandez, D. G. (1994). Good and the bad about women's news in newspapers. *Editor and Publisher,* May 21, pp. 17, 41.

Hetherington, E. M., & Parke, R. D. (1975). *Child psychology: A contemporary viewpoint.* New York: McGraw-Hill.

Hewlett, S. A., & West, C. (1998). *The war against parents: What we can do for America's beleaguered moms and dads.* Boston: Houghton Mifflin.

Heywood, S. (1989). *Fantasy lover.* Ontario, Canada: Harlequin.

Hickman, S. E., & Muehlenhard, C. L. (1997). College women's fears and precautionary behaviors relating to acquaintance rape and stranger rape. *Psychology of Women Quarterly, 21*(4), 527–547.

Hill, J. P. (1988). Adapting to menarche: Famil-ial control and conflict. In M. R. Gunnar & W. A. Collins (Eds.), *Development during the transition to adolescence. Minnesota symposia on child development* (Vol. 21, pp. 43–77). Hillsdale, NJ: Erlbaum.

Hill, J. P., & Holmbeck, G. N. (1987). Familial adaptation to biological change during adolescence. In R. M. Lerner & T. T. Foch (Eds.), *Biological-psychosocial interactions in early adolescence* (pp. 207–223). Hillsdale, NJ: Erlbaum.

Hill, J. P., & Lynch, M. E. (1983). The intensification of gender-related role expectations during early adolescence. In J. Brooks-Gunn & A. C. Petersen (Eds.), *Girls at puberty* (pp. 201–228). New York: Plenum.

Hill, M. (1987). Child-rearing attitudes of black lesbian mothers. In Boston Lesbian Psychologies Collective (Eds.), *Lesbian psychologies* (pp. 215–225). Urbana: University of Illinois Press.

Hillier, L., & Foddy, M. (1993). The role of observer attitudes in judgments of blame in cases of wife assault. *Sex Roles, 29,* 629–644.

Hite, S. (1976). *The Hite report.* New York: Macmillan.

Hite, S. (1987). *The Hite report: Women and love; a cultural revolution in progress.* New York: Knopf.

Ho, C. K. (1990). An analysis of domestic violence in Asian American communities: A multicultural approach to counseling. In L. Brown & M. P. P. Root (Eds.), *Diversity and complexity in feminist therapy and theory* (pp. 129–150). Harrington Park, NY: Haworth Press.

Hochschild, A. R. (1978). *The unexpected community: Portrait of an old-age subculture.* Berkeley, CA: University of California Press.

Hochschild, A. R. (1989). *The second shift: Working parents and the revolution at home.* New York: Viking.

Hockenberry-Eaton, M., Richman, M. J., DiIorio, C., Rivero, T., & Maibach, E. (1996). Mother and adolescent knowledge of sexual development: The effects of gender, age, and sexual experience. *Adolescence, 31*(121), 35–48.

Hoffman, C., & Hurst, N. (1990). Gender stereotypes: Perceptions or rationalization? *Journal of Personality and Social Psychology, 58,* 197–208.

Hoffman, L. W., & Kloska, D. D. (1995). Parents' gender-based attitudes toward marital roles and child rearing: Development and validation of new measures. *Sex Roles, 32,* 273–295.

Hoffnung, M. (1989). Motherhood: Contemporary conflict for women. In J. Freeman (Ed.), *Women: A feminist perspective* (4th ed., pp. 157–175). Mountain View, CA: Mayfield.

Holland, D., & Skinner, D. (1987). Prestige and intimacy: The cultural models behind Americans' talk about gender types. In D. Holland & N. Quinn (Eds.), *Cultural models in language and thought* (pp. 78–111). Cambridge, England: Cambridge University Press.

Hollin, C. R. (1987). Sex roles in adolescence. In D. J. Hargreaves & A. M. Colley (Eds.), *The psychology of sex roles* (pp. 176–197). New York: Hemisphere.

Hollingworth, L. S. (1916). Social devices for impelling women to bear and rear children. *American Journal of Sociology, 22,* 19–29.

Homma-True, R. (1990). Psychotherapeutic issues of Asian American women. *Sex Roles, 22,* 477–486.

Hooijberg, R., & DiTomaso, N. (1996). Leadership in and of demographically diverse organizations. *Leadership Quarterly, 7*(1), 1–19.

hooks, b. (1984). *Feminist theory: From margin to center.* Boston: South End Press.

hooks, b. (1989). *Talking back: Thinking feminist, thinking black.* Boston: South End Press.

Hopkins, J., Marcus, M., & Campbell, S. B. (1984). Postpartum depression: A critical review. *Psychological Bulletin, 95,* 498–515.

Hort, B., Leinbach, M., & Fagot, B. (1991). Is there a coherence among the cognitive components of gender acquisition? *Sex Roles, 24,* 195–207.

Hort, B. E., & Leinbach, M. D. (1993). *Children's use of metaphorical cues in gender typing of objects.* Paper presented at the meeting of the Society for Research on Child Development, New Orleans, LA.

Hossain, Z., & Roopmarine, J. L. (1993). Division of household labor and child care in dual-earner African-American families with infants. *Sex Roles, 29,* 571–584.

Houseknecht, S. K. (1979). Timing of the decision to remain voluntarily childless: Evidence for continuous socialization. *Psychology of Women Quarterly, 4,* 81–86.

Houser, B., & Garvey, C. (1985). Factors that affect nontraditional vocational enrollment among women. *Psychology of Women Quarterly, 9,* 105–118.

Houston, S., & Hwang, N. (1996). Correlates of the objective and subjective experiences of sexual harassment in high school. *Sex Roles, 34,* 189–204.

Howard, J. A., & Hollander, J. A. (Eds.). (1997). *Gendered situations, gendered selves: A gender lens on social psychology.* Thousand Oaks, CA: Sage.

Howe, K. G. (1989). Telling our mothers' story: Changing daughters' perceptions of their mothers in a women's studies course. In R. K. Unger (Ed.), *Representations: Social constructions of gender* (pp. 45–60). Amityville, NY: Baywood.

Howe, L. K. (1977). *Pink collar workers.* New York: Putnam.

Howell, M., & Pugliesi, K. (1988). Husbands who harm: Predicting spousal violence by men. *Journal of Family Violence, 3*(1), 15–27.

Hrdy, S. B. (1988, April). Daughters or sons. *Natural History,* 64–82.

Huesmann, L. R., & Eron, L. (1992). Childhood aggression and adult criminality. In J. McCord (Ed.), *Facts, frameworks, and forecasts: Advances in criminological theory.* Vol. 3. New Brunswick, NJ: Transaction Publishers.

Humphrey, J. A., & White, J. W. (in press). Women's Vulnerability to Sexual Assault from Adolescence to Young Adulthood. *Journal of Adolescent Health.*

Hunt, M. (1974). *Sexual behavior in the 1970s.* Chicago: Playboy Press.

Hunter, G. T. (1974). Pediatrician. In R. B. Kundsin (Ed.), *Women and success: The anatomy of achievement* (pp. 58–61). New York: Morrow.

Hunter, M. S. (1990). Psychological and somatic experience of the menopause: A prospective study. *Psychosomatic Medicine, 52,* 357–367.

Hurlbert, D. F., & Whittaker, K. E. (1991). The role of masturbation in marital and sexual satisfaction: A comparative study of female masturbators and nonmasturbators. *Journal of Sex Education and Therapy, 17,* 272–282.

Hurtig, A. L., & Rosenthal, I. M. (1987). Psychological findings in early treated cases of female pseudohermaphroditism caused by virilizing congenital adrenal hyperplasia. *Archives of Sexual Behavior, 16,* 209–223.

Huselid, B. F., & Cooper, M. L. (1994). Gender roles as mediators of sex differences in expression of pathology. *Journal of Abnormal Psychology, 103,* 595–603.

Huston, A. C. (1983). Sex-typing. In P. H. Mussen (Ed.), *Handbook of child psychology* (Vol. 4; 4th ed., pp. 387–467). New York: Wiley.

Hyde, J. S., Fennema, E., Ryan, M., Frost, L., & Hopp, C. (1990). Gender comparisons of mathematics attitudes and affects: A meta-analysis. *Psychology of Women Quarterly, 14,* 299–324.

Hyde, J. S. (1981). How large are cognitive gender differences? *American Psychologist, 36,* 892–910.

Hyde, J. S. (1990). *Understanding human sexuality* (4th ed.). New York: McGraw-Hill.

Hyde, J. S., & DeLamater, J. (1997). *Understanding human sexuality* (6th ed.). New York: McGraw-Hill.

Hyde, J. S., & Linn, M. C. (Eds.). (1986). *The psychology of gender: Advances through meta-analysis.* Baltimore: Johns Hopkins.

Hyde, J. S., & McKinley, N. M. (1997). Gender differences in cognition: Results from meta-analyses. In P. J. Caplan, M. Crawford, J. S. Hyde, & J. T. E. Richardson, *Gender differences in human cognition* (pp. 30–51). New York: Oxford.

Hyde, J. S., Rosenberg, B. G., & Behrman, J. (1977). "Tomboyism." *Psychology of Women Quarterly, 2,* 73–75.

Idle, T., Wood, E., & Desmarais, S. (1993). Gender role socialization in toy play situations: Mothers and fathers with their sons and daughters. *Sex Roles, 28,* 679–691.

Ihinger-Tallman, M., & Pasley, K. (1987). *Remarriage.* Beverly Hills, CA: Sage.

Imperato-McGinley, J., & Peterson, R. E. (1976). Male pseudohermaphrodism: The complexities of male phenotypic development. *American Journal of Medicine, 61,* 251–272.

Imperato-McGinley, J., Peterson, R. E., Gautier, T., & Sturla, E. (1979). Androgens and the evolution of male-gender identity among male pseudohermaphrodites with 5 alpha-reductase deficiency. *New England Journal of Medicine, 300,* 1233–1237.

Imperato-McGinley, J., Pichardo, M., Gautier, T., Voyer, D., & Bryden, M. P. (1991). Cognitive abilities in androgen-insensitive subjects: Comparison with control males and females from the same kindred. *Clinical Endocrinology, 34,* 341–347.

Island, D., & Letellier, P. (1991). *Men who beat the men who love them: Battered gay men and domestic violence.* Binghamton, NY: Hawthorne Press.

Izraeli, D. N. (1983). Sex effects or structural effects? An empirical test of Kanter's theory of proportions. *Social Forces, 62,* 153–165.

Izraeli, D. N. (1993). "They have eyes and see not"–gender politics in the Diaspora Museum. *Psychology of Women Quarterly, 17,* 515–523.

Jack, D. C., & Dill, D. (1992). The silencing of the self scale schemas of intimacy associated with depression. *Psychology of Women Quarterly, 16,* 97–106.

Jacklin, C. N. (1981). Methodological issues in the study of sex-related differences. *Developmental Review, 1,* 266–273.

Jackson, A. P. (1997). Effects of concerns about child care among single, employed black mothers with preschool children. *American Journal of Community Psychology, 25*(5), 657–673.

Jackson, J. L., Calhoun, K. S., Amick, A. E., Maddever, H. M., & Habif, V. L. (1990). Young adult women who report childhood intrafamiliar sexual abuse: Subsequent adjustment. *Archives of Sexual Behavior, 19,* 211–221.

Jackson, M. (1987). "Facts of life" or the eroticization of women's oppression? Sexology and the social construction of heterosexuality. In P. Caplan (Ed.), *The cultural construction of sexuality* (pp. 52–71). London: Tavistock.

Jackson-Wilson, A. G., & Borgers, S. B. (1993). Disaffiliation revisited: A comparison of homeless and nonhomeless women's perception of family of origin and social supports. *Sex Roles, 28,* 361–377.

Jacobs, A. (1998, September 13). His debut as a woman. *The New York Times Magazine,* pp. 48–51.

Jacobs, J. A. (1992). Women's entry into management: Trends in earnings, authority, and values among salaried managers. Special issue: Process and outcome: Perspectives on the distribution of rewards in organizations. *Administrative Science Quarterly, 37,* 282–301.

Jaffe, P. G., Suderman, M., Reitzel, D., & Killip, S. M. (1992). An evaluation of a secondary school primary prevention program on violence in intimate relationships. *Violence and Victims, 7,* 129–146.

James, J. (1999). The contribution of women's studies programs. In S. Davis, M. Crawford, & J. Sebrechts (Eds.), *Coming into her own: Encouraging educational success in girls and women* (pp. 23–36). San Francisco: Jossey-Bass.

Jamieson, K. H. (1995). *Beyond the double bind: Women and leadership.* New York: Oxford University Press.

Jenkins, R. (1985). *Sex differences in psychiatric morbidity.* Cambridge, England: Cambridge University Press Psychological Medicine Monograph, suppl. 7.

Joffe, H. (1997). Intimacy and love in late modern conditions: Implications for unsafe sexual practices. In J. M. Ussher (Ed.), *Body talk: The material and discursive regulation of sexuality, madness and reproduction* (pp. 159–175). New York: Routledge.

Johansson, C., Mellstrom, D., Lerner, U., & Osterberg, T. (1992). Coffee drinking: A minor risk factor for bone loss and fractures. *Age and Aging, 21,* 20–26.

John, B. A., & Sussman, L. E. (1984–1985). Initiative-taking as a determinant of role-reciprocal organization. *Imagination, Cognition, and Personality, 4,* 277–291.

John, R., Blanchard, P. H., & Hennessy, C. H. (1997). Hidden lives: Aging and contemporary American Indian women. In J. M. Coyle (Ed.), *Handbook on women and aging* (pp. 290–315). Westport, CT: Greenwood Press.

Joiner, G. W., & Kashubeck, S. (1996). Acculturation, body image, self-esteem, and eating-disorder symptomology in adolescent Mexican-American women. *Psychology of Women Quarterly, 20,* 419–435.

Jones, L., & Bigler, R. S. (1996, March). Cognitive-developmental mechanisms in the revision of gender-stereotypic beliefs. Poster session presented at the 14th biennial Conference on Human Development, Birmingham, AL.

Jordan, J. V., Kaplan, A. G., Miller, J. B., Stiver, I. P., & Surrey, J. L. (1991). *Women's growth in connection.* New York: Guilford.

Jorgensen, S. R., & Alexander, S. J. (1983). Research on adolescent pregnancy-risk: Implications for sex education programs. *Theory into Practice, 22,* 125–133.

Joseph, G. I. (1991). Black mothers and daughters: Traditional and new perspectives. In P. Bell-Scott, B. Guy-Sheftall, J. J. Royster, J. Sims-Wood, M. DiCosta-Willis, & L. P. Fultz (Eds.), *Double stitch: Black women write about mothers and daughters* (pp. 94–106). New York: HarperCollins.

Joseph, G. I., & Lewis, J. (1981). *Common differences: Conflicts in black and white feminist perspectives.* Boston: South End Press.

Joseph, J. (1997). Woman battering: A comparative analysis of black and white women. In G. Kaufman Kantor & J. L. Jasinski (Eds.), *Out of darkness: Contemporary perspectives on family violence* (pp. 161–169). Thousand Oaks, CA: Sage.

Jost, J. T. (1997). An experimental replication of the depressed entitlement effect among women. *Psychology of Women Quarterly, 21,* 387–393.

Jost, J. T., & Banaji, M. R. (1994). The role of stereotyping in system-justification and the production of false consciousness. *British Journal of Social Psychology, 33,* 1–27.

Joyce, P. (1997). Mothers of sexually abused children and the concept of collusion: A literature review. *Journal of Child Sexual Abuse, 6,* 75–92.

Jutras, S., & Veilleux, F. (1991). Gender roles and care giving to the elderly: An empirical study. *Sex Roles, 25,* 1–18.

Kahn, A. S., & Jean, P. J. (1983). Integration and elimination or separation and redefinition: The future of the psychology of women. *Signs, 8,* 659–670.

Kahn, A. S., & Yoder, J. D. (1989). The psychology of women and conservatism: Rediscovering social change. *Psychology of Women Quarterly, 13,* 417–432.

Kahn, J., Smith, K., & Roberts, E. (1984). *Familial communication and adolescent sexual behavior.* Final Report to the Office of Adolescent Pregnancy Programs. Cambridge, MA: American Institutes for Research. Cited in J. Brooks-Gunn & F. F. Furstenberg, Jr. (1989).

Kaiser, K. (1990). Cross-cultural perspectives on menopause. In M. Flint, F. Kronenberg, & W. Utian (Eds.), *Multidisciplinary perspectives on menopause. Annals of the New York Academy of Science, 592,* 430–432.

Kakar, S. (1998). The search for middle age in India. In R. A. Shweder (Ed.), *Welcome to middle age: And other cultural fictions* (pp. 75–98). Chicago: University of Chicago Press.

Kane, E. W., & Schippers, M. (1996). Men's and women's beliefs about gender and sexuality. *Gender & Society, 10*(5), 650–665.

Kanekar, S., & Seksaria, V. (1993). Acquaintance versus stranger rape: Testing the ambiguity reduction hypothesis. *European Journal of Social Psychology, 23,* 485–494.

Kanter, R. M. (1977). *Men and women of the corporation.* New York: Basic Books.

Kaplan, A. G., & Surrey, J. L. (1984). The relational self in women: Developmental theory and public policy. In L. E. Walker (Ed.), *Women and mental health policy* (pp. 79–94). Beverly Hills, CA: Sage.

Kaplan, A. G., & Yasinski, L. (1980). Psychodynamic perspectives. In A. M. Brodsky & R. Hare-Mustin (Eds.), *Women and psychotherapy: An assessment of research and practice* (pp. 191–215). New York: Guilford Press.

Kaplan, M. (1983). A woman's view of DSM-III. *American Psychologist, 39,* 786–792.

Kaplan, M. M. (1992). *Mothers' images of motherhood*. New York: Routledge.

Karabenick, S. A., & Knapp, J. R. (1988). Effects of computer privacy on help-seeking. *Journal of Applied Social Psychology, 18,* 461–472.

Karbon, M., Fabes, R. A., Carlo, G., & Martin, C. L. (1992). Preschoolers' beliefs about sex and age differences in emotionality. *Sex Roles, 27,* 377–390.

Karp, S. A., Silber, D. E., Holmstrom, R. W., & Stock, L. J. (1995). Personality of rape survivors and by relation of survivor to perpetrator. *Journal of Clinical Psychology, 51*(5), 587–593.

Karraker, K. H., Vogel, D. A., & Lake, M. A. (1995). Parents' gender stereotyped perceptions of newborns: The eye of the beholder revisited. *Sex Roles, 33,* 687–701.

Katz, B. L. (1991). The psychological impact of stranger versus nonstranger rape on victims' recovery. In A. Parrot & L. Bechhofer, (Eds.), *Acquaintance rape: The hidden crime* (pp. 251–269). New York: Wiley.

Katz, P. A. (1996). Raising feminists. *Psychology of Women Quarterly, 20,* 323–340.

Katz, P. A., & Boswell, S. (1986). Flexibility and traditionality in children's gender roles. *Genetic, Social, & General Psychology Monographs, 112,* 103–147.

Katz, P. A., & Walsh, P. V. (1991). Modification of children's gender stereotyped behavior. *Child Development, 62,* 338–351.

Kaufert, P. L. (1990). Methodological issues in menopause research. In M. Flint, F. Kronenberg, & W. Utian (Eds.), *Multidisciplinary perspectives on menopause. Annals of the New York Academy of Sciences, 592,* 114–122.

Kaufert, P. L., & Gilbert, P. (1986). Women, menopause, and medicalization. *Culture, Medicine & Psychiatry, 10,* 7–21.

Kaw, E. (1994). "Opening" faces: The politics of cosmetic surgery and Asian American women. In N. Sault (Ed.). *Many mirrors: Body image and social relations.* New Brunswick, NJ: Rutgers University Press, pp. 241–265.

Keating, C. T., & Hellman, K. R. (1994). Dominance and deception in children and adults: Are leaders the best misleaders? *Personality and Social Psychology Bulletin, 20,* 312–321.

Keel, P. K., Fulkerson, J. A., & Leon, G. R. (1997). Disordered eating precursors in pre- and early adolescent girls and boys. *Journal of Youth and Adolescence, 26,* 203–216.

Kelley, H. H., Cunningham, J. D., Grisham, J. A., Lefebvre, L. M., Sink, C. R., & Yablon, G. (1978). Sex differences in comments made during conflict within close heterosexual pairs. *Sex Roles, 4,* 473–491.

Kelly, L., & Radford, J. (1996). "Nothing really happened": The invalidation of women's experiences of sexual violence. In M. Hester, L. Kelly, & J. Radford (Eds.), *Women, violence, and male power: Feminist activism, research, and practice.* Buckingham, England: Open University Press.

Kennedy, C. W., & Camden, C. (1983). Interruptions and nonverbal gender differences. *Journal of Nonverbal Behavior, 8,* 91–108.

Kennell, J., Klaus, M., McGrath, S., Robertson, S., & Hinkley, C. (1991). Continuous emotional support during labor in a US hospital. *Journal of the American Medical Association, 265,* 2197–2201.

Kessler, S. J. (1990). The medical construction of gender: Case management of intersexed infants. *Signs, 16,* 3–26.

Kessler, S. J. (1998). *Lessons from the intersexed.* New Brunswick, NJ: Rutgers University Press.

Kiesler, S., Sproull, L., & Eccles, J. S. (1985). Pool halls, chips, and war games: Women in the culture of computing. *Psychology of Women Quarterly, 9,* 451–462.

Kiliansky, S. E., & Rudman, L. A. (1998). Wanting it both ways: Do women approve of benevolent sexism? *Sex Roles, 39,* 333–352.

Kim, E. H. (1986). With silk wings: Asian American women at work. In J. B. Cole (Ed.), *All American women: Lines that divide, ties that bind* (pp. 95–100). New York: Macmillan.

Kimball, M. M. (1995). *Feminist visions of gender similarities and differences.* New York: Harrington Park.

Kimmel, D. C. (1988). Ageism, psychology, and public policy. *American Psychologist, 43,* 175–178.

Kimmel, E. (1999). Feminist teaching: An emergent practice. In S. Davis, M. Crawford, & J. Sebrechts (Eds.), *Coming into her own: Encouraging educational success in girls and women* (pp. 57–76). San Francisco: Jossey-Bass.

Kimmel, E. B. (1989). The experience of feminism. *Psychology of Women Quarterly, 13,* 133–146.

Kimmel, M. S. (1996). *Manhood in America: A cultural history.* New York: Free Press.

Kincaid-Ehlers, E. (1982). Bad maps for an unknown region: Menopause from a literary perspective. In A. M. Voda, M. Dinnerstein, & S. R. O'Donnell (Eds.), *Changing perspectives on menopause* (pp. 24–38). Austin: University of Texas Press.

King, S. (1974). *Carrie*. New York: Doubleday.

Kinsey, A. C., Pomeroy, W. B., & Martin, C. E. (1948). *Sexual behavior in the human male*. Philadelphia: Saunders.

Kinsey, A. C., Pomeroy, W. B., Martin, C. E., & Gebhard, P. H. (1953). *Sexual behavior in the human female*. Philadelphia: Saunders.

Kinsman, S. B., Romer, D., & Schwarz, D. F. (1998). Early sexual initiation: The role of peer norms. *Pediatrics, 102*(5), 1185–1192.

Kinzer, S. (1993, May 29). German court restricts abortion, angering feminists and the East. *New York Times*, p. A1.

Kirchmeyer, C. (1993). Nonwork-to-work spillover: A more balanced view of the experiences and coping of professional women and men. *Sex Roles, 28*, 531–552.

Kirkpatrick, C. (1936). The construction of a belief pattern scale for measuring attitudes toward feminism. *Journal of Social Psychology, 7*, 421–437.

Kirsh, S. J. (1998). Seeing the world through Mortal Kombat–colored glasses: Violent video games and the development of a short-term hostile attribution bias. *Childhood: A Global Journal of Child Research, 5*, 177–184.

Kishor, S. (1993). "May God give sons to all": Gender and child mortality in India. *American Sociological Review, 58*, 247–265.

Kite, M. E., & Deaux, K. (1987). Gender belief systems: Homosexuality and the implicit inversion theory. *Psychology of Women Quarterly, 11*, 83–96.

Kite, M. E., Deaux, K., & Miele, M. (1991). Stereotypes of young and old: Does age outweigh gender? *Psychology and Aging, 6*, 19–27.

Kitzinger, C. (1987). *The social construction of lesbianism*. London: Sage.

Kitzinger, S. (1983). *Women's experience of sex*. London: Dorling Kindersley.

Kline, K. N. (1996). The drama of in utero drug exposure. In R. L. Parrott & C. M. Condit (Eds.), *Evaluating women's health messages* (pp. 61–79). Thousand Oaks: Sage.

Klonoff, E. A., & Landrine, H. (1995). The schedule of sexist events: A measure of lifetime and recent sexist discrimination in women's lives. *Psychology of Women Quarterly, 19*, 439–472.

Knudson-Martin, C., & Mahoney, A. R. (1996). Gender dilemmas and myth in the construction of marital bargains: Issues for marital therapy. *Family Process, 35*(2), 137–153.

Kobrynowicz, D., & Branscombe, N. R. (1997). Who considers themselves victims of discrimination? Individual difference predictors of perceived gender discrimination in women and men. *Psychology of Women Quarterly, 21*, 347–363.

Koch, L. (1990). The fairy tale as a model for women's experience of in vitro fertilization. In H. B. Holmes (Ed.), *Issues in reproductive technology I* (pp. 303–320). New York: Garland.

Koff, E. (1983). Through the looking glass of menarche: What the adolescent girl sees. In S. Golub (Ed.), *Menarche* (pp. 77–86). Lexington, MA: Lexington Books.

Koff, E., Rierdan, J., & Silverstone, E. (1978). Changes in representation of body image as a function of menarcheal status. *Developmental Psychology, 14*, 635–642.

Kohlberg, L. (1966). A cognitive-developmental analysis of children's sex role concepts and attitudes. In E. E. Maccoby (Ed.), *The development of sex differences* (pp. 82–173). Stanford, CA: Stanford University Press.

Kohlberg, L. (1981). *The philosophy of moral development: Essays on moral development*, Vols. I & II. San Francisco: Harper & Row.

Kolata, G. (1983). Math genius may have hormonal basis. *Science, 222*, 1312.

Kolata, G. (1992, February 12). Track federation urges end to gene test for femaleness. *New York Times*.

Kong, M-E. (1997). The portrayal of women's images in magazine advertisements: Goffman's gender analysis revisited. *Sex Roles, 37*, 979–996.

Kortenhaus, C. M., & Demarest, J. (1993). Gender role stereotyping in children's literature: An update. *Sex Roles, 28*, 219–232.

Koss, M. P. (1985). The hidden rape victim: Personality, attitudinal, and situational characteristics. *Psychology of Women Quarterly, 9*, 193–212.

Koss, M. P. (1990). The women's mental health research agenda: Violence against women. *American Psychologist, 45*, 374–380.

Koss, M. P. (1992). The underdetection of rape: Methodological choices influence incidence estimates. *Journal of Social Issues, 48*, 61–75.

Koss, M. P., & Burkhart, B. R. (1989). A conceptual analysis of rape victimization. *Psychology of Women Quarterly, 13*, 27–40.

Koss, M. P., & Cleveland, H. H. (1997). Stepping on toes: Social roots of date rape lead to intractability and politicization. In M. Schwartz (Ed.) *Researching sexual violence against women: Methodological and personal perspectives*, 4–21. Sage Publications, Inc., Thousand Oaks, CA.

Koss, M. P., & Gaines, J. A. (1993). The prediction of sexual aggression by alcohol use, athletic participation, and fraternity affiliation. *Journal of Interpersonal Violence, 8*, 94–108.

Koss, M. P., Gidycz, C. A., & Wisniewski, N. (1987). The scope of rape: Incidence and prevalence of sexual aggression and victimization in a national sample of higher education students. *Journal of Consulting and Clinical Psychology, 55*, 162–170.

Koss, M. P., Goodman, L. A., Browne, A., Fitzgerald, L. F., Keita, G. P., & Russo, N. F. (1994). *No safe haven: Male violence against women at home, at work, and in the community*. Washington, DC: American Psychological Association.

Kosson, D. S., Kelly, J. C., & White, J. W. (1997). Psychopathy-related traits predict self-reported sexual aggression among college men. *Journal of Interpersonal Violence, 12*, 241–254.

Kowalski, R. M. (1992). Nonverbal behaviors and perceptions of sexual intentions: Effects of sexual connotativeness, verbal response, and rape outcome. *Basic and Applied Social Psychology, 13*, 427–445.

Kozlowski, J. (1993). Women, film, and the midlife Sophie's choice: Sink or Sousatzka? In J. C. Callahan (Ed.), *Menopause: A midlife passage* (pp. 3–22). Bloomington: University of Indiana Press.

Kramarae, C., & Treichler, P. A. (1985). *A feminist dictionary*. Boston: Pandora.

Kravetz, D. (1980). Consciousness-raising and self-help. In A. M. Brodsky & R. Hare-Mustin (Eds.), *Women and psychotherapy* (pp. 267–283). New York: Guilford.

Krieger, S. (1982). Lesbian identity and community: Recent social science literature. *Signs, 8*, 91–108.

Krishnan, V. (1987). Preference for sex of children: A multivariate analysis. *Journal of Biosocial Science, 18*, 367–376.

Kronenberg, F. (1990). Hot flashes: Epidemiology and physiology. In M. Flint, F. Kronenberg, & W. Utian (Eds.), *Multidisciplinary perspectives on menopause. Annals of New York Academy of Sciences, 592*, 52–86.

Kuebli, J., & Fivush, R. (1992). Gender differences in parent-child conversations about past emotions. *Sex Roles, 27*, 683–698.

Kunda, A., Sinclair, L., & Griffin, D. (1997). Equal ratings but separate meanings: Stereotypes and the construal of traits. *Journal of Personality and Social Psychology, 72*, 720–734.

Kurdek, L. A. (1988). Perceived social support in gays and lesbians in cohabitating couples. *Journal of Personality and Social Psychology, 54*, 504–509.

Kurdek, L. A. (1993). The allocation of household labor in gay, lesbian, and heterosexual married couples. *Journal of Social Issues, 49*, 127–139.

Kurdek, L. A. (1997). Adjustment to relationship dissolution in gay, lesbian, and heterosexual partners. *Personal Relationships, 4*, 145–161.

Kyle, D. J., & Mahler, H. I. M. (1996). The effects of hair color and cosmetic use on perceptions of a female's ability. *Psychology of Women Quarterly, 20*, 447–455.

Laabs, J. (1998). Sexual harassment: New rules, higher stakes. *Workforce*, 34–42.

Lachman, M. E., & James, J. B. (1997). Charting the course of midlife development. In M. E. Lachman & J. B. James (Eds.), *Multiple paths of midlife development* (pp. 1–17). Chicago: University of Chicago Press.

Lackey, P. N. (1989). Adults' attitudes about assignments of household chores to male and female children. *Sex Roles, 20*, 271–281.

Lafontaine, E., & Tredeau, L. (1986). The frequency, sources, and correlates of sexual harassment among women in traditional male occupations. *Sex Roles 15*, 433–442.

LaFrance, M. (1992). Gender and interruptions: Individual infraction or violation of the social order? *Psychology of Women Quarterly, 16*, 497–512.

La Freniere, P., Strayer, F. F., & Gauthier, R. (1984). The emergence of same-sex affiliative preferences among preschool peers: A developmental/ethological perspective. *Child Development, 55*, 1958–1965.

LaFromboise, T. D., Berman, J. S., & Sohi, B. K. (1994). American Indian Women. In L. Comas-Diaz & B. Greene (Eds.), *Women of color: Integrating ethnic and gender identities in psychotherapy* (pp. 30–71). New York: Guilford.

LaFromboise, T. D., Choney, S. B., James, A., & Running Wolf, P. (1995). American Indian women and psychology. In H. Landrine (Ed.), *Bringing cultural diversity to feminist psychology* (pp. 191–239). Washington, DC: American Psychological Association.

Lakoff, R. (1975). *Language and woman's place.* New York: Harper & Row.

Lakoff, R. (1990). *Talking power: The politics of language.* New York: Basic Books.

Landa, A. (1990). No accident: The voices of voluntarily childless women–An essay on the social construction of fertility choices. In J. P. Knowles & E. Cole (Eds.), *Motherhood: A feminist perspective* (pp. 139–158). New York: Haworth.

Landrine, H. (1985). Race x class stereotypes of women. *Sex Roles, 13,* 65–75.

Landrine, H. (1987). On the politics of madness: A preliminary analysis of the relationship between social roles and psychopathology. *Psychological Monographs, 113*(3), 341–406.

Landrine, H. (1988). Depression and stereotypes of women: Preliminary empirical analyses of the gender-role hypothesis. *Sex Roles, 19,* 527–541.

Landrine, H. (1989). The politics of personality disorder. *Psychology of Women Quarterly, 13,* 325–339.

Landrine, H. (Ed.). (1995). *Bringing cultural diversity to feminist psychology.* Washington, DC: American Psychological Association.

Landrine, H., & Klonoff, E. A. (1997). *Discrimination against women: Prevalence, consequences, remedies.* Thousand Oaks, CA: Sage.

Landrine, H., Klonoff, E. A., & Brown-Collins, A. (1992). Cultural diversity and methodology in feminist psychology: Critique, proposal, empirical example. *Psychology of Women Quarterly, 16,* 145–163.

Landrine, H., Klonoff, E. A., Gibbs, J., Manning, V., & Lund, M. (1995). Physical and psychiatric correlates of gender discrimination: An application of the schedule of sexist events. *Psychology of Women Quarterly, 19,* 473–492.

Laner, M. R. (1979). Growing older female: Heterosexual and homosexual. *Journal of Homosexuality, 4,* 267–275.

Laner, M. R. (1983). Courtship abuse and aggression: Contextual aspects. *Sociological Spectrum, 3,* 69–83.

Langhinrichsen-Rohling J., Neidig, P., & Thorn, G. (1995). Violent marriages: Gender differences in levels of current violence and past abuse. *Journal of Family Violence, 10,* 159–176.

LaPlante, M. N., McCormick, N., & Brannigan, G. G. (1980). Living the sexual script: College students' views of influence in sexual encounters. *Journal of Sex Research, 16,* 338–355.

Laqueur, T. (1990). *Making sex: Body and gender from the Greeks to Freud.* Cambridge, MA: Harvard University Press.

Larkin, J., & Popaleni, K. (1994). Heterosexual courtship violence and sexual harassment: The private and public control of young women. *Feminism & Psychology, 4,* 213–227.

Lauerman, J. (1990, January-February). The time machine. *Harvard Magazine,* pp. 43–46.

Laumann, E. O., Gagnon, J. H., Michael, R. T., & Michaels, S. (1994). *The social organization of sexuality: Sexual practices in the United States.* Chicago: The University of Chicago Press.

Laws, J. L., & Schwartz, P. (1977). *Sexual scripts.* Hinsdale, IL: Dryden.

Laws, S. (1983). The sexual politics of premenstrual tension. *Women's Studies International Forum, 6,* 19–31.

Leaper, C. (1991). Influences and involvement in children's discourse: Age, gender, and partner effects. *Child Development, 62,* 797–811.

Lee, G. R. (1988). Marital intimacy among older persons: The spouse as confidant. *Journal of Family Issues, 9,* 273–284.

Lee, J. (1995). Beyond bean counting. In B. Findlen (Ed.), *Listen up! Voices from the next feminist generation* (pp. 205–211). Seattle: Seal Press.

Lees, S. (1997). *Ruling passions: Sexual violence, reputation and the law.* Buckingham, UK: Open University Press.

Leffler, A., Gillespie, D. L., & Conaty, J. C. (1982). The effects of status differentiation on nonverbal behavior. *Social Psychology Quarterly, 45,* 153–161.

LeGuin, U. K. (1974). *The dispossessed.* New York: Harper & Row.

Leinbach, M. D., & Fagot, B. I. (1991). Attractiveness in young children: Sex-differentiated reactions of adults. *Sex Roles, 25,* 269–284.

Leinbach, M. D., Hort, B. E., & Fagot, B. I. (1997). Bears are for boys: Metaphorical associations in young children's gender stereotypes. *Cognitive Development, 12,* 107–130.

Lembright, M. F., & Riemer, J. W. (1982). Women truckers' problems and the impact of sponsorship. *Work and Occupations, 9,* 457–474.

Lemkau, J. P. (1979). Personality and background characteristics of women in maledominated occupations: A review. *Psychology of Women Quarterly, 4,* 221–240.

Lemkau, J. P. (1983). Women in male-dominated professions: Distinguishing personality and background characteristics. *Psychology of Women Quarterly, 8,* 144–165.

Lemkau, J. P. (1988). Emotional sequelae of abortion: Implications for clinical practice. *Psychology of Women Quarterly, 12,* 461–472.

Lennon, M. C. (1987). Is menopause depressing? An investigation of three perspectives. *Sex Roles, 17,* 1–16.

Leonard, R. (1995). I'm just a girl who can't say "no": A gender difference in children's perception of refusals. *Feminism & Psychology, 5,* 315–328.

Lerman, H. (1986). From Freud to feminist personality theory: Getting there from here. *Psychology of Women Quarterly, 10,* 1–18.

Lerman, H., & Porter, N. (1990). The contribution of feminism to ethics in psychotherapy. In H. Lerman & N. Porter (Eds.), *Feminist ethics in psychotherapy* (pp. 5–13). New York: Springer.

Lerman, H., & Rigby, D. N. (1990). Boundary violations: Misuse of the power of the therapist. In H. Lerman & N. Porter (Eds.), *Feminist ethics in psychotherapy* (pp. 51–59). New York: Springer.

Lerner, R. M., Lerner, J. V., & Tubman, J. T. (1989). Organismic and contextual bases of development in adolescence: A developmental contextual view. In G. R. Adams, R. Montemayor, & T. P. Gullotta (Eds.), *The biology of adolescent behavior and development* (pp. 11–37). Newbury Park, CA: Sage.

LeVay, S. (1991). A difference in hypothalamic structure between heterosexual and homosexual men. *Science, 253,* 1034–1037.

LeVay, S., & Hamer, D. H. (1994). Evidence for a biological influence in male homosexuality. *Scientific American, 270,* 44–49.

Levenson, R. W., Carstensen, L. L., & Gottman, J. M. (1993). Long-term marriage: Age, gender, and satisfaction. *Psychology and Aging, 8,* 301–313.

Levin, I. (1997). The stepparent role from a gender perspective. *Marriage & Family Review, 26*(1/2), 177–190.

Levine, M. P., & Leonard, R. (1984). Discrimination against lesbians in the work force. *Signs, 4,* 700–710.

Levine, R., Sato, S., Hashimoto, T., & Verma, J. (1995). Love and marriage in eleven cultures. *Journal of Cross-Cultural Psychology, 26*(5), 554–571.

Lewin, M., & Tragos, L. M. (1987). Has the feminist movement influenced sex role attitudes? A reassessment after a quarter century. *Sex Roles, 16,* 125–135.

Lewis, C. (1987). Early sex-role socialization. In D. J. Hargreaves & A. M. Colley (Eds.), *The psychology of sex roles* (pp. 95–117). New York: Hemisphere.

Lewis, S. (1979). *Sunday's women: Lesbian life today.* Boston: Beacon.

Lewittes, H. J. (1988). Just being friendly means a lot: Women, friendship, and aging. *Women & Health, 14,* 139–159.

L'Hommedieu, T. (1984). *The divorce experiences of working and middle class women.* Ann Arbor: UMI Research Press.

Lieblich, A. (1985). Sex differences in intelligence test performance of Jewish and Arab school children in Israel. In M. P. Safir, M. S. Mednick, D. Izraeli, & J. Bernard (Eds.), *Women's worlds: From the new scholarship.* New York: Praeger.

Lindahl, L. B., & Heimann, M. (1997). Social proximity in early mother-infant interactions: Implications for gender differences. *Early Development & Parenting, 6,* 83–88.

Linimon, D., Barron, W. L., & Falbo, T. (1984). Gender differences in perception of leadership. *Sex Roles, 11,* 1075–1089.

Lipman-Blumen, J., & Leavitt, H. J. (1976). Vicarious and direct achievement patterns in adulthood. *The Counseling Psychologist, 6,* 26–31.

Lippard, L. (1986). Elizabeth Layton. In J. Alexander, D. Berrow, L. Domitrovich, M. Donnelly, & C. McLean (Eds.), *Woman and aging* (pp. 148–151). Corvallis, OR: Calyx.

Lippman, W. (1922). *Public opinion.* New York: Harcourt.

Lloyd, S. A. (1991). The dark side of courtship. *Family Relations, 40,* 14–20.

Lobel, T. E., Stone, M., & Winch, G. (1997). Masculinity, popularity, and self-esteem among Israeli preadolescent girls. *Sex Roles, 361,* 395–408.

Locher, P., Unger, R. K., Sociedade, P., & Wahl, J. (1993). At first glance: Accessibility of the physical attractiveness stereotype. *Sex Roles, 28,* 729–743.

Lock, M. (1986). Ambiguities of aging: Japanese experience and perceptions of menopause. *Culture, Medicine, and Psychiatry, 10,* 23–46.

Lock, M. (1993). *Encounters with aging: Mythologies of menopause in Japan and North America.* Berkeley & Los Angeles: University of California Press.

Lock, M. (1998). Deconstructing the change: Female maturation in Japan and North America. In R. A. Shweder (Ed.), *Welcome to middle age: And other cultural fictions* (pp. 45–74). Chicago: University of Chicago Press.

Lockheed, M. E. (1985). Sex and social influence: A meta-analysis guided by theory. In J. Berger & M. Zeldich (Eds.), *Status, relations, and rewards*. San Francisco: Jossey-Bass.

Lofland, J. (1969). *Deviance and identity*. Englewood Cliffs, NJ: Prentice-Hall.

Logothetis, M. L. (1993). Disease or development: Women's perceptions of menopause and the need for hormone replacement therapy. In J. C. Callahan (Ed.), *Menopause: A midlife passage* (pp. 123–135). Bloomington: University of Indiana Press.

Loiacano, D. K. (1993). Gay identity issues among Black Americans: Racism, homophobia, and the need for validation. In L. D. Garnets & D. C. Kimmel (Eds.), *Psychological perspectives on lesbian and gay male experiences* (pp. 364–375). New York: Columbia University Press.

Long, J., & Porter, K. L. (1984). Multiple roles of midlife women. In G. Baruch & J. Brooks-Gunn (Eds.), *Women in midlife* (pp. 109–159). New York: Plenum Press.

Long-Scott, E., & Southworth, J. (1992). Norplant: Birth control or control of poor women? *Extra*, Special issue, 17–18.

Lonsway, K. A. (1996). Preventing acquaintance rape through education: What do we know? *Psychology of Women Quarterly, 20,* 229–265.

Lont, C. M. (1990). The roles assigned to females and males in non-music radio programming. *Sex Roles, 22,* 661–668.

Lopez, N. (1987). *Hispanic teenage pregnancy: Overview and implications*. Washington, DC: National Council of La Raza. Reported in Cusick (1987).

LoPiccolo, J., & Stock, W. E. (1986). Treatment of sexual dysfunction. *Journal of Consulting and Clinical Psychology, 54,* 158–167.

Lorber, J. (1993a). Believing is seeing: Biology as ideology. *Gender & Society, 7,* 568–581.

Lorber, J. (1993b). *Paradoxes of gender*. New Haven: Yale University Press.

Lorenzi-Cioldi, F. (1993). They all look alike, but so do we . . . sometimes: Perceptions of in-group and out-group homogeneity as a function of sex and context. *British Journal of Social Psychology, 32,* 111–124.

Lott, B. (1978). Behavioral concordance with sex role ideology related to play areas, creativity, and parental sex-typing of children. *Journal of Personality and Social Psychology, 36,* 1087–1100.

Lott, B. (1987). Sexist discrimination as distancing behavior: I. A laboratory demonstration. *Psychology of Women Quarterly, 11,* 47–58.

Lott, B., & Rocchio, L. M. (1997). Individual and collective action: Social approaches and remedies for sexist discrimination. In H. Landrine & E. A. Klonoff (Eds.), *Discrimination against women: Prevalence, consequences, remedies* (pp. 148–171). Thousand Oaks, CA: Sage.

Lowe, R., & Wittig, M. A. (Eds.). (1989). Achieving pay equity through comparable worth. Special issue of the *Journal of Social Issues, 45.*

Lublin, N. (1998). *Pandora's box*. New York: Rowman & Littlefield.

Lueptow, L. B., Garovich, L., & Lueptow, M. B. (1995). The persistence of gender stereotypes in the face of changing sex roles: Evidence contrary to the sociocultural model. *Ethology & Sociobiology, 16,* 509–530.

Lutz, W. J., & Hock, E. (1998). Factors that influence depressive symptoms in mothers of infants. *Psychology of Women Quarterly, 22(3),* 499–503.

Lykes, M. B., Brabeck, M. M., Ferns, T., & Radan, A. (1993). Human rights and mental health among Latin American women in situations of state-sponsored violence: Bibliographic resources. *Psychology of Women Quarterly, 17,* 525–544.

Lytton, H., & Romney, D. M. (1991). Parents' differential socialization of boys and girls: A meta-analysis. *Psychological Bulletin, 109,* 267–296.

Maccoby, E. E. (1980). *Social development: Psychological growth and the parent-child relationship*. New York: Harcourt Brace Jovanovich.

Maccoby, E. E. (1988). Gender as a social category. *Developmental Psychology, 24,* 755–765.

Maccoby, E. E. (1998). *The two sexes: Growing up apart, coming together*. Cambridge, MA: Belknap Press of Harvard University Press.

Maccoby, E. E., & Jacklin, C. (1974). *The psychology of sex differences*. Stanford, CA: Stanford University Press.

Maccoby, E. E., & Jacklin, C. N. (1987). Gender segregation in childhood. In E. H. Reese (Ed.), *Advances in child development*. New York: Academic Press.

Macdonald, B., & Rich, C. (1983). *Look me in the eye: Old women, aging and ageism*. San Francisco: Spinsters Ink.

MacFarlane, A. (1977). *The psychology of childbirth*. Cambridge, MA: Harvard University Press.

MacKinnon, C. (1979). *Sexual harassment of*

working women. New Haven: Yale University Press.

MacKinnon, C. A. (1994). Sexuality. In A. C. Herrmann & A. J. Stewart (Eds.), *Theorizing feminism: Parallel trends in the humanities and social sciences* (pp. 257–287). Boulder: Westview Press.

MacPherson, K. I. (1985). Osteoporosis and menopause: A feminist analysis of the social construction of a syndrome. *Advances in Nursing Science, 7,* 11–22.

MacPherson, K. I. (1993). The false promises of hormone replacement therapy and current dilemmas. In J. C. Callahan (Ed.), *Menopause: A midlife passage* (pp. 145–159). Bloomington: University of Indiana Press.

Maddux, H. C. (1975). *Menstruation.* New Canaan, CT: Tobey.

Magnusson, D., Strattin, H., & Allen, V. L. (1985). Biological maturation and social development: A longitudinal study of some adjustment processes from mid-adolescence to adulthood. *Journal of Youth and Adolescence, 14,* 267–283.

Major, B. (1994). From social inequality to personal entitlement: The role of social comparisons, legitimacy appraisals, and group membership. In M. P. Zanna (Ed.), *Advances in experimental social psychology,* Vol. 26 (pp. 293–355). New York: Academic Press.

Major, B., Barr, L., Zubek, J., & Babey, S. H. (1999). Gender and self-esteem: A meta-analysis. In W. B. Swann Jr., J. H. Langlois, & L. A. Gilbert (Eds.), *Sexism and stereotypes in modern society: The gender science of Janet Taylor Spence* (pp. 223–253). Washington, DC: American Psychological Association.

Major, B., Cozzarelli, C., Testa, M., & Mueller, P. (1992). Male partners' appraisals of undesired pregnancy and abortion: Implications for women's adjustment to abortion. *Journal of Applied Social Psychology, 22,* 599–614.

Major, B., McFarlin, D. B., & Gagnon, D. (1984). Overworked and underpaid: On the nature of gender differences in personal entitlement. *Journal of Personality and Social Psychology, 47,* 1399–1412.

Makepeace, J. M. (1984). *The severity of courtship violence injuries and individual precautionary measures.* Paper presented at the Second National Family Violence Research Conference, University of New Hampshire, Durham, NH.

Makepeace, J. M. (1986). Gender differences in courtship violence victimization. *Family Relations: Journal of Applied Family and Child Studies, 35,* 383–388.

Makosky, V. P. (1989). Comments on the mommy track. *Division 35 Newsletter, 16,* 7–8.

Malamuth, N. M., Sockloskie, R., Koss, M. P., & Tanaka, J. (1991). The characteristics of aggressors against women: Testing a model using a national sample of college students. *Journal of Consulting and Clinical Psychology, 59,* 670–681.

Malamuth, N. M., & Thornhill, N. W. (1994). Hostile masculinity, sexual aggression, and gender-biased domineeringness in conversations. *Aggressive Behavior, 20,* 185–194.

Malloy, T. E., Fisher, W. A., Albright, L., Misovich, S. J., & Fisher, J. D. (1997). Interpersonal perception of the AIDS risk potential of persons of the opposite sex. *Health Psychology, 16*(5), 480–486.

Malo, C. (1994). Ex-partner, family, friends, and other relationships: Their role within the social network of long-term single mothers. *Journal of Applied Social Psychology, 24,* 60–81.

Malson, H. (1997). Anorexic bodies and the discursive production of feminine excess. In J. M. Ussher (Ed.), *Body talk* (pp. 223–245). London: Routledge.

Maltz, D. N., & Borker, R. A. (1983). A cultural approach to male-female miscommunication. In J. A. Gumperz (Ed.), *Language and social identity* (pp. 196–216). New York: Cambridge University Press.

Mangan, K. S. (1999, March 12). Stanford Law School faces tensions over issues of race and gender. *The Chronicle of Higher Education,* p. A12.

Manning, W. D., & Landale, N. S. (1996). Racial and ethnic differences in the role of cohabitation in premarital childbearing. *Journal of Marriage and the Family, 58,* 63–77.

Mansfield, P. K., Koch, P. B., Henderson, J., Vicary, J. R., Kohn, M., & Young, E. W. (1991). The job climate for women in traditionally male blue-collar occupations. *Sex Roles, 25,* 63–79.

Mantecon, V. H. (1993). Where are the archetypes? Searching for symbols of women's midlife passage. In N. D. Davis, E. Cole, & E. D. Rothblum (Eds.), *Faces of women and aging* (pp. 77–88). Binghamton, NY: Harrington Park Press.

Marecek, J. (1986, March). *Sexual development and girls' self-esteem.* Paper presented at the

Seminar on Girls: Promoting Self-Esteem, sponsored by the Girls' Coalition of Southeastern Pennsylvania, Swarthmore, PA.

Marecek, J. (1989). Introduction to special issue: Theory and method in feminist psychology. *Psychology of Women Quarterly, 13,* 367–378.

Marecek, J. (1993). Silences, gaps, and anxious rhetoric: Gender in abnormal psychology textbooks. *Journal of Theoretical and Philosophical Psychology, 13,* 602–611.

Marecek, J., & Johnson, M. (1980). Gender and the process of therapy. In A. M. Brodsky & R. Hare-Mustin (Eds.), *Women and psychotherapy* (pp. 67–93). New York: Guilford Press.

Marecek, J., & Kravetz, D. (1998). Putting politics into practice: Feminist therapist as feminist praxis. *Women & Therapy, 21,* 17–36.

Markens, S. (1996). The problematic of "experience": A political and cultural critique of PMS. *Gender & Society, 10,* 42–58.

Markides, K. S. (Ed.). (1989). *Aging and health: Perspectives on gender, race, ethnicity, and class.* Newbury Park, CA: Sage.

Markson, E. W. (1997). Sagacious, sinful, or superfluous? The social construction of older women. In J. M. Coyle (Ed.), *Handbook on women and aging* (pp. 53–71). Westport, CT: Greenwood Press.

Markson, E. W., & Taylor, C. A. (1993). Real versus reel world: Older women and the Academy Awards. In N. D. Davis, E. Cole, & E. D. Rothblum (Eds.), *Faces of women and aging* (pp. 157–172). Binghamton, NY: Harrington Park Press.

Marshall, A. (1997). Who's laughing? Hillary Rodham Clinton in political humor. In N. V. Benokraitis (Ed.), *Subtle sexism: Current practice and prospects for change* (pp. 72–90). Thousand Oaks, CA: Sage.

Martin, C. L. (1989). Children's use of gender-related information in making social judgments. *Developmental Psychology, 25,* 80–88.

Martin, C. L. (1990). Attitudes and expectations about children with nontraditional and traditional gender roles. *Sex Roles, 22,* 151–165.

Martin, C. L. (1995). Stereotypes about children with traditional and nontraditional gender roles. *Sex Roles, 33,* 727–751.

Martin, C. L. (1999). A developmental perspective on gender effects and gender concepts. In W. B. Swann Jr., J. H. Langlois, & L. A. Gilbert (Eds.). *Sexism and stereotypes in modern society: The gender science of Janet Taylor Spence* (pp. 45–73). Washington, DC: American Psychological Association.

Martin, C. L., Eisenbud, L., & Rose, H. (1995). Children's gender-based reasoning about toys. *Child Development, 66,* 1453–1471.

Martin, C. L., & Fabes, R. A. (1997, April). Building gender stereotypes in the preschool years. Paper presented at the meetings of the Society for Research on Child Development, Washington, DC.

Martin, C. L., & Little, J. K. (1990). The relation of gender understanding to children's sex-typed preferences and gender stereotypes. *Child Development, 61,* 1427–1439.

Martin, E. (1987). *The woman in the body: A cultural analysis of reproduction.* Boston: Beacon Press.

Martin, K. A. (1996). *Puberty, sexuality, and the self: Girls and boys at adolescence.* London: Routledge.

Martin, S. E. (1988). Think like a man, work like a dog, and act like a lady: Occupational dilemmas of policewomen. In A. Statham, E. M. Miller, & H. O. Mauksch (Eds.), *The worth of women's work: A qualitative synthesis* (pp. 205–224). Albany, NY: State University of New York Press.

Mason, A., & Blankenship, V. (1987). Power and affiliation motivation, stress, and abuse in intimate relationships. *Journal of Personality & Social Psychology, 52,* 203–210.

Mason, D. O., & Lu, Y. (1988). Attitudes toward women's familial roles: Changes in the United States, 1977–1985. *Gender & Society, 2,* 39–57.

Masters, W. H., & Johnson, V. (1966). *Human sexual response.* Boston: Little, Brown.

Masters, W. H., & Johnson, V. (1979). *Homosexuality in perspective.* Boston: Little, Brown.

Mathews, A. M., & Campbell, L. D. (1995). Gender roles, employment, and informal care. In S. Arber & J. Ginn (Eds.), *Connecting gender and aging: A sociological approach* (pp. 129–143). Buckingham, UK: Open University Press.

Mathews, W. S. (1977). Sex-role perception, portrayal, and preference in the fantasy play of young children. *Resources in Education,* August, Document No. ED 136949.

Matthews, A. P. (1996). How evangelical women cope with prescription and description. In C. C. Kroeger, J. R. Beck, et al. (Eds.), *Women, abuse, and the Bible: How scripture can be used to hurt or to heal* (pp. 86–105). Grand Rapids, MI: Baker Books.

Matthews, W. J. (1984). Violence in college students. *College Student Journal, 18,* 150–158.

Mauldin, T., & Meeks, C. B. (1990). Sex differences in children's time use. *Sex Roles, 22,* 537–554.

Mauthner, N. S. (1998). "It's a woman's cry for help": A relational perspective on postnatal depression. *Feminism & Psychology, 8*(3), 325–355.

Maypole, D. E. (1986). Sexual harassment of social workers at work: Injustice within? *Social Work, 31,* 29–34.

Maypole, D. E., & Skaine, R. (1983). Sexual harassment in the workplace. *Social Work, 28,* 385–390.

Mays, V. M., & Cochran, S. D. (1988). Issues in the perception of AIDS risk and risk reduction activities by black and Hispanic/Latina women. *American Psychologist, 43,* 949–957.

Mays, V. M., Coleman, L. M., & Jackson, J. S. (1996). Perceived race-based discrimination, employment status, and job stress in a national sample of black women: Implications for health outcomes. *Journal of Occupational Health Psychology, 1*(3), 319–329.

McCaulay, M., Mintz, L., & Glenn, A. A. (1988). Body image, self-esteem, and depression-proneness: Closing the gender gap. *Sex Roles, 18,* 381–391.

McClelland, D. C., Atkinson, J. W., Clark, R. A., & Lowell, E. L. (1953). *The achievement motive.* Englewood Cliffs, NJ: Prentice-Hall.

McCloskey, L. A., & Coleman, L. M. (1992). Difference without dominance: Children's talk in mixed- and same-sex dyads. *Sex Roles, 27,* 241–257.

McCormick, N. B., & Jesser, C. J. (1983). The courtship game: Power in the sexual encounter. In E. R. Allgeier & N. B. McCormick (Eds.), *Changing boundaries: Gender roles and sexual behavior* (pp. 64–86). Palo Alto, CA: Mayfield.

McCormick, N. B., & Jones, M. A. (1989). Gender differences in nonverbal flirtation. *Journal of Sex Education and Therapy, 15,* 271–282.

McDermid, S. A., Zucker, K. J., Bradley, S. J., & Maing, D. M. (1998). Effect of physical appearance on masculine trait ratings of boys and girls with gender identity disorder. *Archives of Sexual Behavior, 27,* 253–267.

McEwen, B. S. (1981). Neural gonadal steroid actions. *Science, 211,* 1303–1311.

McFarlane, J. M., & Williams, T. M. (1994). Placing premenstrual syndrome in perspective. *Psychology of Women Quarterly, 18,* 339–373.

McGloshen, T. H., & O'Bryant, S. L. (1988). The psychological well-being of older, recent widows. *Psychology of Women Quarterly, 12,* 99–116.

McGoldrick, M., Garcia-Preto, N., Hines, P. M., & Lee, E. (1989). Ethnicity and women. In M. McGoldrick, C. M. Anderson, & F. Walsh (Eds.), *Women in families: A framework of feminist theory* (pp. 169–199). New York: Norton.

McGrath, E., Keita, G. P., Strickland, B. R., & Russo, N. F. (1990). *Women and depression: Risk factors and treatment issues.* Washington, DC: American Psychological Association.

McGrath, J. E. (1986). Continuity and change: Time, method, and the study of social issues. *Journal of Social Issues, 42,* 5–19.

McGuire, J. (1988). Gender stereotypes of parents with two-year-olds and beliefs about gender differences in behavior. *Sex Roles, 19,* 233–240.

McGuire, W. J., McGuire, C. V., & Winton, W. (1979). Effects of household sex composition on the salience of one's gender in the spontaneous self-concept. *Journal of Experimental Social Psychology, 15,* 77–90.

McGuire, W. J., & Padawer-Singer, A. (1976). Trait salience in the spontaneous self-concept. *Journal of Personality and Social Psychology, 33,* 743–754.

McHugh, M. D., Koeske, R. D., & Frieze, I. H. (1986). Issues to consider in conducting nonsexist psychological research: A guide for researchers. *American Psychologist, 41,* 879–890.

McIntosh, P. (1988). *Understanding correspondence between white privilege and male privilege through women's studies work.* (Working paper No. 189). Wellesley, MA: Center for Research on Women, Wellesley College.

McKinley, N. M. (1998). Gender differences in undergraduate's body esteem: The moderating effect of objectified body consciousness and actual/ideal weight discrepancy. *Sex Roles, 39,* 113–123.

McKinley, N. M., & Hyde, J. S. (1996). The objectified body consciousness scale: Development and validation. *Psychology of Women Quarterly, 20,* 181–215.

McLean, C., Carey, M., & White, C. (Eds.). (1996). *Men's ways of being.* Boulder: Westview.

McMahon, M. (1995). *Engendering motherhood.* New York: Guilford.

Media more likely to show women talking about romance than at a job. (1997, May 1). *New York Times,* p. B15.

Mellanby, A. R., Phelps, F. A., Crichton, N. J., & Tripp, J. H. (1996). School sex education, a process for evaluation: Methodology and results. *Health Education Research, 11*(2), 205–214.

Mercer, R. T. (1990). *Parents at risk*. New York: Springer.

Messick, D. M., & Mackie, D. M. (1989). Intergroup relations. *Annual Review of Psychology, 40*, 45–82.

Messner, M. A. (1994). Ah, ya throw like a girl! In M. A. Messner & D. F. Sabo (Eds.), *Sex, violence, and power in sports: Rethinking masculinity* (pp. 28–32). Freedom, CA: The Crossing Press.

Messner, M. A., Duncan, M. C., & Jensen, K. (1993). Separating the men from the girls: The gendered language of televised sports. *Gender & Society, 7*, 121–137.

Meston, C. M., Trapnell, P. D., & Gorzalka, B. B. (1996). Ethnic and gender differences in sexuality: Variations in sexual behavior between Asian and non-Asian university students. *Archives of Sexual Behavior, 25*(1), 33–72.

Middlebrook, D. W. (1998). *Suits me: The double life of Billy Tipton*. Boston, MA: Houghton Mifflin.

Miller, B., & Cafasso, L. (1992). Gender differences in care-giving: Fact or artifact. *American Journal of Psychiatry, 32*, 498–507.

Miller, B. C., Norton, M. C., Curtis, T., Hill, E. J., Schvaneveldt, P., & Young, M. H. (1997). The timing of sexual intercourse among adolescents. *Youth & Society, 29*(1), 54–83.

Miller, D. H. (1996). Medical and psychological consequences of legal abortion in the United States. In R. L. Parrott & C. M. Condit (Eds.), *Evaluating women's health messages* (pp. 17–32). Thousand Oaks: Sage.

Miller, E. K. (1993). Politics and gender: Geraldine Ferraro in the editorial cartoons. In S. T. Hollis, L. Pershing, & M. J. Young (Eds.). *Feminist theory and the study of folklore* (pp. 358–395). Urbana: University of Illinois Press.

Miller, J. B. (1984b). *The development of women's sense of self (Work in Progress Papers No. 84-01)*. Wellesley, MA: Wellesley College, The Stone Center.

Miller, J. B. (1986). *Toward a new psychology of women* (2nd ed.). Boston: Beacon Press.

Miller, J. B. (1991). The development of women's sense of self. In J. V. Jordan, A. C. Kaplan, J. B. Miller, I. P. Stiver, & J. L. Surrey (Eds.), *Women's growth in connection: Writings from the Stone Center* (pp. 11–26). New York: Guilford.

Miller, M., Moen, P., & Dempster-McClain, D. (1991). Motherhood, multiple roles, and maternal well-being: Women of the 1950s. *Gender & Society, 5*, 565–582.

Mills, C. S., & Granoff, B. J. (1992). Date and acquaintance rape among a sample of college students. *Social Work, 37*, 504–509.

Mirowsky, J. (1996). Age and the gender gap in depression. *Journal of Health and Social Behavior, 37*, 362–380.

Mirowsky, J., & Ross, K. E. (1987). Belief in innate sex roles: Sex stratification versus interpersonal influence in marriage. *Journal of Marriage and the Family, 49*, 527–540.

Misovich, S. J., Fisher, J. D., & Fisher, W. A. (1997). Close relationships and elevated HIV risk behavior: Evidence and possible underlying psychological processes. *Review of General Psychology, 1*(1), 72–107.

Mitchell, G., Obradovich, S., Herring, F., Tromborg, C., & Burns, A. L. (1992). Reproducing gender in public places: Adults' attention to toddlers in three public locales. *Sex Roles, 26*, 323–330.

Mitchell, V., & Helson, R. (1990). Women's prime in life: Is it the 50's? *Psychology of Women Quarterly, 14*, 451–470.

Miura, I. (1987). The relationship of computer self-efficacy expectations to computer interest and course enrollment in college. *Sex Roles, 16*, 303–312.

Modleski, T. (1980). The disappearing act: A study of Harlequin romances. *Signs, 5*, 435–448.

Moen, P., Robison, J., & Fields, V. (1994). Women's work and caregiving: A life course approach. *Journal of Gerontology: Social Sciences, 49*, S176–S186.

Moffat, M. (1989). *Coming of age in New Jersey*. New Brunswick, NJ: Rutgers University Press.

Moller, L. C., Hymel, S., & Rubin, K. H. (1992). Sex typing in play and popularity in middle childhood. *Sex Roles, 26*, 331–353.

Moller, L. C., & Serbin, L. A. (1996). Antecedents of toddler gender segregation: Cognitive consonance, gender-typed toy preferences, and behavioral compatability. *Sex Roles, 35*, 445–460.

Molloy, B. M., & Herzberger, S. D. (1998). Body image and self-esteem: A comparison of African-Americans and Caucasian women. *Sex Roles, 38*, 631–643.

Molm, L. D., & Hedley, M. (1992). Gender, power, and social exchange. In C. L. Ridgeway (Ed.), *Gender, interaction, and inequality* (pp. 1–28). New York: Springer-Verlag.

Money, J. (1974). Prenatal hormones and postnatal socialization in gender identity differentiation. In J. K. Cole & R. Dienstbier (Eds.), *Nebraska Symposium on Motivation 1973*, Lincoln: University of Nebraska Press.

Money, J., & Ehrhardt, A. (1972). *Man and woman, boy and girl.* Baltimore: Johns Hopkins University Press.

Money, J., & Mathews, D. (1982). Prenatal exposure to virilizing progestins: An adult follow-up study on 12 young women. *Archives of Sexual Behavior, 11,* 73–83.

Montemayor, R., & Hanson, E. A. (1985). A naturalistic view of conflict between adolescents and their parents and siblings. *Journal of Early Adolescence, 3,* 83–103.

Montgomery, R. J. V., & Kamo, Y. (1989). Parent care by sons and daughters. In J. A. Mancini (Ed.), *Aging parents and adult children* (pp. 213–230). Lexington, MA: Heath.

Mooney, L., & Brabant, S. (1987). Two martinis and a rested woman: "Liberation" in the Sunday comics. *Sex Roles, 17,* 409–420.

Moore, C. L., Dou, H., & Juraska, J. M. (1992). Maternal stimulation affects the number of motor neurons in a sexually dimorphic nucleus of the lumbar spinal cord. *Brain Research, 572,* 42–56.

Morgan, B. L. (1998). A three generational study of tomboy behavior. *Sex Roles, 39,* 787–800.

Morgan, K. P. (1996). Describing the emperor's new clothes: Three myths of educational (in-)equity. In A. Diller, B. Houston, K. P. Morgan, & M. Ayim (Eds.), *The gender questions in education: Theory, pedagogy, and politics* (pp. 105–122). Boulder, CO: Westview Press.

Morgan, K. P. (1998). Women and the knife: Cosmetic surgery and the colonization of women's bodies. In R. Weitz (Ed.), *The politics of women's bodies: Sexuality, appearance, and behavior* (pp. 147–166). New York: Oxford University Press.

Morgan, L. A. (1991). *After marriage ends: Economic consequences for midlife women.* London: Sage.

Mori, D. L., Chaikin, S., & Pliner, P. (1987). "Eating lightly" and the self-presentation of femininity. *Journal of Personality and Social Psychology, 53,* 240–254.

Morokoff, P. (1990, August). Women's sexuality: Expression of self vs. social construction. In C. Travis (chair), The social construction of women's sexuality. Symposium presented at the meeting of the American Psychological Association, Boston.

Morris, J. (1974). *Conundrum.* New York: Harcourt Brace Jovanovich.

Morrow, S. L., & Hawxhurst, D. M. (1998). Feminist therapy: Integrating political analysis in counseling and psychotherapy. *Women & Therapy, 21,* 37–50.

Moss, J. J. (1997, February 4). *Lesbian baiting in the barracks.* The Advocate, 36–40.

Motenko, A. K., & Greenberg, S. (1995). Reframing dependence in old age: A positive transition for families. *Social Work, 40,* 382–390.

Moulton, J. M., Robinson, G. M., & Elias, C. (1978). Sex bias in language use: Neutral pronouns that aren't. *American Psychologist, 33,* 1032–1036.

Moynihan, D. P. (1965). *The Negro family: The case for national action.* Washington, DC: U.S. Department of Labor.

Muehlenhard, C. L., & Hollabough, L. C. (1988). Do women sometimes say no when they mean yes? The prevalence and correlates of women's token resistance to sex. *Journal of Personality and Social Psychology, 54,* 872–879.

Muehlenhard, C. L., & Rodgers, C. S. (1998). Token resistance to sex: New perspectives on an old stereotype. *Psychology of Women Quarterly, 22*(3), 443–463.

Muehlenhard, C. L., & Scardino, T. J. (1985). What will he think? Men's impressions of women who initiate dates and achieve academically. *Journal of Counseling Psychology, 32,* 560–569.

Mueller, K. A., & Yoder, J. D. (1997). Gendered norms for family size, employment, and occupation: Are there personal costs for violating them? *Sex Roles, 36,* 207–220.

Mullen, P. E. (1993). Child sexual abuse and adult mental health: The development of disorder. *Journal of Interpersonal Violence, 8,* 429.

Murray, S. B. (1997). It's safer this way: The subtle and not-so-subtle exclusion of men in child care. In N. Benokraitis (Ed.), *Subtle Sexism* (pp. 135–153). Thousand Oaks, CA: Sage.

Murry-McBride, V. (1996). An ecological analysis of coital timing among middle-class African American adolescent females. *Journal of Adolescent Research, 11*(2), 261–279.

Murstein, B. I. (1986). *Paths to marriage.* Beverly Hills, CA: Sage.

Mwangi, M. W. (1996). Gender roles portrayed in Kenyan television commercials. *Sex Roles, 34,* 205–214.

Myers, D. G. (1986). *Psychology.* New York: Worth.

Nacoste, R. W., & Lehman, D. (1987). Procedural stigma. *Representative Research in Social Psychology, 17,* 25–38.

Nadler, A., & Fisher, J. D. (1986). The role of

threat to self-esteem and perceived control in recipient reaction to help: Theory development and empirical validation. In L. Berkowitz (Ed.), *Advances in Experimental Social Psychology,* Vol. 19. New York: Academic Press.

Nails, D. (1983). Social-scientific sexism: Gilligan's mismeasure of man. *Social Research, 50,* 643–664.

Nanda, S. (1996). Hijras: An alternative sex and gender role in India. In G. Herdt (Ed.), *Third sex, third gender: Beyond sexual dimorphism in culture and history* (pp. 373–417). New York: Zone Books.

Naples, N. A. (1992). Activist mothering: Cross-generational continuity in the community work of women from low-income urban neighborhoods. Special issue: Race, class, and gender. *Gender & Society, 6,* 441–463.

Nash, H. C., & Chrisler, J. C. (1995, August 12). *The psychological adjustment of blue-collar women.* Poster presented at the 103rd annual convention of the American Psychological Association, New York.

Nash, H. C., & Chrisler, J. C. (1997). Is a little (psychiatric) knowledge a dangerous thing? The impact of premenstrual dysphoric disorder on perceptions of premenstrual women. *Psychology of Women Quarterly, 21,* 315–322.

National Committee on Pay Equity. (1998, Fall). Newsnotes. Washington, DC: Author.

Needleman, R., & Nelson, A. (1988). Policy implications: The worth of women's work. In A. Statham, E. M. Miller, & H. O. Mauksch (Eds.), *The worth of women's work: A qualitative synthesis* (pp. 293–307). Albany, NY: State University of New York Press.

Nelson, E. J. (1996). The American experience of childbirth. In R. L. Parrott & C. M. Condit (Eds.), *Evaluating women's health messages* (pp. 109–123). Thousand Oaks: Sage.

Nelson, H. L. (1992). Scrutinizing surrogacy. In H. B. Holmes (Ed.), *Issues in reproductive technology* (pp. 297–302). New York: Garland.

Neppi, T. K., & Murray, A. D. (1997). Social dominance and play patterns among preschoolers: Gender comparisons. *Sex Roles, 36,* 381–393.

Neto, F., & Pinto, I. (1998). Gender stereotypes in Portuguese television advertisements. *Sex Roles, 39,* 153–164.

Nettles, S. M., & Scott-Jones, D. (1987). The role of sexuality and sex equity in the education of minority adolescents. *Peabody Journal of Education, 64,* 183–197.

Neuberg, S. L., Smith, D. M., Hoffman, J. C., & Russell, F. J. (1994). When we observe stigmatized and "normal" individuals interacting: Stigma by association. *Personality and Social Psychology Bulletin, 20,* 196–209.

Nevid, J. S. (1984). Sex differences in factors of romantic attraction. *Sex Roles, 11,* 401–411.

Newson, J., & Newson, E. (1987). Family and sex roles in middle childhood. In D. J. Hargreaves & A. M. Colley (Eds.), *The psychology of sex roles* (pp. 142–158). New York: Hemisphere.

Newton, N. (1970). The effect of psychological environment on childbirth: Combined crosscultural and experimental approach. *Journal of Cross-Cultural Psychology, 1,* 85–90.

Newtson, R. L., & Keith, P. M. (1997). Single women in later life. In J. M. Coyle (Ed.), *Handbook on women and aging* (pp. 385–399). Westport, CT: Greenwood Press.

Nichter, M., & Vuckovic, N. (1994). Fat talk: Body image among adolescent girls. In N. Sault (Ed.), *Many mirrors: Body image and social relations* (pp. 109–131). New Brunswick, NJ: Rutgers University Press.

Nicolson, P. (1990). A brief report of women's expectations of men's behavior in the transition to parenthood: Contradictions and conflicts for counselling psychology practice. Special Issue: Sexual and marital counselling: Perspectives on theory, research and practice. *Counselling Psychology Quarterly, 3,* 353–361.

Nicolson, P. (1993). Motherhood and women's lives. In D. Richardson & V. Robinson (Eds.), *Thinking feminist: Key concepts in women's studies* (pp. 201–224). New York: Guilford.

Nieva, V. F., & Gutek, B. A. (1981). *Women and work: A psychological perspective.* New York: Praeger.

Nigro, G. N., Hill, D. E., Gelbein, M. E., & Clark, C. L. (1988). Changes in the facial prominence of women and men over the last decade. *Psychology of Women Quarterly, 12,* 225–235.

Noble, B. P. (1993, April 18). Worthy child-care pay scales. *New York Times,* 25.

Noll, S. M., & Fredrickson, B. I. (1998). A mediational model linking self-objectification, body shame, and disordered eating. *Psychology of Women Quarterly, 22,* 623–636.

Norris, P. (Ed.). (1997). *Women, media, and politics.* New York: Oxford University Press.

Norton, A. J., & Moorman, J. E. (1987). Current trends in marriage and divorce among

American women. *Journal of Marriage and the Family, 49,* 3–14.

Norton, K. I., Olds, T. S., Olive, S., & Dank, S. (1996). Ken and Barbie at life size. *Sex Roles, 34,* 287–294.

Novak, L. L., & Novack, D. R. (1996). Being female in the eighties and nineties: Conflicts between new opportunities and traditional expectations among white, middle class, heterosexual college women. *Sex Roles, 35,* 57–77.

O'Brien, M., & Huston, A. C. (1985a). Development of sex-typed play in toddlers. *Developmental Psychology, 21,* 866–871.

O'Bryant, S. L. (1988). Sex-differentiated assistance in older widows' support systems. *Sex Roles, 19,* 91–106.

O'Connell, A. N., & Russo, N. F. (Eds.). (1980). Eminent women in psychology: Models of achievement, Special issue. *Psychology of Women Quarterly, 5.*

O'Connor, A. (1995, April). Tomboys. *Allure,* 68–70.

O'Farrell, B., & Harlan, S. L. (1982). Craftworkers and clerks: The effect of male co-worker hostility on women's satisfaction with nontraditional jobs. *Social Problems, 29,* 252–265.

O'Keeffe, N. K., Brockopp, K., & Chew, E. (1986). Teen dating violence. *Social Work, 31,* 465–468.

O'Laughlin, M. A. (1983). Responsibility and moral maturity in the control of fertility–or, a woman's place is in the wrong. *Social Research, 50,* 556–575.

O'Leary, A., & Helgeson, V. S. (1997). Psychosocial factors and women's health: Integrating mind, heart, and body. In S. J. Gallant, G. P. Keita, & R. Royak-Schaler (Eds.), *Health care for women: Psychological, social, and behavioral influences* (pp. 25–40). Washington, DC: American Psychological Association.

O'Leary, K. D., Malone, J., & Tyree, A. (1994). Physical aggression in early marriage: Prerelationship and relationship effects. *Journal of Consulting & Clinical Psychology, 62,* 594–602.

O'Sullivan, C. S. (1991). Acquaintance gang rape on campus. In A. Parrot & L. Bechhofer (Eds.), *Acquaintance rape: The hidden crime* (pp. 140–156). New York: Wiley.

Oakley, A. (1974). *The sociology of housework.* New York: Pantheon.

Oakley, A. (1986). *Telling the truth about Jerusalem.* London: Blackwell.

Oakley, A. (1992). Social support in pregnancy: Methodology and findings of a 1-year follow-up study. *Journal of Reproductive and Infant Psychology, 10,* 219–231.

Obermeyer, C. M. (1996). Fertility norms and son preference in Morocco and Tunisia: Does women's status matter? *Journal of Biosocial Science, 28,* 57–72.

Ofosu, H. B., Lafreniere, K. D., & Senn, C. Y. (1998). Body image perception among women of African descent: A normative context? *Feminism & Psychology, 8,* 303–323.

Ogletree, R. J. (1993). Sexual coercion experience and help-seeking behavior of college women. *Journal of American College Health, 41,* 149–153.

Okun, B. S. (1996). Sex preferences, family planning, and fertility: An Israeli subpopulation in transition. *Journal of Marriage & the Family, 58,* 469–475.

Olday, D., & Wesley, B. (1983). Premarital courtship violence: A summary report. Moorehead State University, Moorehead, KY. Unpublished.

Oliver, M. B., & Hyde, J. S. (1993). Gender differences in sexuality: A meta-analysis. *Psychological Bulletin, 114,* 29–51.

Oliver, S. J., & Toner, B. B. (1990). The influence of gender role typing on the expression of depressive symptoms. *Sex Roles, 22,* 775–790.

Olweus, D. (1993). Victimization by peers: Antecedents and longterm outcomes. In K. H. Rubin & J. B. Asendorpf (Eds.), *Social withdrawal, inhibition, and shyness in childhood.* Hillsdale, NJ: Erlbaum.

Oropesa, R. S. (1996). Normative beliefs about marriage and cohabitation: A comparison of non-Latino Whites, Mexican Americans, and Puerto Ricans. *Journal of Marriage and the Family, 58,* 49–62.

Owen, S. A., & Caudill, S. A. (1996). Contraception and clinical science. In R. L. Parrott & C. M. Condit (Eds.), *Evaluating women's health messages* (pp. 81–94). Thousand Oaks: Sage.

Padavic, I. (1991). Attractions of male blue-collar jobs for Black and White women: Economic need, exposure, and attitudes. *Social Science Quarterly, 72,* 33–49.

Padgett, D. (1988). Aging minority women: Issues in research and health policy. *Women & Health, 14,* 213–225.

Paetzold, R. L., & O'Leary-Kelly, A. M. (1996). The implications of U.S. Supreme Court and circuit court decisions for hostile environment sexual harassment cases. In M. S. Stockdale (Ed.), *Sexual harassment in the* workplace: Perspectives, frontiers, and response strategies (pp. 85–104). Thousand Oaks, CA: Sage.

Paige, K. E., & Paige, J. M. (1981). *The politics of reproductive ritual.* Berkeley: University of California Press.

Palmore, E. B. (1997). Sexism and ageism. In J. M. Coyle (Ed.). *Handbook on women and aging* (pp. 3–13). Westport, CT: Greenwood Press.

Paludi, M. (1997). Sexual harassment in schools. In W. O'Donohue (Ed.), *Sexual harassment theory, research, and treatment* (pp. 225–249). Boston: Allyn & Bacon.

Paludi, M. A., & Bauer, W. D. (1983). Goldberg revisited: What's in an author's name? *Sex Roles, 9,* 387–390.

Paludi, M. A., & Fankell-Hauser, J. (1986). An idiographic approach to the study of women's achievement striving. *Psychology of Women Quarterly, 10,* 89–100.

Paludi, M. A., & Strayer, L. A. (1985). What's in an author's name? Differential evaluations of performance as a function of author's name. *Sex Roles, 10,* 353–361.

Papanek, H. (1973). Men, women, and work: Reflections on the two-person career. *American Journal of Sociology, 78,* 852–870.

Parker, S., Nichter, M., Nichter, M., Vuckovic, N., Sims, C., & Ritenbaugh, C. (1995). Body image and weight concerns among African American and White adolescent females: Differences which make a difference. *Human Organization, 54,* 103–114.

Parlee, M. B. (1975). Review essay: Psychology. *Signs, 1,* 119–138.

Parlee, M. B. (1979). Psychology and women. *Signs, 5,* 121–133.

Parlee, M. B. (1981). Appropriate control groups in feminist research. *Psychology of Women Quarterly, 5,* 637–644.

Parlee, M. B. (1985). Psychology of women in the 80s: Promising problems. *International Journal of Women's Studies, 8,* 193–204.

Parlee, M. B. (1989, March). *The science and politics of PMS research.* Paper presented at the meeting of the Association for Women in Psychology, Newport, RI.

Parlee, M. B. (1990). Integrating biological and social scientific research on menopause. In M. Flint, F. Kronenberg, & W. Utian (Eds.), *Multidisciplinary perspectives on menopause. Annals of the New York Academy of Sciences, 592,* 379–389.

Parsons, T., & Bales, R. F. (1955). *Family, socialization, and interaction process.* Glencoe, IL: Free Press.

Pastor, J., McCormick, J., & Fine, M. (1996). Makin' homes: An urban girl thing. In B. J. R. Leadbeater & N. Way (Eds.), *Urban girls: Resisting stereotypes, creating identities* (pp. 15–34). New York: New York University Press.

Patterson, E. T., & Hale, E. S. (1985). Making sure: Integrating menstrual care practices into activities of daily living. *Advances in Nursing Science, 7,* 18–31.

Payne, B., & Whittington, F. (1976). Older women: An examination of popular stereotypes and research evidence. *Social Problems, 23,* 488–504.

Pearlman, S. F. (1993). Late mid-life astonishment: Disruptions to identity and self-esteem. In N. D. Davis, E. Cole, & E. D. Rothblum (Eds.), *Faces of women and aging* (pp. 1–12). Binghamton, NY: Harrington Park Press.

Pedersen, P., & Thomas, C. D. (1992). Prevalence and correlates of dating violence in a Canadian university sample. *Canadian Journal of Behavioural Science, 24,* 490–501.

Peirce, K. (1990). A feminist theoretical perspective on the socialization of teenage girls through Seventeen Magazine. *Sex Roles, 23,* 491–500.

Peirce, K. (1993). Socialization of teenage girls through teen-magazine fiction: The making of a new woman or an old lady? *Sex Roles, 29,* 59–68.

Pelligrini, A. D., & Perlmutter, J. C. (1989). Classroom contextual effects on children's play. *Developmental Psychology, 25,* 289–296.

Pence, E., & Shepard, M. (1988). Integrating feminist theory and practice: The challenge of the battered women's movement. In K. Yllo & M. Bograd (Eds.), *Feminist perspectives on wife abuse* (pp. 11–26). Berkeley, CA: Sage.

Peplau, L. A. (1983). Roles and gender. In H. H. Kelley et al. (Eds.), *Close relationships.* New York: W. H. Freeman.

Peplau, L. A., & Campbell, S. M. (1989). The balance of power in dating and marriage. In J. Freeman (Ed.), *Women: A feminist perspective* (4th ed., pp. 121–137). Mountain View, CA: Mayfield.

Peplau, L. A., & Cochran, S. D. (1980). Sex differences in values concerning love relationships. Paper presented at American Psychological Association, cited in Peplau, L. A., & Gordon, S. L. (1983). The intimate relationships of lesbians and gay men. In E. R. Allgeier & N. B. McCormick (Eds.), *Changing boundaries: Gender roles and sexual behavior* (pp. 226–244). Palo Alto, CA: Mayfield.

Peplau, L. A., & Cochran, S. D. (1990). A relationship perspective on homosexuality. In D. P. McWhirter, S. A. Sanders, & J. M. Reinisch (Eds.), *Homosexuality/heterosexuality: The Kinsey scales and current research* (pp. 226–244). New York: Oxford University Press.

Peplau, L. A., & Conrad, E. (1989). Beyond nonsexist research: The perils of feminist methods in psychology. *Psychology of Women Quarterly, 13,* 379–400.

Peplau, L. A., & Gordon, S. L. (1983). The intimate relationships of lesbians and gay men. In E. R. Allgeier & N. B. McCormick (Eds.), *Changing boundaries: Gender roles and sexual behavior* (pp. 226–244). Palo Alto, CA: Mayfield.

Peplau, L. A., & Gordon, S. L. (1985). Women and men in love: Gender differences in close heterosexual relationships. In V. E. O'Leary, R. K. Unger, & B. S. Wallston (Eds.), *Women, gender, and social psychology* (pp. 257–292). Hillsdale, NJ: Erlbaum.

Perkins, K. E. (1992). Psychosocial implications of women and retirement. *Social Work, 37,* 526–532.

Perlmutter, E., & Bart, P. B. (1982). Changing news of "The Change": A critical review and suggestions for an attributional approach. In A. M. Voda, M. Dinnerstein, & S. R. O'Donnell (Eds.), *Changing perspectives on menopause* (pp. 185–199). Austin: University of Texas Press.

Perry, D. G., Perry, L. C., & Weiss, R. J. (1989). Sex differences in the consequences that children anticipate for aggression. *Developmental Psychology, 25,* 312–319.

Perry, D. G., White, A. J., & Perry, L. C. (1984). Does early sex-typing result from children's attempts to match their behavior to sex role stereotypes? *Child Development, 55,* 2114–2121.

Perun, P. J., & Bielby, D. D. (1981). Towards a model of female occupational behavior: A human development approach. *Psychology of Women Quarterly, 6,* 234–252.

Peters, D. K., & Cantrell, P. J. (1993). Gender roles and role conflict in feminist lesbian and heterosexual women. *Sex Roles, 28,* 379–392.

Petersen, A. C. (1983). Menarche: Meaning of measures and measuring meaning. In S. Golub (Ed.), *Menarche: The transition from girl to woman* (pp. 63–76). Lexington, MA: Lexington Books.

Petersen, A. C. (1987). The nature of biological-psychosocial interactions: The sample case

of early adolescence. In R. M. Lerner & T. T. Foch (Eds.), *Biological-psychosocial interactions in early adolescence* (pp. 35–61). Hillsdale, NJ: Erlbaum.

Peterson, E. (1974). Consumer specialist. In R. B. Kundsin (Ed.), *Women and success: The anatomy of achievement* (pp. 78–80). New York: William Morrow.

Peterson, R. E., Imperato-McGinley, J., Gautier, T., & Sturla, E. (1977). Male pseudohermaphrodism due to steroid 5 alpha-reductase deficiency. *American Journal of Medicine, 62,* 170–191.

Peterson, R. F., Basta, S. M., & Dykstra, T. A. (1993). Mothers of molested children: Some comparisons of personality characteristics. *Child Abuse and Neglect, 17,* 409–418.

Petrie, T. A., Austin, L. J., Crowley, B. J., Helmcamp, A., Johnson, C. E., Lester, R., Rogers, R., Turner, J., & Walbrick, K. (1996). Sociocultural expectations of attractiveness in males. *Sex Roles, 35,* 581–602.

Phares, V., & Compas, B. E. (1993). Fathers and developmental psychotherapy. *Current Directions in Psychological Science, 2,* 162.

Phelps, G. C., Andrea, R., Rizzo, F. G., Johnston, L., & Main, C. M. (1993). Prevalence of self-induced vomiting and laxative/medication abuse among female adolescents: A longitudinal study. *International Journal of Eating Disorders, 14,* 375–378.

Phillips, L. (1998). *The girls report: What we know & need to know about growing up female.* New York: National Council for Research on Women.

Phillips, R. D., & Gilroy, F. D. (1985). Sex-role stereotypes and clinical judgments of mental health: The Brovermans' findings reexamined. *Sex Roles, 12,* 179–193.

Phillips, S. D., & Imhoff, A. R. (1997). Women and career development: A decade of research. *Annual Review of Psychology, 48,* 31–59.

Phoenix, A., Woollett, A., & Lloyd, E. (Eds.). (1991). *Motherhood: Meanings, practices, and ideologies.* London: Sage.

Pietromonaco, P. R., Manis, J., & Frohart-Lane, K. (1986). Psychological consequences of multiple social roles. *Psychology of Women Quarterly, 10,* 373–382.

Pike, K. M. (1995). Bulimic symptomology in high school girls: Toward a model of cumulative risk. *Psychology of Women Quarterly, 19,* 373–396.

Pike, K. M., & Striegel-Moore, R. H. (1997). Disordered eating and eating disorders. In

S. J. Gallant, G. P. Keita, & R. Royak-Schaler (Eds.), *Health care for women: Psychological, social, and behavioral influence* (pp. 97–114). Washington, DC: American Psychological Association.

Piliavin, J. A., & Unger, R. K. (1985). The helpful but helpless female: Myth or reality? In V. E. O'Leary, R. K. Unger, & B. S. Wallston (Eds.), *Women, gender, and social psychology* (pp. 149–190). Hillsdale, NY: Erlbaum.

Pipher, M. (1994). *Reviving Ophelia: Saving the selves of adolescent girls.* NY: G. P. Putnam's Sons.

Pipher, M. (1999). *Another country: Navigating the emotional terrain of our elders.* New York: Riverhead Books.

Pitts, V. L., & Schwartz, M. D. (1997). Self-blame in hidden rape cases. In M. D. Schwartz (Ed.), *Researching sexual violence against women: Methodological and personal perspectives* (pp. 65–70). Thousand Oaks, CA: Sage.

Pleck, J. H. (1977). The work-family role system. *Social Problems, 24,* 417–427.

Pleck, J. H. (1987). Dual-career families: A comment. *Counseling Psychologist, 15,* 131–133.

Pleck, J. H., Sonenstein, F. L., & Ku, L. C. (1994). Attitudes toward male roles among adolescent males: A discriminant validity analysis. *Sex Roles, 30,* 481–501.

Plous, S., & Neptune, D. (1997). Racial and gender biases in magazine advertising: A content analysis study. *Psychology of Women Quarterly, 21,* 627–644.

Plumb, P., & Cowan, G. (1984). A developmental study of destereotyping and androgynous activity preferences of tomboys, nontomboys, and males. *Sex Roles, 10,* 703–712.

Polakow, V. (1993). *Lives on the edge: Single mothers and their children in the other America.* Chicago: University of Chicago Press.

Police say woman, 21, is killed by ex-husband. (1998, July 26). *New York Times,* p. 1.

Pollack, S. (1990). Lesbian parents: Claiming our visibility. In J. P. Knowles & E. Cole (Eds.), *Motherhood: A feminist perspective* (pp. 181–194). New York: Haworth.

Pollitt, K. (1998). "Fetal rights": A new assault on feminism. In R. Weitz (Ed.), *The politics of women's bodies: Sexuality, appearance, and behavior* (pp. 278–287). New York: Oxford University Press.

Pomerleau, A., Bloduc, D., Malcuit, G., & Cossette, L. (1990). Pink or blue: Environmental gender stereotypes in the first two years of life. *Sex Roles, 22,* 359–367.

Ponse, B. (1978). *Identities in the lesbian world.* Westport, CT: Greenwood Press.

Pooler, W. S. (1991). Sex of child preferences among college students. *Sex Roles, 25,* 569–576.

Pope, K. (1994). *Sexual involvement with therapists: Patient assessment, subsequent treatment, forensics.* Washington, DC: American Psychological Association.

Popenoe, D. (1987). Beyond the nuclear family: A statistical portrait of the changing family in Sweden. *Journal of Marriage and the Family, 49,* 173–183.

Porter, N., & Geis, F. (1981). Women and nonverbal leadership cues: When seeing is not believing. In C. Mayo & N. Henley (Eds.), *Gender and nonverbal behavior* (pp. 39–61). New York: Springer-Verlag.

Porter, N., Geis, F. L., Cooper, E., & Newman, E. (1985). Androgyny and leadership in mixed sex groups. *Journal of Personality and Social Psychology, 49,* 808–823.

Poulin-Dubois, D., Serbin, L. A., & Derbyshire, A. (1998). Toddlers' intermodal and verbal knowledge about gender. *Merrill-Palmer Quarterly, 44,* 338–354.

Poulin-Dubois, D., Serbin, L. A., Kenyon, R., & Derbyshire, A. (1994). Infants' intermodal knowledge about gender. *Developmental Psychology, 30,* 436–442.

Pour-El, M. B. (1974). Mathematician. In R. B. Kundsin (Ed.), *Women and success: The anatomy of achievement* (pp. 36–37). New York: William Morrow.

Powell, A. D., & Kahn, A. S. (1995). Racial differences in women's desire to be thin. *International Journal of Eating Disorders, 17,* 191–195.

Power, T. (1981). Sex typing in infancy: The role of the father. *Infant Mental Health Journal, 2,* 226–240.

Powlishta, K. K. (1995a). Gender bias in children's perception of personality traits. *Sex Role, 32,* 17–28.

Powlishta, K. K. (1995b). Intergroup processes in childhood: Social categorization and sex role development. *Developmental Psychology, 31,* 781–788.

Powlishta, K. K., Serbin, L. A., & Moller, L. C. (1993). The stability of individual differences in gender typing: Implications for understanding gender segregation. *Sex Roles, 29,* 723–737.

Pratto, F. (1996). Sexual politics: The gender gap in the bedroom, the cupboard, and the cabinet. In D. M. Buss & N. M. Malamuth (Eds.), *Sex, power, conflict: Evolutionary and feminist perspectives* (pp. 179–230). New York: Oxford University Press.

Price, S. J., & McKenry, P. C. (1988). *Divorce*. Beverly Hills, CA: Sage.

Prilleltensky, O. (1996). Women with disabilities and feminist therapy. *Women & Therapy, 18,* 87–97.

Pryor, J. B. (1987). Sexual harassment proclivities in men. *Sex Roles, 17,* 269–290.

Pryor, J. B., Giedd, J. L., & Williams, K. B. (1995). A social psychological model for predicting sexual harassment. *Journal of Social Issues, 51,* 69–84.

Pryor, J. B., La Vite, C., & Stoller, L. (1993). A social psychological analysis of sexual harassment: The person/situation interaction. *Journal of Vocational Behavior, 20,* 163–169.

Public Interest Directorate of the American Psychological Association. (1987). Follow-up report to oral presentation of December 2, 1987. Psychological sequelae of abortion.

Pugh, M. D., & Wahrman, R. (1983). Neutralizing sexism in mixed-sex groups: Do women have to be better than men? *American Journal of Sociology, 88,* 746–762.

Purcell, P., & Stewart, L. (1990). Dick and Jane in 1989. *Sex Roles, 22,* 177–185.

Purdy, L. M. (1992). Another look at contract pregnancy. In H. B. Holmes (Ed.), *Issues in reproductive technology* (pp. 303–320). New York: Garland.

Puri, J. (1997). Reading romance novels in post-colonial India. *Gender & Society, 11*(4), 434–452.

Pushkar-Gold, D., Franz, E., Reis, M., & Senneville, C. (1994). The influence of emotional awareness and expressiveness on caregiving burden and health complaints in women and men. *Sex Roles, 31,* 205–224.

Raag, T., & Rackliff, C. L. (1998). Preschoolers' awareness of social expectations of gender relationships to toy choices. *Sex Roles, 38,* 685–700.

Radlove, S. (1983). Sexual response and gender roles. In E. R. Allgeier & N. B. McCormick (Eds.), *Changing boundaries: Gender roles and sexual behavior* (pp. 87–105). Palo Alto, CA: Mayfield.

Radway, J. A. (1984). *Reading the romance: Women, patriarchy, and popular literature.* Chapel Hill, NC: University of North Carolina Press.

Ragsdale, J. D. (1996). Gender, satisfaction level and the use of relational maintenance strategies in marriage. *Communication Monographs, 63*(4), 354–369.

Raines, R. S., Hechtman, S. B., & Rosenthal, R. (1990). Nonverbal behavior and gender as determinants of physical attractiveness. *Journal of Nonverbal Behavior, 14,* 253–267.

Ralston, P. A. (1997). Midlife and older black women. In J. M. Coyle (Ed.), *Handbook on women and aging* (pp. 273–289). Westport, CT: Greenwood Press.

Ramos-McKay, J., Comas-Diaz, L., & Rivera, L. (1988). Puerto Ricans. In L. Comas-Diaz & E. E. H. Griffith (Eds.), *Clinical guidelines in cross-cultural mental health* (pp. 204–232). New York: Wiley.

Randolph, S. M. (1995). African American children in single-mother families. In B. J. Dickerson (Ed.), *African American single mothers* (pp. 117–145). Thousand Oaks: Sage.

Ray, D. C., McKinney, K. A., & Ford, C. V. (1987). Ageism in psychiatrists: Associations with gender, certification, and theoretical orientation. *The Gerontologist, 27,* 82–86.

Raymond, J. G. (1993). *Women as wombs: Reproductive technologies and the battle over women's freedom.* New York: HarperCollins.

Reddin, J. (1997). High-achieving women: Career development patterns. In H. S. Farmer (Ed.), *Diversity & women's career development: From adolescence to adulthood* (pp. 95–126). Thousand Oaks, CA: Sage.

Reese, E., Haden, C. A., & Fivush, R. (1993). Mother-child conversations about the past: Relationship of style and memory over time. *Cognitive Development, 8,* 403–430.

Regan, P. C. (1996). Sexual outcasts: The perceived impact of body weight and gender on sexuality. *Journal of Applied Social Psychology, 26*(20), 1803–1815.

Reid, P. T. (1982). Socialization of black female children. In P. W. Berman & E. R. Ramey (Eds.), *Women: A developmental perspective.* Washington, DC: NIH Publication No. 82-2298.

Reid, P. T. (1993). Poor women in psychological research: Shut up and shut out. *Psychology of Women Quarterly, 17,* 133–150.

Reid, P. T., & Kelly, E. (1994). Research on women of color: From ignorance to awareness. *Psychology of Women Quarterly, 18,* 477–486.

Reid, P. T., Tate, C. C., & Berman, P. W. (1989). Preschool children's self-presentations in situations with infants: Effects of sex and race. *Child Development, 60,* 710–714.

Reid, P. T., & Trotter, K. H. (1993). Children's self-presentations with infants: Gender and ethnic comparisons. *Sex Roles, 29,* 171–181.

Reilly, M. E., & Lynch, J. M. (1990). Power-sharing in lesbian partnerships. *Journal of Homosexuality, 19,* 1–30.

Reineke, M. J. (1989). *Out of order: A critical perspective on women in religion.* In J. Freedman (Ed.), Women: A feminist perspective (4th ed., pp. 395–414). Mountain View, CA: Mayfield.

Reitz, R. (1981). *Menopause: A positive approach.* London: Unwin.

Renzetti, C. M. (1987). New Wave or second stage? Attitudes of college women toward feminism. *Sex Roles, 16,* 265–277.

Renzetti, C. M. (1997). Violence in lesbian and gay relationships. In L. O'Toole, & J. R. Schiffman (Eds.), *Gender violence: Interdisciplinary perspectives* (pp. 285–293). New York: New York University Press.

Reuterman, N. A., & Burcky, W. D. (1989). Dating violence in high school: A profile of the victims. *Psychology: A Journal of Human Behavior, 26,* 1–9.

Rheingold, H. L., & Cook, K. V. (1975). The contents of boys' and girls' rooms as an index of parents' behavior. *Child Development, 46,* 459–463.

Rhoades, J. M. (1989). Social support and the transition to the maternal role. In P. N. Stern (Ed.), *Pregnancy and parenting* (pp. 131–142). New York: Hemisphere.

Rice, F. P. (1984). *The adolescent: Development, relations, and culture.* Boston: Allyn & Bacon.

Rice, J. (1994). Reconsidering research on divorce, family life cycle, and the meaning of family. *Psychology of Women Quarterly, 18,* 559–584.

Rich, A. (1976). *Of woman born: Motherhood as experience and institution.* New York: Norton.

Rich, A. (1980). Compulsory heterosexuality and lesbian existence. *Signs, 5,* 631–660.

Rich, M. K., & Cash, T. F. (1993). The American image of beauty: Media representations of hair color for four decades. *Sex Roles, 29,* 113–124.

Richards, M., Bernal, J., & Brackbill, Y. (1975). Early behavioral differences: Gender or circumcision? *Developmental Psychobiology, 9,* 89–95.

Richardson, D. C., Bernstein, S., & Taylor, S. P. (1979). The effect of situational contingencies on female retaliative behavior. *Journal of Personality and Social Psychology, 37,* 2044–2048.

Rieves, L., & Cash, T. F. (1996). Social developmental factors and women's body-image attitudes. *Journal of Social Behavior and Personality, 11,* 63–78.

Rigby, D. N., & Sophie, J. (1990). Ethical issues and client sexual preference. In H. Lerman & N. Porter (Eds.), *Feminist ethics in psychotherapy* (pp. 165–175). New York: Springer.

Riggs, D. (1993). Relationship problems and dating aggression. *Journal of Interpersonal Violence, 8,* 18–35.

Riggs, D. S., & Caulfield, M. B. (1997). Expected consequences of male violence against their female dating partners. *Journal of Interpersonal Violence, 12,* 229–240.

Riggs, D. S., & O'Leary, K. D. (1989). A theoretical model of courtship aggression. In M. Pirog-Good & J. E. Stets (Eds.), *Violence in dating relationships* (pp. 53–71). New York: Praeger.

Riggs, D. S., & O'Leary, K. D. (1996). Aggression between dating partners: An examination of a causal model of courtship aggression. *Journal of Interpersonal Violence, 11,* 519–540.

Riley, S., & Wrench, D. (1985). Mentoring among women lawyers. *Journal of Applied Social Psychology, 15,* 374–386.

Rind, B., & Tromovitch, P. (1997). A meta-analytic review of findings from national samples on psychological correlates of child sexual abuse. *Journal of Sex Research, 34,* 237–255.

Rintala, D. H., Howland, C. A., Nosek, M. A., Bennett, J. L., Young, M. E., Foley, C. C., Rossi, C. D., & Chanpong, G. (1997). Dating issues for women with physical disabilities. *Sexuality and Disability, 15*(4), 219–242.

Risman, B. J. (1998). *Gender vertigo.* New Haven: Yale University.

Risman, B. J., & Johnson-Sumerford, D. (1998). Doing it fairly: A study of postgender marriages. *Journal of Marriage and the Family, 60,* 23–40.

Roberts, D. E. (1998). The future of reproductive choice for poor women and women of color. In R. Weitz (Ed.), *The politics of women's bodies: Sexuality, appearance, and behavior* (pp. 270–277). New York: Oxford University Press.

Robin, R. W., Chester, B., Rasmussen, J. K., Jaranson, J. M., Goldman, D. (1997). Prevalence and characteristics of trauma and posttraumatic stress disorder in a southwestern American Indian community. *American Journal of Psychiatry, 154,* 1582–1588.

Robinson, C. C., & Morris, J. T. (1986). The gender-stereotyped nature of Christmas toys received by 36-, 48-, and 60-month-old children: A comparison between non-requested and requested toys. *Sex Roles, 15,* 21–32.

Robinson, J. P., & Milkie, M. A. (1998). Back to the basics: Trends in and role determinants of women's attitudes toward housework. *Journal of Marriage and the Family, 60*(1), 205–218.

Rodeheaver, D. (1990). Labor market progeria. *Generations, 14,* 53–58.

Rodin, J., & Langer, E. (1980). Aging labels: The decline of control and the fall of self-esteem. *Journal of Social Issues, 36,* 12–19.

Rodin, J., Silverstein, L. R., Striegel-Moore, R. H. (1984). Women and weight: A normative discontent. In T. B. Sonderegger (Ed.), *Psychology and gender: Nebraska Symposium on Motivation, 1984* (pp. 267–307). Lincoln: University of Nebraska Press.

Rodriguez, C. (1998, November 27). Even in middle school, girls are thinking thin. *The Boston Globe,* pp. B1, B9.

Roff, L. L., & Klemmack, D. L. (1986). Norms for employed daughters' and sons' behavior toward frail older parents. *Sex Roles, 14,* 363–368.

Romkens, R. (1997). Prevalence of wife abuse in the Netherlands. *Journal of Interpersonal Violence, 12,* 99–126.

Roopnarine, J. L. (1986). Mothers' and fathers' behaviors toward the toy play of their infant sons and daughters. *Sex Roles, 14,* 59–68.

Root, M. P. P. (1990). Disordered eating in women of color. *Sex Roles, 22,* 525–536.

Root, M. P. P. (1995). The psychology of Asian women. In H. Landrine (Ed.), *Bringing cultural diversity to feminist psychology: Theory, research, practice* (pp. 265–301). Washington, DC: American Psychological Association.

Rosario, M., Meyer-Bahlburg, H. F. L., Hunter, J., & Exner, T. M. (1996). The psychosexual development of urban lesbian, gay, and bisexual youths. *Journal of Sex Research, 33*(2), 113–126.

Roscoe, B., & Benaske, N. (1985). Courtship violence experienced by abused wives: Similarities in patterns of abuse. *Family Relations, 34,* 419–424.

Roscoe, B., & Kelsey, T. (1986). Dating violence among high school students. *Psychology, 23,* 53–59.

Roscoe, W. (1996). How to become a berdache: Toward a unified analysis of gender diversity. In G. Herdt (Ed.), *Third sex, third gender: Beyond sexual dimorphism in culture and history* (pp. 329–372). New York: Zone Books.

Rose, S., & Frieze, I. H. (1989). Young singles' scripts for a first date. *Gender & Society, 3,* 258–268.

Rosenberg, F. R., & Simmons, R. G. (1975). Sex differences in the self-concept during adolescence. *Sex Roles, 1,* 147–160.

Rosenberg, J., Perlstadt, H., & Phillips, W. R. (1993). Now that we are here: Discrimination, disparagement, and harassment at work and the experience of women lawyers. *Gender & Society, 7,* 415–433.

Rosenberg, R. (1982). *Beyond separate spheres: Intellectual roots of modern feminism.* New Haven: Yale University Press.

Rosenblum, K. E., & Travis, T-M C. (1996). *The meaning of difference: American constructions of race, sex and gender, social class, and sexual orientation.* New York: McGraw-Hill.

Rosenbluth, S. (1997). Is sexual orientation a matter of choice? *Psychology of Women Quarterly, 21*(4), 595–610.

Rosenbluth, S. C., & Steil, J. M. (1995). Predictors of intimacy for women in heterosexual and homosexual couples. *Journal of Social and Personal Relationships, 12*(2), 163–175.

Rosenfeld, M. (1995, December 25). Toys aimed at girls focus on boys. *The Dallas Morning News,* pp. 45A–46A.

Rosenthal, N. B. (1984). Consciousness raising: From revolution to reevaluation. *Psychology of Women Quarterly, 8,* 309–326.

Rosenwasser, S. M., & Patterson, W. (1984–1985). Nontraditional males: Men with primary childcare/household responsibilities. *Psychology and Human Development, 1,* 101–111.

Ross, L., Anderson, D. R., & Wisocki, P. A. (1982). Television viewing and adult sex-role attitudes. *Sex Roles, 8,* 589–592.

Rosser, P. (1992). *The SAT gender gap: ETS responds: A research update.* Washington, DC: Center for Women Policy Studies.

Rosser, P., with the staff of the National Center for Fair and Open Testing (1987). *Sex bias in college admissions tests: Why women lose out* (2nd ed.). Cambridge, MA: National Center for Fair and Open Testing.

Rostosky, S. S., & Travis, C. B. (1996). Menopausal research and the dominance of the biomedical model, 1984–1994. *Psychology of Women Quarterly, 20,* 285–312.

Roter, D. L., & Hall, J. A. (1997). Gender differences in patient-physician communication. In S. J. Gallant, G. P. Keita, & R. Royak-

Schaler (Eds.), *Health care for women: Psychological, social, and behavioral influences* (pp. 57–71). Washington, DC: American Psychological Association.

Roth, S., & Lebowitz, L. (1988). The experience of sexual trauma. *Journal of Traumatic Stress, 1,* 79–107.

Roth, S., Wayland, K., & Woolsey, M. (1990). Victimization history and victim-assailant relationship as factors in recovery from sexual assault. *Journal of Traumatic Stress, 3,* 169–180.

Rothblum, E. D. (1983). Sex-role stereotypes and depression in women. In V. Franks & E. D. Rothblum (Eds.), *The stereotyping of women: Its effects on mental health* (pp. 83–111). New York: Springer.

Rothman, B. K. (1988). *The tentative pregnancy: Prenatal diagnosis and the future of motherhood.* London: Unwin Hyman.

Rousso, H. (1988). Daughters with disabilities: Defective women or minority women? In M. Fine & A. Asch (Eds.), *Women with disabilities: Essays in psychology, culture, and politics* (pp. 139–171). Philadelphia: Temple University Press.

Rubin, G. (1984). Thinking sex: Notes for a radical theory of the politics of sexuality. In C. S. Vance (Ed.), *Pleasure and danger: Exploring female sexuality* (pp. 267–319). Boston: Routledge & Kegan Paul.

Rubin, R. M. (1997). The economic status of older women. In J. M. Coyle (Ed.), *Handbook on women and aging* (pp. 75–92). Westport, CT: Greenwood Press.

Rubin, R. T., Reinisch, J. M., & Haskett, R. F. (1981). Postnatal gonadal steroid effects on human behavior. *Science, 211,* 1318–1324.

Ruble, D. N., Fleming, A. S., Hackel, L. S., & Stangor, C. (1988). Changes in the marital relationship during the transition to first time motherhood: Effects of violated expectations concerning division of household labor. *Journal of Personality and Social Psychology, 85,* 78–87.

Ruddick, S., & Daniels, P. (Eds.). (1977). *Working it out.* New York: Pantheon Books.

Rudman, L. A., & Borgida, E. (1995). The afterglow of construct accessibility: The behavioral consequences of priming men to view women as sexual objects. *Journal of Experimental Social Psychology, 31,* 493–517.

Ruggiero, J. A., & Weston, L. C. (1985). Work options for women in women's magazines: The medium *and* the message. *Sex Roles, 12,* 535–547.

Ruggiero, K. M., & Major, B. N. (1998). Group status and attributions to discrimination: Are low- or high-status group members more likely to blame their failure on discrimination? *Personality and Social Psychology Bulletin, 24,* 821–837.

Ruggiero, K. M., & Taylor, D. M. (1995). Coping with discrimination: How disadvantaged group members perceive the discrimination that confronts them. *Journal of Personality and Social Psychology, 68,* 826–838.

Ruggiero, K. M., & Taylor, D. M. (1997). Why minority group members perceive or do not perceive the discrimination that confronts them: The role of self-esteem and perceived control. *Journal of Personality and Social Psychology, 72,* 373–389.

Russell, M., Lipov, E., Phillips, N., & White, B. (1989, Spring). Psychological profiles of violent and nonviolent maritally distressed couples. *Psychotherapy, 26,* 81–87.

Russett, C. E. (1989). *Sexual science: The Victorian construction of womanhood.* Cambridge, MA: Harvard University Press.

Russo, N. F. (1979). Overview: Sex roles, fertility, and the motherhood mandate. *Psychology of Women Quarterly, 4,* 7–15.

Russo, N. F. (1985). *A women's mental health agenda.* Washington, DC: American Psychological Association.

Russo, N. F., & Denmark, F. L. (1984). Women, psychology, and public policy: Selected issues. *American Psychologist, 39,* 1161–1165.

Russo, N. F., & Dumont, B. A. (1997). A history of Division 35 (Psychology of Women): Origins, issues, activities, future. In D. A. Dewsbury (Ed.), *Unification through division: Histories of the divisions of the American Psychological Association,* Vol. 2. Washington, DC: American Psychological Association.

Rust, P. C. (1993). Neutralizing the political threat of the marginal woman: Lesbians' beliefs about bisexual women. *Journal of Sex Research, 30,* 214–228.

Ruth, S. (1990). *Issues in feminism.* Mountain View, CA: Mayfield.

Ryan, K. M. (1995). Do courtship-violent men have characteristics associated with a "battering personality"? *Journal of Family Violence, 10,* 99–120.

Ryan, W. (1971). *Blaming the victim.* New York: Random House.

Sadker, M., & Sadker, D. (1994). *Failing at fairness: How America's schools cheat girls.* New York: Scribner.

Safir, M. P. (1986). The effects of nature or of nurture on sex differences in intellectual functioning: Israeli findings. *Sex Roles, 14,* 581–590.

Sagrestano, L. M. (1992). Power strategies in interpersonal relationships: The effects of expertise and gender. *Psychology of Women Quarterly, 16,* 481–495.

Sanchez, L. (1993). Women's power and the gendered division of domestic labor in the Third World. *Gender & Society, 7,* 434–459.

Sanchez, L., & Thomson, E. (1997). Becoming mothers and fathers: Parenthood, gender, and the division of labor. *Gender & Society, 11*(6), 747–772.

Sanders, G. S., & Schmidt, T. (1980). Behavioral discrimination against women. *Personality and Social Psychology Bulletin, 6,* 484–488.

Sands, R. G. (1998). Gender and the perception of diversity and intimidation among university students. *Sex Roles, 39,* 801–815.

Sang, B. (1991). Moving toward balance and integration. In B. Sang, J. Warshow, & A. Smith (Eds.), *Lesbians at midlife: The creative transition* (pp. 206–214). San Francisco: Spinsters.

Sanger, S. P., & Alker, H. A. (1972). Dimensions of internal-external locus of control and the women's liberation movement. *Journal of Social Issues, 28,* 115–129.

Sangren, P. S. (1983). Female gender in Chinese religious symbols: Kuan Yin, Ma Tsu, and the "Eternal Mother." *Signs, 9,* 4–25.

Sapiro, V. (1994). *Women in American society: An introduction to women's studies* (3rd ed.). Mountain View, CA: Mayfield.

Sapp, S. G., Harrod, W. J., & Zhao, L. (1996). Leadership emergence in task groups with egalitarian gender role expectations. *Sex Roles, 34,* 65–80.

Sappington, A. A., Pharr, R., Tunstall, A., & Rickert, E. (1997). Relationships among child abuse, date abuse, and psychological problems. *Journal of Clinical Psychology, 53,* 319–329.

Sarantakos, S. (1991). Cohabitation revisited: Paths of change among cohabiting and noncohabiting couples. *Australian Journal of Marriage and Family, 12,* 144–155.

Sargent, J. D., & Blanchflower, D. G. (1994). Obesity and stature in adolescence and earnings in young adulthood. *Annals of Pediatric Adolescent Medicine, 148,* 681–687.

Satterfield, A. T., & Muehlenhard, C. L. (1997). Shaken confidence: The effects of an authority figure's flirtativeness on women's and men's self-rated creativity. *Psychology of Women Quarterly, 21,* 395–416.

Sawyer, R. G., Pinciaro, P. J., Jessell, J. K. (1998). Effects of coercion and verbal consent on university students' perception of date rape. *American Journal of Health Behavior, 22,* 46–53.

Sayers, J. (1997). Adolescent bodies: Boy crazy memories and dreams. In J. M. Ussher (Ed.), *Body talk* (pp. 85–105). London: Routledge.

Scanzoni, L., & Scanzoni, J. (1976). *Men, women, and change: A sociology of marriage and the family.* New York: McGraw-Hill.

Scarborough, E., & Furumoto, L. (1987). *Untold lives: The first generation of American women psychologists.* New York: Columbia University Press.

Scarr, S. (1998). American child care today. *American Psychologist, 53*(2), 95–108.

Scarr, S., Phillips, D., & McCartney, K. (1990). Facts, fantasies and the future of child care in the United States. *Psychological Science, 1,* 26–35.

Schafer, A. T., & Gray, M. W. (1981). Sex and mathematics. *Science, 211,* 231.

Schlesinger, B. (1982). Lasting marriages in the 1980's. *Conciliation Courts Review, 20,* 43–49.

Schlossberg, N. K. (1984). The midlife woman as student. In G. Baruch & J. Brooks-Gunn (Eds.), *Women in midlife* (pp. 315–339). New York: Plenum Press.

Schneider, K. T., Swan, S., & Fitzgerald, L. F. (1997). Job-related and psychological effects of sexual harassment in the workplace: Empirical evidence from two organizations. *Journal of Applied Psychology, 82,* 401–415.

Schneider, M. S. (1986). The relationships of cohabiting lesbian and heterosexual couples: A comparison. *Psychology of Women Quarterly, 10,* 234–239.

Schnitzer, P. K. (1996). "THEY DON'T COME IN!" Stories told, lessons taught about poor families in therapy. *American Journal of Orthopsychiatry, 66,* 572–582.

Schoen, R., & Wooldredge, J. (1989). Marriage choices in North Carolina and Virginia, 1969–71 and 1979–81. *Journal of Marriage and Family, 51,* 465–481.

Schuler, S. R., Hashemi, S. M., Riley, A. P., & Akhter, S. (1996). Credit programs, patriarchy and men's violence against women in rural Bangladesh. *Social Science Medicine, 43,* 1729–1742.

Schulman, G. I., & Hoskins, M. (1986). Perceiving the male versus the female face. *Psychology of Women Quarterly, 10,* 141–154.

Schultz, M. R. (1975). The semantic derogation of women. In B. Thorne & N. Henley (Eds.), *Language and sex: Difference and dom-*

inance (pp. 64–73). Rowley, MA: Newbury House.

Schulz, J. H. (1992). *The economics of aging* (3rd ed.). New York: Auburn House.

Schur, E. M. (1983). *Labeling women deviant: Gender, stigma, and social control.* New York: Random House.

Schuster, M. A., Bell, R. M., & Kanouse, D. E. (1996). The sexual practices of adolescent virgins: Genital sexual activities of high school students who have never had vaginal intercourse. *American Journal of Public Health, 86*(11), 1570–1576.

Schutte, N. S., Malouff, J. M., Post-Gorden, J. C., & Rodasta, A. L. (1988). Effects of playing videogames on children's aggressive and other behaviors. *Journal of Applied Social Psychology, 18,* 454–460.

Schwartz, F. N. (1989). Management women and the new facts of life. *Harvard Business Review, 89,* 65–76.

Schwartz, I. (1993). Affective reactions of American and Swedish women to their first premarital coitus: A cross-cultural comparison. *Journal of Sex Research, 30,* 18–26.

Schwartz, L. A., & Markham, W. T. (1985). Sex stereotyping in children's toy advertisements. *Sex Roles, 12,* 157–170.

Schwartz, M. D. (1989). Asking the right questions: Battered wives are not all passive. *Sociological Viewpoints, 5,* 46–61.

Schwartz, P. (1994). *Peer marriage.* New York: Free Press.

Seagoe, M. V. (1975). *Terman and the gifted.* Los Altos, CA: William Kaufmann.

Searles, P., & Berger, R. J. (1987). The current status of rape reform legislation: An examination of state statutes. *Women's Rights Law Reporter, 10,* 25–43.

Sears, D. O. (1986). College sophomores in the laboratory: Influences of a narrow data base on social psychology's view of human nature. *Journal of Personality and Social Psychology, 51,* 515–530.

Seccombe, K., & Ishu-Kuntz, M. (1991). Perceptions of problems associated with aging: Comparisons among four older age cohorts. *Gerontologist, 31,* 527–533.

Selkow, P. (1984). *Assessing sex bias in testing: A review of the issues and evaluations of 74 psychological and educational tests.* Westport, CT: Greenwood.

Sen, A. (1990, December 20). More than one hundred million women are missing. *New York Review of Books.*

Serbin, L. A., Sprafkin, C., Elman, M., & Doyle, A. B. (1984). The development of sex differentiated patterns of social influence. *Canadian Journal of Social Science, 14,* 350–363.

Settin, J. M. (1982). Clinical judgment in geropsychology practice. *Psychotherapy: Theory, Research, and Practice, 19,* 397–404.

Severne, L. (1982). Psychosocial aspects of the menopause. In A. M. Voda, M. Dinnerstein, & S. R. O'Donnell (Eds.), *Changing perspectives on menopause* (pp. 239–247). Austin: University of Texas Press.

Shachar, S. A., & Gilbert, L. A. (1983). Working lesbians: Role conflicts and coping strategies. *Psychology of Women Quarterly, 7,* 244–256.

Shaffer, J. W. (1963). Masculinity-femininity and other personality traits in gonadal aplasia (Turner's Syndrome). In H. G. Beigel (Ed.), *Advances in sex research.* New York: Harper & Row.

Shakin, M., Shakin, D., & Sternglanz, S. H. (1985). Infant clothing: Sex labeling for strangers. *Sex Roles, 12,* 955–963.

Shea, C. (1994). "Gender gap" on examinations shrank again this year. *Chronicle of Higher Education, 41,* A54.

Sherif, C. W. (1976). *Orientation in social psychology.* New York: Harper & Row.

Sherif, C. W. (1979). Bias in psychology. In J. A. Sherman & E. T. Beck (Eds.), *The prisms of sex: Essays in the sociology of knowledge* (pp. 93–133). Madison: University of Wisconsin Press.

Sherif, C. W. (1982). Needed studies in the concept of gender identity. *Psychology of Women Quarterly, 6,* 375–398.

Sherif, C. W. (1983). Carolyn Wood Sherif (autobiography). In A. O'Connell & N. F. Russo (Eds.), *Models of achievement* (pp. 279–293). New York: Columbia University Press.

Sheriffs, A. C., & McKee, J. P. (1957). Qualitative aspects of beliefs about men and women. *Journal of Personality, 25,* 451–467.

Sherman, J. A. (1982). Continuing in mathematics: A longitudinal study of the attitudes of high school girls. *Psychology of Women Quarterly, 7,* 132–140.

Sherman, J. A. (1983). Factors predicting girls' and boys' enrollment in college preparatory mathematics. *Psychology of Women Quarterly, 7,* 272–281.

Sherman, J. A., & Fennema, E. (1978). Distribution of spatial visualization and mathematical problem solving scores: A test of Stafford's X-linked hypothesis. *Psychology of Women Quarterly, 3,* 157–167.

Sherman, P. J., & Spence, J. T. (1997). A comparison of two cohorts of college students in responses to the male-female relations questionnaire. *Psychology of Women Quarterly, 21,* 265–278.

Shields, S. A. (1975). Functionalism, Darwinism, and the psychology of women: A study in social myth. *American Psychologist, 30,* 739–754.

Shields, S. A. (1982). The variability hypothesis: The history of a biological model of sex difference in intelligence. *Signs, 7,* 769–797.

Shields, S. A., Steinke, P., & Koster, B. A. (1995). The double bind of caregiving: Representation of gendered emotion in American advice literature. *Sex Roles, 33,* 467–488.

Shipman, G. (1971). The psychodynamics of sex education. In R. E. Muuss (Ed.), *Adolescent behavior and society: A book of readings.* New York: Random House.

Showalter, E. (1987). *The female malady: Women, madness, and English culture, 1830–1980.* New York: Pantheon Books.

Shuster, R. (1987). Sexuality as a continuum: The bisexual identity. In Boston Lesbian Psychologies Collective (Eds.), *Lesbian psychologies* (pp. 56–71). Urbana: University of Illinois Press.

Siegel, R. J. (1993). Between midlife and old age: Never too old to learn. In N. D. Davis, E. Cole, & E. D. Rothblum (Eds.), *Faces of women and aging* (pp. 173–185). Binghamton, NY: Harrington Park Press.

Siever, M. D. (1994). Sexual orientation and gender as factors in socioculturally acquired vulnerability to body dissatisfaction and eating disorders. *Journal of Consulting and Clinical Psychology, 62,* 252–260.

Sigelman, C. K., Thomas, D. B., Sigelman, L., & Ribich, F. D. (1986). Gender, physical attractiveness and electability: An experimental investigation of voter biases. *Journal of Applied Social Psychology, 16,* 229–248.

Sigelman, L., & Sigelman, C. K. (1982). Sexism, racism, and ageism in voting behavior: An experimental analysis. *Social Psychology Quarterly, 45,* 263–269.

Sigelman, L., & Welch, S. (1984). Race, gender, and opinion toward black and female presidential candidates. *Public Opinion Quarterly, 48,* 467–475.

Signorella, M. L., Bigler, R. S., & Liben, L. S. (1993). Developmental differences in children's gender-schemata about others: A meta-analytic review. *Developmental Review, 13,* 147–183.

Signorielli, N. (1989). Television and conceptions about sex roles: Maintaining conventionality and the status quo. *Sex Roles, 21,* 341–360.

Signorielli, N., & Lears, M. (1992). Children, television, and conceptions about chores: Attitudes and behaviors. *Sex Roles, 27,* 157–170.

Silverstein, B., Perdue, L., Peterson, B., & Kelly, E. (1986). The role of the mass media in promoting a thin standard of bodily attractiveness for women. *Sex Roles, 14,* 519–532.

Silverstein, B., Peterson, B., & Perdue, L. (1986). Some correlates of the thin standard of bodily attractiveness for women. *International Journal of Eating Disorders, 5,* 895–905.

Silverstein, L. B. (1991). Transforming the debate about child care and maternal employment. *American Psychologist, 46,* 1025–1032.

Silverstein, L. B. (1996). Fathering is a feminist issue. *Psychology of Women Quarterly, 20,* 3–37.

Simmons, R. G., & Blyth, D. A. (1987). *Moving into adolescence: The impact of pubertal change and school context.* New York: Aldine De Gruyter.

Simmons, R. G., Blyth, D. A., Van Cleave, E. F., & Bush, D. M. (1979). Entry into early adolescence: The impact of school structure, puberty, and early dating on self esteem. *American Sociological Review, 44,* 948–967.

Simmons, R. G., Burgeson, R., & Reef, M. J. (1988). In M. R. Gunnar & W. A. Collins (Eds.), *Development during the transition to adolescence* (pp. 123–150). Hillsdale, NJ: Erlbaum.

Simmons, R. G., & Rosenberg, F. R. (1975). Sex, sex-roles, and self-image. *Journal of Youth and Adolescence, 4,* 229–258.

Simon, B. L. (1987). *Never-married women.* Philadelphia: Temple University Press.

Simon-Roper, L. (1996). Victim's response cycle: A model for understanding the incestuous victim-offender relationship. *Journal of Child Sexual Abuse, 5,* 59–79.

Simpson, G. (1996). Factors influencing the choice of law as a career by black women. *Journal of Career Development, 22(3),* 197–209.

Sims, M., Hutchins, T., & Taylor, M. (1998). Gender segregation in young children's conflict behavior in a child care setting. *Child Study Journal, 28,* 1–16.

Singer, J. M., & Stake, J. E. (1986). Mathematics and self-esteem: Implications for women's career choices. *Psychology of Women Quarterly, 10,* 339–351.

Skrypnek, B. J., & Snyder, M. (1982). On the self-perpetuating nature of stereotypes about women and men. *Journal of Experimental Social Psychology, 18,* 277–291.

Slaby, R. G., & Guerra, N. G. (1988). Cognitive mediators of aggression in adolescent offenders: I. Assessment. *Developmental Psychology, 24*, 580–588.

Sleek, S. (1994, August). APA amicus brief affects outcome of Va. court case. *American Psychological Association Monitor, 8*.

Smith, B. (1943). *A tree grows in Brooklyn*. New York: Harper & Row.

Smith, E. A. (1989). A biosocial model of adolescent sexual behavior. In G. R. Adams, R. Montemayor, & T. P. Gullotta (Eds.), *Advances in adolescent development* (pp. 143–167). Newbury Park, CA: Sage.

Smith, M. (1997). Psychology's undervaluation of single motherhood. *Feminism & Psychology, 7*(4), 529–532.

Smith, M. D., & Morra, N. N. (1994). Obscene and threatening telephone calls to women: Data from a Canadian national survey. *Gender & Society, 8*, 584–596.

Smith, P. A., & Midlarsky, E. (1985). Empirically derived conceptions of femaleness and maleness: A current view. *Sex Roles, 12*, 313–328.

Smith, P. H., Smith, J. B., & Earp, J. A. (1999). Beyond the measurement trap: A reconstructed conceptualization and measurement of woman battering. *Psychology of Women Quarterly, 23*, 177–193.

Smith, P. K. (1987). Exploration, play and social development in boys and girls. In D. J. Hargreaves & A. M. Colley (Eds.), *The psychology of sex roles* (pp. 118–141). New York: Hemisphere.

Smith-Lovin, L., & Brody, C. (1989). Interruptions in group discussions: The effects of gender and group composition. *American Sociological Review, 54*, 425–435.

Smith-Rosenberg, C. (1975). The female world of love and ritual: Relations between women in nineteenth-century America. *Signs, 1*, 1–30.

Smith-Rosenberg, C. (1985). *Disorderly conduct: Visions of gender in Victorian America*. New York: Oxford University Press.

Snavely, B. K., & Fairhurst, G. T. (1984). The male nursing student as a token. *Research in Nursing and Health, 7*, 287–294.

Snizek, W. E., & Neil, C. C. (1992). Job characteristics, gender stereotypes, and perceived gender discrimination in the workplace. *Organization Studies, 13*, 403–427.

Snow, J. T., & Harris, M. B. (1985). Maintenance of weight loss: Demographic, behavioral, and attitudinal correlates. *The Journal of Obesity and Weight Regulation, 4*, 234–255.

Snow, J. T., & Harris, M. B. (1986). An analysis of weight and diet content in five women's interest magazines. *The Journal of Obesity and Weight Regulation, 5*, 194–214.

Snow, J. T., & Harris, M. B. (1989). Disordered eating in Southwestern Pueblo Indians and Hispanics. *Journal of Adolescence, 12*, 329–336.

Snow, M. E., Jacklin, C. N., & Maccoby, E. E. (1983). Sex-of-child differences in father-child interaction at one year of age. *Child Development, 54*, 227–232.

Snyder, M., & Swann, W. B., Jr. (1978a). Behavioral confirmation in social interaction: From social perception to social reality. *Journal of Experimental Social Psychology, 14*, 148–162.

Snyder, M., & Swann, W. B., Jr. (1978b). Hypothesis-testing processes in social interaction. *Journal of Personality and Social Psychology, 36*, 1202–1212.

Snyder, M., Tanke, E. D., & Berscheid, E. (1977). Social perception and interpersonal behavior: On the self-fulfilling nature of social stereotypes. *Journal of Personality and Social Psychology, 35*, 656–666.

Snyder, M., & Uranowitz, S. W. (1978). Reconstructing the past: Some cognitive consequences of person perception. *Journal of Personality and Social Psychology, 36*, 941–950.

Snyder, R., & Hasbrouck, L. (1996). Feminist identity, gender traits, and symptoms of disturbed eating among college women. *Psychology of Women Quarterly, 20*, 593–598.

Sohoni, N. K. (1994). Where are the girls? *Ms., 5* (#1), 96.

Sommers-Flanagan, R., Sommers-Flanagan, J., & Davis, B. (1993). What's happening on music television? A gender-role content analysis. *Sex Roles, 28*, 745–753.

Sorenson, S. A. (1996, April). Violence against women: Examining ethnic differences and commonalities. *Evaluation Review, 20*, 123–145.

Sorenson, S. B., & Siegel, J. M. (1992). Gender, ethnicity, and sexual assault: Findings from the Los Angeles epidemiological catchment area study. *Journal of Social Issues, 48*, 93–104.

Sorenson, S. B., Upchurch, D. M., & Shen, H. (1996). Violence and injury in marital arguments: Risk patterns and gender differences. *American Journal of Public Health, 86*, 35–40.

Spanier, G. B. (1983). Married and unmarried cohabitation in the United States: 1980. *Journal of Marriage and the Family, 45*, 277–288.

Spence, J. T., Deaux, K., & Helmreich, R. L. (1985). Sex roles in contemporary American society. In G. Lindzey & E. Aronson (Eds.), *The handbook of social psychology* (3rd ed., pp. 149–178). New York: Random House.

Spence, J. T., & Hahn, D. (1997). The Attitude toward Women Scale and attitude change in college students. *Psychology of Women Quarterly, 21,* 17–34.

Spence, J. T., & Helmreich, R. L. (1983). Achievement-related motives and behaviors. In J. T. Spence (Ed.), *Achievement and achievement motives.* San Francisco: Freeman.

Spielman, S., & Winfeld, L. (1996). Domestic partner benefits: A bottom line discussion. In A. L. & E. D. B. Riggle (Eds.), *Sexual identity on the job: Issues and services* (pp. 53–78). New York: Harrington Park Press.

Sprecher, S. (1985). Sex differences in bases of power in dating relationships. *Sex Roles, 12,* 449–462.

Sprecher, S., Barbee, A., & Schwartz, P. (1995). "Was it good for you, too?": Gender differences in first sexual intercourse experiences. *The Journal of Sex Research, 32,* 3–15.

Spurlock, J. (1984). Black women in the middle years. In G. Baruch & J. Brooks-Gunn (Eds.), *Women in midlife* (pp. 245–260). New York: Plenum Press.

Stack, C. B. (1986). The culture of gender: Women and men of color. *Signs, 11,* 321–324.

Stacy, R. D., Prisbell, M., & Tollefsrud, K. (1992). A comparison of attitudes among college students toward sexual violence committed by strangers and by acquaintances: A research report. *Journal of Sex Education and Therapy, 18,* 257–263.

Stangor, C., Lynch, L., Duan, C., & Glass, B. (1992). Categorization of individuals on the basis of multiple social features. *Journal of Personality and Social Psychology, 62,* 207–218.

Stanley, J. P. (1977). Paradigmatic woman: The prostitute. In D. L. Shores & C. P. Hines (Eds.), *Papers in language variation* (pp. 303–321). University of Alabama: University of Alabama Press.

Stark, E., & Flitcraft, A. (1996). *Women at risk, domestic violence and women's health.* Thousand Oaks, CA: Sage.

Statham, A., Miller, E. M., & Mauksch, H. O. (Eds.). (1988). *The worth of women's work: A qualitative synthesis.* Albany: State University of New York Press.

Stead, B. A., & Zinkhan, G. M. (1986). Service priority in department stores: The effect of customer gender and sex. *Sex Roles, 15,* 601–611.

Steele, B. F. (1986). Notes on the lasting effects of early child abuse throughout the life cycle. *Child Abuse and Neglect, 10,* 283–291.

Steiger, J. (1981). The influence of the feminist subculture in changing sex-role attitudes. *Sex Roles, 7,* 627–634.

Steil, J. M. (1983). Marriage: An unequal partnership. In B. B. Wolman & G. Stricker (Eds.), *Handbook of family and marital therapy* (pp. 49–60). New York: Plenum Press.

Steil, J. M. (1989). Marital relationships and mental health: The psychic costs of inequality. In J. Freeman (Ed.), *Women: A feminist perspective* (4th ed., pp. 138–140). Mountain View, CA: Mayfield.

Steil, J. M. (1994). Supermoms and second shifts: Marital inequality in the 90's. In J. Freeman (Ed.), *Women: A feminist perspective* (5th ed., pp. 149–161). Mountain View, CA: Mayfield.

Steil, J. M. (1997). *Marital equality: Its relationship to the well-being of husbands and wives.* Thousand Oaks, CA: Sage.

Steil, J. M., & Hillman, J. L. (1993). The perceived value of direct and indirect influence strategies: A cross-cultural comparison. *Psychology of Women Quarterly, 17,* 457–462.

Steil, J. M., & Turetsky, B. A. (1987a). Marital influence levels and symptomatology among wives. In F. Crosby (Ed.), *Spouse, parent, worker: On gender and multiple roles* (pp. 74–90). New Haven, CT: Yale University Press.

Steil, J. M., & Turetsky, B. A. (1987b). Is equal better? The relationship between marital equality and psychological symptomatology. In S. Oskamp (Ed.), *Family processes and problems: Social psychological aspects* (pp. 73–97). Beverly Hills, CA: Sage.

Steil, J. M., & Weltman, K. (1991). Marital inequality: The importance of resources, personal attributes, and social norms on career valuing and the allocation of domestic responsibilities. *Sex Roles, 24,* 161–179.

Stein, N. (1995). Sexual harassment in schools: The public performance of gendered violence. *Harvard Educational Review, 65*(2), 145–162.

Steinberg, L., & Silverberg, S. B. (1987). Influences on marital satisfaction during the middle stages of the family life cycle. *Journal of Marriage and the Family, 49,* 751–760.

Steinem, G. (1983). *Outrageous acts and everyday rebellions.* New York: New American Library.

Steinmetz, S. (1977–1978). The battered husband syndrome. *Victimology: An International Journal, 2,* 499–509.

Sterk, H. M. (1996). Contemporary birthing practices. In R. L. Parrott & C. M. Condit (Eds.), *Evaluating women's health messages* (pp. 124–134). Thousand Oaks: Sage.

Stermac, L., Du Mont, J., & Dunn, S. (1998). Violence in known-assailant sexual assaults. *Journal of Interpersonal Violence, 13,* 398–412.

Stern, M., & Karraker, K. H. (1989). Sex stereotyping of infants: A review of gender labeling studies. *Sex Roles, 20,* 501–522.

Stevens, G., & Gardner, S. (1987). But can she command a ship? Acceptance of women by peers at the Coast Guard Academy. *Sex Roles, 16,* 181–188.

Stevens-Long, J., & Commons, M. L. (1992). *Adult life: Developmental processes* (4th ed.). London: Mayfield.

Stewart, A. J., Copeland, A. P., Chester, N. L., Malley, J. E., & Barenbaum, N. B. (1997). *Separating together: How divorce transforms families.* New York: Guilford Press.

Stewart, A. J., & Gold-Steinberg, S. (1990). Midlife women's political consciousness: Case studies of psychosocial development and political commitment. *Psychology of Women Quarterly, 14,* 543–566.

Stiles, D., Gibbons, J. L., Hardardottir, S., & Schnellman, J. (1987). The ideal man or woman as described by young adolescents in Iceland and the United States. *Sex Roles, 17,* 313–320.

Stoltenberg, J. (1989). *Refusing to be a man: Essays on sex and justice.* New York: Penguin Books.

Storms, M. D., Stivers, M. L., Lambers, S. M., & Hill, C. A. (1981). Sexual scripts for women. *Sex Roles, 7,* 699–707.

Straus, M. A., & Gelles, R. J. (1990). *Physical violence in American families: Risk factors and adaptations to violence in 8,145 families.* New Brunswick, NJ: Transaction.

Straus, M. A., Kaufman Kantor, G., & Moore, D. W. (1997). Change in cultural norms approving marital violence from 1968 to 1994. In G. Kaufman Kantor & J. L. Jasinski (Eds.), *Out of darkness: Contemporary perspectives on family violence* (pp. 3–16). Thousand Oaks, CA: Sage.

Stricker, L., Rock, D., & Burton, N. (1992). *Sex differences in SAT predictions of college grades.* New York: The College Board.

Strickland, B. (1988). Sex-related differences in health and illness. *Psychology of Women Quarterly, 12,* 381–399.

Striegel-Moore, R. H., Goldman, S. L., Garvin, V., & Rodin, J. (1996). Within-subjects design: Pregnancy changes both body and mind. In F. E. Donelson (Ed.), *Women's experiences: A psychological perspective* (pp. 430–437). Mountain View, CA: Mayfield.

Striegel-Moore, R. H., & Smolak, L. (1996). The role of race in the development of eating disorders. In L. Smolak, M. Levine, & R. H. Striegel-Moore (Eds.), *The developmental psychopathology of eating disorders: Implications for research, treatment, and prevention* (pp. 259–284). Hillsdale, NJ: Erlbaum.

Strommen, E. F. (1993). "You're a what?": Family member reactions to the disclosure of homosexuality. In L. D. Garnets & D. C. Kimmel (Eds.), *Psychological perspectives on lesbian and gay male experiences* (pp. 248–266). New York: Columbia University Press.

Stueve, A., & O'Donnell, L. (1984). The daughter of aging parents. In G. Baruch & J. Brooks-Gunn (Eds.), *Women in midlife* (pp. 203–225). New York: Plenum Press.

Sugarman, D. B., & Hotaling, G. T. (1989). Dating violence: Prevalence, context, and risk markers. In M. A. Pirog-Good & J. E. Stets (Eds.), *Violence in dating relationships* (pp. 3–32). New York: Praeger.

Suh, M. (1990, September/October). Lesbian battery. *Ms.*

Summit, R. (1983). The child sexual abuse accommodation syndrome. *Child Abuse and Neglect, 7,* 177–193.

A survey finds bias on the front page. (1996, April 17). *New York Times,* p. A17.

Sutherland, E., & Veroff, J. (1985). Achievement motivation and sex roles. In V. E. O'Leary, R. K. Unger, & B. S. Wallston (Eds.), *Women, gender, and social psychology* (pp. 101–128). Hillsdale, NJ: Erlbaum.

Swaab, D. F., & Hofman, M. A. (1990). An enlarged suprachiasmatic nucleus in homosexual men. *Brain Research, 537,* 141–148.

Swan, S., & Wyer, R. S., Jr. (1997). Gender stereotypes and social identity: How being in the minority affects judgments of self and others. *Personality and Social Psychology Bulletin, 23,* 1265–1276.

Swarz, N., Wagner, D., Bannert, M., & Mathes, L. (1987). Cognitive accessibility of sex role concepts and attitudes toward political participation: The impact of sexist advertisements. *Sex Roles, 17,* 593–601.

Swim, J. K., Aikin, K. J., Hall, W. S., & Hunter, B. A. (1995). Sexism and racism: Old-fashioned and modern prejudices. *Journal of Personality and Social Psychology, 68,* 199–214.

Swim, J. K., & Cohen, L. L. (1997). Overt, covert, and subtle sexism: A comparison between the Attitudes toward Women and Modern Sexism Scales. *Psychology of Women Quarterly, 21,* 103–118.

Tajfel, H. (1984). Intergroup relations, social myths, and social justice in social psychology. In H. Tajfel (Ed.), *The social dimension.* Cambridge, England: Cambridge University Press.

Tangri, S., Burt, M., & Johnson, L. (1982). Sexual harassment at work: Three explanatory models. *Journal of Social Issues, 38,* 33–54.

Tannen, D. (1994). *Talking from nine to five.* New York: William Morrow.

Tashakkori, A. (1993). Gender, ethnicity, and the structure of self-esteem: An attitude theory approach. *Journal of Social Psychology, 133,* 479–488.

Tasker, F. L., & Golombok, S. (1997). *Growing up in a lesbian family.* New York: Guilford.

Taylor, C. J., Lambert, C., Perry, J., & Tobin, M. (1999, April 16). *The double standard of aging: Perceptions of similarly and dissimilarly aged couples.* Paper presented at the annual meeting of the Eastern Psychological Association, Providence, Rhode Island.

Taylor, M. G. (1996). The development of children's beliefs about social and biological aspects of gender differences. *Child Development, 67,* 1555–1571.

Taylor, R. L. (1997). Who's parenting? Trends and patterns. In T. Arrendell (Ed.), *Contemporary parenting: Challenges and issues. Understanding families* (vol. 9, pp. 68–91). Thousand Oaks, CA: Sage.

Taylor, S. E. (1983). Adjustment to threatening events: A theory of cognitive adaptation. *American Psychologist, 38,* 1161–1173.

Taylor, S. E., Fiske, S. T., Etcoff, N. L., & Ruderman, A. J. (1978). Categorical and contextual bases of person memory and stereotyping. *Journal of Personality and Social Psychology, 36,* 778–793.

Taylor, S. E., & Langer, E. J. (1977). Pregnancy: A social stigma? *Sex Roles, 3,* 27–35.

Tazeau, Y. N., & Gallagher-Thompson, D. (1993). A look at social support, acculturation, and depression in Mexican-American elderly women. *Focus, 7*(2), 12.

Teachman, J. D., & Polenko, K. A. (1990). Cohabitation and marital stability in the United States. *Social Forces, 69,* 207–220.

Teitelbaum, P. (1989). Feminist theory and standardized testing. In A. M. Jaggar & S. Bordo (Eds.), *Gender/body/knowledge* (pp. 324–335). New Brunswick, NJ: Rutgers University Press.

Tennstedt, C., Cafferata, G. L., & Sullivan, L. (1992). Depression among caregivers of impaired elders. *Journal of Aging and Health, 4,* 58–76.

Terman, L. M., & Oden, M. H. (1959). *Genetic studies of genius. V. The gifted group at midlife: Thirty-five years' follow-up of the superior child.* Stanford, CA: Stanford University Press.

Tevlin, H. E., & Leiblum, S. R. (1983). Sex-role stereotypes and female sexual dysfunction. In V. Franks & E. D. Rothblum (Eds.), *Stereotyping of women: Its effects on mental health* (pp. 129–148). New York: Springer.

Theriault, S. W., & Holmberg, D. (1998). The new old-fashioned girl: Effects of gender and social desirability on reported gender-role ideology. *Sex Roles, 39,* 97–112.

Thibault, J. W., & Kelley, H. H. (1959). *The social psychology of groups.* New York: Wiley.

Thoits, P. A. (1987). Negotiating roles. In F. J. Crosby (Ed.), *Spouse, parent, worker: On gender and multiple roles* (pp. 11–22). New Haven: Yale University Press.

Thomas, V. G., & James, M. D. (1988). Body image, dieting tendencies, and sex role traits in urban black women. *Sex Roles, 18,* 523–529.

Thompson, E. H. (1991). The maleness of violence in dating relationships: An appraisal of stereotypes. *Sex Roles, 24,* 261–278.

Thompson, S. (1986). Pregnancy on purpose. *Village Voice, 31*(51), 31–37. Cited in Cusick (1987). Sexism and early parenting: Cause and effect? *Peabody Journal of Education, 64,* 113–131.

Thompson, S. H., Corwin, S. J., & Sargent, R. G. (1997). Ideal body size beliefs and weight concerns of fourth-grade children. *International Journal of Eating Disorders, 21,* 279–384.

Thompson, S. H., Sargent, R. G., & Kemper, K. A. (1996). Black and white adolescent males' perception of ideal body size. *Sex Roles, 34,* 391–406.

Thompson, S. K. (1975). Gender labels and early sex role development. *Child Development, 46,* 339–347.

Thompson, T. L., & Zerbinos, E. (1995). Gender roles in animated cartoons: Has the picture changed in twenty years? *Sex Roles, 32,* 651–673.

Thompson, T. L., & Zerbinos, E. (1997). Television cartoons: Do children notice it's a boy's world? *Sex Roles, 37,* 415–432.

Thornberry, O. T., Wilson, R. W., & Golden, P. (1986). Health promotion and disease prevention provisional data from the National

Health Interview Survey: United States, January-June, 1985. *Vital and Health Statistics of the National Center for Health Statistics, 119,* 1–16.

Thorne, B. (1986). Girls and boys together, but mostly apart. In W. W. Hartup and Z. Rubin (Eds.), *Relationships and development* (pp. 167–184). Hillsdale, NJ: Erlbaum.

Thorne, B. (1993). *Gender play: Girls and boys in school.* New Brunswick, NJ: Rutgers University Press.

Thorne, B., & Luria, Z. (1986). Sexuality and gender in children's daily worlds. *Social Problems, 33,* 176–190.

Tiefer, L. (1988). A feminist perspective on sexology and sexuality. In M. Gergen (Ed.), *Feminist thought and the structure of knowledge* (pp. 16–26). New York: New York University Press.

Tiefer, L. (1989, August). Feminist transformations of sexology. In M. Crawford (chair), Feminist psychological science: Frameworks, strengths, visions, and a few examples. Symposium conducted at meeting of the American Psychological Association, New Orleans, LA.

Tiefer, L. (1995). *Sex is not a natural act & other essays.* San Francisco: Westview.

Tjaden, P., & Rhownnwa, N. (1998). Prevalence, incidence, and consequences of violence against women: Findings from the National Violence Against Women Survey. *Research Brief, November,* U.S. Department of Justice.

Tjaden, P., & Thoennes, N. (1998). *Stalking in American: Findings from the national violence against women survey.* Denver, CO: Center for Policy Research.

Tobin-Richards, M. H., Boxer, A. M., & Petersen, A. C. (1983). The psychological significance of pubertal change: Sex differences in perceptions of self during early adolescence. In J. Brooks-Gunn & A. C. Petersen (Eds.), *Girls at puberty* (pp. 127–154). New York: Plenum Press.

Todd, J., Friedman, A., & Kariuki, P. W. (1990). Women growing stronger with age: The effect of status in the United States and Kenya. *Psychology of Women Quarterly, 14,* 567–577.

Tolman, R. M. (1989). The development of a measure of psychological maltreatment of women by their male partners. *Violence and Victims, 4,* 159–177.

Tong, R. P. (1998). *Feminist thought* (2nd ed.). Boulder: Westview.

Tontodonato, P., & Crew, B. K. (1992). Dating violence, social learning theory, and gender: A multivariate analysis. *Violence and Victims, 7,* 3–14.

Torrez, D. J. (1997). The health of older women: A diverse experience. In J. Coyle (Ed.), *Handbook of women and aging* (pp. 131–145). Westport, CT: Greenwood.

Tougas, F., Brown, R., Beaton, A. M., & Joly, S. (1995). Neosexism: Plus la change, plus c'est pareil. *Personality and Social Psychology Bulletin, 21,* 842–849.

Travis, C. B. (1988a). *Women and health psychology: Biomedical issues.* Hillsdale, NJ: Erlbaum.

Travis, C. B. (1988b). *Women and health psychology: Mental health issues.* Hillsdale, NJ: Erlbaum.

Treadway, C. R., Kane, F. J., Jarrahi-Zadeh, A., & Lipton, M. A. (1969). A psycho-endocrine study of pregnancy and puerperium. *American Journal of Psychiatry, 125,* 1380–1386.

Trends in Education, APA education directorate news (1995). 2, 2–3.

Trent, K., & South, S. J. (1989). Structural determinants of the divorce rate: A cross-societal analysis. *Journal of Marriage and the Family, 51,* 391–404.

Tronto, J. C. (1987). Beyond gender difference to a theory of care. *Signs, 12,* 644–663.

Trost, J. (1996). Family studies in Sweden. *Marriage & Family Review, 23*(3/4), 723–743.

Tsui, L. (1998). The effects of gender, education, and personal skills self-confidence on income in business management. *Sex Roles, 38,* 363–373.

Tulloch, M. I., & Tulloch, J. C. (1992). Attitudes to domestic violence: School students' responses to a television drama. *Australian Journal of Marriage and Family, 13,* 62–69.

Turk, J. L., & Bell, N. W. (1972). Measuring power in families. *Journal of Marriage and the Family, 34,* 215–223.

Turner-Bowker, D. M. (1996). Gender stereotyped assumptions in children's picture books: Does "Curious Jane" exist in the literature? *Sex Roles, 35,* 461–488.

Twenge, J. M. (1997). Attitudes toward women, 1970–1995: A meta-analysis. *Psychology of Women Quarterly, 21*(1), 35–51.

U.S. Department of Health and Human Services National Center for Health Services (NCHS). (1998). Report finds fewer teen-agers having second babies. (http://www.hhs.gov.)

U.S. Merit Systems Protection Board (USMSPB). (1981). *Sexual harassment in the federal workplace: Is it a problem?* Washington, DC: Office of Merit Systems Review and Studies/Government Printing Office.

U.S. Merit Systems Protection Board (USM-SPB). (1987). *Sexual harassment in the federal workplace: An update*. Washington, DC: Office of Merit Systems Review and Studies/Government Printing Office.

Udry, J. R., Talbert, L., Morris, N. M. (1986). Biosocial foundations for adolescent female sexuality. *Demography, 23*, 217–230.

Ullman, S. E., & Knight, R. A. (1995). Women's resistance strategies to different rapist types. *Criminal Justice and Behavior, 22*, 263–283.

Umberson, D., Wortman, C. B., & Kessler, R. C. (1992). Widowhood and depression: Explaining long-term gender differences in vulnerability. *Journal of Health and Social Behavior, 33*, 10–24.

Unger, R. K. (1976). Male is greater than female: The socialization of status inequality. *The Counseling Psychologist, 6*, 2–9.

Unger, R. K. (1978). The politics of gender: A review of relevant literature. In J. Sherman & F. Denmark (Eds.), *Psychology of women: Future directions of research* (pp. 463–517). New York: Psychological Dimensions.

Unger, R. K. (1979a). *Female and male: Psychological perspectives*. New York: Harper & Row.

Unger, R. K. (1979b). Toward a redefinition of sex and gender. *American Psychologist, 34*, 1085–1094.

Unger, R. K. (1981). Sex as a social reality: Field and laboratory research. *Psychology of Women Quarterly, 5*, 645–653.

Unger, R. K. (1983). Through the looking glass: No Wonderland yet! (The reciprocal relationship between methodology and models of reality.) *Psychology of Women Quarterly, 8*, 9–32.

Unger, R. K. (1984–1985). Explorations in feminist ideology: Surprising consistencies and unexamined conflicts. *Imagination, Cognition, and Personality, 4*, 395–403.

Unger, R. K. (1988). Psychological, feminist, and personal epistemology. In M. M. Gergen (Ed.), *Feminist thought and the structure of knowledge* (pp. 124–141). New York: New York University Press.

Unger, R. K. (1990). Imperfect reflections of reality: Psychology and the construction of gender. In R. Hare-Mustin & J. Marecek (Eds.), *Making a difference: Representations of gender in psychology* (pp. 102–149). New Haven: Yale University Press.

Unger, R. K. (1998a). Positive marginality: Antecedents and consequences. *Journal of Adult Development, 5*, 163–170.

Unger, R. K. (1998b). *Resisting gender: Twenty-five years of feminist psychology*. London: Sage.

Unger, R. K., & Crawford, M. (1989). Methods and values in decisions about gender differences (Review of Alice H. Eagly, *Sex differences in social behavior: A social role interpretation*.) *Contemporary Psychology, 34*, 122–123.

Unger, R. K., & Crawford, M. (1993). Commentary: Sex and gender–The troubled relationship between terms and concepts. *Psychological Science, 4*, 122–124.

Unger, R. K., Draper, R. D., & Pendergrass, M. L. (1986). Personal epistemology and personal experience. *Journal of Social Issues, 42*, 67–79.

Unger, R. K., Hilderbrand, M., & Madar, T. (1982). Physical attractiveness and assumptions about social deviance: Some sex by sex comparisons. *Personality and Social Psychology Bulletin, 8*, 293–301.

Unger, R. K., & Sussman, L. E. (1986). "I and thou": Another barrier to societal change? *Sex Roles, 14*, 629–636.

United Nations. (1991a). *The world's women 1970–1990: Trends and statistics*. New York: United Nations.

United Nations. (1991b). *Women: Challenges to the year 2000*. New York: United Nations.

United Nations. (1995). *The world's women: Trends and statistics*. New York: United Nations.

Urberg, K. A. (1982). The development of the concepts of masculinity and femininity in young children. *Sex Roles, 6*, 659–668.

Ussher, J. (1989). *The psychology of the female body*. London: Routledge.

Valian, V. (1998). *Why so slow? The advancement of women*. Cambridge, MA: MIT Press.

Vance, C. S. (1984). Pleasure and danger: Toward a politics of sexuality. In C. S. Vance (Ed.), *Pleasure and danger: Exploring female sexuality* (pp. 1–27). Boston: Routledge and Kegan Paul.

Vance, E. B., & Wagner, N. N. (1976). Written descriptions of orgasm: A study of sex differences. *Archives of Sexual Behavior, 5*, 87–98.

Vanek, J. (1984). Housewives as workers. In P. Voydanoff (Ed.), *Work and family: Changing roles of men and women* (pp. 89–103). Palo Alto, CA: Mayfield.

Vasquez, M. J. T. (1994). Latinas. In L. Comas-Diaz & B. Greene (Eds.), *Women of color: Integrating ethnic and gender identities in psychotherapy* (pp. 114–138). New York: Guilford.

Vedovato, S., & Vaughter, R. (1980). Psychology of women courses changing sexist and sex-typed attitudes. *Psychology of Women Quarterly, 4,* 587–590.

Vernon, J. A., Williams, J. A., Jr., Phillips, T., & Wilson, J. (1991). Media stereotyping: A comparison of the way elderly women and men are portrayed on prime-time television. *Journal of Women & Aging, 2,* 55–68.

Veroff, J., Wilcox, S., & Atkinson, J. W. (1953). The achievement motive in high school and college age women. *Journal of Abnormal and Social Psychology, 43,* 108–119.

Veroff, J., Young, A. M., & Coon, H. M. (1997). The early years of marriage. In S. Duck (Ed.), *Handbook of personal relationships: Theory, research and interventions* (2nd ed., pp. 431–450). Chichester, England: Wiley.

Vicary, J. R., Klingman, L. R., & Harkness, W. L. (1995). Risk factors associated with date rape and sexual assault of adolescent girls. *Journal of Adolescence, 18,* 289–306.

Vida, V. (Ed.). (1978). *Our right to love: A lesbian resource book.* Englewood Cliffs, NJ: Prentice-Hall.

Vigorito, A. J., & Curry, T. J. (1998). Marketing masculinity: Gender identity and popular magazines. *Sex Roles, 39,* 135–152.

Vinick, B. H., & Ekerdt, D. J. (1992). Couples view retirement activities. In M. Szinovacz, D. J. Ekerdt, & B. H. Vinick (Eds.), *Families and retirement* (pp. 129–144). Newbury Park, CA: Sage.

Vobejda, B. (1994, June 16). Abortion rate slowing in U.S., study concludes. *Washington Post,* p. A13.

Voda, A. M. (1997). *Menopause me and you: The sound of women pausing.* Binghampton, NY: Harrington Park Press.

von Baeyer, C. L., Sherk, D. L., & Zanna, M. P. (1981). Impression management in the job interview: When the female applicant meets the male (chauvinist) interviewer. *Personality and Social Psychology Bulletin, 7,* 45–51.

Vredenburg, K., Krames, L., & Flett, G. L. (1986). Sex differences in the clinical expression of depression. *Sex Roles, 14,* 37–49.

Wahrman, R., & Pugh, M. D. (1972). Competence and conformity: Another look at Hollander's study. *Sociometry, 35,* 376–386.

Wahrman, R., & Pugh, M. D. (1974). Sex, nonconformity, and influence. *Sociometry, 37,* 137–147.

Wajcman, J. (1998). *Managing like a man: Women and men in corporate management.* Cambridge: Polity Press.

Waldo, C. R., Berdahl, J. L., & Fitzgerald, L. F. (1998). Are men sexually harassed? If so, by whom? *Law and Human Behavior, 22,* 59–79.

Walker, L. (1979). *The battered woman.* New York: Harper and Row.

Walker, L. (1993). The battered woman syndrome is a psychological consequence of abuse. In R. J. Gelles & D. R. Loseke (Eds.), *Current controversies on family violence* (pp. 133–153). Newbury Park, CA: Sage.

Walker, L. J. (1984). Sex differences in the development of moral reasoning: A critical review. *Child Development, 55,* 667–691.

Walker, L. J. (1986). Experiential and cognitive sources of moral development in adulthood. *Human Development, 29,* 113–124.

Walkerdine, V. (1996). Working class women: Social and psychological aspects of survival. In S. Wilkinson (Ed.), *Feminism and social psychology: International perspectives* (pp. 145–162). Milton Keynes: Open University Press.

Walkerdine, V. (1998). Popular culture and the eroticization of little girls. In H. Jenkins (Ed.), *The children's culture reader* (pp. 254–264). New York: New York University Press.

Wallen, K. (1996). Nature needs nurture: The interaction of hormonal and social influences on the development of behavioral sex differences in rhesus monkeys. *Hormones and Behavior, 30,* 364–378.

Wallston, B. S., & Grady, K. E. (1985). Integrating the feminist critique and the crisis in social psychology: Another look at research methods. In V. E. O'Leary, R. K. Unger, & B. S. Wallston (Eds.), *Women, gender and social psychology* (pp. 7–34). Hillsdale, NJ: Erlbaum.

Wallston, B. S., & O'Leary, V. E. (1981). Sex makes a difference: Differential perceptions of women and men. In L. Wheeler (Ed.), *Review of personality and social psychology,* Vol. 2 (pp. 9–41). Beverly Hills, CA: Sage.

Walters, E. E., & Kendler, K. S. (1995). Anorexia nervosa and anorexic like symptoms in a population-based female twin sample. *American Journal of Psychiatry, 152,* 64–71.

Walum, L. R. (1974). The changing door ceremony: Notes on the operation of sex roles in everyday life. *Urban Life and Culture, 2,* 506–515.

Walzer, S. (1998). *Thinking about the baby.* Philadelphia: Temple University.

Ward, J. V. (1996). Raising resistors: The role of truth telling in the psychological development of African American girls. In B. J. R. Leadbeater & N. Way (Eds.), *Urban girls:*

Resisting stereotypes, creating identities (pp. 85–99). New York: New York University Press.

Warren, M. P. (1983). Physical and biological aspects of puberty. In J. Brooks-Gunn & A. C. Petersen (Eds.), *Girls at puberty* (pp. 3–28). New York: Plenum Press.

Watson, G., & Williams, J. (1992). Feminist practices in therapy. In J. M. Ussher & P. Nicolson (Eds.), *Gender issues in clinical psychology* (pp. 212–236). London: Routledge.

Watson, M. S., Trasciatti, M. A., & King, C. P. (1996). Our bodies, our risk. In R. L. Parrott & C. M. Condit (Eds.), *Evaluating women's health messages* (pp. 95–108). Thousand Oaks: Sage.

Watts, Barbara. (1996). Legal issues. In M. A. Paludi (Ed.), *Sexual harassment on college campuses: Abusing the ivory power* (pp. 9–24). Albany: State University of New York.

Weatherall, A., & Walton, M. (in press). The metaphorical construction of sexual experience in a speech community of New Zealand university students. *British Journal of Social Psychology.*

Weaver, T. L., Kilpatrick, D. G., Resnick, H. S., Best, C. L., & Saunders, B. E. (1997). An examination of physical assault and childhood victimization histories within a national probability sample of women. In G. Kaufman Kantor & J. L. Jasinski (Eds.), *Out of darkness: Contemporary perspectives on family violence* (pp. 35–48). Thousand Oaks, CA: Sage.

Weber, J. C. (1996). Social class as a correlate of gender identity among lesbian women. *Sex Roles, 35*(5/6), 271–280.

Weber, L. (1998). A conceptual framework for understanding race, class, gender, and sexuality. *Psychology of Women Quarterly, 22,* 13–32.

Weber, L., & Higginbotham, E. (1997). Black and white professional-managerial women's perceptions of racism and sexism in the workplace. In E. Higginbotham & M. Romero (Eds.), *Women and work: Exploring race, ethnicity, and class* (vol. 6, pp. 153–175). Thousand Oaks, CA: Sage.

Weinraub, B. (1994, September 18). Meryl Streep's peculiar career. *New York Times Magazine,* pp. 42–45.

Weinraub, M., Clemens, L. P., Sockloff, A., Ethridge, T., Gracely, E., & Myers, B. (1984). The development of sex role stereotypes in the third year: Relationships to gender labeling, gender identity, sex-typed toy preference, and family characteristics. *Child Development, 55,* 1493–1503.

Weiss, M. R., & Barber, H. (1995). Socialization influences of collegiate female athletes: A tale of two decades. *Sex Roles, 33,* 129–140.

Weisstein, N. (1968). *Kinder, Kirche, Kuche as scientific law: Psychology constructs the female.* Boston: New England Free Press.

Weitz, R., & Gordon, L. (1993). Images of black women among Anglo students. *Sex Roles, 28,* 19–34.

Weitzman, L. (1985). *The divorce revolution.* New York: Free Press.

Weitzman, L. J. (1979). *Sex role socialization.* Palo Alto, CA: Mayfield.

Wells, J. D., Hobfoll, S. E., & Lavin, J. (1997). Resource loss, resource gain, and communal coping during pregnancy among women with multiple roles. *Psychology of Women Quarterly, 21,* 645–662.

Werner, P. D., & LaRussa, G. W. (1985). Persistence and change in sex-role stereotypes. *Sex Roles, 12,* 1089–1100.

Wertz, D. C. (1992). How parents of affected children view selective abortion. In H. B. Holmes (Ed.), *Issues in reproductive technology* (pp. 161–189). New York: Garland.

Wester, S. R., Crown, C. L., Quatman, G. L., & Heesacker, M. (1997). The influence of sexually violent rap music on attitudes of men with little prior exposure. *Psychology of Women Quarterly, 21,* 497–508.

Westney, O. E., Jenkins, R. R., & Benjamin, C. A. (1983). Sociosexual development of preadolescents. In J. Brooks-Gunn & A. C. Petersen (Eds.), *Girls at puberty* (pp. 273–300). New York: Plenum Press.

Whitam, F., Diamond, M., & Martin, J. (1993). Homosexual orientation in twins: A report on 61 pairs and three triplet sets. *Archives of Sexual Behavior, 22,* 187–206.

Whitam, F. L., Daskalos, C., Sobolewski, C. G., & Padilla, P. (1998). The emergence of lesbian sexuality and identity cross-culturally: Brazil, Peru, the Philippines, and the United States. *Archives of Sexual Behavior, 27*(1), 31–56.

Whitbourne, S. (1986). *The me I know: A study of adult identity.* New York: Springer-Verlag.

White, J. W., & Bondurant, B. (1996). Gendered violence. In J. T. Wood (Ed.), *Gendered Relationships* (pp. 197–210). Mountain View, CA: Mayfield.

White, J. W., Bondurant, B., & Travis, C. B. (in press). Social constructions of sexuality. In C. B. Travis & J. W. White (Eds.), *Sexuality,* society and feminism: Psychological perspectives on women. Washington, DC: American Psychological Association.

White, J. W., Holland, L., Mazurek, C., Lyndon, A., Weinstein, A., & Clancey, C. (1998). *Sexual assault experiences among community college students.* Symposium presented at the annual meeting of the North Carolina Coalition Against Sexual Assault, Asheville, NC, October.

White, J. W., & Humphrey, J. A. (1994). *Alcohol/drug use and sexual aggression: Distal and proximal influences.* Paper presented at XI World Meeting: International Society for Research on Aggression. Delray Beach, Florida, July.

White, J. W., & Humphrey, J. A. (1994a, March). *The relationship between perceived justification for forced sexual intercourse and self-reported sexual aggression.* Paper presented at Southeastern Psychological Association, New Orleans.

White, J. W., & Humphrey, J. A. (1995). *Sexual Assault Perpetration and Re-perpetration: From Adolescence to Young Adulthood.* Paper presented at Symposium on Rape and Sexual Assault: Risk Factors and Promising Interventions. National Violence Prevention Conference, Des Moines, Iowa, October 24.

White, J. W., & Humphrey, J. A. (1997). *Vulnerability for sexual assault during adolescence.* Presented at symposium on Factors Related to Sexual Victimization and Revictimization in Women. American Psychological Association, August 19.

White, J. W., & Koss, M. P. (1991). Courtship violence: Incidence in a national sample of higher education students. *Violence and Victims, 6,* 247–256.

White, J. W., & Koss, M. P. (1993). Adolescent sexual aggression within heterosexual relationships: Prevalence, characteristics, and causes. In H. E. Barbarbee, W. L. Marshall, & D. R. Laws (Eds.), *The juvenile sexual offender* (pp. 182–202). New York: Guilford.

White, J. W., Koss, M. P., & Kissling, G. (1991, June). Gender differences in structural models of courtship violence. Poster presented at American Psychological Society, Washington, DC.

White, J. W., & Kowalski, R. M. (1998). Violence against women: An integrative perspective. In R. G. Geen & E. Donnerstein (Eds.), *Perspectives on human aggression.* New York: Academic Press.

White, J. W., & Roufail, M. (1989). Gender and influence strategies of first choice and last resort. *Psychology of Women Quarterly, 13,* 175–189.

Whiting, B. B., & Edwards, C. P. (1973). A cross-cultural analysis of sex differences in the behavior of children aged three through eleven. *Journal of Social Psychology, 91,* 171–188.

Whitley, B. E., Jr. (1985). Sex-role orientation and psychological well-being: Two meta-analyses. *Sex Roles, 12,* 207–225.

Wichstrom, L. (1998). Self-concept development in adolescence: Do American truths hold for Norwegians? In E. Skoe & A. von der Lippe (Eds.), *Personality development in adolescence: A cross-national and lifespan perspective* (pp. 98–122). London: Routledge.

Wichstrom, L. (1999). The emergence of gender difference in depressed mood during adolescence: The role of intensified gender socialization. *Developmental Psychology, 35,* 232–245.

Wiest, W. M. (1977). Semantic differential profiles of orgasm and other experiences among men and women. *Sex Roles, 3,* 399–403.

Wilder, D. A. (1986). Social categorization: Implications for creation and reduction of intergroup bias. In L. Berkowitz (Ed.), *Advances in experimental social psychology,* Vol. 19. Orlando, FL: Academic Press.

Wilkinson, S. (1997a). Feminist psychology. In D. Fox & I. Prilleltensky (Eds.), *Critical psychology: An introduction* (pp. 247–264). London: Sage Publications.

Wilkinson, S. (1997b). Still seeking transformation: Feminist challenges to psychology. In L. Stanley (Ed.), *Knowing feminisms: On academic borders, territories and tribes* (pp. 97–108). Thousand Oaks, CA: Sage.

Wilkinson, S., & Kitzinger, C. (Eds.). (1993). *Heterosexuality: A "feminism and psychology" reader.* London: Sage.

Willemsen, T. M. (1998). Widening the gender gap: Teenage magazines for girls and boys. *Sex Roles, 38,* 851–861.

Williams, J. E., & Best, D. L. (1990). *Measuring sex stereotypes: A multination study.* Newbury Park, CA: Sage.

Williams, L. S. (1992). Biology or society? Parenthood motivation in a sample of Canadian women seeking in vitro fertilization. In H. B. Holmes (Ed.), *Issues in reproductive technology* (pp. 261–274). New York: Garland.

Williams, N. (1990). *The Mexican American fam-*

ily: Tradition and change. New York: General Hall.

Williams, P. J. (1997). My best white friend: Cinderella revisited. In M. Crawford & R. Unger (Eds.), *In our own words: Readings on the psychology of women and gender* (pp. 291–295). New York: McGraw-Hill.

Williams, R., & Wittig, M. A. (1997). "I'm not a feminist but . . .": Factors contributing to the discrepancy between pro-feminist orientation and feminist social identity. *Sex Roles, 37,* 885–904.

Williams, S. S., Kimble, D. L., Covell, N. H., Weiss, L. H., Newton, K. J., Fisher, J. D., & Fisher, W. A. (1992). College students use implicit personality theory instead of safer sex. *Journal of Applied Social Psychology,* 22(12), 921–933.

Williams, W. L. (1986). *The spirit and the flesh: Sexual diversity in American Indian culture.* Boston: Beacon Press.

Williams, W. L. (1987). Women, men, and others: Beyond ethnocentrism in gender theory. *American Behavioral Scientist, 31,* 135–141.

Wilson, A. (1996). How we find ourselves: Identity development and two-spirit people. *Harvard Educational Review, 66*(2), 303–317.

Wilson, B. J., Linz, D., Donnerstein, E., & Stipp, H. (1992). The impact of social issue television programming on attitudes toward rape. *Human Communication Research, 19,* 179–208.

Wilson, J. D., George, F. W., & Griffin, J. E. (1981). The hormonal control of sexual development. *Science, 211,* 1278–1284.

Wilson, M., & Daly, M. (1994). Spousal homicide. *Juristat, 14,* 1–15.

Wilson, R. (1996, February 16). Leading economist stuns field by deciding to become a woman. *The Chronicle of Higher Education,* pp. A17, A19.

Winkel, W., & DeKleuver, E. (1997). Communication aimed at changing cognitions about sexual intimidation: Comparing the impact of a perpetrator-focused versus a victim-focused persuasive strategy. *Journal of Interpersonal Violence, 12,* 513–529.

Witkin, H. A., Mednick, S. A., Schulsinger, F., Bakkestrom, E., Christiansen, K. O., Goodenough, D. R., Hirschhorn, K., Lundsteen, C., Owen, D. R., Philip, J., Rubin, D. B., & Stocking, M. (1976). Criminality in XYY and XYY men. *Science, 193,* 547–555.

Wolf, S. (1985). A multi-factor model of deviant sexuality. *Victimology: An International Journal, 10,* 359–374.

Wolman, C., & Frank, H. (1975). The solo woman in a professional peer group. *American Journal of Orthopsychiatry, 45,* 164–171.

Women's Action Collective. (1992). 75 Reasons why angry Cornell women (your worst nightmare) are exercising their freedom of speech. Women's Action Collective: Author.

Women's Programs Office. (1991). *Graduate faculty interested in psychology of women.* Washington, DC: American Psychological Association.

Wood, A. D., & McHugh, M. C. (1994). Woman battering: The response of the clergy. *Pastoral Psychology, 42,* 185–196.

Wood, K. C., Becker, J. A., & Thompson, J. K. (1996). Body image dissatisfaction in preadolescent children. *Journal of Applied Developmental Psychology, 17,* 85–100.

Wood, W., & Karten, S. J. (1986). Sex differences in interactive style as a product of perceived sex differences in competence. *Journal of Personality and Social Psychology, 50,* 341–347.

Wood, W., & Rhodes, N. (1992). Sex differences in interaction style in task groups. In C. L. Ridgeway (Ed.), *Gender, interaction, and inequality* (pp. 97–121). New York: Springer-Verlag.

Wooley, H. T. (1910). Psychological literature: A review of the recent literature on the psychology of sex. *Psychological Bulletin, 7,* 335–342.

Wooley, S. C., & Wooley, O. W. (1980). Eating disorders: Anorexia and obesity. In A. M. Brodsky & R. Hare-Mustin (Eds.), *Women and psychotherapy* (pp. 135–158). New York: Guilford.

Woollett, A., White, D., & Lyon, L. (1982). Fathers' involvement with their infants: The role of holding. In N. Beail & J. McGuire (Eds.), *Fathers: Psychological perspectives.* London: Junction.

Worell, J. (1988). Women's satisfaction in close relationships. *Clinical Psychology Review, 8,* 477–498.

Worell, J. (1996). Opening doors to feminist research. *Psychology of Women Quarterly, 20,* 469–485.

Workman, J. E., & Johnson, K. K. P. (1991). The role of cosmetics in attributions about sexual harassment. *Sex Roles, 24,* 759–769.

World Wire. (1993, December 21). China proposed eugenics law. *Wall Street Journal,* p. A6.

Worth, D. M., Matthews, P. A., & Coleman, W. R. (1990). Sex role, group affiliation, family background, and courtship violence in college students. *Journal of College Student Development, 31,* 250–254.

Wyatt, G. (1991). Sociocultural context of African American and White American women's rape. *Journal of Social Issues, 48,* 77–92.

Wyatt, G. E. (1985). The sexual abuse of Afro-American and White-American women in childhood. *Child Abuse and Neglect, 9,* 507–519.

Wyatt, G. E., Guthrie, G., & Notgrass, C. M. (1992). Differential effects of women's child sexual abuse and subsequent sexual revictimization. *Journal of Consulting and Clinical Psychology, 60,* 167–173.

Wyatt, G. E., & Riederle, M. H. (1994). Reconceptualizing issues that affect women's sexual decision-making and sexual functioning. *Psychology of Women Quarterly, 18,* 611–626.

Wyche, K. F. (1996). Conceptualization of social class in African American women: Congruence of client-therapist definitions. *Women & Therapy, 18,* 35–43.

Wyche, K. F., & Crosby, F. (Eds.). (1996). *Women's ethnicities: Journeys through psychology.* Boulder, CO: Westview.

Wyche, K. F., & Rice, J. K. (1997). Feminist therapy: From dialogue to tenets. In J. Worell & N. G. Johnson (Eds.), *Shaping the future of feminist psychology: Education, research, and practice* (pp. 57–71). Washington DC: American Psychological Association.

Wynn, R. L., & Fletcher, C. (1987). Sex role development and early educational experiences. In D. B. Carter (Ed.), *Current conceptions of sex roles and sex typing: Theory and research* (pp. 79–88). New York: Praeger.

Yama, M. F., Tovey, S. L., & Fogas, B. S. (1993). Childhood family environment and sexual abuse as predicting of anxiety and depression in adult women. *American Journal of Orthopsychiatry, 63,* 136–141.

Yanovski, S. Z. (1993). Binge eating disorder: Current knowledge and future directions. *Obesity Research, 1,* 305–324.

Yarkin, K. L., Town, J. P., Wallston, B. S. (1982). Blacks and women must try harder: Stimulus persons' race and sex and attributions of causality. *Personality and Social Psychology Bulletin, 8,* 21–30.

Yee, B. W. K. (1990). Gender and family issues in minority groups. *Generations, 14,* 39–42.

Yee, D. (1997). Issues and trends affecting Asian Americans, women, and aging. In J. M. Coyle (Ed.), *Handbook on women and aging* (pp. 316–334). Westport, CT: Greenwood Press.

Yllo, K. (1993). Through a feminist lens: Gender, power, and violence. In R. J. Gelles & D. R. Loseke (Eds.), *Current controversies on family violence* (pp. 47–62). Newbury Park, CA: Sage.

Yoder, J. D. (1985). An academic woman as a token: A case study. *Journal of Social Issues, 41,* 61–72.

Yoder, J. D., Adams, J., Grove, S., & Priest, R. F. (1985). To teach is to learn: Overcoming tokenism with mentors. *Psychology of Women Quarterly, 9,* 119–132.

Yoder, J. D., & Aniakudo, P. (1996). When pranks become harassment: The case of African American women firefighters. *Sex Roles, 35,* 253–269.

Yoder, J. D., & Kahn, A. S. (1992). Toward a feminist understanding of women and power. *Psychology of Women Quarterly, 16,* 381–388.

Yoder, J. D., Schleicher, T. L., & McDonald, T. W. (1998). Empowering token women leaders: The importance of organizationally legitimated credibility. *Psychology of Women Quarterly, 22,* 209–222.

Yoder, J. D., & Sinnett, L. M. (1985). Is it all in the numbers? A case study of tokenism. *Psychology of Women Quarterly, 9,* 413–418.

Young, I. M. (1998). Breasted experience: The look and the feeling. In R. Weitz (Ed.), *The politics of women's bodies: Sexuality, appearance, and behavior* (pp. 125–136). New York: Oxford University Press.

Youngblut, J. M., Singer, L. T., Madigan, E. A., Swegart, L. A., & Rodgers, W. L. (1997). Mother, child, and family factors related to employment of single mothers with LBW preschoolers. *Psychology of Women Quarterly, 21*(2), 247–263.

Zak, A., & McDonald, C. (1997). Satisfaction and trust in intimate relationships: Do lesbians and heterosexual women differ? *Psychological Reports, 80,* 904–906.

Zanna, M. P., & Pack, S. J. (1975). On the self-fulfilling nature of apparent sex differences in behavior. *Journal of Experimental Social Psychology, 11,* 583–591.

Zelnik, M., Kantner, J. F., & Ford, K. (1981). *Sex and pregnancy in adolescence.* Beverly Hills, CA: Sage.

Zernike, K. (1999, March 21). MIT women win a fight against bias. *The Boston Globe,* pp. F1, F4.

Zimmerman, M. K. (1987). The women's health movement: A critique of medical enterprise and the position of women. In B. B. Hess & M. M. Ferree (Eds.), *Analyzing gender* (pp. 442–472). Newbury Park, CA: Sage.

Zinkhan, G. M., & Stoiadin, L. F. (1984). Impact of sex role stereotypes on service priority in department stores. *Journal of Applied Psychology, 69,* 691–693.

Zita, J. N. (1993). Heresy in the female body: The rhetoric of menopause. In J. C. Callahan (Ed.), *Menopause: A midlife passage* (pp. 59–78). Bloomington: University of Indiana Press.

Zlotnick, C., Kohn, R., Peterson, J., & Pearlstein, T. (1998). Partner physical victimization in a national sample of American families. Relationship to psychological functioning, psychosocial factors, and gender. *Journal of Interpersonal Violence, 13,* 156–166.

Zucker, K. J., Wild, J., Bradley, S. J., & Lowry, C. B. (1993). Physical attractiveness of boys with gender identity disorder. *Archives of Sexual Behavior, 22,* 23–36.

Zucker, K. J., Wilson-Smith, D. N., Kurita, J. A., & Stern, A. (1995). Children's appraisals of sex-typed behaviors in their peers. *Sex Roles, 33,* 703–725.

Zuckerman, M., & Kieffer, S. C. (1994). Race differences in faceism: Does facial prominence imply dominance? *Journal of Personality and Social Psychology, 66,* 86–92

Zweig, J. M., Barber, B. L., & Eccles, J. S. (1997). *Journal of Interpersonal Violence, 12,* 291–308.

Credits

Photos

Figure 1.2: Collection of the NY Historical Society; **Figure 2.1:** Dancers of the Third Age; **Figure 2.2:** Noel Quidui/Gamma Liaison; **Figure 2.4 (left):** Lawrence Agron/Archive Photos; **Figure 2.4 (right):** Gamma Liaison; **Figure 2.5 (left):** Reuters/Blake Sell/Archive Photos; **Figure 2.5 (right):** Reuters/Blake Sell/Archive Photos; **Figure 2.6:** © 1999 MAK; **Figure 2.8:** Time, Inc. © 1993 reprinted by permission; **Figure 2.11:** Reuters; **Page 63:** Boston Globe Photos; **Figure 3.1:** Globe Photos/AK; **Figure 3.2:** Michaelangelo Di Battista/New York Times Magazine; **Page 92:** Photograph by Neil Turner; **Figure 3.4:** Red Mertz; **Figure 4.6:** Permission granted by The Women's College Coalition; **Figure 4.7:** Elizabeth Crews/The Image Works; **Page 146:** Greta Pratt; **Figure 5.4:** © 1995 Newsweek, Inc.; **Figure 5.5:** Intersex Society of North America; **Page 168:** Mike Geissinger; **Figure 5.7:** W. Van Cappellon/SABA; **Figure 5.9:** The Philadelphia Inquirer/Barbara Demick; **Figure 6.1:** United Nation (1991). *Women: Challenges to the Year 2000.* NY: United Nations Publications; **Page 215:** Associated Press; **Figure 6.6:** Simons/Sygma; **Figure 6.7:** Nicholas D. Kristor/The New York Times; **Figure 7.4:** Last Resort Design; **Figure 7.7:** Bonnie Burton; **Page 255:** Associated Press Photo; **Page 284:** Associated Press; **Page 325:** Associated Press; **Figure 10.4:** Suzanne Arms/The Image Works; **Figure 10.6:** Michele Maier; **Figure 10.7:** Steve Jacobs/Albany Times Union; **Page 387:** Associated Press; **Page 404:** Associated Press; **Figure 12.1:** 1991 Time Inc. Reprinted by permission; **Figure 12.6:** © 1990 Newsweek, Inc. All rights reserved. Reprinted by permission; **Figure 12.8:** Elizabeth Layton; **Page 475:** Associated Press; **Page 485:** © 1991 Time Inc. Reprinted by permission; **Figure 14.2 (both):** Associated Press; Associated Press; **Page 524:** Corbis/Bettmann-UPI; **Page 569:** Associated Press.

Text

Permission to reprint is gratefully acknowledged for the following:

Page 78: From *Women: A Feminist Perspective*, 4th ed., by Jo Freeman, edited by permission of Mayfield Publishing Company. Copyright © 1989 by Mayfield Publishing Company. **Page 107:** From K.H. Jamison, *Beyond the Double Bind: Women and Leadership.*

Copyright © 1995. Reprinted by permission of Oxford University Press, Inc. **Pages 174, 175–176:** Adapted from John Colapinto, "The True Story of John/Joan," *Rolling Stone,* December 11, 1997, pp. 64, 95. Reprinted by permission of the author. **Page 182:** Kessler, Suanne J., *Lessons from the Intersexed,* copyright © 1998 by Suzanne J. Kessler. Reprinted by permission of Rutgers University Press. **Pages 228–229:** From WORKING IT OUT by Sara Ruddick and Pamela Daniels. Copyright © 1977 by Sara Ruddick and Pamela Daniels. Reprinted by permission of Pantheon Books, a division of Random House, Inc. **Pages 232–233:** From REVIVING OPHELIA by Mary Pipher, Ph.D. Copyright © 1994 by Mary Pipher, Ph.D. Used by permission of Putnam Berkeley, a division of Penguin Putnam, Inc. **Page 238:** From Shipman, G. (1971). The psychodynamics of sex education. In R. E. Muuss (ed.), *Adolescent behavior and society: A book of readings.* New York: Random House, p. 331. **Pages 238, 239, 241, 242, 245:** Copyright © 1996 from *Puberty, Sexuality, and the Self* by Karin A. Martin. Reproduced by permission of Taylor & Francis/Routledge, Inc. http://www.routledge-ny.com. **Page 241:** From Koff, E. (1983). Through the looking glass of menarche: What the adolescent girl sees In S. Golub (ed.), *Menarche,* pp. 77–86. Lexington, MA: Lexington Books, 81. **Page 244:** From Martin, E. (1987). *The woman in the body: A cultural analysis of reproduction.* Boston: Beacon Press, pp. 93–94. **Page 254:** Reprinted by permission of Sage Publications Ltd. From J. Larkin & K. Popaleni, "Heterosexual courtship violence and sexual harassment: the private and public control of young women," *Feminism & Psychology, 4,* p. 220. Copyright © 1994 by Sage Publications Ltd. **Page 261:** From K. Pierce, "Socialization of teenage girls through teen-magazine fiction: The making of a new woman or an old lady" *Sex Roles, 29:* 64. Copyright © 1993 Plenum Publishing Corporation. Reprinted by permission. **Page 276:** Permission granted by Harlequin Books S.A. First published by Mills & Boon ® in Great Britain in 1984. Copyright © 1984 by Rachel Elliot. **Pages 310, 312, 317, 318, 319, and Figure 9.5:** Two figures (#53 and 54) from AMERICAN COUPLES by Philip Blumstein and Pepper Schwartz. Copyright © 1983 by the authors. By permission of William Morrow and Company, Inc. **Page 385:** K. Gieve, *Balancing Acts: On Being a Mother* (1989) Virago. Reprinted by permission of the author. **Pages 481–482:** "With no immediate cause." In *Nappy Edges* by Ntozake Shange, St. Martin's Press, Inc., New York. Copyright © 1972, 1974, 1975, 1976, 1977, 1978 by Ntozake Shange. **Page 529:** From John and Sussman, "Initiative taking as a determinant of role reciprocal orgnization." *Representations: Social Construction of Gender,* edited by Rhoda Unger. Copyright © 1989 Baywood Publishing Company, Inc. Reprinted with permission. **Page 546:** Reprinted by permission of Sage Publications ltd. From Paula J. Caplan. "Delusional dominating personality disorder (DDPD)," *Feminism & Psychology, 1,* pp. 171–174. Copyright © 1991 by Sage Publications Ltd. **Page 550:** Reprinted with the permission of Simon & Schuster, Inc. from THE NEW OURSELVES, GROWING OLDER by Paula Doress Worters and Diana Laskin Siegal. Copyright © 1987, 1994 by Paula Doress Worters and Diana Laskin Siegal.

Name Index

AAUW Educational Foundation, 124
Abrams, D., 227
Abramson, L. M., 411
Abramson, L. Y., 530, 531
Abramson, P. E., 411
Abusharaf, R. M., 282, 283
Achte, K., 455
Acosta, M., 556
Adams, E., 220
Adams, J., 417, 418
Adams, K. L., 24, 284
Adams, M., 332
Adams, R. C., 476, 477
Adams, S., 196
Adams-Price, C., 257
Addelston, J., 59
Adegoke, A., 274
Adelmann, P. K., 462, 464
Ader, D. N., 17
Adler, I., 463
Adler, N. E., 560
Adler, T. F., 126
Adolph, M. A., 443
Affonso, D. D., 366
Agence-France Press., 193
Agor, A. T., 44
Agyei, Y., 158
Aida, Y., 322
Aikin, K. J., 73
Aizenman, M., 498
Akhter, S., 512
Akiyama, H., 477
Alagna, S. W., 545
Alazarov-Por, N., 127
Albert, J. L., 357
Albright, L., 274
Aldous, J., 316
Alexander, P. C., 487
Alexander, S. J., 11, 378
Alfano, D. P., 513
Alington, D. E., 474
Alker, H. A., 112
Alksnis, O., 413
Allan, J. S., 60
Allan, K., 47
Allbritten, W. L., 495

Allen, I. L., 62, 324
Allen, K. R., 354, 360, 361, 362, 394, 395, 413, 434
Allen, L. S., 159
Allen, V. L., 250
Allgood-Merten, B., 258
Allport, G. W., 75
Almquist, E. M., 382, 383
Alpert, D., 430
Altman, M., 292, 294
Amaro, H., 358, 426, 430
American Association of University Women, 506, 509
American Psychiatric Association, 523, 545
Amick, A. E., 487
Amir, M., 499
Ancis, J. R., 55
Anderson, C. M., 291, 476
Anderson, D. R., 54, 464
Anderson, J. V., 226
Anderson, K. J., 95
Anderson, K. L., 513
Anderton, D. L., 507
Andrea, R., 542
Angell, K. E., 530, 531
Angier, N., 151, 155
Angless, T., 516
Aniakudo, P., 508
Anson, O., 463
Antonovsky, A., 458, 463, 480
Antonucci, T. C., 462, 477
Apfelbaum, E., 108, 419
Aragon, A. S., 486
Araoye, M. O., 274
Arato, H., 566
Arber, S., 464
Archer, D., 53, 72
Arendell, T., 338, 339, 340
Argiro, L. G., 104
Arms, S., 367
Arnold, F., 193
Arroyo, J. A., 486
Asch, A., 99, 286
Associated Press, 279

Assunta, M., 224
Astin, H. S., 425
Atkinson, J. W., 421, 422
Attie, I., 246, 250
Atwood, J. D., 380
Auerbach, J., 143
Ault, A., 297
Austin, L. J., 58
Avni, Noga, 495
Azocar, F., 531

Baber, K. M., 354, 360, 361, 362, 394, 395, 413, 434
Babey, S. H., 224, 246
Badgett, M. V. L., 412
Bailey, M. J., 158
Bailey-Werner, B., 68, 70
Baker, N. L., 560
Baker, R., 315
Baker-Ward, L., 196
Bakkestrom, E., 167
Baldwin, L. M., 531
Bales, R. F., 398
Balin, J., 97
Ballinger, S., 450
Banaji, M. R., 74, 83
Bandura, A., 188
Bannert, M., 105
Barak, A., 225, 506
Barbach, L., 475
Barbee, A. P., 60, 275
Barber, B. L., 498, 502
Barber, H., 221
Barbour, M. M., 450
Bardwell, J. R., 219, 227
Barenbaum, N. B., 340
Bargad, A., 565
Bargh, J., 508
Barnett, O. W., 513
Barnett, R. C., 352, 354, 395, 396, 397, 398, 430, 431, 444
Barr, L., 224, 246
Barreca, G., 567
Barrios, M., 53, 72
Barron, W. L., 107
Barshay, J. M., 561

Bart, P. B., 16, 455, 456, 457, 462
Bar-Tal, D., 57
Baruch, G. K., 352, 354, 396, 397, 398, 430, 431, 444, 470, 472
Basow, S. A., 417, 540
Bass, E., 490
Basta, S. M., 488
Bauer, P. J., 209
Bauer, W. D., 411
Bazzini, D. G., 441
Beaton, A. M., 73
Beatty, C. A., 430
Beck, J. C., 545
Beck, R. W., 470
Beck, S. J., 470
Becker, B. J., 122
Becker, E., 272, 274
Becker, H. S., 99
Becker, J. A., 224
Beckett, J., 492, 495
Beckman, L. J., 463
Beckstein, D., 273
Beckwith, B., 135
Begay, C., 460, 467
Begley, S., 446
Behan, P., 160
Behrman, J., 220
Belk, S. S., 304
Bell, C. S., 403
Bell, I. P., 440, 443
Bell, N. W., 317
Bell, R. M., 275
Bem, D. J., 64, 132, 314
Bem, S. L., 27, 64, 132, 314
Benaske, N., 495
Benbow, C. P., 124, 128
Benda, B. B., 272
Benenson, J. F., 197
Benjamin, C. A., 273
Bennett, J. L., 286
Benokraitis, N. V., 97, 101, 402, 405, 412
Bequaert, L., 331, 332
Berardo, D. H., 319
Berch, B., 396, 402

Berdahl, J. L., 507
Berenbaum, S. A., 169
Berger, J., 93
Berger, P. L., 24
Berger, R. J., 502
Berger, R. M., 328
Bergeron, S. M., 543
Bergman, L., 492
Berk, R. A., 516
Berman, J. S., 561
Berman, P. W., 209
Bermant, G., 150
Bernal, J., 195
Bernard, C., 506
Bernard, J., 312, 321, 346,
   349, 429, 430
Bernard, M., 463
Bernat, J. A., 499
Bernstein, S., 90
Berryman-Fink, C., 11
Berscheid, E., 65, 85
Bersoff, D. N., 68, 69, 430
Besnier, N., 183
Best, C. L., 514
Best, D. L., 35, 36, 72, 74
Bethke, N., 494
Betz, N. E., 402, 403, 406,
   408, 409, 412, 420,
   421, 423, 426, 430, 432
Beyene, Y., 447
Biaggio, M., 509, 510
Bianchi, S. M., 310, 313,
   329, 331, 334
Bielby, D. D., 402
Biernat, M., 71, 110
Bigler, R. S., 225, 226
Billingham, R. E., 491, 494
Bing, V. M., 17
Binstock, T., 154
Bird, H. R., 559
Birrell, S. J., 168
Bishop, N., 354, 357
Bitar, N., 47
Bjorkqvist, K., 214
Bjorn, L., 428, 509
Black, J., 298
Black, S. M., 462
Blair, S. L., 395
Blanchard, P. H., 443, 467
Blanchard, R., 178
Blanchflower, D. G., 66
Blankenship, V., 493
Blechman, E. A., 526
Bleier, R., 132, 134, 160,
   161
Block, C. J., 69
Block, J. H., 217
Bloduc, D., 199, 200
Blood, R. O., 317
Blum, L., 143
Blum, R. W., 378
Blumstein, P., 297, 310,
   312, 317, 318, 319,
   325, 326, 327, 330,
   339, 340, 343
Blyth, D. A., 250, 253, 259
Boardman, S. K., 425
Boatwright, K. J., 426
Bodenhausen, G. V., 55
Bogal-Allbritten, 495
Bograd, M., 510
Bohan, J. S., 255, 299, 567,
   572
Bolin, A., 178
Bond, M., 507, 508

Bond, S., 60
Bondurant, B., 285, 483,
   499, 500
Boney-McCoy, S., 486
Bookwala, J., 493
Booth, A., 107
Bordo, S., 251
Borgers, S. B., 558
Borgida, E., 54, 68, 69
Borker, R. A., 213
Bornstein, K., 179
Bose, C. E., 402
Boswell, S. L., 124, 126,
   127, 219
Bouhoutsos, J., 554
Bound, J., 473
Bowker, L., 513
Boxer, A. M., 248, 250
Boyatzis, C. J., 207
Boyd, B., 274
Boyd, J. A., 557, 558
Boyle, P. A., 196
Brabant, S., 43
Brabeck, M. M., 551, 556,
   571
Brackbill, Y., 195
Bradbard, M. R., 2, 202
Braden, A., 426, 427
Bradley, C., 226
Bradley, S. J., 180
Bradshaw, C. K., 556
Bradsher, J. E., 472
Brand, P. A., 511
Brannigan, G. G., 290
Branscombe, N. R., 112
Breedlove, S. M., 157, 158
Breines, W., 489
Brelis, M., 158
Brennan, R. T., 430
Bridges, J. S., 195, 431
Briere, J., 64
Brinkerhoff, D. B., 107
Brockopp, K., 492, 494
Brod, H., 184
Brodsky, A., 565
Brody, C., 94
Brody, L. R., 197
Brogan, D. R., 203
Brohmer, S., 493
Bromberg, J. J., 249
Brooks, L., 506
Brooks-Gunn, J., 187, 192,
   225, 234, 235, 239,
   245, 246, 250, 251,
   257, 258, 259, 272
Broughton, J. M., 143
Broverman, D. M., 38, 547
Broverman, I. K., 38, 547
Brown, B. A., 221, 222, 410
Brown, C. E., 98
Brown, D. R., 473
Brown, E. A., 279
Brown, J. D., 51
Brown, J. K, 457
Brown, L. M., 255, 256
Brown, L. S., 485, 523, 535,
   544, 545, 551, 553
Brown, R., 73
Brown, S., 448
Brown, V., 54
Brown-Collins, A., 71
Browne, A., 489, 510, 512,
   515, 520, 545
Brownell, A., 509, 510
Brownell, K. D., 56

Brownmiller, S., 497
Brush, L. R., 124
Bryant, B. K., 207
Bryden, M. P., 173
Bryer, J. B., 545
Buchman, D. D., 214, 215
Buhl, M., 11
Bumagin, V. E., 444
Buntaine, R. L., 197
Burcky, W. D., 492, 493,
   494
Burgeson, R., 253, 260
Burke, P. J., 369
Burke, R. J., 400, 418, 431
Burkhart, B. R., 501
Burman, E., 485
Burn, S. M., 221
Burns, A. L., 198, 217, 226,
   227
Burns, D. S., 410
Burns, E. A., 459
Burns, J., 537
Burnson, M., 411
Burt, M., 507
Burton, N., 131
Busby, L. J., 42, 47
Buschman, J. K., 11
Bush, D. M., 259
Bush, T. L., 450
Buss, D. M., 72, 150, 311
Butler, D., 97
Butler, L. D., 532
Buzawa, C. G., 516
Buzawa, E. S., 516
Byers, J., 44

Cabaj, R. P., 325
Cafasso, L., 470
Cafferata, G. L., 470
Cahill, B., 220
Caldera, Y. M., 200, 201
Calderone, K. L., 548
Caldwell, M. A., 304, 327
Calhoun, K. S., 487, 499
Califia, P., 178
Camden, C., 94
Campbell, B., 73
Campbell, E. K., 193
Campbell, J. C., 514
Campbell, K. E., 51, 95
Campbell, L. D., 470
Campbell, P. G., 193
Campbell, R., 533
Campbell, S. B., 377
Campbell, S. M., 302, 303
Campenni, C. E., 201
Canetto, S. S., 473, 531
Canino, G. J., 559
Canter, R. J., 422
Cantor, M. G., 52
Cantrell, P. J., 430
Caplan, P. J., 389, 390, 525,
   546, 569
Cardell, M., 327
Carey, C. M., 491, 493
Carey, M., 8
Carleton, R. A., 450
Carli, L. L., 96
Carlo, G., 197
Carlson, B. E., 460
Carmen, E. H., 547
Carp, F. M., 464
Carr, J. G., 531
Carson, D. K., 487
Carstensen, L. L., 324

Cartwright, L. K., 478
Cash, T. F., 53, 55, 58, 59,
   60, 253, 254, 410
Cass, V. C., 299
Cassell, J., 405, 411
Cast, A. D., 369
Cate, C. A., 494
Cauce, A. M., 257, 556
Caudill, S. A., 355
Chacko, T. I., 110
Chaffin, R., 131, 147
Chaikin, S., 539, 540
Chambless, D. L., 526
Champagne, N. M., 534
Chan, C. S., 302
Chandani, A. T., 286
Chanpong, G., 286
Charlesworth, W. R., 212
Chase, S. E., 403
Chavez, D., 43
Cherlin, A. J., 338, 341
Chesler, P., 3, 522, 524, 525
Chester, B., 486
Chester, N. L., 340
Cheung, C., 382
Chew, E., 492, 494
Chi, J. G., 160
Chicago, J., 372
Childs, E. K., 555
Chilman, C. S., 273
Chipman, S. F., 123, 124,
   125
Chodorow, N., 137, 145,
   349
Choney, S. B., 556
Choo, P., 282
Chow, E. N-L., 7, 426
Chrisler, J. C., 427, 441,
   446, 534, 560
Christiansen, K. O., 167
Christopher, F. S., 494
Cialdini, R. B., 105
Clancey, C., 499
Clark, C. L., 54
Clark, M. L., 492, 495
Clark, R. A., 421
Clarkson, F. E., 38, 547
Clayton, S., 413
Cleek, M. G., 335
Clemens, L. P., 217
Clum, G. A., 499
Coates, E. J., 96
Coben, J. H., 514
Coble, C. N., 498
Cochran, S. D., 274, 304,
   327
Cochran, S. W., 219, 227
Code, L. B., 142
Cohen, B. P., 93
Cohen, C. E., 83
Cohen, L. L., 73, 102
Cohen, R., 209
Colapinto, J., 168, 174, 175,
   176, 180
Colby, A., 143
Cole, S. L., 168
Cole, T. R., 436
Coleman, L. M., 210, 420,
   462
Coleman, W. R., 493
Coles, R., 281, 288, 289
Collaer, M. L., 155, 157,
   165, 169, 170, 171

Collins, M. E., 498
Collins, P. H., 51, 382, 383
Collins, R. K. L., 55
Collins, S. K., 405, 422
Coltrane, S., 47
Comas-Diaz, L., 559
Committee on Women in
 Psychology, 544, 546
Commons, M. L., 475
Compas, B. E., 390
Comstock, G., 46
Conaty, J. C., 94
Condon, J., 364
Condry, J. C., Jr., 198
Condry, S. M., 198
Connidis, I. A., 353
Conrad, E., 19, 20
Conway, M., 91
Cook, A. S., 199
Cook, K. V., 200
Cooksey, E. C., 273
Coon, H. M., 321
Cooper, E., 105
Cooper, M. L., 526
Cooper, V. W., 62
Copeland, A. P., 340
Corbett, K., 286
Coriell, M., 560
Corley, M. C., 405
Cornwell, B., 66
Cortina, L. M., 504, 506,
 507, 509
Corwin, S. J., 224
Cossette, L., 199, 200
Costello, C., 334, 338
Costenbader, V. K., 197
Cota, A. A., 64, 91
Courtois, C. A., 486, 487
Covell, N. H., 274
Covey, H. C., 437
Cowan, G., 51, 71, 221,
 260, 262, 451, 506
Coward, R. T., 468
Cox, T. H., Jr., 418
Cozzarelli, C., 357, 359
Craig, R. S., 47
Crandall, C. S., 60, 66
Crawford, M., 3, 4, 18, 19,
 20, 22, 24, 25, 27, 64,
 65, 119, 122, 127, 131,
 132, 147, 256, 305, 383,
 384, 417, 429, 433, 565,
 566, 567
Crew, B. K., 493
Crewdson, J., 490
Crews, D., 150
Crichton, N. J., 292
Crittenden, D., 13
Crocker, J., 66, 102, 103, 111
Crockett, L. J., 248, 250
Croghan, R., 364
Crohan, S. E., 331, 462
Crosbie-Burnett, M., 341
Crosby, F. J., 109, 343, 413,
 429, 430, 431
Crose, R., 459
Croteau, J. M., 413
Crovitz, E., 313, 378
Crowley, B. J., 58
Crowley, M., 39, 40
Crown, C. L., 51
Culbertson, A., 430
Culp, R. E., 199
Cummings, N., 502
Cunningham, J. D., 303

Cunningham, M. R., 60
Curry, T. J., 50
Curtis, T., 272, 273
Cusick, T., 272, 294, 379
Cypress, A., 443

Dabul, A. J., 105
Dahlin, M., 273
Daley, D., 357
Daly, M., 514
D'Amico, R., 404
Damon, W., 143
Dancer, L. S., 395
Daniels, P., 229
Daniluk, J. C., 353, 440,
 475, 476
Dank, S., 58
Dansky, B. S., 509
Darnton, J., 358
Daskalos, C., 302
Datan, N., 458, 480
Daubman, K. A., 88
Davidson, J., 173
Davidson, J. M., 150
Davidson, W., 533
Davis, B., 51
Davis, D. M., 46, 47
Davis, L., 490
Davis, M., 95
Davis, S., 565
de Cubes, M., 379
De Witt, K., 216
Dean, K. E., 499
Dearwater, S. R., 514
Deaux, K., 24, 39, 40, 42,
 56, 67, 68, 69, 120,
 410, 426, 427, 428
DeBlasio, C. L., 104
Deblinger, E., 488
Deddens, J., 428
Dege, K., 456
DeJoy, D. M., 494
DeKeseredy, W. S., 498
DeKleuver, E., 503
DeLamater, J., 266, 271,
 272, 274, 283, 284,
 288, 297, 307, 357,
 374, 376, 377, 378
Delaney, J., 241, 242, 245
Demarest, J., 205
DeMaris, A., 493
DeMeis, D. K., 398
D'Emilio, J., 269, 296, 307
Dempsey, K., 395
Dempster-McClain, D.,
 430
Denmark, F. L., 15, 18, 108,
 406
Derby, C. A., 450
Derbyshire, A., 217
Deschamps, J-C., 91
Desmarais, S., 202
Deutsch, F. M., 66
Devor, H., 155, 177, 178,
 179, 180
Dew, M. A., 66
Dewhurst, A. M., 513
Di Leonardo, M., 398, 399
Diamond, M. A., 150, 152,
 154, 158, 159, 163,
 164, 173, 174, 175,
 176, 182
DiBlasio, F. A., 272
Dickerson, B. J., 380, 381,
 382, 383

Dickson, L., 310
Diebold, J., 68, 70
Dietz, T. L., 215
Dijker, A. J., 112
Dill, D., 531
DiIorio, C., 293
Dion, K. K., 65
Dion, K. L., 64, 91, 111
DiPalma, L. M., 490
Discover Magazine, 246
DiTomaso, N., 419
Dittmann, R. W., 171
Dodson, B., 279
Dolan, E. M., 341
Donaldson, M. A., 487
Donat, P. L. N., 499
Donnerstein, E., 503
Dooling, E. C., 160
Dorans, N. J., 123
Doress, P. B., 450, 454, 466,
 471, 472, 474
Doress-Worters, P. B., 449,
 471, 480
Dornbusch, S. M., 251, 258
Dou, H., 157
Douglas, S. J., 10, 13, 204
Dovidio, J. F., 88, 95, 98
Doyle, A. B., 212
Draper, R. D., 161
Drasgow, F., 504, 507, 508,
 509
Draucker, C. B., 488
Dreher, G. F., 418
Driscoll, J. M., 413
Druen, P. B., 60
Du Mont, J., 483
Duan, C., 80
Duckworth, J., 513
Dumont, B. A., 2, 5
Duncan, G. J., 339, 473
Duncan, L. E., 73
Duncan, M. C., 44
Duncan, P. D., 251, 258
Dungee-Anderson, D.,
 492, 495
Dunkin, K., 206
Dunkle, J. H., 67
Dunlop, E., 455
Dunn, S., 483
Dutton, D. G., 513
Dutton, M. A., 514
Dworkin, A., 204, 294
Dwyer, C. A., 131
Dwyer, E. V., 531
Dwyer, J. W., 468
Dykstra, T. A., 488
Dzur, C., 212

Eagly, A. H., 67, 74, 86, 90,
 105, 108, 122, 418
Earn, B. M., 111
Earp, J. A., 510
East, P. L., 268
Eaton, W. O., 203
Eccles, J. S., 23, 122, 123,
 124, 126, 129, 130,
 135, 216, 421, 425,
 498, 502
Eckes, T., 41
Edelson, M. S., 212
Eder, D., 288, 289, 294
Edleson, J. L., 516
Edman, C. D., 448, 449,
 450, 452
Edwards, C. P., 208, 226

Edwards, J. J., 487
Ehrenreich, B., 536, 537
Ehrhardt, A. A., 166, 169,
 172, 174, 175
Eichler, M., 18
Eisenberg, A. R., 213
Eisenbud, L., 202
Ekerdt, D. J., 464
Ekstrom, B., 455
Eldridge, N. S., 327
Elias, C., 63
Elise, S., 379, 380
Elkind, S. N., 360
Elliot, R., 276
Elliot, S., 534
Ellis, A. L., 413
Ellis, P., 554
Ellyson, S. L., 95, 98, 104
Elman, M., 212
Emmerich, W., 218
Emswiller, T., 410
Endsley, R. C., 2, 202
England, P., 402, 403, 406,
 408, 420
English, D., 536, 537
English, L., 64
Epel, E. S., 56
Equal Employment
 Opportunity
 Commission, 504, 505
Erkut, S., 252
Ernster, V. L., 244
Eron, L. D., 214
Espin, O. M., 60, 283, 284,
 288, 301, 556
Esten, G., 561
Etaugh, C., 201, 217, 410,
 431
Etcoff, N. L., 82, 83
Ethridge, T., 217
Etter-Lewis, G., 42
Evans, C. C., 288, 289, 294
Evans, S. L., 417, 566
Exner, T. M., 299

Fabes, R. A., 197, 207, 208
Facio, E., 467
Faderman, L., 295
Fagot, B. I., 189, 198, 199,
 209, 217, 218, 225
Fain, T. C., 507
Fairhurst, G. T., 416
Falbo, T., 107, 304, 322
Falk, P. J., 385
Faludi, S., 10, 338, 352
Fankell-Hauser, J., 422
Farel, A., 431
Farmer, H. S., 134, 423, 424
Fassinger, R. E., 400, 413,
 430
Faulkner, A. O., 460
Faunce, P. S., 557
Faust, M. G., 246
Fausto-Sterling, A., 152,
 155, 157, 159, 163
Favreau, O. E., 17
Feagin, J. R., 101
Feather, N. T., 532
Federal Bureau of
 Investigation, 513
Federal Glass Ceiling
 Commission, 404
Feeney, J., 321
Fehr, B. J., 95
Feingold, A., 123

Feinman, S., 219
Feiring, C., 206, 207, 250
Feldman, D. C., 408, 409
Feldman, R. S., 96
Feldman, S., 225
Feldman-Summers, S., 410
Fenell, D. L., 323
Fennell, M. P., 221, 222
Fennema, E., 125, 127, 129
Fernandez, M., 512
Fernberger, S. W., 37
Ferns, T., 556, 571
Ferree, M. M., 394, 409, 420, 427, 428
Fidell, L. S., 412, 547, 549
Field, T., 379
Fields, J. P., 252
Fields, V., 469
Findlen, B., 563, 564, 573
Fine, M., 3, 97, 99, 131, 252, 254, 256, 257, 286, 293, 294, 379, 529, 570, 572
Finkel, J. S., 321
Finkelhor, D., 486, 487, 488, 489, 490
Finn, S., 327
Firestein, B. A., 297
First, A., 50
Fisher, E. R., 514
Fisher, J. D., 88, 274, 275
Fisher, W. A., 274, 275
Fiske, A. P., 80, 566
Fiske, S. T., 37, 67, 68, 69, 70, 80, 82, 83, 104, 566
Fitzgerald, L. E., 402, 403, 406, 408, 409, 412, 420, 421, 423, 426, 430, 432
Fitzgerald, L. F., 412, 428, 504, 505, 506, 507, 508, 509, 520, 545
Fivush, R., 196, 197, 218
Flanagan, D., 196, 197
Flanders, L., 348
Fleming, A. S., 321, 364
Fletcher, C., 202
Flett, G. L., 532
Flint, M., 447
Flitcraft, A., 512
Foa, E. B., 483
Foddy, M., 511
Fogas, B. S., 487
Foley, C. C., 286
Follingstad, D. R., 493
Ford, C. V., 547
Ford, K., 272, 273
Ford, M. R., 143
Fordham, S., 256
Foreit, K. G., 44
Forer, B. R., 554
Forrest, L., 426
Forste, R., 329, 330
Forward, J. R., 112
Foschi, M., 104
Foucault, M., 266
Fowers, B. J., 321
Fox, D., 2
Frame, C. L., 499
Francis, P. L., 67
Franco, J. N., 395
Frank, E., 291
Frank, H., 99, 100
Frankel, B. G., 221, 222
Franks, V., 525

Franz, E., 470
Frasher, R. S., 203
Frazier, P. A., 501
Fredrickson, B. I., 543
Fredrickson, B. L., 285
Freedman, E. B., 269, 296, 307
Freedman, R., 57, 58, 60, 447
Freeman, J., 78
Freeman, P. K., 107
Freeman, S., 104
Freud, S., 187
Frey, C., 214
Freyd, J., 485
Friday, N., 295
Fridell, S. R., 180
Friedman, A., 457, 463
Friedman, H., 67
Frieze, I. H., 15, 18, 19, 267, 323, 493
Frijda, N. H., 112
Frintner, M. P., 499
Frisch, R. E., 236, 237, 238
Frohart-Lane, K., 430
Frost, L., 125, 127
Fryer, M. M., 66
Fulkerson, J. A., 541
Funk, J. B., 214, 215
Furnham, A., 47
Furstenberg, F. F., Jr., 272, 379, 380
Furumoto, L., 5, 6, 26, 572
Futterman, R., 126

Gaertner, S. L., 88
Gagnon, D., 111
Gagnon, J. H., 266, 486, 487, 489
Gaines, J. A., 499
Gaiter, D., 423
Galambos, N. L., 260
Galessich, J. M., 417, 566
Gallagher, S., 467
Gallagher-Thompson, D., 533
Galler, R., 286
Galligan, R. F., 274
Gannon, L. R., 17, 445, 446, 447, 448, 449, 450, 452, 455, 476
Garcia, N., 328
Garcia-Falconi, R., 304
Garcia-Preto, N., 227, 559
Gardner, C. B., 506
Gardner, S., 423
Garfinkel, P. E., 58
Garland, A. W., 479
Garland, H., 411
Garner, D. M., 58, 366
Garovich, L., 74
Garst, J., 55
Garvey, C., 427
Garvin, V., 366
Gary, L. E., 473
Gaskill, L. R., 418
Gastil, J., 62, 63
Gauna-Trujillo, B., 366
Gauthier, R., 206
Gautier, T., 172, 173
Gayford, J. J., 495
Gaze, C. E., 55
Gebhard, P. H., 269, 271, 278, 297
Geis, F. L., 54, 95, 97, 105

Gelbein, M. E., 54
Gelfland, M. J., 504, 507, 508, 509
Gelles, R. J., 512, 513
Gelwick, B. P., 507
Genero, N. P., 18, 531
Gentile, D. A., 24
Gentry, M., 31, 289
George, F. W., 155
George, S. M., 383
Gergen, M. M., 461
Gerike, A. E., 441
Gersler, N., 467
Gerson, M., 353
Gerstel, N., 336
Gertz, L. M., 487
Geschwind, N., 160
Ghiz, L., 441
Giarrusso, R., 497
Gibber, J. R., 162
Gibbons, J. L., 56, 260
Gibbs, J., 527
Giddings, P., 383
Gidycz, C. A., 497, 498, 499, 503
Giedd, J. L., 508
Gieve, K., 385
Gilbert, L. A., 18, 327, 343, 395, 417, 418, 429, 430, 435, 552, 554, 566
Gilbert, M. S., 426
Gilbert, P., 452
Giles-Sims, J., 341
Gilgun, J. F., 488
Gillen, B., 67, 410
Gilles, F. H., 160
Gillespie, D. L., 94
Gilligan, C., 141, 145, 146, 255, 256
Gilmore, D. D., 33
Gilroy, F. D., 531, 547
Ginn, J., 464
Ginorio, A., 556
Giroux, H. A., 223
Gitelson, I. B., 260
Giuffre, P. A., 504
Glass, B., 80
Glenn, A. A., 538
Glenn, N. D., 463
Glick, P., 67, 68, 69, 70, 104
Goff, S. B., 126
Goffman, E., 98
Gold, A. R., 227
Gold, R. B., 357
Goldberg, C., 113
Goldberg, P. A., 411
Golden, C., 296, 298, 299
Golden, P., 251
Goldenhar, L. M., 428
Golding, J. M., 533
Goldman, D., 486
Goldman, K., 47
Goldman, S. L., 366
Goldman, W., 85
Goldstein, A. J., 526
Goldstein, D., 511, 513
Gold-Steinberg, S., 479
Golombok, S., 218, 384
Gomez, C. A., 273
Gondlof, E. W., 514, 516, 545
Gonzales, N., 257
Goodchilds, J. D., 497
Goodenough, D. R., 167
Goodman, L. A., 520, 545

Goodman, M., 180
Goodman, M. J., 447
Gordon, C., 77, 90
Gordon, J. S., 516
Gordon, J. W., 154
Gordon, L., 41, 489, 515
Gordon, S. L., 281, 282, 304, 309, 311, 312, 313, 322, 324, 326, 327, 328
Gordon, S. M., 131
Gorski, R. A., 159
Gorzalka, B. B., 268
Gottman, J. M., 212, 324
Gough, K., 309
Gould, S. J., 132, 133
Gove, W. R., 321, 336, 473
Gracely, E., 217
Grady, K. E., 16, 17, 79, 80, 120, 121
Graham, A., 62
Graham, J. A., 209
Graham, L., 196
Grambs, J. D., 459, 464, 465, 466, 477, 478
Granoff, B. J., 498
Gravenkemper, S. A., 422
Graves, D., 257
Gray, J. D., 430
Gray, M. W., 128
Green, J., 488
Green, R., 180
Greenberg, J. H., 411
Greenberg, M., 554
Greenberg, S., 465
Greene, A. L., 257
Greene, B. A., 27, 383, 551, 555, 557, 558, 560, 570
Greene, C. K., 427
Greenfeld, L. A., 485
Greenglass, E. R., 431
Greenspan, M., 550, 551, 552, 553, 554
Greenstein, T. N., 395
Greenwood-Audant, L. M., 336
Gremaux, R., 183
Gretzinger, J., 456
Griffin, D., 71
Griffin, J. E., 155
Griffin, S., 518
Grimm, D. E., 177, 178
Grisham, J., 303
Grogan, S., 55
Gross, R. T., 251, 258
Grossman, A. L., 62
Grossman, F. K., 18
Grossman, M., 455, 456, 457
Grote, N. K., 323
Grove, K., 257
Grove, S., 417, 418
Gruber, J. E., 428, 506, 507, 508, 509
Grundman, E. O., 510
Guerra, N. G., 213
Guilkey, D. K., 273
Guinier, L., 97
Guinn, S., 344
Gullette, M. M., 444, 480
Gutek, B. A., 319, 402, 405, 406, 409, 411, 412, 418, 420, 425, 430, 432, 506, 507, 509
Guthrie, G., 498
Guthrie, I. K., 207

Guthrie, R. V., 5
Gutierrez, L., 556
Gwartney-Gibbs, P. A., 493

Haavind, H., 344
Habif, V. L., 487
Hackel, L. S., 321, 364
Haddock, G., 70
Haden, C. A., 197
Hahn, D., 74
Haiken, E., 286
Haj-Yahia, M. M., 512
Hale, E. S., 244
Hale, G., 513
Hale, K. F., 411
Hall, J. A., 95, 547
Hall, N. L., 357, 365
Hall, R. L., 555
Hall, W. S., 73
Hall-McCorquodale, I., 390
Halpern, D. F., 131, 135
Hamberger, L. K., 512
Hamer, D. H., 158
Hamilton, J. A., 545
Hamilton, L. H., 251
Hamilton, M. C., 63, 64, 192
Hamilton, W. G., 251
Hamm, K. E., 107
Hammer, M., 192
Hammond, J. A., 426, 427
Hankin, B. L., 530, 531
Hanna, R., 56
Hansen, F. J., 547
Hanson, E. A., 256
Hanson, F. J., 321
Hanson, K. A., 503
Hardardottir, S., 56
Harding, S., 132
Hardon, A., 355
Hare-Mustin, R. T., 3, 16, 143, 147, 528
Harkness, W. L., 498
Harlan, S. L., 426, 427, 428
Harlow, H. F., 121, 162
Harnack, L., 395
Harrington, C. C., 425
Harris, B. J., 4
Harris, M. B., 96, 460, 467, 539, 540, 542
Harris, V. R., 558
Harrison, A. A., 56
Harrison, A. W., 421
Harrod, W. J., 98
Harter, S., 531
Hartl, D. L., 165
Hartung, C. M., 523, 525
Hartzler, K., 395
Hasbrouck, L., 543
Hashemi, S. M., 512
Hashimoto, T., 268
Haskett, R. F., 173
Haslam, N., 80, 566
Haslett, B. B., 411
Hatch, L. R., 440
Hatfield, E., 282
Hathaway, C. R., 488
Hatton, B. J., 301, 302
Haug, M. R., 459
Hawes, S. E., 18
Hawxhurst, D. M., 551, 553
Hay, D. H., 197
Hayes, C. D., 378

Hayes, C. L., 464
Hayes, L., 378
Hays, S., 347, 348
Healy, S., 437, 445
Heatherton, T. F., 66
Hebl, M. R., 66
Hecht, M. A., 95
Hechtman, S. B., 54
Hedges, L. V., 122
Hedley, M., 92
Hedlund, R. D., 107
Heesacker, M., 51
Heilman, M. E., 68, 69, 84, 110
Heimann, M., 197
Heisel, M. A., 460
Helgeson, V. S., 549
Hellman, K. R., 96
Helmcamp, A., 58
Helmreich, R. L., 39, 73, 422
Helson, R. M., 228, 462, 475, 477
Helwig, A. A., 206
Hemmer, J. D., 221
Hemstreet, A. H., 560
Henderson, J., 428
Henderson-Daniel, J., 555
Henley, N. M., 7, 9, 24, 63, 64, 78, 88, 93, 433
Henly, J. R., 380
Hennessy, C. H., 443, 467
Henry, C., 25
Henshaw, S. K., 357
Henton, J. M., 494
Henwood, K. L., 466
Herdt, G. H., 173, 174
Herek, G. M., 298
Herman, A., 432
Hernandez, D. G., 44
Hernandez-Sanchez, J., 304
Herring, F., 198
Herzberger, S. D., 60
Heszen, I., 105
Hetherington, E. M., 199
Hewlett, S. A., 313
Heywood, S., 309
Hickman, S. E., 502
Higginbotham, E., 412
Higgins, P. G., 366
Hilderbrand, M., 66
Hill, C. A., 67
Hill, C. E., 462
Hill, D. E., 54
Hill, E. J., 272, 273
Hill, J. P., 257, 258
Hill, M., 384
Hillier, L., 511
Hillman, J. L., 98
Hines, M., 155, 157, 165, 169, 170, 171
Hines, P. M., 227, 559
Hinkley, C., 376
Hiraga, Y., 257
Hirschhorn, K., 167
Hite, S., 277, 278, 289, 295
Ho, C. K., 556
Hobfoll, S. E., 364, 365
Hochschild, A. R., 315, 394, 395, 477, 568
Hochwarter, W. A., 421
Hock, E., 377
Hockenberry-Eaton, M., 293

Hoffman, C. D., 71, 79
Hoffman, J. C., 100
Hoffman, L. W., 225
Hoffman, S. D., 339
Hoffnung, M., 347
Hofman, M. A., 159
Hogg, M. A., 227
Hollabough, L. C., 290
Holland, D., 57
Holland, L., 499
Hollander, J. A., 320
Hollin, C. R., 234
Hollingworth, L. S., 351
Holmbeck, G. N., 257
Holmberg, D., 74
Holmstrom, R. W., 501
Holroyd, J., 554
Homel, R., 217, 226, 227
Homma-True, R., 556
Hooijberg, R., 419
Hooks, B., 293
Hopkins, J., 377
Hopp, C., 125, 127
Hoppe-Graff, S., 214
Horowitz, S. V., 425
Hort, B. E., 217, 218
Hoskins, M., 66
Hossain, Z., 395
Hotaling, G. T., 486, 490, 493, 494
Houseknecht, S. K., 353
Houser, B. B., 427, 463
Housley, P. C., 199
Houston, S., 506
Hovey, M., 512
Howard, J. A., 320
Howe, K. G., 390, 417
Howe, L. K., 409
Howell, M., 513
Howland, C. A., 286
Hrdy, S. B., 193
Hu, N., 158
Hu, S., 158
Hulin, C. L., 504, 507, 508, 509
Hume, A. L., 450
Humphrey, J. A., 498, 499, 500
Hunt, M., 277, 278
Hunter, B. A., 73
Hunter, G. T., 424
Hunter, J., 299
Hunter, M. S., 450
Hurlbert, D. F., 279
Hurrell, J. J., 428
Hurst, N., 79
Hurtig, A. L., 181
Huselid, R. F., 526
Huston, A. C., 200
Hutchins, T., 212
Hwang, N., 506
Hyde, J. S., 18, 55, 122, 124, 125, 127, 128, 131, 132, 133, 135, 220, 266, 271, 272, 274, 277, 278, 283, 284, 291, 297, 307, 357, 374, 376, 377, 378, 565
Hymel, S., 219

Idle, T., 202
Ihinger-Tallman, M., 340, 341
Imhoff, A. R., 394, 419

Imperato-McGinley, J., 172, 173
Iritani, B., 53, 72
Ishu-Kuntz, M., 440
Itzin, C., 463
Izraeli, D. N., 72, 102, 103

Jack, D. C., 531
Jacklin, C. N., 120, 121, 123, 188, 198, 207
Jackson, A. P., 381
Jackson, J. L., 487
Jackson, J. S., 420
Jackson, M., 270, 294
Jackson-Wilson, A. G., 558
Jacobs, A., 177
Jacobs, J. A., 423
Jacobs, J. E., 129, 130, 135
Jaffe, P. G., 495
Jalleh, M., 224
James, A., 556
James, J. B., 437, 475, 565
James, M. D., 542
Jamieson, K. H., 96, 107, 109
Jaranson, J. M., 486
Jarrahi-Zadeh, A., 366, 377
Jean, P. J., 3
Jenkins, R. R., 273, 535
Jennings, S., 54
Jensen, K., 44
Jessell, J. K., 497
Jesser, C. J., 303
Joffe, H., 275
Johan, P., 510, 514
Johansson, C., 449
John, B. A., 80
John, R., 443, 467
Johnson, B. T., 418
Johnson, C. E., 58
Johnson, J., 426, 430
Johnson, K. K. P., 262
Johnson, L., 507
Johnson, P. B., 497
Johnson, S. B., 17
Johnson, V., 270, 277, 292, 297, 366
Johnson-Sumerford, D., 316, 342
Johnston, I. K., 534
Johnston, L., 542
Joiner, G. W., 542
Joly, S., 73
Jones, M. A., 295
Jordan, J. V., 145, 146
Jorgensen, S. R., 378
Joseph, G. I., 257, 266, 283, 294, 295, 301, 349
Joseph, J., 514
Jost, J. T., 74, 83, 111, 419
Joyce, P., 488
Juraska, J. M., 157
Jutras, S., 468

Kaczala, C. M., 126
Kahn, A. S., 3, 27, 258, 565
Kahn, J., 273
Kaiser, K., 457
Kakar, S., 443
Kamo, Y., 468
Kane, E. W., 298
Kane, F. J., 366, 377
Kanekar, S., 501
Kanouse, D. E., 275

Kanter, R. M., 399, 400, 405, 409, 414, 418, 421, 425
Kantner, J. F., 272, 273
Kaplan, A. G., 145, 146, 553
Kaplan, M., 525, 550
Kaplan, M. M., 349
Kappes, M. E., 171
Kappes, M. H., 171
Karabenick, S. A., 89
Karau, S. J., 105, 108, 418
Karbon, M., 197
Kariuki, P. W., 457, 463
Karp, S. A., 501
Karraker, K. H., 196, 199
Karten, S. J., 103
Kashubeck, S., 542
Kasl-Godley, J., 56
Katz, B. L., 501
Katz, P. A., 190, 219, 225, 227
Kaufert, P. L., 447, 452
Kaufman Kantor, G., 511, 515
Kaw, E., 60
Keating, C. T., 96
Keats, J. G., 203
Keel, P. K., 541
Keita, G. P., 520, 533, 545
Keith, P. M., 477
Kelley, F. A., 413
Kelley, G., 498
Kelley, H. H., 303, 318
Kelly, E., 17, 58
Kelly, J. C., 499
Kelly, L., 504
Kelsey, T., 493, 494
Kemper, K. A., 258
Kendler, K. S., 540
Kennedy, C. W., 94, 328
Kennell, J., 376
Kenyon, R., 217
Kessler, R. C., 473
Kessler, S. J., 149, 171, 181, 182
Ketzenberger, K., 426
Kidd, A. H., 511
Kieffer, S. C., 54
Kiesler, S., 216
Kiesler, S. J., 410
Kiger, G., 315
Kiliansky, S. E., 104
Killip, S. M., 495
Kilpatrick, D. G., 509, 514
Kim, E. H., 402, 406
Kimball, M. M., 8, 117, 118, 134, 135, 137, 146, 147
Kimble, D. L., 274, 275
Kimes, D. D., 53, 72
Kimmel, D. C., 437, 440
Kimmel, E. B., 19, 29, 30, 565
Kimmel, M. S., 109
Kincaid-Ehlers, E., 442
King, C. P., 356
King, S., 243, 244
Kinsey, A. C., 269, 271, 278, 297
Kinsman, S. B., 272
Kinzer, S., 358
Kirchmeyer, C., 431
Kirkpatrick, C., 37
Kirsh, S. J., 214
Kishor, S., 193

Kissling, G., 493
Kite, M. E., 42, 67
Kitzinger, C., 296, 297, 300, 570
Kitzinger, S., 365
Klaus, M., 376
Kleiber, D. A., 221
Kleim, D. M., 95
Klemmack, D. L., 468
Kline, K. N., 360
Klingman, L. R., 498
Klonoff, E. A., 71, 408, 411, 412, 527
Kloska, D. D., 225
Knapp, J. R., 89
Knight, R. A., 503
Knott, J. A., 55
Knudson-Martin, C., 317
Kobrynowicz, D., 71, 110, 112, 540
Koch, L., 362
Koch, P. B., 428
Koeske, R. D., 19
Koff, E., 239, 240, 241, 257
Kohl, J. V., 154
Kohlberg, L., 141, 188, 189
Kohn, M., 428
Kohn, R., 510, 514
Kolata, G., 160, 168
Kong, M-E., 47, 50
Koomen, W., 112
Kopsky, W., 492
Kortenhaus, C. M., 205
Koss, M. P., 483, 492, 493, 496, 497, 498, 499, 501, 520, 545
Kosson, D. S., 499
Koster, B. A., 390
Koval, J., 494
Kowalski, R. M., 483, 484, 500
Kozlowski, J., 441
Kramarae, C., 7
Krames, L., 532
Kravetz, D., 551, 565
Krieger, S., 344
Krishnan, V., 192
Krol, P., 545
Kronenberg, F., 447
Ku, L. C., 260
Kuebli, J., 196
Kunda, A., 71
Kuo, E. C., 193
Kurdek, L. A., 326, 328, 339
Kurita, J. A., 220
Kyle, D. J., 65

La Freniere, P., 206
La Vite, C., 508
Laabs, J., 504
Lachman, M. E., 437, 475
Lackey, P. N., 227
Lafontaine, E., 508
LaFrance, M., 95
Lafreniere, K. D., 542
LaFreniere, P., 212
LaFromboise, T. D., 556, 561
Lake, M. A., 196
Lakoff, R., 60, 528, 529
Lambers, S. M., 67
Lambert, C., 440
Landa, A., 353
Landale, N. S., 331

Landrine, H., 41, 71, 408, 411, 412, 524, 525, 527, 560, 572
Laner, M. R., 443, 493
Langer, E. J., 368
Langhinrichsen-Rohling, J., 510
Lanktree, C., 64
LaPlante, M. N., 290
Laqueur, T., 151
Laren, D. S., 473
Larkin, J., 253
Larue, J., 44
LaRussa, G. W., 74
Larwood, L., 412
Lasater, T. M., 450
Latham, L., 498
Lauerman, J., 195
Laumann, E. O., 486, 487, 489
Lavin, J., 364, 365
Laws, J. L., 266
Laws, S., 533, 537, 538
Layman, M. J., 498
Leaper, C., 95, 210
Lears, M., 206
Leavitt, H. J., 400
LeBaron, D., 66
Lebowitz, L., 487
Lee, C. Y., 510
Lee, G. R., 322
Lee, J., 571
Lees, S., 241, 259
Lefebvre, L. M., 303
Leffler, A., 94
LeGuin, U. K., 373
Lehman, D., 111
Lehman, T. C., 88
Leiblum, S. R., 290, 291, 292
Leichty, G., 47
Leinbach, M., 218
Leinbach, M. D., 198, 199, 217, 224
Lembright, M. F., 428
Lemkau, J. P., 359, 423
Lenart, S., 11
Lennon, M. C., 450
Leon, G. R., 541
Leon, I., 207
Leonard, R., 213
Lerman, H., 551, 554, 555
Lerner, J. V., 260
Lerner, R. M., 260
Lerner, U., 449
Leslie, G. R., 319
Lester, R., 58
LeVay, S., 158, 159
Levenson, R. W., 324
Leventhal, E. A., 459
Levin, I., 341
Levine, M. P., 412, 413, 507
Levine, R., 268
Levine, T., 282
Lewin, M., 260
Lewis, C., 195
Lewis, I. A., 486, 490
Lewis, J., 257, 266, 283, 294, 295, 301
Lewis, L. L., 39, 40
Lewis, M., 206, 207, 250
Lewis, P., 85
Lewis, S., 298
L'Hommedieu, T., 338
Liben, L. S., 225

Lichter, D. T., 395
Lieblich, A., 127
Lindahl, L. B., 197
Linimon, D., 107
Linn, M. C., 122, 132, 133, 135
Linz, D., 503
Lipman, S., 411
Lipman-Blumen, J., 400
Lipov, E., 514
Lippard, L., 478
Lippman, J., 488
Lippman, W., 36
Liss, M. B., 201, 217
Little, J. K., 218
Liu, E. S., 382
Livingston, S. A., 123
Lloyd, E., 352
Lloyd, S., 494
Lloyd, S. A., 491
Lobel, T. E., 256
Locher, P., 41
Lock, M., 443, 447, 452
Lockheed, M. E., 212
Lofland, J., 113
Logothetis, M. L., 452, 455
Loiacano, D. K., 301
Lokey, H., 44
Long, J., 461, 462, 463, 467, 473
Long-Scott, E., 355
Lonsway, K. A., 502, 503
Lont, C. M., 261
Lopez, N., 379
LoPiccolo, J., 279
Lorber, J., 45, 46, 168, 348, 381, 391, 394, 402, 403, 404, 405, 415, 417, 428, 433, 434
Lorenzi-Cioldi, F., 83
Lott, B., 94, 221, 411
Lovas, G. S., 197
Lowe, R., 434
Lowell, E. L., 421
Lowery, C. R., 143
Lown, J. M., 341
Lowry, C. B., 180
Lu, Y., 343
Lublin, N., 357, 392
Luchetta, T., 17
Luckmann, T., 24
Lueptow, L. B., 74
Lueptow, M. B., 74
Lund, M., 527
Lundsteen, C., 167
Lupton, M. J., 241, 242, 245
Luria, Z., 209, 210, 211
Lutz, W. J., 377
Lykes, M. B., 556, 571
Lynch, J. M., 327
Lynch, L., 80
Lynch, M. E., 258
Lyndon, A., 499
Lyon, L., 195
Lytton, H., 196

Maas, F., 286
McCarthy, W. J., 7, 9
McCartney, K., 431, 432
McCaulay, M., 538
McClelland, D. C., 421
McCloskey, L. A., 210
Maccoby, E. A., 162, 213
Maccoby, E. E., 120, 123, 188, 189, 198, 203, 207

McCormick, J., 254, 256
McCormick, N., 290
McCormick, N. B., 295, 303
MacCorquodale, P., 288
McCreary, L., 402, 403, 406, 408, 420
McCullough, M., 566
McDermid, S. A., 180
MacDonald, B., 479
McDonald, C., 304
McDonald, T. W., 104, 417
McEwen, B. S., 151
MacFarlane, A., 374, 375
McFarlane, J. M., 534
McFarlin, D. B., 111
McGee, R., 530, 531
McGloshen, T. H., 472
McGoldrick, M., 227, 559
McGrath, E., 533
McGrath, J. E., 28
McGrath, S., 376
McGraw, K. M., 102, 103
McGuire, C. V., 91
McGuire, J., 196
McGuire, W. J., 91
McHenry, P. C., 334, 336, 337, 338
McHugh, M. C., 511
McHugh, M. D., 19
McIntosh, P., 570
McIntosh, W. D., 441
McKee, J. P., 37
McKeen, C. A., 418
McKenna, K. T., 286
Mackie, D. M., 83
McKinley, N. M., 55, 56, 124, 128
McKinney, K. A., 547
MacKinnon, C., 507
MacKinnon, C. A., 282
McLanahan, S., 463
McLean, C., 8
McMahon, M., 347, 350, 369
McMullin, J. A., 353
McNeill-Hawkins, K., 493
Maconachie, M., 516
MacPherson, K. I., 449, 453
Macpherson, P., 252, 257
McPhillip, J. B., 450
Madar, T., 66
Maddever, H. M., 487
Maddux, H. C., 244
Madigan, E. A., 381
Magley, V. J., 504, 505, 507, 508, 509
Magnuson, V., 158
Magnusson, D., 250
Mahler, H. I. M., 65
Mahoney, A. R., 317
Mahoney, C. W., 426, 427
Maibach, E., 293
Main, C. M., 542
Maing, D. M., 180
Major, B., 66, 111, 112, 224, 246, 357, 359, 419
Makepeace, J. M., 493, 494
Makhijani, M., 108, 418
Makosky, V. P., 433
Malamuth, N. M., 499
Malcuit, G., 199, 200
Malley, J. E., 340
Malloy, T. E., 274, 275
Malo, C., 381

Malone, J., 494
Malouff, J. M., 214
Malson, H., 248, 249
Maltz, D. N., 213
Mangan, K. S., 101
Manis, J., 430
Manis, M., 110
Manning, V., 527
Manning, W. D., 331
Mansfield, P. K., 428
Mantecon, V. H., 442
Maoz, B., 458, 480
Marcus, M., 377
Marecek, J., 3, 4, 16, 18, 19, 20, 27, 143, 147, 293, 327, 545, 551
Markens, S., 534
Markham, W. T., 204
Markides, K. S., 437
Marks, F., 252
Markson, E. W., 437, 441
Marshall, A., 399
Marshall, N. L., 430
Martell, R. F., 69
Martin, C. E., 269, 271, 278, 297
Martin, C. L., 197, 202, 207, 208, 218, 220
Martin, E., 244, 448, 454, 455
Martin, J., 158
Martin, K. A., 238, 239, 241, 242, 244, 245, 264
Martin, S. E., 426, 428
Martinez, R., 60
Martinson, B., 395
Mason, A., 493
Mason, D. O., 343
Masters, W. H., 270, 277, 292, 297, 366
Mathes, L., 105
Mathews, A. M., 470
Mathews, D., 170
Mathews, W. S., 187, 192, 203
Mattes, M. A., 446
Matthews, A. P., 313
Matthews, P. A., 493
Matthews, W. J., 494
Mauksch, H. O., 405, 431, 435
Mauldin, T., 216
Mauthner, N. S., 377
Mayberry, L. J., 366
Mayfield, B., 192
Mayo, K., 60
Maypole, D. E., 506, 509
Mays, V. M., 274, 420
Mazurek, C., 499
Mednick, S. A., 167
Meece, J. L., 126
Meeks, C. B., 216
Mellanby, A. R., 292
Mellstrom, D., 449
Meng, K., 7, 9
Mercer, R. T., 383
Messick, D. M., 83
Messner, M. A., 44, 219
Meston, C. M., 268
Meyer-Bahlburg, H. F. L., 169, 299
Michael, R. T., 486, 487, 489
Michaels, S., 486, 487, 489
Michel, Y., 60

Middlebrook, D. W., 179
Midgley, C., 126
Midlarsky, E., 71
Milkie, M. A., 396
Miller, B., 470
Miller, B. C., 272, 273
Miller, D. H., 357, 359
Miller, E. K., 44
Miller, E. M., 431, 435
Miller, J. B., 144, 145, 146, 147, 405, 531, 545, 547
Miller, M., 430
Mills, C. S., 498
Mintz, L., 538
Miranda, J., 531
Mirowsky, J., 312
Misovich, S. J., 274, 275
Mitchell, G., 198
Mitchell, V., 462, 475
Miura, I., 126
Mladinic, A., 67, 74
Modleski, T., 280
Moen, P., 430, 469
Moffat, M., 276, 280, 287, 289
Moffott, T. E., 530, 531
Moller, L. C., 201, 207, 219
Molloy, B. M., 60
Molm, L. D., 92
Money, J., 166, 170, 172, 174, 175, 295
Mongeau, P. A., 491, 493
Montemayor, R., 256
Montgomery, R. JV., 468
Mooney, L., 43
Moore, C. L., 157
Moore, D. W., 511, 515
Moore, K. A., 272, 379, 380
Moore, R. J., 513
Moorman, J. E., 310, 334
Morash, D., 197
Morgan, B. L., 286
Morgan, K. P., 116, 117, 221
Morgan, L. A., 339
Mori, D. L., 540
Morokoff, P., 291, 292
Morra, N. N., 506
Morris, J. T., 201
Morris, N. M., 272
Morrow, S. L., 551, 553
Motenko, A. K., 465
Moulton, J. M., 63
Mount, L., 91
Moynihan, D. P., 383
Muehlenhard, C. L., 105, 290, 303, 502
Mueller, K. A., 353
Mueller, P., 359
Mullen, P. E., 489
Murphy, B. C., 554
Murray, A. D., 207
Murray, S. B., 405
Murry-McBride, V., 273
Murstein, B. I., 330, 331
Mwangi, M. W., 47
Myers, B., 217
Myers, D. G., 118

Nacoste, R. W., 111
Nadler, A., 88
Nails, D., 143
Nallis, M., 207
Nanda, S., 184
Naples, N. A., 383
Nash, H. C., 427, 534

National Committee on Pay Equity, 402, 406, 408
Neale, M., 158
Nederend, S., 221
Needleman, R., 404, 405
Neidig, P., 510
Neil, C. C., 412
Nelson, A., 404, 405
Nelson, B. A., 545
Nelson, E. J., 374, 375
Nelson, H. L., 362
Nelson, T. E., 110
Neppi, T. K., 207
Neptune, D., 47, 50
Neto, F., 47
Nettles, S. M., 273, 379
Neuberg, S. L., 100
Neumark-Sztainer, D., 395
Nevid, J. S., 56, 285
Newman, E., 105
Newson, E., 216, 221
Newson, J., 216, 221
Newton, K. J., 274
Newton, N., 374
Newtson, R. L., 477
Nichter, M., 542, 543
Nicolson, P., 364, 370
Nieva, V. F., 402, 405, 406, 409, 411, 412, 418, 420, 425, 430, 432
Nigro, G. N., 54
Noble, B. P., 405
Nolen-Hoeksema, S., 532
Noll, S. M., 543
Noller, P., 321
Norris, P., 105, 106
Norton, A. J., 310, 334
Norton, K. I., 58
Norton, M. C., 272, 273
Nosek, M. A., 286
Notgrass, C. M., 498
Novack, D. R., 312
Novak, L. L., 312
Noy, A., 225
Nugent, B., 206
Nurss, J. R., 203

Oakley, A., 347, 365, 394, 535
Obermeyer, C. M., 193
Obradovich, S., 198
O'Brien, D., 7, 9
O'Brien, M., 200, 262
O'Bryant, S. L., 468, 470, 472
O'Connell, A. N., 417
O'Connell, M., 413
O'Connor, A., 221
Oden, M. H., 409
O'Donnell, L., 467, 468, 469, 470, 472
O'Donohue, W., 510
O'Farrell, B., 426, 427, 428
Ofosu, H. B., 542
Ogletree, R. J., 501
O'Keeffe, N. K., 492, 494
Okun, B. S., 193
Olasov, B., 483
O'Laughlin, M. A., 142
Olday, D., 493
Olds, T. S., 58
O'Leary, A., 549
O'Leary, K. D., 494

O'Leary, V. E., 41, 411
O'Leary-Kelly, A. M., 506
Oleiniek, L., 473
Olive, S., 58
Oliver, M. B., 278, 291
Oliver, S. J., 532
Olson, K. R., 95
Olweus, D., 483
Omark, D. R., 212
O'Neil, A. K., 221
Orbin, J. A., 104
Oropesa, R. S., 329
Orza, A. M., 431
Osterberg, T., 449
O'Sullivan, C. S., 499
Owen, D. R., 167
Owen, S. A., 355

Pack, S. J., 84
Padavic, I., 427
Padawer-Singer, A., 91
Padgett, D., 460
Padilla, P., 302
Paetzold, R. L., 506
Page, P., 460, 467
Paige, J. M., 235
Paige, K. E., 235
Palazzini, M., 44
Palmore, E. B., 440
Paludi, M. A., 411, 422,
    509, 510
Papanek, H., 399
Pardie, L., 17
Parke, R. D., 199
Parker, J. G., 212
Parker, S., 288, 289, 294,
    543
Parlee, M. B., 3, 5, 16, 19,
    120, 131, 457, 534
Parsons, T., 398
Pasley, K., 340, 341
Pastor, J., 254, 256
Pattatucci, A. M. L., 158
Patterson, E. T., 244
Patterson, M., 44
Patterson, W., 398
Payne, B., 437
Pearlman, S. F., 328, 444
Pearlstein, T., 510, 514
Pearson, T. A., 335
Pedersen, P., 494
Peirce, K., 260, 261
Pelligrini, A. D., 203
Pence, E., 516
Pendergrass, M. L., 161
Peplau, L. A., 19, 20, 281,
    282, 302, 303, 304,
    309, 311, 312, 313, 322,
    324, 326, 327, 328
Perdue, L., 58, 59
Perese, S., 197
Perez, J., 328
Perkins, H. W., 398
Perkins, K. E., 464
Perlmutter, J. C., 203
Perlstadt, H., 506
Perot, A., 506
Perry, D. G., 200, 213
Perry, J., 440
Perry, L. C., 200, 213
Perun, P. J., 402
Peters, D. K., 430
Petersen, A. C., 234, 239,
    242, 248, 250, 259,
    260

Peterson, B. E., 58, 59, 73
Peterson, C., 321
Peterson, E., 422
Peterson, J. L., 272, 379,
    380
Peterson, R. E., 172, 173
Peterson, R. F., 488
Peterson, S. H., 510
Petrakos, H., 197
Petrie, T. A., 58
Phares, V., 390
Pharr, R., 493
Phelps, F. A., 292
Phelps, G. C., 542
Philip, J., 167
Phillips, D., 431, 432
Phillips, L., 224, 248, 250,
    252, 253, 256, 262, 264
Phillips, N., 514
Phillips, R. D., 547
Phillips, S. D., 394, 419
Phillips, T., 441
Phillips, W. R., 506
Phillipson, C., 463
Phoenix, A., 352
Pichardo, M., 173
Pietromonaco, P. R., 430
Pike, K. M., 540, 542
Piliavin, J. A., 87
Pillard, R., 158
Pinciaro, P. J., 497
Pines, A. M., 457
Pinto, I., 47
Pipher, M., 232, 233, 253,
    472
Pitts, V. L., 501
Pizzamiglio, M. T., 91
Pleck, J. H., 260, 316, 428
Pliner, P., 539, 540
Plous, S., 47, 50
Plumb, P., 221, 260
Pogatshnik, L. W., 198
Polakow, V., 380, 381
Polek, D. S., 493
Polenko, K. A., 331
Pollack, S., 385
Pollitt, K., 360
Pomerleau, A., 199, 200
Pomeroy, W. B., 269, 271,
    278, 297
Ponse, B., 298
Pooler, W. S., 192
Popaleni, K., 253
Pope, K., 554
Popenoe, D., 329, 330, 339
Porter, K. L., 461, 462, 463,
    467, 473
Porter, N., 54, 95, 105, 554
Post-Gorden, J. C., 214
Poulin-Dubois, D., 217
Pour-El, M. B., 414
Powell, A. D., 258
Powell, L. C., 570, 572
Power, T., 195
Powlishta, K. K., 191, 201,
    207, 208, 213
Pratto, F., 285
Preston, K. E., 534
Price, S. J., 334, 336, 337,
    338
Priest, R. F., 417, 418
Prilleltensky, I., 2
Prilleltensky, O., 561
Prisbell, M., 501
Pryor, J. B., 508

Public Interest Directorate
    of the American
    Psychological
    Association, 359
Pufall, A., 413
Pugh, M. D., 102, 104
Pugliesi, K., 513
Purcell, D. W., 325
Purcell, P., 205
Purdy, L. M., 362
Puri, J., 279, 281
Pushkar-Gold, D., 470

Quatman, G. L., 51

Raag, T., 201
Rackliff, C. L., 201
Radan, A., 556, 571
Radford, J., 504
Radlove, S., 266, 291, 292
Radway, J. A., 280
Ragsdale, J. D., 398
Rainer, R. K., Jr., 421
Raines, R. S., 54
Rainwater, L., 380
Ralston, P. A., 460, 467
Ramos-McKay, J., 559
Randolph, S. M., 382
Rankin, E., 272, 274
Rasmussen, J. K., 486
Raudenbush, S. W., 430
Ray, D. C., 547
Raymond, J. G., 361, 362
Raymond, P., 508
Reddin, J., 410, 414
Reef, M. J., 253, 260
Reekie, L., 547
Reese, E., 197
Regan, P. C., 285
Reid, P. T., 17, 209, 227,
    379, 558, 572
Reilly, M. E., 327
Reineke, M. J., 34
Reinisch, J. M., 173
Reis, M., 470
Reitz, R., 454
Reitzel, D., 495
Renner, C., 25, 65
Renzetti, C. M., 11, 510
Repetti, R. L., 430
Repper, D. P., 110
Resnick, H. S., 514
Resnick, M. D., 378
Reuterman, N. A., 492,
    493, 494
Rheingold, H. L., 200
Rhoades, J. M., 364
Rhodes, K., 17
Rhodes, N., 103
Rhownnwa, N., 498
Ribich, F. D., 107
Rice, F. P., 491
Rice, J. K., 340, 551
Rich, A., 139, 296, 352, 365,
    368, 371
Rich, C., 479
Rich, M. K., 53
Richards, M., 195, 260
Richardson, D. C., 90
Richman, M. J., 293
Rickel, A. U., 272, 274
Rickert, E., 493
Riederle, M. H., 292
Riemer, J. W., 428
Rierdan, J., 239
Rieves, L., 58, 253, 254

Rigby, D. N., 554, 555
Riggs, D. S., 493, 494
Riley, A. P., 512
Riley, P. J., 315
Riley, S., 417
Rind, B., 486, 490
Rindfuss, R. R., 273
Rintala, D. H., 286
Risman, B. J., 23, 316, 342,
    349
Ritenbaugh, C., 543
Ritter, P. L., 251, 258
Rivera, L., 559
Rivero, T., 293
Rivers, C., 352, 354, 396,
    397, 398, 430, 431
Rizzo, F. G., 542
Roberts, A. R., 60
Roberts, D. E., 354
Roberts, E., 273
Roberts, T., 285
Robertson, S., 376
Robin, R. W., 486
Robinson, C. C., 201
Robinson, G. M., 63
Robinson, J. P., 396
Robison, J., 469
Rocchio, L. M., 411
Rock, D., 131
Rodasta, A. L., 214
Rodeheaver, D., 445
Rodgers, C. S., 290
Rodin, J., 366, 538
Rodriguez, C., 224
Roff, L. L., 468
Rogers, R., 58
Romer, D., 272
Romkens, R., 510
Romney, D. M., 196
Roopnarine, J. L., 200, 395
Root, M. P. P., 51, 526, 542,
    556
Rosario, M., 299
Roscoe, B., 493, 494, 495
Roscoe, W., 182, 183
Rose, H., 202
Rose, S., 267
Rosenberg, B. G., 220
Rosenberg, F. R., 252, 258
Rosenberg, J., 506
Rosenberg, R., 6
Rosenblum, K. E., 22, 25
Rosenbluth, S., 304
Rosenbluth, S. C., 305
Rosenfeld, M., 224
Rosenkrantz, P. S., 38, 547
Rosenthal, I. M., 181
Rosenthal, N. B., 565
Rosenthal, R., 54
Rosenwasser, S. M., 398
Ross, D. F., 198
Ross, K. E., 312
Ross, L., 54
Rosser, P., 131
Rossi, C. D., 286
Rossman, K. M., 418
Rostosky, S. S., 451
Roter, D. L., 547
Roth, S., 487, 501
Rothblum, E. D., 526
Rothman, B. K., 360
Roufail, M., 98
Rousso, H., 286
Rubenstein, D., 291
Rubin, D. B., 167

Rubin, G., 266
Rubin, K. H., 219
Rubin, R. M., 465
Rubin, R. T., 173
Rubinson, L., 499
Rubio-Stipec, M., 559
Ruble, D. N., 239, 321, 364
Ruddick, S., 229
Ruddle, F. H., 154
Ruder, A., 428
Ruderman, A. J., 82, 83
Rudman, L. A., 54, 104
Ruggiero, J. A., 51
Ruggiero, K. M., 112
Running Wolf, 556
Russell, L. G., 344
Russell, M., 514
Russett, C. E., 132
Russo, N. E., 426, 430
Russo, N. F., 2, 5, 15, 18, 350, 406, 417, 483, 520, 533, 545, 547
Rust, P. C., 297, 299
Ruth, S., 370
Rutledge, L. L., 493
Ryan, K. M., 493
Ryan, L., 513
Ryan, M., 11, 125, 127
Ryan, W., 433
Ryan-Finn, K., 257

Sack, A. R., 491
Sadker, D., 23, 124, 125, 131, 421
Sadker, M., 23, 124, 125, 131, 421
Saeed, L., 56
Safir, M. P., 127, 128
Sagrestano, L. M., 98
Sagy, S., 463
St. Ange, M. C., 227
Samelson, M., 258
Samil, R. S., 447
Sanchez, L., 363, 395
Sanchez-Hucles, J., 27, 555, 557, 570
Sanders, G. S., 87
Sands, R. G., 97
Sang, B., 476
Sanger, S. P, 112
Sangren, P. S., 34
Sapiro, V., 205, 380, 381
Sapp, S. G., 98
Sappington, A. A., 493
Sarantakos, S., 339
Sargent, J. D., 66
Sargent, R. G., 224, 258
Sato, S., 268
Satterfield, A. T., 105
Saunders, B. E., 514
Saunders, D. G., 512
Sawyer, R. G., 497
Saxe, L., 57
Sayers, J., 244
Sbordone, R. J., 547
Scanzoni, J., 313
Scanzoni, L., 313
Scarborough, E., 5, 6, 26, 572
Scardino, T. J., 303
Scarr, S., 431, 432
Schafer, A. T., 128
Schellenberg, E. G., 73
Schippers, M., 298

Schlaffer, E., 506
Schleicher, T. L., 104, 417
Schlesinger, B., 321, 323, 324
Schlossberg, N. K., 474
Schmidt, T., 87
Schneider, K. T., 504, 509
Schneider, M. S., 327
Schnellman, J., 56
Schnitzer, P. K., 557
Schoen, R., 312
Schuler, S. R., 512
Schulman, G. I., 66
Schulsinger, F., 167
Schultz, M. R., 60
Schulz, J. H., 465
Schur, E. M., 99
Schuster, M. A., 275
Schutte, N. S., 214
Schvaneveldt, P., 272, 273
Schwartz, D., 58
Schwartz, I., 275
Schwartz, L. A., 204
Schwartz, M. D., 433, 501, 514
Schwartz, P., 266, 275, 297, 310, 312, 313, 315, 316, 317, 318, 319, 325, 326, 327, 330, 339, 340, 342, 343, 344, 345
Schwarz, D. F., 272
Sciaraffa, A., 201
Scott-Jones, D., 273, 379
Seagor, M. V., 410
Seales, L. M., 501
Searles, P., 502
Sears, D. O., 16
Sebrechts, J., 565
Seccombe, K., 440
Sechzer, J. A., 15, 18
Segrist, D., 17
Seksaria, V., 501
Selkow, P., 131
Sen, A., 193
Senn, C. Y., 73, 542, 543
Senneville, C., 470
Serbin, L. A., 201, 207, 212, 217
Severne, L., 456
Shachar, S. A., 430
Shaffer, J. W., 166
Shakin, D., 199
Shakin, M., 199
Shea, C., 124
Shehen, C. L., 319
Shen, H., 513
Shen, Y. C., 395
Shepard, K., 218
Shepard, M., 516
Shepard, S. A., 207
Sherif, C. W., 3, 5, 19, 28, 78
Sheriffs, A. C., 37
Sherk, D. L., 84
Sherman, J. A., 126, 129
Sherman, M. F., 531
Sherman, P. J., 74
Shestakov, D., 516
Shields, S. A., 6, 132, 133, 135, 390
Shin, H-C., 336, 473
Shipman, G., 238
Shkodriani, G. M., 260
Showalter, E., 535, 536, 537

Shrout, P., 559
Shuster, R., 297, 299
Siegal, D. L., 449, 450, 454, 466, 471, 472, 474, 480
Siegel, J. M., 498
Siegel, R. J., 474
Siever, M. D., 543
Sigelman, C. K., 106, 107
Sigelman, L., 106, 107
Sigmundson, H. K., 175
Signorella, M. L., 225
Signorielli, N., 46, 54, 206, 213
Silber, D. E., 501
Silva, P. A., 530, 531
Silver, D., 430
Silverberg, S. B., 321
Silverstein, B., 58, 59
Silverstein, L. B., 41, 390, 391, 432
Silverstein, L. R., 538
Silverstone, E., 239
Simmons, R. G., 250, 252, 253, 258, 259, 260
Simon, B. L., 332, 333
Simon, M. C., 69, 110
Simon, W., 266
Simon-Roper, L., 487
Simpson, G., 424
Simpson, T. L., 486
Sims, C., 543
Sims, M., 212
Sinclair, L., 71
Sing, R., 252
Singer, J. M., 126
Singer, L. T., 381
Sink, C. R., 303
Sinnett, L. M., 416
Skaine, R., 506
Skinner, D., 57
Skover, D. M., 55
Skrypnek, B. J., 85
Skucha, J., 463
Slaby, R. G., 213
Sleek, S., 385
Smith, B., 243
Smith, C., 486, 490, 493
Smith, D. M., 100
Smith, E. A., 272
Smith, J. B., 510
Smith, K., 273
Smith, L., 44
Smith, M., 369, 381, 382
Smith, M. D., 506
Smith, P. A., 71
Smith, P. H., 510
Smith, P. K., 218
Smith, S. M., 441
Smith, V., 143
Smith-Lovin, L., 95
Smith-Rosenberg, C., 295, 536, 537
Smolak, L., 542
Snavely, B. K., 416
Snell, W. E., 304
Snizek, W. E., 412
Snow, J. T., 539, 542
Snow, M. E., 198
Snyder, M., 83, 84, 85
Snyder, R. C., 413, 543
Sobolewski, C. G., 302
Sociedade, P., 41
Sockloff, A., 217
Sockloskie, R., 7, 9, 499
Sohi, B. K., 561

Sohoni, N. K., 193
Sommers-Flanagan, J., 51
Sommers-Flanagan, R., 51
Sonenstein, F. L., 260
Sophie, J., 554
Sorenson, S. A., 514
Sorenson, S. B., 498, 513
South, S. J., 334
Southworth, J., 355
Spain, D., 310, 313, 329, 331, 334
Spanakos, A., 56
Spanier, G. B., 329
Sparkes, K., 227
Spence, J. T., 39, 73, 74, 422
Spielman, S., 413
Sprafkin, C., 212
Sprecher, S., 275, 303
Sproull, L., 216
Spurlock, J., 467, 473
Stack, C. B., 143
Stacy, R. D., 501
Stake, J. E., 126
Stangor, C., 80, 321, 364
Stanley, J. C., 124, 128
Stanley, J. P., 287
Stark, A. C., 25, 65
Stark, E., 512
Starzomski, A., 513
Statham, A., 431, 435
Stead, B. A., 87
Steele, B. F., 486
Steiger, J., 566
Steil, J. M., 98, 305, 310, 313, 314, 317, 318, 320, 321, 322, 327, 343, 344, 429, 430, 431, 432, 515
Stein, N., 254
Stein, R. M., 107
Steinberg, L., 321
Steinem, G., 26, 567
Steinke, S. A., 390
Steinmann, A., 313
Steketee, G. S., 483
Sterk, H. M., 372
Stermac, L., 483
Stern, M., 199
Sternglanz, S. H., 199
Stevens, G., 423
Stevens, L. E., 70, 80
Stevens-Long, J., 475
Stewart, A. J., 340, 479
Stewart, L., 205
Stewart, S., 476
Stiles, D., 56
Stiles, D. A., 260
Stipp, H., 503
Stitt-Gohdes, W. L., 427
Stiver, I. P., 145, 146
Stivers, M. L., 67
Stock, L. J., 501
Stock, W. E., 279
Stockard, J., 258, 493
Stocking, M., 167
Stoiadin, L. F., 87
Stolberg, R., 559
Stoller, L., 508
Stoller, S., 379
Stoltenberg, J., 8
Stone, A. J., 334, 338
Stone, M., 256
Stong, J., 395
Stopeck, M. H., 84
Storms, M. D., 67

Story, M., 395
Strachan, M. D., 55
Strattin, H., 250
Straus, M. A., 511, 512, 513, 515
Strayer, F. F., 206
Strayer, L. A., 411
Stricker, L., 131
Strickland, B. R., 450, 533
Striegel-Moore, R. H., 366, 538, 540, 542
Strommen, E. F., 383
Stueve, A., 467, 468, 469, 470, 472
Sturla, E., 172, 173
Suderman, M., 495
Sugarman, D. B., 493, 494
Suh, M., 511
Sullivan, C. M., 533
Sullivan, L., 470
Summit, R., 487
Surrey, J., 531
Surrey, J. L., 145, 146
Sussman, L. E., 80, 110
Sutherland, E., 422
Swaab, D. F., 159
Swan, S., 102, 504, 505, 506, 507, 509
Swann, W. B., Jr., 84, 85
Swanson, N. G., 428
Swarz, N., 105
Swim, J. K., 73
Swim, J. R., 102

Tajfel, H., 91, 113
Talbert, L., 272
Tanfer, K., 329, 330
Tangri, S., 507
Tanke, E. D., 85
Tannen, D., 57
Tashakkori, A., 258
Tasker, F. L., 384
Tate, C. C., 209
Taylor, C. A., 441
Taylor, C. J., 440
Taylor, D. M., 112
Taylor, M. G., 212, 218
Taylor, R. L., 310, 334, 336
Taylor, S. E., 82, 83, 368, 501
Taylor, S. P., 90
Tazeau, Y. N., 533
Teachman, J. D., 331
Teitelbaum, P., 132
Tennstedt, C., 470
Terman, L. M., 409
Terry, D. J., 274
Testa, M. H., 359
Tevlin, H. E., 290, 291, 292
Thelen, R. E., 510
Theriault, S. W., 74
Thibault, J. S., 318
Thoits, P. A., 343, 344
Thomas, C. D., 494
Thomas, D. B., 107
Thomas, V. G., 124, 542
Thompson, E. H., 493
Thompson, J. K., 224
Thompson, M., 58
Thompson, S., 379
Thompson, S. H., 224, 258
Thompson, S. K., 218
Thompson, T. L., 205, 206
Thomson, E., 363

Thorn, G., 510
Thornberry, O. T., 251
Thorne, B., 208, 209, 210, 211, 213, 214, 245
Tiefer, L., 19, 265, 271
Tjaden, P., 498
Tobin, M., 440
Tobin-Richards, M. H., 248, 250
Todd, J., 457, 463
Tollefsrud, K., 501
Tolman, R. M., 510
Toner, B. B., 532
Tong, R. P., 7
Tontodonato, P., 493
Torrey, J. S., 446
Torrez, D. J., 560
Toth, E., 241, 242, 245
Tougas, F., 73
Tovey, S. L., 487
Town, J. P., 84, 410
Tragos, L. M., 260
Trapnell, P. D., 268
Trasciatti, M. A., 356
Travis, C. B., 145, 285, 447, 451, 546, 547, 548, 549
Travis, T. M. C., 22, 25
Treadway, C. R., 366, 377
Tredeau, L., 508
Treichler, P. A., 7
Trends in Education, 5
Trent, K., 334
Tripp, J. H., 292
Troll, L. E., 474
Tromborg, C., 198
Tromovitch, P., 486, 490
Tronto, J. C., 143
Trost, J., 329, 330
Trotter, K. H., 227
Tsui, L., 408
Tubman, J. T., 260
Tucker, J. S., 62
Tulloch, J. C., 516
Tulloch, M. I., 516
Tunstall, A., 493
Turetsky, B. A., 321, 322, 344
Turk, J. L., 317
Turner, J., 58
Turner-Bowker, D. M., 205
Twenge, J. M., 10, 74
Tyree, A., 494

Udry, J. R., 272
Ullman, J. C., 426, 427, 428
Ullman, S. E., 503
Umberson, D., 473
Underwood, J., 298
Unger, R. K., 2, 5, 17, 18, 19, 20, 21, 22, 24, 27, 28, 41, 42, 56, 66, 79, 87, 93, 112, 119, 120, 133, 135, 157, 160, 161, 213, 227, 228, 332, 352, 353, 422, 458, 526, 571, 573
United Nations, 193, 310, 312, 358, 402, 404
U.S. Department of Health and Human Services, 378
U.S. Merit Systems Protection Board, 506, 507, 509

Upchurch, D. M., 513
Uranowitz, S. W., 83
Urberg, K. A., 219
Ussher, J., 288, 293, 363, 364, 365, 366, 368, 370, 451, 452, 453, 533, 534, 535

Valian, V., 403, 408, 413, 419, 420, 423, 568, 573
Van Cleave, E. F., 259
van der Heuvel, H., 112
van der Kolk, B., 545
Van Zyl, M., 516
Vance, C. S., 266, 307, 518
Vance, E. B., 277
Vanek, J., 394, 395, 397
Vanoss-Martin, B., 273
Vasquez, M. J. T., 556
Vaughter, R., 566
Vedovato, S., 566
Veilleux, F., 468
Verderber, K. S., 11
Verma, J., 268
Vernon, J. A., 441
Veroff, J., 321, 331, 422
Vicary, J. R., 428, 498
Vida, V., 295
Videka-Sherman, L., 460
Vigorito, A. J., 50
Vinick, B. H., 464
Vobejda, B., 357
Voda, A. M., 448, 452
Voelkl, K., 111
Vogel, D. A., 196
Vogel, S. R., 38, 547
von Baeyer, C. L., 84
von Bargen, D., 203
Voyer, D., 173
Vredenburg, K., 532
Vuckovic, N., 542, 543

Wagner, D., 105
Wagner, N. N., 277
Wahl, J., 41
Wahrman, R., 102, 104
Wajcman, J., 400, 403, 404, 405, 408, 414, 417, 420, 429
Walbrick, K., 58
Waldo, C. R., 507
Walker, L., 514, 569
Walker, L. J., 143, 514
Walker, S., 219, 227
Walkerdine, V., 223, 572
Wallen, K., 157, 162
Wallston, B. S., 16, 17, 41, 84, 410, 411
Walsh, P. V., 225
Walster, E., 65
Walters, E. E., 540
Walum, L. R., 87
Walzer, S., 363, 364
Wandersman, A., 274
Ward, J. V., 257
Warren, L. W., 451
Warren, M. P., 236, 251, 258
Watson, G., 550
Watson, M. S., 356
Watts, B., 505
Wayland, K., 501
Weaver, T. L., 514

Weber, J. C., 326, 328
Weber, L., 22, 412
Weinraub, B., 441
Weinraub, M., 217
Weinstein, A., 499
Weis, L., 570, 572
Weiss, L. H., 274
Weiss, M. R., 221
Weiss, R. J., 213
Weisstein, N., 3
Weitz, R., 41
Weitz, S., 95
Weitzman, L. J., 424, 425, 568
Welch, S., 107
Wells, J. D., 364, 365
Wells, M., 492, 495
Weltman, K., 320
Werner, P. D., 74
Wertz, D. C., 360
Wesley, B., 493
West, C., 313
Wester, S. R., 51
Westney, O. E., 273
Weston, L. C., 51
Whalen, P., 413
Wheatstone-Dion, R., 105
Whitam, F., 158
Whitam, F. L., 302
Whitbourne, S., 394, 396
Whitcher-Alagna, S., 88
White, A. J., 200
White, B., 514
White, C., 8
White, D., 195
White, J. W., 98, 285, 483, 484, 492, 493, 498, 499, 500
Whiting, B. B., 208, 226
Whitley, , B. E., Jr., 532
Whittaker, K. E., 279
Whittington, F., 437
Wichstrom, L., 530, 531
Widiger, T. A., 523, 525
Widmayer, S., 379
Wiest, W. M., 277
Wilcox, S., 422
Wild, J., 180
Wilder, D. A., 79
Wiley, D., 273
Wilkinson, S., 4, 5, 570
Willemsen, T. M., 261
Williams, C., 143
Williams, C. L., 504
Williams, J., 550
Williams, J. A., Jr., 441
Williams, J. E., 35, 36, 72, 74
Williams, J. R., 112
Williams, K., 180
Williams, K. B., 508
Williams, K. R., 512
Williams, L. S., 361, 362
Williams, N., 395
Williams, P. J., 283
Williams, R., 11
Williams, S. S., 274, 275
Williams, T. M., 534
Williams, W. L., 183
Willmott, L., 561
Wilson, A., 177, 302
Wilson, B. J., 503
Wilson, D. M., 123, 124, 125

Wilson, J., 441
Wilson, J. D., 155
Wilson, M., 514
Wilson, R. W., 251
Wilson-Smith, D. N., 220
Winch, G., 256
Winfield, L., 413
Wink, P., 477, 478
Winkel, W., 503
Winter, D. G., 73
Winton, W., 39, 40, 91
Wisniewski, N., 497, 498, 499
Wisocki, P. A., 54
Witkin, H. A., 167
Wittig, M. A., 11, 434
Wolf, S., 487
Wolfe, D. M., 317
Wolman, C., 99, 100
Women's Action Collective, 567
Women's Programs Office, 4

Wong, L. M., 570, 572
Wood, A. D., 511
Wood, E., 202
Wood, K. C., 224
Wood, W., 103
Woodward, S., 447
Wooldredge, J., 312
Wooley, H. T., 6
Wooley, O. W., 538, 539
Wooley, S. C., 538, 539
Woollett, A., 195, 352
Woolsey, M., 501
Worell, J., 4, 19, 21, 573
Workman, J. E., 262
World Wire, 358
Worth, D. M., 493
Wortman, C. B., 473
Wosinska, W., 105
Wrench, D., 417
Wu, C., 60
Wyatt, G. E., 292, 486, 498
Wyche, K. F., 551, 555

Wyer, R. S., Jr., 102
Wynn, R. L., 202

Yablon, G., 303
Yama, M. F., 487
Yanovski, S. Z., 541
Yarkin, K. L., 84, 410
Yasinski, L., 553
Yee, D., 460
Yee, P. H. N., 111
Yllo, K., 511
Yoder, J. D., 27, 104, 353, 416, 417, 418, 508, 565
Young, A. M., 321
Young, E. W., 428
Young, I. M., 365
Young, J. L., 451
Young, M. E., 286
Young, M. H., 272, 273
Youngblut, J. M., 381

Zak, A., 304
Zane, N., 379

Zanna, M. P., 70, 84
Zebrowitz, L. A., 67
Zelditch, M., 93
Zellman, G. L., 497
Zelnik, M., 272, 273
Zerbinos, E., 205, 206
Zernike, K., 113, 114
Zhao, L., 98
Zhu, L., 68, 70
Zimmerman, M. K., 451, 452
Zimostrad, S., 513
Zinkhan, G. M., 87
Zita, J. N., 445
Zlotnick, C., 510, 514
Zubek, J., 224, 246
Zucker, K. J., 180, 220
Zuckerman, M., 54
Zweig, J. M., 498, 502

Subject Index

Abortion, 356–360
  anti-abortion protests, 357
  cross-cultural view, 357–358
  legal decisions related to, 357
  pro-choice, 354
  psychological effects, 359–360
  selective abortion, 360
  sex-selective abortion, 193–195
Achievement-oriented women,
    421–426
  achievement motivation, 421–422
  characteristics related to, 423–426
  ethnic/racial groups, 426
  midlife achievement, 474–475
  and mother-daughter relationship,
    228–229, 273, 424
  and singlehood, 332
  and women's expectations,
    419–420
Acquaintance sexual assault, 495–504
  effects on victim, 501–502
  frequency of, 497–498
  gang rape, 499
  miscommunication excuse, 500
  prevention of, 502–504
  rapist, profile of, 498–501
  risk factors, 498
  and sexual precedence, 497
Addams, Jane, 536
Adolescence
  activities and self-esteem, 252
  dating, effects of, 258–259
  difficulties for women, 232–233
  gender role intensification, 258–259
  male/female hostilities, 259–260
  media effects, 260–261
  media support for, 262
  parent-child conflict, 256–257
  puberty, 234–241
  self-esteem decline, 253, 255, 258
  self-silencing during, 255–256
  sexuality in, 271–275
  teen-age mothers, 378–380
Advertising and sexism
  drug advertisements, 548–549
  effects of, 54–56
  magazines, 47–50
  television commercials, 47
Affective traits, types of, 38

Affirmative action, opponents of, 73
Afghanistan, restrictions on women,
    35
African-American women. *See also*
    Racial/ethnic groups; Racism
  achievement-orientation, 257, 426
  adolescent sexuality, 273
  age/aging, 460
  battered women, 514
  body image, 252, 542
  body weight, 60–61, 66, 251
  depression, 532
  gender stereotypes, 41–42
  grandmothers, 467
  health status, 560
  lesbian, 301–302
  marriage, 313
  media stereotyping of, 43, 50, 51, 52
  mental health treatment, 555, 558
  mother-daughter relationship, 257
  motherhood, 349, 382–383
  osteoporosis, 449
  sexuality, 268, 283
  teenage pregnancy, 379
  white beauty standards, 60–61
Age/aging. *See also* Midlife
  cross-cultural view, 442–443
  double standard, 436–441
  family caregiving, 467–472
  grandmotherhood, 466–467
  media discrimination, 440–441, 476
  menopause, 444–457
  and physical attractiveness, 440
  and political activism, 477–479
  racial/ethnic groups, 460
  reentry woman, 474–475
  research bias, 443–444
  retirement, 463–464
  sexist language related to, 437–438
  and sexuality, 440, 475–476
  social construction of, 436–437
  social support, 460, 476–477
  widowhood, 472–474
  women and poverty, 465–466, 473
Aggression, 213–216
  animal studies of, 121, 162
  and computer games, 214–216
  sexually aggressive men, 499–501
  social constructions of, 89–90

Aggression—*Cont.*
  social learning theory, 188,
    213–214
  successful aggression, effects of,
    213–214
Agoraphobia, 526
AIDS, prevention strategy, 275
Albright, Madeline, 108
5-alpha-reductase deficiency, 172–174
Ambivalent sexism, 67–68
  elements of, 68
American Association of Retired
    Persons (AARP), 479
American Association of University
    Women's Educational
    Foundation, 262
American Girl Magazine, 262
American Psychological Association
    (APA)
  Division of the Psychology of
    Women, 5, 6, 19–20
  nonsexist language guidelines, 26
Androcentric, meaning of, 3
Androgen, 154–155
Androgen insensitivity, 171–172
Anorexia nervosa, 535
  characteristics of, 540
Aphrodite, 34
Artemis, 34
Arts-related activities, and self-
    esteem, 252
Ascribed status, 92–93
Asian-American women. *See also*
    Cross-cultural view;
    Racial/ethnic groups
  achievement-orientation, 426
  age/aging, 460
  lesbians, 302
  mental health treatment, 555–556
  osteoporosis risk, 449
  sexuality, 268, 284
  stereotyping in media, 51
  white beauty standards, 60, 61
  in workforce, 402
Association for Women in
    Psychology, 5
Athena, 34
Attitudes toward Women Scale,
    73–74

Attributions
    achievement and women, 410–412
    attributional bias and gender,
        83–84
    blaming the victim, 84
    and gender stereotypes, 65–67
    of homosexuality, 66–67
    meaning and function of, 65
    and physical appearance, 56–57,
        65–67, 85

Backlash, against feminism, 10–14
Baehr, Ninia, contributions of, 325,
    569
Barbie doll, 58, 216, 224, 246
Battered woman's syndrome, 514,
    545
Battered women's movement, 516
Beauty pageants, for children,
    222–223
Beauty standards. *See* Physical
    attractiveness
Behavioral confirmation, meaning of,
    85
Behavioral theory, gender cognition,
    218–219
Benevolent sexism, 67–68
Berdache, 182–183, 302
17-beta-hydroxysteroid
    dehydrogenase deficiency,
    172–174
Bias, in traditional research, 14–18
Binge-eating disorder, 540–541
Biological determinism, and mental
    disorders, 533–535
Biological factors. *See* Genetic factors
Bisexuals
    feminist view of, 297
    self-identification of, 299
    traditional views of, 296–297
Black women. *See* African-American
    women
Blaming the victim, 84, 544
Blond hair, 53, 65
Blue-collar workers, women, 426–428
Bodybuilders, female, 45
Body image
    and adolescent women, 246–250
    African-American women, 252, 542
    and depression, 531
    and eating disorders, 543
    gender-blending lesbians, 179–181
    lesbians, 543
    media stereotype effects, 55–56
    and menarche, 239–241
    and pregnancy, 366–367
    and sexual identity development,
        180
Body-ism, stereotypes in media, 53–54
Body weight
    and African-American women,
        60–61, 66, 251
    distortions, 58
    eating disorders, 59, 249, 525–527,
        538–543
    gain in puberty, 235–237, 246–250
    media influences, 57–58
    and social stigma, 66, 538–540
    thinness, perceived value of,
        248–249
Brain
    gender differences research,
        132–133, 160–161
    lateralization differences, 160–161

Brain—*Cont.*
    of left-handed, 160
    sexual differentiation of, 156–157
    and sexual orientation, 158–159
Breast development
    adolescent feelings about, 245–246
    puberty, 235–236
British Psychological Society,
    Psychology of Women Section, 5
Buechner, Sara, 176–177
Bulimia, characteristics of, 540
Bush, Barbara, 399

Calkins, Mary, 26, 572
Career development
    achievement orientation, 421–426
    expectations of women, 419–420
    lesbians, 426, 430
    math/science/technology careers,
        134–135, 421, 424
    and technology-related skills, 421
    and values, 420–421
Caregiving and women
    and aging parents. *See* Family
        caregiving
    relational work, 398–399, 405
    self-development and women,
        137–139, 349
Cartoons, gender stereotypes in,
    205–206
Central nervous system, sexual
    differentiation in, 156–157
Cesarean births, 374–375
Chase, Cheryl, contributions of, 168,
    570
Chesler, Phyllis, contributions of,
    524, 569
Childbirth, 370–378
    cesarean births, 374–375
    family-centered birth, 375–376
    Lamaze method, 375–376
    medicalization of, 372–375
    postpartum depression, 376–378
    social construction of, 371–372
Childhood sexual abuse, 485–490
    consequences for victim, 488–490,
        544–545
    definition of, 486
    men as perpetrators, 487
    and mothers, 488
    preconditions to abuse, 487
    prevention of, 490
    and racial/ethnic groups, 486
    repressed memories issue, 489
    risk factors for victims, 487–488
    statistical information, 486
Children
    hyperfeminization of, 222–225
    and maternal employment, 431–432
    model of women as, 45–46, 62
    sissies and tomboys, 219–222
Child support, 338
China, abortion in, 358
Chromosomes
    same-sex orientation, 158
    sex determination, 154, 155
Cigarette smoking, and weight
    concerns, 249–250
Civil Rights Act of 1964, Title VII,
    504–505
Clinton, Hillary, 399
    news media focus, 44
Clitoridectomy, 282
Cloning, 150

Clothing, and gender typing,
    198–199
Club Girl Tech, 262
Coalition for Multicultural
    Undergraduate Education, 573
Cockburn, Cynthia, contributions of,
    92, 566
Cognitive factors
    attributions and gender
        stereotypes, 65–67
    gender cognition, 217–219
    gender identity, 188–189
    in sexist language, 63–65
    in social categorization, 82–84
    in stereotyping, 69–70
Cohabitation, 328–331
    break up of relationship, 339
    cross-cultural view, 329–330
    and gender roles, 330
    and later marital satisfaction, 331
    racial/ethnic groups, 329, 331
    reasons for, 330
    trends in U.S., 329
Cohen, Amy, contributions of, 146,
    568
Cohorts
    cohort effects, 458–460
    meaning of, 459
Colorism, 558
Comic strips, gender stereotypes in,
    42–43
Communication. *See also* Language
    conversational dynamics and
        status, 94–95
    tentative speech and women,
        96–97
Computer games, and aggression,
    214–216
Confounding variables, 121–122
Congenital adrenal hyperplasia,
    169–171
Consciousness, feminist, 552
Consciousness-raising groups, 565
Conservatism, view of women, 8, 70,
    313
Contact pregnancy, 362
Contraception, 354–356
    coerced contraception case, 356
    health insurance coverage issue,
        355
    limitations of, 355
Conversational dynamics, and
    status, 94–95
Coping mechanisms, gender-role
    labels for, 100
Coronary heart disease, and
    menopause, 449–450
Corporate wives, 399–401
    cost/benefits of, 400
    and divorce, Wendt case, 401
    types of work of, 399, 400
Cosmetic surgery, 58
Courtship violence, 491–495
    consequences of, 494–495
    definition of, 491–492
    interacting factors, 494
    and nature of relationship,
        493–494
    predictors of, 492–493
    prevalence of, 492
Crawford, Mary, contributions of,
    29–30
Critical psychology, 2
Crone, use of term, 442

Cross-cultural view
  abortion, 357–358
  age/aging of women, 442–443
  cohabitation, 329–330
  depression, 526
  genital mutilation, 282–283
  ideal mate traits, 311–312
  intersex persons, 182–185
  mathematics ability and gender, 127–128
  menopause, 447, 452, 457
  mental illness, 526, 559
  midlife, 458
  osteoporosis, 449
  physical attractiveness, 60–61
  preference for sons, 193–195
  reading romance novels, 281
  sexism in TV commercials, 47
  sex segregation, 208
  sexual harassment, 506
  sexuality, 266–268
  wife abuse, 512
  women leaders, 106, 108–109
  women's power strategies, 304
Cultural feminism, elements of, 8
Cultural influences. *See also* Cross-cultural view; Racial/ethnic groups
  gender stereotypes, 71–73
  sexual scripts, 279–281
Culture-bound syndromes, 559

Daley, Mary, contributions of, 63, 568
Dancel, Genora, contributions of, 325, 569
Dating
  acquaintance sexual assault, 495–504
  in adolescence, 258–259
  courtship violence, 491–495
  egalitarian relationship, 303
  and physical beauty, 56–57
  power differentials in, 302–303
  power strategies in, 303–304
Delusional dominating personality disorder, 546
Dependency. *See also* Power
  and depression, 89, 526, 531–533
Depression, 525–527, 530–535
  cross-cultural view, 526
  and dependency, 89, 526, 531–533
  gender differences, 530–531
  and gender roles, 532
  and learned helplessness, 89, 526
  and menopause, 450–451
  postpartum depression, 376–378
  power issues, 532–533
  racial/ethnic groups, 526, 531, 533, 559
  and relationship needs, 531
Development
  and depression of women, 530–531
  female sense of self, 137–139
  gender identity socialization, 187–206
  new criteria for humans, 145–146
  personality, power-based influences on, 143–145
  sex differentiation, 154–157
Deviance. *See also* Nonconformity
  in group setting, 99–102
  and physical attractiveness, 66–67
  as social construct, 99

Diabetes
  African-American women, 560
  teenagers and weight control, 249
Diagnostic and Statistical Manual of Mental Disorders (DSM-IV), 523, 544
Dihydrotestosterone, 155, 172
Dimorphic behaviors, 151, 157, 162, 234
Disabled women, and sexuality, 286
Distinctive traits, and self-categorization, 91
Divorce, 333–340
  causes of, 334–336
  child support, 338
  economic effects of, 336–339
  prevalence of, 333–334
  psychological adjustment to, 336
  and remarriage, 341
  research bias, 339–340
Dora, Freud's case, 528, 529
Double bind
  for adolescents, 259, 262
  creation of, 96
  and mental illness of women, 527–528
  overcoming, strategies for, 109
  problem for women, 96–98, 104, 109
Double standard
  aging, 436–441
  mental illness diagnosis, 545–546
  for sexuality, 288–289
Drugs, psychotropic, 547–549
Dual-career marriage, 318–320

Eating disorders, 249, 525–527, 538–543
  and age, 540, 541–542
  anorexia nervosa, 540
  binge-eating disorder, 540–541
  and body image, 543
  bulimia, 540
  and children, 224–225
  and fat talk, 542–543
  feminist view, 543
  past era for, 59
  racial/ethnic groups, 542
  and social class, 251–252
  stigma of overweight, 538–540
Education Amendments of 1972, Title IX, 146, 505, 568
Egalitarian relationships
  cohabitation, 330
  commitment and equality as ideals, 341–343
  dating partners, 303
  elements of, 343–344
  family, 225
  lesbian, 326–327
  marriage, 315–316, 318–320, 322
Emotional expression
  gender comparisons, 96, 197–198
  parental emotional vocabulary, 196–198
Employment. *See* Career development; Work
Empowerment
  elements of, 551
  and feminist therapy, 551, 553
Empty-nest syndrome, 461–463
  psychological adjustment to, 462
  and social class, 462–463
  and time era of socialization, 462

Encoding, and social categorization, 82–83
Environmental factors, interaction with genetic factors, 121, 157, 162–163
Equal Rights Amendment, 13
Estrogen, 151, 155
Estrogen replacement therapy, 453–454
  and osteoporosis, 449
  risks of, 453
Ethnicity. *See* Racial/ethnic groups
Eve, biblical, 34
Exercise, and bone loss, 449

Face-ism, stereotypes in media, 53–54
Fairy tales, gender stereotypes in, 204–205
Family caregiving, 467–472
  daughters *versus* sons, 467–468, 470
  psychological adjustment to, 470–472
  and social class, 468–469
  woman in the middle concept, 469–470
Family influences
  egalitarian family influences, 225
  gender flexibility, 226–227
  gender identity socialization, 195–203
  and resistance to gender rules, 225–226, 228–229, 256–257
Female circumcision. *See* Genital mutilation
Feminism & Psychology, 4
Feminism
  backlash against, 10–14
  as contrast to conservatism, 8
  cultural feminism, 8
  definition of, 8
  feminist themes, 21–28, 564
  liberal feminism, 7–8
  men as profeminists, 8
  and older women, 477–479
  radical feminism, 7
  socialist feminism, 7
  third-wave, 563
  women of color feminism, 7
Feminist consciousness, meaning of, 552
Feminist goals
  for psychology, 571–573
  transforming gender, 564–568
  transforming language, 568–570
  for women of color, 570–571
Feminist psychology
  critical psychology, 2
  development of, 2–4, 6
  feminist research, 19–20, 133
  pioneers, 3–4, 6, 26
Feminist therapy, 551–553
  and African-American women, 558
  basic tenets, 552
  empowerment as goal, 551, 553
  evolution of, 551, 565
  compared to nonsexist therapy, 553
Feminization of poverty
  older women, 465–466
  single mothers, 380–381
Ferraro, Geraldine, news media focus, 44
Fetal rights, 360–361

Friendships, and aging, 476–477
Fundamental attribution error, 83–84

Gang rape, 499
Gender
  distinction from sex, 22
  elements of, 21–22, 27
  and identity, 77–78
  and power relations, 22, 78
  social interaction based on, 22–23
  transforming gender as feminist
    goal, 564–568
  use of term, 24
  within-gender comparisons, 26–27
Gender-blending, lesbian women,
  179–181
Gender cognition
  behavioral theory, 218–219
  and gender labels, 217–218
  gender schema theory, 218
Gender constancy, meaning of,
  188–189
Gender comparisons
  aggression, 213–216
  brain studies, 132–133, 160–161
  depression, 530–531
  differences tradition, 117, 135–147
  emotional expression, 96
  history of research, 6, 132–134
  instrumentality, 216–217
  masturbation, 278
  mathematics ability, 123–132
  measurement of, 120–123
  mental disorders, 525–527
  moral reasoning research, 140–143
  mothering research, 137–139
  politics of difference, 146–147
  power and female personality,
    143–145
  psychotropic drug use, 547–549
  research flaws, 120–123
  resolution of issue, 145–147
  romantic love, 281–282
  similarities tradition, 117, 132–135
  statistical factors, 119–120
  status and power indicators, 93–98,
    117
Gender flexibility, 226–230
  family influences, 226–227
  and race, 227
  and social class, 227
Gender harassment, 506
Gender identity socialization,
  187–206
  acquisition of gender-related
    behaviors and age, 190
  clothing and gender typing,
    198–199
  cognitive factors, 188–189
  gender flexibility, 226–230
  of helplessness, 198
  interactive models of, 190–192
  lesbians/bisexuals, 295–302
  and media, 204–206
  parental stereotyping, 195–203
  and play, 202–203
  resistance to, 225–226, 227–229,
    256–257
  social learning theory, 187–188
  and toys, 199–202, 228
Gender labels
  and gender cognition, 217–218
  of nonconformity, 219–220
  of women's roles, 100

Gender preference, for sons,
  192–195
Gender roles
  and depression, 532
  double bind problem, 104, 109
  internalization by women, 109–114
  labels applied to women, 100
  in mixed-group setting, 99–103
  self-categorization, 90–91
  social categorization of, 78–86
  social constructions of, 86–90
  and social power/status, 92–98
  stereotypes. See Gender
    stereotypes
Gender schema theory, gender
  cognition, 218
Gender stereotypes
  age of awareness of, 36, 70–71
  characteristics of, 37–38, 65
  cognitive factors in, 69–70
  cultural factors, 71–73
  decreasing stereotyping, 70
  of feminism, 10–13
  future and change, 74–75
  instrumental and affective traits in,
    38
  measurement of, 38
  in media. See Gender stereotypes
    in media
  and mental illness of women,
    525–527
  and newborn, 195–196
  parental stereotyping and children,
    195–203
  race and class in, 41–42
  and self-fulfilling prophesy, 85–86
  and sexism, 67–69
  subtypes of, 39–41, 69–70
Gender stereotypes in media, 42–56
  and adolescents, 260–262
  ageist images, 440–441, 476
  cartoons, 205–206
  class-based bias, 53
  comic strips, 42–43
  face-ism/body-ism, 53–54
  fairy tales, 204–205
  frequency counts of
    males/females, 205
  gender role acceptance and TV
    viewing, 54–55
  impact of, 54–56
  magazine advertisements, 47–50
  MTV, 51
  in news media, 44
  occupational stereotypes, 206
  physical attractiveness of men
    versus women, 56
  pornography images, 51
  racist images, 42, 50, 51, 52
  slasher films, 261–262
  television, 46–47
  women in sports, 44–46
  women political candidates, 107
  women's magazines, 51–52
Gender-typing, meaning of, 23
Genetic factors
  interaction with social factors, 121,
    157, 162–163
  mathematics ability issue, 128–129
  sex determination, 154, 155
  sexual orientation, 158
Genital mutilation, 282–283
  complications/long-term effects,
    282

Genital mutilation—Cont.
  cross-cultural view, 282–283
  forms of, 282
Genitals, fetal development, 156
Gilligan's theory, moral reasoning,
  141–143
Gilman, Charlotte Perkins, 536
Girls Report: What We Know and Need
  to Know about Growing Up
  Female, 262
Glass ceiling, 404, 412–413
Gonadotropins, 235
Gonads, in utero development,
  154–155
Grandmotherhood, 466–467
  racial/ethnic groups, 467
Gray Panthers, 475, 479
Group setting, 99–103
  exclusion of women from,
    100–102
  indirect power strategies, 97–98
  male labels for women in, 100
  nonconforming women, 99–102
  and self-categorization, 90–91
  and tokenism, 102–103
  women leaders in, 98, 107–108
Growth spurt, puberty, 235, 236
Grrl, 263

Hawaii, same-sex marriage, 325
He, 62–64
Helping behavior, 86–89
  gender comparisons, 86–88
  and self-esteem, 88–89
  and status, 88
Helplessness. See Learned
  helplessness
Hera, 34
Hijiras, 184
Hill, Anita, 507
HIV, transmission and women,
  274
Holliday, Judy, 567
Hollingworth, Leta Stetter, 6, 26, 133,
  351
Homologue, 155
Homosexuality. See also Lesbians
  and brain, 158–159
  genetic factors, 158
  and physical trait descriptions,
    66–67
Hopkins, Nancy, 114, 566
Hopkins v. Price Waterhouse, 68–69,
  566
Hormones
  male/female distinction issue,
    151
  in midlife. See Menopause
  in pregnancy, 366–367
  and puberty, 235
  sex determination, 154–155
Hostile environment sexual
  harassment, 505–506
Hostile sexism, 67
Hot flashes, 447–448
Housework, 394–398
  devaluation of, 396–397
  husband participation in,
    394–395
  time factors, 395–396
Huerta, Dolores, contributions of,
  404, 567, 568, 570
Human rights issues, 571
Hyde Amendment, 357

Hyperfemininity, 222–225
  and beauty pageants, 222–223
  negative effects of, 224–225
Hysteria, 535–536

Identity
  and changes. *See* Psychological
    impact
  gender development. *See* Gender
    identity socialization
  and motherhood, 369–370
Images of women
  invisible women, 33, 72
  older women, 441–443
  religious images, 34–36
Incest. *See also* Childhood sexual
    abuse
  definition of, 486
India
  hijiras, 184
  view of older women, 443
Infants, gender stereotyping of,
    195–196
Infertility treatment, risk to women,
    361–362
Infibulation, 282
Instrumentality, gender differences,
    216–217
Instrumental traits
  and psychological adjustment,
    532
  types of, 38
Interactive models, gender identity,
    190–192
Internalization, of gender norms,
    109–114
Internet
  web sites for adolescents, 262
  web sites for feminists, 571
Intersex persons, 152, 163–164
  case examples, 149, 168
  cross-cultural view, 182–185
  cross-sex rearing, 174–176
  infant genitals of, 170
Intersex Society of North America
    (ISNA), 168, 181
  sexual reassignment, 168, 174–176,
    181–182
  transgendered movement, 164,
    178–179
Intimate relationships. *See also*
    Dating; Marriage; Sexuality
  break-up of, 339
  cohabitation, 328–331
  and equality. *See* Egalitarian
    relationships
  lesbians, 304–305, 324–328
  relationship skills of women,
    305
  romantic love, 279–282
  satisfaction in, 305–306
In vitro fertilization, risk to women,
    361–362
Islam, religious images of women,
    35
Israel, gender differences and
    cognitive ability, 127–128

Jacobi, Mary Putman, 5, 26
James, Alice, 536
Japan, view of older womem, 443
Journals
  on psychology of women, 4
  publication biases, 18

Kali, 442
Kassindja, Fauziuya, contributions
    of, 284, 569
Kinsey studies
  lesbians, 297
  sexuality, 269
Klinefelters syndrome, 167
Koestner, Katie, contributions of, 485,
    568, 569
Kohlberg's theory, moral reasoning,
    140–141
Kuan-Yin, goddess, 34
Kuhn, Maggie, contributions of, 475,
    479, 568, 570

Lamaze method, childbirth, 375–376
Language. *See also* Sexist language
  age-related, 437
  gender-differentiated speech, 210
  meaning and group applied to, 71
  nonsexist, 24, 26, 64–65
  sex-related language, 287
  subjective language, 110
  tentative *versus* assertive, 96–97
  and thought, 24
  transforming language as feminist
    goal, 568–570
Lateralization, brain, 160–161
Latinas
  eating disorders, 252, 542
  grandmothers, 467
  health status, 560
  lesbians, 301
  mental health treatment, 556
  mental illness, 559
  osteoporosis, 449
  sexuality, 283–284
  teenage pregnancy, 379
  in workforce, 402
Layton, Elizabeth, 478
Leadership, 105–109
  effectiveness and gender, 418–419
  legitimacy issue, 98, 108–109
  overcoming double bind, 109
  and role expectations, 108
  visual dominance of women/men,
    98
  women in U.S. politics, 105–107
  women in work setting, 418–419
Learned helplessness
  and depression, 89, 526
  socialization of helplessness, 198
Left-handedness, and brain, 160
Left Hand of Darkness, The (LeGuin), 81
Lesbian relationships, 324–328
  abusive, 511
  breaking up, 339
  endurance over time, factors in,
    326–327
  institutional differences for, 324–325
  loss of life partner, 473–474
  power in, 304–305, 327
  research bias, 328
  satisfaction in, 327–328
  special external pressures, 324, 328
Lesbians, 295–302
  age/aging, 443
  body image, 543
  definitions of, 296
  gender-blending types, 179–181
  historical view, 295–296
  identity development, 298–302
  Kinsey studies, 297
  Masters & Johnson studies, 297

Lesbians—*Cont.*
  mental illness treatment, 554–555
  motherhood of, 383–385
  and racial/ethnic minorities,
    301–302
  societal views of, 297–298
  in work/career development, 400,
    412–413, 426, 430
Liberal feminism, elements of, 7–8
Lightner, Candy, 387
Lilith, biblical, 34
Love. *See also* Intimate relationships
  romantic love, 279–282

Mabry, Linda, 101
McCloskey, Deirdre, 176–177
Machismo, 284
Magazines
  for adolescents, 260–261
  advertisements, sexism of, 47–50
  ageist practices of, 441
  beauty standard for women, 53,
    57–58
  women's, gender-role
    stereotyping, 51–52
Marianismo, 284
Marriage
  and age, 310
  and birth of child, 363–364
  divorce, 333–340
  dual-career marriage and equality,
    318–320
  egalitarian, 315–316, 318–320, 322,
    343–344
  endurance over time, factors in,
    323–324
  ideal mate, characteristics of,
    311–312
  marital satisfaction and inequality,
    322–323
  marital satisfaction over time, 321
  marriage gradient, 312
  modern, 313–315
  power in, 317–318, 322–323
  and psychological well-being,
    321–322
  remarriage, 340–341
  research bias, 316–317
  same-sex. *See* Lesbian
    relationships
  traditional, 313
  use of husband's name, 25
Mary, mother of Jesus, 34
Masochism, feminist perspective,
    544–545
Massachusetts Institute of
    Technology (MIT), gender bias
    case, 113, 114
Masters & Johnson research
  lesbians, 297
  sexuality, 269–270
Masturbation, 277–279
  gender comparisons, 278
  Kinsey findings, 269
  methods, 278
  and sexual satisfaction, 279
Mathematics ability, 123–132
  biological basis issue, 128–129
  classroom interaction factors,
    124–125
  confidence/expectation factors,
    125–126
  cross-cultural view, 127–128
  math for men concept, 126–127

Mathematics ability—*Cont.*
SAT scores, 123–124, 131–132
social effects of gender research, 129–132
women's participation in math/science careers, 134–135, 421, 424
Media. *See* Gender stereotypes in media
Men. *See also* Gender comparisons
abusive men, profile of, 513
ambivalent sexism of, 67–68
delusional dominating personality disorder, 546
eating disorders, 540, 541
fathering as feminist issue, 390–391
gender nonconformity, 219–220
homosexual, 158–159
language applied to, 61–63
magazine images of, 50, 53–54, 71–72
mental illness, 526, 537
mothering skills of, 349–350
nonverbal indicators of status, 93–94
physical attractiveness, 56, 66, 246, 248
preference for sons, 192–195
profeminist, 8
sexual harassers, profile of, 508
sexually aggressive, 499–501
sissies, 219–220
subtypes of, 40
Menarche, 234–235, 237–241
and body fat, 236
and body image, 239–241
cultural views of, 241–244
female ambivalence about, 238–239
and social class, 237–238
Menopause, 444–457
average age of, 445
coronary heart disease, 449–450
cross-cultural view, 447, 452, 457
and depression, 450–451
estrogen replacement therapy, 453–454
hot flashes, 447–448
language related to, 454
medicalization of, 446–447, 451–454
osteoporosis, 448–449
and power/status, 456–457
and social class, 456
social construction of, 445–447
subjective reports of, 455–456
Menstruation
menarche, 234–235, 237–241
negative associations, 242–244, 534
Mental illness
agoraphobia, 526
culture-bound syndromes, 559
depression, 525–527, 530–535
diagnosis and gender bias, 523–525, 545–546
and double bind, 527–528
eating disorders, 525–527, 538–543
gender comparisons, theories of, 525–527
labeling issue, 544–545
masochism, 544
nervous disorders, 535–538
and physical health, 560

Mental illness—*Cont.*
posttraumatic stress disorder, 545
power issues, 523, 528–530
racial/ethnic groups, 526, 559
reproduction-related disorders, 533–535, 536
self-defeating personality disorder, 544–545
social construction of, 522–523
Mental illness treatment, 549–559
abuse of power, 528–530
and African-American women, 558
feminist therapy, 551–553
historical view, 528, 529, 536
and invisible women, 560–561
lesbian clients/therapists, 554–555
neutrality myth, 550–551
poor clients, 529–530, 557–558
practitioner and gender bias, 547
psychotropic drugs, 547–549
racial/ethnic groups, 555–557
sexual abuse by therapist, 554
therapist gender, impact of, 528–530, 553–554
traditional, feminist critique of, 549–551
Mentors, in work setting, 417–418
Meta-analysis
gender comparisons, 122–123
procedure in, 122
Metropolitan Community Church, 325
Midlife
cohort effects, 458–460
cross-cultural view, 458
empty-nest syndrome, 461–463
menopause, 444–457
role transitions, 461
Mitchell, Silas Weir, 536
Moderator variable, 122
Mommy track, 433
Montague, Helen, 133
Moral reasoning, 140–143
Gilligan's theory, 141–143
Kohlberg's theory, 140–141
Morris, Jan, 176, 178
Motherhood, 137–139
abortion issue, 356–360
African-American women, 349, 382–383
animal studies, 162
body image and pregnancy, 366–367
childbirth, 370–378
child-free women, decision making of, 352–354
commonalities among women, 385–388
contraception issues, 354–356
future view, 390–391
having children, decision making about, 348–350
lesbian mothers, 383–385
and marital relationship, 363–364
motherhood mandate, 350, 352
myths related to, 347–348, 442
pregnancy, 366–370
psychological adjustment, 363–370
reproductive technology issues, 360–362
role changes, coping with, 364–365
scapegoating of mothers issue, 389–390

Motherhood—*Cont.*
self-development and females, 137–139, 349
and self-identity, 369–370
and sexuality, 365–366
single mothers, 380–382
societal control of, 354–363
teen-age mothers, 378–380
working mothers, 428–432
Mothers
and childhood sexual abuse, 488
-daughter conflicts in adolescence, 257
and high-achieving women, 228–229, 273, 424
influence for African-American women, 257
and sex education, 292–293
Mothers Against Drunk Driving (MADD), 387
Motivation, and achievement. *See* Achievement-oriented women
Moynihan Report, 383
Ms., use of word, 26, 64–65
Ms. Foundation, 262
MTV, sexist images of, 51
Music videos, sexist images of, 51

Nancy Drew, as role model, 228
National Council for Research on Women, 262
Native Americans
berdache, 182–183, 302
eating disorders, 542
grandmothers, 467
invisible women, 560–561
power of older women, 442–443
Neosexism, 73
Nervous disorders, 535–538
historical view, 535–536
Neurasthenia, 536
News media, gender stereotypes in, 44
Nonconformity
deviance as, 99–102
gender flexibility, 226–230
and high-achieving women, 228–230
resistance to gender socialization, 225–226, 227–229
and stigma, 98–99
tomboys, 220–222
women in group setting, 99–102
Nonsexist language
APA guidelines, 26
Ms., 24, 64–65
Nonsexist research
elements of, 18–21
and social change, 27–28
Nonverbal behavior
gender comparisons, 93–94
indicators of status, 93–94
types of gestures, 94

Occupational stereotypes, in media, 206
Older Women's League (OWL), 479
Old Maid stereotype, 331–332
Olympics
chromosomal testing of women, 168
coverage of women, 45–46
Orgasm, subjective experience of, 276–277

Osteoporosis, 448–449
  cross-cultural view, 449
  and estrogen replacement therapy, 449
  risk factors, 448–449

Parenthood. *See* Motherhood
Parts of a Sexual Profile (PRIMO), 152, 154
Pat character, 81, 82
Peers
  and adolescents, 259–260
  same-sex peers, 206–212
  and teen sexual behavior, 273
Peterson, Kelli, contributions of, 255, 567
P-FLAG, 325
Physical attractiveness
  and African-American women, 60–61
  and aging, 440
  and body weight, 57–58, 66
  cross-cultural view, 60–61, 72
  and hyperfemininity, 222–225
  and male/female relationships, 56–57
  male *versus* female standards, 56, 57
  and sexual desirability, 285–286
  social attributions related to, 65–67, 85
  social importance of, 56–57
  and stereotyping, 41
  taking care of looks, 57
  teasing in childhood/adolescence, 254
Physical health, and mental health, 560
Pink-collar employment, 409
Play
  and gender-typed behaviors, 202–203
  sex segregation, 206–212
  toys, 199–202
Pledged virgins, 183–184
Political activism, of older persons, 477–479
Pornography, race-based sexism, 51
Postpartum depression, 376–378, 534
Posttraumatic stress disorder, feminist perspective, 545
Poverty
  and mental illness treatment, 529–530, 557–558
  older women, 465–466, 473
  and single mothers, 380–381
Power
  and dating relationships, 302–303
  and depression, 532–533
  and female personality development, 143–145
  and gender, 22, 78
  indirect power strategies, 97–98, 303–304
  and lesbian relationships, 304–305, 327
  in marriage, 317–318
  and mental illness of women, 523, 528–530
  social power, 92
  and status, 92–98
  and wife abuse, 510–512
  women at midlife, 456–457
  in words/language, 62, 96–97

Pregnancy, 366–370. *See also* Motherhood
  hormonal changes in, 366–367
  reactions to pregnant women, 367–369
Premenstrual syndrome, social construction of, 533– 534, 537–538
Prenatal period
  preference for males, 192–195
  sex determination. *See* Sex differentiation
Procedural stigma, 110–111
Pro-choice, 354
Profeminists, 8
Professional women, exclusion from group, 100–102
Progestins, 155
Psychological impact. *See also* Mental illness; Mental illness treatment
  abortion, 359–360
  acquaintance sexual assault, 501–502
  breaking up relationship, 339
  childbirth, 376–378
  childhood sexual abuse, 488–490
  divorce, 336
  empty-nest syndrome, 462–463
  family caregiving, 470–472
  loss of lesbian life partner, 473–474
  marriage, 321–322
  menopause, 450–451
  motherhood, 363–370
  retirement, 464
  sexual harassment, 509
  widowhood, 472–473
  wife abuse, 514–515
  work involvement, 431
Psychology
  effects on women's movement on, 4–6
  feminist goals for, 571–573
Psychology of Women Quarterly, 4
Psychotherapy. *See* Mental illness treatment
Psychotropic drugs, 547–549
  gender differences in use, 547–549
Puberty, 234–241
  age on onset, 235
  breast development, 245–246
  early and late maturation, 250–251, 272–273
  girls compared to boys, 234
  individual variation in, 235
  menarche, 234–235, 237–241
  and race, 251–253
  and social class, 251–253
  weight gain in, 235–237, 246–250
Puerto Rican syndrome, 559

Quid pro quo sexual harassment, 505

Racial/ethnic groups
  achievement-oriented women, 426
  age/aging, 460
  childhood sexual abuse, 486
  cohabitation, 329, 331
  depression, 526, 531, 533
  eating disorders, 542
  feminist goals for, 570–571
  gender flexibility, 227
  gender stereotypes, 41–42
  gender stereotypes in media, 51, 52

Racial/ethnic groups—*Cont.*
  grandmotherhood, 467
  lesbians, 301–302
  mental illness, 526, 559
  mental illness treatment, 555–557
  response to puberty, 251–253
  sexual harassment, 507
  sexuality, 268, 283–285
  teen-age mothers, 379
  work, 402
Racism
  in academic studies, 5–6
  colorism, 558
Radical feminism, elements of, 7
Ramsey, JonBenet, 222–223
Rape. *See* Violence against women
Rap music, 51
Reentry woman, 474–475
Reframing, sexist language, 109
Relationships. *See also* Intimate relationships
  and aging, 476–477
  needs of women and depression, 531
  relational work of women, 398–399, 405
Religion, images of women, 34–36
Remarriage, 340–341
  marital satisfaction, 341
  reasons for, 341
Reno, Janet, 108
Repressed memories, of sexual abuse, 489
Reproductive technology, social/ethical issues related to, 361–363
Research
  cohort effects, 458–460
  confounding variables, 121–122
  first research on women, 132
  gender comparisons research, 120–123
  meta-analysis, 122–123
  nonsexist research, 18–21
  retrospective research, 425
  sex research, 269–271
  traditional, process of, 14–18
Rest cure, 536
Retirement, 463–464
  psychological adjustment to, 464
Retrospective research, method of, 425
Reward, based on sexual category, 110–111
Richards, Rene, 176
Roe v. Wade, 357
Role conflict, working mothers, 429–430
Role models
  female therapists, 554
  of high-achieving women, 228
  working mothers as, 432
  in work setting, 417–418
Role overload, working mothers, 429
Romance novels, 279–281
Romantic love, 279–282
  gender comparisons, 281–282
  and romance novels, 279–281

Safe sex, women's neglect of, 273–275
St. Elizabeth, 442
Same-sex peers. *See* Sex segregation